OXFORD

ATLAS
OF THE
UNITED
STATES

H. J. DE BLIJ, EDITOR

EDITOR H. J. de Blij, Distinguished Professor
of Geography, Michigan State University

OXFORD UNIVERSITY PRESS
EDITORIAL/RESEARCH Ben Keene
GAZETTEER DESIGN Nora Wertz

BOARD OF ADVISORS
Chair: Peter O. Muller, Professor of Geography,
University of Miami

Adrián Guillermo Aguilar, Professor and Director
of the Institute of Geography, Universidad Nacional
Autonoma de Mexico

Patricia Gober, Professor of Geography and
Co-Director of the Decision Center for a Desert City
at Arizona State University

Richard E. Groop, Professor and Chair of the
Department of Geography, Michigan State University

Glen M. MacDonald, Professor and Chair of the
Department of Geography, University of California,
Los Angeles

Ian MacLachlan, Associate Professor of Geography,
University of Lethbridge, Canada

Barney Warf, Professor and Chair of the Department
of Geography, Florida State University

Published by Oxford University Press, Inc.
198 Madison Avenue
New York, NY, 10016
http://www.oup.com/us/atlas

Cartography by Philip's

Philip's, a division of Octopus Publishing Group Ltd
2–4 Heron Quays
London E14 4JP, UK
http://www.philips-maps.co.uk

Cartography and Placename Index copyright © 2006 Philip's

Text copyright © 2006 Oxford University Press, Inc.

OXFORD   Oxford is a registered trademark
UNIVERSITY PRESS   of Oxford University Press

Library of Congress Cataloging-in-Publication Data available

ISBN-13 978–0–19–522044–5
ISBN-10 0–19–522044–7

Printed in Hong Kong

REFERENCES AND ACKNOWLEDGEMENTS
The publishers wish to thank various government agencies and others for
providing many of the figures used in this atlas. While every effort has been
made to secure permission, we apologize if in any case we have failed to trace
the copyright holder.

NORTH AMERICAN GEOGRAPHY
p. 11   Adapted from *Modern Physical Geography*, 2nd ed., Thompson
             & Turk, Saunders, 1997.
p. 12–13 After Orme, *The Physical Geography of North America*, Oxford,
             2002.
p. 17 (top) Adapted from "Groundwater Resources" Map Supplement
             © 1993, National Geographic Society.
p. 21   Adapted from *North American Terrestrial Vegetation*, 2nd ed.,
             Barbour & Billings, Cambridge, 1999.
p. 22   After J. L. Hough, *Geology of the Great Lakes*, University of
             Illinois, 1958.
p. 23   After Orme, *The Physical Geography of North America*, Oxford,
             2002.
p. 24   From H. Driver et al, *Indiana University Publications in Anthropology
             and Linguistics*, 1953.
p. 25   After Greenberg and the 1998 Britannica Book of the Year.
p. 26   Adapted from *World Atlas of the Past, The Age of Discovery*,
             volume 3, Haywood, Oxford, 2000.
p. 35   Adapted from *La Agricultura en Mexico*, Hurtada & Calderon,
             UNAM, 2003.
p. 45   After Gaustad and Barlow, *New Historical Atlas of Religion in
             America*, Oxford, 2001.
p. 47   Adapted from "Federal Lands" Map Supplement © 1996 National
             Geographic Society.

UNITED STATES GAZETTEER
The "At a Glance" sections of the atlas were compiled from data collected
by the U.S. Census Bureau. All rights reserved. This information is published
with the permission of the aforementioned agency.

All photographs that appear in the Gazetteer are part of the Photodisc image
collection copyright Getty Images, Inc. 2004.

SATELLITE IMAGERY
pp. 8, 50–51, front and rear endpapers
Courtesy of NPA Group, Edenbridge, Kent, UK (www.satmaps.com)

CITY MAPS
The following city maps utilize base data supplied courtesy of
MapQuest.com, Inc. (© MapQuest):
Baltimore, Charlotte, Cincinnati, Cleveland, Dallas–Fort Worth, Denver,
Detroit, Houston, Indianapolis, Las Vegas, Memphis, Milwaukee,
Minneapolis–St. Paul, New Orleans, Norfolk, Orlando, Philadelphia,
Phoenix, Pittsburgh, Portland, St. Louis, Salt Lake City, San Antonio,
San Diego, Seattle, Tampa & St. Petersburg.

FOREWORD

Incorporating computer-derived maps that have been generated using the very latest digital cartographic techniques, the *Atlas of the United States* exemplifies a finely produced, serious work of reference for home, school, or library use. Large-scale maps show all 50 states from the lowest point to the highest elevation with exceptional clarity. Capturing everything from creek beds to county lines, this atlas offers up-to-date, precise political and topographical information unavailable elsewhere in print.

HOW TO USE THIS ATLAS

This atlas is divided into a number of sections that are explained in brief below.

U.S. & NORTH AMERICAN STATISTICS

U.S. statistical data showing comparative rankings of state sizes and city populations, together with lists of National Parks, National Scenic Byways, National Seashores, Lakeshores, and Rivers, complement lists of dimensions of North American geographical features, including mountains, rivers, islands, and lakes.

NORTH AMERICAN GEOGRAPHY

This richly informative section comprises 40 pages of thematic maps, charts, graphs, and diagrams that explain key concepts relating to the continent's physical, cultural, economic, and political geography. Explanatory text on each page describes the patterns shown by this illuminating set of data.

UNITED STATES MAPS

An outstanding collection of over 130 pages of distinctive Oxford cartography, these highly acclaimed physical maps combine relief shading with layer-colored contours to give a striking visual picture of the country's surface. Roads, railroads, canals, and airports are accurately depicted on the maps, while towns, cities, National Parks, and Indian Reservations are clearly marked.

UNITED STATES CITY MAPS

A detailed selection of maps for 34 urban areas in the U.S., useful for planning trips as well as for comparative studies of cities nationwide. Parks and points of interest are located along with public buildings, places of worship, rail and subway stations.

UNITED STATES GAZETTEER

Arranged in alphabetical order, this section comprises brief summaries of each state and its capital city, illustrated with color photographs, maps, and flags.

INDEX TO MAPS

The index to the maps, with more than 30,000 placenames, includes geographical features as well as towns and cities, with both latitude/longitude and letter/figure grid references.

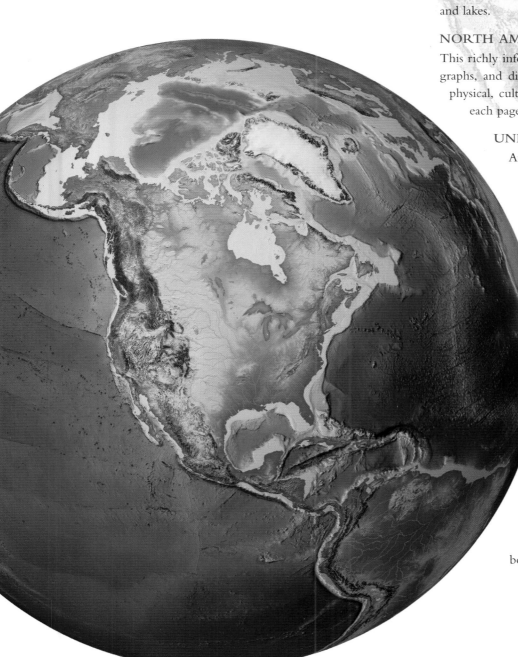

CONTENTS

U.S. & North American
Statistics   6–7

NORTH AMERICAN GEOGRAPHY

North America:
Satellite image   8

North America:
Political   9

Physical Geography
and Geology   10–11

Tectonic Provinces
and Physiography   12–13

Energy and Minerals   14–15

Surface Water
and Drainage   16–17

Climate and Weather   18–19

Soil and Vegetation   20–21

Pleistocene Land Cover
and Glaciation   22–23

Indigenous Peoples   24–25

Early Settlement
and Expansion   26–27

Population and
Social Diversity   28–29

Immigration and
Population Change   30–31

Urbanization   32–33

Land Use and
Agriculture   34–35

United States:
Manufacturing
Industries   36–37

United States:
Service Industries   38–39

Trade and
Telecommunications   40–41

Highways and
Railroads   42–43

Languages and
Religions   44–45

National Parks and
Federal Lands   46–47

Maritime Zones
and Claims   48

UNITED STATES

Map symbols   49

United States:
Satellite image   50–51

United States
1:10 700 000   52–53

Eastern United
States   54–55
1:5 300 000

Middle United
States   56–57
1:5 300 000

Western United
States   58–59
1:5 300 000

Alabama   60
1:2 200 000

Alaska   61
1:8 900 000

Arizona   62
1:2 200 000

Arkansas   63
1:2 200 000

California   64–65
1:2 200 000

Colorado   66
1:2 200 000

Florida   67
1:2 200 000

Georgia   68
1:2 200 000

Hawai'i   69
1:2 200 000

Idaho   70
1:2 200 000

Illinois   71
1:2 200 000

Indiana   72
1:2 200 000

Iowa   73
1:2 200 000

Kansas   74
1:2 200 000

Louisiana   75
1:2 200 000

Maine   76
1:2 200 000

Maryland, Delaware
and District of
Columbia   77
1:1 100 000

Massachusetts,
Connecticut and
Rhode Island   78
1:1 100 000

Michigan   79
1:2 200 000

Minnesota   80
1:2 200 000

Mississippi   81
1:2 200 000

Missouri   82
1:2 200 000

Montana   83
1:3 300 000

Nebraska   84
1:2 200 000

Nevada   85
1:2 200 000

New Hampshire
and Vermont   86
1:1 100 000

New Jersey   87
1:1 100 000

New Mexico   88
1:2 300 000

New York   89
1:2 200 000

North Carolina and
South Carolina   90
1:2 700 000

North Dakota and
South Dakota   91
1:2 700 000

Ohio   92
1:2 200 000

Oklahoma   93
1:2 200 000

Oregon   94
1:2 200 000

Pennsylvania   95
1:2 200 000

Tennessee and
Kentucky   96–97
1:2 200 000

Texas   98–99
1:2 700 000

Utah   100
1:2 200 000

Washington   101
1:2 200 000

West Virginia
and Virginia   102
1:2 200 000

Wisconsin 103
1:2 200 000

Wyoming 104
1:2 200 000

**Puerto Rico and
the U.S. Pacific
Territories** 105

U.S. Outlying Areas
1:84 400 000

Puerto Rico and the
Virgin Islands
1:1 530 000

Northern Marianas
1:17 800 000

Guam
1:890 000

Saipan and Tinian
(Northern Marianas)
1:890 000

Samoan Islands
1:22 200 000

Tutuila (American Samoa)
1:890 000

Manua Islands
(American Samoa)
1:890 000

UNITED STATES CITY MAPS

Atlanta 106

Baltimore 107

Boston 106

Charlotte 107

Chicago 108

Cincinnati 107

Cleveland 107

Dallas–Fort Worth 109

Denver 109

Detroit 109

Houston 110

Indianapolis 110

Las Vegas 110

Los Angeles 110–111

Memphis 112

**Miami–Fort
Lauderdale** 112

Milwaukee 112

Minneapolis–St. Paul 113

New Orleans 113

New York 114–115

Norfolk 115

Orlando 115

Philadelphia 116

Phoenix 116

Pittsburgh 116

Portland 116

St. Louis 117

Salt Lake City 117

San Antonio 117

San Diego 117

San Francisco 118

Seattle 118

**Tampa and
St. Petersburg** 119

Washington 119

UNITED STATES GAZETTEER
120–168

INDEX TO MAPS
169–208

U.S. & North American Statistics

UNITED STATES OF AMERICA

See page 9 for a political map

State	Area (sq. km)	Area (sq. miles)	Population	Capital
Alabama	131,426	50,744	4,500,752	Birmingham
Alaska	1,481,353	571,951	648,818	Juneau
Arizona	294,313	113,635	5,580,811	Phoenix
Arkansas	134,856	52,068	2,725,714	Little Rock
California	403,934	155,959	35,484,453	Sacramento
Colorado	268,630	103,718	4,550,688	Denver
Connecticut	12,549	4,845	3,483,372	Hartford
Delaware	5,061	1,954	817,491	Dover
Florida	139,671	53,927	17,019,068	Tallahassee
Georgia	149,977	57,906	8,684,715	Atlanta
Hawai'i	16,636	6,423	1,257,608	Honolulu
Idaho	214,315	82,747	1,366,332	Boise
Illinois	143,963	55,584	12,653,544	Springfield
Indiana	92,896	35,867	6,195,643	Indianapolis
Iowa	144,701	55,869	2,944,062	Des Moines
Kansas	211,901	81,815	2,723,507	Topeka
Kentucky	102,896	39,728	4,117,827	Frankfort
Louisiana	112,826	43,562	4,496,334	Baton Rouge
Maine	79,933	30,862	1,305,728	Augusta
Maryland	25,315	9,774	5,508,909	Annapolis
Massachusetts	20,306	7,840	6,433,422	Boston
Michigan	147,122	56,804	10,079,985	Lansing
Minnesota	206,190	79,610	5,059,375	St. Paul
Mississippi	121,489	46,907	2,881,281	Jackson
Missouri	178,415	68,886	5,704,484	Jefferson City
Montana	376,980	145,552	917,621	Helena
Nebraska	199,098	76,872	1,739,291	Lincoln
Nevada	284,449	109,826	2,241,154	Carson City
New Hampshire	23,227	8,968	1,287,687	Concord
New Jersey	19,210	7,417	8,638,396	Trenton
New Mexico	314,312	121,356	1,874,614	Sante Fe
New York	122,284	47,214	19,190,115	Albany
North Carolina	126,161	48,711	8,407,248	Raleigh
North Dakota	178,648	68,976	633,837	Bismarck
Ohio	106,055	40,948	11,435,798	Columbus
Oklahoma	177,848	68,667	3,511,532	Oklahoma City
Oregon	248,632	95,997	3,559,596	Salem
Pennsylvania	116,076	44,817	12,365,455	Harrisburg
Rhode Island	2,707	1,045	1,076,164	Providence
South Carolina	77,982	30,109	4,147,152	Columbia
South Dakota	196,542	75,885	764,309	Pierre
Tennessee	106,752	41,217	5,841,748	Nashville
Texas	678,054	261,797	22,118,509	Austin
Utah	212,753	82,144	2,351,467	Salt Lake City
Vermont	23,958	9,250	619,107	Montpelier
Virginia	102,548	39,594	7,386,330	Richmond
Washington	172,349	66,544	6,131,445	Olympia
West Virginia	62,362	24,078	1,810,354	Charleston
Wisconsin	140,663	54,310	5,472,299	Madison
Wyoming	251,489	97,100	501,242	Cheyenne

LARGEST CITIES OF THE UNITED STATES

See pages 32–33 for maps of Urbanization

Metropolitan area	Population
New York-Northern New Jersey-Long Island (NY-NJ-PA)	18,323,002
Los Angeles-Long Beach-Santa Ana (CA)	12,365,627
Chicago-Naperville-Joliet (IL-IN-WI)	9,098,316
Philadelphia-Camden-Wilmington (PA-NJ-DE)	5,687,147
Dallas-Fort Worth-Arlington (TX)	5,161,544
Miami-Fort Lauderdale-Miami Beach (FL)	5,007,564
Washington-Arlington-Alexandria (DC-VA-MD)	4,796,183

Metropolitan area	Population
Houston-Baytown-Sugar Land (TX)	4,715,407
Detroit-Warren-Livonia (MI)	4,452,557
Boston-Cambridge-Quincy (MA-NH)	4,391,344
Atlanta-Sandy Springs-Marietta (GA)	4,247,981
San Francisco-Oakland-Fremont (CA)	4,123,740
Riverside-San Bernardino-Ontario (CA)	3,254,821
Phoenix-Mesa-Scottsdale (AZ)	3,251,876
Seattle-Tacoma-Bellevue (WA)	3,043,878
Minneapolis-St. Paul-Bloomington (MN-WI)	2,968,806
San Diego-Carlsbad-San Marcos (CA)	2,813,833

Metropolitan area	Population
St. Louis (MO-IL)	2,698,687
Baltimore-Towson (MD)	2,552,994
Pittsburgh (PA)	2,431,087
Tampa-St. Petersburg-Clearwater (FL)	2,395,997
Denver-Aurora (CO)	2,179,240
Cleveland-Elyria-Mentor (OH)	2,148,143
Cincinnati-Middletown (OH-KY-IN)	2,009,632
Portland-Vancouver-Beaverton (OR-WA)	1,927,881

The city population figures are taken from the most recent census or estimate available and represent the urban agglomeration.

NATIONAL SCENIC BYWAYS OF THE UNITED STATES

See page 42 for a map of Highways

A1A Scenic and Historic Coastal Byway (FL)
Acadia Byway (ME)
Alaska's Marine Highway (AK)
Amish Country Byway (OH)
Arroyo Seco Historic Parkway (CA)
Ashley River Road (SC)
Beartooth Highway (MT, WY)
Big Sur Coast Highway-Route 1 (CA)
Billy the Kid Trail (NM)
Blue Ridge Parkway (VA, NC)
Brandywine Valley Scenic Byway (DE)
CanalWay Ohio Scenic Byway (OH)
Cascade Lakes Scenic Byway (OR)
Catoctin Mountain Scenic Byway (MD)
Cherohala Skyway (TN)
Cherokee Foothills Scenic Highway (SC)
Chesapeake Country Scenic Byway (MD)
Chinook Scenic Byway (WA)
The Coal Heritage Trail (WV)
Colonial Parkway (VA)
Colorado River Headwaters Byway (CO)
Connecticut River Byway (CT)
Connecticut State Route 169 (CT)
Copper Country Trail (MI)
Coronado Trail Scenic Byway (AZ)
Coulee Corridor Scenic Byway (WA)
Country Music Highway (KY)
Creole Nature Trail (LA)
Crowley's Ridge Parkway (MO, AR)
Death Valley Scenic Byway (CA)
Dinosaur Diamond Prehistoric Highway (UT, CO)
Ebbetts Pass Scenic Byway (CA)
Edge of the Wilderness (MN)
El Camino Real (NM)

The Energy Loop: Huntington & Eccles Canyons Scenic Byways (UT)
Flaming Gorge-Uintas Scenic Byway (UT)
Flint Hills Scenic Byway (KS)
Frontier Pathways Scenic and Historic Byway (CO)
George Washington Memorial Parkway (VA)
Geronimo Trail Scenic Byway (NM)
Glenn Highway (AK)
Gold Belt Tour Scenic and Historic Byway (CO)
Grand Mesa Scenic and Historic Byway (CO)
Grand Rounds Scenic Byway (MN)
The Great River Road (AR, MN, IA, IL, WI, MS)
Hells Canyon Scenic Byway (OR)
Highland Scenic Highway (WV)
Highway 12-A Journey Through Time Scenic Byway (UT)
Historic Bluff Country Scenic Byway (MN)
Historic Columbia River Highway (OR)
The Historic National Road (MD, WV, IN, PA, IL, OH)
Historic Route 66 (AZ, NM, IL)
Illinois River Road: Route of the Voyageurs (IL)
Indian River Lagoon Scenic Highway (FL)
International Selkirk Loop (ID, WA)
Jemez Mountain Trail (NM)
Kaibab Plateau-North Rim Parkway (AZ)
Kancamagus Scenic Byway (NH)
Lake Erie Coastal Ohio Trail (OH)
Lakes to Locks Passage: The Great Northeastern Journey (NY)

Lake Tahoe-Eastshore Drive (NV)
Las Vegas Strip (NV)
Lincoln Highway (IL)
Little Dixie Highway of the Great River Road (MO)
Loess Hills Scenic Byway (IA)
Logan Canyon Scenic Byway (UT)
McKenzie Pass-Santiam Pass Scenic Byway (OR)
Meeting of the Great Rivers Scenic Route (IL)
Merritt Parkway (CT)
Midland trail (WV)
Minnesota River Valley Scenic Byway (MN)
Mohawk Towpath Byway (NY)
Mountains to Sound Greenway-I-90 (WA)
Mt. Hood Scenic Byway (OR)
Natchez Trace Parkway (AL, MS, TN)
Native American Scenic Byway (SD, ND)
Nebo Loop Scenic Byway (UT)
North Shore Scenic Drive (MN)
Northwest Passage Scenic Byway (ID)
Ohio River Scenic Byway (IN, IL, OH)
Old Canada Road Scenic Byway (ME)
Outback Scenic Byway (OR)
Pacific Coast Scenic Byway (OR)
Paul Bunyan Scenic Byway (MN)
Payette River Scenic Byway (ID)
Pend Oreille Scenic Byway (ID)
Peter Norbeck Scenic Byway (SD)
Pioneer Historic Byway (ID)
Pyramid Lake Scenic Byway (NV)
Rangeley Lakes Scenic Byway (ME)
Red River Gorge Scenic Byway (KY)
Red Rock Scenic Road (AZ)
River Road Scenic Byway (MI)

Rogue-Umpqua Scenic Byway (OR)
Russell-Brasstown National Scenic Byway (GA)
San Juan Skyway (CO)
San Luis Obispo North Coast Highway-Route 1 (CA)
Santa Fe Trail (NM, CO)
Savannah River Scenic Byway (SC)
Schoodic Scenic Byway (ME)
Seaway Trail (NY, PA)
Selma to Montgomery March Byway (AL)
The Seward Highway (AK)
Sheyenne River Valley Scenic Byway (ND)
Sky Island Scenic Byway (AZ)
Skyline Drive (VA)
Staunton-Parkersburg Turnpike (VA)
Stevens Pass Greenway (WA)
Strait of Juan de Fuca Highway-SR112 (WA)
Talimena Scenic Drive (OK, AR)
Talladega Scenic Drive (AL)
Tioga Road/Big Oak Flat Road (CA)
Top of the Rockies (CO)
Trail of the Ancients (UT, CO)
Trail of the Mountain Spirits Scenic Byway (NM)
Trail Ridge Road/Beaver Meadow Road (CO)
Turquoise Trail (NM)
Volcanic Legacy Scenic Byway (OR, CA)
Washington Heritage Trail (WV)
West Cascades Scenic Byway (OR)
Western Heritage Historic Byway (ID)
Wetlands and Wildlife Scenic Byway (KS)
White Mountain Trail (NH)
Wilderness Road Heritage Highway (KY)
Woodward Avenue-M-1 (MI)

NATIONAL PARKS OF THE UNITED STATES

See page 46 for a map of National Parks

Acadia National Park (ME)
Arches National Park (UT)
Badlands National Park (SD)
Big Bend National Park (TX)
Biscayne National Park (FL)
Black Canyon of the Gunnison National Park (CO)
Bryce Canyon National Park (UT)
Canyonlands National Park (UT)
Capitol Reef National Park (UT)
Carlsbad Caverns National Park (NM)
Channel Islands National Park (CA)
Congaree National Park (SC)
Crater Lake National Park (OR)
Cuyahoga Valley National Park (OH)
Death Valley National Park (CA)
Denali National Park and Preserve (AK)
Dry Tortugas National Park (FL)
Everglades National Park (FL)
Gates of the Arctic National Park and Preserve (AK)
Glacier Bay National Park and Preserve (AK)
Glacier National Park (MT)
Grand Canyon National Park (AZ)
Grand Teton National Park (WY)
Great Basin National Park (NV)
Great Sand Dunes National Park and Preserve (CO)
Great Smoky Mountains National Park (NC)
Guadalupe Mountains National Park (TX)
Haleakala National Park (HI)
Hawai'i Volcanoes National Park (HI)

Hot Springs National Park (AR)
Isle Royale National Park (MI)
Joshua Tree National Park (CA)
Katmai National Park and Preserve (AK)
Kenai Fjords National Park (AK)
Kobuk Valley National Park (AK)
Lake Clark National Park and Preserve (AK)
Lassen Volcanic National Park (CA)
Mammoth Cave National Park (KY)
Mesa Verde National Park (CO)
Mount Rainier National Park (WA)
National Park of American Samoa
North Cascades National Park (WA)
Olympic National Park (WA)
Petrified Forest National Park (AZ)
Redwood National and State Parks (CA)
Rocky Mountain National Park (CO)
Saguaro National Park (AZ)
Sequoia and Kings Canyon National Parks (CA)
Shenandoah National Park (VA)
Theodore Roosevelt National Park (ND)
Virgin Islands National Park
Voyageurs National Park (MN)
Wind Cave National Park (SD)
Wrangell-St. Elias National Park and Preserve (AK)
Yellowstone National Park (WY)
Yosemite National Park (CA)
Zion National Park (UT)

U.S. NATIONAL SEASHORES, LAKESHORES, & RIVERS

See page 16 for a map of Surface Water and Drainage

Alganak Wild River (AK)
Apostle Island National Lakeshore (WI)
Assateague Island National Seashore (MD, VA)
Big South Fork National River & Recreation Area (KY, TN)
Bluestone National Scenic River (WV)
Buffalo National River (AR)
Canaveral National Seashore (FL)
Cape Cod National Seashore (MA)
Cape Hatteras National Seashore (NC)
Cape Lookout National Seashore (NC)
Cumberland Island National Seashore (GA)
Delaware National Scenic River (NJ, PA)
Fire Island National Seashore (NY)
Gulf Islands National Seashore (FL, MS)
Indiana Dunes National Lakeshore (IN)
Mississippi National River and Recreation Area (MN)
Missouri National Recreational River (SD)
New River Gorge National River (WV)
Niobrara National Scenic River (NE)
Obed Wild & Scenic River (TN)
Ozark National Scenic Riverways (MO)
Padre Island National Seashore (TX)
Pictured Rocks National Lakeshore (MI)
Point Reyes National Seashore (CA)
Rio Grande Wild and Scenic River (TX)
Saint Croix National Scenic River (WI)
Sleeping Bear Dunes National Lakeshore (MI)
Upper Delaware Scenic & Recreational River (PA, NY)

NORTH AMERICAN LANDSCAPES

See page 10 for a map of Physical Geography

HIGHEST MOUNTAINS

Name	meters	feet	Country
Mt. McKinley (Denali)	6,194	20,322	U.S.
Mt. Logan	5,959	19,551	Canada
Pico de Orizaba (Citlaltepetl)	5,610	18,406	Mexico
Mt. St Elias	5,489	18,009	U.S./Canada
Popocatépetl	5,452	17,887	Mexico
Mt. Foraker	5,304	17,402	U.S.
Iztaccíhuatl	5,230	17,159	Mexico
Mt. Lucania	5,226	17,146	Canada
Mt. King	5,173	16,972	Canada
Mt. Steele	5,073	16,644	Canada
Mt. Bona	5,005	16,421	U.S.
Mt. Blackburn	4,996	16,391	U.S.
Mt. Sanford	4,949	16,237	U.S.
Mt. Wood	4,842	15,886	Canada
Mt. Vancouver	4,785	15,699	Canada

LONGEST RIVERS

Name	km	miles	Feeds into
Mississippi-Missouri	5,971	3,710	Gulf of Mexico
Mackenzie	4,240	2,630	Arctic Ocean
Missouri	4,088	2,540	Mississippi
Mississippi	3,782	2,350	Gulf of Mexico
Yukon	3,185	1,980	Pacific Ocean
Rio Grande	3,030	1,880	Gulf of Mexico
Arkansas	2,340	1,450	Mississippi
Colorado	2,330	1,445	Pacific Ocean
Red	2,040	1,270	Mississippi
Columbia	1,950	1,210	Pacific Ocean
Saskatchewan	1,940	1,205	Lake Winnipeg
Snake	1,674	1,040	Columbia
Platte	1,594	990	Missouri
Ohio	1,579	981	Mississippi
Pecos	1,491	926	Rio Grande

LARGEST ISLANDS

Name	sq. km	sq. miles	Country
Baffin	508,000	196,100	Canada
Victoria	212,200	81,900	Canada
Ellesmere	212,000	81,800	Canada
Newfoundland	108,860	42,031	Canada
Banks	70,028	27,038	Canada
Devon	55,247	21,331	Canada
Axel Heiberg	43,178	16,671	Canada
Melville	42,149	16,274	Canada
Southampton	41,214	15,913	Canada
Prince of Wales	33,339	12,872	Canada
Vancouver	31,285	12,079	Canada
Somerset	24,786	9,570	Canada
Bathurst	16,042	6,194	Canada
Prince Patrick	15,848	6,119	Canada
King William	13,111	5,062	Canada

LARGEST LAKES

Name	sq. km	sq. miles	Country
Lake Superior	82,350	31,800	Canada/U.S.
Lake Huron	59,600	23,010	Canada/U.S.
Lake Michigan	58,000	22,400	U.S.
Great Bear Lake	31,800	12,280	Canada
Great Slave Lake	28,500	11,000	Canada
Lake Erie	25,700	9,900	Canada/U.S.
Lake Winnipeg	24,400	9,400	Canada
Lake Ontario	19,500	7,500	Canada/U.S.
Lake Athabasca	7,920	3,058	Canada
Lake Reindeer	6,330	2,444	Canada
Lake Winnipegosis	5,403	2,086	Canada
Lake Nettiling	5,051	1,950	Canada
Lake Nipigon	4,843	1,870	Canada
Lake Manitoba	4,706	1,817	Canada
Great Salt Lake	4,662	1,800	U.S.

NORTH AMERICAN RECORDS

See pages 18–19 for maps of Climate and Weather

Highest Temperature	°C	°F	Date
Death Valley, California	56.7	134	July 10, 1913

Lowest Temperature	°C	°F	Date
Snag, Yukon Territory	−63	−81.4	February 3, 1947

Highest Annual Rainfall	cm	inches	Date
Henderson Lake, British Columbia	650.2	256	1990

Lowest Annual Rainfall	cm	inches	Date
Batagues, Mexico	3	1.2	1990

Largest Volcanic Eruption	VEI*	Ash Dispersal	Date
Katmai, Alaska	6	120,000 sq. km (46,000 sq. mi)	1912

Deadliest Volcanic Eruption	VEI*	Deaths	Date
El Chichón, Mexico	5	2,000	1982

Largest Earthquake	Magnitude	Deaths	Date
Prince William Sound, Alaska	9.2	125	March 28, 1964

Most Snowfall (single season)	cm	inches	Date
Mt. Baker Ski Area, Washington	2,895.6	1,140	July 1998 – June 1999

Highest Wind Speed	km/h	mph	Date
Mt. Washington, New Hampshire	372	231	April 12, 1934

Largest Hailstone	Diameter	Circumference	Date
Aurora, Nebraska	17.8 cm (7 inches)	47.6 cm (18.75 inches)	June 22, 2003

Volcanic Explosivity Index

NORTH
AMERICAN
GEOGRAPHY

PHYSICAL GEOGRAPHY AND GEOLOGY

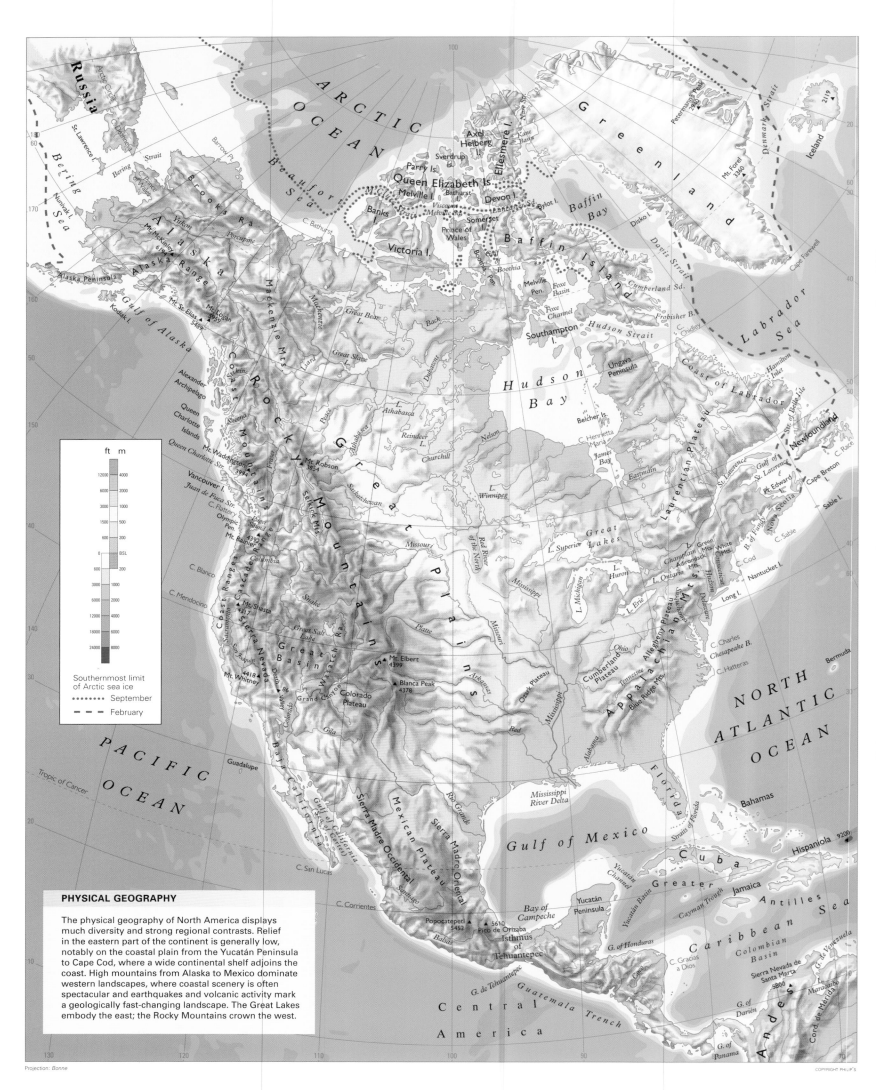

ft m

12000 — 4000
6000 — 2000
3000 — 1000
1500 — 500
600 — 200
0 — BSL
600 — 200
3000 — 1000
6000 — 2000
12000 — 4000
18000 — 6000
24000 — 8000

Southernmost limit
of Arctic sea ice
• • • • • • September
– – – – – February

ARCTIC OCEAN

PACIFIC OCEAN

NORTH ATLANTIC OCEAN

Gulf of Mexico

Caribbean Sea

PHYSICAL GEOGRAPHY

The physical geography of North America displays
much diversity and strong regional contrasts. Relief
in the eastern part of the continent is generally low,
notably on the coastal plain from the Yucatán Peninsula
to Cape Cod, where a wide continental shelf adjoins the
coast. High mountains from Alaska to Mexico dominate
western landscapes, where coastal scenery is often
spectacular and earthquakes and volcanic activity mark
a geologically fast-changing landscape. The Great Lakes
embody the east; the Rocky Mountains crown the west.

Projection: *Bonne*

COPYRIGHT PHILIP'S

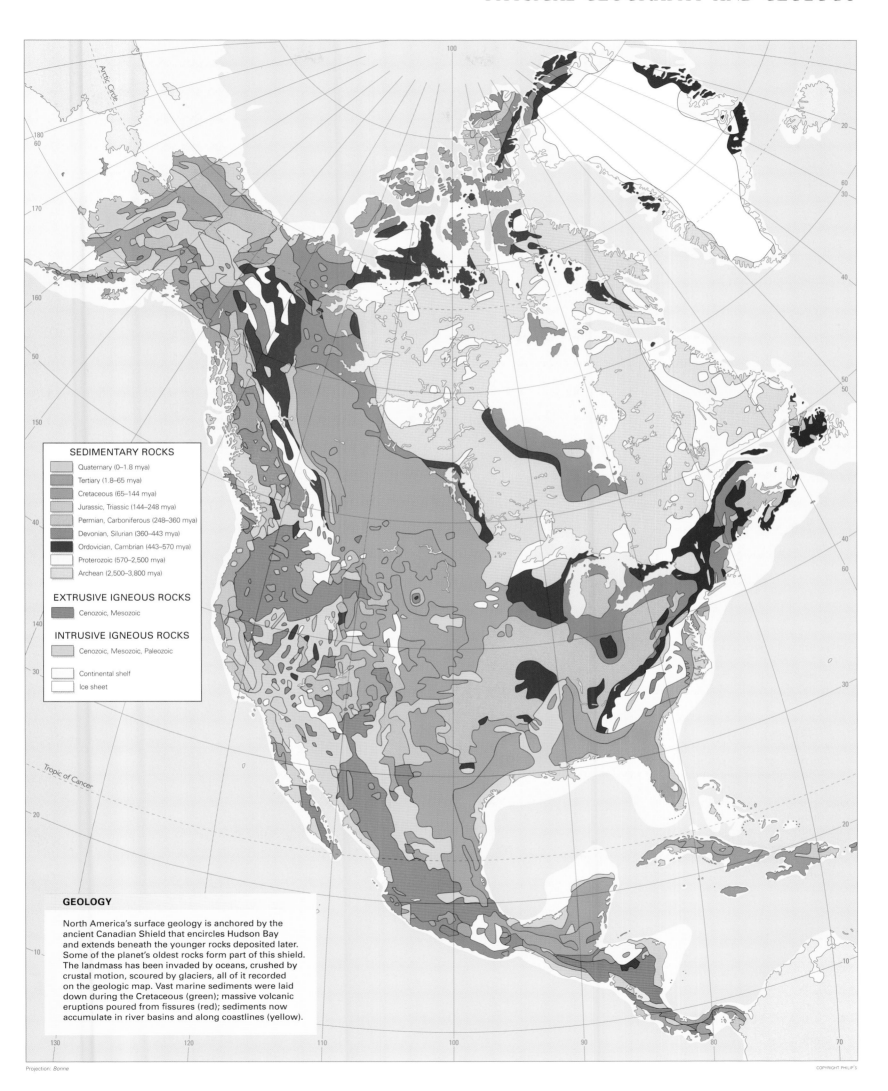

SEDIMENTARY ROCKS

Quaternary (0–1.8 mya)
Tertiary (1.8–65 mya)
Cretaceous (65–144 mya)
Jurassic, Triassic (144–248 mya)
Permian, Carboniferous (248–360 mya)
Devonian, Silurian (360–443 mya)
Ordovician, Cambrian (443–570 mya)
Proterozoic (570–2,500 mya)
Archean (2,500–3,800 mya)

EXTRUSIVE IGNEOUS ROCKS

Cenozoic, Mesozoic

INTRUSIVE IGNEOUS ROCKS

Cenozoic, Mesozoic, Paleozoic

Continental shelf
Ice sheet

GEOLOGY

North America's surface geology is anchored by the
ancient Canadian Shield that encircles Hudson Bay
and extends beneath the younger rocks deposited later.
Some of the planet's oldest rocks form part of this shield.
The landmass has been invaded by oceans, crushed by
crustal motion, scoured by glaciers, all of it recorded
on the geologic map. Vast marine sediments were laid
down during the Cretaceous (green); massive volcanic
eruptions poured from fissures (red); sediments now
accumulate in river basins and along coastlines (yellow).

Projection: *Bonne*

COPYRIGHT PHILIP'S

TECTONIC PROVINCES AND PHYSIOGRAPHY

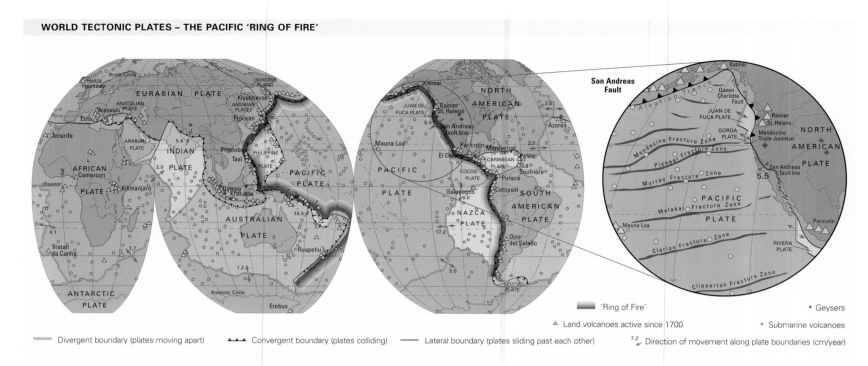

'Ring of Fire'

△ Land volcanoes active since 1700

• Geysers

○ Submarine volcanoes

——— Divergent boundary (plates moving apart)　　▲▲▲ Convergent boundary (plates colliding)　　——— Lateral boundary (plates sliding past each other)　　7.2↗ Direction of movement along plate boundaries (cm/year)

TECTONIC PROVINCES

The familiar outline of North America shown on atlas maps marks the current interface between land and surface water, but a substantial part of the landmass lies submerged during the current glacier-melting warm period. As this map indicates, approximately one-quarter of the continent lies under water today.

The ancient, crystalline core or *shield* of North America, shown in yellow on the adjacent map, extends far beyond its exposed, glacially-scoured limits. Younger sediments of the Interior Plains, creating the Great Plains and the Central Lowlands, and including glacial deposits laid down during the Pleistocene, cover much of it. The recent, Cenozoic sediments of the Coastal Plain facing the Atlantic Ocean and the Gulf of Mexico also form the ocean floor to the continental slope.

As the map of World Tectonic Plates (above) shows, the North American landmass rests on the North American tectonic plate, one of eight major, slow-moving lithospheric plates forming most of the Earth's crust (the remainder is made up by numerous smaller plates such as the Juan de Fuca and Gorda Plates off Washington and Oregon).

The eastern boundary of the North American tectonic plate is marked by the divergent Mid-Atlantic Ridge, where new rock emerges molten from below and where the North American and Eurasian/African plates are pulling apart.

On its western margin, the North American plate is converging with the Pacific Plate in a process called *subduction* where the continental plate overrides the heavier oceanic plate and pushes it downward, resulting in the mountainous, earthquake-prone and volcano-studded landscapes that extend from Alaska to Central America. The San Andreas Fault is a manifestation of this gigantic collision.

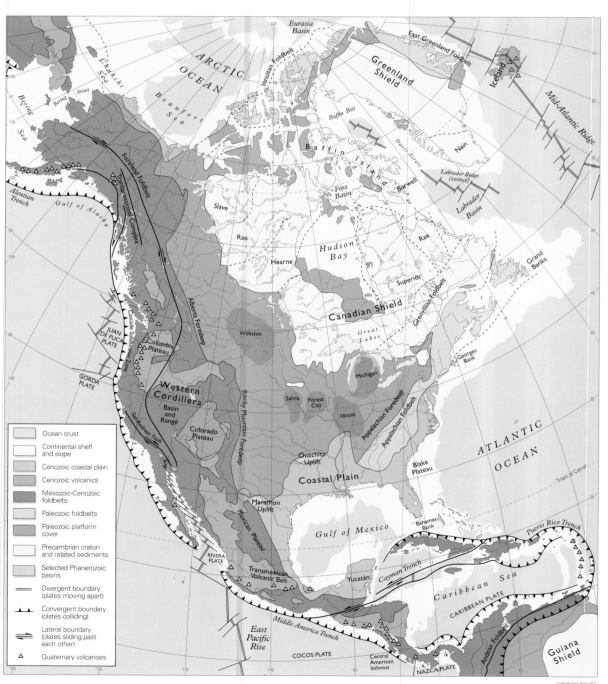

Ocean crust

Continental shelf and slope

Cenozoic coastal plain

Cenozoic volcanics

Mesozoic-Cenozoic foldbelts

Paleozoic foldbelts

Paleozoic platform cover

Precambrian craton and related sediments

Selected Phanerozoic basins

——— Divergent boundary (plates moving apart)

▲▲▲ Convergent boundary (plates colliding)

——— Lateral boundary (plates sliding past each other)

△ Quaternary volcanoes

COPYRIGHT PHILIP'S

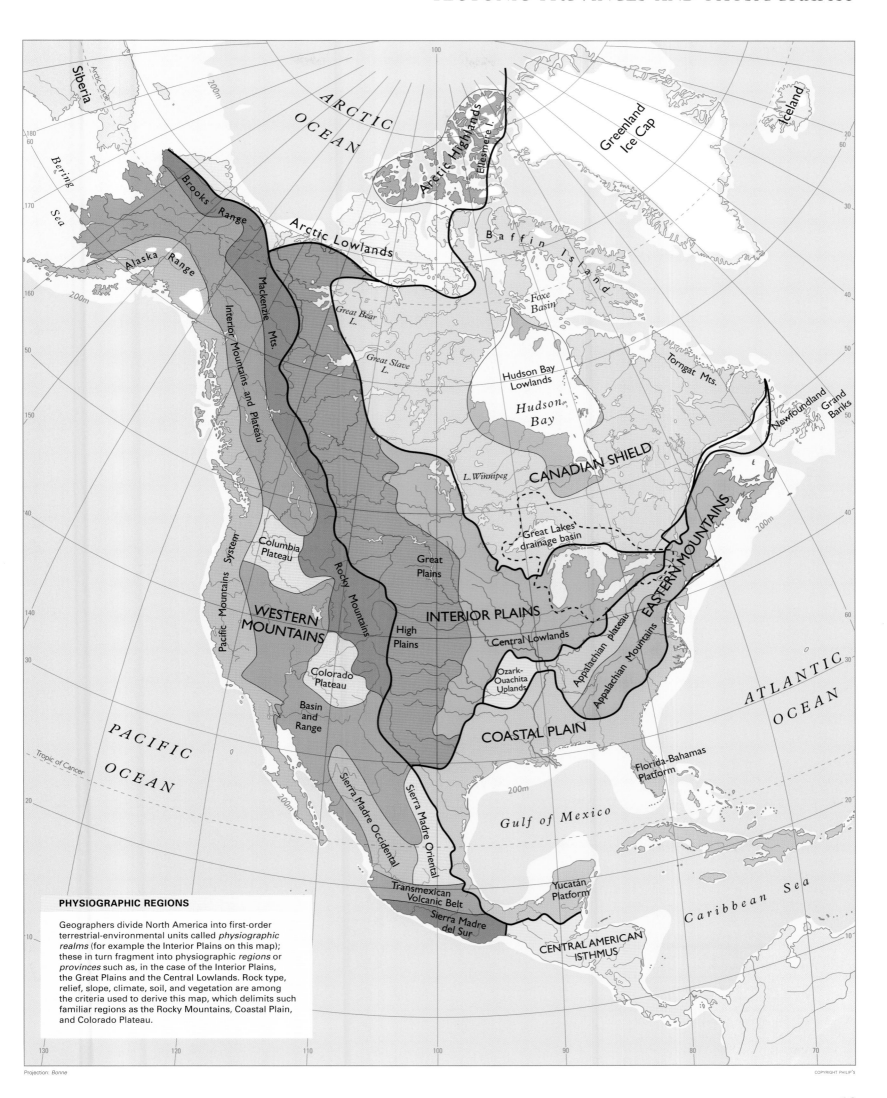

PHYSIOGRAPHIC REGIONS

Geographers divide North America into first-order
terrestrial-environmental units called *physiographic
realms* (for example the Interior Plains on this map);
these in turn fragment into physiographic *regions* or
provinces such as, in the case of the Interior Plains,
the Great Plains and the Central Lowlands. Rock type,
relief, slope, climate, soil, and vegetation are among
the criteria used to derive this map, which delimits such
familiar regions as the Rocky Mountains, Coastal Plain,
and Colorado Plateau.

Projection: Bonne

ENERGY AND MINERALS

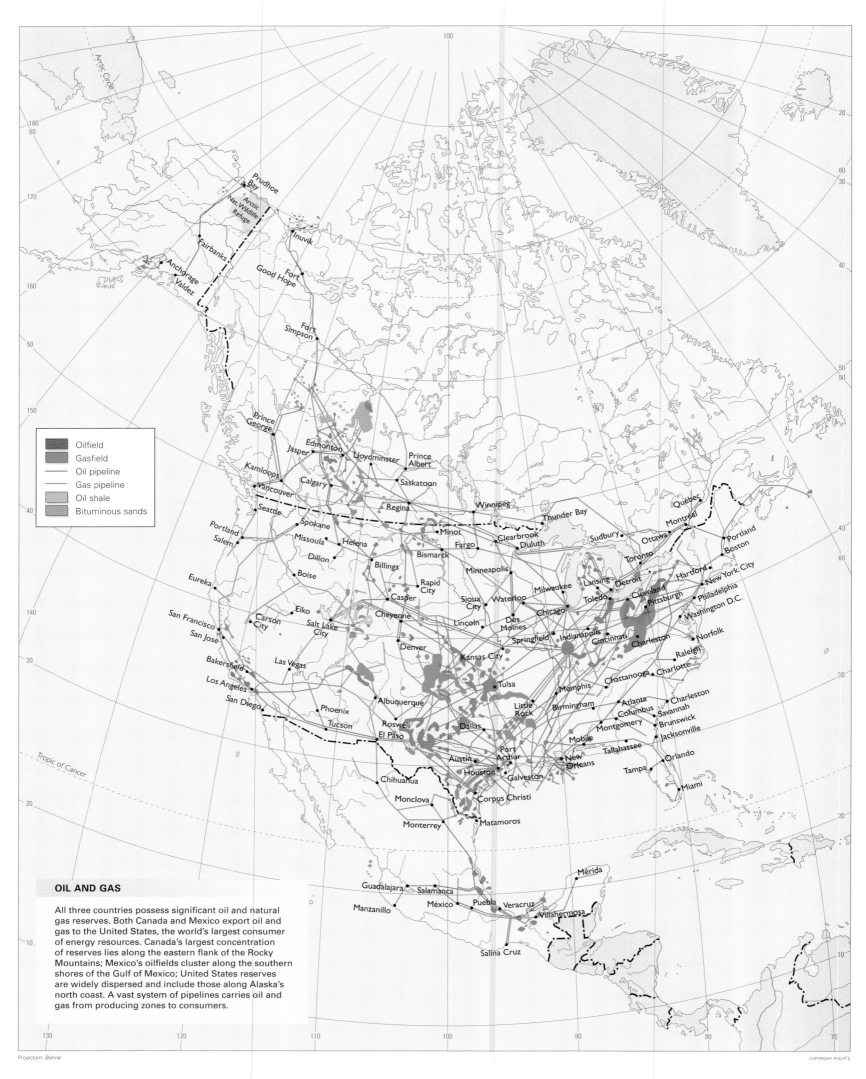

Prudhoe Bay
Arctic Nat. Wildlife Refuge
Inuvik
Fairbanks
Anchorage
Valdez
Good Hope
Fort Simpson
Prince George
Edmonton
Jasper
Lloydminster
Prince Albert
Kamloops
Calgary
Saskatoon
Vancouver
Regina
Winnipeg
Seattle
Thunder Bay
Quebec
Portland
Spokane
Minot
Clearbrook
Montreal
Salem
Missoula
Helena
Fargo
Duluth
Sudbury
Ottawa
Portland
Dillon
Bismarck
Toronto
Boston
Boise
Billings
Minneapolis
Milwaukee
Lansing
Detroit
Hartford
New York City
Eureka
Rapid City
Sioux City
Waterloo
Toledo
Cleveland
Pittsburgh
Philadelphia
Casper
Des Moines
Chicago
Indianapolis
Cincinnati
Washington D.C.
San Francisco
Carson City
Elko
Salt Lake City
Cheyenne
Lincoln
Springfield
Charleston
Norfolk
San Jose
Denver
Kansas City
Raleigh
Bakersfield
Las Vegas
Charlotte
Los Angeles
Tulsa
Memphis
Chattanooga
San Diego
Phoenix
Albuquerque
Little Rock
Birmingham
Atlanta
Columbus
Charleston
Savannah
Tucson
Roswell
Dallas
Montgomery
Brunswick
El Paso
Mobile
Tallahassee
Jacksonville
Austin
Port Arthur
New Orleans
Houston
Galveston
Tampa
Orlando
Chihuahua
Corpus Christi
Miami
Monclova
Monterrey
Matamoros
Mérida
Guadalajara
Salamanca
Manzanillo
México
Puebla
Veracruz
Villahermosa
Salina Cruz

Legend

- Oilfield
- Gasfield
- Oil pipeline
- Gas pipeline
- Oil shale
- Bituminous sands

OIL AND GAS

All three countries possess significant oil and natural gas reserves. Both Canada and Mexico export oil and gas to the United States, the world's largest consumer of energy resources. Canada's largest concentration of reserves lies along the eastern flank of the Rocky Mountains; Mexico's oilfields cluster along the southern shores of the Gulf of Mexico; United States reserves are widely dispersed and include those along Alaska's north coast. A vast system of pipelines carries oil and gas from producing zones to consumers.

Projection: Bonne

COPYRIGHT PHILIP'S

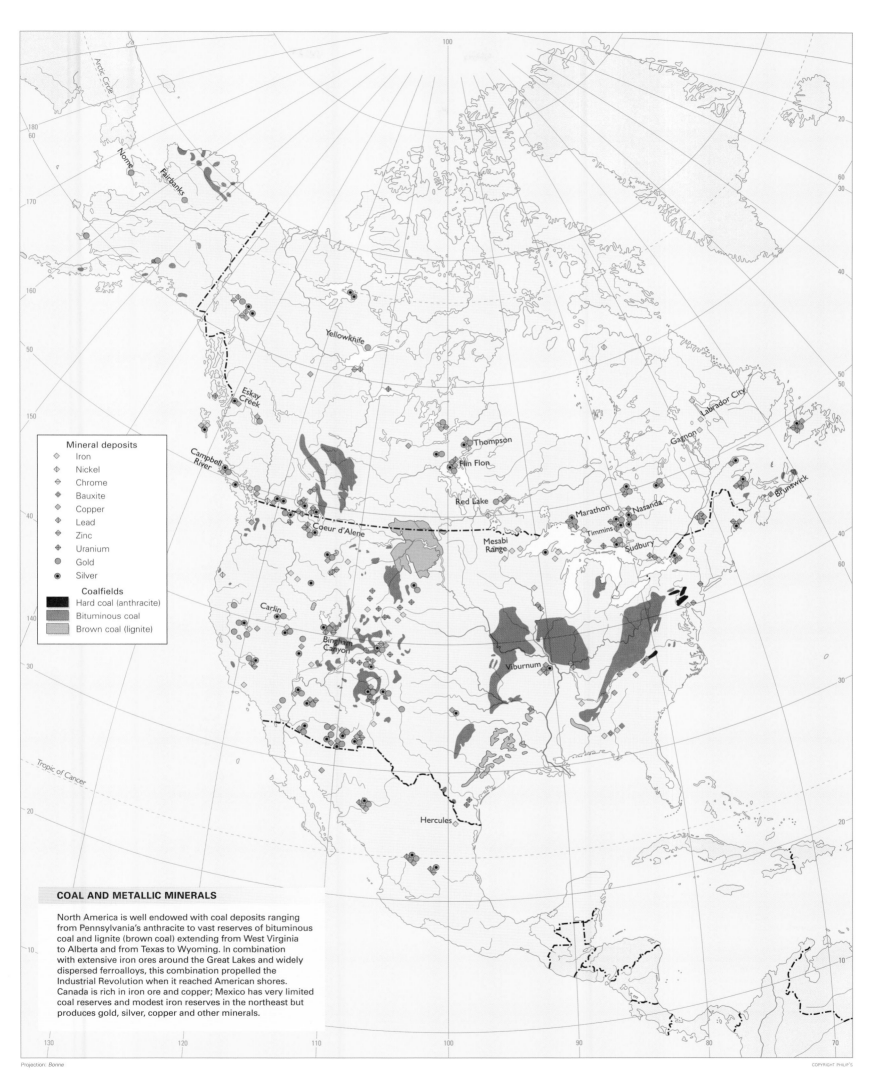

Mineral deposits
◇ Iron
◈ Nickel
◇ Chrome
◇ Bauxite
◇ Copper
◇ Lead
◇ Zinc
✦ Uranium
● Gold
◉ Silver

Coalfields
Hard coal (anthracite)
Bituminous coal
Brown coal (lignite)

COAL AND METALLIC MINERALS

North America is well endowed with coal deposits ranging
from Pennsylvania's anthracite to vast reserves of bituminous
coal and lignite (brown coal) extending from West Virginia
to Alberta and from Texas to Wyoming. In combination
with extensive iron ores around the Great Lakes and widely
dispersed ferroalloys, this combination propelled the
Industrial Revolution when it reached American shores.
Canada is rich in iron ore and copper; Mexico has very limited
coal reserves and modest iron reserves in the northeast but
produces gold, silver, copper and other minerals.

Projection: *Bonne*

COPYRIGHT PHILIP'S

SURFACE WATER AND DRAINAGE

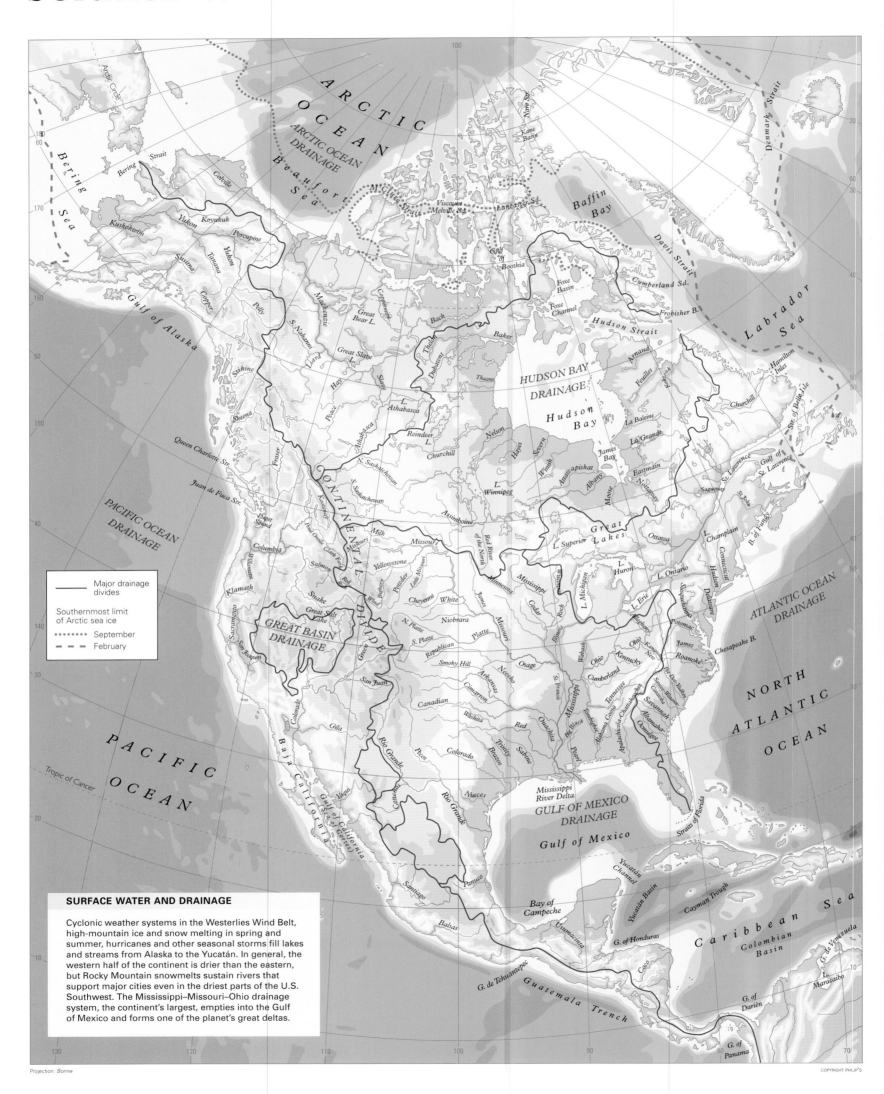

ARCTIC OCEAN

ARCTIC OCEAN DRAINAGE

Bering Strait

Bering Sea

Beaufort Sea

Gulf of Alaska

PACIFIC OCEAN DRAINAGE

Queen Charlotte Str.

Juan de Fuca Str.

PACIFIC OCEAN

Tropic of Cancer

Baja California

Gulf of California (Sea of Cortés)

Kuskokwim
Yukon
Koyukuk
Porcupine
Yukon
Tanana
Susitna
Copper
S. Nahanni
Liard
Hay
Peace
Pelly
Stikine
Skeena
Fraser
Kootenay
Pend Oreille
Clark Fork
Puget Sound
Columbia
Willamette
Klamath
Salmon
Snake
Sacramento
San Joaquin
Gila
Colorado
Yaqui
Santiago
Balsas

Mackenzie
Great Bear L.
Great Slave L.
Slave
Athabasca
L. Athabasca
Reindeer L.
N. Saskatchewan
S. Saskatchewan
CopPermine
Back
Thelon
Dubawnt
Thaane
Baker
Churchill
Nelson
L. Winnipeg
Assiniboine
Milk
Missouri
Red River of the North
Yellowstone
Powder
Bighorn
Wind
Green
Great Salt Lake
GREAT BASIN DRAINAGE
CONTINENTAL DIVIDE
Cheyenne
White
Niobrara
N. Platte
S. Platte
Republican
Smoky Hill
Canadian
Cimarron
Wichita
Red
Pecos
Rio Grande
Colorado
Nueces
Conchos
Rio Grande
Pánuco
Usumacinta
G. de Tehuantepec

M'Clure Strait
Viscount Melville Sd.
Lancaster Sd.
Gulf of Boothia
Foxe Basin
Foxe Channel
Hudson Strait
Baffin Bay
Cumberland Sd.
Frobisher B.
Kane Basin
New Str.
Davis Strait
Denmark Strait

HUDSON BAY DRAINAGE

Hudson Bay

James Bay
Hayes
Severn
Winisk
Attawapiskat
Albany
Moose
Nottaway
Eastmain
La Baleine
La Grande
Arnaud
Feuilles
Koksoak
Churchill
Saguenay
St. John
St. Lawrence
Gulf of St. Lawrence
Ottawa
L. Champlain
Connecticut
Hudson
Delaware
Susquehanna
Potomac
Chesapeake B.
James
Roanoke
New
Kanawha
Kentucky
Cumberland
Tennessee
Ohio
Wabash
Illinois
Rock
Cedar
Minnesota
Mississippi
Iowa
Des Moines
St. Francis
Arkansas
Neosho
Osage
Canadian
Ouachita
Big Black
Yazoo
Mississippi
Alabama
Coosa
Tallapoosa
Chattahoochee
Apalachicola
Flint
Savannah
Altamaha
Oconee
Ocmulgee
Pearl
Sabine
Trinity
Brazos

Great Lakes
L. Superior
L. Michigan
L. Huron
L. Erie
L. Ontario

ATLANTIC OCEAN DRAINAGE

NORTH ATLANTIC OCEAN

B. of Fundy

Labrador Sea
Hamilton Inlet
Str. of Belle Isle

GULF OF MEXICO DRAINAGE

Mississippi River Delta

Gulf of Mexico

Straits of Florida

Bay of Campeche

Yucatán Channel

Yucatán Basin

Cayman Trough

Caribbean Sea

Colombian Basin

G. de Venezuela

L. Maracaibo

G. of Darién

G. of Panama

G. of Honduras

Coco

Guatemala Trench

Legend

	Major drainage divides
	Southernmost limit of Arctic sea ice
·······	September
– – –	February

Projection: Bonne

SURFACE WATER AND DRAINAGE

Cyclonic weather systems in the Westerlies Wind Belt, high-mountain ice and snow melting in spring and summer, hurricanes and other seasonal storms fill lakes and streams from Alaska to the Yucatán. In general, the western half of the continent is drier than the eastern, but Rocky Mountain snowmelts sustain rivers that support major cities even in the driest parts of the U.S. Southwest. The Mississippi–Missouri–Ohio drainage system, the continent's largest, empties into the Gulf of Mexico and forms one of the planet's great deltas.

GROUNDWATER

Rivers contain but a small fraction (0.03 percent) of all the planet's freshwater. Ten times as much is held in lakes, but by far the greatest proportion (about 75 percent) is locked in glaciers. Most of what remains is hidden beneath the ground as groundwater and comes to the surface by natural processes in springs or by artificial means through wells.

Rainwater or meltwater percolating downward under the influence of gravity saturates the pores between grains in sedimentary rock, creating subsurface reservoirs or aquifers that vary widely in extent and volume. Permanent aquifers are replenished by nature, but they are subject to overuse and depletion.

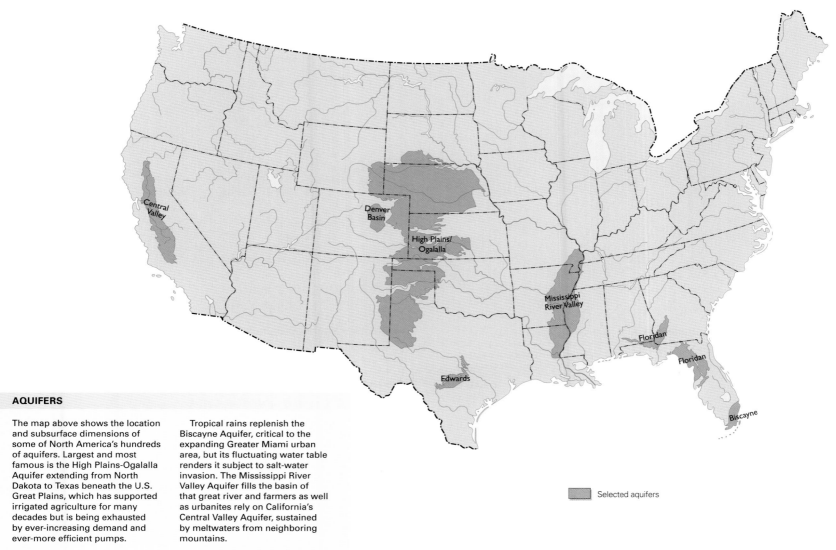

AQUIFERS

The map above shows the location and subsurface dimensions of some of North America's hundreds of aquifers. Largest and most famous is the High Plains-Ogalalla Aquifer extending from North Dakota to Texas beneath the U.S. Great Plains, which has supported irrigated agriculture for many decades but is being exhausted by ever-increasing demand and ever-more efficient pumps.

Tropical rains replenish the Biscayne Aquifer, critical to the expanding Greater Miami urban area, but its fluctuating water table renders it subject to salt-water invasion. The Mississippi River Valley Aquifer fills the basin of that great river and farmers as well as urbanites rely on California's Central Valley Aquifer, sustained by meltwaters from neighboring mountains.

Selected aquifers

WATER SUPPLY AND SUBSIDENCE IN MEXICO CITY

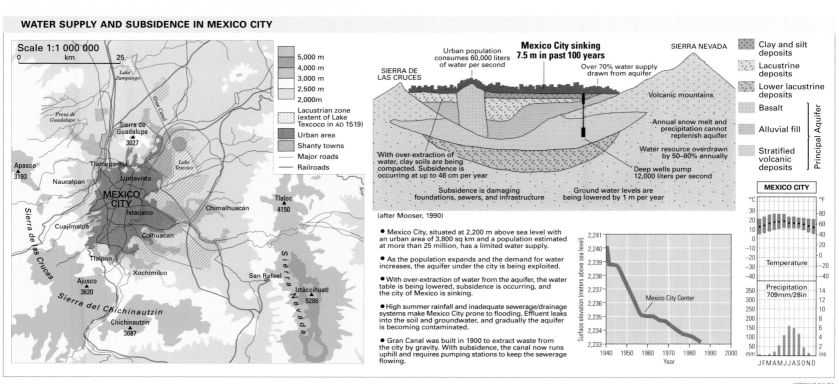

(after Mooser, 1990)

- Mexico City, situated at 2,200 m above sea level with an urban area of 3,800 sq km and a population estimated at more than 25 million, has a limited water supply.

- As the population expands and the demand for water increases, the aquifer under the city is being exploited.

- With over-extraction of water from the aquifer, the water table is being lowered, subsidence is occurring, and the city of Mexico is sinking.

- High summer rainfall and inadequate sewerage/drainage systems make Mexico City prone to flooding. Effluent leaks into the soil and groundwater, and gradually the aquifer is becoming contaminated.

- Gran Canal was built in 1900 to extract waste from the city by gravity. With subsidence, the canal now runs uphill and requires pumping stations to keep the sewerage flowing.

COPYRIGHT PHILIP'S

17

CLIMATE AND WEATHER

ATLANTIC HURRICANES

Typical hurricane tracks

THE 10 COSTLIEST U.S. HURRICANES

Rank	Hurricane	Year	Damage (US$ million)
1	Katrina (AL, LA, MS)	2005	200,000
2	Andrew (SE FL, SE LA)	1992	34,955
3	Charley (FL)	2004	15,000
4	Hugo (SC)	1989	9,740
5	Agnes (FL, NE USA)	1972	8,602
6	Betsy (SE FL, SE LA)	1965	8,517
7	Camille (MS, SE LA, VA)	1969	6,992
8	Diane (NE USA)	1955	5,541
9	Frederic (AL, MS)	1979	4,965
10	Floyd (NC & NE USA)	1999	4,667

Hurricanes in the Atlantic zone tend to track westward in the low-latitude Trade Wind Belt and then recurve northward and eventually northeastward as they come under the influence of the westerly winds of the middle latitudes. This map underscores the vulnerability of the U.S. southeast coast to hurricane impacts, as well as the Caribbean region and the entire rim of the Gulf of Mexico. Although some storm systems survive as far north as Newfoundland, they tend to weaken (and wind speeds decline) as they reach cooler environs.

TORNADO ZONES

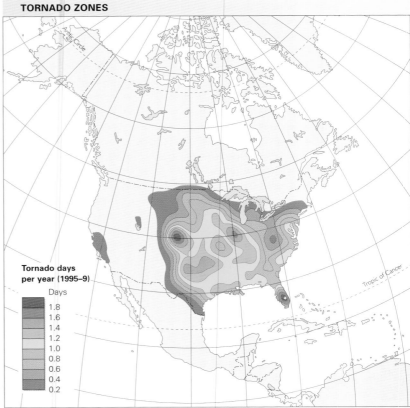

Tornado days per year (1995–9)

Days
1.8
1.6
1.4
1.2
1.0
0.8
0.6
0.4
0.2

MONTHLY TORNADO OCCURRENCES

Three-year average, 2001–3

January	4	July	94
February	16	August	78
March	41	September	73
April	127	October	87
May	222	November	105
June	133	December	61
		Total	**1,039**

The "Tri-State Tornado" on March 18, 1925 – early in the season – swept across Missouri, Illinois, and Indiana and killed 689 persons in 45 minutes.

No landmass on Earth suffers as severely from tornado impacts as does North America, where topography and weather systems combine to create the conditions favorable to tornado development. Clashing airmasses and heat-generated, violent thunderstorms produce twisting funnel clouds 330–1,650 ft (100–500 meters) in diameter around pressure centers that may be 100–200 millibars below the surrounding air. This triggers winds of 100–300 mph (150–450 kph) with devastating effect on the surface they traverse.

AIR MASSES AND WEATHER MAKERS

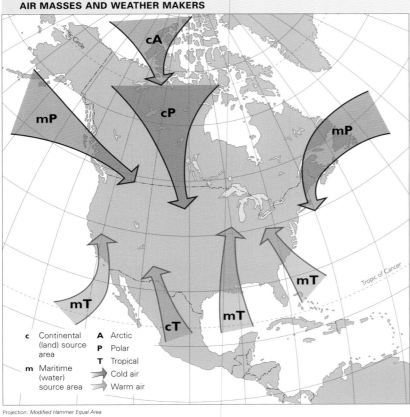

cA

mP

cP

mP

mT

mT

cT

mT

c Continental (land) source area

m Maritime (water) source area

A Arctic
P Polar
T Tropical

→ Cold air
→ Warm air

Projection: *Modified Hammer Equal Area*

Weather conditions in all parts of the world result from a combination of factors among which the properties of air masses are critical. When large parcels of air (1,500 km across or more) remain relatively stationary for several days over cold, warm, moist, or dry surface environments, they take on the characteristics of these surfaces. Then, when they are steered away from their source regions by the general atmospheric circulation, they carry those conditions to other locales, where they form powerful weather makers. In this way, dry arctic cold penetrates the heart of North America in winter, warm tropical air reaches Canada during the summer, and rain from moist Pacific air drenches the slopes of British Columbia, Washington, and Oregon.

The key properties of air masses are signaled by a two-letter acronym that reflects their continental (c) or their maritime (m) sources and, in the case of North America, their Arctic (A), polar (P), or tropical (T) origins. For example, "cT" air, dry and hot, originates in northern Mexico and is drawn into the U.S. Southwest, and "mP" air, comparatively moist but cold, flows from beyond the Labrador Sea into the northeastern corner of the continent.

When air masses move, they bring the weather conditions of their source areas to distant regions, so that frigid arctic conditions may prevail for several successive winter days in the U.S. Midwest while oppressive, humid summer heat can blanket Canada north of the Great Lakes in summer.

When air masses with strongly contrasting properties collide, their frontal contact can generate strong storms punctuated by dangerous tornadoes. In North America, this hazard is amplified by the continent's topography: nothing interferes with the movement of air masses between the Rocky Mountains to the west and the Appalachians to the east, creating an unmatched arena of air-mass collision and associated storms whose cumulative cost, in lives and damage, is incalculable.

The maps and charts on page 19 display the contrasting continental January and July temperatures and climographs for selected stations across the realm. The annual precipitation map (bottom left) reveals the rain-shadow effect of the western mountains, where orographic rainfall drenches western slopes, and arid conditions on the mountains' lee side.

The map of climatic regions (bottom right) summarizes the prevailing conditions into ten regional categories. Deserts and highlands prevail in the west, humid and warm-summer conditions in the southeast, and cold-winter conditions from the U.S. Midwest northward. Polar environments in the far north, a dry-summer Mediterranean regime along the west coast, and equatorial conditions in eastern Mexico complete this variable regional picture. In the United States, only the tip of Florida is truly tropical.

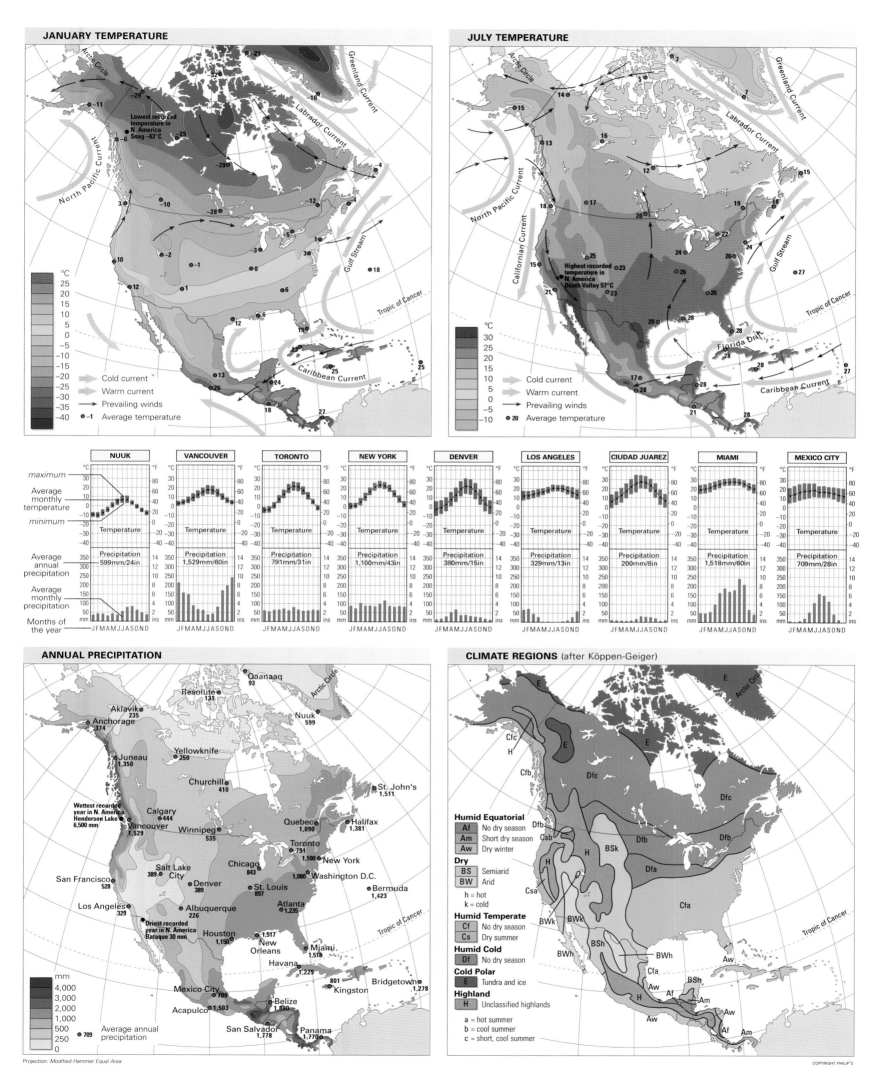

JANUARY TEMPERATURE

°C
25
20
15
10
5
0
–5
–10
–15
–20
–25
–30
–35
–40

Cold current
Warm current
Prevailing winds
–1 Average temperature

Lowest recorded temperature in N. America Snag –63°C

JULY TEMPERATURE

°C
30
25
20
15
10
5
0
–5
–10

Cold current
Warm current
Prevailing winds
20 Average temperature

Highest recorded temperature in N. America Death Valley 57°C

Climate graphs

	NUUK	VANCOUVER	TORONTO	NEW YORK	DENVER	LOS ANGELES	CIUDAD JUAREZ	MIAMI	MEXICO CITY

maximum
Average monthly temperature
minimum
Average annual precipitation
Average monthly precipitation
Months of the year

Precipitation 599mm/24in — Precipitation 1,529mm/60in — Precipitation 791mm/31in — Precipitation 1,100mm/43in — Precipitation 380mm/15in — Precipitation 329mm/13in — Precipitation 200mm/8in — Precipitation 1,518mm/60in — Precipitation 709mm/28in

ANNUAL PRECIPITATION

Qaanaaq 93
Resolute 131
Aklavik 235
Anchorage 374
Nuuk 599
Juneau 1,350
Yellowknife 250
Churchill 410
St. John's 1,511
Wettest recorded year in N. America Henderson Lake 6,500 mm
Calgary 444
Vancouver 1,529
Winnipeg 535
Quebec 1,090
Halifax 1,381
Toronto 791
Salt Lake City 389
Chicago 843
New York 1,080
Washington D.C.
San Francisco 528
Denver 389
St. Louis 897
Bermuda 1,423
Los Angeles 329
Albuquerque 226
Atlanta 1,235
Driest recorded year in N. America Bataque 30 mm
Houston 1,150
New Orleans 1,517
Miami 1,518
Havana 1,225
Mexico City 709
Belize 1,890
Kingston 801
Bridgetown 1,278
Acapulco 1,503
San Salvador 1,778
Panama 1,770

mm
4,000
3,000
2,000
1,000
500
250
0
709 Average annual precipitation

Projection: Modified Hammer Equal Area

CLIMATE REGIONS (after Köppen-Geiger)

Humid Equatorial
Af No dry season
Am Short dry season
Aw Dry winter

Dry
BS Semiarid
BW Arid
h = hot
k = cold

Humid Temperate
Cf No dry season
Cs Dry summer

Humid Cold
Df No dry season

Cold Polar
E Tundra and ice

Highland
H Unclassified highlands

a = hot summer
b = cool summer
c = short, cool summer

COPYRIGHT PHILIP'S

SOIL AND VEGETATION

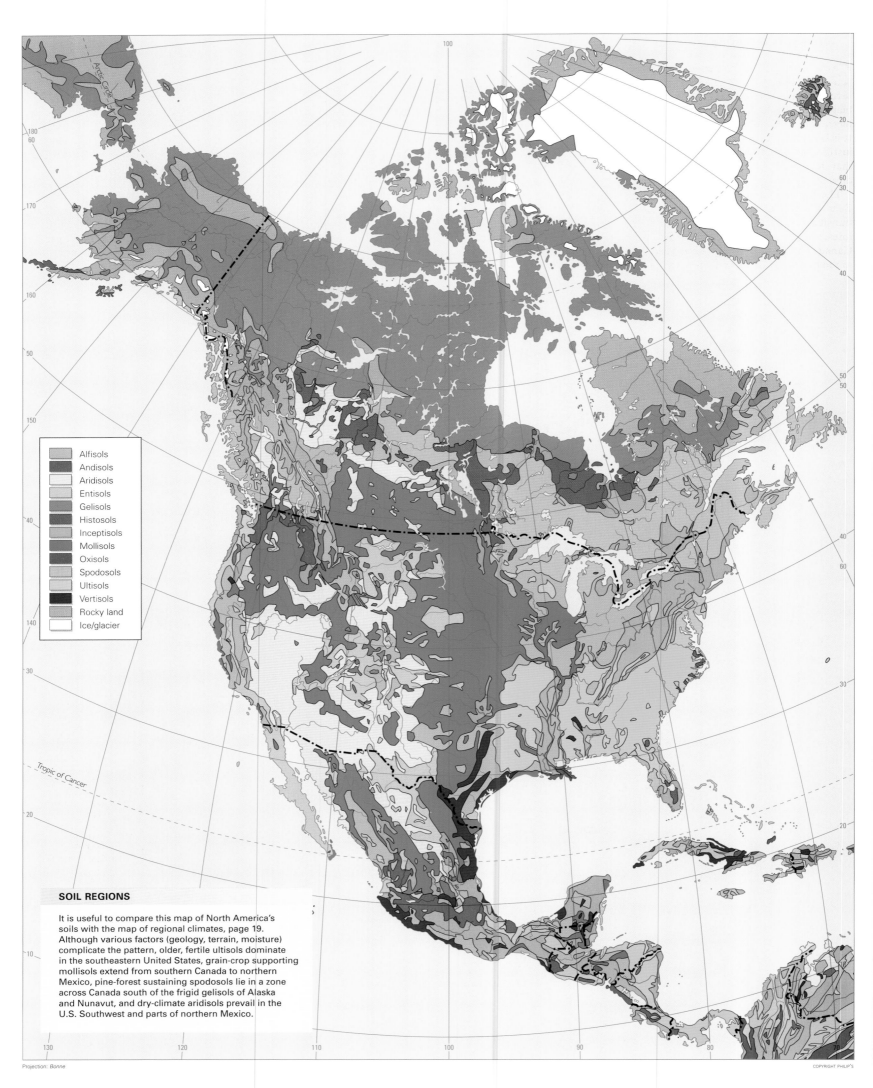

Alfisols
Andisols
Aridisols
Entisols
Gelisols
Histosols
Inceptisols
Mollisols
Oxisols
Spodosols
Ultisols
Vertisols
Rocky land
Ice/glacier

SOIL REGIONS

It is useful to compare this map of North America's
soils with the map of regional climates, page 19.
Although various factors (geology, terrain, moisture)
complicate the pattern, older, fertile ultisols dominate
in the southeastern United States, grain-crop supporting
mollisols extend from southern Canada to northern
Mexico, pine-forest sustaining spodosols lie in a zone
across Canada south of the frigid gelisols of Alaska
and Nunavut, and dry-climate aridisols prevail in the
U.S. Southwest and parts of northern Mexico.

Projection: Bonne

COPYRIGHT PHILIP'S

VEGETATION REGIONS OF NORTH AMERICA

Generalizing vegetation spatially is problematic, and botanists and geographers have devised several schemes to represent the broadest assemblages of plants in North America. The map on this page, therefore, is only one such approximation. It is based on the notion of the *biome*, the broadest justifiable assemblage of plants (and animals) that forms an ecological unit of subcontinental dimensions.

The lines on the map, however, do not represent clear breaks on the ground. They reflect broad transition zones. The taiga (northern coniferous forest) that extends from Newfoundland across Canada to Alaska thins out as it yields southward to the mixed deciduous forests of the U.S. Midwest and Northeast and to the grasslands of the central plains. To the north the taiga becomes patchy, its trees stunted as it surrenders to the Arctic tundra.

In the south, Mexico's tropical forests flank Pacific and Gulf shores to a latitude close to the Tropic of Cancer, but toward the interior, rising elevation influences the pattern and temperate coniferous forests dominate. Deserts and highland biomes dominate northern Mexico, although the grasslands of the interior plains reach across the U.S. border in the northwest.

In the eastern United States, the mixed temperate deciduous forests of the coastal plain yield to the oak-pine forests of the Appalachians; in the west, the forests and alpine assemblages of the Rocky Mountains separate the grasses of the interior Great Plains from the diverse biomes fronting the Pacific Ocean.

The Pacific Coastal-Cascadian forests extend from Alaska to northern California, where the distinctive Mediterranean biome (grasslands, chaparral, and woodlands) prevails. Toward the interior the forests of the Sierra Nevada flank this biome, and to the south the Mojave and Sonoran Deserts dominate.

The biome mapped as the Central Prairies and Plains can be subdivided on the basis of the height of its grasses. In general, tall-grass prairie prevails in the east of this region, and short-grass prairie in the drier west.

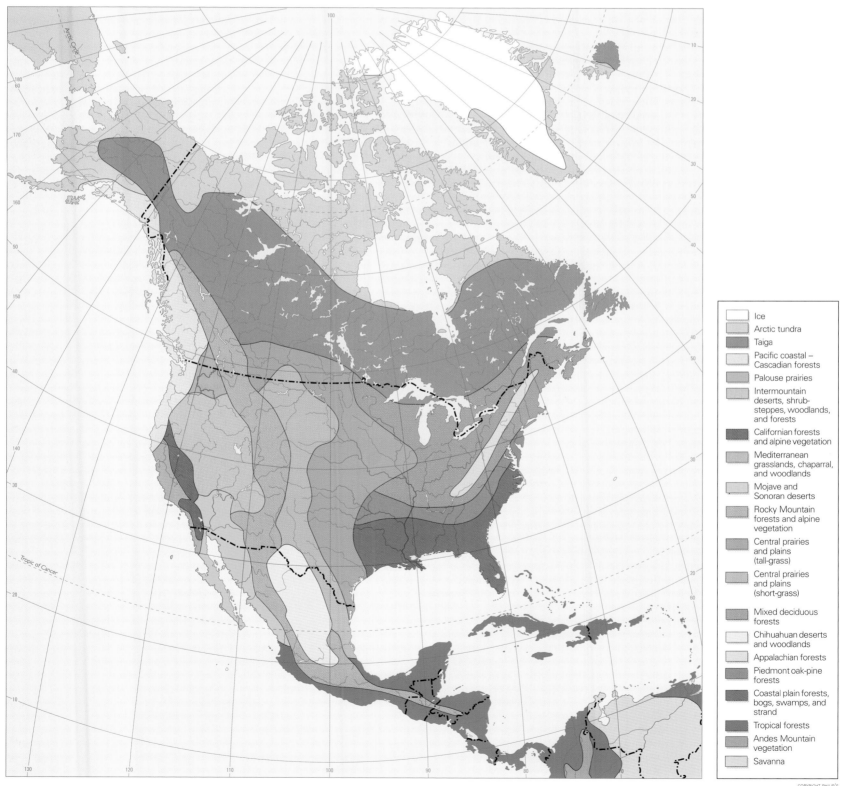

Ice
Arctic tundra
Taiga
Pacific coastal – Cascadian forests
Palouse prairies
Intermountain deserts, shrub-steppes, woodlands, and forests
Californian forests and alpine vegetation
Mediterranean grasslands, chaparral, and woodlands
Mojave and Sonoran deserts
Rocky Mountain forests and alpine vegetation
Central prairies and plains (tall-grass)
Central prairies and plains (short-grass)
Mixed deciduous forests
Chihuahuan deserts and woodlands
Appalachian forests
Piedmont oak-pine forests
Coastal plain forests, bogs, swamps, and strand
Tropical forests
Andes Mountain vegetation
Savanna

COPYRIGHT PHILIP'S

PLEISTOCENE LAND COVER AND GLACIATION

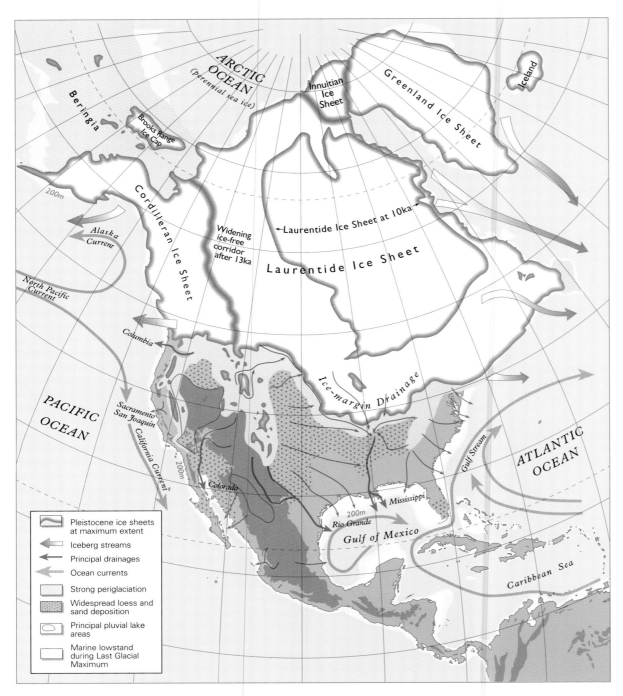

PLEISTOCENE LAND COVER

PLEISTOCENE LAND COVER

Planet Earth has been subject to the vagaries of rapidly changing environmental conditions throughout its 4,650-million-year existence. Long periods of global warmth, ample moisture, luxuriant vegetation, and exuberant animal life were abrogated by sudden declines in temperature, spreading droughts, and floral and faunal dislocation accompanied by mass extinctions. When an ice age commences, glacial ice forms over ever-larger areas in high latitudes, permanent ice develops on high mountains in all latitudes, oceans cool, sea level drops, and precipitation declines in many parts of the world. The process can be quite sudden, forcing plant life to shift to lower latitudes and lesser altitudes and animals to move to new ranges and niches.

Ice ages last for tens of millions of years, but they are not uniformly or continuously frigid. Extremely cold periods or glaciations, when ice advances from polar zones and mountaintops, are interrupted by warmer interglacials, when the ice recedes and life spreads poleward again. Glaciations tend to be much longer than full-scale interglacials, but the short warm spells occur even during glacial times.

The Earth is experiencing an ice age today, the Late Cenozoic Ice Age. The Antarctic ice sheet began to form about 35 million years ago (mya); high-elevation glaciers appeared some 23 mya, North Polar ice became permanent around 12 mya, and global cooling continued until, 1.8 mya, the Pleistocene epoch brought the conditions that prevail today.

The Pleistocene has been marked by a series of lengthy glaciations, each lasting over 100,000 years and marked by comparatively brief mild spells, separated by interglacials lasting 10,000 years or longer. The previous interglacial, the Eemian, ended about 120,000 years ago and produced temperatures even warmer

---

GREAT LAKES FORMATION

The continental glaciers that advanced and receded several times during the Pleistocene epoch repeatedly transformed the landscape of the northern and central parts of North America. Eroding as they went, they picked up vast amounts of bedrock, crushed it into particles ranging from boulders to silt, and carried it hundreds of kilometers from its source. In the process, the sediment-laden ice moved into pre-existing stream valleys, widening and deepening them. Eventually the melting and receding glaciers dropped their sedimentary loads, burying the

bedrock below and leaving ridges called *terminal moraines* where their forward motion stopped.

When such moraines lay astride glacier-enlarged valleys and basins, the dammed-up meltwater formed lakes among which the five North American Great Lakes are the most extensive. The maps below show the approximate position of the ice at two stages during the recession, approximately 13,000 and 10,000 years ago. As the ice receded, the water bodies expanded, and for a time ancient

Lake Algonquin encompassed present-day Lake Michigan as well as a vast Lake Huron. Ancient Lake Iroquois, the future Lake Ontario, drained via the Hudson River into the Atlantic.

Just after the ice had melted away completely, in the early Holocene, ancient Lake Nipissing drained via the Ottawa River into the St. Lawrence River. The Great Lakes will continue to change in response to human activity, crustal rebound following the disappearance of the ice, and climate variation.

Glacial retreat (Woodfordian substage)

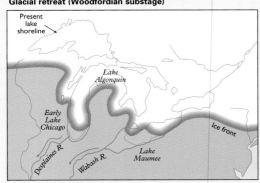

Glacial retreat (Post-Valderan)

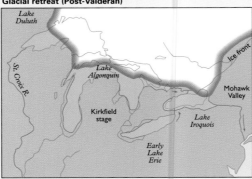

Post-Glacial Great Lakes

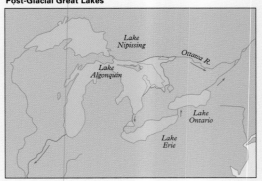

than those of today. The Eemian inter-glacial was followed by the Wisconsinan glaciation, when great ice sheets covered the Midwest and pushed as far south as the Ohio River valley. About 18,000 years ago, global warming began to melt the Wisconsinan's glaciers, and after a brief return to frigid temperatures the current interglacial – the Holocene – began approximately 10,000 years ago.

What was North America like when the Pleistocene ice sheets spread over the northern one-third of the continent? Reconstructing Pleistocene-glacial environments is a complicated process, and the map on this page is but an approximation of what may have happened (*see right*). In the low-relief east, a zone of tundra vegetation adjoined the ice. To the west, in the mountains and along the cold Pacific shores, desert, semidesert, and steppe prevailed because glaciation causes aridity as well as frigidity. The spruce forests of present-day Canada migrated south to the Appalachians (today's Blue Ridge forests are remnants of that shift)

and into the Mississippi Valley, thinning out westward and yielding to arid steppe in the southern Great Plains. Deciduous forests stood in Florida and along the Gulf coast to the west. Pine forests covered the Southwest and parts of present-day Mexico; savanna vegetation extended from the Yucatán Peninsula to Costa Rica. The only area of tropical forest to survive on the landmass was in Panama.

This process has occurred numerous times during the Pleistocene's 1.8 million years, and it is likely to take place again. But the end of the Holocene will be sharply different from the end of the Eemian interglacial, when the Earth had a minuscule human population and North America had none at all. Today the planet has 6.4 billion inhabitants and North America's three most populous countries count 430 million, their activities affecting atmosphere and oceans and playing a role in modifying climate. Imagine the dislocation even a partial return to the conditions reflected by the map at right would cause!

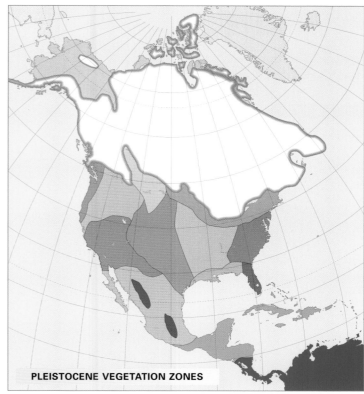

PLEISTOCENE VEGETATION ZONES

Ice	
Polar desert	
Tundra	
Desert	
Semidesert	
Dry steppe	
Open spruce woodland	
Spruce forest	
Pine woodland and semidesert mosaic	
Woodland	
Oak scrub	
Mixed forest	
Savanna	
Tropical forest	

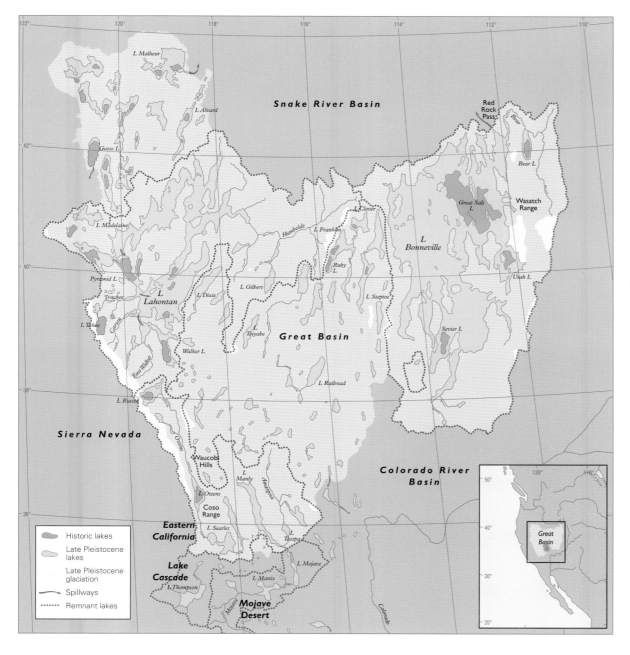

Historic lakes
Late Pleistocene lakes
Late Pleistocene glaciation
Spillways
Remnant lakes

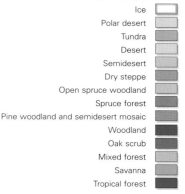

THE PLUVIAL LAKES

The continental glaciers, as the map on this page shows, never reached Utah, Nevada, Oregon, or California. But even there the glacial episodes had far-reaching effects. As the climate map on page 19 shows, much of the U.S. Southwest and Far West is arid today. But during the glaciations, precipitation in these areas was substantial, and more than 100 lakes, known as pluvial lakes, formed as a result.

The remnant of the largest of these, Lake Bonneville, still survives as the Great Salt Lake in Utah. Glacial Lake Bonneville at one stage was approximately as large as Lake Michigan is today. It reached a maximum depth of 300 meters and overflowed northward through Idaho into the Snake River and hence into the Columbia River and the Pacific Ocean.

Climate change during and following deglaciation desiccated the area, however, lake levels dropped, and the salinity of the water increased as rainfall declined. The dimensions of former Lake Bonneville, and the other pluvial lakes of the region, can be deduced from the shoreline terraces they left behind, visible on the slopes of the mountains that encircled them. Today, water remains in only a few basins of the once-plentiful pluvial lakes.

INDIGENOUS PEOPLES

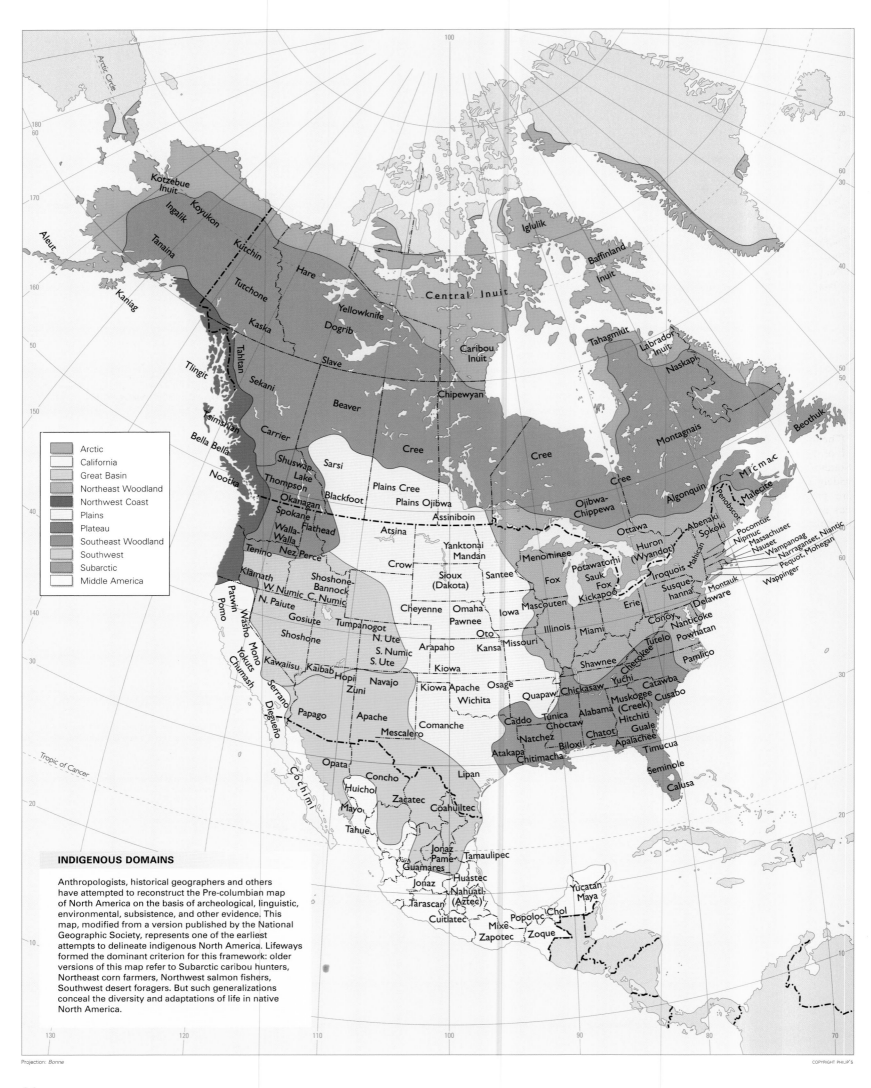

Legend:
- Arctic
- California
- Great Basin
- Northeast Woodland
- Northwest Coast
- Plains
- Plateau
- Southeast Woodland
- Southwest
- Subarctic
- Middle America

INDIGENOUS DOMAINS

Anthropologists, historical geographers and others have attempted to reconstruct the Pre-columbian map of North America on the basis of archeological, linguistic, environmental, subsistence, and other evidence. This map, modified from a version published by the National Geographic Society, represents one of the earliest attempts to delineate indigenous North America. Lifeways formed the dominant criterion for this framework: older versions of this map refer to Subarctic caribou hunters, Northeast corn farmers, Northwest salmon fishers, Southwest desert foragers. But such generalizations conceal the diversity and adaptations of life in native North America.

Projection: Bonne

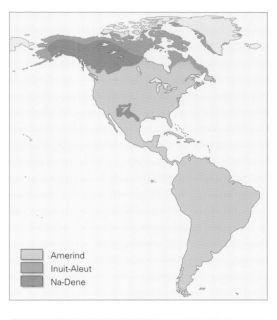

First-Nation reserves or settlements inhabited by 1,000 or more persons

Inuit communities populated by 500 or more persons

Amerind
Inuit-Aleut
Na-Dene

ETHNOLINGUISTIC REGIONS

The American linguist Joseph Greenberg has proposed that North America's indigenous languages represent three major language families, each corresponding to a major wave of migration into North America from East Asia. The oldest, largest, and most widely dispersed family is the Amerind, which spread from the shores of Hudson Bay to the coasts of Tierra del Fuego. The next oldest, second-largest, but much less widely dispersed family is the Na-Dene, whose languages are spoken by the First Nations of northwest Canada and part of Alaska, and by the Apache and Navajo. Last to bring their languages to North America were the Inuit-Aleut, still concentrated today along Arctic and near-Arctic shores.

LAND AND PEOPLE

The maps above and below display the distribution of native populations in Canada and the United States respectively. The aboriginal rights of Canada's widely dispersed First Nations and Inuit peoples are protected by the federal government, which has recently moved to endorse limited tribal self-government in northern British Columbia and has made territorial concessions in the far north. In the U.S., the relentless westward push of white settlement devastated indigenous society, eventually leaving what remained of the country's Native American nations with about 4 percent of U.S. territory in the form of mostly impoverished reservations, concentrated in the southwest and scattered across the north.

Ojibwa Reservations
1 Red Lake
2 White Earth
3 Leech Lake
4 Fond du Lac
5 Red Cliff
6 Bad River
7 Lac Courte Oreilles

New Mexico Pueblos
8 Zuni
9 Ramah (Navajo)
10 Laguna
11 Zia
12 Canoncito (Navajo)
13 Acoma

Native American reservations populated by 500 or more persons

Alaska Native Villages populated by 500 or more Alaska Natives (American Indians, Inuits, and Aleuts)

Counties or Metropolitan Statistical Areas with 500 or more Native Americans

EARLY SETTLEMENT AND EXPANSION

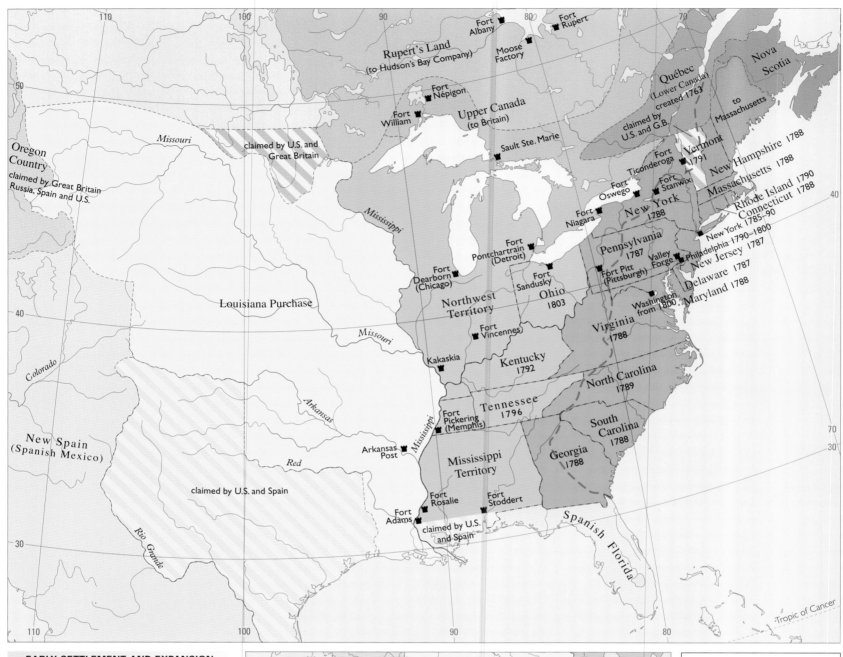

EARLY SETTLEMENT AND EXPANSION

European settlement and land alienation uprooted Native American peoples and drove them westward even as Europeans fought among themselves for political primacy. The French acquired a vast sphere of influence from Québec to Louisiana; the major British holding consisted of 13 colonies along the east coast extending from Maine to Georgia, and New Spain extended Spanish sway from Mexico into California and beyond. In the 13 colonies, anti-British resentment rose over the imposition of taxes and restrictions on overseas trade, as well as Britain's delimitation of the so-called Proclamation Line, which prohibited white settlement west of the Appalachians.

France's defeat in 1763 allowed the British to organize Canada, but the colonies rebelled and proclaimed independence in 1776. Expansion westward resumed, and in 1803 Napoleon, needing money to finance his European war effort, sold Louisiana to the young republic. The stage was set for the Union's final push to the Pacific and the ouster of the Spanish from "New Spain."

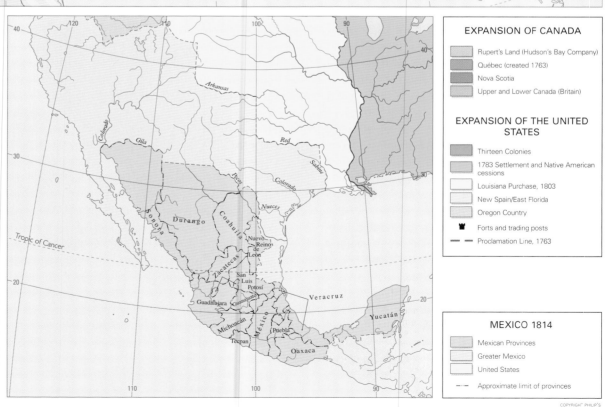

EXPANSION OF CANADA

Rupert's Land (Hudson's Bay Company)

Québec (created 1763)

Nova Scotia

Upper and Lower Canada (Britain)

EXPANSION OF THE UNITED STATES

Thirteen Colonies

1783 Settlement and Native American cessions

Louisiana Purchase, 1803

New Spain/East Florida

Oregon Country

♛ Forts and trading posts

– – – Proclamation Line, 1763

MEXICO 1814

Mexican Provinces

Greater Mexico

United States

– · – Approximate limit of provinces

COPYRIGHT PHILIP'S

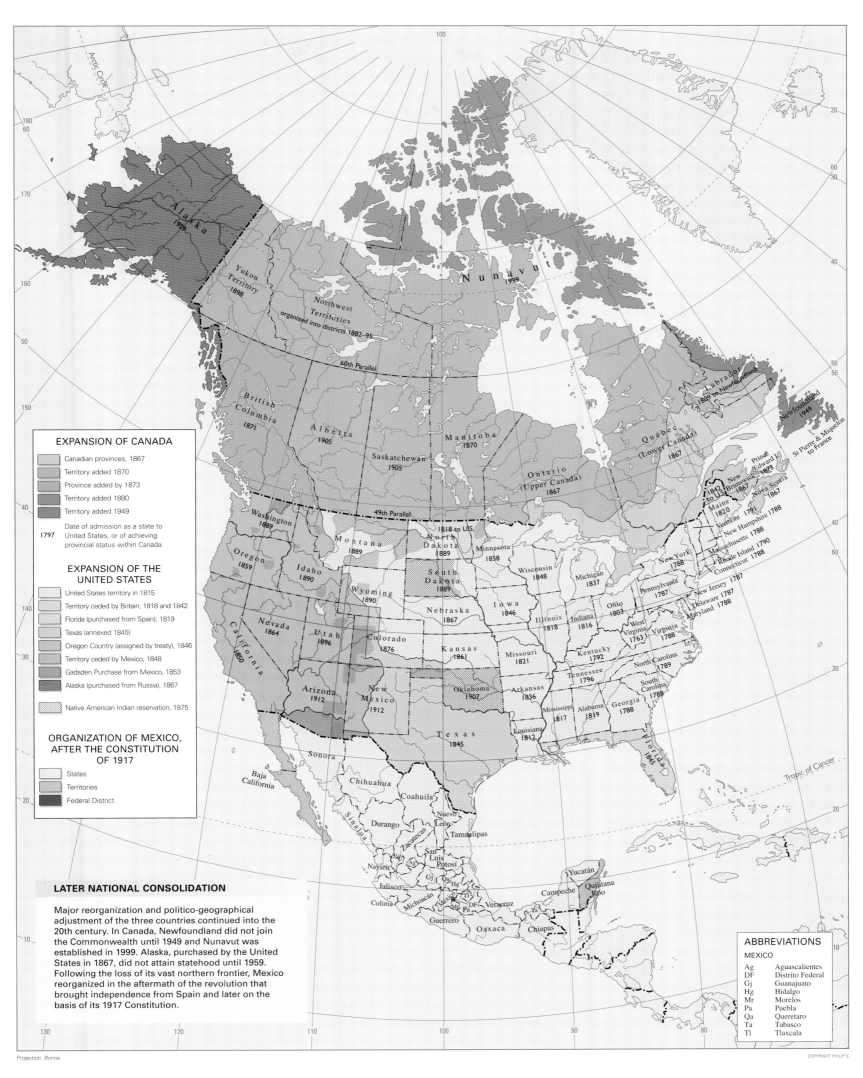

EXPANSION OF CANADA

Canadian provinces, 1867

Territory added 1870

Province added by 1873

Territory added 1880

Territory added 1949

1797   Date of admission as a state to
United States, or of achieving
provincial status within Canada

**EXPANSION OF THE
UNITED STATES**

United States territory in 1815

Territory ceded by Britain, 1818 and 1842

Florida (purchased from Spain), 1819

Texas (annexed 1845)

Oregon Country (assigned by treaty), 1846

Territory ceded by Mexico, 1848

Gadsden Purchase from Mexico, 1853

Alaska (purchased from Russia), 1867

Native American Indian reservation, 1875

**ORGANIZATION OF MEXICO,
AFTER THE CONSTITUTION
OF 1917**

States

Territories

Federal District

LATER NATIONAL CONSOLIDATION

Major reorganization and politico-geographical
adjustment of the three countries continued into the
20th century. In Canada, Newfoundland did not join
the Commonwealth until 1949 and Nunavut was
established in 1999. Alaska, purchased by the United
States in 1867, did not attain statehood until 1959.
Following the loss of its vast northern frontier, Mexico
reorganized in the aftermath of the revolution that
brought independence from Spain and later on the
basis of its 1917 Constitution.

ABBREVIATIONS

MEXICO

Ag	Aguascalientes
DF	Distrito Federal
Gj	Guanajuato
Hg	Hidalgo
Mr	Morelos
Pa	Puebla
Qa	Queretaro
Ta	Tabasco
Tl	Tlaxcala

Projection: *Bonne*

COPYRIGHT PHILIP'S

POPULATION AND SOCIAL DIVERSITY

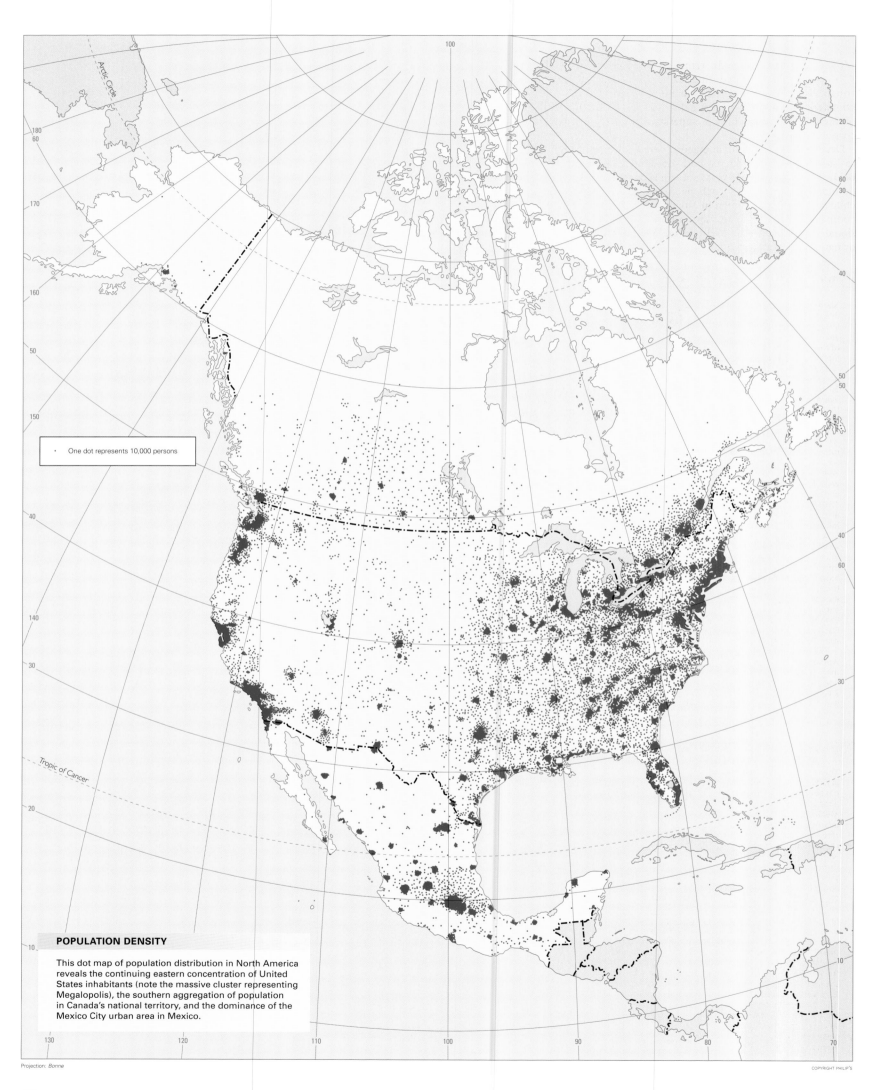

One dot represents 10,000 persons

Arctic Circle

Tropic of Cancer

POPULATION DENSITY

This dot map of population distribution in North America
reveals the continuing eastern concentration of United
States inhabitants (note the massive cluster representing
Megalopolis), the southern aggregation of population
in Canada's national territory, and the dominance of the
Mexico City urban area in Mexico.

Projection: *Bonne*

WOMEN IN THE U.S.

American women made remarkable progress during the 20th century but face daunting challenges in the quest for genuine equality of opportunity. They achieved breakthroughs in occupations such as law and medicine that were once the exclusive domain of men, and several female superstars now lead "Fortune 500" corporations.

Despite these highly visible gains, women are less likely than men to hold a bachelor's degree and more likely to live in households below the poverty level. Most are concentrated in low-wage, female-dominated occupations such as secretary, waitress, teacher, and childcare provider. Women in North America continue to constitute comparatively small minorities on university faculties and in professional associations, and they are far from achieving parity in local or national political arenas.

NORTH AMERICA: LIFE EXPECTANCY

North American women live longer and healthier lives than they did 100 years ago. At the dawn of the 20th century, the life expectancy of the typical Mexican woman was little more than 30 years, while the average Canadian and U.S. woman lived only into her late forties.

Major causes of death were influenza, typhoid, tuberculosis, cholera, and, of course, childbirth. Year-to-year fluctuations were high, as in the conspicuous trough in 1918 (see center graph at right), marking a major influenza outbreak.

Advances in sanitation as well as medical care, immunization against infectious diseases, and higher standards of living brought consistency to the annual regime and extended life expectancy to today's 82 years in Canada, 80 in the U.S., and 78 in Mexico.

The gender gap – women's advantage over men in life expectancy – has grown from around 2 years in 1900 to between 5 and 6 years today.

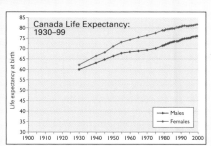

NORTH AMERICA: FERTILITY RATE AND LABOR FORCE

The rising status of women is linked to better control of reproduction and greater economic autonomy. As Mexico modernized and urbanized, its total fertility rate – the number of children that a typical woman has as she passes through her reproductive years – plummeted from almost 7 in 1970 to around 2.5 today. With fewer children, women are far more likely to work outside the home. Mexican women now comprise one-third of the nation's workforce. Female labor force participation in the U.S. rose from just 25 percent immediately after World War II to almost 60 percent today as society's views of acceptable roles for women changed.

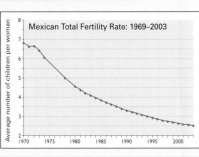

WOMEN IN NORTH AMERICA

Women in Provincial Assemblies: 2003

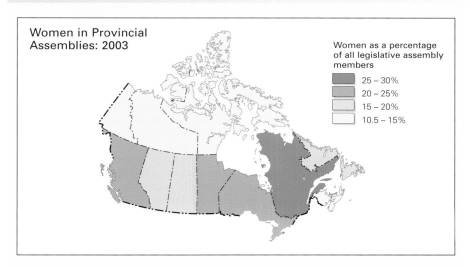

Women as a percentage of all legislative assembly members

- 25 – 30%
- 20 – 25%
- 15 – 20%
- 10.5 – 15%

Women in State Legislatures: 2001

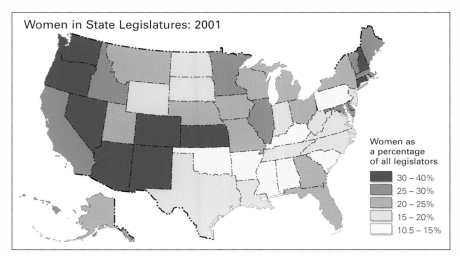

Women as a percentage of all legislators

- 30 – 40%
- 25 – 30%
- 20 – 25%
- 15 – 20%
- 10.5 – 15%

Municipalities governed by women: 1998

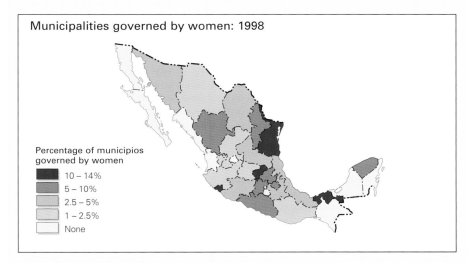

Percentage of municipios governed by women

- 10 – 14%
- 5 – 10%
- 2.5 – 5%
- 1 – 2.5%
- None

Canada did not enfranchise women until 1918, the United States in 1920, and Mexico in 1953, so that male domination of political institutions and networks, well established and deeply entrenched, will take some considerable time to overcome.

However, sweeping political and social change has opened the political process to the women of North America. Women represent a majority of the electorate, and they are choosing in increasing numbers to orchestrate political events, run campaigns, join movements, and seek elective office.

The year 1992 was dubbed "The Year of the Woman" in the U.S., as a record number of women were elected to Congress. Today, there are 62 women in the U.S. House of Representatives and 14 in the Senate. The Canadian House of Commons has 63 women,

and there are 35 in the Senate. Women who achieve national office often cut their teeth by holding office at the regional level.

In the U.S., women have the greatest success in being elected to state legislatures in New England and the West, while in Canada the women of Québec occupy proportionately more legislative positions than those in the Yukon, Northwest Territories, or Nunavut.

During the past 15 years, Mexico's political process has been opened to groups, including women, who previously had little say in policy-making and the electoral process. Women are especially influential at the local or municipio level where their involvement in government is tied to meeting daily needs or by crises in the neighborhood or local community.

IMMIGRATION AND POPULATION CHANGE

IMMIGRATION

International migration – people moving across national borders – is on the rise due to the globalization of the world economy, growing inequalities between the rich and the poor, continuing demographic pressure in high-growth countries, and widespread civil war and ethnic strife. North America figures prominently in the global migration system because it includes major origin and destination regions for international movements. Mexico sends between 200,000 and 300,000 documented migrants to the United States each year. The U.S. and Canada, which together account for just 5 percent of the world's population, are destinations for one-half of the world's immigrants.

Global migrants do not move randomly around the world but in well-defined streams that connect particular origins and destinations. Immigrants rely on friends and relatives from their native countries for information about potential destinations and help in finding jobs and places to live. Living together in an ethnic enclave allows immigrants to speak a familiar language, enjoy native foods, join social clubs, and find work in immigrant-owned businesses. Low-skilled migrants are especially dependent upon family members to provide help in finding work and establishing a new life, and are therefore very likely to concentrate near already established immigrants.

Streams of international migrants to the U.S. and Canada are strongly focused on large gateway cities and metropolitan regions. Almost 95 percent of new immigrants to the United States settle initially in one of the nation's metropolitan regions. Cities and suburbs of Southern California and the New York City area capture nearly one-quarter of new arrivals, followed by the Miami, Chicago, and Washington, DC areas. The tendency for immigrants to concentrate in large urban regions is even more prevalent in Canada as one-half of all international migrants settle in the Toronto area, 14 percent in the vicinity of Montreal, and 13 percent in Vancouver. The channelized nature of international migration streams accounts for the fact that different source areas contribute migrants to cities across the continent, creating unique blends of culture, religion, language, architecture, and cuisine.

MEXICO POPULATION

Mexican migration to the United States began in earnest with the recruitment of rural workers for farm work to replace American men drafted into World Wars I and II. Migration continued as employers came to depend upon cheap Mexican labor and Mexicans came to depend upon income earned in the U.S. Liberalization of U.S. immigration policy in the mid 1960s accelerated northward migration. Americans are now moving southward, albeit in much smaller numbers, as retirees settle in amenity-rich communities along the Pacific coast and the Lake Chapala Riviera located in the state of Jalisco.

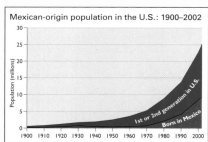

Mexican-origin population in the U.S.: 1900–2002

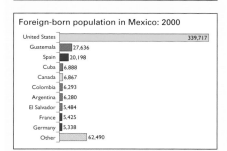

Foreign-born population in Mexico: 2000

United States	339,717
Guatemala	27,636
Spain	20,198
Cuba	6,888
Canada	6,867
Colombia	6,293
Argentina	6,280
El Salvador	5,484
France	5,425
Germany	5,338
Other	62,490

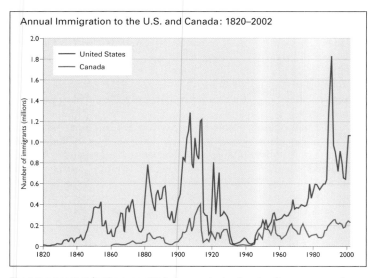

Annual Immigration to the U.S. and Canada: 1820–2002

There is precedent for the current influx of immigrants to North America from across the world. Large numbers of Europeans entered the U.S. and Canada during the late-19th and early 20th centuries. Immigration was severely restricted by government policy after World War I, and during the Great Depression of the 1930s few Europeans wanted to immigrate.

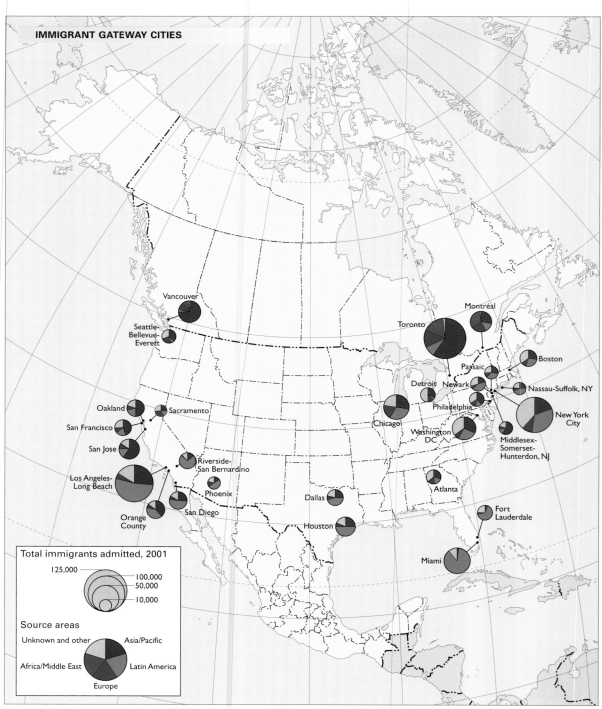

IMMIGRANT GATEWAY CITIES

Total immigrants admitted, 2001

125,000
100,000
50,000
10,000

Source areas
Unknown and other
Africa/Middle East
Europe
Asia/Pacific
Latin America

COPYRIGHT PHILIP'S

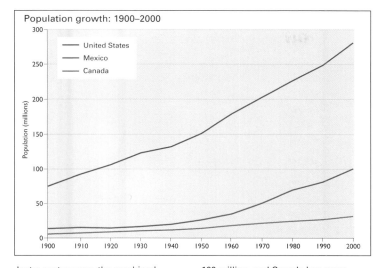

Population growth: 1900–2000

Just a century ago, the combined population of the United States, Mexico, and Canada was about 100 million. Today that total exceeds 425 million. The U.S. population approaches 300 million; Mexico's tops 100 million, and Canada has more than 30 million inhabitants. Population projections suggest that, by 2025, the U.S. population will near 350 million, Mexico's will surpass 130 million, and Canada's will reach 36 million.

POPULATION CHANGE

The populations of the three largest North American countries continue to grow, albeit at different rates and for different reasons. In 2004, Mexico's annual rate of natural increase was by far the highest, 2.1 percent, substantially higher than the world average (1.2 percent). This demographic picture is reflected by the country's age-distribution pyramid (*below*), with the numbers of youngsters in the population far exceeding those in the older categories. At present, Mexico's population is doubling in only 33 years. Canada, by contrast, is growing at a rate of only 0.4 percent, with a doubling time of 175 years.

As the population pyramids of Canada and the United States indicate, older people make up a far larger percentage of the population than is the case in Mexico. The U.S. and Canadian pyramids also evince the longer life expectancy of women in these maturing populations.

While Mexico's rate of natural increase fairly accurately reflects the overall growth rate of the population, the United States and to a lesser degree Canada are growing faster than the figures suggest because of immigration. In the case of the United States, documented and undocumented immigration combined may be boosting the overall growth rate to above 1.0 percent.

Long-term population gains and losses in North America result from economic, environmental, and social conditions. Hardships in the heartland, the Canadian Maritimes, the U.S. Northeast, and rural Mexico are driving people to the cities. The southward and westward "sunbelt" migration continues. And Nevada is gaining so fast because life in California, for many, is not what it used to be.

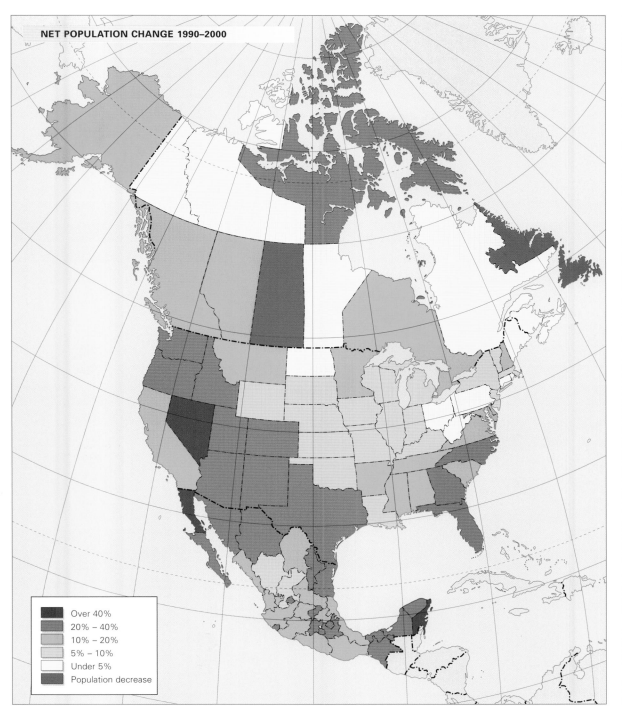

NET POPULATION CHANGE 1990–2000

Over 40%
20% – 40%
10% – 20%
5% – 10%
Under 5%
Population decrease

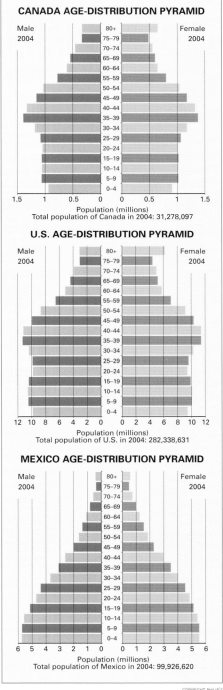

CANADA AGE-DISTRIBUTION PYRAMID

Male 2004   Female 2004

Population (millions)
Total population of Canada in 2004: 31,278,097

U.S. AGE-DISTRIBUTION PYRAMID

Male 2004   Female 2004

Population (millions)
Total population of U.S. in 2004: 282,338,631

MEXICO AGE-DISTRIBUTION PYRAMID

Male 2004   Female 2004

Population (millions)
Total population of Mexico in 2004: 99,926,620

URBANIZATION

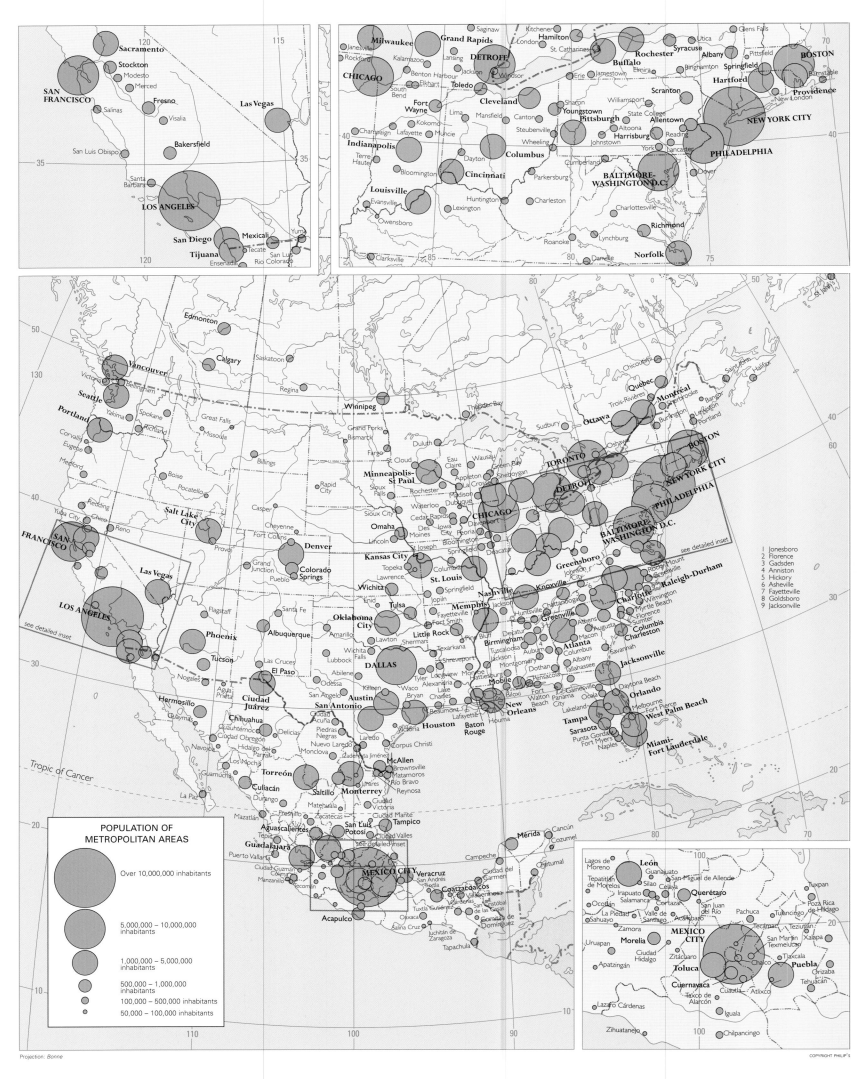

POPULATION OF METROPOLITAN AREAS

Over 10,000,000 inhabitants

5,000,000 – 10,000,000 inhabitants

1,000,000 – 5,000,000 inhabitants

500,000 – 1,000,000 inhabitants

100,000 – 500,000 inhabitants

50,000 – 100,000 inhabitants

1 Jonesboro
2 Florence
3 Gadsden
4 Anniston
5 Hickory
6 Asheville
7 Fayetteville
8 Goldsboro
9 Jacksonville

Projection: Bonne

COPYRIGHT PHILIP'S

MEGALOPOLIS

The United States is an urbanized society: more than 75 percent of its inhabitants live in cities and towns, and migration to the metropolitan areas continues. These two maps illustrate the consequences. On the Atlantic seaboard, metropolitan areas have grown so large that they have coalesced, creating a nearly continuous urbanized area from Boston, Massachusetts in the north to Richmond and Norfolk, Virginia in the south. The famed geographer Jean Gottmann was the first to call this vast built-up corridor *megalopolis*, and later the prefix *Bosnywash* was attached to it for Boston-New York-

Washington, three of the region's largest urban complexes.

The megalopolis phenomenon is not unique to the northeastern United States, nor to North America: other highly urbanized regions of the world are experiencing the same process, including Western Europe, Japan, and Pacific-Rim China. In North America, megalopolitan development is taking place in the Midwest from Chicago to Pittsburgh, in Canada along "Main Street" from Windsor to Québec, in California from San Francisco to San Diego, in the Northwest from Vancouver to Portland

anchored by Seattle, in Florida from Miami to Orlando, and in Mexico around the capital, Mexico City, which now lies at the heart of a fast-growing megalopolis.

In addition, secondary megalopolitan coalescence is taking place in such areas as the Colorado Piedmont. This map illustrates the progress of the urbanizing Rocky Mountain front around Denver and several smaller nearby cities and towns over the past half-century. Already, Boulder is part of the Denver metropolitan area, and Denver expands southward even as Colorado Springs grows northward.

BOSNYWASH MEGALOPOLIS

INCIPIENT COLORADO MEGALOPOLIS

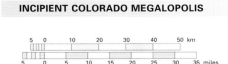

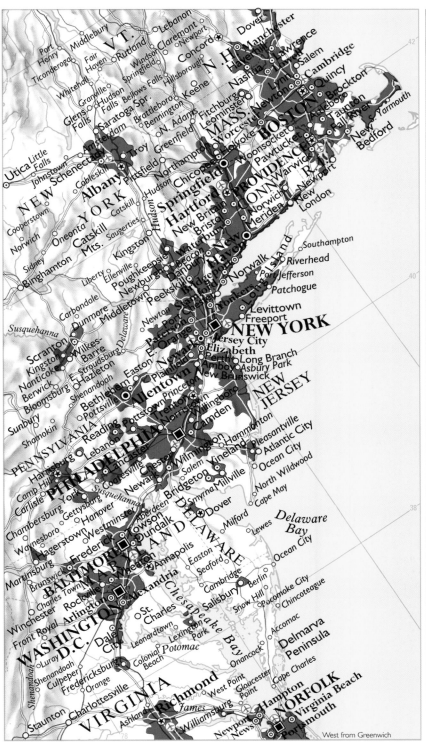

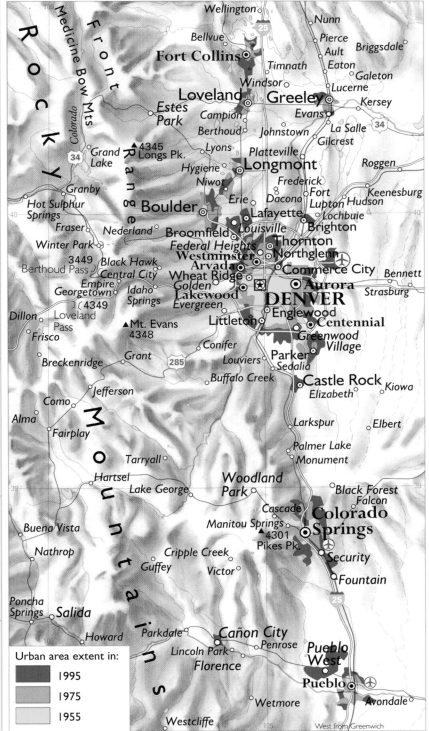

Urban area extent in:
- 1995
- 1975
- 1955

West from Greenwich

COPYRIGHT PHILIP'S

LAND USE AND AGRICULTURE

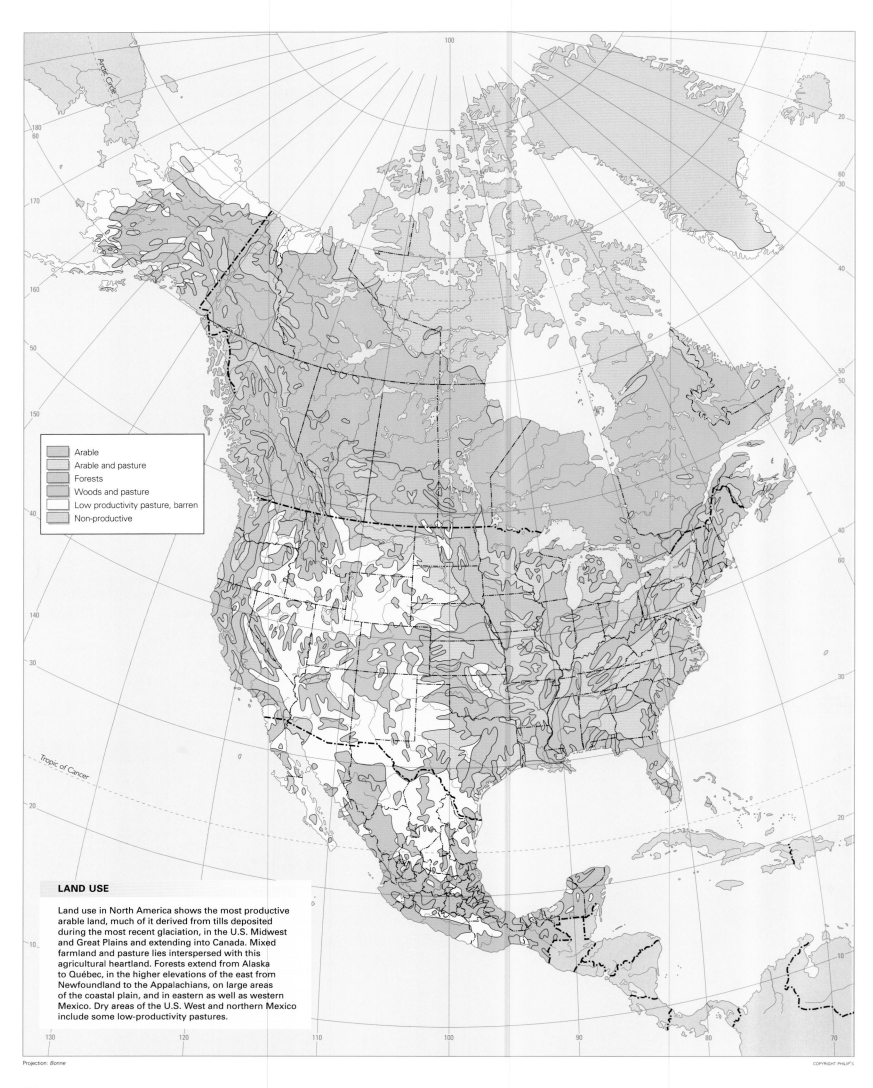

Arable
Arable and pasture
Forests
Woods and pasture
Low productivity pasture, barren
Non-productive

LAND USE

Land use in North America shows the most productive arable land, much of it derived from tills deposited during the most recent glaciation, in the U.S. Midwest and Great Plains and extending into Canada. Mixed farmland and pasture lies interspersed with this agricultural heartland. Forests extend from Alaska to Québec, in the higher elevations of the east from Newfoundland to the Appalachians, on large areas of the coastal plain, and in eastern as well as western Mexico. Dry areas of the U.S. West and northern Mexico include some low-productivity pastures.

Projection: *Bonne*

COPYRIGHT PHILIP'S

CATTLE

◄ The largest herds of beef cattle in the United States and Canada are on the pastures of the Great Plains from Texas to Alberta east of the Rocky Mountains; dairy cattle are raised near Canada's eastern cities, in Wisconsin and in the U.S. East from Virginia and Kentucky to Florida. Mexico's large herds are concentrated in four areas.

CORN

► The U.S. Corn Belt is still clearly delimited on this map, but the primacy of corn in this area is declining as soybean production increases. Mexico's comparatively small production comes from states in the center and south of the country, and almost all of Canada's corn is grown in southern Ontario and Québec.

HOGS

◄ Factory-farm hog raising marks the large principal production zone in the U.S. Midwest, but North Carolina has become a major producer. Mexico's main production areas are along the northwest and southeast coasts and west of the capital. Canada's production is scattered.

SOYBEANS

► Almost all soybean production in North America comes from a U.S. area larger than the Corn Belt and extending from the Canadian border to southern Louisiana. Soybean production has increased significantly over the past two decades.

POULTRY

◄ North Americans have a huge appetite for poultry, supporting a large fast-food industry in which chicken is a staple. Production in all three countries is scattered widely though U.S. production is concentrated in a zone from southern Pennsylvania to eastern Texas.

WHEAT

► The U.S. and Canada are two of the world's largest wheat producers. The spring wheat belt extends from Canada to Montana and the Dakotas; the winter wheat belt centers on Kansas. Mexico's relatively small production comes from Michoacan and coastal Sonora and Sinaloa.

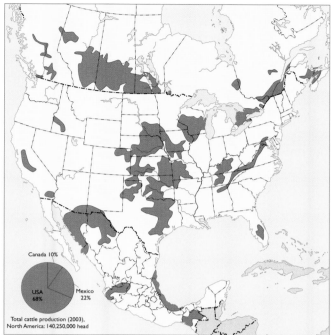

Canada 10%
USA 68%
Mexico 22%
Total cattle production (2003), North America: 140,250,000 head

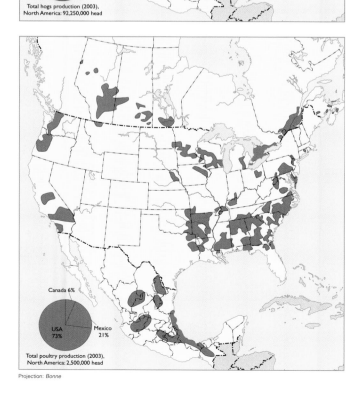

Canada 16%
USA 64%
Mexico 20%
Total hogs production (2003), North America: 92,250,000 head

Canada 6%
USA 73%
Mexico 21%
Total poultry production (2003), North America: 2,500,000 head

Projection: Bonne

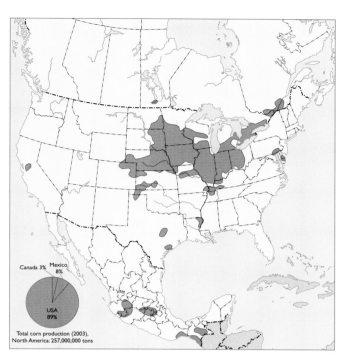

Canada 3%
Mexico 8%
USA 89%
Total corn production (2003), North America: 257,000,000 tons

Canada 3%
USA 97%
Total soybeans production (2003), North America: 77,250,000 tons

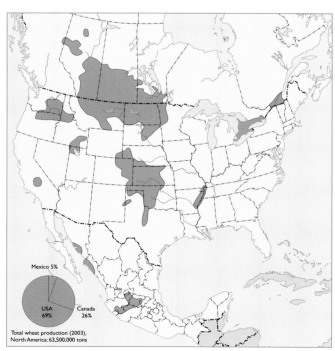

Mexico 5%
USA 69%
Canada 26%
Total wheat production (2003), North America: 63,500,000 tons

UNITED STATES: MANUFACTURING INDUSTRIES

THE CHANGING MAP OF INDUSTRY

The geography of North America's industrial production has long been dominated by a "Manufacturing Belt" whose durability was ensured by proximity to industrial resources, including iron and coal, and by its easy access to the continent's largest and richest market. But today the distribution of North American industry is changing as interregional transport methods and costs modulate, market proximity matters less, energy derives increasingly from oil and gas, high-technology manufacturing depends less on low-skill labor, and foreign competition forces business decisions that close plants and relocate production facilities. In the process, venerable operations such as the steel industry suffer from obsolescence and contraction. Parts of the old Manufacturing Belt became a Rust Belt.

But, as this series of maps focusing on the United States experience illustrate, a new industrial era has dawned, sometimes referred to as the "Post-industrial Revolution." High-technology, white-collar, office-based activities lead this postindustrial economy, whose geographic imprint is dispersed, not clustered as was the case in the days when heavy manufacturing anchored the industrial map. Climatic amenities have also played a role, and the Sunbelt continues to attract industrial growth.

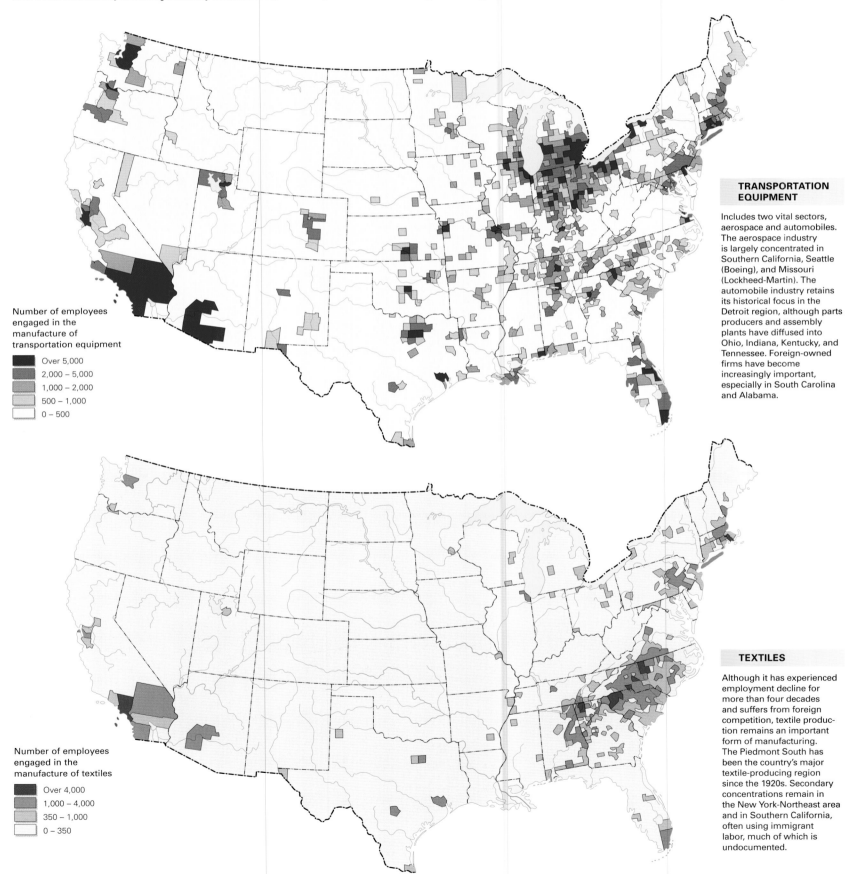

Number of employees engaged in the manufacture of transportation equipment

- Over 5,000
- 2,000 – 5,000
- 1,000 – 2,000
- 500 – 1,000
- 0 – 500

TRANSPORTATION EQUIPMENT

Includes two vital sectors, aerospace and automobiles. The aerospace industry is largely concentrated in Southern California, Seattle (Boeing), and Missouri (Lockheed-Martin). The automobile industry retains its historical focus in the Detroit region, although parts producers and assembly plants have diffused into Ohio, Indiana, Kentucky, and Tennessee. Foreign-owned firms have become increasingly important, especially in South Carolina and Alabama.

Number of employees engaged in the manufacture of textiles

- Over 4,000
- 1,000 – 4,000
- 350 – 1,000
- 0 – 350

TEXTILES

Although it has experienced employment decline for more than four decades and suffers from foreign competition, textile production remains an important form of manufacturing. The Piedmont South has been the country's major textile-producing region since the 1920s. Secondary concentrations remain in the New York-Northeast area and in Southern California, often using immigrant labor, much of which is undocumented.

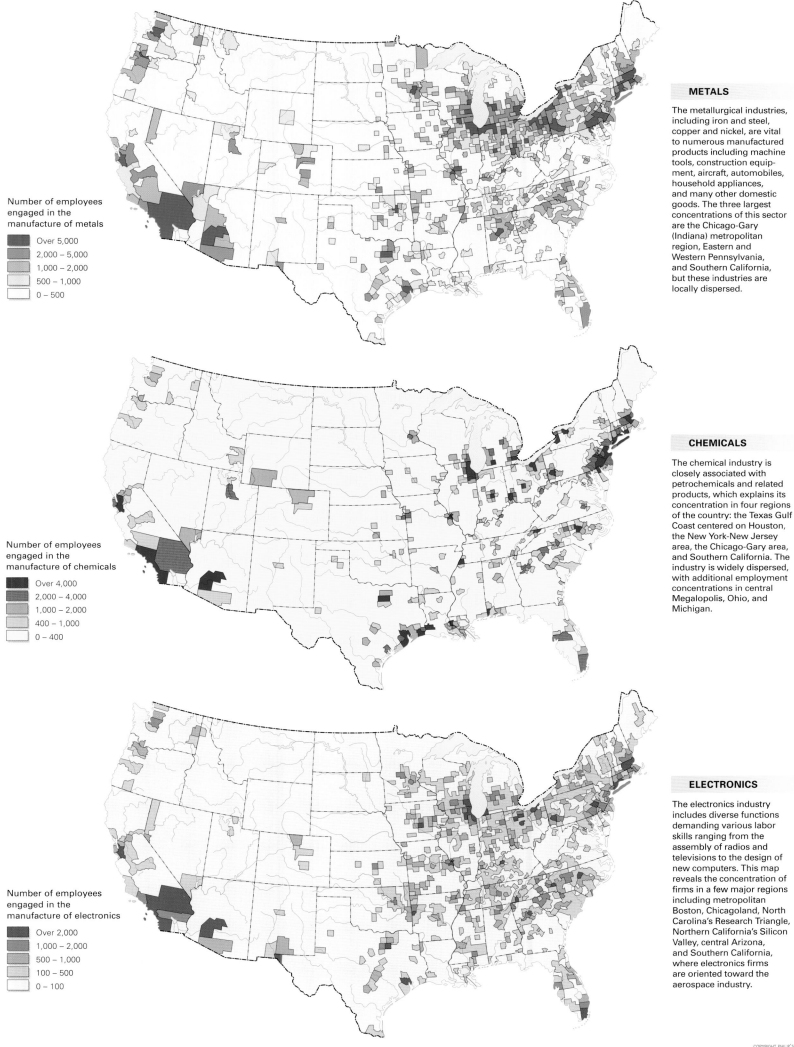

METALS

The metallurgical industries, including iron and steel, copper and nickel, are vital to numerous manufactured products including machine tools, construction equipment, aircraft, automobiles, household appliances, and many other domestic goods. The three largest concentrations of this sector are the Chicago-Gary (Indiana) metropolitan region, Eastern and Western Pennsylvania, and Southern California, but these industries are locally dispersed.

Number of employees engaged in the manufacture of metals

- Over 5,000
- 2,000 – 5,000
- 1,000 – 2,000
- 500 – 1,000
- 0 – 500

CHEMICALS

The chemical industry is closely associated with petrochemicals and related products, which explains its concentration in four regions of the country: the Texas Gulf Coast centered on Houston, the New York-New Jersey area, the Chicago-Gary area, and Southern California. The industry is widely dispersed, with additional employment concentrations in central Megalopolis, Ohio, and Michigan.

Number of employees engaged in the manufacture of chemicals

- Over 4,000
- 2,000 – 4,000
- 1,000 – 2,000
- 400 – 1,000
- 0 – 400

ELECTRONICS

The electronics industry includes diverse functions demanding various labor skills ranging from the assembly of radios and televisions to the design of new computers. This map reveals the concentration of firms in a few major regions including metropolitan Boston, Chicagoland, North Carolina's Research Triangle, Northern California's Silicon Valley, central Arizona, and Southern California, where electronics firms are oriented toward the aerospace industry.

Number of employees engaged in the manufacture of electronics

- Over 2,000
- 1,000 – 2,000
- 500 – 1,000
- 100 – 500
- 0 – 100

UNITED STATES: SERVICE INDUSTRIES

SERVICE INDUSTRIES

conomic activity is often grouped into four categories, of which the primary (extractive) and secondary (manufacturing) have been mapped in earlier parts of this thematic section.

The tertiary and quaternary activities form the subject of pages 38 and 39. These are the hallmark activities of the postindustrial era: the service industries, representing a large array of functions ranging from retailing and finance to education and administration, and the information industries, which collect, process, manipulate, and disseminate knowledge.

Over the past 200 years, each of these activities has successively dominated U.S. and Canadian economic geography. Agriculture and mining, then manufacturing, then services, and now the quaternary (information) industries, still rising, have been the leading employers of North American labor.

Today in the United States, 2 percent of workers are in agriculture, 15 percent in manufacturing, 18 percent in services, and 65 percent in information industries. The maps on these pages illustrate the spatial aspects of contemporary tertiary and quaternary industries.

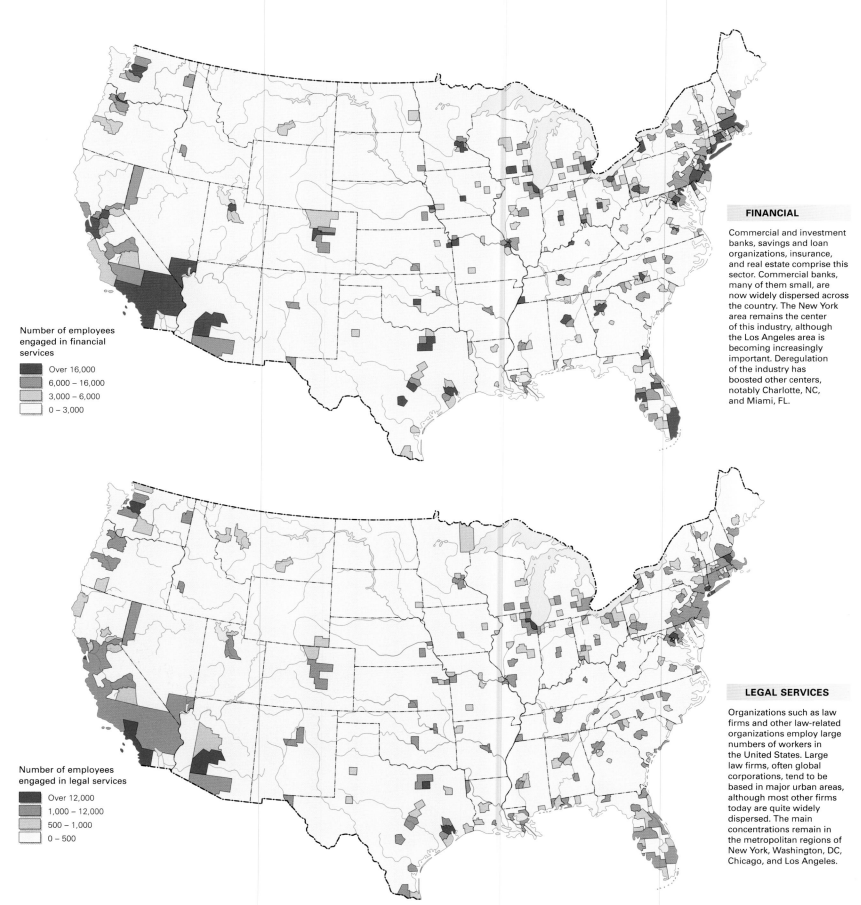

FINANCIAL

Commercial and investment banks, savings and loan organizations, insurance, and real estate comprise this sector. Commercial banks, many of them small, are now widely dispersed across the country. The New York area remains the center of this industry, although the Los Angeles area is becoming increasingly important. Deregulation of the industry has boosted other centers, notably Charlotte, NC, and Miami, FL.

Number of employees engaged in financial services

- Over 16,000
- 6,000 – 16,000
- 3,000 – 6,000
- 0 – 3,000

LEGAL SERVICES

Organizations such as law firms and other law-related organizations employ large numbers of workers in the United States. Large law firms, often global corporations, tend to be based in major urban areas, although most other firms today are quite widely dispersed. The main concentrations remain in the metropolitan regions of New York, Washington, DC, Chicago, and Los Angeles.

Number of employees engaged in legal services

- Over 12,000
- 1,000 – 12,000
- 500 – 1,000
- 0 – 500

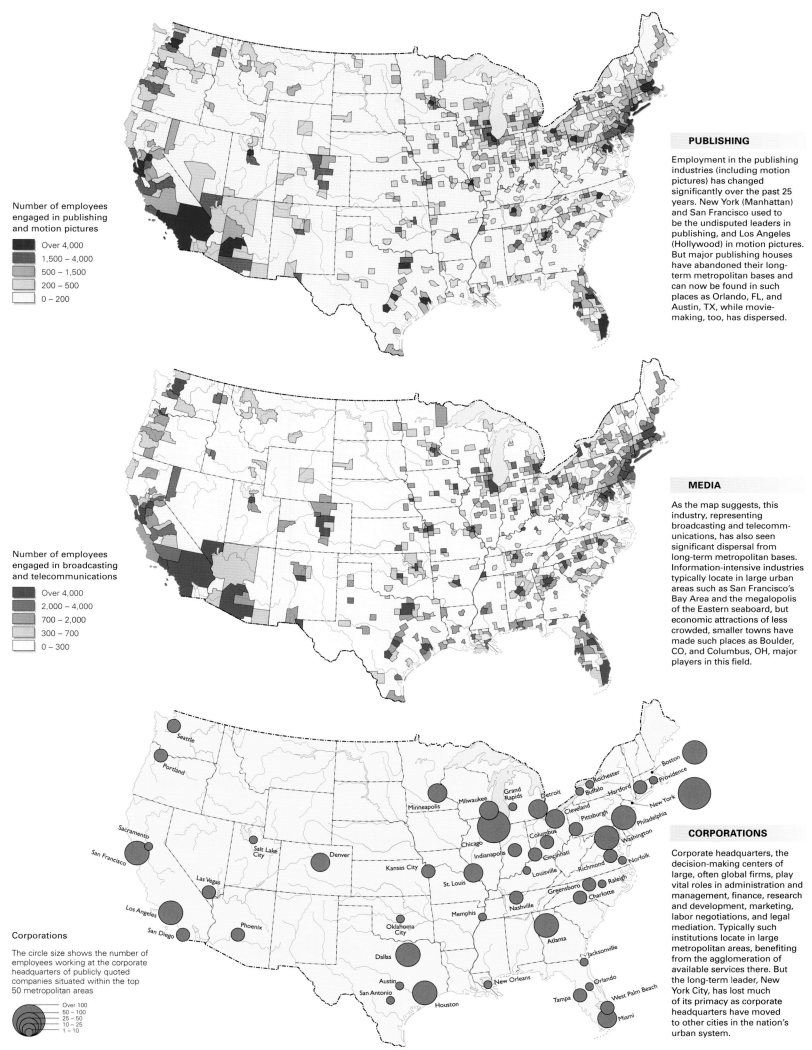

PUBLISHING

Employment in the publishing industries (including motion pictures) has changed significantly over the past 25 years. New York (Manhattan) and San Francisco used to be the undisputed leaders in publishing, and Los Angeles (Hollywood) in motion pictures. But major publishing houses have abandoned their long-term metropolitan bases and can now be found in such places as Orlando, FL, and Austin, TX, while movie-making, too, has dispersed.

Number of employees engaged in publishing and motion pictures

- Over 4,000
- 1,500 – 4,000
- 500 – 1,500
- 200 – 500
- 0 – 200

MEDIA

As the map suggests, this industry, representing broadcasting and telecommunications, has also seen significant dispersal from long-term metropolitan bases. Information-intensive industries typically locate in large urban areas such as San Francisco's Bay Area and the megalopolis of the Eastern seaboard, but economic attractions of less crowded, smaller towns have made such places as Boulder, CO, and Columbus, OH, major players in this field.

Number of employees engaged in broadcasting and telecommunications

- Over 4,000
- 2,000 – 4,000
- 700 – 2,000
- 300 – 700
- 0 – 300

CORPORATIONS

Corporate headquarters, the decision-making centers of large, often global firms, play vital roles in administration and management, finance, research and development, marketing, labor negotiations, and legal mediation. Typically such institutions locate in large metropolitan areas, benefiting from the agglomeration of available services there. But the long-term leader, New York City, has lost much of its primacy as corporate headquarters have moved to other cities in the nation's urban system.

Corporations

The circle size shows the number of employees working at the corporate headquarters of publicly quoted companies situated within the top 50 metropolitan areas

- Over 100
- 50 – 100
- 25 – 50
- 10 – 25
- 1 – 10

TRADE AND TELECOMMUNICATIONS

IMPORTS AND EXPORTS

Proximity remains a powerful factor in trade relationships among countries, as these diagrams representing imports and exports of the three major countries of North America suggest. For all three countries, immediate neighbors are the leading sources of imports as well as the top destinations for exports. This is especially true of Canada and Mexico: for both, the U.S. is by far the leading trade partner. Even for the United States, Canada and Mexico rank first and second in terms of exports; Canada still outranks China in terms of imports, with Mexico a close third.

NAFTA (North American Free Trade Agreement), of course, played a major role in strengthening these relationships, and as the pie charts show, transport equipment and machinery form the largest trade category. Among exports-producing states of the U.S., California and Texas lead, followed by three Midwestern states (automobiles), New York State, and Washington State (aircraft).

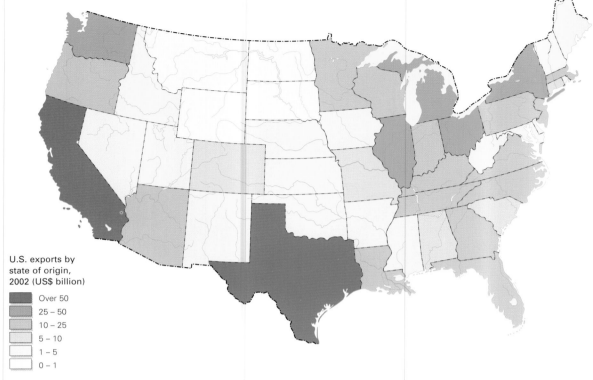

U.S. exports by state of origin, 2002 (US$ billion)

- Over 50
- 25 – 50
- 10 – 25
- 5 – 10
- 1 – 5
- 0 – 1

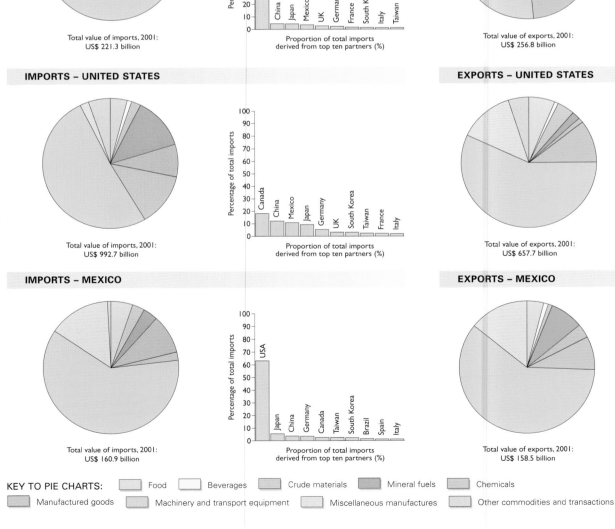

IMPORTS – CANADA

Total value of imports, 2001: US$ 221.3 billion

Percentage of total imports — USA, China, Japan, Mexico, UK, Germany, France, South Korea, Italy, Taiwan

Proportion of total imports derived from top ten partners (%)

EXPORTS – CANADA

Total value of exports, 2001: US$ 256.8 billion

Percentage of total exports — USA, Japan, UK, China, Germany, Mexico, South Korea, France, Belgium, Netherlands

Proportion of total exports sent to top ten partners (%)

IMPORTS – UNITED STATES

Total value of imports, 2001: US$ 992.7 billion

Percentage of total imports — Canada, China, Mexico, Japan, Germany, UK, South Korea, Taiwan, France, Italy

Proportion of total imports derived from top ten partners (%)

EXPORTS – UNITED STATES

Total value of exports, 2001: US$ 657.7 billion

Percentage of total exports — Canada, Mexico, Japan, UK, China, Germany, South Korea, Netherlands, Taiwan, France

Proportion of total exports sent to top ten partners (%)

IMPORTS – MEXICO

Total value of imports, 2001: US$ 160.9 billion

Percentage of total imports — USA, Japan, China, Germany, Canada, Taiwan, South Korea, Brazil, Spain, Italy

Proportion of total imports derived from top ten partners (%)

EXPORTS – MEXICO

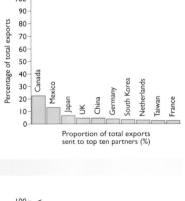

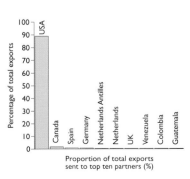

Total value of exports, 2001: US$ 158.5 billion

Percentage of total exports — USA, Canada, Spain, Germany, Netherlands Antilles, Netherlands, UK, Venezuela, Colombia, Guatemala

Proportion of total exports sent to top ten partners (%)

KEY TO PIE CHARTS: Food · Beverages · Crude materials · Mineral fuels · Chemicals · Manufactured goods · Machinery and transport equipment · Miscellaneous manufactures · Other commodities and transactions

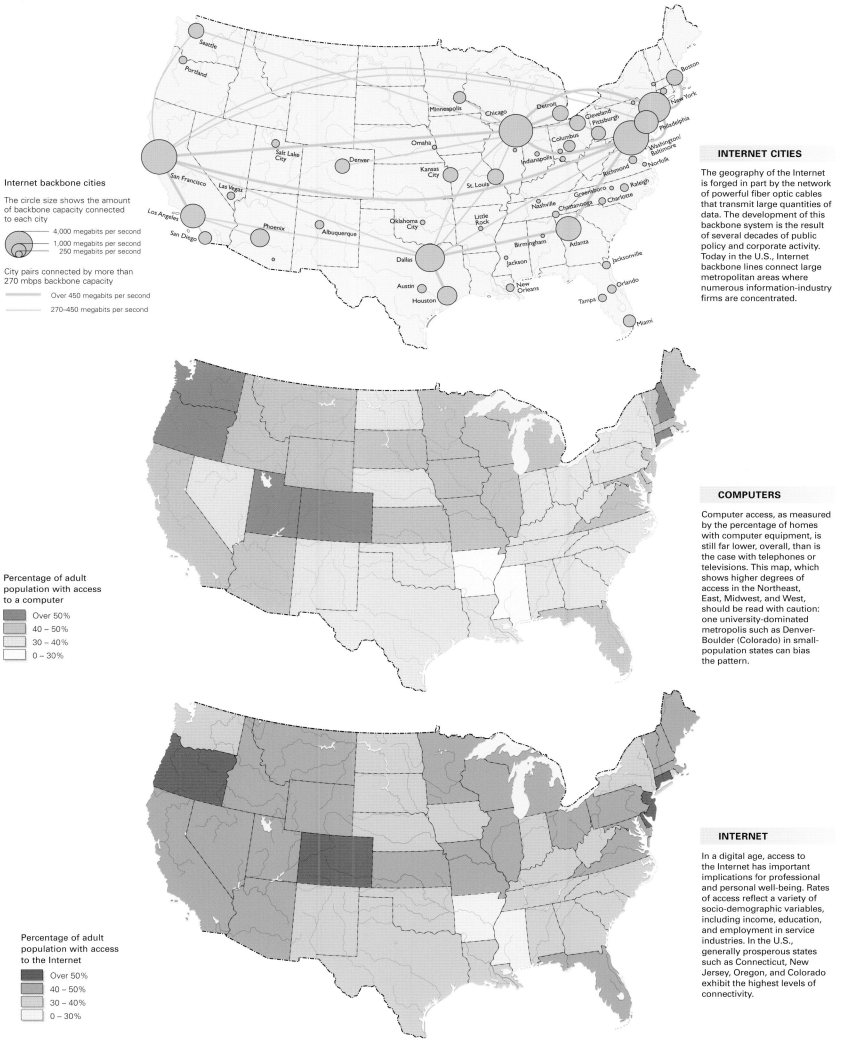

Internet backbone cities

The circle size shows the amount of backbone capacity connected to each city

- 4,000 megabits per second
- 1,000 megabits per second
- 250 megabits per second

City pairs connected by more than 270 mbps backbone capacity

Over 450 megabits per second

270–450 megabits per second

INTERNET CITIES

The geography of the Internet is forged in part by the network of powerful fiber optic cables that transmit large quantities of data. The development of this backbone system is the result of several decades of public policy and corporate activity. Today in the U.S., Internet backbone lines connect large metropolitan areas where numerous information-industry firms are concentrated.

Percentage of adult population with access to a computer

- Over 50%
- 40 – 50%
- 30 – 40%
- 0 – 30%

COMPUTERS

Computer access, as measured by the percentage of homes with computer equipment, is still far lower, overall, than is the case with telephones or televisions. This map, which shows higher degrees of access in the Northeast, East, Midwest, and West, should be read with caution: one university-dominated metropolis such as Denver-Boulder (Colorado) in small-population states can bias the pattern.

Percentage of adult population with access to the Internet

- Over 50%
- 40 – 50%
- 30 – 40%
- 0 – 30%

INTERNET

In a digital age, access to the Internet has important implications for professional and personal well-being. Rates of access reflect a variety of socio-demographic variables, including income, education, and employment in service industries. In the U.S., generally prosperous states such as Connecticut, New Jersey, Oregon, and Colorado exhibit the highest levels of connectivity.

HIGHWAYS AND RAILROADS

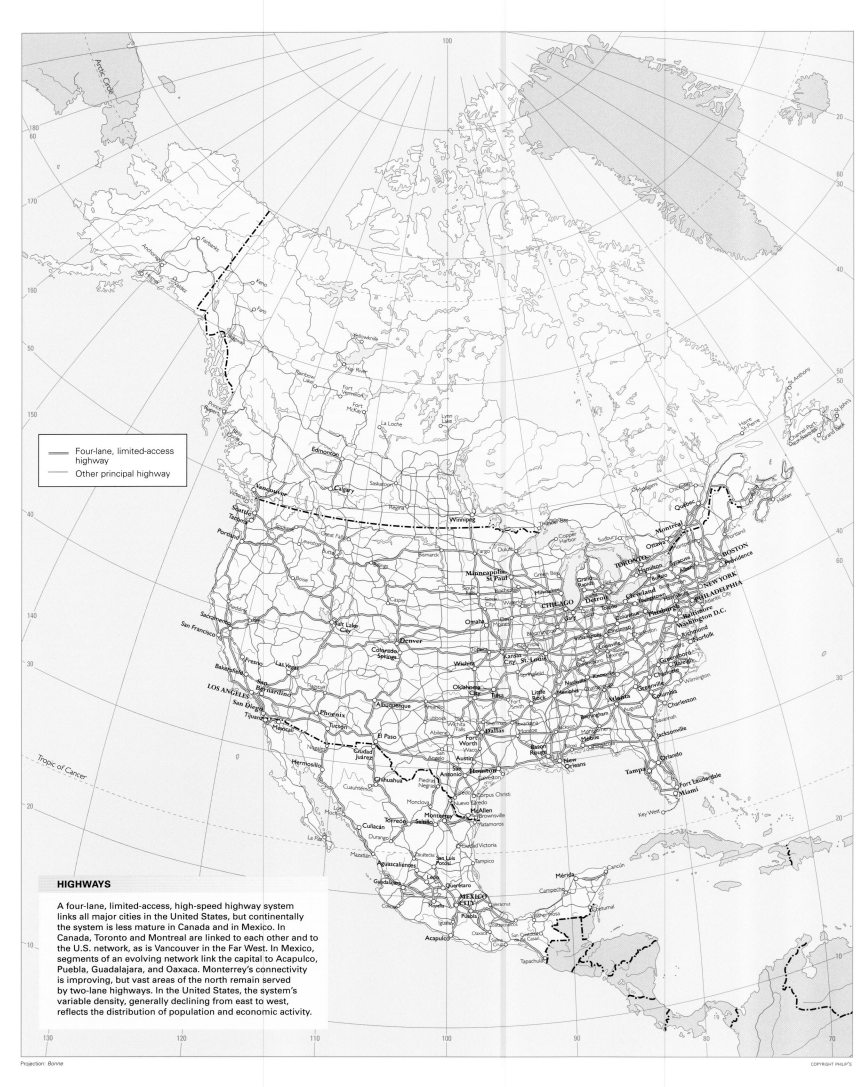

Four-lane, limited-access
highway

Other principal highway

HIGHWAYS

A four-lane, limited-access, high-speed highway system
links all major cities in the United States, but continentally
the system is less mature in Canada and in Mexico. In
Canada, Toronto and Montreal are linked to each other and to
the U.S. network, as is Vancouver in the Far West. In Mexico,
segments of an evolving network link the capital to Acapulco,
Puebla, Guadalajara, and Oaxaca. Monterrey's connectivity
is improving, but vast areas of the north remain served
by two-lane highways. In the United States, the system's
variable density, generally declining from east to west,
reflects the distribution of population and economic activity.

Projection: Bonne

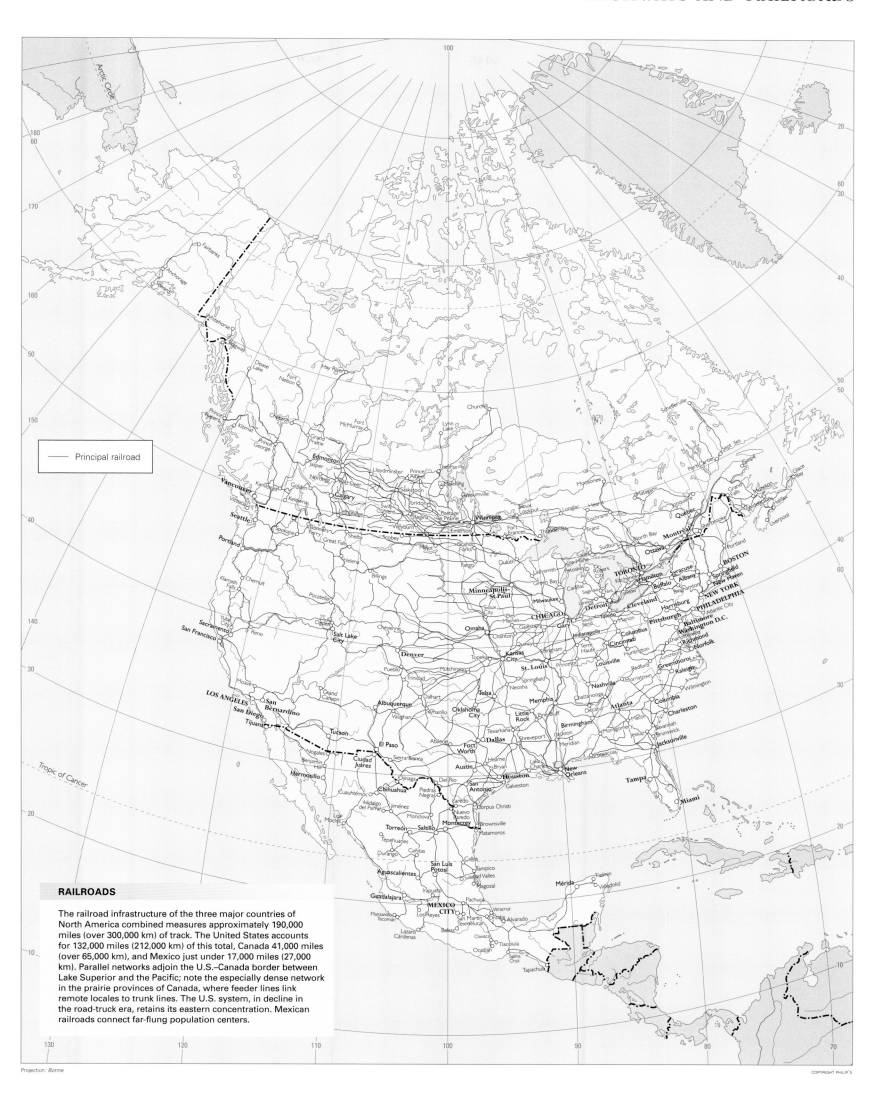

Principal railroad

RAILROADS

The railroad infrastructure of the three major countries of North America combined measures approximately 190,000 miles (over 300,000 km) of track. The United States accounts for 132,000 miles (212,000 km) of this total, Canada 41,000 miles (over 65,000 km), and Mexico just under 17,000 miles (27,000 km). Parallel networks adjoin the U.S.–Canada border between Lake Superior and the Pacific; note the especially dense network in the prairie provinces of Canada, where feeder lines link remote locales to trunk lines. The U.S. system, in decline in the road-truck era, retains its eastern concentration. Mexican railroads connect far-flung population centers.

Projection: Bonne

COPYRIGHT PHILIP'S

LANGUAGES AND RELIGIONS

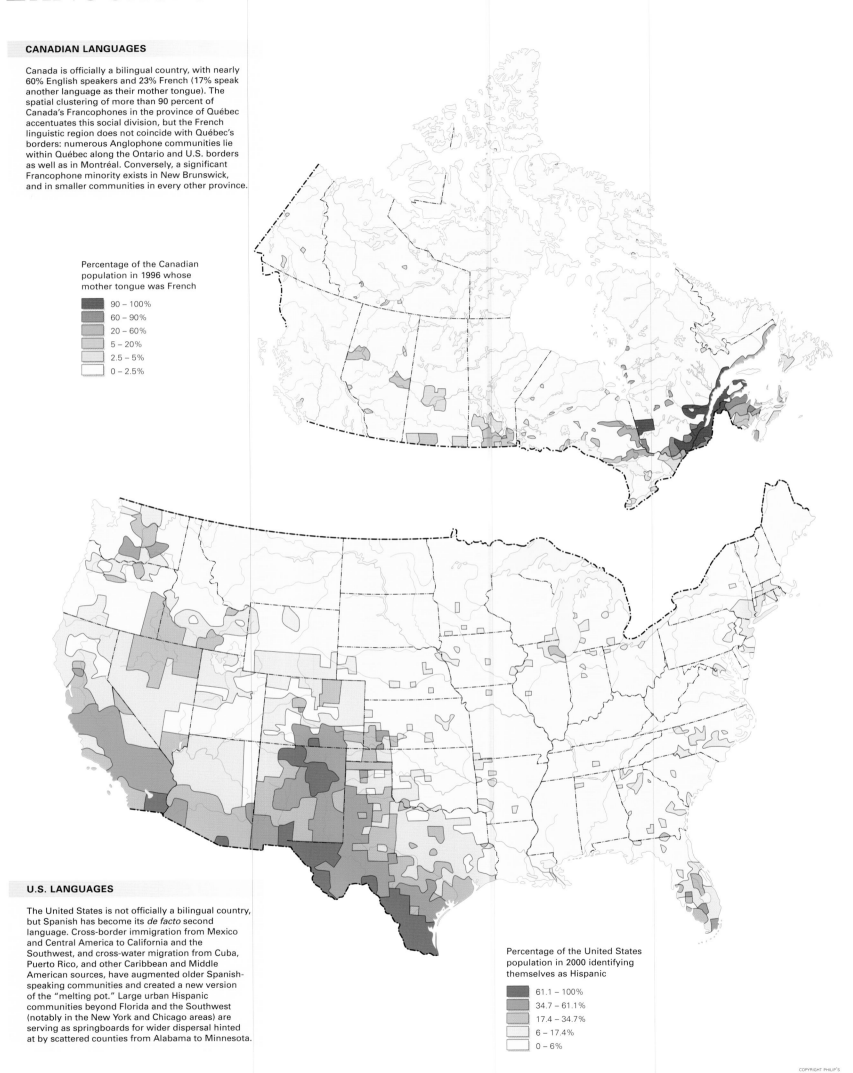

CANADIAN LANGUAGES

Canada is officially a bilingual country, with nearly 60% English speakers and 23% French (17% speak another language as their mother tongue). The spatial clustering of more than 90 percent of Canada's Francophones in the province of Québec accentuates this social division, but the French linguistic region does not coincide with Québec's borders: numerous Anglophone communities lie within Québec along the Ontario and U.S. borders as well as in Montréal. Conversely, a significant Francophone minority exists in New Brunswick, and in smaller communities in every other province.

Percentage of the Canadian population in 1996 whose mother tongue was French

- 90 – 100%
- 60 – 90%
- 20 – 60%
- 5 – 20%
- 2.5 – 5%
- 0 – 2.5%

U.S. LANGUAGES

The United States is not officially a bilingual country, but Spanish has become its *de facto* second language. Cross-border immigration from Mexico and Central America to California and the Southwest, and cross-water migration from Cuba, Puerto Rico, and other Caribbean and Middle American sources, have augmented older Spanish-speaking communities and created a new version of the "melting pot." Large urban Hispanic communities beyond Florida and the Southwest (notably in the New York and Chicago areas) are serving as springboards for wider dispersal hinted at by scattered counties from Alabama to Minnesota.

Percentage of the United States population in 2000 identifying themselves as Hispanic

- 61.1 – 100%
- 34.7 – 61.1%
- 17.4 – 34.7%
- 6 – 17.4%
- 0 – 6%

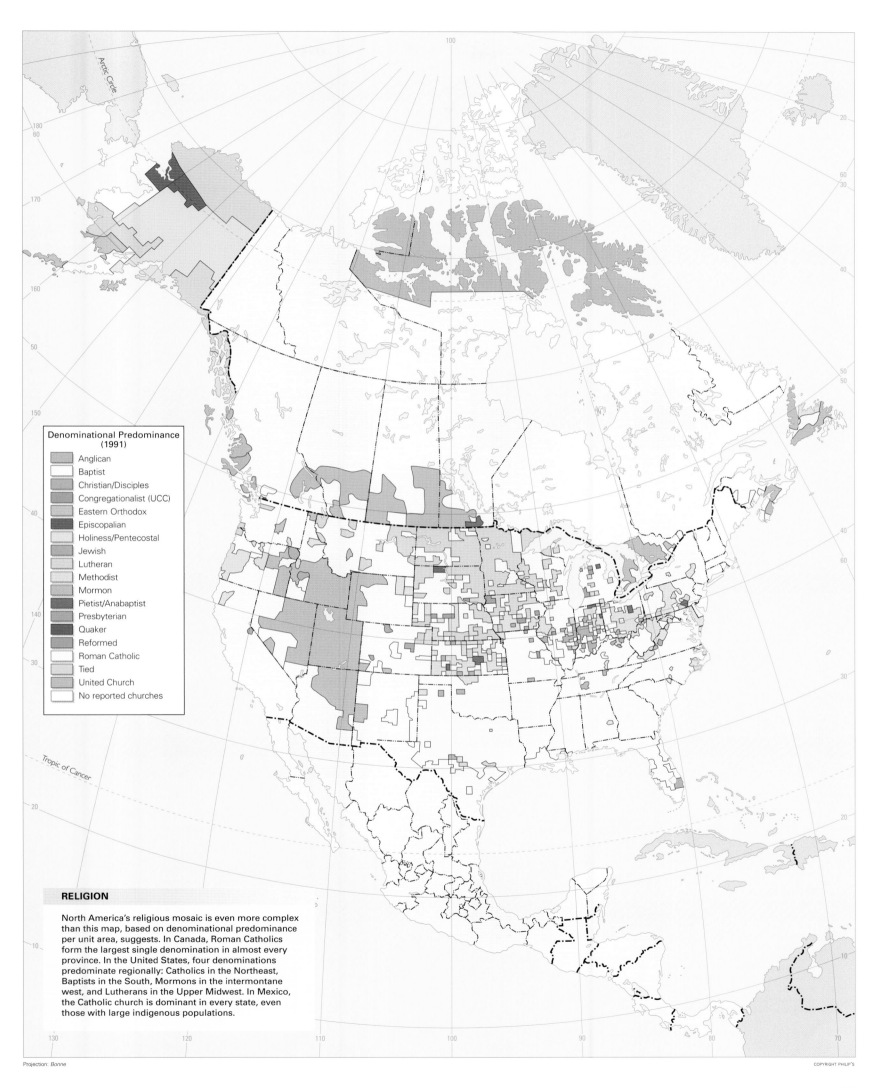

Denominational Predominance
(1991)

- Anglican
- Baptist
- Christian/Disciples
- Congregationalist (UCC)
- Eastern Orthodox
- Episcopalian
- Holiness/Pentecostal
- Jewish
- Lutheran
- Methodist
- Mormon
- Pietist/Anabaptist
- Presbyterian
- Quaker
- Reformed
- Roman Catholic
- Tied
- United Church
- No reported churches

RELIGION

North America's religious mosaic is even more complex than this map, based on denominational predominance per unit area, suggests. In Canada, Roman Catholics form the largest single denomination in almost every province. In the United States, four denominations predominate regionally: Catholics in the Northeast, Baptists in the South, Mormons in the intermontane west, and Lutherans in the Upper Midwest. In Mexico, the Catholic church is dominant in every state, even those with large indigenous populations.

Projection: Bonne

National Parks and Federal Lands

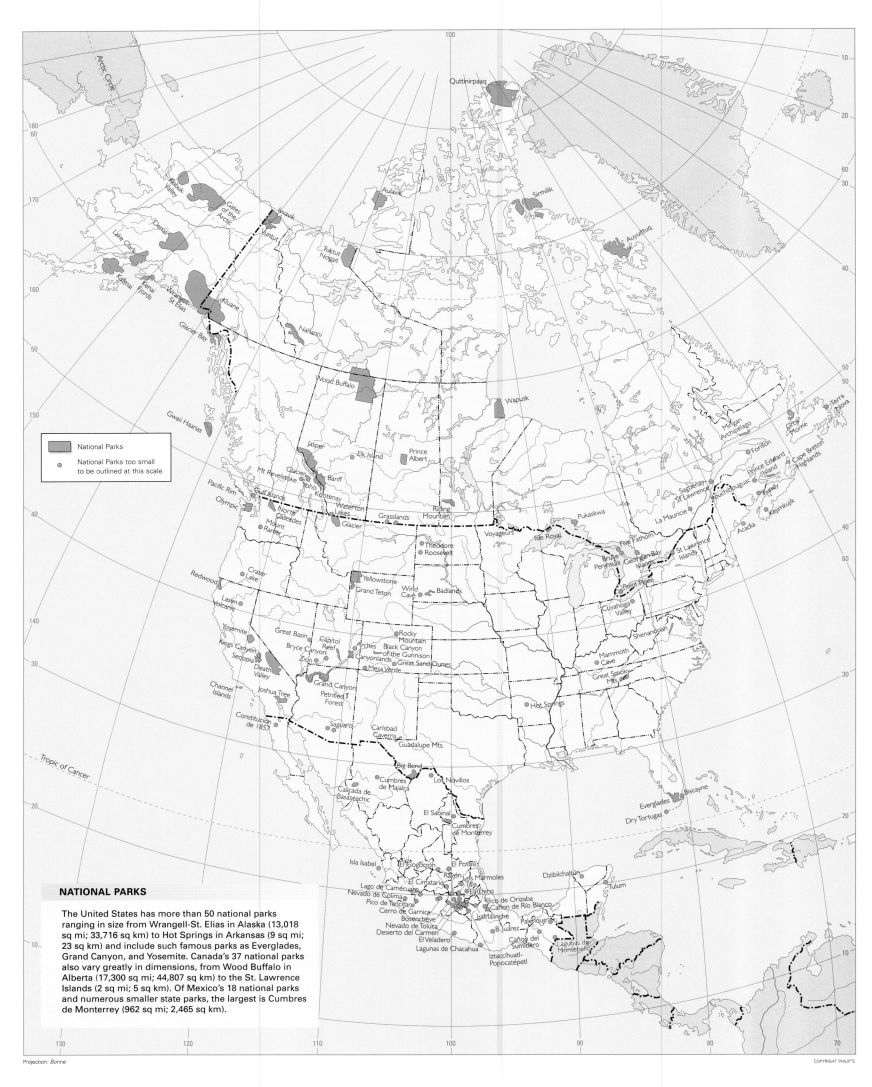

NATIONAL PARKS

The United States has more than 50 national parks ranging in size from Wrangell-St. Elias in Alaska (13,018 sq mi; 33,716 sq km) to Hot Springs in Arkansas (9 sq mi; 23 sq km) and include such famous parks as Everglades, Grand Canyon, and Yosemite. Canada's 37 national parks also vary greatly in dimensions, from Wood Buffalo in Alberta (17,300 sq mi; 44,807 sq km) to the St. Lawrence Islands (2 sq mi; 5 sq km). Of Mexico's 18 national parks and numerous smaller state parks, the largest is Cumbres de Monterrey (962 sq mi; 2,465 sq km).

Projection: *Bonne*

COPYRIGHT PHILIP'S

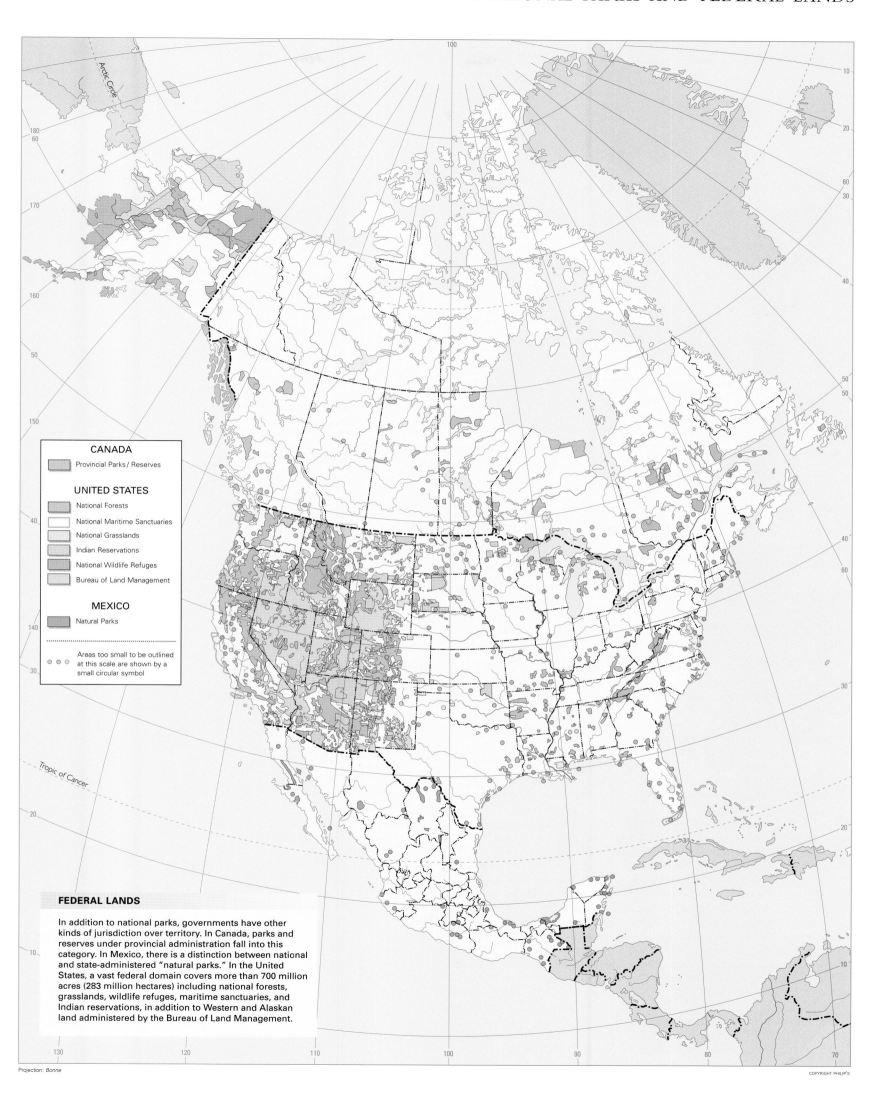

CANADA
■ Provincial Parks / Reserves

UNITED STATES
■ National Forests
□ National Maritime Sanctuaries
■ National Grasslands
■ Indian Reservations
■ National Wildlife Refuges
■ Bureau of Land Management

MEXICO
■ Natural Parks

○ ○ ○ Areas too small to be outlined at this scale are shown by a small circular symbol

FEDERAL LANDS

In addition to national parks, governments have other kinds of jurisdiction over territory. In Canada, parks and reserves under provincial administration fall into this category. In Mexico, there is a distinction between national and state-administered "natural parks." In the United States, a vast federal domain covers more than 700 million acres (283 million hectares) including national forests, grasslands, wildlife refuges, maritime sanctuaries, and Indian reservations, in addition to Western and Alaskan land administered by the Bureau of Land Management.

Projection: Bonne

COPYRIGHT PHILIP'S

MARITIME ZONES AND CLAIMS

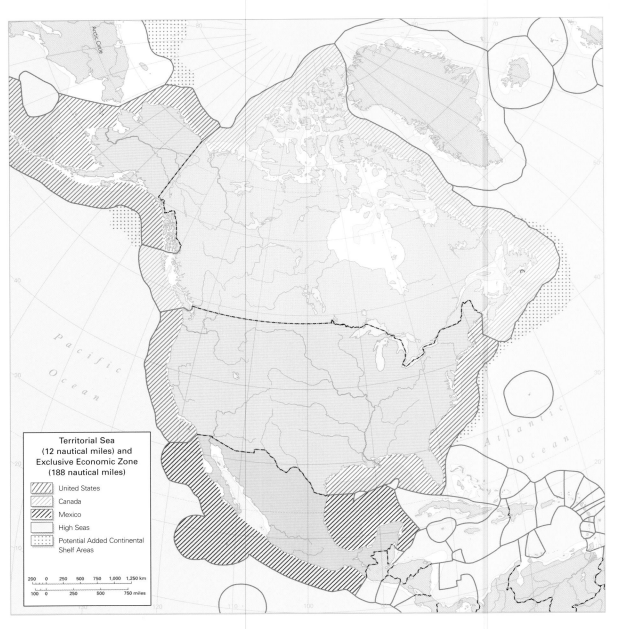

**Territorial Sea
(12 nautical miles) and
Exclusive Economic Zone
(188 nautical miles)**

- United States
- Canada
- Mexico
- High Seas
- Potential Added Continental Shelf Areas

200 0 250 500 750 1,000 1,250 km
100 0 250 500 750 miles

MARITIME ZONES

Claims to resources in and beneath the sea, coupled with concerns over ocean pollution and national security, have led to the extension of national jurisdiction over adjacent waters and the *subsoil* below. This is an ongoing process that started centuries ago when European coastal countries heavily dependent on fishing closed off bays and estuaries to fishing boats from other countries, leading to the notion of the *territorial sea*, a continuous offshore zone where a coastal state claimed all the rights it had on its territory.

In the 17th and 18th centuries, such territorial seas were 3, 4 or at most 6 nautical miles wide (1 nautical mile = 1.15 statute miles or 1.85 km). Beyond lay the *high seas*, free and open to all.

During the 19th century, European states were more concerned with consolidating their colonial empires than expanding their maritime claims, but the 20th century was the scene of a "scramble for the oceans," and not just the oceans but also the subsoil and its resources. After the United States laid claim to the continental shelf down to a depth of 100 fathoms (600 feet), unleashing the scramble, the United Nations convened a series of conferences to control the contest, which had cold-war overtones.

These conferences produced a convention, still not signed by the United States by 2004, that awarded all states sovereign rights over a 12-mile territorial sea and an *Exclusive Economic Zone* (EEZ) extending to 200 miles offshore, within which states have rights to resources but also conservation responsibilities.

MARITIME CLAIMS

Canada, the United States, and Mexico all have lengthy coastlines on open waters, and the three large nations of North America benefited greatly from the United Nations Convention on the Law of the Sea (UNCLOS) that awarded coastal states a 200-mile EEZ.

The map above shows the approximate maritime areas under each state's jurisdiction. Because islands have their own EEZs, offshore possessions effectively extend EEZs seaward, as is the case off the west coast of mainland Mexico. On its east coast, Mexico's EEZ is hemmed in by Cuba and Guatemala, but Mexico has a large share of the resources of the Gulf of Mexico.

The United States has a full-width EEZ from north Florida northward to the Canadian border, an equally wide EEZ in the west, and a vast maritime sphere off Alaska and the Aleutian Islands. The U.S. EEZ meets that of Russia in the Bering Strait.

Canada's western EEZ is confined to a section off British Columbia between the southern end of the Alaska Peninsula and the Juan de Fuca Strait, but its eastern and northern EEZ encompasses a vast maritime area from Nova Scotia to the border with Alaska.

In recent years, the United Nations has begun to authorize states to extend their claims to the continental shelves beyond the 200-mile limit if they can prove that these extensions are "natural prolongations" of their landmasses.

As our map shows, the United States and Canada would be leading beneficiaries of this new provision. In the case of Canada, it would help mitigate a problem created by the delimitation of the 200-mile EEZ off its east coast (map at right). The shallow Grand Bank is bisected by the EEZ boundary, leaving the "Nose" and "Tail" of the Bank outside its jurisdiction, creating disputes with foreign countries over fishing activities and causing management problems.

The push for maritime claims is not over yet, but the international order achieved by the United Nations has controlled the process, has established strict rules for claimants and has saved what remains of the high seas from unrestricted invasion.

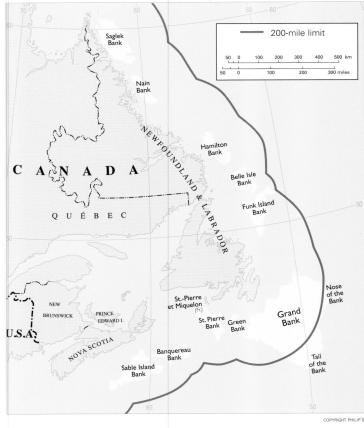

200-mile limit

50 0 100 200 300 400 500 km
50 0 100 200 300 miles

UNITED STATES

STATE MAPS

Settlements
(number of inhabitants)

- ■ **NEW YORK** — Over 5,000,000
- ■ **SEATTLE** — 2,000,000 – 5,000,000
- ■ **SACRAMENTO** — 1,000,000 – 2,000,000
- ◉ **Albuquerque** — 500,000 – 1,000,000
- ⊙ **Omaha** — 250,000 – 500,000
- ⊙ **Abilene** — 100,000 – 250,000
- ⊙ **Charleston** — 50,000 – 100,000
- ⊙ Sandusky — 20,000 – 50,000
- ○ *Twentynine Palms* — 10,000 – 20,000
- ○ Pecos — 5,000 – 10,000
- ○ *Deadwood* — Less than 5,000
- ▢ — Extent of urban areas (over 1,000,000 inhabitants)

Population figures for settlements are from the U.S. Census 2000 Summary file. Population figures for settlements with over 500,000 inhabitants are for urban areas.

Administration

- International boundaries
- State boundaries
- County boundaries (parishes in Louisiana and census areas in Alaska)
- CALHOUN — County names
- *NAVAJO IND. RES.* — Indian reservations
- *MESA VERDE NAT. PARK* — National parks *
- *NANTAHALA NAT. FOREST* — National forests and grasslands
- *FORT A.P. HILL* — Military and federal reserves
- **WASHINGTON D.C.** ■ — National capital
- **PHOENIX** ⊡ — State capitals with over 1,000,000 inhabitants
- **Dover** ⊛ — State capitals with less than 1,000,000 inhabitants
- ■ *JOHN F. KENNEDY SPACE CENTER* — Selected points of interest

* Includes national monuments, national preserves, national recreation areas, national scenic areas, national memorials, national historic sites, national seashores, national wildlife refuges, and selected state parks.

Communications

- Limited-access highways
- Limited-access highways under construction
- Other highways
- (70) Interstate route numbers
- (40) U.S. route numbers
- (13) State route numbers
- Principal railroads (Amtrak)
- Other railroads
- Railroad tunnels
- JFK ✈ Principal airports (with location identifiers)
- ✈ Other airports
- Transportation canals and aqueducts

CITY MAPS

- Free limited-access highways (with interchange)
- Toll limited-access highways
- Tunnels
- Primary divided highways
- Primary undivided highways
- Secondary divided highways
- Secondary undivided highways
- Other roads
- (70) Interstate route numbers
- (40) U.S. route numbers
- (13) State route numbers
- Railroads
- Union Terminal □ — Principal railroad stations
- ✈ Principal airports
- ✈ Other airports
- □ City centers
- City center map coverage
- Urban areas
- **Lynn** / **Clifton** / Swampscott — Suburbs (size of type indicates relative populations)
- Woodlands and parks
- ▪ Zoo — Points of interest

CITY CENTER MAPS

- Free limited-access highways
- Toll limited-access highways
- Through routes
- Secondary routes
- Divided highways
- Other roads
- Tunnels
- Railroads
- Central Sta. — Railroad stations
- Ⓢ Ⓜ — Subway stations
- Urban areas
- **BEACON HILL** — Suburbs
- Woodlands and parks
- □ — Public buildings
- † — Churches
- ✝ — Cathedrals
- Museum — Points of interest

STATE MAPS
Physical features

- Perennial streams and rivers
- Intermittent streams and rivers
- Perennial lakes and reservoirs
- Intermittent lakes
- Dry lakes
- Swamps and marshes
- Reservoirs (with dams)
- Permanent ice and glaciers
- ▲ 4301 — Elevations in meters
- ▼ 2731 — Sea and lake depths in meters
- *1134* — Height of lake surface above sea level in meters
- C. Fear — Capes, points and mountain passes
- **Blue Ridge** — Islands, peninsulas, mountain ranges and peaks
- *Tennessee* — Rivers, lakes, bays, straits, glaciers, marshes and deserts
- *Columbia Plateau* — Plateaus, basins and valleys

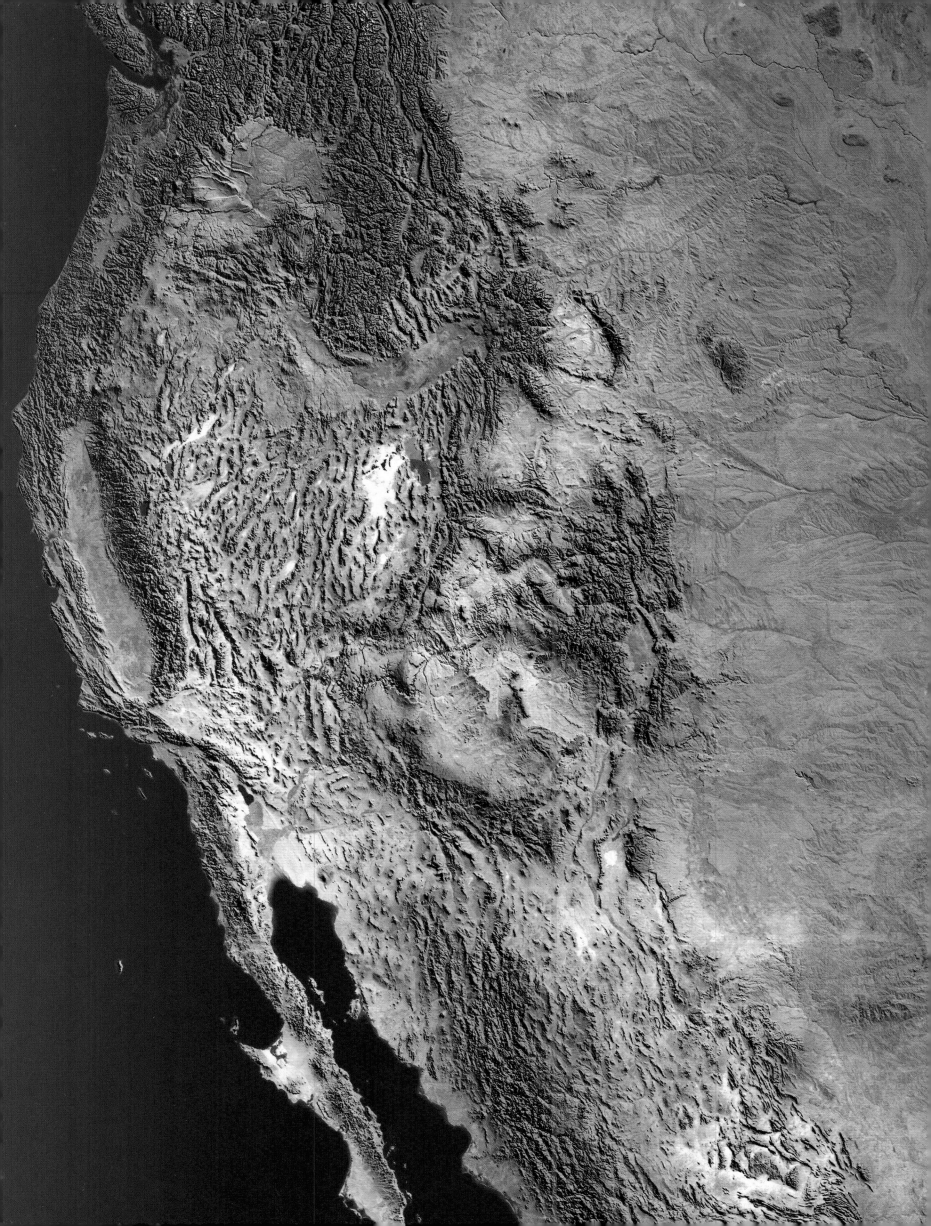

1:10 700 000

Projection: Albers' Equal Area with two standard parallels

West from Greenwich

HAWAI'I
1:8 900 000

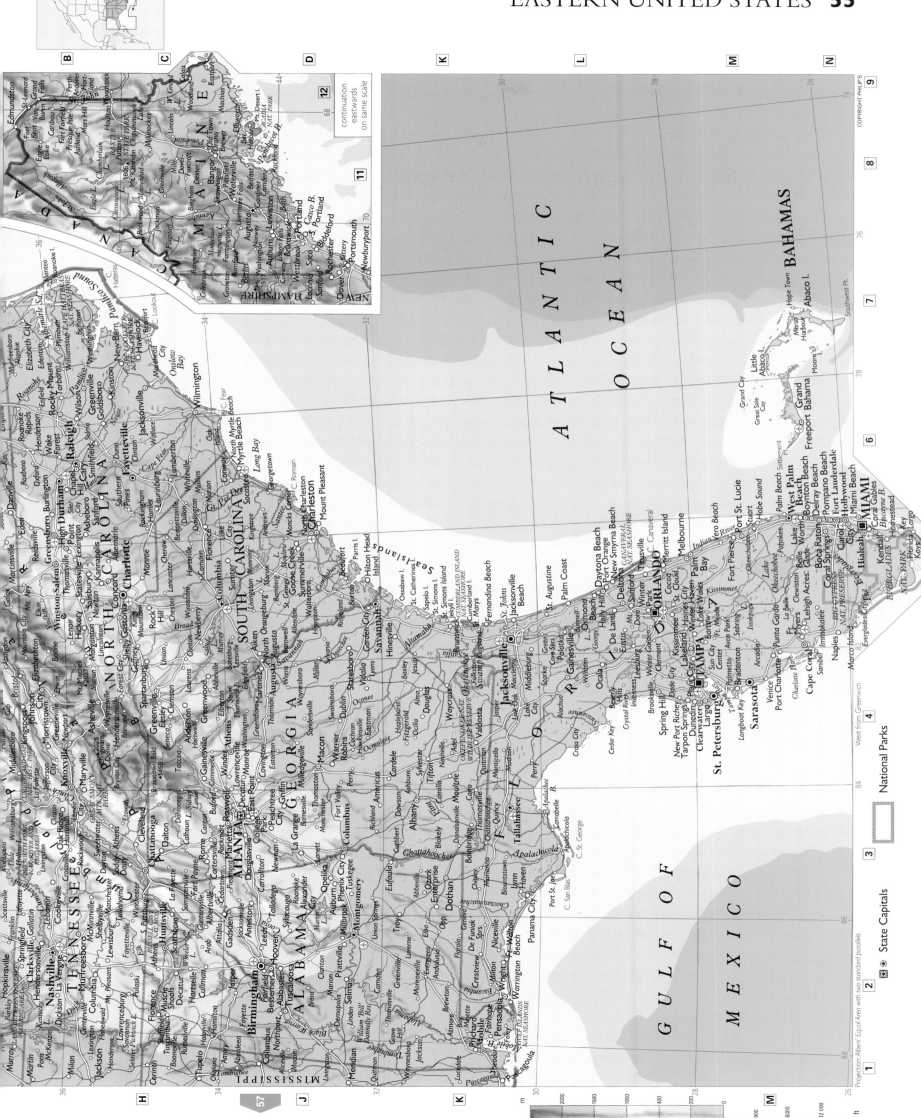

ATLANTIC

OCEAN

BAHAMAS

GULF OF

MEXICO

State Capitals

National Parks

continuation
eastwards
on same scale

COPYRIGHT PHILIP'S

Projection: Albers' Equal Area with two standard parallels

West from Greenwich

1:5 300 000

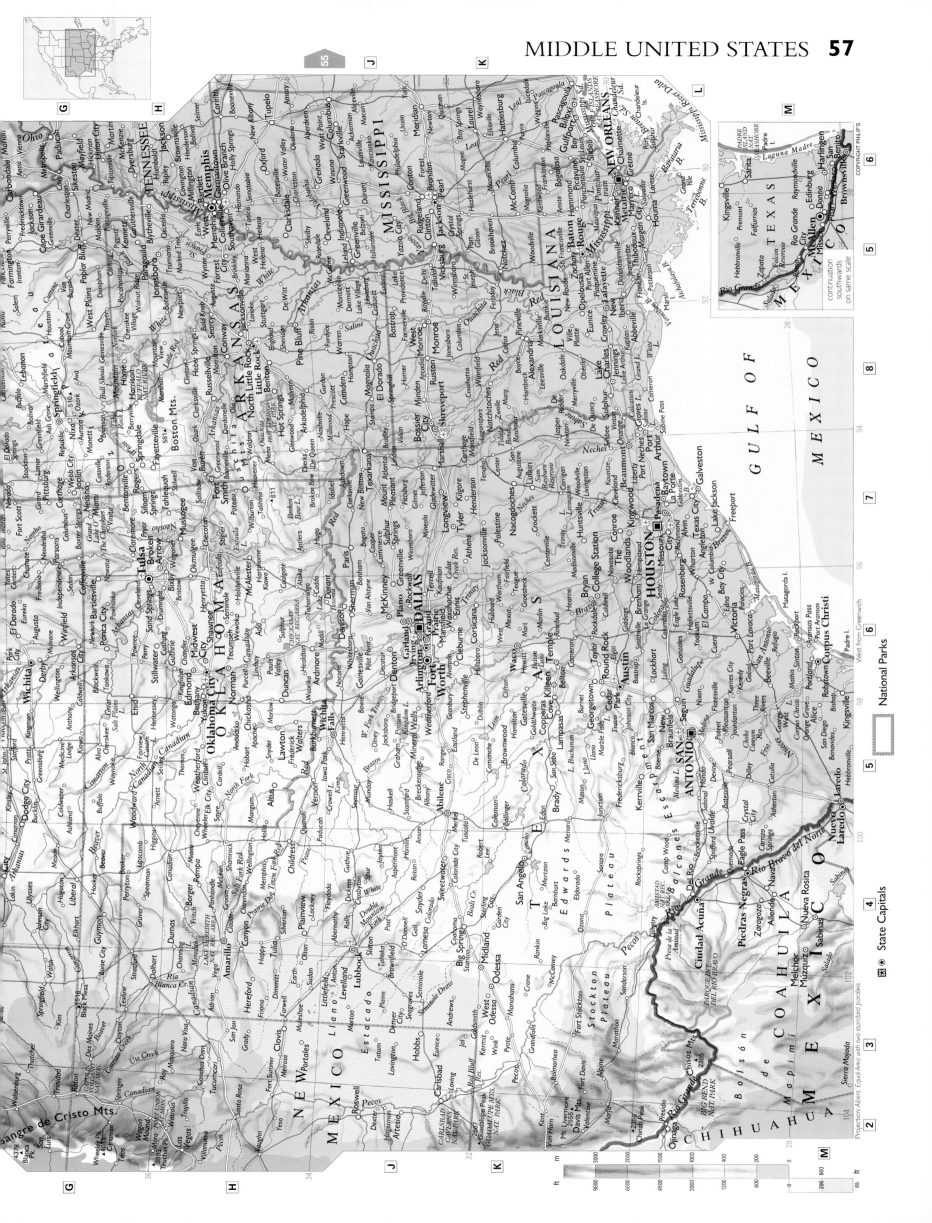

National Parks

State Capitals

50 0 50 100 150 200 km
50 0 50 100 150 miles

1:5 300 000

A B C D 56 E F

B C D

10 9 108 110 8 112 7 114 6 116 5 118 4 120 3 122 2 1

SASKATCHEWAN

ALBERTA

BRITISH COLUMBIA

MONTANA

NORTH DAKOTA

WYOMING

IDAHO

OREGON

WASHINGTON

NEVADA

UTAH

Rocky Mountains

Bighorn Mountains

Absaroka Range

Wind River Range

Medicine Bow Mts.

Park Ra.

Bitterroot Range

Salmon River Mountains

Sawtooth Range

Columbia Plateau

Great Salt Lake

Great Salt Lake Desert

Uinta Mountains

Wasatch Range

Great Basin

Toiyabe Ra.

Ruby Mts.

Shoshone Mountains

Stillwater Ra.

Warner Mts.

Cascade Range

Blue Mountains

Wallowa Mts.

Columbia Basin

Olympic Mts.

Coast Ranges

VANCOUVER

SEATTLE

PORTLAND

SACRAMENTO

Spokane

Helena

Missoula

Butte

Great Falls

Billings

Boise

Salt Lake City

Ogden

Provo

Pocatello

Idaho Falls

Casper

Laramie

Reno

Carson City

Eugene

Salem

Medford

Redding

Klamath Falls

Bend

Yakima

Tacoma

Olympia

Bellingham

Victoria

Nanaimo

PACIFIC RIM NAT. PARK

YELLOWSTONE NAT. PARK

GRAND TETON NAT. PARK

CRATERS OF THE MOON NAT. MON.

Juan de Fuca Strait

Puget Sound

Columbia

Snake

Missouri

Salmon

Humboldt

Pyramid L.

Lake Tahoe

Walker L.

Goose L.

Summer L.

Harney L.

Malheur L.

Upper Klamath L.

Flaming Gorge Res.

Fort Peck Lake

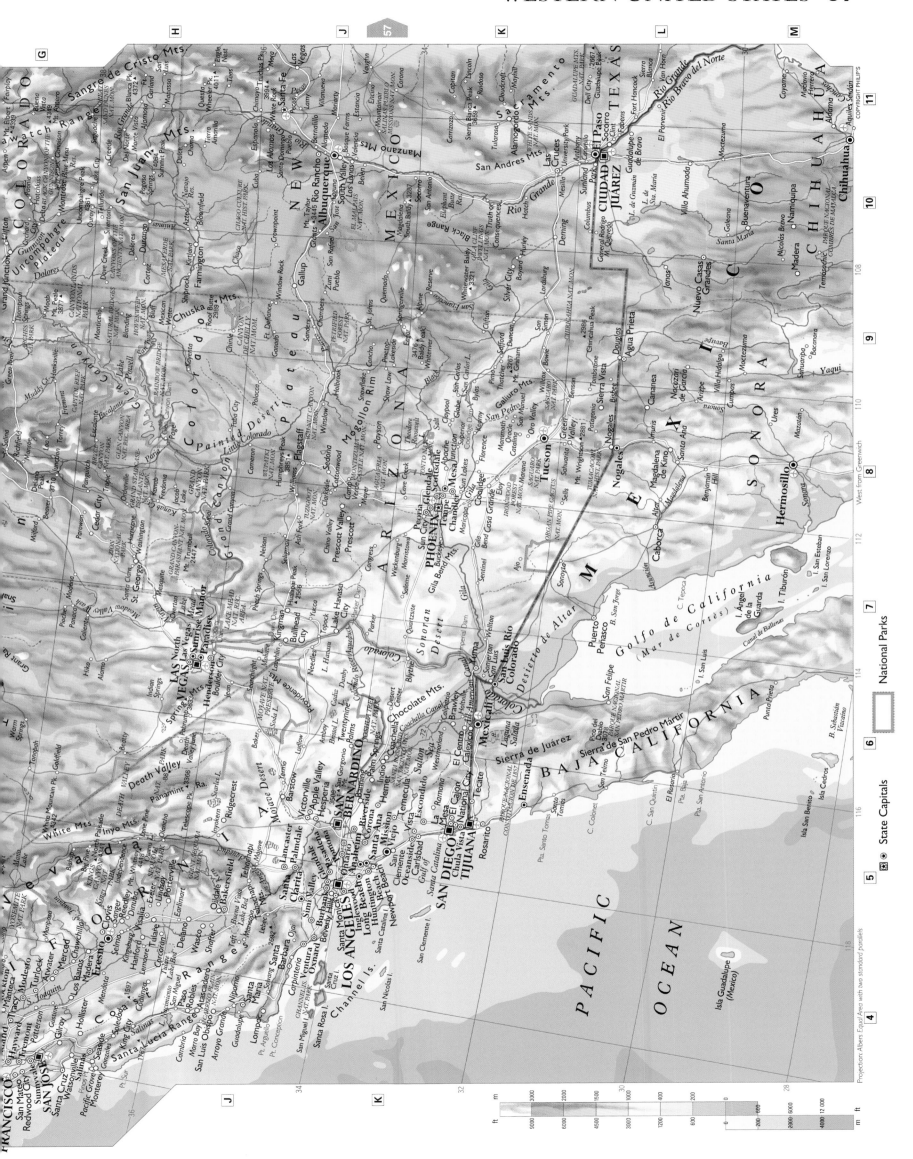

Projection: Albers Equal Area with two standard parallels

West from Greenwich

National Parks

State Capitals

1:2 200 000

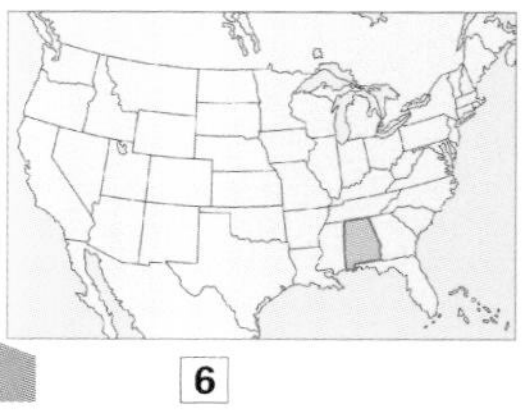

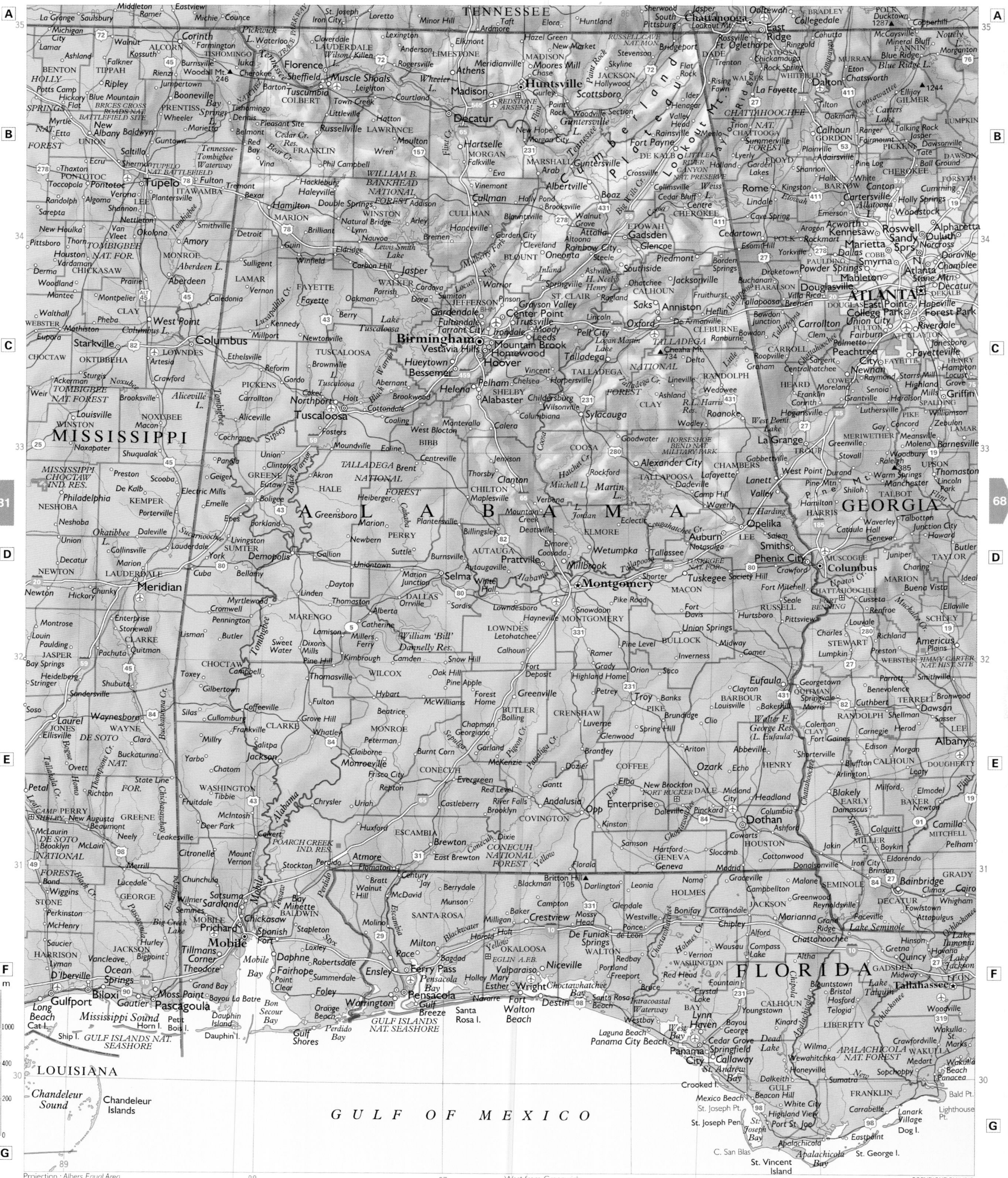

Projection : Albers Equal Area

West from Greenwich

COPYRIGHT PHILIP'S

TENNESSEE

MISSISSIPPI

ALABAMA

GEORGIA

FLORIDA

LOUISIANA

GULF OF MEXICO

Huntsville
Decatur
Florence · Muscle Shoals · Sheffield · Tuscumbia
Athens
Chattanooga
Rome
Gadsden
Anniston
Birmingham
Bessemer · Hoover · Homewood · Mountain Brook · Vestavia Hills
Tuscaloosa · Northport
Atlanta
Columbus
Montgomery
Selma
Demopolis
Meridian
Auburn · Opelika
Phenix City
Dothan
Enterprise · Dothan
Andalusia
Brewton
Atmore
Mobile · Prichard · Chickasaw · Saraland
Pensacola
Fort Walton Beach · Destin
Panama City · Panama City Beach
Tallahassee
Biloxi · Gulfport · Pascagoula
Gulf Shores

GULF ISLANDS NAT. SEASHORE

Chandeleur Sound · Chandeleur Islands

Dauphin I. · Petit Bois I. · Horn I. · Ship I. · Cat I.

Mississippi Sound

Mobile Bay

TALLADEGA NATIONAL FOREST

WILLIAM B. BANKHEAD NATIONAL FOREST

TOMBIGBEE NAT. FOR.

CONECUH NATIONAL FOREST

APALACHICOLA NAT. FOREST

DE SOTO NATIONAL FOREST

EGLIN A.F.B.

FORT RUCKER

REDSTONE ARSENAL

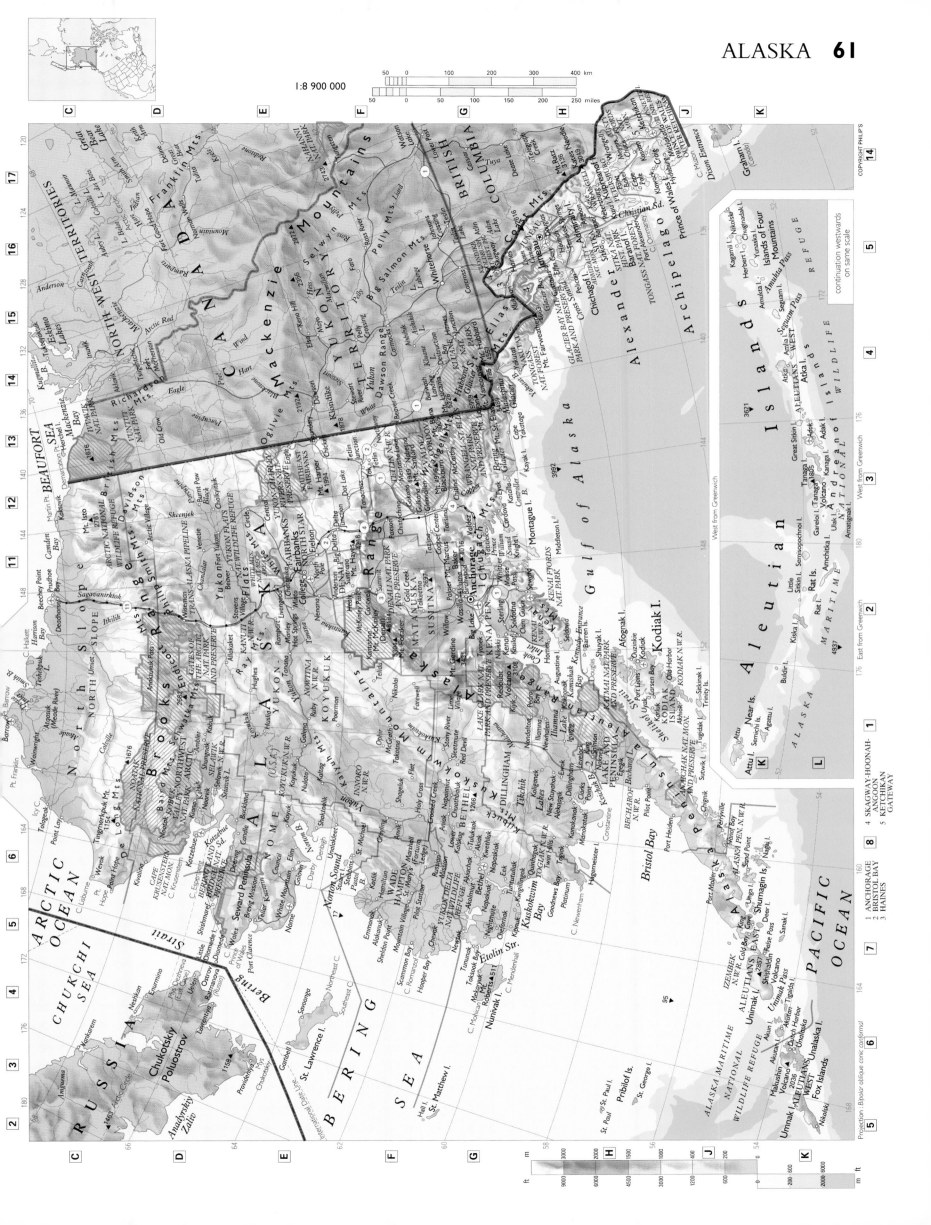

1:2 200 000

10 0 10 20 30 40 50 60 70 80 90 km
10 0 10 20 30 40 50 60 miles

NEVADA
CLARK

Littlefield
Colorado City
Moccasin
Fredonia
UTAH
L. Powell
VERMILION CLIFFS
Rainbow Plateau
Monument Pass 1609
Monument Valley
Mexican Water
Teec Nos Pas
Pastora Pk. 2869

Mesquite
Mt. Bangs 2442
Bunkerville
Virgin Mts.
PIPE SPRING NAT. MON.
Kaibab
Kanab Plateau
Kaibab Plateau
Paria Plateau
PARIA CANYON NAT. MON.
Page
Navajo Cr.
Dennehotso
Rock Point
Red Rock
Roof Butte 2869

Logandale
Overton
GRAND CANYON-PARASHANT NAT. MON.
Hurricane Cliffs
Mt. Trumbull 2447
GRAND CANYON
NATIONAL
Point Imperial 2683
North Rim
COCONINO
Echo Cliffs
Kaibito Plateau
Black Mesa
Kayenta
Marsh Pass 2041
Navajo
Round Rock
Lukachukai
Matthews Pk. 2899
Tsaile

Lake Mead
Jumbo Pk. 1757
Shivwits Plateau
GRAND CANYON NAT. REC. AREA
Supai
HAVASUPAI IND. RES.
Grand Canyon
Tusayan
Tuba City
Moenkopi
Painted Desert
Shonto
Tonalea
Pinon
CANYON DE CHELLY NAT. MON.
Chinle

Hoover Dam
LAKE MEAD NAT. REC. AREA
Colorado
GRAND CANYON NATIONAL PARK
Kaibab
Cameron
Moenkopi Wash
Hotevilla
NAVAJO
HOPI
Polacca
Kykotsmovi Village
Second Mesa
Keams Canyon
Steamboat Canyon
Ganado
HUBBELL TRADING POST NAT. HIST. SITE
Fort Defiance
Window Rock

Black Mts.
Dolan Springs
Red L.
Mt. Tipton 2179
Cerbat Mts.
MOHAVE
HUALAPAI INDIAN RESERVATION
Peach Springs
Coconino Plateau
Aubrey Cliffs
WUPATKI NAT. MON.
Dilkon
INDIAN
RESERVATION
Lupton

Lake Mohave
Chloride
Truxton
Nelson
Seligman
San Francisco Mts.
Humphreys Pk. 3851
SUNSET CRATER VOLCANO NAT. MON.
NAVAJO INDIAN
Chambers
Houk
Sanders

Davis Dam
Bullhead City
Riviera
Kingman
Hualapai Pk. 2566
Valentine
Hackberry
Ash Fork
Williams
Bill Williams Mt
KAIBAB NATIONAL
Bellemont
Flagstaff
WALNUT CANYON NAT. MON.
COCONINO
Winslow
Joseph City
Holbrook
PETRIFIED FOREST NAT. PARK
Navajo
APACHE

FORT MOJAVE IND. RES.
Oatman
Hualapai Mts.
Mohon Pk. 2285
Aquarius Mts.
Juniper Mts.
Big Chino Wash
Drake
Paulden
Mountainaire
Mormon Lake
Hutch Mt. 2601
Happy Jack
Clear Cr.
Chevelon Cr.
ZUNI INDIAN RESERVATION
Zion Res.

Topock
Mohave Valley
L. Havasu 1554
Chino Valley
Clarkdale
Jerome
Cottonwood
TUZIGOOT NAT. MON.
Cornville
MONTEZUMA CASTLE NAT. MON.
Sedona
NATIONAL
Snowflake
Concho
St. Johns
Lyman Lake

Lake Havasu City
CHEMEHUEVI IND. RES.
Parker Dam
Bagdad
Skull Valley
PRESCOTT
Prescott
Prescott Valley
Dewey
Humboldt
Camp Verde
Lake Montezuma
FOREST
APACHE
Baker Butte 2461
SITGREAVES
Heber
NATIONAL
Taylor
Show Low
FOREST
Springerville
Eagar

CALIFORNIA
Colorado
Parker
Bill Williams R. N.W.R.
BILL WILLIAMS RIVER N.W.R. 1197
Buckskin Mts. 1197
Alamo L.
Hillside
Kirkland
Kirkland Junction
Yarnell
YAVAPAI
2345
Spruce Mt.
Mayer
AGUA FRIA NAT. MON.
Verde R.
Pine
Mogollon Plateau
Mogollon Rim
Payson
Tonto Cr.
Pinetop-Lakeside
McNary
White Mts.
Baldy Pk. 3476
Whiteriver
Nutrioso
Alpine

LA PAZ
Bouse
Harcuvar Mts. 1598
Aguila
Vulture Mts. 1115
Morristown
Black Canyon City
Horseshoe Res.
TONTO 2409
Cibecue
FORT APACHE INDIAN RESERVATION
White R.

ARIZONA
Poston
COLORADO RIVER IND. RES.
Quartzsite
Vicksburg
Hope
Harquahala Mts. 1732
Salome
Wenden
Wickenburg
60
Wittmann
Cave Creek
Carefree
Bartlett Res.
Mazatzal Mts.
NATIONAL
Aztec Pk. 2345
Theodore Roosevelt L.
Roosevelt
GILA
Black R.
Rose Pk. 2678

Ehrenberg
Bouse Wash
KOFA
Signal Pk. 1487
KOFA NAT. WILDLIFE REFUGE
Eagletail Mts.
1006
Surprise
Sun City West
Sun City
El Mirage
Peoria
Paradise Valley
Glendale
Scottsdale
FORT McDOWELL IND. RES.
Fountain Hills
Apache L.
Apache Junction
Tortilla Flat
FOREST
TONTO NAT. MON.
2334
Superior
Claypool
Miami
Globe
Peridot
San Carlos
SAN CARLOS INDIAN RESERVATION

Cibola
Trigo Mts.
Chocolate Mts.
Castle Dome Pk. 1155
Gila Bend Mts.
966
PHOENIX
Goodyear
Avondale
Tolleson
Tempe
Mesa
Gilbert
Chandler
Sun Lakes
GILA RIVER
Queen Creek
60
San Carlos L.
Coolidge Dam
Bylas
Gila R.
Morenci
Clifton
GREENLEE

Martinez Lake
Imperial Res.
SONORAN
YUMA
YUMA PROVING GROUND
Buckeye
Palo Verde
Arlington
MARICOPA
HOHOKAM PIMA
Guadalupe
Komatke
SONORAN
Mobile
GILA RIVER INDIAN RES.
Sacaton
Olberg
Florence
CASA GRANDE RUINS NAT. MON.
Kearny
Hayden
Winkelman
Dudleyville
GRAHAM
Pima
Safford
Solomon
Duncan

Imperial Dam
Yuma
Somerton
Gadsden
San Luis
Gila R. 960
YUMA
Roll
Wellton
Tacna
Dateland
Sentinel
BARRY M. GOLDWATER AIR FORCE RANGE
Gila Bend
GILA BEND IND. RES.
Stanfield
Casa Grande
Eloy
Picacho
Picacho Pass 549
La Palma
PINAL
Table Mt. 1877
Mt. Graham 3267
Pinaleno Mts.
San Simon
Franklin

Yuma Desert
Mohawk Mts.
846
Granite Mts.
Growler Mts.
Ajo
Desert
Sauceda Mts.
1252
Sand Tank Mts.
Table Top 1333
ORGAN PIPE NAT. MON.
Chuichu
Arizona City
Santa Rosa Wash
Marana
Rillito
Catalina
Oracle
San Manuel 2336
Santa Catalina Mts. 2791
CORONADO NAT. FOREST
Mammoth
San Pedro R.

MEXICO
SONORA
Gran Desierto de Altar
Rio Sonoyta
Sonoyta
Lukeville
1206
CABEZA PRIETA N.W.R.
Sierra Pinta
899
ORGAN PIPE CACTUS NAT. MON.
Mt. Ajo 1465
Anegam
Silver Bell
IRONWOOD FOREST NAT. MON.
Santa Rosa
TOHONO O'ODHAM INDIAN RESERVATION
1459
Sil Nakya
PIMA
Comobabi Mts.
Pisinimo
Sells
Cartero
Oro Valley
SAGUARO NAT. PARK
Tucson
South Tucson
TOHONO O'ODHAM (SAN XAVIER) IND. RES.
Vail
SAGUARO NAT. PARK
Willcox
San Simon
FORT BOWIE NAT. HIST. SITE
Willcox Playa
Bowie
COCHISE
Dragoon
CHIRICAHUA NAT. MON.
Portal
Chiricahua Pk. 2986

Cawlic
Topawa
Baboquivari Pk. 2356
BUENOS AIRES N.W.R.
Sahuarita
Green Valley
Keystone Pk. 1892
Mt. Wrightson 2881
Tubac
TUMACACORI NAT. HIST. PARK
Patagonia
Tombstone
Elfrida
McNeal
Naco
Douglas

SONORA
Sasabe
Nogales
SANTA CRUZ
Sierra Vista
Hereford
Bisbee
FORT HUACHUCA
Huachuca City
Pearce
Pirtleville

Projection: Albers Equal Area
West from Greenwich
COPYRIGHT PHILIP'S

0 200 400 1000 1500 2000 3000 m
0 600 1200 3000 4500 6000 9000 ft

1:2 200 000

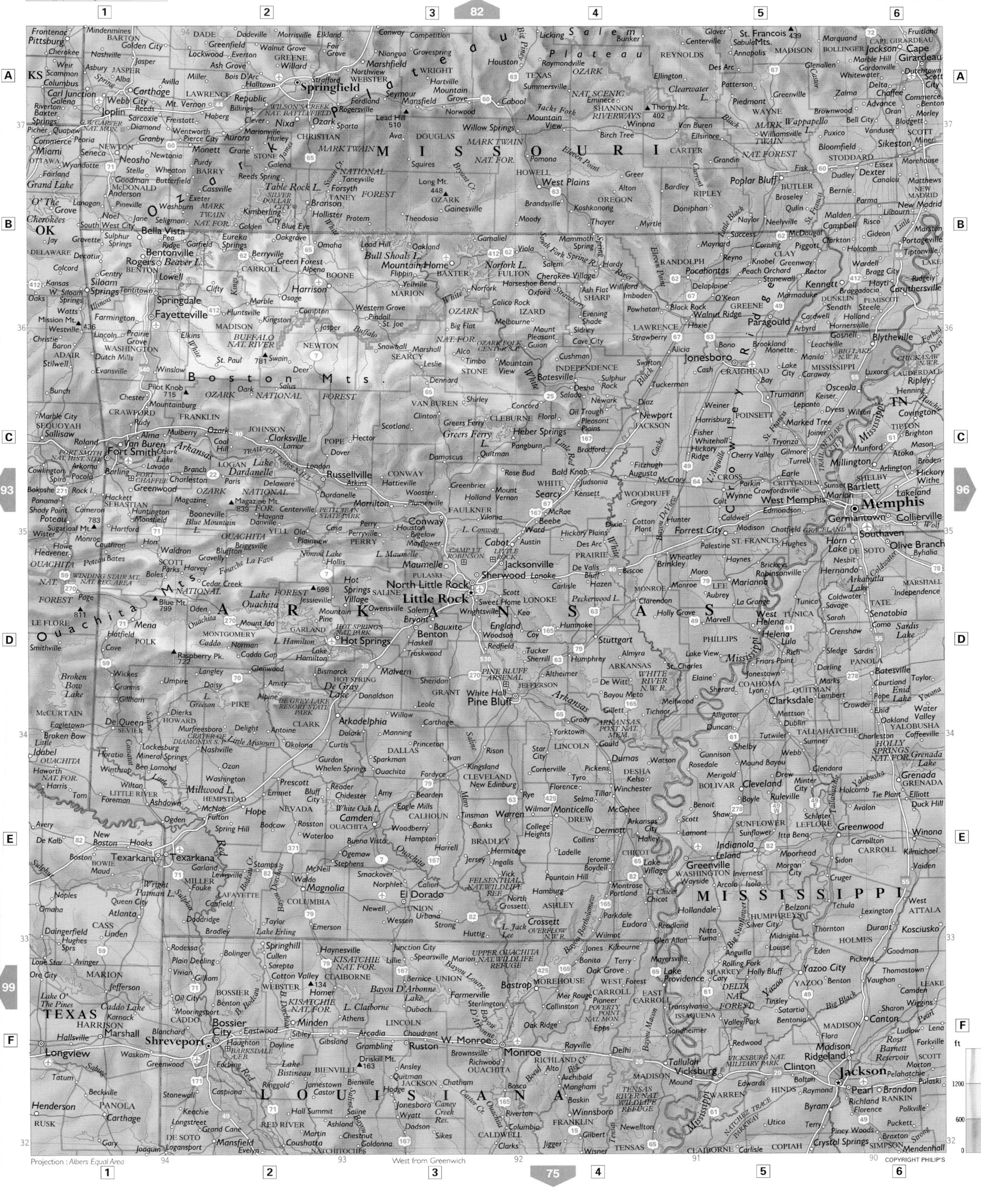

10 0 10 20 30 40 50 60 70 80 100 km
10 0 10 20 30 40 50 60 miles

MISSOURI

KS

OK

TENNESSEE (TN)

A R K A N S A S

MISSISSIPPI

TEXAS

LOUISIANA

Ozark Plateau

Salem Plateau

MARK TWAIN NATIONAL FOREST

OZARK NATIONAL FOREST

Boston Mts.

Ouachita Mts.

OUACHITA NATIONAL FOREST

BUFFALO NAT. RIVER

Springfield

Joplin

Fayetteville

Fort Smith

Little Rock

North Little Rock

Hot Springs

Pine Bluff

Texarkana

El Dorado

Jonesboro

West Memphis

Memphis

Shreveport

Bossier City

Monroe

W. Monroe

Ruston

Jackson

Vicksburg

Greenville

Pilot Knob 715

Magazine Mt. 839

Blue Mt. 799

Rich Mt. 811

Sugarloaf Mt. 783

Mt. Magazine

Driskill Mt. 163

Thorny Mt. 402

Lead Hill 510

Long Mt. 448

Ozark 781

Mt. 436

Poplar Bluff

Cape Girardeau

Projection : Albers Equal Area   West from Greenwich   COPYRIGHT PHILIP'S

ft m
1200 400
600 200

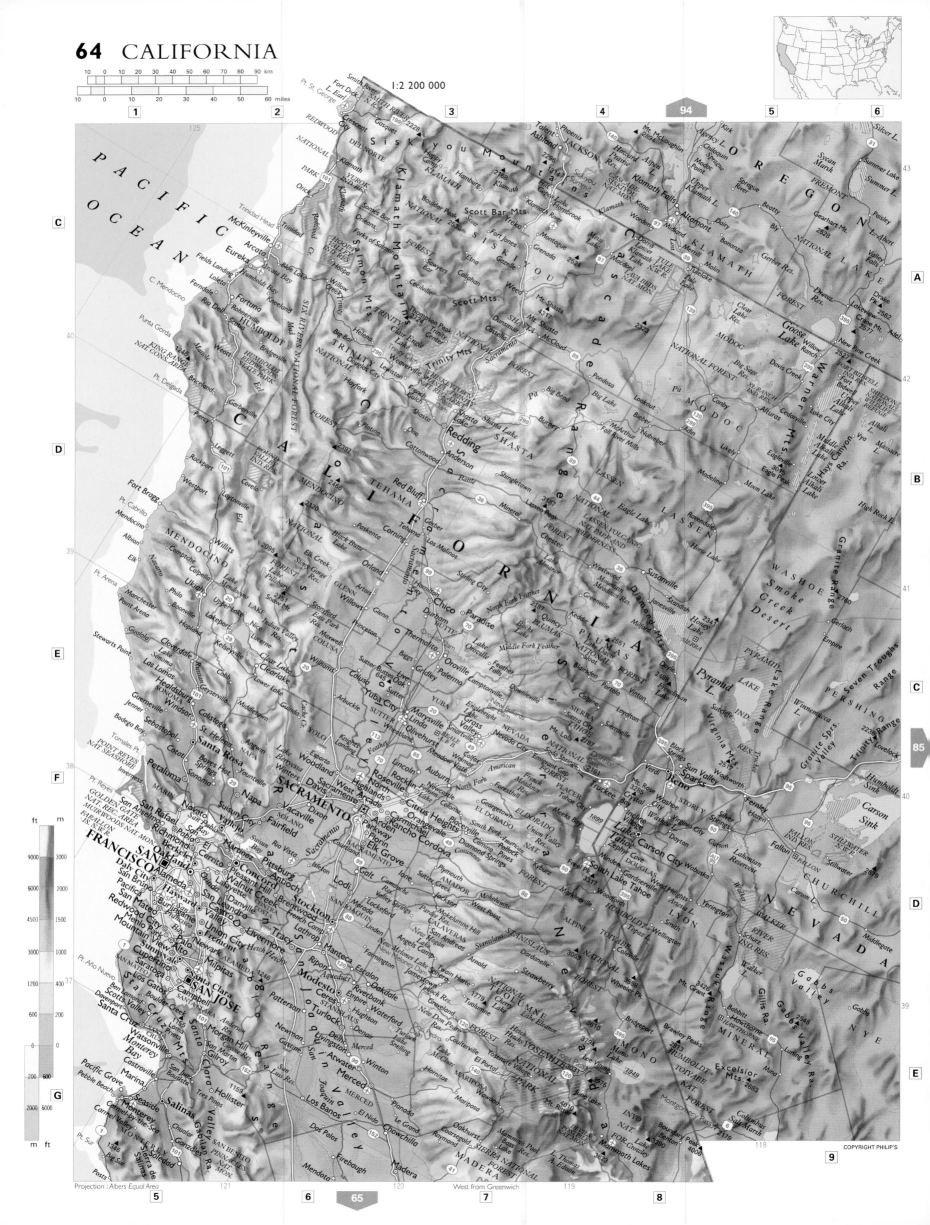

G H J K L M

PACIFIC OCEAN

NEVADA

MEXICO BAJA CALIFORNIA

ARIZONA YUMA

Channel Islands

San Miguel Island
Santa Rosa Island
Santa Cruz Island
Anacapa I.
San Nicolas Island
San Clemente Island
Santa Catalina
Santa Barbara Channel
Gulf of Santa Catalina
Outer Santa Barbara Passage
San Clemente Passage

CHANNEL ISLANDS NAT. PARK

Salinas Valley
Gabilan Ra.
Soledad
Gonzales
Greenfield
King City
San Lucas
San Ardo
San Miguel
Paso Robles
Templeton
Atascadero
San Luis Obispo
Pismo Beach
Arroyo Grande
Nipomo
Santa Maria
Orcutt
Guadalupe
Lompoc
Vandenberg A.F.B.
Solvang
Buellton
Santa Ynez
Los Olivos
Goleta
Santa Barbara
Montecito
Carpinteria
Ventura
Oxnard
Port Hueneme
Camarillo
Thousand Oaks
Simi Valley
Fillmore
Santa Paula
El Rio
Ojai
Oak View

Morro Bay
Los Osos
Cambria
Cayucos
San Simeon
Grover Beach

SANTA LUCIA RANGE
LOS PADRES NAT. FOR.
SAN RAFAEL MTS.
SANTA YNEZ MTS.
Pt. Conception

Fresno
Clovis
Madera
Mendota
Firebaugh
Tranquillity
Highway City
Kerman
San Joaquin
Selma
Kingsburg
Parlier
Reedley
Dinuba
Sanger
Centerville
Orange Cove
Hanford
Lemoore
Corcoran
Visalia
Exeter
Lindsay
Porterville
Woodlake
Three Rivers
Springville
Delano
McFarland
Wasco
Shafter
Buttonwillow
Greenacres
BAKERSFIELD
Oildale
Arvin
Lamont
Taft
Maricopa
Tehachapi
Mojave
Rosamond
Lancaster
Palmdale
Littlerock
California City
Edwards

SEQUOIA NATIONAL PARK
KINGS CANYON NATIONAL PARK
SEQUOIA NAT. FOR.
SIERRA NATIONAL FOREST
INYO NATIONAL FOREST
GIANT SEQUOIA NAT. MON.

Mt. Whitney 4418
Independence
Lone Pine
Big Pine
Bishop
Owens L.

DEATH VALLEY NATIONAL PARK
Death Valley
PANAMINT RANGE
ARGUS RANGE
COSO RANGE
SALINE VALLEY
PANAMINT VALLEY
Ridgecrest
China Lake
Trona
Johannesburg
Red Mountain
Randsburg

MOJAVE DESERT
Barstow
Victorville
Hesperia
Adelanto
Apple Valley
Yermo
Newberry Springs
Ludlow
Amboy
Essex
Needles

SAN BERNARDINO NATIONAL FOREST
SAN BERNARDINO
Redlands
Riverside
Colton
Corona
Fontana
Rancho Cucamonga
Ontario
Upland
Claremont
Pomona
Chino
Moreno Valley
Perris
Hemet
San Jacinto
Beaumont
Banning
Palm Springs
Cathedral City
Palm Desert
Indio
Coachella
Mecca
JOSHUA TREE NAT. PARK
Twentynine Palms
Yucca Valley
Joshua Tree
Desert Hot Springs
Blythe
Salton Sea

LOS ANGELES
Burbank
Glendale
Pasadena
Alhambra
Azusa
Covina
West Covina
Beverly Hills
Santa Monica
Inglewood
Compton
Downey
Norwalk
Whittier
Torrance
Redondo Beach
Long Beach
Westminster
Garden Grove
Anaheim
Fullerton
Orange
Santa Ana
Irvine
Costa Mesa
Newport Beach
Huntington Beach
Lake Elsinore
Sun City
Temecula
Fallbrook
San Clemente
San Juan Capistrano
Dana Point
Laguna Beach
Mission Viejo
Oceanside
Carlsbad
Vista
San Marcos
Encinitas
Escondido
Ramona
Poway
Santee
Lakeside
El Cajon
La Mesa
SAN DIEGO
Coronado
National City
Chula Vista
Imperial Beach
TIJUANA
Rosarito
Tecate
Mexicali
Calexico
El Centro
Brawley
Holtville
Imperial
Niland
Westmorland

PACIFIC OCEAN

Projection: Albers Equal Area

West from Greenwich

COPYRIGHT PHILIP'S

1:2 200 000

KANSAS

NEBRASKA

WYOMING

UTAH

NEW MEXICO

OKLAHOMA

COLORADO

DENVER

Colorado Springs

Pueblo

Fort Collins

Greeley

Boulder

Aurora

Lakewood

Arvada

Westminster

Longmont

Loveland

Grand Junction

Montrose

Durango

Alamosa

Trinidad

Sterling

Fort Morgan

Craig

Steamboat Springs

Aspen

Glenwood Springs

Leadville

Salida

Cañon City

ROCKY MOUNTAINS

Rocky Mtn. Nat. Park

Sangre de Cristo Mountains

San Juan Mountains

San Luis Valley

Sawatch Range

Front Range

Park Range

Medicine Bow Mts.

Flat Tops

Grand Mesa

Uncompahgre Plateau

Colorado Plateau

Book Cliffs

Roan Cliffs

Danforth Hills

Pawnee National Grassland

Comanche National Grassland

Mt. Elbert 4399

Pikes Peak 4301

Blanca Peak 4372

Mesa Verde National Park

Projection: Albers Equal Area
COPYRIGHT PHILIP'S

See page 78 for Connecticut and page 77 for Delaware and District of Columbia

1:2 200 000

10 0 10 20 30 40 50 60 70 80 100 km
10 0 10 20 30 40 50 60 miles

ATLANTIC OCEAN

GEORGIA

GULF OF MEXICO

FLORIDA

ft / m elevation legend:
600 / 200, 0, 200 / 600, m / ft

Major cities and places

Tallahassee, Jacksonville, Gainesville, Ocala, Orlando, TAMPA, St. Petersburg, Clearwater, Sarasota, Bradenton, Lakeland, Kissimmee, Melbourne, Palm Bay, Vero Beach, Fort Pierce, Port St. Lucie, Okeechobee, W. Palm Bch., Palm Beach, Boca Raton, Deerfield Bch., Pompano Bch., Fort Lauderdale, Hollywood, Hialeah, MIAMI, Miami Beach, Coral Gables, Homestead, Naples, Fort Myers, Cape Coral, Punta Gorda, Port Charlotte, Cape Canaveral, Cocoa Beach, Titusville, Daytona Beach, Ormond Beach, St. Augustine, Palm Coast, Flagler Beach, Jacksonville Beach, Fernandina Beach, St. Marys, Key West, Key Largo, Islamorada, Marathon, Big Pine Key

Counties and features

APALACHICOLA NAT. FOREST, OSCEOLA NAT. FOREST, OCALA NATIONAL FOREST, LOWER SUWANNEE NAT. WILDLIFE REFUGE, ST. MARKS N.W.R., MERRITT ISLAND N.W.R., JOHN F. KENNEDY SPACE CENTER, CAPE CANAVERAL, CANAVERAL NAT. SEASHORE, EVERGLADES NATIONAL PARK, BIG CYPRESS NAT. PRESERVE, BISCAYNE NAT. PARK, DE SOTO NAT. MEM., TIMUCUAN ECOLOG. & HIST. PRESERVE, CASTILLO DE SAN MARCOS NAT. MON., FORT MATANZAS NAT. MON., GULF ISLANDS NAT. SEASHORE, BIG CYPRESS IND. RES., MICCOSUKEE IND. RES., ARTHUR R. MARSHALL LOXAHATCHEE NATIONAL WILDLIFE REFUGE, BRIGHTON IND. RES., GREAT WHITE HERON NAT. WILDLIFE REFUGE, KEY WEST NAT. WILDLIFE REFUGE, NATIONAL KEY DEER REFUGE, CYPRESS NAT. PRESERVE

Lake Okeechobee, Lake Seminole, Lake George, Lake Apopka, Lake Kissimmee, Lake Placid, Lake Istokpoga, Apalachee Bay, Tampa Bay, Charlotte Harbor, Biscayne Bay, Florida Bay, Straits of Florida, Florida Keys, Walt Disney World

Inset maps

ALABAMA — FLORIDA (panhandle): Pensacola, Panama City, Fort Walton Beach, Destin, Crestview, Marianna, Niceville, Milton, EGLIN A.F.B., TYNDALL A.F.B.

continuation westwards on same scale
continuation southwards on same scale

West from Greenwich

Projection: Albers Equal Area

COPYRIGHT PHILIP'S

1:2 200 000

10 0 10 20 30 40 50 60 70 80 90 km
10   0   10   20   30   40   50 60 miles

TENNESSEE

NORTH CAROLINA

SOUTH CAROLINA

GEORGIA

ALABAMA

FLORIDA

ATLANTIC OCEAN

Gulf of Mexico

Chattanooga · East Ridge · Dalton · Rome · Calhoun · Cartersville · Marietta · Roswell · Alpharetta · Gainesville · **Atlanta** · Decatur · East Point · College Park · Douglasville · Carrollton · Newnan · Griffin · LaGrange · Columbus · Phenix City · Auburn · Opelika · Americus · Albany · Dothan · Bainbridge · Thomasville · Valdosta · Tifton · Moultrie · Douglas · Waycross · Brunswick · St. Simons I. · Jekyll I. · Savannah · Statesboro · Dublin · Vidalia · Macon · Warner Robins · Perry · Fort Valley · Milledgeville · Athens · Augusta · Greenville · Spartanburg · Greenwood · Columbia · Aiken · Orangeburg · Tallahassee · Jacksonville · Cumberland Island · St. Marys · Kingsland

OKEFENOKEE NAT. WILDLIFE REFUGE · Okefenokee Swamp

CHATTAHOOCHEE NAT. FOREST · OCONEE NAT. FOREST · APALACHICOLA NAT. FOREST · SUMTER NAT. FOREST

ft / m elevation scale: 4500 / 1500 · 3000 / 1200 · 1500 / 400 · 600 / 200 · 0

1:2 200 000

COPYRIGHT PHILIP'S

HAWAIIAN ISLANDS

1:17 600 000

HAWAI'I

Tropic of Cancer

Kaua'i
KAUAI COUNTY
O'ahu
HONOLULU COUNTY
Moloka'i
KALAWAO COUNTY
Maui
MAUI COUNTY
Lāna'i
Kaho'olawe
HAWAI'I COUNTY

Lehua I.
Ni'ihau
Ka'ula I.
Nihoa

H a w a i i a n   I s l a n d s

Necker I.

Gardner Pinnacles

French Frigate Shoals

Maro Reef

Laysan I.

Lisianski I.

Pearl and Hermes Reef

Midway Is.
HONOLULU COUNTY

Kure I.

P A C I F I C   O C E A N

P A C I F I C   O C E A N

P A C I F I C   O C E A N

Projection: Albers Equal Area

West from Greenwich

Kaua'i

KAUAI COUNTY
Princeville
Hanalei
Kīlauea
Kapa'a
Kōloa
Kekaha
Kalāheo
Waimea
Līhu'e
Hā'ena
Nāpali Coast
Nā Pali Kōke'e SETE PARK
Waimea Canyon
Wai'ale'ale 1569
Kawaikini 1598
Hanapēpē
Puhi
Nāwiliwili Pt.
Hanamā'ulu
Makahuena Pt.
Ha'ena

Ka'ula I.
Lehua I.
Ni'ihau
Pu'uwai
Pānī'au 390
Kawaihoa Pt.
Kaulakahi Channel

Kaua'i Channel

O'ahu
Kahuku Pt.
Lā'ie
Hau'ula
Wai'anae
Nānākuli
Waialua
Hale'iwa
Wahiawā
Waipahu
Ka'ena Pt.
Ka'ala 1231
Barbers Pt.
'Ewa Beach
Kailua
Kāne'ohe
Waimānalo
Honolulu
HNL
Pearl Harbor
HONOLULU COUNTY

Kaiwi Channel
Kaua'i Channel
▼3026

P A C I F I C   O C E A N

Moloka'i
KALAUPAPA NAT. HIST. PARK
KALAWAO COUNTY
Ho'olehua
Kala'e
Kaunakakai
Kualapu'u
Maunaloa
'Ilio Pt.
Mo'omomi
Kamalō
Lā'au Pt.
Kalohi Channel
Makapu'u Pt.

Lāna'i
Lāna'i City 1027
Lāna'ihale
Kaumālapa'u
Pālāoa Pt.
Kaunolū

Kaho'olawe
Lua Makika 450
Lae 'o Kealaikahiki
Kealaikahiki Channel
Kaho'olawe Channel

Maui
MAUI COUNTY
Kahului
Wailuku
Lahaina
Kīhei
Hāna
Pā'ia
Makawao
Nāpili
Kā'anapali
Mā'alaea
Wailea-Mākena
Pu'u Kukui 1765
Haleakalā 3055
HALEAKALĀ NAT. PARK
ROAD TO HANA
Haiku-Pauwela
Waihe'e
Kahakuloa
Honokōhau
Honokahua
Olowalu
'Ulupalakua
Kaupō
Kula
Pu'u 'Ula'ula
Ranch
Nakalele Pt.
Pā'ilolo Channel
Hālawa Channel

▼446
▼1340

Hawai'i
HAWAI'I COUNTY
Hilo
Mauna Kea 4205
Mauna Loa 4169
Hualālai 2521
Kīlauea 1243
HAWAI'I VOLCANOES NATIONAL PARK
KOHALA FOR. RES.
KOHALA FOREST RES.
Waimea (Kamuela)
Waikoloa
Kailua
Kealakekua
Captain Cook
Honomū
Pepeekeo
Papa'ikou
Pa'auilo
Honoka'a
Kukuihaele
Honaunau
Keaau
Kea'au
Pāhoa
Volcano
Glenwood
Mountain View
Kurtistown
Pāhala
Nā'ālehu
Honalo
Kula
Kaunā Pt.
Kalae
Ka Lae
'O'ōkala
Honomū
Pepe'ekeo
Kapoho
Kumukahi
Opihikao
Kalapana
Kehena
Hōnaunau
Holualoa
Kealia
Pu'u 'ō'ōke'o 2096
PUNA FOR. RES.
KA'Ū FOREST RES.
PU'UHONUA O HŌNAUNAU NAT. HISTORICAL PARK
KALOKO-HONOKŌHAU NAT. HISTORICAL PARK
PU'UKOHOLĀ HEIAU NAT. HISTORIC SITE
Kawaihae Bay
Kiholo Bay
Keāhole
Keāhole Pt.
Ka Lae
Kaūnā Pt.
Pōhue Bay
Kealaikahiki
Miloli'i
'Upolu Pt.
Māhukona
Hāwī
Honoka'a
'Alenuihāhā Channel
Laupāhoehoe
Hilo Bay
Leleiwi Pt.
Cape Kumukahi

P A C I F I C   O C E A N

O'AHU
1:440 000
Projection: Lambert's Conformal Conic

KO'OLAULOA DISTRICT
Kahuku
Lā'ie
Hau'ula
Punalu'u
Kahana
Ka'a'awa
Kualoa Pt.
POLYNESIAN CULTURAL CENTER
Sunset Beach
Waimea
Pūpūkea
Kawailoa
Hale'iwa
Waialua
Mokulē'ia
WAIALUA DISTRICT
HONOLULU COUNTY
'EWA DISTRICT
Schofield Barracks
Wahiawā
Mililani Town
Waipahu
Pearl City
Waimalu
'Aiea
Pearl Harbor
HICKAM HOUSING
HICKAM AFB
Honouliuli
'Ewa Villages
'Ewa Beach
Waimānalo
Makakilo City
Kapolei
Nānākuli
Mā'ili
Wai'anae
Mākaha
WAI'ANAE DISTRICT
MĀKUA MILITARY RESERVE
LUALUALEI NAVAL RESERVE
HONOULIULI FOREST RESERVE
PAHOLE NAT. AREA RESERVE
Ka'ena Pt.
Mōkua
Kepuhi Pt.
Pōka'ī Bay
Makaiwa Pt.
Barbers Pt.
Kalaeloa
Kahe Pt.
Ka'ena 1231
Pu'u Hāpapa 944
KOLOLAUPOKO DISTRICT
Kāne'ohe
He'eia
Kahalu'u
Kailua
Waimānalo
Waimānalo Beach
Maunawili
Mōkapu Peninsula
Mōkapu Pt.
Kāne'ohe Bay
Kailua Bay
Mokoli'i I.
Mōkōlea Rock
Mokulua Is.
Mānana I.
Makapu'u Pt.
KO'OLAU POKO
Pu'u Konahuanui 946
Pali
Honolulu
Waikīkī
Diamond Head
Koko Head
Hanauma Bay
Kāhala
Maunalua Bay
Niu Valley
Kuli'ou'ou
Kapahulu
'Aina Haina
HONOLULU WATERSHED FOREST RESERVE
HONOLULU FOREST RESERVE
'IOLANI PALACE
BISHOP MUSEUM
Tantalus
Mānoa
Kaimukī
Sand I.
Māmala Bay
Kāhala
Kapāpa I.
Waiāhole
Pūpūkea

Mōkapu Peninsula
Mōkapu Pt.

WAIANAE RANGE
KO'OLAU RANGE
Pu'u Ka'ala

m / ft
9000 3000
6000 2000
4500 1500
3000 1000
1200 400
600 200
0
-200 -600
2000 6000
m ft

1:2 200 000

10 0 10 20 30 40 50 60 70 80 90 km
10 0 10 20 30 40 50 60 miles

continuation northwards on same scale

BRITISH COLUMBIA   CANADA

Projection : Albers Equal Area   West from Greenwich   COPYRIGHT PHILIP'S

NEVADA   UTAH

MONTANA

OREGON

WASHINGTON

IDAHO

Boise
Pullman
Moscow
Lewiston
Clarkston
Coeur d'Alene
Sandpoint
Missoula
Nampa
Caldwell
Meridian
Twin Falls
Pocatello
Idaho Falls
Blackfoot
Mountain Home
McCall
Salmon
Grangeville
Orofino

CLEARWATER NATIONAL FOREST
NEZPERCE NATIONAL FOREST
PAYETTE NATIONAL FOREST
BOISE NATIONAL FOREST
SALMON NATIONAL FOREST
CHALLIS NATIONAL FOREST
SAWTOOTH NATIONAL FOREST
TARGHEE NATIONAL FOREST
CARIBOU NATIONAL FOREST
ST. JOE NATIONAL FOREST
KANIKSU NATIONAL FOREST
COEUR D'ALENE NATIONAL FOREST
CABINET MTS
FRANK CHURCH RIVER OF NO RETURN WILDERNESS
SAWTOOTH WILDERNESS
BITTERROOT NATIONAL FOREST
SELWAY-BITTERROOT WILDERNESS

Snake River
Salmon River
Clearwater River
Columbia Plateau
Owyhee
Seven Devils Mts
Sawtooth Range
Boulder Mts
Pioneer Mts
Lost River Range
Lemhi Range
Beaverhead Mts
Bitterroot Range
Selkirk Mts
Purcell Mts
Salish Mts
Smoky Mts

Borah Peak 3859
Hyndman Peak 3681
Scott Peak 3473
May Mt. 3344
Diamond Pk 3716
Mt. McGuire 3073
Trapper Pk. 3096
Lolo Peak 2785
Naomi Peak 3042
Cache Peak 3151
Monument Pk. 2457
Black Pine Pk. 2861

CITY OF ROCKS NATIONAL RESERVE
CRATERS OF THE MOON NATIONAL MONUMENT
HAGERMAN FOSSIL BEDS NATIONAL MONUMENT
SNAKE RIVER BIRDS OF PREY N.C.A.
YELLOWSTONE NATIONAL PARK
HELLS CANYON NAT. REC. AREA
WALLOWA-WHITMAN NATIONAL FOREST
DUCK VALLEY INDIAN RESERVATION
FORT HALL INDIAN RESERVATION
NEZ PERCE IND. RES.
COEUR D'ALENE IND. RES.
KALISPEL IND. RES.
CURLEW NAT. GRASSLANDS

American Falls Reservoir
Palisades Reservoir
Blackfoot Reservoir
Bear Lake
Cascade Reservoir
Brownlee Reservoir
Dworshak Reservoir
L. Pend Oreille
Coeur d'Alene L.

ft m
9000 3000
6000 2000
4500 1500
3000 1000
1200 400
600 200

1:2 200 000

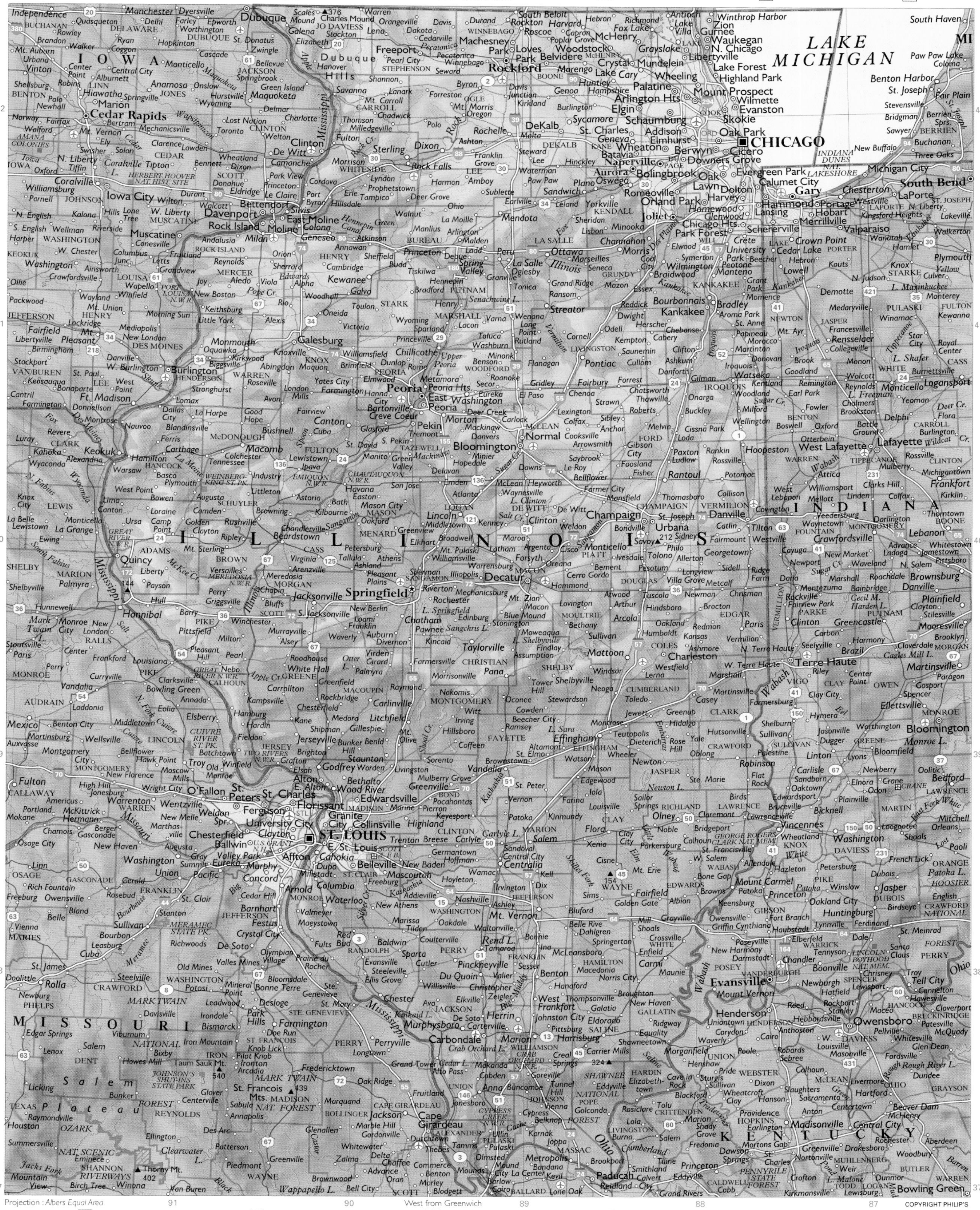

LAKE
MICHIGAN

IOWA

ILLINOIS

INDIANA

MISSOURI

KENTUCKY

MI

CHICAGO

St. Louis

Rockford

Peoria

Springfield

Decatur

Champaign

Bloomington

Normal

Quincy

Danville

Terre Haute

Evansville

Owensboro

Bowling Green

South Bend

Lafayette

Cedar Rapids

Iowa City

Davenport

Dubuque

Galesburg

Burlington

Hannibal

Rolla

Paducah

Cairo

ft   m
3000 1000
1200   400
600   200
0   0

1:2 200 000

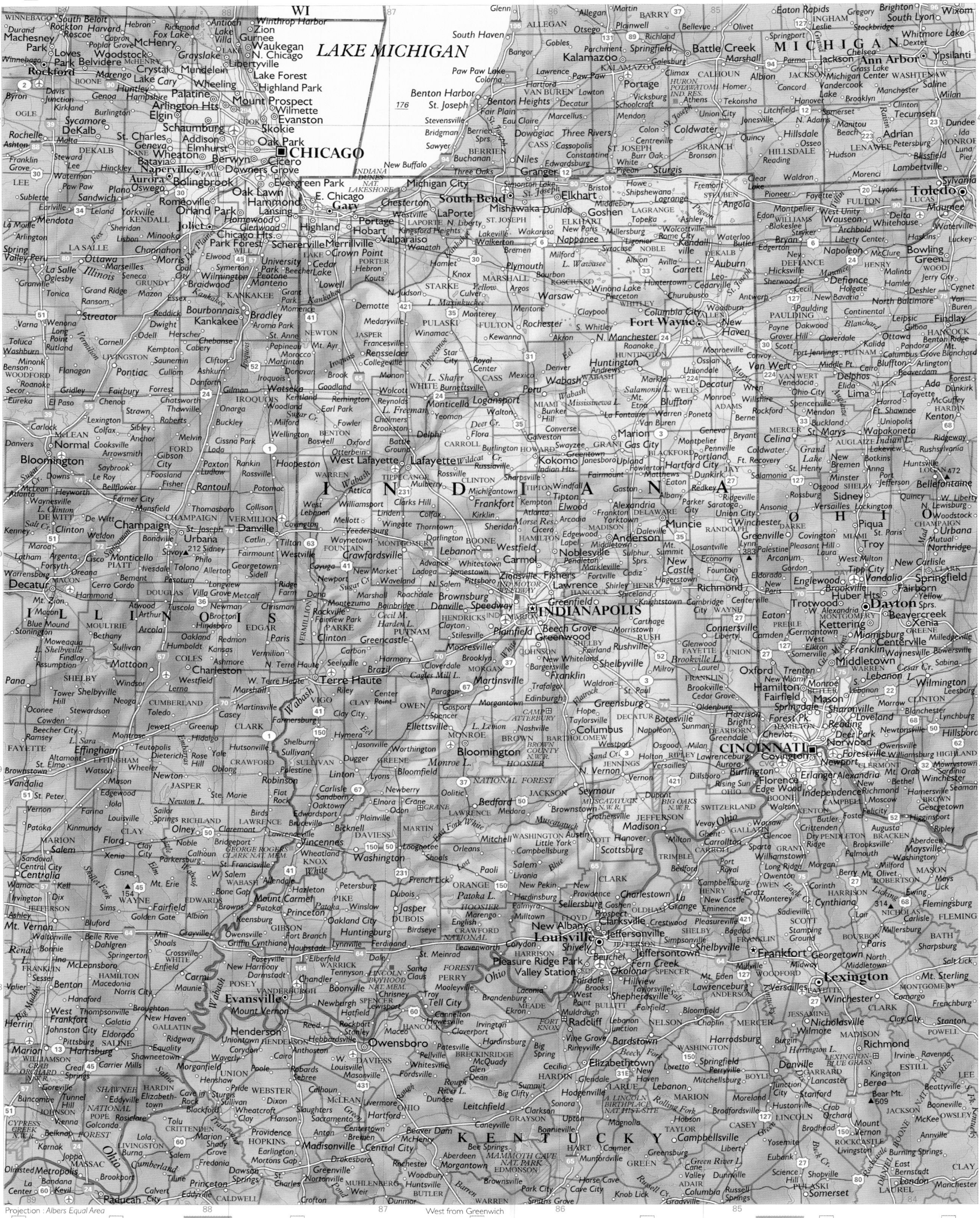

10 0 10 20 30 40 50 60 70 80 90 km

10 0 10 20 30 40 50 60 miles

LAKE MICHIGAN

WISCONSIN
MICHIGAN
INDIANA
ILLINOIS
OHIO
KENTUCKY

CHICAGO
Fort Wayne
INDIANAPOLIS
Terre Haute
Bloomington
Evansville
Louisville
CINCINNATI
Dayton
Lexington
Toledo

HOOSIER NATIONAL FOREST

Projection : Albers Equal Area

West from Greenwich

1:2 200 000

Projection: Albers Equal Area

West from Greenwich

COPYRIGHT PHILIPS

IOWA

WISCONSIN

ILLINOIS

MINNESOTA

NEBRASKA

MISSOURI

SD · KS

1:2 200 000

10 0 10 20 30 40 50 60 70 80 90 km

10 0 10 20 30 40 50 60 miles

Projection: Albers Equal Area

West from Greenwich

See page 96 for Kentucky

1:2 200 000

10 0 10 20 30 40 50 60 70 80 100 km
10 0 10 20 30 40 50 60 miles

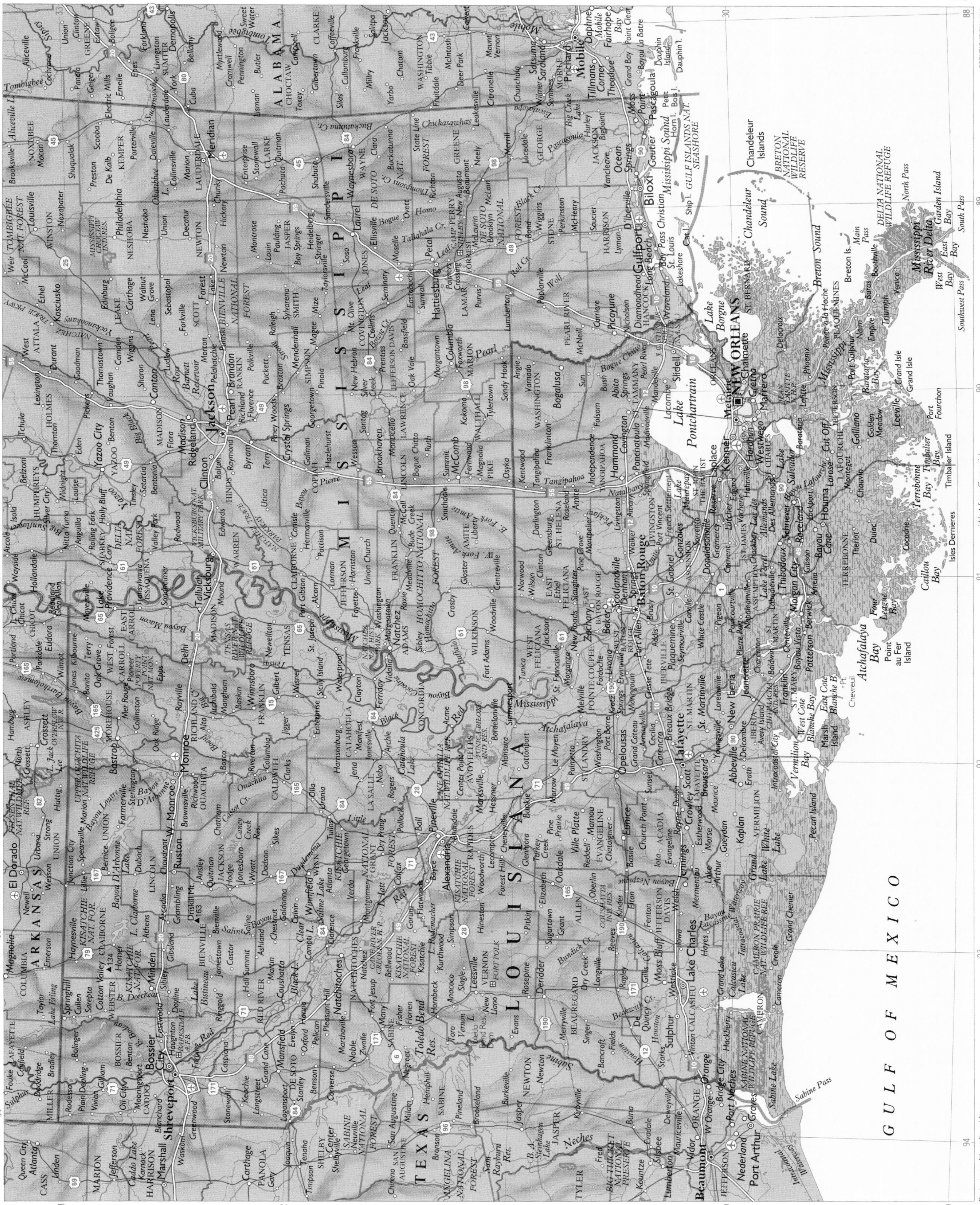

ALABAMA

MISSISSIPPI

LOUISIANA

ARKANSAS

TEXAS

GULF OF MEXICO

New Orleans
Baton Rouge
Shreveport
Jackson
Mobile
Biloxi
Gulfport
Monroe
W. Monroe
Lafayette
Lake Charles
Alexandria
Natchitoches
Meridian
Hattiesburg
Vicksburg
Natchez
Houma
Beaumont
Port Arthur

Lake Pontchartrain
Lake Borgne
Lake Maurepas
Chandeleur Sound
Breton Sound
Mississippi River Delta
Atchafalaya Bay
Mississippi Sound
Toledo Bend Res.

DELTA NATIONAL WILDLIFE REFUGE
BRETON NATIONAL WILDLIFE RESERVE
GULF ISLANDS NAT. SEASHORE
Chandeleur Islands

West from Greenwich

Projection: Albers Equal Area

1:2 200 000

10 0 10 20 30 40 50 60 70 80 90 km
10 0 10 20 30 40 50 60 miles

CANADA

QUÉBEC

NEW BRUNSWICK

Québec · Lévis · Beauport
Ste-Foy · Charny

AROOSTOOK

Edmundston · Madawaska · Van Buren · Fort Kent · Caribou · Presque Isle · Fort Fairfield · Houlton

Mt. Carleton ▲ 820
MOUNT CARLETON PROV. PARK

SOMERSET · PISCATAQUIS · PENOBSCOT

BAXTER STATE PARK
Mt. Katahdin ▲ 1606

Moosehead L. · Millinocket · East Millinocket

M A I N E

Moosehead · Greenville · Dover-Foxcroft · Milo

WASHINGTON

Saint John

Bangor · Brewer · Old Town · Orono

Calais · Eastport · Lubec

VERMONT

White Mts. · Mt. Washington ▲ 1917

NEW HAMPSHIRE

Franklin · Blue Mts. · Rangeley

KENNEBEC · FRANKLIN · OXFORD · ANDROSCOGGIN

Augusta · Waterville · Lewiston · Auburn

KNOX · WALDO · HANCOCK · LINCOLN · SAGADAHOC

Belfast · Camden · Rockland · Bar Harbor

ACADIA NAT. PARK
Mount Desert I.

CUMBERLAND · YORK

Portland · South Portland · Biddeford · Saco · Sanford

Casco Bay · Cape Elizabeth · Old Orchard Beach

Gulf of Maine

Bay of Fundy

NOVA SCOTIA
Yarmouth

ATLANTIC OCEAN

MASSACHUSETTS

BOSTON · Cambridge · Quincy · Worcester · Lowell · Lawrence · Haverhill

Massachusetts Bay

Cape Cod

ft m
4500 1500
3000 1000
1200 400
600 200
0 0
200 600
m ft

Projection: Albers Equal Area
West from Greenwich

COPYRIGHT PHILIP'S

1:1 100 000

5 0 10 20 30 40 km
5 0 5 10 15 20 25 miles

ATLANTIC OCEAN

NEW JERSEY

PENNSYLVANIA

DELAWARE

MARYLAND

VIRGINIA

WEST VIRGINIA

PHILADELPHIA

Wilmington

Dover

BALTIMORE

WASHINGTON D.C.

Annapolis

Chesapeake Bay

Delaware Bay

Delmarva Peninsula

Eastern Shore

Tangier Sound

Assateague Island

Chincoteague

Cumberland

ALLEGANY

GARRETT

West from Greenwich

COPYRIGHT PHILIP'S

Projection: Lambert's Conformal Conic

continuation westwards on same scale

NATIONAL FOREST

1:1 100 000

Gulf of Maine

Massachusetts Bay

ATLANTIC OCEAN

Long Island Sound

Long Island

NEW HAMPSHIRE

VERMONT

MASSACHUSETTS

CONNECTICUT

RHODE ISLAND

NEW YORK

BOSTON

WORCESTER

Springfield

PROVIDENCE

Hartford

New Haven

Bridgeport

Cape Cod

Cape Cod Bay

Cape Cod National Seashore

Nantucket Island

Martha's Vineyard

Buzzards Bay

Narragansett Bay

Rhode Island Sound

Block Island Sound

Block Island (R.I.)

Montauk Point

West from Greenwich

Projection: Lambert's Conformal Conic

1:2 200 000

10 0 10 20 30 40 50 60 70 80 90 100 km
10 0 10 20 30 40 50 60 miles

LAKE SUPERIOR

extension north-westwards on same scale

CANADA
ONTARIO

Isle Royale
KEWEENAW
Windigo ISLE ROYAL NAT PARK
GRAND PORTAGE IND. RES.
Grand Portage
MN
Hovland
Cumberland Pt.
MICHIGAN
LAKE SUPERIOR

extension westwards on same scale

Apostle Islands
Outer I.
APOSTLE ISLANDS NAT LAKESHORE
Stockton I.
Michigan I.
ASHLAND
LAKE SUPERIOR
Fourteen Mile Pt.
ONTONAGON IND. RES.
Ontonagon
Silver City
PORCUPINE MOUNTAINS WILDERNESS STATE PARK
Porcupine Mts.
White Pine
Greenland
Mass City
Rockland
GOGEBIC RANGE
Ironwood
Bessemer
Wakefield
Ramsay
GOGEBIC
Iron Belt
OTTAWA NATIONAL FOREST
Marenisco
Watersmeet
Bond Falls Flowage
LAC VIEUX DESERT IND. RES.
Lac Vieux Desert
WISCONSIN
VILAS
Phelps

MICHIGAN

LAKE MICHIGAN

LAKE HURON

WISCONSIN

CANADA
ONTARIO

DETROIT
Windsor
CANADA
ONTARIO
LAKE ERIE

MILWAUKEE

CHICAGO

Green Bay

Grand Rapids

Lansing

Projection : Albers Equal Area

COPYRIGHT Philip's

1:2 200 000

10 0 10 20 30 40 50 60 70 80 90 km
10 0 10 20 30 40 50 60 miles

MANITOBA

CANADA

ONTARIO

Lake of the Woods
Angle Inlet
RED LAKE INDIAN RES.
Lake of the Woods Prov. Park

LAKE OF THE WOODS
RED LAKE INDIAN RESERVATION

KOOCHICHING

Rainy Lake
VOYAGEURS NAT. PARK
Lac La Croix
QUETICO PROV. PARK
BOUNDARY WATERS CANOE AREA WILDERNESS

Fort Frances
International Falls
Ranier

BOIS FORTE (NETT LAKE) IND. RES.
BOIS FORTE (DEER CREEK) INDIAN RES.

Mesabi Iron Range
Vermilion Range
ST. LOUIS

CHIPPEWA NATIONAL FOREST
ITASCA

SUPERIOR NAT. FOREST
Sawtooth Mountains
SUPERIOR NATIONAL FOREST

LEECH LAKE INDIAN RESERVATION
Lake Winnibigoshish

Hibbing
Virginia
Eveleth

LAKE SUPERIOR
APOSTLE IS. NAT. LAKESHORE

ITASCA STATE PARK
WHITE EARTH INDIAN RESERVATION
MAHNOMEN INDIAN RESERVATION
TAMARAC N.W.R.

Duluth
Superior

MINNESOTA

Fargo
Moorhead

Brainerd
Cuyuna Range

CASS
AITKIN
CROW WING

Mille Lacs Lake
MILLE LACS IND. RES.

PILLSBURY STATE FOREST
Camp Ripley
Fort Ripley

St. Cloud

BAYFIELD
CHEQUAMEGON
ASHLAND
CHIPPEWA NATIONAL FOREST

ST. CROIX NAT. SCENIC RIVERWAY
PINE

MORRISON
TODD
STEVENS
POPE
DOUGLAS

BENTON
SHERBURNE
ISANTI
CHISAGO

Minneapolis
St. Paul
Bloomington
Burnsville

WISCONSIN

SD
ND

LAC QUI PARLE
CHIPPEWA
BIG STONE
TRAVERSE
YELLOW MEDICINE

LOWER SIOUX IND. RES.
UPPER SIOUX IND. RES.

RENVILLE
MEEKER
WRIGHT
HENNEPIN
CARVER
SCOTT
DAKOTA

Red Wing

REDWOOD
LYON
LINCOLN
MURRAY
COTTONWOOD
BROWN
NICOLLET
SIBLEY
RICE
GOODHUE

New Ulm
Mankato
Faribault
Owatonna
Rochester
OLMSTED

PIPESTONE NAT. MON.
ROCK
NOBLES
JACKSON
MARTIN
FARIBAULT
FREEBORN
MOWER
FILLMORE
HOUSTON

Worthington
Fairmont
Albert Lea
Austin
La Crosse
Winona

Projection: Albers Equal Area
West from Greenwich
COPYRIGHT PHILIP'S

Northern Light Lake
ONTARIO
continuation eastwards on same scale
BOUNDARY WATERS CANOE AREA WILDERNESS
GRAND PORTAGE IND. RES.
Grand Portage
COOK
Misquah Hills
Sawtooth Mts.
Grand Marais
LAKE SUPERIOR

ft m
1200 400
600 200
0 0
200 600
m ft

1:2 200 000

Projection: Albers' Equal Area   West from Greenwich   COPYRIGHT PHILIP'S

TENNESSEE

ARKANSAS

MISSISSIPPI

ALABAMA

LOUISIANA

FLORIDA

GULF OF MEXICO

Major cities and features: Memphis, Little Rock, Pine Bluff, Jackson, Vicksburg, Natchez, Hattiesburg, Meridian, Columbus, Tupelo, Corinth, Greenville, Greenwood, Clarksdale, Cleveland, Oxford, Starkville, Laurel, Gulfport, Biloxi, Pascagoula, Mobile, Baton Rouge, New Orleans, Lafayette, Monroe, Tuscaloosa, Pensacola.

Lake Pontchartrain, Lake Borgne, Mississippi Sound, Chandeleur Sound, Chandeleur Islands, Breton National Wildlife Reserve, Gulf Islands Nat. Seashore.

1:2 200 000

1:3 300 000

Projection: Albers' Equal Area

West from Greenwich

COPYRIGHT PHILIP'S

SASKATCHEWAN

ALBERTA

BRITISH COLUMBIA

NORTH DAKOTA

WYOMING

IDAHO

MONTANA

Great Falls
Helena
Butte
Bozeman
Billings
Missoula
Kalispell
Miles City
Glendive
Lewistown
Havre

FORT PECK INDIAN RESERVATION

BLACKFEET INDIAN RESERVATION

FORT BELKNAP RESERVATION

ROCKY BOY'S IND. RES.

NORTHERN CHEYENNE IND. RES.

CROW INDIAN RESERVATION

WIND RIVER IND. RES.

CHARLES M. RUSSELL REFUGE

UPPER MISSOURI BREAKS NAT. MON.

GLACIER NATIONAL PARK

YELLOWSTONE NATIONAL PARK

GRAND TETON NATIONAL PARK

BIGHORN NATIONAL FOREST

CUSTER NATIONAL FOREST

GALLATIN NATIONAL FOREST

BEAVERHEAD NATIONAL FOREST

LEWIS AND CLARK NATIONAL FOREST

FLATHEAD NATIONAL FOREST

KOOTENAI NATIONAL FOREST

LOLO NATIONAL FOREST

BITTERROOT NATIONAL FOREST

SHOSHONE NATIONAL FOREST

Rocky Mountains

Bighorn Mts

Absaroka Range

Beartooth Range

Beaverhead Mts

Lemhi Range

Sawtooth Mts

Bitterroot Range

Cabinet Mts

Little Rocky Mts

Bears Paw Mts

Big Snowy Mts

Judith Mts

Crazy Mts

Wind River Range

Missouri

Yellowstone

Powder River

Musselshell

Milk River

1:2 200 000

10 0 10 20 30 40 50 60 70 80 90 km
10 0 10 20 30 40 50 60 miles

COPYRIGHT PHILIP'S

Projection: Albers Equal Area

West from Greenwich

SOUTH DAKOTA

IOWA

Missouri

NEBRASKA

KANSAS

continuation westwards on same scale

Sand Hills

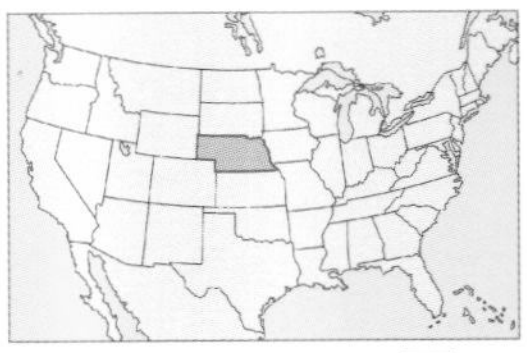

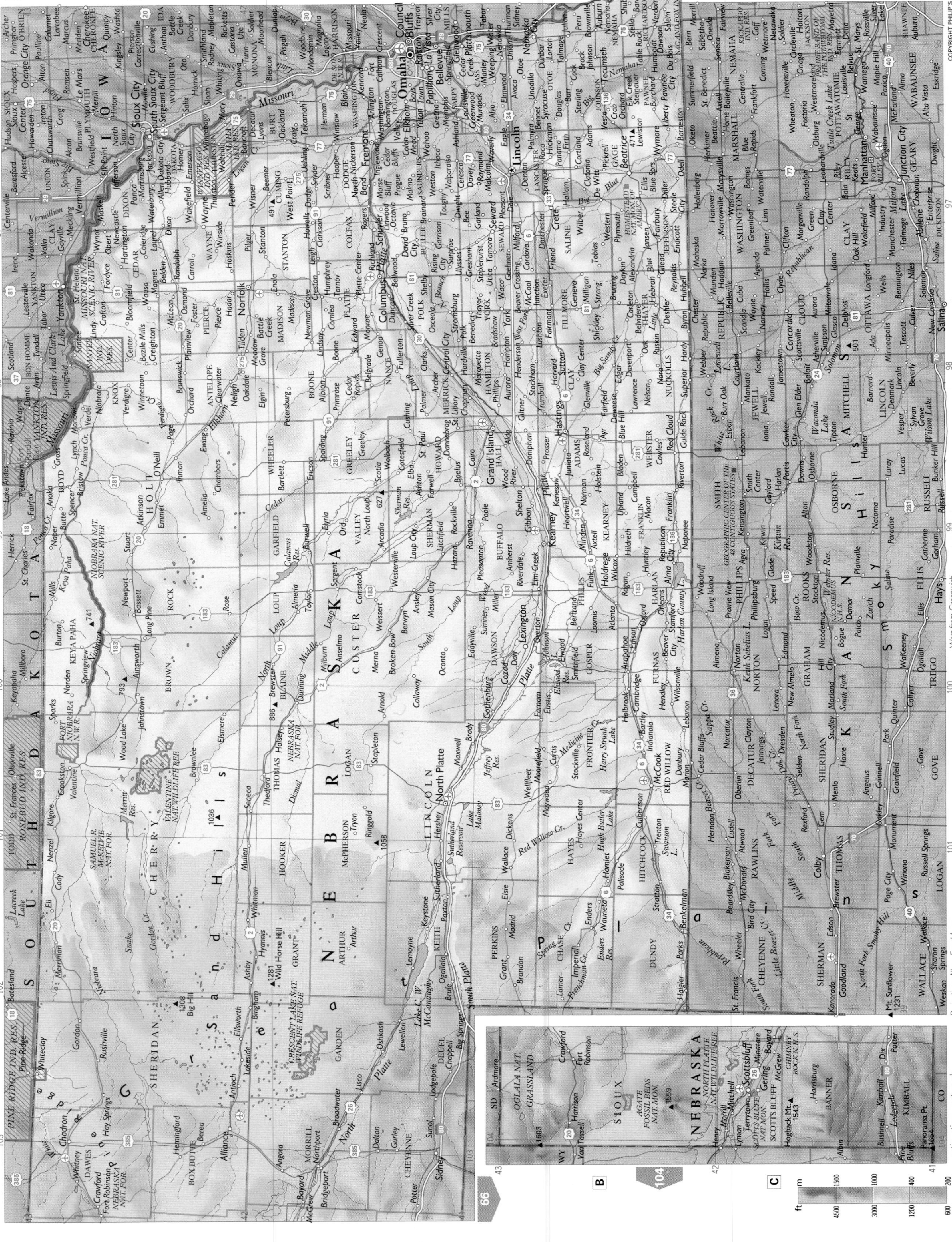

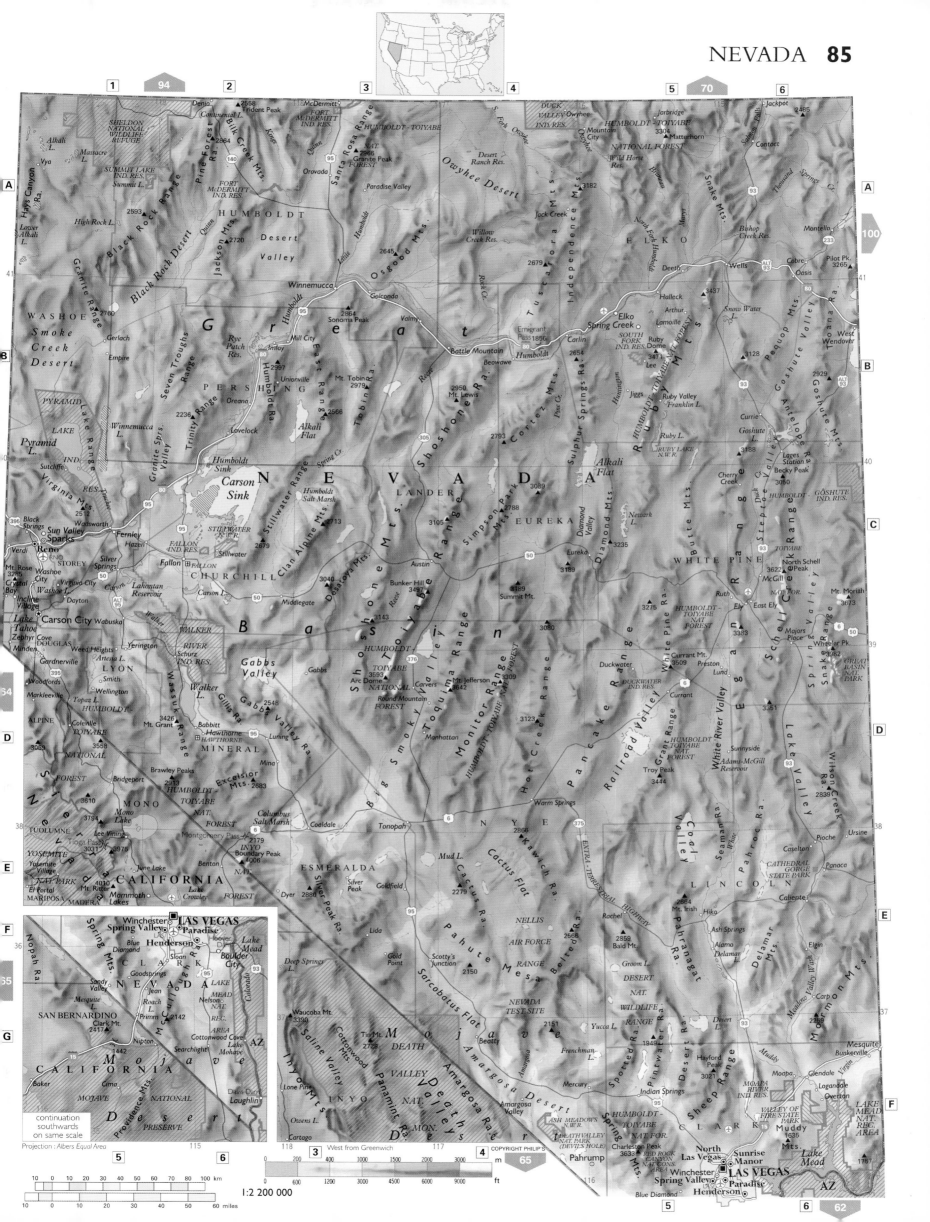

continuation
southwards
on same scale

Projection : Albers Equal Area

West from Greenwich

COPYRIGHT PHILIP'S

0   200   400   600   800   1000   1500   2000   3000   m

0   600   1200   3000   4500   6000   9000   ft

1:2 200 000

10   0   10   20   30   40   50   60   70   80   100 km

10   0   10   20   30   40   50   60 miles

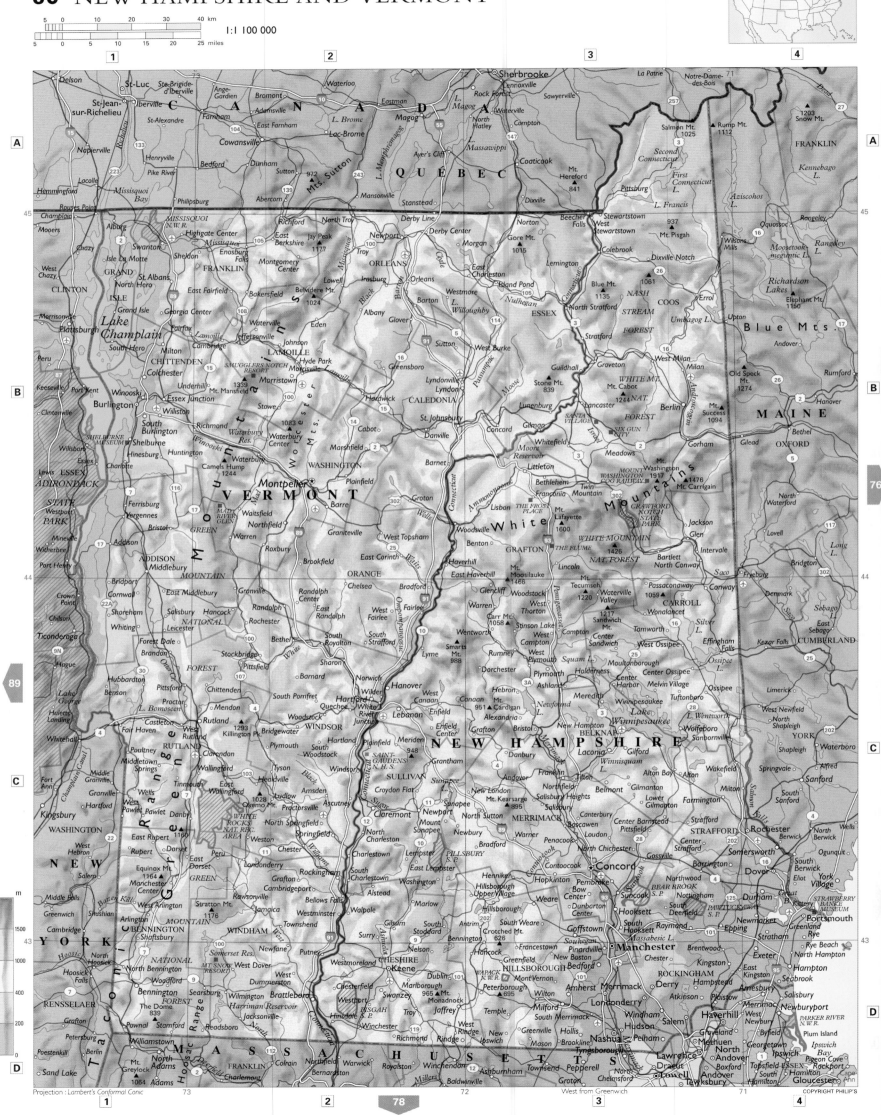

1:1 100 000

Projection : Lambert's Conformal Conic

West from Greenwich

COPYRIGHT PHILIP'S

1:1 100 000

5 0 10 20 30 40 km
5 0 5 10 15 20 25 miles

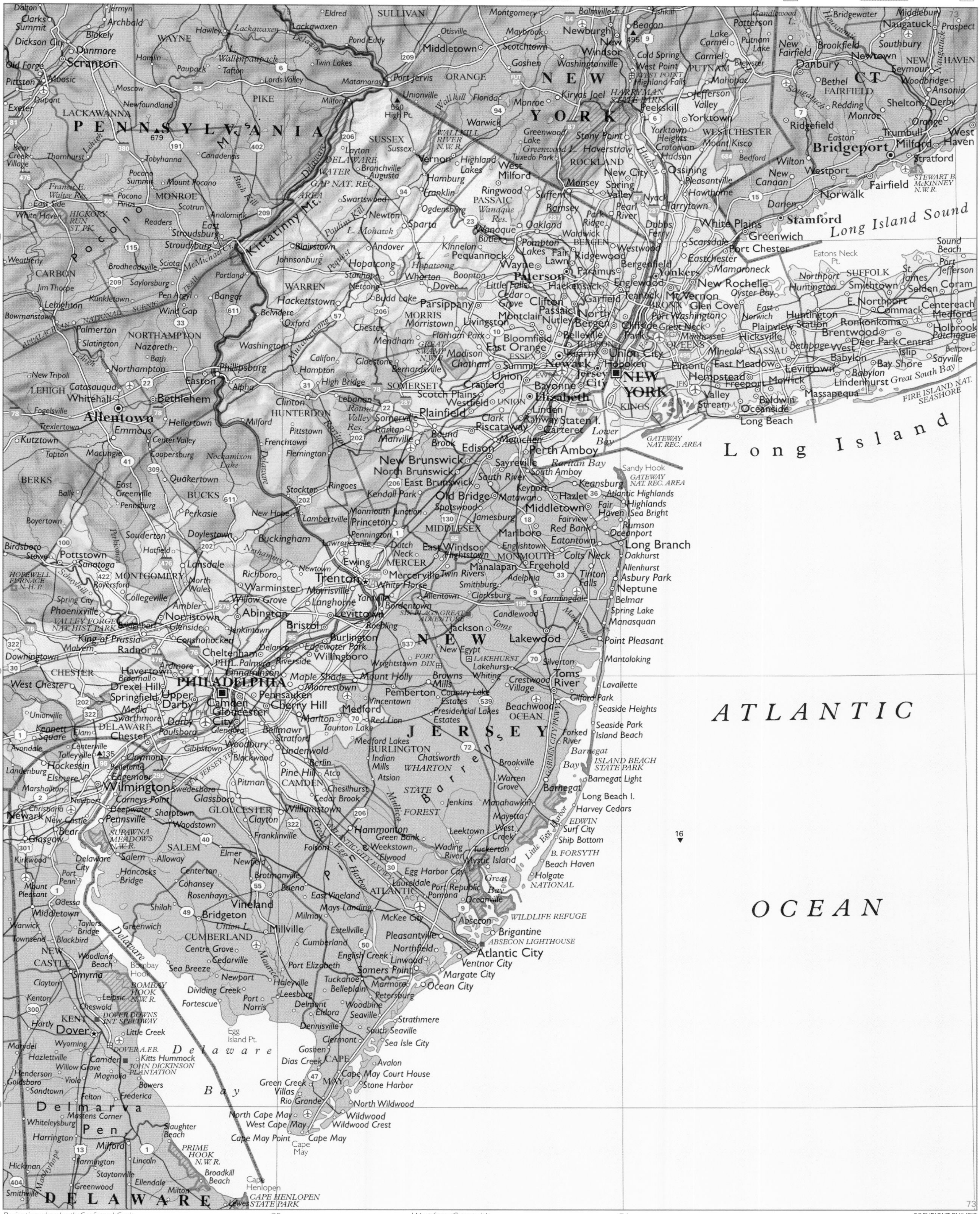

PENNSYLVANIA

NEW YORK

NEW JERSEY

DELAWARE

CT

Long Island Sound

Long Island

ATLANTIC

OCEAN

Delaware Bay

Delmarva Pen

PHILADELPHIA

NEW YORK

Newark

Trenton

Atlantic City

Cape May

Projection : Lambert's Conformal Conic

West from Greenwich

COPYRIGHT PHILIP'S

1:2 300 000

COLORADO

Counties and regions:
UNION · COLFAX · KIOWA · TAOS · MORA · HARDING · RIO ARRIBA · SAN JUAN · McKINLEY · SANDOVAL · SAN MIGUEL · QUAY · SANTA FE · GUADALUPE · CURRY · TORRANCE · VALENCIA · DE BACA · ROOSEVELT · SOCORRO · LINCOLN · CIBOLA · CATRON · CHAVES · SIERRA · OTERO · EDDY · LEA · GRANT · DONA ANA · LUNA · HIDALGO

NEW MEXICO

Major places:
Raton · Farmington · Shiprock · Gallup · Grants · Santa Fe · Los Alamos · Espanola · Taos · Las Vegas · Albuquerque · Bernalillo · Rio Rancho · Socorro · Tucumcari · Santa Rosa · Fort Sumner · Clovis · Portales · Roswell · Artesia · Carlsbad · Hobbs · Lovington · Ruidoso · Alamogordo · Tularosa · Cloudcroft · Truth or Consequences · Elephant Butte · Silver City · Deming · Lordsburg · Las Cruces · El Paso · CIUDAD JUAREZ

TEXAS · CHIHUAHUA · MEXICO · HUDSPETH · CULBERSON · REEVES · LOVING

Reservations and national areas:
NAVAJO INDIAN RESERVATION · UTE MT. IND. RES. · JICARILLA APACHE IND. RES. · CARSON NATIONAL FOREST · SANTA FE NAT. FOREST · CIBOLA NAT. FOREST · GILA NATIONAL FOREST · APACHE SITGREAVES NAT. FOREST · MESCALERO APACHE IND. RES. · ZUNI IND. RES. · ACOMA IND. RES. · LAGUNA IND. RES. · ISLETA IND. RES. · LINCOLN NATIONAL FOREST · GUADALUPE MTS. NAT. PARK · CARLSBAD CAVERNS NAT. PARK · WHITE SANDS MISSILE RANGE · WHITE SANDS NAT. MON. · FORT BLISS MILITARY RES. · CHACO CULTURE NAT. HIST. PARK · BANDELIER NAT. MON. · KIOWA NATIONAL GRASSLANDS · CAPULIN VOLCANO NAT. MON. · EL MALPAIS NAT. MON. · EL MORRO NAT. MON. · SALINAS PUEBLO MISSIONS NAT. MON. · GILA CLIFF DWELLINGS NAT. MON. · FORT UNION NAT. MON. · AZTEC RUINS NAT. MON.

Mountains/peaks (with elevations in metres):
Ship Rock 2188 · Mt. Taylor 3445 · Wheeler Peak 4011 · Baldy Pk. 3792 · Agua Fria Pk. 3639 · Truchas Pk. 3994 · Laughlin Pk. 2688 · Sierra Blanca Pk. 3659 · Capitan Pk. 3073 · South Baldy 3287 · Mt. Withington 3033 · Magdalena Mts. · Cebolleta Pk. 2671 · Alegros Mt. 3122 · San Jose 2809 · Tularosa Mts. 2983 · Whitewater Baldy 3321 · Black Mt. 2819 · Reeds Pk. 3053 · Cookes Pk. 2563 · Burro Pk. 2449 · Guadalupe Peak 2667 · Pelloncillo Mts. 2601 · Big Hatchet Pk. 2550 · Sierra Pk. 2611 · Wind Mt. 2219 · 2140 · 2166

Rivers and features:
Rio Grande · Rio Chama · Rio Puerco · Rio Salado · Pecos · Canadian · Rio Hondo · Rio Felix · Rio Peñasco · San Juan · Rio Bravo del Norte · Gila · Mimbres · Jornado del Muerto · Plains of San Agustin · Llano Estacado · San Juan Basin · North Plains · Diablo Bolson

Projection: Albers Equal Area

COPYRIGHT PHILIP'S

Underlined settlements give their name to the county in which they stand.

1 PETROGLYPH NAT. MON.   6 SAN FELIPE IND. RES.
2 POJOAQUE IND. RES.   7 SANDIA IND. RES.
3 NAMBE IND. RES.   8 SANTA ANA IND. RES.
4 TESUQUE IND. RES.   9 SANTA CLARA IND. RES.
5 SAN ILDEFONSO IND. RES.   10 SANTO DOMINGO IND. RES.

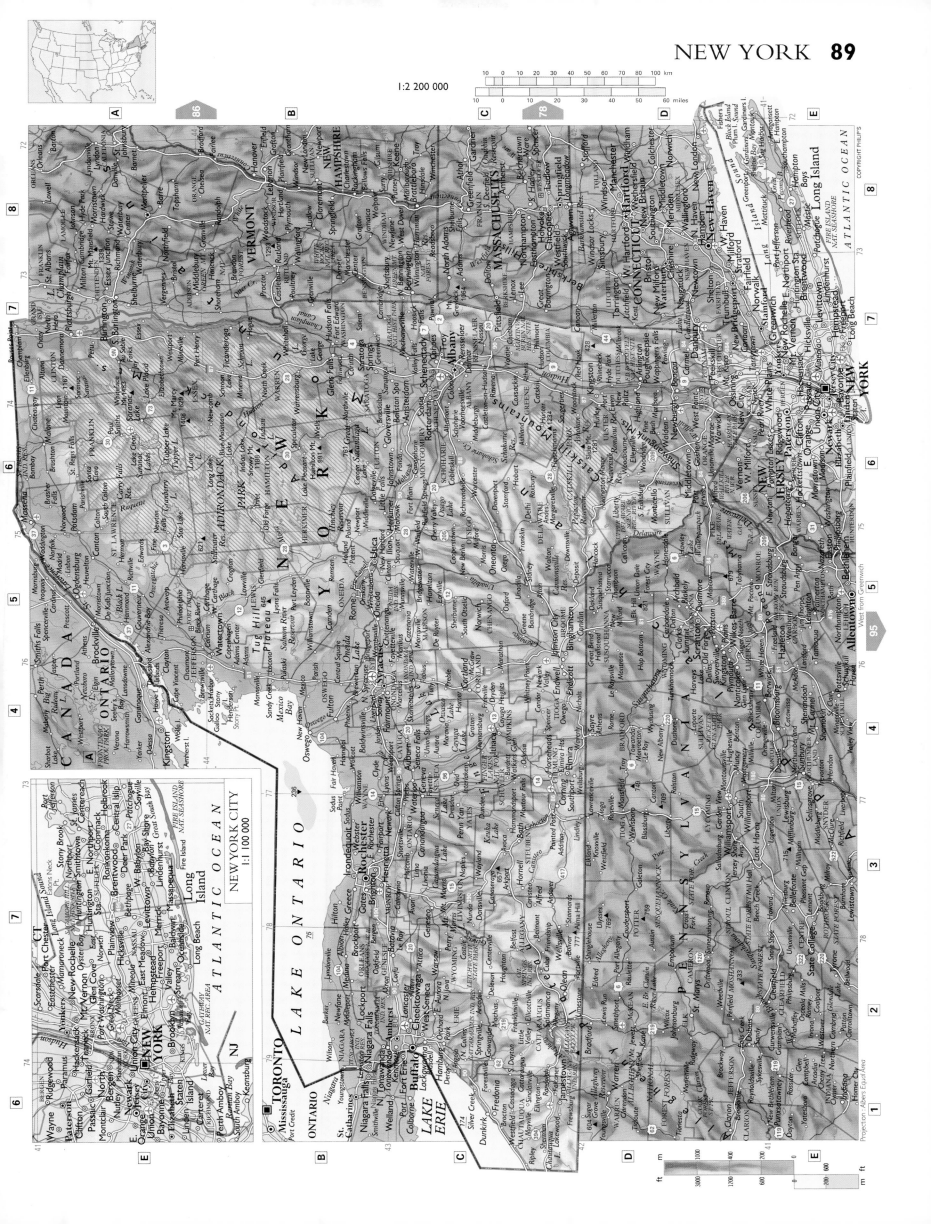

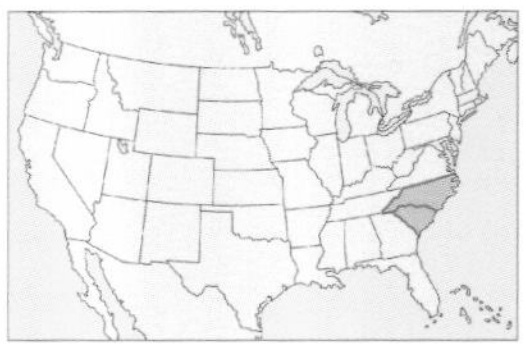

1:2 700 000

West from Greenwich

Underlined settlements give their name

COPYRIGHT PHILIP'S

Projection: Albers Equal Area

continuation westwards on same scale

ATLANTIC OCEAN

V I R G I N I A

N O R T H   C A R O L I N A

S O U T H   C A R O L I N A

G E O R G I A

TENNESSEE

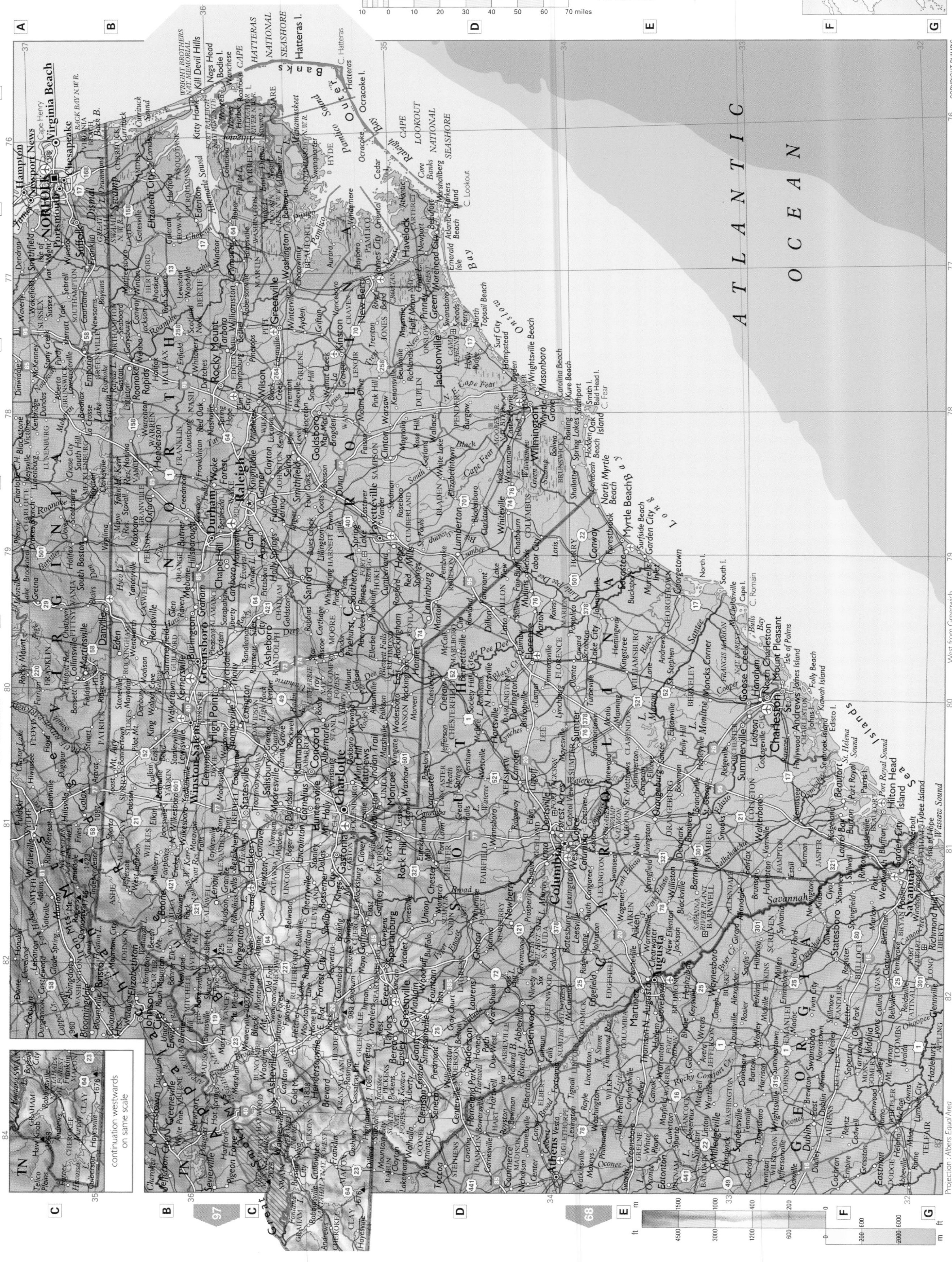

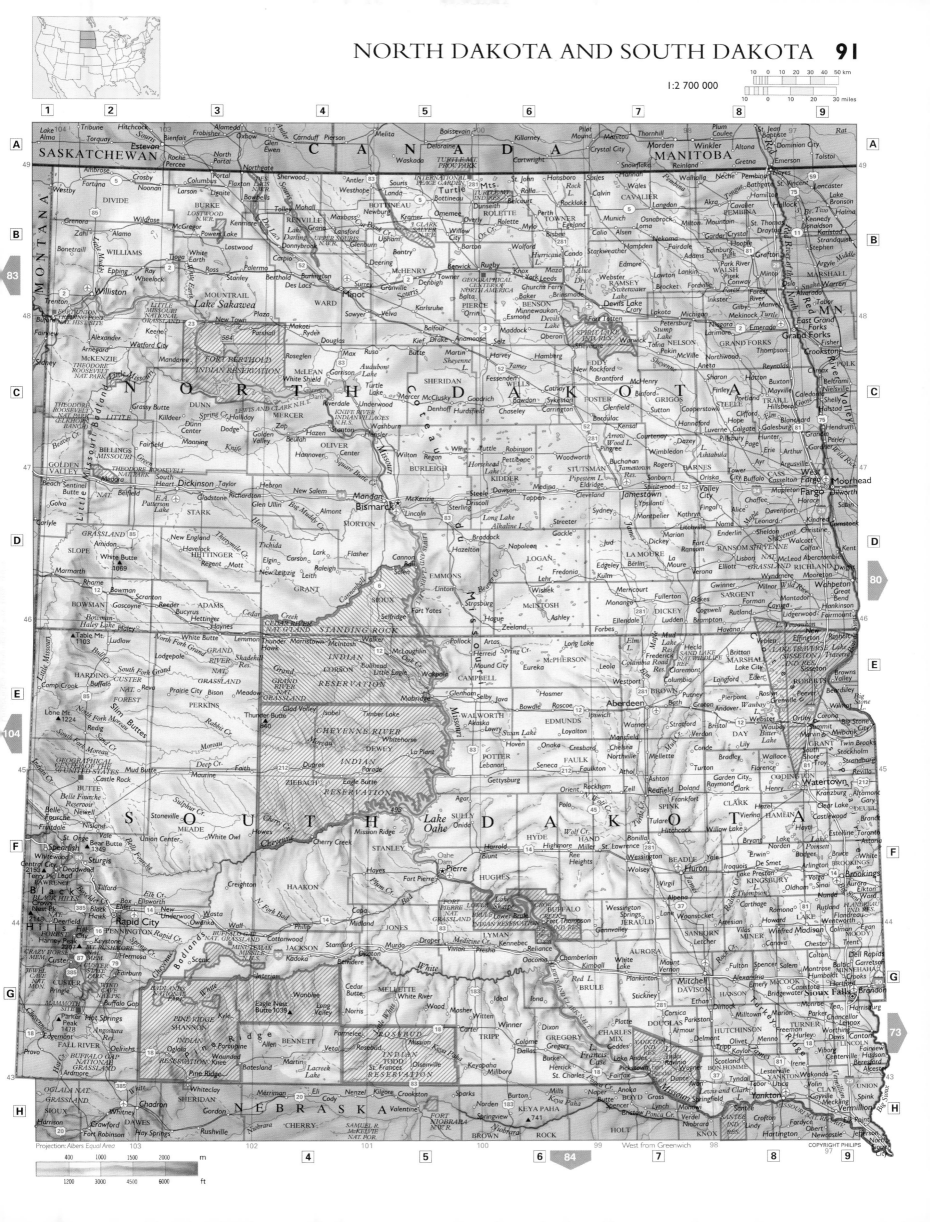

SASKATCHEWAN

CANADA

MANITOBA

MONTANA

NORTH DAKOTA

SOUTH DAKOTA

NEBRASKA

MN

10 0 10 20 30 40 50 60 70 80 90 km

1:2 200 000

10 0 10 20 30 40 50 60 miles

MICHIGAN

ONTARIO

CANADA

LAKE ERIE

DETROIT

Windsor

CLEVELAND

Akron

Youngstown

PA

Toledo

Fort Wayne

OHIO

IN

Columbus

Dayton

Cincinnati

PITTSBURGH

WEST VIRGINIA

Charleston

Huntington

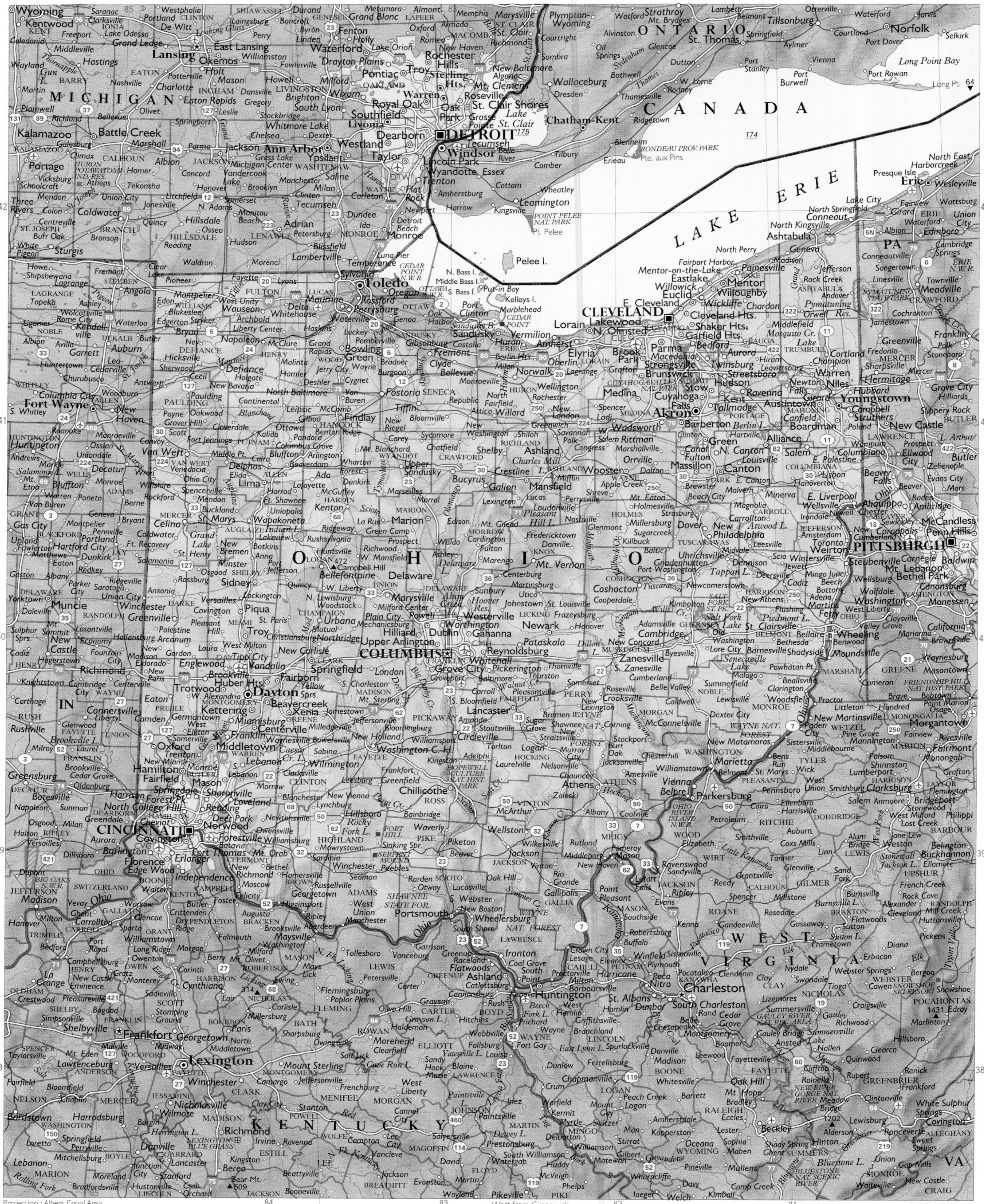

Parkersburg

KENTUCKY

Lexington

Frankfort

VA

Projection : Albers Equal Area

West from Greenwich

COPYRIGHT PHILIP'S

1:2 200 000

Projection: Albers Equal Area

West from Greenwich

continuation westwards on same scale

1:2 200 000

10 0 10 20 30 40 50 60 70 80 90 km
10 0 10 20 30 40 50 60 miles

West from Greenwich

Projection: Albers Equal Area

PACIFIC OCEAN

WASHINGTON

ID

NV

CA

Portland
Salem
Eugene
Bend
Medford
Klamath Falls
Pendleton
La Grande
Baker City
Burns

Wallowa-Whitman National Forest
Umatilla National Forest
Ochoco National Forest
Deschutes National Forest
Malheur National Forest
Fremont National Forest
Winema National Forest
Umpqua National Forest
Siskiyou National Forest
Willamette National Forest
Mount Hood National Forest
Siuslaw National Forest

Great Sandy Desert
High Desert
Low Desert
Harney Basin
Catlow Valley
Alvord Desert
Steens Mountain
Owyhee Mts.
Columbia River

Permanent Ice

ft m
9000 3000
6000 2000
4500 1500
3000 1000
1200 400
600 200
0 0
ft m

See page 78 for Rhode Island, page 90 for
South Carolina and page 91 for South Dakota

1:2 200 000

1. HOPEWELL FURNACE NAT. HIST. PARK
2. VALLEY FORGE NAT. HIST. PARK
3. ALLEGHENY PORTAGE RAILROAD NAT. HIST. SITE

Underlined settlements give their name
to the county in which they stand.

West from Greenwich

Projection : Albers Equal Area

1:2 200 000

See page 78 for Rhode Island, page 90 for
South Carolina and page 91 for South Dakota

Projection: Albers Equal Area

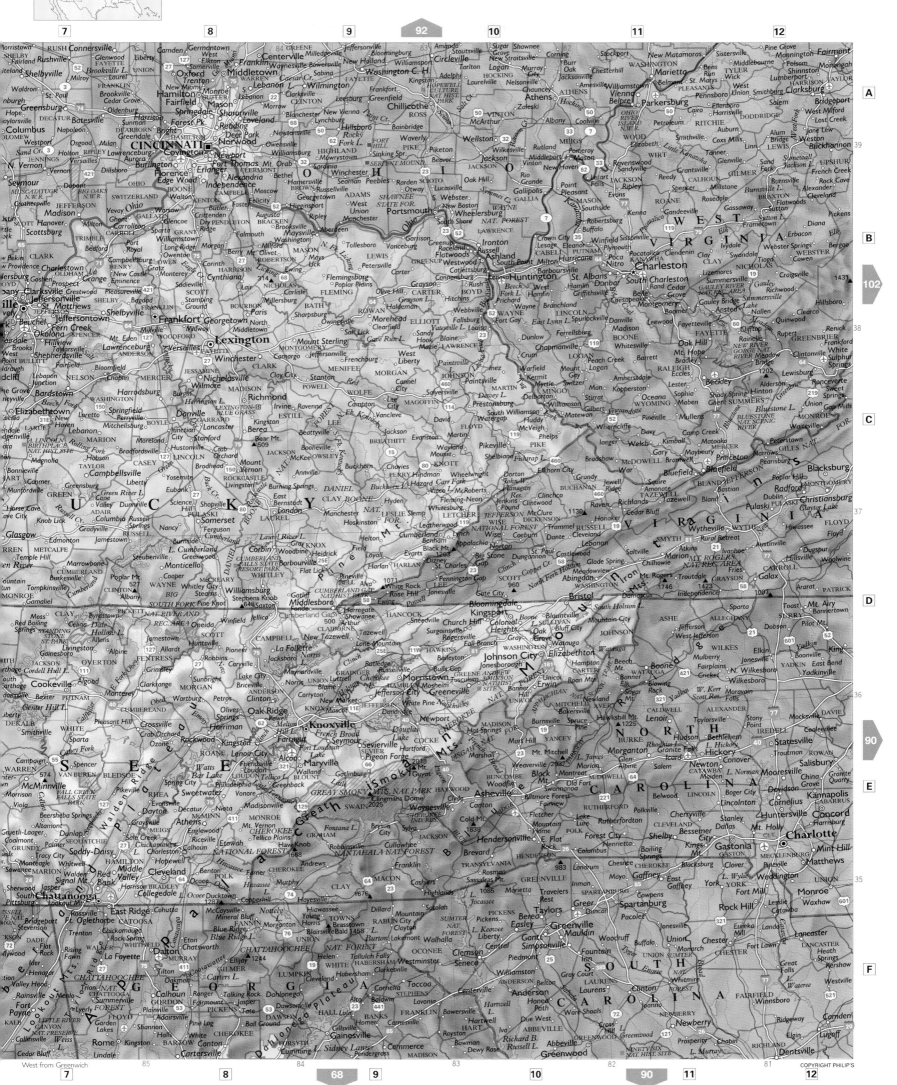

1:2 700 000

continuation northwards on same scale

continuation southwards on same scale

OKLAHOMA

NEW MEXICO

T E X A S

MEXICO

CHIHUAHUA

COAHUILA

TAMAULIPAS

NUEVO LEÓN

GULF OF MEXICO

Projection : Albers Equal Area

West from Greenwich

El Paso, Ciudad Juárez, Amarillo, Lubbock, Midland, Odessa, San Angelo, Del Rio, Laredo, Nuevo Laredo, Corpus Christi, McAllen, Reynosa, Brownsville, Matamoros, Big Spring, Sweetwater, Hobbs, Portales, Plainview

BIG BEND NATIONAL PARK

PADRE ISLAND NATIONAL SEASHORE

Padre I.

Rio Grande / Rio Bravo del Norte

Davis Mountains, Guadalupe Mts. Nat. Park, Stockton Plateau, Edwards Plateau

Sierra Madre Oriental

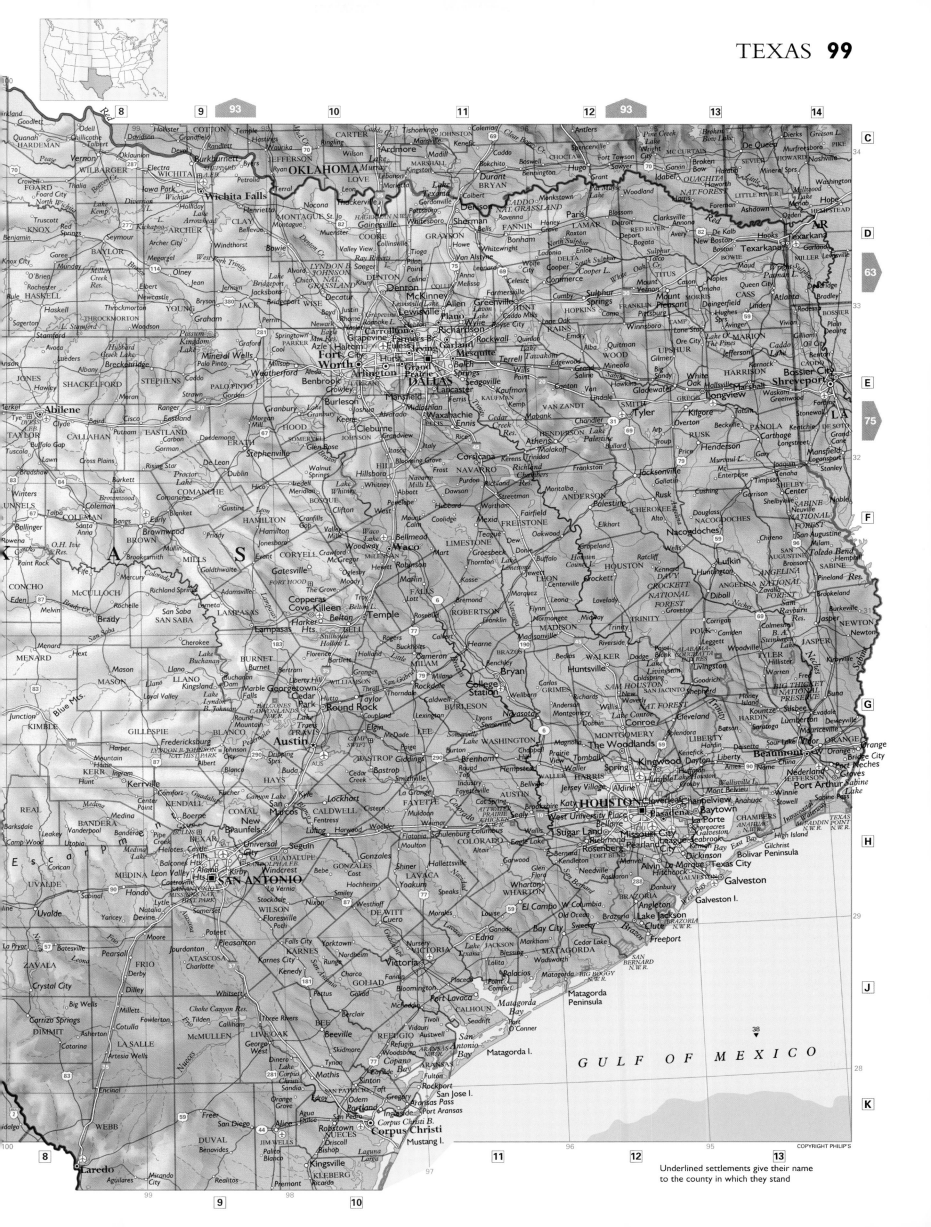

GULF OF MEXICO

COPYRIGHT PHILIP'S

Underlined settlements give their name
to the county in which they stand

1:2 200 000

Projection: Albers Equal Area

West from Greenwich

COPYRIGHT PHILIP'S

States and regions: IDAHO, WYOMING, NEVADA, ARIZONA, COLORADO

Major features and places:

Great Salt Lake, Great Salt Lake Desert, Great Basin, Sevier Desert, Escalante Desert, San Rafael Desert

Salt Lake City, Ogden, Provo, Orem, Logan, Brigham City, Cedar City, St. George, Vernal, Price, Moab, Kanab, Green River, Nephi, Richfield, Delta, Tooele, Layton, Clearfield, Bountiful, Murray, Sandy, West Valley City

Counties: BOX ELDER, CACHE, RICH, WEBER, MORGAN, SUMMIT, DAGGETT, DAVIS, TOOELE, SALT LAKE, UTAH, WASATCH, DUCHESNE, UINTAH, JUAB, SANPETE, CARBON, EMERY, MILLARD, SEVIER, BEAVER, PIUTE, WAYNE, GRAND, IRON, GARFIELD, SAN JUAN, WASHINGTON, KANE

National Forests / Parks: WASATCH-CACHE NATIONAL FOREST, ASHLEY NATIONAL FOREST, UINTA NATIONAL FOREST, MANTI-LA SAL NATIONAL FOREST, FISHLAKE NATIONAL FOREST, DIXIE NATIONAL FOREST, GREAT BASIN NATIONAL PARK, ZION NATIONAL PARK, BRYCE CANYON NATIONAL PARK, CAPITOL REEF NATIONAL PARK, CANYONLANDS NATIONAL PARK, ARCHES NATIONAL PARK, DINOSAUR NATIONAL MONUMENT, FLAMING GORGE NATIONAL RECREATION AREA, GLEN CANYON NATIONAL RECREATION AREA, GRAND STAIRCASE-ESCALANTE NATIONAL MONUMENT, CEDAR BREAKS NATIONAL MONUMENT, NATURAL BRIDGES NATIONAL MONUMENT, RAINBOW BRIDGE NATIONAL MONUMENT

Indian Reservations: UINTAH AND OURAY INDIAN RESERVATION, NAVAJO NATION INDIAN RESERVATION, SKULL VALLEY IND. RES., GOSHUTE IND. RES., PAIUTE IND. RES.

Mountain ranges and peaks: Uinta Mountains, Wasatch Range, Kings Peak 4123, Mt. Peale 3877, Mt. Lena, Delano Peak 3710, Mt. Nebo, Mt. Ellen, Navajo Mt. 3166, Abajo Peak 3463, Mt. Pennell 3466, Notch Peak 2943, Ibapah Pk. 3684, Swasey Peak 2947, Wheeler Pk. 3982

Great Salt Lake, Utah Lake, Sevier Lake, Bear Lake, Flaming Gorge Reservoir, Strawberry Res., Scofield Res., Otter Creek Res., L. Powell

Scale bar: ft / m — 9000 / 3000, 6000 / 2000, 4500 / 1500, 3000 / 1000, 1200 / 400

FOUR CORNERS

See page 86 for Vermont and page 102 for Virginia

1:2 200 000

10 0 10 20 30 40 50 60 70 80 100 km
10 0 10 20 30 40 50 60 miles

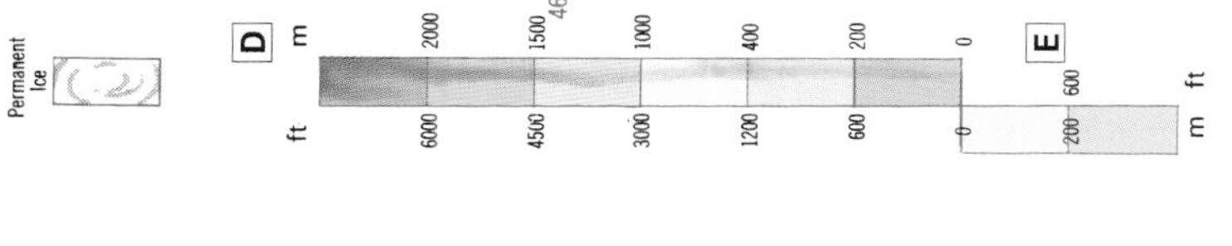

COPYRIGHT PHILIP'S

BRITISH COLUMBIA

CANADA

ID

WASHINGTON

OREGON

PACIFIC OCEAN

Strait of Juan de Fuca

Vancouver Island

Puget Sound

Seattle

Tacoma

Olympia

Spokane

Vancouver

Portland

Yakima

Walla Walla

Pendleton

Lewiston

Projection: Albers Equal Area

m ft
2000 6000
1500 4500
1000 3000
600 1800
400 1200
200 600
0 0

Underlined settlements give their name
to the county in which they stand

1:2 200 000

COPYRIGHT PHILIP'S

West from Greenwich

Projection: Albers Equal Area

continuation westwards
on same scale

1:2 200 000

10 0 10 20 30 40 50 60 70 80 100 km
10 0 10 20 30 40 50 60 miles

LAKE SUPERIOR

MINNESOTA

MICHIGAN

WISCONSIN

IOWA

ILLINOIS

LAKE MICHIGAN

Apostle Islands
APOSTLE ISLANDS NAT. LAKESHORE

Duluth
Superior
Ashland
Bayfield
Washburn
CHEQUAMEGON
NATIONAL FOREST
Hayward
Rice Lake
Eau Claire
Chippewa Falls
Menomonie
La Crosse
Sparta
Tomah
Wisconsin Dells
Baraboo
Madison
Janesville
Beloit
Rochester
Dubuque
Cedar Rapids
Rockford
CHICAGO
MILWAUKEE
Racine
Kenosha
Waukesha
Oshkosh
Fond du Lac
Appleton
Neenah
Menasha
Green Bay
Manitowoc
Sheboygan
Marinette
Menominee
Wausau
Stevens Point
Wisconsin Rapids
Marshfield
Rhinelander
Merrill
Antigo
Shawano
Oconto
Sturgeon Bay
DOOR
Escanaba
Iron Mountain
Marquette
Ironwood
Houghton
NICOLET NATIONAL FOREST
MENOMINEE IND. RES.
LAC DU FLAMBEAU INDIAN RES.
BAD RIVER INDIAN RES.
HURON MTS.

Projection: Albers Equal Area
West from Greenwich
COPYRIGHT PHILIP'S

ft m
1200 400
600 200
0 0
200 600
m ft

1:2 200 000

10 0 10 20 30 40 50 60 70 80 90 km

10 0 10 20 30 40 50 60 miles

Projection: Albers Equal Area

West from Greenwich 107

COPYRIGHT PHILIP'S

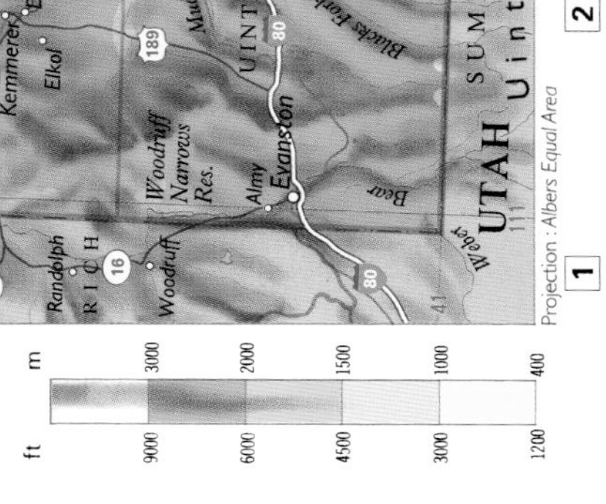

MONTANA

IDAHO

UTAH

COLORADO

NE

SD

WYOMING

YELLOWSTONE NATIONAL PARK

GRAND TETON NATIONAL PARK

BIGHORN NATIONAL FOREST

SHOSHONE NATIONAL FOREST

BRIDGER NATIONAL FOREST

MEDICINE BOW NATIONAL FOREST

THUNDER BASIN NATIONAL GRASSLAND

WIND RIVER INDIAN RESERVATION

FLAMING GORGE NATIONAL REC. AREA

Cheyenne

Casper

Laramie

Rock Springs

Green River

Gillette

Sheridan

Cody

Jackson

Evanston

Rawlins

Douglas

Buffalo

Powell

Worland

Thermopolis

Riverton

Lander

Pinedale

Kemmerer

Wheatland

Torrington

Newcastle

Sundance

Lusk

m 3000 2000 1500 1000 400

ft 9000 6000 4500 3000 1200

U.S. OUTLYING AREAS
1:84 400 000
Projection: Mercator

Sea of Okhotsk
Kamchatka
Bering Sea
Sakhalin
Kuril Is.

ALASKA (U.S.A.)
West from Greenwich
Arctic Circle
Anchorage

CANADA
Hudson Bay

Gulf of Alaska

North America

Edmonton
Vancouver
Winnipeg
Seattle
Montreal
Toronto

A s i a
CHINA
Vladivostok

P A C I F I C

Beijing
N. KOREA
S. KOREA
Seoul
JAPAN
Tokyo
Osaka
Shanghai
Taipei
TAIWAN

U N I T E D   S T A T E S
San Francisco
Los Angeles
Phoenix
Houston

Detroit
Chicago
Washington D.C.
Atlanta
Boston
New York
Philadelphia

ATLANTIC OCEAN

O C E A N

Midway Is. (U.S.A.)
Tropic of Cancer
Honolulu
HAWAI'I
Wake I. (U.S.A.)
Johnston I. (U.S.A.)

Monterrey
MEXICO
Mexico
Guadalajara
Gulf of Mexico
Miami
Havana
CUBA
BAHAMAS
Guantanamo Bay (U.S.A.)
DOM. REP.
Navassa I. (U.S.A.)
HAITI
Virgin Is. (U.S.A.)
PUERTO RICO (U.S.A.)

Manila
PHILIPPINES
Mindanao

NORTHERN MARIANAS (U.S.A.)
GUAM (U.S.A.)
FEDERATED STATES OF MICRONESIA
PALAU
MARSHALL IS.

Howland I. (U.S.A.)
Baker I. (U.S.A.)
Palmyra Is. (U.S.A.)
Jarvis I. (U.S.A.)

GUATEMALA
EL SALVADOR
BELIZE
HONDURAS
NICARAGUA
COSTA RICA
PANAMA
Caribbean Sea
Caracas
VENEZUELA
GUYANA
COLOMBIA
Bogotá
ECUADOR
Guayaquil
PERU
BRAZIL
South America

INDONESIA
Celebes
PAPUA NEW GUINEA
NAURU
KIRIBATI
Equator

SOLOMON IS.
TUVALU
Tokelau Is. (N.Z.)

AUSTRALIA
VANUATU
FIJI
TONGA
SAMOA
AMERICAN SAMOA (U.S.A.)
FRENCH POLYNESIA

PUERTO RICO AND THE VIRGIN IS.
1:1 530 000

A T L A N T I C   O C E A N

Ruffling Pt.
The Settlement
Anegada
East Pt.

VIRGIN ISLANDS (U.K.)

Pta. Agujereada
Pta. Higuero
Isabela
Quebradillas
Camuy
Hatillo
Arecibo
Barceloneta
Vega Baja
Levittown
Cataño
San Juan
Carolina
Rio Grande

Aguadilla
Moca
Aguada
PARQUE DE LAS CAVERNAS DEL RIO CAMUY
OBSERVATORIO DE ARECIBO
Manatí
Vega Alta
Bayamón
Trujillo Alto
Guaynabo
Luquillo
Fajardo

Rincón
San Sebastián
Lares
Florida
Ciales
Corozal
Comerío
Gurabo
Sierra de Luquillo
EL YUNQUE
Ceiba

Mayagüez
Añasco
Maricao
P U E R T O   R I C O
Utuado
Cerro de Punta 1338
Adjuntas
Villalba
Barranquitas
Caguas
Juncos
Las Piedras
Humacao

Hormigueros
Cabo Rojo
San German
Sabana Grande
Mts. de Uroyan
Yauco
Juana Diaz
Coamo
Cayey
Cidra
Yabucoa

Parguera
Guánica
Guayanilla
Ponce
Salinas
Guayama
Patillas
Maunabo

Pta. Aguila
Santa Isabel
I. Caja de Muertos

Dewey
Culebra
Isabel Segunda
Esperanza
Vieques
Pta. Puerca
Pta. Arenas

Jost Van Dyke I.
Hans Lollik I.
Guana I.
Great Camanoe
Beef
Virgin Gorda
Spanish Town
Tortola
521
Road Town
Peter I.
Charlotte Amalie
Cruz Bay
VIRGIN IS. NAT. PARK
St. Thomas I.
St. John I.

VIRGIN ISLANDS (U.S.A.)

C A R I B B E A N   S E A

Christiansted
Frederiksted
Mt. Eagle 353
East Pt.
Southwest Pt.
St. Croix I. (U.S.A.)
West from Greenwich

NORTHERN MARIANAS
1:17 800 000

Farallon de Pajaros
Maug Is.
Asuncion
Agrihan
Pagan
Alamagan
Guguan
Sarigan
Anatahan
Farallon de Medinilla
Saipan
Tinian
Rota
Agana
9650
GUAM (U.S.A.)

NORTHERN MARIANAS (U.S.A.)
Mariana Islands
Mariana Trench
PACIFIC OCEAN

GUAM
1:890 000

Ritidian Pt.
Pati Pt.
ANDERSEN A.F.B.
Mt. Santa Rosa
Yigo
Dededo 252
Tumon Bay
Tamuning
Agana
GUAM
Barrigada
Orote Peninsula
Piti
WAR IN THE PACIFIC N.H.P.
Yona
Pago Bay
Agat
Santa Rita
Mt. Lamlam 406
Talofofo
Umatac
Merizo
Inarajan
Cocos I.
PACIFIC OCEAN

SAIPAN & TINIAN (NORTHERN MARIANAS)
1:890 000

Sabaneta Pt.
Tanapag
Garapan
Capitol Hill
Mt. Tagpochau 465
Chalan Kanoa
Bahia Laulau
Saipan
Saipan Channel
Tahgong Pt.
Naftan Pt.
Tinian
Masalog Pt.
Diablo Pt.
San Jose 178
Tinian Channel
Carolinas Pt.
PACIFIC OCEAN

SAMOAN ISLANDS
1:22 200 000

PACIFIC OCEAN
KIRIBATI
International Date Line
Tokelau Is. (N.Z.)
SAMOA
Savai'i
Apia
Upolu
Tutuila
Manua Is.
AMERICAN SAMOA
Vava'u Group
Ha'apai Group
TONGA
Niue (N.Z.)
International Date Line

TUTUILA (AMER. SAMOA)
1:890 000

PACIFIC OCEAN
Vatia
Aua
Cape Matatula
Tula
Pago Pago
Fagasa
652
Nu'uuli
Amanave
Leone
Futiga
Aunuu
C. Taputapu
Steps Pt.
Pago Pago Harbor

MANUA IS. (AMER. SAMOA)
1:890 000

PACIFIC OCEAN
Olosega
Pumafua Mt. 639
Ofu 484
Luma
Leusoalii
Lata Mt. 931
Siufaalele Pt.
Tau

ft m
3000 1000
1200 400
600 200
0
200 600
1000 3000
2000 6000
4000 12000
m ft

COPYRIGHT PHILIP'S

10 0 10 20 30 km
10 0 10 20 miles
1:1 530 000

100 0 100 200 300 400 500 600 700 800 km
100 0 100 200 300 400 500 miles
1:17 800 000

5 0 5 10 km
5 0 5 10 miles
1:890 000

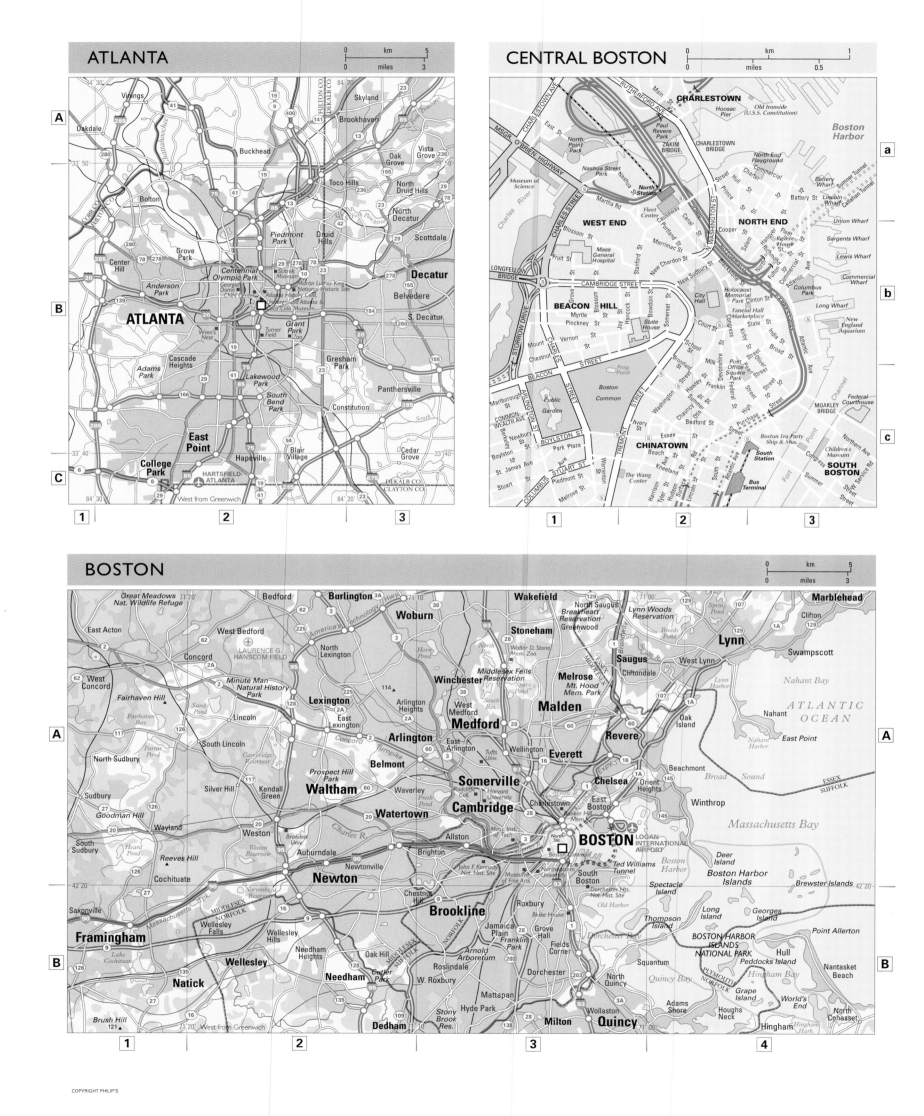

ATLANTA

CENTRAL BOSTON

BOSTON

BALTIMORE

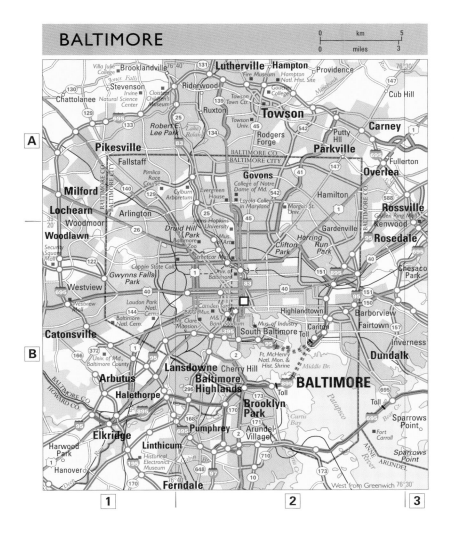

CHARLOTTE

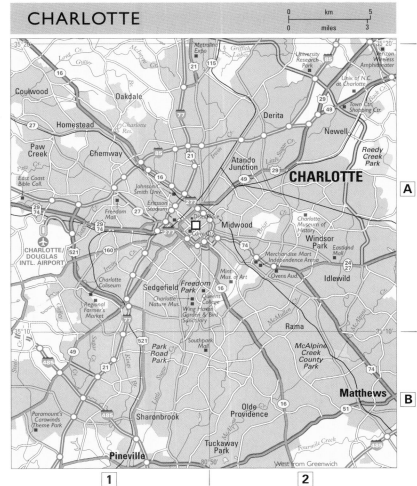

CINCINNATI

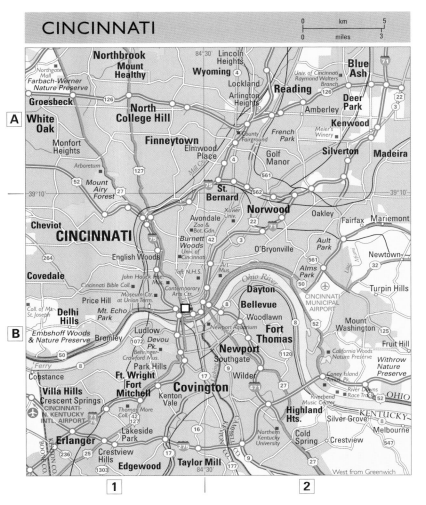

CLEVELAND

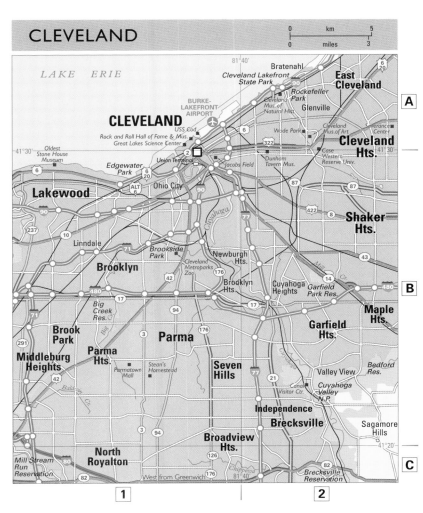

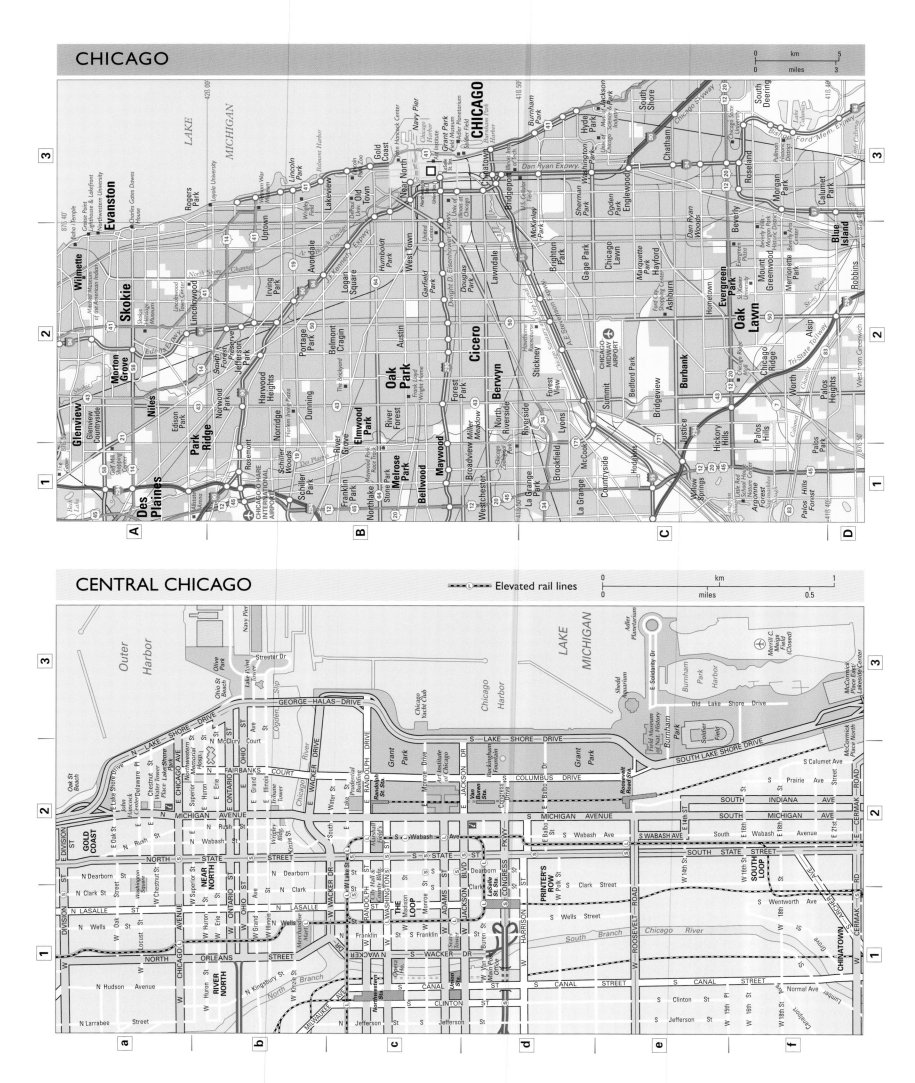

CHICAGO

CENTRAL CHICAGO

⊏⊐L Elevated rail lines

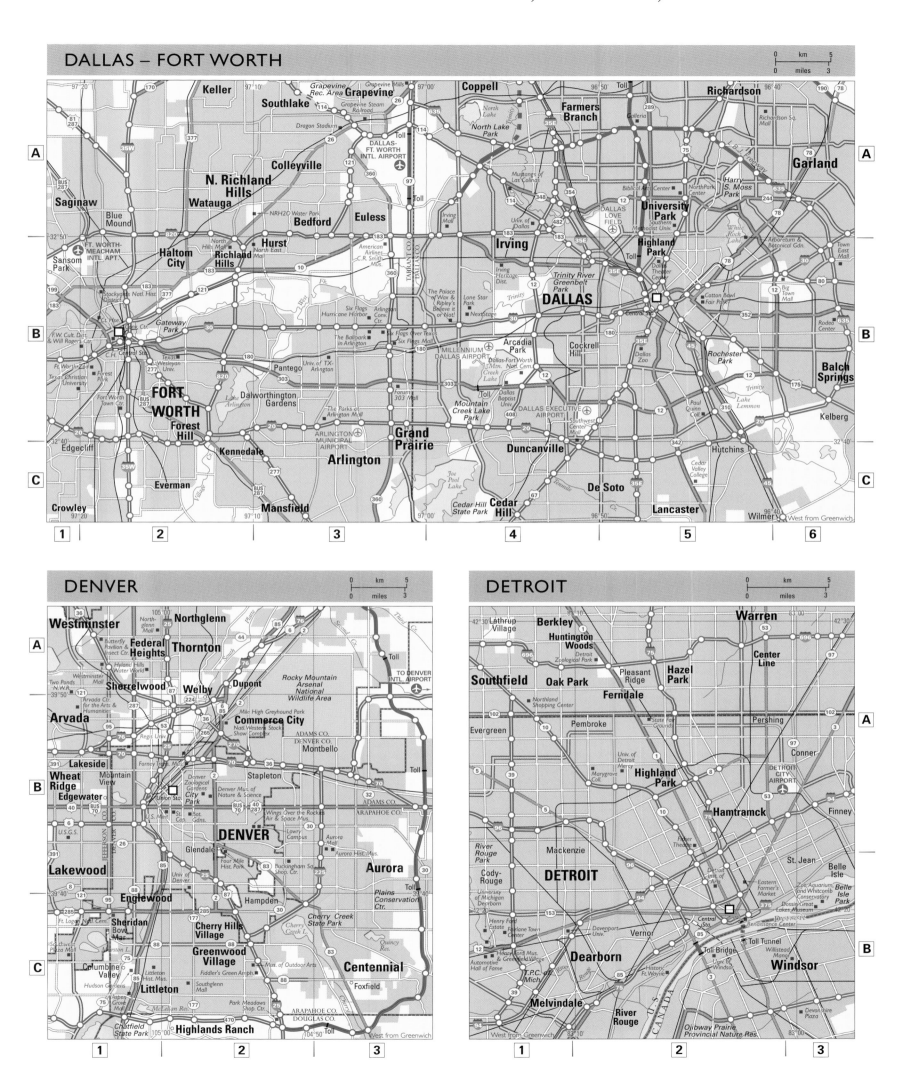

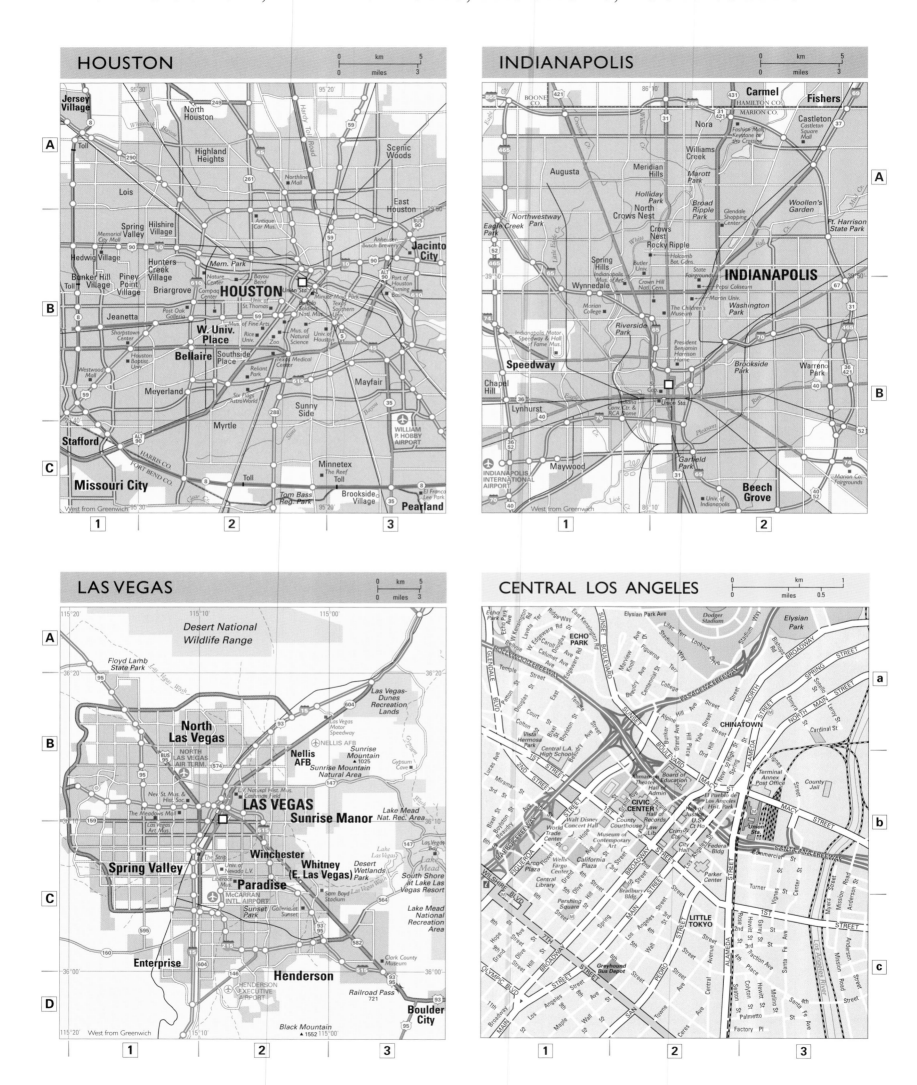

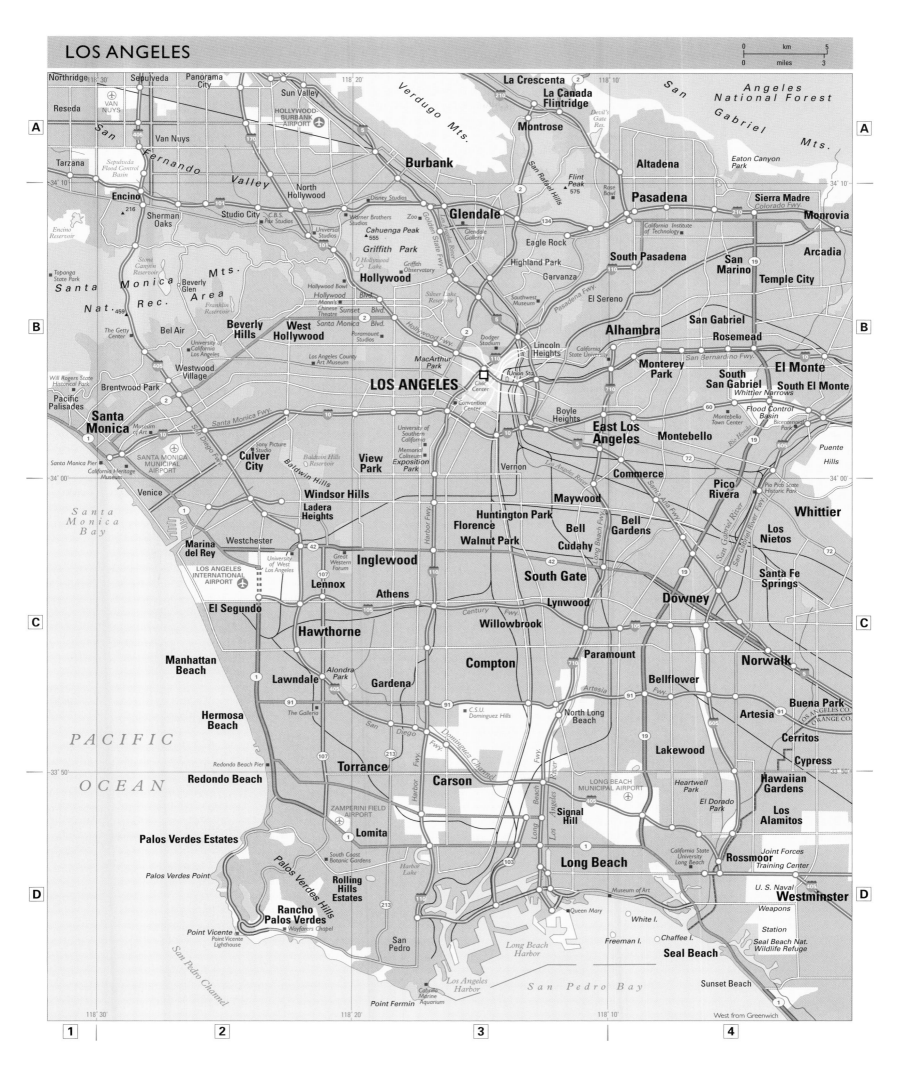

LOS ANGELES

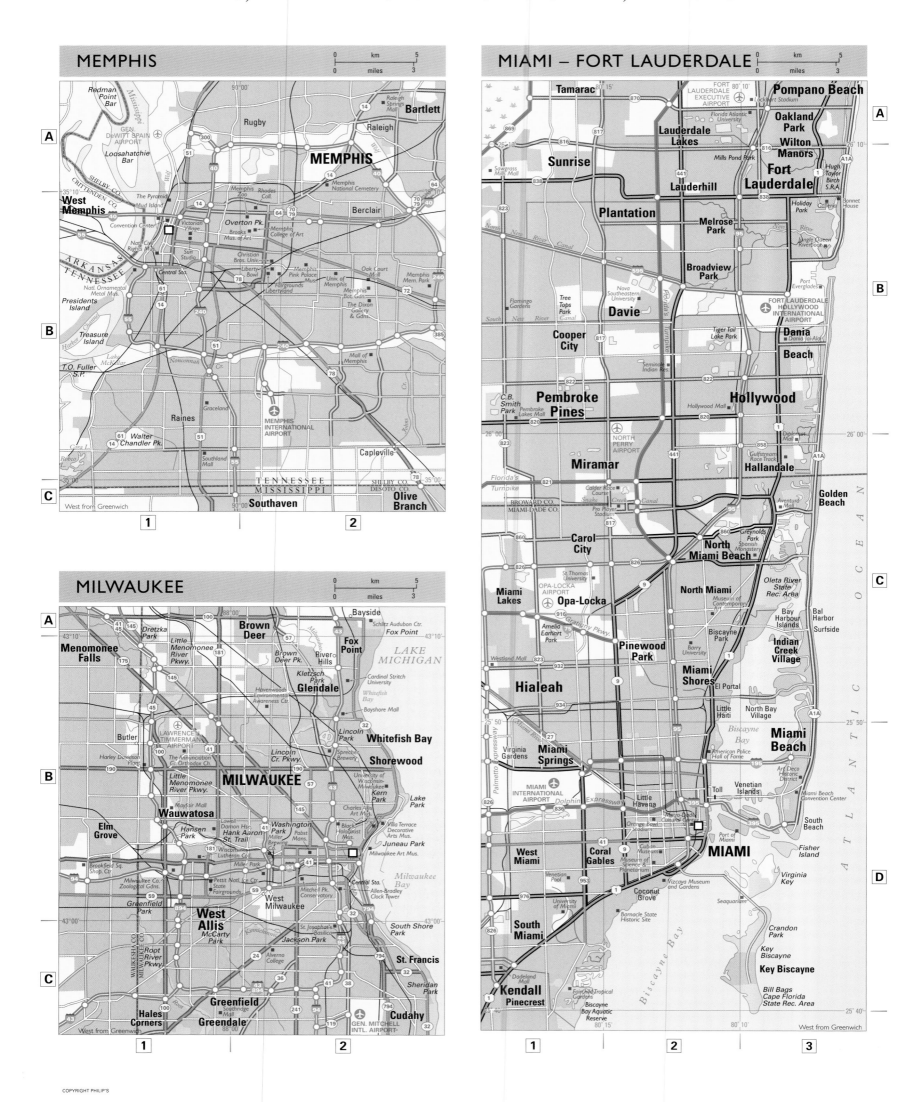

MINNEAPOLIS – ST. PAUL

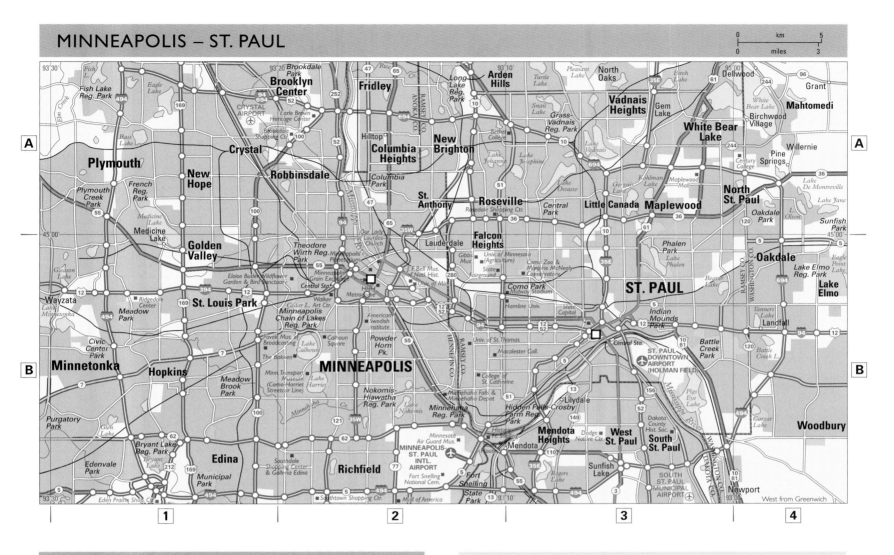

NEW ORLEANS

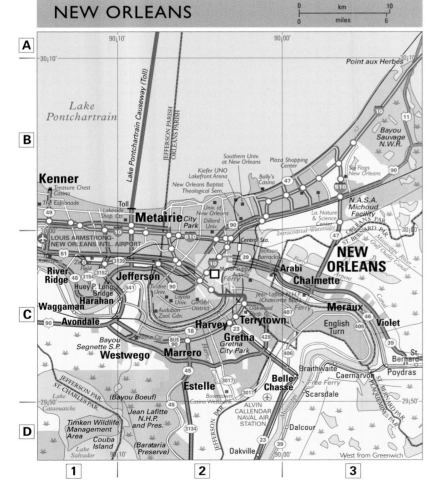

CENTRAL NEW ORLEANS

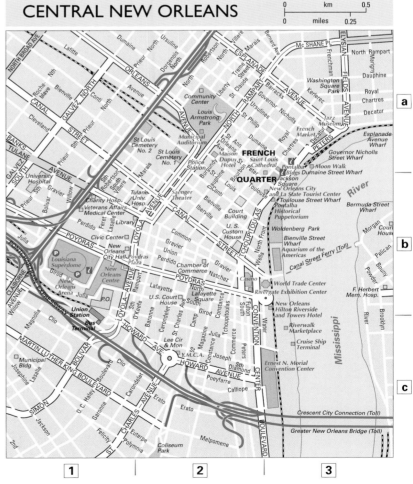

Note: Maps represent the topography of the city of New Orleans before storm surges from Hurricane Katrina caused severe flooding in August 2005.

COPYRIGHT PHILIP'S

NEW YORK

CENTRAL NEW YORK

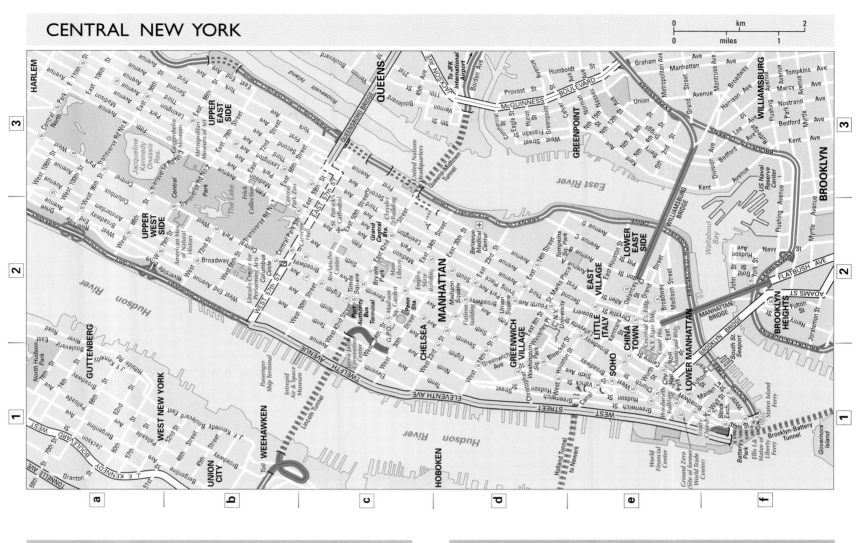

NORFOLK

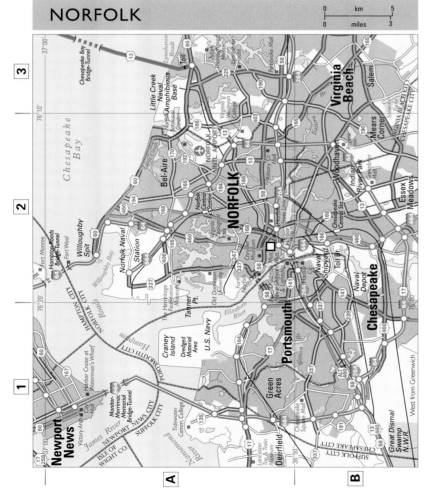

ORLANDO

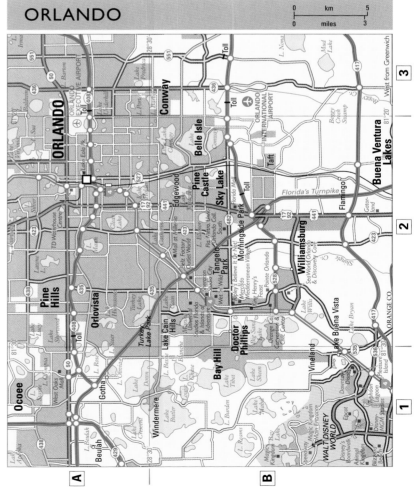

PHILADELPHIA

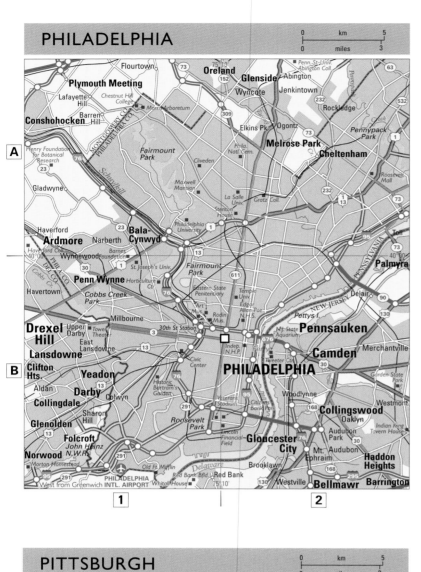

PHOENIX

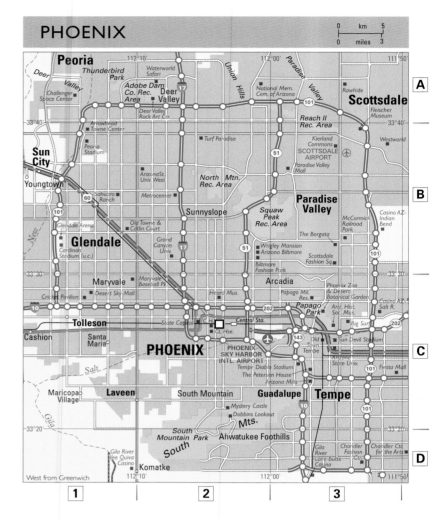

PITTSBURGH

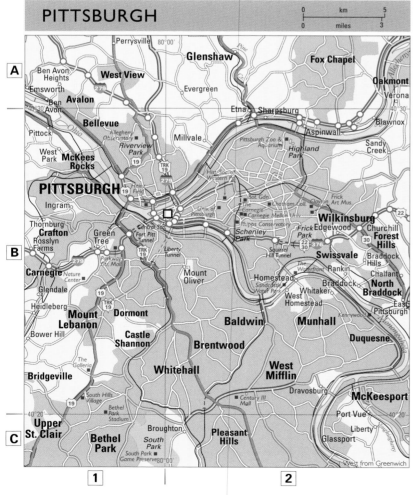

PORTLAND

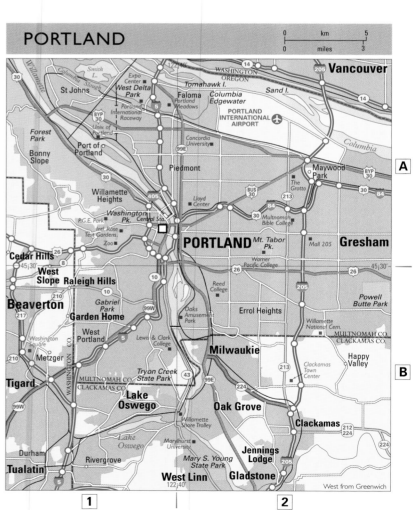

ST. LOUIS

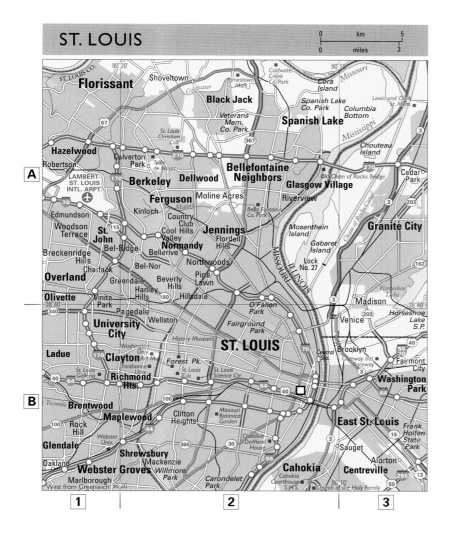

SALT LAKE CITY

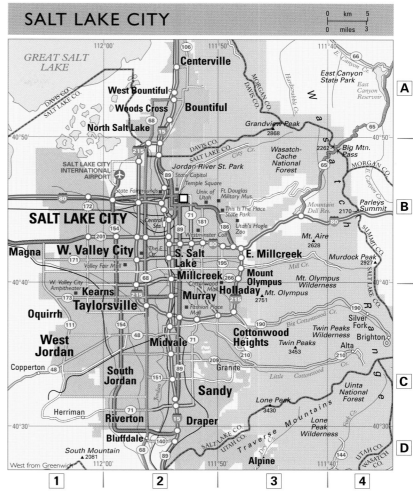

SAN ANTONIO

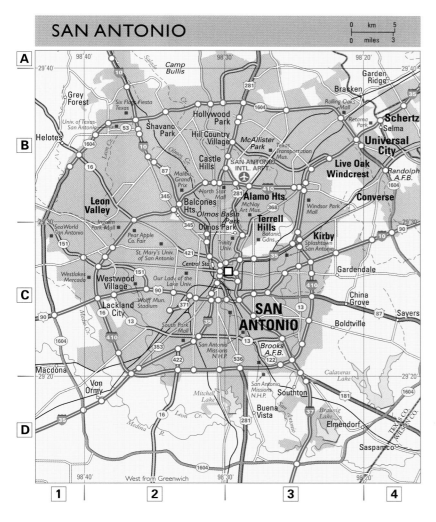

SAN DIEGO

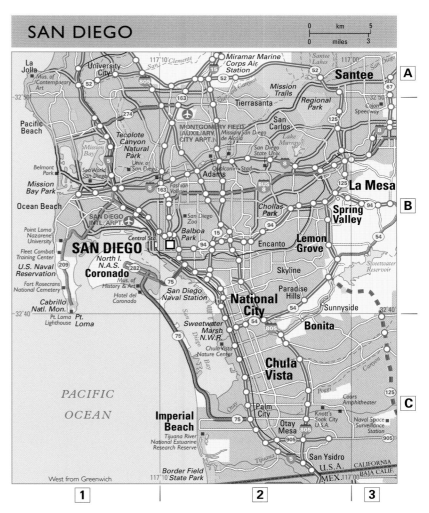

COPYRIGHT PHILIP'S

SAN FRANCISCO

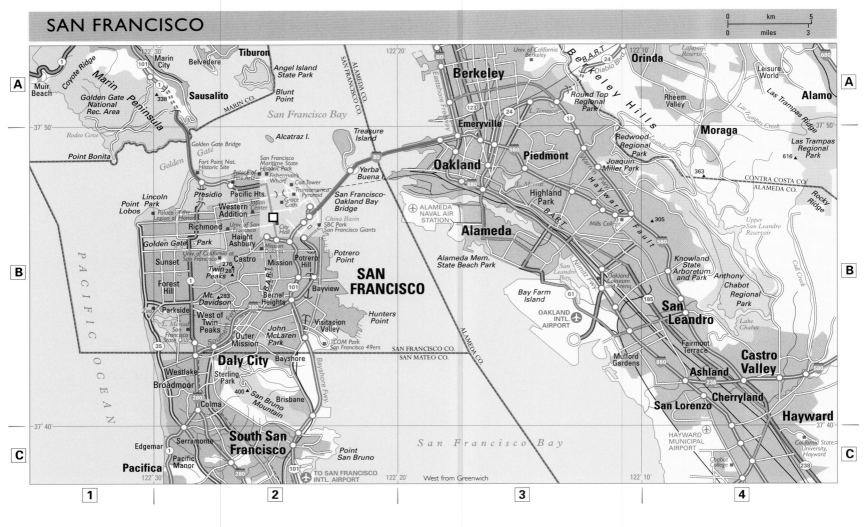

km 5
miles 3

A

Muir Beach · Coyote Ridge · Marin Peninsula · Marin City · Belvedere · Tiburon · Angel Island State Park · Blunt Pt · Univ. of California Berkeley · Berkeley · 24 · Diablo Blvd · Orinda · Lafayette Reservoir · Leisure World · Alamo

Sausalito · 338 · Rodeo Cove · San Francisco Bay · Treasure Island · Emeryville · 123 · 24 · 13 · Round Top Regional Park · Rheem Valley · Las Trampas Creek · Moraga · Las Trampas Ridge · Las Trampas Regional Park

Point Bonita · Golden Gate Bridge · Alcatraz I. · Oakland · Piedmont · Redwood Regional Park · 616 · 363 · CONTRA COSTA CO. · ALAMEDA CO. · Rocky Ridge

B

Lincoln Park · Point Lobos · Presidio · Pacific Hts. · Western Addition · Richmond · Haight Ashbury · Castro · Mission · Potrero Hill · Potrero Point · Alameda · Highland Park · Mills College · 305 · Knowland State Arboretum and Park · Anthony Chabot Regional Park · Upper San Leandro Reservoir

Golden Gate Park · Sunset · Twin Peaks · 276 · Mt. Davidson 283 · Bernal Heights · Bayview · SAN FRANCISCO · Hunters Point · Alameda Mem. State Beach Park · Bay Farm Island · 61 · OAKLAND INTL. AIRPORT · Oakland Coliseum and Arena · 185 · San Leandro Bay · San Leandro

Forest Hill · Parkside · Zoo · West of Twin Peaks · Outer Mission · John McLaren Park · Visitacion Valley · 3COM Park San Francisco 49ers · SAN FRANCISCO CO. · SAN MATEO CO. · Mulford Gardens · 880 · Fairmont Terrace · Ashland · 238 · Castro Valley · 580

C

Daly City · Bayshore · 400 · San Bruno Mountain · Brisbane · San Francisco Bay · San Lorenzo · Cherryland · Hayward

Westlake · Broadmoor · Sterling Park · Colma · 280 · Edgemar · Serramonte · Pacific Manor · South San Francisco · Point San Bruno · 101 · TO SAN FRANCISCO INTL. AIRPORT · West from Greenwich · HAYWARD MUNICIPAL AIRPORT · Chabot College · 238 · California State University, Hayward

Pacifica

CENTRAL SAN FRANCISCO

km 0.5
miles 0.25

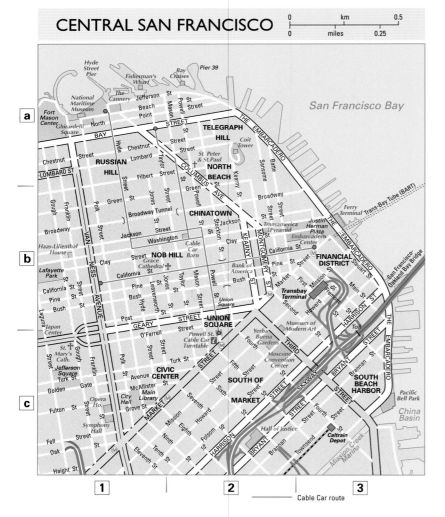

Cable Car route

SEATTLE

km 5
miles 3

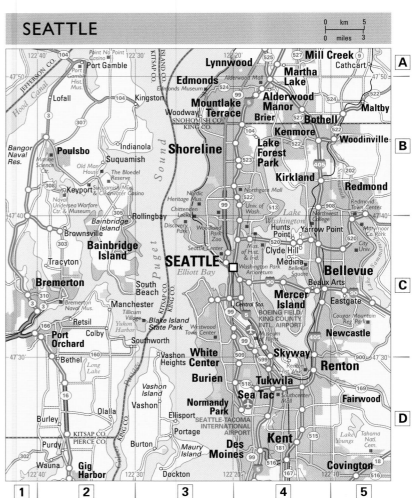

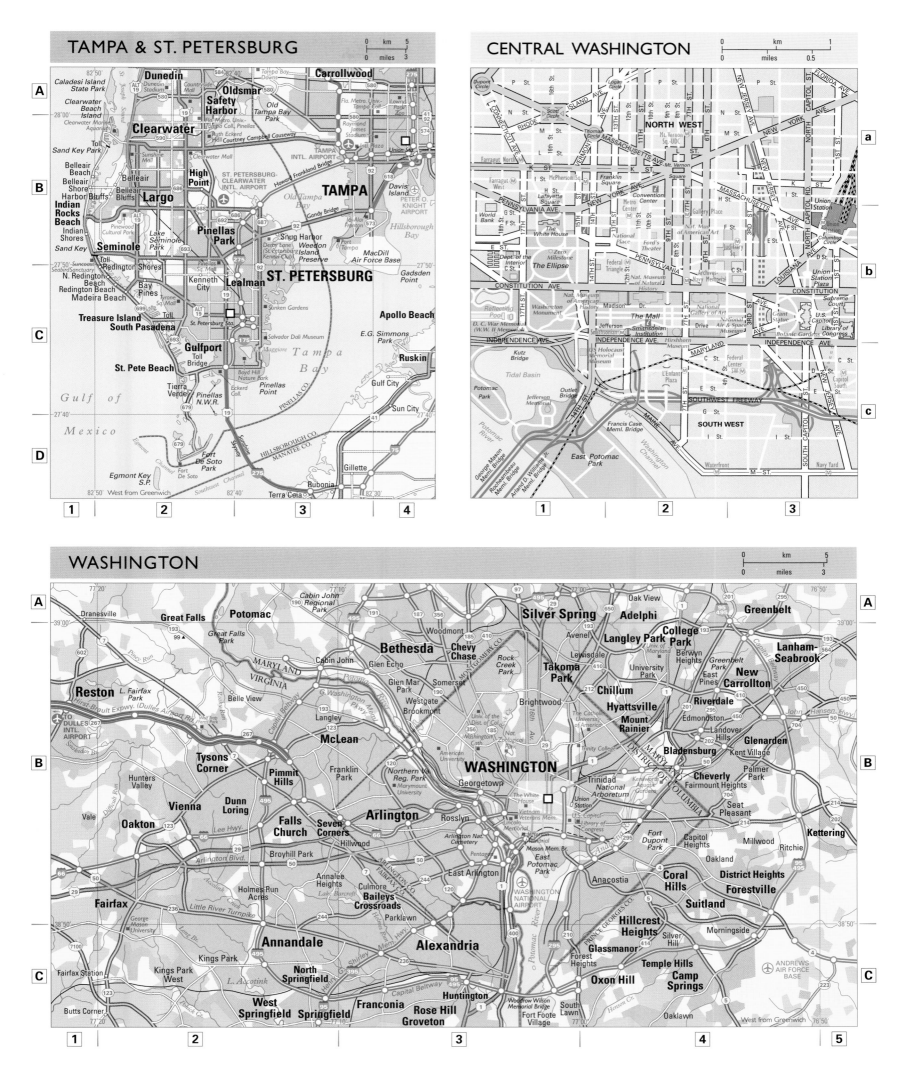

TAMPA & ST. PETERSBURG

CENTRAL WASHINGTON

WASHINGTON

Alabama

Statehood: December 14, 1819
Nickname: The Heart of Dixie
State bird: Yellowhammer
State flower: Camellia
State tree: Southern pine
State motto: We dare defend our rights
State capital: Montgomery
Population of capital: 201,568 (2000)

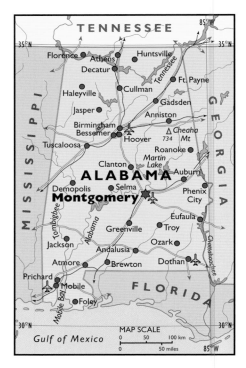

Settled by the French in 1702, this Southeastern state in the chief cotton-growing region of the United States was acquired by Britain in 1763. Originally, Creek and Choctaw territory, most of Alabama was ceded to the fledgling country after the American Revolution (1776–83), and it was admitted into the Union as the 22nd state in 1819. Following secession in 1861 as one of the original six states of the Confederacy, Alabama was readmitted to the Union in 1868. Birmingham is the largest metropolis and a major center for manufacturing as well as telecommunications. In the 1960s, the civil rights movement took shape in Birmingham and Montgomery. Huntsville and Mobile are the other main cities in this state of 67 counties.

The Northern part of the state lies in the heavily wooded Appalachian Highlands, which have coal, iron ore, and other mineral deposits, while much of the rest of Alabama's geography consists of swampland on the Gulf coastal plain, crossed by a wide strip of rich, fertile soil. The Mobile River, its tributaries, and the canalized Tombigbee River form the chief river system. The principal crops are peanuts, soybeans, and corn, with cotton decreasingly important. Industries include chemicals, textiles, electronics, metal, and paper products.

A crimson St. Andrew's cross on a white background, the state flag of Alabama is patterned after the Confederate flag and was adopted in 1895.

Montgomery

Made state capital in 1847, Montgomery later became the first capital of the Confederate States of America. Jefferson Davis was inaugurated president and occupied the first white house of the Confederacy here near the confluence of the Coosa and Tallapoosa rivers. It subsequently grew in importance and in the 1950s, was the scene of the beginnings of the civil-rights movement. It was in this city in the southeastern part of the state that Rosa Parks refused to give up her seat on a segregated city bus, sparking a bus boycott led by the Rev. Martin Luther King, Jr. Textiles, fertilizers, furniture, air conditioning and heating unit manufacturing comprise the local industry.

Alabama at a Glance

People	Alabama	USA
Population, 2003 estimate	4,500,752	290,809,777
Population percent change, April 1, 2000–July 1, 2001	1.2	1.2
Population, 2000	4,447,100	281,421,906
Persons under 5 years old, percent, 2000	6.7%	6.8%
Persons under 18 years old, percent, 2000	25.3%	25.7%
Persons 65 years old and over, percent, 2000	13.0%	12.4%
Female persons, percent, 2000	51.7%	50.9%
White persons, percent, 2000 (a)	71.1%	75.1%
African American persons, percent, 2000 (a)	26.0%	12.3%
Native American persons, percent, 2000 (a)	0.5%	0.9%
Asian persons, percent, 2000 (a)	0.7%	3.6%
Native Hawaiian and Other Pacific Islander, percent, 2000 (a)	Z	0.1%
Persons of Hispanic or Latino origin, percent, 2000 (b)	1.7%	12.5%
White persons, not of Hispanic/Latino origin, percent, 2000	70.3%	69.1%
Foreign born persons, percent, 2000	2.0%	11.1%
Language other than English spoken at home, percent age 5+, 2000	3.9%	17.9%
High school graduates, percent of persons age 25+, 2000	75.3%	80.4%
Bachelor's degree or higher, percent of persons age 25+, 2000	19.0%	24.4%
Persons with a disability, age 5+, 2000	945,705	49,746,248
Homeownership rate, 2000	72.5%	66.2%
Median value of owner-occupied housing units, 2000	$85,100	$119,600
Households, 2000	1,737,080	105,480,101
Persons per household, 2000	2.49	2.59
Median household money income, 1999	$34,135	$41,994
Per capita money income, 1999	$18,189	$21,587
Persons below poverty, percent, 1999	16.1%	12.4%

Business	Alabama	USA
Private nonfarm establishments, 1999	100,507	7,008,444
Private nonfarm employment, 1999	1,633,909	110,705,661
Private nonfarm employment, percent change 1990–99	21.7%	18.4%
Nonemployer establishments, 1999	219,932	16,152,604
Manufacturers shipments, 1997 ($1,000)	67,970,076	3,842,061,405
Retail sales, 1997 ($1,000)	36,623,327	2,460,886,012
Retail sales per capita, 1997	$8,477	$9,190
Minority-owned firms, percent of total, 1997	9.9%	14.6%
Women-owned firms, percent of total, 1997	24.4%	26.0%
Federal funds and grants, 2001 ($1,000)	31,700,462	1,763,896,019
Local government employment – full-time equivalent, 1997	175,369	10,227,429

Geography	Alabama	USA
Land area, 2000 (square miles)	50,744	3,537,438
Persons per square mile, 2000	87.6	79.6

(a) Includes persons reporting only one race.
(b) Hispanics may be of any race, so also are included in applicable race categories.
Z: Value greater than zero but less than half unit of measure shown.

Source: U.S. Census Bureau State & County QuickFacts

Alaska

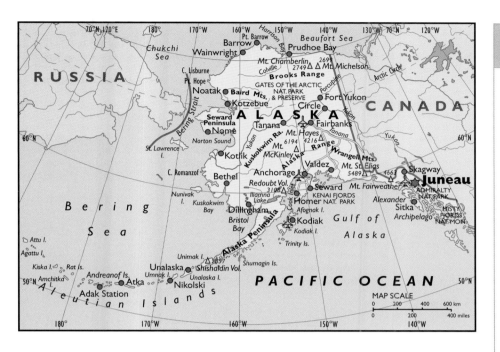

Statehood: January 3, 1959
Nickname: The Last Frontier
State bird: Willow ptarmigan
State flower: Forget-me-not
State tree: Sitka spruce
State motto: North to the future
State capital: Juneau
Population of capital: 30,711 (2000)

Separated from the rest of continental United States by the Canadian province of British Columbia, and from Russia by the Bering Strait, Alaska is the westernmost, northernmost, and easternmost state because the furthest Aleutian Islands cross the 180th meridian. Until Captain James Cook explored the region in search of a Northwest Passage, the maritime lifestyle of the Aleut, Athabaskan, and Inuit people remained unknown to Europeans. In 1867 the United States purchased Alaska from Russia for $7.2 million dollars. Fishing initially drew settlers and in the decade following the gold rush of the 1890s the population doubled. Alaska, partitioned into 25 census divisions, became the 49th state of the Union in 1959. The capital Juneau is considerably smaller than Fairbanks or Anchorage.

About twenty-five percent of the state lies inside the Arctic Circle and Alaska has more coastline than the rest of the states combined. Despite its latitude, however, glaciers only cover about five percent of Alaska. Between the Brooks Range and the Coast Range, the Alaska mountains include Mount McKinley (Denali), the highest peak in North America. The chief river is the Yukon. The Alaskan economy is based on fish, natural gas, timber, quartz, and (primarily) oil. Numerous national parks such as Glacier Bay encourage tourism. Because of its strategic position and oil reserves, Alaska has been developed as a military area linked to the rest of the United States via the 1,500 mile-long (2,450 km) Alaska Highway. Although by far the largest state by area in the U.S., it has the third smallest population after Wyoming and Vermont. Native Americans (mainly Inuit-Aleut) account for approximately fifteen percent of the total population.

The flag was adopted when Alaska gained its statehood. The blue field represents the sea, the sky and the mountain lakes while the stars in the shape of the Big Dipper allude to the state's gold resources. The eighth and largest star stands for the North Star, conveying Alaska's geographic position.

Juneau

A seaport on the Gastineau Channel, Juneau grew rapidly after the 1880 discovery of gold by the town's namesake, Joseph Juneau, and another prospector, Richard Harris. Made capital of the Alaska territory in 1900, the city is home to mining, timber, salmon canning, and tourist industries.

Alaska at a Glance

People	Alaska	USA
Population, 2003 estimate	648,818	290,809,777
Population percent change,		
April 1, 2000–July 1, 2001	1.3%	1.2%
Population, 2000	626,932	281,421,906
Persons under 5 years old, percent, 2000	7.6%	6.8%
Persons under 18 years old, percent, 2000	30.4%	25.7%
Persons 65 years old and over, percent, 2000	5.7%	12.4%
Female persons, percent, 2000	48.3%	50.9%
White persons, percent, 2000 (a)	69.3%	75.1%
African American persons,		
percent, 2000 (a)	3.5%	12.3%
Native American persons,		
percent, 2000 (a)	15.6%	0.9%
Asian persons, percent, 2000 (a)	4.0%	3.6%
Native Hawaiian and Other Pacific Islander,		
percent, 2000 (a)	0.5%	0.1%
Persons of Hispanic or Latino origin,		
percent, 2000 (b)	4.1%	12.5%
White persons, not of Hispanic/Latino origin,		
percent, 2000	67.6%	69.1%
Foreign born persons, percent, 2000	5.9%	11.1%
Language other than English spoken at home,		
percent age 5+, 2000	14.3%	17.9%
High school graduates, percent of persons		
age 25+, 2000	88.3%	80.4%
Bachelor's degree or higher,		
percent of persons age 25+, 2000	24.7%	24.4%
Persons with a disability, age 5+, 2000	83,220	49,746,248
Homeownership rate, 2000	62.5%	66.2%
Median value of owner-occupied		
housing units, 2000	$144,200	$119,600
Households, 2000	221,600	105,480,101
Persons per household, 2000	2.74	2.59
Median household money income, 1999	$51,571	$41,994
Per capita money income, 1999	$22,660	$21,587
Persons below poverty, percent, 1999	9.4%	12.4%

Business	Alaska	USA
Private nonfarm establishments, 1999	18,433	7,008,444
Private nonfarm employment, 1999	198,459	110,705,661
Private nonfarm employment,		
percent change 1990–99	25.8%	18.4%
Nonemployer establishments, 1999	48,441	16,152,604
Manufacturers shipments, 1997 ($1,000)	3,304,952	3,842,061,405
Retail sales, 1997 ($1,000)	6,251,372	2,460,886,012
Retail sales per capita, 1997	$10,268	$9,190
Minority-owned firms, percent of total, 1997	16.7%	14.6%
Women-owned firms, percent of total, 1997	25.9%	26.0%
Federal funds and grants, 2001 ($1,000)	6,403,171	1,763,896,019
Local government employment –		
full-time equivalent, 1997	23,132	10,227,429

Geography	Alaska	USA
Land area, 2000 (square miles)	571,951	3,537,438
Persons per square mile, 2000	1.1	79.6

(a) Includes persons reporting only one race.
(b) Hispanics may be of any race, so also are included in applicable race categories.
Z: Value greater than zero but less than half unit of measure shown.

Source: U.S. Census Bureau State & County QuickFacts

Arizona

Bordering Mexico in the southwestern part of the country, Arizona became the 48th state of the Union in 1912 after 64 years as a territory when Mexico yielded most of the land presently within its boundaries to the United States at the end of the Mexican War (1846–48). Today the state is made up of 15 counties; many like Apache, Navajo and Yuma have taken the names of the Indian tribes that once claimed the land as their own. Most of the largest cities, with the exception of Tucson, cluster around the capital in the south.

The Colorado Plateau occupies the northern part of the state, and is cut by many steep canyons, most notably the Grand Canyon, through which the Colorado River flows. Arizona's mineral resources, grazing and farmland have long been mainstays of the economy and while mining and agriculture are still important, manufacturing has been the most profitable sector since the 1950s. The state has many scenic attractions including the Petrified Forest, Fort Apache, Hoover Dam, as well as the reconstructed London Bridge at Lake Havasu and tourism is now a major source of income. Arizona also has one of the largest Native American populations in the nation (255,879 in 2000) with Indian reservations comprising twenty-eight percent of the land area. Between 1990 and 1998, Arizona's population grew by 30 percent, one of the fastest rates in the country.

Full of symbolism, Arizona's flag displays thirteen rays of red and gold that simultaneously represent the setting sun and the original colonies. The colors themselves reflect those of Spain, while the blue on the bottom half of the banner matches that on the national flag. The star at the center borrows its color from the state's chief mineral. It was adopted in 1917.

Phoenix

Founded on the Salt River in 1870, the city expanded after agriculture in the area had been made possible by using water from the river for irrigation. It became the capital in 1889 and computer parts, aircraft, fabricated metals, machinery, textiles, clothing, and food products are now the leading industries along with many high-tech companies. The dry climate makes Phoenix a popular winter resort.

Arizona at a Glance

People	Arizona	USA
Population, 2003 estimate	5,580,811	290,809,777
Population percent change, April 1, 2000–July 1, 2001	3.4%	1.2%
Population, 2000	5,130,632	281,421,906
Persons under 5 years old, percent, 2000	7.5%	6.8%
Persons under 18 years old, percent, 2000	26.6%	25.7%
Persons 65 years old and over, percent, 2000	13.0%	12.4%
Female persons, percent, 2000	50.1%	50.9%
White persons, percent, 2000 (a)	75.5%	75.1%
African American persons, percent, 2000 (a)	3.1%	12.3%
Native American persons, percent, 2000 (a)	5.0%	0.9%
Asian persons, percent, 2000 (a)	1.8%	3.6%
Native Hawaiian and Other Pacific Islander, percent, 2000 (a)	0.1%	0.1%
Persons of Hispanic or Latino origin, percent, 2000 (b)	25.3%	12.5%
White persons, not of Hispanic/Latino origin, percent, 2000	63.8%	69.1%
Foreign born persons, percent, 2000	12.8%	11.1%
Language other than English spoken at home, percent age 5+, 2000	25.9%	17.9%
High school graduates, percent of persons age 25+, 2000	81.0%	80.4%
Bachelor's degree or higher, percent of persons age 25+, 2000	23.5%	24.4%
Persons with a disability, age 5+, 2000	902,252	49,746,248
Homeownership rate, 2000	68.0%	66.2%
Median value of owner-occupied housing units, 2000	$121,300	$119,600
Households, 2000	1,901,327	105,480,101
Persons per household, 2000	2.64	2.59
Median household money income, 1999	$40,558	$41,994
Per capita money income, 1999	$20,275	$21,587
Persons below poverty, percent, 1999	13.9%	12.4%

Business	Arizona	USA
Private nonfarm establishments, 1999	112,545	7,008,444
Private nonfarm employment, 1999	1,838,277	110,705,661
Private nonfarm employment, percent change 1990–99	48.7%	18.4%
Nonemployer establishments, 1999	260,743	16,152,604
Manufacturers shipments, 1997 ($1,000)	43,030,348	3,842,061,405
Retail sales, 1997 ($1,000)	43,960,933	2,460,886,012
Retail sales per capita, 1997	$9,657	$9,190
Minority-owned firms, percent of total, 1997	13.2%	14.6%
Women-owned firms, percent of total, 1997	27.0%	26.0%
Federal funds and grants, 2001 ($1,000)	30,375,935	1,763,896,019
Local government employment – full-time equivalent, 1997	165,331	10,227,429

Geography	Arizona	USA
Land area, 2000 (square miles)	113,635	3,537,438
Persons per square mile, 2000	45.2	79.6

(a) Includes persons reporting only one race.

(b) Hispanics may be of any race, so also are included in applicable race categories.

Z: Value greater than zero but less than half unit of measure shown.

Source: U.S. Census Bureau State & County QuickFacts

Arkansas

Statehood: June 15, 1836
Nickname: The Land of Opportunity
State bird: Mockingbird
State flower: Apple Blossom
State tree: Pine tree
State motto: The people rule
State capital: Little Rock
Population of capital: 183,133 (2000)

Bounded on the East by the Mississippi River, Arkansas was acquired as part of the Louisiana Purchase in 1803 and was admitted to the Union as the 25th state in 1836. The Quapaw people, called the Arkansea by other local tribes, give their name to the state. Arkansas was one of the 11 Confederate states during the American Civil War. Despite containing 75 counties, Arkansas has few large cities; Fort Smith and Pine Bluff are only a fraction of the size of the capital.

In the East and South the land is low and flat, providing excellent farmland for cotton, rice, and soybeans. The hilly, higher land in the northwest, including the Ouachita Mountains and the Ozark Plateau meets the plains of the state at Little Rock. Like all of the state's rivers, the principal waterway, the Arkansas, drains into the Mississippi. Forests are extensive and economically important. Bauxite processing, timber and chemicals are the main industries. Noted for its resistance to black equality in the 1960s, former president Bill Clinton served five terms as governor of Arkansas. Hot Springs National Park, America's most famous mineral water spa, and the oldest area in the National Park system, has long been a destination for tourists and health seekers.

The diamond design of the flag adopted by Arkansas in 1913 is meant to recall the state's unique status as the only producer of the precious gem in the country. The 25 stars around the diamond point to the timing of Arkansas's statehood. Of the stars in the center, the uppermost signifies its membership in the Confederate States of America, while the three below stand for Spain, France and the United States.

Little Rock

Founded on the banks of the river by the same name in 1814, Arkansas's largest city became the state capital in 1821. French explorers began calling the spot Little Rock to distinguish it from other outcroppings further up the river. In 1957, federal troops enforced a U.S. Supreme Court ruling against racial segregation in schools. The main industries are electronics, textiles and consumer goods.

Arkansas at a Glance

People	Arkansas	USA
Population, 2003 estimate	2,725,714	290,809,777
Population percent change,		
April 1, 2000–July 1, 2001	0.7%	1.2%
Population, 2000	2,673,400	281,421,906
Persons under 5 years old, percent, 2000	6.8%	6.8%
Persons under 18 years old, percent, 2000	25.4%	25.7%
Persons 65 years old and over, percent, 2000	14.0%	12.4%
Female persons, percent, 2000	51.2%	50.9%
White persons, percent, 2000 (a)	80.0%	75.17%
African American persons,		
percent, 2000 (a)	15.7%	12.3%
Native American persons,		
percent, 2000 (a)	0.7%	0.9%
Asian persons, percent, 2000 (a)	0.8%	3.6%
Native Hawaiian and Other Pacific Islander,		
percent, 2000 (a)	0.1%	0.1%
Persons of Hispanic or Latino origin,		
percent, 2000 (b)	3.2%	12.5%
White persons, not of Hispanic/Latino origin,		
percent, 2000	78.6%	69.1%
Foreign born persons, percent, 2000	2.8%	11.1%
Language other than English spoken at home,		
percent age 5+, 2000	5.0%	17.9%
High school graduates, percent of persons		
age 25+, 2000	75.3%	80.4%
Bachelor's degree or higher,		
percent of persons age 25+, 2000	16.7%	24.4%
Persons with a disability, age 5+, 2000	576,471	49,746,248
Homeownership rate, 2000	69.4%	66.2%
Median value of owner-occupied		
housing units, 2000	$72,800	$119,600
Households, 2000	1,042,696	105,480,101
Persons per household, 2000	2.49	2.59
Median household money income, 1999	$32,182	$41,994
Per capita money income, 1999	$16,904	$21,587
Persons below poverty, percent, 1999	15.8%	12.4%

Business	Arkansas	USA
Private nonfarm establishments, 1999	62,737	7,008,444
Private nonfarm employment, 1999	954,948	110,705,661
Private nonfarm employment,		
percent change 1990–99	27.2%	18.4%
Nonemployer establishments, 1999	151,948	16,152,604
Manufacturers shipments, 1997 ($1,000)	45,185,963	3,842,061,405
Retail sales, 1997 ($1,000)	21,643,695	2,460,886,012
Retail sales per capita, 1997	$8,575	$9,190
Minority-owned firms, percent of total, 1997	6.7%	14.6%
Women-owned firms, percent of total, 1997	22.0%	26.0%
Federal funds and grants, 2001 ($1,000)	16,632,110	1,763,896,019
Local government employment –		
full-time equivalent, 1997	90,806	10,227,429

Geography	Arkansas	USA
Land area, 2000 (square miles)	52,068	3,537,438
Persons per square mile, 2000	51.3	79.6

(a) Includes persons reporting only one race.

(b) Hispanics may be of any race, so also are included in applicable race categories.

Z: Value greater than zero but less than half unit of measure shown.

Source: U.S. Census Bureau State & County QuickFacts

California

CALIFORNIA REPUBLIC

Statehood: September 9, 1850
Nickname: The Golden State
State bird: California valley quail
State flower: Golden poppy
State tree: California redwood
State motto: Eureka!
State capital: Sacramento
Population of capital: 407,018 (2000)

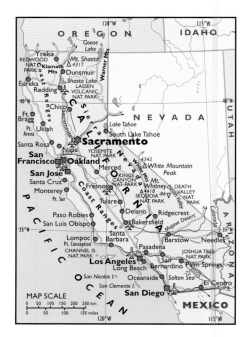

The largest state by population and the third largest in area, California sits on the Pacific coast of the United States. The Spanish explored the coast in 1542, but the first European settlement did not appear until 1769, with the founding of a Franciscan mission at San Diego. The area became part of Mexico, and huge cattle ranches were established. Settlers later migrated from the East and, during the Mexican War, United States forces occupied California in 1846, which was ceded to the United States at the war's end. After gold was discovered at Sutter's Mill in 1848, the Gold Rush swelled the population from 15,000 to 250,000 in just four years and California joined the Union as the 31st state. In the 20th century, the discovery of oil and development of service industries encouraged further growth. Sacramento, as state capital nonetheless ranks behind Los Angeles, San Diego, San Jose, San Francisco, and Oakland in size. Fifty-eight counties divide the state.

In the West, coastal ranges run North to South, paralleled by the Sierra Nevada Mountains in the East; between them lies the fertile Central Valley, drained by the Sacramento and San Joaquin Rivers. Death Valley and the Mojave Desert occupy the Southeast. California is the leading producer of many crops, including a wide variety of fruits and vegetables but poultry, fishing, and dairy produce are also important farming activities. Forests cover approximately forty percent of the land and support a sizable timber industry. Deposits of oil, natural gas, and a variety of ores are valuable in manufacturing, the largest economic sector. Vital industries include aircraft, aerospace equipment, electronic components, entertainment, missiles, wine, and tourism.

Patterned after the flag flown by American settlers revolting against Mexico in 1846, the state flag was adopted in 1911. The single red star is meant to reflect the lone star of Texas and the grizzly bear was chosen due to its predominance at the time.

Sacramento

An inland port on the Sacramento River in central California, Sacramento was the focal point of the 1848 gold rush, and became the state capital in 1854. A 43 mi (69 km) channel links the city to an arm of San Francisco Bay, and it also benefits from a large U.S. Army depot and the McClellan Air Base. Industries of note are missile development, transportation equipment, food processing, and building materials.

California at a Glance

People	California	USA
Population, 2003 estimate	35,484,453	290,809,777
Population percent change, April 1, 2000–July 1, 2001	1.9%	1.2%
Population, 2000	33,871,648	281,421,906
Persons under 5 years old, percent, 2000	7.3%	6.8%
Persons under 18 years old, percent, 2000	27.3%	25.7%
Persons 65 years old and over, percent, 2000	10.6%	12.4%
Female persons, percent, 2000	50.2%	50.9%
White persons, percent, 2000 (a)	59.5%	75.1%
African American persons, percent, 2000 (a)	6.7%	12.3%
Native American persons, percent, 2000 (a)	1.0%	0.9%
Asian persons, percent, 2000 (a)	10.9%	3.6%
Native Hawaiian and Other Pacific Islander, percent, 2000 (a)	0.3%	0.1%
Persons of Hispanic or Latino origin, percent, 2000 (b)	32.4%	12.5%
White persons, not of Hispanic/Latino origin, percent, 2000	46.7%	69.1%
Foreign born persons, percent, 2000	26.2%	11.1%
Language other than English spoken at home, percent age 5+, 2000	39.5%	17.9%
High school graduates, percent of persons age 25+, 2000	76.8%	80.4%
Bachelor's degree or higher, percent of persons age 25+, 2000	26.6%	24.4%
Persons with a disability, age 5+, 2000	5,923,361	49,746,248
Homeownership rate, 2000	56.9%	66.2%
Median value of owner-occupied housing units, 2000	$211,500	$119,600
Households, 2000	11,502,870	105,480,101
Persons per household, 2000	2.87	2.59
Median household money income, 1999	$47,493	$41,994
Per capita money income, 1999	$22,711	$21,587
Persons below poverty, percent, 1999	14.2%	12.4%

Business	California	USA
Private nonfarm establishments, 1999	784,935	7,008,444
Private nonfarm employment, 1999	12,356,363	110,705,661
Private nonfarm employment, percent change 1990–99	9.2%	18.4%
Nonemployer establishments, 1999	2,050,809	16,152,604
Manufacturers shipments, 1997 ($1,000)	379,612,443	3,842,061,405
Retail sales, 1997 ($1,000)	263,118,346	2,460,886,012
Retail sales per capita, 1997	$8,167	$9,190
Minority-owned firms, percent of total, 1997	28.8%	14.6%
Women-owned firms, percent of total, 1997	27.3%	26.0%
Federal funds and grants, 2001 ($1,000)	188,516,866	1,763,896,019
Local government employment – full-time equivalent, 1997	1,194,169	10,227,429

Geography	California	USA
Land area, 2000 (square miles)	155,959	3,537,438
Persons per square mile, 2000	217.2	79.6

(a) Includes persons reporting only one race.

(b) Hispanics may be of any race, so also are included in applicable race categories.

Z: Value greater than zero but less than half unit of measure shown.

Source: U.S. Census Bureau State & County QuickFacts

Colorado

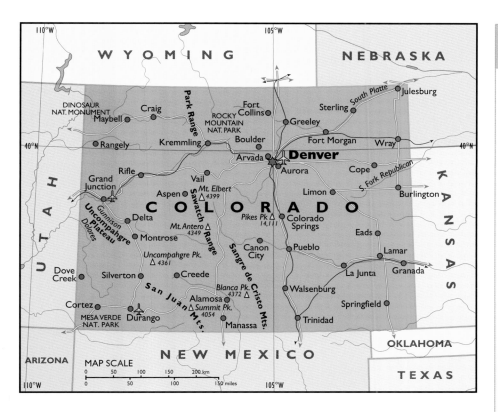

Statehood: August 1, 1876
Nickname: Centennial State
State bird: Lark bunting
State flower: White and lavender columbine
State tree: Colorado blue spruce
State motto: Nothing without the deity
State capital: Denver
Population of capital: 554,636 (2000)

The United States acquired the eastern portion of this Western state from France in the Louisiana Purchase and Mexico relinquished the remainder after the Mexican War (1848). The discovery of gold and silver encouraged immigration, and Colorado became a territory in 1861. Major cities include Colorado Springs, Boulder, Ft. Collins, and Pueblo as well as Denver, the seat of government, and fall along the eastern edge of the Rocky Mountains. The state's 63 counties allude to its history with Spanish (Huerfano, Mesa), English (Kit Carson, Fremont), and Native American (Arapahoe, Cheyenne) names.

It is the highest state in the U.S., with an average elevation of 6,800 ft (2,073 m) and over 1,000 peaks over 10,000 ft (3,048 m) within its borders. The Rocky Mountains cover the western half of the state, and the Great Plains occupy the east. Major rivers are the Colorado, the Río Grande, the Arkansas, and the South Platte. Agricultural activity includes sheep and cattle rearing on the Plains and sugar beet, corn and hay farming aided by irrigation. Key industries are transportation and electrical equipment, mining, telecommunications, chemicals and tourism at sites like Rocky Mountain National Park and Mesa Verde National Park.

Consisting of three alternating stripes of equal width, the state flag's colors are meant to evoke the blue sky and the white snow. Adopted in 1911, the red "C" in the center stands for the name Spanish explorers gave the reddish hued Colorado River. The golden circle within the letter symbolizes gold.

Denver

Resting at the foot of the Rocky Mountains at an altitude of 5,280 ft (1,608 m), Denver is nicknamed the "Mile High City." Founded in 1858, it became state capital in 1867. Like other western cities, its prosperity was boosted with the discovery of gold and silver, along with the construction of the Denver Pacific Railroad in 1870. Denver is the site of many government agencies, including a U.S. Mint and other places of note are the Denver Art Museum, the Boettcher Botanical Gardens. After World War II, Denver's dramatic growth and high altitude led to serious pollution problems. Exploitation of oil deposits created further growth in the 1970s, but the worldwide slump in prices in the early 1980s temporarily caused the economy to stagnate. Denver International Airport, one of the largest in the world, and the city's proximity to the Rockies as well as the Aspen ski resort have turned the capital into a major tourist center. Denver is a processing, shipping, and distribution center that many high-technology industries, especially aerospace and electronics, also call home.

Colorado at a Glance

People	Colorado	USA
Population, 2003 estimate	4,550,688	290,809,777
Population percent change, April 1, 2000–July 1, 2001	2.7%	1.2%
Population, 2000	4,301,261	281,421,906
Persons under 5 years old, percent, 2000	6.9%	6.8%
Persons under 18 years old, percent, 2000	25.6%	25.7%
Persons 65 years old and over, percent, 2000	9.7%	12.4%
Female persons, percent, 2000	49.6%	50.9%
White persons, percent, 2000 (a)	82.8%	75.1%
African American persons, percent, 2000 (a)	3.8%	12.3%
Native American persons, percent, 2000 (a)	1.0%	0.9%
Asian persons, percent, 2000 (a)	2.2%	3.6%
Native Hawaiian and Other Pacific Islander, percent, 2000 (a)	0.1%	0.1%
Persons of Hispanic or Latino origin, percent, 2000 (b)	17.1%	12.5%
White persons, not of Hispanic/Latino origin, percent, 2000	74.5%	69.1%
Foreign born persons, percent, 2000	8.6%	11.1%
Language other than English spoken at home, percent age 5+, 2000	15.1%	17.9%
High school graduates, percent of persons age 25+, 2000	86.9%	80.4%
Bachelor's degree or higher, percent of persons age 25+, 2000	32.7%	24.4%
Persons with a disability, age 5+, 2000	638,654	49,746,248
Homeownership rate, 2000	67.3%	66.2%
Median value of owner-occupied housing units, 2000	$166,600	$119,600
Households, 2000	1,658,238	105,480,101
Persons per household, 2000	2.53	2.59
Median household money income, 1999	$47,203	$41,994
Per capita money income, 1999	$24,049	$21,587
Persons below poverty, percent, 1999	9.3%	12.4%

Business	Colorado	USA
Private nonfarm establishments, 1999	133,743	7,008,444
Private nonfarm employment, 1999	1,821,717	110,705,661
Private nonfarm employment, percent change 1990–99	46.0%	18.4%
Nonemployer establishments, 1999	325,432	16,152,604
Manufacturers shipments, 1997 ($1,000)	40,012,820	3,842,061,405
Retail sales, 1997 ($1,000)	40,536,034	2,460,886,012
Retail sales per capita, 1997	$10,417	$9,190
Minority-owned firms, percent of total, 1997	9.0%	14.6%
Women-owned firms, percent of total, 1997	28.0%	26.0%
Federal funds and grants, 2001 ($1,000)	24,344,658	1,763,896,019
Local government employment – full-time equivalent, 1997	153,146	10,227,429

Geography	Colorado	USA
Land area, 2000 (square miles)	103,718	3,537,438
Persons per square mile, 2000	41.5	79.6

(a) Includes persons reporting only one race.

(b) Hispanics may be of any race, so also are included in applicable race categories.

Z: Value greater than zero but less than half unit of measure shown.

Source: U.S. Census Bureau State & County QuickFacts

Connecticut

Statehood: January 9, 1788
Nickname: Constitution State
State bird: Robin
State flower: Mountain laurel
State tree: White oak
State motto: He who transplanted still sustains
State capital: Hartford
Population of capital: 121,578 (2000)

The English first settled one of the original Thirteen Colonies, Connecticut, in the 1630s. Puritans flocked to the area, and in 1662 the colony received a charter from King Charles II. Connecticut was the fifth state to ratify the Constitution and was admitted to the Union in 1788. By chance, numerous inventions came into being in Connecticut, from the Algonquin word *quinnitukqut*, or beside the long tidal river, around the time of the Industrial Revolution. Eli Whitney and Samuel Colt perfected firearms manufacturing here and Noah Webster published the first American dictionary in New Haven in 1806. The state capital and largest city is Hartford, followed by Stamford, Bridgeport and New Haven. Only eight counties divide this small state.

The Connecticut River, the longest waterway in New England, separates the western and eastern highlands. The state economy is based primarily on manufacturing but fishing is also important. Industries include transport equipment, machinery, chemicals, and metallurgy. Dairy produce, eggs and tobacco are the main farm products. Mystic Seaport, once a shipyard of considerable importance, has restored many of its 18th- and 19th-century buildings and now attracts thousands of visitors annually. Connecticut is also one of the most heavily suburbanized states in the country.

A white shield on a field of blue, the flag bears the state motto under three grapevines that represent the first settlements of English colonists who moved from Massachusetts in the 1630s. In 1895, these "transplanted" citizens of Connecticut adopted the flag flown today.

Hartford

Dozens of insurance companies, the first of which opened in 1794, have their headquarters here along the Connecticut River. Founded by Dutch settlers in 1623, Hartford is also home to the oldest continually published newspaper in the United States, the Hartford *Courant* that began in 1764 as the Connecticut Courant. Manufactures include precision instruments, electrical equipment and computers as well as firearms.

Connecticut at a Glance

People	Connecticut	USA
Population, 2003 estimate	3,483,372	290,809,777
Population percent change, April 1, 2000–July 1, 2001	0.6%	1.2%
Population, 2000	3,405,565	281,421,906
Persons under 5 years old, percent, 2000	6.6%	6.8%
Persons under 18 years old, percent, 2000	24.7%	25.7%
Persons 65 years old and over, percent, 2000	13.8%	12.4%
Female persons, percent, 2000	51.6%	50.9%
White persons, percent, 2000 (a)	81.6%	75.1%
African American persons, percent, 2000 (a)	9.1%	12.3%
Native American persons, percent, 2000 (a)	0.3%	0.9%
Asian persons, percent, 2000 (a)	2.4%	3.6%
Native Hawaiian and Other Pacific Islander, percent, 2000 (a)	Z	0.1%
Persons of Hispanic or Latino origin, percent, 2000 (b)	9.4%	12.5%
White persons, not of Hispanic/Latino origin, percent, 2000	77.5%	69.1%
Foreign born persons, percent, 2000	10.9%	11.1%
Language other than English spoken at home, percent age 5+, 2000	18.3%	17.9%
High school graduates, percent of persons age 25+, 2000	84.0%	80.4%
Bachelor's degree or higher, percent of persons age 25+, 2000	31.4%	24.4%
Persons with a disability, age 5+, 2000	546,813	49,746,248
Homeownership rate, 2000	66.8%	66.2%
Median value of owner-occupied housing units, 2000	$166,900	$119,600
Households, 2000	1,301,670	105,480,101
Persons per household, 2000	2.53	2.59
Median household money income, 1999	$53,935	$41,994
Per capita money income, 1999	$28,766	$21,587
Persons below poverty, percent, 1999	7.9%	12.4%

Business	Connecticut	USA
Private nonfarm establishments, 1999	92,454	7,008,444
Private nonfarm employment, 1999	1,530,539	110,705,661
Private nonfarm employment, percent change 1990–99	3.3%	18.4%
Nonemployer establishments, 1999	211,724	16,152,604
Manufacturers shipments, 1997 ($1,000)	46,938,210	3,842,061,405
Retail sales, 1997 ($1,000)	34,938,893	2,460,886,012
Retail sales per capita, 1997	$10,690	$9,190
Minority-owned firms, percent of total, 1997	7.2%	14.6%
Women-owned firms, percent of total, 1997	25.5%	26.0%
Federal funds and grants, 2001 ($1,000)	22,741,764	1,763,896,019
Local government employment – full-time equivalent, 1997	104,338	10,227,429

Geography	Connecticut	USA
Land area, 2000 (square miles)	4,845	3,537,438
Persons per square mile, 2000	702.9	79.6

(a) Includes persons reporting only one race.

(b) Hispanics may be of any race, so also are included in applicable race categories.

Z: Value greater than zero but less than half unit of measure shown.

Source: U.S. Census Bureau State & County QuickFacts

Delaware

Statehood: December 7, 1787
Nickname: The First State
State bird: Blue hen chicken
State flower: Peach blossom
State tree: American holly
State motto: Liberty and independence
State capital: Dover
Population of capital: 32,135 (2000)

Discovered by Henry Hudson in 1609, this state on the Atlantic coast, occupying a peninsula between Chesapeake and Delaware Bays was named for the British Governor of Virginia, Baron De la Warr. Settled by Swedes in 1638, the Dutch, under Peter Stuyvesant, conquered the territory by 1655. Although the Dutch briefly recaptured Delaware in 1673, it was effectively under English control from 1664 to 1776. One of the original thirteen states, it was also the first to ratify the Constitution in 1789. Despite being a slave state, it maintained a fragile loyalty to the Union during the Civil War. The two largest cities, Wilmington and Newark, lie within the megalopolis on the northeastern seaboard and are clustered in the northernmost of Delaware's three counties.

After Rhode Island, Delaware is the second smallest state by area, and most of its land is coastal plain. Tidal marshes teeming with wildlife opposite New Jersey give way to sandy beaches in the south. The highest point in the state is only about 440 ft (135 m) above sea level.

Emptying into the Atlantic, the Delaware River, an important shipping route from Philadelphia, forms part of the eastern boundary. Industries include chemicals, rubber, plastics, and metallurgy while agricultural products include cereal crops, soya, poultry, and dairy goods.

Delaware's flag, adopted in 1913, proudly displays the date on which it became the first state against the blue and buff colors that George Washington wore as general of the continental army. Within the central diamond, a farmer, an ox, wheat, and corn affirm the importance of agriculture in the history of the state while the soldier and the ship are symbols of the Revolution and commerce. The state motto appears between the two standing figures.

Dover

Founded in 1683, Dover was laid out by William Penn alongside the St. Jones River in 1717 and has been state capital since 1777. Dover contains fine examples of Georgian architecture and serves as a shipping and canning center for the surrounding agricultural region. It is also the site of Dover Air Force Base. Industries include lumber, paints, paper, synthetic polymers, adhesives, and chemicals.

Delaware at a Glance

People	Delaware	USA
Population, 2003 estimate	817,491	290,809,777
Population percent change, April 1, 2000–July 1, 2001	1.6%	1.2%
Population, 2000	783,600	281,421,906
Persons under 5 years old, percent, 2000	6.6%	6.8%
Persons under 18 years old, percent, 2000	24.8%	25.7%
Persons 65 years old and over, percent, 2000	13.0%	12.4%
Female persons, percent, 2000	51.4%	50.9%
White persons, percent, 2000 (a)	74.6%	75.1%
African American persons, percent, 2000 (a)	19.2%	12.3%
Native American persons, percent, 2000 (a)	0.3%	0.9%
Asian persons, percent, 2000 (a)	2.1%	3.6%
Native Hawaiian and Other Pacific Islander, percent, 2000 (a)	Z	0.1%
Persons of Hispanic or Latino origin, percent, 2000 (b)	4.8%	12.5%
White persons, not of Hispanic/Latino origin, percent, 2000	72.5%	69.1%
Foreign born persons, percent, 2000	5.7%	11.1%
Language other than English spoken at home, percent age 5+, 2000	9.5%	17.9%
High school graduates, percent of persons age 25+, 2000	82.6%	80.4%
Bachelor's degree or higher, percent of persons age 25+, 2000	25.0%	24.4%
Persons with a disability, age 5+, 2000	131,794	49,746,248
Homeownership rate, 2000	72.3%	66.2%
Median value of owner-occupied housing units, 2000	$130,400	$119,600
Households, 2000	298,736	105,480,101
Persons per household, 2000	2.54	2.59
Median household money income, 1999	$47,381	$41,994
Per capita money income, 1999	$23,305	$21,587
Persons below poverty, percent, 1999	9.2%	12.4%

Business	Delaware	USA
Private nonfarm establishments, 1999	23,381	7,008,444
Private nonfarm employment, 1999	360,735	110,705,661
Private nonfarm employment, percent change 1990–99	16.0%	18.4%
Nonemployer establishments, 1999	39,181	16,152,604
Manufacturers shipments, 1997 ($1,000)	13,397,302	3,842,061,405
Retail sales, 1997 ($1,000)	8,236,970	2,460,886,012
Retail sales per capita, 1997	$11,206	$9,190
Minority-owned firms, percent of total, 1997	9.4%	14.6%
Women-owned firms, percent of total, 1997	24.1%	26.0%
Federal funds and grants, 2001 ($1,000)	4,245,638	1,763,896,019
Local government employment – full-time equivalent, 1997	18,865	10,227,429

Geography	Delaware	USA
Land area, 2000 (square miles)	1,954	3,537,438
Persons per square mile, 2000	401.1	79.6

(a) Includes persons reporting only one race.

(b) Hispanics may be of any race, so also are included in applicable race categories.

Z: Value greater than zero but less than half unit of measure shown.

Source: U.S. Census Bureau State & County QuickFacts

Florida

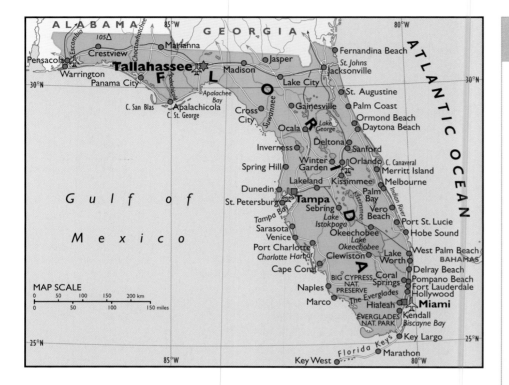

Statehood: March 3, 1845
Nickname: Sunshine State
State bird: Mockingbird
State flower: Orange blossom
State tree: Sabal palm
State motto: In God we trust
State capital: Tallahassee
Population of capital: 150,624 (2000)

Occupying a peninsula and adjoining mainland between the Atlantic Ocean and the Gulf of Mexico in the extreme Southeast of the United States, Florida was first visited by Europeans in 1513. The Spanish built the first permanent European settlement in the United States at St. Augustine on the northwestern coast. Its 17th-century walls stand as the oldest masonry fort in the nation. The land then passed to the English at the end of the French and Indian Wars (1689–1763) before returning to Spain in 1783. In 1819, the United States purchased Florida and in nearly twenty years, settlers forced the majority of the native Seminole population to move west. Although the state seceded from the Union in 1861, it was little affected by the Civil War. It developed rapidly after 1880, when forest clearing and drainage schemes were begun. The most populous cities in this state of 67 counties are Jacksonville, Orlando, Tampa, St. Petersburg and Miami, where Florida's historic ties with Cuba are particularly evident.

Much of Florida forms a long peninsula with tens of thousands of lakes, many rivers, and vast areas of wetland, the largest of which is the Everglades. Lake Okeechobee, the biggest lake in the southern United States feeds into the 40-mile wide marsh populated with a diverse array of rare flora and fauna. Stretching west from its south-

ern tip, a chain of small coral islands known as Florida Keys is North America's largest reef system and one of the three biggest attractions in the state along with Everglades National Park and Walt Disney World in Orlando. Aside from tourism that attracts close to 50 million visitors each year, major industry concentrates on the John F. Kennedy Space Center at Cape Canaveral. Chief agricultural products are citrus fruits, sugarcane, and vegetables.

A red diagonal cross frames the state seal on Florida's flag. Adopted in 1899, the central seal depicts a steamboat sailing in front of the sun, a sabal palm (the state tree), as well as a Seminole woman scattering flowers. The image is encircled by the state motto.

Tallahassee

First discovered by Europeans in 1539, Tallahassee was the site of a Spanish mission before becoming the capital of Florida Territory in 1824. During the American Civil War, it was the only Confederate capital city east of the Mississippi River that was not captured by the Union army. Florida State University and Florida A & M University are located here along with businesses associated with chemicals, timber, paper, and tourism.

Florida at a Glance

People	Florida	USA
Population, 2003 estimate	17,019,068	290,809,777
Population percent change, April 1, 2000–July 1, 2001	2.6%	1.2%
Population, 2000	15,982,378	281,421,906
Persons under 5 years old, percent, 2000	5.9%	6.8%
Persons under 18 years old, percent, 2000	22.8%	25.7%
Persons 65 years old and over, percent, 2000	17.6%	12.4%
Female persons, percent, 2000	51.2%	50.9%
White persons, percent, 2000 (a)	78.0%	75.1%
African American persons, percent, 2000 (a)	14.6%	12.3%
Native American persons, percent, 2000 (a)	0.3%	0.9%
Asian persons, percent, 2000 (a)	1.7%	3.6%
Native Hawaiian and Other Pacific Islander, percent, 2000 (a)	0.1%	0.1%
Persons of Hispanic or Latino origin, percent, 2000 (b)	16.8%	12.5%
White persons, not of Hispanic/Latino origin, percent, 2000	65.4%	69.1%
Foreign born persons, percent, 2000	16.7%	11.1%
Language other than English spoken at home, percent age 5+, 2000	23.1%	17.9%
High school graduates, percent of persons age 25+, 2000	79.9%	80.4%
Bachelor's degree or higher, percent of persons age 25+, 2000	22.3%	24.4%
Persons with a disability, age 5+, 2000	3,274,566	49,746,248
Homeownership rate, 2000	70.1%	66.2%
Median value of owner-occupied housing units, 2000	$105,500	$119,600
Households, 2000	6,337,929	105,480,101
Persons per household, 2000	2.46	2.59
Median household money income, 1999	$38,819	$41,994
Per capita money income, 1999	$21,557	$21,587
Persons below poverty, percent, 1999	12.5%	12.4%

Business	Florida	USA
Private nonfarm establishments, 1999	424,089	7,008,444
Private nonfarm employment, 1999	5,954,982	110,705,661
Private nonfarm employment, percent change 1990–99	29.3%	18.4%
Nonemployer establishments, 1999	1,031,053	16,152,604
Manufacturers shipments, 1997 ($1,000)	77,477,510	3,842,061,405
Retail sales, 1997 ($1,000)	151,191,241	2,460,886,012
Retail sales per capita, 1997	$10,297	$9,190
Minority-owned firms, percent of total, 1997	22.0%	14.6%
Women-owned firms, percent of total, 1997	25.9%	26.0%
Federal funds and grants, 2001 ($1,000)	99,998,376	1,763,896,019
Local government employment – full-time equivalent, 1997	543,525	10,227,429

Geography	Florida	USA
Land area, 2000 (square miles)	53,927	3,537,438
Persons per square mile, 2000	296.4	79.6

(a) Includes persons reporting only one race.

(b) Hispanics may be of any race, so also are included in applicable race categories.

Z: Value greater than zero but less than half unit of measure shown.

Source: U.S. Census Bureau State & County QuickFacts

Georgia

Statehood: January 2, 1788
Nickname: Empire State of the South
State bird: Brown thrasher
State flower: Cherokee rose
State tree: Live oak
State motto: Wisdom, Justice and Moderation
State capital: Atlanta
Population of capital: 416,474 (2000)

First settled in 1732 and named after King George II, Georgia, on the Atlantic coast of the Southeast, was one of the original six states of the Confederacy in the Civil War. Ravaged by the armies of General William T. Sherman in 1864, Georgia was readmitted to the Union in 1870. Before the war broke out however, the discovery of gold at Dahlonega in 1828 sparked the first gold rush and prompted the government to establish a mint in Lumpkin County, one of 159 counties in the state. Outside of the Atlanta metropolitan area, where nearly half of the state's residents live, the other major cities are Columbus, Macon, and Savannah, the location of Georgia's first settlement.

A broad coastal plain encompasses the south and east of the state while the center consists of the hilly Piedmont. The Blue Ridge Mountains and the Appalachian, drained by the Savannah, Ogeechee, and Altamaha Rivers lie beyond the Piedmont in the North. Cotton, once the chief crop, has declined in favor of tobacco, peaches, peanuts, livestock, and poultry. Textiles have been a major industry, but chemicals, paper and timber, and the manufacture of ships, aircraft and truck bodies are becoming increasingly significant. The Confederate Memorial at Stone Mountain, Okefenokee National Wildlife Refuge and the Little White House at Warm Springs attract tourists to Georgia.

Georgia's new state flag, adopted in 2003, abandoned the Confederate banner in favor of three red and white stripes with the state seal in the upper left corner against a blue field. Three pillars supporting an arch on the seal represent the three branches of government while the thirteen stars that encircle it refer to the state's position as one of the original colonies. The man with a drawn sword drawn defends the Constitution, whose principles are wisdom, justice and moderation.

Atlanta

Creek and Cherokee land until the early 1800s, the city of Terminus, as it was known, was founded in 1837 at the eastern end of the Western and Atlantic Railroad. It became Marthasville in 1843, Atlanta two years later, and the permanent state capital in 1887. It served as a Confederate supply depot and communications center during the American Civil War and on September 2, 1864 fell to General Sherman, whose army razed the city. Atlanta was rapidly rebuilt and soon recovered its importance as a transport and cotton manufacturing center. Now the headquarters of Coca-Cola, Atlanta also contains the High Museum of Art and Emory University. The textile, chemicals, iron and steel, and electronics industries dominate the local economy.

Georgia at a Glance

People	Georgia	USA
Population, 2003 estimate	8,684,715	290,809,777
Population percent change, April 1, 2000–July 1, 2001	2.4%	1.2%
Population, 2000	8,186,453	281,421,906
Persons under 5 years old, percent, 2000	7.3%	6.8%
Persons under 18 years old, percent, 2000	26.5%	25.7%
Persons 65 years old and over, percent, 2000	9.6%	12.4%
Female persons, percent, 2000	50.8%	50.9%
White persons, percent, 2000 (a)	65.1%	75.1%
African American persons, percent, 2000 (a)	28.7%	12.3%
Native American persons, percent, 2000 (a)	0.3%	0.9%
Asian persons, percent, 2000 (a)	2.1%	3.6%
Native Hawaiian and Other Pacific Islander, percent, 2000 (a)	0.1%	0.1%
Persons of Hispanic or Latino origin, percent, 2000 (b)	5.3%	12.5%
White persons, not of Hispanic/Latino origin, percent, 2000	62.6%	69.1%
Foreign born persons, percent, 2000	7.1%	11.1%
Language other than English spoken at home, percent age 5+, 2000	9.9%	17.9%
High school graduates, percent of persons age 25+, 2000	78.6%	80.4%
Bachelor's degree or higher, percent of persons age 25+, 2000	24.3%	24.4%
Persons with a disability, age 5+, 2000	1,456,812	49,746,248
Homeownership rate, 2000	67.5%	66.2%
Median value of owner-occupied housing units, 2000	$111,200	$119,600
Households, 2000	3,006,369	105,480,101
Persons per household, 2000	2.65	2.59
Median household money income, 1999	$42,433	$41,994
Per capita money income, 1999	$21,154	$21,587
Persons below poverty, percent, 1999	13.0%	12.4%

Business	Georgia	USA
Private nonfarm establishments, 1999	197,759	7,008,444
Private nonfarm employment, 1999	3,363,797	110,705,661
Private nonfarm employment, percent change 1990–99	34.6%	18.4%
Nonemployer establishments, 1999	452,567	16,152,604
Manufacturers shipments, 1997 ($1,000)	124,526,834	3,842,061,405
Retail sales, 1997 ($1,000)	72,212,484	2,460,886,012
Retail sales per capita, 1997	$9,646	$9,190
Minority-owned firms, percent of total, 1997	15.6%	14.6%
Women-owned firms, percent of total, 1997	25.6%	26.0%
Federal funds and grants, 2001 ($1,000)	47,320,410	1,763,896,019
Local government employment – full-time equivalent, 1997	324,480	10,227,429

Geography	Georgia	USA
Land area, 2000 (square miles)	57,906	3,537,438
Persons per square mile, 2000	141.4	79.6

(a) Includes persons reporting only one race.

(b) Hispanics may be of any race, so also are included in applicable race categories.

Z: Value greater than zero but less than half unit of measure shown.

Source: U.S. Census Bureau State & County QuickFacts

Hawai'i

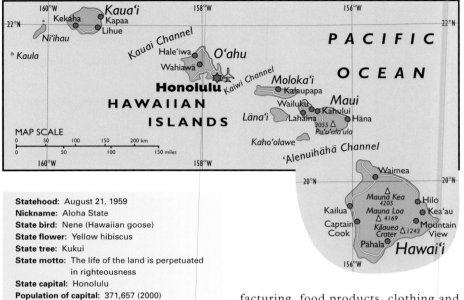

Statehood: August 21, 1959
Nickname: Aloha State
State bird: Nene (Hawaiian goose)
State flower: Yellow hibiscus
State tree: Kukui
State motto: The life of the land is perpetuated in righteousness
State capital: Honolulu
Population of capital: 371,657 (2000)

Southwest of California and separated from the continental United States by 2,400 miles of ocean, Hawai'i is comprised of 137 volcanic islands and atolls altogether. Settled by Polynesians in the 9th century, dubbed the Sandwich Islands by Captain James Cook, and unified under King Kamehameha in the late 18th century, Hawai'i then endured missionaries, disease and sugarcane plantations before becoming a republic in 1894. It was not until 1898 that Hawai'i became a U.S. territory, and statehood was not achieved until 1959, 18 years after the bombing of Pearl Harbor on December 7, 1941. Although there are eight major islands, divided into five counties, three out of four Hawaiians and the capital city can be found on Oahu.

A tropical paradise to tourists worldwide, Hawai'i is home to Mount Waialele, the wettest place on Earth. The moist climate as well as Hawai'i's geographic and reproductive isolation, means that ninety percent of the flowering plants found there today do not grow naturally any other place on Earth. Nevertheless, it is interesting to note that none of the flora or fauna is native to the islands; they were all carried from elsewhere by wind or water. Natural vegetation aside, Hawai'i is a land of volcanic beaches and smoking craters, and in fact, Hawai'i, the largest island, continues to grow in size due to volcanoes such as Kilauea island, the most active on the planet. The world's tallest sea cliffs at 3,250 ft (990 m) can be found on the island of Moloka'i. Surfing or *hele nalu* (wave sliding) as it is known in Hawaiian, is the signature sport of the islands, first introduced to the world by Duke Kahanamoku in the early 1900s. The biggest industries are tourism and agriculture, which concentrates on sugarcane, bananas, pineapple, taro and macadamia nuts, as well as coffee and cattle to a lesser degree. As for manu-

facturing, food products, clothing and refined petroleum are particularly important to the economy of this state.

The red, white and blue stripes on the state flag represent the eight main islands and the Union Jack of Great Britain is emblazoned in the upper left corner to honor Hawai'i's friendship with the British. The flag was adopted in 1959.

Honolulu

A key port of entry for both people and commercial goods, Honolulu handles approximately eight million tons of cargo each year. Honolulu became the capital of the kingdom of Hawai'i in 1845 and remained the capital after the annexation of the islands under President McKinley. Landmarks include the Iolani Palace (the only royal residence on U.S. soil), Waikiki Beach, the USS *Arizona* Memorial at Pearl Harbor, and Diamond Head Crater. The headquarters of the U.S. Navy's Pacific fleet can be found here, as well as several colleges and universities. Tourism is the most important economic activity, followed by sugar refining and pineapple canning.

Hawai'i at a Glance

People	Hawai'i	USA
Population, 2003 estimate	1,257,608	290,809,777
Population percent change, April 1, 2000–July 1, 2001	1.1%	1.2%
Population, 2000	1,211,537	281,421,906
Persons under 5 years old, percent, 2000	6.5%	6.8%
Persons under 18 years old, percent, 2000	24.4%	25.7%
Persons 65 years old and over, percent, 2000	13.3%	12.4%
Female persons, percent, 2000	49.8%	50.9%
White persons, percent, 2000 (a)	24.3%	75.1%
African American persons, percent, 2000 (a)	1.8%	12.3%
Native American persons, percent, 2000 (a)	0.3%	0.9%
Asian persons, percent, 2000 (a)	41.6%	3.6%
Native Hawaiian and Other Pacific Islander, percent, 2000 (a)	9.4%	0.1%
Persons of Hispanic or Latino origin, percent, 2000 (b)	7.2%	12.5%
White persons, not of Hispanic/Latino origin, percent, 2000	22.9%	69.1%
Foreign born persons, percent, 2000	17.5%	11.1%
Language other than English spoken at home, percent age 5+, 2000	26.6%	17.9%
High school graduates, percent of persons age 25+, 2000	84.6%	80.4%
Bachelor's degree or higher, percent of persons age 25+, 2000	26.2%	24.4%
Persons with a disability, age 5+, 2000	199,819	49,746,248
Homeownership rate, 2000	56.5%	66.2%
Median value of owner-occupied housing units, 2000	$272,700	$119,600
Households, 2000	403,240	105,480,101
Persons per household, 2000	2.92	2.59
Median household money income, 1999	$49,820	$41,994
Per capita money income, 1999	$21,525	$21,587
Persons below poverty, percent, 1999	10.7%	12.4%

Business	Hawai'i	USA
Private nonfarm establishments, 1999	29,569	7,008,444
Private nonfarm employment, 1999	419,047	110,705,661
Private nonfarm employment, percent change 1990–99	–3.1%	18.4%
Nonemployer establishments, 1999	72,610	16,152,604
Manufacturers shipments, 1997 ($1,000)	3,192,532	3,842,061,405
Retail sales, 1997 ($1,000)	11,317,752	2,460,886,012
Retail sales per capita, 1997	$9,516	$9,190
Minority-owned firms, percent of total, 1997	57.7%	14.6%
Women-owned firms, percent of total, 1997	27.5%	26.0%
Federal funds and grants, 2001 ($1,000)	9,722,242	1,763,896,019
Local government employment – full-time equivalent, 1997	14,319	10,227,429

Geography	Hawai'i	USA
Land area, 2000 (square miles)	6,423	3,537,438
Persons per square mile, 2000	188.6	79.6

(a) Includes persons reporting only one race.

(b) Hispanics may be of any race, so also are included in applicable race categories.

Z: Value greater than zero but less than half unit of measure shown.

Source: U.S. Census Bureau State & County QuickFacts

Idaho

Statehood: July 3, 1890
Nickname: Gem State
State bird: Mountain bluebird
State flower: Mock orange
State tree: Western white pine
State motto: It is forever
State capital: Boise
Population of capital: 185,787 (2000)

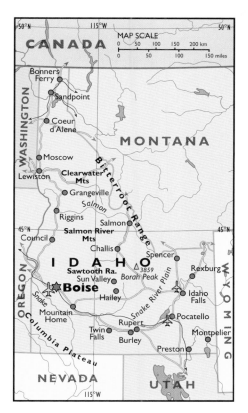

The discovery of gold in 1860 brought many immigrants to this northwestern state, although Mormons established the first permanent settlement at Franklin in the same year. Idaho was admitted to the Union as the 43rd state in 1890 and soon began to develop its resources. Pocatello and Idaho Falls in the southern part of the state follow Boise, the most populous city. The names of the 44 counties are often taken from the native tribes such as the Shoshone, Kootenai and the Nez Perce, who resisted the early white communities until 1877.

The terrain is dominated by the Rocky Mountains, including the Bitterroot Range and is drained chiefly by the Snake River, whose waters are used for irrigation and to generate hydroelectricity. In addition to cattle raising, the agricultural economy relies of the production of hay, wheat and sugar beet, and potatoes in particular. Lumbering and the mining of silver, lead, cobalt, mercury, antimony and zinc are the largest industries. The state's tourist destinations are primarily natural attractions: Craters of the Moon and Hagerman Fossil Beds National Monuments, Nez Perce National Historic Park, Sun Valley ski resort and City of Rocks National Reserve.

Carrying the state seal on a blue field, Idaho's state flag was adopted in 1907. Within the seal, a woman holding the scales of justice represents liberty and equality while the miner alludes to the state's wealth of mineral resources. The elk, conifer and cornucopias stand for wildlife, timber and agriculture respectively.

Boise

Founded in the Boise River valley in 1863 as a supply post for gold miners, the state capital is now a trade center for the agricultural region of southwestern Idaho and eastern Oregon. Farming yields sugar beets, potatoes, wheat, alfalfa, and onions and steel, sheet metal, furniture, electrical equipment, and timber products are the main industrial commodities. Despite its French name, Boise is home to the only Basque Museum in the United States.

Idaho at a Glance

People	Idaho	USA
Population, 2003 estimate	1,366,332	290,809,777
Population percent change,		
April 1, 2000–July 1, 2001	2.1%	1.2%
Population, 2000	1,293,953	281,421,906
Persons under 5 years old, percent, 2000	7.5%	6.8%
Persons under 18 years old, percent, 2000	28.5%	25.7%
Persons 65 years old and over, percent, 2000	11.3%	12.4%
Female persons, percent, 2000	49.9%	50.9%
White persons, percent, 2000 (a)	91.0%	75.1%
African American persons,		
percent, 2000 (a)	0.4%	12.3%
Native American persons,		
percent, 2000 (a)	1.4%	0.9%
Asian persons, percent, 2000 (a)	0.9%	3.6%
Native Hawaiian and Other Pacific Islander,		
percent, 2000 (a)	0.1%	0.1%
Persons of Hispanic or Latino origin,		
percent, 2000 (b)	7.9%	12.5%
White persons, not of Hispanic/Latino origin,		
percent, 2000	88.0%	69.1%
Foreign born persons, percent, 2000	5.0%	11.1%
Language other than English spoken at home,		
percent age 5+, 2000	9.3%	17.9%
High school graduates, percent of persons		
age 25+, 2000	84.7%	80.4%
Bachelor's degree or higher,		
percent of persons age 25+, 2000	21.7%	24.4%
Persons with a disability, age 5+, 2000	200,498	49,746,248
Homeownership rate, 2000	72.4%	66.2%
Median value of owner-occupied		
housing units, 2000	$106,300	$119,600
Households, 2000	469,645	105,480,101
Persons per household, 2000	2.69	2.59
Median household money income, 1999	$37,572	$41,994
Per capita money income, 1999	$17,841	$21,587
Persons below poverty, percent, 1999	11.8%	12.4%

Business	Idaho	USA
Private nonfarm establishments, 1999	36,975	7,008,444
Private nonfarm employment, 1999	434,461	110,705,661
Private nonfarm employment,		
percent change 1990–99	44.7%	18.4%
Nonemployer establishments, 1999	83,083	16,152,604
Manufacturers shipments, 1997 ($1,000)	16,952,872	3,842,061,405
Retail sales, 1997 ($1,000)	11,649,609	2,460,886,012
Retail sales per capita, 1997	$9,623	$9,190
Minority-owned firms, percent of total, 1997	4.7%	14.6%
Women-owned firms, percent of total, 1997	23.5%	26.0%
Federal funds and grants, 2001 ($1,000)	7,528,906	1,763,896,019
Local government employment –		
full-time equivalent, 1997	46,035	10,227,429

Geography	Idaho	USA
Land area, 2000 (square miles)	82,747	3,537,438
Persons per square mile, 2000	15.6	79.6

(a) Includes persons reporting only one race.
(b) Hispanics may be of any race, so also are included in applicable race categories.
Z: Value greater than zero but less than half unit of measure shown.

Source: U.S. Census Bureau State & County QuickFacts

Illinois

Statehood: December 3, 1818
Nickname: Prairie State
State bird: Cardinal
State flower: Native violet
State tree: Oak
State motto: State sovereignty, national union
State capital: Springfield
Population of capital: 111,454 (2000)

The French, attracted by the fur trade, first explored Illinois, on the eastern bank of the Mississippi River, in 1673. Ceded to the British in 1763, it was occupied by American troops during the American Revolution and became a state in 1818. By the early 19th century, nearly all of the Sauk, Fox and Illinois people living in the area had vanished and with the advent of the railroad in the latter part of the century, the population surged.

A massive fire in October of 1871 destroyed most of Chicago's wooden buildings, but the city quickly recovered. The steel plow, barbed wire and the Pullman sleeping car, accomplishments of innovative citizens, were invented here. After the transport and distribution center of Chicago, Peoria, Rockford, and the capital are the largest cities in this state of 102 counties.

Generally flat, the land is drained by rivers flowing to the Mississippi in the west like the Rock, the Illinois and the Kaskaskia. While much of the economy activity is located in northern Illinois, the state has fertile soil that supports crops such as corn, soybeans, hay, oats, and barley and livestock farming is also important. Coal and other mineral deposits are found in the south. The Art Institute of Chicago, the Sears Tower, the Frank Lloyd Wright Home and Studio and many other tourist attractions, with the exception of Lincoln Home National Historic Site, are clustered in the Windy City.

Featuring a simple design, the state seal

occupies most of the white background of the flag of Illinois. The laurel and the rising sun represent progress on this banner, adopted in 1915.

Springfield

Founded in 1818, this landlocked city became state capital in 1837. It was named for a spring on the land of its first resident, Elisha Kelly. Abraham Lincoln lived here for 17 years before he left to occupy the White House. The center of a fertile farming area, Springfield's industries include machinery, consumer goods, electronics, and fertilizers.

Illinois at a Glance

People	Illinois	USA
Population, 2003 estimate	12,653,544	290,809,777
Population percent change, April 1, 2000–July 1, 2001	0.5%	1.2%
Population, 2000	12,419,293	281,421,906
Persons under 5 years old, percent, 2000	7.1%	6.8%
Persons under 18 years old, percent, 2000	26.1%	25.7%
Persons 65 years old and over, percent, 2000	12.1%	12.4%
Female persons, percent, 2000	51.0%	50.9%
White persons, percent, 2000 (a)	73.5%	75.1%
African American persons, percent, 2000 (a)	15.1%	12.3%
Native American persons, percent, 2000 (a)	0.2%	0.9%
Asian persons, percent, 2000 (a)	3.4%	3.6%
Native Hawaiian and Other Pacific Islander, percent, 2000 (a)	Z	0.1%
Persons of Hispanic or Latino origin, percent, 2000 (b)	12.3%	12.5%
White persons, not of Hispanic/Latino origin, percent, 2000	67.8%	69.1%
Foreign born persons, percent, 2000	12.3%	11.1%
Language other than English spoken at home, percent age 5+, 2000	19.2%	17.9%
High school graduates, percent of persons age 25+, 2000	81.4%	80.4%
Bachelor's degree or higher, percent of persons age 25+, 2000	26.1%	24.4%
Persons with a disability, age 5+, 2000	1,999,717	49,746,248
Homeownership rate, 2000	67.3%	66.2%
Median value of owner-occupied housing units, 2000	$130,800	$119,600
Households, 2000	4,591,779	105,480,101
Persons per household, 2000	2.63	2.59
Median household money income, 1999	$46,590	$41,994
Per capita money income, 1999	$23,104	$21,587
Persons below poverty, percent, 1999	10.7%	12.4%

Business	Illinois	USA
Private nonfarm establishments, 1999	306,899	7,008,444
Private nonfarm employment, 1999	5,342,675	110,705,661
Private nonfarm employment, percent change 1990–99	15.0%	18.4%
Nonemployer establishments, 1999	665,553	16,152,604
Manufacturers shipments, 1997 ($1,000)	200,019,991	3,842,061,405
Retail sales, 1997 ($1,000)	108,002,177	2,460,886,012
Retail sales per capita, 1997	$8,992	$9,190
Minority-owned firms, percent of total, 1997	12.5%	14.6%
Women-owned firms, percent of total, 1997	27.2%	26.0%
Federal funds and grants, 2001 ($1,000)	65,035,608	1,763,896,019
Local government employment – full-time equivalent, 1997	459,893	10,227,429

Geography	Illinois	USA
Land area, 2000 (square miles)	55,584	3,537,438
Persons per square mile, 2000	223.4	79.6

(a) Includes persons reporting only one race.

(b) Hispanics may be of any race, so also are included in applicable race categories.

Z: Value greater than zero but less than half unit of measure shown.

Source: U.S. Census Bureau State & County QuickFacts

Indiana

Statehood: December 11, 1816
Nickname: Hoosier State
State bird: Cardinal
State flower: Peony
State tree: Tulip tree
State motto: Crossroads of America
State capital: Indianapolis
Population of capital: 791,926 (2000)

Indiana, located in the Midwest, was explored by the French in the early 18th century, and ceded to the British in 1763. It passed to the United States after the American Revolution and the westward flow of trappers, traders and farmers pushed the Miami, Potawatomi, Delaware and other native peoples out of the territory. The state remained a rural area until the late 19th century when steel mills and oil refineries attracted immigrants from Eastern Europe. Indianapolis is by far the largest city, but Gary, South Bend, Fort Wayne and Evansville are also sizable urban areas. Known as the Hoosier State, Indiana is divided into 92 counties.

Glacial advances during the last ice age left the northern portion of the state low, flat and interspersed with small bodies of water and deposited dark, fertile soil across the center of Indiana. Access via interstate highways, long-distance railroads, and major waterways ensures efficient distribution of the state's agricultural and manufacturing products. The area is a rich farming region and the development of heavy industry in the northwest has also made Indiana a leading producer of machinery. Industries include grain, soybeans, livestock, coal, limestone, steel, electrical machinery, and motor vehicles. Indiana Dunes National Lakeshore, Lincoln Boyhood National Memorial, Turkey Run State Park and George Rogers Clark National Historic Park are among the major landmarks.

A gold flaming torch, symbol of liberty and enlightenment, occupies most of the flag adopted in 1917. Nineteen stars, the largest of which represents the state itself, are arranged in a circular fashion on a blue field.

Indianapolis

Built on a specially selected site on the White River in central Indiana, Indianapolis became the state capital in 1825 and resembles the wheel pattern used in the design of Washington, D.C. It is home to the Motor Speedway, where the Indianapolis 500 motor race has been held each year since 1911. The city is the major cereal and livestock market in a fertile agricultural area and its industries include electronic equipment, vehicle parts, pharmaceuticals, as well as printing and publishing.

Indiana at a Glance

People	Indiana	USA
Population, 2003 estimate	6,195,643	290,809,777
Population percent change, April 1, 2000–July 1, 2001	0.6%	1.2%
Population, 2000	6,080,485	281,421,906
Persons under 5 years old, percent, 2000	7.0%	6.8%
Persons under 18 years old, percent, 2000	25.9%	25.7%
Persons 65 years old and over, percent, 2000	12.4%	12.4%
Female persons, percent, 2000	51.0%	50.9%
White persons, percent, 2000 (a)	87.5%	75.1%
African American persons, percent, 2000 (a)	8.4%	12.3%
Native American persons, percent, 2000 (a)	0.3%	0.9%
Asian persons, percent, 2000 (a)	1.0%	3.6%
Native Hawaiian and Other Pacific Islander, percent, 2000 (a)	Z	0.1%
Persons of Hispanic or Latino origin, percent, 2000 (b)	3.5%	12.5%
White persons, not of Hispanic/Latino origin, percent, 2000	85.8%	69.1%
Foreign born persons, percent, 2000	3.1%	11.1%
Language other than English spoken at home, percent age 5+, 2000	6.4%	17.9%
High school graduates, percent of persons age 25+, 2000	82.1%	80.4%
Bachelor's degree or higher, percent of persons age 25+, 2000	19.4%	24.4%
Persons with a disability, age 5+, 2000	1,054,757	49,746,248
Homeownership rate, 2000	71.4%	66.2%
Median value of owner-occupied housing units, 2000	$94,300	$119,600
Households, 2000	2,336,306	105,480,101
Persons per household, 2000	2.53	2.59
Median household money income, 1999	$41,567	$41,994
Per capita money income, 1999	$20,397	$21,587
Persons below poverty, percent, 1999	9.5%	12.4%

Business	Indiana	USA
Private nonfarm establishments, 1999	146,528	7,008,444
Private nonfarm employment, 1999	2,580,408	110,705,661
Private nonfarm employment, percent change 1990–99	20.0%	18.4%
Nonemployer establishments, 1999	312,840	16,152,604
Manufacturers shipments, 1997 ($1,000)	142,270,702	3,842,061,405
Retail sales, 1997 ($1,000)	57,241,650	2,460,886,012
Retail sales per capita, 1997	$9,748	$9,190
Minority-owned firms, percent of total, 1997	5.5%	14.6%
Women-owned firms, percent of total, 1997	25.9%	26.0%
Federal funds and grants, 2001 ($1,000)	32,166,145	1,763,896,019
Local government employment – full-time equivalent, 1997	220,747	10,227,429

Geography	Indiana	USA
Land area, 2000 (square miles)	35,867	3,537,438
Persons per square mile, 2000	169.5	79.6

(a) Includes persons reporting only one race.

(b) Hispanics may be of any race, so also are included in applicable race categories.

Z: Value greater than zero but less than half unit of measure shown.

Source: U.S. Census Bureau State & County QuickFacts

Iowa

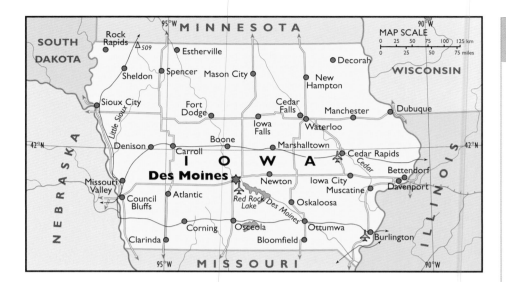

Statehood: December 28, 1846
Nickname: Hawkeye State
State bird: Eastern goldfinch
State flower: Wild rose
State tree: Oak
State motto: Our liberties we prize
and our rights we will maintain
State capital: Des Moines
Population of capital: 198,682 (2000)

Located in the Midwest between the Missouri and Mississippi Rivers, Iowa was first explored by Europeans in 1673 and claimed for France by La Salle in 1682. The region inhabited by the Iowa people was sold to the U.S. in the Louisiana Purchase of 1803 and admitted to the Union in 1846 as the 29th state.

Industrial development was encouraged after World War II and today the Mesquakie tribe is the only native community remaining within state borders. Once characterized by small farming communities, the expansion of agribusiness has steadily encouraged those living in the nation's breadbasket to move to urban areas. Des Moines, Davenport, Cedar Rapids and Sioux City are the largest cities in a state with 99 counties.

Originally prairie that was plowed to create farmland, the region is known for its deep, fertile topsoil. Hilly topography along the Nebraska border contrasts with millions of acres of fields in the east. Nearly ninety percent of the land is farmed, corn, soybean and other cereals being the dominant cash crops, and Iowa stands second only to Texas in the raising of prime cattle. Industries, too, revolve around agriculture and include food processing as well as farm machinery. Fort Dodge Historical Museum, the Amana Colonies, Herbert Hoover National Historic Site, Effigy Mounds National Monument and Living History Farms are some of the main sites of interest.

Adopted in 1921, the Iowa flag shows an eagle with a banner bearing the state motto in its beak. Vertical red, white and blue stripes appear behind the bird.

Des Moines

Near the confluence of the Des Moines and Raccoon Rivers, Des Moines was founded in 1843 as a military garrison, and is now an industrial and transportation center for the Corn Belt. Named either for the native burial mounds or the Trappist Monks that lived at the mouth of the river, the city's industries include mechanical and aerospace engineering, chemical production, insurance, and plastic products.

Iowa at a Glance

People	Iowa	USA
Population, 2003 estimate	2,944,062	290,809,777
Population percent change,		
April 1, 2000–July 1, 2001	−0.1%	1.2%
Population, 2000	2,926,324	281,421,906
Persons under 5 years old, percent, 2000	6.4%	6.8%
Persons under 18 years old, percent, 2000	25.1%	25.7%
Persons 65 years old and over, percent, 2000	14.9%	12.4%
Female persons, percent, 2000	50.9%	50.9%
White persons, percent, 2000 (a)	93.9%	75.1%
African American persons,		
percent, 2000 (a)	2.1%	12.3%
Native American persons,		
percent, 2000 (a)	0.3%	0.9%
Asian persons, percent, 2000 (a)	1.3%	3.6%
Native Hawaiian and Other Pacific Islander,		
percent, 2000 (a)	Z	0.1%
Persons of Hispanic or Latino origin,		
percent, 2000 (b)	2.8%	12.5%
White persons, not of Hispanic/Latino origin,		
percent, 2000	92.6%	69.1%
Foreign born persons, percent, 2000	3.1%	11.1%
Language other than English spoken at home,		
percent age 5+, 2000	5.8%	17.9%
High school graduates, percent of persons		
age 25+, 2000	86.1%	80.4%
Bachelor's degree or higher,		
percent of persons age 25+, 2000	21.2%	24.4%
Persons with a disability, age 5+, 2000	446,665	49,746,248
Homeownership rate, 2000	72.3%	66.2%
Median value of owner-occupied		
housing units, 2000	$82,500	$119,600
Households, 2000	1,149,276	105,480,101
Persons per household, 2000	2.46	2.59
Median household money income, 1999	$39,469	$41,994
Per capita money income, 1999	$19,674	$21,587
Persons below poverty, percent, 1999	9.1%	12.4%

Business	Iowa	USA
Private nonfarm establishments, 1999	81,213	7,008,444
Private nonfarm employment, 1999	1,239,354	110,705,661
Private nonfarm employment,		
percent change 1990–99	23.0%	18.4%
Nonemployer establishments, 1999	169,753	16,152,604
Manufacturers shipments, 1997 ($1,000)	62,413,687	3,842,061,405
Retail sales, 1997 ($1,000)	26,723,822	2,460,886,012
Retail sales per capita, 1997	$9,362	$9,190
Minority-owned firms, percent of total, 1997	2.3%	14.6%
Women-owned firms, percent of total, 1997	25.3%	26.0%
Federal funds and grants, 2001 ($1,000)	17,401,265	1,763,896,019
Local government employment –		
full-time equivalent, 1997	112,667	10,227,429

Geography	Iowa	USA
Land area, 2000 (square miles)	55,869	3,537,438
Persons per square mile, 2000	52.4	79.6

(a) Includes persons reporting only one race.

(b) Hispanics may be of any race, so also are included in applicable race categories.

Z: Value greater than zero but less than half unit of measure shown.

Source: U.S. Census Bureau State & County QuickFacts

Kansas

Statehood: January 29, 1861
Nickname: Sunflower State
State bird: Western meadowlark
State flower: Sunflower
State tree: Cottonwood
State motto: To the stars through difficulties
State capital: Topeka
Population of capital: 122,377 (2000)

First visited by Spanish explorers in the 16th century, Kansas passed from France to the new United States under the Louisiana Purchase of 1803. It was Native American territory until 1854, when the creation of the Territory of Kansas opened up Wichita, Pawnee, Kansas and Osage lands for settlement. The Oregon and Sante Fe Trails, along with several others, pass through Kansas and carried thousands farther west. Those that stopped were forced to choose between becoming a free state or a slave state following the passage of the Kansas-Nebraska Act in 1854. After seven years of violent conflict, earning it the nickname of "Bleeding Kansas," the territory was admitted to the Union as a free state

in 1861. Clustered in the east, Wichita, and Kansas City in addition to Topeka, are the four sizable metropolitan areas. Divided into 102 counties, Kansans elected the country's first female mayor.

Part of the Great Plains, the landscape rises from prairie in the east to semiarid high plains in the west and is drained by the Kansas, Smoky Hill, Arkansas and Neosho Rivers. The country's leading producer of wheat, Kansas also grows corn, hay, sugar beets and sorghum in abundance. Beginning in the 1860s cattle raising became economically significant along with manufacturing at the turn of the century. Industries include aircraft equipment, chemicals, petroleum products, and machinery. The Eisenhower Center, Dodge City, the cowboy capital, and Fort Scott and Fort Larned National Historic Sites are the some of the main tourist draws.

The state seal, depicting the sun rising over a farmer plowing his field, a steamboat on the river, a wagon train and a buffalo hunt, sits in the center of a deep blue background. Thirty-four stars within the seal mark the entrance of Kansas into the Union as the 34th state. The sunflower at the top of the flag adopted in 1927 refers to the state flower.

Topeka

West of Kansas City on the Kansas River, Topeka was founded in 1854 by settlers from New England, and became the state capital seven years later. A major transport center for cattle and wheat. The city was once the general headquarters for the Atchison, Topeka and Santa Fe Railroad. The Menninger Clinic, world famous for its treatment of mental illness, is located in the city. Printing, rubber goods, grain milling, steel products, and footwear all contribute significantly to the local economy.

Kansas at a Glance

People	Kansas	USA
Population, 2003 estimate	2,723,507	290,809,777
Population percent change, April 1, 2000–July 1, 2001	0.2%	1.2%
Population, 2000	2,688,418	281,421,906
Persons under 5 years old, percent, 2000	7.0%	6.8%
Persons under 18 years old, percent, 2000	26.5%	25.7%
Persons 65 years old and over, percent, 2000	13.3%	12.4%
Female persons, percent, 2000	50.6%	50.9%
White persons, percent, 2000 (a)	86.1%	75.1%
African American persons, percent, 2000 (a)	5.7%	12.3%
Native American persons, percent, 2000 (a)	0.9%	0.9%
Asian persons, percent, 2000 (a)	1.7%	3.6%
Native Hawaiian and Other Pacific Islander, percent, 2000 (a)	Z	0.1%
Persons of Hispanic or Latino origin, percent, 2000 (b)	7.0%	12.5%
White persons, not of Hispanic/Latino origin, percent, 2000	83.1%	69.1%
Foreign born persons, percent, 2000	5.0%	11.1%
Language other than English spoken at home, percent age 5+, 2000	8.7%	17.9%
High school graduates, percent of persons age 25+, 2000	86.0%	80.4%
Bachelor's degree or higher, percent of persons age 25+, 2000	25.8%	24.4%
Persons with a disability, age 5+, 2000	429,687	49,746,248
Homeownership rate, 2000	69.2%	66.2%
Median value of owner-occupied housing units, 2000	$83,500	$119,600
Households, 2000	1,037,891	105,480,101
Persons per household, 2000	2.51	2.59
Median household money income, 1999	$40,624	$41,994
Per capita money income, 1999	$20,506	$21,587
Persons below poverty, percent, 1999	9.9%	12.4%

Business	Kansas	USA
Private nonfarm establishments, 1999	74,486	7,008,444
Private nonfarm employment, 1999	1,111,884	110,705,661
Private nonfarm employment, percent change 1990–99	24.4%	18.4%
Nonemployer establishments, 1999	155,052	16,152,604
Manufacturers shipments, 1997 ($1,000)	46,296,431	3,842,061,405
Retail sales, 1997 ($1,000)	22,571,918	2,460,886,012
Retail sales per capita, 1997	$8,627	$9,190
Minority-owned firms, percent of total, 1997	5.5%	14.6%
Women-owned firms, percent of total, 1997	25.6%	26.0%
Federal funds and grants, 2001 ($1,000)	16,698,766	1,763,896,019
Local government employment – full-time equivalent, 1997	118,302	10,227,429

Geography	Kansas	USA
Land area, 2000 (square miles)	81,815	3,537,438
Persons per square mile, 2000	32.9	79.6

(a) Includes persons reporting only one race.

(b) Hispanics may be of any race, so also are included in applicable race categories.

Z: Value greater than zero but less than half unit of measure shown.

Source: U.S. Census Bureau State & County QuickFacts

Kentucky

Statehood: June 1, 1792
Nickname: Bluegrass State
State bird: Kentucky cardinal
State flower: Goldenrod
State tree: Tulip poplar
State motto: United we stand, divided we fall
State capital: Frankfort
Population of capital: 27,741 (2000)

Ceded to Britain by France in 1763, the territory now known as Kentucky was a fertile hunting ground for the Chicksaw, Cherokee and the Shawnee. Admitted to the Union in 1792, its loyalties were divided at the outbreak of the Civil War, and both sides invaded the state. A growing interest in coal, oil, and especially horse racing slowly helped the state recover economically, as did roads linking it to Cincinnati in the north and Nashville in the south. The dense grass that blooms each spring has given the state its nickname and its most enduring tradition: the Kentucky Derby. Since 1875 three-year-old horses have been racing around the one-mile track at Churchill Downs the first Saturday in May. Sectioned into 120 counties, Kentucky has two major cities, Louisville and Lexington.

Most of the state is rolling plain drained by the Ohio, Kentucky and Tennessee Rivers. In the southeast, the Pine Mountains, part of the Cumberlands, dominate the rugged appalachian plateau region. Tobacco is the chief crop, followed by hay,

corn, and soybeans. Kentucky is noted for breeding thoroughbred racehorses and cattle raising to a lesser degree. Industries include electrical equipment, machinery, chemicals, and metals. Kentucky is also one of the major bituminous coal producers in the United States. Mammoth Cave National Park, Big South Fork National River and Recreation Area, Cumberland Gap National Historic Park, Abraham Lincoln Birthplace National Historic Site, and Shaker Village are some of the tourist attractions in Kentucky.

A frontiersman and a statesman embrace on Kentucky's flag, enacting the state motto. Adopted in 1918, sprigs of Goldenrod and the words "Commonwealth of Kentucky" placed against a blue background encircle the central image.

Frankfort

First settled in 1779, Frankfort was made the capital in 1792 as a compromise to the larger cities it lies between. Notable buildings here along the Kentucky River include the campus of Kentucky State College, "Liberty Hall," reportedly designed by Thomas Jefferson, and the Old Capitol. Tobacco, textiles, electronic parts, and furniture follow whisky distilling in their economic importance to the capital of the Bluegrass State.

Kentucky at a Glance

People	Kentucky	USA
Population, 2003 estimate	4,117,827	290,809,777
Population percent change, April 1, 2000–July 1, 2001	0.6%	1.2%
Population, 2000	4,041,769	281,421,906
Persons under 5 years old, percent, 2000	6.6%	6.8%
Persons under 18 years old, percent, 2000	24.6%	25.7%
Persons 65 years old and over, percent, 2000	12.5%	12.4%
Female persons, percent, 2000	51.1%	50.9%
White persons, percent, 2000 (a)	90.1%	75.1%
African American persons, percent, 2000 (a)	7.3%	12.3%
Native American persons, percent, 2000 (a)	0.2%	0.9%
Asian persons, percent, 2000 (a)	0.7%	3.6%
Native Hawaiian and Other Pacific Islander, percent, 2000 (a)	Z	0.1%
Persons of Hispanic or Latino origin, percent, 2000 (b)	1.5%	12.5%
White persons, not of Hispanic/Latino origin, percent, 2000	89.3%	69.1%
Foreign born persons, percent, 2000	2.0%	11.1%
Language other than English spoken at home, percent age 5+, 2000	3.9%	17.9%
High school graduates, percent of persons age 25+, 2000	74.1%	80.4%
Bachelor's degree or higher, percent of persons age 25+, 2000	17.1%	24.4%
Persons with a disability, age 5+, 2000	874,156	49,746,248
Homeownership rate, 2000	70.8%	66.2%
Median value of owner-occupied housing units, 2000	$86,700	$119,600
Households, 2000	1,590,647	105,480,101
Persons per household, 2000	2.47	2.59
Median household money income, 1999	$33,672	$41,994
Per capita money income, 1999	$18,093	$21,587
Persons below poverty, percent, 1999	15.8%	12.4%

Business	Kentucky	USA
Private nonfarm establishments, 1999	89,946	7,008,444
Private nonfarm employment, 1999	1,469,315	110,705,661
Private nonfarm employment, percent change 1990–99	23.9%	18.4%
Nonemployer establishments, 1999	222,304	16,152,604
Manufacturers shipments, 1997 ($1,000)	86,636,107	3,842,061,405
Retail sales, 1997 ($1,000)	33,332,675	2,460,886,012
Retail sales per capita, 1997	$8,530	$9,190
Minority-owned firms, percent of total, 1997	4.5%	14.6%
Women-owned firms, percent of total, 1997	23.4%	26.0%
Federal funds and grants, 2001 ($1,000)	25,835,136	1,763,896,019
Local government employment – full-time equivalent, 1997	134,740	10,227,429

Geography	Kentucky	USA
Land area, 2000 (square miles)	39,728	3,537,438
Persons per square mile, 2000	101.7	79.6

(a) Includes persons reporting only one race.

(b) Hispanics may be of any race, so also are included in applicable race categories.

Z: Value greater than zero but less than half unit of measure shown.

Source: U.S. Census Bureau State & County QuickFacts

Louisiana

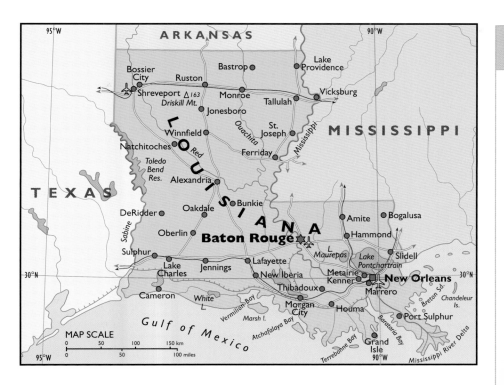

Around 1699, French colonists wrested control from Atapaka and Chitimacha Indians, founded Louisiana on the Gulf of Mexico and named it for their king, Louis XIV. Regained by France in 1800 after spending time under the Spanish crown, Napoleon then sold the territory to Thomas Jefferson three years later. It joined the Confederacy at the start of the Civil War, but was readmitted to the Union in 1868. The discovery of oil and natural gas in the early 20th century provided a great boost to the economy. Racial discrimination, however, left the large African-American community—approximately one third of the population—politically powerless until the 1960s. New Orleans, Shreveport, Monroe, Alexandria and Lafayette are the major cities to be found among 64 parishes, or county-like administrative divisions.

Louisiana consists of two main regions: the Mississippi alluvial plain and the Gulf coastal plain. The Mississippi Delta in the southeast covers close to 13,000 square miles (33,700 sq km), about one quarter of the state's total area. And at 7,721 miles (12,426 km) long, the tidal shoreline and the multitude of waterways have converted nearly fifteen percent of the state into swamp. The subtropical climate and low-lying land combined with heavy rainfall make this region prone to flooding, as on August 29, 2005, when Hurricane Katrina made landfall, breaching the levee system protecting greater New Orleans.

Although almost half of the state is forested, north of the marshes, prairies stretch to the Texas border. A leading producer of soybeans, sweet potatoes, rice, cotton and sugarcane, Louisiana is one of the nation's leading mineral producers. Petroleum and coal account for more than ninety-five percent of mining income. Fishing is another major industry, particularly shrimps and crayfish. The French Quarter in New Orleans, Jean Lafitte National Historic Park and the Poverty Point National Monument attract the most tourists.

A mother pelican, symbolizing the state's role as a guardian, dominates the flag. The only other element interrupting the blue field is a banner carrying the state motto.

Baton Rouge

Founded on the Mississippi River in 1719 by French colonists, Baton Rouge was named after a red post marking the dividing line between two Indian tribes. Ceded to Britain by France in 1763, and to the United States with the Louisiana Purchase, it became the state capital in 1849. The city contains both Louisiana State University and Southern University, and is the site of many food-processing industries as well as a large petrochemical complex. Other industries include natural gas, chemicals, plastics, pharmaceuticals and seafood.

Louisiana at a Glance

People	Louisiana	USA
Population, 2003 estimate	4,496,334	290,809,777
Population percent change, April 1, 2000–July 1, 2001	−0.1%	1.2%
Population, 2000	4,468,976	281,421,906
Persons under 5 years old, percent, 2000	7.1%	6.8%
Persons under 18 years old, percent, 2000	27.3%	25.7%
Persons 65 years old and over, percent, 2000	11.6%	12.4%
Female persons, percent, 2000	51.6%	50.9%
White persons, percent, 2000 (a)	63.9%	75.1%
African American persons, percent, 2000 (a)	32.5%	12.3%
Native American persons, percent, 2000 (a)	0.6%	0.9%
Asian persons, percent, 2000 (a)	1.2%	3.6%
Native Hawaiian and Other Pacific Islander, percent, 2000 (a)	Z	0.1%
Persons of Hispanic or Latino origin, percent, 2000 (b)	2.4%	12.5%
White persons, not of Hispanic/Latino origin, percent, 2000	62.5%	69.1%
Foreign born persons, percent, 2000	2.6%	11.1%
Language other than English spoken at home, percent age 5+, 2000	9.2%	17.9%
High school graduates, percent of persons age 25+, 2000	74.8%	80.4%
Bachelor's degree or higher, percent of persons age 25+, 2000	18.7%	24.4%
Persons with a disability, age 5+, 2000	880,047	49,746,248
Homeownership rate, 2000	67.9%	66.2%
Median value of owner-occupied housing units, 2000	$85,000	$119,600
Households, 2000	1,656,053	105,480,101
Persons per household, 2000	2.62	2.59
Median household money income, 1999	$32,566	$41,994
Per capita money income, 1999	$16,912	$21,587
Persons below poverty, percent, 1999	19.6%	12.4%

Business	Louisiana	USA
Private nonfarm establishments, 1999	101,020	7,008,444
Private nonfarm employment, 1999	1,579,949	110,705,661
Private nonfarm employment, percent change 1990–99	24.3%	18.4%
Nonemployer establishments, 1999	228,628	16,152,604
Manufacturers shipments, 1997 ($1,000)	80,423,978	3,842,061,405
Retail sales, 1997 ($1,000)	35,807,894	2,460,886,012
Retail sales per capita, 1997	$8,229	$9,190
Minority-owned firms, percent of total, 1997	14.1%	14.6%
Women-owned firms, percent of total, 1997	23.9%	26.0%
Federal funds and grants, 2001 ($1,000)	27,816,445	1,763,896,019
Local government employment – full-time equivalent, 1997	169,976	10,227,429

Geography	Louisiana	USA
Land area, 2000 (square miles)	43,562	3,537,438
Persons per square mile, 2000	102.6	79.6

(a) Includes persons reporting only one race.

(b) Hispanics may be of any race, so also are included in applicable race categories.

Z: Value greater than zero but less than half unit of measure shown.

Source: U.S. Census Bureau State & County QuickFacts

Maine

Statehood: March 15, 1820
Nickname: Pine Tree State
State bird: Chickadee
State flower: White pine cone and flower
State tree: White pine
State motto: I direct
State capital: Augusta
Population of capital: 18,560 (2000)

Inhabited by Algonquin and Abenaki Indians, Maine was explored by John Cabot in 1498 although Vikings are thought to have landed on the coast much earlier. The first British settlement, Fort St. George, was established in 1607 but quickly abandoned and firm colonization began in the 1620s as the rest of New England was populated. French and Native American resistance hindered further British settlement and in 1652 it fell under the administration of the Massachusetts Bay Company before becoming part of Massachusetts proper in 1691. It was not until 1820 however, that Maine entered the Union as the 23rd state. Portland, Lewiston and Bangor are the largest cities in this sparsely populated state of 16 counties.

The landscape is generally rolling country with the thickly wooded Longfellow Mountains in the west and more than 2,000 lakes scattered across the landscape. The biggest rivers are the St. John, the Penobscot, the Kennebec, and the St. Croix. Initial economic development was steady, based on numerous ports and its timber resources for shipbuilding. With poor soil, a short growing season, geographic remoteness, and three-quarters of Maine forested, the major economic sector at present is the manufacture of paper and wood products. Broiler chickens and blueberries are the major agricultural products while lobsters are the mainstay of the modern fishing industry. Tourism has also become important as East Coast urbanites seek the natural beauty found at places such as Acadia

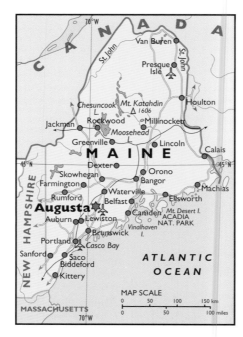

National Park, earning Maine another nickname: "vacationland."

The flag adopted in 1909 displays the coat of arms against a blue background. The sailor and the farmer illustrate the first occupations in the state and the North Star above the moose and the state tree pictured symbolizes the motto.

Augusta

Founded by settlers from Plymouth as a trading post in 1628, Augusta, on the Kennebec River, was incorporated in 1797. A dam built across the river in 1837 led to a shift in Augusta's industry from shipping to the manufacture of textiles, paper, steel, and more recently, computers and electronics. The city also benefits from tourists passing through on their way to scenic vacation spots further up the Maine coast.

Maine at a Glance

People	Maine	USA
Population, 2003 estimate	1,305,728	290,809,777
Population percent change, April 1, 2000–July 1, 2001	0.9%	1.2%
Population, 2000	1,274,923	281,421,906
Persons under 5 years old, percent, 2000	5.5%	6.8%
Persons under 18 years old, percent, 2000	23.6%	25.7%
Persons 65 years old and over, percent, 2000	14.4%	12.4%
Female persons, percent, 2000	51.3%	50.9%
White persons, percent, 2000 (a)	96.9%	75.1%
African American persons, percent, 2000 (a)	0.5%	12.3%
Native American persons, percent, 2000 (a)	0.6%	0.9%
Asian persons, percent, 2000 (a)	0.7%	3.6%
Native Hawaiian and Other Pacific Islander, percent, 2000 (a)	Z	0.1%
Persons of Hispanic or Latino origin, percent, 2000 (b)	0.7%	12.5%
White persons, not of Hispanic/Latino origin, percent, 2000	96.5%	69.1%
Foreign born persons, percent, 2000	2.9%	11.1%
Language other than English spoken at home, percent age 5+, 2000	7.8%	17.9%
High school graduates, percent of persons age 25+, 2000	85.4%	80.4%
Bachelor's degree or higher, percent of persons age 25+, 2000	22.9%	24.4%
Persons with a disability, age 5+, 2000	237,910	49,746,248
Homeownership rate, 2000	71.6%	66.2%
Median value of owner-occupied housing units, 2000	$98,700	$119,600
Households, 2000	518,200	105,480,101
Persons per household, 2000	2.39	2.59
Median household money income, 1999	$37,240	$41,994
Per capita money income, 1999	$19,533	$21,587
Persons below poverty, percent, 1999	10.9%	12.4%

Business	Maine	USA
Private nonfarm establishments, 1999	38,878	7,008,444
Private nonfarm employment, 1999	475,149	110,705,661
Private nonfarm employment, percent change 1990–99	12.1%	18.4%
Nonemployer establishments, 1999	96,884	16,152,604
Manufacturers shipments, 1997 ($1,000)	14,097,609	3,842,061,405
Retail sales, 1997 ($1,000)	12,737,087	2,460,886,012
Retail sales per capita, 1997	$10,229	$9,190
Minority-owned firms, percent of total, 1997	2.2%	14.6%
Women-owned firms, percent of total, 1997	24.0%	26.0%
Federal funds and grants, 2001 ($1,000)	8,180,498	1,763,896,019
Local government employment – full-time equivalent, 1997	46,260	10,227,429

Geography	Maine	USA
Land area, 2000 (square miles)	30,862	3,537,438
Persons per square mile, 2000	41.3	79.6

(a) Includes persons reporting only one race.

(b) Hispanics may be of any race, so also are included in applicable race categories.

Z: Value greater than zero but less than half unit of measure shown.

Source: U.S. Census Bureau State & County QuickFacts

Maryland & Washington, D.C.

Maryland

District of Columbia

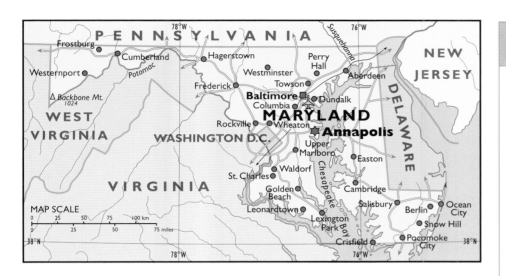

Statehood: April 28, 1788
Nickname: Old Line State
State bird: Baltimore Oriole
State flower: Black Eyed Susan
State tree: White Oak
State motto: Manly deeds, womanly words
State capital: Annapolis
Population of capital: 35, 838 (2000)

The first European settlements here on the Atlantic coast were founded circa 1634 but dozens of Indian groups like the Susquehannock, Patuxent, Assateague and Potomac, had hunted and fished Maryland's waterways for centuries. One of the original Thirteen Colonies, its citizens were active in the cause for independence. During the Civil War, Maryland was one of the border states that did not secede from the Union, but its citizens served on both sides of the conflict. Baltimore, the largest city, forms its own administrative division along with 23 counties.

The Alleghenies mark the western half of the state but the Chesapeake Bay and its coastal marshlands dominate Maryland geography. Cattle and poultry are the most important livestock while corn, hay, tobacco and soybeans are the chief crops. Industries include iron and steel, shipbuilding, transport equipment (particularly aircraft), chemical, electrical machinery, and fishing. Harper's Ferry National Park, Chesapeake and Ohio Canal National Park, Antietam National Battlefield and the Goddard Space Flight Center attract the most visitors.

The state flag borrows its design from two English families. The Crosslands coat of arms bore the red and white design, while the Calverts, a black and yellow. It was adopted in 1904.

Annapolis

A port at the mouth of the Severn River on the Chesapeake Bay, Annapolis, named in honor of Queen Anne, was founded in 1649 by Puritans from Virginia, and in 1694 was laid out as the state capital. The site of the signing of the peace treaty ending the American Revolution, it has many buildings dating from the colonial period. George Bancroft founded the U.S. Naval Academy here in 1845. Local industries such as seafood packing, sail and boat-making rely on the Chesapeake Bay and the Atlantic.

Washington, D.C.

The nation's capital, the District of Columbia occupies the eastern bank of the Potomac River, yet its metropolitan area extends far into the neighboring states of Maryland and Virginia. The site was chosen as the seat of government in 1791, and the French engineer Pierre Charles L'Enfant planned the city. Construction of the White House began in 1793, and the Capitol building the following year. In 1800, Congress moved from Philadelphia to Washington, but during the War of 1812, the British occupied the city and burned many public buildings, including the White House and the Capitol. The main governmental buildings for the legislative, judicial, and administrative center of the country include the Library of Congress, the Pentagon, the Supreme Court, and the Capitol which contains the Senate and the House of Representatives.

Maryland & DC at a Glance

People	MD	DC	USA
Population, 2003 estimate	5,508,909	563,384	290,809,777
Population percent change, April 1, 2000–July 1, 2001	1.5%	0.0%	1.2%
Population, 2000	5,296,486	572,059	281,421,906
Persons under 5 years old, percent, 2000	6.7%	5.7%	6.8%
Persons under 18 years old, percent, 2000	25.6%	20.1%	25.7%
Persons 65 years old and over, percent, 2000	11.3%	12.2%	12.4%
Female persons, percent, 2000	51.7%	52.9%	50.9%
White persons, percent, 2000 (a)	64.0%	30.8%	75.1%
African American persons, percent, 2000 (a)	27.9%	60.0%	12.3%
Native American persons, percent, 2000 (a)	0.3%	0.3%	0.9%
Asian persons, percent, 2000 (a)	4.0%	2.7%	3.6%
Native Hawaiian and Other Pacific Islander, percent, 2000 (a)	Z	0.1%	0.1%
Persons of Hispanic or Latino origin, percent, 2000 (b)	4.3%	7.9%	12.5%
White persons, not of Hispanic/Latino origin, percent, 2000	62.1%	27.8%	69.1%
Foreign born persons, percent, 2000	9.8%	12.9%	11.1%
Language other than English spoken at home, percent age 5+, 2000	12.6%	16.8%	17.9%
High school graduates, percent of persons age 25+, 2000	83.8%	77.8%	80.4%
Bachelor's degree or higher, percent of persons age 25+, 2000	31.4%	39.1%	24.4%
Persons with a disability, age 5+, 2000	854,345	115,980	49,746,248
Homeownership rate, 2000	67.7%	40.8%	66.2%
Median value of owner-occupied housing units, 2000	$146,000	$157,200	$119,600
Households, 2000	1,980,859	248,338	105,480,101
Persons per household, 2000	2.61	2.16	2.59
Median household money income, 1999	$52,868	$40,127	$41,994
Per capita money income, 1999	$25,614	$28,659	$21,587
Persons below poverty, percent, 1999	8.5%	20.2%	12.4%

Business	MD	DC	USA
Private nonfarm establishments, 1999	127,431	19,469	7,008,444
Private nonfarm employment, 1999	1,988,950	404,372	110,705,661
Private nonfarm employment, percent change 1990–99	9.8%	–5.3%	18.4%
Nonemployer establishments, 1999	307,535	31,486	16,152,604
Manufacturers shipments, 1997 ($1,000)	36,505,948	320,234	3,842,061,405
Retail sales, 1997 ($1,000)	46,428,206	2,788,831	2,460,886,012
Retail sales per capita, 1997	$9,116	$5,274	$9,190
Minority-owned firms, percent of total, 1997	20.6%	33.6%	14.6%
Women-owned firms, percent of total, 1997	28.9%	30.9%	26.0%
Federal funds and grants, 2001 ($1,000)	48,163,883	30,940,658	1,763,896,019
Local government employment – full-time equivalent, 1997	171,635	46,246	10,227,429

Geography	MD	DC	USA
Land area, 2000 (square miles)	9,774	61	3,537,438
Persons per square mile, 2000	541.9	9,316.4	79.6

(a) Includes persons reporting only one race.

(b) Hispanics may be of any race, so also are included in applicable race categories.

Z: Value greater than zero but less than half unit of measure shown.

Source: U.S. Census Bureau State & County QuickFacts

Massachusetts

The Pilgrims founded the Plymouth Colony, the first settlement in New England, in 1620 on Massachusetts Bay. English Puritans, led by John Winthrop, established the city of Boston in 1630, and it became the center of the Massachusetts Bay Colony. The state played a leading role in events leading up to the American Revolution, and was the scene of the first major armed conflict at the Battle of Bunker Hill. Massachusetts prospered after achieving statehood in 1788 and 14 counties were eventually created. Apart from Boston, the biggest cities are Worcester, Springfield, Cambridge, and New Bedford.

The eastern portion of the state is a low-lying coastal plain while the Connecticut River valley and the Berkshire hills mark the uplands of the interior. The principal rivers are the Housatonic, Merrimack, and the Connecticut, New England's longest waterway. A once highly industrialized region, Massachusetts is one of the most densely populated states in the nation. Agricultural produce includes cranberries, tobacco, hay, vegetables, and dairy products. Manufacturing centers around the Boston metropolitan area; electronic equipment, plastics, footwear, paper, machinery, metal and rubber goods, printing and publishing, and fishing are the largest employers.

The state flag features a blue shield emblazoned with a Massachuset Indian on a white field. The state motto appears in Latin on the banner around the shield. The white star in the upper left corner represents the state as one of the original thirteen while the arm and sword above symbolizes the first part of the motto.

Boston

A principal seaport at the mouth of the Charles River on Massachusetts Bay, Boston is the largest city in New England. By 1700, Boston was the largest city in the British American colonies and the largest port in the British Empire outside the mother country. It had the first free public school (1635), the first public library (1653), as well as the first newspaper (1707) in the Americas. The city lay at the heart of the struggle for American independence. Faneuil Hall (1742), a meeting place for the revolutionaries, is known as the "Cradle of Liberty," and incidents such as the Boston Massacre (1770) and the Boston Tea Party (1773) were early warnings of American resistance to British rule. In the 19th century, Boston was the center of Transcendentalism, the first truly distinctive national cultural movement, and remains the world headquarters for the Church of Christian Science. The first subway system in the United States opened in Boston in 1895. Historic sites include Paul Revere's House, the oldest wooden building in Boston, the Old South Meeting House, the State Capitol built by Charles Bulfinch, Boston Athenaeum, and the Museum of Fine Arts. Printing and publishing, health care, banking and insurance, shipbuilding, electronics, fishing, and clothing manufacturing are the key industries.

Massachusetts at a Glance

People	Massachusetts	USA
Population, 2003 estimate	6,433,422	290,809,777
Population percent change, April 1, 2000–July 1, 2001	0.5%	1.2%
Population, 2000	6,349,097	281,421,906
Persons under 5 years old, percent, 2000	6.3%	6.8%
Persons under 18 years old, percent, 2000	23.6%	25.7%
Persons 65 years old and over, percent, 2000	13.5%	12.4%
Female persons, percent, 2000	51.8%	50.9%
White persons, percent, 2000 (a)	84.5%	75.1%
African American persons, percent, 2000 (a)	5.4%	12.3%
Native American persons, percent, 2000 (a)	0.2%	0.9%
Asian persons, percent, 2000 (a)	3.8%	3.6%
Native Hawaiian and Other Pacific Islander, percent, 2000 (a)	Z	0.1%
Persons of Hispanic or Latino origin, percent, 2000 (b)	6.8%	12.5%
White persons, not of Hispanic/Latino origin, percent, 2000	81.9%	69.1%
Foreign born persons, percent, 2000	12.2%	11.1%
Language other than English spoken at home, percent age 5+, 2000	18.7%	17.9%
High school graduates, percent of persons age 25+, 2000	84.8%	80.4%
Bachelor's degree or higher, percent of persons age 25+, 2000	33.2%	24.4%
Persons with a disability, age 5+, 2000	1,084,746	49,746,248
Homeownership rate, 2000	61.7%	66.2%
Median value of owner-occupied housing units, 2000	$185,700	$119,600
Households, 2000	2,443,580	105,480,101
Persons per household, 2000	2.51	2.59
Median household money income, 1999	$50,502	$41,994
Per capita money income, 1999	$25,952	$21,587
Persons below poverty, percent, 1999	9.3%	12.4%

Business	Massachusetts	USA
Private nonfarm establishments, 1999	173,267	7,008,444
Private nonfarm employment, 1999	2,971,052	110,705,661
Private nonfarm employment, percent change 1990–99	7.2%	18.4%
Nonemployer establishments, 1999	404,333	16,152,604
Manufacturers shipments, 1997 ($1,000)	77,876,576	3,842,061,405
Retail sales, 1997 ($1,000)	58,578,048	2,460,886,012
Retail sales per capita, 1997	$9,579	$9,190
Minority-owned firms, percent of total, 1997	7.3%	14.6%
Women-owned firms, percent of total, 1997	26.6%	26.0%
Federal funds and grants, 2001 ($1,000)	44,178,642	1,763,896,019
Local government employment – full-time equivalent, 1997	213,917	10,227,429

Geography	Massachusetts	USA
Land area, 2000 (square miles)	7,840	3,537,438
Persons per square mile, 2000	809.8	79.6

(a) Includes persons reporting only one race.

(b) Hispanics may be of any race, so also are included in applicable race categories.

Z: Value greater than zero but less than half unit of measure shown.

Source: U.S. Census Bureau State & County QuickFacts

Michigan

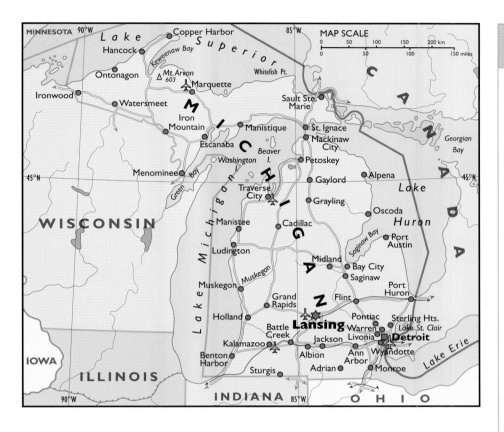

Statehood: January 26, 1837
Nickname: Wolverine State
State bird: Robin
State flower: Apple blossom
State tree: White pine
State motto: If you seek a pleasant peninsula, look around you
State capital: Lansing
Population of capital: 119,128 (2000)

First explored by the French in the 17th century, who traded for furs with the Chippewa, Ottawa and Potawatomi, this region bordered by four of the Great Lakes was surrendered to Britain after the Seven Years' War. The British finally left the area in 1796, and Michigan became a territory shortly thereafter, achieving full statehood in 1837. In 1825 the opening of the Erie Canal aided its growth, but the real industrial boom came with the development of the motor vehicle industry in the early 20th century. The largest cities are Detroit, Grand Rapids, Warren, Flint, Lansing, Sterling, Ann Arbor and Livonia. The Wolverine State is divided into 83 counties.

Michigan is made up of two peninsulas separated by the Straits of Mackinac, connecting Lakes Michigan and Huron. The Upper Peninsula has swampland on its northeastern shores and the Huron Mountains in the west. The rocky landscape yields natural resources like copper, iron ore and timber. The abundantly forested Lower Peninsula also contains deposits of oil, gypsum, sandstone, and limestone. In the south, near Battle Creek, cereal crops are cultivated and livestock rearing is important. The Lower Peninsula also holds most of Michigan's population. Industries include motor vehicles, primary and fabricated metals, chemicals, and food products. The appeal of the lakes and the natural beauty of places like Mackinac Island, Isle Royale National Park (the largest isle in Lake Superior) and Pictured Rocks National Lakeshore attract numerous visitors each summer.

An elk, a moose and an eagle hold a shield emblazoned with the Latin word *Tuebor* (I will defend) on the state flag. Set against a blue background the shield contains an image of a man standing on a peninsula with one hand raised in a gesture of peace and the other holding a rifle, in reference to defense. The mottoes of the nation and the state appear above and below the shield respectively. Michigan adopted their flag in 1911.

Lansing

This city in southern Michigan was first settled in the 1840s, it was made the state capital in 1847. Lansing didn't start to grow significantly until Ransom Eli Olds started manufacturing and selling his Oldsmobiles here along the Grand River in 1897. Lansing continues to produce motor vehicles, metal goods, machinery, plastic products and building materials. East Lansing is the home to one of the state's two premier universities, Michigan State University.

Michigan at a Glance

People	Michigan	USA
Population, 2003 estimate	10,079,985	290,809,777
Population percent change, April 1, 2000–July 1, 2001	0.5%	1.2%
Population, 2000	9,938,444	281,421,906
Persons under 5 years old, percent, 2000	6.8%	6.8%
Persons under 18 years old, percent, 2000	26.1%	25.7%
Persons 65 years old and over, percent, 2000	12.3%	12.4%
Female persons, percent, 2000	51.0%	50.9%
White persons, percent, 2000 (a)	80.2%	75.1%
African American persons, percent, 2000 (a)	14.2%	12.3%
Native American persons, percent, 2000 (a)	0.6%	0.9%
Asian persons, percent, 2000 (a)	1.8%	3.6%
Native Hawaiian and Other Pacific Islander, percent, 2000 (a)	Z	0.1%
Persons of Hispanic or Latino origin, percent, 2000 (b)	3.3%	12.5%
White persons, not of Hispanic/Latino origin, percent, 2000	78.6%	69.1%
Foreign born persons, percent, 2000	5.3%	11.1%
Language other than English spoken at home, percent age 5+, 2000	8.4%	17.9%
High school graduates, percent of persons age 25+, 2000	83.4%	80.4%
Bachelor's degree or higher, percent of persons age 25+, 2000	21.8%	24.4%
Persons with a disability, age 5+, 2000	1,711,231	49,746,248
Homeownership rate, 2000	73.8%	66.2%
Median value of owner-occupied housing units, 2000	$115,600	$119,600
Households, 2000	3,785,661	105,480,101
Persons per household, 2000	2.56	2.59
Median household money income, 1999	$44,667	$41,994
Per capita money income, 1999	$22,168	$21,587
Persons below poverty, percent, 1999	10.5%	12.4%

Business	Michigan	USA
Private nonfarm establishments, 1999	236,456	7,008,444
Private nonfarm employment, 1999	3,996,300	110,705,661
Private nonfarm employment, percent change 1990–99	17.1%	18.4%
Nonemployer establishments, 1999	506,038	16,152,604
Manufacturers shipments, 1997 ($1,000)	214,900,655	3,842,061,405
Retail sales, 1997 ($1,000)	93,706,078	2,460,886,012
Retail sales per capita, 1997	$9,576	$9,190
Minority-owned firms, percent of total, 1997	7.6%	14.6%
Women-owned firms, percent of total, 1997	27.2%	26.0%
Federal funds and grants, 2001 ($1,000)	51,632,490	1,763,896,019
Local government employment – full-time equivalent, 1997	332,671	10,227,429

Geography	Michigan	USA
Land area, 2000 (square miles)	56,804	3,537,438
Persons per square mile, 2000	175	79.6

(a) Includes persons reporting only one race.
(b) Hispanics may be of any race, so also are included in applicable race categories.
Z: Value greater than zero but less than half unit of measure shown.

Source: U.S. Census Bureau State & County QuickFacts

Minnesota

Statehood: May 11, 1858
Nickname: Gopher State
State bird: Common loon
State flower: Pink and white lady-slipper
State tree: Norway pine
State motto: Star of the North
State capital: St. Paul
Population of capital: 287,151 (2000)

French fur trader Daniel Greysolon, sieur Duluth reached this area along the existing Canadian border in 1679 and found it inhabited by Dakota and Ojibwa Indians. After the French and Indian War (1754–63), the land east of the Mississippi passed to Britain, then to the U.S. following the Revolutionary War. The lands west of the Mississippi were among those acquired with the Louisiana Purchase. Organized as a territory in 1849, Minnesota acquired statehood in 1858 and over time 87 counties took shape. Minneapolis, sitting on the same side of the river as the capital, and Duluth, the westernmost Atlantic seaport, are the major cities.

The state's terrain varies from the southern prairies to the northern forests. Northeast of Lake Itasca, the source of the Mississippi, lie several smaller mountain chains: the Misquah Hills and the Mesabi and Vermillion Ranges, which hold small deposits of iron ore. The numerous lakes in the north empty into the Mississippi, Minnesota, and St. Croix Rivers. Many farms raise beef and dairy cattle while wheat and corn are the major crops. Since the 1950s, manufacturing has replaced agriculture as the main economic activity. Industries include electronic equipment, machinery, paper products, chemicals, printing and publishing. Tourists to the Land of 10,000 Lakes who don't stop at the Mall of America often visit Voyageurs National Park, Mississippi National River and Recreational Area in addition to the Pipestone and Grand Portage National Monuments.

Nineteen stars surround the seal on the state flag of Minnesota. Within the seal a wreath of lady slippers, the state flower, encloses an image of a farmer plowing and a Native American on horseback, representing the state's heritage. The year Minnesota became the 32nd state appears above while 1819, the year Ft. Snelling was established on the present site of Minneapolis, and 1893, the year the original flag was adopted, flank the seal. The largest star on this current flag, adopted in 1957, stands for the North Star.

St. Paul

In 1849 the town formerly known as Pig's Eye, after a local saloon, was made capital of the Minnesota territory. When Minnesota joined the Union in 1858, St. Paul became the state capital, developing rapidly as a river port and transportation center on the eastern bank of the Mississippi. Today it is a major manufacturing and distribution hub with industries ranging from computers and electronics, to printing and automobile assembly.

Minnesota at a Glance

People	Minnesota	USA
Population, 2003 estimate	5,059,375	290,809,777
Population percent change, April 1, 2000–July 1, 2001	1.1%	1.2%
Population, 2000	4,919,479	281,421,906
Persons under 5 years old, percent, 2000	6.7%	6.8%
Persons under 18 years old, percent, 2000	26.2%	25.7%
Persons 65 years old and over, percent, 2000	12.1%	12.4%
Female persons, percent, 2000	50.5%	50.9%
White persons, percent, 2000 (a)	89.4%	75.1%
African American persons, percent, 2000 (a)	3.5%	12.3%
Native American persons, percent, 2000 (a)	1.1%	0.9%
Asian persons, percent, 2000 (a)	2.9%	3.6%
Native Hawaiian and Other Pacific Islander, percent, 2000 (a)	Z	0.1%
Persons of Hispanic or Latino origin, percent, 2000 (b)	2.9%	12.5%
White persons, not of Hispanic/Latino origin, percent, 2000	88.2%	69.1%
Foreign born persons, percent, 2000	5.3%	11.1%
Language other than English spoken at home, percent age 5+, 2000	8.5%	17.9%
High school graduates, percent of persons age 25+, 2000	87.9%	80.4%
Bachelor's degree or higher, percent of persons age 25+, 2000	27.4%	24.4%
Persons with a disability, age 5+, 2000	679,236	49,746,248
Homeownership rate, 2000	74.6%	66.2%
Median value of owner-occupied housing units, 2000	$122,400	$119,600
Households, 2000	1,895,127	105,480,101
Persons per household, 2000	2.52	2.59
Median household money income, 1999	$47,111	$41,994
Per capita money income, 1999	$23,198	$21,587
Persons below poverty, percent, 1999	7.9%	12.4%

Business	Minnesota	USA
Private nonfarm establishments, 1999	137,305	7,008,444
Private nonfarm employment, 1999	2,338,642	110,705,661
Private nonfarm employment, percent change 1990–99	27.6%	18.4%
Nonemployer establishments, 1999	313,444	16,152,604
Manufacturers shipments, 1997 ($1,000)	76,244,894	3,842,061,405
Retail sales, 1997 ($1,000)	48,097,982	2,460,886,012
Retail sales per capita, 1997	$10,260	$9,190
Minority-owned firms, percent of total, 1997	3.7%	14.6%
Women-owned firms, percent of total, 1997	26.4%	26.0%
Federal funds and grants, 2001 ($1,000)	24,935,394	1,763,896,019
Local government employment – full-time equivalent, 1997	188,845	10,227,429

Geography	Minnesota	USA
Land area, 2000 (square miles)	79,610	3,537,438
Persons per square mile, 2000	61.8	79.6

(a) Includes persons reporting only one race.

(b) Hispanics may be of any race, so also are included in applicable race categories.

Z: Value greater than zero but less than half unit of measure shown.

Source: U.S. Census Bureau State & County QuickFacts

Mississippi

Statehood: December 10, 1817
Nickname: Magnolia State
State bird: Mockingbird
State flower: Magnolia
State tree: Magnolia
State motto: By valor and arms
State capital: Jackson
Population of capital: 184,256 (2000)

Hernando de Soto of Spain first wandered through the region in the early 1540s, but the French coastal settlements allowed them to claim the semitropical land on the Gulf of Mexico in 1682. Louisiana passed to the British after the French and Indian War and in 1798, when the U.S. government established the Territory of Mississippi, the Choctaw and other tribes were displaced by incoming settlers. The 29th state seceded from the Union in 1861 and was the site of several Civil War battles.

Haunted by the legacy of slavery, racial segregation lasted until the 1960s, when the state was a focus of the civil rights movement. The capital and largest city is Jackson and other major cities are Meridian, Biloxi, Vicksburg, and Laurel. This low-lying state, broken into 82 counties, was hard hit by Katrina, a Category 4 tropical storm, in August 2005.

The topography slopes westward from Alabama and the hills in the northeast to the delta, a fertile plain between the Mississippi and Yazoo Rivers. Pine forests cover most of the southern part of the state as far as the sandy coastal plain. Primarily an agricultural state, Mississippi is among the leading producers of cotton in the U.S. but hay, peanuts, pecans, rice and soybeans have grown in importance, as has dairy farming. Valuable reserves of oil and natural gas exist in small quantities. Other industries include clothing, wood products, and chemicals. Vicksburg National Military Park, Tupelo National Battlefield, the Mississippi Petrified Forest

and the Natchez Trace Parkway are a few of the best-known landmarks.

The state flag, with three broad stripes of blue, white and red, was adopted in 1894 and still bears the Confederate "southern cross" in the upper left corner. The stars stand for the eleven states in the Confederacy, in addition to Kentucky and Missouri.

Jackson

Located in southwestern Mississippi, Jason was established as a trading post in the 1790s by Louis LeFleur, a French Canadian. Later assuming the name of President Andrew Jackson, the city on the Pearl River was chosen as state capital in 1821. Glass, furniture, textiles, and more recently natural gas are some of the primary industries.

Mississippi at a Glance

People	Mississippi	USA
Population, 2003 estimate	2,881,281	290,809,777
Population percent change, April 1, 2000–July 1, 2001	0.5%	1.2%
Population, 2000	2,844,658	281,421,906
Persons under 5 years old, percent, 2000	7.2%	6.8%
Persons under 18 years old, percent, 2000	27.3%	25.7%
Persons 65 years old and over, percent, 2000	12.1%	12.4%
Female persons, percent, 2000	51.7%	50.9%
White persons, percent, 2000 (a)	61.4%	75.1%
African American persons, percent, 2000 (a)	36.3%	12.3%
Native American persons, percent, 2000 (a)	0.4%	0.9%
Asian persons, percent, 2000 (a)	0.7%	3.6%
Native Hawaiian and Other Pacific Islander, percent, 2000 (a)	Z	0.1%
Persons of Hispanic or Latino origin, percent, 2000 (b)	1.4%	12.5%
White persons, not of Hispanic/Latino origin, percent, 2000	60.7%	69.1%
Foreign born persons, percent, 2000	1.4%	11.1%
Language other than English spoken at home, percent age 5+, 2000	3.6%	17.9%
High school graduates, percent of persons age 25+, 2000	72.9%	80.4%
Bachelor's degree or higher, percent of persons age 25+, 2000	16.9%	24.4%
Persons with a disability, age 5+, 2000	607,570	49,746,248
Homeownership rate, 2000	72.3%	66.2%
Median value of owner-occupied housing units, 2000	$71,400	$119,600
Households, 2000	1,046,434	105,480,101
Persons per household, 2000	2.63	2.59
Median household money income, 1999	$31,330	$41,994
Per capita money income, 1999	$15,853	$21,587
Persons below poverty, percent, 1999	19.9%	12.4%

Business	Mississippi	USA
Private nonfarm establishments, 1999	59,834	7,008,444
Private nonfarm employment, 1999	948,883	110,705,661
Private nonfarm employment, percent change 1990–99	31.2%	18.4%
Nonemployer establishments, 1999	130,932	16,152,604
Manufacturers shipments, 1997 ($1,000)	39,658,260	3,842,061,405
Retail sales, 1997 ($1,000)	20,774,508	2,460,886,012
Retail sales per capita, 1997	$7,605	$9,190
Minority-owned firms, percent of total, 1997	13.1%	14.6%
Women-owned firms, percent of total, 1997	22.8%	26.0%
Federal funds and grants, 2001 ($1,000)	20,211,644	1,763,896,019
Local government employment – full-time equivalent, 1997	122,256	10,227,429

Geography	Mississippi	USA
Land area, 2000 (square miles)	46,907	3,537,438
Persons per square mile, 2000	60.6	79.6

(a) Includes persons reporting only one race.

(b) Hispanics may be of any race, so also are included in applicable race categories.

Z: Value greater than zero but less than half unit of measure shown.

Source: U.S. Census Bureau State & County QuickFacts

Missouri

Statehood: August 10, 1821
Nickname: "Show me" State
State bird: Eastern bluebird
State flower: Hawthorn
State tree: Flowering dogwood
State motto: The welfare of the people
State capital: Jefferson City
Population of capital: 39,636 (2000)

The French were the first Europeans to settle this area west of the Mississippi River in the mid-18th century, lured by stories from the Osage and Shawnee Indians of precious metals. In 1812, shortly after acquiring this midwestern region as part of the Louisiana Purchase, the U.S. government established the Missouri Territory, and it became a major corridor for westward migration. In 1821 Missouri was admitted to the Union without restrictions on slavery, where it remained throughout the prolonged conflict. A year before the violence of the Civil War bitterly divided the sympathies of its citizens the first Pony Express rider departed St. Joseph for California. St. Louis, Kansas City, Independence, Columbia and Springfield have the largest populations in this state of 114 counties.

Geographically, Missouri is divided into two parts: north of the Missouri River farmers grow corn, cotton and vegetables and raise livestock in prairie country. South of the river are the foothills and the Ozark Plateau. A small wheat-growing area is in the southwest and in the southeast the Missouri, Mississippi, and Ohio

Rivers converge to create a floodplain crowded with cotton fields. The chief mineral resources are coal, lead, zinc, and iron ore. Missouri's economy is based on manufacturing for example, transportation equipment, food processing, chemicals, printing and publishing, fabricated metals, as well as electrical machinery. Wilson's Creek National Battlefield, George Washington Carver National Monument and the Harry S. Truman and Ulysses S. Grant National Historic Sites and the 630-foot Gateway Arch in St. Louis bring many sightseers to the "Show Me" state.

Demonstrating its loyalty to the Union, the Missouri state flag adopted a red, white and blue design in 1913. The coat of arms, placed in the center of the flag, shows two grizzly bears symbolizing strength and bravery supporting a shield with additional references to the state and the Federal government. Twenty-four stars around the seal signify Missouri's position as the 24th state.

Jefferson City

Chosen as state capital in 1821 and named after the nation's third president, Jefferson City lies on the Missouri River. The Capitol building (1911–18) contains a number of finely painted murals by Thomas Hart Benton and N. C. Wyeth. The production of shoes, clothing, dairy products, and electrical appliances drives the local economy.

Missouri at a Glance

People	Missouri	USA
Population, 2003 estimate	5,704,484	290,809,777
Population percent change, April 1, 2000–July 1, 2001	0.6%	1.2%
Population, 2000	5,595,211	281,421,906
Persons under 5 years old, percent, 2000	6.6%	6.8%
Persons under 18 years old, percent, 2000	25.5%	25.7%
Persons 65 years old and over, percent, 2000	13.5%	12.4%
Female persons, percent, 2000	51.4%	50.9%
White persons, percent, 2000 (a)	84.9%	75.1%
African American persons, percent, 2000 (a)	11.2%	12.3%
Native American persons, percent, 2000 (a)	0.4%	0.9%
Asian persons, percent, 2000 (a)	1.1%	3.6%
Native Hawaiian and Other Pacific Islander, percent, 2000 (a)	0.1%	0.1%
Persons of Hispanic or Latino origin, percent, 2000 (b)	2.1%	12.5%
White persons, not of Hispanic/Latino origin, percent, 2000	83.8%	69.1%
Foreign born persons, percent, 2000	2.7%	11.1%
Language other than English spoken at home, percent age 5+, 2000	5.1%	17.9%
High school graduates, percent of persons age 25+, 2000	81.3%	80.4%
Bachelor's degree or higher, percent of persons age 25+, 2000	21.6%	24.4%
Persons with a disability, age 5+, 2000	973,637	49,746,248
Homeownership rate, 2000	70.3%	66.2%
Median value of owner-occupied housing units, 2000	$89,900	$119,600
Households, 2000	2,194,594	105,480,101
Persons per household, 2000	2.48	2.59
Median household money income, 1999	$37,934	$41,994
Per capita money income, 1999	$19,936	$21,587
Persons below poverty, percent, 1999	11.7%	12.4%

Business	Missouri	USA
Private nonfarm establishments, 1999	144,874	7,008,444
Private nonfarm employment, 1999	2,350,965	110,705,661
Private nonfarm employment, percent change 1990–99	16.8%	18.4%
Nonemployer establishments, 1999	310,678	16,152,604
Manufacturers shipments, 1997 ($1,000)	93,115,478	3,842,061,405
Retail sales, 1997 ($1,000)	51,269,881	2,460,886,012
Retail sales per capita, 1997	$9,482	$9,190
Minority-owned firms, percent of total, 1997	6.5%	14.6%
Women-owned firms, percent of total, 1997	25.2%	26.0%
Federal funds and grants, 2001 ($1,000)	39,190,881	1,763,896,019
Local government employment – full-time equivalent, 1997	201,609	10,227,429

Geography	Missouri	USA
Land area, 2000 (square miles)	68,886	3,537,438
Persons per square mile, 2000	81.2	79.6

(a) Includes persons reporting only one race.

(b) Hispanics may be of any race, so also are included in applicable race categories.

Z: Value greater than zero but less than half unit of measure shown.

Source: U.S. Census Bureau State & County QuickFacts

Montana

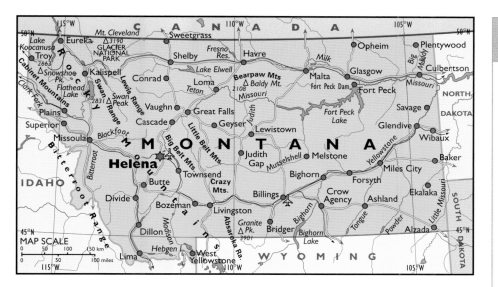

Statehood: November 8, 1889
Nickname: Treasure State
State bird: Western meadowlark
State flower: Bitterroot
State tree: Ponderosa pine
State motto: Oro y Plata (Gold and Silver)
State capital: Helena
Population of capital: 25,780 (2000)

Until the United States acquired this northwestern area in the Louisiana Purchase, Montana was relatively unexplored yet supported an array of indigenous cultures such as the Crow, Blackfoot, Cheyenne and Flathead. Although Lewis and Clark followed the Missouri River through the region en route to the Pacific Ocean in 1805, boomtowns did not appear until mid-century. The discovery of gold in 1852 brought a rush of immigrants and the Territory of Montana was organized in 1864. The opening of the Northern Pacific Railroad in 1883 provided a stimulus to further growth and development. With the exception of Billings, the other cities—Helena, Missoula and Great Falls—are concentrated in the west where some of the smallest of the 56 counties are also located.

The western section of Montana is dominated by dozens of mountain ranges, collectively called the Rocky Mountains, whereas the east is part of the Great Plains, drained by the Missouri and Yellowstone Rivers. Sheep and cattle are raised on the wide prairie (Big Sky Country), and the main crops: wheat, hay, barley, and sugar beet are grown in the same terrain using irrigation. The Rocky Mountains have large mineral deposits including copper, silver, gold, zinc, lead, and manganese. Oil, natural gas, and coal are found in the southeast. Industries include timber, food processing, and petroleum products but tourism is also important to the state economy. Yellowstone and Glacier National Park, as well as Custer Battlefield National

Monument lure millions of visitors to Montana's frontier.

Beneath the word Montana against a blue background, the image of mountain peaks and the Great Falls alludes to the state's remote terrain. The centralized seal also contains mining and farming implements together with the Spanish state motto: *Oro y plata.*

Helena

Dubbed Last Chance by prospecting settlers in about 1864, Helena's population by 1868 had grown to 7,500 and $16 million worth of gold had been mined in the surrounding area. In 1875 this city in the western part of the state was made the capital of the Montana Territory, becoming the state capital in 1889. Mineral smelting is still a prominent industry here alongside the production of consumer goods, concrete and sheet metal products.

Montana at a Glance

People	Montana	USA
Population, 2003 estimate	917,621	290,809,777
Population percent change, April 1, 2000–July 1, 2001	0.2%	1.2%
Population, 2000	902,195	281,421,906
Persons under 5 years old, percent, 2000	6.1%	6.8%
Persons under 18 years old, percent, 2000	25.5%	25.7%
Persons 65 years old and over, percent, 2000	13.4%	12.4%
Female persons, percent, 2000	50.2%	50.9%
White persons, percent, 2000 (a)	90.6%	75.1%
African American persons, percent, 2000 (a)	0.3%	12.3%
Native American persons, percent, 2000 (a)	6.2%	0.9%
Asian persons, percent, 2000 (a)	0.5%	3.6%
Native Hawaiian and Other Pacific Islander, percent, 2000 (a)	0.1%	0.1%
Persons of Hispanic or Latino origin, percent, 2000 (b)	2.0%	12.5%
White persons, not of Hispanic/Latino origin, percent, 2000	89.5%	69.1%
Foreign born persons, percent, 2000	1.8%	11.1%
Language other than English spoken at home, percent age 5+, 2000	5.2%	17.9%
High school graduates, percent of persons age 25+, 2000	87.2%	80.4%
Bachelor's degree or higher, percent of persons age 25+, 2000	24.4%	24.4%
Persons with a disability, age 5+, 2000	145,732	49,746,248
Homeownership rate, 2000	69.1%	66.2%
Median value of owner-occupied housing units, 2000	$99,500	$119,600
Households, 2000	358,667	105,480,101
Persons per household, 2000	2.45	2.59
Median household money income, 1999	$33,024	$41,994
Per capita money income, 1999	$17,151	$21,587
Persons below poverty, percent, 1999	14.6%	12.4%

Business	Montana	USA
Private nonfarm establishments, 1999	31,365	7,008,444
Private nonfarm employment, 1999	288,358	110,705,661
Private nonfarm employment, percent change 1990–99	30.0%	18.4%
Nonemployer establishments, 1999	69,327	16,152,604
Manufacturers shipments, 1997 ($1,000)	4,866,279	3,842,061,405
Retail sales, 1997 ($1,000)	7,779,112	2,460,886,012
Retail sales per capita, 1997	$8,853	$9,190
Minority-owned firms, percent of total, 1997	3.6%	14.6%
Women-owned firms, percent of total, 1997	23.9%	26.0%
Federal funds and grants, 2001 ($1,000)	6,617,863	1,763,896,019
Local government employment – full-time equivalent, 1997	32,676	10,227,429

Geography	Montana	USA
Land area, 2000 (square miles)	145,552	3,537,438
Persons per square mile, 2000	6.2	79.6

(a) Includes persons reporting only one race.

(b) Hispanics may be of any race, so also are included in applicable race categories.

Z: Value greater than zero but less than half unit of measure shown.

Source: U.S. Census Bureau State & County QuickFacts

Nebraska

Statehood: March 1, 1867
Nickname: The Cornhusker State
State bird: Western meadowlark
State flower: Goldenrod
State tree: Cottonwood
State motto: Equality before the law
State capital: Lincoln
Population of capital: 225,581 (2000)

This region was acquired under the Louisiana Purchase of 1803 and was unexplored until the Lewis and Clark Expedition passed through the Great Plains in 1804. The Oto Indian word for the Platte River, *nebrathka*, meaning "flat water" appeared in publications shortly before the territory of Nebraska was officially created. By the time admittance to the Union occurred in 1867, hundreds of thousands of pioneers were using the Oregon Trail to cross the state on their way west. Omaha, the largest city, and the majority of the total population have remained near the Missouri River, which forms the eastern border with Iowa and Missouri. A few of the 93 counties in Nebraska take their names from tribes like the Cheyenne and the Pawnee that once roamed the vast grasslands.

The land rises gradually from the east to the foothills of the Rocky Mountains in the west, and is drained chiefly by the Platte River, a tributary of the Missouri. The eastern half of the state is devoted to agriculture where farmers grow grain and raise cattle and pigs. Nebraska's economy is overwhelmingly agricultural. Industries include food processing, oil, and sand, gravel, and stone quarrying. The Homestead, Scotts Bluff and Agate Fossil Beds National Monuments, and Chimney Rock National Historic Site, visible from miles away, are the main landmarks.

The state seal of Nebraska, in gold, rests on the blue field of the flag adopted in 1925. Inside the seal, a steamboat ascending the Missouri River, a smith with hammer and anvil, a settler's cabin, sheaves of wheat and stalks of corn, and finally a train heading towards the Rocky Mountains in the background symbolize the mechanical arts, agriculture and transportation. The state motto floats above the scene.

Lincoln

Founded in 1856 as Lancaster, its name was changed in honor of Abraham Lincoln. The city was made state capital when Nebraska joined the Union in 1867 and it is currently the second-largest city in the state. Home to the University of Nebraska, Lincoln is a center for livestock and grain, and more recently, finance and insurance. Food processing, automotive part production and construction material manufacturing are among the key industries based in and around Lincoln.

Nebraska at a Glance

People	Nebraska	USA
Population, 2003 estimate	1,739,291	290,809,777
Population percent change, April 1, 2000–July 1, 2001	0.1%	1.2%
Population, 2000	1,711,263	281,421,906
Persons under 5 years old, percent, 2000	6.8%	6.8%
Persons under 18 years old, percent, 2000	26.3%	25.7%
Persons 65 years old and over, percent, 2000	13.6%	12.4%
Female persons, percent, 2000	50.7%	50.9%
White persons, percent, 2000 (a)	89.6%	75.1%
African American persons, percent, 2000 (a)	4.0%	12.3%
Native American persons, percent, 2000 (a)	0.9%	0.9%
Asian persons, percent, 2000 (a)	1.3%	3.6%
Native Hawaiian and Other Pacific Islander, percent, 2000 (a)	Z	0.1%
Persons of Hispanic or Latino origin, percent, 2000 (b)	5.5%	12.5%
White persons, not of Hispanic/Latino origin, percent, 2000	87.3%	69.1%
Foreign born persons, percent, 2000	4.4%	11.1%
Language other than English spoken at home, percent age 5+, 2000	7.9%	17.9%
High school graduates, percent of persons age 25+, 2000	86.6%	80.4%
Bachelor's degree or higher, percent of persons age 25+, 2000	23.7%	24.4%
Persons with a disability, age 5+, 2000	250,534	49,746,248
Homeownership rate, 2000	67.4%	66.2%
Median value of owner-occupied housing units, 2000	$88,000	$119,600
Households, 2000	666,184	105,480,101
Persons per household, 2000	2.49	2.59
Median household money income, 1999	$39,250	$41,994
Per capita money income, 1999	$19,613	$21,587
Persons below poverty, percent, 1999	9.7%	12.4%

Business	Nebraska	USA
Private nonfarm establishments, 1999	48,968	7,008,444
Private nonfarm employment, 1999	733,905	110,705,661
Private nonfarm employment, percent change 1990–99	25.0%	18.4%
Nonemployer establishments, 1999	102,137	16,152,604
Manufacturers shipments, 1997 ($1,000)	27,859,177	3,842,061,405
Retail sales, 1997 ($1,000)	16,529,333	2,460,886,012
Retail sales per capita, 1997	$9,981	$9,190
Minority-owned firms, percent of total, 1997	3.3%	14.6%
Women-owned firms, percent of total, 1997	24.1%	26.0%
Federal funds and grants, 2001 ($1,000)	10,771,411	1,763,896,019
Local government employment – full-time equivalent, 1997	75,377	10,227,429

Geography	Nebraska	USA
Land area, 2000 (square miles)	76,872	3,537,438
Persons per square mile, 2000	22.3	79.6

(a) Includes persons reporting only one race.
(b) Hispanics may be of any race, so also are included in applicable race categories.
Z: Value greater than zero but less than half unit of measure shown.

Source: U.S. Census Bureau State & County QuickFacts

Nevada

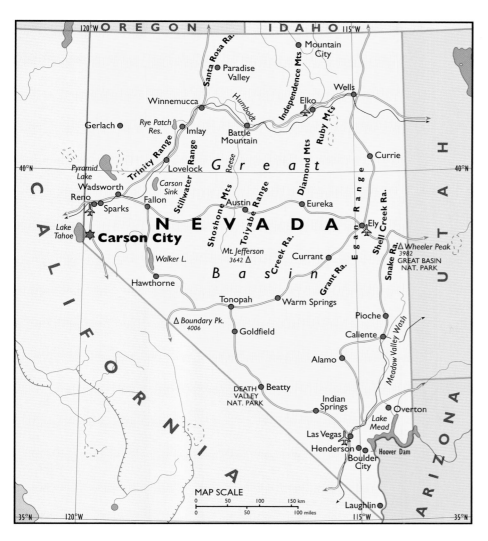

The United States acquired this western region in 1848 at the end of the Mexican War. When gold and silver were found in 1859, settlers flocked to the mountainous terrain inhabited by the Shoshone, Paiute and Washoe Indians. Nevada became the 36th state five years later. Mormon Station (now Genoa) just across the California border was the first permanent town, yet Las Vegas and Reno have evolved into the most populous cities since the legalization of gambling. Sixteen counties and the independent capital make up the state's administrative divisions.

Much of the state lies in the Great Basin, but the Sierra Nevada chain rises steeply from its western edge. Despite the Oasis created by Lake Mead in the southeast, Nevada's extremely dry climate and steep slopes have hindered the development of an agricultural economy. Hay and alfalfa are principal crops, sheep and cattle grazing are also important to the farming sector and additional wealth comes from mineral deposits of copper, lead, silver, gold, zinc, and tungsten. In Las Vegas and Reno, gambling and tourism provide the biggest source of revenue. Other less significant industries include chemicals, timber, electrical machinery, and glass products. In addition to glittering casinos, visitors are drawn to Nevada to see Lake Tahoe, the Hoover Dam, Great Basin National Park, and dusty, lonely ghost towns.

Nevada's blue flag displays a simple silver star, above which the words "Battle Born" allude to its entrance into the Union during the Civil War. The flag was adopted in 1929 and also depicts a half wreath of sagebrush, the state flower.

Carson City

The capital of Nevada, located south of Reno, grew rapidly after silver was discovered at the Comstock Lode in 1859. Nestled between Lake Tahoe and the Pine Nut Mountains, Carson City was named for Kit Carson, a legendary scout and frontiersman. Gambling is the main industry.

Nevada at a Glance

People	Nevada	USA
Population, 2003 estimate	2,241,154	290,809,777
Population percent change,		
April 1, 2000–July 1, 2001	5.4%	1.2%
Population, 2000	1,998,257	281,421,906
Persons under 5 years old, percent, 2000	7.3%	6.8%
Persons under 18 years old, percent, 2000	25.6%	25.7%
Persons 65 years old and over, percent, 2000	11.0%	12.4%
Female persons, percent, 2000	49.1%	50.9%
White persons, percent, 2000 (a)	75.2%	75.1%
African American persons,		
percent, 2000 (a)	6.8%	12.3%
Native American persons,		
percent, 2000 (a)	1.3%	0.9%
Asian persons, percent, 2000 (a)	4.5%	3.6%
Native Hawaiian and Other Pacific Islander,		
percent, 2000 (a)	0.4%	0.1%
Persons of Hispanic or Latino origin,		
percent, 2000 (b)	19.7%	12.5%
White persons, not of Hispanic/Latino origin,		
percent, 2000	65.2%	69.1%
Foreign born persons, percent, 2000	15.8%	11.1%
Language other than English spoken at home,		
percent age 5+, 2000	23.1%	17.9%
High school graduates, percent of persons		
age 25+, 2000	80.7%	80.4%
Bachelor's degree or higher,		
percent of persons age 25+, 2000	18.2%	24.4%
Persons with a disability, age 5+, 2000	375,910	49,746,248
Homeownership rate, 2000	60.9%	66.2%
Median value of owner-occupied		
housing units, 2000	$142,000	$119,600
Households, 2000	751,165	105,480,101
Persons per household, 2000	2.62	2.59
Median household money income, 1999	$44,581	$41,994
Per capita money income, 1999	$21,989	$21,587
Persons below poverty, percent, 1999	10.5%	12.4%

Business	Nevada	USA
Private nonfarm establishments, 1999	46,890	7,008,444
Private nonfarm employment, 1999	854,358	110,705,661
Private nonfarm employment,		
percent change 1990–99	59.2%	18.4%
Nonemployer establishments, 1999	106,416	16,152,604
Manufacturers shipments, 1997 ($1,000)	6,361,782	3,842,061,405
Retail sales, 1997 ($1,000)	18,220,790	2,460,886,012
Retail sales per capita, 1997	$10,874	$9,190
Minority-owned firms, percent of total, 1997	11.7%	14.6%
Women-owned firms, percent of total, 1997	25.7%	26.0%
Federal funds and grants, 2001 ($1,000)	9,623,557	1,763,896,019
Local government employment –		
full-time equivalent, 1997	56,607	10,227,429

Geography	Nevada	USA
Land area, 2000 (square miles)	109,826	3,537,438
Persons per square mile, 2000	18.2	79.6

(a) Includes persons reporting only one race.

(b) Hispanics may be of any race, so also are included in applicable race categories.

Z: Value greater than zero but less than half unit of measure shown.

Source: U.S. Census Bureau State & County QuickFacts

New Hampshire

Statehood: June 21, 1788
Nickname: The Granite State
State bird: Purple finch
State flower: Purple lilac
State tree: White birch
State motto: Live free or die
State capital: Concord
Population of capital: 40,687 (2000)

The first settlements in New Hampshire were made in 1623, along its small coastline. Early colonists interacted with the Pennacook and Abenaki tribes who relied on ocean resources for their way of life. Shipbuilding, weaving and granite mining brought the state considerable wealth in the 18th and 19th centuries and the beautifully restored mansions in the southeast reflect this prosperous period. In a state with just ten counties, Manchester and Nashua in the south are the largest cities.

Much of the land is mountainous and forested. Mount Washington, the tallest peak in the White Mountains, is known for its fierce winds, which have been recorded at speeds of over 200 miles per hour. The principal rivers are the Connecticut, which forms the border with Vermont, and the Merrimack, fed by countless smaller tributaries and more than 1,000 lakes. Characteristic of the northeast, farming is restricted by poor, stony soil and is mostly concentrated in the Connecticut Valley. Dairy and garden produce, hay, apples, and potatoes are the chief agricultural products. New Hampshire was formerly highly industrialized and relies on some hydroelectric power. Industries include electrical

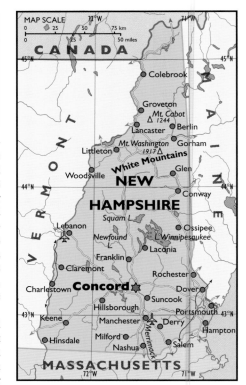

machinery, paper and wood products, printing and publishing, leather goods, and textiles. The Green Mountain Railroad, the Saint-Gaudens National Historic Site, and Canterbury Shaker Village encourage tourists to explore the history of the Granite State.

Surrounded by a wreath of laurel leaves and nine stars symbolizing its place as the 9th state to enter the United States, the seal appears in the center of the blue New Hampshire flag. Adopted in 1909, the centralized seal shows the frigate *Raleigh*, built at Portsmouth in 1776, one of the first 13 warships the Continental Congress commissioned for a new American navy.

Concord

Founded as a trading post on the Merrimack River, Concord was settled in 1727. It was the scene of New Hampshire's ratification of the Constitution as the ninth and deciding state in June of 1788, and designated state capital in 1808. Quarries north of the city produced the white granite used for the construction of the Library of Congress in Washington, D.C. and the Museum of Modern Art in New York City. A center for insurance and metal manufacturing, its industries include electrical equipment, publishing and printing.

New Hampshire at a Glance

People	New Hampshire	USA
Population, 2003 estimate	1,287,687	290,809,777
Population percent change, April 1, 2000–July 1, 2001	1.9%	1.2%
Population, 2000	1,235,786	281,421,906
Persons under 5 years old, percent, 2000	6.1%	6.8%
Persons under 18 years old, percent, 2000	25.0%	25.7%
Persons 65 years old and over, percent, 2000	12.0%	12.4%
Female persons, percent, 2000	50.8%	50.9%
White persons, percent, 2000 (a)	96.0%	75.1%
African American persons, percent, 2000 (a)	0.7%	12.3%
Native American persons, percent, 2000 (a)	0.2%	0.9%
Asian persons, percent, 2000 (a)	1.3%	3.6%
Native Hawaiian and Other Pacific Islander, percent, 2000 (a)	Z	0.1%
Persons of Hispanic or Latino origin, percent, 2000 (b)	1.7%	12.5%
White persons, not of Hispanic/Latino origin, percent, 2000	95.1%	69.1%
Foreign born persons, percent, 2000	4.4%	11.1%
Language other than English spoken at home, percent age 5+, 2000	8.3%	17.9%
High school graduates, percent of persons age 25+, 2000	87.4%	80.4%
Bachelor's degree or higher, percent of persons age 25+, 2000	28.7%	24.4%
Persons with a disability, age 5+, 2000	193,893	49,746,248
Homeownership rate, 2000	69.7%	66.2%
Median value of owner-occupied housing units, 2000	$133,300	$119,600
Households, 2000	474,606	105,480,101
Persons per household, 2000	2.53	2.59
Median household money income, 1999	$49,467	$41,994
Per capita money income, 1999	$23,844	$21,587
Persons below poverty, percent, 1999	6.5%	12.4%

Business	New Hampshire	USA
Private nonfarm establishments, 1999	37,180	7,008,444
Private nonfarm employment, 1999	528,902	110,705,661
Private nonfarm employment, percent change 1990–99	20.3%	18.4%
Nonemployer establishments, 1999	86,589	16,152,604
Manufacturers shipments, 1997 ($1,000)	19,813,107	3,842,061,405
Retail sales, 1997 ($1,000)	15,812,027	2,460,886,012
Retail sales per capita, 1997	$13,477	$9,190
Minority-owned firms, percent of total, 1997	2.8%	14.6%
Women-owned firms, percent of total, 1997	23.6%	26.0%
Federal funds and grants, 2001 ($1,000)	6,313,708	1,763,896,019
Local government employment – full-time equivalent, 1997	38,830	10,227,429

Geography	New Hampshire	USA
Land area, 2000 (square miles)	8,968	3,537,438
Persons per square mile, 2000	137.8	79.6

(a) Includes persons reporting only one race.

(b) Hispanics may be of any race, so also are included in applicable race categories.

Z: Value greater than zero but less than half unit of measure shown.

Source: U.S. Census Bureau State & County QuickFacts

New Jersey

Statehood: December 18, 1787
Nickname: The Garden State
State bird: Eastern goldfinch
State flower: Purple violet
State tree: Red oak
State motto: Liberty and Prosperity
State capital: Trenton
Population of capital: 85,403 (2000)

Settlement of New Jersey, ancestral home of the Leni-Lenape Indians, began in the 1620s, when the Dutch founded the colony of New Netherland (later New York) on the Atlantic coast. In 1664, the British acquired the territory from the Netherlands, and separated the land between the Hudson and Delaware Rivers, naming it after the island of Jersey in the English Channel. The third state to ratify the Constitution in 1787, New Jersey introduced the world to the first steam-powered locomotive, the electric telegraph, the boardwalk, the picture postcard and the incandescent electric bulb. Divided into 21 counties, the state currently has one of the highest population densities in the U.S. with the majority of its citizens living in urban areas such as Newark, Elizabeth, Jersey City, and Paterson.

The Kittatinny Mountains in the north of the state form part of the Appalachian highland region and southeast of the Appalachians lie the fertile Piedmont plains. Pine and oak forests, cedar swamps and marshes characterize the southernmost section of the state. More than half of the state is coastal plain and the white sandy beaches of its barrier islands beckon vacationers each summer. The agricultural economy relies on a variety of crops as well as cattle and poultry raising. New Jersey is overwhelmingly industrial, however, and chemicals, pharmaceuticals, rubber goods, textiles, electronic equipment, missile components, copper smelting, and oil refining number among the most important industries. Principal landmarks include the Delaware Water Gap, Edison National Historic Site, Morristown National Historic Park, and Pinelands National Reserve.

A variation of the state seal, the flag was adopted in 1896 and displays the coat of arms against a buff background. Three plows on the shield in the center symbolize agriculture, as does the horse head above. Ceres, the Roman goddess of grain, holding a cornucopia, and Liberty, carrying the liberty cap on her staff, stand on either side of the shield. The helmet denotes New Jersey's sovereignty and the banner beneath the coat of arms bears the year of independence along with the state motto.

Trenton

Located on the Delaware River, the state capital was first settled by English Quakers in the 1670s. The city takes its name from William Trent, a wealthy colonial merchant who became New Jersey's first Chief Justice in 1723. A monument in Trenton commemorates the 1776 battle in which George Washington crossed the frozen Delaware River to defeat Hessian troops during the American Revolution. Once thriving industries include ceramics, automobile parts, plastics, metal products, rubber goods, and textiles.

New Jersey at a Glance

People	New Jersey	USA
Population, 2003 estimate	8,638,396	290,809,777
Population percent change,		
April 1, 2000–July 1, 2001	0.8%	1.2%
Population, 2000	8,414,350	281,421,906
Persons under 5 years old, percent, 2000	6.7%	6.8%
Persons under 18 years old, percent, 2000	24.8%	25.7%
Persons 65 years old and over, percent, 2000	13.2%	12.4%
Female persons, percent, 2000	51.5%	50.9%
White persons, percent, 2000 (a)	72.6%	75.1%
African American persons,		
percent, 2000 (a)	13.6%	12.3%
Native American persons,		
percent, 2000 (a)	0.2%	0.9%
Asian persons, percent, 2000 (a)	5.7%	3.6%
Native Hawaiian and Other Pacific Islander,		
percent, 2000 (a)	Z	0.1%
Persons of Hispanic or Latino origin,		
percent, 2000 (b)	13.3%	12.5%
White persons, not of Hispanic/Latino origin,		
percent, 2000	66.0%	69.1%
Foreign born persons, percent, 2000	17.5%	11.1%
Language other than English spoken at home,		
percent age 5+, 2000	25.5%	17.9%
High school graduates, percent of persons		
age 25+, 2000	82.1%	80.4%
Bachelor's degree or higher,		
percent of persons age 25+, 2000	29.8%	24.4%
Persons with a disability, age 5+, 2000	1,389,811	49,746,248
Homeownership rate, 2000	65.6%	66.2%
Median value of owner-occupied		
housing units, 2000	$170,800	$119,600
Households, 2000	3,064,645	105,480,101
Persons per household, 2000	2.68	2.59
Median household money income, 1999	$55,146	$41,994
Per capita money income, 1999	$27,006	$21,587
Persons below poverty, percent, 1999	8.5%	12.4%

Business	New Jersey	USA
Private nonfarm establishments, 1999	231,823	7,008,444
Private nonfarm employment, 1999	3,440,721	110,705,661
Private nonfarm employment,		
percent change 1990–99	6.8%	18.4%
Nonemployer establishments, 1999	471,485	16,152,604
Manufacturers shipments, 1997 ($1,000)	97,060,800	3,842,061,405
Retail sales, 1997 ($1,000)	79,914,892	2,460,886,012
Retail sales per capita, 1997	$9,922	$9,190
Minority-owned firms, percent of total, 1997	15.6%	14.6%
Women-owned firms, percent of total, 1997	23.7%	26.0%
Federal funds and grants, 2001 ($1,000)	46,239,529	1,763,896,019
Local government employment –		
full-time equivalent, 1997	298,363	10,227,429

Geography	New Jersey	USA
Land area, 2000 (square miles)	7,417	3,537,438
Persons per square mile, 2000	1,134.4	79.6

(a) Includes persons reporting only one race.
(b) Hispanics may be of any race, so also are included in applicable race categories.
Z: Value greater than zero but less than half unit of measure shown.

Source: U.S. Census Bureau State & County QuickFacts

New Mexico

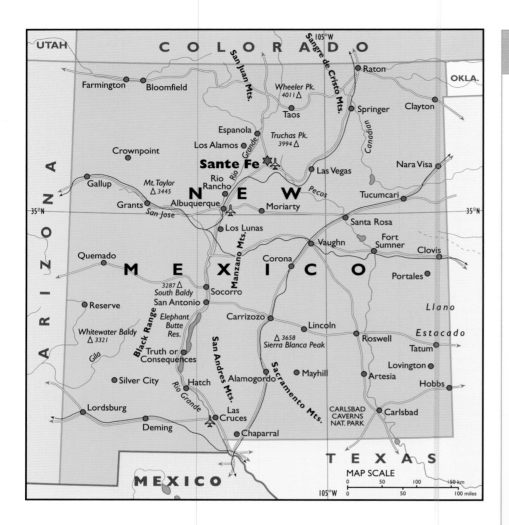

Soon after Francisco Coronado crossed into present-day New Mexico in 1540, the first permanent Spanish settlers followed suit, competing with Navajo, Apache, Zuni, and Kiowa tribes for land. The U.S. acquired this southwestern region with the Mexican Cession and the Texas annexation, adding the last piece with the Gadsden Purchase in 1853. In 1912, New Mexico entered the Union as the 47th state. Heavily involved in energy research, the first atomic bomb was detonated near Alamogordo in 1945. Although Santa Fe gained its foothold in the north before Albuquerque, the metropolis on the river has surpassed the population of the capital city. Thirty-two counties divide the state.

The Sangre de Cristo and the Sierra Nacimiento Mountains in the north flank the Río Grande, which runs north to south through the state. Semiarid plains typify the south and southwest and the remaining terrain includes colorful desert, forested mountains, and stark mesa. The Pecos and Río Grande Rivers provide irrigation for fields of cotton, hay, and wheat. Dairy produce and chili peppers are also rather important to agriculture. A large proportion of the state's wealth comes from mineral deposits, including uranium, manganese, copper, silver, turquoise, oil, coal, and natural gas. Carlsbad Caverns National Park and Chaco Culture National Historic Park are perennially fascinating destinations for tourists.

Adopted in 1925, the New Mexico state flag borrows its red and yellow colors from Spain and the sun symbol from the Zia people. Four groups of four rays represent the cardinal directions, the seasons, the hours of the day, and the stages of life.

Santa Fe

The oldest capital city in the country, Santa Fe was founded at the foot of the Sangre de Cristo Mountains circa 1609 by the Spanish, and served as a center of trade for more than 200 years. Mexico's independence in 1821 opened trade with the United States and the city functioned as the western terminus of the Santa Fe Trail. In 1846, U.S. troops captured the city, and in 1850 the region became an official territory. Today, it is primarily an administrative, tourist, and resort center.

New Mexico at a Glance

People	New Mexico	USA
Population, 2003 estimate	1,874,614	290,809,777
Population percent change, April 1, 2000–July 1, 2001	0.6%	1.2%
Population, 2000	1,819,046	281,421,906
Persons under 5 years old, percent, 2000	7.2%	6.8%
Persons under 18 years old, percent, 2000	28.0%	25.7%
Persons 65 years old and over, percent, 2000	11.7%	12.4%
Female persons, percent, 2000	50.8%	50.9%
White persons, percent, 2000 (a)	66.8%	75.1%
African American persons, percent, 2000 (a)	1.9%	12.3%
Native American persons, percent, 2000 (a)	9.5%	0.9%
Asian persons, percent, 2000 (a)	1.1%	3.6%
Native Hawaiian and Other Pacific Islander, percent, 2000 (a)	0.1%	0.1%
Persons of Hispanic or Latino origin, percent, 2000 (b)	42.1%	12.5%
White persons, not of Hispanic/Latino origin, percent, 2000	44.7%	69.1%
Foreign born persons, percent, 2000	8.2%	11.1%
Language other than English spoken at home, percent age 5+, 2000	36.5%	17.9%
High school graduates, percent of persons age 25+, 2000	78.9%	80.4%
Bachelor's degree or higher, percent of persons age 25+, 2000	23.5%	24.4%
Persons with a disability, age 5+, 2000	338,430	49,746,248
Homeownership rate, 2000	70.0%	66.2%
Median value of owner-occupied housing units, 2000	$108,100	$119,600
Households, 2000	677,971	105,480,101
Persons per household, 2000	2.63	2.59
Median household money income, 1999	$34,133	$41,994
Per capita money income, 1999	$17,261	$21,587
Persons below poverty, percent, 1999	18.4%	12.4%

Business	New Mexico	USA
Private nonfarm establishments, 1999	42,918	7,008,444
Private nonfarm employment, 1999	541,386	110,705,661
Private nonfarm employment, percent change 1990–99	29.5%	18.4%
Nonemployer establishments, 1999	99,319	16,152,604
Manufacturers shipments, 1997 ($1,000)	17,906,091	3,842,061,405
Retail sales, 1997 ($1,000)	14,984,454	2,460,886,012
Retail sales per capita, 1997	$8,697	$9,190
Minority-owned firms, percent of total, 1997	28.5%	14.6%
Women-owned firms, percent of total, 1997	29.4%	26.0%
Federal funds and grants, 2001 ($1,000)	16,586,876	1,763,896,019
Local government employment – fulltime equivalent, 1997	69,941	10,227,429

Geography	New Mexico	USA
Land area, 2000 (square miles)	121,356	3,537,438
Persons per square mile, 2000	15	79.6

(a) Includes persons reporting only one race.

(b) Hispanics may be of any race, so also are included in applicable race categories.

Z: Value greater than zero but less than half unit of measure shown.

Source: U.S. Census Bureau State & County QuickFacts

New York

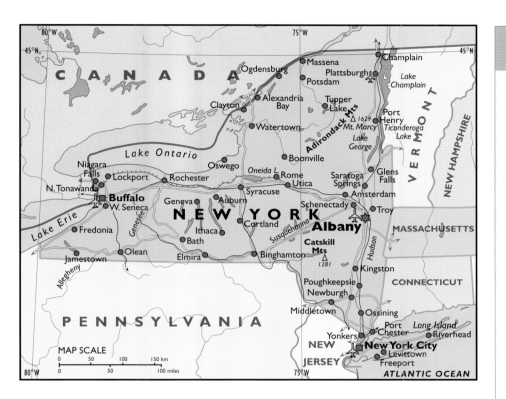

Statehood: July 26, 1788
Nickname: The Empire State
State bird: Bluebird
State flower: Rose
State tree: Sugar maple
State motto: Ever upward
State capital: Albany
Population of capital: 95,658 (2000)

Although Giovanni da Verrazano sailed past Manhattan Island in 1524, Henry Hudson explored New York Bay, and in 1609 sailed up the river that now bears his name. The Dutch established New Netherland colony in the Hudson Valley, but in 1664, this Algonquin and Iroquois land bounded by Canada, the Great Lakes and the Atlantic Ocean was seized by the British and renamed for the duke of York, eventually becoming one of the original Thirteen Colonies. The opening of the Erie Canal in 1825 was an enormous stimulus to New York's growth. New York City is by far the largest city in this state of 62 counties.

Much of the state is mountainous, the Adirondacks in the northeast and the Catskills in the southeast being the principal ranges. The west consists of the rolling Appalachian Plateau sloping down to Lake Ontario and the St. Lawrence River Valley. The Hudson and its tributary, the Mohawk, are the chief rivers. Throughout the history of the United States, New York's economic strength and large population have given it great influence in national affairs and for a time made it the leading manufacturing and commercial state in the country. Agricultural production concentrates on cattle, fruit and vegetable farming. Industries include clothing, chemicals, processed foods, communications, finance, advertising and publishing.

The coat of arms appears on the state flag against a dark blue background. Liberty and Justice flank a shield that bears an image of the sun rising over the Hudson. The eagle resting on a globe above the shield represents the western hemisphere and the crown at the feet of Liberty denotes independence from the English throne.

Albany

The Dutch settled here along the Hudson River in 1614 and Albany replaced New York as state capital in 1797. An administrative center with fine old buildings, it developed in the 1820s with the building of the Erie Canal, linking it to the Great Lakes, and remains an important river port. The largest industries are paper, brewing, machine tools, metal products, and textiles.

New York at a Glance

People	New York	USA
Population, 2003 estimate	19,190,115	290,809,777
Population percent change, April 1, 2000–July 1, 2001	0.2%	1.2%
Population, 2000	18,976,457	281,421,906
Persons under 5 years old, percent, 2000	6.5%	6.8%
Persons under 18 years old, percent, 2000	24.7%	25.7%
Persons 65 years old and over, percent, 2000	12.9%	12.4%
Female persons, percent, 2000	51.8%	50.9%
White persons, percent, 2000 (a)	67.9%	75.1%
African American persons, percent, 2000 (a)	15.9%	12.3%
Native American persons, percent, 2000 (a)	0.4%	0.9%
Asian persons, percent, 2000 (a)	5.5%	3.6%
Native Hawaiian and Other Pacific Islander, percent, 2000 (a)	Z	0.1%
Persons of Hispanic or Latino origin, percent, 2000 (b)	15.1%	12.5%
White persons, not of Hispanic/Latino origin, percent, 2000	62.0%	69.1%
Foreign born persons, percent, 2000	20.4%	11.1%
Language other than English spoken at home, percent age 5+, 2000	28.0%	17.9%
High school graduates, percent of persons age 25+, 2000	79.1%	80.4%
Bachelor's degree or higher, percent of persons age 25+, 2000	27.4%	24.4%
Persons with a disability, age 5+, 2000	3,606,147	49,746,248
Homeownership rate, 2000	53.0%	66.2%
Median value of owner-occupied housing units, 2000	$148,700	$119,600
Households, 2000	7,056,860	105,480,101
Persons per household, 2000	2.61	2.59
Median household money income, 1999	$43,393	$41,994
Per capita money income, 1999	$23,389	$21,587
Persons below poverty, percent, 1999	14.6%	12.4%

Business	New York	USA
Private nonfarm establishments, 1999	485,954	7,008,444
Private nonfarm employment, 1999	7,135,960	110,705,661
Private nonfarm employment, percent change 1990–99	0.9%	18.4%
Nonemployer establishments, 1999	1,168,595	16,152,604
Manufacturers shipments, 1997 ($1,000)	146,720,195	3,842,061,405
Retail sales, 1997 ($1,000)	139,303,944	2,460,886,012
Retail sales per capita, 1997	$7,678	$9,190
Minority-owned firms, percent of total, 1997	19.6%	14.6%
Women-owned firms, percent of total, 1997	26.1%	26.0%
Federal funds and grants, 2001 ($1,000)	116,366,112	1,763,896,019
Local government employment – full-time equivalent, 1997	860,168	10,227,429

Geography	New York	USA
Land area, 2000 (square miles)	47,214	3,537,438
Persons per square mile, 2000	401.9	79.6

(a) Includes persons reporting only one race.
(b) Hispanics may be of any race, so also are included in applicable race categories.
Z: Value greater than zero but less than half unit of measure shown.

Source: U.S. Census Bureau State & County QuickFacts

North Carolina

Statehood: November 21, 1789
Nickname: The Tar Heel State
State bird: Cardinal
State flower: Flowering dogwood
State tree: Pine
State motto: To be, rather than to seem
State capital: Raleigh
Population of capital: 276,093 (2000)

The first English colony in North America was founded in 1585 on Roanoke Island off the Atlantic coast of the eastern seaboard. Thwarted by a resistant native population, a second group of colonists had mysteriously disappeared by the time a supply ship returned in 1590 and permanent settlers did not move into the region from Virginia until the 1650s. Finally subduing the Tuscarora and Roanoke Indians, among others, North Carolina was the 12th state to join the Union and the last state to secede. Coincidentally, brothers Wilbur and Orville Wright found success not far from this failed community, and watched as their flyer, the first powered aircraft, took flight in December of 1903 in Kitty Hawk. Charlotte, Winston-Salem, Greensboro, Wilmington and the Research Triangle encompassing Durham, Chapel Hill and Raleigh are the largest urban areas. The pine forests that still cover many of the state's 100 counties produced large quantities of tar, pitch and turpentine, as well as the unusual nickname.

North Carolina's low-lying coastal plain is characterized by swamps and forested dunes. Its hilly western edge rises steadily towards the Tennessee border to form the highest mountain ranges in the eastern U.S., the Blue Ridge and Great Smoky Mountains. The leading producer of tobacco in the U.S., North Carolina farms also raise corn, soybeans, peanuts, pigs, turkeys and chickens. Industries include textiles, timber, fishing, tourism, electrical machinery, and chemicals. Mineral resources include phosphate, feldspar, mica and kaolin. Beaches along the Outer Banks, Cape Hatteras and

Cape Lookout National Seashores, along with Blue Ridge National Parkway, Old Salem and Biltmore, the largest private home in the country, encourage tourism in North Carolina.

The two dates on the red, white and blue state flag adopted in 1885 display two declarations of independence. Above the white star is a gilt scroll reading May 20, 1775, when Mecklenberg County declared its independence from Great Britain. On April 12, 1776, North Carolina voted for independence at the Constitutional Convention.

Raleigh

Founded in the east central part of the state in 1792 as the capital, Raleigh was named for Sir Walter Raleigh, the poet, courtier and adventurer who fought against the Spanish Armada after colony on Roanoke Island failed. Historically at the center of the cotton and tobacco trade, its modern industries include food processing, textiles, chemicals, and electronic equipment. A number of colleges and universities cluster in and around Raleigh.

North Carolina at a Glance

People	North Carolina	USA
Population, 2003 estimate	8,407,248	290,809,777
Population percent change, April 1, 2000–July 1, 2001	1.7%	1.2%
Population, 2000	8,049,313	281,421,906
Persons under 5 years old, percent, 2000	6.7%	6.8%
Persons under 18 years old, percent, 2000	24.4%	25.7%
Persons 65 years old and over, percent, 2000	12.0%	12.4%
Female persons, percent, 2000	51.0%	50.9%
White persons, percent, 2000 (a)	72.1%	75.1%
African American persons, percent, 2000 (a)	21.6%	12.3%
Native American persons, percent, 2000 (a)	1.2%	0.9%
Asian persons, percent, 2000 (a)	1.4%	3.6%
Native Hawaiian and Other Pacific Islander, percent, 2000 (a)	Z	0.1%
Persons of Hispanic or Latino origin, percent, 2000 (b)	4.7%	12.5%
White persons, not of Hispanic/Latino origin, percent, 2000	70.2%	69.1%
Foreign born persons, percent, 2000	5.3%	11.1%
Language other than English spoken at home, percent age 5+, 2000	8.0%	17.9%
High school graduates, percent of persons age 25+, 2000	78.1%	80.4%
Bachelor's degree or higher, percent of persons age 25+, 2000	22.5%	24.4%
Persons with a disability, age 5+, 2000	1,540,365	49,746,248
Homeownership rate, 2000	69.4%	66.2%
Median value of owner-occupied housing units, 2000	$108,300	$119,600
Households, 2000	3,132,013	105,480,101
Persons per household, 2000	2.49	2.59
Median household money income, 1999	$39,184	$41,994
Per capita money income, 1999	$20,307	$21,587
Persons below poverty, percent, 1999	12.3%	12.4%

Business	North Carolina	USA
Private nonfarm establishments, 1999	201,706	7,008,444
Private nonfarm employment, 1999	3,324,155	110,705,661
Private nonfarm employment, percent change 1990–99	24.1%	18.4%
Nonemployer establishments, 1999	445,159	16,152,604
Manufacturers shipments, 1997 ($1,000)	161,900,477	3,842,061,405
Retail sales, 1997 ($1,000)	72,356,763	2,460,886,012
Retail sales per capita, 1997	$9,740	$9,190
Minority-owned firms, percent of total, 1997	10.8%	14.6%
Women-owned firms, percent of total, 1997	24.5%	26.0%
Federal funds and grants, 2001 ($1,000)	44,557,095	1,763,896,019
Local government employment – full-time equivalent, 1997	293,505	10,227,429

Geography	North Carolina	USA
Land area, 2000 (square miles)	48,711	3,537,438
Persons per square mile, 2000	165.2	79.6

(a) Includes persons reporting only one race.
(b) Hispanics may be of any race, so also are included in applicable race categories.
Z: Value greater than zero but less than half unit of measure shown.

Source: U.S. Census Bureau State & County QuickFacts

North Dakota & South Dakota

North Dakota   South Dakota

Statehood: November 2, 1889
Nickname: The Flickertail State
State bird: Western meadowlark
State flower: Wild prairie rose
State tree: American elm
State motto: Liberty and union, now and
          forever, one and inseparable
State capital: Bismarck
Population of capital: 55,532 (2000)

Statehood: November 2, 1889
Nickname: The Sunshine State
State bird: Ring-necked pheasant
State flower: American pasqueflower
State tree: Black Hills spruce
State motto: Under God the people rule
State capital: Pierre
Population of capital: 13,876 (2000)

French explorers first ventured into the northern territory occupied by the Mandan, Hidatsa, Arikara and Sioux (Dakota) tribes in 1738. The United States acquired the western half of the area from France in the Louisiana Purchase, and the rest from Britain in 1818, when the boundary with Canada was fixed. Dakota was later divided into North and South Dakota, which both entered the Union in 1889. Fargo and Grand Forks, both just across the Minnesota state line, are the largest cities. North Dakota is divided into 53 counties. The region is low-lying and drained by the Missouri and Red Rivers. The most prominent geographical feature however is the windswept Badlands in the western part of the state. Wheat, barley, rye, oats, sunflowers, and flaxseed are the chief crops. Cattle raising, as well as coal, petroleum, and natural gas mining are key important economic activities.

Bismarck

Bismarck, overlooking the Missouri River, originated in the 1830s, became a distribution center for grain and cattle and was later an important stop on the Northern Pacific Railroad. By borrowing the name of the German Chancellor, residents hoped to attract German capital to use in railroad construction. Livestock raising, dairying, and woodworking are the largest employers. The University of Mary and Bismarck State College are also here, adding to the population.

French trappers claimed this region on the northern Plains for France in the 1740s, and the U.S. acquired part of the land in 1803. The Dakota Territory was formed in 1861 and in 1874, the discovery of gold in the Black Hills led to an increase in population, subsequently causing the territory to be divided into two states. In 1890, the war that pitted Sioux and Cheyenne against the U.S. Army came to an end at Wounded Knee. Partitioned into 66 counties, today the largest populations can be found in Sioux Falls and Rapid City. The land rises gradually from the east to the Black Hills (featuring Mount Rushmore) in the west and the Badlands in the southwest, with the Missouri River bisecting the state. One-fifth of the area west of the Missouri River is semiarid plain, mostly covered by Native American Reservations, while the remainder is divided into large cattle and sheep ranches. Agriculture is a dominant economic activity; major crops include wheat, corn, oats, sunflowers and soybeans. The largest producer of gold in the country, South Dakota also mines tin, beryllium, stone, sand, and gravel. Industry is concentrated in meat-packing and food processing.

Pierre

Originally the capital of the Aricara Indians, and also on the Missouri River opposite Fort Pierre, Pierre started as a trading post in the early 19th century before being converted into a railroad terminus in 1880. It became the permanent state capital in 1904 and its economy is based on government services and agriculture.

The Dakotas at a Glance

People	ND	SD	USA
Population, 2003 estimate	633,837	764,309	290,809,777
Population percent change,			
April 1, 2000–July 1, 2001	–1.2%	0.2%	1.2%
Population, 2000	642,200	754,844	281,421,906
Persons under 5 years old, percent, 2000	6.1%	6.8%	6.8%
Persons under 18 years old, percent, 2000	25.0%	26.8%	25.7%
Persons 65 years old and over, percent, 2000	14.7%	14.3%	12.4%
Female persons, percent, 2000	50.1%	50.4%	50.9%
White persons, percent, 2000 (a)	92.4%	88.7%	75.1%
African American persons,			
percent, 2000 (a)	0.6%	0.6%	12.3%
Native American persons,			
percent, 2000 (a)	4.9%	8.3%	0.9%
Asian persons, percent, 2000 (a)	0.6%	0.6%	3.6%
Native Hawaiian and Other Pacific Islander,			
percent, 2000 (a)	Z	Z	0.1%
Persons of Hispanic or Latino origin,			
percent, 2000 (b)	1.2%	1.4%	12.5%
White persons, not of Hispanic/Latino origin,			
percent, 2000	91.7%	88.0%	69.1%
Foreign born persons, percent, 2000	1.9%	1.8%	11.1%
Language other than English spoken at home,			
percent age 5+, 2000	6.3%	6.5%	17.9%
High school graduates, percent of persons			
age 25+, 2000	83.9%	84.6%	80.4%
Bachelor's degree or higher,			
percent of persons age 25+, 2000	22.0%	21.5%	24.4%
Persons with a disability, age 5+, 2000	97,817	114,619	49,746,248
Homeownership rate, 2000	66.6%	68.2%	66.2%
Median value of owner-occupied			
housing units, 2000	$74,400	$79,600	$119,600
Households, 2000	257,152	290,245	105,480,101
Persons per household, 2000	2.41	2.5	2.59
Median household money income, 1999	$34,604	$35,282	$41,994
Per capita money income, 1999	$17,769	$17,562	$21,587
Persons below poverty, percent, 1999	11.9%	13.2%	12.4%

Business	ND	SD	USA
Private nonfarm establishments, 1999	20,380	23,693	7,008,444
Private nonfarm employment, 1999	250,292	295,139	110,705,661
Private nonfarm employment,			
percent change 1990–99	27.3%	37.2%	18.4%
Nonemployer establishments, 1999	38,921	47,469	16,152,604
Manufacturers shipments, 1997 ($1,000)	5,115,890	12,305,468	3,842,061,405
Retail sales, 1997 ($1,000)	6,702,134	11,707,133	2,460,886,012
Retail sales per capita, 1997	$10,457	$16,018	$9,190
Minority-owned firms, percent of total, 1997	2.8%	2.5%	14.6%
Women-owned firms, percent of total, 1997	22.5%	21.5%	26.0%
Federal funds and grants, 2001 ($1,000)	5,948,331	5,806,982	1,763,896,019
Local government employment –			
full-time equivalent, 1997	21,221	26,567	10,227,429

Geography	ND	SD	USA
Land area, 2000 (square miles)	68,976	75,885	3,537,438
Persons per square mile, 2000	9.3	9.9	79.6

(a) Includes persons reporting only one race.
(b) Hispanics may be of any race, so also are included in applicable race categories.
Z: Value greater than zero but less than half unit of measure shown.

Source: U.S. Census Bureau State & County QuickFacts

Ohio

As the first residents of Ohio, the Hopewell and Adena people built elaborate earthen mounds resembling animals and geometric shapes. The British likely encountered examples of ancient architecture when they acquired the land south of Lake Erie at the end of the French and Indian War. Ceded to the U.S. after the American Revolution, Ohio became part of Northwest Territory in 1787, joining the Union in 1803. Heavy migration from New England in the 19th century allowed industry to take hold, and railways and factories soon interrupted rural landscapes. The largest cities in this state of 88 counties include Columbus, the capital, along with Cleveland, Cincinnati, Toledo, Akron and Dayton.

Mostly low-lying with wooded hills in the south, the Buckeye State is intersected by numerous rivers, chiefly the Ohio, Scioto, Miami and Muskingum. Ohio's larger farms produce hay, corn, wheat, soybeans, and dairy foods, and cattle and pigs are raised. The state is highly industrialized and Ohio produces sandstone, oil, natural gas, clay, salt,

lime, and gravel. Its lake ports handle large amounts of copper ore, coal and oil. Industries include vehicle and aircraft manufacturing, transportation equipment, and primary and fabricated metals. Cedar Point, the Rock and Roll Hall of Fame, the Cuyahoga Valley National Recreation Area, the homes of several presidents and numerous acclaimed museums number among the most popular tourist attractions.

The only state with a two-pointed pennant, Ohio adopted its unique flag in 1902. Seventeen stars represent Ohio as the 17th state, while the white "O," set against a blue field, stands for both the Buckeye and the Native American name of the state. The colors were chosen to match the stars and stripes of Old Glory, the flag of the United States.

Columbus

Founded in 1812, Columbus grew rapidly alongside the Scioto River with the arrival of the railroad in 1850. A major transport, industrial and trading center for a rich agricultural region, Columbus also has numerous universities and colleges including Ohio State University. The Battelle Memorial Institute (1929) conducts scientific, technological and economic research. The home offices of many machinery, aircraft, printing and publishing industries can be found in Columbus.

Ohio at a Glance

People	Ohio	USA
Population, 2003 estimate	11,435,798	290,809,777
Population percent change, April 1, 2000–July 1, 2001	0.2%	1.2%
Population, 2000	11,353,140	281,421,906
Persons under 5 years old, percent, 2000	6.6%	6.8%
Persons under 18 years old, percent, 2000	25.4%	25.7%
Persons 65 years old and over, percent, 2000	13.3%	12.4%
Female persons, percent, 2000	51.4%	50.9%
White persons, percent, 2000 (a)	85.0%	75.1%
African American persons, percent, 2000 (a)	11.5%	12.3%
Native American persons, percent, 2000 (a)	0.2%	0.9%
Asian persons, percent, 2000 (a)	1.2%	3.6%
Native Hawaiian and Other Pacific Islander, percent, 2000 (a)	Z	0.1%
Persons of Hispanic or Latino origin, percent, 2000 (b)	1.9%	12.5%
White persons, not of Hispanic/Latino origin, percent, 2000	84.0%	69.1%
Foreign born persons, percent, 2000	3.0%	11.1%
Language other than English spoken at home, percent age 5+, 2000	6.1%	17.9%
High school graduates, percent of persons age 25+, 2000	83.0%	80.4%
Bachelor's degree or higher, percent of persons age 25+, 2000	21.1%	24.4%
Persons with a disability, age 5+, 2000	1,909,489	49,746,248
Homeownership rate, 2000	69.1%	66.2%
Median value of owner-occupied housing units, 2000	$103,700	$119,600
Households, 2000	4,445,773	105,480,101
Persons per household, 2000	2.49	2.59
Median household money income, 1999	$40,956	$41,994
Per capita money income, 1999	$21,003	$21,587
Persons below poverty, percent, 1999	10.6%	12.4%

Business	Ohio	USA
Private nonfarm establishments, 1999	270,766	7,008,444
Private nonfarm employment, 1999	4,867,368	110,705,661
Private nonfarm employment, percent change 1990–99	14.6%	18.4%
Nonemployer establishments, 1999	591,150	16,152,604
Manufacturers shipments, 1997 ($1,000)	241,902,924	3,842,061,405
Retail sales, 1997 ($1,000)	102,938,830	2,460,886,012
Retail sales per capita, 1997	$9,181	$9,190
Minority-owned firms, percent of total, 1997	6.3%	14.6%
Women-owned firms, percent of total, 1997	26.2%	26.0%
Federal funds and grants, 2001 ($1,000)	61,704,785	1,763,896,019
Local government employment – full-time equivalent, 1997	421,092	10,227,429

Geography	Ohio	USA
Land area, 2000 (square miles)	40,948	3,537,438
Persons per square mile, 2000	277.3	79.6

(a) Includes persons reporting only one race.

(b) Hispanics may be of any race, so also are included in applicable race categories.

Z: Value greater than zero but less than half unit of measure shown.

Source: U.S. Census Bureau State & County QuickFacts

Oklahoma

Statehood: November 16, 1907
Nickname: The Sooner State
State bird: Scissor-tailed flycatcher
State flower: Mistletoe
State tree: Redbud
State motto: Labor conquers all things
State capital: Oklahoma City
Population of capital: 506,132 (2000)

Formerly hunting grounds for the Osage, Arapaho, Comanche and Apache tribes, much of the area that would become Oklahoma was acquired by the U.S. from France in the Louisiana Purchase of 1803. Designated as an Indian territory in 1834, hundreds of thousands of Native Americans living east of the Mississippi were relocated to Oklahoma. In 1889, after the discovery of valuable oil and coal deposits, and pressured by a rapidly expanding population, the government sponsored a land rush. Desperate for fields to farm, thousands of homesteaders clamored to claim parcels of land shortly after noon on April 22nd. The Sooners, as people who jumped the gun were called, earned the state the nickname that lasts to this day. In the 1930s, the newly formed state was one of those hardest hit by the Dust Bowl phenomenon. Apart from Oklahoma City, the other important city is Tulsa. Seventy-seven counties break the state into administrative divisions.

Starting with Black Mesa in the western panhandle, which scrapes against the foothills of the Rockies, Oklahoma extends across the Great Plains to the Ouachita Mountains and their numerous lakes, spilling over the state boundary from neighboring Arkansas. The river by the same name, running through the northeastern corner of the state and the Red River, forming the southern border with Texas, are Oklahoma's main waterways. Wheat and cotton are the leading crops, but livestock generates more revenue and the capital city continues to be one of the world's largest cattle markets. Although many minerals exist within Oklahoma's borders, oil and natural gas form the basis of Oklahoma's economic wealth. Landmarks include the Chickasaw National Recreation Area, the National Cowboy Hall of Fame, the Will Rogers Home and Memorial and the Cherokee Cultural Center.

A calumet pipe and an olive branch, symbols of peace, cross an Osage warrior's shield on the state flag. Set against a sky blue background, the shield is adorned with eagle feathers and small crosses that represent stars. Oklahoma's flag was adopted in 1925.

Oklahoma City

The capital and largest city of Oklahoma is located in the center of the state on the North Canadian River. The area was settled in 1889 and the city made the state capital in 1910, prospering with the discovery of one of the country's richest oil deposits in 1928. It was the site of a terrorist bomb in April 1995, which killed 168 people and injured 400 others. Industries include oil-refining, meatpacking, grain milling, cotton processing, steel products, electronic equipment, and aircraft manufacturing.

Oklahoma at a Glance

People	Oklahoma	USA
Population, 2003 estimate	3,511,532	290,809,777
Population percent change, April 1, 2000–July 1, 2001	0.3%	1.2%
Population, 2000	3,450,654	281,421,906
Persons under 5 years old, percent, 2000	6.8%	6.8%
Persons under 18 years old, percent, 2000	25.9%	25.7%
Persons 65 years old and over, percent, 2000	13.2%	12.4%
Female persons, percent, 2000	50.9%	50.9%
White persons, percent, 2000 (a)	76.2%	75.1%
African American persons, percent, 2000 (a)	7.6%	12.3%
Native American persons, percent, 2000 (a)	7.9%	0.9%
Asian persons, percent, 2000 (a)	1.4%	3.6%
Native Hawaiian and Other Pacific Islander, percent, 2000 (a)	0.1%	0.1%
Persons of Hispanic or Latino origin, percent, 2000 (b)	5.2%	12.5%
White persons, not of Hispanic/Latino origin, percent, 2000	74.1%	69.1%
Foreign born persons, percent, 2000	3.8%	11.1%
Language other than English spoken at home, percent age 5+, 2000	7.4%	17.9%
High school graduates, percent of persons age 25+, 2000	80.6%	80.4%
Bachelor's degree or higher, percent of persons age 25+, 2000	20.3%	24.4%
Persons with a disability, age 5+, 2000	676,098	49,746,248
Homeownership rate, 2000	68.4%	66.2%
Median value of owner-occupied housing units, 2000	$70,700	$119,600
Households, 2000	1,342,293	105,480,101
Persons per household, 2000	2.49	2.59
Median household money income, 1999	$33,400	$41,994
Per capita money income, 1999	$17,646	$21,587
Persons below poverty, percent, 1999	14.7%	12.4%

Business	Oklahoma	USA
Private nonfarm establishments, 1999	84,854	7,008,444
Private nonfarm employment, 1999	1,171,356	110,705,661
Private nonfarm employment, percent change 1990–99	24.5%	18.4%
Nonemployer establishments, 1999	217,991	16,152,604
Manufacturers shipments, 1997 ($1,000)	37,453,197	3,842,061,405
Retail sales, 1997 ($1,000)	27,065,555	2,460,886,012
Retail sales per capita, 1997	$8,166	$9,190
Minority-owned firms, percent of total, 1997	10.2%	14.6%
Women-owned firms, percent of total, 1997	24.0%	26.0%
Federal funds and grants, 2001 ($1,000)	22,671,563	1,763,896,019
Local government employment – full-time equivalent, 1997	129,462	10,227,429

Geography	Oklahoma	USA
Land area, 2000 (square miles)	68,667	3,537,438
Persons per square mile, 2000	50.3	79.6

(a) Includes persons reporting only one race.
(b) Hispanics may be of any race, so also are included in applicable race categories.
Z: Value greater than zero but less than half unit of measure shown.

Source: U.S. Census Bureau State & County QuickFacts

Oregon

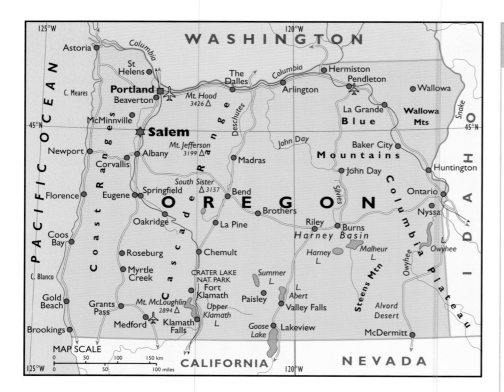

Statehood: February 14, 1859
Nickname: The Beaver State
State bird: Western meadowlark
State flower: Oregon grape
State tree: Douglas fir
State motto: She flies with her own wings
State capital: Salem
Population of capital: 136,924 (2000)

The Hudson Bay Company set up out-posts here on the Pacific coast in the 1790s, and from 1842, the fur trade and the Oregon Trail brought more settlers. The Oregon Territory was formed in 1848, and was admitted to the Union in 1859. The major cities, Portland and Eugene, as well as the state capital line up along the Willamette River in the northwest. Some of the state's 36 counties, such as Tillamook and Umatilla, take the name of the indigenous people who inhabited them before European explorers arrived.

The Columbia River to the north marks the boundary with Washington, while the Columbia Plateau in the east separates the state from neighboring Idaho. The forested slopes of the Coast Ranges and the Cascade Range, containing Mt. Hood, the highest peak, dominate the state. Between the two lies the fertile Willamette Valley. Agricultural revenue comes from cattle, dairy produce, wheat, fruit and salmon farming. Oregon's coastal conifers produce more than twenty percent of the softwood timber logged in the United States. Whereas the Oregon Trail brought many pioneers to the state in the 19th century, Crater Lake National Park, the John Day Fossil Beds and the Oregon Shakespeare Festival bring tourists to Oregon today.

The 33 stars around the seal on the blue state flag signify that Oregon was the 33rd state. Adopted in 1925, the blue flag has a different image on each side. The shield on the front depicts the setting sun over the Pacific, a plow, a pickaxe and wheat, symbols of the state's natural resources, and a covered wagon emerging from a forest. A beaver, the state animal appears on the reverse.

Salem

Founded in 1840 by Methodist missionaries, Salem was made territorial capital in 1851 and state capital in 1859. The industries clustered here on the Willamette River include timber, paper, textiles, food canning, meat packing, and high-technology equipment.

Oregon at a Glance

People	Oregon	USA
Population, 2003 estimate	3,559,596	290,809,777
Population percent change,		
April 1, 2000–July 1, 2001	1.5%	1.2%
Population, 2000	3,421,399	281,421,906
Persons under 5 years old, percent, 2000	6.5%	6.8%
Persons under 18 years old, percent, 2000	24.7%	25.7%
Persons 65 years old and over, percent, 2000	12.8%	12.4%
Female persons, percent, 2000	50.4%	50.9%
White persons, percent, 2000 (a)	86.6%	75.1%
African American persons,		
percent, 2000 (a)	1.6%	12.3%
Native American persons,		
percent, 2000 (a)	1.3%	0.9%
Asian persons, percent, 2000 (a)	3.0%	3.6%
Native Hawaiian and Other Pacific Islander,		
percent, 2000 (a)	0.2%	0.1%
Persons of Hispanic or Latino origin,		
percent, 2000 (b)	8.0%	12.5%
White persons, not of Hispanic/Latino origin,		
percent, 2000	83.5%	69.1%
Foreign born persons, percent, 2000	8.5%	11.1%
Language other than English spoken at home,		
percent age 5+, 2000	12.1%	17.9%
High school graduates, percent of persons		
age 25+, 2000	85.1%	80.4%
Bachelor's degree or higher,		
percent of persons age 25+, 2000	25.1%	24.4%
Persons with a disability, age 5+, 2000	593,301	49,746,248
Homeownership rate, 2000	64.3%	66.2%
Median value of owner-occupied		
housing units, 2000	$152,100	$119,600
Households, 2000	1,333,723	105,480,101
Persons per household, 2000	2.51	2.59
Median household money income, 1999	$40,916	$41,994
Per capita money income, 1999	$20,940	$21,587
Persons below poverty, percent, 1999	11.6%	12.4%

Business	Oregon	USA
Private nonfarm establishments, 1999	99,945	7,008,444
Private nonfarm employment, 1999	1,332,403	110,705,661
Private nonfarm employment,		
percent change 1990–99	31.0%	18.4%
Nonemployer establishments, 1999	212,334	16,152,604
Manufacturers shipments, 1997 ($1,000)	47,665,990	3,842,061,405
Retail sales, 1997 ($1,000)	33,396,849	2,460,886,012
Retail sales per capita, 1997	$10,297	$9,190
Minority-owned firms, percent of total, 1997	6.2%	14.6%
Women-owned firms, percent of total, 1997	27.6%	26.0%
Federal funds and grants, 2001 ($1,000)	18,401,222	1,763,896,019
Local government employment –		
full-time equivalent, 1997	117,999	10,227,429

Geography	Oregon	USA
Land area, 2000 (square miles)	95,997	3,537,438
Persons per square mile, 2000	35.6	79.6

(a) Includes persons reporting only one race.

(b) Hispanics may be of any race, so also are included in applicable race categories.

Z: Value greater than zero but less than half unit of measure shown.

Source: U.S. Census Bureau State & County QuickFacts

Pennsylvania

Statehood: December 12, 1787
Nickname: The Keystone State
State bird: Ruffed grouse
State flower: Mountain laurel
State tree: Hemlock
State motto: Virtue, liberty, and independence
State capital: Harrisburg
Population of capital: 48,950 (2000)

Swedish and Dutch settlements were made in the Middle Atlantic along the Delaware River in the mid-17th century but by 1664, the English controlled the area. William Penn received a charter from Charles II for the region and chose a Latin name, "Penn's Woods." One of the 13 original states, the Declaration of Independence was signed and the Constitution ratified in Philadelphia, which was also the national capital from 1790 to 1800. The Union victory at the Battle of Gettysburg in July 1863 was a turning point in the Civil War. The Keystone State introduced the first labor union, the first commercial oil well and the first limited access expressway in the United States. Pennsylvania's large population is concentrated in its largest cities: Philadelphia, Pittsburgh, Scranton, Allentown, Lancaster, Erie and Harrisburg. Sixty-seven counties fall within the state's borders.

Apart from small low-lying areas in the northwest and southeast, Pennsylvania is composed of mountain ridges and rolling hills with narrow valleys. The Delaware, Susquehanna and Allegheny Rivers are the longest in the state. Farming is concentrated to the south and east of the Alleghenies and the Appalachians where the principal crops are cereals, tobacco, potatoes, and fruit, besides some dairy farming. Pennsylvania has rich deposits of coal and iron ore and has long been a producer of steel, which today accounts for a decreasing percentage of the country's total output. Industries include chemicals, cement, electrical machinery, and metal goods. With an abundance of historic places, Gettysburg National Military Park, Valley Forge National Historic Park, Steamtown National Historic Site, and Independence National Park in Philadelphia are just some of the top attractions.

The Pennsylvania State Legislature adopted its flag in 1907. It displays the coat of arms on a blue background held by two horses and an eagle. Within the seal a tall ship, a plow and three bundles of wheat are pictured. A stalk of corn and an olive branch appear above the state motto.

Harrisburg

John Harris built a trading post here on the Susquehanna River in 1718, and by 1785 his son had established a town. Later the scene of the Harrisburg Convention, it became the state capital in 1812. When a disaster at the Three Mile Island power plant was narrowly avoided in 1979, the U.S. reassessed its nuclear safety standards. The local textile, machinery, and electronic equipment industries are no longer overshadowed by the chocolate production in nearby Hershey.

Pennsylvania at a Glance

People	Pennsylvania	USA
Population, 2003 estimate	12,365,455	290,809,777
Population percent change, April 1, 2000–July 1, 2001	0.0%	1.2%
Population, 2000	12,281,054	281,421,906
Persons under 5 years old, percent, 2000	5.9%	6.8%
Persons under 18 years old, percent, 2000	23.8%	25.7%
Persons 65 years old and over, percent, 2000	15.6%	12.4%
Female persons, percent, 2000	51.7%	50.9%
White persons, percent, 2000 (a)	85.4%	75.1%
African American persons, percent, 2000 (a)	10.0%	12.3%
Native American persons, percent, 2000 (a)	0.1%	0.9%
Asian persons, percent, 2000 (a)	1.8%	3.6%
Native Hawaiian and Other Pacific Islander, percent, 2000 (a)	Z	0.1%
Persons of Hispanic or Latino origin, percent, 2000 (b)	3.2%	12.5%
White persons, not of Hispanic/Latino origin, percent, 2000	84.1%	69.1%
Foreign born persons, percent, 2000	4.1%	11.1%
Language other than English spoken at home, percent age 5+, 2000	8.4%	17.9%
High school graduates, percent of persons age 25+, 2000	81.9%	80.4%
Bachelor's degree or higher, percent of persons age 25+, 2000	22.4%	24.4%
Persons with a disability, age 5+, 2000	2,111,771	49,746,248
Homeownership rate, 2000	71.3%	66.2%
Median value of owner-occupied housing units, 2000	$97,000	$119,600
Households, 2000	4,777,003	105,480,101
Persons per household, 2000	2.48	2.59
Median household money income, 1999	$40,106	$41,994
Per capita money income, 1999	$20,880	$21,587
Persons below poverty, percent, 1999	11.0%	12.4%

Business	Pennsylvania	USA
Private nonfarm establishments, 1999	293,491	7,008,444
Private nonfarm employment, 1999	4,986,591	110,705,661
Private nonfarm employment, percent change 1990–99	8.4%	18.4%
Nonemployer establishments, 1999	614,594	16,152,604
Manufacturers shipments, 1997 ($1,000)	172,193,216	3,842,061,405
Retail sales, 1997 ($1,000)	109,948,462	2,460,886,012
Retail sales per capita, 1997	$9,150	$9,190
Minority-owned firms, percent of total, 1997	5.9%	14.6%
Women-owned firms, percent of total, 1997	24.2%	26.0%
Federal funds and grants, 2001 ($1,000)	79,310,064	1,763,896,019
Local government employment – full-time equivalent, 1997	365,556	10,227,429

Geography	Pennsylvania	USA
Land area, 2000 (square miles)	44,817	3,537,438
Persons per square mile, 2000	274	79.6

(a) Includes persons reporting only one race.
(b) Hispanics may be of any race, so also are included in applicable race categories.
Z: Value greater than zero but less than half unit of measure shown.

Source: U.S. Census Bureau State & County QuickFacts

Rhode Island

Statehood: May 29, 1790
Nickname: Ocean State
State bird: Rhode Island Red
State flower: Violet
State tree: Red maple
State motto: Hope
State capital: Providence
Population of capital: 173,618 (2000)

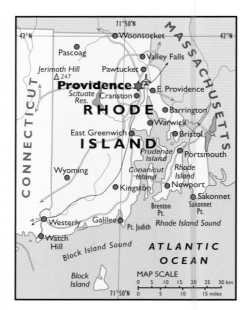

Located on the Atlantic coast, Rhode Island is the smallest U.S. state with only five counties. People from Massachusetts seeking religious freedom, led by Roger Williams, first settled the region in 1636, purchasing land from the Narragansett and other local tribes. It was granted a royal charter in 1663 and was occupied by British troops during the American Revolution after declaring independence before any of the other colonies. Despite being the first state to outlaw slavery, during the 18th century, Rhode Island merchants amassed fortunes participating in the Triangle Trade. By the 19th century, however, manufacturing had evolved into the most profitable business. Warwick, Pawtucket, and Cranston are scattered around the largest city and capital, Providence.

Rhode Island's low-lying position on the coast has left it vulnerable to hurricanes and flooding throughout its history. The highest point in the state, Jeremoth Hill, is a mere 812 feet above sea level. Much of the landscape is forested, dotted with small lakes as well as some dairy and poultry farms. Potatoes, hay, apples, oats, and corn are the chief crops, but fishing is a more significant source of revenue. Lobster, clams, Atlantic cod and flounder are a few of the products that contribute to an established maritime industry. Other industries include textiles, fabricated metals, silverware, machinery, electrical equipment and tourism. Visitors often stop at The Breakers, a famous seaside mansion built for Cornelius Vanderbilt, Samuel Slater's cotton mill in Pawtucket, and Touro Synagogue, the oldest in the country.

Featuring a rather simple design, the Rhode Island flag places an anchor ringed by thirteen stars representing the original colonies on a white background. The state motto appears on a blue ribbon beneath the image. It was adopted in 1897.

Providence

Providence was founded in 1636 as a refuge for religious dissenters from Massachusetts and became a port on Providence Bay in northeastern Rhode Island, enjoying great prosperity through trade with the West Indies. The city played an active role in the War for Independence and the Industrial Revolution and is now a center for jewelry, electrical equipment, silverware, machine tools, and plastic manufacturing. More than ten colleges are in Providence.

Rhode Island at a Glance

People	Rhode Island	USA
Population, 2003 estimate	1,076,164	290,809,777
Population percent change, April 1, 2000–July 1, 2001	1.0%	1.2%
Population, 2000	1,048,319	281,421,906
Persons under 5 years old, percent, 2000	6.1%	6.8%
Persons under 18 years old, percent, 2000	23.6%	25.7%
Persons 65 years old and over, percent, 2000	14.5%	12.4%
Female persons, percent, 2000	52.0%	50.9%
White persons, percent, 2000 (a)	85.0%	75.1%
African American persons, percent, 2000 (a)	4.5%	12.3%
Native American persons, percent, 2000 (a)	0.5%	0.9%
Asian persons, percent, 2000 (a)	2.3%	3.6%
Native Hawaiian and Other Pacific Islander, percent, 2000 (a)	0.1%	0.1%
Persons of Hispanic or Latino origin, percent, 2000 (b)	8.7%	12.5%
White persons, not of Hispanic/Latino origin, percent, 2000	81.9%	69.1%
Foreign born persons, percent, 2000	11.4%	11.1%
Language other than English spoken at home, percent age 5+, 2000	20.0%	17.9%
High school graduates, percent of persons age 25+, 2000	78.0%	80.4%
Bachelor's degree or higher, percent of persons age 25+, 2000	25.6%	24.4%
Persons with a disability, age 5+, 2000	195,806	49,746,248
Homeownership rate, 2000	60.0%	66.2%
Median value of owner-occupied housing units, 2000	$133,000	$119,600
Households, 2000	408,424	105,480,101
Persons per household, 2000	2.47	2.59
Median household money income, 1999	$42,090	$41,994
Per capita money income, 1999	$21,688	$21,587
Persons below poverty, percent, 1999	11.9%	12.4%

Business	Rhode Island	USA
Private nonfarm establishments, 1999	28,240	7,008,444
Private nonfarm employment, 1999	405,445	110,705,661
Private nonfarm employment, percent change 1990–99	3.0%	18.4%
Nonemployer establishments, 1999	57,664	16,152,604
Manufacturers shipments, 1997 ($1,000)	10,482,011	3,842,061,405
Retail sales, 1997 ($1,000)	7,505,754	2,460,886,012
Retail sales per capita, 1997	$7,605	$9,190
Minority-owned firms, percent of total, 1997	5.9%	14.6%
Women-owned firms, percent of total, 1997	24.6%	26.0%
Federal funds and grants, 2001 ($1,000)	6,988,588	1,763,896,019
Local government employment – full-time equivalent, 1997	29,102	10,227,429

Geography	Rhode Island	USA
Land area, 2000 (square miles)	1,045	3,537,438
Persons per square mile, 2000	1,003.2	79.6

(a) Includes persons reporting only one race.

(b) Hispanics may be of any race, so also are included in applicable race categories.

Z: Value greater than zero but less than half unit of measure shown.

Source: U.S. Census Bureau State & County QuickFacts

South Carolina

MAP SCALE

ATLANTIC OCEAN

Statehood: May 23, 1788
Nickname: The Palmetto State
State bird: Carolina wren
State flower: Carolina jessamine
State tree: Palmetto
State motto: Prepared in mind and resources
State capital: Columbia
Population of capital: 116,278 (2000)

Although a Spanish expedition explored the coastline more than 100 years earlier, the English were the first Europeans to permanently settle the area beginning in 1663. South Carolina became a royal province in 1729, and a plantation society evolved based on rice, indigo, and cotton, compelling Catawba, Yamasee and other native peoples to fight or move westward. One of the original 13 states, it was the first to secede from the Union, and the opening shots of the Civil War were fired at Fort Sumter. In 1865, Union troops devastated South Carolina, leaving a long road ahead towards reconstruction and racial equality. The state capital and largest city is Columbia, followed by Greenville and Charleston, the main port. South Carolina has 46 counties.

The land rises from the swampy coastal plain to the rolling hills of the Piedmont plateau, jutting up against the Blue Ridge Mountains in the northwest. Many rivers, including the Savannah, which forms most of the Georgia border, drain the region and once powered textile mills whose operation depended on sprawling cotton plantations. Today major crops include tobacco, soybeans, corn, sweet potatoes, peaches and peanuts. Timber and fishing are other sources of employment, but tourism is now the state's second biggest source of income after textiles and clothing. Resorts such as Myrtle Beach and Hilton Head attract tourists seeking relaxation, while Fort Sumter National Monument, Cowpens National Battlefield appeal to people fascinated by the state's military history.

South Carolina's Revolutionary War recruits often wore a silver crescent moon, a shape that graces the State flag, on their hats. At the center of the blue flag adopted in 1861 is a palmetto, which refers to the resilience of the fort on Sullivan Island built from the tough logs of this tree.

Columbia

At the junction of the Broad and Saluda Rivers in the center of the state, Columbia was founded as the capital in 1786, a compromise between two different economic realities in the Piedmont and on the coast. Nearly destroyed by General William Sherman on his march to the sea, it is home to the University of South Carolina, Columbia College, Allen University and the Woodrow Wilson Museum. Textile, paper, pharmaceutical and electronic equipment manufacturers are located within the city limits along with a number of notable antebellum houses.

South Carolina at a Glance

People	South Carolina	USA
Population, 2003 estimate	4,147,152	290,809,777
Population percent change, April 1, 2000–July 1, 2001	1.3%	1.2%
Population, 2000	4,012,012	281,421,906
Persons under 5 years old, percent, 2000	6.6%	6.8%
Persons under 18 years old, percent, 2000	25.2%	25.7%
Persons 65 years old and over, percent, 2000	12.1%	12.4%
Female persons, percent, 2000	51.4%	50.9%
White persons, percent, 2000 (a)	67.2%	75.1%
African American persons, percent, 2000 (a)	29.5%	12.3%
Native American persons, percent, 2000 (a)	0.3%	0.9%
Asian persons, percent, 2000 (a)	0.9%	3.6%
Native Hawaiian and Other Pacific Islander, percent, 2000 (a)	Z	0.1%
Persons of Hispanic or Latino origin, percent, 2000 (b)	2.4%	12.5%
White persons, not of Hispanic/Latino origin, percent, 2000	66.1%	69.1%
Foreign born persons, percent, 2000	2.9%	11.1%
Language other than English spoken at home, percent age 5+, 2000	5.2%	17.9%
High school graduates, percent of persons age 25+, 2000	76.3%	80.4%
Bachelor's degree or higher, percent of persons age 25+, 2000	20.4%	24.4%
Persons with a disability, age 5+, 2000	810,857	49,746,248
Homeownership rate, 2000	72.2%	66.2%
Median value of owner-occupied housing units, 2000	$94,900	$119,600
Households, 2000	1,533,854	105,480,101
Persons per household, 2000	2.53	2.59
Median household money income, 1999	$37,082	$41,994
Per capita money income, 1999	$18,795	$21,587
Persons below poverty, percent, 1999	14.1%	12.4%

Business	South Carolina	USA
Private nonfarm establishments, 1999	96,440	7,008,444
Private nonfarm employment, 1999	1,561,727	110,705,661
Private nonfarm employment, percent change 1990–99	23.3%	18.4%
Nonemployer establishments, 1999	200,265	16,152,604
Manufacturers shipments, 1997 ($1,000)	70,797,020	3,842,061,405
Retail sales, 1997 ($1,000)	33,634,264	2,460,886,012
Retail sales per capita, 1997	$8,874	$9,190
Minority-owned firms, percent of total, 1997	11.8%	14.6%
Women-owned firms, percent of total, 1997	24.7%	26.0%
Federal funds and grants, 2001 ($1,000)	24,674,761	1,763,896,019
Local government employment – full-time equivalent, 1997	143,952	10,227,429

Geography	South Carolina	USA
Land area, 2000 (square miles)	30,109	3,537,438
Persons per square mile, 2000	133.2	79.6

(a) Includes persons reporting only one race.
(b) Hispanics may be of any race, so also are included in applicable race categories.
Z: Value greater than zero but less than half unit of measure shown.

Source: U.S. Census Bureau State & County QuickFacts

Tennessee

Statehood: June 1, 1796
Nickname: The Volunteer State
State bird: Mockingbird
State flower: Iris
State tree: Tulip-poplar
State motto: Agriculture and Commerce
State capital: Nashville
Population of capital: 569,891 (2000)

The first European to enter the area in 1540 was a Spaniard, Hernando De Soto. The French followed a century later, but their claim was ceded to Britain in 1763, and the first permanent settlement between the Appalachian Mountains and the Mississippi River was established in 1769. Taking its name from a Yuchi word *tana-see*, which translates as "meeting place," Tennessee became the 16th State of the Union in 1796. Andrew Jackson forcibly relocated most of the large population of Cherokee to Oklahoma by 1839. Tennessee's enthusiastic response to the request for volunteers during the Mexican War (1846–48) earned it the nickname of the "Volunteer State," and during the Civil War, it was the site of more than 400 battles, many of which, like Shiloh and Chattanooga, were among the bloodiest. The last state to secede, in 1866 it became the first Southern state to be readmitted to the Union.

A melting pot for American music from blues to rockabilly, Tennessee has also been influenced by Christian fundamentalism, and the teaching of evolution was banned throughout its 95 counties from 1925 to 1967. In addition to the capital, the main cities are Memphis, Chattanooga, and Knoxville.

The Great Smoky Mountains, part of the Appalachian chain, and the Cumberland Plateau dominate the east while the fertile floodplains of west Tennessee, a production center for cotton, tobacco and soybeans, are defined by the Mississippi and Tennessee Rivers. Central Tennessee is a bluegrass region famed for its horse breeding and livestock rearing. Mineral deposits include zinc and coal and major industries include chemicals, automobile assembly, electrical equipment, foodstuffs, and tourism. Great Smoky Mountains National Park, Cherokee National Forest, Big South Fork National River and Recreation Area, Fort Donelson and Stones River National Battlefields, and the Shiloh, Chickamauga, and Chattanooga National Military Parks are the chief landmarks.

Adopted in 1905 and echoing the colors of the national flag, the state flag is crimson with a central blue circle containing three stars. Bound together in an unbroken circle they represent three regions: mountains in the east, highlands in the middle and lowlands in the west. A blue bar relieves some of the sameness of the red field when the flag hangs limp.

Nashville

A port on the Cumberland River, Fort Nasborough was settled in 1779 and changed its name before becoming the state capital in 1843. During the Civil War, it was the scene of a decisive Union victory. The city merged with Davidson County in 1963 and is now the center of country music, and home of the Country Music Hall of Fame, the Grand Ole Opry House and an entertainment complex called Opryland USA. Seat of several institutions of highter education, Nashville has many neo-classical buildings and the music and publishing industries are key to the economy.

Tennessee at a Glance

People	Tennessee	USA
Population, 2003 estimate	5,841,748	290,809,777
Population percent change, April 1, 2000–July 1, 2001	0.9%	1.2%
Population, 2000	5,689,283	281,421,906
Persons under 5 years old, percent, 2000	6.6%	6.8%
Persons under 18 years old, percent, 2000	24.6%	25.7%
Persons 65 years old and over, percent, 2000	12.4%	12.4%
Female persons, percent, 2000	51.3%	50.9%
White persons, percent, 2000 (a)	80.2%	75.1%
African American persons, percent, 2000 (a)	16.4%	12.3%
Native American persons, percent, 2000 (a)	0.3%	0.9%
Asian persons, percent, 2000 (a)	1.0%	3.6%
Native Hawaiian and Other Pacific Islander, percent, 2000 (a)	Z	0.1%
Persons of Hispanic or Latino origin, percent, 2000 (b)	2.2%	12.5%
White persons, not of Hispanic/Latino origin, percent, 2000	79.2%	69.1%
Foreign born persons, percent, 2000	2.8%	11.1%
Language other than English spoken at home, percent age 5+, 2000	4.8%	17.9%
High school graduates, percent of persons age 25+, 2000	75.9%	80.4%
Bachelor's degree or higher, percent of persons age 25+, 2000	19.6%	24.4%
Persons with a disability, age 5+, 2000	1,149,693	49,746,248
Homeownership rate, 2000	69.9%	66.2%
Median value of owner-occupied housing units, 2000	$93,000	$119,600
Households, 2000	2,232,905	105,480,101
Persons per household, 2000	2.48	2.59
Median household money income, 1999	$36,360	$41,994
Per capita money income, 1999	$19,393	$21,587
Persons below poverty, percent, 1999	13.5%	12.4%

Business	Tennessee	USA
Private nonfarm establishments, 1999	131,116	7,008,444
Private nonfarm employment, 1999	2,338,780	110,705,661
Private nonfarm employment, percent change 1990–99	25.1%	18.4%
Nonemployer establishments, 1999	335,266	16,152,604
Manufacturers shipments, 1997 ($1,000)	98,503,080	3,842,061,405
Retail sales, 1997 ($1,000)	50,813,221	2,460,886,012
Retail sales per capita, 1997	$9,448	$9,190
Minority-owned firms, percent of total, 1997	7.8%	14.6%
Women-owned firms, percent of total, 1997	24.0%	26.0%
Federal funds and grants, 2001 ($1,000)	36,757,793	1,763,896,019
Local government employment – full-time equivalent, 1997	194,274	10,227,429

Geography	Tennessee	USA
Land area, 2000 (square miles)	41,217	3,537,438
Persons per square mile, 2000	138	79.6

(a) Includes persons reporting only one race.

(b) Hispanics may be of any race, so also are included in applicable race categories.

Z: Value greater than zero but less than half unit of measure shown.

Source: U.S. Census Bureau State & County QuickFacts

Texas

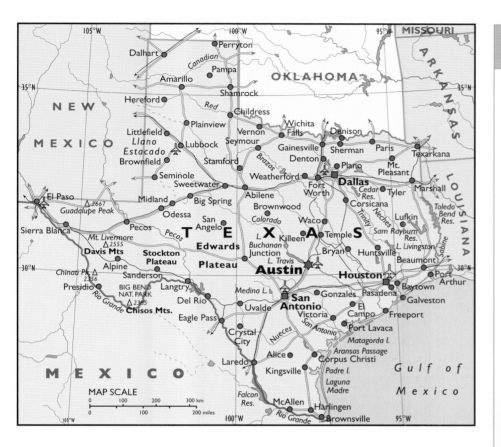

Statehood: December 29, 1845
Nickname: The Lone Star State
State bird: Mockingbird
State flower: Bluebonnet
State tree: Pecan
State motto: Friendship
State capital: Austin
Population of capital: 656,562 (2000)

Spaniards explored the region bounded by the Gulf of Mexico and the Río Grande in the early 16th century, and it became part of the colony of Mexico. Missionaries tried with limited success to convert Caddo, Concho and other Native American groups to Christianity and by the time Mexico achieved independence in 1821, many Americans had begun to settle in Texas. In 1836, they revolted against Mexican rule, rallied around a defeat at the Alamo, forced the army to surrender, and established the Republic of Texas. The following year, the U.S. recognized Sam Houston's republic and Texas was admitted to the Union as the 28th state. In 1873, the invention of barbed wire brought the short-lived era of cowboys and cattle drives to an end. Austin and most of the other major cities including Fort Worth, San Antonio, Dallas, and Houston are in the east. The second largest state in the country has 254 counties, many with names alluding to a persistent Hispanic influence.

Beginning with the southeast, the Texas terrain moves from barrier islands to cypress swamps, past pine-covered hills and the cliffs of the Balcones Escarpment across an expansive prairie to end at the New Mexico border with the Llano Estacado. Cotton, rice and citrus fruits are key cash crops and the timber industry contributes noticeably to the economy. Millions of cattle and sheep roam the rangeland of the Río Grande Valley, from where the land rises into the Davis and Guadalupe Mountains of West Texas and the Great Plains area of the Panhandle in the north. Rich oil and gas fields, some of which are offshore, anchor the state's economy. Other mainstay industries include oil refining, food processing, aircraft manufacturing, and telecommunications. Big Bend and Guadeloupe National Parks, the Johnson Space Center in Houston, and Padre Island National Seashore are some of the many attractions to be found in Texas.

The red, white and blue flag of Texas reflects the colors of the national banner representing bravery, purity and loyalty respectively. It was adopted in 1839.

Austin

Settled as Waterloo in 1835, the city was renamed four years later for Stephen Austin, the "father of Texas." A number of fine examples of 19th-century architecture, including the Capitol building were built here on the Colorado River. The market center for a farming and ranching area, Austin, as a location for high-tech electronics, furniture, machinery, building materials, and food processing industries, hosts national conventions.

Texas at a Glance

People	Texas	USA
Population, 2003 estimate	22,118,509	290,809,777
Population percent change, April 1, 2000–July 1, 2001	2.3%	1.2%
Population, 2000	20,851,820	281,421,906
Persons under 5 years old, percent, 2000	7.8%	6.8%
Persons under 18 years old, percent, 2000	28.2%	25.7%
Persons 65 years old and over, percent, 2000	9.9%	12.4%
Female persons, percent, 2000	50.4%	50.9%
White persons, percent, 2000 (a)	71.0%	75.1%
African American persons, percent, 2000 (a)	11.5%	12.3%
Native American persons, percent, 2000 (a)	0.6%	0.9%
Asian persons, percent, 2000 (a)	2.7%	3.6%
Native Hawaiian and Other Pacific Islander, percent, 2000 (a)	0.1%	0.1%
Persons of Hispanic or Latino origin, percent, 2000 (b)	32.0%	12.5%
White persons, not of Hispanic/Latino origin, percent, 2000	52.4%	69.1%
Foreign born persons, percent, 2000	13.9%	11.1%
Language other than English spoken at home, percent age 5+, 2000	31.2%	17.9%
High school graduates, percent of persons age 25+, 2000	75.7%	80.4%
Bachelor's degree or higher, percent of persons age 25+, 2000	23.2%	24.4%
Persons with a disability, age 5+, 2000	3,605,542	49,746,248
Homeownership rate, 2000	63.8%	66.2%
Median value of owner-occupied housing units, 2000	$82,500	$119,600
Households, 2000	7,393,354	105,480,101
Persons per household, 2000	2.74	2.59
Median household money income, 1999	$39,927	$41,994
Per capita money income, 1999	$19,617	$21,587
Persons below poverty, percent, 1999	15.4%	12.4%

Business	Texas	USA
Private nonfarm establishments, 1999	467,087	7,008,444
Private nonfarm employment, 1999	7,763,815	110,705,661
Private nonfarm employment, percent change 1990–99	32.4%	18.4%
Nonemployer establishments, 1999	1,236,927	16,152,604
Manufacturers shipments, 1997 ($1,000)	297,657,003	3,842,061,405
Retail sales, 1997 ($1,000)	182,516,112	2,460,886,012
Retail sales per capita, 1997	$9,430	$9,190
Minority-owned firms, percent of total, 1997	23.9%	14.6%
Women-owned firms, percent of total, 1997	25.0%	26.0%
Federal funds and grants, 2001 ($1,000)	112,530,383	1,763,896,019
Local government employment – full-time equivalent, 1997	850,380	10,227,429

Geography	Texas	USA
Land area, 2000 (square miles)	261,797	3,537,438
Persons per square mile, 2000	79.6	79.6

(a) Includes persons reporting only one race.

(b) Hispanics may be of any race, so also are included in applicable race categories.

Z: Value greater than zero but less than half unit of measure shown.

Source: U.S. Census Bureau State & County QuickFacts

Utah

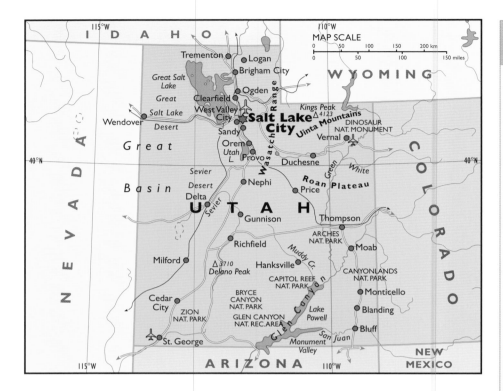

Statehood: January 4, 1896
Nickname: The Beehive State
State bird: Sea gull
State flower: Sego lily
State tree: Blue spruce
State motto: Industry
State capital: Salt Lake City
Population of capital: 181,743 (2000)

The Ute and Shoshone, replacing the Anasazi, lived among the mesas, plateaus and sandy wastes for centuries before the first Spaniards crossed into their territory. Another part of the region given to the U.S. at the end of the Mexican War, Utah was admitted to the Union in 1896. The influence of the Church of Jesus Christ of the Latter-Day Saints is strong in the state, and in 1857–58 there were conflicts between federal troops and the Mormons. Mining, then the transcontinental railroad, which was completed at Promontory in 1869, altered the peaceful religious community. Salt Lake City, the capital and single largest city in the state, is very close to the two other cities: Provo and Ogden. Divided into 29 sizable counties, Utah retains much of the wilderness encountered by Spanish explorers Escalante and Dominguez.

In the north, the Wasatch Range separates the mountainous east from the Great Basin, which includes the Great Salt Lake. Although large rivers such as the Green, the Colorado and Sevier run through the state and hay, barley, wheat, beans, and sugar beet are grown with the aid of irrigation, the semiarid climate hinders widespread agriculture. The chief farming activity is livestock raising. Mining is also important: there are rich deposits of cop-

per, petroleum, coal, molybdenum, silver, lead, and gold. With many ski resorts, monuments, and national parks like Canyonlands, Arches, Grand Staircase and Zion, tourism is vital to the economy.

The state flag, adopted in 1913, shows two dates: 1847, the year Mormon settlers arrived, and 1896, the year Utah was added as the 45th state. Beneath the protective wings of a bald eagle, symbol of the United States, the seal rests in the center of the blue flag, displaying a beehive for industry (the state motto), and the sego lily for peace.

Salt Lake City

Founded southeast of Great Salt Lake in 1847 by Brigham Young, Salt Lake City, the world headquarters of the Mormon Church, grew rapidly to become capital of the territory and then the state of Utah. Zinc, gold, silver, lead, and copper are mined in the surrounding Wasatch Range. The city has developed into a headquarters for industries as varied as missiles, rocket engines, oil-refining, tourism, printing and publishing.

Utah at a Glance

People	Utah	USA
Population, 2003 estimate	2,351,467	290,809,777
Population percent change, April 1, 2000–July 1, 2001	1.6%	1.2%
Population, 2000	2,233,169	281,421,906
Persons under 5 years old, percent, 2000	9.4%	6.8%
Persons under 18 years old, percent, 2000	32.2%	25.7%
Persons 65 years old and over, percent, 2000	8.5%	12.4%
Female persons, percent, 2000	49.9%	50.9%
White persons, percent, 2000 (a)	89.2%	75.1%
African American persons, percent, 2000 (a)	0.8%	12.3%
Native American persons, percent, 2000 (a)	1.3%	0.9%
Asian persons, percent, 2000 (a)	1.7%	3.6%
Native Hawaiian and Other Pacific Islander, percent, 2000 (a)	0.7%	0.1%
Persons of Hispanic or Latino origin, percent, 2000 (b)	9.0%	12.5%
White persons, not of Hispanic/Latino origin, percent, 2000	85.3%	69.1%
Foreign born persons, percent, 2000	7.1%	11.1%
Language other than English spoken at home, percent age 5+, 2000	12.5%	17.9%
High school graduates, percent of persons age 25+, 2000	87.7%	80.4%
Bachelor's degree or higher, percent of persons age 25+, 2000	26.1%	24.4%
Persons with a disability, age 5+, 2000	298,686	49,746,248
Homeownership rate, 2000	71.5%	66.2%
Median value of owner-occupied housing units, 2000	$146,100	$119,600
Households, 2000	701,281	105,480,101
Persons per household, 2000	3.13	2.59
Median household money income, 1999	$45,726	$41,994
Per capita money income, 1999	$18,185	$21,587
Persons below poverty, percent, 1999	9.4%	12.4%

Business	Utah	USA
Private nonfarm establishments, 1999	53,809	7,008,444
Private nonfarm employment, 1999	889,355	110,705,661
Private nonfarm employment, percent change 1990–99	55.8%	18.4%
Nonemployer establishments, 1999	134,513	16,152,604
Manufacturers shipments, 1997 ($1,000)	24,014,379	3,842,061,405
Retail sales, 1997 ($1,000)	19,964,601	2,460,886,012
Retail sales per capita, 1997	$9,666	$9,190
Minority-owned firms, percent of total, 1997	5.1%	14.6%
Women-owned firms, percent of total, 1997	24.8%	26.0%
Federal funds and grants, 2001 ($1,000)	11,377,441	1,763,896,019
Local government employment – full-time equivalent, 1997	63,884	10,227,429

Geography	Utah	USA
Land area, 2000 (square miles)	82,144	3,537,438
Persons per square mile, 2000	27.2	79.6

(a) Includes persons reporting only one race.

(b) Hispanics may be of any race, so also are included in applicable race categories.

Z: Value greater than zero but less than half unit of measure shown.

Source: U.S. Census Bureau State & County QuickFacts

Vermont

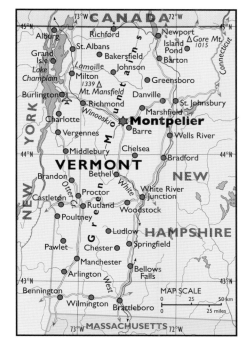

Traveling south from Québec in 1609, Samuel de Champlain discovered the lake that now bears his name, but permanent European settlements in the region did not appear until 1724. These first farms and villages probably interacted with Iroquois and Mahican people who hunted and fished in the same territory. Land grant disputes with New Hampshire and New York persisted for many years until Vermont declared its independence in 1777, retaining this unrecognized status until it was finally admitted to the Union in 1791. Perhaps in response to the growing popularity of winter sports, an enterprising Vermonter built the first ski tow in Woodstock, near the Ottauquechee River and the birthplace of Calvin Coolidge. Burlington is the major city in this state of 14 counties.

The Green Mountains range north to south, and dominate the terrain. Lake Champlain, the largest in New England, separates the state from New York, forming most of the western border of Vermont. The Connecticut River runs along the entire border with New Hampshire. Heavily forested with limited arable land, dairy farming is by far the most important agricultural activity in Vermont. Mineral resources include granite, slate, marble and asbestos while the biggest industries include pulp and paper production, food processing, computer component manufacturing, and maple syrup production. Outdoor enthusiasts might travel to the state to ski at Stowe or Killington or hike the undeveloped wilderness and return home having learned about Vermont's history from the Bennington Museum or the Billings Farm.

The Vermont coat of arms shows a pine tree, a cow and sheaves of grain in the foreground and the Green Mountains behind them. A stag's head is positioned at the top of the shield with the motto below. Vermont adopted the image for its deep blue flag in 1923.

Montpelier

First settled in the 1780s, Montpelier became state capital in 1805. Admiral George Dewey, who defeated the Spanish at Manilsa Bay in 1898, was born in the city limits. Tourism, machinery, granite quarrying, timber, maple sugar and syrup, and plastics industries can be found here at the confluence of the Winooski and North Branch Rivers.

Vermont at a Glance

People	Vermont	USA
Population, 2003 estimate	619,107	290,809,777
Population percent change, April 1, 2000–July 1, 2001	0.7%	1.2%
Population, 2000	608,827	281,421,906
Persons under 5 years old, percent, 2000	5.6%	6.8%
Persons under 18 years old, percent, 2000	24.2%	25.7%
Persons 65 years old and over, percent, 2000	12.7%	12.4%
Female persons, percent, 2000	51.0%	50.9%
White persons, percent, 2000 (a)	96.8%	75.1%
African American persons, percent, 2000 (a)	0.5%	12.3%
Native American persons, percent, 2000 (a)	0.4%	0.9%
Asian persons, percent, 2000 (a)	0.9%	3.6%
Native Hawaiian and Other Pacific Islander, percent, 2000 (a)	Z	0.1%
Persons of Hispanic or Latino origin, percent, 2000 (b)	0.9%	12.5%
White persons, not of Hispanic/Latino origin, percent, 2000	96.2%	69.1%
Foreign born persons, percent, 2000	3.8%	11.1%
Language other than English spoken at home, percent age 5+, 2000	5.9%	17.9%
High school graduates, percent of persons age 25+, 2000	86.4%	80.4%
Bachelor's degree or higher, percent of persons age 25+, 2000	29.4%	24.4%
Persons with a disability, age 5+, 2000	97,167	49,746,248
Homeownership rate, 2000	70.6%	66.2%
Median value of owner-occupied housing units, 2000	$111,500	$119,600
Households, 2000	240,634	105,480,101
Persons per household, 2000	2.44	2.59
Median household money income, 1999	$40,856	$41,994
Per capita money income, 1999	$20,625	$21,587
Persons below poverty, percent, 1999	9.4%	12.4%

Business	Vermont	USA
Private nonfarm establishments, 1999	21,598	7,008,444
Private nonfarm employment, 1999	246,320	110,705,661
Private nonfarm employment, percent change 1990–99	14.4%	18.4%
Nonemployer establishments, 1999	49,696	16,152,604
Manufacturers shipments, 1997 ($1,000)	7,803,041	3,842,061,405
Retail sales, 1997 ($1,000)	5,898,646	2,460,886,012
Retail sales per capita, 1997	$10,020	$9,190
Minority-owned firms, percent of total, 1997	3.1%	14.6%
Women-owned firms, percent of total, 1997	25.2%	26.0%
Federal funds and grants, 2001 ($1,000)	3,733,752	1,763,896,019
Local government employment – full-time equivalent, 1997	17,841	10,227,429

Geography	Vermont	USA
Land area, 2000 (square miles)	9,250	3,537,438
Persons per square mile, 2000	65.8	79.6

(a) Includes persons reporting only one race.

(b) Hispanics may be of any race, so also are included in applicable race categories.

Z: Value greater than zero but less than half unit of measure shown.

Source: U.S. Census Bureau State & County QuickFacts

Virginia

Statehood: June 25, 1788
Nickname: Old Dominion
State bird: Cardinal
State flower: Dogwood flower
State tree: Dogwood
State motto: This always to tyrants
State capital: Richmond
Population of capital: 197,790 (2000)

The first permanent British settlement in North America was at Jamestown in 1607. Overcoming disease, harsh weather and violent confrontations with the Mattaponi, Chickahominy, Monacan and Rappahannock tribes, Virginia evolved into an aristocratic plantation society based on vast tobacco holdings. Virginia's military and political leaders were at the forefront of the Revolution and during the Civil War Richmond acted as the capital of the Confederacy. The main battleground of the war with over 400 engagements and the location of General Lee's surrender to General Grant at Appomattox, Virginia gained readmittance to the Union in 1870. More than 110 years later, citizens of Old Dominion elected the country's first black governor. The majority of the population is distributed between Virginia's largest cities: Alexandria, Richmond, Newport News, and Norfolk. Forty-one independent cities and 95 counties, many named after places in England lie within state borders.

The most northerly of the southern states, Virginia's geography is split between coastal plain and the Appalachian Plateau. In the west, the Piedmont rises to the Blue Ridge Mountains, where extensive forests and limestone caves add to the natural beauty. An important part of the state economy, Virginia's farms yield tobacco, peanuts, grain, vegetables, and fruits as well as some livestock. Industries include chemicals, shipbuilding, fishing, and transportation equipment. Stone, sand, and gravel are quarried but coal is the most important mineral deposit. The homes of numerous statesmen (Virginia is also known as the Mother of Presidents), his-

toric Jamestown and Williamsburg, numerous Civil War battlefields, and Skyline Drive in the Blue Ridge Mountains make this state a popular tourist destination.

Set on a blue field, the two figures, triumphant Virtue and defeated Tyranny pictured inside the seal enact the state motto. The Virginia Legislature adopted the flag in 1931.

Richmond

Settlers arrived here on the James River in about 1637 but the town served as a trading post before it was made state capital in 1780. Previous capitals at Jamestown and Williamsburg were short lived. In 1775 Patrick Henry, a fiery delegate who attended the Continental Congress uttered his famous words "Give me liberty or give me death," at St. John's Church in Richmond. During the Civil War, it became capital of the Confederate States until it fell to Union forces in 1865 after a prolonged siege. The tobacco industry has been an important source of revenue since the colonial period, joined more recently by metal product, textile, clothing, chemical, and publishing companies. Today large schools such as the University of Richmond and Virgina Commonwealth University share space downtown with numerous landmarks.

Virginia at a Glance

People	Virginia	USA
Population, 2003 estimate	7,386,330	290,809,777
Population percent change, April 1, 2000–July 1, 2001	1.5%	1.2%
Population, 2000	7,078,515	281,421,906
Persons under 5 years old, percent, 2000	6.5%	6.8%
Persons under 18 years old, percent, 2000	24.6%	25.7%
Persons 65 years old and over, percent, 2000	11.2%	12.4%
Female persons, percent, 2000	51.0%	50.9%
White persons, percent, 2000 (a)	72.3%	75.1%
African American persons, percent, 2000 (a)	19.6%	12.3%
Native American persons, percent, 2000 (a)	0.3%	0.9%
Asian persons, percent, 2000 (a)	3.7%	3.6%
Native Hawaiian and Other Pacific Islander, percent, 2000 (a)	0.1%	0.1%
Persons of Hispanic or Latino origin, percent, 2000 (b)	4.7%	12.5%
White persons, not of Hispanic/Latino origin, percent, 2000	70.2%	69.1%
Foreign born persons, percent, 2000	8.1%	11.1%
Language other than English spoken at home, percent age 5+, 2000	11.1%	17.9%
High school graduates, percent of persons age 25+, 2000	81.5%	80.4%
Bachelor's degree or higher, percent of persons age 25+, 2000	29.5%	24.4%
Persons with a disability, age 5+, 2000	1,155,083	49,746,248
Homeownership rate, 2000	68.1%	66.2%
Median value of owner-occupied housing units, 2000	$125,400	$119,600
Households, 2000	2,699,173	105,480,101
Persons per household, 2000	2.54	2.59
Median household money income, 1999	$46,677	$41,994
Per capita money income, 1999	$23,975	$21,587
Persons below poverty, percent, 1999	9.6%	12.4%

Business	Virginia	USA
Private nonfarm establishments, 1999	173,550	7,008,444
Private nonfarm employment, 1999	2,791,977	110,705,661
Private nonfarm employment, percent change 1990–99	20.3%	18.4%
Nonemployer establishments, 1999	360,974	16,152,604
Manufacturers shipments, 1997 ($1,000)	83,814,009	3,842,061,405
Retail sales, 1997 ($1,000)	62,569,924	2,460,886,012
Retail sales per capita, 1997	$9,293	$9,190
Minority-owned firms, percent of total, 1997	14.9%	14.6%
Women-owned firms, percent of total, 1997	27.5%	26.0%
Federal funds and grants, 2001 ($1,000)	71,257,343	1,763,896,019
Local government employment – full-time equivalent, 1997	253,219	10,227,429

Geography	Virginia	USA
Land area, 2000 (square miles)	39,594	3,537,438
Persons per square mile, 2000	178.8	79.6

(a) Includes persons reporting only one race.

(b) Hispanics may be of any race, so also are included in applicable race categories.

Z: Value greater than zero but less than half unit of measure shown.

Source: U.S. Census Bureau State & County QuickFacts

Washington

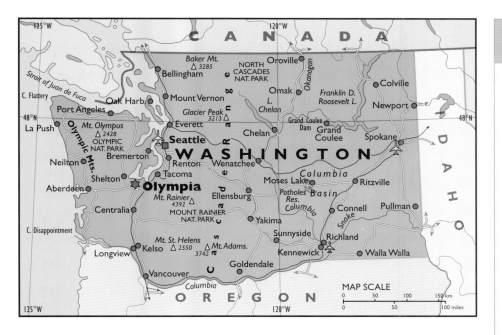

Statehood: November 11, 1889
Nickname: The Evergreen State
State bird: Willow goldfinch
State flower: Coast rhododendron
State tree: Western hemlock
State motto: Alki (Chinook word
for "by and by")
State capital: Olympia
Population of capital: 42,514 (2000)

Spanish explorers discovered the mouth of the Columbia River in 1775 and in 1792, British navigator George Vancouver mapped Puget Sound. Robert Gray sailed down the Sound and established the U.S. claim to the region. The Lewis and Clark Expedition, then the establishment of an American Fur Company trading post in 1811 strengthened this claim. From 1821 to 1846, the Hudson Bay Company administered the region, which was still inhabited by dozens of tribes like the Makah, Tulalip, Spokane, and Yakima. A treaty with the British fixed the boundary with Canada, and in 1847 most of the present state became part of the Oregon Territory. In 1853, Washington Territory was created and exploitation of its forests and fisheries attracted settlement. Spokane, on Hangman Creek in the east, along with Seattle and Tacoma, which hug the western shore, are the most populous cities. Washington is divided into 39 counties.

The Columbia Plateau, the volcanic Cascade Range, including Mount Rainier and Mount St. Helens, and Puget Sound dominate Washington's geography. The coastal region to the west of the range is one of the wettest areas in the country, supporting a dense temperate rain forest. In contrast, the region to the east of the Cascades is mostly treeless plain with low rainfall. An important wheat-producing area, the plateau is dependent on irrigation from the Columbia River, which is also one of the world's best sources of hydroelectricity. Washington is the leading producer of apples in the U.S.; other commercial activities include food processing, timber, aluminum, aerospace, and computer technology. Mounts Rainier and St. Helens, North Cascades National Park, the Whitman Mission and Fort Vancouver National Historic Site stand as examples of Washington's rich history and natural beauty.

The green background of the state flag represents the large fir, spruce and cedar forests in Washington. The centralized seal, showing George Washington, makes the flag the only banner in the nation with a picture of a president.

Olympia

A port on the southern tip of the Puget Sound, Olympia was made capital of Washington Territory in 1853. Development was spurred with the coming of the railroad in the 1880s and its port was expanded during both World Wars. Agriculture, food canning, brewing, oyster fishing, and lumbering generate the most revenue for the city.

Washington at a Glance

People	Washington	USA
Population, 2003 estimate	6,131,445	290,809,777
Population percent change, April 1, 2000–July 1, 2001	1.6%	1.2%
Population, 2000	5,894,121	281,421,906
Persons under 5 years old, percent, 2000	6.7%	6.8%
Persons under 18 years old, percent, 2000	25.7%	25.7%
Persons 65 years old and over, percent, 2000	11.2%	12.4%
Female persons, percent, 2000	50.2%	50.9%
White persons, percent, 2000 (a)	81.8%	75.1%
African American persons, percent, 2000 (a)	3.2%	12.3%
Native American persons, percent, 2000 (a)	1.6%	0.9%
Asian persons, percent, 2000 (a)	5.5%	3.6%
Native Hawaiian and Other Pacific Islander, percent, 2000 (a)	0.4%	0.1%
Persons of Hispanic or Latino origin, percent, 2000 (b)	7.5%	12.5%
White persons, not of Hispanic/Latino origin, percent, 2000	78.9%	69.1%
Foreign born persons, percent, 2000	10.4%	11.1%
Language other than English spoken at home, percent age 5+, 2000	14.0%	17.9%
High school graduates, percent of persons age 25+, 2000	87.1%	80.4%
Bachelor's degree or higher, percent of persons age 25+, 2000	27.7%	24.4%
Persons with a disability, age 5+, 2000	981,007	49,746,248
Homeownership rate, 2000	64.6%	66.2%
Median value of owner-occupied housing units, 2000	$168,300	$119,600
Households, 2000	2,271,398	105,480,101
Persons per household, 2000	2.53	2.59
Median household money income, 1999	$45,776	$41,994
Per capita money income, 1999	$22,973	$21,587
Persons below poverty, percent, 1999	10.6%	12.4%

Business	Washington	USA
Private nonfarm establishments, 1999	162,932	7,008,444
Private nonfarm employment, 1999	2,209,129	110,705,661
Private nonfarm employment, percent change 1990–99	25.4%	18.4%
Nonemployer establishments, 1999	321,766	16,152,604
Manufacturers shipments, 1997 ($1,000)	78,852,486	3,842,061,405
Retail sales, 1997 ($1,000)	52,472,866	2,460,886,012
Retail sales per capita, 1997	$9,363	$9,190
Minority-owned firms, percent of total, 1997	9.6%	14.6%
Women-owned firms, percent of total, 1997	27.5%	26.0%
Federal funds and grants, 2001 ($1,000)	36,903,358	1,763,896,019
Local government employment – full-time equivalent, 1997	185,152	10,227,429

Geography	Washington	USA
Land area, 2000 (square miles)	66,544	3,537,438
Persons per square mile, 2000	88.6	79.6

(a) Includes persons reporting only one race.
(b) Hispanics may be of any race, so also are included in applicable race categories.
Z: Value greater than zero but less than half unit of measure shown.

Source: U.S. Census Bureau State & County QuickFacts

West Virginia

Statehood: June 20, 1863
Nickname: The Mountain State
State bird: Cardinal
State flower: Rhododendron
State tree: Sugar maple
State motto: Mountaineers are always free
State capital: Charleston
Population of capital: 53,421 (2000)

In 1727, Germans established the first settlement at New Mecklenburg (now Shepherdstown) in the Appalachian Mountains. This land lay at the edge of the territory claimed by the Adena mound building culture and several structures survive today. English settlers crossing the Appalachian and Allegheny Mountains led to the French and Indian War. The region was then part of Virginia, but political and economic disagreements especially regarding slavery arose between western Virginians and the dominant eastern inhabitants. When Virginia seceded in May 1861 to join the Confederacy, there was much opposition in the west, and West Virginia was admitted to the Union as the 35th state. Charleston, Morgantown, Huntington and Wheeling contain the majority of West Virginia's population, the rest of which is dispersed across 55 counties.

West Virginia, mountainous and rugged, has two narrow projections: the Northern Panhandle extending north between Ohio and Pennsylvania and the Eastern Panhandle cutting between Maryland and Virginia. Harpers Ferry in the eastern corner lies on the bank of the Potomac River, which forms much of the state's northern border while the Ohio River forms most of the western border. Hay, tobacco, corn, and apples are the principal crops, but West Virginia also has rich mineral deposits, and is the leading producer of bituminous coal in the U.S. Some sixty-five percent of the land is forested. Industries include glass, chemicals, steel, machinery, and tourism, drawing people to Harpers Ferry, Blackwater Falls State Park, or any of the various caverns in the west.

Adopted in 1929, the state flag depicts a miner and a farmer standing in front of a pair of rifles and a red liberty cap that demonstrate their readiness to fight for freedom. The date of West Virginia's statehood is shown on a rock in the center of the seal and rhododendron, the state flower, surrounds the image. The white flag has a blue border.

Charleston

At the junction of the Elk and Kanawha Rivers, Charleston grew around Fort Lee in the 1780s. It is an important trade and transport center for the industrialized Kanawha Valley. A center for salt production in the 19th century, local industry has since shifted to concentrate on chemicals, glass, metallurgy, timber, and oil, gas, and coal in particular. Daniel Boone lived here at the end of the 18th century.

West Virginia at a Glance

People	West Virginia	USA
Population, 2003 estimate	1,810,354	290,809,777
Population percent change,		
April 1, 2000–July 1, 2001	−0.4%	1.2%
Population, 2000	1,808,344	281,421,906
Persons under 5 years old, percent, 2000	5.6%	6.8%
Persons under 18 years old, percent, 2000	22.3%	25.7%
Persons 65 years old and over, percent, 2000	15.3%	12.4%
Female persons, percent, 2000	51.4%	50.9%
White persons, percent, 2000 (a)	95.0%	75.1%
African American persons,		
percent, 2000 (a)	3.2%	12.3%
Native American persons,		
percent, 2000 (a)	0.2%	0.9%
Asian persons, percent, 2000 (a)	0.5%	3.6%
Native Hawaiian and Other Pacific Islander,		
percent, 2000 (a)	Z	0.1%
Persons of Hispanic or Latino origin,		
percent, 2000 (b)	0.7%	12.5%
White persons, not of Hispanic/Latino origin,		
percent, 2000	94.6%	69.1%
Foreign born persons, percent, 2000	1.1%	11.1%
Language other than English spoken at home,		
percent age 5+, 2000	2.7%	17.9%
High school graduates, percent of persons		
age 25+, 2000	75.2%	80.4%
Bachelor's degree or higher,		
percent of persons age 25+, 2000	14.8%	24.4%
Persons with a disability, age 5+, 2000	410,781	49,746,248
Homeownership rate, 2000	75.2%	66.2%
Median value of owner-occupied		
housing units, 2000	$72,800	$119,600
Households, 2000	736,481	105,480,101
Persons per household, 2000	2.4	2.59
Median household money income, 1999	$29,696	$41,994
Per capita money income, 1999	$16,477	$21,587
Persons below poverty, percent, 1999	17.9%	12.4%

Business	West Virginia	USA
Private nonfarm establishments, 1999	41,451	7,008,444
Private nonfarm employment, 1999	545,495	110,705,661
Private nonfarm employment,		
percent change 1990–99	13.1%	18.4%
Nonemployer establishments, 1999	81,212	16,152,604
Manufacturers shipments, 1997 ($1,000)	18,293,309	3,842,061,405
Retail sales, 1997 ($1,000)	14,057,933	2,460,886,012
Retail sales per capita, 1997	$7,743	$9,190
Minority-owned firms, percent of total, 1997	3.8%	14.6%
Women-owned firms, percent of total, 1997	27.1%	26.0%
Federal funds and grants, 2001 ($1,000)	12,540,808	1,763,896,019
Local government employment –		
full-time equivalent, 1997	59,926	10,227,429

Geography	West Virginia	USA
Land area, 2000 (square miles)	24,078	3,537,438
Persons per square mile, 2000	75.1	79.6

(a) Includes persons reporting only one race.

(b) Hispanics may be of any race, so also are included in applicable race categories.

Z: Value greater than zero but less than half unit of measure shown.

Source: U.S. Census Bureau State & County QuickFacts

Wisconsin

Statehood: May 29, 1848
Nickname: The Badger State
State bird: Robin
State flower: Wood violet
State tree: Sugar maple
State motto: Forward
State capital: Madison
Population of capital: 208,054 (2000)

Explorer Jean Nicolet claimed the region for France in 1634, but Britain seized the land southwest of the Great Lakes and east of the Mississippi River in 1763. At the end of the Revolutionary War, Britain ceded it to the United States but settlement of the rugged hills between Lake Superior and Lake Michigan was slow. In 1836, the U.S. government established the Territory of Wisconsin. The first state to establish primary elections, Wisconsin also contains the birthplace of the Ringling Brothers Circus at Baraboo. Madison, Milwaukee and Green Bay are the largest metropolitan areas in the Badger State. The names of many of Wisconsin's native tribes are preserved in the designations given to its waterways and its 72 counties: Winnebago, Menominee, Kickapoo and Oneida.

Primarily rolling plain, Wisconsin's landscape is dotted with numerous glacial lakes as it slopes gradually down from the Gogebic range in the north. Meandering rivers such as the St. Croix, the Chippewa, and state's namesake, have carved the terrain into interesting rock formations. Wisconsin is the leading producer of milk, butter, and cheese in the nation with hundreds of factories statewide. The chief crops are hay, corn, oats, fruit, and vegetables. Wisconsin's most valuable resource however, is timber—forty-five percent of the land is forested. Zinc, lead, copper, iron, sand, and gravel mining in the north along with food processing, farm machinery manufacturing, brewing, and tourism are the primary sources of employment. Numerous landmarks like the Apostle Islands National Lakeshore, the St. Croix National Scenic Riverway, the National Railroad Museum and the Wisconsin Maritime Museum encourage sightseers to visit the state more than once.

A seal replete with symbolism sits between the word "Wisconsin" and the date of statehood, "1848," on the blue state flag. Divided into quarters, the coat of arms displays representations of mining, sailing, manufacturing and agriculture. A sailor and a miner stand on either side, with a badger, the state animal, above. Beneath the scene a cornucopia and a stack of lead stand for the state's resources.

Madison

On an isthmus between Lakes Mendota and Monona, Madison was founded as the state capital in 1836, named for President James Madison, and incorporated as a city in 1856. The second-largest urban area in Wisconsin is an educational and manufacturing center in a dairy-farming region. The production of medical equipment, along with agricultural machinery, meat and dairy products, supports the economy.

Wisconsin at a Glance

People	Wisconsin	USA
Population, 2003 estimate	5,472,299	290,809,777
Population percent change, April 1, 2000–July 1, 2001	0.7%	1.2%
Population, 2000	5,363,675	281,421,906
Persons under 5 years old, percent, 2000	6.4%	6.8%
Persons under 18 years old, percent, 2000	25.5%	25.7%
Persons 65 years old and over, percent, 2000	13.1%	12.4%
Female persons, percent, 2000	50.6%	50.9%
White persons, percent, 2000 (a)	88.9%	75.1%
African American persons, percent, 2000 (a)	5.7%	12.3%
Native American persons, percent, 2000 (a)	0.9%	0.9%
Asian persons, percent, 2000 (a)	1.7%	3.6%
Native Hawaiian and Other Pacific Islander, percent, 2000 (a)	Z	0.1%
Persons of Hispanic or Latino origin, percent, 2000 (b)	3.6%	12.5%
White persons, not of Hispanic/Latino origin, percent, 2000	87.3%	69.1%
Foreign born persons, percent, 2000	3.6%	11.1%
Language other than English spoken at home, percent age 5+, 2000	7.3%	17.9%
High school graduates, percent of persons age 25+, 2000	85.1%	80.4%
Bachelor's degree or higher, percent of persons age 25+, 2000	22.4%	24.4%
Persons with a disability, age 5+, 2000	790,917	49,746,248
Homeownership rate, 2000	68.4%	66.2%
Median value of owner-occupied housing units, 2000	$112,200	$119,600
Households, 2000	2,084,544	105,480,101
Persons per household, 2000	2.5	2.59
Median household money income, 1999	$43,791	$41,994
Per capita money income, 1999	$21,271	$21,587
Persons below poverty, percent, 1999	8.7%	12.4%

Business	Wisconsin	USA
Private nonfarm establishments, 1999	139,646	7,008,444
Private nonfarm employment, 1999	2,368,404	110,705,661
Private nonfarm employment, percent change 1990–99	21.5%	18.4%
Nonemployer establishments, 1999	264,657	16,152,604
Manufacturers shipments, 1997 ($1,000)	117,382,992	3,842,061,405
Retail sales, 1997 ($1,000)	50,520,463	2,460,886,012
Retail sales per capita, 1997	$9,715	$9,190
Minority-owned firms, percent of total, 1997	3.7%	14.6%
Women-owned firms, percent of total, 1997	24.4%	26.0%
Federal funds and grants, 2001 ($1,000)	26,645,345	1,763,896,019
Local government employment – full-time equivalent, 1997	201,633	10,227,429

Geography	Wisconsin	USA
Land area, 2000 (square miles)	54,310	3,537,438
Persons per square mile, 2000	98.8	79.6

(a) Includes persons reporting only one race.

(b) Hispanics may be of any race, so also are included in applicable race categories.

Z: Value greater than zero but less than half unit of measure shown.

Source: U.S. Census Bureau State & County QuickFacts

Wyoming

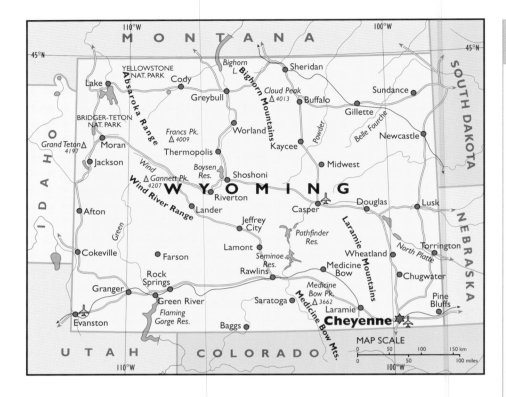

Statehood: July 10, 1890
Nickname: The Equality State
State bird: Meadowlark
State flower: Indian paintbrush
State tree: Cottonwood
State motto: Equal rights
State capital: Cheyenne
Population of capital: 53,001 (2000)

Beginning with the Louisiana Purchase of 1803, the U.S. gradually acquired the entire territory of Wyoming through treaties. The fur trade aided 19th-century development, as did westward migration along the Oregon Trail. The 1860s marked the first dramatic arrival of new settlers, first with the Bozeman Trail, and then with the arrival of the railroad in 1868. While the state did relocate most of the Native American population to reservations by the 1870s, it also passed the first equal rights laws in the nation, ensuring women could vote and hold office. The next 20 years were marked by a rise of vigilante groups formed to deal with cattle rustlers and outlaws. In 1890, Wyoming became the 44th state of the Union. Ranked last in population in the nation, the cities of Cheyenne, Casper and Laramie contain less than half a million inhabitants combined. Wyoming is divided into 23 counties.

Steep mountains and 10 million acres of forest dominate the landscape of Wyoming. The Wind River, and Absaroka ranges, as part of the Rockies cross the state from northwest to southeast offering a route west to pioneers at South Pass. In the east lie the rolling grasslands of high plains country. The north of the state where the Crow, Sioux, and Cheyenne hunted buffalo, is also primarily tall grass plain. Today, fertile farmland and cattle ranches cover the same country. Many rivers, including the North Platte and the Snake, flow down from the mountains. While cattle ranching, sheep, and wheat farming remain important to the economy, Wyoming is a top oil-producing state. Other important mineral resources include coal, bentonite and uranium. Tourism is a vital industry, with the state's natural beauty annually attracting more than seven million visitors. Yellowstone, the largest National Park in the country, occupies the entire northwestern corner of the state. Grand Teton National Park, Devil's Tower National Monument and Fort Laramie National Historic Site also compel tourists to linger in Wyoming.

The state seal is branded on the white silhouette of a buffalo on Wyoming's flag, adopted in 1917. It shows a woman, representing equal rights, with a rancher and a miner on either side. A banner curling around two columns reads: Livestock, Grains, Mines, and Oil. The red border refers to Native Americans and the blood of pioneers.

Cheyenne

Founded in 1867 as a banking and transportation center for freight and livestock, Cheyenne gained a degree of fame due to its connections with figures such as Buffalo Bill, Calamity Jane, and Wild Bill Hickock. Logging, packing plants, and oil refineries have risen in economic importance in the 20th century.

Wyoming at a Glance

People	Wyoming	USA
Population, 2003 estimate	501,242	290,809,777
Population percent change, April 1, 2000–July 1, 2001	0.1%	1.2%
Population, 2000	493,782	281,421,906
Persons under 5 years old, percent, 2000	6.3%	6.8%
Persons under 18 years old, percent, 2000	26.1%	25.7%
Persons 65 years old and over, percent, 2000	11.7%	12.4%
Female persons, percent, 2000	49.7%	50.9%
White persons, percent, 2000 (a)	92.1%	75.1%
African American persons, percent, 2000 (a)	0.8%	12.3%
Native American persons, percent, 2000 (a)	2.3%	0.9%
Asian persons, percent, 2000 (a)	0.6%	3.6%
Native Hawaiian and Other Pacific Islander, percent, 2000 (a)	0.1%	0.1%
Persons of Hispanic or Latino origin, percent, 2000 (b)	6.4%	12.5%
White persons, not of Hispanic/Latino origin, percent, 2000	88.9%	69.1%
Foreign born persons, percent, 2000	2.3%	11.1%
Language other than English spoken at home, percent age 5+, 2000	6.4%	17.9%
High school graduates, percent of persons age 25+, 2000	87.9%	80.4%
Bachelor's degree or higher, percent of persons age 25+, 2000	21.9%	24.4%
Persons with a disability, age 5+, 2000	77,143	49,746,248
Homeownership rate, 2000	70.0%	66.2%
Median value of owner-occupied housing units, 2000	$96,600	$119,600
Households, 2000	193,608	105,480,101
Persons per household, 2000	2.48	2.59
Median household money income, 1999	$37,892	$41,994
Per capita money income, 1999	$19,134	$21,587
Persons below poverty, percent, 1999	11.4%	12.4%

Business	Wyoming	USA
Private nonfarm establishments, 1999	17,909	7,008,444
Private nonfarm employment, 1999	169,188	110,705,661
Private nonfarm employment, percent change 1990–99	28.1%	18.4%
Nonemployer establishments, 1999	35,195	16,152,604
Manufacturers shipments, 1997 ($1,000)	2,955,070	3,842,061,405
Retail sales, 1997 ($1,000)	4,530,537	2,460,886,012
Retail sales per capita, 1997	$9,438	$9,190
Minority-owned firms, percent of total, 1997	4.3%	14.6%
Women-owned firms, percent of total, 1997	22.6%	26.0%
Federal funds and grants, 2001 ($1,000)	3,583,585	1,763,896,019
Local government employment – full-time equivalent, 1997	27,423	10,227,429

Geography	Wyoming	USA
Land area, 2000 (square miles)	97,100	3,537,438
Persons per square mile, 2000	5.1	79.6

(a) Includes persons reporting only one race.

(b) Hispanics may be of any race, so also are included in applicable race categories.

Z: Value greater than zero but less than half unit of measure shown.

Source: U.S. Census Bureau State & County QuickFacts

INDEX

How to use the index

The index contains the names of the places and features shown on the maps covering the United States. Each name is followed by an additional entry in italics giving the state, province or region within which it is located.

The alphabetical order of names composed of two or more words is governed primarily by the first word and then by the second. This is an example of the rule:

Middle River *MD* . . . 39°20N 76°27W **77 A4**
Middle River *MN* . . . 48°26N 96°10W **80 B2**
Middle Valley *TN* . . . 35°12N 85°11W **97 E7**
Middle Village *NY* . 40°43N 73°52W **114 B3**
Middleboro *MA* . . . . 41°54N 70°55W **78 C4**

Physical features composed of a proper name (Erie) and a description (Lake) are positioned alphabetically by the proper name. The description is positioned after the proper name and is usually abbreviated:

Erie, L. *N. Amer.* . . . . 42°15N 81°0W **92 B5**

Where a description forms part of a settlement or administrative name, however, it is always written in full and put in its true alphabetical position:

Mount Olive *IL* . . . . . . 39°4N 89°44W **71 D4**

Names beginning with M' and Mc are indexed as if they were spelled Mac. Names beginning St. are alphabetized under Saint, but Sant', Santa and San are all spelled in full and are alphabetized accordingly.

The geographical coordinates that follow the name give the latitude and longitude of each place. The first coordinate indicates latitude – the distance north or south of the Equator. The second coordinate indicates longitude – the distance east or west of the Greenwich Meridian. Both latitude and longitude are measured in degrees and minutes (there are 60 minutes in a degree).

The latitude is followed by N(orth) or S(outh) and the longitude by E(ast) or W(est).

The number in bold type that follows the geographical coordinates refers to the number of the map page where that feature or place will be found. This is usually the largest scale at which the place or feature appears.

The letter and figure that are in bold type immediately after the page number give the grid square on the map page, within which the feature is situated. The letter represents the latitude and the figure the longitude. A lower-case letter immediately after the page number refers to an inset map on that page.

In some cases the feature itself may fall within the specified square, while the name is outside. This is usually the case only with features that are larger than a grid square.

Rivers are indexed to their mouths or confluences, and carry the symbol → after their names. The following symbols are also used in the index: ■ country, ☒ overseas territory or dependency, ☐ state or province, ☆ county, △ national park, ⌓ other park (national monuments and recreation areas, state and provincial parks, and wildlife reserves), and ✈ (DCA) principal airport (and location identifier).

Abbreviations

AK – Alaska
AL – Alabama
Amer. – America(n)
AR – Arkansas
AZ – Arizona
B. – Baie, Bahía, Bay
C. – Cabo, Cap, Cape
CA – California
CO – Colorado
CT – Connecticut
DC – District of Columbia
DE – Delaware
E. – East
FL – Florida
G. – Golfe, Golfo, Gulf
GA – Georgia
Harb. – Harbor, Harbour
Hd. – Head
HI – Hawai'i
Hts. – Heights
I.(s). – Île, Isla, Island, Isle
IA – Iowa
ID – Idaho
IL – Illinois
IN – Indiana
KS – Kansas
KY – Kentucky
L. – Lac, Lago, Lake
LA – Louisiana
MA – Massachusetts
MD – Maryland
ME – Maine
MI – Michigan
MN – Minnesota
MO – Missouri
MS – Mississippi
MT – Montana
Mt.(s). – Mont, Montaña, Mount, Mountain
N. – Nord, Norte, North, Northern
Nat. – National
NC – North Carolina
ND – North Dakota
NE – Nebraska
NH – New Hampshire
NJ – New Jersey
NM – New Mexico
NV – Nevada
NY – New York
OH – Ohio
OK – Oklahoma
OR – Oregon
P. – Pass
PA – Pennsylvania
Pac. Oc. – Pacific Ocean
Pass. – Passage
Pen. – Peninsula, Péninsule
Pk. – Peak
Plat. – Plateau
Pt. – Point
Pta. – Punta
R. – Rio, River
Range – Range
Recr. – Recreational
Res. – Reserve, Reservoir
RI – Rhode Island
S. – South, Southern
Sa. – Serra, Sierra
SC – South Carolina
SD – South Dakota
Sd. – Sound
Sprs. – Springs
St. – Saint
Sta. – Santa
Ste. – Sainte
Sto. – Santo
Str. – Strait, Stretto
Terr. – Territory, Territoire
TN – Tennessee
TX – Texas
UT – Utah
VA – Virginia
VT – Vermont
W. – West
WA – Washington
WI – Wisconsin
WV – West Virginia
WY – Wyoming

A

Abajo Peak *UT* . . . 37°51N 109°27W **100 F6**
Abbaye, Pt. *MI* . . . . . . 46°58N 88°8W **79 C3**
Abbeville *AL* . . . . . . 31°34N 85°15W **60 E5**
Abbeville *GA* . . . . . . 31°59N 83°18W **68 E3**
Abbeville *LA* . . . . 29°58N 92°8W **75 E3**
Abbeville *MS* . . . . . . 34°30N 89°30W **81 B4**
Abbeville *SC* . . . . 34°11N 82°23W **90 D3**
Abbeville County ☆
SC . . . . 34°15N 82°30W **90 D3**
Abbotsford *WI* . . . . 44°57N 90°19W **103 D3**
Abbott *NM* . . . . 36°18N 104°16W **88 A6**
Abbott *TX* . . . . 31°53N 97°4W **99 F10**
Abbottstown *PA* . . . . 39°53N 76°59W **77 A4**
Abercrombie *ND* . . . 46°27N 96°44W **91 D9**
Aberdeen *AL* . . . . . . 33°49N 88°33W **81 C5**
Aberdeen *ID* . . . . . . 42°57N 112°50W **70 G6**
Aberdeen *KY* . . . . . . 37°15N 86°41W **96 C6**
Aberdeen *MD* . . . . . . 39°31N 76°10W **77 A4**
Aberdeen *NC* . . . . 35°8N 79°26W **90 C6**
Aberdeen *OH* . . . . . . 38°39N 83°46W **92 E3**
Aberdeen *SD* . . . . . . 45°28N 98°29W **91 E7**
Aberdeen *WA* . . . . 46°59N 123°50W **101 D2**
Aberdeen L. *MS* . . . . 33°50N 88°31W **81 C5**
Aberdeen Proving Ground
MD . . . . 39°29N 76°10W **77 A4**
Abernant *AL* . . . . 33°17N 87°12W **60 C3**
Abernathy *TX* . . . . . 33°50N 101°51W **98 D6**
Abert, L. *OR* . . . . . . 42°38N 120°14W **94 E5**
Abilene *KS* . . . . 38°55N 97°13W **74 C6**
Abilene *TX* . . . . 32°28N 99°43W **99 E8**
Abingdon *IL* . . . . 40°48N 90°24W **71 C3**
Abingdon *VA* . . . . . 36°43N 81°59W **102 E3**
Abington *CT* . . . . 41°52N 72°1W **78 C2**
Abington *MA* . . . . 42°6N 70°57W **78 B4**
Abington *PA* . . . . 40°7N 75°7W **116 A2**
Abiquiu *NM* . . . . . . 36°13N 106°19W **88 A4**
Abiquiu Res. *NM* . . 36°16N 106°27W **88 A4**
Abita Springs *LA* . . . . 30°29N 90°2W **75 D5**
Abraham Lincoln Birthplace Nat.
Historic Site ⌓ *KY* 37°32N 85°44W **97 C7**
Absaroka Range
WY . . . . 44°45N 109°50W **104 B3**
Absarokee *MT* . . . . 45°31N 109°27W **83 E8**
Absecon *NJ* . . . . 39°26N 74°30W **87 C2**
Absecon Lighthouse
NJ . . . . 39°22N 74°27W **87 C2**
Acadia Nat. Park △
ME . . . . 44°20N 68°13W **76 D5**
Acadia Parish ☆ *LA*. 30°13N 92°22W **75 D3**
Accident *MD* . . . . 39°38N 79°19W **77 A1**
Accokeek *MD* . . . . 38°40N 77°2W **77 B3**
Accomac *VA* . . . . . . 37°43N 75°40W **102 D9**
Accomack County ☆
VA . . . . 37°45N 75°40W **102 D9**
Accotink, L. *VA* . . . 38°47N 77°13W **119 C2**
Accotink Cr. → *VA* 38°51N 77°15W **119 B2**
Achille *OK* . . . . 33°50N 96°23W **93 E7**
Ackerman *MS* . . . . . . 33°19N 89°11W **81 C4**
Ackley *IA* . . . . 42°33N 93°3W **73 C5**
Acme *LA* . . . . 31°17N 91°49W **75 C4**
Acoma Indian Reservation
NM . . . . 34°45N 107°30W **88 C3**
Acomita *NM* . . . . 35°3N 107°34W **88 B3**
Acton *MA* . . . . 42°29N 71°26W **78 B3**
Acushnet *MA* . . . . . . 41°41N 70°55W **78 C4**
Acworth *GA* . . . . 34°4N 84°41W **68 B2**
Ada *KS* . . . . 39°9N 97°53W **74 B6**
Ada *MN* . . . . 47°18N 96°31W **80 C2**
Ada *OH* . . . . 40°46N 83°49W **92 C3**
Ada *OK* . . . . 34°46N 96°41W **93 D7**
Ada County ☆ *ID* . . 43°30N 116°15W **70 F2**
Adair *IA* . . . . 41°30N 94°39W **73 D4**
Adair *OK* . . . . 36°26N 95°16W **93 B8**
Adair County ☆ *IA* . 41°20N 94°30W **73 D4**
Adair County ☆ *KY* . . 37°5N 85°20W **97 C7**
Adair County ☆ *MO* 40°10N 92°35W **82 A4**
Adair County ☆ *OK* 35°55N 94°45W **93 C9**
Adairsville *GA* . . . . . 34°22N 84°56W **68 B2**
Adairville *KY* . . . . . . 36°40N 86°51W **96 D6**
Adak *AK* . . . . 51°45N 176°45W **61 L3**
Adak I. *AK* . . . . 51°45N 176°45W **61 L3**
Adams *CA* . . . . 32°45N 117°7W **117 B2**
Adams *MA* . . . . 42°38N 73°7W **78 B1**
Adams *MN* . . . . 43°34N 92°43W **80 G6**
Adams *ND* . . . . 48°25N 98°5W **91 B7**
Adams *NY* . . . . 43°49N 76°1W **89 B4**
Adams *NE* . . . . 40°28N 96°31W **84 D9**
Adams *OK* . . . . 36°45N 101°5W **93 B2**
Adams *OR* . . . . 45°46N 118°34W **94 B7**
Adams *TN* . . . . 36°35N 87°4W **96 D5**
Adams *WI* . . . . 43°57N 89°49W **103 E4**
Adams, Mt. *WA* . . 46°12N 121°30W **101 D4**
Adams Center *NY* . . . 43°52N 76°0W **89 B5**
Adams County ☆
CO . . . . 39°50N 104°10W **66 C6**
Adams County ☆ *ID* 45°0N 116°30W **70 E2**
Adams County ☆ *IL* . 40°0N 91°10W **71 D2**
Adams County ☆ *IN* . 40°45N 85°0W **72 C6**
Adams County ☆ *IA* . 41°0N 94°40W **73 D4**
Adams County ☆ *MS* 31°23N 91°24W **81 E2**
Adams County ☆
ND . . . . 46°0N 102°30W **91 D3**
Adams County ☆ *NE* 40°30N 98°30W **84 D7**
Adams County ☆
OH . . . . 38°48N 83°33W **92 E3**
Adams County ☆ *PA* 39°50N 77°14W **95 E5**
Adams County ☆
WA . . . . 47°0N 118°30W **101 C7**
Adams County ☆ *WI* 44°0N 89°50W **103 E4**
Adams-McGill Res.
NV . . . . 38°22N 115°7W **85 D5**
Adams Park *GA* . . . 33°43N 84°27W **106 B2**
Adams Pt. *MI* . . . . . . 45°25N 83°43W **79 D8**
Adams Shore *MA* . . 42°15N 70°59W **106 B4**
Adamstown *PA* . . . . . . 40°15N 76°3W **95 D6**
Adamsville *OH* . . . . . . 40°4N 81°53W **92 C5**
Adamsville *RI* . . . . . . 41°30N 71°10W **78 C3**
Adamsville *TN* . . . . . 35°14N 88°23W **96 E4**
Adamsville *TX* . . . . . 31°18N 98°10W **99 F9**
Addieville *IL* . . . . 38°23N 89°29W **71 E4**
Addington *OK* . . . . . 34°15N 97°58W **93 D6**
Addis *LA* . . . . 30°21N 91°16W **75 D4**
Addison *AL* . . . . 34°12N 87°11W **60 B3**
Addison *IL* . . . . 41°55N 88°0W **71 B5**
Addison *NY* . . . . 42°1N 77°14W **89 C3**
Addison *OH* . . . . 38°53N 82°9W **92 E4**
Addison *VT* . . . . 44°8N 73°20W **86 B1**
Addison County ☆ *VT* 44°0N 73°15W **86 B1**
Addy *WA* . . . . 48°21N 117°50W **101 B8**
Adel *GA* . . . . 31°8N 83°25W **68 E3**
Adel *IA* . . . . 41°37N 94°1W **73 D4**
Adel *OR* . . . . 42°11N 119°54W **94 E6**
Adelanto *CA* . . . . . . 34°35N 117°22W **65 J9**
Adelphi *MD* . . . . 39°0N 76°58W **119 A4**
Adelphi *OH* . . . . 39°28N 82°45W **92 D4**
Adelphia *NJ* . . . . 40°13N 74°15W **87 B2**
Adena *OH* . . . . 40°13N 80°53W **92 C6**
Adin *CA* . . . . 41°12N 120°57W **64 B6**
Adirondack Mts. *NY* . . 44°0N 74°0W **89 B7**
Adirondack Park ⌓
NY . . . . 44°0N 74°20W **89 B6**
Adjuntas
Puerto Rico . . . . 18°10N 66°43W **105 G16**
Adler Planetarium
IL . . . . 41°51N 87°36W **108 B3**
Admiralty I. *AK* . . 57°30N 134°30W **61 H14**
Admiralty Inlet *WA* 48°8N 122°58W **101 B3**
Admiralty Island Nat. Monument ⌓
U.S.A. . . . . 57°40N 134°10W **61 H14**
Adobe Creek Res.
CO . . . . 38°14N 103°17W **66 D7**
Adobe Dam County Recreation
Area *AZ* . . . . 33°41N 112°9W **116 A1**
Adrian *GA* . . . . 32°33N 82°35W **68 D4**
Adrian *MI* . . . . 41°54N 84°2W **79 H7**
Adrian *MN* . . . . 43°38N 95°56W **80 G3**
Adrian *MO* . . . . 38°24N 94°21W **82 C2**
Adrian *OR* . . . . 43°45N 117°4W **94 D8**
Adrian *TX* . . . . 35°16N 102°40W **98 B5**
Advance *IN* . . . . 40°0N 86°40W **72 D4**
Advance *MO* . . . . 37°6N 89°55W **82 D7**
Aetna *KS* . . . . 37°5N 98°58W **74 D5**
Affton *MO* . . . . 38°33N 90°20W **82 C6**
Afognak I. *AK* . . . . 58°15N 152°30W **61 G9**
Afton *CA* . . . . 35°2N 116°23W **65 H10**
Afton *IA* . . . . 41°2N 94°12W **73 D4**
Afton *NY* . . . . 42°14N 75°32W **89 C5**
Afton *OK* . . . . 36°42N 94°58W **93 B9**
Afton *WY* . . . . 42°44N 110°56W **104 D2**
Agana *Guam* . . . . 13°28N 144°45E **105 b**
Agar *SD* . . . . 44°50N 100°5W **91 F5**
Agassiz Nat. Wildlife Refuge ⌓
MN . . . . 48°21N 95°57W **80 B3**
Agassiz Pool *MN* . . . 48°20N 95°59W **80 B3**
Agat *Guam* . . . . 13°25N 144°40E **105 b**
Agate *CO* . . . . 39°28N 103°57W **66 C7**
Agate Fossil Beds Nat.
Monument ⌓ *NE* 42°20N 103°50W **84 B2**
Agattu I. *AK* . . . . 52°25N 173°35E **61 K1**
Agawam *MA* . . . . 42°5N 72°37W **78 B2**
Agawam *MT* . . . . 48°0N 112°10W **83 C5**
Agency *IA* . . . . 41°0N 92°18W **73 E6**
Agency L. *OR* . . . . . 42°33N 121°58W **94 E4**
Agenda *KS* . . . . 39°43N 97°26W **74 B6**
Agra *KS* . . . . 39°46N 99°7W **74 B4**
Agra *OK* . . . . 35°54N 96°53W **93 C7**
Agrihan *N. Marianas* 18°46N 145°40E **105 a**
Agua Dulce *TX* . . . . 27°47N 97°55W **99 K10**
Agua Fria *NM* . . . . . . 35°39N 106°1W **88 B4**
Agua Fria → *AZ* . . 33°23N 112°22W **62 D3**
Agua Fria Nat. Monument ⌓
AZ . . . . 34°14N 112°0W **62 C3**
Agua Fria Pk. *NM* . 36°22N 105°13W **88 A5**
Agua Nueva *TX* . . . . 26°54N 98°36W **98 L9**
Aguada
Puerto Rico . . . . 18°23N 67°11W **105 G15**
Aguadilla
Puerto Rico . . . . 18°26N 67°10W **105 G15**
Aguila *AZ* . . . . 33°57N 113°11W **62 D2**
Aguila, Punta
Puerto Rico . . . . 17°57N 67°13W **105 H15**
Aguilar *CO* . . . . 37°24N 104°39W **66 E6**
Aguilares *TX* . . . . 27°27N 99°5W **98 K8**
Agujereada, Pta.
Puerto Rico . . . . . 18°30N 67°8W **105 G15**
Ahoskie *NC* . . . . 36°17N 76°59W **90 B9**
'Āhuimanu *HI* . . . . 21°26N 157°50W **69 K14**
Ahwatukee Foothills
AZ . . . . 33°20N 111°59W **116 D2**
'Aiea *HI* . . . . 21°23N 157°56W **69 K14**
Aiken *SC* . . . . 33°34N 81°43W **90 E4**
Aiken County ☆ *SC* . 33°30N 81°40W **90 E4**
Ailey *GA* . . . . 32°11N 82°34W **68 D4**
Ainsworth *IA* . . . . . . 41°17N 91°33W **73 D7**
Ainsworth *NE* . . . . . . 42°33N 99°52W **84 B6**
Aire, Mt. *UT* . . . . . 40°43N 111°41W **117 B3**
Airway Heights
WA . . . . 47°39N 117°36W **101 C8**
Aitkin *MN* . . . . 46°32N 93°42W **80 D5**
Aitkin County ☆ *MN* 46°30N 93°25W **80 D5**
Aix, Mt. *WA* . . . . . 46°47N 121°15W **101 D4**
Ajo *AZ* . . . . 32°22N 112°52W **62 E3**
Ajo Mt. *AZ* . . . . 32°5N 112°45W **62 E3**
Ak-Chin = Maricopa Indian
Reservation *AZ* . . . 33°0N 112°1W **62 E3**
Akaska *SD* . . . . 45°20N 100°7W **91 E5**
Akeley *MN* . . . . 47°0N 94°44W **80 C4**
Akhiok *AK* . . . . 56°57N 154°10W **61 H9**
Akiachak *AK* . . . . . 60°55N 161°26W **61 F7**
Akiak *AK* . . . . 60°55N 161°13W **61 F7**
Akolmiut *AK* . . . . . 60°55N 162°20W **61 F7**
Akra *ND* . . . . 48°47N 97°44W **91 B8**
Akron *AL* . . . . 32°53N 87°45W **60 D3**
Akron *CO* . . . . 40°10N 103°13W **66 B7**
Akron *IN* . . . . 41°2N 86°1W **72 B4**
Akron *IA* . . . . 42°50N 96°33W **73 C2**
Akron *NY* . . . . 43°1N 78°30W **89 B2**
Akron *OH* . . . . 41°5N 81°31W **92 B5**
Akron *PA* . . . . 40°9N 76°12W **95 D6**
Akun I. *AK* . . . . 54°11N 165°32W **61 J6**
Akutan *AK* . . . . 54°8N 165°46W **61 J6**
Akutan I. *AK* . . . . . . 54°7N 165°55W **61 J6**
Alabama ☐ *U.S.A.* . . . . 33°0N 87°0W **60 D4**
Alabama → *AL* . . . . . 31°8N 87°57W **60 E3**
Alabama-Coushatta Indian
Reservation *TX* . . 30°43N 94°42W **99 G13**
Alabaster *AL* . . . . . . 33°15N 86°49W **60 C4**
Alachua *FL* . . . . 29°47N 82°30W **67 B6**
Alachua County ☆
FL . . . . 29°45N 82°20W **67 B6**
Aladdin *WY* . . . . . . 44°38N 104°11W **104 B8**
Alakanuk *AK* . . . . . 62°41N 164°37W **61 E6**
'Alaläkeiki Channel
HI . . . . 20°30N 156°30W **69 C5**
Alamagan
N. Marianas . . . . . . 17°36N 145°50E **105 a**
Alamance County ☆
NC . . . . 36°0N 79°25W **90 C6**
Alameda *CA* . . . . . 37°46N 122°15W **118 B3**
Alameda *NM* . . . . . . 35°11N 106°37W **88 B4**
Alameda County ☆
CA . . . . 37°40N 121°50W **64 F5**
Alameda Memorial State Beach
Park *CA* . . . . 37°45N 122°16W **118 B3**
Alameda Naval Air Station
CA . . . . 37°47N 122°19W **118 B3**
Alamito → *TX* . . . . 29°45N 104°18W **98 H3**
Alamo *CA* . . . . 37°51N 122°1W **118 A4**
Alamo *GA* . . . . 32°9N 82°47W **68 D4**
Alamo *ND* . . . . 48°35N 103°28W **91 B2**
Alamo *NM* . . . . 34°25N 107°31W **88 C3**
Alamo *NV* . . . . 37°22N 115°10W **85 E5**
Alamo *TN* . . . . 35°47N 89°7W **96 E3**
Alamo → *CA* . . . . 33°13N 115°37W **65 K11**
Alamo Heights *TX* . 29°29N 98°27W **117 B3**
Alamo Indian Reservation
NM . . . . 34°20N 107°30W **88 C3**
Alamo L. *AZ* . . . . . 34°10N 113°35W **62 C2**
Alamogordo *NM* . . 32°54N 105°57W **88 E5**
Alamosa *CO* . . . . . . 37°28N 105°52W **66 E5**
Alamosa → *CO* . . . 37°22N 105°46W **66 E5**
Alamosa → *NM* . . . 33°25N 107°15W **88 D3**
Alamosa County ☆
CO . . . . 37°40N 105°40W **66 E5**
Alamosa Cr. → *NM* 34°20N 104°10W **88 C6**
Alanreed *TX* . . . . . . 35°13N 100°44W **98 B7**
Alanson *MI* . . . . 45°27N 84°47W **79 D7**
Alapaha *GA* . . . . 31°23N 83°13W **68 E3**
Alapaha → *GA* . . . . . 30°27N 83°6W **68 F3**
Alaska ☐ *U.S.A.* . . . . . 64°0N 154°0W **61 D9**
Alaska, G. of
Pac. Oc. . . . . 58°0N 145°0W **61 G11**
Alaska Maritime Nat. Wildlife
Refuge ⌓ *AK* . . . . . 52°0N 174°0W **61 L4**
Alaska Peninsula *AK* . 56°0N 159°0W **61 H8**
Alaska Peninsula Nat. Wildlife
Refuge ⌓ *AK* . . . . . . 56°0N 159°0W **61 J8**
Alaska Range *AK* . . 62°50N 151°0W **61 E10**
Alava, C. *WA* . . . . 48°10N 124°44W **101 B1**
Alba *MO* . . . . 37°14N 94°25W **82 D2**
Alba *TX* . . . . 32°48N 95°38W **99 E12**
Albany *GA* . . . . 31°35N 84°10W **68 E2**
Albany *IN* . . . . 40°18N 85°14W **72 C5**
Albany *KY* . . . . 36°42N 85°8W **97 D7**
Albany *LA* . . . . 30°30N 90°35W **75 D5**
Albany *MN* . . . . 45°38N 94°34W **80 E4**
Albany *MO* . . . . 40°15N 94°20W **82 A2**
Albany *NY* . . . . 42°39N 73°45W **89 C7**
Albany *OH* . . . . 39°14N 82°12W **92 D4**
Albany *OK* . . . . 33°53N 96°10W **93 E7**
Albany *OR* . . . . 44°38N 123°6W **94 C2**
Albany *TX* . . . . 32°44N 99°18W **99 E8**
Albany *VT* . . . . 44°43N 72°23W **86 B2**
Albany *WI* . . . . 42°42N 89°26W **103 F4**
Albany *WY* . . . . 41°11N 106°8W **104 E6**
Albany County ☆ *NY* 42°30N 74°0W **89 C7**
Albany County ☆
WY . . . . 41°50N 105°40W **104 E7**

Albany Int. ✈ (ALB)
NY ..... 42°45N 73°48W 89 C7
Albemarle NC ..... 35°21N 80°12W 90 C5
Albemarle County ☆
VA ..... 38°02N 78°30W 102 C4
Albemarle Sd. NC ..... 36°05N 76°00W 90 B9
Albert KS ..... 38°27N 99°1W 74 C4
Albert OK ..... 35°14N 98°25W 93 C5
Albert TX ..... 30°12N 98°36W 99 G8
Albert City IA ..... 42°47N 94°57W 73 C4
Albert Lea MN ..... 43°39N 93°22W 80 D3
Alberta AL ..... 32°14N 87°25W 00 D3
Alberta MI ..... 46°39N 88°29W 79 C3
Alberta VA ..... 36°52N 77°53W 102 E7
Alberton MT ..... 47°0N 114°29W 83 D3
Albertson NY ..... 40°46N 73°40W 114 B6
Albertville AL ..... 34°16N 86°13W 00 B4
Albertville MN ..... 45°14N 93°39W 80 E5
Albia IA ..... 41°2N 92°48W 73 D6
Albin WY ..... 41°25N 104°6W 104 E8
Albion CA ..... 39°14N 123°46W 64 D3
Albion ID ..... 42°25N 113°35W 70 G6
Albion IL ..... 38°23N 88°4W 71 E5
Albion IN ..... 41°24N 85°25W 72 B5
Albion IA ..... 42°7N 92°59W 73 C6
Albion ME ..... 44°32N 69°27W 76 D4
Albion MI ..... 42°15N 84°45W 79 G7
Albion NY ..... 43°15N 78°12W 89 B2
Albion NE ..... 41°42N 98°0W 84 C7
Albion OK ..... 34°40N 95°6W 93 D8
Albion PA ..... 41°53N 80°22W 95 C2
Albion WA ..... 46°48N 117°15W 101 D8
Albion, Mts. U.S.A. ..... 42°13N 113°43W 70 G5
Albright WV ..... 39°30N 79°39W 102 B5
Albuquerque Int. ✈ (ABQ)
NM ..... 35°3N 106°36W 88 B4
Alburg VT ..... 44°59N 73°18W 86 B1
Alburnett IA ..... 42°9N 91°37W 73 C7
Alcalde NM ..... 36°5N 106°3W 88 A4
Alcester SD ..... 43°1N 96°38W 91 G9
Alcoa TN ..... 35°48N 83°59W 97 E9
Alcolu SC ..... 33°45N 80°13W 90 D5
Alcona County ☆ MI 44°40N 83°40W 79 E8
Alcorn MS ..... 31°53N 91°8W 81 E2
Alcorn County ☆ MS 34°56N 88°31W 81 B5
Alcova WY ..... 42°34N 106°43W 104 D6
Alcova Res. WY ..... 42°33N 106°43W 104 D6
Alda NE ..... 40°52N 98°28W 84 D7
Aldan PA ..... 39°55N 75°17W 116 B1
Alden IA ..... 42°31N 93°23W 73 C5
Alden KS ..... 38°15N 98°19W 74 C5
Alden MN ..... 43°40N 93°34W 80 G5
Alden NY ..... 42°54N 78°30W 89 C2
Aldene NJ ..... 40°39N 74°16W 114 C1
Alder MT ..... 45°19N 112°6W 83 E5
Alder L. WA ..... 46°48N 122°18W 101 D3
Alderson OK ..... 34°55N 95°41W 93 D8
Alderson WV ..... 37°44N 80°38W 102 D4
Alderwood Manor
WA ..... 47°49N 122°16W 118 B4
Aldie VA ..... 38°59N 77°39W 77 B3
Aldine TX ..... 29°56N 95°23W 99 H12
Aledo IL ..... 41°12N 90°45W 71 B3
Aledo TX ..... 32°42N 97°36W 99 E10
Alegros Mt. NM ..... 34°9N 108°11W 88 C2
Aleknagik AK ..... 59°17N 158°36W 61 G8
'Alenuihāhā Channel
HI ..... 20°30N 156°0W 69 C5
Alesia MD ..... 39°43N 76°51W 77 A4
Aleutian Is. Pac. Oc. .. 52°0N 175°0W 61 K3
Aleutian Range AK .. 60°0N 154°0W 61 G9
Aleutians East ☆
AK ..... 54°51N 163°25W 61 J7
Aleutians West ☆
AK ..... 52°15N 177°0W 61 J4
Alex OK ..... 34°55N 97°47W 93 D6
Alexander GA ..... 33°1N 81°53W 68 C5
Alexander IA ..... 42°48N 93°29W 73 C5
Alexander KS ..... 38°28N 99°33W 74 C4
Alexander ME ..... 45°5N 67°23W 76 C6
Alexander ND ..... 47°51N 103°39W 91 C2
Alexander WV ..... 38°47N 80°23W 102 C4
Alexander Arch. AK . 56°0N 136°0W 61 J14
Alexander City AL.. 32°56N 85°58W 60 D5
Alexander County ☆
NC ..... 35°50N 81°10W 90 C4
Alexandria IN ..... 40°16N 85°41W 72 C5
Alexandria LA ..... 31°18N 92°27W 75 C3
Alexandria MN ..... 45°53N 95°22W 80 E3
Alexandria MO ..... 40°27N 91°28W 82 A5
Alexandria NH ..... 43°37N 71°47W 86 C3
Alexandria NE ..... 40°15N 97°23W 84 D8
Alexandria PA ..... 40°34N 78°6W 95 D4
Alexandria SD ..... 43°39N 97°47W 91 G8
Alexandria TN ..... 36°5N 86°2W 96 D6
Alexandria VA ..... 38°49N 77°3W 119 C3
Alexandria Bay NY.. 44°20N 75°55W 89 A5
Alexis IL ..... 41°4N 90°33W 71 B3
Alfalfa OK ..... 34°51N 98°36W 93 C5
Alfalfa County ☆ OK 36°45N 98°15W 93 B5
Alford FL ..... 30°42N 85°24W 67 A3
Alfred ME ..... 43°29N 70°43W 76 E3
Alfred NY ..... 42°16N 77°48W 89 C3
Alger County ☆ MI .. 46°20N 86°50W 79 C5
Algodones NM ..... 35°23N 106°29W 88 B4
Algoma MS ..... 34°11N 89°2W 81 B4
Algoma WI ..... 44°36N 87°26W 103 D6
Algona IA ..... 43°4N 94°14W 73 B4
Algonac MI ..... 42°37N 82°32W 79 G9
Algonquin IL ..... 42°10N 88°18W 71 A5
Algood TN ..... 36°12N 85°17W 97 D7
Alhambra CA ..... 34°5N 118°7W 111 J8
Aibates Flint Quarries Nat.
Monument □ TX 35°34N 101°41W 98 B5
Alice ND ..... 46°46N 97°33W 91 D8
Alice TX ..... 27°45N 98°5W 99 K9
Alice, L. ND ..... 48°20N 99°7W 91 B6
Aliceville AL ..... 33°8N 88°9W 60 C2
Aliceville WI ..... 38°9N 95°33W 74 C8
Aliceville L. U.S.A... 33°15N 88°17W 60 C2
Alicia AR ..... 35°54N 91°5W 63 C4
Aline OK ..... 36°31N 98°27W 93 B5
Aliquippa PA ..... 40°37N 80°15W 95 D2
Alkali Flat NV ..... 40°24N 117°21W 85 B3
Alkali Flat NV ..... 40°0N 115°58W 85 C5
Alkali L. NV ..... 41°42N 119°51W 85 A1
Alkali L. OR ..... 42°58N 120°2W 94 E5
Alkali L. ND ..... 46°40N 99°4W 91 D6
All American Canal
CA ..... 32°45N 115°15W 65 L11
Allagash ME ..... 47°5N 69°3W 76 A4
Allagash → ME ..... 47°5N 69°3W 76 A4
Allagash L. ME ..... 46°18N 69°35W 76 B4
Allakaket AK ..... 66°34N 152°39W 61 C9
Allamakee County ☆
IA ..... 43°15N 91°20W 73 B7
Allamoore TX ..... 31°5N 105°0W 98 E3
Allardt TN ..... 36°23N 84°53W 97 D8
Allatoona L. GA ..... 34°10N 84°4W 68 B2
Allegan MI ..... 42°32N 85°51W 79 G6
Allegan County ☆
MI ..... 42°35N 85°50W 79 G6
Allegany NY ..... 42°6N 78°30W 89 C2
Allegany → PA ..... 43°26N 124°2W 94 D1

Allegany County ☆
MD ..... 39°40N 78°40W 77 A2
Allegany County ☆
NY ..... 42°15N 78°0W 89 C3
Allegany Indian Reservation
NY ..... 42°6N 78°55W 89 C2
Allegany State Park ☆
NY ..... 42°3N 78°48W 89 C2
Alleghany County ☆
NC ..... 36°25N 81°10W 90 B4
Alleghany County ☆
VA ..... 37°50N 80°0W 102 D4
Allegheny → PA ..... 40°27N 80°1W 95 D2
Allegheny County ☆
PA ..... 40°25N 80°0W 95 D3
Allegheny Mts. WV.. 38°15N 80°10W 102 C4
Allegheny Nat. Forest
PA ..... 41°45N 79°5W 95 C3
Allegheny Plateau
PA ..... 41°30N 78°30W 95 C4
Allegheny Portage Railroad Nat.
Historic Site □ PA.. 40°28N 78°51W 95 D4
Allegheny Res. PA.. 41°50N 79°0W 95 C3
Allemands, L. des LA 29°55N 90°35W 75 E5
Allen KS ..... 38°39N 96°10W 74 C7
Allen NE ..... 42°25N 96°51W 84 B9
Allen OK ..... 34°53N 96°25W 93 D7
Allen TX ..... 33°6N 96°40W 99 D11
Allen County ☆ IN .. 41°5N 85°5W 72 B5
Allen County ☆ KS .. 37°50N 95°15W 74 D8
Allen County ☆ KY .. 36°45N 86°10W 96 E5
Allen County ☆ OH .. 40°46N 84°6W 92 C2
Allen Parish ☆ LA .. 30°37N 92°46W 75 D3
Allendale IL ..... 38°32N 87°43W 71 E6
Allendale SC ..... 33°1N 81°18W 90 E4
Allendale County ☆
SC ..... 33°0N 81°20W 90 E4
Allenhurst NJ ..... 40°15N 73°59W 87 B3
Allensville KY ..... 36°43N 87°4W 96 D5
Allentown NJ ..... 40°11N 74°35W 87 B2
Allentown PA ..... 40°37N 75°29W 87 B1
Allerton IL ..... 39°55N 87°56W 71 D6
Allerton IA ..... 40°42N 93°22W 73 E5
Allerton, Pt. MA ... 42°18N 70°53W 106 A6
Alley Pond Park NY 40°44N 73°43W 114 B4
Alliance NE ..... 42°6N 102°52W 84 B3
Alliance OH ..... 40°55N 81°6W 92 C5
Alligator MS ..... 34°6N 90°43W 81 B3
Alligator → NC ..... 35°55N 76°7W 90 C9
Alligator Alley = Everglades
Parkway FL ..... 26°10N 81°0W 67 E7
Alligator L = New L.
NC ..... 35°39N 76°21W 90 C9
Allison CO ..... 37°2N 107°29W 66 E3
Allison IA ..... 42°45N 92°48W 73 C6
Allison TX ..... 35°36N 100°6W 98 B7
Allons TN ..... 36°27N 85°21W 97 D7
Allouez WI ..... 39°34N 75°22W 87 C1
Alloway NJ ..... 39°34N 75°22W 87 C1
Allstate Arena IL.. 42°2N 87°54W 108 A1
Allston MA ..... 42°21N 71°7W 106 A3
Allyn WA ..... 47°23N 122°50W 101 C3
Alma AR ..... 35°29N 94°13W 63 C1
Alma CO ..... 39°17N 106°4W 66 C4
Alma GA ..... 31°33N 82°28W 68 E4
Alma KS ..... 39°1N 96°17W 74 B7
Alma MI ..... 43°23N 84°39W 79 F7
Alma MO ..... 39°6N 93°33W 82 B3
Alma NM ..... 33°23N 108°54W 88 D1
Alma NE ..... 40°6N 99°22W 84 D6
Alma WI ..... 44°20N 91°55W 103 D2
Alma Center WI ..... 44°26N 90°55W 103 D3
Alma Hill NY ..... 42°3N 78°0W 89 C3
Almanor, L. CA ..... 40°14N 121°9W 64 C5
Almena KS ..... 39°54N 99°43W 74 B4
Almena WI ..... 45°25N 92°2W 103 C1
Almeria NE ..... 41°50N 99°31W 84 C6
Almira WA ..... 47°43N 118°56W 101 C7
Almo KY ..... 36°42N 88°16W 96 D4
Almon GA ..... 33°37N 83°56W 68 C3
Almond WI ..... 44°16N 89°25W 103 D4
Almont CO ..... 38°40N 106°51W 66 D4
Almont MI ..... 42°55N 83°3W 79 G8
Almont ND ..... 46°44N 101°30W 91 D4
Alms Park OH ..... 39°6N 84°25W 107 B2
Almyra AR ..... 34°24N 91°27W 63 D4
Alness WV ..... 41°19N 111°0W 104 F2
Ainyra AR ..... 34°24N 91°25W 63 D4
Aloha OR ..... 45°29N 122°52W 94 B3
Alondra Park CA .. 33°52N 118°20W 111 C2
Alorton IL ..... 38°35N 90°7W 117 B3
Alpaugh CA ..... 35°53N 119°29W 65 H7
Alpena AR ..... 36°18N 93°18W 63 B2
Alpena SD ..... 44°11N 98°22W 91 F7
Alpena County ☆ MI. 45°0N 83°40W 79 E8
Alpha IL ..... 41°12N 90°23W 71 B3
Alpha MI ..... 46°3N 88°23W 79 C3
Alpha NJ ..... 40°40N 75°9W 87 B1
Alpharetta GA ..... 34°5N 84°18W 68 B2
Alpine AZ ..... 33°51N 109°9W 62 D6
Alpine CA ..... 34°14N 93°23W 63 D2
Alpine CA ..... 32°50N 116°46W 65 L10
Alpine NJ ..... 40°57N 73°57W 114 A3
Alpine TN ..... 36°24N 85°13W 97 D7
Alpine TX ..... 30°22N 103°40W 98 G4
Alpine UT ..... 40°27N 111°46W 100 C3
Alpine WY ..... 43°11N 111°3W 104 C1
Alpine County ☆
CA ..... 38°40N 119°50W 64 E7
Alsea → OR ..... 44°26N 124°5W 94 C1
Alsen ND ..... 48°38N 98°42W 91 B7
Alsey IL ..... 39°34N 90°26W 71 D3
Alsip IL ..... 41°40N 87°44W 108 D2
Alstead NH ..... 43°9N 72°22W 86 C2
Alta IA ..... 42°40N 95°18W 73 C3
Alta UT ..... 40°35N 111°38W 117 C4
Alta WY ..... 43°45N 111°2W 104 C1
Alta Vista IA ..... 43°12N 92°25W 73 B6
Alta Vista KS ..... 38°52N 96°29W 74 C7
Altadena CA ..... 34°11N 118°8W 111 A4
Altair TX ..... 29°34N 96°27W 99 H11
Altamaha → GA .. 31°20N 81°20W 68 E5
Altamaha Sound GA .. 31°19N 81°17W 68 E5
Altamont IL ..... 39°4N 88°45W 71 D5
Altamont KS ..... 37°12N 95°18W 74 D8
Altamont MO ..... 39°53N 94°5W 82 B2
Altamont NY ..... 42°42N 74°2W 89 C6
Altamont OR ..... 42°12N 121°44W 94 E4
Altamont SD ..... 44°50N 96°42W 91 F9
Altamont TN ..... 35°26N 85°44W 97 E7
Altamont UT ..... 40°22N 110°17W 100 C5
Altavista VA ..... 37°6N 79°17W 102 D5
Altha FL ..... 30°34N 85°8W 67 A3
Altheimer AR ..... 34°19N 91°51W 63 D4
Alto GA ..... 34°28N 83°35W 68 B3
Alto LA ..... 32°22N 91°52W 75 B4
Alto NM ..... 33°23N 105°41W 88 D5
Alto Pass IL ..... 37°34N 89°19W 71 F4
Alton IL ..... 38°53N 90°11W 71 E3
Alton IA ..... 42°59N 96°1W 73 C2
Alton KS ..... 39°28N 98°57W 74 B5
Alton MO ..... 36°42N 91°24W 82 E6
Alton NH ..... 43°27N 71°13W 86 C3
Alton Bay NH ..... 43°27N 71°13W 86 C3
Altona MN ..... 44°53N 73°39W 89 A7
Altoona AL ..... 34°2N 86°20W 60 B4
Altoona IA ..... 41°39N 93°28W 73 D5
Altoona KS ..... 37°32N 95°40W 74 D8

Altoona PA ..... 40°31N 78°24W 95 D4
Altoona WI ..... 44°48N 91°26W 103 D2
Alturas CA ..... 41°29N 120°32W 64 B6
Altus OK ..... 34°38N 99°20W 93 D4
Altus, L. OK ..... 34°53N 99°18W 93 D4
Alum Bridge WV.... 39°2N 80°40W 102 B4
Alum Creek L. OH .. 40°11N 82°57W 92 C4
Alva FL ..... 26°43N 81°37W 67 E7
Alva KY ..... 36°44N 83°23W 97 F8
Alva OK ..... 36°48N 98°40W 93 B5
Alvarado MN ..... 48°10N 97°0W 80 B2
Alvarado TX ..... 32°24N 97°13W 99 E10
Alvaton KY ..... 36°53N 86°21W 96 E5
Alvin TX ..... 29°26N 95°15W 99 H12
Alvin Callendar Naval Air Station
LA ..... 29°50N 90°1W 113 D2
Alvo NE ..... 40°52N 96°23W 84 D9
Alvord IA ..... 43°20N 96°18W 73 B2
Alvord TX ..... 33°22N 97°42W 99 D10
Alvord L. OR ..... 42°23N 118°36W 94 E7
Alzada MT ..... 45°2N 104°25W 83 E9
Amador County ☆
CA ..... 38°25N 120°45W 64 E6
Amagansett NY ..... 40°59N 72°9W 78 D2
Amana IA ..... 41°48N 91°52W 73 D7
Amana Colonies IA .. 41°48N 91°56W 73 D7
Amanave
Amer. Samoa .... 14°20S 170°50W 105 e
Amanda OH ..... 39°39N 82°45W 92 D4
Amargosa → CA .. 36°14N 116°51W 65 G10
Amargosa Desert
CA ..... 36°40N 116°30W 85 F4
Amargosa Range
NV ..... 36°39N 116°24W 85 F4
Amargosa Valley
NV ..... 36°39N 116°24W 85 F4
Amarillo TX ..... 35°13N 101°50W 98 B6
Amasa MI ..... 46°14N 88°27W 79 C3
Amatignak I. AK .. 51°16N 179°6W 61 L3
Amazonia MO ..... 39°53N 94°54W 82 B2
Amber OK ..... 35°9N 97°53W 93 C6
Amberg WI ..... 45°30N 88°9W 103 C6
Amberley OH ..... 39°12N 84°25W 107 A2
Ambler AK ..... 67°5N 157°52W 61 C8
Ambler PA ..... 40°9N 75°13W 87 B1
Amboy CA ..... 34°33N 115°45W 65 J11
Amboy IL ..... 41°44N 89°20W 71 B4
Amboy MN ..... 43°53N 94°10W 80 G4
Amboy WA ..... 45°55N 122°26W 101 D4
Ambridge PA ..... 40°36N 80°14W 95 D2
Ambrose GA ..... 31°36N 83°1W 68 E3
Ambrose ND ..... 48°57N 103°29W 91 B2
Ambrosia Lake NM .. 35°26N 107°54W 88 B3
Amchitka I. AK .. 51°32N 179°0E 61 L2
Amelia LA ..... 29°40N 91°6W 75 E4
Amelia NE ..... 42°14N 98°55W 84 B7
Amelia County ☆
VA ..... 37°21N 77°59W 102 D7
Amelia Court House
VA ..... 37°21N 77°59W 102 D7
Amelia Earhart Park
FL ..... 25°53N 80°16W 112 C1
Amelia I. FL ..... 30°40N 81°25W 67 A7
Amenia NY ..... 41°51N 73°33W 78 C1
American Corners
MD ..... 38°47N 75°51W 77 B5
American Falls ID .. 42°47N 112°51W 70 G6
American Falls Dam
ID ..... 42°47N 112°52W 70 G6
American Falls Res.
ID ..... 42°47N 112°52W 70 G6
American Fork UT.. 40°23N 111°48W 100 C4
American Samoa ☑
Pac. Oc. .... 14°20S 170°40W 105 d
American University
DC ..... 38°56N 77°5W 119 B3
Americus GA ..... 32°4N 84°14W 68 D2
Americus KS ..... 38°30N 96°16W 74 C7
Americus MO ..... 38°47N 91°54W 82 C4
Amery WI ..... 45°19N 92°22W 103 C1
Ames IA ..... 42°2N 93°37W 73 C5
Ames NE ..... 36°15N 98°11W 93 B5
Ames TX ..... 30°3N 94°45W 99 G13
Amesbury MA ..... 42°51N 70°56W 78 B4
Amesville OH ..... 39°24N 81°57W 92 D5
Amherst ME ..... 44°50N 68°22W 76 D5
Amherst MA ..... 42°23N 72°31W 78 B2
Amherst NH ..... 42°52N 71°38W 86 D3
Amherst NY ..... 42°59N 78°48W 89 C2
Amherst NE ..... 40°46N 99°16W 84 D6
Amherst OH ..... 41°24N 82°14W 92 B4
Amherst TX ..... 34°1N 102°25W 98 C5
Amherst VA ..... 37°35N 79°3W 102 D5
Amherst County ☆
VA ..... 37°38N 79°5W 102 D5
Amherst Junction
WI ..... 44°28N 89°19W 103 D4
Amherstdale WV ..... 37°47N 81°49W 102 D3
Amidon ND ..... 46°29N 103°19W 91 D2
Amistad NM ..... 35°55N 103°9W 88 B7
Amistad Nat. Recr. Area
TX ..... 29°32N 101°12W 98 H6
Amistad Res. TX .. 29°28N 101°0W 98 H6
Amite LA ..... 30°44N 90°30W 75 D5
Amite → LA ..... 30°11N 90°43W 75 E5
Amite County ☆ MS 31°10N 90°49W 81 E3
Amity AR ..... 34°16N 93°28W 63 D2
Amity OR ..... 45°7N 123°12W 94 B2
Amlia I. AK ..... 52°4N 173°30W 61 K4
Ammon ID ..... 43°28N 111°58W 70 F7
Ammonoonsuc →
NH ..... 44°10N 72°2W 86 B2
Amonate VA ..... 37°12N 81°38W 102 D3
Amoret MO ..... 38°15N 94°35W 82 C2
Amorita OK ..... 36°56N 98°18W 93 B5
Amory MS ..... 33°59N 88°29W 81 C5
Amsden VT ..... 43°25N 72°30W 86 C2
Amsterdam NY ..... 42°56N 74°11W 89 C6
Amsterdam OH ..... 40°28N 80°56W 92 C6
Amukta I. AK ..... 52°30N 171°16W 61 K5
Amukta Pass AK .. 52°0N 171°0W 61 K5
Amy AR ..... 33°44N 92°49W 63 E3
Anacapa I. CA ..... 34°1N 119°26W 65 J7
Anaconda LA ..... 31°15N 93°21W 75 C2
Anaconda MT ..... 46°8N 112°57W 83 D5
Anaconda Ra. MT.. 45°50N 113°25W 83 E4
Anacortes WA ..... 48°30N 122°37W 101 B3
Anacostia → DC.. 38°52N 77°1W 119 B4
Anacostia DC ..... 38°51N 76°59W 119 B4
Anadarko OK ..... 35°4N 98°15W 93 C5
Anaheim CA ..... 33°50N 117°55W 65 K9
Anahola HI ..... 22°9N 159°19W 69 A2
Anahuac TX ..... 29°46N 94°41W 99 H13
'Anahulu → HI .. 21°37N 158°6W 69 J13
Anaichak Nat. Monument and
Preserve □ AK.. 56°50N 158°15W 61 H8
Anaktuvuk Pass AK 68°8N 151°45W 61 C9
Analomink PA ..... 41°3N 75°13W 87 A1
Anamoose ND ..... 47°53N 100°15W 91 C5
Anamosa IA ..... 42°7N 91°17W 73 C7
Anasco Puerto Rico 18°17N 67°8W 105 G15
Anatahan
N. Marianas .... 16°21N 145°40E 105 a
Anatone WA ..... 46°8N 117°8W 101 D8
Anceney MT ..... 45°52N 111°21W 83 E6
Ancho NM ..... 33°55N 105°45W 88 D5
Anchor IL ..... 40°34N 88°32W 71 C5
Anchorage AK ..... 61°13N 149°54W 61 F10

Anchorage ☆ AK .. 61°10N 149°15W 61 F10
Anchorage ✈ (ANC)
AK ..... 61°10N 150°0W 61 F10
Ancram NY ..... 42°3N 73°38W 78 B1
Andale KS ..... 37°48N 97°38W 74 D6
Andalusia AL ..... 31°18N 86°29W 60 A2
Andalusia IL ..... 41°26N 90°43W 71 B3
Andersen Air Force Base
Guam .... 13°35N 144°55E 105 b
Anderson AL ..... 34°55N 87°16W 60 B3
Anderson AK ..... 64°25N 149°15W 61 D10
Anderson CA ..... 40°27N 122°18W 64 C4
Anderson IN ..... 40°10N 85°41W 72 C5
Anderson MO ..... 36°39N 94°27W 82 E2
Anderson SC ..... 34°31N 82°39W 90 C3
Anderson TX ..... 30°29N 95°59W 99 G12
Anderson County ☆
KS ..... 38°15N 95°15W 74 C8
Anderson County ☆
KY ..... 38°0N 85°0W 97 C8
Anderson County ☆
SC ..... 34°30N 82°40W 90 D3
Anderson County ☆
TN ..... 36°6N 84°8W 97 D8
Anderson Park NM .. 31°46N 95°38W 99 F12
Anderson Ranch Res.
ID ..... 43°22N 115°27W 70 F3
Anderson Res. CA .. 37°10N 121°38W 64 F5
Andersonville Nat. Historic Site □
GA ..... 32°11N 84°8W 68 D2
Andes NY ..... 42°12N 74°47W 89 C6
Andes, L. SD ..... 43°11N 98°27W 91 G7
Andover CT ..... 41°44N 72°23W 78 C2
Andover KS ..... 37°43N 97°7W 74 D6
Andover ME ..... 44°38N 70°45W 86 B4
Andover MN ..... 45°17N 93°23W 80 E5
Andover NH ..... 43°26N 71°49W 86 C3
Andover NJ ..... 40°59N 74°45W 87 B2
Andover NY ..... 42°10N 77°48W 89 C3
Andover OH ..... 41°36N 80°34W 92 B6
Andover SD ..... 45°25N 97°54W 91 E8
Andreanof Is. AK.. 51°30N 176°0W 61 L4
Andrew County ☆
MO ..... 40°0N 94°45W 82 B2
Andrew Johnson Nat. Historic
Site → TN ..... 36°10N 82°50W 97 D10
Andrews IN ..... 40°52N 85°36W 72 C5
Andrews NC ..... 35°12N 83°49W 90 C2
Andrews SC ..... 33°27N 79°34W 90 D6
Andrews TX ..... 32°19N 102°33W 98 E5
Andrews County ☆
TX ..... 32°19N 102°33W 98 E5
Androscoggin → ME 43°58N 69°52W 76 E4
Androscoggin County ☆
ME ..... 44°10N 70°10W 76 D3
Anegada
Br. Virgin Is. .. 18°45N 64°20W 105 G18
Anegam AZ ..... 32°22N 112°2W 62 E3
Aneta ND ..... 47°41N 97°59W 91 C8
Aneth UT ..... 37°13N 109°11W 100 E6
Angel Fire NM ..... 36°24N 105°17W 88 A5
Angel Island State Park
CA ..... 37°52N 122°25W 118 A2
Angeles Nat. Forest
CA ..... 34°15N 118°0W 65 J9
Angelina → TX .. 30°54N 94°12W 99 F13
Angelina County ☆
TX ..... 31°21N 94°44W 99 F13
Angelina Nat. Forest
TX ..... 31°7N 94°15W 99 F13
Angels Camp CA .. 38°4N 120°32W 64 E6
Angie LA ..... 30°58N 89°49W 68 E1
Angier NC ..... 35°31N 78°44W 90 C7
Angle Inlet MN ..... 49°21N 95°4W 80 A3
Angleton TX ..... 29°10N 95°26W 99 H12
Angola DE ..... 38°40N 75°15W 77 B5
Angola IN ..... 41°38N 85°0W 72 B6
Angola NY ..... 42°38N 79°2W 89 C1
Angoon AK ..... 57°30N 134°35W 61 H14
Angora NE ..... 41°51N 103°8W 84 C2
Angostura Res. SD. 43°21N 103°26W 91 G2
Anguilla MS ..... 32°59N 90°50W 81 D3
Anguilla ■ W. Indies 18°14N 63°5W 105 G17
Aniak AK ..... 61°35N 159°32W 61 F8
Animas NM ..... 31°57N 108°49W 88 F2
Animas → NM .. 36°43N 108°13W 88 A2
Animas Mts. NM .. 31°33N 108°47W 88 F2
Animas Peak NM .. 31°35N 108°47W 88 F2
Anita IA ..... 41°27N 94°46W 73 D4
Ankeny IA ..... 41°44N 93°36W 73 D5
Anmoore WV ..... 39°16N 80°18W 102 B4
Ann, C. MA ..... 42°38N 70°35W 78 B4
Ann Arbor MI ..... 42°17N 83°45W 79 G8
Anna IL ..... 37°28N 89°15W 71 F4
Anna OH ..... 40°24N 84°11W 92 C2
Anna TX ..... 33°21N 96°33W 99 D11
Anna, L. VA ..... 38°4N 77°45W 102 C7
Annabella UT ..... 38°43N 112°4W 100 E3
Annada MO ..... 39°16N 90°50W 82 B6
Annandale NY ..... 42°2N 73°55W 78 B1
Annandale MN ..... 45°16N 94°8W 80 E4
Annandale VA ..... 38°50N 77°11W 119 C2
Annapolis MD ..... 38°59N 76°30W 77 B4
Annapolis IL ..... 39°6N 87°44W 71 D6
Annawan IL ..... 41°24N 89°55W 71 B4
Anne Arundel County ☆
MD ..... 39°0N 76°40W 77 A4
Annette Island Indian Reservation
AK ..... 55°9N 131°28W 61 J15
Anniston AL ..... 33°39N 85°50W 60 C4
Annona TX ..... 33°35N 94°55W 99 D13
Annville PA ..... 40°20N 76°31W 95 D6
Año Nuevo, Pt. CA 37°7N 122°20W 64 F4
Anoka MN ..... 45°12N 93°23W 80 E5
Anoka County ☆ MN 45°15N 93°15W 80 E5
Anselmo NE ..... 41°37N 99°52W 84 C6
Ansley LA ..... 32°24N 92°42W 75 B3
Ansley NE ..... 41°18N 99°23W 84 C6
Anson TX ..... 32°45N 99°54W 98 D8
Anson County ☆ NC .. 35°0N 80°0W 90 D5
Ansonia CT ..... 41°21N 73°5W 78 C1
Ansonia OH ..... 40°13N 84°38W 92 C2
Ansonville NC ..... 35°6N 80°7W 90 D5
Ansted WV ..... 38°8N 81°6W 102 C3
Antelope OR ..... 44°55N 120°43W 94 C5
Antelope County ☆
NE ..... 42°15N 98°0W 84 B7
Antelope Hills OK.. 35°25N 99°48W 93 C4
Antelope Hills WY.. 42°20N 108°25W 104 D4
Antelope I. UT ..... 40°15N 112°10W 100 C3
Antelope Range NV 40°40N 116°20W 85 B4
Antelope Res. OR.. 42°54N 117°14W 94 E8
Antero, Mt. CO .... 38°40N 106°15W 66 D4
Antero Res. CO .... 38°56N 105°55W 66 D4
Anthon IA ..... 42°23N 95°52W 73 C3
Anthony FL ..... 29°18N 82°7W 67 B6
Anthony KS ..... 37°9N 98°2W 74 D5
Anthony NM ..... 32°0N 106°36W 88 E4
Anthony Chabot Regional Park
CA ..... 37°51N 122°9W 118 B4
Anthoston KY ..... 37°46N 87°32W 96 C5

Antigo WI ..... 45°9N 89°9W 103 C4
Antimony UT ..... 38°6N 112°0W 100 E4
Antioch CA ..... 38°1N 121°48W 64 E5
Antioch IL ..... 42°29N 88°6W 71 A5
Antioch NE ..... 42°4N 102°35W 84 B3
Antler ND ..... 48°59N 101°17W 91 B4
Antlers OK ..... 34°14N 95°37W 93 D8
Antoine AR ..... 34°2N 93°25W 63 D2
Anton TX ..... 33°49N 102°10W 98 C5
Anton KY ..... 37°21N 87°24W 96 C5
Anton Chico NM .... 35°12N 105°9W 88 B5
Antonino KS ..... 38°51N 99°22W 74 C4
Antonio B. Won Pat Int. ✈ (GUM)
Guam .... 13°29N 144°48E 105 b
Antonito CO ..... 37°5N 106°0W 66 E5
Antrim NH ..... 43°2N 71°56W 86 C3
Antrim County ☆ MI. 45°0N 85°10W 79 E6
Antwerp NY ..... 44°12N 75°37W 89 A5
Antwerp OH ..... 41°11N 84°45W 92 B1
Anvik AK ..... 62°39N 160°13W 61 E7
Anza Borrego Desert State Park ☆
CA ..... 33°0N 116°26W 65 L10
Apache OK ..... 34°54N 98°22W 93 C5
Apache County ☆
AZ ..... 35°0N 109°30W 62 B6
Apache Creek NM.. 33°50N 108°37W 88 D2
Apache Junction
AZ ..... 33°25N 111°33W 62 D4
Apache L. AZ ..... 33°36N 111°21W 62 D4
Apache Mts. TX .. 31°12N 104°35W 98 F3
Apache Sitgreaves Nat. Forest
AZ ..... 34°30N 110°30W 62 C5
Apalache B. FL .... 30°0N 84°0W 67 B5
Apalachicola FL .... 29°43N 84°59W 67 B4
Apalachicola → FL .. 29°43N 84°58W 67 B4
Apalachicola B. FL .. 29°40N 85°0W 67 B4
Apalachicola Nat. Forest
FL ..... 30°10N 85°0W 67 A4
Apex NC ..... 35°44N 78°51W 90 C7
Apishapa → CO .. 38°8N 103°57W 66 D7
Aplington IA ..... 42°35N 92°53W 73 C6
Apollo PA ..... 40°35N 79°34W 95 D3
Apollo Beach FL .. 27°46N 82°24W 119 C4
Apopka FL ..... 28°40N 81°31W 67 C7
Apopka, L. FL ..... 28°37N 81°37W 115 A1
Apostle Is. WI ..... 47°0N 90°40W 103 A3
Apostle Islands Nat. Lakeshore
WI ..... 46°55N 91°0W 103 B3
Appalachia VA ..... 36°54N 82°47W 102 E2
Appalachian Mts. VA. 38°0N 80°0W 54 G6
Appalachian Nat. Scenic Trail
U.S.A. ..... 44°34N 83°50W 68 B3
Appanoose County ☆
IA ..... 40°45N 92°50W 73 E6
Apple → IL ..... 42°11N 90°14W 71 A3
Apple → WI ..... 45°9N 92°45W 103 C1
Apple Creek OH .. 40°45N 81°51W 92 C5
Apple Creek → IL .. 39°22N 90°37W 71 D3
Apple Valley CA .. 34°32N 117°14W 65 J9
Applegate MI ..... 43°21N 82°38W 79 F9
Appleton MN ..... 45°12N 96°1W 80 E2
Appleton WI ..... 44°16N 88°25W 103 D5
Appleton City MO .. 38°11N 94°2W 82 C2
Appling GA ..... 33°33N 82°19W 68 C4
Appling County ☆
GA ..... 31°45N 82°15W 68 E4
Appomattox VA .... 37°21N 78°50W 102 D6
Appomattox → VA .. 37°19N 77°17W 102 D7
Appomattox County ☆
VA ..... 37°22N 78°49W 102 D6
Aquarius Mts. AZ.. 34°45N 113°20W 62 C2
Aquarius Plateau
UT ..... 38°0N 111°40W 100 F4
Aquasco MD ..... 38°35N 76°43W 77 B4
Arab AL ..... 34°19N 86°30W 60 B3
Arabela NM ..... 33°35N 105°10W 88 D5
Arabi GA ..... 30°58N 83°44W 68 E3
Arabi LA ..... 29°57N 90°0W 113 C3
Arago, C. OR ..... 43°20N 124°30W 94 D1
Aragon GA ..... 34°2N 85°3W 68 B1
Aransas County ☆
TX ..... 28°5N 96°28W 99 J11
Aransas Nat. Wildlife Refuge →
TX ..... 28°15N 96°54W 99 J11
Aransas Pass TX.. 27°55N 97°9W 99 K10
Arapaho OK ..... 35°34N 98°58W 93 C5
Arapaho Nat. Forest
CO ..... 39°30N 106°15W 66 C4
Arapahoe CO ..... 38°51N 102°11W 66 D8
Arapahoe NE ..... 40°18N 99°54W 84 D6
Arapahoe WY ..... 42°58N 108°29W 104 D4
Arapahoe County ☆
CO ..... 39°40N 104°15W 66 C6
Ararat VA ..... 36°36N 80°31W 102 E5
Arbon ID ..... 42°27N 112°34W 70 G6
Arbuckle CA ..... 39°1N 122°3W 64 D4
Arbuckle L. FL .... 27°42N 81°24W 67 D7
Arbuckle Mts. OK .. 34°20N 97°10W 93 D6
Arbutus MD ..... 39°15N 76°42W 107 B1
Arbyrd MO ..... 36°3N 90°2W 82 E6
Arc Dome NV ..... 38°51N 117°22W 85 D3
Arcade GA ..... 34°5N 83°34W 68 B3
Arcade NY ..... 42°32N 78°25W 89 C2
Arcadia AZ ..... 33°28N 111°55W 116 C3
Arcadia FL ..... 27°13N 81°52W 67 D7
Arcadia IN ..... 40°11N 86°1W 72 C4
Arcadia LA ..... 32°33N 92°55W 75 B3
Arcadia NE ..... 41°25N 99°8W 84 C6
Arcadia OK ..... 35°40N 97°20W 93 C6
Arcadia Park TX .. 32°44N 96°54W 109 B4
Arcanum OH ..... 39°59N 84°33W 92 C2
Arcata CA ..... 40°52N 124°5W 64 C2
Arcata B. CA ..... 40°54N 124°5W 64 C2
Archbald LA ..... 32°21N 91°47W 75 B4
Archbold OH ..... 41°31N 84°18W 92 B2
Archdale NC ..... 35°56N 79°57W 90 C6
Archer FL ..... 29°32N 82°32W 67 B6
Archer NE ..... 41°10N 98°8W 84 C7
Archer City TX .... 33°36N 98°38W 99 D9
Archer County ☆ TX 33°35N 98°40W 99 D9
Arches Nat. Park ☆
UT ..... 38°45N 109°25W 100 E6
Archie LA ..... 31°35N 91°58W 75 C4
Archie MO ..... 38°29N 94°21W 82 C2
Archuleta County ☆
CO ..... 37°10N 107°0W 66 E4
Arco ID ..... 43°38N 113°18W 70 F5
Arco MN ..... 44°23N 96°11W 80 F2
Arcola IL ..... 39°41N 88°18W 71 D5
Arcola MS ..... 33°16N 90°53W 81 C3
Arcola MO ..... 37°33N 93°53W 82 D3
Arctic Village AK .. 68°8N 145°32W 61 B10
Arden CA ..... 38°36N 121°23W 64 E5
Arden Hills MN ..... 45°5N 93°9W 113 A2
Ardenvoir WA ..... 47°47N 120°22W 101 C5
Ardmore AL ..... 34°59N 86°52W 60 B4
Ardmore OK ..... 34°10N 97°8W 93 D6
Ardmore PA ..... 40°2N 75°17W 116 A1
Ardmore SD ..... 43°1N 103°40W 91 G2
Ardmore TN ..... 35°0N 86°51W 96 F6

Arecibo
Puerto Rico .... 18°29N 66°43W 105 G16
Aredale IA ..... 42°50N 93°0W 73 C5
Arena WI ..... 43°10N 89°55W 103 E4
Arena, Pt. CA ..... 38°57N 123°44W 64 E3
Arenac County ☆
MI ..... 44°0N 83°55W 79 E8
Arenas, Pta.
Puerto Rico .... 18°7N 65°35W 105 G17
Arenzville IL ..... 39°53N 90°22W 71 D3
Argenta = North Little Rock
AR ..... 34°45N 92°16W 63 D3
Argenta IL ..... 39°59N 88°49W 71 D5
Argonia KS ..... 37°16N 97°46W 74 D6
Argonne WI ..... 45°40N 88°53W 103 C5
Argos IN ..... 41°14N 86°15W 72 B4
Arguello, Pt. CA .. 34°35N 120°39W 65 J6
Argus Range CA .. 36°10N 117°40W 65 G9
Argusville ND ..... 47°3N 96°56W 91 C9
Argyle MN ..... 48°20N 96°49W 80 B2
Argyle WI ..... 42°42N 89°52W 103 F4
Ariel WA ..... 45°57N 122°34W 101 E3
Arikaree → U.S.A. 40°1N 101°56W 66 B9
Arimo ID ..... 42°34N 112°10W 70 G6
Arion IA ..... 41°57N 95°27W 73 D3
Ariton AL ..... 31°36N 85°43W 60 E5
Arizona City AZ .. 32°45N 111°40W 62 E4
Arizona □ U.S.A... 34°0N 112°0W 62 C4
Arkabutla L. MS.. 34°46N 90°8W 81 B3
Arkadelphia AR .. 34°7N 93°4W 63 D2
Arkansas □ U.S.A... 35°0N 92°30W 63 D3
Arkansas → AR .. 33°47N 91°4W 63 E4
Arkansas City AR .. 33°37N 91°12W 63 E4
Arkansas County ☆
AR ..... 34°18N 91°20W 63 D4
Arkansas Junction
NM ..... 32°42N 103°21W 88 E7
Arkansas Post Nat. Memorial
AR ..... 34°1N 91°20W 63 D4
Arkoma OK ..... 35°21N 94°26W 93 C9
Arkport NY ..... 42°24N 77°42W 89 C3
Arlee MT ..... 47°10N 114°5W 83 C3
Arley AL ..... 34°4N 87°13W 60 B3
Arlington AZ ..... 33°20N 112°46W 62 D3
Arlington CO ..... 38°20N 103°21W 66 D7
Arlington GA ..... 31°26N 84°44W 68 E2
Arlington IL ..... 41°29N 89°15W 71 B4
Arlington IN ..... 42°45N 91°10W 73 C7
Arlington KS ..... 37°54N 98°11W 74 D5
Arlington MA ..... 42°24N 71°10W 106 A2
Arlington MN ..... 44°36N 94°5W 80 F4
Arlington NY ..... 41°42N 73°54W 89 C7
Arlington NE ..... 41°27N 96°21W 84 C9
Arlington OR ..... 45°43N 120°12W 94 B5
Arlington SD ..... 44°22N 97°8W 91 F8
Arlington TN ..... 35°18N 89°40W 96 E3
Arlington TX ..... 32°44N 97°7W 109 B3
Arlington VT ..... 43°5N 73°9W 86 C1
Arlington VA ..... 38°53N 77°7W 119 C3
Arlington WA ..... 48°12N 122°8W 101 B4
Arlington WY ..... 41°36N 106°12W 104 E6
Arlington, L. TX .. 32°43N 97°11W 109 B2
Arlington Heights
MA ..... 42°25N 71°10W 106 A2
Arlington Heights
OH ..... 39°12N 84°27W 107 A2
Arlington Heights
TX ..... 32°39N 97°5W 109 B3
Arlington Municipal ✈
TX ..... 32°39N 97°5W 109 B3
Arlington Nat. Cemetery
VA ..... 38°52N 77°4W 119 B3
Arma KS ..... 37°33N 94°42W 74 D9
Armada MI ..... 42°51N 82°53W 79 G9
Armijo NM ..... 35°4N 106°39W 88 C4
Armington IL ..... 40°20N 89°47W 71 C4
Armona CA ..... 36°19N 119°42W 65 G7
Armour SD ..... 43°19N 98°21W 91 G7
Armstrong IA ..... 43°24N 94°29W 73 B4
Armstrong MO ..... 39°16N 92°42W 82 B4
Armstrong OK ..... 34°3N 96°21W 93 D7
Armstrong TX ..... 26°56N 97°47W 98 L10
Armstrong County ☆
PA ..... 40°45N 79°25W 95 D3
Armstrong County ☆
TX ..... 35°0N 101°20W 98 C6
Arnaudville LA ..... 30°24N 91°56W 75 D4
Arnegard ND ..... 47°49N 103°27W 91 C2
Arnett OK ..... 36°8N 99°46W 93 B4
Arnold CA ..... 38°15N 120°21W 64 E6
Arnold MD ..... 39°2N 76°30W 77 A4
Arnold MN ..... 46°3N 92°6W 80 D7
Arnold MO ..... 38°26N 90°23W 82 C6
Arnold NE ..... 41°26N 100°12W 84 C5
Arnold Arboretum
MA ..... 42°18N 71°8W 106 B3
Arnold Engineering Development
Center TN ..... 35°21N 86°2W 96 E6
Arnolds Park IA .. 43°22N 95°8W 73 B3
Arock OR ..... 42°55N 117°32W 94 E8
Aroma Park IL ..... 41°5N 87°48W 71 B6
Aroostook → ME .. 45°48N 67°45W 76 C6
Aroostook County ☆
ME ..... 47°0N 69°0W 76 B5
Arp TX ..... 32°14N 95°4W 99 E12
Arpin WI ..... 44°33N 90°2W 103 D3
Arrey NM ..... 32°48N 107°19W 88 E3
Arriba CO ..... 39°17N 103°17W 66 C7
Arrington KS ..... 39°24N 95°32W 74 B8
Arrow Cr. → MT.. 47°43N 109°50W 83 C6
Arrow Rock MO .. 39°4N 92°57W 82 B4
Arrow Wood L. ND. 47°14N 98°50W 91 C7
Arrowhead, L. TX . 33°46N 98°25W 99 D9
Arrowood Res. ID. 43°36N 115°56W 70 F3
Arrowsmith IL ..... 40°27N 88°38W 71 C5
Arroyo del Macho →
NM ..... 33°49N 104°7W 88 D6
Arroyo Grande CA .. 35°7N 120°35W 65 H6
Arroyo Hondo NM .. 36°32N 105°40W 88 A5
Art Institute IL .... 41°52N 87°37W 108 B3
Artas SD ..... 45°53N 99°49W 91 E6
Artesia CA ..... 33°51N 118°4W 111 C4
Artesia MS ..... 33°25N 88°39W 81 C5
Artesia L. NV ..... 38°56N 119°22W 85 D1
Artesia Wells TX.. 28°17N 99°17W 98 J8
Arthur IL ..... 39°43N 88°28W 71 D5
Arthur ND ..... 47°6N 97°13W 91 C8
Arthur NE ..... 41°35N 101°41W 84 C4
Arthur TN ..... 36°33N 83°40W 97 D9
Arthur County ☆
NE ..... 41°35N 101°40W 84 C4
Arthur R. Marshall-Loxahatchee
Nat. Wildlife Refuge →
FL ..... 26°27N 80°14W 67 E8
Artois CA ..... 39°37N 122°12W 64 D4
Arundel Village MD 39°13N 76°36W 107 B2
Arvada CO ..... 39°48N 105°5W 109 B1
Arvada WY ..... 44°39N 106°8W 104 B6
Arvin CA ..... 35°12N 118°50W 65 H8
Arvon, Mt. MI ..... 46°45N 88°9W 79 C3
Asbury IA ..... 42°31N 90°45W 73 C8
Asbury Park NJ .. 40°13N 74°1W 87 B3

Ascension Parish ☆
   LA .... 30°14N 90°55W **75 D5**
Ascutney VT .... 43°24N 72°25W **86 C2**
Ash Flat AR .... 36°13N 91°37W **63 B4**
Ash Fork AZ .... 35°13N 112°29W **62 B3**
Ash Grove MO .... 37°19N 93°35W **82 D3**
Ash Meadows Nat. Wildlife
   Refuge △ NV . 36°25N 116°19W **85 F4**
Ash Springs NV ..... 37°28N 115°12W **85 E5**
Ashaway RI .... 41°25N 71°47W **78 C3**
Ashburn GA .... 31°43N 83°39W **68 E3**
Ashburn IL .... 41°45N 87°43W **108 C2**
Ashburn VA .... 39°3N 77°29W **77 A3**
Ashburnham MA ... 42°38N 71°55W **78 B3**
Ashby MN .... 46°6N 95°49W **80 D3**
Ashby NE .... 42°1N 101°56W **84 B4**
Ashdown AR .... 33°40N 94°8W **63 E1**
Ashe County ☆ NC .. 36°25N 81°31W **90 B4**
Asheboro NC .... 35°43N 79°49W **90 C6**
Asher OK .... 34°59N 96°56W **93 D7**
Asherton TX .... 28°27N 99°46W **99 J8**
Asherville KS .... 39°24N 97°59W **74 B6**
Asheville NC .... 35°36N 82°33W **90 C3**
Ashfield MA .... 42°32N 72°48W **78 B2**
Ashford AL .... 31°11N 85°14W **60 E5**
Ashford WA .... 46°46N 122°2W **101 D3**
Ashkum IL .... 40°53N 87°57W **71 C6**
Ashland ☆ .... 33°16N 85°50W **60 C5**
Ashland CA .... 37°41N 122°6W **118 B4**
Ashland IL .... 39°53N 90°1W **71 D3**
Ashland KS .... 37°11N 99°46W **74 D4**
Ashland KY .... 38°28N 82°38W **97 B10**
Ashland LA .... 32°9N 93°6W **75 B2**
Ashland ME .... 46°38N 68°24W **76 B5**
Ashland MA .... 42°16N 71°28W **78 B3**
Ashland MS .... 34°50N 89°11W **81 B4**
Ashland MO .... 38°47N 92°16W **82 C4**
Ashland MT .... 45°36N 106°16W **83 E11**
Ashland NH .... 43°42N 71°38W **86 C3**
Ashland NY .... 42°18N 74°20W **89 C6**
Ashland NE .... 41°3N 96°23W **84 D9**
Ashland OH .... 40°52N 82°19W **92 C4**
Ashland OK .... 34°46N 96°4W **93 D7**
Ashland OR .... 42°12N 122°43W **94 E3**
Ashland VA .... 37°46N 77°29W **102 D7**
Ashland WI .... 46°35N 90°53W **103 B3**
Ashland City TN .... 36°17N 87°4W **96 B5**
Ashland County ☆
   OH .... 40°52N 82°19W **92 C4**
Ashland County ☆
   WI .... 46°35N 90°45W **103 B3**
Ashley IL .... 38°20N 89°11W **71 E4**
Ashley IN .... 41°32N 85°4W **72 B5**
Ashley MI .... 43°11N 84°29W **79 F7**
Ashley ND .... 46°2N 99°22W **91 D6**
Ashley OH .... 40°25N 82°57W **92 C4**
Ashley County ☆ AR 33°14N 91°48W **63 E4**
Ashley Cr. → FL .... 28°20N 109°17W **100 C6**
Ashley Nat. Forest
   UT .... 40°55N 110°0W **100 C5**
Ashmore IL .... 39°32N 88°1W **71 D5**
Ashtabula OH .... 41°52N 80°47W **92 A6**
Ashtabula L. ND .... 47°2N 98°5W **91 C7**
Ashtabula County ☆
   OH .... 41°40N 80°52W **92 B6**
Ashton IA .... 43°4N 111°27W **70 E7**
Ashton IL .... 41°52N 89°13W **71 B4**
Ashton IA .... 43°19N 95°47W **73 B3**
Ashton NE .... 41°15N 98°48W **84 C7**
Ashton RI .... 41°56N 71°26W **78 C3**
Ashton SD .... 44°59N 98°31W **91 F7**
Ashuelot → NH ..... 43°0N 72°29W **86 D2**
Ashville AL .... 33°50N 86°15W **60 C4**
Ashville FL .... 30°37N 83°9W **67 A5**
Ashville PA .... 40°34N 78°33W **95 D4**
Ashwood OR .... 44°44N 120°45W **94 C5**
Askov MN .... 46°12N 92°47W **80 D6**
Asotin WA .... 46°20N 117°3W **101 D4**
Asotin County ☆
   WA .... 46°8N 117°8W **101 D4**
Aspen CO .... 39°11N 106°49W **66 C4**
Aspen Hill MD ...... 39°5N 77°5W **77 A3**
Aspen L. OR .... 42°17N 122°0W **94 E3**
Aspermont TX ...... 33°8N 100°14W **98 E5**
Aspinwall PA .... 40°29N 79°54W **116 B2**
Assaria KS .... 38°41N 97°36W **74 C6**
Assateague I. MD ... 38°15N 75°10W **77 B5**
Assateague Island Nat. Seashore
   MD .... 38°15N 75°10W **77 B5**
Assawompset Pond
   MA .... 41°50N 70°55W **78 C4**
Assinippi MA .... 42°10N 70°51W **78 B4**
Assonet MA .... 41°48N 71°4W **78 C3**
Assumption IL ...... 39°31N 89°3W **71 D4**
Assumption Parish ☆
   LA .... 30°0N 91°0W **75 E4**
Astatula FL .... 28°43N 81°44W **67 C7**
Astoria IL .... 40°14N 90°21W **71 C3**
Astoria NY .... 40°46N 73°55W **114 B3**
Astoria OR .... 46°11N 123°50W **94 A3**
Astoria SD .... 44°34N 96°33W **91 F9**
Asuncion
   N. Marianas .. 19°40N 145°24E **105 a**
Atacosa → TX ..... 29°16N 98°44W **99 H9**
Atando Junction
   NC .... 35°15N 80°49W **107 A2**
Atascadero CA ..... 35°29N 120°40W **65 H6**
Atascosa County ☆
   TX .... 28°55N 98°33W **99 J9**
Atchafalaya → LA .. 29°53N 91°28W **75 E4**
Atchafalaya B. LA .. 29°25N 91°25W **75 F4**
Atchison KS .... 39°34N 95°7W **74 B8**
Atchison County ☆
   KS .... 39°30N 95°15W **74 B8**
Atchison County ☆
   MO .... 40°25N 95°25W **82 A1**
Atco NJ .... 39°46N 74°53W **87 C2**
Athena FL .... 29°59N 83°30W **67 B6**
Athena OR .... 45°49N 118°30W **94 B7**
Athens AL .... 34°48N 86°58W **60 B4**
Athens CA .... 33°55N 118°16W **111 C3**
Athens GA .... 33°57N 83°23W **68 C3**
Athens IL .... 39°58N 89°44W **71 D4**
Athens LA .... 32°39N 93°1W **75 B2**
Athens MI .... 42°5N 85°14W **79 G6**
Athens NY .... 42°16N 73°49W **89 C7**
Athens OH .... 39°20N 82°6W **92 D4**
Athens PA .... 41°57N 76°31W **95 C6**
Athens TN .... 35°27N 84°36W **97 B8**
Athens TX .... 32°12N 95°51W **99 E12**
Athens WV .... 37°25N 80°58W **103 C3**
Athens County ☆ OH 39°20N 82°6W **92 D4**
Athol ID .... 47°57N 116°42W **70 B2**
Athol MA .... 42°36N 72°14W **78 B2**
Athol SD .... 45°1N 98°36W **91 E7**
Atka AK .... 52°12N 174°12W **61 K4**
Atka I. AK .... 52°7N 174°30W **61 K4**
Atkins AR .... 35°14N 92°56W **63 C3**
Atkins VA .... 36°20N 81°25W **102 E3**
Atkinson IL .... 41°13N 91°47W **68 E5**
Atkinson NH .... 42°50N 71°9W **86 D3**
Atkinson County ☆
   GA .... 31°15N 82°50W **68 E4**
Atlanta GA .... 33°45N 84°23W **106 B2**
Atlanta ID .... 43°48N 115°8W **70 F3**
Atlanta IL .... 40°16N 89°14W **71 C4**
Atlanta IN .... 40°13N 86°2W **72 C4**
Atlanta KS .... 37°26N 96°46W **74 D7**
Atlanta LA .... 31°48N 92°45W **75 C3**
Atlanta MI .... 45°0N 84°9W **79 E7**

Atlanta MO .... 39°54N 92°29W **82 B4**
Atlanta NE .... 40°22N 99°28W **84 D6**
Atlanta TX .... 33°7N 94°10W **99 D13**
Atlanta Hartsfield Int. ✈ (ATL)
   GA .... 33°38N 84°26W **106 D2**
Atlanta Zoo GA .... 33°44N 84°22W **106 B2**
Atlantic IA .... 41°24N 95°1W **73 D3**
Atlantic NC .... 34°54N 76°20W **90 D9**
Atlantic VA .... 37°54N 75°30W **77 C5**
Atlantic Beach FL .. 30°20N 81°24W **67 A7**
Atlantic Beach NC .. 34°42N 76°44W **90 D9**
Atlantic Beach NY .. 40°35N 73°45W **114 C4**
Atlantic City NJ .... 39°21N 74°27W **87 C2**
Atlantic City WY ... 42°30N 108°45W **104 D3**
Atlantic County ☆
   NJ .... 39°30N 74°40W **87 B2**
Atlantic Highlands NJ 40°25N 74°3W **87 B2**
Atlantic Pk. WY .... 42°37N 109°0W **104 D3**
Atmore AL .... 31°2N 87°29W **60 E3**
Atoka OK .... 34°23N 96°8W **93 D7**
Atoka TN .... 35°26N 89°47W **96 B2**
Atoka County ☆ OK. 34°25N 96°0W **93 D8**
Atoka Res. OK ..... 34°25N 96°0W **93 D7**
Atomic City ID .... 43°27N 112°49W **70 F6**
Atqasuk AK .... 70°28N 157°24W **61 A8**
Atqasuk → AK ..... 70°52N 155°55W **61 A9**
Atsion NJ .... 39°44N 74°44W **87 C2**
Attala County ☆ MS . 33°4N 89°35W **81 C4**
Attalla AL .... 34°1N 86°6W **60 B4**
Attapulgus GA ..... 30°45N 84°29W **68 E2**
Attica IN .... 40°18N 87°15W **72 C3**
Attica KS .... 37°15N 98°13W **74 D5**
Attica NY .... 42°52N 78°17W **89 C2**
Attica OH .... 41°4N 82°53W **92 B3**
Attleboro MA ...... 41°57N 71°17W **78 C3**
Attu AK .... 52°56N 173°15E **61 K1**
Attu I. AK .... 52°55N 172°55E **61 K1**
Atwater CA .... 29°43N 96°20W **99 H11**
Atwater CA .... 37°21N 120°37W **64 F6**
Atwater MN .... 45°8N 94°47W **80 E4**
Atwood IL .... 39°48N 88°28W **71 D5**
Atwood KS .... 39°48N 101°3W **74 B2**
Atwood OK .... 34°57N 96°20W **93 D7**
Atwood TN .... 35°59N 88°41W **96 E4**
Atwood L. OH ...... 40°33N 81°13W **92 C5**
Au Gres MI .... 44°3N 83°42W **79 E8**
Au Sable MI .... 44°25N 83°20W **79 E8**
Au Sable → MI ..... 44°25N 83°20W **79 E8**
Au Sable Forks NY . 44°27N 73°41W **89 A7**
Au Sable Pt. MI .... 46°40N 86°8W **79 C5**
Au Sable Pt. MI .... 44°20N 83°20W **79 E8**
Aua Amer. Samoa .. 14°16N 170°40W **105 e**
Auburn AR .... 34°43N 90°54W **63 D5**
Auburn CA .... 38°54N 121°4W **64 E5**
Auburn GA .... 34°1N 83°50W **68 C3**
Auburn IL .... 39°36N 89°45W **71 D4**
Auburn IN .... 41°22N 85°4W **72 B5**
Auburn IL .... 42°15N 94°53W **73 C4**
Auburn KS .... 38°54N 95°49W **74 C8**
Auburn KY .... 36°52N 86°43W **96 D6**
Auburn ME .... 44°6N 70°14W **76 D3**
Auburn MA .... 42°12N 71°50W **78 B3**
Auburn NY .... 43°36N 84°4W **79 F7**
Auburn NY .... 42°56N 76°34W **89 C6**
Auburn NE .... 40°23N 95°51W **84 D10**
Auburn WV .... 39°6N 80°51W **102 B4**
Auburn WA .... 47°18N 122°14W **101 C3**
Auburndale FL ..... 28°4N 81°48W **67 C7**
Auburndale MA .... 42°20N 71°14W **106 A2**
Auburndale WI ..... 44°38N 90°0W **103 D4**
Auburntown TN .... 35°57N 86°5W **96 E6**
Aucilla → FL ...... 30°5N 83°58W **67 A5**
Audrain County ☆
   MO .... 39°10N 91°50W **82 B5**
Audubon IA .... 41°43N 94°56W **73 D3**
Audubon MN .... 46°52N 95°59W **80 D3**
Audubon NJ .... 39°53N 79°4W **116 B2**
Audubon County ☆
   IA .... 41°40N 94°50W **73 D3**
Audubon L. ND ..... 47°36N 101°10W **91 C4**
Augila → OH .... 40°53N 79°5W **116 B2**
Auglaize → OH ..... 41°17N 84°21W **92 B2**
Auglaize County ☆
   OH .... 40°34N 84°12W **92 C2**
Augusta AR .... 35°17N 91°22W **63 C4**
Augusta GA .... 33°28N 81°58W **68 C5**
Augusta IL .... 40°14N 90°57W **71 C3**
Augusta IN .... 39°53N 86°12W **108 A1**
Augusta KS .... 37°41N 96°59W **74 D7**
Augusta KY .... 38°47N 84°0W **97 B8**
Augusta ME .... 44°19N 69°47W **76 D4**
Augusta MO .... 38°34N 90°53W **82 C6**
Augusta NJ .... 41°8N 74°44W **87 A2**
Augusta WV .... 39°18N 78°38W **77 A2**
Augusta WI .... 44°41N 91°7W **103 D2**
Augusta County ☆ VA 38°9N 79°4W **102 C5**
Augusta I. AK ..... 59°22N 133°6W **61 G9**
Aullville MO .... 39°1N 93°41W **82 B3**
Ault CO .... 40°35N 104°44W **66 B6**
Ault Park OH ...... 39°4N 84°24W **107 B2**
Aulneau County ☆
   VA .... 38°50N 77°6W **119 B3**
Aunuu Amer. Samoa 14°20S 170°31W **105 e**
Aurelia IA .... 42°43N 95°26W **73 B2**
Aurora CO .... 39°43N 104°49W **109 B3**
Aurora IL .... 41°45N 88°19W **71 B5**
Aurora IL .... 39°4N 84°54W **72 D6**
Aurora IN .... 39°4N 84°54W **72 D6**
Aurora KS .... 42°37N 91°44W **73 C7**
Aurora KS .... 39°27N 97°32W **74 B6**
Aurora KY .... 36°47N 88°9W **96 D4**
Aurora ME .... 44°52N 68°20W **76 C5**
Aurora MN .... 47°32N 92°14W **80 C6**
Aurora MO .... 36°58N 93°43W **82 E3**
Aurora NC .... 35°18N 76°47W **90 C9**
Aurora NY .... 42°45N 76°42W **89 C4**
Aurora NE .... 40°52N 98°0W **84 D7**
Aurora OH .... 41°21N 81°20W **92 B5**
Aurora SD .... 44°17N 96°41W **91 F9**
Aurora WV .... 39°19N 79°33W **77 A1**
Aurora County ☆ SD 43°43N 98°29W **91 G7**
Austin IN .... 35°0N 92°0W **63 D4**
Austin IN .... 41°53N 87°45W **108 B2**
Austin IL .... 38°45N 85°49W **72 E5**
Austin MN .... 43°40N 92°58W **80 G6**
Austin MT .... 46°39N 112°15W **83 D5**
Austin NV .... 39°30N 117°4W **85 C4**
Austin PA .... 41°38N 78°6W **95 C4**
Austin Bergstrom Int. ✈ (AUS)
   TX .... 30°12N 97°41W **99 G10**
Austin County ☆
   TX .... 29°57N 96°15W **99 H11**
Austintown OH .... 41°6N 80°46W **92 B6**
Austinville VA ...... 36°51N 80°55W **102 E4**
Austwell TX .... 28°23N 96°51W **99 J11**
Autauga County ☆
   AL .... 32°26N 86°39W **60 D4**
Autaugaville AL .... 32°26N 86°39W **60 D4**
Auxvasse MO ...... 39°1N 91°54W **82 B5**
Ava IL .... 37°53N 89°30W **71 E4**
Ava MO .... 36°57N 92°40W **82 E4**
Avalon CA .... 33°21N 118°20W **65 K8**
Avalon MS .... 33°39N 90°5W **81 C3**
Avalon NJ .... 39°6N 74°43W **87 C2**
Avalon PA .... 40°30N 80°4W **116 A1**
Avalon, L. NM ..... 32°27N 104°15W **88 E6**
Avant OK .... 36°29N 96°3W **93 B7**
Avard OK .... 36°42N 98°42W **93 B5**
Avawatz Mts. CA .. 35°40N 116°30W **65 H10**

Avenal CA .... 36°0N 120°8W **65 H6**
Avenel MD .... 38°59N 76°59W **119 B4**
Avenue MD .... 38°16N 76°46W **77 B4**
Avera GA .... 33°12N 82°32W **68 C4**
Avery ID .... 47°15N 115°49W **70 B3**
Avery TX .... 33°33N 94°47W **99 D13**
Avery County ☆ NC . 36°5N 82°0W **90 B4**
Avery Island LA .... 29°55N 91°54W **75 E4**
Avilla IN .... 41°22N 85°14W **72 B5**
Avilla MO .... 37°8N 94°8W **82 D2**
Avinger TX .... 32°54N 94°33W **99 E13**
Avis PA .... 41°11N 77°19W **95 C5**
Avoca IA .... 41°29N 95°20W **73 D3**
Avoca MN .... 43°57N 95°39W **80 G3**
Avoca NY .... 42°24N 77°25W **89 C3**
Avoca TX .... 32°52N 99°43W **98 E6**
Avon CO .... 39°38N 106°31W **66 C4**
Avon CT .... 41°49N 72°50W **78 C2**
Avon IL .... 40°40N 90°26W **71 C3**
Avon MT .... 46°36N 112°36W **83 D5**
Avon NY .... 42°55N 77°45W **89 C3**
Avon SD .... 43°0N 98°4W **91 H7**
Avon Park FL ..... 27°36N 81°31W **67 D7**
Avon Park Air Force Range
   FL .... 27°38N 81°33W **67 D7**
Avondale AZ .... 33°26N 112°21W **62 D3**
Avondale CO .... 38°14N 104°21W **66 D6**
Avondale LA .... 41°56N 87°41W **108 B2**
Avondale LA .... 29°54N 90°12W **113 C1**
Avondale PA .... 39°50N 75°47W **77 A5**
Avonmore PA ...... 40°32N 79°28W **95 D3**
Avoyelles Parish ☆ LA 31°0N 92°0W **75 C3**
Axial CO .... 40°17N 107°47W **66 B3**
Axson GA .... 31°17N 82°44W **68 E4**
Axtell KS .... 39°52N 96°15W **74 B7**
Axtell NE .... 40°29N 99°8W **84 D6**
Ayden NC .... 35°28N 77°25W **90 C8**
Ayer MA .... 42°34N 71°35W **78 B3**
Ayr ND .... 47°3N 97°29W **91 C8**
Ayr NE .... 40°26N 98°26W **84 D7**
Ayrshire IA .... 43°2N 94°50W **73 B4**
Azdscohos L. ME .. 45°0N 71°0W **86 B4**
Azle TX .... 32°54N 97°32W **99 E10**
Aztec AZ .... 32°49N 113°27W **62 E2**
Aztec NM .... 36°49N 107°59W **88 A3**
Aztec Peak AZ ..... 33°49N 110°54W **62 D5**
Aztec Ruins Nat. Monument →
   NM .... 36°50N 108°0W **88 A3**
Azusa CA .... 34°8N 117°52W **65 J9**

B

B.A. Steinhagen L.
   TX .... 30°50N 94°15W **99 G13**
B. Everett Jordan L.
   NC .... 35°30N 79°0W **90 C6**
Babb MT .... 48°51N 113°27W **83 B4**
Babbitt MN .... 47°41N 91°54W **80 C7**
Babbitt NV .... 38°32N 118°39W **85 D2**
Babboquivari Peak
   AZ .... 31°46N 111°36W **62 F4**
Babson Park FL .... 27°49N 81°32W **67 D7**
Babylon NY .... 40°42N 73°19W **87 B3**
Baca County ☆ CO . 37°15N 102°30W **66 D8**
Bachelor, Mt. OR .. 43°59N 121°41W **94 D4**
Back Bay Nat. Wildlife Refuge
   VA .... 36°39N 75°56W **102 E9**
Backbone Mt. MD .. 39°12N 79°28W **77 A1**
Backus MN .... 46°49N 94°31W **80 D4**
Bacon County ☆ GA 31°30N 82°30W **68 E4**
Baconton GA ...... 31°23N 84°10W **68 E2**
Bad → SD .... 44°21N 100°22W **91 F5**
Bad Axe MI .... 43°48N 83°0W **79 F9**
Bad River Indian Reservation
   WI .... 46°30N 90°45W **103 B3**
Baden PA .... 40°38N 80°14W **95 D2**
Badger IA .... 42°37N 94°9W **73 C4**
Badger MN .... 48°47N 96°1W **80 B2**
Badger SD .... 44°29N 97°12W **91 F8**
Badger Cr. → CO .. 40°17N 103°42W **66 B7**
Badger Pk. MT ..... 45°40N 106°33W **83 E11**
Badin NC .... 35°24N 80°6W **90 C5**
Badlands SD ...... 43°55N 102°30W **91 G3**
Badlands Nat. Park △
   SD .... 43°38N 102°56W **91 G3**
Badwater Cr. →
   WY .... 43°17N 108°8W **104 C4**
Baffin B. TX .... 27°18N 97°30W **98 K10**
Bagdad AZ .... 34°34N 113°11W **62 C3**
Bagdad FL .... 30°36N 87°2W **67 A1**
Bagdad KY .... 38°16N 85°3W **97 B7**
Baggs WY .... 41°2N 107°39W **104 E5**
Bagley MN .... 47°32N 95°24W **80 C3**
Baha'i Temple IL ... 42°4N 87°41W **108 A2**
Bahia County ☆ TX 34°50N 105°21W **104 D6**
Bailey, Harbor WI .. 45°4N 87°8W **103 C6**
Baileys Crossroads
   VA .... 38°50N 77°6W **119 B3**
Baileys Harbor WI .. 45°4N 87°8W **103 C6**
Baileyton TN ...... 36°20N 82°50W **97 D10**
Baileyville KS ...... 39°51N 96°11W **74 B7**
Bainbridge GA ..... 30°55N 84°35W **68 F2**
Bainbridge IN ...... 39°46N 86°49W **72 D4**
Bainbridge NY ..... 42°18N 75°29W **89 C5**
Bainbridge OH ..... 39°14N 83°16W **92 D3**
Bainbridge Island
   WA .... 47°38N 122°32W **118 C2**
Bainville MT .... 48°8N 104°13W **83 B13**
Baird TX .... 32°24N 99°24W **99 E8**
Baird Mts. AK ..... 67°0N 160°0W **61 C7**
Bairoil WY .... 42°15N 107°33W **104 D5**
Baisley Pond NY ... 40°40N 73°47W **114 B4**
Baker FL .... 30°48N 86°41W **67 A2**
Baker ID .... 45°6N 113°44W **70 D5**
Baker LA .... 30°35N 91°10W **75 D4**
Baker MT .... 46°22N 104°17W **83 D13**
Baker ND .... 48°10N 99°39W **91 B6**
Baker OK .... 36°52N 101°1W **93 B2**
Baker, Mt. WA ..... 48°50N 121°49W **101 B4**
Baker Butte AZ .... 34°27N 111°24W **62 C4**
Baker City OR ..... 44°47N 117°50W **94 C8**
Baker County ☆ FL . 30°20N 82°20W **67 A6**
Baker County ☆ GA . 31°20N 84°30W **68 E2**
Baker County ☆ OR 44°40N 117°50W **94 C8**
Baker I. Pac. Oc. .. 0°10N 176°35W **105 D6**
Bakerhill AL .... 31°47N 85°18W **60 D5**
Bakersfield CA ..... 35°22N 119°2W **65 J7**
Bakersfield VT ..... 44°47N 72°48W **86 B2**
Bakersville NC ..... 36°1N 82°10W **90 B3**
Bal Harbor FL ..... 25°53N 80°7W **112 C3**
Bala KS .... 39°19N 96°57W **74 B7**
Bala-Cynwyd PA ... 40°0N 75°13W **116 A1**
Balaton MN .... 44°14N 95°53W **80 F3**
Balboa Park CA .... 32°43N 117°9W **117 B2**
Balch Springs TX .. 32°43N 96°37W **109 B6**
Balcones Canyonlands Nat.
   Wildlife Refuge △
   TX .... 30°33N 98°0W **99 G10**
Balcones Escarpment
   TX .... 29°30N 99°15W **98 H7**
Balcones Heights
   TX .... 29°29N 98°33W **117 B2**
Bald Head I. NC .... 33°52N 77°59W **90 E8**
Bald Knob AR ..... 35°19N 91°34W **63 C4**

Bald Knob VA ..... 37°56N 79°51W **102 D5**
Bald Knoll WY ..... 42°22N 110°28W **104 D2**
Bald Mt. OR ...... 43°16N 121°21W **94 D4**
Bald Pt. FL .... 29°57N 84°20W **67 B4**
Baldwin FL .... 30°18N 81°59W **67 A7**
Baldwin GA .... 34°30N 83°32W **68 B3**
Baldwin IL .... 38°11N 89°51W **71 E4**
Baldwin LA .... 29°50N 91°33W **75 E4**
Baldwin MI .... 43°54N 85°51W **79 F6**
Baldwin NY .... 40°39N 73°36W **114 C5**
Baldwin PA .... 40°21N 79°58W **116 B2**
Baldwin WI .... 44°58N 92°22W **103 D1**
Baldwin, L. FL ..... 28°34N 81°19W **115 A3**
Baldwin City KS ... 38°47N 95°11W **74 C8**
Baldwin County ☆
   AL .... 30°53N 87°46W **60 F3**
Baldwin County ☆ GA 33°5N 83°10W **68 C3**
Baldwin Hills CA ... 34°0N 118°21W **111 B2**
Baldwin Hills Res.
   CA .... 34°0N 118°21W **111 B2**
Baldwinsville NY ... 43°10N 76°20W **89 B4**
Baldwinville MA .... 42°37N 72°5W **78 B2**
Baldwyn MS .... 34°31N 88°38W **81 B5**
Baldy Pk. AZ ...... 33°54N 109°34W **62 D6**
Baldy Pk. NM ..... 36°38N 105°13W **88 A5**
Baler L. WA .... 48°44N 121°38W **101 B4**
Balfour ND .... 47°57N 100°32W **91 C5**
Ball Club MN ...... 47°19N 93°47W **80 C4**
Ball Ground GA .... 34°20N 84°23W **68 B2**
Ballantine MT ..... 45°57N 108°9W **83 E9**
Ballard UT .... 40°17N 109°35W **100 C6**
Ballard County ☆ KY . 37°0N 89°0W **96 D4**
Ballenger Creek MD 39°22N 77°26W **77 A3**
Ballinger TX .... 31°45N 99°57W **98 F6**
Ballston Spa NY ... 43°0N 73°51W **89 C7**
Balltown L. AL ..... 42°38N 90°51W **73 C8**
Balm MO .... 38°36N 90°33W **82 C6**
Bally PA .... 40°24N 75°35W **87 B1**
Balmorhea TX ..... 30°59N 103°45W **98 G4**
Balmville NY ...... 41°32N 74°1W **87 A2**
Balsam Lake WI ... 45°27N 92°27W **103 C1**
Balta ND .... 48°10N 100°2W **91 B5**
Baltic CT .... 41°37N 72°5W **78 C2**
Baltic OH .... 40°26N 81°42W **92 C5**
Baltic SD .... 43°46N 96°44W **91 G9**
Baltimore MD ..... 39°17N 76°36W **107 B2**
Baltimore OH ...... 39°51N 82°36W **92 D4**
Baltimore County ☆
   MD .... 39°20N 76°40W **77 A4**
Baltimore Highlands
   MD .... 39°13N 76°38W **107 B2**
Baltimore Washington Int. ✈
   (BWI) MD .... 39°11N 76°40W **77 A4**
Bamberg SC .... 33°18N 81°2W **90 E4**
Bamberg County ☆
   SC .... 33°10N 81°0W **90 E4**
Bancroft ID .... 42°43N 111°53W **70 G7**
Bancroft IA .... 43°18N 94°13W **73 B4**
Bancroft LA .... 42°53N 84°4W **79 G7**
Bancroft MI .... 42°53N 84°4W **79 G7**
Bandana KY .... 37°9N 88°56W **96 C4**
Bandelier Nat. Monument →
   NM .... 35°50N 106°25W **88 B4**
Bandera County ☆
   TX .... 29°48N 99°15W **99 H8**
Bandon OR .... 43°7N 124°25W **94 D1**
Bangor ME .... 44°48N 68°46W **76 D5**
Bangor MI .... 42°19N 86°7W **79 G5**
Bangor PA .... 40°52N 75°13W **87 B1**
Bangor Naval Reserve
   WA .... 47°43N 122°44W **118 B1**
Bangs, Mt. AZ ..... 36°48N 113°51W **62 A2**
Banister → VA ..... 36°42N 78°48W **102 E6**
Banks AL .... 31°49N 85°51W **60 E5**
Banks ID .... 44°5N 116°7W **70 F2**
Banks OR .... 45°37N 123°7W **94 B2**
Banks County ☆ GA . 34°20N 83°30W **68 B3**
Banks L. GA .... 31°2N 83°6W **68 E3**
Banks L. WA .... 47°47N 119°19W **101 C6**
Bannack AZ .... 45°12N 112°59W **83 E5**
Banner MS .... 34°5N 89°23W **81 B4**
Banner WY .... 44°36N 106°52W **104 B6**
Banner County ☆
   NE .... 41°30N 103°40W **84 C2**
Banner Elk NC ..... 36°10N 81°52W **90 B4**
Bannertown NC .... 36°29N 80°35W **90 B5**
Banning CA .... 33°56N 116°53W **65 K10**
Bannock County ☆
   ID .... 42°30N 112°10W **70 G6**
Bannock Cr. → ID .. 42°53N 112°40W **70 G6**
Bannock Range ID. 42°40N 112°30W **70 G6**
Bantam CT .... 41°43N 73°15W **78 C1**
Bapchule AZ ...... 33°12N 111°50W **62 D4**
Bar Harbor ME .... 44°23N 68°13W **76 D5**
Bar Nunn WY ..... 42°52N 106°21W **104 D6**
Baraboo WI .... 43°28N 89°45W **103 E4**
Baraga MI .... 46°47N 88°30W **79 C3**
Baraga County ☆ MI 46°40N 88°20W **79 C3**
Baranof AK .... 57°5N 134°50W **61 H14**
Baranof I. AK ...... 57°0N 135°0W **61 H14**
Baratararia LA ..... 29°44N 90°8W **75 E5**
Barataria B. LA .... 29°20N 89°55W **75 E6**
Barataria Preserve
   LA .... 29°47N 90°7W **113 D2**
Barber, L. FL ...... 30°36N 81°19W **115 A3**
Barber County ☆ KS 37°15N 98°40W **74 D5**
Barbers Pt. HI ..... 21°18N 158°7W **69 K13**
Barberton OH ..... 41°1N 81°39W **92 B5**
Barberville FL ..... 29°11N 81°26W **67 B7**
Barbour County ☆
   AL .... 31°53N 85°27W **60 E5**
Barbour County ☆
   WV .... 39°9N 80°3W **102 B4**
Barbourmeade KY .. 38°18N 85°41W **97 B7**
Barboursville WV .. 38°24N 82°18W **102 C2**
Barbourville KY .... 36°52N 83°53W **97 D9**
Barceloneta
   Puerto Rico .. 18°27N 66°32W **105 G16**
Barclay MD .... 39°9N 75°52W **77 A5**
Barcroft, L. VA ..... 38°52N 77°9W **119 B3**
Bardley MO .... 36°42N 91°7W **82 E5**
Bardstown KY ..... 37°49N 85°28W **97 C7**
Bardwell KY .... 36°52N 89°1W **96 D3**
Barga MN .... 47°35N 91°55W **101 B3**
Bargersville IN .... 39°31N 86°10W **72 D4**
Baring MO .... 40°15N 92°12W **82 A4**
Barkamsted Res.
   CT .... 41°53N 72°58W **78 C2**
Barkley, L. TN ..... 36°0N 88°0W **96 C4**
Barksdale TX ...... 29°44N 100°2W **98 H6**
Barksdale Air Force Base
   LA .... 32°29N 93°42W **75 B2**
Barling AR .... 35°20N 94°18W **63 C1**
Barlow KY .... 37°3N 89°2W **96 D3**
Barlow PA .... 39°45N 77°14W **77 A3**
Barnard KS .... 39°11N 98°3W **74 B5**
Barnard MO .... 40°10N 94°50W **82 A2**
Barnegat NJ .... 39°45N 74°14W **87 C2**
Barnegat Light NJ . 39°46N 74°6W **87 C2**
Barnes KS .... 39°43N 96°52W **74 B7**
Bay AR .... 35°45N 90°34W **63 C4**

Barnes County ☆ ND . 47°0N 98°0W **91 C7**
Barneston NE ...... 40°5N 96°38W **84 D9**
Barnesville GA ..... 33°3N 84°9W **68 C2**
Barnesville MD .... 39°13N 77°23W **77 A3**
Barnesville MN .... 46°43N 96°28W **80 D2**
Barnesville OH ..... 39°59N 81°11W **92 D5**
Barnet VT .... 44°18N 72°3W **86 B2**
Barnett MO .... 38°23N 92°41W **82 C4**
Barney GA .... 31°1N 83°31W **68 E3**
Barnhart TX .... 31°8N 101°10W **98 F6**
Barnhart TX .... 31°8N 101°10W **98 F6**
Barnstable MA ..... 41°42N 70°18W **78 C4**
Barnstable County ☆
   MA .... 41°40N 70°15W **78 C4**
Barnstable Harbor
   MA .... 41°43N 70°18W **78 C4**
Barnum MN .... 46°30N 92°42W **80 D6**
Barnum WY .... 43°40N 106°55W **104 C6**
Barnwell SC .... 33°15N 81°23W **90 E4**
Barnwell County ☆
   SC .... 33°15N 81°30W **90 E4**
Baron OK .... 35°55N 94°36W **93 C9**
Barques, Pt. Aux MI . 44°4N 82°58W **79 E9**
Barques, Pt. Aux MI . 45°48N 86°21W **79 C5**
Barranquitas
   Puerto Rico .. 18°11N 66°19W **105 G16**
Barre MA .... 42°25N 72°6W **78 B2**
Barre VT .... 44°12N 72°30W **86 B2**
Barren → KY ...... 37°7N 86°57W **96 C6**
Barren County ☆ KY 36°57N 85°57W **97 D7**
Barren Hill PA ..... 40°5N 75°15W **116 A1**
Barren Is. AK ..... 58°55N 152°15W **61 G9**
Barren River L. KY . 36°54N 86°8W **96 D6**
Barrett MN .... 45°55N 95°53W **80 E3**
Barrett WV .... 37°53N 81°40W **102 D3**
Barrigada Guam ... 13°28N 144°48E **105 b**
Barrineau Park FL .. 30°42N 87°26W **67 A1**
Barrington NH ..... 43°12N 70°59W **86 C4**
Barrington NJ ..... 39°52N 75°4W **116 B2**
Barrington RI ...... 41°44N 71°18W **78 C3**
Barron WI .... 45°24N 91°51W **103 C2**
Barron County ☆
   WI .... 45°25N 91°50W **103 C2**
Barrow, Pt. AK .... 71°23N 156°29W **61 A8**
Barrow County ☆ GA 34°0N 83°40W **68 C3**
Barry IL .... 39°42N 91°2W **71 D2**
Barry County ☆ MI . 42°35N 85°25W **79 G6**
Barry County ☆ MO 36°40N 93°45W **82 E3**
Barry M. Goldwater Air Force
   Range AZ .... 32°38N 113°33W **62 E2**
Barryton MI .... 43°45N 85°9W **79 F6**
Barstow TX .... 31°28N 103°24W **98 F4**
Barstow CA .... 34°54N 117°1W **65 J9**
Bartholomew, Bayou
   LA .... 32°43N 92°4W **75 B3**
Bartholomew County ☆
   IN .... 39°10N 85°55W **72 D5**
Bartlesville OK .... 36°45N 95°59W **93 B8**
Bartlett KS .... 37°3N 95°13W **74 D8**
Bartlett NH .... 44°5N 71°17W **86 B3**
Bartlett NE .... 41°53N 98°33W **84 C7**
Bartlett TX .... 35°12N 89°52W **112 A2**
Bartlett Res. AZ ... 33°49N 111°38W **62 C4**
Bartley NE .... 40°15N 100°18W **84 D5**
Bartley WV .... 37°23N 81°40W **102 D3**
Barton MD .... 39°34N 79°2W **77 A1**
Barton VT .... 44°45N 72°11W **86 B2**
Barton, L. FL ...... 28°33N 81°18W **115 A3**
Barton County ☆ KS 38°30N 98°40W **74 C5**
Bartonville IL ...... 40°39N 89°39W **71 C4**
Bartonville TX ..... 37°8N 80°17W **102 D4**
Bartow FL .... 27°54N 81°50W **67 D7**
Bartow GA .... 32°53N 82°29W **68 D4**
Bartow County ☆
   GA .... 34°20N 84°50W **68 B2**
Bartonville IL ...... 40°39N 89°39W **71 C4**
Barwick GA .... 30°54N 83°44W **68 F3**
Basalt CO .... 39°22N 107°2W **66 C3**
Basalt ID .... 43°19N 112°10W **70 F6**
Basaslt MT .... 46°16N 112°16W **83 D5**
Bashan L. MN ..... 48°7N 91°54W **80 B7**
Basin MT .... 46°16N 112°16W **83 D5**
Basin WY .... 44°23N 108°2W **104 B4**
Basinger FL .... 27°23N 81°2W **67 D7**
Baskahegan L. ME . 45°28N 67°45W **76 C6**
Baskin LA .... 32°16N 91°45W **75 B4**
Bass Lake MN ..... 45°35N 93°25W **113 A1**
Bassett NE .... 42°35N 99°32W **84 B6**
Bassett VA .... 36°46N 79°59W **102 E5**
Basswood L. MN .. 48°7N 91°30W **80 B7**
Bastian VA .... 37°7N 81°11W **102 D3**
Bastrop LA .... 32°47N 91°55W **75 B4**
Bastrop TX .... 30°7N 97°19W **99 G10**
Bastrop County ☆
   TX .... 30°10N 97°20W **99 G10**
Batavia IL .... 41°51N 88°19W **71 B5**
Batavia NY .... 43°0N 78°11W **89 B2**
Batavia OH .... 39°5N 84°11W **92 D2**
Batchtown IL ...... 39°2N 90°43W **71 D3**
Bates County ☆ MO 38°15N 94°20W **82 C2**
Batesburg-Leesville
   SC .... 33°54N 81°33W **90 E4**
Batesville IN ...... 39°18N 85°13W **72 D5**
Batesville AR ...... 35°46N 91°39W **63 B4**
Batesville TX ...... 28°58N 99°37W **99 J8**
Bath IL .... 40°11N 90°8W **71 C3**
Bath ME .... 43°55N 69°49W **76 E4**
Bath NY .... 42°20N 77°19W **89 C3**
Bath PA .... 40°44N 75°24W **87 B1**
Bath SD .... 45°28N 98°20W **91 E7**
Bath County ☆ KY . 38°8N 83°45W **97 B8**
Bath County ☆ VA . 38°0N 79°50W **102 C5**
Bathgate ND ...... 48°53N 97°29W **91 B8**
Baton Rouge LA ... 30°27N 91°11W **75 D4**
Batson TX .... 30°15N 94°40W **99 G13**
Battle → CA .... 40°21N 122°11W **64 C4**
Battle Creek IA .... 42°19N 95°37W **73 C3**
Battle Creek MI .... 42°19N 85°11W **79 G6**
Battle Creek NE ... 42°0N 97°36W **84 C8**
Battle Creek L. MN 44°56N 92°58W **113 B4**
Battle Creek Park
   MN .... 44°56N 93°1W **113 B3**
Battle Ground IN .. 40°31N 86°50W **72 C4**
Battle Ground WA . 45°47N 122°32W **101 E3**
Battle Lake MN .... 46°17N 95°43W **80 D3**
Battle Mountain NV 40°38N 116°56W **85 B5**
Battle Mt. WY ..... 42°2N 106°57W **104 E5**
Baudette MN ...... 48°43N 94°36W **80 B4**
Bauxite AR .... 34°33N 92°30W **63 D3**
Bavaria KS .... 38°48N 97°45W **74 C6**
Baxley GA .... 31°47N 82°21W **68 E4**
Baxter IA .... 41°49N 93°9W **73 D5**
Baxter KS .... 39°11N 98°3W **74 B5**
Baxter MN .... 46°22N 94°17W **80 D4**
Baxter TN .... 36°9N 85°38W **97 D7**
Baxter VT .... 44°43N 72°2W **86 B2**
Baxter Estates NY . 40°50N 73°41W **114 A4**
Baxter Springs KS . 37°2N 94°44W **74 D9**
Baxter State Park △
   U.S.A. .... 46°5N 68°57W **76 B5**
Bay AR .... 35°45N 90°34W **63 C4**

Bay, L. FL .... 28°25N 81°34W **115 A2**
Bay City MI .... 43°36N 83°54W **79 F8**
Bay City OR .... 45°31N 123°53W **94 B2**
Bay City TX .... 28°59N 95°58W **99 J12**
Bay County ☆ FL .. 30°20N 85°45W **67 A3**
Bay County ☆ MI .. 43°45N 84°5W **79 F7**
Bay Farm Island
   CA .... 37°43N 122°12W **118 B3**
Bay Harbour Islands
   FL .... 25°53N 80°7W **112 C3**
Bay Minette AL .... 28°28N 81°30W **115 B1**
Bay Mills Indian Reservation
   MI .... 46°26N 84°15W **79 C7**
Bay Minette AL .... 30°53N 87°46W **60 F3**
Bay Park NY .... 40°37N 73°40W **114 C5**
Bay Pines FL ...... 27°48N 82°46W **119 C2**
Bay Port MI .... 43°51N 83°23W **79 F8**
Bay Ridge NY ..... 40°37N 74°1W **114 C2**
Bay Shore NY ..... 40°43N 73°15W **87 B3**
Bay St. Louis MS .. 30°19N 89°20W **81 F4**
Bay Springs MS ... 31°59N 89°17W **81 E4**
Bay Springs L. MS . 34°31N 88°20W **81 B5**
Bay View MD ...... 39°39N 75°58W **77 A5**
Bayamón
   Puerto Rico .. 18°24N 66°9W **105 G16**
Bayard IA .... 41°51N 94°33W **73 D4**
Bayard NM .... 32°46N 108°8W **88 E2**
Bayard NE .... 41°45N 103°20W **84 C2**
Bayard WV .... 39°16N 79°22W **77 A1**
Bayboro NC .... 35°9N 76°46W **90 C9**
Bayfield CO .... 37°14N 107°36W **66 E3**
Bayfield WI .... 46°49N 90°49W **103 B3**
Bayfield County ☆
   WI .... 46°25N 91°15W **103 B2**
Bayfield Ridge WI . 46°45N 91°25W **103 B2**
Baylor County ☆ TX 33°35N 99°16W **99 D8**
Bayonet Point FL .. 28°20N 82°41W **67 C6**
Bayonne NJ .... 40°40N 74°6W **114 B2**
Bayou Boeuf LA ... 29°50N 90°35W **113 C2**
Bayou Cane LA .... 29°37N 90°45W **75 E5**
Bayou D'Arbonne L.
   LA .... 32°43N 92°21W **75 B3**
Bayou de Chien →
   KY .... 36°35N 89°12W **96 D3**
Bayou DeView →
   AR .... 34°48N 91°18W **63 D4**
Bayou George FL .. 30°16N 85°33W **67 A3**
Bayou La Batre AL . 30°24N 88°15W **60 F2**
Bayou Meto AR .... 34°13N 91°31W **63 D4**
Bayou Pierre → MS . 31°55N 91°11W **81 E2**
Bayou Sauvage Nat. Wildlife
   Refuge △ LA .. 30°1N 89°53W **113 B3**
Bayou Segnette State Park
   LA .... 29°53N 90°10W **113 C1**
Bayou Vista LA .... 29°41N 91°16W **75 E4**
Bayport FL .... 28°32N 82°39W **67 C6**
Bayshore CA ...... 37°42N 122°24W **118 B2**
Bayshore FL .... 26°43N 81°50W **67 E7**
Bayside NY .... 40°46N 73°46W **114 B4**
Bayside TX .... 28°6N 97°13W **99 J10**
Bayside WI .... 43°10N 87°54W **112 A2**
Bayview CA .... 37°48N 97°26W **99 G10**
Bayview TX .... 30°48N 97°26W **99 G10**
Bayview CA .... 47°59N 116°34W **70 B2**
Bazaar KS .... 38°13N 96°33W **74 C7**
Bazile Mills KS .... 42°31N 97°53W **84 B8**
Bazine KS .... 38°27N 99°42W **74 C4**
Beach ND .... 46°58N 104°0W **91 D2**
Beach City OH ..... 40°39N 81°35W **92 C5**
Beach Haven NJ ... 39°34N 74°14W **87 C2**
Beachmont MA .... 38°8N 76°24W **77 B4**
Beachwood NJ .... 39°56N 74°12W **87 C2**
Beachville MD ..... 38°8N 76°24W **77 B4**
Beacon IA .... 41°17N 92°41W **73 D6**
Beacon NY .... 41°30N 73°58W **87 A3**
Beacon Hill FL ..... 29°56N 85°23W **67 B3**
Beadle County ☆ SD 44°22N 98°13W **91 F7**
Beagle KS .... 38°25N 94°57W **74 C9**
Beale Air Force Base
   CA .... 39°7N 121°19W **64 D5**
Beallsville OH ...... 39°51N 81°2W **92 D5**
Beals Cr. → TX .... 32°10N 100°51W **98 E7**
Bear DE .... 39°38N 75°39W **77 A5**
Bear Brook State Park
   NH .... 43°6N 71°21W **86 C3**
Bear Cr. → AL ..... 33°11N 88°5W **60 C2**
Bear Cr. → WY .... 41°41N 104°13W **104 E8**
Bear Creek WI ..... 44°32N 88°44W **103 D5**
Bear Creek → MD . 39°13N 76°30W **107 B2**
Bear Creek Village
   PA .... 41°11N 75°45W **87 A1**
Bear Lake MI ...... 44°25N 86°9W **79 E5**
Bear Lake County ☆
   ID .... 42°20N 111°15W **70 G7**
Bear Lake Nat. Wildlife Refuge △
   ID .... 42°10N 111°18W **70 G7**
Bear Peak WY ..... 43°34N 109°13W **104 C3**
Bear River City UT 41°37N 112°8W **100 B3**
Bear River Range
   WY .... 42°9N 111°36W **70 G7**
Bear Tooth Pass
   WY .... 44°58N 109°28W **104 B3**
Bearden AR .... 33°43N 92°37W **63 E3**
Bearden OK .... 35°21N 96°23W **93 C7**
Beardsley MN ..... 45°33N 96°43W **80 E2**
Beardsley WY ..... 33°49N 101°14W **74 D2**
Beardstown IL ..... 40°1N 90°26W **71 C3**
Bearmouth MT .... 46°48N 113°20W **83 D4**
Bearpaw Mts. MT . 48°12N 109°30W **83 B8**
Bears Ears UT ..... 37°38N 109°51W **100 F6**
Beartooth Mts. MT 45°10N 109°48W **104 A3**
Beartooth Pass MT 45°0N 109°28W **104 B3**
Beatrice AL .... 31°44N 87°13W **60 E4**
Beatrice NE .... 40°16N 96°45W **84 D9**
Beattie KS .... 39°52N 96°25W **74 B7**
Beatty NV .... 36°54N 116°46W **85 E4**
Beatty OR .... 42°27N 121°16W **94 E4**
Beattyville KY ..... 37°35N 83°42W **97 C9**
Beaufort NC .... 34°43N 76°40W **90 D9**
Beaufort SC .... 32°26N 80°40W **90 F5**
Beaufort County ☆
   NC .... 35°30N 76°50W **90 C9**
Beaufort County ☆
   SC .... 32°30N 80°50W **90 F5**
Beaumont CA ...... 33°57N 116°59W **65 K10**
Beaumont MS ..... 31°10N 88°55W **81 E5**
Beaumont TX ...... 30°5N 94°6W **99 G13**
Beauregard Parish ☆
   LA .... 30°50N 93°20W **75 D2**
Beaux Arts WA .... 47°35N 122°11W **118 C4**
Beaver AK .... 66°22N 147°24W **61 C11**
Beaver KS .... 38°38N 98°40W **74 C5**
Beaver OH .... 39°2N 82°50W **92 D3**
Beaver OR .... 45°17N 123°49W **94 B2**
Beaver UT .... 38°17N 112°38W **100 E3**
Beaver → AZ ...... 36°54N 113°30W **62 B1**
Beaver → UT ...... 39°10N 112°57W **100 D3**
Beaver Bay MN .... 47°16N 91°18W **80 C7**
Beaver City NE .... 40°8N 99°50W **84 D6**
Beaver County ☆
   OK .... 36°45N 100°25W **93 B3**
Beaver County ☆ PA 40°45N 80°20W **100 E2**
Beaver County ☆
   UT .... 38°20N 113°10W **100 E2**
Beaver Cr. → MT .. 48°27N 107°18W **83 B10**
Beaver Cr. → ND .. 47°20N 103°39W **91 C2**

Beaver Cr. → ND . 46°15N 100°32W **91** D5
Beaver Cr. → NE... 40°7N 99°29W **84** D6
Beaver Cr. → TX .. 33°53N 98°49W **99** D9
Beaver Creek → WY 43°38N 108°26W **104** D4
Beaver Creek MN.. 43°37N 96°22W **80** G2
Beaver Crossing NE. 40°47N 97°17W **84** D8
Beaver Dam KY ... 37°24N 86°52W **96** C4
Beaver Dam WI ... 43°28N 88°50W **103** E5
Beaver Dam L. WI . 43°31N 88°53W **103** E5
Beaver I. MI ..... 45°40N 85°33W **79** D6
Beaver Lake MN .. 36°25N 93°51W **63** B2
Beaver Lake MN .. 44°58N 93°0W **113** B3
Beavercreek OH ... 39°43N 84°11W **92** D2
Beaverdam OH .... 40°50N 83°59W **92** C3
Beaverhead → MT. 45°5N 112°10W **83** E4
Beaverhead County ☆
　MT .... 45°5N 113°10W **83** E4
Beaverhead Mts. ID. 45°0N 113°20W **70** E7
Beaverhead Nat. Forest ○
　MT .... 45°10N 113°12W **83** E4
Beaverton MI ..... 43°53N 84°29W **79** F7
Beaverton MT..... 48°26N 107°15W **83** B10
Beaverton OR ..... 45°29N 122°48W **116** B1
Bebe TX.......... 29°25N 97°38W **99** H10
Becharof L. AK.... 57°56N 156°23W **61** H8
Becharof Nat. Wildlife Refuge ○
　AK .... 58°0N 156°15W **61** H8
Beck L. IL .... 42°4N 87°52W **108** A1
Becker County ☆
　MN .... 46°50N 95°50W **80** D3
Beckham County ☆
　OK .... 35°15N 99°40W **93** C4
Beckley WV ...... 37°47N 81°11W **102** D3
Beckville TX ..... 32°15N 94°27W **99** E13
Beckwith Cr. → CA. 41°20N 120°20W **78** F5
Becky Pk. NV .... 39°58N 114°36W **85** C6
Bedford IN .... 38°52N 86°29W **72** E4
Bedford IA .... 40°40N 94°44W **73** E4
Bedford KY....... 38°36N 85°19W **97** B7
Bedford MA ...... 42°27N 71°15W **106** A2
Bedford NH ...... 42°55N 71°32W **86** D3
Bedford NY....... 41°12N 73°38W **117** B5
Bedford PA .... 40°1N 78°30W **95** B6
Bedford TX .... 32°50N 97°8W **109** A3
Bedford VA .... 37°20N 79°31W **102** D5
Bedford County ☆ PA 40°0N 78°30W **95** E4
Bedford County ☆
　TN .... 35°29N 86°28W **96** E6
Bedford County ☆
　VA .... 37°20N 79°31W **102** D5
Bedford Park IL ... 41°46N 87°46W **108** C2
Bedford Park NY .. 40°52N 73°52W **114** A3
Bedford Reservation ○
　OH .... 41°22N 81°33W **107** B2
Bedford Stuyvesant
　NY............ 40°41N 73°56W **114** B3
Bedias TX .... 30°45N 95°55W **99** G11
Bedrock CO ...... 38°19N 108°54W **66** D2
Bee NE.......... 41°0N 97°4W **84** C8
Bee County ☆ TX . 28°24N 97°54W **99** J10
Bee Ridge FL ..... 27°17N 82°29W **67** D6
Bee Springs KY ... 37°17N 86°17W **96** C4
Beebe AR .... 35°4N 91°53W **63** C4
Beech → TN....... 35°37N 88°2W **96** E4
Beech Bottom WV . 40°14N 80°39W **102** A4
Beech Creek PA ... 41°5N 77°36W **95** C5
Beech Fork → KY .. 37°46N 85°41W **97** C7
Beech Fork L. WV . 38°18N 82°25W **102** C2
Beech Grove IN ... 39°43N 86°5W **110** B2
Beech Mountain NC 36°12N 81°53W **90** B4
Beecher IL .... 41°21N 87°38W **71** B6
Beecher City IL ... 39°11N 88°47W **71** D5
Beecher Falls VT .. 45°1N 71°31W **86** A3
Beechey Point AK . 70°29N 149°8W **61** A10
Beechgrove TN .... 35°38N 86°14W **96** E6
Beechwood MI .... 46°10N 88°6W **79** B2
Beef I.
　Br. Virgin Is. .. 18°26N 64°30W **105** G18
Beeler KS .... 38°26N 100°12W **74** C3
Beemer NE .... 41°56N 96°48W **84** C9
Beersheba Springs
　TN .... 35°28N 85°39W **97** E7
Beeville TX .... 28°24N 97°45W **99** J10
Beggs OK .... 35°56N 96°4W **93** C7
Bejou MN .... 47°26N 95°55W **80** C3
Bekabito NM ..... 36°50N 109°1W **98** A1
Bel Air CA .... 34°4N 118°27W **111** B2
Bel Air MD .... 39°32N 76°21W **77** A4
Bel Aire KS ...... 37°46N 97°16W **74** D6
Bel-Aire VA ...... 36°55N 76°13W **115** A2
Bel Alton MD ..... 38°28N 76°59W **77** B4
Bel-Nor MO ...... 38°42N 90°19W **117** A2
Bel-Ridge MO .... 38°42N 90°19W **117** A2
Belcamp MD ...... 39°28N 76°14W **77** A4
Belchertown MA .. 42°17N 72°24W **78** B2
Belcourt ND ...... 48°50N 99°45W **91** B6
Belden NE........ 42°25N 97°13W **84** B8
Belding MI .... 43°6N 85°14W **79** F6
Belen NM .... 34°40N 106°46W **88** C4
Belews L. NC ..... 36°15N 80°5W **90** B5
Belfair WA .... 47°27N 122°50W **101** C3
Belfast ME .... 44°26N 69°1W **76** D4
Belfast NY .... 42°21N 78°7W **89** C2
Belfast TN .... 35°25N 86°42W **96** E6
Belfield ND ...... 46°53N 103°12W **91** D2
Belfry MT .... 45°9N 109°1W **83** E8
Belgium WI ...... 43°30N 87°51W **103** E6
Belgrade ME ...... 44°27N 69°50W **76** D4
Belgrade MN ..... 45°27N 95°0W **80** E3
Belgrade MT ...... 45°47N 111°11W **83** E6
Belgrade NE ...... 41°28N 98°4W **84** C7
Belhaven NC ..... 35°33N 76°37W **90** C9
Belington WV .... 39°2N 79°56W **102** B5
Belknap IL .... 37°19N 88°56W **71** F5
Belknap County ☆
　NH .... 43°30N 71°30W **86** C3
Bell CA .... 33°58N 118°11W **111** C3
Bell FL .... 29°45N 82°52W **67** B6
Bell Buckle TN ... 35°35N 86°21W **96** E6
Bell City KY ..... 36°31N 88°30W **96** D4
Bell City MO ..... 37°1N 89°49W **82** D7
Bell County ☆ KY . 36°45N 83°40W **97** D9
Bell County ☆ TX . 31°3N 97°28W **99** F10
Bell Gardens CA .. 33°58N 118°9W **111** C4
Bell Ranch NM ... 35°32N 104°6W **88** B6
Bella Vista AR ... 36°28N 94°16W **63** B1
Bellaire MI .... 44°59N 85°13W **79** E6
Bellaire KY....... 40°42N 73°45W **114** B4
Bellaire OH ...... 40°1N 80°45W **92** C6
Bellaire TX .... 29°42N 95°27W **110** B2
Bellamy AL .... 32°27N 88°8W **60** D2
Belle MO .... 38°17N 91°43W **82** C5
Belle WV .... 38°14N 81°33W **102** C3
Belle → MI .... 42°43N 82°30W **79** G9
Belle-Chasse LA .. 29°51N 90°0W **63** D8
Belle Fourche SD . 44°40N 103°51W **91** F2
Belle Fourche →
　SD .... 44°26N 102°18W **91** F3
Belle Fourche Res.
　SD .... 44°43N 103°41W **91** F2
Belle Glade FL ... 26°41N 80°40W **67** E8
Belle Harbor NY .. 40°34N 73°51W **114** C3
Belle Haven VA .. 37°33N 75°49W **102** D9
Belle Isle FL ..... 28°27N 81°12W **115** B2
Belle Isle MI ..... 42°20N 82°58W **109** A3
Belle Plaine IA ... 41°54N 92°17W **73** D6
Belle Plaine KS ... 37°24N 97°17W **74** D6
Belle Plaine MN .. 44°37N 93°46W **80** F5
Belle Rive IL ..... 38°14N 88°45W **71** E5
Belle Valley OH .. 39°47N 81°33W **92** D5

Belle View VA .... 38°57N 77°14W **119** B2
Bellair FL .... 27°56N 82°48W **119** B1
Bellair Beach FL .. 27°55N 82°49W **119** B1
Bellair Bluffs FL .. 27°55N 82°49W **119** B2
Bellair Shore FL .. 27°54N 82°50W **119** B1
Bellefontaine OH .. 40°22N 83°46W **92** C3
Bellefontaine Neighbors
　MO .... 38°44N 90°13W **117** A2
Bellefonte DE ..... 39°47N 75°30W **77** A5
Bellefonte PA ..... 40°55N 77°47W **95** D5
Bellemont AZ ..... 35°14N 111°50W **62** B4
Belleplain NJ ..... 39°16N 74°48W **77** E2
Bellerive MO ..... 38°42N 90°18W **117** A2
Bellerose NY ..... 40°43N 73°42W **114** B4
Belleview FL ..... 29°4N 82°3W **67** B6
Belleville IL ...... 38°31N 89°59W **71** E4
Belleville KS ..... 39°50N 97°38W **74** B6
Belleville NJ ..... 40°47N 74°9W **114** B2
Belleville WI ..... 42°52N 89°32W **103** F4
Bellevue ID ...... 43°28N 114°16W **70** F4
Bellevue IA ...... 42°16N 90°26W **73** C8
Bellevue KY ...... 39°6N 84°28W **107** B3
Bellevue MI ...... 38°42N 76°11W **77** B4
Bellevue NE ...... 41°27N 85°1W **79** G6
Bellevue NE ...... 41°9N 95°54W **84** C10
Bellevue OH ...... 41°17N 82°51W **92** B4
Bellevue PA ...... 40°29N 80°3W **116** B1
Bellevue WA ..... 47°37N 122°12W **118** C5
Bellflower CA .... 33°52N 118°6W **111** C4
Bellflower IL ..... 40°20N 88°32W **71** C5
Bellflower MO .... 39°0N 91°21W **82** B5
Bellingham MA ... 42°5N 71°28W **78** B3
Bellingham MN ... 45°8N 96°17W **80** E2
Bellingham WA ... 48°46N 122°29W **101** B3
Bellmawr NJ ..... 39°52N 75°5W **116** B2
Bellmead TX ..... 31°35N 97°6W **99** F10
Bellows Falls VT .. 43°8N 72°27W **86** C2
Bellport NY ...... 40°46N 72°56W **87** B6
Bells TN .... 35°43N 89°5W **96** E3
Bellton DE .... 33°37N 96°25W **99** D11
Bellvue CO .... 40°38N 105°11W **77** B5
Bellville GA ...... 32°9N 81°59W **68** D5
Bellville TX ...... 29°57N 96°15W **99** H11
Bellvue CO .... 40°38N 105°10W **66** B5
Bellwood IL ...... 41°52N 87°53W **108** B1
Bellwood LA ...... 31°23N 93°12W **75** C2
Bellwood NE ...... 41°21N 97°14W **84** C8
Bellwood PA ...... 40°36N 78°20W **95** D4
Belmar NJ .... 40°11N 74°2W **87** B2
Belmond IA ...... 42°51N 93°37W **73** C5
Belmont CA ...... 37°31N 122°16W **118** A2
Belmont KS ...... 37°31N 98°28W **74** D5
Belmont MA ...... 42°23N 71°10W **106** A2
Belmont MA ...... 34°31N 88°13W **81** B5
Belmont MS ...... 34°31N 88°13W **81** B5
Belmont NH ...... 43°27N 71°29W **86** C3
Belmont NY ...... 39°23N 81°16W **102** B3
Belmont WI ...... 42°44N 90°20W **103** F3
Belmont County ☆ OH 40°1N 81°4W **92** C5
Belmont Cragin IL . 41°55N 87°45W **108** B2
Belmont Harbor IL 41°56N 87°38W **108** B3
Beloit KS .... 39°28N 98°6W **74** B5
Beloit WI .... 42°31N 89°2W **103** F4
Belpre KS .... 37°57N 99°6W **74** D4
Belpre OH .... 39°17N 81°34W **92** D4
Belt MT .... 47°23N 110°55W **83** C7
Belted Ra. NV .... 37°22N 116°8W **85** E4
Belton MO .... 38°49N 94°32W **82** C2
Belton SC .... 34°31N 82°30W **90** D3
Belton TX .... 31°3N 97°28W **99** F10
Belton L. TX ..... 31°6N 97°28W **99** F10
Beltrami MN ..... 47°33N 95°58W **80** C3
Beltrami County ☆
　MN .... 47°45N 94°50W **80** C4
Beltsville MD ..... 39°2N 76°54W **77** B3
Belvedere CA ..... 37°52N 122°27W **118** A2
Belvedere GA ..... 33°45N 84°16W **106** B3
Belvidere IL ...... 42°15N 88°50W **71** A5
Belvidere NJ ..... 40°50N 75°5W **87** B1
Belvidere NE ..... 40°15N 97°33W **84** D8
Belvidere SD ..... 43°50N 101°16W **91** G4
Belvidere Mt. VT . 44°46N 72°33W **86** B2
Belview MN ...... 44°36N 95°20W **80** F4
Belvue KS .... 39°13N 96°11W **74** B7
Belwood NC ...... 35°29N 81°31W **90** C4
Belzoni MS .... 33°11N 90°29W **81** C3
Bement IL .... 39°55N 88°34W **71** D5
Bemidji MN ...... 47°28N 94°53W **80** C4
Bemis WV .... 38°49N 79°45W **102** C5
Ben Avon Heights
　PA............ 40°30N 80°4W **116** A1
Ben Hill County ☆
　GA .... 31°45N 83°10W **68** E3
Ben Lomond CA .. 37°5N 122°5W **64** E4
Ben Lomond CA .. 37°5N 122°5W **64** E4
Ben Wheeler TX .. 32°26N 95°38W **99** E12
Bena MN .... 47°21N 94°12W **80** C4
Benavides TX ..... 27°36N 98°25W **98** K9
Benbrook TX ..... 30°45N 96°27W **99** G11
Benchley TX ..... 30°45N 96°27W **99** G11
Bend OR .... 44°4N 121°19W **94** C4
Benedict KS ...... 37°38N 95°45W **74** D8
Benedict MD ..... 38°31N 76°41W **77** B4
Benedict NE ...... 41°0N 97°36W **84** C8
Benevolence GA .. 31°53N 84°44W **68** E2
Benewah County ☆
　ID .... 47°5N 116°35W **70** B2
Benham KY .... 36°58N 82°57W **97** D10
Benjamin TX ..... 33°35N 99°48W **99** D8
Benkelman NE .... 40°3N 101°32W **84** D3
Benld IL .... 39°6N 89°48W **71** D4
Bennet NE .... 40°41N 96°30W **84** D9
Bennett CO .... 39°46N 104°26W **66** C6
Bennett IA .... 41°43N 90°59W **73** D8
Bennett County ☆
　SD .... 43°45N 101°45W **91** G4
Bennettsville SC .. 34°37N 79°41W **90** C6
Bennington ID .... 42°24N 111°19W **70** G7
Bennington KS ... 39°2N 97°36W **74** B6
Bennington NH ... 43°0N 71°55W **86** C3
Bennington VT ... 42°22N 96°9W **84** C9
Bennington OK ... 33°58N 96°2W **93** E7
Bennington VT ... 42°53N 73°12W **86** D1
Bennington County ☆
　VT............ 43°0N 73°10W **86** D1
Benoit MS .... 33°39N 91°8W **81** C2
Bens Run WV .... 39°28N 81°6W **102** B3
Bensley VA .... 37°27N 77°27W **102** D7
Benson AZ .... 31°58N 110°18W **62** F5
Benson IL .... 40°51N 89°7W **71** C4
Benson LA .... 31°52N 93°42W **75** C2
Benson MN .... 45°19N 95°36W **80** E3
Benson NC .... 35°23N 78°33W **90** C7
Benson VT .... 43°42N 73°18W **86** C1
Benson County ☆ ND 48°5N 99°20W **91** B6
Benton AR .... 34°34N 92°35W **63** C3
Benton CA .... 37°48N 118°32W **64** F8
Benton IL .... 38°0N 88°55W **71** E5
Benton IA .... 40°42N 94°22W **73** E4
Benton KY........ 36°52N 88°21W **96** D4
Benton LA .... 32°41N 93°44W **75** B2
Benton MS .... 32°50N 90°16W **81** D3
Benton MO .... 37°6N 89°34W **82** D7
Benton PA .... 41°12N 76°23W **95** C7
Benton TN .... 35°10N 84°39W **97** E8

Benton WI .... 42°34N 90°23W **103** F3
Benton City MO .. 39°8N 91°46W **82** B5
Benton City WA .. 46°16N 119°29W **101** D6
Benton County ☆ AR 36°22N 94°13W **63** B1
Benton County ☆ IN 40°35N 87°20W **72** C3
Benton County ☆ IA . 42°0N 92°0W **73** C6
Benton County ☆ MN 45°43N 93°50W **80** E5
Benton County ☆ MS 34°50N 89°11W **81** B4
Benton County ☆
　MO .... 38°20N 93°15W **82** C3
Benton County ☆
　OR .... 44°30N 123°20W **94** C2
Benton County ☆ TN . 36°4N 88°6W **96** D4
Benton County ☆
　WA .... 46°25N 119°25W **101** D6
Benton Harbor MI . 42°6N 86°27W **79** G5
Benton Heights MI 42°7N 86°24W **79** G5
Benton L. MT ..... 47°40N 111°20W **83** C6
Benton Lake Nat. Wildlife
　Refuge ○ MT .. 47°40N 111°20W **83** C6
Benton Ridge OH . 41°0N 83°48W **92** C3
Bentonia MS ..... 32°38N 90°22W **81** D3
Bentonite Spur WY 44°52N 104°9W **104** B8
Bentonville AR ... 36°22N 94°13W **63** B1
Bentonville OH ... 38°38N 78°19W **77** B2
Bent's Old Fort Nat. Historic Site ○
　CO .... 38°6N 103°5W **66** D7
Benwood WV ..... 40°1N 80°44W **102** A4
Benzie County ☆ MI 44°30N 86°0W **79** E5
Beowawe NV ..... 40°35N 116°29W **85** B4
Berclair TN ...... 35°8N 89°54W **112** D2
Berclair TX ...... 28°32N 97°36W **99** J10
Berea KY .... 37°34N 84°17W **97** C8
Berea OH .... 41°23N 102°59W **84** B3
Berea SC .... 34°50N 82°25W **90** D3
Beresford SD ..... 43°5N 96°47W **91** G9
Bergen NY .... 43°5N 77°57W **89** B3
Bergen County ☆ NJ 40°55N 73°59W **114** A3
Berger MO .... 38°41N 91°20W **82** C5
Bergland MI ...... 46°36N 89°34W **79** C2
Bergoo WV .... 38°29N 80°18W **102** C4
Bergstrom-Austin Int. ✈ (AUS)
　TX .... 30°12N 97°41W **99** G10
Bering Glacier AK . 60°20N 143°30W **61** F12
Bering Land Bridge Nat.
　Preserve ○ AK . 66°20N 165°0W **61** C6
Bering Strait Pac. Oc. 65°30N 169°0W **61** D5
Berino NM .... 32°4N 106°37W **88** E4
Berkeley CA ...... 37°51N 122°16W **118** A3
Berkeley MO ..... 38°45N 90°19W **117** A2
Berkeley County ☆ SC 33°15N 80°0W **90** E6
Berkeley County ☆
　WV .... 39°25N 78°0W **77** A2
Berkeley Hills CA . 37°52N 122°14W **118** A3
Berkeley Springs WV 39°38N 78°14W **77** A2
Berkley MI .... 42°30N 83°11W **109** A1
Berks County ☆ PA. 40°25N 76°0W **95** D6
Berkshire County ☆
　MA .... 42°25N 73°15W **78** B1
Berkshire Hills MA . 42°25N 73°10W **78** B1
Berlin CT .... 41°37N 72°45W **78** C2
Berlin GA .... 31°4N 83°37W **68** E3
Berlin MD .... 38°20N 75°13W **77** B5
Berlin NH .... 44°28N 71°11W **86** B3
Berlin NJ .... 39°48N 74°56W **87** C2
Berlin NY .... 42°42N 73°23W **78** B1
Berlin PA .... 39°55N 78°57W **95** E4
Berlin WI .... 43°58N 88°57W **103** E5
Berlin Heights OH . 41°20N 82°30W **92** B4
Berlin L. OH ..... 41°3N 81°0W **92** B5
Bern NM .... 35°24N 105°19W **88** B5
Bernal NM .... 35°24N 105°19W **88** B5
Bernal Heights CA 37°44N 122°24W **118** B2
Bernalillo NM .... 35°18N 106°33W **88** B4
Bernalillo County ☆
　NM .... 35°0N 106°45W **88** B4
Bernardo NM ..... 34°25N 106°50W **88** C4
Bernardston MA .. 42°40N 72°33W **78** B2
Bernardsville NJ .. 40°43N 74°34W **87** B2
Berne IN .... 40°39N 84°57W **72** C6
Bernice LA .... 32°49N 92°39W **75** B3
Bernice OK .... 36°34N 94°57W **93** B9
Bernie MO .... 36°40N 89°58W **82** E7
Berrien County ☆
　GA .... 31°15N 83°10W **68** E3
Berrien County ☆ MI 42°0N 86°25W **79** H5
Berrien Springs MI. 41°57N 86°20W **79** H5
Berry KY .... 38°31N 84°23W **97** B8
Berrydale FL ..... 30°53N 87°3W **67** A1
Berryessa, L. CA .. 38°31N 122°6W **64** E4
Berryville AR .... 36°22N 93°34W **63** B2
Berryville VA ..... 39°9N 77°59W **77** A3
Bertha MN .... 46°16N 95°4W **80** D4
Berthold ND ..... 48°19N 101°44W **91** B4
Berthoud CO ..... 40°19N 105°5W **66** C5
Berthoud Pass CO . 39°48N 105°47W **66** C5
Bertie County ☆ NC 36°0N 77°0W **90** B8
Bertram IA .... 41°57N 91°33W **73** D7
Bertram TX ...... 30°45N 98°3W **99** G9
Bertrand MO ..... 36°55N 89°27W **82** E7
Bertrand NE ..... 40°32N 99°38W **84** D6
Berwick LA ...... 29°42N 91°13W **75** E4
Berwick ME ...... 43°16N 70°52W **86** D3
Berwick ND ...... 48°22N 100°15W **91** B5
Berwick PA .... 41°3N 76°14W **95** C6
Berwyn IL .... 41°50N 87°47W **108** B2
Berwyn NE ...... 41°22N 99°30W **84** C6
Berwyn Heights MD 38°59N 76°55W **119** B4
Beryl UT .... 37°54N 113°40W **100** F2
Bessemer AL ..... 33°24N 86°58W **60** C4
Bessemer MI ..... 46°29N 90°3W **79** C1
Bessemer PA ..... 40°59N 80°30W **92** B6
Bessemer City NC . 35°17N 81°17W **90** C4
Bessie, L. FL ..... 28°29N 81°31W **115** B1
Bessie TX .... 31°13N 101°37W **98** F5
Bethalto IL .... 38°55N 90°2W **71** E3
Bethany MO ..... 39°39N 88°45W **71** D5
Bethany MO ..... 40°16N 94°2W **82** A2
Bethany OK ...... 35°31N 97°38W **93** C6
Bethany Beach DE . 38°32N 75°3W **77** B5
Bethel CT .... 41°22N 73°25W **78** C1
Bethel ME .... 44°25N 70°47W **86** B4
Bethel MN .... 45°24N 93°16W **80** E5
Bethel NC .... 35°48N 77°22W **90** C8
Bethel OH .... 38°58N 84°5W **92** E2
Bethel PA .... 34°22N 94°51W **93** D9
Bethel PA .... 40°28N 76°18W **95** D6
Bethel VT .... 43°50N 72°38W **86** C2
Bethel WA .... 47°29N 122°37W **118** D2
Bethel Acres OK .. 35°22N 97°3W **93** C6
Bethel Park PA ... 40°20N 80°2W **116** B1
Bethel Springs TN. 35°14N 88°36W **96** E4
Bethesda OH ..... 40°1N 81°4W **92** C5
Bethesda → OH ... 35°57N 78°50W **90** C7
Bethlehem CT .... 41°38N 73°13W **78** C1
Bethlehem GA .... 33°56N 83°44W **68** C3
Bethlehem NC .... 35°48N 75°57W **90** B5
Bethlehem PA .... 40°37N 75°23W **95** D7
Bethpage NY ..... 40°44N 73°30W **87** B3
Bethune CO ..... 39°18N 102°26W **66** C8
Betsie, Pt. MI .... 44°41N 86°15W **79** E5
Bettendorf IA .... 41°32N 90°30W **73** D8
Betterton MD .... 39°22N 76°4W **77** A4

Beulah CO .... 38°5N 104°59W **66** D6
Beulah MI .... 28°32N 81°34W **115** A1
Beulah MI .... 44°38N 86°6W **79** E5
Beulah ND ...... 47°16N 101°47W **91** C4
Beulah WY ...... 44°33N 104°5W **104** B8
Beulah, L. FL .... 28°32N 81°33W **115** A1
Beulah Res. OR .. 43°55N 118°9W **94** D7
Beulahville NC ... 34°55N 77°46W **90** D8
Beulaville VA .... 37°51N 77°11W **77** C3
Beverly IL .... 41°42N 87°39W **108** C3
Beverly KS ...... 39°1N 97°58W **74** B6
Beverly MA ...... 42°33N 70°53W **78** B4
Beverly WV ...... 38°51N 79°53W **102** C5
Beverly WA ...... 46°50N 119°56W **101** D6
Beverly Arts Center
　IL .... 41°41N 87°40W **108** C4
Beverly Glen CA . 34°6N 118°26W **111** B2
Beverly Hills CA . 34°5N 118°24W **111** B2
Beverly Hills FL .. 28°55N 82°28W **67** C6
Beverly Hills MO . 38°42N 90°19W **117** A2
Beverly Hills -Morgan Park
　Historic District
　IL .... 41°41N 87°40W **108** C2
Bevier MO .... 39°45N 92°34W **82** B4
Bexar AL .... 34°11N 88°9W **60** B2
Bexar County ☆ TX . 29°25N 98°30W **99** H9
Bibb County ☆ AL . 32°57N 87°8W **60** D3
Bibb County ☆ GA . 32°50N 83°45W **68** D3
Bicentennial Park CA 34°1N 118°1W **111** B4
Bicknell IN .... 38°47N 87°19W **72** E3
Bicknell UT ...... 38°20N 111°33W **100** E4
Biddeford ME .... 43°30N 70°28W **76** E3
Bieber CA .... 41°7N 121°8W **64** B5
Bienville LA ...... 32°22N 92°59W **75** B3
Bienville Nat. Forest
　MS .... 32°10N 89°25W **81** D4
Bienville Parish ☆ LA 32°20N 93°0W **75** B2
Big → MO .... 38°28N 90°37W **82** C6
Big Antelope Cr. →
　OR .... 42°28N 117°13W **94** E8
Big Baldy ID ..... 44°47N 115°13W **70** E3
Big Baldy Mountain
　MT .... 46°59N 110°39W **83** D7
Big Bar CA ...... 40°45N 123°15W **64** C3
Big Bay MI ...... 46°49N 87°44W **79** C4
Big Bay de Noc MI . 45°45N 86°40W **79** D5
Big Bear City CA . 34°16N 116°51W **65** J10
Big Bear Lake CA . 34°15N 116°56W **65** J10
Big Belt Mts. MT . 46°30N 111°25W **83** D6
Big Bend CA ..... 41°1N 121°55W **64** B5
Big Bend Dam SD . 44°1N 99°23W **91** F6
Big Bend Nat. Park ○
　TX .... 29°20N 103°5W **98** H4
Big Black → MS .. 32°3N 91°4W **81** D2
Big Blue → MS ... 35°35N 96°34W **74** B7
Big Boggy Nat. Wildlife Refuge ○
　TX .... 28°17N 95°52W **99** J12
Big Bow KS ...... 37°34N 101°34W **74** D2
Big Cabin OK .... 36°32N 95°14W **93** B8
Big Canyon → TX . 29°45N 101°8W **98** H6
Big Chino Wash →
　AZ .... 34°52N 112°28W **62** C3
Big Clifty KY ..... 37°33N 86°9W **96** C6
Big Coal → WV .. 38°16N 81°48W **102** C3
Big Cr. → LA .... 32°10N 91°53W **75** B4
Big Creek ID ..... 45°8N 115°20W **70** E3
Big Creek L. AL .. 30°43N 88°20W **60** F2
Big Creek Reservation ○
　OH .... 41°26N 81°45W **107** B1
Big Cypress Indian Reservation ○
　FL .... 26°18N 81°10W **67** E7
Big Cypress Nat. Preserve ○
　FL .... 26°0N 81°10W **67** F7
Big Cypress Swamp
　FL .... 26°15N 81°30W **67** F7
Big Darby Cr. →
　OH .... 39°37N 82°58W **92** D3
Big Delta AK ..... 64°10N 145°51W **61** D11
Big Eau Pleine Res.
　WI .... 44°44N 89°46W **103** D4
Big Falls MN ..... 48°12N 93°48W **80** B5
Big Falls WI ..... 44°37N 89°1W **103** D4
Big Flat AR ...... 36°1N 92°24W **63** B3
Big Fork → MN .. 48°31N 93°43W **80** B5
Big Hatchet Peak
　NM .... 31°38N 108°24W **88** F2
Big Hill NE ...... 42°33N 102°3W **84** B3
Big Hole → MT .. 45°34N 112°2W **83** E5
Big Hole Nat. Battlefield-Nez Perce
　Nat. Historic Park ○
　MT .... 45°39N 113°39W **83** E4
Big Horn WY .... 44°41N 106°59W **104** B6
Big Horn County ☆
　MT .... 45°25N 107°45W **83** E10
Big Horn County ☆
　WY .... 44°45N 108°0W **104** B4
Big Horn Mts. = Bighorn Mts.
　WY .... 44°25N 107°0W **104** B6
Big Island VA .... 37°32N 79°22W **102** D5
Big L. CA .... 41°7N 121°25W **64** B5
Big L. ME .... 45°17N 67°41W **76** C6
Big Lake AK ..... 61°20N 150°20W **61** F10
Big Lake MN ..... 45°20N 93°45W **80** E5
Big Lake TX ...... 31°12N 101°28W **98** F6
Big Lake Nat. Wildlife Refuge ○
　AR .... 35°54N 90°7W **63** B5
Big Lookout Mt.
　OR .... 44°36N 117°17W **94** C8
Big Lost → ID ... 43°36N 112°44W **70** F6
Big Muddy → IL . 37°33N 89°32W **71** F4
Big Muddy Cr. →
　MT .... 48°8N 104°36W **83** B13
Big Nemaha → NE . 40°1N 95°32W **84** D10
Big Oak Nat. Wildlife Refuge ○
　FL .... 30°8N 85°26W **72** E5
Big Otter → VA .. 37°29N 79°23W **102** D5
Big Pine CA ...... 37°10N 118°17W **65** G7
Big Pine Key FL .. 24°40N 81°21W **67** G7
Big Piney WY .... 42°32N 110°7W **104** D2
Big Rapids MI .... 43°42N 85°29W **79** F6
Big Rib → WI .... 44°49N 89°41W **103** D4
Big Rock TN ..... 36°35N 87°46W **96** D5
Big Sable Pt. MI .. 44°3N 86°1W **79** E5
Big Sage Res. CA . 41°35N 120°38W **64** B6
Big Sand Lake FL . 28°26N 81°29W **115** B2
Big Sandy MT .... 48°11N 110°7W **83** B7
Big Sandy TN .... 36°14N 88°5W **96** D4
Big Sandy TX .... 32°35N 95°7W **99** E13
Big Sandy WY ... 42°38N 109°28W **104** D3
Big Sandy → AZ . 34°19N 113°3W **62** C2
Big Sandy → TX . 38°25N 82°36W **97** B10
Big Sandy Cr. →
　WY .... 38°5N 109°38W **104** E3
Big Sandy Cr. = Sandy Cr. →
　CO .... 38°7N 102°29W **66** D8
Big Sandy Res.
　WY .... 42°15N 109°29W **104** D4
Big Satilla Cr. → GA 31°27N 82°3W **68** E4
Big Sheep Mt. MT 47°10N 105°40W **83** C12
Big Sioux → SD .. 42°29N 96°27W **91** H9
Big Sky MT ...... 45°17N 111°22W **83** E6
Big Smoky Valley
　NV............ 38°30N 117°10W **85** D3
Big Snowy Mts. MT 46°45N 109°30W **83** D8

Big South Fork Nat. River and
　Recr. Area ○ TN . 36°27N 84°47W **97** E8
Big Southern Butte
　ID .... 43°23N 113°1W **70** F5
Big Spring KY .... 37°48N 86°9W **96** C6
Big Spring TX .... 32°15N 101°28W **98** E6
Big Springs NE ... 41°4N 102°5W **84** C3
Big Stone City SD . 45°18N 96°28W **91** E9
Big Stone County ☆
　MN .... 45°25N 96°15W **80** E2
Big Stone Gap VA . 36°52N 82°47W **102** E2
Big Stone L. MN .. 45°18N 96°27W **80** E2
Big Stone Nat. Wildlife Refuge ○
　MN .... 45°25N 96°15W **80** E2
Big Sunflower → MS 32°40N 90°40W **81** D3
Big Sur CA ...... 36°15N 121°48W **64** F4
Big Swamp → NC . 34°28N 78°57W **90** D7
Big Thicket Nat. Preserve ○
　TX .... 30°12N 94°7W **99** G13
Big Timber MT ... 45°50N 109°57W **83** E8
Big Trails WY .... 43°46N 107°19W **104** C5
Big Water UT .... 37°5N 111°40W **100** F4
Big Wells TX ..... 28°35N 99°34W **99** J8
Big Wills Cr. → AL . 33°59N 86°0W **60** C5
Big Wood → ID .. 42°52N 114°54W **70** G4
Bigelow AR ...... 35°0N 92°38W **63** C3
Bigelow MN ...... 43°30N 95°42W **80** G3
Bigfork MN ...... 47°45N 93°39W **80** C5
Bigfork MT ...... 48°4N 114°4W **83** B3
Biggs CA .... 39°25N 121°43W **64** D5
Biggs OR .... 45°40N 120°50W **94** B5
Biggsville IL ..... 40°51N 90°52W **71** C3
Bighorn MT ..... 46°10N 107°27W **83** D10
Bighorn → MT ... 46°10N 107°28W **83** D10
Bighorn Basin WY . 44°0N 108°0W **104** B6
Bighorn Canyon Nat. Recr. Area ○
　MT .... 45°10N 108°0W **83** E9
Bighorn L. U.S.A. . 44°55N 108°15W **104** B4
Bighorn Mts. WY . 44°25N 107°0W **104** B6
Bighorn Nat. Forest ○
　WY .... 44°30N 107°30W **104** B5
Biglerville PA .... 39°56N 77°15W **95** E5
Bigpoint MS ..... 30°35N 88°29W **81** F5
Bijou Cr. → CO .. 40°17N 104°0W **66** B6
Bilk Creek Mts. NV 41°50N 118°27W **85** A4
Bill WY .... 43°15N 105°16W **104** C7
Bill Baggs Cape Florida State Recr.
　Area ○ FL ..... 25°40N 80°9W **112** D3
Bill Williams → AZ . 34°18N 114°4W **62** C1
Bill Williams Mt.
　AZ .... 35°12N 112°12W **62** B3
Bill Williams River Nat. Wildlife
　Refuge ○ AZ .. 34°20N 114°5W **62** C1
Billerica MA ..... 42°34N 71°16W **78** B3
Billings MO ...... 37°4N 93°33W **82** D3
Billings MT ...... 45°47N 108°30W **83** E9
Billings OK ...... 36°32N 97°27W **93** B6
Billings County ☆
　ND .... 47°0N 103°15W **91** C2
Billingsley AL .... 32°40N 86°43W **60** D4
Billsburg MO .... 39°21N 75°40W **77** B5
Billy Chinook, L.
　OR .... 44°36N 121°17W **94** C4
Billy Clapp L. WA 47°28N 119°20W **101** C6
Biloxi MS .... 30°24N 88°53W **81** F5
Biltmore Forest NC 35°34N 82°33W **90** C3
Binford ND ...... 47°34N 98°21W **91** C7
Bingen WA ...... 45°43N 121°28W **101** E4
Binger OK .... 35°18N 98°21W **93** C5
Bingham IL ...... 39°6N 89°14W **71** D5
Bingham ME ..... 45°3N 69°53W **76** C4
Bingham NE ..... 33°55N 106°21W **88** D4
Bingham NE ..... 42°1N 102°5W **84** B3
Bingham Canyon
　UT............ 40°32N 112°9W **100** C3
Bingham County ☆
　ID .... 43°15N 112°30W **70** F6
Binghamton NY .. 42°6N 75°55W **89** C4
Biola CA .... 36°48N 120°1W **65** G6
Birch Bay WA .... 48°55N 122°45W **101** B3
Birch L. MN ..... 47°45N 91°51W **80** C7
Birch L. MN ..... 47°43N 95°4W **80** C4
Birch Lake MN ... 46°18N 93°53W **80** D5
Birch Run MI .... 43°15N 83°48W **79** F8
Birch Tree MO ... 36°59N 91°30W **82** E5
Birchwood WI .... 45°40N 91°33W **103** C2
Birchwood Village
　MN .... 45°3N 92°58W **113** A4
Bird City KS ..... 39°45N 101°32W **74** B2
Bird Island MN .. 44°46N 94°54W **80** F4
Birds IL .... 38°50N 87°40W **71** E6
Birdsboro PA ..... 40°16N 75°48W **87** B1
Birdseye IN ...... 38°19N 86°42W **72** E4
Birdsville MD .... 38°54N 76°36W **77** B4
Birmingham AL .. 33°31N 86°48W **60** C4
Birmingham MI .. 42°33N 83°13W **109** A1
Birmingham MT .. 45°25N 107°45W **83** E10
Birmingham ✈ (BHM)
　AL .... 33°34N 86°45W **60** C4
Birnamwood WI .. 44°56N 89°13W **103** D4
Bisbee AZ .... 31°27N 109°55W **62** F6
Bisbee ND .... 48°37N 99°23W **91** B6
Biscay MN .... 44°46N 94°16W **80** F4
Biscayne, Key FL . 25°42N 80°10W **67** F8
Biscayne B. FL ... 25°40N 80°12W **67** F8
Biscayne Bay Aquatic Reserve
　FL .... 25°33N 80°13W **112** D1
Biscayne Nat. Park ○
　FL .... 25°25N 80°12W **67** F8
Biscayne Park FL . 25°52N 80°10W **112** C2
Biscoe AR .... 34°49N 91°25W **63** C4
Biscoe NC .... 35°22N 79°47W **90** C6
Bishop GA .... 33°49N 83°26W **68** C3
Bishop TX .... 27°35N 97°48W **98** K10
Bishop Creek Res.
　HI .... 42°15N 114°55W **85** A6
Bishop Museum
　HI .... 21°20N 157°52W **69** K14
Bishops Head MD . 38°16N 76°5W **77** B4
Bishopville FL .... 38°22N 75°12W **77** B5
Bishopville SC ... 34°13N 80°15W **90** D5
Bismarck AR ..... 34°19N 93°10W **63** D2
Bismarck IL ...... 40°16N 87°37W **71** C6
Bismarck MO ..... 37°46N 90°38W **82** D6
Bismarck ND ..... 46°48N 100°47W **91** C5
Bison KS .... 38°31N 99°12W **74** C4
Bison OK .... 36°12N 97°53W **93** B6
Bisteneau, L. LA .. 32°20N 93°25W **75** B2
Bitely MI .... 43°45N 85°43W **79** F6
Bithlo FL .... 28°33N 81°6W **67** C7
Bitter Cr. → WY . 41°31N 109°27W **104** E3
Bitter Creek WY .. 41°33N 108°33W **104** E4
Bitter L. SD ..... 45°17N 97°19W **91** E8
Bitterroot → MT .. 46°52N 114°7W **83** C3
Bitterroot Nat. Forest ○
　ID .... 45°52N 114°10W **70** D4
Bitterroot Range ID. 46°0N 114°20W **70** D4
Bitterroot Mts. MT 39°37N 79°14W **77** A1
Biwabik MN ..... 47°32N 92°21W **80** C6
Bixby MO .... 37°40N 91°7W **82** D5
Bixby OK .... 35°57N 95°53W **93** C7
Black → AK ..... 66°42N 144°42W **61** C11
Black → AR ..... 35°38N 91°20W **63** B4
Black → LA ..... 31°16N 91°50W **75** C4
Black → MI ..... 42°59N 82°27W **79** G9
Black → NY ..... 43°59N 76°4W **89** A4
Black → SC ..... 33°24N 79°15W **90** E6
Black → VT ..... 43°37N 72°23W **86** C2

Black → VT ...... 43°16N 72°27W **86** C2
Black → WI ..... 43°57N 91°22W **103** E3
Black Bear Cr. → OK
　............... 36°57N 96°38W **93** B7
Black Butte L. CA . 39°49N 122°21W **64** D4
Black Canyon City AZ 34°3N 112°9W **62** C3
Black Canyon of the Gunnison Nat.
　Park ○ CO .... 38°30N 107°35W **66** D3
Black Cr. → MS .. 30°39N 88°39W **81** F5
Black Cr. → NC .. 34°18N 79°7W **90** C6
Black Cr. → SC .. 35°38N 77°56W **90** C8
Black Creek WI .. 44°29N 88°27W **103** D5
Black Diamond → Pittsburg
　CA .... 38°2N 121°53W **64** E5
Black Diamond WA 47°19N 89°45W **103** E3
Black Earth WI .. 43°8N 89°45W **103** E4
Black Forest CO .. 39°0N 104°43W **66** C6
Black Hawk CO .. 39°48N 105°30W **66** C5
Black Hawk SD .. 44°9N 103°19W **91** F2
Black Hawk County ☆
　IA .... 42°25N 92°20W **73** C6
Black Hills SD ... 44°0N 103°45W **91** F2
Black Hills Nat. Forest ○
　SD .... 44°10N 103°50W **91** F2
Black Jack MO ... 38°47N 90°16W **117** A2
Black Kettle Nat. Grassland ○
　OK .... 35°35N 99°45W **93** C4
Black L. LA ...... 31°57N 93°3W **75** C2
Black L. NY ...... 44°31N 75°36W **89** A5
Black Mesa AZ ... 36°30N 110°15W **62** A5
Black Mesa OK .. 36°58N 102°58W **93** B1
Black Mountain NC 35°37N 82°19W **90** C3
Black Mt. KY .... 36°54N 82°54W **97** D10
Black Mt. NM ... 33°23N 108°14W **88** D2
Black Mt. NV .... 35°55N 115°2W **110** D2
Black Mt. OR ... 45°13N 119°17W **94** B6
Black Mt. TX. ... 29°38N 100°20W **98** H7
Black Pine Mts. ID. 42°8N 113°0W **70** G6
Black Pine Pt. ID. 42°8N 113°8W **70** G5
Black Range NM . 33°15N 107°50W **88** D3
Black River WY .. 44°1N 75°48W **89** A5
Black River Falls
　WI .... 44°18N 90°51W **103** D3
Black Rock AR ... 36°7N 91°6W **63** B4
Black Rock MT ... 44°29N 108°27W **104** B4
Black Rock Desert
　NV .... 41°10N 118°50W **85** A2
Black Rock Range
　NV .... 41°20N 119°8W **85** A1
Black Springs NV . 39°37N 119°51W **85** C1
Black Squirrel Cr. →
　CO .... 38°25N 104°15W **66** D6
Black Warrior → AL 32°32N 87°51W **60** D3
Blackbeard Island Nat. Wildlife
　Refuge ○ GA .. 31°30N 81°12W **68** E5
Blackbird DE ..... 39°21N 75°40W **77** A5
Blackburn MO ... 39°6N 93°30W **82** B3
Blackburn OK ... 36°23N 96°38W **93** B7
Blackburn, Mt. AK 61°44N 143°26W **61** F12
Blackduck MN ... 47°44N 94°33W **80** C4
Blackfeet Indian Reservation ○
　MT .... 48°45N 113°0W **83** B5
Blackfoot ID ..... 43°11N 112°21W **70** F6
Blackfoot → ID .. 43°8N 112°30W **70** F6
Blackfoot Res. ID. 42°55N 111°39W **70** G7
Blackford KY .... 37°29N 87°23W **96** C3
Blackford County ☆
　IN .... 40°30N 85°20W **72** C5
Blackhall Mt. WY . 41°2N 106°41W **104** E6
Blackman NV .... 36°56N 86°38W **97** A2
Blacks Fork →
　WY .... 41°25N 109°37W **104** E3
Blacksburg SC ... 35°7N 81°31W **90** C4
Blacksburg VA ... 37°14N 80°25W **102** D4
Blackshear GA ... 31°18N 82°14W **68** E4
Blackshear, L. GA 31°51N 83°55W **68** E3
Blackstone MA ... 42°1N 71°30W **78** B3
Blackstone VA ... 37°5N 78°0W **102** D6
Blacktail Mts. MT. 44°59N 112°33W **83** F5
Blackville SC .... 33°22N 81°16W **90** D4
Blackwater → MD . 38°29N 76°4W **77** B4
Blackwater → MD . 38°21N 76°1W **77** B4
Blackwater MO .. 38°59N 92°59W **82** C3
Blackwater VA ... 36°38N 82°57W **97** D10
Blackwater → TX . 33°40N 100°47W **98** D7
Blackwater → VA . 36°24N 76°55W **90** B8
Blackwater Falls State Park ○
　WV .... 39°7N 79°30W **102** B5
Blackwater Nat. Wildlife Refuge ○
　MD .... 38°26N 76°5W **77** B4
Blackwell OK .... 36°48N 97°17W **93** B6
Blackwell TX .... 32°5N 100°19W **98** E7
Blackwells Corner
　CA .... 35°37N 119°47W **65** H7
Blackwood NJ ... 39°48N 75°4W **87** C1
Bladen NE .... 40°19N 98°36W **84** D7
Bladen County ☆ NC 34°36N 78°30W **90** D7
Bladenboro NC ... 34°33N 78°48W **90** D7
Bladensburg MD . 38°55N 76°55W **119** B4
Blain PA .... 40°20N 77°31W **95** D5
Blaine KY .... 38°2N 82°51W **97** B10
Blaine TN .... 36°9N 83°42W **97** D9
Blaine WA .... 48°59N 122°45W **101** B3
Blaine County ☆ ID. 43°30N 114°0W **70** F4
Blaine County ☆ MT 48°30N 108°40W **83** B9
Blaine County ☆ NE 42°0N 99°55W **84** C6
Blaine County ☆ OK 35°50N 98°25W **93** C5
Blair NE .... 41°33N 96°8W **84** C9
Blair OK .... 34°47N 99°20W **93** D4
Blair WI .... 44°18N 91°14W **103** D2
Blair County ☆ PA . 40°30N 114°0W **95** D4
Blair Village GA .. 33°40N 84°23W **106** C2
Blairs VA .... 36°41N 79°23W **102** E5
Blairsburg IA .... 42°29N 93°39W **73** C5
Blairsden CA ..... 39°47N 120°37W **64** D6
Blairstown IA .... 41°55N 92°5W **73** D6
Blairstown NJ ... 40°59N 74°57W **87** B2
Blairsville GA .... 34°53N 83°58W **68** B3
Blairsville PA .... 40°26N 79°16W **95** D3
Blake House MA .. 42°19N 71°4W **106** B3
Blake Island State Park ○
　WA .... 47°32N 122°39W **118** C3
Blake Pt. MI ..... 48°11N 88°25W **79** A3
Blakely GA .... 31°23N 84°56W **68** E2
Blakely PA .... 41°31N 75°37W **95** C7
Blakeman KS .... 39°49N 101°7W **74** B2
Blakeslee OH .... 41°32N 84°44W **92** B2
Blalock OR ...... 45°42N 120°22W **94** B5
Blalock CO ...... 37°27N 105°31W **66** E5
Blanca CO .... 37°27N 105°31W **66** E5
Blanca Peak CO .. 37°35N 105°29W **66** E5
Blanchard ID .... 48°1N 116°59W **70** A2
Blanchard IA .... 40°35N 95°13W **73** E3
Blanchard ND .... 47°21N 97°15W **91** C8
Blanchard OK .... 35°8N 97°39W **93** C6
Blanchardville WI 42°49N 89°52W **103** F4
Blanche, L. FL ... 28°22N 81°33W **115** B1
Blanchester OH .. 39°17N 83°59W **92** D3
Blanco NM ...... 36°43N 107°50W **88** A3
Blanco TX .... 30°6N 98°25W **99** G9
Blanco → CO .... 29°51N 97°55W **99** H10
Blanco, C. OR ... 42°51N 124°34W **94** E1

Blanco County ☆ *TX* 30°17N 98°25W **99 G9**
Bland *MO* 38°18N 91°38W **82 C5**
Bland *VA* 37°6N 81°7W **102 D3**
Bland County ☆ *VA*. 37°6N 81°7W **102 D3**
Blandford *MA* 42°11N 72°56W **78 B2**
Blandinsville *IL* 40°33N 90°52W **71 C3**
Blaney Park *MI* 46°9N 85°55W **79 C6**
Blanket *TX* 31°49N 98°47W **99 F9**
Blasdell *NY* 42°48N 78°50W **89 C2**
Blawnox *PA* 40°29N 79°51W **116 B2**
Bleckley County ☆
   GA 32°25N 83°15W **68 D3**
Bledsoe *TX* 33°38N 103°1W **98 D4**
Bledsoe County ☆
   TN 35°36N 85°11W **97 E7**
Blencoe *IA* 41°56N 96°5W **73 D2**
Blessing *TX* 28°52N 96°13W **99 J11**
Blewett Falls L. *NC* 35°3N 79°59W **90 C6**
Bliss *ID* 42°56N 114°57W **70 G4**
Blissfield *IL* 41°50N 83°52W **79 H8**
Blissfield *OH* 40°24N 81°58W **92 C5**
Blitchton *GA* 32°12N 81°26W **68 D5**
Block I. *RI* 41°11N 71°35W **78 C3**
Block Island Sd. *RI*. 41°5N 71°40W **78 C3**
Blocker *OK* 35°4N 95°34W **93 C8**
Blockton *IA* 40°37N 94°29W **73 E4**
Blodgett *MO* 37°0N 89°32W **82 D6**
Bloodsworth I. *MD* 38°10N 76°3W **77 B4**
Bloody Mt. *CA* 37°34N 118°54W **65 F8**
Bloom = Chicago Heights
   IL 41°30N 87°38W **71 B6**
Bloomer *WI* 45°6N 91°29W **103 C2**
Bloomfield *IN* 39°1N 86°57W **72 D4**
Bloomfield *IA* 40°45N 92°25W **73 E6**
Bloomfield *KY* 37°55N 85°19W **97 C7**
Bloomfield *MO* 36°53N 89°56W **82 E7**
Bloomfield *NJ* 40°48N 74°11W **114 B1**
Bloomfield *NM* 36°43N 107°59W **88 A3**
Bloomfield *NE* 42°36N 97°39W **84 B8**
Blooming Grove *TX* 32°6N 96°43W **99 E11**
Blooming Prairie *MN*. 43°52N 93°3W **80 G5**
Bloomingburg *OH*. 39°36N 83°24W **92 D3**
Bloomingdale *TN*. 36°34N 82°32W **97 D10**
Bloomington *ID* 42°11N 111°24W **70 G7**
Bloomington *IL* 40°28N 89°0W **71 C4**
Bloomington *IN* 39°10N 86°32W **72 D4**
Bloomington *MN* 44°50N 93°17W **80 F5**
Bloomington *TX* 28°39N 96°54W **99 J11**
Bloomington *WI* 42°53N 90°55W **103 E2**
Bloomsburg *PA* 41°0N 76°27W **95 D6**
Bloomsdale *MO* 38°1N 90°13W **82 C6**
Bloomville *OH* 41°3N 83°1W **92 B3**
Blossburg *PA* 41°41N 77°4W **95 C5**
Blossom *TX* 33°40N 95°23W **99 D12**
Blossom Point Proving Grounds
   MD 38°26N 77°5W **77 B3**
Blount County ☆ *AL* 33°57N 86°28W **60 C4**
Blount County ☆ *TN* 35°46N 83°58W **97 E9**
Blountstown *FL* 30°27N 85°3W **67 A3**
Blountsville *AL* 34°5N 86°35W **60 C4**
Blountville *TN* 36°32N 82°19W **97 D10**
Blowing Rock *NC* 36°8N 81°41W **90 B4**
Bloxom *VA* 37°50N 75°37W **77 C5**
Blue → *IN* 38°11N 86°19W **72 C4**
Blue Ash *OH* 39°13N 84°22W **107 A2**
Blue Cypress L. *FL* 27°44N 80°45W **67 D8**
Blue Diamond *NV* 36°3N 115°24W **85 F5**
Blue Earth *MN* 43°38N 94°6W **80 G4**
Blue Earth County ☆
   MN 44°5N 94°0W **80 F3**
Blue Eye *MO* 36°30N 93°24W **82 E3**
Blue Hill *ME* 44°25N 68°35W **76 D5**
Blue Hill *NE* 40°20N 98°27W **84 D7**
Blue Island *IL* 41°40N 87°40W **108 D2**
Blue Knob *PA* 40°18N 78°34W **95 D4**
Blue Knob State Park ○
   PA 40°16N 78°34W **95 D4**
Blue Lake *CA* 40°53N 123°59W **64 C3**
Blue Mesa Res. *CO* 38°28N 107°20W **66 B3**
Blue Mound *IL* 39°42N 89°7W **71 D4**
Blue Mound *KS* 38°5N 95°0W **74 C9**
Blue Mound *TX* 32°51N 97°20W **109 A2**
Blue Mountain *CO* 40°15N 108°52W **66 A2**
Blue Mountain *MS* 34°40N 89°2W **81 B4**
Blue Mountain L. *AR* 35°2N 93°53W **63 C2**
Blue Mountain Lake
   NY 43°51N 74°27W **89 B6**
Blue Mountain Pass
   OR 42°18N 117°49W **94 E8**
Blue Mt. *AR* 34°41N 94°3W **63 D1**
Blue Mt. *NH* 44°47N 71°28W **86 B3**
Blue Mt. *PA* 40°30N 76°30W **95 D6**
Blue Mts. *ME* 44°50N 70°35W **76 D3**
Blue Mts. *OR* 45°0N 118°20W **94 C7**
Blue Mts. *TX* 30°34N 99°27W **99 G8**
Blue Rapids *KS* 39°41N 96°39W **74 B8**
Blue Ridge *GA* 34°52N 84°20W **68 B2**
Blue Ridge *VA* 36°40N 80°50W **102 E4**
Blue Ridge L. *GA* 34°53N 84°17W **68 B2**
Blue Ridge Parkway
   VA 36°40N 80°39W **102 E4**
Blue River *OR* 44°9N 122°20W **94 C3**
Blue River *WI* 43°11N 90°34W **103 E3**
Blue Springs *MO* 39°1N 94°17W **82 B3**
Blue Springs *NE* 40°9N 96°40W **84 D9**
Bluefield *VA* 37°15N 81°17W **102 D3**
Bluefield *WV* 37°16N 81°13W **102 D3**
Bluejacket *OK* 36°48N 95°4W **93 B8**
Bluejoint L. *OR* 42°42N 119°38W **94 E6**
Bluestone → *WV* 37°37N 80°55W **102 D4**
Bluestone L. *WV* 37°38N 80°53W **102 D4**
Bluestone Nat. Scenic River ○
   WV 37°33N 81°0W **102 D3**
Bluewater *NM* 35°15N 107°59W **88 B3**
Bluff *UT* 37°17N 109°33W **100 F4**
Bluff City *AR* 33°43N 93°8W **63 E2**
Bluff City *KS* 37°5N 97°53W **74 D6**
Bluff City *TN* 36°28N 82°16W **97 D10**
Bluffdale *UT* 40°29N 111°56W **117 D2**
Bluffs *IL* 39°45N 90°32W **71 D3**
Bluffton *AR* 34°54N 93°36W **63 D2**
Bluffton *GA* 31°31N 84°52W **68 E2**
Bluffton *IN* 40°44N 85°11W **72 C5**
Bluffton *MN* 46°28N 95°14W **80 D3**
Bluffton *OH* 40°54N 83°54W **92 C3**
Bluffton *SC* 32°14N 80°52W **90 F5**
Bluford *IL* 38°20N 88°45W **71 E5**
Blunt *SD* 44°31N 99°59W **91 F6**
Blunt Pt. *CA* 37°51N 122°28W **118 A2**
Bly *OR* 42°24N 121°3W **94 E4**
Blyn *WA* 48°1N 123°0W **101 B2**
Blythe *CA* 33°37N 114°36W **65 L2**
Blythe *GA* 33°17N 82°12W **68 C4**
Blytheville *AR* 35°56N 89°55W **63 C6**
Boalsburg *PA* 40°47N 77°49W **95 D5**
Boardman *OH* 41°2N 80°40W **92 B6**
Boardman *OR* 45°51N 119°43W **94 B6**
Boardman Bombing Range
   OR 45°48N 119°45W **94 B6**
Boardwalk *NJ* 39°21N 74°25W **87 B3**
Boaz *AL* 34°12N 86°10W **60 C4**
Boaz *WI* 43°20N 90°32W **103 E3**
Bobtown *PA* 39°46N 79°59W **95 E3**
Boca Grande *FL* 26°45N 82°16W **67 E6**
Boca Raton *FL* 26°21N 80°5W **67 E8**
Bock *MN* 45°47N 93°33W **80 E5**
Bodcau, Bayou →
   LA 32°13N 93°30W **75 B2**
Bodcaw *AR* 33°33N 93°25W **63 E2**
Bode *IA* 42°52N 94°17W **73 C4**
Bodega Bay *CA* 38°20N 123°4W **64 E3**
Bodie *CA* 38°12N 119°1W **65 F7**
Bodie I. *NC* 35°54N 75°35W **90 C10**

Boeing Field = King County Int. ✈
   (BFI) *WA* 47°31N 122°18W **118 C4**
Boelus *NE* 41°5N 98°43W **84 C7**
Boerne *TX* 29°47N 98°44W **99 H9**
Bogalusa *LA* 30°47N 89°52W **75 D6**
Bogard *MO* 39°27N 93°32W **82 B3**
Bogata *TX* 33°28N 95°13W **99 D12**
Boger City *NC* 35°28N 81°13W **90 C4**
Boggy Creek Swamp
   FL 28°22N 81°19W **115 B2**
Bogota *MN* 40°52N 74°2W **114 A2**
Bogota *TN* 36°10N 89°26W **96 D3**
Bogue *KS* 39°22N 99°41W **74 B4**
Bogue Chitto *MS* 31°26N 90°27W **81 D3**
Bogue Chitto → *LA* 30°34N 89°50W **75 D6**
Bogue Homo → *MS* 31°6N 89°13W **81 C5**
Boiling Spring Lakes
   NC 34°2N 78°4W **90 D7**
Boiling Springs *NC*. 35°15N 81°40W **90 C4**
Bois Blanc I. *MI* 45°46N 84°27W **79 D7**
Bois D'Arc *MO* 37°18N 93°21W **82 D3**
Bois de Sioux → *ND* 46°16N 96°36W **91 D9**
Boise Forte (Deer Creek) Indian
   Reservation *MN*. 47°48N 93°23W **80 C5**
Boise Forte (Nett Lake) Indian
   Reservation *MN*. 48°5N 93°5W **80 B5**
Boise *ID* 43°37N 116°13W **70 F2**
Boise → *ID* 43°49N 117°1W **70 F1**
Boise → (BOI) *ID*. 43°34N 116°14W **70 F2**
Boise City *OK* 36°44N 102°31W **93 B1**
Boise County ☆ *ID*. 44°0N 115°45W **70 F3**
Boise Mts. *ID* 43°45N 115°30W **70 F3**
Boise Nat. Forest *ID* 44°5N 115°30W **70 F3**
Boistfort Pk. *WA*. 46°29N 123°12W **101 D2**
Bokchito *OK* 34°1N 96°9W **93 D7**
Bokoshe *OK* 35°11N 94°47W **93 C9**
Bolckow *MO* 40°7N 94°50W **82 A2**
Boldtville *TX* 29°28N 98°21W **117 C3**
Boles *AR* 34°47N 94°3W **63 D1**
Boley *OK* 35°29N 96°29W **93 C7**
Boligee *AL* 32°45N 88°2W **60 D2**
Bolingbroke *GA* 32°57N 83°48W **68 D3**
Bolingbrook *IL* 41°42N 88°4W **71 B5**
Bolinger *LA* 32°57N 93°41W **75 B2**
Bolivar *MO* 37°37N 93°25W **82 D3**
Bolivar *NY* 42°4N 78°10W **89 C2**
Bolivar *TN* 35°12N 89°0W **96 E4**
Bolivar *WV* 39°19N 77°43W **77 A3**
Bolivar, Mt. *OR* 42°51N 123°56W **94 E2**
Bolivar County ☆ *MS* 33°50N 90°43W **81 C3**
Bolivar Peninsula
   TX 29°27N 94°39W **99 H13**
Bolivia *NC* 34°4N 78°9W **90 D7**
Bolling *AL* 31°43N 86°42W **60 E4**
Bollinger County ☆
   MO 37°20N 90°0W **82 D6**
Bolton *GA* 33°48N 84°28W **106 B2**
Bolton *MS* 32°21N 90°28W **81 D3**
Bombay *NY* 44°56N 74°34W **89 A6**
Bombay Hook DE... 39°21N 75°30W **77 A5**
Bombay Hook Nat. Wildlife
   Refuge ○ *DE* 39°16N 75°27W **77 A5**
Bomoseen, L. *VT*. 43°39N 73°13W **86 C1**
Bon Air *VA* 37°31N 77°34W **102 D7**
Bon Homme County ☆
   SD 43°0N 97°50W **91 G8**
Bon Secour B. *AL*. 30°15N 87°58W **60 F3**
Bona, Mt. *AK* 61°23N 141°45W **61 F12**
Bonaire *GA* 32°33N 83°36W **68 D3**
Bonanza *CO* 38°18N 106°8W **66 B3**
Bonanza *OR* 42°12N 121°24W **94 E4**
Bonanza Pk. *WA*. 48°14N 120°52W **101 B5**
Bonaparte *IA* 40°42N 91°48W **73 E7**
Bonaparte, Mt. *WA*. 48°45N 119°8W **101 B6**
Bond *CO* 39°53N 106°42W **66 A4**
Bond *MS* 30°54N 89°10W **81 F4**
Bond County ☆ *IL*. 38°50N 89°25W **71 E4**
Bond Falls Flowage
   MI 46°30N 89°15W **79 C2**
Bondurant *IA* 41°42N 93°28W **73 D5**
Bondurant *WY* 43°12N 110°24W **104 C2**
Bondville *IL* 40°7N 88°22W **71 C5**
Bone Gap *IL* 38°27N 88°0W **71 E6**
Bonetraill *ND* 48°26N 103°51W **91 B2**
Bonham *TX* 33°35N 96°11W **99 D11**
Bonifay *FL* 30°47N 85°41W **67 A3**
Bonita *SD* 43°52N 94°40W **73 E4**
Bonita *CA* 32°39N 117°1W **117 C2**
Bonita *LA* 32°55N 91°40W **75 B4**
Bonita, Pt. *CA* 37°48N 122°31W **118 B1**
Bonita Springs *FL*. 26°21N 81°47W **67 E7**
Bonneauville *PA*. 39°48N 77°8W **77 A3**
Bonner County ☆
   ID 48°20N 116°30W **70 A2**
Bonner Springs *KS*. 39°4N 94°53W **74 B9**
Bonners Ferry *ID*. 48°42N 116°19W **70 A2**
Bonneville County ☆
   ID 43°20N 111°30W **70 F7**
Bonneville Dam
   U.S.A. 45°38N 121°56W **94 B4**
Bonneville Pk. *ID*. 42°55N 111°38W **70 G7**
Bonneville Salt Flats
   UT 40°45N 113°50W **100 C2**
Bonney Lake *WA*. 47°11N 122°11W **101 C3**
Bonnie *IL* 38°12N 88°54W **71 E5**
Bonnieville *KY* 37°23N 85°54W **97 C7**
Bonny Res. *CO* 39°37N 102°11W **66 C8**
Bonny Slope *OR* 45°32N 122°46W **116 A1**
Bono *AR* 35°55N 90°48W **63 C5**
Book Cliffs *CO* 39°20N 108°45W **66 C2**
Book Cliffs *UT* 39°20N 109°0W **100 D6**
Booker *TX* 36°27N 100°32W **98 B5**
Booker T. Washington Nat.
   Monument ○ *VA*. 37°7N 79°44W **102 D5**
Boone *WV* 38°0N 81°42W **102 D3**
Boone *CO* 38°15N 104°15W **66 C6**
Boone *IA* 42°4N 93°53W **73 C5**
Boone *NC* 36°13N 81°41W **90 B4**
Boone *NE* 41°38N 97°55W **84 C8**
Boone → *IA* 42°19N 93°56W **73 C5**
Boone County ☆ *AR*. 36°14N 93°7W **63 B2**
Boone County ☆ *IL*. 42°20N 89°0W **71 A4**
Boone County ☆ *IN*. 40°5N 86°30W **72 C4**
Boone County ☆ *IA*. 42°0N 94°0W **73 C4**
Boone County ☆ *KY*. 38°55N 84°45W **97 B8**
Boone County ☆ *MO*. 39°0N 92°20W **82 C4**
Boone County ☆ *NE*. 41°40N 98°0W **84 C8**
Boone County ☆ *WV*. 38°4N 81°41W **102 D3**
Boone L. *TN* 36°26N 82°26W **97 D10**
Boones Mill *VA* 37°7N 79°57W **102 D5**
Booneville *AR* 35°8N 93°55W **63 C2**
Booneville *KY* 37°29N 83°41W **97 C9**
Booneville *MS* 34°39N 88°34W **81 B5**
Boonsboro *MD* 39°30N 77°39W **77 A3**
Boonton *NJ* 40°54N 74°25W **87 A2**
Boonville *CA* 39°1N 123°22W **64 D3**
Boonville *IN* 38°3N 87°16W **72 E3**
Boonville *MO* 38°58N 92°44W **82 C4**
Boonville *NC* 36°14N 80°43W **90 B5**
Boonville *NY* 43°29N 75°20W **89 B5**
Boothbay Harbor
   ME 43°51N 69°38W **76 E4**
Boothville *LA* 29°20N 89°25W **75 E6**
Boquillas *TX* 29°11N 102°58W **98 H4**
Borah Peak *ID* 44°8N 113°47W **70 E5**
Bordeaux *TX* 36°12N 86°50W **96 H6**
Bordelonville *LA* 31°6N 91°55W **75 C4**
Border County ☆
   TX 32°46N 101°27W **98 E6**
Border Springs *AL* 34°9N 87°32W **60 B4**
Bordentown *NJ* 40°9N 74°43W **87 B2**

Border *WY* 42°11N 111°3W **104 D1**
Border Field State Park ○
   CA 32°32N 117°7W **117 C2**
Bordulac *ND* 47°23N 98°58W **91 C7**
Borger *TX* 35°39N 101°24W **98 B6**
Borgne, L. *LA* 30°1N 89°42W **75 D6**
Boron *CA* 35°0N 117°39W **65 H9**
Borrego Springs
   CA 33°15N 116°23W **65 K10**
Borup *MN* 47°11N 96°30W **80 C2**
Boscawen *NH* 43°19N 71°37W **86 C3**
Bosco *LA* 32°17N 92°5W **75 B3**
Boscobel *WI* 43°8N 90°42W **103 E3**
Bosler *WY* 41°35N 105°42W **104 D7**
Bosque *NM* 34°34N 106°47W **88 C4**
Bosque County ☆
   TX 31°56N 97°39W **99 F10**
Bosque Farms *NM* . 35°51N 106°42W **88 B4**
Bossier City *LA* 32°31N 93°44W **75 B2**
Bossier Parish ☆ *LA* 32°42N 93°44W **75 B2**
Boston *GA* 30°47N 83°47W **68 F3**
Boston *MA* 42°22N 71°3W **106 A3**
Boston *TX* 33°27N 94°25W **99 D13**
Boston Harbor *MA*. 42°20N 70°58W **106 A4**
Boston Harbor Islands
   MA 42°19N 70°57W **106 A4**
Boston Harbor Islands Nat. Park △
   MA 42°18N 70°57W **106 B4**
Boston Logan Int. ✈ (BOS)
   MA 42°22N 71°1W **106 A3**
Boston Mts. *AR* 35°42N 93°15W **63 C2**
Bostwick *FL* 29°46N 81°38W **67 B7**
Bostwick *GA* 33°44N 83°31W **68 C3**
Boswell *IN* 40°31N 87°23W **72 C3**
Boswell *OK* 34°2N 95°52W **93 D8**
Boswell *PA* 40°10N 79°2W **95 D3**
Bosworth *MO* 39°28N 93°20W **82 B3**
Botetourt County ☆
   VA 37°32N 79°41W **102 D5**
Bothell *WA* 47°45N 122°12W **118 B4**
Botkins *OH* 40°28N 84°11W **92 C2**
Bottineau *ND* 48°50N 100°27W **91 A5**
Bottineau County ☆
   ND 48°55N 101°0W **91 B5**
Boulder *CO* 40°1N 105°17W **66 B5**
Boulder *MT* 46°14N 112°7W **83 D5**
Boulder *UT* 37°55N 111°25W **100 F4**
Boulder City *NV* 35°42N 109°43W **104 D3**
Boulder City *NV* 35°58N 114°49W **85 F6**
Boulder County ☆
   CO 40°10N 105°15W **66 B5**
Boulder Creek *CA*. 37°7N 122°7W **64 F4**
Boulder Dam = Hoover Dam
   U.S.A. 36°1N 114°44W **62 A1**
Boulder L. *WY* 43°0N 109°40W **104 D3**
Boulder Mts. *ID* 43°53N 114°30W **70 F4**
Boulder Peak *CA* 41°35N 123°5W **64 B3**
Bound Brook *NJ*. 40°34N 74°32W **87 B2**
Boundary *AK* 64°5N 141°1W **61 D12**
Boundary County ☆
   ID 48°45N 116°25W **70 A2**
Boundary Peak *NV* 37°51N 118°21W **85 E2**
Boundary Waters Canoe Area
   Wilderness ○ *MN*. 47°57N 91°13W **80 C7**
Bourbeuse → *MO* 38°24N 90°53W **82 C6**
Bourbon *IN* 41°18N 86°7W **72 B4**
Bourbon *MO* 38°9N 91°15W **82 C5**
Bourbon County ☆
   KS 37°45N 94°45W **74 D9**
Bourbon County ☆
   KY 38°10N 84°15W **97 B8**
Bourbonnais *IL* 41°9N 87°52W **71 B6**
Bouse *AZ* 33°56N 114°0W **62 D1**
Bouse Wash → *AZ* 34°3N 114°20W **62 C1**
Bovey *MN* 47°17N 93°25W **80 C5**
Bovill *ID* 46°51N 116°20W **70 D2**
Bovina *TX* 34°31N 102°53W **98 C5**
Bow *WA* 48°34N 122°24W **101 B3**
Bow Center *NH* 43°10N 71°34W **86 C3**
Bow Cr. → *KS* 39°39N 99°8W **74 B4**
Bow Mar *CO* 39°37N 105°2W **109 C1**
Bowbells *ND* 48°48N 102°15W **91 A3**
Bowden *WV* 38°55N 79°43W **102 C5**
Bowdoin L. *MT*. 45°27N 99°9W **83 B8**
Bowdoin Nat. Wildlife Refuge ○
   MT 48°24N 107°39W **83 B10**
Bowdon *GA* 33°32N 85°15W **68 C1**
Bowdon *ND* 47°28N 99°43W **91 C6**
Bowdon Junction *GA* 33°40N 85°9W **68 C1**
Bowen *IL* 40°14N 91°4W **71 C2**
Bowens *MD* 38°30N 76°8W **77 B4**
Bower Hill *PA* 40°22N 80°5W **116 B1**
Bowers *DE* 39°4N 75°24W **77 A5**
Bowersville *GA* 34°22N 83°5W **68 B3**
Bowersville *OH* 39°35N 83°44W **92 D3**
Bowie *AZ* 32°16N 109°29W **62 E6**
Bowie *MD* 39°0N 76°47W **77 B4**
Bowie *TX* 33°34N 97°51W **99 D10**
Bowie County ☆
   TX 33°27N 94°25W **99 D13**
Bowie *AZ* 32°19N 109°29W **62 E6**
Bowlegs *OK* 35°9N 96°40W **93 C7**
Bowling Green *FL*. 27°38N 81°50W **67 D7**
Bowling Green *KY*. 36°59N 86°27W **96 D6**
Bowling Green *MO* . 39°21N 91°12W **82 B5**
Bowling Green *OH*. 41°23N 83°39W **92 B3**
Bowling Green *VA*. 38°3N 77°21W **77 B3**
Bowls *MN* 45°49N 94°24W **80 E4**
Bowman *GA* 34°12N 83°2W **68 B3**
Bowman *ND* 46°11N 103°24W **91 D2**
Bowman *SC* 33°21N 80°41W **90 E5**
Bowman County ☆
   ND 46°2N 103°30W **91 D2**
Bowman-Haley Lake
   ND 45°59N 103°14W **91 E2**
Bowmanstown *PA*. 40°48N 75°40W **87 B1**
Bowmont *ID* 43°27N 116°32W **70 F2**
Bowring *OK* 36°53N 96°7W **93 B7**
Bowstring L. *MN*. 47°33N 93°55W **80 C5**
Box Butte County ☆
   NE 42°15N 103°0W **84 B2**
Box Elder *SD* 44°7N 103°4W **91 F2**
Box Elder County ☆
   UT 41°30N 113°0W **100 B3**
Boxelder *SD* 44°11N 102°27W **91 F3**
Boxelder Cr. → *SD* 45°59N 103°0W **91 D2**
Boxford *MA* 42°40N 71°0W **78 B4**
Boxholm *IA* 42°10N 94°6W **73 C4**
Boy River *MN* 47°10N 94°7W **80 C4**
Boyce *LA* 31°23N 92°40W **75 C3**
Boyce *VA* 39°6N 78°4W **77 A2**
Boyceville *WI* 45°3N 92°2W **103 C1**
Boyd *FL* 30°11N 83°37W **68 F4**
Boyd *MN* 44°51N 95°54W **80 F3**
Boyd *TX* 33°5N 97°34W **99 D10**
Boyd County ☆ *KY*. 38°20N 82°40W **97 B10**
Boyd County ☆ *NE*. 42°50N 98°40W **84 B7**
Boydell *AR* 33°37N 91°15W **63 E5**
Boyden *IA* 43°12N 96°0W **73 B3**
Boyer → *IA* 41°27N 95°53W **73 D3**
Boyertown *PA* 40°20N 75°38W **87 B1**
Boyes *MT* 45°16N 105°2W **83 E12**
Boyes Hot Springs
   CA 38°19N 122°29W **118 A1**
Boykin *GA* 31°6N 84°41W **68 E2**
Boykins *VA* 36°35N 77°12W **102 E7**
Boyle *MS* 33°42N 90°44W **81 C3**
Boyle County ☆ *KY*. 37°39N 84°51W **97 C8**
Boyle Heights *CA*. 34°1N 118°12W **111 B3**

Boyne City *MI* 45°13N 85°1W **79 D6**
Boyne Falls *MI* 45°10N 84°55W **79 D7**
Boynton *OK* 35°39N 95°39W **93 C8**
Boynton Beach *FL*. 26°32N 80°4W **67 E8**
Boys Town *NE* 41°16N 96°8W **84 C9**
Boysen Res. *WY*. 43°25N 108°11W **104 C4**
Bozeman *MT* 45°41N 111°2W **83 E6**
Bozman *MD* 38°46N 76°16W **77 B4**
Bracey *VA* 36°36N 78°9W **102 E6**
Bracken *TX* 29°36N 98°19W **117 B3**
Bracken County ☆ *KY* 38°40N 84°5W **97 B8**
Brackettville *TX*. 29°19N 100°25W **98 H7**
Braddock *ND* 46°34N 100°6W **91 D5**
Braddock *PA* 40°24N 79°52W **116 B2**
Braddock Heights
   MD 39°25N 77°30W **77 A3**
Braddock Hills *PA* 40°25N 79°51W **116 B2**
Braddyville *IA* 40°35N 95°2W **73 E3**
Bradate *TN* 35°23N 89°34W **96 E3**
Bradenton *FL* 27°30N 82°34W **67 D6**
Bradford *AR* 35°25N 91°27W **63 C4**
Bradford *IL* 41°11N 89°39W **71 B4**
Bradford *NH* 43°17N 71°56W **86 C3**
Bradford *PA* 41°58N 78°38W **95 C4**
Bradford *RI* 41°24N 71°45W **78 C3**
Bradford *TN* 36°5N 88°49W **96 D4**
Bradford *VT* 43°59N 72°9W **86 C2**
Bradford County ☆
   FL 30°0N 82°10W **67 B6**
Bradford County ☆
   PA 41°50N 76°30W **95 C6**
Bradfordsville *KY*. 37°30N 85°9W **97 C7**
Bradford Mt. *CT*. 41°55N 73°18W **78 C1**
Bradshaw *IA* 42°48N 94°25W **73 C4**
Bradshaw *NE* 40°53N 97°45W **84 D8**
Bradshaw *WV* 37°21N 81°48W **102 D3**
Brady *MT* 48°2N 111°51W **83 B6**
Brady *NE* 41°1N 100°22W **84 C5**
Brady *TX* 31°9N 99°20W **99 F8**
Brady Cr. → *TX* 31°8N 98°59W **99 F9**
Bragg City *MO* 36°16N 89°55W **82 E7**
Braggs *OK* 35°40N 95°12W **93 C8**
Braggadocio *MO* 36°5N 89°50W **82 E7**
Bragg's Spur = West Memphis
   AR 35°8N 90°11W **112 B1**
Braidwood *IL* 41°16N 88°13W **71 B5**
Brainard *NE* 41°11N 97°0W **84 C8**
Brainerd *MN* 46°22N 94°12W **80 D4**
Braintree *MA* 42°13N 71°0W **78 B4**
Braithwaite *LA* 29°51N 89°59W **113 C3**
Braman *OK* 36°56N 97°20W **93 B6**
Bramwell *WV* 37°20N 81°19W **102 D3**
Branch *LA* 30°10N 92°32W **75 D3**
Branch County ☆ *MI*. 41°50N 85°5W **79 H6**
Branchland *WV* 38°13N 82°12W **102 C2**
Branchville *NJ* 41°9N 74°45W **87 A2**
Branchville *SC* 33°15N 80°49W **90 E5**
Brandeis University
   MA 42°21N 71°17W **106 A2**
Brandenburg *KY*. 38°0N 86°10W **96 C6**
Brandon *CO* 38°27N 102°26W **66 C8**
Brandon *FL* 27°56N 82°17W **67 D6**
Brandon *IA* 42°19N 92°0W **73 C7**
Brandon *MN* 45°58N 95°36W **80 E3**
Brandon *MS* 32°16N 89°59W **81 D4**
Brandon *NE* 40°48N 101°55W **84 D4**
Brandon *SD* 43°35N 96°35W **91 G9**
Brandon *VT* 43°48N 73°6W **86 C1**
Brandon *WI* 43°44N 88°47W **103 E4**
Brandonville *WV* 39°40N 79°37W **102 B5**
Brandsville *MO* 36°39N 91°42W **82 E5**
Brandt *SD* 44°40N 96°38W **91 F9**
Brandy Pk. *OR* 42°36N 123°53W **94 E2**
Brandywine *MD* 38°42N 76°51W **77 B4**
Brandywine *WV* 38°38N 79°15W **102 C5**
Branford *CT* 41°17N 72°49W **78 C2**
Branford *FL* 29°58N 82°56W **67 B6**
Branscomb *CA* 39°39N 123°38W **64 D3**
Branson *MO* 36°39N 93°13W **82 E3**
Brantford *ND* 47°36N 98°55W **91 C7**
Brantley *AL* 31°35N 86°16W **60 E4**
Brantley County ☆
   GA 31°10N 82°0W **68 E5**
Brantley L. *NM* 32°32N 104°22W **88 E6**
Brashear *MO* 40°9N 92°23W **82 A4**
Brasher Falls *NY* 44°49N 74°47W **89 A6**
Brasstown Bald *GA* 34°53N 83°49W **68 B3**
Brassua L. *ME* 45°40N 69°55W **76 C4**
Bratenahl *OH* 41°32N 81°37W **107 A2**
Bratt *FL* 30°58N 87°27W **60 F2**
Brattleboro *VT* 42°51N 72°34W **86 D2**
Braunig Lake *TX* 29°14N 98°22W **117 D3**
Brave *PA* 39°43N 80°15W **102 C5**
Bravo del Norte, Rio = Grande,
   Rio → *N. Amer.*. 25°58N 97°9W **98 M10**
Brawley *CA* 32°59N 115°31W **65 L12**
Brawley Peaks *NV*. 38°5N 118°36W **85 D2**
Brawley Wash →
   AZ 32°34N 111°26W **62 E4**
Braxton *MS* 32°1N 89°58W **81 D4**
Braxton County ☆
   WV 38°43N 80°39W **102 C4**
Bray *OK* 34°38N 97°49W **93 D6**
Braymer *MO* 39°35N 93°48W **82 B3**
Brayton *IA* 41°33N 94°56W **73 D4**
Brazeau *MO* 37°42N 89°39W **82 D6**
Brazoria *TX* 29°3N 95°34W **99 H12**
Brazoria County ☆
   TX 29°10N 95°26W **99 H12**
Brazoria Nat. Wildlife Refuge ○
   TX 29°3N 95°15W **99 H12**
Brazos → *TX* 28°53N 95°23W **99 J12**
Brazos County ☆
   TX 30°40N 96°22W **99 G11**
Breakers, The *RI* 41°28N 71°18W **78 C3**
Breakheart Reservation
   MA 42°28N 71°1W **106 A3**
Breaks Interstate Park ○
   U.S.A. 37°17N 82°18W **97 C10**
Breathitt County ☆
   KY 37°30N 83°20W **97 C9**
Breaux Bridge *LA*. 30°16N 91°54W **75 D4**
Breckenridge *CO* 39°29N 106°3W **66 C4**
Breckenridge *MI*. 43°24N 84°28W **79 G7**
Breckenridge *MN*. 46°16N 96°35W **80 D2**
Breckenridge *MO*. 39°46N 93°48W **82 B3**
Breckenridge *TX*. 32°45N 98°54W **99 E9**
Breckenridge Hills
   MO 38°42N 90°22W **117 A1**
Breckinridge *OK* 36°26N 97°44W **93 B6**
Breckinridge County ☆
   KY 37°45N 86°25W **96 C6**
Brecksville *OH* 41°18N 81°38W **107 C2**
Brecksville Reservation
   OH 41°18N 81°36W **107 C2**
Breda *IA* 42°11N 94°59W **73 C4**

Breeds Pond *MA* 42°28N 70°58W **106 A4**
Breese *IL* 38°37N 89°32W **71 E4**
Breezy Point *NY* 40°33N 73°56W **114 C3**
Bremen *IL* 33°59N 86°58W **60 C4**
Bremen *GA* 33°43N 85°9W **68 C1**
Bremen *IN* 41°27N 86°9W **72 B4**
Bremen *KY* 37°22N 87°13W **96 C5**
Bremen *OH* 39°42N 82°26W **92 D4**
Bremer County ☆ *IA* 42°50N 92°20W **73 C6**
Bremerton *WA* 47°34N 122°37W **118 C2**
Bremond *TX* 31°10N 96°41W **99 F11**
Brendon *TX* 30°10N 96°24W **99 G11**
Brent *AL* 32°56N 87°10W **60 D3**
Brentwood *MO* 38°37N 90°20W **117 B1**
Brentwood *NH* 42°58N 71°6W **86 D4**
Brentwood *PA* 40°47N 73°15W **87 B3**
Brentwood *TN* 36°2N 86°47W **96 D6**
Brentwood Park *PA* 40°21N 79°58W **116 B2**
Brewer *ME* 44°48N 68°46W **76 D5**
Brewerton *NY* 43°14N 76°9W **89 B4**
Brewster *KS* 39°22N 101°23W **74 B2**
Brewster *MA* 41°46N 70°5W **78 C4**
Brewster *MN* 43°42N 95°28W **80 G3**
Brewster *NY* 41°24N 73°36W **78 C1**
Brewster *NE* 41°56N 99°52W **84 C6**
Brewster *OH* 40°43N 81°36W **92 C5**
Brewster *WA* 48°6N 119°47W **101 B6**
Brewster County ☆
   TX 30°0N 103°0W **98 H4**
Brewster Is. *MA* 42°20N 70°55W **106 A4**
Brewton *AL* 31°7N 87°4W **60 E3**
Brewton *GA* 32°36N 82°48W **68 D4**
Brian Head *UT* 37°41N 112°50W **100 F3**
Briargrove *TX* 29°44N 95°29W **110 B2**
Briartown *OK* 35°18N 95°14W **93 C8**
Briceland *CA* 40°7N 123°54W **64 C2**
Bricely *MN* 43°54N 93°49W **80 G5**
Bricelyn *MN* 43°34N 93°49W **80 G5**
Brices Cross Roads Nat. Battlefield
   Site ○ *MS* 34°30N 88°44W **81 B5**
Briceville *TN* 36°11N 84°11W **97 D8**
Brickeys *AR* 34°52N 90°36W **63 D5**
Brickyard, The *IL* 41°55N 87°47W **108 B2**
Bridge *ID* 42°8N 113°20W **70 G5**
Bridge *OR* 43°1N 124°0W **94 D2**
Bridge City *TX* 30°1N 93°51W **99 G14**
Bridgeboro *LA* 31°24N 83°59W **68 E3**
Bridgehampton *NY*. 40°56N 72°19W **78 C2**
Bridgeport *CA* 38°15N 119°14W **64 F7**
Bridgeport *CT* 41°11N 73°12W **78 C1**
Bridgeport *IL* 38°50N 87°46W **71 E6**
Bridgeport *IL* 38°43N 87°46W **71 E6**
Bridgeport *NJ* 39°47N 75°21W **87 B2**
Bridgeport *NY* 43°9N 75°58W **89 B5**
Bridgeport *NE* 41°40N 103°6W **84 C2**
Bridgeport *OK* 35°33N 98°23W **93 C5**
Bridgeport *TX* 33°13N 97°45W **99 D10**
Bridgeport *WV* 39°17N 80°15W **102 B4**
Bridgeport *WY* 42°40N 109°40W **101 C6**
Bridgeport, L. *TX*. 33°13N 97°50W **99 D10**
Bridger *MT* 45°18N 108°55W **83 E9**
Bridger Peak *WY* 41°11N 107°2W **104 E5**
Bridger-Teton Nat. Forest
   WY 43°5N 110°5W **104 C2**
Bridgeton *IN* 39°26N 75°14W **87 C1**
Bridgeton *MO* 38°29N 75°14W **73 B1**
Bridgeview *IL* 41°45N 87°48W **108 C2**
Bridgeville *CA* 40°25N 123°50W **64 C3**
Bridgeville *DE* 38°45N 75°36W **77 B5**
Bridgeville *PA* 40°21N 80°6W **116 B1**
Bridgewater *CT* 41°32N 73°22W **78 C1**
Bridgewater *IA* 41°15N 94°40W **73 D4**
Bridgewater *MA* 41°59N 70°58W **78 C4**
Bridgewater *ME* 46°25N 67°51W **76 B6**
Bridgewater *SD* 43°33N 97°30W **91 G8**
Bridgewater *VT* 43°35N 72°38W **86 C2**
Bridgman *MI* 41°57N 86°33W **79 H5**
Bridgton *ME* 44°3N 70°42W **86 B4**
Bridport *VT* 43°59N 73°17W **86 C1**
Brier *WA* 47°47N 122°16W **118 B4**
Brier Cr. → *GA* 32°44N 81°26W **68 D5**
Brigantine *NJ* 39°24N 74°22W **87 C2**
Briggs *TX* 30°53N 97°57W **99 G10**
Briggsdale *CO* 40°38N 104°20W **66 B6**
Briggsville *AR* 34°56N 93°30W **63 D2**
Brigham City *UT* 41°31N 112°1W **100 B3**
Bright *IN* 39°13N 84°51W **72 D6**
Brighton *CO* 39°59N 104°49W **66 C6**
Brighton *IA* 41°10N 91°49W **73 D7**
Brighton *IL* 39°2N 90°8W **71 D3**
Brighton *MI* 42°32N 83°47W **79 G8**
Brighton *TN* 35°29N 89°43W **96 E3**
Brighton *UT* 40°36N 111°34W **117 C4**
Brighton Indian Reservation
   FL 27°0N 81°15W **67 D7**
Brighton Park *IL* 41°48N 87°41W **108 C2**
Brightwood *DC* 38°57N 77°1W **119 B3**
Brillant *AL* 34°1N 87°46W **60 B3**
Brillion *WI* 44°11N 88°4W **103 D5**
Brimfield *IL* 40°50N 89°53W **71 C4**
Brimfield *MA* 42°7N 72°12W **78 B2**
Brimley *MI* 46°24N 84°34W **79 C7**
Brimson *MN* 47°17N 91°52W **80 C7**
Brinkley *AR* 34°53N 91°12W **63 D4**
Brinnon *WA* 47°41N 122°54W **101 C2**
Brinsmade *ND* 48°11N 99°19W **91 B6**
Brinson *GA* 30°59N 84°44W **68 F2**
Brisbie *CA* 37°40N 122°25W **118 B2**
Briscoe *TX* 35°35N 100°17W **98 B5**
Briscoe County ☆
   TX 34°28N 101°13W **98 C7**
Bristol *CO* 38°7N 102°19W **66 C8**
Bristol *CT* 41°40N 72°57W **78 C2**
Bristol *FL* 30°26N 84°59W **67 A4**
Bristol *IN* 41°43N 85°49W **72 B5**
Bristol *MD* 38°47N 76°40W **77 B4**
Bristol *NH* 43°36N 71°44W **86 C3**
Bristol *RI* 41°40N 71°16W **78 C3**
Bristol *SD* 45°21N 97°45W **91 F8**
Bristol *TN* 36°36N 82°11W **97 D10**
Bristol *VA* 36°36N 82°11W **102 E2**
Bristol *VT* 44°8N 73°5W **86 B1**
Bristol B. *AK* 58°0N 160°0W **61 H8**
Bristol Bay ☆ *AK*. 58°45N 156°50W **61 G8**
Bristol County ☆ *RI*. 41°41N 71°20W **78 C3**
Bristol County ☆ *MA* 41°43N 71°3W **78 C3**
Bristol L. *CA* 34°28N 115°41W **65 J11**
Bristol Mts. *CA* 34°30N 115°50W **65 J11**
Bristow *IA* 42°51N 92°54W **73 C6**
Bristow *OK* 35°50N 96°23W **93 C7**
Bristow *VA* 38°43N 77°32W **77 B3**
British Virgin Is. ☒
   W. Indies. 18°30N 64°30W **105 G18**
Britt *IA* 43°6N 93°48W **73 B5**
Britton *SD* 45°48N 97°45W **91 E8**
Bristol Hill *FL* 30°59N 86°17W **60 F2**
Broad → *GA* 33°59N 82°39W **68 C4**

Broad → *SC* 34°1N 81°4W **90 D4**
Broad Ripple Park
   IN 39°52N 86°7W **72 D4**
Broad Sd. *MA* 42°23N 70°56W **106 A4**
Broadalbin *NY* 43°4N 74°12W **89 B6**
Broadbent *OR* 43°1N 124°9W **94 D1**
Broadhurst *GA* 31°32N 81°56W **68 E5**
Broadkill Beach *DE*. 38°47N 75°10W **77 B5**
Broadmoor *CA* 37°41N 122°29W **118 B2**
Broadus *MT* 45°27N 105°25W **83 E12**
Broadview *IL* 41°51N 87°52W **108 B1**
Broadview *NM* 34°49N 103°13W **88 C7**
Broadview Heights
   OH 41°18N 81°41W **107 B1**
Broadview Park *FL*. 26°5N 80°12W **112 B2**
Broadwater *NE* 41°36N 102°52W **84 C3**
Broadwater County ☆
   MT 46°25N 111°30W **83 D6**
Broadwell *IL* 38°37N 78°48W **102 C6**
Broadwell *IL* 40°4N 89°27W **71 C4**
Brock *NE* 40°29N 95°58W **84 D10**
Brocket *ND* 48°13N 98°21W **91 B7**
Brockport *NY* 43°13N 77°56W **89 B3**
Brockton *MA* 42°5N 71°1W **78 B3**
Brockton *MT* 48°9N 104°55W **83 B13**
Brockway *MT* 47°18N 105°45W **83 C12**
Brockway *PA* 41°15N 78°47W **95 C4**
Brocton *NY* 42°23N 79°26W **89 C1**
Brodhead *KY* 37°24N 84°25W **97 C8**
Brodhead *WI* 42°37N 89°22W **103 F4**
Brodheadsville *PA*. 40°55N 75°24W **87 B1**
Brodnax *VA* 36°43N 78°2W **102 E6**
Brogan *OR* 44°15N 117°31W **94 C8**
Brogden *NC* 35°18N 78°2W **90 C7**
Brokaw *WI* 45°2N 89°39W **103 C4**
Broken Arrow *OK*. 36°3N 95°48W **93 B8**
Broken Bow *NE* 41°24N 99°38W **84 C6**
Broken Bow *OK* 34°2N 94°44W **93 D9**
Broken Bow Lake *OK* 34°9N 94°40W **93 D9**
Bromide *OK* 34°22N 96°30W **93 D7**
Bromley *OH* 39°4N 84°33W **107 B1**
Bronaugh *MO* 37°41N 94°28W **82 D2**
Bronson *FL* 29°27N 82°39W **67 B6**
Bronson *KS* 37°54N 95°4W **74 D8**
Bronson *MI* 41°52N 85°12W **79 H6**
Bronson *TX* 31°21N 94°1W **99 F13**
Bronte *TX* 31°53N 100°18W **98 F7**
Bronwood *GA* 31°50N 84°22W **68 E2**
Bronx *NY* 40°51N 73°52W **114 B3**
Bronx County ☆ *NY* 40°50N 73°52W **114 B3**
Bronxville *NY* 40°56N 73°49W **114 A3**
Brook *IN* 40°52N 87°22W **72 C3**
Brook Park *OH* 41°23N 81°48W **107 B1**
Brookdale Park *MN*. 45°3N 93°19W **114 A2**
Brooke County ☆
   WV 40°16N 80°37W **102 A4**
Brookesmith *TX* 31°33N 99°7W **99 F8**
Brookfield *IL* 41°48N 87°50W **108 C1**
Brookfield *MA* 42°13N 72°6W **78 B2**
Brookfield *MO* 39°47N 93°4W **82 B3**
Brookfield *OH* 41°14N 80°35W **92 B6**
Brookfield *VT* 44°4N 72°38W **86 B2**
Brookfield *WI* 43°3N 88°9W **103 E5**
Brookford *NC* 35°41N 81°22W **90 C4**
Brookhaven *GA* 33°52N 84°19W **106 A2**
Brookhaven *MS* 31°35N 90°26W **81 E3**
Brookings *OR* 42°3N 124°17W **94 E1**
Brookings *SD* 44°19N 96°48W **91 F9**
Brookings County ☆
   SD 44°19N 96°48W **91 F9**
Brookland = West Columbia
   SC 33°59N 81°4W **90 D4**
Brookland *AR* 35°54N 90°35W **63 C5**
Brooklandville *MD* 39°25N 76°40W **107 A1**
Brooklawn *NJ* 39°52N 75°7W **116 B2**
Brooklet *GA* 32°23N 81°40W **68 D5**
Brooklet *NH* 42°44N 71°40W **86 B3**
Brooklet *OR* 42°19N 71°8W **106 B2**
Brooklyn *CT* 41°48N 71°57W **78 C3**
Brooklyn *IL* 38°39N 90°10W **117 B2**
Brooklyn *IA* 41°44N 92°27W **73 D6**
Brooklyn *MS* 31°3N 89°11W **81 E4**
Brooklyn *OH* 41°26N 81°44W **107 B1**
Brooklyn *WA* 46°47N 123°31W **101 D2**
Brooklyn Center *MN* 45°4N 93°19W **113 A2**
Brooklyn Heights
   NY 40°41N 73°59W **114 B3**
Brooklyn Heights
   OH 41°26N 81°41W **107 B1**
Brooklyn Park *MD*. 39°13N 76°37W **107 B2**
Brooklyn Park *MN*. 45°6N 93°23W **80 E5**
Brookmont *MD* 38°57N 77°7W **119 B2**
Brookneal *VA* 37°3N 78°57W **102 D6**
Brookport *IL* 37°8N 88°38W **71 F5**
Brooks *KY* 38°4N 85°43W **97 B7**
Brooks *MN* 47°49N 96°0W **80 C2**
Brooks Air Force Base
   TX 29°20N 98°25W **117 C3**
Brooks County ☆ *GA*. 30°50N 83°45W **68 F3**
Brooks County ☆ *TX*. 27°0N 98°5W **99 K9**
Brooks Range *AK*. 68°0N 152°0W **61 C9**
Brookshire *TX* 29°47N 95°57W **99 H12**
Brookside Park *IN*. 39°47N 86°6W **110 B2**
Brookside Village
   TX 29°35N 95°13W **110 C3**
Brookston *IN* 40°36N 86°52W **72 C4**
Brookston *MN* 46°52N 92°36W **80 D6**
Brooksville *FL* 28°33N 82°23W **67 C6**
Brooksville *KY* 38°41N 84°4W **97 B8**
Brooksville *MS* 33°14N 88°35W **81 C5**
Brookview *MD* 38°36N 75°47W **77 B5**
Brookville *IN* 39°25N 85°1W **72 D6**
Brookville *KS* 38°46N 97°52W **74 C6**
Brookville *NJ* 40°49N 74°18W **87 A2**
Brookville *OH* 39°50N 84°25W **92 D2**
Brookville L. *IN* 39°28N 85°0W **72 D6**
Brookwood *AL* 33°15N 87°18W **60 C3**
Broomall *PA* 39°58N 75°21W **116 B2**
Broome County ☆ *NY* 42°5N 75°45W **89 C5**
Broomes Island *MD*. 38°25N 76°33W **77 B4**
Broomfield *CO* 39°55N 105°5W **96 C5**
Brooten *MN* 45°30N 95°8W **80 E3**
Broseley *MO* 36°40N 90°15W **82 E6**
Browerville *MN* 46°5N 94°52W **80 D4**
Brown, Pt. *WA* 46°15N 124°10W **101 D1**
Brown City *MI* 43°12N 82°59W **79 F9**
Brown County ☆ *IL*. 39°55N 90°45W **71 D3**
Brown County ☆ *IN*. 39°10N 86°15W **72 D4**
Brown County ☆ *KS*. 39°45N 95°35W **74 B9**
Brown County ☆ *MN*. 44°15N 94°45W **80 F4**
Brown County ☆ *NE*. 42°30N 100°0W **84 B6**
Brown County ☆ *OH*. 38°55N 83°55W **92 E3**
Brown County ☆ *SD*. 45°37N 98°19W **91 E7**
Brown County ☆ *TX*. 31°50N 99°0W **99 F8**
Brown County ☆ *WI*. 44°30N 88°0W **103 D6**
Brown County State Park ○
   IN 39°7N 86°16W **72 D4**

Brown Deer WI .... 43°9N 87°57W 112 A2
Brown Deer Park WI 43°9N 87°57W 112 B2
Brownell KS ...... 38°38N 99°44W 74 C4
Brownfield TX .... 33°11N 102°17W 98 D5
Browning IL .... 40°8N 90°22W 71 C3
Browning MT ...... 48°34N 113°1W 83 B4
Brownlee NE ...... 42°17N 100°37W 84 C4
Brownlee Res. ID .. 44°50N 116°54W 70 E2
Browns IL .... 38°23N 87°59W 71 E6
Browns Mills NJ ... 39°58N 74°34W 87 C2
Browns Park Nat. Wildlife
  Refuge ○ CO .... 40°50N 108°55W 66 B2
Browns Valley MN .. 45°36N 96°50W 80 E2
Brownsburg IN ..... 39°51N 86°24W 72 D4
Brownsdale MN .... 43°45N 92°52W 80 G6
Brownstown IL .... 39°0N 88°57W 71 E5
Brownstown IN .... 38°53N 86°3W 72 E4
Brownsville KY .... 37°12N 86°16W 97 C6
Brownsville LA .... 32°29N 92°9W 75 B3
Brownsville MN .... 43°42N 91°17W 80 G7
Brownsville OR .... 44°24N 122°59W 94 C3
Brownsville PA .... 40°1N 79°53W 95 D3
Brownsville TN .... 35°36N 89°16W 96 E3
Brownsville TX .... 25°54N 97°30W 98 M10
Brownsville WA .... 47°39N 122°36W 118 C2
Brownton MN ..... 44°44N 94°21W 80 F4
Browntown WI ..... 42°35N 89°48W 103 F4
Brownville AL ..... 33°24N 87°52W 60 C3
Brownville NE ..... 45°18N 69°2W 76 C4
Brownville NY ..... 44°0N 75°59W 89 A4
Brownville Junction
  ME .... 45°21N 69°3W 76 C4
Brownwood MO .... 37°5N 89°57W 82 D7
Brownwood TX .... 31°43N 98°59W 99 F9
Brownwood, L. TX.. 31°50N 99°0W 99 F8
Broxton GA .... 31°38N 82°53W 68 E4
Broyhill Park VA .. 38°52N 77°12W 119 B2
Bruce FL .... 30°28N 85°58W 67 A3
Bruce MS .... 33°59N 89°21W 81 C4
Bruce SD .... 44°26N 96°54W 91 F9
Bruce WI .... 45°28N 91°16W 103 C2
Bruceton TN ...... 36°3N 88°15W 96 D4
Bruceton Mills WV. 39°40N 79°38W 102 B5
Bruceville IN ..... 38°46N 87°25W 72 E3
Bruceville MD .... 38°40N 75°59W 77 B5
Bruin PA .... 41°3N 79°43W 95 C3
Bruin Pt. UT ..... 39°39N 110°21W 100 D5
Brule NE .... 41°6N 101°53W 84 C4
Brule → WI ...... 45°57N 88°12W 103 C5
Brule County ☆ SD 43°45N 99°9W 91 G6
Brule L. MN ...... 46°58N 90°50W 80 B8
Brumley MO ...... 38°5N 92°29W 82 C4
Brundidge AL ..... 31°43N 85°49W 60 E5
Bruneau ID .... 42°53N 115°48W 70 G3
Bruneau → ID .... 42°56N 115°57W 70 G3
Bruning NE .... 40°20N 97°34W 84 D8
Bruno MN .... 46°17N 92°40W 80 D6
Bruno NE .... 41°17N 96°58W 84 C9
Brunson SC .... 32°56N 81°11W 90 F4
Brunsville IA ..... 42°49N 96°16W 73 C2
Brunswick GA ..... 31°10N 81°30W 68 E5
Brunswick ME ..... 43°55N 69°58W 76 E4
Brunswick MD ..... 39°19N 77°38W 77 A3
Brunswick MO ..... 39°26N 93°8W 82 B4
Brunswick NE ..... 42°20N 97°58W 84 B8
Brunswick OH ..... 41°14N 81°51W 92 B5
Brunswick County ☆
  NC .... 34°0N 78°20W 90 D7
Brunswick County ☆
  VA .... 36°46N 77°51W 102 E7
Brunswick Naval Air Station
  ME .... 43°53N 69°57W 76 E4
Brush CO .... 40°15N 103°37W 66 B7
Brush Creek TN ... 36°7N 86°2W 96 D6
Brush Hill MA .... 42°15N 71°22W 106 B1
Brushton NY ...... 44°50N 74°31W 89 A6
Brusly LA .... 30°23N 91°14W 75 D4
Brussels WI ...... 44°44N 87°37W 103 D6
Bryan OH .... 41°28N 84°33W 92 B2
Bryan TX .... 30°40N 96°22W 99 G11
Bryan, L. FL ..... 28°22N 81°29W 115 B2
Bryan County ☆ GA 32°0N 81°25W 68 D5
Bryan County ☆ OK. 34°0N 96°15W 93 E7
Bryans Road MD .. 38°38N 77°4W 77 B3
Bryant AR .... 34°36N 92°29W 63 D3
Bryant IN .... 40°32N 84°58W 72 C6
Bryant SD .... 44°35N 97°28W 91 F8
Bryant Cr. → MO.. 36°36N 92°17W 82 E4
Bryant Lake MN ... 44°52N 93°25W 113 B1
Bryant Lake Regional Park ○
  MN .... 44°52N 93°25W 113 B1
Bryantown MD ..... 38°36N 76°52W 77 B4
Bryce Canyon Nat. Park △
  UT .... 37°30N 112°10W 100 F3
Bryson TX .... 33°10N 98°23W 99 D9
Bryson City NC ... 35°26N 83°27W 90 C2
Buchanan GA ...... 33°48N 85°11W 68 C1
Buchanan MI ...... 41°50N 86°22W 79 F6
Buchanan ND ..... 47°4N 98°50W 91 C7
Buchanan VA ...... 37°32N 79°41W 102 D5
Buchanan, L. TX .. 30°45N 98°25W 99 G9
Buchanan County ☆
  IA .... 42°30N 91°50W 73 C7
Buchanan County ☆
  MO .... 39°40N 94°50W 82 B2
Buchanan County ☆
  VA .... 37°17N 82°6W 102 D2
Buchanan Dam TX . 30°45N 98°25W 99 G9
Buchon, Pt. CA ... 35°15N 120°54W 65 H6
Buck Cr. KY ...... 36°59N 84°29W 97 D8
Buck Grove IA .... 41°55N 95°23W 73 D3
Buckatunna MS ... 31°32N 88°32W 81 E5
Buckatunna Cr. →
  MS .... 31°30N 88°32W 81 E5
Buckeye AZ .... 33°22N 112°35W 62 D3
Buckeye IA .... 42°25N 93°23W 73 C5
Buckeystown MD .. 39°20N 77°26W 77 A3
Buckfield ME ..... 44°17N 70°22W 76 D3
Buckhannon WV ... 39°0N 80°8W 102 C4
Buckhead GA ...... 33°51N 84°24W 106 A2
Buckholts TX ..... 30°52N 97°7W 99 G10
Buckhorn KY ...... 37°21N 83°28W 97 C9
Buckhorn NM ..... 33°2N 108°42W 88 D2
Buckhorn L. KY ... 37°21N 83°28W 97 C9
Buckingham CO ... 40°37N 103°58W 66 B7
Buckingham PA ... 40°19N 75°4W 87 B1
Buckingham VA .... 37°33N 78°33W 102 D6
Buckingham County ☆
  VA .... 37°40N 78°40W 102 D6
Buckland AK ...... 65°59N 161°8W 61 D7
Buckland OH ...... 40°37N 84°16W 92 C2
Buckley IL .... 40°36N 88°2W 71 C5
Buckley MI .... 44°30N 85°41W 79 D6
Buckley WA .... 47°10N 122°2W 101 C4
Bucklin KS .... 37°33N 99°38W 74 D4
Bucklin MO ...... 39°47N 92°53W 82 B4
Buckman MN ...... 45°54N 94°6W 80 E4
Bucks County ☆ PA. 40°15N 75°10W 95 D7
Bucks L. CA ...... 39°54N 121°12W 64 D5
Buckskin Mts. AZ.. 34°10N 113°50W 62 D2
Bucksport ME ..... 44°34N 68°47W 76 D5
Bucoda WA .... 46°48N 122°52W 101 D3
Bucyrus KS .... 38°44N 94°44W 74 C9
Bucyrus ND ...... 46°4N 102°47W 91 D3
Bucyrus OH .... 40°48N 82°59W 92 C5
Buda IL .... 41°20N 89°41W 71 B4
Buda TX .... 30°5N 97°51W 99 G10
Budd Lake NJ ..... 40°52N 74°44W 87 B2
Budds Creek MD .. 38°23N 76°51W 77 B4
Bude MS .... 31°28N 90°51W 81 E3

Buechel KY .... 38°12N 85°39W 97 B7
Buena NJ .... 39°31N 74°56W 87 D2
Buena Park CA .... 33°52N 117°59W 111 C4
Buena Ventura Lakes
  FL .... 28°21N 81°21W 115 B2
Buena Vista AR ... 33°29N 92°57W 63 E3
Buena Vista CA ... 38°51N 106°8W 66 D4
Buena Vista GA ... 32°19N 84°31W 68 D2
Buena Vista TN ... 29°16N 98°27W 117 D3
Buena Vista VA ... 37°44N 79°21W 102 D5
Buena Vista County ☆
  IA .... 42°45N 95°10W 73 C3
Buena Vista Lake Bed
  CA .... 35°12N 119°18W 65 H7
Buenos Aires Nat. Wildlife
  Refuge ○ AZ ... 31°30N 111°30W 62 F4
Bueyeros NM ...... 35°59N 103°41W 88 B7
Buffalo IA .... 41°26N 90°43W 73 D8
Buffalo KS .... 37°42N 95°42W 74 D8
Buffalo MN .... 45°10N 93°53W 80 E5
Buffalo MO .... 37°39N 93°6W 82 D3
Buffalo ND .... 46°55N 97°33W 91 D8
Buffalo NY .... 42°53N 78°53W 89 C2
Buffalo OK .... 36°50N 99°38W 93 B4
Buffalo SC .... 34°43N 81°41W 90 D4
Buffalo SD .... 45°35N 103°33W 91 E2
Buffalo TX .... 31°28N 96°4W 99 F11
Buffalo WV .... 38°37N 81°59W 102 C3
Buffalo WY .... 44°21N 106°42W 104 B6
Buffalo → AR .... 36°10N 92°6W 63 B4
Buffalo → MN .... 47°6N 96°49W 80 C2
Buffalo → MS .... 31°4N 91°34W 81 E2
Buffalo → TN .... 36°0N 87°50W 96 E5
Buffalo Bill Res.
  WY .... 44°30N 109°11W 104 B3
Buffalo Center IA. 43°23N 93°57W 73 B5
Buffalo County ☆ SD. 44°0N 99°5W 91 G6
Buffalo County ☆
  WI .... 44°20N 91°50W 103 D2
Buffalo Creek CO. 39°23N 105°16W 66 C5
Buffalo Gap SD ... 43°30N 103°19W 91 G2
Buffalo Gap TX ... 32°17N 99°50W 99 E8
Buffalo Gap Nat. Grassland
  SD .... 43°30N 103°30W 91 G2
Buffalo Hump ID . 45°37N 115°42W 70 D3
Buffalo L. TX .... 34°52N 102°12W 98 C5
Buffalo L. WI .... 43°47N 89°25W 103 E4
Buffalo Nat. River ○
  AR .... 36°14N 92°36W 63 B3
Buffalo Niagara Int. ✕ (BUF)
  NY .... 42°56N 78°44W 89 C2
Buford GA .... 34°10N 84°0W 68 B3
Buford ND .... 48°0N 103°59W 91 C2
Buford WY .... 41°7N 105°18W 104 E7
Buhl ID .... 42°36N 114°46W 70 G4
Buhl MN .... 47°30N 92°45W 80 C6
Buhler KS .... 38°8N 97°46W 74 C6
Buies Creek NC ... 35°25N 78°44W 90 C7
Buldir I. AK ..... 52°21N 175°56E 61 K1
Bull Cr. → SD .... 45°40N 103°18W 91 E2
Bull L. WY .... 43°13N 109°3W 104 C3
Bull Mts. MT ..... 46°8N 109°0W 83 D9
Bull Shoals L. AR. 36°22N 92°35W 63 B3
Bullard GA .... 32°38N 83°30W 68 D3
Bullard TX .... 32°8N 95°19W 99 E12
Bullhead SD ...... 45°45N 101°5W 91 E4
Bullhead City AZ. 35°8N 114°32W 62 B1
Bullitt County ☆ KY. 38°0N 85°40W 97 C7
Bulloch County ☆
  GA .... 32°20N 81°45W 68 D5
Bullock County ☆ AL. 32°9N 85°43W 60 D5
Bulls B. SC ...... 32°59N 79°35W 90 F6
Bulls Gap TN ..... 36°15N 83°5W 97 D9
Bully Cr. → OR .. 43°58N 117°14W 94 D8
Bumpus Mills TN . 36°36N 87°50W 96 D5
Buna TX .... 30°26N 93°58W 99 G14
Buncombe MO .... 38°47N 92°48W 82 C4
Buncombe OK ..... 35°41N 94°46W 93 C9
Buncombe County ☆
  NC .... 35°30N 82°30W 90 C3
Bundick Cr. → LA. 30°36N 92°57W 75 D3
Bunker MO .... 37°27N 91°13W 82 D5
Bunker Hill IL ... 39°3N 89°57W 71 D4
Bunker Hill IN ... 40°40N 86°6W 72 C4
Bunker Hill KS ... 38°53N 98°42W 74 C4
Bunker Hill NV ... 39°15N 117°8W 85 C3
Bunker Hill OR ... 43°22N 124°12W 94 D1
Bunker Hill WV ... 39°20N 78°3W 77 A2
Bunker Hill Memorial
  MA .... 42°22N 71°4W 106 A3
Bunker Hill Village
  TX .... 29°46N 95°31W 110 B1
Bunkerville NV ... 36°46N 114°8W 85 F6
Bunkie LA .... 30°57N 92°11W 75 D3
Bunnell FL .... 29°28N 81°16W 67 B7
Buras LA .... 29°21N 89°32W 75 E6
Burbank CA .... 34°12N 118°18W 111 A3
Burbank IL .... 41°44N 87°46W 108 C2
Burbank OK .... 36°42N 96°44W 93 B7
Burbank WA .... 46°12N 119°1W 101 D6
Burbank ✕ (BUR)
  CA .... 34°12N 118°21W 65 J8
Burchard NE ...... 40°9N 96°21W 84 D9
Burden KS .... 37°19N 96°45W 74 D7
Burden, L. FL .... 28°27N 81°33W 115 B1
Burdett KS .... 38°12N 99°32W 74 C4
Burdett NY .... 42°25N 76°51W 89 C4
Burdick KS .... 38°34N 96°51W 74 C7
Burghardt County ☆ IL. 41°45N 87°56W 71 B4
Burgaw NC .... 34°33N 77°56W 90 D8
Burgdorf ID ...... 45°17N 115°55W 70 D3
Burgess VA .... 37°53N 76°21W 77 C4
Burgess Junction
  WY .... 44°46N 107°32W 104 B5
Burgin KY .... 37°45N 84°46W 97 C8
Burgoon OH .... 41°16N 83°15W 92 B3
Burien WA .... 47°28N 122°20W 118 D3
Burkburnett TX .. 34°6N 98°34W 99 C9
Burke SD .... 43°11N 99°18W 91 G6
Burke County ☆ GA. 33°0N 82°0W 68 C4
Burke County ☆ NC. 35°45N 81°40W 90 C4
Burke County ☆
  ND .... 48°55N 102°30W 91 B3
Burke-Lakefront ✕ (BKL)
  OH .... 41°31N 81°41W 107 A1
Burkesville KY ... 36°48N 85°22W 97 D7
Burkett TX .... 32°0N 99°8W 99 E8
Burkettsville OH. 40°21N 84°39W 92 C2
Burkeville TX .... 31°0N 93°40W 99 F14
Burkeville VA .... 37°11N 78°12W 102 D6
Burkittsville MD. 39°22N 77°38W 77 A3
Burleigh County ☆
  ND .... 47°0N 100°30W 91 C5
Burleson TX ...... 32°33N 97°19W 99 E10
Burleson County ☆
  TX .... 30°32N 96°42W 99 G11
Burley ID .... 42°32N 113°48W 70 G5
Burley WA .... 47°25N 122°37W 118 D2
Burlingame CA .... 37°35N 122°21W 64 F4
Burlingame KS .... 38°45N 95°50W 74 C8
Burlington CO .... 39°18N 102°16W 66 C8
Burlington IA .... 40°49N 91°14W 73 D7
Burlington KS .... 38°12N 95°45W 74 C8
Burlington KY .... 39°2N 84°43W 97 A8
Burlington MA .... 42°30N 71°13W 106 A2
Burlington NC .... 36°6N 79°26W 90 B6

Burlington ND .... 48°17N 101°26W 91 B4
Burlington NJ .... 40°4N 74°51W 87 B2
Burlington OH .... 36°54N 98°23W 93 B5
Burlington VT .... 44°29N 73°12W 86 B1
Burlington WA .... 48°28N 122°20W 101 B3
Burlington WI .... 42°41N 88°17W 103 F5
Burlington WY .... 44°27N 108°26W 104 B4
Burlington County ☆
  NJ .... 39°50N 74°45W 87 C2
Burlington Junction
  MO .... 40°27N 95°4W 82 A1
Burnet TX .... 30°45N 98°14W 99 G9
Burnet County ☆ TX 30°45N 98°15W 99 G9
Burnett County ☆
  WI .... 45°50N 92°20W 103 C1
Burnett Woods OH. 39°8N 84°31W 107 B1
Burnettsville IN.. 40°46N 86°36W 72 C4
Burney CA .... 40°53N 121°40W 64 C5
Burnham ME .... 44°42N 69°26W 76 D4
Burnham PA .... 40°38N 77°34W 95 D5
Burnham IL .... 41°49N 87°35W 108 C3
Burnham Park Harbor
  IL .... 41°48N 87°37W 108 C3
Burning Springs KY 37°15N 83°49W 97 C9
Burns CO .... 39°52N 106°53W 66 C4
Burns KS .... 38°5N 96°53W 74 C7
Burns OR .... 43°35N 119°3W 94 D6
Burns TN .... 36°3N 87°19W 96 D5
Burns WY .... 41°12N 104°21W 104 E8
Burns Flat OK .... 35°21N 99°10W 93 D5
Burns Junction OR. 42°47N 117°51W 94 E8
Burns Paiute Indian Reservation
  OR .... 43°35N 119°6W 94 D6
Burnside KY ...... 36°59N 84°36W 97 D8
Burnsville AL .... 32°28N 86°53W 60 D4
Burnsville MN .... 44°47N 93°17W 80 F5
Burnsville MS .... 34°51N 88°19W 81 B5
Burnsville NC .... 35°55N 82°18W 90 C3
Burnsville WV .... 38°52N 80°40W 102 C4
Burnsville L. WV . 38°50N 80°37W 102 C4
Burnt → OR ...... 44°22N 117°14W 94 C8
Burnt Corn AL .... 31°33N 87°0W 60 E3
Burnt Pk. AK ..... 66°54N 143°44W 61 C12
Burntfork WY ..... 41°2N 109°59W 104 E3
Burr NE .... 40°33N 96°19W 84 D9
Burr Oak KS ...... 39°52N 98°18W 74 B5
Burr Oak MI ...... 41°51N 85°19W 79 H6
Burr Oak OH ...... 39°33N 82°4W 92 D4
Burrel CA .... 36°29N 119°59W 65 G7
Burris WY .... 43°22N 109°16W 104 C3
Burro Pk. NM ..... 32°35N 108°26W 88 E2
Burrton KS .... 38°2N 97°41W 74 C6
Burt IA .... 43°12N 94°13W 73 B4
Burt County ☆ NE. 41°50N 96°15W 84 C9
Burt L. MI .... 45°28N 84°40W 79 D7
Burton MI .... 43°0N 83°40W 79 G8
Burton OH .... 41°28N 81°9W 92 B5
Burton SC .... 32°26N 80°43W 90 F5
Burton TX .... 30°11N 96°42W 99 G11
Burton WA .... 47°23N 122°27W 118 D3
Burton, L. GA .... 34°50N 83°33W 68 B3
Burtrum MN .... 45°52N 94°41W 80 E4
Burwell NE .... 41°47N 99°8W 84 C6
Bush LA .... 30°36N 89°54W 75 D6
Bush Kill → PA .. 41°5N 75°0W 87 A1
Bushkill PA ...... 41°6N 75°0W 87 A1
Bushnell FL ...... 28°40N 82°7W 67 C6
Bushnell IL ...... 40°33N 90°31W 71 C3
Bushnell NE ...... 41°14N 103°54W 84 C2
Bushong KS .... 38°39N 96°15W 74 C7
Bushton KS .... 38°31N 98°24W 74 C5
Bushwood MD ...... 38°18N 76°47W 77 B4
Bussey IA .... 41°12N 92°53W 73 D6
Bustamante TX .... 29°52N 98°53W 98 L8
Butler AL .... 32°5N 88°13W 60 D2
Butler GA .... 32°33N 84°14W 68 D2
Butler IN .... 41°26N 84°52W 72 B6
Butler KY .... 38°47N 84°22W 97 B8
Butler MO .... 38°16N 94°20W 82 C2
Butler NJ .... 41°0N 74°20W 87 B2
Butler OK .... 35°38N 99°11W 93 C4
Butler PA .... 40°52N 79°54W 95 C3
Butler WI .... 43°6N 88°4W 112 A1
Butler, L. FL .... 28°29N 81°33W 115 B1
Butler County ☆ AL 31°50N 86°38W 60 E4
Butler County ☆ IA 42°45N 92°48W 73 C6
Butler County ☆ KS 37°45N 96°45W 74 D6
Butler County ☆ KY 37°15N 86°45W 97 C6
Butler County ☆ MO 36°45N 90°25W 82 E6
Butler County ☆ NE 41°15N 97°0W 84 C8
Butler County ☆ OH 39°24N 84°34W 92 D2
Butler County ☆ PA 41°0N 80°0W 95 C3
Butner NC .... 36°8N 78°45W 90 B7
Butte MT .... 46°0N 112°32W 83 D5
Butte ND .... 47°50N 100°40W 91 C5
Butte NE .... 42°55N 98°51W 84 B7
Butte City CA .... 39°40N 121°45W 64 D5
Butte County ☆ CA 39°40N 121°45W 64 D5
Butte County ☆ ID 43°50N 113°0W 70 F5
Butte County ☆ SD 45°0N 103°30W 91 E2
Butte Falls OR ... 42°33N 122°34W 94 E3
Butte Mts. NV .... 39°50N 115°5W 85 C5
Butterfield MN ... 43°58N 94°48W 80 G4
Butternut WI ..... 46°0N 90°30W 103 B3
Butternut → WI .. 46°1N 90°30W 103 B3
Buttonwillow CA .. 35°24N 119°28W 65 H7
Butts Corner VA .. 38°46N 77°19W 119 C2
Butts County ☆ GA 33°20N 84°0W 68 C3
Buxton ND .... 47°36N 97°6W 91 C8
Buxton OR .... 45°43N 123°11W 94 B2
Buzzards B. MA ... 41°30N 70°45W 78 C4
Buzzards Bay MA . 41°45N 70°37W 78 C4
Byars OK .... 34°53N 97°3W 93 D6
Byers CO .... 39°43N 104°14W 66 C6
Byers KS .... 37°48N 98°52W 74 D5
Byers TX .... 34°4N 98°11W 99 C9
Byesville OH ..... 39°58N 81°32W 92 D5
Byfield MA .... 42°46N 70°57W 78 B4
Byhalia MS .... 34°52N 89°41W 81 B4
Bylas AZ .... 33°8N 110°7W 62 D5
Bynum MT .... 47°59N 112°19W 83 C5
Bynum TX .... 31°58N 96°59W 99 F10
Byrdstown TN ..... 36°34N 85°8W 97 D7
Byromville GA .... 32°12N 83°45W 68 D3
Byron CA .... 37°52N 121°38W 65 G6
Byron GA .... 32°39N 83°46W 68 D3
Byron IL .... 42°8N 89°15W 71 A4
Byron MN .... 44°2N 92°17W 80 F6
Byron ME .... 44°43N 70°38W 76 D3
Byron OK .... 36°54N 98°16W 93 B5
Byron WY .... 44°48N 108°30W 104 B4

C

C.B.S. Fox Studios
  CA .... 34°9N 118°24W 111 B2
C.J. Strike Res. ID. 42°59N 115°58W 70 G3
C.N.N. Center GA. 33°45N 84°23W 106 B2
C.W. McConaughy, L.
  NE .... 41°14N 101°40W 84 C4
Caballo NM .... 32°59N 107°18W 88 E3
Caballo Res. NM .. 32°54N 107°18W 88 E3
Cabarrus County ☆
  NC .... 35°20N 80°30W 90 C5
Cabazon CA .... 33°55N 116°47W 65 K10

Cabell County ☆ WV 38°26N 82°8W 102 C2
Cabery IL .... 41°0N 88°12W 71 C5
Cabeza Prieta Nat. Wildlife
  Refuge ○ AZ ... 32°15N 113°20W 62 E2
Cabin Branch
  MD .... 39°12N 76°34W 107 B2
Cabin John MD .... 38°58N 77°10W 119 B2
Cabin John Regional Park ○
  MD .... 39°1N 77°10W 119 A2
Cabo Rojo
  Puerto Rico .... 18°5N 67°9W 105 G15
Cabool MO .... 37°7N 92°6W 82 D4
Cabot AR .... 34°59N 92°1W 63 D3
Cabot VT .... 44°23N 72°18W 86 B2
Cabrillo, Pt. CA . 39°21N 123°50W 64 E1
Cabrillo Nat. Monument ○
  CA .... 32°40N 117°14W 117 B1
Cacapon → WV .... 39°37N 78°16W 77 A2
Cache OK .... 34°38N 98°38W 93 D5
Cache → AR ...... 34°43N 91°20W 63 D4
Cache → IL ...... 37°14N 89°10W 71 F4
Cache County ☆
  UT .... 41°40N 111°45W 100 B4
Cache la Poudre →
  CO .... 40°25N 104°36W 66 B6
Cache Peak ID .... 42°11N 113°40W 70 G5
Cachuma, L. CA ... 34°35N 119°59W 65 J7
Cactus TX .... 36°3N 101°59W 98 A6
Cactus Flat NV ... 37°45N 116°40W 85 E4
Cactus Ra. NV .... 37°40N 116°50W 85 E4
Caddo OK .... 34°7N 96°16W 93 D7
Caddo TX .... 32°43N 98°40W 99 E8
Caddo → OK ...... 35°10N 98°20W 93 C5
Caddo → AR ...... 34°10N 93°3W 63 D2
Caddo Cr. → OK .. 34°14N 96°59W 93 D7
Caddo Gap AR .... 34°24N 93°37W 63 D2
Caddo L. LA ...... 32°43N 93°55W 75 B2
Caddo Mills TX ... 33°4N 96°14W 99 D11
Caddo Nat. Grassland
  TX .... 33°44N 95°57W 99 D12
Caddo Parish ☆ LA 32°45N 93°58W 75 B2
Caddoa CO .... 38°4N 102°56W 66 D8
Cadillac MI ...... 44°15N 85°24W 79 E6
Cadiz IN .... 39°57N 85°29W 72 D5
Cadiz KY .... 36°52N 87°50W 96 D5
Cadiz OH .... 40°22N 81°0W 92 C6
Cadiz L. CA ...... 34°18N 115°24W 65 J11
Cadley GA .... 33°32N 82°40W 68 C4
Cadott WI .... 44°57N 91°9W 103 D2
Cadwell GA .... 32°20N 83°3W 68 D3
Caernarvon LA .... 29°51N 89°54W 113 C3
Cagles Mill L. IN. 39°36N 86°55W 72 D4
Caguas Puerto Rico 18°14N 66°2W 105 G16
Cahaba → AL ..... 32°20N 87°56W 60 D3
Cahokia IL .... 38°34N 90°11W 117 B2
Cahone CO .... 37°39N 108°49W 66 E2
Cahuenga Park CA. 34°8N 118°19W 111 B3
Cahuilla Indian Reservation
  CA .... 33°31N 116°43W 65 K10
Caillou B. LA .... 29°3N 91°0W 75 E5
Cain, L. FL ...... 28°28N 81°28W 115 B2
Caineville UT .... 38°20N 111°1W 100 E4
Cainsville MO .... 40°26N 93°47W 82 A3
Cairo GA .... 30°52N 84°13W 68 F2
Cairo IL .... 37°0N 89°11W 71 F4
Cairo NE .... 41°0N 98°36W 84 C7
Cairo KY .... 37°24N 87°39W 96 C5
Cairo NY .... 42°18N 74°0W 89 C6
Cairo OH .... 40°50N 84°5W 92 C2
Cairo WV .... 39°13N 81°9W 102 B3
Caja de Muertos, I.
  Puerto Rico .... 17°54N 66°32W 105 H16
Cajon Summit CA . 34°21N 117°27W 65 J9
Calabash NC ...... 33°53N 78°34W 90 D7
Caladesi Island State Park
  FL .... 28°1N 82°49W 119 A2
Calais ME .... 45°11N 67°17W 76 D6
Calamus → NE .... 41°48N 99°9W 84 C6
Calamus Res. NE . 41°50N 99°9W 84 C6
Calapooia → OR .. 44°38N 123°8W 94 C2
Calaveras County ☆
  CA .... 38°15N 120°40W 64 E6
Calaveras Lake TX 29°16N 98°18W 117 C4
Calcasieu → LA .. 30°5N 93°18W 75 D2
Calcasieu L. LA .. 29°55N 93°18W 75 E2
Calcasieu Parish ☆
  LA .... 30°14N 93°23W 75 D2
Calcium NY .... 44°1N 75°51W 89 A5
Caldwell AR ...... 35°5N 90°49W 63 C5
Caldwell ID ...... 43°40N 116°41W 70 F2
Caldwell KS ...... 37°2N 97°37W 74 D6
Caldwell NJ ...... 40°50N 74°16W 114 A1
Caldwell OH ...... 39°45N 81°31W 92 D5
Caldwell TX ...... 30°32N 96°42W 99 G11
Caldwell County ☆
  KY .... 37°10N 87°50W 96 C5
Caldwell County ☆
  MO .... 39°40N 94°0W 82 B3
Caldwell County ☆
  NC .... 36°0N 81°30W 90 C4
Caldwell County ☆
  TX .... 29°53N 97°40W 99 H10
Caldwell Parish ☆ LA 32°0N 92°0W 75 B3
Caledonia MN ..... 43°38N 91°30W 80 G7
Caledonia MS ..... 33°41N 88°20W 81 C5
Caledonia ND ..... 47°28N 96°53W 91 C9
Caledonia NY ..... 42°58N 77°51W 89 C3
Caledonia County ☆
  VT .... 44°30N 72°10W 86 B2
Calera AL .... 33°6N 86°45W 60 C4
Calera OK .... 33°52N 96°29W 93 E7
Calexico CA ...... 32°40N 115°30W 65 L11
Calfkiller → TN . 35°49N 85°29W 97 E7
Calhoun CO .... 39°2N 104°18W 66 C6
Calhoun GA .... 34°30N 84°57W 68 B2
Calhoun IL .... 38°39N 88°3W 71 E5
Calhoun KY .... 37°32N 87°16W 96 C5
Calhoun LA .... 32°30N 92°20W 75 B3
Calhoun MO .... 38°28N 93°38W 82 C3
Calhoun TN .... 35°18N 84°45W 97 E8
Calhoun, L. MN .. 44°56N 93°18W 113 B2
Calhoun City MS . 33°51N 89°19W 81 C4
Calhoun County ☆ AL 33°47N 86°0W 60 C4
Calhoun County ☆
  FL .... 30°30N 85°15W 67 A3
Calhoun County ☆
  GA .... 31°30N 84°40W 68 E2
Calhoun County ☆
  IA .... 42°25N 94°40W 73 C4
Calhoun County ☆ MI 42°15N 85°0W 79 G7
Calhoun County ☆
  MS .... 33°56N 89°20W 81 C4
Calhoun County ☆
  SC .... 33°45N 80°50W 90 E5
Calhoun County ☆
  TX .... 28°37N 96°38W 99 J11
Calhoun County ☆
  WV .... 38°55N 81°6W 102 C3
Calhoun Falls SC. 34°6N 82°36W 90 D3
Calico Rock AR ... 36°7N 92°9W 63 B3
Caliente CA ...... 35°17N 118°38W 65 H8
Caliente NV ...... 37°37N 114°31W 85 E6
Califon NJ .... 40°43N 74°50W 87 B2
California MD ..... 38°18N 76°32W 77 B4

California MO ..... 38°38N 92°34W 82 C4
California PA ..... 40°4N 79°54W 95 D3
California □ U.S.A. 37°30N 119°30W 64 F7
California Aqueduct
  CA .... 35°52N 117°12W 65 K9
California City CA. 35°10N 117°55W 65 H9
California Coastal Nat.
  Monument ○ CA . 36°19N 121°46W 65 G5
California Inst. of Tech.
  CA .... 34°8N 118°8W 111 B4
California Los Angeles, University
  of CA .... 34°4N 118°27W 111 B2
California State University
  CA .... 34°4N 118°10W 111 B2
California State University
  CA .... 33°52N 117°12W 65 K9
Calmar IA .... 43°11N 91°52W 73 B7
Caloosahatchee → FL 26°31N 82°1W 67 E6
Calpella CA ...... 39°14N 123°12W 64 D3
Calpine CA .... 39°40N 120°27W 64 D6
Calumet IA .... 42°57N 95°33W 73 C3
Calumet MI .... 47°14N 88°27W 79 B5
Calumet MN .... 47°19N 93°17W 80 C5
Calumet City IL .. 41°37N 87°32W 71 B6
Calumet County ☆
  WI .... 44°5N 88°10W 103 E5
Calumet L. IL .... 41°41N 87°35W 108 C3
Calumet Park IL .. 41°40N 87°39W 108 C3
Calumet Sag Channel →
  IL .... 41°40N 87°47W 108 C2
Calvert AL .... 31°9N 88°1W 60 E2
Calvert MD .... 39°42N 75°58W 77 A5
Calvert TX .... 30°59N 96°40W 99 G11
Calvert City KY .. 37°2N 88°21W 96 C4
Calvert County ☆
  MD .... 38°30N 76°35W 77 B4
Calverton MD ..... 35°11N 95°39W 93 C8
Calverton Park MO 38°45N 90°18W 117 A2
Calvin LA .... 31°58N 92°47W 75 C3
Calvin ND .... 48°51N 98°56W 91 B7
Calvin OK .... 34°58N 96°15W 93 D7
Calwa CA .... 36°42N 119°46W 65 G7
Camanche IA ...... 41°47N 90°15W 73 D8
Camanche Res. IA. 41°47N 90°15W 73 D8
Camano I. WA ..... 48°10N 122°30W 101 B3
Camargo IL .... 39°48N 88°10W 71 D5
Camargo KY .... 38°0N 83°53W 97 C9
Camarillo CA ..... 34°13N 119°2W 65 J7
Camas WA .... 45°35N 122°24W 101 E3
Camas County ☆ ID 43°30N 114°50W 70 F4
Camas Nat. Wildlife Refuge ○
  ID .... 43°55N 112°15W 70 F6
Camas Valley OR . 43°2N 123°40W 94 D2
Cambria CA .... 35°34N 121°5W 65 H5
Cambria WI .... 43°33N 89°7W 103 E4
Cambria County ☆
  PA .... 40°30N 78°52W 95 D4
Cambria Heights
  NY .... 40°41N 73°44W 114 B4
Cambridge ID ..... 44°34N 116°41W 70 E2
Cambridge IL ..... 41°18N 90°12W 71 B3
Cambridge IA ..... 41°54N 93°32W 73 C5
Cambridge KS ..... 37°19N 96°40W 74 D7
Cambridge MA ..... 42°23N 71°7W 106 A3
Cambridge MD ..... 38°34N 76°5W 77 B5
Cambridge MN ..... 45°34N 93°13W 80 E5
Cambridge NE ..... 40°17N 100°10W 84 D5
Cambridge NY ..... 43°2N 73°22W 78 A1
Cambridge OH ..... 40°2N 81°35W 92 C5
Cambridge VT ..... 44°39N 72°53W 86 B2
Cambridge City IN 39°49N 85°10W 72 D5
Cambridge Res. MA 42°24N 71°16W 106 A2
Cambridgeport VT. 43°10N 72°36W 86 C2
Camden AL .... 31°59N 87°17W 60 E3
Camden DE .... 39°7N 75°25W 77 A5
Camden IL .... 40°9N 90°46W 71 C3
Camden IN .... 40°10N 86°32W 72 C4
Camden ME .... 44°13N 69°4W 76 D4
Camden MS .... 32°47N 89°54W 81 D4
Camden NC .... 36°20N 76°10W 90 B8
Camden NJ .... 39°55N 75°7W 116 B2
Camden NY .... 43°20N 75°45W 89 B5
Camden OH .... 39°38N 84°39W 92 D2
Camden SC .... 34°16N 80°36W 90 D5
Camden TN .... 36°4N 88°6W 96 D4
Camden Bay AK ... 70°10N 145°15W 61 A11
Camden County ☆ GA 31°0N 81°45W 68 F5
Camden County ☆
  MO .... 38°0N 92°45W 82 C4
Camden County ☆
  NC .... 36°20N 76°10W 90 B9
Camden County ☆
  NJ .... 39°45N 75°0W 87 C2
Camdenton MO .... 38°1N 92°45W 82 C4
Cameron AZ .... 35°53N 111°25W 62 B4
Cameron LA .... 29°48N 93°20W 75 E2
Cameron MO .... 39°44N 94°14W 82 B2
Cameron OK .... 35°8N 94°32W 93 C9
Cameron MT .... 45°13N 111°41W 83 E6
Cameron TX .... 30°51N 96°59W 99 G11
Cameron WI .... 45°25N 91°44W 103 C2
Cameron County ☆
  PA .... 41°30N 78°5W 95 C4
Cameron County ☆
  TX .... 26°12N 97°42W 98 L10
Cameron Parish ☆
  LA .... 29°58N 93°10W 75 E2
Cameron Prairie Nat. Wildlife
  Refuge ○ LA ... 29°54N 92°50W 75 E3
Camilla GA .... 31°14N 84°12W 68 E2
Camino CA .... 38°44N 120°41W 64 E6
Camp Atterbury IN 39°20N 86°4W 72 D4
Camp Blanding Training Site
  FL .... 29°56N 81°57W 67 B7
Camp Bullis TX .. 29°38N 98°35W 117 B3
Camp Coulter = Powell
Camp County ☆ TX 33°0N 94°59W 99 E13
Camp Creek WV ... 37°30N 81°6W 102 D3
Camp Crook SD ... 45°33N 103°59W 91 E2
Camp Douglas WI. 43°55N 90°16W 103 E3
Camp Edwards and Otis A.N.G.
  Base MA .... 41°39N 70°32W 78 C4
Camp Grayling MI. 44°47N 79°7W 79 E7
Camp Hill AL ..... 32°48N 85°39W 60 D5
Camp Hill PA ..... 40°14N 76°55W 95 D6
Camp Houston OK. 36°49N 99°7W 93 B4

Camp J.T. Robinson
  AR .... 34°52N 92°21W 63 D3
Camp Lejeune Marine Corps Base
  NC .... 34°43N 77°22W 90 D8
Camp Pendleton
  CA .... 33°13N 117°24W 65 K9
Camp Point IL .... 40°3N 91°4W 71 C2
Camp Ripley MN .. 46°9N 94°22W 80 D4
Camp Roberts CA . 35°47N 120°48W 65 H6
Camp Shelby Training Site
  MS .... 31°11N 89°15W 81 E4
Camp Springs MD. 38°48N 76°55W 119 C4
Camp Swift TX ... 30°18N 97°20W 99 G10
Camp Verde AZ ... 34°34N 111°51W 62 C4
Camp Wood TX ... 29°40N 100°1W 99 H7
Campaign TN ..... 35°45N 85°37W 97 E7
Campbell CA ...... 37°17N 121°57W 64 F5
Campbell FL ...... 28°16N 81°27W 115 C2
Campbell MN ..... 46°6N 96°24W 80 D2
Campbell MO ..... 36°30N 90°4W 82 E6
Campbell NE ..... 40°18N 98°44W 84 D7
Campbell OH ..... 41°5N 80°37W 92 C6
Campbell County ☆
  KY .... 38°55N 84°20W 97 B8
Campbell County ☆
  SD .... 45°55N 100°0W 91 E6
Campbell County ☆
  TN .... 36°23N 84°7W 97 D8
Campbell County ☆
  VA .... 37°15N 79°5W 102 D5
Campbell County ☆
  WY .... 44°15N 105°30W 104 B7
Campbell Hill OH. 40°22N 83°43W 92 C3
Campbellsburg IN. 38°39N 86°16W 72 E4
Campbellsburg KY 38°31N 85°12W 97 B7
Campbellsport WI 43°36N 88°17W 103 E5
Campbellsville KY 37°21N 85°20W 97 C7
Campbellton FL .. 30°57N 85°24W 67 A3
Campion CO ...... 40°18N 105°5W 66 B5
Campo CO .... 37°6N 102°35W 66 E8
Campo Indian Reservation
  CA .... 32°37N 116°23W 65 L10
Campti LA .... 31°54N 93°7W 75 C2
Campton FL ...... 30°53N 86°31W 67 A2
Campton GA ...... 33°52N 83°43W 68 C3
Campton KY ...... 37°44N 83°33W 97 C9
Campton NH ...... 43°50N 71°39W 86 C3
Camptonville CA . 39°27N 121°3W 64 D5
Campville FL ..... 29°40N 82°7W 67 B6
Camuy
  Puerto Rico .... 18°29N 66°51W 105 G16
Canaan CT .... 42°2N 73°20W 78 B1
Canaan NH .... 43°40N 72°1W 86 C2
Canadensis PA ... 41°12N 75°15W 87 A1
Canadian TX ..... 35°55N 100°23W 98 B7
Canadian → OK .. 35°27N 95°3W 93 C8
Canadian County ☆
  OK .... 35°35N 98°0W 93 C6
Canajoharie NY .. 42°54N 74°35W 89 C6
Canal Fulton OH . 40°53N 81°36W 92 C5
Canal Point FL .. 26°52N 80°38W 67 E8
Canalou MO ...... 36°46N 89°41W 82 E7
Canandaigua NY .. 42°54N 77°17W 89 C3
Canandaigua L. NY 42°47N 77°19W 89 C3
Canaseraga NY ... 42°27N 77°45W 89 C3
Canaveral, C. FL . 28°27N 80°32W 67 C8
Canaveral Nat. Seashore ○
  FL .... 28°28N 80°34W 67 C8
Canby CA .... 41°27N 120°52W 64 B6
Canby MN .... 44°43N 96°16W 80 F2
Canby OR .... 45°16N 122°42W 94 B3
Candle AK .... 65°55N 161°56W 61 D7
Candler County ☆ GA 32°30N 82°0W 68 D4
Candlewood, L. CT 41°33N 73°23W 78 B1
Cando ND .... 48°32N 99°12W 91 B6
Cando NC .... 35°18N 79°45W 90 C6
Candor NY .... 42°14N 76°21W 89 C4
Cane River Creole Nat. Historical
  Park ○ LA ..... 31°40N 93°1W 75 C2
Cane Valley KY ... 37°11N 85°19W 97 C7
Caney KS .... 37°1N 95°56W 74 D8
Caney OK .... 34°14N 96°13W 93 D7
Caney → U.S.A. .. 36°20N 95°42W 74 E8
Caney Creek Res.
  TX .... 32°13N 92°50W 75 B3
Caney Fork → TN 36°15N 85°57W 97 D7
Caneyville KY .... 37°26N 86°29W 96 C6
Canfield AR ...... 33°11N 93°38W 63 E2
Canfield OH ...... 41°2N 80°46W 92 C6
Canisteo NY ...... 42°16N 77°36W 89 C3
Canisteo → NY .. 42°7N 77°8W 89 C3
Canistota SD ..... 43°36N 97°18W 91 G8
Canjilon NM ...... 36°29N 106°26W 88 A4
Cannon Air Force Base
  MS .... 35°23N 104°12W 88 B6
Cannon Ball ND .. 46°25N 100°38W 91 D5
Cannon Beach OR . 45°53N 123°58W 94 B2
Cannon County ☆ TN 35°50N 86°4W 96 E6
Cannon Falls MN . 44°31N 92°54W 80 F6
Cannonball → ND 46°26N 100°35W 91 D5
Cannonsburg KY .. 38°23N 82°42W 97 B10
Cannonville UT ... 37°34N 112°3W 100 F3
Canobie Lake NH . 42°49N 71°17W 78 B3
Cañon City CO ... 38°27N 105°14W 66 D5
Cañon Largo →
  NM .... 36°43N 107°49W 88 A3
Canoncito Indian Reservation
  NM .... 35°10N 107°0W 88 B3
Canonsburg PA ... 40°16N 80°11W 95 D3
Canoochee → GA 31°59N 81°19W 68 E5
Canova SD .... 43°53N 97°30W 91 G8
Canterbury CT ... 41°41N 71°57W 78 C3
Canterbury NH ... 43°20N 71°34W 86 C3
Cantil CA .... 35°18N 117°58W 65 H9
Canton CT .... 41°49N 72°54W 78 C2
Canton GA .... 34°14N 84°29W 68 B2
Canton IL .... 40°33N 90°2W 71 C3
Canton KS .... 38°23N 97°26W 74 C6
Canton KY .... 36°48N 87°58W 96 D5
Canton MA .... 42°9N 71°9W 78 B3
Canton MN .... 43°32N 91°56W 80 G7
Canton MS .... 32°37N 90°2W 81 D3
Canton MO .... 40°8N 91°32W 82 A5
Canton NY .... 44°36N 75°10W 89 A5
Canton NC .... 35°32N 82°50W 90 C3
Canton OH .... 40°48N 81°23W 92 C5
Canton OK .... 36°3N 98°35W 93 B5
Canton PA .... 41°39N 76°51W 95 C6
Canton SD .... 43°18N 96°35W 91 G9
Canton TX .... 32°33N 95°52W 99 E12
Cantonment FL ... 30°37N 87°20W 67 A1
Cantril IA .... 40°39N 92°4W 73 E6
Cantwell AK ...... 63°24N 148°57W 61 E10
Canute OK .... 35°25N 99°17W 93 C4
Canutillo TX ..... 31°55N 106°36W 98 F1
Canyon TX .... 34°59N 101°55W 98 C6
Canyon City OR .. 44°23N 118°57W 94 C7
Canyon County ☆
  ID .... 43°38N 116°42W 70 F2
Canyon Creek MT 46°49N 112°16W 83 D5
Canyon De Chelly Nat.
  Monument ○ AZ. 36°10N 109°20W 62 A6

Canyon Ferry L. MT . . . . 46°39N 111°44W **83 D6**
Canyon L. TX . . . 29°52N 98°12W **99 H9**
Canyon Village WY . . . . . 44°46N 110°32W **104 B2**
Canyonlands Nat. Park △ UT . . . 38°15N 110°0W **100 E6**
Canyons of the Ancients Nat. Monument △ CO 37°30N 108°55W **66 E2**
Canyonville OR . . 42°56N 123°17W **94 E2**
Cap Rock Escarpment TX . . . . 33°25N 101°11W **98 D6**
Capa SD . . . . . 44°7N 100°59W **91 F5**
Capac MI . . . . . 43°1N 82°56W **79 F9**
Cape Canaveral FL. 28°24N 80°36W **67 C8**
Cape Canaveral Air Station FL . . . . 28°28N 80°34W **67 C8**
Cape Charles VA . . 37°16N 76°1W **102 D8**
Cape Cod B. MA . . 41°50N 70°20W **78 C4**
Cape Cod Nat. Seashore △ MA . . . . 41°56N 70°6W **78 C4**
Cape Coral FL . . . . 26°33N 81°57W **67 E7**
Cape Elizabeth ME . . 43°34N 70°12W **76 E3**
Cape Fear ~ NC . . . 33°53N 78°1W **90 E7**
Cape Girardeau MO . 37°19N 89°32W **82 D7**
Cape Girardeau County ☆ MO . . . . 37°25N 89°40W **82 D7**
Cape Hatteras Nat. Seashore ○ NC . . . . 35°30N 75°28W **90 C10**
Cape Henlopen State Park △ DE . . . . 38°46N 75°5W **77 B5**
Cape L. SC . . . . 33°2N 79°21W **90 E6**
Cape Krusenstern Nat. Monument △ U.S.A . . . 67°30N 163°30W **61 C7**
Cape Lisburne = Wevok AK . . . . 68°53N 166°13W **61 B6**
Cape Lookout Nat. Seashore △ NC . . . . 35°45N 76°25W **90 C9**
Cape May NJ . . . . 38°56N 74°56W **87 D2**
Cape May County ☆ NJ . . . . 39°10N 74°45W **87 C2**
Cape May Court House U.S.A. . . . 39°5N 74°50W **87 C2**
Cape May Point NJ . 38°56N 74°58W **87 D2**
Cape Pole AK . . 55°58N 133°48W **61 J14**
Cape St. Claire MD . . 39°3N 76°25W **77 A4**
Cape Vincent NY . . . 44°8N 76°20W **89 A4**
Cape Yakataga AK 60°4N 142°27W **61 F12**
Capitan NM . . . . 33°35N 105°35W **88 D3**
Capitan Grande Indian Reservation CA . . 32°54N 116°43W **65 L10**
Capitan Mts. NM . . . 33°36N 105°22W **88 D3**
Capitan Pk. NM . . . 33°35N 105°16W **88 D3**
Capitol Heights MD 38°52N 76°55W **119 B4**
Capitol Hill N. Marianas . . . 15°13N 145°45E **105 c**
Capitol Reef Nat. Park △ UT . . . 38°15N 111°10W **100 E4**
Capitol View SC . . . 33°58N 80°50W **90 D5**
Capitola FL . . . . 30°27N 84°54W **67 A4**
Capleville TN . . . . 35°1N 89°53W **112 B2**
Capon Bridge WV . . . 39°18N 78°26W **77 A2**
Caprock NM . . . . 33°24N 103°43W **88 D7**
Capron IL . . . . 42°24N 88°44W **71 A5**
Capron OK . . . . 36°54N 98°35W **93 B5**
Captain Cook HI . . 19°30N 155°55W **69 D6**
Captiva FL . . . . 26°31N 82°11W **67 E6**
Capulin Pk. NM . . . 33°56N 106°46W **88 A4**
Capulin Volcano Nat. Monument △ U.S.A.. 36°47N 103°58W **88 A7**
Caratunk ME . . . . 45°8N 69°59W **76 C4**
Caraway AR . . . . 35°46N 90°19W **63 C5**
Carbon IN . . . . 39°36N 87°6W **72 D3**
Carbon TX . . . . 41°3N 94°50W **73 D4**
Carbon TX . . . . 32°16N 98°50W **99 E9**
Carbon County ☆ MT . . . . 45°10N 109°0W **83 E9**
Carbon County ☆ PA 41°0N 75°50W **95 D7**
Carbon County ☆ UT . . . 39°40N 110°30W **100 D5**
Carbon County ☆ WY . . . . 42°0N 107°0W **104 E4**
Carbon Hill AL . . 33°53N 87°32W **60 C3**
Carbonado WA . . 47°5N 122°3W **101 C3**
Carbondale CO . . 39°24N 107°13W **66 C3**
Carbondale IL . . . . 37°44N 89°13W **71 F4**
Carbondale KS . . . . 38°49N 95°41W **74 C8**
Carbondale PA . . . . 41°35N 75°30W **95 C7**
Cardiff CO . . . . 39°31N 107°19W **66 C3**
Cardigan, Mt. NH . . 43°40N 71°54W **86 C3**
Cardington OH . . . . 40°30N 82°54W **92 C4**
Cardwell MO . . . . 36°3N 90°17W **82 E6**
Carefree AZ . . . . 33°50N 111°55W **62 D4**
Carencro LA . . . . 30°19N 92°3W **75 D3**
Caret VA . . . . 38°1N 76°59W **102 C7**
Carey ID . . . . 43°19N 113°57W **70 F5**
Carey OH . . . . 40°57N 83°23W **92 C3**
Caribou ME . . . . 46°52N 68°1W **76 B5**
Caribou County ☆ ID . . . . 42°50N 111°30W **70 G7**
Caribou Nat. Forest ID . . . . 42°50N 111°5W **70 G7**
Caribou Range ID . 43°10N 111°15W **70 F7**
Carl Blackwell L. OK 36°8N 97°11W **93 B6**
Carl Junction MO . . 37°11N 94°34W **82 D2**
Carleton MI . . . . 42°4N 83°23W **79 G8**
Carleton NE . . . . 40°18N 97°41W **84 D8**
Carlile WY . . . . 44°29N 104°48W **104 B8**
Carlin NV . . . . 40°43N 116°7W **85 B4**
Carlinville IL . . . . 39°17N 89°53W **71 D4**
Carlisle AR . . . . 34°47N 91°45W **63 D4**
Carlisle IN . . . . 38°58N 87°24W **72 E3**
Carlisle IA . . . . 41°30N 93°29W **73 D5**
Carlisle KY . . . . 38°19N 84°1W **97 B8**
Carlisle MS . . . . 32°0N 90°47W **81 E3**
Carlisle PA . . . . 40°12N 77°12W **95 D5**
Carlisle WA . . . . 47°10N 124°0W **101 C1**
Carlisle County ☆ KY 36°50N 89°0W **96 D14**
Carlock IL . . . . 40°35N 89°8W **71 C4**
Carlos MN . . . . 45°58N 95°18W **80 E3**
Carlos TX . . . . 30°36N 96°5W **99 G11**
Carlsbad CA . . . . 33°10N 117°21W **65 K9**
Carlsbad NM . . . . 32°25N 104°14W **88 E6**
Carlsbad TX . . . . 31°36N 100°38W **98 F7**
Carlsbad Caverns Nat. Park △ NM . . . . 32°10N 104°35W **88 E6**
Carlshend MI . . . . 46°19N 87°13W **79 C4**
Carlstadt NJ . . . . 40°50N 74°6W **114 A2**
Carlton MN . . . . 46°40N 92°25W **80 D6**
Carlton OR . . . . 45°18N 123°11W **94 B2**
Carlton County ☆ MN . . . . 46°35N 92°45W **80 D6**
Carlyle IL . . . . 38°37N 89°22W **71 E4**
Carlyle MT . . . . 46°40N 104°4W **83 D13**
Carlyle L. IL . . . . 38°37N 89°21W **71 E4**
Carmel IN . . . . 39°58N 86°7W **110 A2**
Carmel NY . . . . 41°26N 73°41W **87 A3**
Carmel-by-the-Sea CA . . . . 36°33N 121°55W **64 G3**
Carmel Valley CA . . 36°29N 121°43W **64 G5**
Carmen ID . . . . 45°15N 113°54W **70 D5**
Carmen OK . . . . 36°35N 98°28W **93 B5**
Carmi IL . . . . 38°5N 88°10W **71 E5**
Carmichael CA . . . . 38°38N 121°19W **64 E3**
Carnegie OK . . . . 35°6N 98°36W **93 C5**
Carnegie PA . . . . 40°24N 80°5W **116 B1**
Carneiro KS . . . . 38°44N 98°2W **74 C6**
Carnesville GA . . . . 34°22N 83°14W **68 B3**
Carney MD . . . . 39°23N 76°31W **107 A2**
Carney MI . . . . 45°35N 87°34W **79 D4**
Carney OK . . . . 35°48N 97°1W **93 C6**
Carneys Point NJ . . 39°43N 75°28W **87 C1**

Caro MI . . . . . 43°29N 83°24W **79 F8**
Caroga Lake NY . . 43°8N 74°29W **89 B6**
Carol City FL . . . . 25°56N 80°14W **112 C1**
Carolina Puerto Rico . . 18°23N 65°58W **105 G17**
Carolina IL . . . . 41°28N 71°40W **78 C3**
Carolina Beach NC . . 34°2N 77°54W **90 D8**
Carolinas Pt. N. Marianas . . . 14°55N 145°38E **105 c**
Caroline CA . . . . 43°14N 85°48W **79 F6**
Caroline County ☆ MD . . . . 38°50N 75°50W **77 B5**
Caroline County ☆ VA . . . . 38°3N 77°21W **102 C7**
Carondelet Park MO . . . . 38°33N 90°15W **117 B2**
Carp NV . . . . . 37°7N 114°29W **85 E6**
Carpenter IA . . . . 43°25N 93°1W **73 B5**
Carpenter WY . . . . 41°3N 104°22W **104 E8**
Carpenterville OR . . 42°13N 124°17W **94 E1**
Carpinteria CA . . . . 34°24N 119°31W **65 J7**
Carr CO . . . . 40°54N 104°53W **66 B6**
Carr Fork L. KY . . . 37°14N 83°0W **97 C9**
Carr, Mt. NH . . . . 43°52N 71°50W **86 C3**
Carrabassett ME . . 45°5N 70°13W **76 C3**
Carrabelle FL . . . . 29°51N 84°40W **67 B4**
Carraboro NC . . . . 35°55N 79°5W **90 C6**
Carrier OK . . . . 36°29N 98°2W **93 B5**
Carrier Mills IL . . . . 37°41N 88°38W **71 F5**
Carriere MS . . . . 30°37N 89°39W **81 F4**
Carrigain, Mt. NH . . . 44°6N 71°26W **86 B3**
Carrington ND . . . . 47°27N 99°8W **91 C6**
Carrizo Cr. ~ NM. 36°55N 103°55W **88 A7**
Carrizo Plain Nat. Monument △ U.S.A. . . . 35°11N 119°47W **65 H7**
Carrizo Springs TX . . 28°31N 99°52W **99 J8**
Carrizo Wash ~ AZ . . . . 34°36N 109°26W **88 C1**
Carroll IA . . . . 42°4N 94°52W **73 C4**
Carroll NE . . . . 42°1N 97°12W **84 B8**
Carroll OH . . . . 39°48N 82°43W **92 D5**
Carroll County ☆ AR 36°22N 93°34W **63 B2**
Carroll County ☆ GA 33°35N 85°10W **68 C1**
Carroll County ☆ IL. 42°0N 90°0W **71 A4**
Carroll County ☆ IN 40°35N 86°35W **72 C4**
Carroll County ☆ IA. 42°0N 94°50W **73 C4**
Carroll County ☆ KY. 38°40N 85°5W **97 B7**
Carroll County ☆ MD 39°30N 77°0W **77 A4**
Carroll County ☆ MS 33°30N 89°55W **81 C4**
Carroll County ☆ MO . . . . 39°25N 93°30W **82 B3**
Carroll County ☆ NH 43°50N 71°15W **86 C3**
Carroll County ☆ OH 40°35N 81°5W **92 D6**
Carroll County ☆ TN. 36°0N 88°26W **96 E4**
Carroll County ☆ VA . . . . 36°55N 80°50W **102 E4**
Carrollton PA . . . . 39°44N 77°23W **77 A3**
Carrolls WA . . . . 46°4N 122°52W **101 D3**
Carrollton AL . . . . 33°15N 88°6W **60 C2**
Carrollton GA . . . . 33°35N 85°5W **68 C1**
Carrollton IL . . . . 39°18N 90°24W **71 D3**
Carrollton KY . . . . 38°41N 85°11W **97 B7**
Carrollton MI . . . . 43°28N 83°55W **79 F8**
Carrollton MS . . . . 33°30N 89°55W **81 C4**
Carrollton MO . . . . 39°22N 93°30W **82 B3**
Carrollton OH . . . . 40°34N 81°5W **92 D6**
Carrollton TX . . . . 32°57N 96°55W **99 E11**
Carrollton VA . . . . 36°58N 76°34W **102 E7**
Carrolltown PA . . . . 40°36N 78°43W **95 D4**
Carrollwood FL . . . . 28°2N 82°29W **119 A3**
Carry Falls Res. NY. 44°31N 74°45W **89 A6**
Carson CA . . . . 33°49N 118°16W **111 D3**
Carson IA . . . . 41°14N 95°25W **73 D3**
Carson ND . . . . 46°25N 101°34W **91 D4**
Carson WA . . . . 45°44N 121°49W **101 E4**
Carson ~ NV . . . . 39°45N 118°40W **85 D3**
Carson City MI . . . . 43°11N 84°51W **79 F7**
Carson City NV . . . . 39°10N 119°46W **85 C1**
Carson County ☆ TX . . . . 35°20N 101°25W **98 B6**
Carson L. NV . . . . 39°18N 118°43W **85 C2**
Carson Nat. Forest NC . . . . 36°20N 79°15W **90 B6**
Cat I. MS . . . . 30°14N 89°6W **81 F4**
Carson Sink NV . . 39°50N 118°25W **85 C2**
Carta Valley TX . . 29°48N 100°41W **98 H7**
Cartago CA . . . . 36°19N 118°2W **65 G8**
Carter KY . . . . 38°26N 83°8W **97 B9**
Carter OK . . . . 35°13N 99°30W **93 C4**
Carter WY . . . . 41°26N 110°26W **104 E2**
Carter County ☆ KY. 38°20N 83°0W **97 B9**
Carter County ☆ MT . . . . 45°30N 104°30W **83 E13**
Carter County ☆ OK 34°15N 97°15W **93 D6**
Carter County ☆ TN . . . . 36°17N 82°10W **97 D10**
Carter Mt. WY . . . 44°12N 109°25W **104 B3**
Carteret NJ . . . . 40°34N 74°13W **114 C1**
Carteret County ☆ NC . . . . 34°50N 76°30W **90 D9**
Carters L. GA . . . 34°37N 84°40W **68 B2**
Cartersville VA . . . . 37°40N 78°6W **102 D6**
Carterville IL . . . . 37°46N 89°5W **71 F4**
Carthage AR . . . . 34°4N 92°33W **63 D3**
Carthage IL . . . . 40°25N 91°8W **71 C2**
Carthage MS . . . . 32°44N 89°34W **81 D4**
Carthage MO . . . . 37°11N 94°19W **82 D2**
Carthage NY . . . . 43°59N 75°37W **89 B5**
Carthage SD . . . . 44°10N 97°43W **91 F8**
Carthage TN . . . . 36°15N 85°57W **97 D7**
Carthage TX . . . . 32°9N 94°20W **99 E13**
Carthersville MO . 36°11N 89°39W **82 E7**
Carver MA . . . . 41°53N 70°46W **78 C4**
Carver County ☆ MN 44°50N 93°45W **80 F5**
Carver Lake MN . . 44°54N 92°58W **113 B4**
Carvers NV . . . . 38°47N 117°11W **85 D3**
Carville LA . . . . 30°13N 91°6W **75 D4**
Cary IL . . . . 42°13N 88°14W **71 A5**
Cary MS . . . . 32°49N 90°56W **81 D3**
Cary NC . . . . 35°47N 78°46W **90 C7**
Caryville TN . . . . 36°18N 84°13W **97 D8**
Casa Blanca NM . . 35°3N 107°28W **88 B3**
Casa Grande AZ . . 32°53N 111°45W **62 E4**
Casa Grande Ruins Nat. Monument △ AZ. 33°0N 111°32W **62 E4**
Cascade Heights GA . . . . 33°43N 84°26W **106 B2**
Cascade CO . . . . 38°54N 104°58W **66 D6**
Cascade ID . . . . 44°31N 116°2W **70 E2**
Cascade IA . . . . 42°18N 91°0W **73 C8**
Cascade MT . . . . 47°16N 111°42W **83 C6**
Cascade County ☆ MT . . . . 47°20N 111°30W **83 C6**
Cascade Head OR . . 45°3N 124°1W **94 B1**
Cascade-Siskiyou Nat. Monument △ OR 42°4N 122°30W **94 C3**
Cascade OR . . . . 44°24N 122°29W **94 C3**
Casco ME . . . . 43°57N 70°31W **76 E3**
Casco WI . . . . 44°34N 87°37W **103 D6**
Casco B. ME . . . . 43°45N 70°0W **76 E4**
Caselton NV . . . . 37°55N 114°29W **85 E6**
Caseville MI . . . . 43°56N 83°9W **79 F8**
Casey IL . . . . 39°18N 87°59W **71 D6**
Casey IA . . . . 41°31N 94°32W **73 D4**
Casey County ☆ KY. 37°20N 85°0W **97 C8**

Cash AR . . . . 35°48N 90°56W **63 C5**
Cashie ~ NC . . . . 35°53N 76°49W **90 C8**
Cashiers NC . . . . 35°6N 83°6W **90 C2**
Cashion AZ . . . . 33°26N 112°17W **116 C1**
Cashion OK . . . . 35°48N 97°41W **93 C6**
Cashmere WA . . . . 47°31N 120°28W **101 C5**
Cashton WI . . . . 43°43N 90°47W **103 E4**
Casmalia CA . . . . 34°50N 120°32W **65 J6**
Casnovia MI . . . . 43°14N 85°48W **79 F6**
Cason TX . . . . 33°2N 94°49W **99 D13**
Casper WY . . . . 42°51N 106°19W **104 D6**
Caspian MI . . . . 46°4N 88°38W **79 C3**
Caspiana LA . . . . 32°17N 93°33W **75 B2**
Cass WV . . . . 38°24N 79°55W **102 C5**
Cass ~ MI . . . . 43°23N 83°59W **79 F8**
Cass City MI . . . . 43°36N 83°11W **79 F8**
Cass County ☆ IL. 40°0N 90°15W **71 D3**
Cass County ☆ IN.. 40°45N 86°20W **72 C4**
Cass County ☆ IA. 41°20N 94°55W **73 D4**
Cass County ☆ MI. 41°50N 86°0W **79 H5**
Cass County ☆ MN. 47°0N 94°10W **80 D4**
Cass County ☆ MO. 38°40N 94°20W **82 C2**
Cass County ☆ ND. 47°0N 97°0W **91 D8**
Cass County ☆ NE. 40°50N 96°10W **84 D9**
Cass County ☆ TX. 33°1N 94°22W **99 D13**
Cass L. MN . . . . 47°27N 94°29W **80 C4**
Cass Lake MN . . . . 47°23N 94°37W **80 C4**
Cassadaga NY . . . . 42°20N 79°19W **89 C1**
Casselberry FL . . . . 28°41N 81°20W **67 C7**
Casselman PA . . . . 39°53N 79°13W **77 A1**
Casselton ND . . . . 46°54N 97°13W **91 D8**
Cassia County ☆ ID 42°20N 113°30W **70 G5**
Cassoday KS . . . . 38°3N 96°38W **74 C7**
Cassopolis MI . . . . 41°55N 86°1W **79 H5**
Cassville MO . . . . 36°41N 93°52W **82 E3**
Cassville PA . . . . 40°18N 78°2W **95 D4**
Cassville WI . . . . 42°43N 90°59W **103 F3**
Castaic CA . . . . 34°32N 118°37W **65 J8**
Castalia IA . . . . 43°7N 91°41W **73 B7**
Castalia OH . . . . 41°24N 82°49W **92 B4**
Castalia NC . . . . 42°4N 95°55W **73 C3**
Castella CA . . . . 41°9N 122°19W **64 B4**
Castile NY . . . . 42°38N 78°3W **89 C2**
Castillo de San Marcos Nat. Monument △ U.S.A. . . . 29°54N 81°19W **67 B7**
Castle OK . . . . 35°28N 96°23W **93 C7**
Castle Dale UT . . 39°13N 111°1W **100 D4**
Castle Danger MN . . 47°7N 91°30W **80 C7**
Castle Dome Peak AZ 33°3N 114°9W **62 D1**
Castle Hayne NC . . 34°21N 77°54W **90 D8**
Castle Hills TX . . 29°31N 98°30W **99 H9**
Castle Mts. MT . . 46°28N 110°46W **83 D7**
Castle Peak CO . . 39°1N 106°52W **66 C4**
Castle Pk. ID . . 44°1N 114°42W **70 F4**
Castle Rock CO . . 39°22N 104°51W **66 C6**
Castle Rock SD . . 44°57N 103°25W **91 F2**
Castle Rock WA . . 46°17N 122°54W **101 D3**
Castle Rock L. WI. 43°52N 89°57W **103 E4**
Castle Shannon PA . . 40°21N 80°1W **116 B1**
Castle Valley UT . 38°38N 109°25W **100 E6**
Castleberry AL . . 31°18N 87°1W **60 E3**
Castleford ID . . 42°31N 114°52W **70 G4**
Castleton IN . . 39°54N 86°3W **110 A2**
Castleton VT . . 43°37N 73°11W **86 C1**
Castleton Corners NY . . . . 40°36N 74°8W **114 C2**
Castleton-on-Hudson NY . . . . 42°32N 73°45W **89 C7**
Castlewood CO . . 44°44N 97°2W **91 F8**
Castlewood VA . . 36°53N 82°17W **102 E2**
Castolon TX . . 29°8N 103°31W **98 H4**
Castor LA . . 32°15N 93°10W **75 B2**
Castor ~ MO . . 36°51N 89°44W **82 E7**
Castor Cr. ~ LA . . 31°47N 92°22W **75 C3**
Castro CA . . . . 37°45N 122°6W **118 B2**
Castro County ☆ TX . . . . 34°33N 102°19W **98 C5**
Castro Valley CA . . 37°41N 122°5W **118 B3**
Castroville CA . . 36°46N 121°45W **64 G5**
Castroville TX . . 29°21N 98°53W **99 H9**
Caswell County ☆ NC . . . . 36°20N 79°15W **90 B6**
Cat I. MS . . . . 30°14N 89°6W **81 F4**
Catahoula L. LA . . 31°31N 92°7W **75 C3**
Catahoula Parish ☆ LA . . . . 31°35N 91°58W **75 C4**
Catalina AZ . . . . 32°30N 110°50W **62 E5**
Cataño Puerto Rico 18°27N 66°7W **105 G16**
Cataouatche, L. LA 29°50N 90°14W **113 C1**
Cataract IN . . . . 39°30N 86°53W **72 D4**
Cataract L. IN . . 39°29N 86°55W **72 D4**
Catarina TX . . . . 28°21N 99°37W **99 J8**
Catasauqua PA . . 40°39N 75°29W **87 B1**
Catawba SC . . . . 34°51N 80°55W **90 D5**
Catawba WI . . . . 45°32N 90°32W **103 C3**
Catawba ~ SC . . 34°28N 80°53W **90 D5**
Catawba County ☆ NC . . . . 35°40N 81°10W **90 C4**
Catawissa PA . . . . 40°57N 76°28W **95 D6**
Cathay ND . . . . 47°33N 99°25W **91 C6**
Cathcart WA . . . . 47°51N 122°5W **118 A5**
Cathedral Pk. MT . . 45°11N 85°37W **79 D6**
Cathedral City CA 33°38N 116°28W **65 K10**
Cathedral Gorge State Park △ NV . . . . 37°49N 114°25W **85 E6**
Cathedral Mt. TX . . 30°11N 103°40W **98 G4**
Catherine AL . . . . 32°11N 87°28W **60 D3**
Catherine KS . . . . 38°56N 99°13W **74 C4**
Catherine, L. AR . . 34°28N 91°24W **115 B2**
Catlettsburg KY . . 38°25N 82°36W **97 B6**
Catlow Valley OR . . 42°20N 119°5W **94 E6**
Catoctin Mountain Park △ MD . . . . 39°39N 77°28W **77 A3**
Catoctin Mt. MD . . 39°16N 76°43W **107 B1**
Catonsville MD . . 39°16N 76°43W **107 B1**
Catoosa OK . . . . 36°11N 95°45W **93 B8**
Catoosa County ☆ GA . . . . 34°50N 85°10W **68 B1**
Caton County ☆ NM . . . . 34°0N 108°15W **88 D2**
Catskill NY . . . . 42°14N 73°52W **89 C7**
Catskill Mts. NY . . 42°10N 74°25W **89 C6**
Catskill Park △ U.S.A. 42°8N 74°39W **89 C6**
Cattaraugus NY . . 42°20N 78°52W **89 C2**
Cattaraugus County ☆ NY . . . . 42°30N 78°45W **89 C1**
Cattaraugus Indian Reservation NY . . . . 42°30N 79°9W **89 B2**
Caucomgomoc L. ME 46°13N 69°36W **76 B4**
Causey NM . . . . 33°53N 103°8W **88 D7**
Cauthron AR . . . . 34°55N 94°18W **63 D1**
Cavalier ND . . . . 48°48N 97°37W **91 B8**
Cavalier County ☆ ND . . . . 48°55N 98°30W **91 B7**
Cave City AR . . . . 35°57N 91°33W **63 C4**
Cave City KY . . . . 37°8N 85°58W **97 C7**
Cave Creek AZ . . 33°50N 111°57W **62 D4**
Cave in Rock IL . . 37°28N 88°10W **71 F5**
Cave Junction OR . . 42°10N 123°39W **94 E2**
Cave Spring GA . . 34°6N 85°20W **68 B1**
Cave Spring VA . . 37°47N 79°53W **102 D5**
Cavernas del Río Camuy, Parque de las △ Puerto Rico. 18°20N 66°50W **105 G16**
Cawker City KS . . 39°31N 98°26W **74 B5**
Cayce KY . . . . 36°33N 89°2W **96 D3**
Cayce SC . . . . 33°58N 81°4W **90 D4**

Cayey Puerto Rico. 18°7N 66°10W **105 G16**
Cayucos CA . . . . 35°27N 120°54W **65 H6**
Cayuga IN . . . . 39°57N 87°28W **72 D3**
Cayuga County ☆ NY 42°45N 76°45W **89 C4**
Cayuga Heights NY. 42°28N 76°30W **89 C4**
Cayuga L. NY . . . . 42°41N 76°41W **89 C4**
Cazenovia NY . . . . 42°56N 75°51W **89 C5**
Cearfoss MD . . . . 39°42N 77°46W **77 A3**
Cebolla NM . . . . 36°32N 106°29W **88 A4**
Cebolleta NM . . . . 35°12N 107°23W **88 B3**
Cecil GA . . . . 32°11N 93°33W **75 B2**
Cecil OR . . . . 41°13N 84°36W **92 B1**
Cecil OR . . . . 45°37N 119°58W **94 B6**
Cecil County ☆ MD. 39°30N 76°0W **77 A5**
Cecilia KY . . . . 37°40N 85°57W **97 C7**
Cecilia LA . . . . 30°20N 91°51W **75 D4**
Ceilton MD . . . . 39°24N 75°52W **77 A5**
Cedar ~ IA . . . . 41°9N 123°8W **64 B3**
Cedar ~ MI . . . . 45°25N 87°26W **79 D4**
Cedar ~ NE . . . . 42°40N 97°56W **84 C8**
Cedar ~ WA . . . . 47°30N 122°13W **101 C3**
Cedar Bluff AL . . 34°13N 85°37W **60 B5**
Cedar Bluff VA . . 37°5N 81°46W **102 D3**
Cedar Bluff Res. KS. 38°47N 99°43W **74 C4**
Cedar Bluffs KS . . 39°59N 100°34W **74 B3**
Cedar Bluffs NE . . 41°24N 96°37W **84 C9**
Cedar Breaks Nat. Monument △ UT . . . . 37°40N 112°50W **100 F3**
Cedar Brook NJ . . 39°43N 74°54W **87 C2**
Cedar Butte SD . . 43°35N 101°1W **91 G4**
Cedar City MO . . 38°36N 92°11W **82 C4**
Cedar City UT . . 37°41N 113°4W **100 F2**
Cedar County ☆ IA. 41°45N 91°10W **73 D7**
Cedar County ☆ MO. 37°45N 93°50W **82 D3**
Cedar County ☆ NE. 42°40N 97°15W **84 B8**
Cedar Cr. ~ ND . . 46°8N 101°19W **91 D4**
Cedar Creek AZ . . 34°47N 93°51W **63 D2**
Cedar Creek NE . . 41°2N 96°5W **84 C9**
Cedar Creek TX . . 30°5N 97°30W **99 G10**
Cedar Creek Res. AL 34°33N 87°50W **60 B3**
Cedar Creek Res. TX 32°11N 96°4W **99 E11**
Cedar Falls IA . . 42°32N 92°27W **73 C6**
Cedar Grove FL . . 30°10N 85°38W **67 A3**
Cedar Grove GA . . 33°40N 84°16W **106 C3**
Cedar Grove IN . . 39°22N 84°56W **72 D6**
Cedar Grove WI . . 43°33N 87°49W **103 E6**
Cedar Grove WV . . 38°13N 81°26W **102 C3**
Cedar Grove WV . . 33°34N 87°49W **103 E6**
Cedar Grove Res. NJ . . . . 40°51N 74°12W **114 A1**
Cedar Hill MO . . 38°21N 90°39W **82 C6**
Cedar Hill TN . . 36°33N 87°0W **96 D5**
Cedar Hill State Park △ TX . . . . 32°36N 96°59W **109 C4**
Cedar Hills OR . . 45°30N 122°47W **116 A1**
Cedar I. NC . . . . 34°57N 76°20W **90 D9**
Cedar Key FL . . 29°8N 83°2W **67 B5**
Cedar L. IL . . . . 37°37N 89°18W **71 F4**
Cedar L. TX . . . . 32°49N 102°17W **98 E5**
Cedar Lake IN . . 41°22N 87°26W **72 B3**
Cedar Lake MN . . 44°57N 93°38W **113 B2**
Cedar Mills MN . . 44°57N 94°31W **80 F4**
Cedar Mts. UT . . 40°10N 112°30W **100 C3**
Cedar Park IL . . 38°45N 90°6W **117 A3**
Cedar Park TX . . 30°30N 97°49W **99 G10**
Cedar Point KS . . 38°16N 96°49W **74 C7**
Cedar Point Nat. Wildlife Refuge △ OH . . . . 41°41N 83°19W **92 B3**
Cedar Point OH . . 41°29N 82°41W **92 B4**
Cedar Rapids IA . . 41°59N 91°40W **73 D7**
Cedar Rapids NE . . 41°34N 98°9W **84 C7**
Cedar River MT . . 46°58N 106°9W **83 C11**
Cedar River Nat. Grassland ND . . . . 46°0N 101°45W **91 E4**
Cedar Springs MI . . 43°13N 85°33W **79 F6**
Cedar Vale KS . . 37°6N 96°30W **74 D7**
Cedarburg WI . . 43°18N 87°59W **103 E6**
Cedardale AK . . 34°47N 93°51W **63 D2**
Cedarhurst NY . . 40°37N 73°42W **114 C4**
Cedartown GA . . 34°1N 85°15W **68 B1**
Cedarvale NM . . 34°21N 105°36W **88 D5**
Cedarville CA . . 41°32N 120°10W **64 B6**
Cedarville IL . . 42°23N 89°38W **71 A4**
Cedarville MD . . 38°40N 76°47W **77 B4**
Cedarville MI . . 46°0N 84°22W **79 D7**
Cedarville NJ . . 39°18N 75°12W **87 C1**
Cedarville OH . . 39°45N 83°49W **92 D3**
Cedarville WV . . 38°34N 79°87W **102 C4**
Ceiba Puerto Rico. 18°16N 65°39W **105 G17**
Celeste TX . . . . 33°18N 96°12W **99 D11**
Celestine IN . . . . 38°27N 86°45W **72 E4**
Celina OH . . . . 40°33N 84°35W **92 C2**
Celina TN . . . . 36°33N 85°30W **97 D7**
Celina TX . . . . 33°19N 96°47W **99 D11**
Cement OK . . . . 34°56N 98°8W **93 C5**
Centennial CO . . 39°34N 104°52W **109 C3**
Centennial WY . . 41°18N 106°8W **104 E6**
Centennial Mts. ID . . 44°35N 111°55W **70 E7**
Centennial Olympic Park GA . . . . 33°46N 84°23W **106 B2**
Centennial Wash ~ AZ . . . . 33°17N 112°48W **62 D3**
Center CO . . . . 37°45N 106°6W **66 E4**
Center GA . . . . 34°3N 83°25W **68 B3**
Center MO . . . . 39°30N 91°32W **82 B5**
Center NE . . . . 42°37N 97°53W **84 B8**
Center ND . . . . 47°7N 101°18W **91 C4**
Center TX . . . . 31°48N 94°11W **99 F13**
Center Barnstead NH 43°19N 71°15W **86 C3**
Center City MN . . 45°24N 92°49W **80 E6**
Center Cross VA . . 37°48N 76°47W **77 C4**
Center Harbor NH. 43°42N 71°27W **86 C3**
Center Hill GA . . 33°46N 84°29W **106 B2**
Center Hill L. TN . . 36°8N 85°49W **97 D7**
Center Line MI . . 42°29N 83°1W **109 A2**
Center Moriches NH. 43°45N 71°19W **86 C3**
Center Ossipee NH. 43°45N 71°9W **86 C3**
Center Point AL . . 33°38N 86°41W **60 C4**
Center Point IA . . 42°11N 91°46W **73 C7**
Center Point LA . . 31°15N 92°13W **75 C3**
Center Point TX . . 29°57N 99°2W **99 H8**
Center Sandwich NH 43°39N 71°25W **86 C3**
Center Strafford NH 43°17N 71°10W **86 C3**
Center Valley PA . . 40°32N 75°24W **87 B1**
Centerburg OH . . 40°18N 82°42W **92 C4**
Centereach NY . . 40°52N 73°6W **78 D1**
Centerfield UT . . 39°8N 111°49W **100 D4**
Centerton AR . . 36°22N 94°17W **63 B1**
Centertown MO . . 38°38N 92°25W **82 C4**
Centerville AL . . 35°4N 85°55W **97 E7**
Centerville AR . . 35°7N 93°10W **63 C2**
Centerville CA . . 36°44N 119°30W **65 G7**
Centerville IN . . 39°49N 85°0W **72 D6**
Centerville IA . . 40°44N 92°52W **73 E6**
Centerville KS . . 38°13N 95°1W **74 C8**
Centerville MO . . 37°26N 90°58W **82 D6**
Centerville PA . . 40°2N 79°59W **95 D3**
Centerville PA . . 39°50N 78°39W **77 A2**
Centerville SC . . 34°32N 82°42W **90 D3**
Centerville SD . . 43°7N 96°58W **91 G9**
Centerville TN . . 35°47N 87°28W **96 E5**
Centerville TX . . 31°16N 95°59W **99 F12**

Centerville UT . . 40°55N 111°52W **117 A2**
Centrahoma OK . . 34°37N 96°21W **93 D7**
Central AK . . . . 65°35N 144°48W **61 D11**
Central SC . . . . 34°44N 82°47W **90 D3**
Central TX . . . . 35°48N 89°32W **96 E3**
Central UT . . . . 37°25N 113°49W **100 F2**
Central, Cordillera Puerto Rico . . 18°8N 66°35W **105 G16**
Central City CO . . 39°48N 105°31W **66 C5**
Central City IA . . 38°33N 89°8W **71 E4**
Central City KY . . 37°18N 87°7W **96 C5**
Central City NE . . 41°7N 98°0W **84 C8**
Central City PA . . 40°7N 78°48W **95 D4**
Central City SD . . 44°22N 103°46W **91 F2**
Central Islip NY . . 40°47N 73°12W **87 B3**
Central Park MN . . 45°1N 93°7W **113 A3**
Central Park WA . . 46°58N 123°41W **101 D2**
Central Point OR . . 42°23N 122°55W **94 E3**
Central Square NY . . 43°17N 76°9W **89 B4**
Centralhatchee GA . . 33°22N 85°6W **68 C1**
Centralia IL . . . . 38°32N 89°8W **71 E4**
Centralia KS . . . . 39°44N 96°8W **74 B7**
Centralia MO . . . . 39°13N 92°8W **82 B4**
Centralia WA . . . . 46°48N 95°21W **93 B8**
Centralia WA . . . . 46°43N 122°58W **101 D3**
Centre AL . . . . 34°9N 85°41W **60 B5**
Centre County ☆ PA. 41°0N 78°0W **95 D5**
Centre Grove NJ . . 39°29N 75°8W **87 C1**
Centreville AL . . 32°57N 87°8W **60 D3**
Centreville IL . . 38°34N 90°7W **117 B3**
Centreville MD . . 39°3N 76°4W **77 A4**
Centreville MS . . 31°5N 91°4W **81 E2**
Centreville VA . . 38°50N 77°26W **77 B3**
Century FL . . . . 30°58N 87°16W **67 A1**
Cerab Mts. AZ . . 35°30N 114°10W **62 B1**
Ceres CA . . . . 37°35N 120°57W **64 F6**
Cereso VT . . . . 41°3N 86°39W **72 C4**
Cereze Canyon NM. 36°39N 107°42W **88 A3**
Cerrillos CA . . . . 35°26N 106°8W **88 B4**
Cerritos CA . . . . 33°51N 118°3W **111 C4**
Cerro Gordo IL . . 39°53N 88°44W **71 D5**
Cerro Gordo County ☆ IA . . . . 43°5N 93°15W **73 B5**
Cerro Vista Peak NM . . . . 36°14N 105°25W **88 A5**
Cesar Creek L. OH. 39°29N 84°3W **92 D2**
Ceylon MN . . . . 43°32N 94°38W **80 G4**
Chabot, L. CA . . 37°43N 122°7W **118 B4**
Chackbay LA . . . . 29°53N 90°48W **75 E5**
Chaco ~ NM . . 36°46N 108°39W **88 A3**
Chaco Canyon Nat. Monument △ NM . . . . 36°6N 108°0W **88 A3**
Chaco Culture Nat. Historical Park ~ U.S.A.. 36°3N 107°58W **88 A3**
Chacuaco ~ CO . . 37°19N 103°50W **66 E7**
Chadbourn NC . . 34°19N 78°50W **90 D7**
Chadron NE . . . . 42°50N 103°0W **84 B3**
Chadwick IL . . 42°1N 89°53W **71 A4**
Chaffee MO . . 37°11N 89°40W **82 D7**
Chaffee NY . . 46°46N 97°21W **91 D8**
Chaffee County ☆ CO . . . . 38°45N 106°10W **66 D4**
Chaffee I. CA . . 33°44N 118°8W **111 D4**
Chagrin Falls OH . . 41°26N 81°53W **92 B5**
Chain of Lakes Regional Park ☆ MN . . . . 44°56N 93°19W **113 B2**
Chain O' Lakes State Park △ IL . . . . 42°29N 88°9W **71 A5**
Chaires FL . . . . 30°26N 84°7W **67 A4**
Chalan Kanoa N. Marianas . . 15°9N 145°42E **105 c**
Chalfant PA . . 40°24N 79°50W **116 B2**
Chalk Mts. TX . . 30°3N 103°18W **98 H4**
Chalkyitsik AK . . 66°39N 143°43W **61 C12**
Challis ID . . 44°30N 114°14W **70 E4**
Challis Nat. Forest ID . . . . 44°0N 113°40W **70 E5**
Chalmers IN . . 40°40N 86°52W **72 C4**
Chalmette LA . . 29°56N 89°57W **113 C3**
Chama CO . . 37°10N 105°23W **66 E5**
Chama NM . . 36°54N 106°35W **88 A4**
Chama ~ NM . . 36°10N 106°10W **88 A4**
Chamberino NM . . 32°3N 106°41W **88 F4**
Chamberlain SD . . 43°49N 99°20W **91 G6**
Chamberlain L. ME . . 46°14N 69°19W **76 B4**
Chambers AZ . . 35°11N 109°26W **62 B6**
Chambers County ☆ AL . . . . 32°54N 85°24W **60 D5**
Chambers County ☆ TX . . . . 29°47N 94°35W **99 H13**
Chambers I. WI . . 45°11N 87°22W **103 C6**
Chambersburg PA . . 39°56N 77°40W **95 E5**
Chamblee GA . . 33°53N 84°18W **106 A3**
Chamisal NM . . 36°10N 105°44W **88 A5**
Chamois MO . . 38°41N 91°46W **82 C5**
Chamokane Cr. ~ WA . . . . 47°51N 117°51W **101 C8**
Champaign IL . . 40°7N 88°15W **71 C5**
Champaign County ☆ IL . . . . 40°10N 88°10W **71 C5**
Champaign County ☆ OH . . . . 40°7N 83°45W **92 C3**
Champion MI . . 46°31N 87°58W **79 C4**
Champion OH . . 41°19N 80°51W **92 B6**
Champion Creek Res. TX . . . . 32°17N 100°52W **98 E7**
Champlain NY . . 44°59N 73°27W **86 B1**
Champlain, L. U.S.A. 44°35N 73°20W **86 B1**
Champlain Canal NY 43°30N 73°27W **86 C1**
Chanceford PA . . 43°20N 96°59W **91 G9**
Chancellor SD . . 43°22N 96°59W **91 G9**
Chandalar ~ AK . . 66°37N 146°0W **61 C11**
Chandler AZ . . 29°55N 85°57W **75 E7**
Chandler Sd. LA . . 29°55N 89°21W **75 E7**
Chandler IN . . 38°3N 87°22W **72 E3**
Chandler OK . . 35°42N 96°53W **93 C7**
Chandler TX . . 32°18N 95°29W **99 E12**
Chandlerville IL . . 40°3N 90°9W **71 C3**
Chandeleur Is. LA . . 29°55N 88°57W **75 E8**
Chaneysville PA . . 39°49N 78°19W **77 A2**
Changi ND . . 47°10N 99°41W **91 C6**
Channel Is. CA . . 33°40N 119°15W **65 K7**
Channel Islands Nat. Park △ CA . . . . 34°0N 119°24W **65 K7**
Channelview TX . . 29°47N 95°8W **109 A4**
Channing MI . . 46°9N 88°5W **79 C3**
Channing TX . . 35°41N 102°20W **98 B5**
Chantilly VA . . 38°53N 77°26W **77 B3**
Chantote KS . . 37°41N 95°27W **74 D8**
Chaparral NM . . 32°3N 106°24W **88 F4**
Chapel Hill IN . . 39°46N 86°16W **110 B1**
Chapel Hill NC . . 35°55N 79°4W **90 C6**
Chapel Hill TN . . 35°38N 86°41W **96 E6**
Chapin = Edinburg TX . . . . 26°18N 98°10W **98 L9**
Chapin IL . . . . 39°46N 90°24W **71 D3**
Chapin SC . . . . 34°10N 81°21W **90 D4**
Chapin KY . . . . 37°55N 82°30W **97 C10**
Chapman KS . . . . 38°58N 97°1W **74 C6**
Chapman NE . . . . 41°1N 98°9W **84 C7**
Chapman Ranch TX. 27°35N 97°33W **99 K10**
Chapmanville WV . . 37°59N 82°1W **102 D2**
Chappaquiddick Island MA . . . . 41°22N 70°30W **78 C4**
Chappell NE . . . . 41°6N 102°28W **84 C3**
Chappell Hill TX . . 30°9N 96°15W **99 G11**
Chaptico MD . . . . 38°21N 76°49W **77 B4**
Charco TX . . . . 28°44N 97°37W **99 J10**

Chardon OH . . . . 41°35N 81°12W **92 B5**
Charenton LA . . . . 29°53N 91°32W **75 E4**
Charing GA . . . . 32°28N 84°22W **68 D2**
Chariton IA . . . . 41°1N 93°19W **73 D5**
Chariton ~ MO . . 39°19N 92°58W **82 B4**
Chariton County ☆ MO . . . . 39°30N 93°0W **82 B4**
Charity MO . . . . 37°33N 93°1W **82 D3**
Charity I. MI . . . . 44°2N 83°26W **79 E8**
Charlack MO . . . . 38°42N 90°20W **117 A1**
Charlemont MA . . 42°38N 72°52W **78 B2**
Charleroi PA . . . . 40°9N 79°57W **95 D3**
Charles ~ MA . . 42°22N 71°3W **78 B4**
Charles, C. VA . . 37°7N 75°58W **102 D7**
Charles City IA . . 43°4N 92°41W **73 B6**
Charles City VA . . 37°21N 77°4W **102 D7**
Charles City County ☆ VA . . . . 37°21N 77°4W **102 D7**
Charles Gates Dawes House IL . . . . 42°2N 87°40W **108 A2**
Charles Mill L. OH . . 40°45N 82°22W **92 C4**
Charles Mix County ☆ SD . . . . 43°15N 98°42W **91 G7**
Charles Mound IL . . 42°30N 90°14W **71 A3**
Charles Town WV . . 39°17N 77°52W **77 A3**
Charleston AR . . 35°18N 94°5W **63 C1**
Charleston IL . . 39°30N 88°10W **71 D5**
Charleston MS . . 34°1N 90°4W **81 B3**
Charleston MO . . 36°55N 89°21W **82 E7**
Charleston OR . . 43°20N 124°21W **94 D1**
Charleston SC . . 32°46N 79°56W **90 E6**
Charleston TN . . 35°17N 84°45W **97 E8**
Charleston UT . . 40°28N 111°28W **100 C4**
Charleston WV . . 38°21N 81°38W **102 C3**
Charleston County ☆ SC . . . . 32°50N 80°0W **90 F5**
Charleston Int. ✈ (CHS) SC . . . . 32°54N 80°2W **90 F5**
Charleston Peak NV 36°16N 115°42W **85 F5**
Charlestown IN . . 38°27N 85°40W **72 E5**
Charlestown MA . . 42°22N 71°4W **106 A3**
Charlestown MD . . 39°35N 75°59W **77 A5**
Charlestown NH . . 43°14N 72°25W **86 C2**
Charlestown RI . . 41°23N 71°45W **78 C3**
Charlevoix MI . . 45°19N 85°16W **79 D6**
Charlevoix, I. MI . . 45°16N 85°8W **79 D6**
Charlevoix County ☆ MI . . . . 45°15N 85°0W **79 D6**
Charlo MT . . . . 47°26N 114°10W **83 C3**
Charlotte IA . . . . 41°58N 90°28W **73 C8**
Charlotte MI . . . . 42°34N 84°50W **79 G7**
Charlotte NC . . 35°13N 80°50W **107 A2**
Charlotte TN . . 36°11N 87°21W **96 D5**
Charlotte TX . . 28°52N 98°43W **99 J9**
Charlotte VT . . 44°19N 73°16W **86 B1**
Charlotte Amalie U.S. Virgin Is.. 18°21N 64°56W **105 G18**
Charlotte County ☆ FL . . . . 26°50N 82°0W **67 E7**
Charlotte County ☆ VA . . . . 37°0N 78°55W **102 D6**
Charlotte Court House VA . . . . 37°3N 78°39W **102 D6**
Charlotte-Douglas Int. ✈ (CLT) NC . . . . 35°14N 80°56W **107 A1**
Charlotte Hall MD . . 38°26N 76°45W **77 B4**
Charlotte Harbor FL . . 26°57N 82°4W **67 E6**
Charlotte Res. NC. 35°16N 80°53W **107 A1**
Charlottesville VA . . 38°2N 78°30W **102 C6**
Charlton MA . . 42°8N 78°30W **78 B3**
Charlton County ☆ GA . . . . 30°50N 82°10W **68 F4**
Charter Oak IA . . 42°4N 95°36W **73 C3**
Chase AL . . . . 34°47N 86°33W **60 B4**
Chase KS . . . . 38°21N 98°21W **74 C5**
Chase MD . . . . 39°22N 76°22W **77 A5**
Chase, L. FL . . 28°28N 81°31W **115 B2**
Chase City VA . . 36°48N 78°28W **102 E6**
Chase County ☆ KS . . . . 38°15N 96°45W **74 C7**
Chase County ☆ NE . . . . 40°30N 101°40W **84 D4**
Chaseburg WI . . 43°40N 91°6W **103 E2**
Chaseley ND . . 47°27N 99°49W **91 C6**
Chaska MN . . 44°47N 93°36W **80 F5**
Chassahowitzka FL. 28°43N 82°34W **67 C6**
Chastaigier LA . . 30°34N 92°19W **75 D3**
Chatanika AK . . 65°7N 147°28W **61 D11**
Chateaugay NY . . 44°56N 74°5W **89 A6**
Chatfield AR . . 35°0N 90°24W **63 C5**
Chatfield MN . . 43°51N 92°11W **80 G6**
Chatfield State Park △ CO . . . . 39°32N 105°4W **109 C1**
Chatham IL . . . . 41°45N 87°36W **108 C2**
Chatham IL . . . . 39°40N 89°42W **71 D4**
Chatham LA . . . . 32°18N 92°27W **75 B3**
Chatham MA . . . . 41°41N 69°58W **78 C5**
Chatham MI . . . . 46°21N 86°56W **79 C5**
Chatham NJ . . . . 40°44N 74°23W **87 B2**
Chatham NY . . . . 42°21N 73°36W **78 B1**
Chatham PA . . . . 39°51N 75°49W **77 A5**
Chatham VA . . . . 36°50N 79°24W **102 E5**
Chatham County ☆ GA . . . . 32°0N 81°10W **68 E5**
Chatham County ☆ NC . . . . 35°45N 79°10W **90 C6**
Chatom AL . . . . 31°28N 88°16W **60 E2**
Chatsworth GA . . 34°46N 84°46W **68 B2**
Chatsworth IL . . 40°45N 88°18W **71 C5**
Chatsworth NJ . . 42°55N 96°31W **73 B2**
Chatsworth WA . . 38°49N 74°32W **87 C2**
Chattahoochee FL . . 30°42N 84°51W **67 A4**
Chattahoochee ~ GA . . . . 30°54N 84°57W **68 F2**
Chattahoochee County ☆ GA . . . . 32°20N 84°50W **68 D2**
Chattahoochee Nat. Forest GA . . . . 34°35N 84°0W **68 B2**
Chattanooga OK . . 34°25N 98°39W **93 D5**
Chattanooga TN . . 35°3N 85°19W **97 E7**
Chattaroy WA . . 47°53N 117°21W **101 C8**
Chattolanee MD . . 39°24N 76°44W **107 A1**
Chattooga ~ GA . . . . 34°30N 85°15W **68 B1**
Chattooga County ☆ GA . . . . 34°30N 85°20W **68 B1**
Chatuga L. U.S.A. 35°0N 83°40W **68 A3**
Chaumont NY . . 44°4N 76°8W **89 B4**
Chauncey OH . . 39°24N 82°8W **92 D5**
Chautauqua KS . . 37°1N 96°11W **74 D7**
Chautauqua County ☆ KS . . . . 37°15N 96°15W **74 D7**
Chautauqua County ☆ NY . . . . 42°10N 79°15W **89 C1**
Chautauquan Nat. Wildlife Refuge ~ IL . . 40°23N 89°59W **71 C4**
Chauvin LA . . . . 29°26N 90°36W **75 E5**
Chaves County ☆ NM . . . . 33°15N 104°30W **88 D6**
Chazy NY . . . . 44°53N 73°26W **86 B1**
Cheaha Mt. AL . . 33°29N 85°49W **60 C5**
Cheat Bridge WV . . 38°37N 79°52W **102 C5**
Cheatham County ☆ TN . . . . 36°17N 87°4W **96 D5**
Chebanse IL . . . . 41°0N 87°54W **71 C6**
Cheboygan MI . . 45°39N 84°29W **79 D7**
Cheboygan County ☆ MI . . . . 45°30N 84°30W **79 D7**
Check VA . . . . 37°2N 80°10W **102 D4**

Checotah OK ..... 35°28N 95°31W 93 C8
Cheektowaga NY ☆ 42°54N 78°45W 89 C2
Cheesman L. CO .. 39°33N 105°16W 66 C5
Cefornak AK ..... 60°13N 164°12W 61 F6
Chehalis AK ..... 46°40N 122°58W 101 D3
Chehalis → WA .. 46°57N 123°50W 101 D2
Chehalis Indian Reservation
  WA .... 46°49N 123°12W 101 D2
Chelan WA ...... 47°51N 120°1W 101 C5
Chelan, L. WA ... 48°11N 120°30W 101 B5
Chelan County ☆
  WA .... 48°0N 120°30W 101 C5
Chelan Falls WA .. 47°48N 119°59W 101 C6
Chelatchie WA ... 45°55N 122°25W 101 E3
Chelmsford WA .. 42°36N 71°21W 78 B3
Chelsea AL ...... 33°20N 86°38W 60 E4
Chelsea IA ...... 41°55N 92°24W 73 D6
Chelsea MA ...... 42°23N 71°1W 106 A3
Chelsea MI ...... 42°19N 84°1W 79 G7
Chelsea OK ...... 36°32N 95°26W 93 B8
Chelsea VT ...... 43°59N 72°27W 86 C2
Cheltenham MD ... 38°42N 76°50W 77 B4
Cheltenham PA ☆ 40°3N 75°5W 116 A2
Chemehuevi Indian Reservation
  CA .... 34°30N 114°25W 65 J12
Chemquasabamticook L.
  ME .... 46°30N 69°37W 76 B4
Chemult OR ..... 43°14N 121°47W 94 D4
Chemung County ☆
  NY .... 42°10N 76°45W 89 C4
Chemway NC ..... 35°16N 80°53W 107 A1
Chenango → NY .. 42°6N 75°55W 89 C5
Chenango County ☆
  NY .... 42°30N 75°40W 89 C5
Chenes, Pointe aux
  MI .... 45°55N 84°54W 79 D7
Cheney KS ...... 37°38N 97°47W 74 D6
Cheney WA ...... 47°30N 117°35W 101 C8
Cheney Res. KS .. 37°43N 97°48W 74 D6
Cheneyville LA .. 31°1N 92°17W 75 C3
Chenoa OK ...... 40°45N 88°43W 71 C8
Chenoweth OR ... 45°37N 121°13W 94 B4
Chepachet RI .... 41°55N 71°40W 78 C3
Chequamegon B.
  U.S.A. ..... 46°39N 90°51W 103 B3
Chequamegon Nat. Forest
  WI .... 46°10N 91°0W 103 B3
Chequamegon Pt.
  WI .... 46°42N 90°45W 103 B3
Cheraw CO ...... 38°6N 103°31W 66 D7
Cheraw SC ...... 34°42N 79°53W 90 D6
Cheriton VA ..... 37°17N 75°58W 102 D9
Cherokee AL ..... 34°45N 87°58W 60 B3
Cherokee IA ..... 42°45N 95°33W 73 C3
Cherokee KS ..... 37°21N 94°49W 93 B5
Cherokee OK ..... 36°45N 98°21W 93 B6
Cherokee TX ..... 30°59N 98°43W 99 G9
Cherokee County ☆
  AL .... 34°9N 85°41W 60 B5
Cherokee County ☆
  GA .... 34°20N 84°20W 68 B2
Cherokee County ☆
  IA .... 42°45N 95°35W 73 C3
Cherokee County ☆
  KS .... 37°15N 94°45W 74 D9
Cherokee County ☆
  NC .... 35°10N 84°10W 90 C1
Cherokee County ☆
  OK .... 36°0N 95°0W 93 B9
Cherokee County ☆
  SC .... 35°0N 81°40W 90 C4
Cherokee County ☆
  TX .... 31°58N 95°17W 99 F12
Cherokee Indian Reservation
  NC .... 35°30N 83°20W 90 C2
Cherokee L. TN ☆ 36°10N 83°30W 97 D9
Cherokee Nat. Forest
  TN .... 36°0N 82°40W 97 E10
Cherokee Village AR 36°18N 91°31W 63 B4
Cherokees, Grand Lake O' The
  OK .... 36°44N 95°5W 93 B9
Cherry Co. ☆ NE 42°30N 101°0W 84 B4
Cherry Cr. → SD .. 39°45N 105°0W 109 B2
Cherry Cr. → SD .. 44°36N 101°30W 91 C4
Cherry Creek NV .. 39°54N 114°53W 85 C6
Cherry Creek SD .. 44°36N 101°30W 91 C4
Cherry Creek L.
  CO .... 39°39N 104°51W 109 C2
Cherry Creek State Park
  CO .... 39°38N 104°51W 109 C2
Cherry Hill MD .. 39°15N 76°38W 107 B2
Cherry Hill NJ ... 39°56N 75°2W 87 C1
Cherry Hills Village
  CO .... 39°38N 104°57W 109 C2
Cherry L. CA..... 37°59N 119°55W 64 F7
Cherry Tree PA .. 40°44N 78°48W 95 D4
Cherry Valley AR . 35°24N 90°45W 63 C5
Cherry Valley NY . 42°48N 74°45W 89 C6
Cherryfield ME .. 44°36N 67°56W 76 D6
Cherryland CA ... 37°40N 122°6W 118 B4
Cherryvale KS ... 37°16N 95°33W 74 D8
Cherryville NC .. 35°23N 81°23W 90 C4
Chesaco Park MD . 39°18N 76°29W 107 B3
Chesaning MI ... 43°11N 84°7W 79 F7
Chesapeake VA ☆. 36°49N 76°16W 115 B1
Chesapeake WV .. 38°13N 81°32W 102 C3
Chesapeake B. .. 38°0N 76°10W 115 A3
Chesapeake Bay Bridge-Tunnel
  VA .... 37°2N 76°5W 115 A3
Chesapeake Beach
  MD .... 38°41N 76°32W 77 B4
Chesapeake City MD 39°32N 75°49W 77 A5
Chesapeake Ranche Estates
  MD .... 38°21N 76°25W 77 B4
Chesaw WA ...... 48°57N 119°3W 101 B6
Chesdin, L. VA .. 37°20N 77°40W 102 D7
Cheshire CT ..... 41°30N 72°54W 78 C2
Cheshire MA ..... 42°34N 73°10W 78 B1
Cheshire County ☆
  NH .... 43°0N 72°15W 86 D2
Chesnut NJ ..... 39°44N 74°52W 87 C2
Chesnee SC ..... 35°9N 81°52W 90 C4
Chester AR ...... 35°41N 94°11W 63 C1
Chester CA ...... 40°19N 121°14W 64 D5
Chester GA ...... 32°24N 83°9W 68 D3
Chester IL ...... 37°55N 89°49W 71 F4
Chester MA ...... 42°17N 72°59W 78 B2
Chester MT ...... 48°31N 110°58W 83 B7
Chester NH ...... 42°55N 71°15W 86 D3
Chester NJ ...... 40°47N 74°42W 87 B2
Chester NE ...... 40°1N 97°37W 84 D8
Chester OK ...... 36°13N 98°55W 93 B5
Chester PA ...... 39°51N 75°22W 77 A5
Chester SC ...... 34°43N 81°12W 90 D4
Chester SD ...... 43°54N 97°7W 91 G9
Chester VA ...... 37°21N 77°27W 102 D7
Chester VT ...... 43°16N 72°36W 86 C2
Chester WV ...... 40°37N 80°34W 102 A4
Chester → MD ... 39°3N 76°15W 77 A4
Chester County ☆
  PA .... 39°59N 75°50W 95 E7
Chester County ☆
  SC .... 34°30N 81°10W 90 D4
Chester County ☆
  TN .... 35°20N 88°45W 96 E4
Chesterfield IL .. 39°15N 90°4W 71 D3
Chesterfield MO .. 38°40N 90°35W 82 C6
Chesterfield SC .. 34°44N 80°5W 90 D5
Chesterfield County ☆
  VA .... 37°23N 77°31W 102 D7

Chesterfield Court House
  VA .... 37°23N 77°31W 102 D7
Chesterhill OH ... 39°29N 81°52W 92 D5
Chesterton IN ... 41°37N 87°4W 72 B3
Chesterville MD .. 39°13N 76°4W 107 A5
Chesterville MD .. 39°17N 75°55W 77 A5
Chestnut LA ..... 32°3N 93°1W 75 B2
Chestnut Hill MA . 42°19N 71°10W 106 B2
Chesuncook L. ME . 46°0N 69°21W 76 C4
Cheswold DE .... 39°13N 75°35W 77 A5
Chetco → OR .... 42°3N 124°16W 94 E1
Chetek WI ...... 45°19N 91°39W 103 C2
Chetumal MD .... 38°55N 76°54W 119 B4
Chevak AK ...... 61°32N 165°35W 61 F6
Chevelon Cr. → AZ 34°55N 110°35W 62 C5
Chevreuil, Pt. LA . 29°1N 91°33W 75 E4
Chevy Chase MD .. 38°59N 77°4W 119 B3
Chewaucan → OR . 42°48N 120°11W 101 B8
Chewelah WA ... 48°17N 117°43W 101 B8
Chewuch → WA .. 48°29N 120°11W 101 B5
Cheyenne OK .... 35°37N 99°40W 93 C4
Cheyenne → SD .. 44°41N 101°18W 91 F4
Cheyenne WY ... 41°8N 104°49W 104 E8
Cheyenne Bottoms
  KS .... 38°27N 98°40W 74 C5
Cheyenne County ☆
  CO .... 38°50N 102°35W 66 D8
Cheyenne County ☆
  KS .... 39°45N 101°45W 74 B2
Cheyenne County ☆
  NE .... 41°15N 103°0W 84 C3
Cheyenne River Indian Reservation
  SD .... 45°0N 101°0W 91 E4
Cheyenne Wells CO 38°49N 102°21W 66 D8
Chicago IL ...... 41°52N 87°38W 108 B3
Chicago, University of
  IL .... 41°47N 87°35W 108 C3
Chicago Harbor IL . 41°52N 87°36W 108 C3
Chicago Heights IL . 41°30N 87°38W 71 B6
Chicago Lawn IL .. 41°47N 87°40W 108 C3
Chicago-Midway ✈ (MDW)
  IL .... 41°47N 87°45W 108 C2
Chicago O'Hare Int. ✈ (ORD)
  IL .... 41°59N 87°54W 108 B2
Chicago Ridge IL .. 41°41N 87°46W 108 C2
Chicago Sanitary and Ship Canal
  IL .... 41°59N 87°45W 108 C2
Chicago State University
  IL .... 41°43N 87°36W 108 C3
Chicago Zoo IL ... 41°50N 87°50W 108 B3
Chicagof I. AK ... 57°30N 135°30W 61 H14
Chickahominy →
  VA .... 37°14N 76°53W 102 D8
Chickamauga GA .. 34°52N 85°18W 68 B1
Chickamauga L. TN 35°16N 85°17W 97 E7
Chickasaw AL .... 30°46N 88°5W 60 F2
Chickasaw County ☆
  IA .... 43°5N 92°20W 73 B6
Chickasaw County ☆
  MS .... 33°54N 89°0W 81 C5
Chickasawhay → MS 30°59N 88°44W 81 E5
Chickasha OK .... 35°3N 97°58W 93 C6
Chickasaw Nat. Recr. Area
  OK .... 34°26N 97°0W 93 D7
Chickasaw Nat. Wildlife Refuge
  TN .... 35°49N 89°38W 96 E3
Chickasha OK .... 35°3N 97°58W 93 C6
Chico CA .... 39°44N 121°50W 64 D5
Chico TX .... 33°18N 97°48W 99 D10
Chicopee GA ..... 34°15N 83°51W 68 B3
Chicopee MA ..... 42°9N 72°37W 78 B2
Chicopee → MA .. 42°9N 72°37W 78 B2
Chicot AR .... 33°12N 91°17W 63 E4
Chicot County ☆ AR 33°12N 91°17W 63 E4
Chidester AR ..... 33°42N 93°1W 63 E2
Chief Joseph Dam
  WA .... 48°0N 119°38W 101 B6
Chiefland FL ..... 29°29N 82°52W 67 B6
Chignik AK ...... 56°18N 158°24W 61 H8
Chikaskia → OK .. 36°37N 97°15W 93 B6
Childersburg AL .. 33°16N 86°21W 60 C4
Childress TX ..... 34°25N 100°13W 98 C7
Childress County ☆
  TX .... 34°25N 100°15W 98 C7
Chilhowie VA .... 36°48N 81°41W 102 E3
Chililí NM ...... 34°53N 106°14W 88 C4
Chillicothe IL .... 40°55N 89°29W 71 C4
Chillicothe MO ... 39°48N 93°33W 82 B3
Chillicothe OH ... 39°20N 82°59W 92 D4
Chillicothe TX ... 34°15N 99°31W 99 C8
Chillum MD ..... 38°56N 76°58W 119 B4
Chilmark MA .... 41°21N 70°45W 78 C4
Chilocco OK ..... 36°59N 97°4W 93 B6
Chiloquin OR .... 42°35N 121°52W 94 E4
Chilson NY ...... 43°53N 73°32W 86 C1
Chilton WI ...... 44°2N 88°10W 103 D5
Chilton County ☆
  AL .... 32°51N 86°38W 60 D4
Chimacum WA ... 48°0N 105°56W 88 E5
Chimney Rock CO . 37°13N 107°18W 66 E3
Chimney Rock Nat. Historic Site
  NE .... 41°42N 103°21W 84 C2
China TX .... 30°3N 94°20W 99 G13
China Basin CA ... 37°46N 122°23W 118 c3
China Grove NC .. 35°34N 80°35W 90 C5
China Grove TX .. 29°23N 98°20W 117 C5
China L. CA ...... 35°43N 117°20W 65 H9
Chinati Mts. TX .. 29°57N 104°30W 98 H3
Chinati Peak TX .. 29°57N 104°29W 98 H3
Chincoteague VA .. 37°56N 75°23W 77 C5
Chincoteague Bay
  MD .... 38°15N 75°15W 77 B5
Chincoteague I. VA . 37°56N 75°23W 77 C5
Chincoteague Nat. Wildlife
  Refuge ⌂ VA .. 37°56N 75°19W 102 D9
Chinle AZ .... 36°9N 109°33W 62 A6
Chinle → UT .... 37°12N 109°43W 100 F6
Chino Valley AZ .. 34°45N 112°27W 62 C3
Chinook MT ...... 48°35N 109°14W 83 B8
Chinook WA ..... 46°16N 123°57W 101 D2
Chinook, L. OR ... 44°33N 121°22W 94 C4
Chinook Pass WA .. 46°52N 121°32W 101 D4
Chipley FL ...... 30°47N 85°32W 67 A3
Chipola → FL .... 30°1N 85°5W 67 A3
Chippewa → MN .. 44°58N 94°17W 79 F7
Chippewa → MN .. 44°56N 95°44W 80 F3
Chippewa → WI .. 44°25N 92°5W 103 D1
Chippewa, L. WI .. 45°57N 91°12W 103 C2
Chippewa County ☆
  MI .... 46°20N 84°40W 79 C7
Chippewa County ☆
  MN .... 45°0N 95°35W 80 F3
Chippewa County ☆
  WI .... 45°4N 91°24W 103 D2
Chippewa Falls WI . 44°56N 91°24W 103 D2
Chippewa Nat. Forest
  MN .... 47°45N 94°0W 80 C4
Chiputneticook Lakes
  N. Amer. ... 45°35N 67°43W 76 C6
Chireno TX ...... 31°30N 94°21W 99 F13
Chiricahua Mts. AZ . 32°0N 109°15W 62 F6
Chiricahua Nat. Monument
  AZ .... 32°0N 109°20W 62 E6
Chiricahua Peak AZ 31°51N 109°18W 62 F6
Chisago County ☆
  MN .... 45°30N 92°55W 80 E6
Chisholm ME .... 44°29N 70°12W 76 D3

Chisholm MN .... 47°29N 92°53W 80 C6
Chisos Mts. TX ... 29°5N 103°15W 98 H4
Chistochina AK ... 62°34N 144°40W 61 E11
Chitina AK ...... 61°31N 144°26W 61 F11
Chitina → AK ... 61°31N 144°26W 61 F11
Chittenango NY .. 43°3N 75°52W 89 B5
Chittenden VT ... 43°42N 72°55W 86 C2
Chittenden County ☆
  VT .... 44°30N 73°10W 86 B1
Chivington CO ... 38°26N 102°32W 66 D8
Chloride AZ ..... 35°25N 114°12W 62 B1
Chocolate Mountain Naval Aerial
  Gunnery CA .. 33°14N 115°10W 65 K11
Chocolate Mts. AZ . 33°15N 114°30W 62 D1
Chocowinity NC .. 35°31N 77°6W 90 C8
Choctaw OK ..... 35°31N 97°17W 93 C6
Choctaw Bluff AL . 31°22N 87°46W 60 E3
Choctaw County ☆
  AL .... 32°0N 88°10W 60 E2
Choctaw County ☆
  MS .... 33°19N 89°11W 81 C4
Choctaw County ☆
  OK .... 34°0N 95°30W 93 D8
Choctawhatchee →
  FL .... 30°25N 86°8W 67 A2
Choctawhatchee B.
  FL .... 30°20N 86°20W 67 A2
Choke Canyon Res.
  TX .... 28°30N 98°20W 99 J9
Chokio MN ...... 45°34N 96°10W 80 E2
Chokoloskee FL .. 25°49N 81°22W 67 F7
Cholame CA ...... 35°44N 120°18W 65 H6
Chollas Park CA .. 32°44N 117°3W 117 B2
Choptank MD .... 38°41N 75°57W 77 B5
Choptank → MD .. 38°38N 76°13W 77 B4
Choteau MT ..... 47°49N 112°11W 83 C5
Choudrant LA .... 32°32N 92°31W 75 B3
Chouteau OK .... 36°11N 95°21W 93 B8
Chouteau County ☆
  MT .... 47°55N 110°30W 83 C7
Chowan → NC ... 36°10N 76°40W 90 B9
Chowan County ☆
  NC .... 36°10N 76°40W 90 B9
Chowchilla CA ... 37°7N 120°16W 64 F6
Chrisman IL ..... 39°48N 87°41W 71 D6
Chrisney IN ..... 38°1N 87°2W 72 E3
Christian County ☆
  IL .... 39°30N 89°15W 71 D4
Christian County ☆
  KY .... 36°50N 87°30W 96 D5
Christian County ☆
  MO .... 37°0N 93°10W 82 E3
Christian Sd. AK .. 55°56N 134°40W 61 J14
Christie CA ...... 35°57N 94°43W 93 C9
Christine ND .... 46°35N 96°48W 91 D9
Christopher IL ... 37°59N 89°3W 71 F4
Christoval TX .... 31°12N 100°30W 98 F7
Chrome NJ ...... 40°34N 74°13W 114 C1
Chromo CO ...... 37°2N 106°50W 66 E4
Chrysler AL ..... 31°18N 87°42W 60 E3
Chualar CA ...... 36°34N 121°31W 64 G5
Chuathbaluk AL .. 61°40N 159°15W 61 F8
Chubbuck ID .... 42°55N 112°28W 70 G6
Chuckawalla Mts.
  CA .... 33°30N 115°20W 65 K11
Chugach Mts. AK . 60°45N 147°0W 61 F11
Chuginadak I. AK . 52°50N 169°45W 61 K5
Chugwater WY ... 41°46N 104°50W 104 E8
Chula GA .... 31°33N 83°32W 68 E3
Chula MO .... 39°55N 93°29W 82 B3
Chula Vista CA ... 32°38N 117°5W 117 C2
Chunchula AL .... 30°55N 88°12W 60 F2
Chunky MS ...... 32°20N 88°56W 81 D5
Chupadera Mesa
  NM .... 33°52N 106°14W 88 D4
Church Creek MD . 38°30N 76°10W 77 B4
Church Hill MD .. 39°9N 75°59W 77 A5
Church Hill TN ... 36°31N 82°43W 97 D10
Church Point LA .. 30°24N 92°13W 75 D3
Church Rock NM .. 35°32N 108°36W 88 C2
Churchill County ☆
  NV .... 39°30N 118°30W 85 C2
Churchs Ferry ND . 48°16N 99°12W 91 B6
Churchville MD .. 39°34N 76°15W 77 A4
Churdan IA ...... 42°9N 94°29W 73 C4
Churubusco IN ... 41°14N 85°19W 72 B5
Chuska Mts. NM .. 36°15N 108°50W 88 A2
Cibecue AZ ...... 34°12N 110°29W 62 C5
Cibola AZ .... 33°17N 114°42W 62 D1
Cibola County ☆ NM 35°0N 108°0W 88 C2
Cibola Nat. Forest
  NM .... 33°52N 106°14W 88 D4
Cicero IL .... 41°51N 87°44W 108 B2
Cicero IN .... 40°7N 86°1W 72 C4
Cidra Puerto Rico .. 18°11N 66°10W 105 G16
Cima CA .... 35°14N 115°30W 65 H11
Cimarron KS ..... 37°48N 100°21W 74 D3
Cimarron NM .... 36°31N 104°55W 88 A6
Cimarron → OK .. 36°10N 96°16W 93 B7
Cimarron City OK . 35°48N 97°36W 93 C6
Cimarron County ☆
  OK .... 36°45N 102°30W 93 A1
Cimarron Nat. Grassland
  KS .... 37°15N 102°2W 74 D1
Cincinnati IA ..... 40°38N 92°56W 73 E6
Cincinnati OH .... 39°9N 84°27W 107 B2
Cincinnati Municipal ✈ (LUK)
  OH .... 39°6N 84°25W 107 B2
Cincinnati-Northern Kentucky
  Int. ✈ (CVG) KY 39°3N 84°40W 107 B1
Circle AK .... 65°50N 144°4W 61 D11
Circle MT .... 47°25N 105°35W 83 C12
Circle Cliffs UT .. 37°52N 111°15W 100 F4
Circleville KS .... 39°31N 95°52W 100 F4
Circleville OH .... 39°36N 82°57W 92 D4
Circleville UT .... 38°10N 112°16W 100 E3
Circleville WV ... 38°40N 79°30W 102 C5
Circleville Mt. UT . 38°12N 112°24W 100 E3
Cisco IL .... 40°1N 88°44W 71 C5
Cisco TX .... 32°23N 98°59W 99 E9
Cisco UT .... 38°58N 109°19W 100 E6
Cisne IL .... 38°31N 88°26W 71 E5
Cissna Park IL ... 40°34N 87°54W 71 C6
Cistern TX ...... 29°49N 97°13W 99 H10
Citra FL .... 29°25N 82°7W 67 B6
Citronelle AL .... 31°6N 88°14W 60 E2
Citrus County ☆ FL 28°50N 82°27W 67 C6
Citrus Heights CA . 38°42N 121°17W 64 E5
City Island NY ... 40°50N 73°47W 114 A4
City of Rocks Nat. Reserve →
  ID .... 42°5N 113°42W 70 G5
City Park FL ..... 39°44N 104°56W 109 B2
City Park LA ..... 30°0N 90°0W 113 B2
Civic Center Park
  LA .... 44°56N 93°27W 113 B3
Clackamas → OR . 45°22N 122°36W 94 B3

Clackamas County ☆
  OR .... 45°15N 122°15W 94 B3
Claflin KS ...... 38°31N 98°32W 74 C5
Claiborne AL .... 31°33N 87°31W 60 E3
Claiborne MD .... 38°50N 76°17W 77 B4
Claiborne County ☆
  MS .... 31°58N 90°59W 81 E3
Claiborne County ☆
  TN .... 36°27N 83°34W 97 D9
Claiborne Parish ☆
  LA .... 32°48N 93°4W 75 B2
Clair Engle L. CA . 40°48N 122°46W 64 C4
Clairton PA ..... 40°18N 79°53W 95 D3
Clallam Bay WA .. 48°15N 124°16W 101 B1
Clallam County ☆
  WA .... 48°0N 124°0W 101 C2
Clam Gulch AK ... 60°15N 151°23W 61 F10
Clan Alpine Mts.
  NV .... 39°40N 117°55W 85 C3
Clancy MT ...... 46°28N 111°59W 83 D6
Clanton AL ...... 32°51N 86°38W 60 D4
Clara City MN ... 44°58N 95°22W 80 F3
Clarcona FL ..... 28°38N 81°31W 67 E11
Clare IA .... 42°35N 94°21W 73 C4
Clare MI .... 43°49N 84°46W 79 F7
Clare County ☆ MI 43°55N 84°55W 79 F7
Clarement IL ..... 38°43N 87°58W 71 E6
Claremont NH ... 43°23N 72°20W 86 C2
Claremont VA .... 37°14N 76°58W 102 D8
Claremore OK ... 36°19N 95°36W 93 B8
Clarence IA ...... 41°53N 91°4W 73 C7
Clarence LA ..... 31°49N 93°2W 75 C2
Clarence, Port AK . 65°15N 166°40W 61 D6
Clarendon AR .... 34°42N 91°19W 63 D4
Clarendon PA .... 41°47N 79°6W 95 C3
Clarendon TX .... 34°56N 100°53W 98 C7
Clarendon County ☆
  SC .... 33°45N 80°10W 90 E5
Clareton WY .... 43°42N 104°42W 104 C8
Clarinda IA ...... 40°44N 95°2W 73 E3
Clarington OH ... 39°46N 80°52W 92 D6
Clarion IA .... 42°44N 93°44W 73 C5
Clarion PA ...... 41°13N 79°23W 95 C3
Clarion → PA .... 41°7N 79°41W 95 C3
Clarion County ☆ PA 41°15N 79°23W 95 C3
Clarissa MN ..... 46°8N 94°57W 80 D4
Clarita OK ...... 34°29N 96°26W 93 D7
Clark MO .... 39°17N 92°21W 82 C4
Clark SD .... 44°53N 97°44W 91 F8
Clark WY .... 44°54N 109°9W 104 B3
Clark Canyon Res.
  MT .... 44°57N 112°56W 83 F5
Clark County ☆ AR 33°55N 93°9W 63 E2
Clark County ☆ ID 44°15N 112°30W 70 E6
Clark County ☆ IL 39°20N 87°45W 71 D6
Clark County ☆ IN 38°30N 85°40W 72 E5
Clark County ☆ KS 37°15N 99°45W 74 D4
Clark County ☆ KY 38°0N 84°10W 97 C8
Clark County ☆ MO 40°25N 91°40W 82 A5
Clark County ☆ NV 36°10N 115°10W 85 F5
Clark County ☆ OH 39°55N 83°49W 92 D3
Clark County ☆ SD 44°45N 97°45W 91 F8
Clark County ☆
  WA .... 45°55N 122°25W 101 E4
Clark County ☆ WI 44°50N 90°40W 103 D3
Clark Fork ID .... 48°9N 116°11W 70 A2
Clark Fork → ID .. 48°9N 116°15W 70 A2
Clark Mt. CA .... 35°32N 115°35W 65 H11
Clarkdale AZ .... 34°46N 112°3W 62 C3
Clarke County ☆ AL 31°42N 87°47W 60 E3
Clarke County ☆ GA 33°57N 83°23W 68 C3
Clarke County ☆ IA 41°0N 93°45W 73 E5
Clarke County ☆ MS 32°0N 88°44W 81 D5
Clarke County ☆ VA 39°9N 77°59W 102 B7
Clarkesville GA ... 34°37N 83°31W 68 B3
Clarkfield MN ... 44°48N 95°48W 80 F3
Clarkia ID ...... 47°1N 116°15W 70 B2
Clarkrange TN ... 36°11N 85°1W 97 D7
Clarks LA .... 32°2N 92°8W 75 B3
Clarks → KY .... 37°38N 88°33W 96 C4
Clarks Fork Yellowstone →
  WY .... 45°32N 108°50W 83 E9
Clarks Grove MN . 43°46N 93°20W 80 G5
Clarks Hill IN ... 40°15N 86°43W 72 C4
Clarks Hill L. → J. Strom Thurmond
  L. GA ...... 33°40N 82°12W 68 C4
Clarks Point AK .. 58°51N 158°33W 61 G8
Clarks Summit PA . 41°30N 75°42W 87 A1
Clarksburg CA ... 38°26N 121°31W 118 A3
Clarksburg MO ... 38°40N 92°40W 82 C4
Clarksburg TN ... 40°12N 74°27W 87 B2
Clarksburg VA ... 35°52N 88°24W 96 E4
Clarksburg WV ... 39°17N 80°30W 102 B4
Clarksdale MO ... 39°49N 94°33W 82 B2
Clarksdale MS ... 34°12N 90°35W 81 B3
Clarkson KY ..... 37°30N 86°13W 96 C5
Clarkson NE ..... 41°43N 97°7W 84 C8
Clarkston UT .... 41°55N 112°3W 100 B3
Clarkston WA .... 46°25N 117°3W 101 D8
Clarksville IN ... 38°17N 85°45W 72 E5
Clarksville MI ... 42°50N 85°15W 79 G6
Clarksville OH ... 39°24N 83°59W 92 D3
Clarksville TN ... 36°32N 87°21W 96 D5
Clarksville TX ... 33°37N 95°3W 99 D12
Clarksville VA ... 36°37N 78°34W 102 E6
Clarkton NC ..... 34°29N 78°39W 90 D7
Clatonia NE ..... 40°28N 96°51W 84 D9
Clatskanie OR ... 46°6N 123°12W 94 A2
Clatsop County ☆
  OR .... 46°0N 123°40W 94 A2
Claude TX .... 35°7N 101°22W 98 B6
Claxton GA ...... 32°10N 81°55W 68 D5
Clay KY .... 37°29N 87°49W 96 C5
Clay County ☆ AL 33°16N 85°50W 60 C5
Clay County ☆ AR 36°19N 90°34W 63 B5
Clay County ☆ FL . 30°0N 81°45W 67 B7
Clay County ☆ GA 31°30N 85°0W 68 E2
Clay County ☆ IA 43°0N 95°10W 73 B3
Clay County ☆ IL 38°45N 88°30W 71 E5
Clay County ☆ IN 39°20N 87°10W 72 D3
Clay County ☆ KS 39°20N 97°10W 74 B6
Clay County ☆ KY 37°10N 83°35W 97 D8
Clay County ☆ MN 46°50N 96°30W 80 D2
Clay County ☆ MO 39°20N 94°20W 82 B2
Clay County ☆ MS 33°36N 88°50W 81 C5
Clay County ☆ NC 35°5N 83°45W 90 C2
Clay County ☆ NE 40°30N 98°0W 84 D7
Clay County ☆ SD 42°55N 96°58W 91 H9
Clay County ☆ TN 36°30N 85°30W 97 D7
Clay County ☆ TX 33°49N 98°12W 99 D9
Clay County ☆ WV 38°27N 81°5W 102 C3
Clay Springs AZ .. 34°22N 110°18W 62 C5
Claymont DE .... 39°48N 75°27W 77 A5
Claypool AZ ..... 33°25N 110°51W 62 D5
Claypool IN ..... 41°8N 85°53W 72 B5
Claysburg PA .... 40°7N 78°27W 95 D5
Claysville PA .... 40°7N 80°25W 95 D2
Clayton AL ...... 31°53N 85°27W 60 E5
Clayton CA ...... 37°56N 121°56W 118 A5
Clayton DE ...... 39°17N 75°38W 77 A5

Clayton GA ...... 34°53N 83°23W 68 B3
Clayton ID ...... 44°16N 114°24W 70 E4
Clayton IL ...... 40°2N 90°55W 71 C3
Clayton IN ...... 39°41N 86°31W 72 D4
Clayton KS ...... 39°44N 100°11W 74 B3
Clayton LA ...... 31°43N 91°33W 75 C4
Clayton MN ..... 42°38N 96°22W 80 E2
Clayton MO ..... 38°38N 90°19W 117 B5
Clayton NC ..... 35°39N 78°28W 90 C7
Clayton MT ..... 46°46N 113°43W 83 D4
Clayton NC ..... 35°0N 78°23W 90 C7
Clayton NJ ...... 40°38N 74°55W 87 B2
Clayton NY ..... 44°14N 76°5W 89 A4
Clayton OK ..... 34°35N 95°21W 93 D8
Clayton WI ..... 45°20N 92°10W 103 C1
Clayton County ☆
  GA .... 33°30N 84°20W 68 C2
Clayton County ☆ IA 42°50N 91°20W 73 C7
Clayton Lake ME . 46°36N 69°32W 76 B4
Clayton L. VA .... 37°5N 80°35W 102 D4
Cle Elum WA .... 47°12N 120°56W 101 C5
Clear → AZ ...... 34°59N 110°38W 62 C5
Clear County ☆ IL 35°15N 89°25W 71 E4
Clear L. CA ...... 39°2N 122°50W 64 D4
Clear L. IA ...... 43°8N 93°23W 73 B5
Clear L. IA ...... 31°53N 93°0W 75 C3
Clear L. UT ...... 39°7N 112°38W 100 D3
Clear Lake IA .... 41°44N 84°50W 73 B6
Clear Lake IA .... 43°8N 93°23W 73 B5
Clear Lake MN ... 45°27N 94°0W 80 E5
Clear Lake SD ... 44°45N 96°41W 91 F9
Clear Lake Res. CA 41°56N 121°5W 64 C5
Clear Spring MD . 39°39N 77°56W 77 A3
Clearbrook MN ... 47°42N 95°26W 80 C3
Clearfield KY .... 38°10N 83°26W 97 B9
Clearfield PA .... 41°2N 78°27W 95 C4
Clearfield UT .... 41°7N 112°2W 100 B3
Clearfield County ☆
  PA .... 41°0N 78°35W 95 D4
Clearlake MO .... 38°57N 122°38W 64 D4
Clearmont MO ... 40°31N 95°2W 82 A1
Clearmont WY ... 44°38N 106°23W 104 B6
Clearwater NM ... 35°20N 96°11W 93 C7
Clearwater FL ... 27°59N 82°48W 119 B2
Clearwater KS ... 37°30N 97°30W 74 D6
Clearwater NE ... 42°10N 98°11W 84 B7
Clearwater SC ... 33°30N 81°54W 90 E4
Clearwater → ID . 46°31N 116°23W 70 C2
Clearwater → MN . 45°44N 95°54W 80 E3
Clearwater Beach Island
  FL .... 27°59N 82°49W 119 A2
Clearwater County ☆
  ID .... 46°50N 115°30W 70 C3
Clearwater County ☆
  MN .... 47°30N 95°20W 80 C3
Clearwater L. ID .. 46°5N 90°47W 82 D6
Clearwater Mts. ID. 46°5N 115°30W 70 C3
Clearwater Nat. Forest
  ID .... 46°40N 115°5W 70 C3
Cleburne TX ..... 32°21N 97°23W 99 E10
Cleburne County ☆
  AR .... 35°30N 92°2W 63 C3
Cleburne County ☆
  AL .... 33°39N 85°35W 60 C5
Cleghorn IA ..... 42°49N 95°43W 73 C3
Clemmons NC ... 36°2N 80°23W 90 B5
Clements KS ..... 38°18N 96°44W 74 C7
Clements MD .... 38°18N 76°43W 77 B4
Clemmons SC .... 44°23N 95°3W 80 F3
Clemson SC ..... 34°41N 82°50W 90 D3
Clendenin WV ... 38°29N 81°21W 102 C3
Cleo Springs OK . 36°26N 98°29W 93 B5
Clermont FL ..... 28°33N 81°46W 67 C7
Clermont IA ..... 43°0N 91°39W 73 B7
Clermont County ☆
  OH .... 39°5N 84°11W 92 D2
Cleveland AL ... 33°59N 86°35W 60 C4
Cleveland GA .... 34°36N 83°46W 68 B3
Cleveland MN ... 44°19N 93°50W 80 F5
Cleveland MS .... 33°45N 90°43W 81 C3
Cleveland ND .... 46°54N 99°7W 91 C6
Cleveland OH ... 41°29N 81°41W 107 A1
Cleveland OK ... 36°19N 96°28W 93 B7
Cleveland TN ... 35°10N 84°53W 97 E8
Cleveland TX .... 30°21N 95°5W 99 G12
Cleveland UT .... 39°21N 110°51W 100 D5
Cleveland WI .... 43°55N 87°45W 103 D5
Cleveland, Mt. MT . 48°56N 113°51W 83 B4
Cleveland County ☆
  AR .... 33°58N 92°11W 63 E3
Cleveland County ☆
  NC .... 35°10N 97°20W 93 C6
Cleveland Heights
  OH .... 41°31N 81°33W 107 A2
Cleveland Hopkins Int. ✈ (CLE)
  OH .... 41°25N 81°51W 92 B5
Cleveland Nat. Forest
  CA .... 32°45N 116°40W 65 L10
Clever MO ...... 37°2N 93°28W 82 D3
Clewiston FL .... 26°45N 80°56W 67 E8
Cliff NM .... 32°58N 108°36W 88 E2
Clifford MI ...... 43°19N 83°11W 79 F8
Clifford ND ..... 47°21N 97°24W 91 C8
Cliffside Park NJ .. 40°49N 73°59W 114 B3
Cliffton WV ..... 38°0N 80°56W 102 D4
Clifton AZ ...... 33°3N 109°18W 62 D6
Clifton CO ...... 39°7N 108°22W 66 C2
Clifton ID .... 42°11N 112°0W 70 G7
Clifton IL .... 40°56N 87°56W 71 C6
Clifton KS ...... 39°34N 97°17W 74 B6
Clifton NJ ...... 40°37N 74°4W 114 B2
Clifton TN ...... 35°18N 88°1W 96 E4
Clifton TX ...... 31°47N 97°35W 99 F10
Clifton Forge VA . 37°50N 79°50W 102 D5
Clifton Heights MO 38°36N 90°17W 117 B2
Clifton Heights PA . 39°56N 75°17W 116 B4
Clifton Park MD .. 39°19N 76°34W 107 B2
Clifton Springs NY . 42°58N 77°8W 89 C3
Climax GA ...... 30°53N 84°26W 68 F2
Climax MI ...... 42°14N 85°20W 79 G6
Climax MN ...... 47°37N 96°49W 80 C2
Climax NC ...... 35°53N 79°42W 90 C6
Climax NY ...... 42°24N 73°56W 89 C7
Climax SD ...... 44°36N 96°30W 91 C8
Clinch → TN .... 35°53N 84°29W 97 E8
Clinch County ☆ GA 31°0N 82°45W 68 F4
Clinchco VA ..... 37°10N 82°21W 102 E2
Clinchport VA .... 36°42N 82°45W 102 E2
Clines Corners NM . 35°1N 105°40W 88 C5
Clingmans Dome TN 35°34N 83°30W 97 E9
Clint TX .... 31°35N 106°14W 98 F1
Clinton AL ...... 32°58N 88°0W 60 D1
Clinton CT ...... 41°17N 72°32W 78 C2
Clinton IA ...... 41°51N 90°12W 73 D8
Clinton IL ...... 40°9N 88°57W 71 C5
Clinton IN ...... 39°40N 87°24W 72 D3
Clinton KY ...... 36°40N 89°0W 96 D3

Clinton LA ...... 30°52N 91°1W 75 D4
Clinton ME ..... 44°38N 69°30W 76 D3
Clinton MA ..... 42°25N 71°41W 78 B3
Clinton MD ..... 38°46N 76°54W 77 B4
Clinton MI ...... 42°4N 83°58W 79 G8
Clinton MN ..... 45°28N 96°26W 80 E2
Clinton MO ..... 38°22N 93°46W 82 C3
Clinton MT ..... 46°46N 113°43W 83 D4
Clinton NC ..... 35°0N 78°23W 90 C7
Clinton NJ ...... 40°38N 74°55W 87 B2
Clinton NY ...... 43°3N 75°23W 89 B5
Clinton OH ...... 40°56N 81°38W 92 C5
Clinton SC ...... 34°29N 81°53W 90 D4
Clinton TN ...... 36°6N 84°8W 97 D8
Clinton WI ...... 42°34N 88°52W 103 F5
Clinton, L. IL .... 40°9N 88°45W 71 C5
Clinton County ☆ IL 38°35N 89°25W 71 E4
Clinton County ☆ IN 40°20N 86°30W 72 C4
Clinton County ☆ IA 41°55N 90°30W 73 D8
Clinton County ☆
  KY .... 36°45N 85°10W 97 D7
Clinton County ☆ MI 42°50N 84°40W 79 G7
Clinton County ☆
  MO .... 39°35N 94°25W 82 B2
Clinton County ☆
  NY .... 44°50N 73°40W 89 A7
Clinton County ☆
  OH .... 39°27N 83°50W 92 D3
Clinton County ☆ PA 41°10N 77°50W 95 C5
Clintondale NY ... 41°42N 74°5W 87 B3
Clintonville WI ... 44°37N 88°46W 103 D5
Clintwood VA .... 37°9N 82°28W 102 E2
Clio AL .... 31°43N 85°37W 60 E5
Clio MI .... 43°11N 83°44W 79 F8
Clio SC .... 34°35N 79°33W 90 D6
Clive IA .... 41°36N 93°43W 73 D5
Clontarf MN ..... 45°23N 95°40W 80 E3
Cloquet MN ..... 46°43N 92°28W 80 D6
Cloquet → MN ... 46°52N 92°35W 80 D6
Cloud County ☆ KS 39°30N 97°45W 74 B6
Cloud Peak WY .. 44°23N 107°11W 104 B6
Cloudcroft NM ... 32°58N 105°45W 88 E5
Clover SC .... 35°7N 81°14W 90 C4
Cloverdale CA .... 38°48N 123°1W 64 E3
Cloverdale IN .... 39°31N 86°48W 72 D4
Cloverdale OH ... 41°1N 84°18W 92 B2
Cloverleaf TX .... 29°46N 95°9W 119 H12
Cloverport KY ... 37°50N 86°38W 96 C5
Clovis CA .... 36°49N 119°42W 64 G7
Clovis NM .... 34°24N 103°12W 88 D7
Clute TX .... 29°1N 95°24W 99 H12
Clutier IA .... 42°4N 92°24W 73 C6
Clyattville GA ... 30°42N 83°19W 68 F3
Clyde KS .... 39°36N 97°24W 74 B6
Clyde NC .... 35°32N 82°55W 90 C3
Clyde OH .... 41°18N 82°59W 92 B4
Clyde TX .... 32°24N 99°30W 98 E8
Clyde → VT ..... 44°56N 72°13W 86 B2
Clyde Hill WA ... 47°37N 122°13W 118 C4
Clyde Park MT ... 45°53N 110°37W 83 E7
Clymer NY ...... 42°1N 79°37W 89 C1
Clymer PA ...... 40°40N 79°1W 95 D3
Clyo GA .... 32°29N 81°16W 68 D5
Coachella CA .... 33°41N 116°10W 65 K10
Coachella Canal
  CA .... 32°43N 114°57W 65 L12
Coahoma TX ..... 32°18N 101°18W 98 E6
Coahoma County ☆
  MS .... 34°12N 90°35W 81 B3
Coal City IL ..... 41°17N 88°17W 71 B5
Coal County ☆ OK 34°40N 96°15W 93 D7
Coal Grove OH ... 38°30N 82°39W 92 E4
Coal Hill AR ..... 35°26N 93°40W 63 C2
Coal Valley NV ... 37°57N 115°18W 85 D5
Coaldale CO ..... 38°22N 105°45W 66 D5
Coaldale OK ..... 38°2N 117°54W 85 D3
Coalgate OK ..... 34°32N 96°13W 93 D7
Coaling AL ...... 33°10N 87°20W 60 C3
Coalinga CA ..... 36°9N 120°21W 65 G6
Coalmont CO .... 40°34N 106°27W 66 B4
Coalmont TN .... 35°20N 85°42W 97 E7
Coalport PA ..... 40°45N 78°32W 95 D5
Coalville UT ..... 40°55N 111°24W 100 C3
Coamo Puerto Rico . 18°5N 66°22W 105 G16
Coarsegold CA ... 37°16N 119°42W 64 F7
Coast Ranges CA . 39°0N 123°0W 64 D3
Coast Ranges OR . 44°0N 123°40W 94 D2
Coatesville IN ... 39°41N 86°40W 72 D4
Coatesville PA ... 39°59N 75°50W 95 E7
Coats KS .... 37°31N 98°50W 74 D5
Coats NC .... 35°25N 78°40W 90 C7
Cobalt ID .... 45°6N 114°14W 70 D4
Cobb CA .... 38°49N 122°43W 64 E4
Cobb KY .... 36°59N 87°47W 96 D5
Cobb County ☆ GA 33°50N 84°40W 68 C2
Cobb Island MD .. 38°16N 76°51W 77 B4
Cobbs Creek Park
  PA .... 39°58N 75°15W 116 B4
Cobden IL .... 37°32N 89°15W 71 F4
Cobden MN ...... 44°17N 94°51W 80 F4
Cobleskill NY .... 42°41N 74°29W 89 C6
Cobre NV .... 41°7N 114°24W 85 A6
Coburg IA .... 40°55N 95°16W 73 E3
Coburg OR ...... 44°8N 123°4W 94 C2
Coburn Gore ME . 45°27N 70°48W 76 C3
Coburn Mt. ME .. 45°28N 70°6W 76 C3
Cochise AZ ...... 32°7N 109°55W 62 E6
Cochise County ☆
  AZ .... 32°0N 109°30W 62 F6
Cochiti Indian Reservation
  NM .... 35°38N 106°22W 88 B4
Cochituate MA ... 42°19N 71°21W 106 A1
Cochituate, L. MA . 42°16N 71°21W 106 B1
Cochran GA ...... 32°23N 83°21W 68 D3
Cochran TX ...... 36°51N 77°54W 102 E7
Cochran County ☆
  TX .... 33°37N 102°48W 98 D5
Cochrane AL ..... 33°4N 88°15W 60 C2
Cochrane WI ..... 44°14N 91°50W 103 D2
Cochranton PA ... 41°31N 80°3W 95 C2
Cochranville PA .. 39°55N 75°55W 95 E7
Cockeysville MD .. 39°29N 76°39W 77 A4
Cockrell Hill TX .. 32°44N 96°53W 109 E8
Coco FL .... 28°21N 80°44W 67 C8
Cocoa Beach FL .. 28°19N 80°37W 67 C8
Cocodrie LA ..... 29°15N 90°40W 75 E5
Cocodrie, Bayou →
  LA .... 31°11N 91°41W 75 C4
Cocolalla ID ..... 48°6N 116°37W 70 A2
Coconino County ☆
  AZ .... 36°0N 112°0W 62 B4
Coconino Nat. Forest
  AZ .... 34°45N 111°20W 62 C4
Coconino Plateau
  AZ .... 35°45N 112°40W 62 B3
Coconut Grove FL . 25°42N 80°15W 112 D2
Cocos I. Guam ... 13°14N 144°39E 105 b
Cod, C. MA ..... 42°5N 70°10W 78 B4
Codington County ☆
  SD .... 44°54N 97°9W 91 F8
Cody NE .... 42°56N 101°15W 84 B4
Cody WY .... 44°32N 109°3W 104 B3
Cody-Rouge MI .. 42°21N 83°13W 109 A1

Coeburn VA ...... 36°57N 82°28W 102 E2
Coeur d'Alene ID .. 47°41N 116°46W 70 B2
Coeur d'Alene → ID 47°45N 116°0W 70 B2
Coeur d'Alene Indian Reservation
  ID .... 47°10N 116°55W 70 B2
Coeur d'Alene L.
  U.S.A. ...... 47°32N 116°49W 70 B2
Coeur d'Alene Mts.
  U.S.A. ...... 47°45N 116°0W 70 B2
Coeur d'Alene Nat. Forest
  ID .... 47°55N 116°15W 70 B2
Coffee County ☆ AL 31°23N 85°56W 60 E5
Coffee County ☆ GA 31°30N 82°50W 68 E4
Coffee County ☆ TN. 35°29N 86°5W 96 E6
Coffeen IL .... 39°5N 89°24W 71 D4
Coffeeville AL ... 31°45N 88°5W 60 E2
Coffeeville MS ... 33°59N 89°41W 81 C4
Coffey MO ...... 40°7N 94°9W 82 A3
Coffey County ☆ KS 38°15N 95°45W 74 C8
Coffeyville KS.... 37°2N 95°37W 74 D8
Cogar OK .... 35°20N 98°8W 93 C5
Cogdell GA ...... 31°10N 82°43W 68 E4
Coggon IA .... 42°17N 91°32W 73 C7
Cogswell ND ..... 46°7N 97°47W 91 C9
Cohagen MT ..... 47°3N 106°37W 83 C11
Cohansey NJ ..... 39°21N 75°22W 87 C1
Cohasset MA ..... 42°14N 70°48W 78 B4
Cohasset MN ..... 47°16N 93°38W 80 C5
Cohocton → NY... 42°9N 77°6W 89 C3
Cohoes NY .... 42°46N 73°42W 78 B1
Cohutta GA ...... 34°58N 84°57W 68 B2
Coin IA .... 40°40N 95°14W 73 E3
Cokato MN ...... 45°5N 94°11W 80 E5
Coke County ☆ TX 31°54N 100°29W 98 F7
Coker AL .... 33°15N 87°41W 60 C3
Cokeville WY .... 42°5N 110°57W 104 D2
Colbert GA ...... 34°2N 83°13W 68 B3
Colbert OK ...... 33°51N 96°30W 93 E7
Colbert County ☆
  AL .... 34°44N 87°42W 60 B3
Colbourne MD ... 38°15N 75°26W 77 B5
Colburn ID ...... 48°24N 116°32W 70 A2
Colby KS .... 39°24N 101°3W 74 B2
Colby WA .... 47°31N 122°27W 118 E2
Colby WI .... 44°55N 90°19W 103 D3
Colchester CT .... 41°35N 72°20W 78 C2
Colchester IL .... 40°25N 90°48W 71 C3
Colchester VT .... 44°33N 73°9W 86 B1
Colcord OK ...... 36°16N 94°42W 93 A9
Cold Bay AK ..... 55°12N 162°42W 61 J7
Cold Mt. NC ..... 35°25N 82°51W 90 C6
Cold Spring KY .. 39°1N 84°26W 107 B2
Cold Spring MN .. 45°27N 94°26W 80 E4
Cold Spring NY .. 41°25N 73°57W 87 A3
Cold Springs Cr. →
  WY .... 44°32N 104°6W 104 B8
Coldspring TX.... 30°36N 95°8W 99 G12
Coldwater KS .... 37°16N 99°20W 74 D4
Coldwater MI .... 41°57N 85°0W 79 H6
Coldwater MS .... 34°41N 89°59W 81 B4
Coldwater OH .... 40°29N 84°38W 92 C2
Coldwater → MS .. 34°18N 90°12W 81 B3
Coldwater Cr. →
  OK .... 36°40N 101°10W 93 B2
Cole OK .... 35°8N 97°33W 93 C6
Cole Camp MO ... 38°28N 93°12W 82 C3
Cole County ☆ MO 38°30N 92°15W 82 C4
Colebrook NH .... 44°54N 71°30W 86 B3
Coleman FL ...... 28°48N 82°4W 67 C6
Coleman GA ...... 31°40N 84°54W 68 E2
Coleman MI ...... 43°46N 84°35W 79 F7
Coleman TX ...... 31°50N 99°26W 93 D7
Coleman WI ...... 45°4N 88°2W 103 C5
Coleman County ☆
  TX .... 31°50N 99°30W 99 F8
Colerain NC ...... 36°12N 76°46W 90 B9
Coleraine MN .... 47°17N 93°27W 80 C5
Coles County ☆ IL. 39°30N 88°15W 71 D5
Coles Point VA ... 38°9N 76°38W 77 B4
Colesburg IA ..... 42°38N 91°12W 73 C6
Colesville MD .... 39°5N 77°0W 77 A4
Coleville CA ..... 38°34N 119°30W 64 E7
Colfax CA .... 39°6N 120°57W 64 D6
Colfax IL .... 40°34N 88°37W 71 C5
Colfax IA .... 41°41N 93°14W 73 D5
Colfax LA .... 31°31N 92°42W 75 C3
Colfax ND .... 46°28N 96°53W 91 D9
Colfax WA .... 46°53N 117°22W 101 D8
Colfax WI .... 45°0N 91°44W 103 C2
Colfax County ☆
  NM .... 36°30N 104°30W 88 A6
Colfax County ☆ NE. 41°30N 97°0W 84 C8
Colgate ND ...... 47°15N 97°39W 91 C9
Collbran CO ..... 39°14N 107°58W 66 C3
College AK ...... 64°52N 147°49W 61 D11
College Corner OH. 39°34N 84°49W 92 D2
College Heights AR. 33°35N 91°48W 63 D5
College Park GA .. 33°39N 84°27W 106 C2
College Park MD .. 38°59N 76°55W 119 B4
College Place WA. 46°3N 118°23W 101 D7
College Point NY .. 40°47N 73°50W 114 B3
College Station TX. 30°37N 96°21W 99 G11
Collegedale TN ... 35°4N 85°3W 97 E7
Collegeville IN ... 40°55N 87°9W 72 C3
Collegeville PA .. 40°11N 75°27W 87 B2
Colleton County ☆ SC 33°0N 80°40W 90 F5
Colleyville TX.... 32°52N 97°9W 109 A3
Collier County ☆ FL. 26°0N 81°30W 67 E6
Collierville TN ... 35°3N 89°40W 96 E3
Collin County ☆ TX. 33°6N 96°40W 99 D11
Collingswood NJ. 39°55N 75°4W 116 B1
Collingsworth County ☆
  TX .... 35°0N 100°15W 98 C7
Collins AR .... 33°32N 91°34W 63 E4
Collins GA .... 32°11N 82°7W 68 D4
Collins IA .... 41°54N 93°18W 73 D5
Collins MS .... 31°39N 89°33W 81 E4
Collins MO ...... 37°54N 93°37W 82 D3
Collins → TN ..... 35°23N 85°34W 97 E7
Collinston LA .... 32°41N 91°52W 75 B4
Collinsville AL ... 34°16N 85°52W 60 B5
Collinsville CT ... 41°49N 72°55W 78 C2
Collinsville IL ... 38°40N 89°59W 71 D4
Collinsville MS ... 32°30N 88°51W 81 D5
Collinsville OK ... 36°22N 95°50W 93 B7
Collinsville TX ... 33°34N 96°55W 99 D11
Collinsville VA ... 36°43N 79°55W 102 E5
Collinwood TN ... 35°10N 87°44W 96 E5
Collison IL .... 40°13N 87°48W 71 C6
Collyer KS .... 39°2N 100°7W 74 B3
Colma CA .... 37°40N 122°27W 118 B2
Colman SD ...... 43°59N 96°49W 91 D9
Colmesneil TX ... 30°54N 94°25W 99 G13
Colo IA .... 42°1N 93°19W 73 D5
Coloma CA ...... 38°48N 120°53W 64 E6
Coloma MI ...... 42°11N 86°19W 79 G5
Coloma WI ...... 44°2N 89°31W 103 D4
Colome SD ...... 43°16N 99°43W 91 G6
Colon MI .... 41°57N 85°19W 79 H6
Colon NE .... 41°18N 96°37W 84 C9
Colona CO ...... 38°20N 107°47W 66 D3
Colona IL .... 41°29N 90°21W 71 B3
Colonia NJ ...... 40°34N 74°18W 114 C1
Colonial Beach VA. 38°15N 76°58W 77 B4
Colonial Heights
  TN .... 36°29N 82°30W 97 D10
Colonial Heights
  VA .... 37°15N 77°25W 102 D7

Colonial Nat. Historical Park ○
  VA .... 37°13N 76°31W 102 D8
Colonie NY ...... 42°43N 73°50W 89 C7
Colony KS .... 38°4N 95°22W 74 C8
Colony OK .... 35°23N 98°41W 93 C5
Colorado □ U.S.A.. 39°30N 105°30W 66 C5
Colorado →
  N. Amer. ..... 31°45N 114°40W 59 L6
Colorado → TX ... 28°36N 95°59W 99 J12
Colorado City AZ.. 36°59N 112°59W 62 A3
Colorado City TX.. 32°24N 100°52W 98 E7
Colorado County ☆
  TX .... 29°42N 96°33W 99 H11
Colorado Nat. Monument ○
  CO .... 39°4N 108°42W 66 C2
Colorado Plateau AZ. 37°0N 111°0W 62 A5
Colorado River Aqueduct
  CA .... 33°33N 117°23W 65 K9
Colorado River Indian Reservation
  AZ .... 33°55N 114°25W 62 D1
Colorado Springs
  CO .... 38°50N 104°49W 66 D6
Colorado Springs Peterson Field ✈
  (COS) CO .... 38°49N 104°43W 66 D6
Colquitt GA ...... 31°10N 84°44W 68 E2
Colquitt County ☆
  GA .... 31°15N 83°50W 68 E3
Colrain MA ...... 42°41N 72°42W 78 B2
Colstrip MT ...... 45°53N 106°38W 83 E11
Colt AR .... 35°8N 90°49W 63 C5
Colter Bay Village
  WY .... 43°54N 110°38W 104 C2
Colter Peak WY .. 44°18N 110°7W 104 B2
Colton CA .... 34°4N 117°20W 65 J9
Colton NY .... 44°33N 74°56W 89 A6
Colton SD .... 43°47N 96°56W 91 G9
Colton UT .... 39°51N 111°0W 100 D5
Colton WA .... 46°34N 117°8W 101 D8
Colts Neck NJ ... 40°17N 74°11W 87 B2
Columbia AL ..... 31°18N 85°7W 60 E5
Columbia CT ..... 41°42N 72°18W 78 C2
Columbia IL ..... 38°27N 90°12W 71 D3
Columbia KY ..... 37°6N 85°18W 97 C7
Columbia LA ..... 32°6N 92°5W 75 B3
Columbia MD ..... 39°14N 76°50W 77 A4
Columbia MS ..... 31°15N 89°50W 81 E4
Columbia MO ..... 38°57N 92°20W 82 C4
Columbia NC ..... 35°55N 76°15W 90 C9
Columbia NJ ..... 40°56N 75°6W 87 B1
Columbia PA ..... 40°2N 76°30W 95 D6
Columbia SC ..... 34°0N 81°2W 90 D4
Columbia SD ..... 45°37N 98°19W 91 E7
Columbia TN ..... 35°37N 87°2W 96 E5
Columbia →
  N. Amer. ..... 46°15N 124°5W 101 D1
Columbia, District of □
  U.S.A. .... 38°55N 77°0W 77 B4
Columbia Basin WA 46°45N 119°5W 101 D6
Columbia Bottom
  MO .... 38°48N 90°9W 117 A3
Columbia City IN . 41°10N 85°29W 72 B5
Columbia City OR. 45°53N 122°49W 94 B3
Columbia County ☆
  AR .... 33°16N 93°14W 63 E2
Columbia County ☆
  FL .... 30°15N 82°40W 67 A6
Columbia County ☆
  GA .... 33°30N 82°10W 68 C4
Columbia County ☆
  NY .... 42°10N 73°40W 89 C7
Columbia County ☆
  OR .... 45°55N 123°0W 94 B2
Columbia County ☆
  PA .... 41°10N 76°20W 95 C6
Columbia County ☆
  WA .... 46°15N 117°50W 101 D8
Columbia County ☆
  WI .... 43°30N 89°20W 103 E4
Columbia Edgewater
  OR .... 45°35N 122°48W 116 A2
Columbia Falls ME. 44°39N 67°44W 76 D6
Columbia Falls MT. 48°23N 114°11W 83 B3
Columbia Heights
  MN .... 45°2N 93°14W 113 A2
Columbia Park MN. 45°3N 93°15W 113 A2
Columbia Plateau
  U.S.A. .... 44°0N 117°30W 58 D5
Columbia River Gorge Nat. Scenic
  Area → WA... 45°42N 121°55W 101 E4
Columbia Road Res.
  SD .... 45°40N 98°18W 91 E7
Columbiana AL ... 33°11N 86°36W 60 C4
Columbiana OH ... 40°53N 80°42W 92 C6
Columbiana County ☆
  OH .... 40°46N 80°46W 92 C6
Columbiaville MI. 43°9N 83°25W 79 F8
Columbine CO ... 40°56N 106°59W 66 B4
Columbine Valley
  CO .... 39°36N 105°1W 109 C1
Columbus IN ..... 39°13N 85°55W 72 D5
Columbus KS ..... 37°10N 94°50W 74 D9
Columbus KY ..... 36°46N 89°6W 96 D3
Columbus MS ..... 33°30N 88°25W 81 C5
Columbus MT ..... 45°38N 109°15W 83 E8
Columbus NC ..... 35°15N 82°12W 90 C3
Columbus ND ..... 48°54N 102°47W 91 B3
Columbus NM ..... 31°50N 107°38W 88 F3
Columbus NE ..... 41°26N 97°22W 84 C8
Columbus OH ..... 39°58N 83°0W 92 D4
Columbus TX ..... 29°42N 96°33W 99 H11
Columbus WI ..... 43°21N 89°1W 103 E4
Columbus Air Force Base
  MS .... 33°38N 88°26W 81 C5
Columbus County ☆
  NC .... 34°15N 78°45W 90 D7
Columbus Grove OH 40°55N 84°4W 92 C2
Columbus Int. ✈ (CMH)
  OH .... 40°0N 82°53W 92 D4
Columbus Junction
  IA .... 41°17N 91°22W 73 D7
Columbus L. MS .. 33°31N 88°29W 81 C5
Columbus Salt Marsh
  NV .... 38°5N 118°5W 85 D2
Colusa CA .... 39°13N 122°1W 64 D4
Colusa County ☆
  CA .... 39°15N 122°15W 64 D4
Colville WA ...... 48°33N 117°54W 101 B8
Colville → AK ... 70°25N 150°30W 61 A10
Colville → WA ... 48°37N 118°5W 101 B7
Colville Indian Reservation
  WA .... 48°15N 119°0W 101 B7
Colville Nat. Forest
  WA .... 48°50N 117°15W 101 B8
Colvos Passage
  WA .... 47°29N 122°31W 118 D2
Colwell IA .... 43°9N 92°36W 73 B6
Colwich KS ...... 37°47N 97°32W 74 D6
Colwyn PA .... 39°54N 75°15W 116 B1
Comal County ☆ TX 29°53N 98°19W 99 H9
Comanche OK .... 34°22N 97°58W 93 E6
Comanche TX .... 31°54N 98°36W 98 F9
Comanche County ☆
  KS .... 37°15N 99°15W 74 D4
Comanche County ☆
  OK .... 34°40N 98°25W 93 D5
Comanche County ☆
  TX .... 31°55N 98°35W 98 F9
Comanche Nat. Grassland
  CO .... 37°20N 103°0W 66 E8
Combahee → SC .. 32°31N 80°31W 90 F5
Comer AL .... 32°2N 85°23W 60 D5
Comer GA .... 34°4N 83°8W 68 B3

Comerío
  Puerto Rico ... 18°12N 66°12W 105 G16
Comfort TX ...... 29°58N 98°55W 99 H9
Comfrey MN ..... 44°7N 94°54W 80 F4
Commack NY ..... 40°51N 73°18W 87 B3
Commerce CA .... 34°0N 118°9W 111 B4
Commerce GA .... 34°12N 83°28W 68 B3
Commerce MO ... 37°9N 89°27W 82 D7
Commerce OK .... 36°56N 94°53W 93 B9
Commerce TX .... 33°15N 95°54W 99 D12
Commerce City
  CO .... 39°48N 104°56W 109 B2
Como CO .... 39°19N 105°54W 66 C5
Como MS .... 34°31N 89°56W 81 B4
Como TX .... 33°3N 95°28W 99 D12
Como Park MN ... 44°58N 93°9W 113 B3
Comobabi Mts. AZ. 32°0N 111°45W 62 E4
Compass Lake FL .. 30°36N 85°24W 67 A3
Competition MO .. 37°29N 92°26W 82 D4
Comptche CA ..... 39°16N 123°35W 64 D3
Compton AR ...... 36°6N 93°18W 63 B2
Compton CA ...... 33°53N 118°13W 111 C3
Comstock MI ..... 46°40N 96°45W 80 D2
Comstock NE ..... 41°33N 99°14W 84 C6
Comstock TX ..... 29°41N 101°10W 98 H6
Comstock Park MI. 43°2N 85°40W 79 F6
Conanicut I. RI ... 41°32N 71°21W 78 C3
Conasauga → GA .. 34°33N 84°55W 68 B2
Concan TX .... 29°30N 99°42W 99 H8
Conception, Pt. CA. 34°27N 120°28W 65 J4
Conception Junction
  MO .... 40°16N 94°42W 82 A2
Conchas NM ..... 35°23N 104°18W 88 B6
Conchas Dam NM. 35°22N 104°11W 88 B6
Concho AZ .... 34°28N 109°36W 62 C6
Concho → TX .... 31°34N 99°43W 98 F8
Concho County ☆ TX 31°30N 99°51W 99 F8
Conconully WA ... 48°34N 119°45W 101 B6
Concord AR ...... 35°40N 91°51W 63 C4
Concord CA ...... 37°59N 122°2W 64 F4
Concord MA ..... 42°27N 71°20W 106 A1
Concord MI ...... 42°11N 84°38W 79 G7
Concord MO ..... 38°32N 90°23W 82 C6
Concord NC ...... 35°25N 80°35W 90 C5
Concord NH ...... 43°12N 71°32W 86 C3
Concord VT ...... 44°26N 71°53W 86 B3
Concordia KS .... 39°34N 97°40W 74 B6
Concordia MO ... 38°59N 93°34W 82 C3
Concordia Parish ☆
  LA .... 31°38N 91°33W 75 C4
Concrete WA ..... 48°32N 121°45W 101 B4
Conda ID .... 42°44N 111°32W 70 G7
Conde SD .... 45°9N 98°6W 91 E7
Condon MT ...... 47°34N 113°45W 83 C4
Condon OR ...... 45°14N 120°11W 94 B5
Conecuh → FL .... 30°58N 87°13W 67 A1
Conecuh County ☆
  AL .... 31°26N 86°57W 60 E4
Conecuh Nat. Forest
  AL .... 31°2N 86°45W 60 E4
Conejos CO ...... 37°5N 106°1W 66 E4
Conejos → CO ... 37°18N 105°44W 66 E5
Conejos County ☆
  CO .... 37°10N 106°0W 66 E4
Conesville IA .... 41°23N 91°21W 73 D7
Coney Island NY .. 40°34N 73°57W 114 C3
Confluence PA ... 39°49N 79°21W 77 A1
Confusion Range
  UT .... 39°20N 113°40W 100 D2
Congaree → SC ... 33°44N 80°38W 90 E5
Congaree Swamp Nat.
  Monument ○
  U.S.A. .... 33°47N 80°47W 90 E5
Conger MN ...... 43°37N 93°32W 80 G5
Congress AZ ..... 34°9N 112°51W 62 C3
Congress OH ..... 40°56N 82°3W 92 C4
Conifer CO ...... 39°31N 105°18W 66 C5
Conklin NY ...... 42°2N 75°49W 89 C5
Conlen TX .... 36°14N 102°15W 98 A5
Conley GA .... 33°40N 84°17W 106 C3
Conneaut OH ..... 41°57N 80°34W 92 B6
Conneaut Lake PA. 41°36N 80°18W 95 C2
Conneautville PA. 41°45N 80°22W 95 C2
Connecticut □ U.S.A. 41°30N 72°45W 78 C2
Connecticut → U.S.A. 41°16N 72°20W 78 C2
Connell WA ...... 46°40N 118°52W 101 D7
Connellsville PA .. 40°1N 79°35W 95 D3
Conner MT ...... 45°56N 114°7W 83 E3
Connersville IN .. 39°39N 85°8W 72 D5
Connerville OK ... 34°27N 96°38W 93 D7
Conover NC ...... 35°42N 81°13W 90 C4
Conowingo MD ... 39°40N 76°11W 77 A4
Conrad IA .... 42°14N 92°52W 73 C6
Conrad MT ...... 48°10N 111°57W 83 B6
Conrath WI ...... 45°22N 91°2W 103 C2
Conroe TX .... 30°19N 95°27W 99 G12
Conroe, L. TX ... 30°21N 95°37W 99 G12
Conshohocken PA. 40°4N 75°18W 116 A1
Constance KY .... 39°4N 84°38W 107 B1
Constantine MI .. 41°50N 85°40W 79 H6
Constantine, C. AK 58°24N 158°54W 61 G8
Constitution GA .. 33°42N 84°20W 106 B2
Contact NV ...... 41°46N 114°45W 85 A6
Continental AZ ... 31°51N 110°58W 62 E5
Continental OH ... 41°6N 84°16W 92 C2
Continental Divide
  NM .... 35°25N 108°19W 88 B2
Continental L. NV. 41°54N 118°43W 85 A2
Contoocook NH ... 43°13N 71°45W 86 C3
Contoocook → NH. 43°27N 71°35W 86 C3
Contra Costa County ☆
  CA .... 37°50N 121°50W 64 F5
Contreras NM .... 34°23N 106°49W 88 C4
Controller B. AK .. 60°7N 144°15W 61 F11
Convent LA ...... 30°1N 90°50W 75 D6
Convention Center
  CA .... 34°3N 118°16W 111 B3
Converse IN ..... 40°35N 85°52W 72 C5
Converse LA ..... 31°47N 93°42W 75 C2
Converse TX ..... 29°31N 98°18W 117 B4
Converse County ☆
  WY .... 43°0N 105°45W 104 D7
Convoy OH .... 40°55N 84°43W 92 C2
Conway AR ...... 35°5N 92°26W 63 C3
Conway FL ...... 28°30N 81°19W 115 B2
Conway KS ...... 38°22N 97°47W 74 C6
Conway MO ..... 37°30N 92°49W 82 D4
Conway NC ...... 36°26N 77°14W 90 B8
Conway NH ...... 43°59N 71°7W 86 C3
Conway SC ...... 33°51N 79°3W 90 E6
Conway TX ...... 35°13N 101°23W 98 B6
Conway, L. FL ... 28°28N 81°21W 115 B2
Conway County ☆
  AR .... 35°10N 92°38W 63 C3
Conway Springs KS 37°24N 97°39W 74 D6
Conyers GA ...... 33°40N 84°1W 68 C2
Cook MN .... 47°51N 92°41W 80 C6
Cook NE .... 40°30N 96°9W 84 D9
Cook County ☆ GA. 31°10N 83°30W 68 E3
Cook County ☆ IL. 41°50N 87°50W 72 B3
Cook County ☆ MN 47°50N 90°30W 80 C8
Cook Forest State Park ○
  PA .... 41°19N 79°9W 95 C3
Cook Inlet AK .... 60°0N 152°0W 61 G10
Cooke City MT ... 45°1N 109°56W 83 E8
Cooke County ☆ TX 33°38N 97°8W 99 D10
Cookes Peak NM . 32°32N 107°44W 88 E3
Cookeville TN .... 36°10N 85°30W 97 D7

Cooks MI .... 45°55N 86°29W 79 D5
Cooks Hammock FL 29°56N 83°17W 67 B5
Cooksville IL ..... 40°33N 88°43W 71 C5
Cool TX .... 31°26N 97°45W 99 F10
Cool Valley MO .. 38°43N 90°18W 117 A2
Cooleemee NC ... 35°49N 80°33W 90 C5
Coolidge AZ ..... 32°59N 111°31W 62 E4
Coolidge GA ..... 31°1N 83°52W 68 E3
Coolidge KS ..... 38°3N 102°1W 74 C1
Coolidge TX ..... 31°45N 96°39W 99 F11
Coolidge Dam AZ. 33°10N 110°32W 62 D5
Coolin ID .... 48°29N 116°51W 70 A2
Coolville OH ..... 39°13N 81°48W 92 D5
Coon Rapids IA .. 41°53N 94°41W 73 D4
Coon Rapids MN. 45°9N 93°19W 80 E5
Coon Valley WI .. 43°42N 91°1W 103 E2
Cooper TX .... 33°23N 95°42W 99 D12
Cooper → SC .... 32°50N 79°56W 90 F6
Cooper City FL ... 26°3N 80°16W 112 B1
Cooper County ☆
  MO .... 38°50N 92°49W 82 C4
Cooper L. TX .... 33°19N 95°42W 99 D12
Cooperdale OH ... 40°13N 82°3W 92 D4
Coopersburg PA .. 40°31N 75°23W 87 B1
Coopersville MI .. 43°4N 85°57W 79 F6
Coos Bay OR ..... 43°22N 124°13W 94 D1
Coos County ☆ NH 44°40N 71°15W 86 B3
Coos County ☆ OR 43°15N 124°0W 94 D1
Coosa → AL ..... 32°30N 86°16W 60 D4
Coosa County ☆ AL 32°56N 86°13W 60 D4
Coosada AL ...... 32°29N 86°20W 60 D4
Coosawattee → GA 34°35N 84°55W 68 B2
Copake NY .... 42°7N 73°33W 78 B1
Copalis Beach WA. 47°7N 124°10W 101 C1
Copan OK .... 36°54N 95°56W 93 B8
Copan L. OK ..... 36°58N 95°57W 93 B8
Copano B. TX .... 28°6N 97°0W 99 J10
Copco L. CA ..... 41°59N 122°20W 94 A4
Cope CO .... 39°40N 102°51W 66 C8
Copeland ID ..... 48°53N 116°31W 70 A2
Copeland KS ..... 37°33N 100°38W 74 D2
Copemish MI ..... 44°29N 85°55W 79 E6
Copenhagen NY .. 43°54N 75°41W 89 B5
Copiah County ☆ MS 31°52N 90°27W 81 E3
Coppell TX .... 32°57N 97°0W 109 A4
Copper → AK .... 60°18N 145°3W 61 F11
Copper Butte WA. 48°42N 118°28W 101 B7
Copper Center AK. 61°57N 145°18W 61 F11
Copper Cove TX . 31°8N 97°54W 99 F10
Copperhill TN .... 35°0N 84°15W 97 E8
Copperopolis CA. 37°59N 120°39W 64 E6
Copperton UT .... 40°33N 112°7W 100 C4
Copperville AZ ... 34°7N 109°16W 62 C6
Coquille OR ...... 43°11N 124°11W 94 D1
Coquille → OR ... 43°15N 124°12W 94 D1
Cora WY .... 42°56N 109°59W 104 D3
Cora MO .... 38°49N 90°11W 117 A2
Cora L. TN ...... 35°0N 90°7W 112 B1
Coral Gables FL .. 25°43N 80°16W 112 D2
Coral Hills MD ... 38°51N 76°55W 119 B4
Coral Springs FL. 26°16N 80°16W 112 B1
Coralville IA ..... 41°40N 91°35W 73 D7
Coralville L. IA ... 41°42N 91°33W 73 D7
Coram MT .... 48°25N 114°3W 83 B3
Coram NY .... 40°52N 73°0W 78 D2
Coraopolis PA ... 40°31N 80°10W 95 D2
Corbin KS .... 37°8N 97°33W 74 D6
Corbin KY .... 36°57N 84°6W 97 C8
Corbin MT ...... 46°23N 112°4W 83 D5
Corcoran CA ..... 36°6N 119°33W 65 G7
Cordele GA ...... 31°58N 83°47W 68 E3
Cordell OK ...... 35°17N 98°59W 93 C5
Cordell Hull L. TN. 36°17N 85°56W 97 D7
Cordova AL ...... 33°46N 87°11W 60 C3
Cordova AK ...... 60°33N 145°45W 61 F11
Cordova IL .... 41°41N 90°19W 71 B3
Cordova NE ...... 40°43N 97°21W 84 D8
Core Banks NC ... 34°45N 76°15W 90 D9
Corfu NY .... 42°58N 78°24W 89 C2
Corinna ME ...... 44°55N 69°16W 76 D4
Corinne UT ...... 41°33N 112°7W 100 B3
Corinth KY ...... 38°30N 84°34W 97 B8
Corinth MS ...... 34°56N 88°31W 81 B5
Corinth NY ...... 43°15N 73°49W 89 B7
Corinth VT ...... 44°2N 72°16W 86 C2
Corliss WI .... 42°43N 88°13W 103 F5
Cornelia GA ..... 34°31N 83°32W 68 B3
Cornelius NC ..... 35°29N 80°52W 90 C5
Cornelius OR ..... 45°31N 123°0W 94 B2
Cornell IL .... 40°59N 88°44W 71 C5
Cornell WI .... 45°10N 91°9W 103 C2
Cornersville TN .. 35°22N 86°50W 96 E6
Cornerville AR ... 33°51N 91°56W 63 E4
Corning AR ...... 36°25N 90°35W 63 B6
Corning CA ...... 39°56N 122°11W 64 D4
Corning IA ...... 40°59N 94°44W 73 E4
Corning KS ...... 39°40N 96°2W 74 B7
Corning NY ...... 42°9N 77°3W 89 C3
Corning OH ...... 39°36N 82°5W 92 D4
Cornish ME ...... 43°48N 70°48W 76 D3
Cornish NH ...... 43°29N 72°17W 86 C2
Cornlea NE ...... 41°41N 97°4W 84 C8
Cornucopia OR ... 45°0N 117°11W 94 B8
Cornudas TX ..... 31°47N 105°28W 98 F2
Cornville AZ ..... 34°43N 111°55W 62 C4
Cornwall CT ..... 41°50N 73°20W 78 C1
Cornwall NY ..... 41°27N 74°1W 78 D1
Cornwall VT ..... 43°57N 73°12W 86 C1
Cornwall Bridge CT 41°49N 73°22W 78 C1
Cornwell FL ...... 27°23N 81°6W 67 D7
Corona CA .... 33°53N 117°34W 65 K9
Corona SD .... 45°20N 96°46W 91 E9
Coronado CA ..... 32°41N 117°10W 117 B1
Coronado Nat. Forest
  AZ .... 32°10N 110°20W 62 E5
Coronado Nat. Monument ○
  AZ .... 31°20N 110°20W 62 F5
Corozal
  Puerto Rico ... 18°21N 66°19W 105 G16
Corpus Christi TX. 27°47N 97°24W 99 K10
Corpus Christi, L. TX 28°2N 97°52W 99 J10
Corpus Christi B.
  TX .... 27°47N 97°22W 99 K10
Corrales NM ..... 35°14N 106°36W 88 B4
Correctionville IA. 42°29N 95°47W 73 C3
Correll MN ...... 45°14N 96°10W 80 E2
Corrigan TX ..... 31°0N 94°52W 99 G13
Corriganville MD. 39°45N 78°47W 77 A2
Corry PA .... 41°55N 79°39W 95 C3
Corryton TN ..... 36°9N 83°47W 97 D9
Corsica SD ...... 43°25N 98°24W 91 G7
Corsicana TX .... 32°6N 96°28W 99 E11
Corson County ☆ SD 45°30N 101°0W 91 E4
Cortaro AZ ...... 32°21N 111°10W 62 E4
Cortez CO .... 37°21N 108°35W 66 E2
Cortez Mts. NV .. 40°20N 116°20W 85 B4
Cortland IL ...... 41°55N 88°41W 71 B5
Cortland NE ..... 40°30N 96°42W 84 D9
Cortland NY ..... 42°36N 76°11W 89 C4
Cortland OH ..... 41°20N 80°44W 92 B6
Cortland County ☆
  NY .... 42°35N 76°5W 89 C4
Corum OK .... 34°13N 98°5W 93 D6
Corunna MI ...... 42°59N 84°7W 79 G7
Corvallis MT ..... 46°19N 114°6W 83 D3
Corvallis OR ..... 44°34N 123°16W 94 C2
Corwin KS .... 37°11N 98°18W 74 D5
Corwith IA ...... 42°59N 93°57W 73 C5
Corydon IN ...... 38°13N 86°7W 72 E4
Corydon IA ...... 40°46N 93°19W 73 E5

Corydon KY ..... 37°44N 87°43W 96 C5
Coryell County ☆
  TX .... 31°26N 97°45W 99 F10
Coshocton OH ... 40°16N 81°51W 92 C5
Coshocton County ☆
  OH .... 40°16N 81°51W 92 C5
Cosmopolis WA .. 46°57N 123°46W 101 D2
Coso Junction CA. 36°3N 117°57W 65 G8
Coso Range CA ... 36°9N 117°44W 65 G9
Cossatot → AR ... 33°48N 94°9W 63 E1
Cost TX .... 29°22N 97°32W 99 H10
Costa Mesa CA ... 33°38N 117°55W 65 K9
Costilla NM ...... 36°59N 105°32W 88 A5
Costilla County ☆
  CO .... 37°15N 105°30W 66 E5
Cosumnes → CA .. 38°16N 121°26W 64 E5
Cotati CA .... 38°20N 122°42W 64 E4
Coteau des Prairies
  ND .... 45°20N 97°50W 91 E8
Coteau du Missouri
  ND .... 47°0N 100°0W 91 C5
Cotesfield NE .... 41°22N 98°38W 84 C7
Cottage Grove MN. 44°50N 92°57W 80 F6
Cottage Grove OR. 43°48N 123°3W 94 D2
Cottageville SC .. 32°56N 80°29W 90 F5
Cotton GA .... 31°10N 84°4W 68 E2
Cotton County ☆
  OK .... 34°15N 98°20W 93 D5
Cotton Plant AR .. 35°0N 91°15W 63 C4
Cotton Valley LA. 32°49N 93°25W 75 B2
Cottondale AL .... 33°11N 87°27W 60 C3
Cottondale FL .... 30°48N 85°23W 67 A3
Cottonport LA .... 30°59N 92°3W 75 D3
Cottonwood AL .. 31°3N 85°18W 60 E5
Cottonwood AZ .. 34°45N 112°1W 62 C3
Cottonwood CA .. 40°23N 122°17W 64 C4
Cottonwood ID .. 46°3N 116°21W 70 C2
Cottonwood MN .. 44°37N 95°40W 80 F3
Cottonwood SD .. 43°58N 101°54W 91 G4
Cottonwood → KS. 38°23N 96°3W 74 C7
Cottonwood → MN 44°17N 94°25W 80 F4
Cottonwood County ☆
  MN .... 44°0N 95°10W 80 F3
Cottonwood Cr. →
  NV .... 35°29N 114°41W 85 G6
Cottonwood Cr. →
  TX .... 35°29N 114°41W 98 C7
Cottonwood Falls KS 38°22N 96°32W 74 C7
Cottonwood Heights
  UT .... 40°37N 111°48W 117 C3
Cottonwood Mt. OR 44°10N 117°40W 94 C8
Cottonwood Mts.
  CA .... 36°55N 117°40W 65 G9
Cotuit MA .... 41°37N 70°26W 78 C4
Cotulla TX ...... 28°26N 99°14W 99 J8
Couba Island LA . 29°48N 90°12W 113 D1
Couderay WI ..... 45°48N 91°18W 103 C2
Coudersport PA .. 41°46N 78°1W 95 C4
Cougar WA ...... 46°3N 122°18W 101 D3
Cougar Res. OR .. 44°7N 122°14W 94 C3
Coulee City WA .. 47°37N 119°17W 101 C6
Coulee Dam WA .. 47°58N 118°58W 101 C7
Coulee Dam Nat. Recr. Area =
  Lake Roosevelt Nat. Recr.
  Area → WA... 48°5N 118°14W 101 B7
Coulterville CA ... 37°43N 120°12W 64 F6
Coulterville IL ... 38°11N 89°36W 71 D4
Coulwood NC .... 35°17N 80°56W 107 A1
Counce TN ...... 35°3N 88°16W 96 E4
Council AK ...... 64°53N 163°41W 61 D7
Council ID .... 44°44N 116°26W 70 E2
Council Bluffs IA. 41°16N 95°52W 73 D3
Council Grove KS. 38°40N 96°29W 74 C7
Council Grove Lake
  KS .... 38°41N 96°33W 74 C7
Council Hill OK .. 35°31N 95°42W 93 C8
Country Club Hills
  MO .... 38°43N 90°16W 117 A2
Country Homes WA 47°45N 117°24W 101 C8
Country Lake Estates
  NJ .... 39°55N 74°32W 87 C2
Countryside IL ... 41°47N 87°52W 108 C1
County Art Museum
  CA .... 34°4N 118°21W 111 B3
Coupeville WA ... 48°13N 122°41W 101 B3
Coupland TX ..... 30°28N 97°23W 99 G10
Courtenay ND .... 47°13N 98°34W 91 C7
Courtland AL ..... 34°40N 87°19W 60 B3
Courtland CA ..... 38°20N 121°34W 64 E5
Courtland KS ..... 39°47N 97°54W 74 B6
Courtland MN .... 44°16N 94°20W 80 F4
Courtland MS .... 34°14N 89°57W 81 B4
Courtland VA ..... 36°43N 77°4W 102 E7
Courtright Res. CA. 37°5N 118°58W 64 F8
Coushatta LA ..... 32°1N 93°21W 75 B2
Coushatta Indian Reservation
  LA .... 30°31N 92°47W 75 D3
Cove AR .... 34°26N 94°25W 63 D1
Cove OR .... 45°18N 117°49W 94 B8
Cove Fort UT .... 38°36N 112°35W 100 D3
Cove Point MD ... 38°23N 76°24W 77 B4
Covedale OH ..... 39°7N 84°36W 107 B1
Covelo CA .... 39°48N 123°15W 64 D3
Covert MI .... 42°18N 86°16W 79 G5
Coventry CT ..... 41°48N 72°22W 78 C2
Coventry RI ..... 41°41N 71°34W 78 C3
Coventry VT ..... 44°52N 72°16W 86 B2
Coverdale GA .... 31°38N 83°58W 68 E3
Covington GA .... 33°36N 83°51W 68 C3
Covington IN ..... 40°9N 87°24W 72 C2
Covington KY .... 39°5N 84°30W 107 B1
Covington LA ..... 30°29N 90°6W 75 D6
Covington OH .... 40°7N 84°21W 92 C2
Covington TN .... 35°34N 89°39W 96 E3
Covington VA .... 37°47N 79°59W 102 D4
Covington WA .... 47°20N 122°6W 118 D5
Covington County ☆
  AL .... 31°18N 86°29W 60 E4
Covington County ☆
  MS .... 31°39N 89°33W 81 E4
Cow Cr. → KS ... 37°59N 97°56W 74 D6
Cow Cr. → OR ... 42°55N 123°22W 94 D2
Cowan TN .... 35°10N 86°1W 96 E6
Coward SC ...... 33°58N 79°45W 90 E6
Cowarts AL ...... 31°12N 85°18W 60 E5
Cowden IL .... 39°15N 88°52W 71 D5
Cowdrey CO ..... 40°52N 106°19W 66 B4
Cowen WV .... 38°25N 80°34W 102 C4
Coweta OK ...... 35°57N 95°39W 93 C8
Coweta County ☆
  GA .... 33°20N 84°50W 68 C2
Cowgill MO ...... 39°34N 93°55W 82 B3
Cowiche WA ..... 46°39N 120°46W 101 D5
Cowley WY ...... 44°53N 108°28W 104 B4
Cowley County ☆ KS 37°15N 96°58W 74 D7
Cowlic AZ .... 31°59N 111°59W 62 F4
Cowlington OK ... 35°17N 94°54W 93 C9
Cowlitz → WA ... 46°6N 122°55W 101 D3
Cowpens SC ..... 35°1N 81°48W 90 C4
Cox City OK ..... 34°53N 97°44W 93 D6
Cox's Mills WV .. 39°3N 80°50W 102 B4
Coxsackie NY .... 42°21N 73°48W 89 C7
Coy AL .... 32°3N 87°23W 60 D3
Coyanosa Draw →
  TX .... 31°18N 103°6W 98 F4
Coyle OK .... 35°57N 97°14W 93 C6
Coyote NM ...... 36°10N 106°37W 88 A4

Coyote Canyon NM 35°46N 108°37W 88 B2
Coyote L. CA .... 35°4N 116°46W 65 H10
Coyote Res. CA .. 37°7N 121°33W 64 F5
Coyote Ridge CA. 37°25N 122°33W 118 A1
Coyote Wash → AZ 32°41N 114°8W 62 E1
Coyville KS ...... 37°41N 95°54W 74 D8
Cozad NE .... 40°52N 99°59W 84 D6
Crab Cr. → WA .. 47°1N 119°19W 101 C6
Crab Orchard KY. 37°28N 84°30W 97 C8
Crab Orchard NE. 40°20N 96°25W 84 D9
Crab Orchard TN. 35°55N 84°53W 97 E8
Crab Orchard L. IL 37°43N 89°9W 71 F4
Crab Orchard Nat. Wildlife
  Refuge → IL .. 37°42N 89°4W 71 F4
Crabtree OR ..... 44°38N 122°54W 94 C2
Crafton PA ...... 40°26N 80°3W 116 B2
Craig AK .... 55°29N 133°9W 61 J14
Craig CO .... 40°31N 107°33W 66 B3
Craig IA .... 42°54N 96°19W 73 C2
Craig MO .... 40°11N 95°22W 82 A1
Craig MT .... 47°5N 111°58W 83 C6
Craig NE .... 41°47N 96°22W 84 C9
Craig County ☆ OK 36°45N 95°10W 93 B8
Craig County ☆ VA 37°25N 80°5W 102 D4
Craig Pass WY ... 44°26N 110°43W 104 B2
Craighead County ☆
  AR .... 35°50N 90°42W 63 C5
Craigmont ID .... 46°15N 116°29W 70 C2
Craigsville VA .... 38°5N 79°23W 102 C5
Craigsville WV ... 38°20N 80°39W 102 C4
Cranberry L. NY .. 44°11N 74°50W 89 A6
Crandon WI ...... 45°34N 88°54W 103 C5
Crandon Park FL . 25°42N 80°9W 112 D2
Crane MO .... 36°54N 93°34W 82 D3
Crane OR .... 43°25N 118°35W 94 D7
Crane TX .... 31°24N 102°21W 98 F5
Crane County ☆ TX 31°24N 102°21W 98 F5
Crane Mt. OR ... 42°4N 120°13W 94 E5
Crane Naval Weapons Support
  Center IN .... 38°51N 86°50W 72 E4
Crane Prairie Res.
  OR .... 43°45N 121°47W 94 D4
Cranfills Gap TX . 31°46N 97°50W 99 F10
Cranford NJ ..... 40°40N 74°18W 87 B2
Cranston RI ...... 41°47N 71°26W 78 C3
Crapo MD .... 38°18N 76°9W 77 B4
Crary ND .... 48°4N 98°38W 91 B7
Crater L. OR ..... 42°56N 122°6W 94 E3
Crater Lake OR .. 42°54N 122°8W 94 E3
Crater Lake Nat. Park ○
  OR .... 42°55N 122°10W 94 E3
Crater of Diamonds State Park ○
  AR .... 34°2N 93°40W 63 D2
Craters of the Moon Nat.
  Monument ○ ID. 43°25N 113°30W 70 F5
Craven County ☆ NC 35°15N 77°10W 90 C8
Crawford CO ..... 38°42N 107°37W 66 D3
Crawford MS ..... 33°18N 88°37W 81 C5
Crawford NE ..... 42°41N 103°25W 84 B2
Crawford OK ..... 35°50N 99°48W 93 C4
Crawford TX ..... 31°32N 97°27W 99 F10
Crawford County ☆
  AR .... 35°20N 94°18W 63 C1
Crawford County ☆
  GA .... 32°50N 84°0W 68 D3
Crawford County ☆
  IL .... 39°0N 87°45W 71 D6
Crawford County ☆
  IN .... 38°15N 86°25W 72 E4
Crawford County ☆
  IA .... 42°0N 95°20W 73 C3
Crawford County ☆
  KS .... 37°30N 94°45W 74 D9
Crawford County ☆
  MI .... 44°45N 84°40W 79 E7
Crawford County ☆
  MO .... 38°0N 91°20W 82 D5
Crawford County ☆
  OH .... 40°48N 82°59W 92 C4
Crawford County ☆
  PA .... 41°40N 80°10W 95 C2
Crawford County ☆
  WI .... 43°15N 90°50W 103 E3
Crawford Notch State Park ○
  NH .... 44°11N 71°24W 86 B3
Crawfordsville AR. 35°14N 90°20W 63 C5
Crawfordsville IN. 40°2N 86°54W 72 C4
Crawfordsville IA. 41°12N 91°32W 73 D7
Crawfordville FL . 30°11N 84°23W 67 A4
Crawfordville GA . 33°33N 82°54W 68 C4
Crazy Horse Memorial
  SD .... 43°49N 103°35W 91 G2
Crazy Mts. MT ... 46°12N 110°20W 83 D7
Crazy Woman Cr. →
  WY .... 44°29N 106°8W 104 B6
Creagerstown MD. 39°37N 77°22W 77 A3
Creal Springs IL .. 37°37N 88°50W 71 F5
Creede CO .... 37°51N 106°56W 66 E4
Creedmoor NC ... 36°7N 78°41W 90 B7
Creek County ☆ OK 35°58N 96°25W 93 C7
Creighton MO ... 38°30N 94°4W 82 C2
Creighton NE .... 42°28N 97°54W 84 B8
Crellin MD .... 39°25N 79°29W 77 A1
Crenshaw MS ..... 34°30N 90°12W 81 B3
Crenshaw County ☆
  AL .... 31°43N 86°16W 60 E4
Creole LA .... 29°49N 93°7W 75 E2
Cresaptown MD .. 39°36N 78°50W 77 A2
Cresbard SD ..... 45°10N 98°57W 91 E7
Crescent OK ..... 35°57N 97°36W 93 C6
Crescent OR ..... 43°28N 121°42W 94 D4
Crescent, L. FL ... 28°30N 81°33W 115 A1
Crescent, L. WA .. 48°4N 123°49W 101 B2
Crescent Beach FL 29°46N 81°15W 67 B7
Crescent City CA . 41°45N 124°12W 64 B2
Crescent City FL . 29°26N 81°31W 67 B7
Crescent Junction
  UT .... 38°57N 109°49W 100 E6
Crescent L. FL ... 29°26N 81°31W 67 B7
Crescent Lake Nat. Wildlife
  Refuge → NE . 41°45N 102°27W 84 C3
Crescent Springs KY 39°3N 84°34W 107 B1
Cresco IA .... 43°23N 92°7W 73 B6
Cresskill NJ ...... 40°56N 73°57W 114 A3
Cresson PA ...... 40°28N 78°36W 95 D4
Cresson TX ...... 32°32N 97°37W 99 E10
Crested Butte CO. 38°52N 106°59W 66 D4
Crestline CA ..... 34°14N 117°17W 65 J9
Creston IA .... 41°4N 94°22W 73 D4
Creston NE ...... 41°42N 97°22W 84 C8
Creston WA ...... 47°46N 118°31W 101 C7
Creston WY ...... 41°42N 107°45W 104 E5
Crestview FL ..... 30°46N 86°34W 67 A2
Crestview KY ..... 39°3N 84°35W 107 B2
Crestview Hills KY. 39°1N 84°35W 107 B1
Crestwood IL ..... 41°39N 87°45W 108 C2
Crestwood Village
  NJ .... 39°56N 74°22W 87 C2
Creswell NC ...... 35°53N 76°23W 90 C9
Creswell OR ...... 43°55N 123°1W 94 D2
Crete IL .... 41°27N 87°38W 71 B6
Crete NE .... 40°38N 96°58W 84 D8
Creve Coeur IL ... 40°38N 89°36W 71 C4
Cricket NC .... 36°9N 81°11W 90 B4
Cricket Mts. UT .. 39°0N 112°58W 100 D3
Crimora VA ...... 38°9N 78°51W 102 C6
Criner OK .... 34°58N 97°34W 93 D6

Cripple Creek CO . 38°45N 105°11W 66 D5
Crisfield MD . 37°59N 75°51W 77 C5
Crisp County ☆ GA . 31°50N 83°50W 68 E3
Crisp Pt. MI . 46°45N 85°16W 79 C6
Crittenden KY . 38°47N 84°36W 97 B8
Crittenden County ☆
AR . 35°14N 90°20W 63 C5
Crittenden County ☆
KY . 37°20N 88°5W 96 C4
Crivitz WI . 45°14N 88°1W 103 C6
Croatan Nat. Forest
NC . 34°50N 77°5W 90 D8
Crocheron MD . 38°15N 76°3W 77 B4
Crocker MO . 37°57N 92°16W 82 D4
Crockett TX . 31°19N 95°27W 99 F12
Crockett County ☆
TN . 35°49N 89°14W 96 E3
Crockett County ☆
TX . 30°45N 101°30W 98 G6
Crofton KY . 37°3N 87°29W 96 C5
Crofton MD . 39°1N 76°42W 77 A4
Crofton NE . 42°44N 97°30W 84 B8
Croghan NY . 43°54N 75°24W 89 B5
Cromwell AL . 32°14N 88°17W 60 D2
Cromwell CT . 41°36N 72°39W 78 C2
Cromwell MN . 46°41N 92°53W 80 D6
Cromwell OK . 35°22N 96°29W 93 C7
Crook CO . 40°52N 102°48W 66 B8
Crook County ☆
OR . 44°10N 120°20W 94 C5
Crook County ☆
WY . 44°44N 104°30W 104 B8
Crooked ➤ OR . 44°32N 121°16W 94 C4
Crooked I. FL . 29°59N 85°31W 67 B2
Crooked L. FL . 27°48N 81°35W 67 D7
Crooked River Nat. Grassland
OR . 44°33N 121°7W 94 C4
Crooks SD . 43°40N 96°37W 91 G9
Crookston MN . 47°47N 96°37W 80 C2
Crookston NE . 42°56N 100°45W 84 B5
Crooksville OH . 39°46N 82°6W 92 D4
Croom MD . 38°45N 76°46W 77 B4
Cropsey IL . 40°37N 88°29W 71 C5
Crosby MN . 46°29N 93°58W 80 D5
Crosby MS . 31°17N 91°4W 81 E2
Crosby ND . 48°55N 103°18W 91 B2
Crosby TX . 29°55N 95°4W 99 H12
Crosby, Mt. WY . 43°52N 109°20W 104 C3
Crosby County ☆
TX . 33°40N 101°14W 98 D6
Crosbyton TX . 33°40N 101°14W 98 D6
Cross Anchor SC . 34°38N 81°51W 90 D4
Cross City FL . 29°38N 83°7W 67 B5
Cross County ☆ AR . 35°14N 90°47W 63 C5
Cross Creeks Nat. Wildlife
Refuge ➤ TN . 36°26N 87°42W 96 D5
Cross Fork PA . 41°29N 77°49W 95 C5
Cross Hill SC . 34°18N 81°59W 90 D4
Cross L. ME . 47°7N 68°20W 76 A5
Cross Lake MN . 46°40N 94°7W 80 D4
Cross Plains TN . 36°33N 86°42W 96 D6
Cross Plains TX . 32°8N 99°11W 99 E8
Cross Sound AK . 58°0N 135°0W 61 C4
Cross Timbers MO . 38°1N 93°14W 82 C3
Cross Village MI . 45°39N 85°2W 79 D6
Crossett AR . 33°8N 91°58W 63 E4
Crossroads NM . 33°31N 103°20W 98 D7
Crossville AL . 34°17N 86°0W 60 B5
Crossville IL . 38°10N 88°4W 71 E5
Crossville TN . 35°57N 85°2W 97 E7
Croswell MI . 43°16N 82°37W 79 F9
Crotched Mt. NH . 42°59N 71°52W 86 C3
Crothersville IN . 38°48N 85°50W 72 E5
Croton-on-Hudson
NY . 41°12N 73°55W 87 A3
Crouch ID . 44°7N 115°58W 70 E3
Crow Agency MT . 45°36N 107°28W 83 E10
Crow Cr. ➤ CO . 40°23N 104°29W 66 B6
Crow Creek Indian Reservation
SD . 44°3N 99°25W 91 F6
Crow Indian Reservation
MT . 45°25N 108°0W 83 E10
Crow Wing ➤ MN . 46°19N 94°0W 80 D4
Crow Wing County ☆
MN . 46°30N 94°0W 80 D4
Crowder MS . 34°11N 90°8W 81 B3
Crowder OK . 35°7N 95°40W 93 C8
Crowell TX . 33°59N 99°43W 99 D8
Crowheart WY . 43°19N 109°12W 104 C3
Crowley CO . 38°12N 103°51W 66 D7
Crowley LA . 30°13N 92°22W 75 D3
Crowley TX . 32°34N 97°21W 109 C1
Crowley, L. CA . 37°35N 118°42W 64 F8
Crowley County ☆
CO . 38°15N 103°45W 66 D7
Crowley Ridge AR . 35°45N 90°45W 63 C5
Crown City OH . 38°36N 82°17W 92 E4
Crown Point IN . 41°25N 87°22W 72 B3
Crown Point NY . 43°57N 73°26W 86 C1
Crownpoint NM . 35°41N 108°9W 98 B2
Crows Nest IN . 39°51N 86°10W 110 A2
Crows Nest Pk. SD . 44°3N 103°58W 91 E2
Croydon Flat NH . 43°25N 72°12W 86 C2
Crozet VA . 38°4N 78°42W 102 D6
Cruger MS . 33°19N 90°14W 81 C3
Crum WV . 37°54N 82°27W 102 D2
Crump L. OR . 42°17N 119°50W 94 E6
Crumpton MD . 39°14N 75°55W 77 A5
Cruz Bay
U.S. Virgin Is. . 18°20N 64°48W 105 G18
Crystal MN . 45°2N 93°21W 113 A1
Crystal ND . 48°36N 97°40W 91 B8
Crystal B. FL . 28°50N 82°45W 67 C6
Crystal Bay NV . 39°15N 120°0W 85 C1
Crystal City MO . 38°13N 90°23W 82 C6
Crystal City TX . 28°41N 99°50W 99 J8
Crystal Falls MI . 46°5N 88°20W 79 C3
Crystal Hill VA . 36°51N 78°55W 102 E6
Crystal L. MI . 44°40N 86°10W 79 E5
Crystal Lake FL . 30°26N 85°42W 67 A1
Crystal Lake IL . 42°14N 88°19W 71 A5
Crystal Lake IA . 43°13N 93°47W 73 B5
Crystal River FL . 28°54N 82°35W 67 C6
Crystal Springs MS . 31°59N 90°21W 81 D3
Cub Hill MD . 39°24N 76°30W 107 A2
Cuba AL . 32°26N 88°23W 60 D2
Cuba IL . 40°30N 90°12W 71 C3
Cuba KS . 39°48N 97°27W 74 B6
Cuba MO . 38°4N 91°24W 82 C5
Cuba NM . 36°1N 107°4W 98 A3
Cuba NY . 42°13N 78°17W 89 C2
Cuba City WI . 42°36N 90°26W 103 F3
Cubero NM . 35°5N 107°31W 98 B3
Cucharas ➤ CO . 37°55N 104°32W 66 E6
Cuchillo NM . 33°14N 107°22W 98 C3
Cuckoo VA . 37°57N 77°54W 102 D7
Cudahy CA . 33°57N 118°11W 111 C3
Cudahy WI . 42°57N 87°51W 112 C2
Cuddeback L. CA . 35°18N 117°29W 65 H9
Cuero TX . 29°6N 97°17W 99 H10
Cuervo NM . 35°2N 104°25W 98 B6
Cuivre ➤ MO . 38°56N 90°41W 82 C6
Cuivre River State Park
MO . 39°2N 90°56W 82 B6
Culberson County ☆
TX . 31°30N 104°30W 98 F3
Culbertson MT . 48°9N 104°31W 83 B13
Culbertson NE . 40°14N 100°50W 84 D5
Culdesac ID . 46°23N 116°40W 70 C2

Culebra
Puerto Rico . 18°19N 65°18W 105 G17
Cullen LA . 32°58N 93°27W 75 B2
Cullison KS . 37°38N 98°54W 74 D5
Cullman AL . 34°11N 86°51W 60 B4
Cullman County ☆
AL . 34°11N 86°51W 60 B4
Culloden GA . 32°52N 84°6W 68 D2
Cullom IL . 40°53N 88°16W 71 C5
Cullomburg AL . 31°43N 88°18W 60 D2
Cullowhee NC . 35°19N 83°11W 90 D2
Culmore VA . 38°51N 77°8W 119 B3
Culp Creek OR . 43°42N 122°50W 94 D3
Culpeper VA . 38°30N 78°0W 102 C6
Culpeper County ☆
VA . 38°28N 78°0W 102 C6
Culver IN . 41°13N 86°25W 72 B4
Culver KS . 38°58N 97°46W 74 C6
Culver OR . 44°32N 121°13W 94 C4
Culver City CA . 34°1N 118°24W 111 B2
Culverton GA . 33°19N 82°54W 68 C4
Cumberland KY . 36°59N 82°59W 97 D10
Cumberland MD . 39°39N 78°46W 77 A2
Cumberland VA . 37°30N 78°15W 102 D6
Cumberland County ☆
IL . 39°15N 88°15W 71 D5
Cumberland County ☆
KY . 36°45N 85°25W 97 D7
Cumberland County ☆
ME . 43°50N 70°30W 76 E3
Cumberland County ☆
NC . 35°0N 78°45W 90 D7
Cumberland County ☆
NJ . 39°20N 75°10W 87 C1
Cumberland County ☆
PA . 40°5N 77°10W 95 D5
Cumberland County ☆
TN . 36°0N 85°0W 97 D7
Cumberland County ☆
VA . 37°30N 78°15W 102 D6
Cumberland Falls State Park
KY . 36°50N 84°20W 97 D8
Cumberland Gap KY . 36°36N 83°41W 97 D9
Cumberland Gap Nat. Historical
Park ➤ KY . 36°36N 83°40W 97 D9
Cumberland Hill RI . 41°59N 71°28W 78 C3
Cumberland I. GA . 30°50N 81°25W 68 F5
Cumberland Island Nat.
Seashore ➤ GA . 30°12N 81°24W 68 F5
Cumberland Plateau
U.S.A. . 36°0N 85°0W 97 E7
Cumberland Pt. MI . 47°51N 89°14W 79 B2
Cumby TX . 33°8N 95°50W 99 D12
Cuming County ☆
NE . 41°50N 96°40W 84 C9
Cumming GA . 34°12N 84°8W 68 B2
Cunningham KS . 37°39N 98°26W 74 D5
Cupertino CA . 37°19N 122°2W 64 F4
Cuprum ID . 45°5N 116°41W 70 D2
Curecanti Nat. Recr. Area
CO . 38°24N 107°25W 66 D3
Curlew IA . 42°59N 94°44W 73 C4
Curlew WA . 48°53N 118°36W 101 B7
Curlew Nat. Grasslands
ID . 42°13N 112°45W 70 G6
Curran MI . 44°43N 83°48W 79 E8
Currant NV . 38°44N 115°28W 85 D5
Currant Mt. NV . 38°55N 115°23W 85 D5
Current ➤ AR . 36°15N 90°55W 63 B5
Currie MN . 44°3N 95°40W 80 F3
Currie NV . 40°16N 114°45W 85 B6
Currituck NC . 36°27N 76°1W 90 B9
Currituck County ☆
NC . 36°20N 76°0W 90 B10
Currituck Sd. NC . 36°20N 75°52W 90 B10
Curry County ☆
NM . 34°30N 103°15W 88 C7
Curry County ☆ OR . 42°30N 124°20W 94 E1
Curryville MO . 39°21N 91°21W 82 B5
Curtin OR . 43°43N 123°12W 94 D2
Curtis AR . 34°0N 93°2W 63 D3
Curtis NE . 40°38N 100°31W 84 D5
Curtis Bay MD . 39°13N 76°33W 107 B2
Curtis Creek ➤ MD 39°13N 76°33W 107 B2
Curwensville PA . 40°58N 78°32W 95 D4
Cushing IA . 42°28N 95°41W 73 C3
Cushing NE . 41°19N 98°22W 84 C7
Cushing OK . 35°59N 96°46W 93 C7
Cushman AR . 35°53N 91°45W 63 C4
Cushman OR . 43°59N 124°3W 94 D1
Cushman, L. WA . 47°25N 123°13W 101 C2
Cusick WA . 48°20N 117°18W 101 B8
Cusseta GA . 32°18N 84°47W 68 D2
Custer MT . 46°8N 107°33W 83 D10
Custer SD . 43°46N 103°36W 91 G2
Custer WA . 48°55N 122°38W 101 B3
Custer City OK . 35°40N 98°53W 93 C5
Custer County ☆
CO . 38°10N 105°20W 66 D5
Custer County ☆ ID . 44°0N 114°0W 70 E4
Custer County ☆
MT . 46°23N 105°30W 83 D12
Custer County ☆ NE . 41°30N 99°40W 84 C6
Custer County ☆ OK . 35°40N 99°0W 93 C5
Custer Nat. Forest
MT . 45°15N 109°50W 83 E8
Custer Nat. Forest
SD . 45°30N 103°15W 91 E2
Custer State Park ➤
SD . 43°42N 103°22W 91 G2
Cut Bank MT . 48°38N 112°20W 83 B5
Cut Bank Cr. ➤
ND . 48°10N 100°45W 91 B5
Cut Bank Cr. ➤
MT . 48°29N 112°14W 83 B5
Cut Off LA . 29°33N 90°20W 75 E5
Cuthbert GA . 31°46N 84°48W 68 E2
Cutler CA . 36°31N 119°17W 65 G7
Cutler IL . 38°2N 89°34W 71 E4
Cutler ME . 44°40N 67°12W 76 D6
Cutler Park MA . 42°17N 71°12W 106 B2
Cutler Ridge FL . 25°35N 80°20W 67 F8
Cutlerville MI . 42°50N 85°40W 79 G6
Cuttyhunk I. MA . 41°25N 70°56W 78 D4
Cuyahoga ➤ OH . 41°30N 81°41W 107 B1
Cuyahoga County ☆
OH . 41°23N 81°43W 92 B5
Cuyahoga Falls OH . 41°8N 81°29W 92 B5
Cuyahoga Heights
OH . 41°26N 81°39W 107 B2
Cuyahoga Valley Nat. Park ➤
U.S.A. . 41°14N 81°33W 107 B2
Cuyama ➤ CA . 34°58N 120°18W 65 J6
Cuyama State Park ➤
CA . 32°56N 116°33W 65 L10
Cuyapaipe Indian Reservation
CA . 32°51N 116°23W 65 L10
Cuyuna Range MN . 46°29N 93°30W 80 D5
Cygnet OH . 41°14N 83°39W 92 B3
Cylinder IA . 43°5N 94°33W 73 B4
Cynthiana IN . 38°11N 87°43W 72 E3
Cynthiana KY . 38°23N 84°18W 97 B8

Cypress CA . 33°49N 118°2W 111 C3
Cypress IL . 37°22N 89°1W 71 F4
Cypress Creek Nat. Wildlife
Refuge ➤ IL . 37°18N 89°8W 71 F4
Cyril OK . 34°54N 98°12W 93 D5
Cyrus MN . 45°37N 95°44W 80 E3

D

Dacoma OK . 36°40N 98°34W 93 B5
Dacono CO . 40°5N 104°56W 66 B6
Dacula GA . 33°59N 83°54W 68 C3
Dade City FL . 28°22N 82°11W 67 C6
Dade County ☆ GA . 34°53N 85°31W 68 B1
Dade County ☆ MO . 37°25N 93°50W 82 D3
Dadeville AL . 32°50N 85°46W 60 D5
Dadeville MO . 37°29N 93°41W 82 D3
Dafter MI . 46°22N 84°26W 79 C7
Dagget MD . 45°28N 87°36W 79 D4
Daggett County ☆
UT . 40°55N 109°30W 100 C6
Dagsboro DE . 38°33N 75°15W 77 B5
Dahlgren IL . 38°12N 88°41W 71 E5
Dahlgren VA . 38°20N 77°3W 77 B3
Dahlonega GA . 34°32N 83°59W 68 B3
Dahlonega Plat. GA . 34°30N 84°0W 68 B3
Dailey WV . 38°48N 79°54W 102 C5
Daingerfield TX . 33°2N 94°44W 99 D13
Dairy OR . 42°14N 121°31W 94 E4
Daisetta TX . 30°7N 94°39W 99 G13
Daisy AR . 34°14N 93°45W 63 D2
Daisy GA . 32°8N 81°51W 68 D5
Dakota MN . 43°55N 91°22W 80 G7
Dakota City IA . 42°43N 94°12W 73 C4
Dakota City NE . 42°25N 96°25W 84 B9
Dakota County ☆ MN . 44°45N 93°0W 80 F5
Dakota County ☆
NE . 42°30N 96°30W 84 B9
Dalark AR . 34°2N 92°53W 63 D3
Dalcour LA . 29°48N 89°59W 113 F3
Dale IN . 38°10N 86°59W 72 E4
Dale OK . 35°24N 97°3W 93 C6
Dale VA . 38°38N 77°19W 77 B3
Dale County ☆ AL . 31°28N 85°39W 60 E5
Dale Hollow L. TN . 36°35N 85°27W 97 D7
Daleville AL . 31°19N 85°43W 60 E5
Daleville IN . 40°7N 85°33W 72 D5
Daleville MS . 32°34N 88°41W 81 D5
Dalhart TX . 36°4N 102°31W 98 A5
Dalkeith FL . 30°0N 85°9W 67 A3
Dallam County ☆
TX . 36°15N 102°30W 98 A5
Dallas NC . 35°19N 81°11W 90 D4
Dallas OR . 44°55N 123°19W 94 C2
Dallas PA . 41°20N 75°58W 95 C7
Dallas SD . 43°14N 99°31W 91 G6
Dallas TX . 32°47N 96°48W 109 B4
Dallas WV . 45°16N 96°5W 91 G9
Dallas Center IA . 41°41N 93°58W 73 D4
Dallas City IL . 40°38N 91°10W 71 C2
Dallas County ☆ AL . 32°25N 87°1W 60 D3
Dallas County ☆ AR . 33°58N 92°38W 63 E3
Dallas County ☆ IA . 41°40N 94°0W 73 D4
Dallas County ☆ MO . 37°40N 93°0W 82 D3
Dallas County ☆ TX 32°50N 96°50W 99 E11
Dallas-Fort Worth Int. ✈ (DFW)
TX . 32°53N 97°2W 109 A3
Dallastown PA . 39°54N 76°38W 77 A4
Dalles, The OR . 45°36N 121°10W 94 B4
Dalles Dam, The
WA . 45°37N 121°8W 101 E4
Dalton GA . 34°46N 84°58W 68 B2
Dalton MA . 42°28N 73°11W 78 B1
Dalton MN . 46°10N 95°55W 80 D3
Dalton NE . 41°25N 102°58W 84 C3
Dalton OH . 40°48N 81°42W 92 C5
Dalton PA . 41°32N 75°44W 87 A1
Dalton Gardens ID . 47°43N 116°46W 70 B2
Dalworthington Gardens
TX . 32°43N 97°9W 109 A3
Daly City CA . 37°42N 122°27W 118 B2
Damar KS . 39°19N 99°35W 74 B4
Damascus AR . 35°22N 92°25W 63 C3
Damascus GA . 31°18N 84°43W 68 E2
Damascus MD . 39°17N 77°12W 77 A3
Damascus VA . 36°38N 81°47W 102 E3
Dameron MD . 38°11N 76°22W 77 B4
Dan ➤ VA . 36°32N 78°50W 102 E6
Dan Ryan Woods
IL . 41°44N 87°40W 108 C2
Dana IN . 39°48N 87°30W 72 D3
Dana Point CA . 33°28N 117°42W 65 K9
Danbury CT . 41°24N 73°28W 78 C2
Danbury NC . 36°25N 80°12W 90 C4
Danbury NH . 43°32N 71°52W 86 C3
Danbury NE . 40°3N 100°25W 84 D5
Danbury TX . 29°14N 95°21W 99 H12
Danbury WI . 46°0N 92°22W 80 D6
Danby VT . 43°20N 72°59W 86 C2
Dane County ☆ WI . 43°0N 89°29W 103 E4
Danforth IL . 40°49N 87°59W 71 C6
Danforth ME . 45°40N 67°52W 76 C6
Danforth Hills CO . 40°15N 108°0W 66 B2
Dania Beach FL . 26°3N 80°8W 112 B3
Daniel WY . 42°52N 110°4W 104 D2
Daniel Boone Nat. Forest
KY . 38°30N 84°0W 97 C8
Daniels County ☆
MT . 48°40N 105°20W 83 B12
Daniels Pass UT . 40°18N 111°10W 100 C4
Danielson CT . 41°48N 71°53W 78 C3
Danielsville GA . 34°8N 83°13W 68 B3
Danish West Indies = Virgin Is.
(U.S.) ☒
W. Indies . 18°20N 65°0W 105 G18
Dannebrog NE . 41°7N 98°33W 84 C7
Dannemora NY . 44°43N 73°44W 89 A7
Dansville NY . 42°34N 77°42W 89 C3
Dante SD . 43°2N 98°11W 91 G7
Dante VA . 36°59N 82°18W 102 E2
Danvers IL . 40°32N 89°11W 71 C4
Danvers MA . 42°34N 70°56W 78 B4
Danvers MN . 45°17N 95°45W 80 E3
Danville AR . 35°3N 93°24W 63 D2
Danville CA . 37°49N 122°0W 64 F5
Danville GA . 32°37N 83°15W 68 D3
Danville IL . 40°8N 87°37W 71 C6
Danville IN . 39°46N 86°32W 72 D4
Danville KS . 37°17N 97°54W 74 D6
Danville KY . 37°39N 84°46W 97 C8
Danville PA . 40°58N 76°37W 95 D6
Danville VA . 36°36N 79°23W 102 E5
Danville VT . 44°25N 72°8W 86 B3
Danville WA . 48°59N 118°30W 101 B7

Dardanelle AR . 35°13N 93°9W 63 C2
Dardanelle CA . 38°20N 119°50W 64 E7
Dardanelle, L. AR . 35°14N 93°10W 63 C2
Dare County ☆ NC . 35°45N 75°40W 90 C10
Darfur MN . 44°3N 94°50W 80 F4
Darien CT . 41°5N 73°28W 78 C1
Darien GA . 31°23N 81°26W 68 E5
Darien WI . 42°36N 88°42W 103 F5
Darke County ☆ OH . 40°6N 84°38W 92 C2
Darling MS . 34°22N 90°16W 81 B3
Darling, L. ND . 48°27N 101°35W 91 B4
Darlington FL . 30°57N 86°3W 67 A2
Darlington IN . 40°6N 86°47W 72 C4
Darlington LA . 30°53N 90°49W 75 D5
Darlington SC . 34°18N 79°52W 90 D6
Darlington WI . 42°41N 90°7W 103 F3
Darmstadt IN . 38°6N 87°35W 72 E3
Darnell AR . 34°47N 91°28W 63 D4
Darnestown MD . 39°6N 77°18W 77 A3
Darr NE . 40°40N 99°47W 84 D6
Darrington WA . 48°15N 121°36W 101 B4
Darrouzett TX . 36°27N 100°20W 98 A7
Dartmouth MA . 41°34N 71°1W 78 D3
Dasher GA . 30°45N 83°13W 68 F3
Dassel MN . 45°5N 94°19W 80 E4
Dateland AZ . 32°48N 113°33W 62 E2
Datil NM . 34°9N 107°51W 88 C3
Dauphin PA . 40°20N 76°55W 95 D6
Dauphin County ☆
PA . 40°20N 76°50W 95 D6
Dauphin I. AL . 30°15N 88°11W 60 F2
Dauphin Island AL . 30°15N 88°6W 60 F2
Davenport CA . 37°1N 122°12W 64 F4
Davenport FL . 28°10N 81°36W 67 C7
Davenport IA . 41°32N 90°35W 73 D8
Davenport ND . 46°43N 97°4W 91 D8
Davenport NE . 40°19N 97°49W 84 D8
Davenport OK . 35°42N 96°46W 93 C7
Davenport WA . 47°39N 118°9W 101 C7
Davey NE . 40°59N 96°40W 84 D9
David KY . 37°36N 82°54W 97 C10
Davidson MD . 39°5N 76°38W 77 B4
Davidson NC . 35°30N 80°50W 90 C5
Davidson OK . 34°14N 99°5W 93 D4
Davidson, Mt. CA . 37°44N 122°27W 118 B2
Davidson County ☆
NC . 35°45N 80°10W 90 C5
Davidson County ☆
TN . 36°10N 86°47W 96 D6
Davidsonville MD . 38°55N 76°38W 77 B4
Davie FL . 26°3N 80°14W 112 B2
Davie County ☆ NC . 35°55N 80°40W 90 C5
Daviess County ☆ IN . 38°40N 87°5W 72 E3
Daviess County ☆ KY . 37°40N 87°5W 96 C4
Daviess County ☆ MO . 40°0N 94°0W 82 B3
Davis CA . 38°33N 121°44W 64 E5
Davis IL . 42°25N 89°24W 71 A4
Davis OK . 34°30N 97°7W 93 D6
Davis SD . 43°16N 96°59W 91 G9
Davis WV . 39°8N 79°28W 102 C5
Davis, Lake CA . 39°53N 120°29W 64 D6
Davis City IA . 40°38N 93°49W 73 E5
Davis County ☆ IA . 40°45N 92°25W 73 E6
Davis County ☆ UT . 41°0N 112°5W 100 C3
Davis Creek CA . 41°44N 120°22W 64 B6
Davis Dam U.S.A. . 35°12N 114°34W 62 D1
Davis Island TX . 27°55N 82°27W 119 B4
Davis Junction IL . 42°6N 89°6W 71 A4
Davis Mts. TX . 30°50N 103°55W 98 G4
Davisboro GA . 32°59N 82°36W 68 D4
Davison MI . 43°2N 83°31W 79 F8
Davison County ☆ SD 43°43N 98°0W 91 F8
Davisville MO . 37°49N 91°11W 82 D5
Davy WV . 37°29N 81°39W 102 D3
Davy Crockett Nat. Forest
TX . 31°22N 95°2W 99 F12
Dawes County ☆ NE . 42°45N 103°0W 84 B2
Dawn TX . 34°55N 102°12W 98 C5
Dawson GA . 31°46N 84°27W 68 E2
Dawson MN . 44°56N 96°3W 80 F2
Dawson ND . 46°52N 99°45W 91 D6
Dawson NE . 40°8N 95°50W 84 D10
Dawson TX . 31°54N 96°43W 99 F11
Dawson County ☆
GA . 34°25N 84°10W 68 B2
Dawson County ☆
MT . 47°15N 105°0W 83 C13
Dawson Springs KY . 37°10N 87°41W 96 C5
Dawsonville GA . 34°25N 84°7W 68 B2
Day County ☆ SD . 45°20N 97°31W 91 E8
Daykin NE . 40°19N 97°18W 84 D8
Dayton IN . 40°22N 86°46W 72 C4
Dayton KY . 39°6N 84°28W 107 B2
Dayton NV . 39°14N 119°36W 85 C1
Dayton OH . 39°45N 84°12W 92 D2
Dayton PA . 40°53N 79°15W 95 D3
Dayton TN . 35°30N 85°1W 97 E7
Dayton VA . 38°25N 78°56W 102 C6
Dayton WA . 46°19N 117°59W 101 D8
Dayton WY . 44°53N 107°16W 104 B5
Dayton Int. ✈ (DAY)
OH . 39°54N 84°13W 92 D2
Daytona Beach FL . 29°13N 81°1W 67 B7
Dayville OR . 44°28N 119°32W 94 C6
Dazey ND . 47°11N 98°12W 91 C7
De Armanville AL . 33°38N 85°45W 60 C5
De Baca County ☆
NM . 34°15N 104°30W 88 C6
De Bary FL . 28°54N 81°18W 67 C7
De Beque CO . 39°20N 108°13W 66 C2
De Forest WI . 43°15N 89°20W 103 E4
De Funiak Springs FL . 30°43N 86°7W 67 A2
De Gray Lake ➤ AR . 34°13N 93°7W 63 D2
De Gray Lake Resort State Park
AR . 34°15N 93°10W 63 D2
DeKalb MS . 32°46N 88°39W 81 D5
DeKalb TX . 33°31N 94°37W 99 D13
De Kalb County ☆
AL . 34°26N 85°43W 60 B5
DeKalb County ☆
MO . 39°50N 94°25W 82 B2
De Kalb Junction NY 44°30N 75°17W 89 A5
De Land FL . 29°2N 81°18W 67 C7
De Leon TX . 32°7N 98°32W 99 E9
De Long Mts. AK . 68°10N 163°30W 61 B7
De Montreville, L.
MN . 45°1N 92°56W 113 A4
De Pere WI . 44°27N 88°4W 103 D5
De Queen AR . 34°2N 94°21W 63 D1
De Ruyter NY . 42°45N 75°53W 89 C5
De Smet ID . 47°9N 116°57W 70 C2
De Smet SD . 44°23N 97°33W 91 F8
De Smet, L. WY . 44°29N 106°45W 104 B6
De Soto IA . 41°32N 94°1W 73 D4
De Soto KS . 38°59N 94°58W 74 C9
De Soto MO . 38°8N 90°34W 82 C6
De Soto TX . 32°35N 96°51W 109 C5

De Soto WI . 43°25N 91°12W 103 E2
De Soto City FL . 27°27N 81°24W 67 D7
De Soto County ☆
FL . 27°15N 81°45W 67 D7
De Soto County ☆ MS 34°53N 90°1W 81 B3
De Soto Nat. Forest MS . 31°0N 89°0W 81 E4
De Soto Nat. Memorial
FL . 27°31N 82°39W 67 D6
De Soto Nat. Wildlife Refuge ➤
IA . 41°30N 96°1W 73 D2
De Soto Parish ☆ LA . 32°2N 93°43W 75 B2
De Tour Village MI . 46°0N 83°56W 79 C8
De Valls Bluff AR . 34°47N 91°28W 63 D4
De Witt AR . 34°18N 91°20W 63 D4
De Witt IA . 41°49N 90°33W 73 D8
De Witt MI . 42°51N 84°34W 79 G7
De Witt NE . 40°24N 96°55W 84 D9
De Witt County ☆ IL . 40°10N 88°55W 71 C5
De Witt County ☆
TX . 29°6N 97°17W 99 H10
Dead L. FL . 30°5N 85°10W 67 A3
Deadhorse AK . 70°11N 148°27W 61 A10
Deadwood SD . 44°23N 103°44W 91 F2
Deal NJ . 40°15N 74°0W 87 B3
Deale MD . 38°47N 76°33W 77 B4
Dealcambre LA . 29°57N 91°58W 75 E4
Deary ID . 46°48N 116°32W 70 C2
Dearborn MO . 39°32N 94°46W 82 B2
Dearborn County ☆
IN . 39°10N 85°0W 72 D6
Death Valley Junction
CA . 36°20N 116°25W 65 G10
Death Valley Nat. Park ➤
CA . 36°29N 117°6W 65 G9
Deatsville AL . 32°37N 86°24W 60 D4
Deaver WY . 44°54N 108°36W 104 B4
Deblois ME . 44°45N 68°1W 76 D5
Decatur AL . 34°36N 86°59W 60 B4
Decatur GA . 33°46N 84°16W 106 B3
Decatur IL . 39°51N 88°57W 71 D5
Decatur IN . 40°50N 84°56W 72 C6
Decatur MS . 32°26N 89°7W 81 D4
Decatur NE . 42°0N 96°15W 84 C9
Decatur TN . 35°31N 84°47W 97 E8
Decatur TX . 33°14N 97°35W 99 D10
Decatur City IA . 40°45N 93°50W 73 E5
Decatur County ☆ GA 31°0N 84°30W 68 F2
Decatur County ☆ IN . 39°20N 85°30W 72 D6
Decatur County ☆
IA . 40°45N 93°45W 73 E5
Decatur County ☆
KS . 39°45N 100°20W 74 B3
Decatur County ☆ TN 35°35N 88°7W 96 E4
Deception, Mt. WA 47°49N 123°14W 101 C2
Decherd TN . 35°13N 86°5W 96 E6
Deckerville MI . 43°32N 82°44W 79 F9
Declo ID . 42°32N 113°40W 70 G5
Decorah IA . 43°18N 91°48W 73 B7
Dededo Guam . 13°31N 144°50E 105 b
Dedham IA . 41°55N 94°49W 73 D4
Dedham MA . 42°15N 71°10W 106 B2
Dee OR . 45°33N 121°37W 94 B4
Deep ➤ SD . 45°11N 102°15W 91 E3
Deep Creek L. MD . 39°31N 79°24W 77 A1
Deep Creek Range
UT . 39°50N 113°50W 100 D2
Deep Fork ➤ OK . 35°28N 95°55W 93 C8
Deep River CT . 41°23N 72°26W 78 C2
Deep River IA . 41°35N 92°22W 73 D6
Deep Run ➤ MD . 37°24N 76°40W 107 B8
Deep Springs L. CA . 37°20N 118°3W 65 F8
Deepstep GA . 33°1N 82°58W 68 C4
Deepwater MO . 38°16N 93°47W 82 C3
Deepwater NJ . 39°41N 75°29W 87 C1
Deer Cr. ➤ IN . 40°34N 86°41W 72 C4
Deer Cr. ➤ OH . 39°27N 83°0W 92 D3
Deer Creek IL . 40°38N 89°20W 71 C4
Deer Creek ➤ OH . 39°27N 83°1W 92 D3
Deer Isle ME . 44°14N 68°41W 76 D5
Deer Lodge MT . 46°24N 112°44W 83 D5
Deer Lodge County ☆
MT . 46°0N 113°0W 83 E4
Deer Grove IL . 41°37N 89°42W 71 B4
Deer I. AK . 54°55N 162°18W 61 J7
Deer I. ME . 44°13N 68°41W 76 D5
Deer Park FL . 28°6N 80°54W 67 C8
Deer Park MD . 39°26N 79°18W 77 A1
Deer Park NY . 40°46N 73°20W 87 B3
Deer Park WA . 47°57N 117°28W 101 C8
Deer Trail CO . 39°37N 104°2W 66 C6
Deer Valley AZ . 33°41N 112°4W 116 A1
Deer Valley AZ . 33°43N 112°12W 116 A1
Deerfield KS . 37°59N 101°8W 74 D2
Deerfield VA . 38°13N 79°24W 102 C5
Deerfield Beach FL . 26°19N 80°6W 67 E8
Deerfield ➤ MA . 42°33N 72°37W 78 B2
Deerlodge Nat. Forest
MT . 46°20N 113°0W 83 D4
Deersville OH . 40°18N 81°11W 92 C5
Deerwood MN . 46°29N 93°54W 80 D5
Deeth NV . 41°4N 115°17W 85 A5
Defiance IA . 41°49N 95°20W 73 D3
Defiance OH . 41°17N 84°22W 92 B2
Defiance County ☆
OH . 41°23N 84°32W 92 B2
Del City OK . 35°27N 97°26W 93 C6
Del Mar CA . 32°58N 117°16W 65 L9
Del Norte CO . 37°41N 106°21W 66 E4
Del Norte County ☆
CA . 41°40N 124°0W 64 B3
Del Rio TX . 29°22N 100°54W 98 H7
Delano CA . 35°46N 119°15W 65 H7
Delano MN . 45°3N 93°47W 80 E5
Delano Peak UT . 38°22N 112°22W 100 E3
Delaplaine AR . 36°14N 90°44W 63 B5
Delaplane VA . 38°55N 77°55W 77 B3

Delavan IL . 40°22N 89°33W 71 C4
Delavan KS . 38°40N 96°49W 74 C7
Delavan WI . 42°38N 88°39W 103 F5
Delaware AR . 35°17N 93°19W 63 C2
Delaware OH . 40°18N 83°4W 92 C3
Delaware OK . 36°47N 95°39W 93 B8
Delaware ☐ U.S.A. . 39°15N 75°20W 77 A5
Delaware ➤ DE . 39°15N 75°20W 77 A5
Delaware B. DE . 39°0N 75°10W 77 A5
Delaware City DE . 39°35N 75°36W 77 A5
Delaware County ☆
IN . 40°15N 85°25W 72 C5
Delaware County ☆
IA . 42°30N 91°20W 73 C7
Delaware County ☆
NY . 42°15N 75°0W 89 D6
Delaware County ☆
OH . 40°18N 83°4W 92 C3
Delaware County ☆
OK . 36°25N 94°50W 93 B9
Delaware County ☆
PA . 39°55N 75°23W 95 E7
Delaware Cr. ➤
TX . 32°2N 104°0W 98 F3
Delaware Mts. TX . 31°45N 104°50W 98 F3
Delaware Seashore State Park ➤
DE . 38°38N 75°4W 77 B5
Delaware Water Gap Nat. Recr.
Area ➤ NJ . 41°0N 74°55W 87 A2
Delbarton WV . 37°43N 82°11W 102 D2
Delcambre LA . 29°57N 91°58W 75 E4
Delevan NY . 42°29N 78°29W 89 C2
Delgada, Pt. CA . 40°2N 124°5W 64 C1
Delhi CA . 37°26N 120°46W 64 F6
Delhi IA . 42°26N 91°20W 73 C7
Delhi LA . 32°28N 91°30W 75 B4
Delhi NY . 42°17N 74°55W 89 C6
Delhi Hills OH . 39°5N 84°36W 107 B1
Delia KS . 39°15N 95°59W 74 B8
Delight AR . 34°3N 93°31W 63 D2
Dell MT . 44°44N 112°42W 83 F5
Dell City TX . 31°56N 105°12W 98 F2
Dell Rapids SD . 43°50N 96°43W 91 G9
Dellwood MO . 45°6N 92°57W 113 A4
Dellwood MN . 38°47N 90°17W 113 B5
Delmar DE . 38°27N 75°35W 77 B5
Delmar IA . 42°0N 90°37W 73 C8
Delmar NY . 42°37N 73°55W 89 C7
Delmarva Peninsula
MD . 38°45N 75°45W 77 B5
Delmont NJ . 39°13N 74°57W 87 C2
Delmont SD . 43°16N 98°10W 91 G7
Deloit IA . 42°6N 95°19W 73 C3
Delphi IN . 40°36N 86°41W 72 C4
Delphos KS . 39°17N 97°46W 74 B6
Delphos OH . 40°51N 84°21W 92 C2
Delray WV . 39°12N 78°36W 102 B6
Delray Beach FL . 26°28N 80°4W 67 E8
Delta AL . 33°26N 85°42W 60 C5
Delta CO . 38°44N 108°4W 66 D2
Delta MO . 37°12N 89°44W 82 D7
Delta OH . 41°34N 84°0W 92 B2
Delta UT . 39°21N 112°35W 100 D3
Delta County ☆ CO . 38°50N 107°50W 66 D3
Delta County ☆ MI . 46°0N 87°0W 79 D3
Delta County ☆ TX . 33°23N 95°42W 99 D12
Delta Junction AK . 64°2N 145°44W 61 D11
Delta Nat. Forest MS 32°50N 90°55W 81 D3
Delta Nat. Wildlife Refuge ➤
LA . 29°15N 89°15W 75 E6
Deltona FL . 28°54N 81°16W 67 C7
Demarcation Pt.
AK . 69°41N 141°18W 61 B12
Deming NM . 32°16N 107°46W 88 E3
Deming WA . 48°50N 122°13W 101 B3
Demopolis AL . 32°31N 87°50W 60 D3
Demorest GA . 34°34N 83°33W 68 B3
Demotte IN . 41°12N 87°12W 72 B3
Dempsey OK . 35°31N 99°49W 93 C4
Denair CA . 37°32N 120°48W 64 F6
Denali = McKinley, Mt.
AK . 63°4N 151°0W 61 E10
Denali ☆ AK . 61°13N 149°52W 61 E10
Denali Nat. Park and Preserve ➤
AK . 63°30N 152°0W 61 E10
Denbigh ND . 48°19N 100°35W 91 B5
Denbigh, C. AK . 64°23N 161°32W 61 D7
Dendron VA . 37°3N 76°56W 102 D8
Denham MN . 46°22N 92°57W 80 D6
Denhoff ND . 47°29N 100°16W 91 C5
Denham Springs LA . 30°29N 90°57W 75 D5
Denio NV . 41°59N 118°38W 85 A2
Denison IA . 42°1N 95°21W 73 C3
Denison KS . 39°24N 95°38W 74 B8
Denison TX . 33°45N 96°33W 99 D11
Denmark ME . 43°58N 70°48W 76 E2
Denmark SC . 33°19N 81°9W 90 D4
Denmark WI . 44°21N 87°50W 103 D6
Dennehotso AZ . 36°51N 109°51W 62 A6
Dennis KS . 37°21N 95°25W 74 D8
Dennis MA . 41°44N 70°12W 78 C4
Dennis Port MA . 41°39N 70°8W 78 C4
Dennison MN . 44°25N 93°2W 80 F5
Dennison OH . 40°24N 81°19W 92 C5
Dennisville NJ . 39°12N 74°49W 87 C2
Dent MN . 46°33N 95°43W 80 D3
Dent County ☆ MO . 37°35N 91°30W 82 D5
Denton GA . 31°44N 82°42W 68 E4
Denton KS . 39°44N 95°16W 74 B8
Denton MD . 38°53N 75°50W 77 B5
Denton NC . 35°38N 80°6W 90 C5
Denton TX . 33°13N 97°8W 99 D10
Denton County ☆
TX . 33°15N 97°10W 99 D10
Dentsville SC . 34°4N 80°58W 90 D5
Dentsville MD . 38°28N 76°51W 77 B4
Denver CO . 39°42N 104°59W 109 B2
Denver IA . 42°40N 92°20W 73 C6
Denver NC . 35°32N 81°2W 90 C4
Denver PA . 40°14N 76°8W 95 D6
Denver City TX . 32°58N 102°50W 98 E5
Denver County ☆
CO . 39°45N 105°0W 66 C6
Denver Int. ✈ (DEN)
CO . 39°51N 104°40W 66 C6
DePaul University
IL . 41°55N 87°39W 108 B3
Depoe Bay OR . 44°49N 124°4W 94 C1
Deport TX . 33°32N 95°19W 99 D12
Deposit NY . 42°4N 75°25W 89 C5
Depue IL . 41°19N 89°18W 71 B4
Derby CT . 41°19N 73°5W 78 C2
Derby KS . 37°33N 97°16W 74 D6
Derby NY . 42°41N 78°58W 89 C2
Derby TX . 28°46N 98°8W 99 J9
Derby Line VT . 45°0N 72°6W 86 B2
Deridder LA . 30°51N 93°17W 75 D2
Derita NC . 35°17N 80°47W 107 A2
Derma MS . 33°51N 89°17W 81 C4
Dermott AR . 33°32N 91°26W 63 E4
Dernieres, Isles LA . 29°2N 90°50W 75 E5
Derry NH . 42°53N 71°19W 86 D3

Des Allemands *LA* . . 29°49N 90°28W **75 E5**
Des Arc *AR* . . . . . . 34°58N 91°30W **63 D4**
Des Arc *MO* . . . . . . 37°17N 90°38W **82 D6**
Des Lacs *ND* . . . . . . 48°16N 101°34W **91 B5**
Des Lacs ~ *ND* . . . . . 48°17N 100°20W **91 B5**
Des Lacs Nat. Wildlife Refuge
  ND . . . . 48°46N 102°0W **91 B5**
Des Moines *IA* . . . . . 41°35N 102°37W **73 D5**
Des Moines *NM* . . . . 36°46N 103°50W **88 A7**
Des Moines *WA* . . . . 47°24N 122°19W **118 D4**
Des Moines ~ *IA* . . . . 40°23N 91°25W **73 E7**
Des Moines ✈ (DSM)
  IA . . . . 41°32N 93°40W **73 D5**
Des Moines County ☆
  IA . . . . 40°55N 91°10W **73 E7**
Des Plaines *IL* . . . . . 42°2N 87°54W **108 A1**
Des Plaines ~ *IL* . . . . 41°23N 88°15W **71 B5**
Desatoya Mts. *NV* . . . 39°20N 117°40W **85 C8**
Descanso *CA* . . . . . 32°51N 116°37W **65 L10**
Deschutes ~ *OR* . . . . 44°0N 121°30W **94 D4**
Deschutes County ☆
  OR . . . . 44°0N 121°30W **94 D4**
Deschutes Nat. Forest
  OR . . . . 43°40N 121°20W **94 D4**
Desdemona *TX* . . . . . 32°16N 98°33W **99 J8**
Deseret *UT* . . . . . . 39°17N 112°39W **100 D3**
Deseret Peak *UT* . . . . 40°28N 112°38W **100 C3**
Desert Center *CA* . . . 33°43N 115°24W **65 K11**
Desert Hot Springs
  CA . . . . 33°58N 116°30W **65 K10**
Desert L. *NV* . . . . . 36°59N 115°14W **85 F5**
Desert Nat. Wildlife Range ☆
  NV . . . . 37°8N 115°52W **110 A2**
Desert Peak *UT* . . . . 41°11N 113°22W **100 B2**
Desert Ra. *NV* . . . . . 36°55N 115°25W **85 F5**
Desert Ranch Res.
  NV . . . . 41°42N 116°33W **85 A4**
Desert Valley *NV* . . . 41°10N 118°58W **85 A5**
Desert Wetlands Park
  NV . . . . 36°7N 115°2W **110 C3**
Desha *AR* . . . . 35°44N 91°41W **63 C4**
Desha County ☆ *AR* . . 33°48N 91°16W **63 E4**
Deshler *NE* . . . . . . 40°9N 97°44W **84 D8**
Deshler *OH* . . . . . . 41°13N 83°54W **92 B3**
Desloge *MO* . . . . . . 37°51N 90°32W **82 D6**
Destin *FL* . . . . 30°24N 86°30W **67 A2**
Detour, Pt. *MI* . . . . . 45°40N 86°40W **79 D5**
Detroit *MI* . . . . 34°2N 88°10W **60 B2**
Detroit *MI* . . . . 42°19N 83°12W **109 A2**
Detroit *OR* . . . . . . 44°44N 122°9W **94 C3**
Detroit Beach *MI* . . . 41°56N 83°19W **79 H8**
Detroit City ✈ (DET)
  MI . . . . 42°24N 83°0W **109 A2**
Detroit Lakes *MN* . . . 46°49N 95°51W **80 D3**
Detroit Metropolitan Wayne
  County ✈ (DTW)
  MI . . . . 42°13N 83°21W **79 G8**
Deuel County ☆ *NE* . . 41°10N 102°20W **84 C3**
Deuel County ☆ *SD* . . 44°45N 96°41W **91 G8**
Devereux *GA* . . . . . 33°13N 83°5W **68 C3**
Devils Den *CA* . . . . . 35°46N 119°58W **65 H7**
Devils Hole = Death Valley Nat.
  Park △ *U.S.A.* . . . 36°29N 116°54W **65 G9**
Devils L. *ND* . . . . . 48°2N 98°58W **91 B7**
Devils L. *TX* . . . . . 29°34N 100°54W **98 H1**
Devils Lake *ND* . . . . 48°7N 98°52W **91 B7**
Devil's Lake State Park
  WI . . . . 43°25N 89°42W **103 E4**
Devils Playground
  CA . . . . 35°0N 115°50W **65 J11**
Devils Postpile Nat. Monument △
  CA . . . . 37°37N 119°5W **64 F7**
Devils Tower *WY* . . . 44°35N 104°42W **104 B8**
Devils Tower Nat. Monument △
  WY . . . . 44°48N 104°55W **104 B8**
Devine *TX* . . . . 29°8N 98°54W **99 H9**
Devol *OK* . . . . 34°11N 98°35W **93 D6**
Devon *KS* . . . . 37°55N 94°49W **74 D9**
Devou *MT* . . . . 48°28N 111°29W **83 B6**
Devou Park *KY* . . . . 39°4N 84°32W **107 B1**
Dew *TX* . . . . 31°36N 96°9W **99 F11**
Dewar *OK* . . . . 35°28N 95°56W **93 C8**
Deweese *NE* . . . . . . 40°21N 98°8W **84 D7**
Dewey *Puerto Rico* 18°18N 65°18W **105 G17**
Dewey *AZ* . . . . 34°32N 112°15W **62 C3**
Dewey *OK* . . . . 36°48N 95°56W **93 B8**
Dewey Beach *DE* . . . . 38°42N 75°5W **77 B5**
Dewey County ☆ *OK* . 36°0N 99°0W **93 C5**
Dewey County ☆ *SD* . 45°0N 101°0W **91 E5**
Dewey L. *KY* . . . . . 37°44N 82°44W **97 C10**
Deweyville *TX* . . . . . 30°18N 93°45W **99 G14**
Dewy Rose *GA* . . . . 34°10N 82°57W **68 B4**
Dexter *GA* . . . . . . 32°27N 83°4W **68 D3**
Dexter *KS* . . . . 37°11N 96°43W **74 D7**
Dexter *KY* . . . . . . 36°44N 88°17W **96 D4**
Dexter *ME* . . . . . . 45°1N 69°18W **76 C4**
Dexter *MI* . . . . 42°20N 83°53W **79 G8**
Dexter *MN* . . . . . . 43°43N 92°42W **80 G6**
Dexter *MO* . . . . . . 36°48N 89°57W **82 E7**
Dexter *NM* . . . . . . 33°12N 104°22W **88 D6**
Dexter City *OH* . . . . 39°39N 81°28W **92 D5**
Diablo, Sierra *TX* . . . 31°15N 105°0W **98 F3**
Diablo Bolson *TX* . . . 31°45N 105°25W **98 F2**
Diablo Pt. *N. Marianas* 15°0N 145°35E **105 c**
Diablo Range *CA* . . . 37°20N 121°25W **64 F5**
Diagonal *IA* . . . . . . 40°49N 94°20W **73 E4**
Diamond *MO* . . . . . 36°59N 94°19W **82 E2**
Diamond, L. *OR* . . . . 43°10N 122°9W **94 D3**
Diamond Head *HI* . . . 21°16N 157°49W **69 K14**
Diamond Lake *UT* . . . 40°16N 120°33W **64 C6**
Diamond Mts. *CA* . . . 40°16N 120°33W **64 C6**
Diamond Mts. *NV* . . . 39°40N 115°50W **85 C5**
Diamond Pk. *CO* . . . 40°59N 108°50W **66 B2**
Diamond Pk. *ID* . . . . 44°8N 113°5W **70 E3**
Diamond Springs
  CA . . . . 38°42N 120°49W **64 E6**
Diamond Valley *NV* . . 39°46N 115°58W **85 C5**
Diamondhead *MS* . . . 30°24N 89°22W **81 F4**
Diamondville *WY* . . . 41°47N 110°32W **104 E2**
Diana *WV* . . . . . . 38°34N 80°27W **102 C4**
Dias Creek *NJ* . . . . 39°8N 74°53W **87 C2**
Diaz *AR* . . . . 35°38N 91°16W **63 C4**
Dibble *OK* . . . . . . 35°2N 97°38W **93 C6**
D'Iberville *MS* . . . . 30°26N 88°54W **81 F5**
Diboll *TX* . . . . . . 31°11N 94°47W **99 F13**
Dickens *NE* . . . . . . 40°49N 101°2W **84 D4**
Dickens *TX* . . . . . . 33°37N 100°50W **98 D7**
Dickens County ☆
  TX . . . . 33°40N 100°50W **98 D7**
Dickenson County ☆
  VA . . . . 37°10N 82°22W **102 D2**
Dickey *ND* . . . . . . 46°32N 98°27W **91 D7**
Dickey County ☆ *ND* . 46°2N 98°30W **91 D7**
Dickeyville *WI* . . . . 42°38N 90°36W **103 E3**
Dickinson *ND* . . . . . 46°53N 102°47W **91 D3**
Dickinson *TX* . . . . . 29°28N 95°3W **99 H12**
Dickinson County ☆
  IA . . . . 43°20N 95°10W **73 B3**
Dickinson County ☆
  KS . . . . 38°50N 97°10W **74 C6**
Dickinson County ☆
  MI . . . . 46°0N 87°50W **79 C4**
Dickson *OK* . . . . . . 34°11N 96°59W **93 D7**
Dickson *TN* . . . . . . 36°5N 87°23W **96 D5**
Dickson City *PA* . . . 41°28N 75°36W **87 A1**
Dickson County ☆
  TN . . . . 36°11N 87°21W **96 D5**
Diehlstadt *MO* . . . . 36°58N 89°26W **82 E7**
Dierks *AR* . . . . . . 34°7N 94°1W **63 D1**
Dieterich *IL* . . . . . 39°4N 88°23W **71 D5**
Dietrich *ID* . . . . . . 42°55N 114°16W **70 G4**

Difficult Run ~ *VA* . . 38°55N 77°18W **119 B2**
Dighton *KS* . . . . . . 38°29N 100°28W **74 C3**
Dike *IA* . . . . 42°28N 92°38W **73 C5**
Dilia *NM* . . . . 35°12N 105°4W **88 B5**
Dilkon *AZ* . . . . . . 35°23N 110°19W **62 B5**
Dill City *OK* . . . . . 35°17N 99°8W **93 C4**
Dillard *GA* . . . . . . 34°58N 83°23W **68 B3**
Dilley *TX* . . . . 28°40N 99°10W **99 J8**
Dillingham *AK* . . . . 59°3N 158°28W **61 G8**
Dillingham ☆ *AK* . . . 60°0N 156°0W **61 F8**
Dillon *CO* . . . . . . 39°37N 106°4W **66 C4**
Dillon *MT* . . . . . . 45°13N 112°38W **83 E5**
Dillon *SC* . . . . . . 34°25N 79°22W **90 D6**
Dillon County ☆ *SC* . 34°20N 79°20W **90 D6**
Dillon L. *OH* . . . . . 40°0N 82°6W **92 D4**
Dillsboro *IN* . . . . . 39°1N 85°4W **72 D5**
Dillsburg *PA* . . . . . 40°7N 77°2W **95 D5**
Dillwyn *VA* . . . . . . 37°32N 78°27W **102 D6**
Dilworth *MN* . . . . . 46°53N 96°42W **80 D2**
Dimmit County ☆ *TX* 28°27N 99°46W **99 J8**
Dimmitt *TX* . . . . . 34°33N 102°19W **98 D5**
Dimock *SD* . . . . . . 43°29N 97°59W **91 G8**
Dinero *TX* . . . . . . 28°14N 97°58W **99 J10**
Dinnebito Wash ~
  AZ . . . . 35°29N 111°14W **62 B4**
Dinosaur *CO* . . . . . 40°15N 109°1W **66 B1**
Dinosaur Nat. Monument △
  CO . . . . 40°30N 108°45W **66 B2**
Dinuba *CA* . . . . . . 36°32N 119°23W **65 G7**
Dinwiddie *VA* . . . . . 37°5N 77°35W **102 D6**
Dinwiddie County ☆
  VA . . . . 37°5N 77°35W **102 D7**
Diomede *AK* . . . . . 65°47N 169°0W **61 D3**
Dirty Devil ~ *UT* . . . 37°58N 110°24W **100 F5**
Disappointment, C.
  WA . . . . 46°18N 124°5W **101 D1**
Disautel *WA* . . . . . 48°22N 119°14W **101 B6**
Dishman *WA* . . . . . 47°39N 117°17W **101 C8**
Dismal ~ *NE* . . . . . 41°50N 100°5W **84 C5**
Dismal Swamp ~ *VA* . 36°40N 76°20W **102 E8**
Disney *OK* . . . . . . 36°29N 95°1W **93 B8**
Disney Studios *CA* . . 34°9N 118°19W **111 B3**
Disneyland *CA* . . . . 33°49N 117°55W **65 K9**
Dispatanta *VA* . . . . 37°8N 77°14W **102 D7**
District Heights *MD* . 38°52N 76°54W **77 C10**
District of Columbia □
  U.S.A. . . . . . . 38°55N 77°0W **77 B4**
Divernon *IL* . . . . . 39°34N 89°39W **71 D4**
Diversion L. *TX* . . . . 33°49N 98°56W **99 D9**
Divide *CO* . . . . . . 38°57N 105°9W **66 C5**
Divide County ☆
  ND . . . . 48°55N 103°30W **91 B2**
Dividing Creek *NJ* . . 39°16N 75°6W **87 C1**
Dix *IL* . . . . 38°27N 88°56W **71 E5**
Dix *NE* . . . . 41°14N 103°29W **84 C2**
Dix ~ *KY* . . . . . . 37°49N 84°43W **97 C8**
Dixfield *ME* . . . . . 44°32N 70°28W **76 D3**
Dixie *AR* . . . . 31°9N 86°44W **60 G4**
Dixie *WA* . . . . . . 46°8N 118°9W **101 D7**
Dixie Nat. Forest
  UT . . . . 37°45N 112°15W **100 F3**
Dixie Union *GA* . . . 31°20N 82°28W **68 E4**
Dixmont *ME* . . . . . 44°41N 69°10W **76 D4**
Dixon *CA* . . . . . . 38°27N 121°49W **64 E5**
Dixon *IL* . . . . 41°50N 89°29W **71 B4**
Dixon *IA* . . . . 41°45N 90°47W **73 D8**
Dixon *KY* . . . . . . 37°31N 87°41W **96 C5**
Dixon *MO* . . . . . . 37°59N 92°6W **82 D4**
Dixon *MT* . . . . . . 47°19N 114°19W **83 C3**
Dixon *NE* . . . . . . 42°24N 97°2W **84 B8**
Dixon *NM* . . . . . . 36°12N 105°53W **88 A5**
Dixon County ☆ *NE* . 42°30N 96°50W **84 B9**
Dixon Entrance
  U.S.A. . . . . . . 54°30N 132°0W **61 J14**
Dixons Mills *AL* . . . 32°4N 87°47W **60 D3**
Dixville Notch *NH* . . 44°50N 71°18W **86 B3**
Dizney *KY* . . . . . . 36°51N 83°7W **97 D9**
Dobbin *TX* . . . . . . 30°22N 95°46W **99 G12**
Dobbs Ferry *NY* . . . 41°1N 73°52W **87 A3**
Dobey Sound *GA* . . . 31°23N 81°16W **68 E5**
Dobson *NC* . . . . . 36°24N 80°43W **90 B5**
Dockton *WA* . . . . . 47°22N 122°27W **118 D3**
Doctor Phillips *FL* . . 28°26N 81°29W **115 B2**
Doctors Inlet *FL* . . . 30°6N 81°47W **67 A7**
Doddridge *AR* . . . . 33°6N 93°55W **63 E2**
Doddridge County ☆
  WV . . . . 39°17N 80°44W **102 B4**
Dodge *ND* . . . . . . 47°18N 102°12W **91 C3**
Dodge *NE* . . . . . . 41°43N 96°53W **84 C9**
Dodge *TX* . . . . . . 30°45N 95°24W **99 G12**
Dodge Center *MN* . . 44°2N 92°52W **80 F6**
Dodge City *KS* . . . . 37°45N 100°1W **74 D3**
Dodge Plains *NY* . . . 41°43N 73°35W **78 C1**
Dodge County ☆ *GA* 32°10N 83°10W **68 D3**
Dodge County ☆ *MN* 44°0N 92°50W **80 G6**
Dodge County ☆ *NE* . 41°30N 96°40W **84 C9**
Dodge County ☆
  WI . . . . 43°20N 88°45W **103 E5**
Dodger Stadium *CA* 34°4N 118°14W **111 B3**
Dodgeville *WI* . . . . 42°58N 90°8W **103 E3**
Dodson *LA* . . . . . . 32°5N 92°39W **75 C3**
Dodson *TX* . . . . . . 34°48N 100°1W **93 D4**
Doe Run *MO* . . . . . 37°45N 90°30W **82 D6**
Doerun *GA* . . . . . . 31°19N 83°55W **68 E2**
Dog I. *FL* . . . . 29°48N 84°36W **67 B4**
Dolan Springs *AZ* . . 35°36N 114°16W **62 B1**
Doland *SD* . . . . . . 44°54N 98°6W **91 F7**
Doles *GA* . . . . . . 31°42N 83°53W **68 E2**
Dolgeville *NY* . . . . 43°6N 74°46W **89 B6**
Dolliver *IA* . . . . . . 43°28N 94°37W **73 B4**
Dolores *CO* . . . . . . 37°28N 108°30W **66 E2**
Dolores ~ *UT* . . . . 38°49N 109°17W **100 E6**
Dolores County ☆
  CO . . . . 37°45N 108°30W **66 E2**
Dolton *IL* . . . . . . 41°38N 87°36W **108 C2**
Dome, The *VT* . . . . 42°45N 73°12W **86 D1**
Don Pedro Dam *CA* . 37°43N 120°24W **64 E6**
Dona Ana *NM* . . . . 32°23N 106°49W **88 E4**
Dona Ana County ☆
  NM . . . . 32°20N 107°0W **88 E4**
Donahue *IA* . . . . . 41°42N 90°41W **73 D8**
Donaldson *AR* . . . . 34°14N 92°55W **63 D3**
Donaldson *MN* . . . . 48°35N 96°53W **80 B2**
Donalsonville *GA* . . . 31°3N 84°53W **68 E1**
Donaldsonville *LA* . . 36°0N 90°59W **75 D5**
Doncaster *MD* . . . . 38°30N 77°15W **77 B3**
Dongan Hills *NY* . . . 40°35N 74°5W **114 C2**
Donie *TX* . . . . 31°29N 96°13W **99 F11**
Doniphan *KS* . . . . . 39°38N 95°5W **74 B8**
Doniphan *MO* . . . . 36°37N 90°50W **82 E6**
Doniphan *NE* . . . . . 40°46N 98°22W **84 D7**
Doniphan County ☆
  KS . . . . 39°45N 95°10W **74 B8**
Donley County ☆ *TX* 35°0N 100°45W **98 B7**
Donna *TX* . . . . . . 26°9N 98°4W **98 L1**
Donnelly *ID* . . . . . 44°44N 116°5W **70 E2**
Donnelly *MN* . . . . . 45°42N 96°1W **80 E2**
Donner Pass *CA* . . . 39°19N 120°20W **64 D6**
Donner und Blitzen ~
  OR . . . . 43°17N 118°49W **94 D7**
Donnybrook *ND* . . . 48°31N 101°53W **91 B4**
Donora *PA* . . . . . . 40°11N 79°52W **95 D3**
Donovan *IL* . . . . . 40°53N 87°37W **71 C6**
Doolittle *MO* . . . . . 37°56N 91°53W **82 D4**
Dooly County ☆ *GA* . 32°10N 83°50W **68 D3**
Doon *IA* . . . . 43°17N 96°14W **73 B2**
Door County ☆ *WI* . 45°0N 87°15W **103 C6**
Door Peninsula *WI* . . 44°45N 87°25W **103 D6**
Dora *AL* . . . . 33°44N 87°5W **60 C3**
Dora *NM* . . . . 33°56N 103°20W **88 D7**
Dora ~ *IA* . . . . . . 43°10N 123°19W **94 D2**
Doran *MN* . . . . . . 46°11N 96°29W **80 D2**
Doraville *GA* . . . . . 33°54N 84°17W **106 B3**
Dorcas *WV* . . . . . . 38°56N 79°6W **102 C5**
Dorchester ~
  LA . . . . 32°10N 93°25W **75 B2**
Dorchester *MA* . . . . 42°17N 71°4W **106 B3**
Dorchester *NH* . . . . 43°44N 71°56W **86 C3**
Dorchester *NE* . . . . 40°39N 97°7W **84 D8**
Dorchester *WI* . . . . 45°0N 90°20W **103 C4**
Dorchester B. *MA* . . 42°18N 71°1W **106 B3**
Dorchester County ☆
  MD . . . . 38°20N 76°0W **77 B4**
Dorchester County ☆
  SC . . . . 33°10N 80°30W **90 E5**
Dorchester Heights Nat. Historical
  Site ☆ *MA* . . . . 42°20N 71°2W **106 B3**
Dorena *OR* . . . . . . 43°43N 122°52W **94 D3**
Dormont *PA* . . . . . 40°23N 80°2W **116 B1**
Dorrance *KS* . . . . . 38°51N 98°35W **74 C5**
Dorris *CA* . . . . . . 41°58N 121°55W **64 B5**
Dorris *VA* . . . . . . 43°15N 73°6W **86 C1**
Dorthes *NC* . . . . . 36°1N 77°51W **90 B8**
Dorton *KY* . . . . . . 37°17N 82°35W **97 C10**
Dos Palos *CA* . . . . . 36°59N 120°37W **64 G6**
Du Quoin *IL* . . . . . 38°1N 89°14W **71 E4**
Dot Lake *AK* . . . . . 63°40N 144°4W **61 E11**
Dothan *AL* . . . . . . 31°13N 85°24W **60 E5**
Doty *WA* . . . . . . 46°38N 123°17W **101 C2**
Double Mountain Fork ~
  TX . . . . 33°16N 100°0W **98 D7**
Double Springs *AL* . . 34°9N 87°24W **60 B3**
Doubletop Pk. *WY* . . 43°21N 110°17W **104 C2**
Dougherty *IA* . . . . . 42°55N 93°3W **73 C5**
Dougherty *OK* . . . . 34°24N 97°3W **93 D6**
Dougherty County ☆
  GA . . . . 31°30N 84°10W **68 E2**
Douglas *AK* . . . . . 58°17N 134°24W **61 G14**
Douglas *AZ* . . . . . 31°21N 109°33W **62 F6**
Douglas *GA* . . . . . 31°31N 82°51W **68 E4**
Douglas *MA* . . . . . 42°3N 71°45W **86 D3**
Douglas *MI* . . . . . 42°39N 86°14W **79 B10**
Douglas *ND* . . . . . 48°19N 101°30W **91 B4**
Douglas *NE* . . . . . 40°36N 96°23W **84 D9**
Douglas *WY* . . . . . 42°45N 105°24W **104 D7**
Douglas City *CA* . . . 40°39N 122°57W **64 C4**
Douglas County ☆
  CO . . . . 39°15N 105°0W **66 C6**
Douglas County ☆
  IL . . . . 39°45N 88°15W **71 D5**
Douglas County ☆
  KS . . . . 38°50N 95°15W **74 C8**
Douglas County ☆
  MN . . . . 45°50N 95°20W **80 E3**
Douglas County ☆
  MO . . . . 36°55N 92°30W **82 E4**
Douglas County ☆
  NV . . . . 38°55N 119°45W **85 D1**
Douglas County ☆
  OR . . . . 43°15N 123°0W **94 D3**
Douglas County ☆
  SD . . . . 43°25N 98°24W **91 G7**
Douglas County ☆
  WA . . . . 47°50N 119°45W **101 C6**
Douglas L. *TN* . . . . 35°58N 83°32W **97 EF9**
Douglas Park *IL* . . . 41°51N 87°42W **108 B2**
Douglass *KS* . . . . . 37°31N 97°1W **74 D6**
Douglass *TX* . . . . . 31°40N 94°53W **99 F13**
Douglaston *NY* . . . . 40°46N 73°44W **114 B4**
Douglasville *GA* . . . 33°45N 84°45W **68 C2**
Dousman *WI* . . . . . 43°1N 88°29W **103 E5**
Dove Creek *CO* . . . 37°46N 108°54W **66 E1**
Dover *DE* . . . . . . 39°10N 75°32W **77 A5**
Dover *ID* . . . . 48°15N 116°36W **70 A2**
Dover *NH* . . . . . . 43°12N 70°56W **86 C4**
Dover *NJ* . . . . . . 40°53N 74°34W **87 B2**
Dover *OH* . . . . . . 40°32N 81°29W **92 C5**
Dover *TN* . . . . . . 36°29N 87°50W **96 D5**
Dover Air Force Base
  DE . . . . 39°7N 75°29W **77 A5**
Dover Downs International
  Speedway *DE* . . . 39°14N 75°35W **77 A5**
Dover-Foxcroft *ME* . 45°11N 69°13W **76 C4**
Dover Plains *NY* . . . 41°43N 73°35W **78 C1**
Dow City *IA* . . . . . 41°56N 95°30W **73 D3**
Dowagiac *MI* . . . . . 41°59N 86°6W **79 H5**
Down, L. *FL* . . . . . 28°30N 81°31W **115 A1**
Downers Grove *IL* . . 41°48N 88°1W **71 B5**
Downey *CA* . . . . . 33°56N 118°9W **111 C4**
Downey *ID* . . . . . . 42°26N 112°7W **70 G6**
Downieville *CA* . . . . 39°34N 120°50W **64 D6**
Downing *MO* . . . . . 40°29N 92°22W **82 A4**
Downingtown *PA* . . 40°0N 75°42W **87 B1**
Downs *IL* . . . . . . 40°24N 88°52W **71 C5**
Downs *KS* . . . . . . 39°30N 98°32W **74 B5**
Downsville *MD* . . . . 39°35N 77°48W **77 A3**
Downsville *NY* . . . . 42°5N 75°0W **89 C5**
Doyle *CA* . . . . . . 40°2N 120°6W **64 C6**
Doylestown *OH* . . . 40°58N 81°41W **92 C5**
Doylestown *PA* . . . . 40°21N 75°10W **95 D7**
Doyleville *CO* . . . . 38°25N 106°35W **66 D4**
Doyline *LA* . . . . . . 32°32N 93°25W **75 B2**
Dozier *AL* . . . . . . 31°30N 86°28W **60 E4**
Dragerton *UT* . . . . 39°33N 110°25W **100 D5**
Dragoon *AZ* . . . . . 32°2N 110°2W **62 E5**
Drain *OR* . . . . . . 43°40N 123°19W **94 D2**
Drake *ND* . . . . . . 47°55N 100°23W **91 C5**
Drake Pk. *OR* . . . . 42°19N 120°7W **94 E5**
Drakes Branch *VA* . . 36°59N 78°36W **102 E6**
Drakesboro *KY* . . . . 37°13N 87°3W **96 C5**
Draketown *GA* . . . . 33°50N 85°3W **68 C1**
Dranesville *VA* . . . . 39°0N 77°20W **119 A1**
Draper *SD* . . . . . . 43°52N 100°30W **91 G5**
Dravosburg *PA* . . . . 40°21N 79°53W **116 B2**
Drayden *MD* . . . . . 38°11N 76°28W **77 B4**
Drayton *ND* . . . . . 48°34N 97°11W **91 B8**
Drayton Plains *MI* . . 42°41N 83°23W **79 G8**
Dresden *OH* . . . . . 40°7N 82°1W **92 C4**
Dresden *TN* . . . . . 36°18N 88°42W **96 D3**
Dresser *WI* . . . . . . 45°22N 92°38W **103 C1**
Dretzka Park *WI* . . . 43°10N 88°4W **112 A1**
Drew *MS* . . . . . . 33°49N 90°32W **81 C3**
Drew County ☆ *AR* . 33°35N 91°45W **63 E4**
Drews Res. *OR* . . . . 42°7N 120°37W **94 E5**
Drexel *MO* . . . . . . 38°29N 94°37W **82 C2**
Drexel Hill *PA* . . . . 39°56N 75°17W **116 B1**
Driftwood *PA* . . . . 41°20N 78°8W **95 C5**
Driggs *ID* . . . . . . 43°44N 111°6W **70 F7**
Dripping Springs *TX* . 30°12N 98°5W **99 G9**

Driscoll *ND* . . . . . 46°51N 100°9W **91 C5**
Driscoll *TX* . . . . . 27°41N 97°45W **98 K10**
Driskill Mt. *LA* . . . . 32°25N 92°54W **75 B3**
Druid Hill Park *MD* . 39°19N 76°38W **107 D4**
Druid Hills *GA* . . . . 33°47N 84°21W **106 B2**
Drummond *ID* . . . . 43°59N 111°20W **70 F7**
Drummond *MT* . . . . 46°40N 113°9W **83 D4**
Drummond *OK* . . . . 36°18N 98°2W **93 B5**
Drummond *WI* . . . . 46°20N 91°15W **103 B3**
Drummond, L. *VA* . . 36°36N 76°28W **102 E8**
Drummond I. *MI* . . . 46°1N 83°39W **79 C6**
Drury *MD* . . . . . . 39°48N 76°42W **82 D7**
Dry Cr. ~ *OR* . . . . 43°34N 117°21W **94 D8**
Dry Cr. ~ *WY* . . . . 44°31N 108°3W **104 B4**
Dry Devils ~ *TX* . . . 29°47N 100°59W **98 H1**
Dry Falls Dam *WA* . 47°37N 119°19W **101 C6**
Dry Fork Cheyenne ~
  WY . . . . 43°26N 105°3W **104 C7**
Dry L. *ND* . . . . . . 48°16N 98°59W **91 B7**
Dry Prong *LA* . . . . 31°35N 92°32W **75 C3**
Dry Ridge *KY* . . . . 38°41N 84°35W **97 B8**
Dryden *NY* . . . . . . 42°30N 76°18W **89 C4**
Dryden *TX* . . . . . . 30°3N 102°7W **98 G5**
Du Bay, L. *WI* . . . . 44°40N 89°39W **103 D4**
Du Bois *NE* . . . . . . 40°2N 96°4W **84 D9**
Du Page County ☆ *IL* 41°50N 88°5W **71 B5**
Du Quoin *IL* . . . . . 38°1N 89°14W **71 E4**
Duback *LA* . . . . . . 32°42N 92°39W **75 B3**
Dublin *GA* . . . . . . 32°32N 82°54W **68 D4**
Dublin *MD* . . . . . . 39°39N 76°16W **77 A4**
Dublin *NH* . . . . . . 42°52N 72°5W **86 D2**
Dublin *OH* . . . . . . 40°5N 83°7W **92 C3**
Dublin *TX* . . . . . . 32°5N 98°21W **99 E9**
Dublin *VA* . . . . . . 37°6N 80°41W **102 D4**
Dubois *ID* . . . . . . 44°10N 112°14W **70 E6**
Dubois *IN* . . . . . . 38°27N 86°48W **72 E4**
Dubois *WY* . . . . . . 43°33N 109°38W **104 C3**
Dubois County ☆ *IN* 38°20N 86°50W **72 E4**
Dubuque *IA* . . . . . . 42°30N 90°41W **73 C8**
Dubuque County ☆
  IA . . . . 42°30N 90°50W **73 C8**
Duchesne *UT* . . . . 40°10N 110°24W **100 C5**
Duchesne ~ *UT* . . . 40°5N 109°41W **100 C6**
Duchesne County ☆
  UT . . . . 40°20N 110°30W **100 C5**
Duck ~ *TN* . . . . . 36°2N 87°52W **96 D5**
Duck Cr. ~ *NV* . . . 41°55N 116°27W **85 A4**
Duck Hill *MS* . . . . . 33°38N 89°43W **81 C4**
Duck River *TN* . . . . 35°43N 87°16W **96 E5**
Duck Valley Indian Reservation
  NV . . . . 41°53N 116°8W **70 H2**
Ducktown *TN* . . . . . 35°3N 84°23W **97 E8**
Duckwater *NV* . . . . 38°56N 115°43W **85 D5**
Duckwater Indian Reservation
  NV . . . . 38°56N 115°43W **85 D5**
Dudley *GA* . . . . . . 32°32N 83°5W **68 D3**
Dudley *MO* . . . . . . 36°46N 90°8W **82 E6**
Dudley *PA* . . . . . . 40°12N 78°10W **95 D4**
Dudleyville *AZ* . . . . 32°54N 110°42W **62 E5**
Due West *SC* . . . . . 34°20N 82°23W **90 D3**
Dugdemona ~ *LA* . . 31°47N 92°22W **75 C3**
Dugger *IN* . . . . . . 39°4N 87°18W **72 D3**
Dugspur *VA* . . . . . 36°50N 80°37W **102 E4**
Dugway *UT* . . . . . . 40°13N 112°45W **100 C3**
Dugway Proving Ground
  UT . . . . 40°3N 113°1W **100 C2**
Duke *OK* . . . . 34°40N 99°34W **93 D4**
Dukes County ☆ *MA* 41°23N 70°31W **78 C4**
Dulac *LA* . . . . 29°23N 90°42W **75 E5**
Dulce *NM* . . . . . . 36°56N 107°0W **88 A3**
Dulles Int. ✈ (IAD)
  VA . . . . 38°57N 77°27W **102 C7**
Duluth *GA* . . . . . . 34°0N 84°9W **68 B2**
Duluth *MN* . . . . . . 46°47N 92°6W **80 D6**
Dumas *AR* . . . . . . 33°53N 91°29W **63 E4**
Dumas *TX* . . . . . . 35°52N 101°58W **98 B6**
Dumfries *VA* . . . . . 38°34N 77°20W **77 B3**
Dumont *IA* . . . . . . 42°45N 92°58W **73 C6**
Dumont *MN* . . . . . 45°43N 96°26W **80 E2**
Dumont *NJ* . . . . . . 40°56N 73°59W **114 A3**
Dunbar *NE* . . . . . . 40°38N 96°1W **84 D9**
Dunbar *PA* . . . . . . 39°58N 79°37W **95 E3**
Dunbar *WV* . . . . . . 38°22N 81°44W **102 C3**
Dunbarton Center *NH* 43°8N 71°38W **86 C3**
Duncan *AZ* . . . . . . 32°43N 109°6W **62 E6**
Duncan *MS* . . . . . . 34°3N 90°45W **81 B3**
Duncan *OK* . . . . . . 34°30N 97°57W **93 D6**
Duncan *SC* . . . . . . 34°56N 82°9W **90 D3**
Duncannon *PA* . . . . 40°23N 77°2W **95 D5**
Duncanville *TX* . . . . 32°39N 96°54W **109 C4**
Duncombe *IA* . . . . . 42°28N 94°0W **73 C4**
Dundalk *MD* . . . . . 39°15N 76°31W **107 B2**
Dundas *MN* . . . . . . 44°26N 93°12W **80 F5**
Dundas ~ *FL* . . . . . 30°15N 83°15W **67 A5**
Dundee *FL* . . . . . . 28°1N 81°37W **67 C6**
Dundee *MI* . . . . . . 41°57N 83°40W **79 H8**
Dundee *MN* . . . . . . 43°51N 95°28W **80 G3**
Dundee *NY* . . . . . . 42°32N 76°59W **89 C4**
Dundy County ☆
  NE . . . . 40°15N 101°45W **84 D4**
Dunedin *FL* . . . . . . 28°1N 82°46W **67 C5**
Dunes City *OR* . . . . 43°53N 124°7W **94 D1**
Dungannon *VA* . . . . 36°50N 82°28W **102 E2**
Dungeness *WA* . . . . 48°9N 123°7W **101 B2**
Dunkerton *IA* . . . . . 42°34N 92°9W **73 C6**
Dunkirk *IN* . . . . . . 40°23N 85°13W **72 C5**
Dunkirk *MT* . . . . . . 48°29N 111°40W **83 B6**
Dunkirk *NY* . . . . . . 42°29N 79°20W **89 C1**
Dunkirk *OH* . . . . . . 40°48N 83°39W **92 C3**
Dunklin County ☆
  MO . . . . 36°20N 90°0W **82 E6**
Dunlap *IL* . . . . . . 40°52N 89°40W **71 C4**
Dunlap *IA* . . . . . . 41°51N 95°36W **73 D3**
Dunlap *KS* . . . . . . 38°35N 96°22W **74 C7**
Dunlap *TN* . . . . . . 35°23N 85°23W **97 E7**
Dunlow *WV* . . . . . 38°1N 82°26W **102 C2**
Dunmor *KY* . . . . . 37°4N 86°59W **96 C6**
Dunmore *PA* . . . . . 41°25N 75°38W **87 A1**
Dunn *NC* . . . . 35°19N 78°37W **90 C7**
Dunn Center *ND* . . . 47°21N 102°37W **91 C3**
Dunn County ☆ *ND* . 47°21N 102°37W **91 C3**
Dunn County ☆ *WI* . 44°55N 91°50W **103 D2**
Dunn Loring *VA* . . . 38°54N 77°13W **119 B2**
Dunnell *MN* . . . . . . 43°34N 94°47W **80 G4**
Dunning *NE* . . . . . 41°50N 100°6W **84 C5**
Dunnville *KY* . . . . . 37°12N 85°51W **97 C7**
Dunnville *WI* . . . . . 44°46N 91°54W **103 D2**
Dunsmuir *CA* . . . . . 41°13N 122°16W **64 B4**
Dunseith *ND* . . . . . 48°50N 100°3W **91 B5**
Duo *TX* . . . . 36°20N 87°9W **96 D5**
Dupo *IL* . . . . 38°31N 90°13W **75 E5**
Dupont *CO* . . . . . . 39°51N 104°57W **109 J12**
Dupont *IN* . . . . . . 38°54N 85°31W **72 D5**
Dupont *OH* . . . . . . 41°4N 84°17W **92 B2**
Dupont *WA* . . . . . . 47°6N 122°38W **118 E3**
Dupree *SD* . . . . . . 45°4N 101°35W **91 E4**
Dupuyer *MT* . . . . . 48°13N 112°30W **83 B5**
Duquesne *PA* . . . . . 40°22N 79°51W **116 B2**
Duran *NM* . . . . . . 34°28N 105°24W **88 C5**
Durand *IL* . . . . . . 42°26N 89°20W **71 A4**
Durand *MI* . . . . . . 42°55N 83°59W **79 G8**
Durand *WI* . . . . . . 44°38N 91°58W **103 D2**
Durango *CO* . . . . . 37°16N 107°53W **66 E3**
Durant *IA* . . . . . . 41°36N 90°54W **73 D8**
Durant *MS* . . . . . . 33°4N 89°51W **81 C4**
Durant *OK* . . . . . . 33°59N 96°25W **93 E7**
Durbin *WV* . . . . . . 38°33N 79°50W **102 C5**
Durham *CA* . . . . . . 39°39N 121°48W **64 D5**
Durham *CT* . . . . . . 41°29N 72°41W **78 C2**
Durham *KS* . . . . . . 38°30N 97°15W **74 C6**
Durham *NC* . . . . . . 35°59N 78°54W **90 C7**
Durham *NH* . . . . . . 43°8N 70°56W **86 C4**
Durham County ☆ *NC* 36°2N 78°55W **90 C7**
Dushore *PA* . . . . . 41°31N 76°24W **95 C6**
Duson *LA* . . . . . . 30°14N 92°11W **75 D3**
Dustin *OK* . . . . . . 35°12N 96°1W **93 C7**
Dusty *WA* . . . . . . 46°51N 117°38W **101 D8**
Dutch Harbor *AK* . . 53°53N 166°32W **61 K6**
Dutch John *UT* . . . . 40°55N 109°24W **100 B6**
Dutch Mills *AR* . . . . 35°52N 94°29W **63 C1**
Dutch Neck *NJ* . . . . 40°17N 74°40W **87 B2**
Dutchess County ☆
  NY . . . . 41°45N 73°45W **89 D7**
Dutchtown *MO* . . . . 37°18N 89°42W **82 D7**
Dutton *MT* . . . . . . 47°51N 111°43W **83 C6**
Dutton, Mt. *UT* . . . . 38°0N 112°13W **100 E3**
Duval County ☆ *FL* . 30°30N 81°30W **67 A7**
Duval County ☆ *TX* . 27°50N 98°30W **98 K9**
Duvall *WA* . . . . . . 47°45N 121°59W **101 C4**
Duxbury *MA* . . . . . 42°2N 70°40W **78 B4**
Dwight *IL* . . . . . . 41°5N 88°26W **71 B5**
Dwight *KS* . . . . . . 38°50N 96°36W **74 C7**
Dwight *ND* . . . . . . 46°18N 96°44W **91 D9**
Dwight *NE* . . . . . . 41°5N 97°1W **84 C8**
Dworshak Res. *ID* . . 46°48N 116°0W **70 C2**
Dyer *NV* . . . . 37°41N 118°5W **85 E2**
Dyer *TN* . . . . 36°4N 88°59W **96 D4**
Dyersburg *TN* . . . . 36°3N 89°23W **96 D3**
Dyersville *IA* . . . . . 42°29N 91°8W **73 C7**
Dyess *AR* . . . . . . 35°35N 90°13W **63 C5**
Dyess Air Force Base
  TX . . . . 32°25N 99°51W **99 E8**
Dyke *VA* . . . . 38°15N 78°32W **102 C6**
Dysart *IA* . . . . 42°10N 92°18W **73 C6**

E

E.G. Simmons Park
  FL . . . . 27°46N 82°28W **119 C4**
E.V. Spence Res.
  TX . . . . 31°58N 100°40W **98 F7**
Eads *CO* . . . . 38°29N 102°47W **66 D8**
Eagar *AZ* . . . . 34°6N 109°17W **62 C6**
Eagle *AK* . . . . 64°47N 141°12W **61 D12**
Eagle *CO* . . . . 39°39N 106°50W **66 C4**
Eagle *ID* . . . . 43°42N 116°21W **70 F2**
Eagle *NE* . . . . 40°49N 96°26W **84 D9**
Eagle *WI* . . . . 42°53N 88°29W **103 E5**
Eagle ~ *CO* . . . . . . 39°39N 107°4W **66 C3**
Eagle, Mt.
  U.S. Virgin Is. . . 17°46N 64°49W **105 H18**
Eagle Bend *MN* . . . 46°10N 95°2W **80 D3**
Eagle Butte *SD* . . . 45°0N 101°10W **91 H4**
Eagle Cr. ~ *OK* . . . 35°56N 98°53W **93 C5**
Eagle Creek Park
  IN . . . . 39°52N 86°18W **110 A1**
Eagle Grove *IA* . . . . 42°40N 93°54W **73 C5**
Eagle L. *CA* . . . . . 40°39N 120°45W **64 C6**
Eagle L. *ME* . . . . . 46°20N 69°22W **76 B4**
Eagle L. *TX* . . . . . 29°35N 96°20W **99 H11**
Eagle Lake *FL* . . . . 27°59N 81°45W **67 C6**
Eagle Lake *ME* . . . . 47°3N 68°36W **76 B5**
Eagle Lake *MN* . . . . 44°10N 93°54W **80 F5**
Eagle Lake *TX* . . . . 29°35N 96°20W **99 H11**
Eagle Mountain
  CA . . . . 33°49N 115°27W **65 K11**
Eagle Mountain Res.
  TX . . . . 32°53N 97°28W **99 E10**
Eagle Mt. *NM* . . . . 47°54N 90°34W **80 C8**
Eagle Mts. *TX* . . . . 30°55N 105°5W **98 G2**
Eagle Nest *NM* . . . . 36°33N 105°16W **88 A5**
Eagle Nest Butte
  SD . . . . 43°27N 101°39W **91 G4**
Eagle Pass *TX* . . . . 28°43N 100°30W **98 J7**
Eagle Peak *CA* . . . . 41°17N 120°12W **64 B6**
Eagle Pk. *CA* . . . . 37°5N 119°1W **65 F7**
Eagle Point ~
  MN . . . . 44°58N 92°54W **113 B4**
Eagle Point *OR* . . . 42°28N 122°48W **94 E3**
Eagle Point Lake
  MN . . . . 45°5N 92°55W **103 C1**
Eagle River *WI* . . . . 45°55N 89°15W **103 C4**
Eagle Rock *CA* . . . . 34°8N 118°12W **111 B3**
Eagle Rock *VA* . . . . 37°38N 79°48W **102 D5**
Eagletail Mts. *AZ* . . 33°20N 113°30W **62 D2**
Eagleville *CA* . . . . . 41°19N 120°7W **64 B6**
Eagleville *OK* . . . . . 34°2N 94°34W **93 D9**
Eagleville *TN* . . . . . 35°45N 86°39W **96 E6**
Eakly *OK* . . . . 35°18N 98°34W **93 C5**
Earl, L. *CA* . . . . . . 41°50N 124°11W **64 B2**
Earl Park *IN* . . . . . 40°42N 87°25W **72 C3**
Earle *AR* . . . . 35°16N 90°28W **63 C5**
Earleville *MD* . . . . 39°24N 75°54W **77 A5**
Earlham *IA* . . . . . . 41°30N 94°7W **73 D4**
Earlimart *CA* . . . . . 35°53N 119°16W **65 H7**
Earling *IA* . . . . . . 41°38N 95°25W **73 D3**
Earlington *KY* . . . . 37°16N 87°30W **96 C5**
Earlsboro *OK* . . . . 35°19N 96°47W **93 C7**
Earlton *KS* . . . . . . 37°35N 95°28W **74 D8**
Earlville *IL* . . . . . . 41°35N 88°55W **71 B5**
Earlville *NY* . . . . . 42°44N 75°33W **89 C5**
Early *TX* . . . . 31°46N 98°58W **99 F9**
Early County ☆ *GA* . 31°20N 84°55W **68 E1**
Earth *TX* . . . . 34°14N 102°24W **98 D5**
Easley *SC* . . . . . . 34°50N 82°36W **90 D3**
East ~ *NY* . . . . . . 40°47N 73°58W **114 B3**
East Acton *MA* . . . 42°28N 71°24W **106 A1**
East Alton *IL* . . . . 38°53N 90°7W **117 A3**
East Arlington *MA* . 42°24N 71°9W **106 A3**
East Arlington *VT* . 43°3N 73°9W **86 C1**
East Arm Grand Traverse B.
  MI . . . . 44°55N 85°29W **79 E6**
East Atlantic Beach
  NY . . . . 40°35N 73°42W **114 C4**
East Aurora *NY* . . . 42°46N 78°37W **89 C2**
East B. *TX* . . . . . . 29°30N 94°43W **99 H13**
East B. *LA* . . . . . . 29°0N 89°12W **75 F6**
East Baton Rouge Parish ☆
  LA . . . . 30°30N 91°5W **75 D4**
East Bend *NC* . . . . 36°13N 80°31W **90 B5**
East Berkshire *VT* . 44°56N 72°42W **86 B2**
East Berlin *PA* . . . 39°56N 76°59W **95 D6**
East Bernard *TX* . . 29°32N 96°4W **99 H11**
East Bernstadt *KY* . 37°9N 84°12W **97 C8**
East Boston *MA* . . 42°22N 71°0W **106 A3**
East Brady *PA* . . . 40°59N 79°37W **95 D3**
East Branch Clarion River L.
  PA . . . . 41°35N 78°35W **95 C4**
East Brewton *AL* . . 31°6N 87°4W **60 E3**
East Bridgewater *MA* 42°2N 70°58W **78 B4**

East Brunswick *NJ* . 40°25N 74°23W **87 B2**
East Canton *OH* . . . 40°47N 81°17W **92 C5**
East Canyon Res.
  UT . . . . 40°55N 111°36W **117 A4**
East Canyon State Park
  UT . . . . 40°54N 111°35W **117 A4**
East Carbon *UT* . . . 39°35N 110°25W **100 D5**
East Carroll Parish ☆
  LA . . . . 32°45N 91°15W **75 B4**
East Charleston *VT* . 44°49N 71°59W **86 B3**
East Chicago *IN* . . . 41°38N 87°27W **72 B3**
East Cleveland *OH* . 41°31N 81°34W **107 A2**
East Corinth *VT* . . . 44°5N 72°12W **86 B2**
East Cote Blanche B.
  LA . . . . 29°34N 91°38W **75 E4**
East Dismal Swamp
  NC . . . . 35°43N 76°41W **90 C9**
East Dorset *VT* . . . 43°13N 73°0W **86 C2**
East Douglas *MA* . . 42°4N 71°43W **78 B3**
East Dublin *GA* . . . 32°32N 82°52W **68 D4**
East Dubuque *IL* . . 42°30N 90°39W **71 A3**
East Elmhurst *NY* . 40°45N 73°52W **114 B3**
East Ely *NV* . . . . . 39°15N 114°53W **85 C6**
East Fairfield *VT* . . 44°47N 72°55W **86 B2**
East Feliciana Parish ☆
  LA . . . . 30°47N 91°8W **75 D4**
East Flat Rock *NC* . 35°17N 82°25W **90 C3**
East Fork Amite ~
  U.S.A. . . . . . . 31°0N 90°50W **81 E3**
East Fork Bruneau ~
  ID . . . . 42°34N 115°38W **70 G3**
East Fork Obey ~
  TN . . . . 36°27N 85°9W **97 D7**
East Fork Sevier ~
  UT . . . . 38°14N 112°12W **100 E3**
East Fork White ~
  IN . . . . 38°33N 87°14W **72 E3**
East Fultonham *OH* . 39°51N 82°8W **92 D4**
East Gaffney *SC* . . 35°5N 81°38W **90 C4**
East Glacier Park
  MT . . . . 48°27N 113°13W **83 B4**
East Granby *CT* . . . 41°57N 72°44W **78 B2**
East Grand Forks *MN* 47°56N 97°1W **80 C1**
East Grand Rapids
  MI . . . . 42°58N 85°37W **79 G6**
East Greenville *PA* . 40°24N 75°30W **87 B1**
East Greenwich *RI* . 41°40N 71°27W **78 C3**
East Haddam *CT* . . 41°27N 72°28W **78 C2**
East Hampton *CT* . . 41°35N 72°31W **78 C2**
East Hampton *NY* . 40°58N 72°11W **78 D2**
East Hartford *CT* . . 41°46N 72°39W **78 B2**
East Haven *CT* . . . 41°17N 72°52W **78 C2**
East Haverhill *NH* . 44°3N 71°58W **86 B3**
East Helena *MT* . . 46°35N 111°56W **83 D6**
East Hills *NY* . . . . 40°47N 73°37W **114 B5**
East Holden *ME* . . 44°44N 68°38W **76 D5**
East Hope *ID* . . . . 48°14N 116°17W **70 A2**
East Houston *TX* . . 29°49N 95°16W **110 A3**
East Jordan *MI* . . . 45°10N 85°7W **79 D6**
East Kingston *NH* . 42°55N 71°2W **86 D3**
East Lansdowne *PA* 39°56N 75°15W **116 B1**
East Lansing *MI* . . 42°44N 84°29W **79 G7**
East Las Vegas = Whitney
  NV . . . . 36°4N 115°5W **110 C2**
East Lempster *NH* . 43°13N 72°13W **86 C2**
East Lexington *MA* . 42°27N 71°12W **106 A2**
East Liberty *OH* . . 40°20N 83°35W **92 C3**
East Liverpool *OH* . 40°37N 80°35W **92 C6**
East Longmeadow
  MA . . . . 42°4N 72°31W **78 B2**
East Los Angeles
  CA . . . . 34°1N 118°10W **111 B3**
East Lyme *CT* . . . . 41°22N 72°14W **78 C2**
East Lynn L. *WV* . . 38°10N 82°23W **102 C2**
East Lynne *MO* . . . 38°41N 94°14W **82 C2**
East Meadow *NY* . 40°43N 73°33W **114 B5**
East Middlebury *VT* 43°58N 73°6W **86 C1**
East Millcreek *UT* . 40°41N 111°48W **117 B3**
East Millinocket *ME* 45°38N 68°35W **76 C5**
East Milwaukee = Shorewood
  WI . . . . 43°5N 87°53W **112 B2**
East Moline *IL* . . . 41°32N 90°26W **71 B3**
East Naples *FL* . . . 26°8N 81°46W **67 E7**
East New Market
  MD . . . . 38°36N 75°56W **77 B5**
East New York *NY* . 40°40N 73°53W **114 B3**
East Newark *NJ* . . 40°45N 74°9W **114 B1**
East Nishnabotna ~
  IA . . . . 40°53N 95°38W **73 E3**
East Northport *NY* . 40°53N 73°20W **78 D1**
East Norwich *NY* . 40°51N 73°32W **87 B3**
East Olympia *WA* . 46°58N 122°50W **101 D3**
East Orange *NJ* . . 40°46N 74°12W **114 B1**
East Palatka *FL* . . 29°39N 81°36W **67 B7**
East Palestine *OH* . 40°50N 80°33W **92 C6**
East Park Res. *CA* . 39°37N 122°31W **64 D4**
East Paterson *NJ* . 40°54N 74°7W **114 A2**
East Peoria *IL* . . . 40°40N 89°34W **71 C4**
East Peru *IA* . . . . 41°14N 93°56W **73 D5**
East Petersburg *PA* 40°6N 76°21W **95 D6**
East Pines *MD* . . . 38°57N 76°54W **119 B4**
East Point *GA* . . . 33°41N 84°25W **106 B2**
East Potomac Park
  DC . . . . 38°52N 77°1W **119 B3**
East Prairie *MO* . . 36°47N 89°23W **82 E7**
East Prospect *PA* . 39°58N 76°32W **95 E6**
East Providence *RI* 41°49N 71°23W **78 C3**
East Pt.
  Br. Virgin Is. . . 18°40N 64°18W **105 G18**
East Pt.
  U.S. Virgin Is. . 17°45N 64°34W **105 H18**
East Randolph *VT* . 43°57N 72°33W **86 C2**
East Range *NV* . . 40°30N 117°57W **85 B3**
East Ridge *TN* . . . 34°59N 85°13W **97 F7**
East River ~ *NY* . . 40°45N 73°58W **114 C3**
East Rochester *NY* . 43°7N 77°29W **89 B3**
East Rockaway *NY* . 40°38N 73°40W **114 C4**
East Rockingham
  NC . . . . 34°55N 79°45W **90 D6**
East Rupert *VT* . . 43°16N 73°8W **86 C1**
East Rutherford *NJ* 40°50N 74°5W **114 A2**
East St. Louis *IL* . . 38°37N 90°9W **117 B3**
East Sebago *ME* . . 43°51N 70°38W **86 B4**
East Shoreham *NY* . 40°57N 72°53W **78 D2**
East Side *PA* . . . . 41°4N 75°46W **87 A1**
East Spring Cr. ~
  CO . . . . 39°40N 109°40W **100 D6**
East Stroudsburg *PA* 41°1N 75°11W **95 C7**
East Tavaputs Plateau
  UT . . . . 39°40N 109°40W **100 D6**
East Tawas *MI* . . . 44°17N 83°29W **79 E8**
East Troy *WI* . . . . 42°47N 88°24W **103 E5**
East Vineland *NJ* . . 39°30N 74°55W **87 C2**
East Wallingford *VT* 43°27N 72°51W **86 C2**
East Wareham *MA* . 41°46N 70°40W **78 C4**
East Wenatchee
  WA . . . . 47°25N 120°18W **101 C5**
East Williston *NY* . 40°45N 73°38W **114 B5**
East Windsor *NJ* . . 40°17N 74°34W **87 B2**
East Youngstown = Campbell
  OH . . . . 41°5N 80°37W **92 B6**
Eastanollee *GA* . . . 34°29N 83°19W **68 B3**
Eastchester *NY* . . 40°57N 73°49W **114 A3**
Eastchester Bay *NY* 40°50N 73°48W **114 A4**
Eastern Neck Nat. Wildlife
  Refuge ☆ *MD* . . 39°2N 76°14W **77 A4**
Eastern Shore *MD* . 38°35N 75°50W **77 B5**

Eastgate WA ..... 47°34N 122°9W 118 C5
Eastham MA ..... 41°50N 69°58W 78 C5
Easthampton MA .. 42°16N 72°40W 78 B2
Eastlake MI ..... 44°15N 86°18W 79 E6
Eastlake OH ..... 41°40N 81°26W 92 B5
Eastland TX ..... 32°24N 98°49W 99 E9
Eastland County ☆
  TX. ..... 32°25N 98°50W 99 E9
Eastman GA ..... 32°12N 83°11W 68 D3
Eastman WI ..... 43°10N 91°1W 103 E2
Easton CA ..... 36°39N 119°47W 65 G7
Easton CT ..... 41°15N 73°18W 78 C1
Easton IL ..... 40°14N 89°50W 71 C4
Easton KS ..... 39°21N 95°7W 74 B8
Easton MD ..... 38°47N 76°5W 87 B4
Easton MN ..... 43°46N 93°54W 80 G5
Easton MO ..... 39°43N 94°39W 82 B2
Easton PA ..... 40°41N 75°13W 87 B1
Easton WA ..... 47°14N 121°11W 101 C4
Eastover NC ..... 35°6N 78°47W 90 C7
Eastover SC ..... 33°52N 80°41W 90 E5
Eastpoint FL ..... 29°44N 84°53W 67 B4
Eastport ID ..... 48°59N 116°10W 70 A2
Eastport ME ..... 44°56N 67°0W 76 D6
Eastport MI ..... 45°6N 85°13W 79 D6
Eastsound WA .... 48°42N 122°55W 101 B3
Eastview TN ..... 35°5N 88°33W 96 E4
Eastville VA ..... 37°21N 75°57W 102 D9
Eastwood LA ..... 32°33N 93°34W 75 B2
Eaton CO ..... 40°32N 104°42W 66 B6
Eaton IN ..... 40°21N 85°21W 72 C5
Eaton OH ..... 39°45N 84°38W 92 D2
Eaton Canyon Park
  CA ..... 34°10N 118°5W 111 A3
Eaton Rapids MI .. 42°31N 84°39W 79 G7
Eatons Neck Pt. NY. 40°57N 73°24W 78 D1
Eatonton GA ..... 33°20N 83°23W 68 C3
Eatontown NJ .... 40°19N 74°4W 87 B2
Eatonville WA .... 46°52N 122°16W 101 D3
Eau Claire MI .... 41°59N 86°18W 79 H5
Eau Claire WI .... 44°49N 91°30W 103 D2
Eau Claire → WI .. 44°55N 89°35W 103 D4
Eau Claire County ☆
  WI. ..... 44°45N 91°20W 103 D2
Eau Galle WI ..... 44°42N 92°1W 103 D1
Ebensburg PA .... 40°29N 78°44W 95 D4
Ebey's Landing Nat. Historical
  Reserve ○ WA . 48°12N 122°41W 101 B3
Ebony VA ..... 36°37N 77°59W 102 E7
Eccles WV ..... 37°47N 81°16W 102 D3
Echeechotee → GA 32°39N 83°36W 68 D3
Echo AL ..... 31°29N 85°28W 60 E5
Echo MN ..... 44°37N 95°25W 80 F3
Echo OR ..... 45°45N 119°12W 94 B6
Echo Bay NY ..... 40°54N 73°46W 114 A4
Echo Cliffs AZ .... 36°30N 111°35W 62 A4
Echols County ☆ GA. 30°45N 83°0W 68 F4
Eckley CO ..... 40°7N 102°29W 66 B8
Eclectic AL ..... 32°38N 86°2W 60 D4
Economy = Ambridge
  PA. ..... 40°36N 80°14W 95 D2
Economy IN ..... 39°59N 85°5W 72 C4
Ecru MS ..... 34°21N 89°2W 81 B4
Ector County ☆ TX 31°46N 102°37W 98 F5
Edcouch TX ..... 26°18N 97°58W 98 L10
Eddy County ☆ ND. 47°50N 99°0W 91 C7
Eddy County ☆ NM 32°30N 104°20W 88 E6
Eddyville IL ..... 37°30N 88°35W 71 F5
Eddyville IA ..... 41°9N 92°38W 73 D6
Eddyville KY ..... 37°3N 88°4W 96 C4
Eddyville NE ..... 41°1N 99°38W 84 C6
Eden = Bar Harbor
  ME ..... 44°23N 68°13W 76 D5
Eden MS ..... 32°59N 90°20W 81 D3
Eden NC ..... 36°29N 79°53W 90 B6
Eden SD ..... 45°37N 97°25W 91 E8
Eden TX ..... 31°13N 99°51W 99 F8
Eden VT ..... 44°42N 72°33W 86 B2
Eden WI ..... 43°42N 88°22W 103 E5
Eden WY ..... 42°3N 109°26W 104 D3
Eden Res. WY. .... 42°14N 109°21W 104 D3
Eden Valley MN ... 45°19N 94°33W 80 E4
Edenton NC ..... 36°4N 76°39W 90 B9
Edenvale Park MN. 44°52N 93°27W 113 B1
Edesville MD ..... 39°9N 76°13W 77 A4
Edgar NE ..... 40°22N 97°58W 84 D8
Edgar WI ..... 44°55N 89°59W 103 D4
Edgar County ☆ IL. 39°40N 87°45W 71 D7
Edgar Springs MO . 37°42N 91°52W 82 D5
Edgard LA ..... 30°3N 90°34W 75 E6
Edgartown MA .... 41°23N 70°31W 78 C4
Edgecliff TX ..... 32°39N 97°20W 109 C1
Edgecombe County ☆
  NC. ..... 35°50N 77°30W 90 C8
Edgefield SC ..... 33°47N 81°56W 90 E4
Edgefield County ☆
  SC. ..... 33°50N 82°0W 90 E4
Edgeley ND ..... 46°22N 98°43W 91 D7
Edgemar CA ..... 37°39N 122°29W 118 C2
Edgemere MD ..... 39°14N 76°27W 77 A4
Edgemont SD ..... 43°18N 103°50W 91 G2
Edgerton KS ..... 38°46N 95°1W 74 C8
Edgerton MN ..... 43°53N 96°8W 80 G2
Edgerton MO ..... 39°30N 94°38W 82 B2
Edgerton OH ..... 41°27N 84°45W 92 B2
Edgerton WI ..... 42°50N 89°4W 103 F4
Edgerton WY ..... 43°25N 106°15W 104 C6
Edgewater CO ..... 39°45N 105°3W 109 B1
Edgewater FL ..... 28°59N 80°54W 67 C8
Edgewater Park OH 41°29N 81°43W 107 B1
Edgewater NJ ..... 40°4N 74°54W 87 B2
Edgewood FL ..... 28°29N 81°22W 115 B2
Edgewood IL ..... 38°55N 88°40W 71 E5
Edgewood IN ..... 39°41N 86°8W 72 D4
Edgewood IA ..... 42°39N 91°24W 73 C7
Edgewood KY ..... 39°1N 84°34W 107 B1
Edgewood MD ..... 39°25N 76°18W 77 A4
Edgewood NM ..... 35°4N 106°11W 88 B4
Edgewood TX ..... 32°42N 95°53W 99 E12
Edina MN ..... 44°53N 93°20W 113 B1
Edina MO ..... 40°10N 92°11W 82 A4
Edinboro PA ..... 41°52N 80°8W 95 C2
Edinburg IL ..... 39°39N 89°23W 71 D4
Edinburg MS ..... 32°48N 89°20W 81 D4
Edinburg ND ..... 48°30N 97°52W 91 B8
Edinburg TX ..... 26°18N 98°10W 98 L9
Edinburgh IN ..... 39°21N 85°58W 72 D4
Edison GA ..... 31°34N 84°44W 68 E2
Edison NJ ..... 40°31N 74°25W 87 B2
Edison NE ..... 40°17N 99°47W 84 D6
Edison Park IL .... 42°1N 87°48W 108 A2
Edisto → SC ..... 32°29N 80°21W 90 F5
Edisto I. SC ..... 32°35N 80°20W 90 F5
Edmond KS ..... 39°37N 99°50W 74 B4
Edmond OK ..... 35°39N 97°29W 93 C8
Edmonds WA ..... 47°48N 122°23W 118 B3
Edmondson AR .... 35°6N 90°19W 63 C5
Edmondson TX .... 34°17N 101°54W 98 C6
Edmonson County ☆
  KY. ..... 37°10N 86°15W 96 C6
Edmonton KY ..... 36°59N 85°37W 97 D7
Edmore MI ..... 43°25N 85°3W 79 F6
Edmore ND ..... 48°25N 98°27W 91 B7
Edmunds County ☆
  SD. ..... 45°27N 99°20W 91 E6

Edmundson MO ... 38°44N 90°21W 117 A1
Edna KS ..... 37°4N 95°22W 74 D8
Edna TX ..... 28°59N 96°39W 99 J11
Edray WV ..... 38°16N 80°6W 102 C4
Edroy TX ..... 27°59N 97°41W 98 K10
Edson KS ..... 39°20N 101°33W 74 B2
Edwall WA ..... 47°30N 117°57W 101 C8
Edward Arthur Patterson L.
  CA ..... 34°52N 117°56W 65 J9
Edwards CA ..... 34°50N 117°40W 65 J9
Edwards MS ..... 32°20N 90°36W 81 D3
Edwards NY ..... 44°20N 75°15W 89 A5
Edwards → IL ..... 41°9N 90°59W 71 B3
Edwards Air Force Base
  CA ..... 34°52N 117°56W 65 J9
Edwards County ☆ IL. 38°25N 88°0W 71 E5
Edwards County ☆
  KS. ..... 37°50N 99°15W 74 D4
Edwards County ☆
  TX. ..... 30°10N 100°13W 98 G7
Edwards Plateau
  TX. ..... 30°45N 101°20W 98 G6
Edwardsburg MI .. 41°48N 86°6W 79 H5
Edwardsport IN ... 38°49N 87°15W 72 E3
Edwardsville IL ... 38°49N 89°58W 71 E4
Eek AK ..... 60°14N 162°2W 61 F7
Eel → CA ..... 40°38N 124°20W 64 C2
Eel → IN ..... 39°7N 86°57W 72 D4
Eel → IN ..... 40°45N 86°22W 72 C4
Effie MN ..... 47°50N 93°38W 80 C5
Effigy Mounds Nat. Monument ○
  IA ..... 43°5N 91°11W 73 B7
Effingham IL ..... 39°7N 88°33W 71 D5
Effingham KS ..... 39°31N 95°24W 74 B8
Effingham County ☆
  GA ..... 32°20N 81°15W 68 D5
Effingham County ☆
  IL. ..... 39°5N 88°35W 71 D5
Effingham Falls NH . 43°47N 71°5W 86 C3
Egan Range WY ... 39°35N 114°55W 85 C6
Egegik AK ..... 58°13N 157°22W 61 G8
Egeland ND ..... 48°38N 99°6W 91 B6
Egg Harbor WI ... 45°3N 87°17W 103 C6
Egg Harbor City NJ . 39°32N 74°39W 87 C2
Egg Island Pt. NJ .. 39°11N 75°8W 87 C1
Eglin Air Force Base
  FL. ..... 30°28N 86°32W 67 A2
Egmont Channel
  FL. ..... 27°36N 82°47W 119 D2
Egmont Key State Park
  FL. ..... 27°36N 82°46W 119 D2
Egnar CO ..... 37°55N 108°56W 66 E2
Ehrenberg AZ .... 33°36N 114°31W 62 D1
Eielson AK ..... 64°40N 147°4W 61 D11
Eklutna AK ..... 61°27N 149°22W 61 F10
Ekron KY ..... 37°56N 86°11W 96 C5
Ekwok AK ..... 59°22N 157°30W 61 G8
El Cajon CA ..... 32°48N 116°58W 65 L10
El Campo TX ..... 29°12N 96°16W 99 H11
El Capitan Res. CA 32°53N 116°49W 65 L10
El Centro CA ..... 32°48N 115°34W 65 L11
El Cerrito CA ..... 37°55N 122°19W 64 F4
El Dorado AR ..... 33°12N 92°40W 63 E3
El Dorado KS ..... 37°49N 96°52W 74 D7
El Dorado County ☆
  CA ..... 38°45N 120°40W 64 E6
El Dorado L. KS ... 37°51N 96°49W 74 D7
El Dorado Park CA 33°48N 118°5W 111 D4
El Dorado Springs
  MO ..... 37°52N 94°1W 82 D2
El Indio TX ..... 28°31N 100°19W 98 J7
El Malpais Nat. Monument ○
  U.S.A. ..... 34°53N 108°0W 88 C2
El Mirage AZ ..... 33°36N 112°19W 62 D3
El Mirage L. CA ... 34°39N 117°37W 65 J9
El Monte CA ..... 34°4N 118°1W 111 B4
El Morro Nat. Monument ○
  NM ..... 35°2N 108°21W 88 B2
El Nido CA ..... 37°8N 120°29W 64 F6
El Paso = Derby KS . 37°33N 97°16W 74 D6
El Paso IL ..... 40°44N 89°1W 71 C4
El Paso TX ..... 31°45N 106°29W 98 F1
El Paso County ☆
  CO ..... 38°50N 104°30W 66 D6
El Paso County ☆ TX 31°55N 106°15W 98 F1
El Paso Int. × (ELP)
  TX. ..... 31°48N 106°23W 98 F1
El Portal CA ..... 37°41N 119°47W 64 F7
El Portal FL ..... 25°51N 80°11W 112 C2
El Porvenir NM ... 35°43N 105°25W 88 B5
El Reno OK ..... 35°32N 97°57W 93 C6
El Rio CA ..... 34°14N 119°10W 65 J7
El Rito NM ..... 36°21N 106°11W 88 A4
El Segundo CA .... 33°55N 118°24W 111 C2
El Sereno CA ..... 34°5N 118°10W 111 B3
El Vado Res. NM .. 36°36N 106°44W 88 A4
El Yunque
  Puerto Rico .. 18°19N 65°48W 105 G17
Elaine AR ..... 34°19N 90°51W 63 D5
Elam PA ..... 39°51N 75°32W 77 A5
Elba AL ..... 31°25N 86°4W 60 E4
Elba ID ..... 42°14N 113°34W 70 G5
Elba MN ..... 44°5N 92°1W 80 F6
Elba NE ..... 41°17N 98°34W 84 C7
Elberfeld IN ..... 38°10N 87°27W 72 E3
Elberon IA ..... 42°0N 92°19W 73 C6
Elbert, Mt. CO .... 39°13N 106°27W 66 D4
Elbert TX ..... 33°15N 99°0W 99 D9
Elbert County ☆
  CO ..... 39°20N 104°15W 66 C6
Elbert County ☆ GA 34°10N 82°50W 68 B4
Elberta AL ..... 44°37N 86°14W 79 E6
Elberta UT ..... 39°57N 111°57W 100 D4
Elberton GA ..... 34°7N 82°52W 68 B4
Elbing KS ..... 38°3N 97°8W 74 C6
Elbow Lake MN ... 45°59N 95°58W 80 E2
Elburn IL ..... 41°54N 88°28W 108 A1
Elcho WI ..... 45°27N 89°11W 103 D4
Elderon WI ..... 44°47N 89°15W 103 D4
Eldersburg MD .... 39°24N 76°57W 77 A4
Eldon IA ..... 40°55N 92°13W 73 D6
Eldon MO ..... 38°21N 92°35W 82 C4
Eldon WA ..... 47°33N 123°3W 101 C2
Eldora IA ..... 42°22N 93°5W 73 C5
Eldora NJ ..... 39°12N 74°52W 87 C2
Eldorado IL ..... 37°49N 88°26W 71 F5
Eldorado OH ..... 39°54N 84°41W 92 D2
Eldorado TX ..... 30°52N 100°36W 98 G7
Eldorado at Santa Fe
  NM ..... 35°32N 105°56W 88 B5
Eldorendo GA ..... 31°3N 84°39W 68 E2
Eldred IL ..... 39°19N 90°34W 71 D3
Eldred PA ..... 41°58N 78°23W 95 C4
Eldridge CA ..... 38°22N 122°30W 64 E4
Eldridge IA ..... 41°39N 90°35W 73 D8
Eldridge MO ..... 37°50N 92°45W 82 D4
Eldridge ND ..... 46°54N 98°51W 91 D7
Eleanor WV ..... 38°32N 81°56W 102 C3
Eleanor, L. CA .... 37°59N 119°53W 64 F7
Eleao HI ..... 21°27N 157°52W 69 K14
Electra TX ..... 34°2N 98°55W 99 C9
Electra L. CO ..... 37°33N 107°48W 66 E3
Electric City WA .. 47°56N 119°2W 101 C6
Electric Mills MS .. 32°46N 88°28W 81 D5

Elephant Butte NM. 33°9N 107°11W 88 D3
Elephant Butte Lake State Park
  NM ..... 33°38N 107°1W 88 D3
Elephant Butte Res.
  NM ..... 33°9N 107°11W 88 D3
Elevation Mt. ME .. 44°46N 70°47W 86 A3
Eleva WI ..... 44°35N 91°28W 103 D2
Eleven Point → AR . 36°9N 91°5W 63 B4
Elevenmile Canyon Res.
  CO ..... 38°54N 105°29W 66 D5
Elfin Cove AK ..... 58°12N 136°22W 61 G13
Elfrida AZ ..... 31°41N 109°41W 62 F6
Elgin IL ..... 42°2N 88°17W 71 A5
Elgin IA ..... 42°57N 91°38W 73 C7
Elgin KS ..... 37°0N 96°17W 74 E7
Elgin MN ..... 44°8N 92°15W 80 F6
Elgin ND ..... 46°24N 101°51W 91 D4
Elgin NE ..... 41°59N 98°5W 84 C7
Elgin OK ..... 34°47N 98°18W 93 D5
Elgin OR ..... 45°34N 117°55W 94 B8
Elgin SC ..... 34°10N 80°48W 90 D5
Elgin TX ..... 30°21N 97°22W 99 G10
Elgin Res. TX ..... 28°42N 99°59W 99 J8
Eli NE ..... 42°58N 103°18W 84 B2
Elida NM ..... 33°57N 103°39W 88 D7
Elida OH ..... 40°47N 84°12W 92 C2
Elim AK ..... 64°37N 162°15W 61 D7
Eliot ME ..... 43°9N 70°47W 76 E3
Elizabeth CO ..... 39°22N 104°36W 66 C6
Elizabeth IL ..... 42°19N 90°13W 71 A3
Elizabeth LA ..... 30°52N 92°48W 75 D3
Elizabeth MN ..... 46°23N 96°8W 80 D2
Elizabeth NJ ..... 40°39N 74°12W 114 C3
Elizabeth WV ..... 39°4N 81°24W 102 B3
Elizabeth, C. WA .. 47°21N 124°19W 101 C1
Elizabeth City NC.. 36°18N 76°14W 90 B9
Elizabeth Islands MA 41°29N 70°50W 78 C4
Elizabeth River
  VA ..... 36°52N 76°20W 115 A1
Elizabethton TN ... 36°21N 82°13W 97 D10
Elizabethtown IL ... 37°27N 88°18W 71 F5
Elizabethtown KY .. 37°42N 85°52W 97 C7
Elizabethtown NC .. 34°38N 78°37W 90 D7
Elizabethtown NY .. 44°13N 73°36W 89 A7
Elizabethtown PA .. 40°9N 76°36W 95 D6
Elizabethville PA ... 40°33N 76°49W 95 D6
Elk CA ..... 39°8N 123°43W 64 D3
Elk → AL ..... 34°46N 87°16W 60 B3
Elk → KS ..... 37°15N 95°41W 74 D8
Elk → MD ..... 39°26N 76°1W 77 A4
Elk → WV ..... 38°21N 81°38W 102 C3
Elk Basin WY ..... 44°59N 108°52W 104 B4
Elk City ID ..... 45°50N 115°26W 70 D3
Elk City KS ..... 37°18N 95°55W 74 D8
Elk City OK ..... 35°25N 99°25W 93 C4
Elk City Lake KS .. 37°30N 96°1W 74 D7
Elk County ☆ KS .. 37°30N 96°16W 74 D7
Elk County ☆ PA .. 41°35N 78°45W 95 C4
Elk Cr. → SD ..... 44°14N 102°22W 91 F3
Elk Creek CA ..... 39°36N 122°32W 64 D4
Elk Creek NE ..... 40°17N 96°8W 84 D9
Elk Falls KS ..... 37°22N 96°11W 74 D7
Elk Garden WV ... 39°23N 79°9W 77 A1
Elk Grove CA ..... 38°25N 121°22W 64 E5
Elk Hill PA ..... 41°42N 75°32W 95 C7
Elk Horn IA ..... 41°36N 95°3W 73 D3
Elk L. MI ..... 44°50N 85°20W 79 E6
Elk Mound WI .... 44°52N 91°42W 103 D2
Elk Mountain WY . 41°41N 106°25W 104 E6
Elk Mt. WY ..... 41°38N 106°32W 104 E6
Elk Neck MD ..... 39°31N 75°57W 77 A5
Elk Point SD ..... 42°41N 96°41W 91 H9
Elk Rapids MI .... 44°54N 85°25W 79 E6
Elk Ridge UT ..... 40°1N 111°41W 100 C4
Elk River ID ..... 46°47N 116°11W 70 C2
Elk River MN ..... 45°18N 93°35W 80 E5
Elkader IA ..... 42°51N 91°24W 73 C7
Elkhart IL ..... 40°1N 89°29W 71 C4
Elkhart IN ..... 41°41N 85°58W 72 B5
Elkhart KS ..... 37°0N 101°54W 74 D2
Elkhart TX ..... 31°38N 95°35W 99 F12
Elkhart County ☆ IN 41°35N 85°50W 72 B5
Elkhart Lake WI ... 43°50N 88°1W 103 E5
Elkhorn NE ..... 41°17N 96°14W 84 C9
Elkhorn WI ..... 42°40N 88°33W 103 F5
Elkhorn → NE .... 41°8N 96°19W 84 C9
Elkhorn City KY ... 37°18N 82°21W 97 D10
Elkin NC ..... 36°15N 80°51W 90 B5
Elkins AR ..... 36°0N 94°0W 63 B2
Elkins NM ..... 33°42N 104°4W 88 D6
Elkins WV ..... 38°55N 79°51W 102 C5
Elkins Park PA .... 40°4N 75°7W 116 A2
Elkland MO ..... 37°27N 93°2W 82 D3
Elkland PA ..... 41°59N 77°19W 95 C5
Elkmont AL ..... 34°56N 86°58W 60 B4
Elko GA ..... 32°20N 83°42W 68 D3
Elko MN ..... 44°34N 93°19W 80 F5
Elko NV ..... 40°50N 115°46W 85 B5
Elko County ☆ NV. 41°10N 115°20W 85 B5
Elkol WY ..... 41°43N 110°37W 104 E2
Elkridge MD ..... 39°12N 76°42W 77 A4
Elkton KY ..... 36°49N 87°9W 96 D5
Elkton MD ..... 39°37N 75°49W 77 A5
Elkton MI ..... 43°49N 83°11W 79 F8
Elkton OR ..... 43°40N 123°34W 94 D2
Elkton SD ..... 44°14N 96°29W 91 F9
Elkton TN ..... 35°3N 86°53W 96 E6
Elkton VA ..... 38°25N 78°37W 102 C6
Elkville IL ..... 37°55N 89°14W 71 F4
Ellamore WV ..... 38°55N 80°5W 102 C4
Ellaville GA ..... 32°14N 84°19W 68 D2
Ellenboro WV ..... 39°16N 81°3W 102 B3
Ellendale DE ..... 38°48N 75°26W 77 B5
Ellendale MN ..... 43°52N 93°18W 80 G5
Ellendale ND ..... 46°0N 98°32W 91 D7
Ellenor, L. FL ..... 28°28N 81°25W 115 B2
Ellensburg WA .... 46°59N 120°34W 101 D5
Ellenton GA ..... 31°11N 83°35W 68 E3
Ellenville NY ..... 41°43N 74°24W 89 D6
Ellerbe NC ..... 35°4N 79°46W 90 C6
Ellettsville IN ..... 39°14N 86°38W 72 D4
Ellicott City MD ... 39°16N 76°48W 77 A4
Ellicottville NY .... 42°17N 78°40W 89 C2
Ellijay GA ..... 34°42N 84°29W 68 B2
Ellington CT ..... 41°54N 72°28W 78 C2
Ellington MO ..... 37°14N 90°58W 82 D6
Ellington NY ..... 42°13N 79°6W 89 C1
Ellinwood KS ..... 38°21N 98°35W 74 C5
Elliott IA ..... 41°9N 95°10W 73 D3
Elliott, L. NJ ..... 40°41N 74°2W 114 C3
Elliott MD ..... 38°38N 75°59W 77 B5
Elliott MS ..... 33°41N 89°45W 81 C4
Elliott ND ..... 46°24N 97°49W 91 D8
Elliott Bay WA .... 47°36N 122°21W 118 C3
Elliott County ☆ KY. 38°5N 83°5W 97 B9
Elliott Key FL ..... 25°27N 80°12W 67 G8
Elliott Knob VA ... 38°10N 79°19W 102 C5
Ellis ID ..... 44°42N 114°3W 70 E4
Ellis KS ..... 38°56N 99°34W 74 C4
Ellis NE ..... 40°13N 96°54W 84 D9
Ellis County ☆ KS . 38°45N 99°15W 74 C4
Ellis County ☆ OK. 36°20N 99°45W 93 B4
Ellis County ☆ TX. 32°20N 96°48W 99 E11
Ellis Grove IL ..... 38°1N 89°55W 71 E4
Elliston MT ..... 46°33N 112°26W 83 D4
Ellisville MS ..... 31°36N 89°12W 81 E4
Elloree SC ..... 33°32N 80°34W 90 E5

Ellsinore MO ..... 36°56N 90°45W 82 E6
Ellston IA ..... 40°51N 94°7W 73 E4
Ellsworth IA ..... 42°19N 93°35W 73 C5
Ellsworth KS ..... 38°44N 98°14W 74 C5
Ellsworth ME ..... 44°33N 68°25W 76 D5
Ellsworth MI ..... 45°10N 85°15W 79 D6
Ellsworth MN ..... 43°31N 96°1W 80 G2
Ellsworth NE ..... 42°4N 102°17W 84 B3
Ellsworth SD ..... 44°9N 103°4W 91 F2
Ellsworth WI ..... 44°44N 92°29W 103 D1
Ellsworth County ☆
  KS. ..... 38°45N 98°15W 74 C5
Ellwood City PA ... 40°52N 80°17W 95 D2
Elm → ND ..... 47°11N 96°20W 91 C9
Elm → SD ..... 44°21N 102°42W 91 F3
Elm City NC ..... 35°48N 77°52W 90 C8
Elm Cr. → TX ..... 28°42N 99°59W 99 J8
Elm Creek NE ..... 40°43N 99°22W 84 D6
Elm Fork Red →
  U.S.A. ..... 34°53N 99°19W 93 D4
Elm Grove WI ..... 43°2N 88°4W 112 B1
Elm L. SD ..... 45°51N 98°42W 91 E7
Elma IA ..... 43°15N 92°26W 73 B6
Elma WA ..... 47°0N 123°25W 101 C2
Elma Center NY ... 42°46N 78°38W 108 C3
Elmdale KS ..... 38°22N 96°39W 74 C6
Elmendorf TX ..... 29°15N 98°19W 117 D3
Elmer MO ..... 39°57N 92°39W 82 B4
Elmer NJ ..... 39°36N 75°10W 87 C1
Elmer OK ..... 34°29N 99°21W 93 D4
Elmira ID ..... 48°29N 116°27W 70 A2
Elmira MI ..... 45°4N 84°51W 79 E7
Elmira NY ..... 42°6N 76°48W 89 C4
Elmira Heights NY . 42°8N 76°50W 89 C4
Elmo KS ..... 38°41N 97°14W 74 C6
Elmo MT ..... 47°50N 114°21W 83 C3
Elmo UT ..... 39°23N 110°49W 100 D5
Elmodel GA ..... 31°21N 84°29W 68 E2
Elmont NY ..... 40°42N 73°42W 114 B4
Elmont KS ..... 39°10N 95°44W 74 B8
Elmora MN ..... 43°30N 94°5W 80 G4
Elmore MN ..... 43°30N 94°5W 80 G4
Elmore City OK ... 34°37N 97°24W 93 D6
Elmore County ☆
  AL. ..... 32°32N 86°13W 60 D4
Elmore County ☆
  ID. ..... 43°30N 115°30W 70 F3
Elmsford NY ..... 41°3N 73°49W 114 A3
Elmwood IL ..... 40°47N 89°58W 71 C3
Elmwood NE ..... 40°50N 96°18W 84 D9
Elmwood OK ..... 36°37N 100°31W 93 B3
Elmwood WI ..... 44°47N 92°9W 103 D1
Elmwood Park IL .. 41°55N 87°48W 108 B2
Elmwood Park NJ . 40°54N 74°7W 114 B2
Elmwood Place OH 39°11N 84°29W 107 A2
Elnora IN ..... 38°53N 87°5W 72 E3
Elon NC ..... 36°6N 79°30W 90 B6
Eloro AZ ..... 32°45N 111°33W 62 E4
Elrosa MN ..... 45°34N 94°57W 80 E4
Elroy WI ..... 43°45N 90°16W 103 E3
Elsa TX ..... 26°18N 97°59W 98 L10
Elsah IL ..... 38°57N 90°22W 71 E3
Elsberry MO ..... 39°10N 90°47W 82 B6
Elsie MI ..... 43°5N 84°23W 79 F7
Elsie NE ..... 40°51N 101°23W 84 D4
Elsie OR ..... 45°52N 123°36W 94 B2
Elsinore UT ..... 38°41N 112°9W 100 D3
Elsmere DE ..... 39°44N 75°35W 77 A5
Elsmere KY ..... 39°0N 84°36W 107 B1
Elsmere NE ..... 42°10N 100°11W 84 B5
Elsworth, L. OK ... 34°49N 98°22W 93 D5
Eltinville NY ..... 40°33N 74°10W 114 C1
Elton LA ..... 30°29N 92°42W 75 D3
Eltopia WA ..... 46°27N 119°1W 101 D6
Elverson PA ..... 40°9N 75°50W 95 D7
Elwell, L. = Tiber Res.
  MT ..... 48°19N 111°6W 83 B6
Elwood IL ..... 41°24N 88°7W 71 B5
Elwood IN ..... 40°17N 85°50W 72 C5
Elwood NE ..... 40°36N 99°52W 84 D6
Elwood NJ ..... 39°35N 74°43W 87 C2
Elwood Res. NE ... 40°29N 99°55W 84 D6
Ely IA ..... 41°52N 91°35W 73 D7
Ely MN ..... 47°55N 91°51W 80 C7
Ely NV ..... 39°15N 114°54W 85 C6
Elyria NE ..... 41°41N 99°0W 84 C6
Elyria OH ..... 41°22N 82°7W 92 B4
Emanuel County ☆
  GA ..... 32°40N 82°20W 68 D4
Embarras → IL .... 38°39N 87°37W 71 E6
Embarrass → MN .. 47°40N 88°42W 103 D5
Emblem WY ..... 44°30N 108°23W 104 B4
Embshoff Woods & Nature
  Preserve ○ OH .. 39°8N 84°34W 107 B1
Emden IL ..... 40°18N 89°29W 71 C4
Emelle AL ..... 32°44N 88°19W 60 D2
Emerado ND ..... 47°55N 97°22W 91 C8
Emerald Isle NC ... 34°41N 76°57W 90 D8
Emerson AR ..... 33°6N 93°11W 63 E2
Emerson GA ..... 34°8N 84°45W 68 B2
Emerson IA ..... 41°1N 95°24W 73 D3
Emerson NE ..... 42°17N 96°44W 84 B9
Emerson L. CA .... 34°27N 116°23W 65 J10
Emery UT ..... 38°55N 111°15W 100 D4
Emery County ☆
  UT. ..... 39°0N 110°40W 100 D5
Emeryville CA ..... 37°49N 122°17W 118 A3
Emigrant Gap CA .. 39°19N 120°38W 64 D6
Emigrant Pass NV . 40°39N 116°16W 85 B4
Emily MN ..... 46°44N 93°58W 80 D5
Eminence KY ..... 38°22N 85°11W 97 B7
Eminence MO ..... 37°9N 91°21W 82 D5
Emiquon Nat. Wildlife Refuge ○
  IL. ..... 40°20N 90°7W 71 C3
Emlenton PA ..... 41°11N 79°43W 95 C3
Emmalena KY ..... 37°20N 83°0W 97 C9
Emmaus PA ..... 40°32N 75°30W 87 B1
Emmet AR ..... 33°44N 93°28W 63 E2
Emmet NE ..... 42°28N 98°49W 84 B7
Emmet County ☆ IA 43°20N 94°40W 73 B4
Emmet County ☆ MI 45°30N 84°55W 79 D7
Emmetsburg IA ... 43°7N 94°41W 73 B4
Emmett ID ..... 43°52N 116°30W 70 F2
Emmett KS ..... 39°19N 96°3W 74 B7
Emmett MI ..... 42°59N 82°46W 79 G8
Emmitsburg MD ... 39°42N 77°20W 77 A3
Emmonak AK ..... 62°47N 164°31W 61 E6
Emmons County ☆
  ND. ..... 46°20N 100°20W 91 D5
Emmorton MD ..... 39°30N 76°20W 77 A4
Emory TX ..... 32°52N 95°46W 99 E12
Emory → TN ..... 35°56N 84°33W 96 E7
Emory Peak TX ... 29°15N 103°18W 98 H4
Empire CA ..... 37°38N 120°54W 64 F6
Empire CO ..... 39°46N 105°41W 66 C5
Empire GA ..... 32°21N 83°18W 68 D3
Empire LA ..... 29°23N 89°36W 75 E6
Empire MI ..... 44°49N 86°4W 79 E6
Empire NV ..... 40°35N 119°21W 85 B1
Empire Res. CO ... 40°16N 104°12W 66 B6
Emporia KS ..... 38°25N 96°11W 74 C7
Emporia VA ..... 36°42N 77°32W 102 E7
Emporium PA ..... 41°31N 78°14W 95 C4
Emsworth PA ..... 40°30N 80°5W 116 A1
Encampment WY .. 41°12N 106°47W 104 E6

Encanto CA ..... 32°42N 117°2W 117 B2
Encinal TX ..... 28°2N 99°21W 98 J8
Encinitas CA ..... 33°3N 117°17W 65 K9
Encino NM ..... 34°9N 105°28W 88 C5
Encino TX ..... 26°56N 98°8W 98 L9
Encino Res. CA .... 34°8N 118°30W 111 B1
Endeavor WI ..... 43°43N 89°28W 103 E4
Enderlin ND ..... 46°38N 97°36W 91 D8
Enders NE ..... 40°27N 101°32W 84 D4
Enders Res. NE ... 40°25N 101°31W 84 D4
Endicott NY ..... 42°6N 76°4W 89 C4
Endicott WA ..... 46°56N 117°41W 101 D8
Endicott Mts. AK .. 68°0N 152°0W 61 C9
Endwell NY ..... 42°6N 76°2W 89 C4
Enfield CT ..... 41°58N 72°36W 78 C2
Enfield IL ..... 38°6N 88°20W 71 E5
Enfield NC ..... 36°11N 77°41W 90 B8
Enfield NH ..... 43°39N 72°9W 86 C2
Enfield Center NH . 43°38N 72°8W 86 C2
Engadine MI ..... 46°7N 85°34W 79 C6
England AR ..... 34°33N 91°58W 63 D4
Engle NM ..... 33°4N 107°2W 88 D3
Englebright L. CA . 39°14N 121°16W 64 D5
Englewood CO .... 39°38N 104°59W 109 C1
Englewood FL ..... 26°58N 82°21W 67 E6
Englewood KS .... 37°2N 99°59W 74 D3
Englewood NJ ..... 40°54N 73°58W 114 A3
Englewood OH .... 39°53N 84°18W 92 D2
Englewood TN .... 35°26N 84°29W 97 E8
Englewood Cliffs
  NJ ..... 40°53N 73°59W 114 A3
English IN ..... 38°20N 86°28W 72 E4
English Creek NJ .. 39°20N 74°42W 87 C2
English Turn LA ... 29°53N 89°27W 113 C3
English Woods OH . 39°8N 84°33W 107 B1
Englishtown NJ ... 40°18N 74°22W 87 B2
Enid MS ..... 34°8N 89°55W 81 B4
Enid OK ..... 36°24N 97°53W 93 B6
Enid L. MS ..... 34°9N 89°54W 81 B4
Enigma GA ..... 31°24N 83°20W 68 E3
Enloe TX ..... 33°26N 95°39W 99 D12
Ennis MT ..... 45°21N 111°44W 83 E6
Ennis TX ..... 32°20N 96°38W 99 E11
Enoch UT ..... 37°47N 113°2W 100 F2
Enochs TX ..... 33°51N 102°49W 98 C5
Enola NE ..... 41°56N 97°30W 84 C8
Enon OH ..... 39°52N 83°56W 92 D3
Enosburg Falls VT . 44°55N 72°48W 86 B2
Ensenada NM ..... 36°44N 106°32W 88 A4
Ensign KS ..... 37°39N 100°14W 74 D3
Ensley FL ..... 30°31N 87°16W 67 A1
Enterprise KS ..... 38°54N 97°7W 74 C6
Enterprise MS ..... 32°10N 88°49W 81 D5
Enterprise OR ..... 45°25N 117°17W 94 B8
Enterprise UT ..... 37°34N 113°43W 100 F2
Enterprise County ☆ NV 40°0N 116°10W 85 C4
Enumclaw WA .... 47°12N 121°59W 101 C4
Enville TN ..... 35°23N 88°26W 96 E4
Eola MO ..... 39°14N 91°1W 82 B5
Eolia MO ..... 39°14N 91°1W 82 B5
Epes AL ..... 32°42N 88°7W 60 D2
Ephraim UT ..... 39°22N 111°35W 100 D4
Ephrata PA ..... 40°11N 76°11W 95 D6
Ephrata WA ..... 47°19N 119°33W 101 C6
Epping ND ..... 48°17N 103°21W 91 B2
Epping NH ..... 43°2N 71°4W 86 D4
Eppley Airfield, Omaha × (OMA)
  NE ..... 41°18N 95°53W 84 C10
Epps LA ..... 32°36N 91°29W 75 B4
Epworth IA ..... 42°27N 90°56W 73 C8
Equality IL ..... 37°44N 88°20W 71 F5
Equinox Mt. VT ... 43°11N 73°6W 86 C1
Erath LA ..... 29°58N 92°2W 75 E3
Erath County ☆ TX. 32°13N 98°12W 99 E9
Erbacon WV ..... 38°33N 80°35W 102 C4
Erda UT ..... 40°37N 112°18W 100 C3
Erhard MN ..... 46°29N 96°6W 80 D2
Erick OK ..... 35°13N 99°52W 93 C4
Ericson NE ..... 41°47N 98°41W 84 C7
Eridu FL ..... 30°18N 83°45W 67 A5
Erie CO ..... 40°3N 105°3W 66 B5
Erie IL ..... 41°39N 90°5W 71 B3
Erie KS ..... 37°34N 95°15W 74 D8
Erie PA ..... 42°8N 80°5W 95 B2
Erie, L. N. Amer. .. 42°15N 81°0W 92 B5
Erie Canal NY .... 43°5N 78°43W 89 B2
Erie County ☆ NY. 42°50N 78°45W 89 C2
Erie County ☆ OH. 41°24N 82°33W 92 B4
Erie County ☆ PA.. 41°55N 80°0W 95 B2
Erie Nat. Wildlife Refuge ○
  PA ..... 41°36N 80°0W 95 C3
Erin TN ..... 36°19N 87°42W 96 D5
Erin Springs OK ... 34°49N 97°36W 93 D6
Erlanger KY ..... 39°1N 84°36W 107 B1
Erling, L. AR ..... 33°3N 93°32W 63 E2
Errol NH ..... 44°47N 71°8W 86 B3
Errol Heights OR . 45°28N 122°36W 116 B2
Erskine MN ..... 47°40N 96°0W 80 C2
Erving MA ..... 42°36N 72°24W 78 B2
Erwin NC ..... 35°20N 78°41W 90 C7
Erwin SD ..... 44°29N 97°27W 91 F8
Erwin TN ..... 36°9N 82°25W 97 D10
Erwinville LA ..... 30°32N 91°24W 75 D4
Esbon KS ..... 39°49N 98°26W 74 B5
Escalante UT ..... 37°47N 111°36W 100 E4
Escalante → UT ... 37°24N 110°57W 100 F5
Escalante Desert
  UT. ..... 37°50N 113°20W 100 F2
Escalon CA ..... 37°48N 121°0W 64 F6
Escambia → FL ... 30°32N 87°11W 67 A1
Escambia County ☆
  AL. ..... 31°7N 87°4W 60 E3
Escambia County ☆
  FL. ..... 30°30N 87°20W 67 A1
Escanaba MI ..... 45°45N 87°4W 79 D4
Escanaba → MI ... 45°47N 87°3W 79 D4
Escatawpa → MS . 30°36N 88°33W 81 F5
Escondido CA ..... 33°7N 117°5W 65 K9
Eskridge KS ..... 38°52N 96°6W 74 C7
Esmeralda County ☆
  NV. ..... 37°50N 117°45W 85 E3
Esmond ND ..... 48°2N 99°46W 91 B6
Esmont VA ..... 37°50N 78°37W 102 D6
Esom Hill GA ..... 33°57N 85°23W 68 C1
Espanola FL ..... 29°31N 81°19W 67 B7
Espanola NM ..... 35°59N 106°5W 88 B4
Esparto CA ..... 38°42N 122°1W 64 E4
Esperance → CA .. 66°33N 163°36W 61 C7
Esperanza
  Puerto Rico .. 18°6N 65°28W 105 G17
Essex CA ..... 34°44N 115°15W 65 J12
Essex CT ..... 41°21N 72°24W 78 C2
Essex IL ..... 41°11N 88°11W 71 B5
Essex IA ..... 40°50N 95°18W 73 E3
Essex MD ..... 39°19N 76°29W 77 A4
Essex MO ..... 36°48N 89°49W 82 E7
Essex MT ..... 48°17N 113°37W 83 B4
Essex NY ..... 44°19N 73°21W 89 A7
Essex VT ..... 44°29N 73°7W 86 B1
Essex County ☆ NJ. 40°45N 74°15W 87 B2
Essex County ☆ NY 44°10N 73°45W 89 A7
Essex County ☆ VT 44°45N 71°45W 86 B3
Essex Fells NJ .... 40°49N 74°17W 114 B1
Essex Junction VT . 44°29N 73°7W 86 B1

Essex Meadows VA 36°45N 76°14W 115 B2
Essexville MI ..... 43°37N 83°50W 79 F8
Estacada OR ..... 45°17N 122°20W 94 B3
Estancia NM ..... 34°46N 106°4W 88 C4
Estelle LA ..... 29°50N 90°6W 113 C2
Estelline SD ..... 44°35N 96°54W 91 F9
Estelline TX ..... 34°33N 100°26W 98 C7
Estellville NJ ..... 39°23N 74°45W 87 C2
Estero FL ..... 26°26N 81°49W 67 E7
Estes Park CO .... 40°23N 105°31W 66 B5
Estherwood LA ... 30°11N 92°28W 75 D3
Estill SC ..... 32°45N 81°15W 90 F4
Estill County ☆ KY. 37°40N 84°0W 97 C9
Estill Springs TN .. 35°16N 86°8W 96 E6
Etchison MD ..... 39°15N 77°8W 77 A3
Ethan SD ..... 43°33N 97°59W 91 G8
Ethel MO ..... 39°52N 92°45W 82 B4
Ethel MS ..... 33°7N 89°28W 81 C4
Ethel WA ..... 46°33N 122°45W 101 D3
Ethelsville AL ..... 33°25N 88°13W 60 C2
Ethete WY ..... 43°2N 108°46W 104 D4
Ethridge MT ..... 48°34N 112°8W 83 B5
Ethridge TN ..... 35°19N 87°18W 96 E5
Etna CA ..... 41°27N 122°54W 64 B4
Etna ME ..... 44°49N 69°7W 76 D4
Etna OH ..... 39°58N 82°41W 92 C4
Etna PA ..... 40°30N 79°56W 116 B2
Etna UT ..... 41°40N 113°58W 100 B2
Etna WY ..... 43°5N 111°0W 104 C2
Etolin Strait AK ... 60°20N 165°15W 61 F6
Eton GA ..... 34°50N 84°46W 68 B2
Etowah TN ..... 35°20N 84°32W 97 E8
Etowah → AL .... 34°20N 86°0W 60 B4
Etowah County ☆ AL. 34°0N 86°0W 60 B4
Etta MS ..... 34°28N 89°14W 81 B4
Etter TX ..... 35°47N 101°57W 98 A6
Ettrick WI ..... 44°10N 91°16W 103 D2
Eubank KY ..... 37°17N 84°40W 97 C8
Euclid OH ..... 41°34N 81°32W 92 B5
Eudora AR ..... 33°7N 91°16W 63 E4
Eudora KS ..... 38°57N 95°6W 74 C8
Eufaula AL ..... 31°54N 85°9W 60 E5
Eufaula L. OK .... 35°18N 95°21W 93 C8
Eufaula OK ..... 35°17N 95°35W 93 C8
Eugene MO ..... 38°21N 92°24W 82 C4
Eugene OR ..... 44°5N 123°4W 94 C2
Euless TX ..... 32°50N 97°4W 109 A3
Eulonia GA ..... 31°32N 81°26W 68 E5
Eunice LA ..... 30°30N 92°25W 75 D3
Eunice NM ..... 32°26N 103°10W 88 E7
Eupora MS ..... 33°32N 89°16W 81 C4
Eureka CA ..... 40°47N 124°9W 64 C2
Eureka IL ..... 40°43N 89°16W 71 C4
Eureka KS ..... 37°49N 96°17W 74 D7
Eureka MT ..... 48°53N 115°3W 83 B2
Eureka NV ..... 39°31N 115°58W 85 C5
Eureka SD ..... 45°46N 99°38W 91 E6
Eureka UT ..... 39°58N 112°7W 100 D3
Eureka County ☆ NV 40°0N 116°10W 85 C4
Eureka Springs AR. 36°24N 93°44W 63 B2
Eustace TX ..... 32°19N 96°1W 99 E11
Eustis FL ..... 28°51N 81°41W 67 C7
Eustis ME ..... 45°13N 70°29W 76 C3
Eustis NE ..... 40°40N 100°2W 84 D5
Eustis, L. FL ..... 28°50N 81°44W 67 C7
Eutaw AL ..... 32°50N 87°53W 60 D3
Eutawville SC ..... 33°24N 80°21W 90 E5
Eva AL ..... 34°20N 86°46W 60 B4
Evadale TX ..... 30°21N 94°5W 99 G13
Evan MN ..... 44°21N 94°50W 80 F4
Evangeline LA ..... 30°16N 92°34W 75 D3
Evangeline Parish ☆
  LA ..... 30°47N 92°25W 75 D3
Evans CO ..... 40°23N 104°41W 66 B6
Evans GA ..... 33°32N 82°8W 68 C4
Evans LA ..... 30°59N 93°30W 75 D2
Evans, Mt. CO .... 39°35N 105°39W 66 C5
Evansdale IA ..... 42°30N 92°17W 73 C6
Evanston IL ..... 42°3N 87°41W 108 A2
Evanston WY ..... 41°16N 110°58W 104 E2
Evansville AR ..... 35°48N 94°30W 63 B2
Evansville IL ..... 38°5N 89°56W 71 E4
Evansville IN ..... 37°58N 87°35W 72 F3
Evansville MN .... 46°0N 95°41W 80 D3
Evansville WI ..... 42°47N 89°18W 103 F4
Evansville WY ..... 42°52N 106°16W 104 D6
Evant TX ..... 31°29N 98°9W 99 F9
Evarts KY ..... 36°52N 83°12W 97 D9
Eveleth MN ..... 47°28N 92°32W 80 C6
Evelyn LA ..... 31°59N 93°27W 75 C2
Evening Shade AR . 36°4N 91°37W 63 B4
Evensville TN ..... 35°34N 84°57W 97 E8
Everest KS ..... 39°41N 95°26W 74 B8
Everett GA ..... 31°24N 81°38W 68 E5
Everett PA ..... 40°1N 78°23W 95 D4
Everett WA ..... 47°59N 122°12W 101 C3
Everett, Mt. MA .. 42°6N 73°26W 78 B1
Everglades, The FL. 25°50N 81°0W 67 F8
Everglades City FL. 25°52N 81°23W 67 F7
Everglades Nat. Park △
  FL. ..... 25°30N 81°0W 67 F8
Everglades Parkway
  FL. ..... 26°10N 81°0W 67 E7
Evergreen AL ..... 31°26N 86°57W 60 E4
Evergreen CO ..... 39°38N 105°19W 66 C5
Evergreen MT ..... 48°14N 114°17W 83 B3
Evergreen Park IL . 41°43N 87°42W 108 C2
Everly IA ..... 43°10N 95°19W 73 B3
Everson WA ..... 48°55N 122°20W 101 B3
Ewan WA ..... 47°7N 117°44W 101 C8
Ewell MD ..... 37°59N 76°2W 77 B4
Ewing KY ..... 38°26N 83°53W 97 B8
Ewing MO ..... 40°0N 91°43W 82 A5
Ewing NE ..... 42°16N 98°21W 84 B7
Ewing VA ..... 36°38N 83°26W 102 E1
Excello MO ..... 39°38N 92°22W 82 B4
Excelsior Mts. NV. 38°15N 118°15W 85 D2
Excelsior Springs MO 39°20N 94°13W 82 B2
Exeland WI ..... 45°40N 91°15W 103 C2
Exeter CA ..... 36°18N 119°9W 65 G7
Exeter MO ..... 36°40N 93°56W 82 E3
Exeter NE ..... 40°39N 97°27W 84 D8
Exeter NH ..... 42°59N 70°57W 86 D4
Exeter PA ..... 41°19N 75°49W 87 A1
Exeter RI ..... 41°35N 71°32W 78 C3
Exira IA ..... 41°35N 94°52W 73 D4
Exmore VA ..... 37°32N 75°50W 102 D9
Experiment = Highland Mills
Experiment GA .... 33°16N 84°17W 68 C2
Exposition Park CA 34°0N 118°17W 111 B3
Eyak AK ..... 60°32N 145°36W 61 F11
Eyota MN ..... 43°59N 92°14W 80 G6

F

F.D. Roosevelt Nat. Historic Site
NY ...... 41°46N 73°56W **89 D7**
Fabens TX ...... 31°30N 106°10W **98 F1**
Fabius NY ...... 42°50N 75°59W **89 C5**
Faceville GA ...... 30°45N 84°38W **68 F2**
Fagasa Amer. Samoa 14°17S 170°43W **105 e**
Fair Bluff NC ...... 34°19N 79°2W **90 D6**
Fair Grove MO ...... 37°23N 93°9W **82 D3**
Fair Haven MI ...... 40°22N 74°2W **87 B2**
Fair Haven NY ...... 43°19N 76°42W **89 B4**
Fair Haven VT ...... 43°36N 73°16W **86 C1**
Fair Lawn NJ ...... 40°56N 74°7W **114 A2**
Fair Oaks OK ...... 36°17N 95°50W **93 B8**
Fair Plain MI ...... 42°5N 86°27W **79 G5**
Fair Play MO ...... 37°38N 93°35W **82 D3**
Fairbank IA ...... 42°38N 92°3W **73 C6**
Fairbank MD ...... 38°41N 76°20W **77 B4**
Fairbanks AK ...... 64°51N 147°43W **61 D11**
Fairbanks FL ...... 29°44N 82°16W **67 B6**
Fairbanks North Star ☆
AK ...... 64°50N 146°25W **61 D11**
Fairborn OH ...... 39°49N 84°2W **92 D2**
Fairburn GA ...... 33°34N 84°35W **68 C2**
Fairburn SD ...... 43°41N 103°13W **91 G2**
Fairbury IL ...... 40°45N 88°31W **71 C5**
Fairbury NE ...... 40°8N 97°11W **84 D8**
Fairchance PA ...... 39°49N 79°45W **95 E3**
Fairchild WI ...... 44°36N 90°58W **103 D3**
Fairchild Air Force Base
WA ...... 47°38N 117°35W **101 C8**
Fairdale KY ...... 38°6N 85°46W **97 B7**
Fairdale ND ...... 48°30N 98°14W **91 B7**
Fairfax IA ...... 41°55N 91°47W **73 D7**
Fairfax MN ...... 44°32N 94°43W **80 F4**
Fairfax OH ...... 39°8N 84°23W **107 B2**
Fairfax OK ...... 36°34N 96°42W **93 B7**
Fairfax SC ...... 32°59N 81°15W **90 F4**
Fairfax SD ...... 43°2N 98°53W **91 G7**
Fairfax VA ...... 38°50N 77°19W **119 B2**
Fairfax VT ...... 44°40N 73°1W **86 B1**
Fairfax County ☆
VA ...... 38°51N 77°18W **102 C7**
Fairfax Station VA ... 38°48N 77°19W **119 C2**
Fairfield AL ...... 33°29N 86°55W **68 C2**
Fairfield CA ...... 38°15N 122°3W **64 E4**
Fairfield CT ...... 41°9N 73°16W **78 C1**
Fairfield ID ...... 43°21N 114°44W **70 F4**
Fairfield IL ...... 38°23N 88°22W **71 E5**
Fairfield IA ...... 40°56N 91°57W **73 E7**
Fairfield KY ...... 37°56N 85°23W **97 C7**
Fairfield ME ...... 44°35N 69°36W **76 D4**
Fairfield MT ...... 47°37N 111°59W **83 C6**
Fairfield ND ...... 47°8N 103°14W **91 C2**
Fairfield NJ ...... 40°53N 74°18W **114 A1**
Fairfield NE ...... 40°26N 98°6W **84 D7**
Fairfield OH ...... 39°20N 84°34W **92 D2**
Fairfield PA ...... 39°47N 77°22W **77 A3**
Fairfield TX ...... 31°44N 96°10W **99 F11**
Fairfield WA ...... 47°23N 117°10W **101 C8**
Fairfield County ☆
CT ...... 41°15N 73°20W **78 C1**
Fairfield County ☆
OH ...... 39°43N 82°36W **92 D4**
Fairfield County ☆
SC ...... 34°25N 81°10W **90 D4**
Fairground Park
MO ...... 38°39N 90°13W **117 B2**
Fairgrove MI ...... 43°32N 83°33W **79 F8**
Fairhaven MA ...... 41°39N 70°55W **78 C4**
Fairhaven WA ...... 48°43N 122°29W **101 A3**
Fairhaven Bay MA ... 42°25N 71°21W **106 A1**
Fairhaven Hill MA ... 42°26N 71°21W **106 A1**
Fairhope AL ...... 30°31N 87°54W **60 F3**
Fairhope PA ...... 39°50N 78°48W **77 A2**
Fairland IN ...... 39°35N 85°52W **72 D8**
Fairland MD ...... 39°5N 76°57W **77 A4**
Fairland OK ...... 36°45N 94°51W **93 B9**
Fairlee MD ...... 39°13N 76°10W **77 A4**
Fairlee VT ...... 43°54N 72°9W **86 C2**
Fairmont MN ...... 43°39N 94°28W **80 G4**
Fairmont NC ...... 34°30N 79°7W **90 D6**
Fairmont NE ...... 40°38N 97°35W **84 D8**
Fairmont OK ...... 36°21N 97°43W **93 B6**
Fairmont WV ...... 39°29N 80°9W **102 B4**
Fairmont City IL ... 38°38N 90°4W **117 B3**
Fairmont Terrace
CA ...... 37°42N 122°6W **118 B4**
Fairmount GA ...... 34°26N 84°42W **68 B2**
Fairmount IL ...... 40°3N 87°56W **71 C6**
Fairmount IN ...... 40°25N 85°39W **72 C5**
Fairmount MD ...... 38°6N 75°48W **77 B5**
Fairmount ND ...... 46°3N 96°36W **91 D9**
Fairmount NY ...... 43°3N 76°11W **89 C4**
Fairmount Heights
MD ...... 38°54N 76°54W **119 B4**
Fairmount Park PA ... 40°1N 75°11W **116 A1**
Fairplains NC ...... 36°12N 81°9W **90 B4**
Fairplay CO ...... 39°15N 106°2W **66 C4**
Fairport NY ...... 43°6N 77°27W **89 B3**
Fairport Harbor OH ... 41°45N 81°17W **92 B5**
Fairtown MD ...... 39°16N 76°31W **107 B2**
Fairview IL ...... 40°38N 90°10W **71 C4**
Fairview KS ...... 39°50N 95°44W **74 B8**
Fairview MI ...... 44°44N 84°3W **79 E7**
Fairview MT ...... 47°51N 104°3W **83 C13**
Fairview NC ...... 35°31N 82°24W **90 C3**
Fairview NJ ...... 40°48N 73°59W **114 B3**
Fairview NJ ...... 40°23N 74°5W **87 B2**
Fairview OK ...... 36°16N 98°29W **93 B5**
Fairview OR ...... 45°32N 122°26W **94 B3**
Fairview PA ...... 42°2N 80°15W **95 B2**
Fairview SD ...... 43°13N 96°29W **91 G9**
Fairview TN ...... 35°59N 87°7W **96 E5**
Fairview UT ...... 39°38N 111°26W **100 D4**
Fairview WV ...... 39°36N 80°15W **102 B4**
Fairview, L. FL ...... 28°35N 81°24W **115 A2**
Fairview Park IN ... 39°41N 87°25W **72 D3**
Fairweather, Mt.
AK ...... 58°55N 137°32W **61 G13**
Faison NC ...... 35°7N 78°8W **90 C7**
Faith SD ...... 45°2N 102°2W **91 E3**
Faithorn MI ...... 45°41N 87°45W **79 D4**
Fajardo
Puerto Rico ... 18°20N 65°39W **105 G17**
Falcon CO ...... 38°56N 104°37W **66 D6**
Falcon, C. OR ...... 45°46N 123°59W **98 L3**
Falcon Hts. TX ...... 26°34N 99°10W **98 L8**
Falcon Res. TX ...... 26°44N 99°12W **99 J8**
Falfurrias TX ...... 27°14N 98°9W **99 J9**
Falkner MS ...... 34°51N 88°56W **61 B4**
Falkville AL ...... 34°22N 86°55W **60 B4**
Fall → KS ...... 37°24N 95°40W **74 D8**
Fall Branch TN ...... 36°25N 82°37W **97 D10**
Fall Creek WI ...... 44°46N 91°17W **103 D2**
Fall Creek Falls State Park
TN ...... 35°39N 85°20W **97 E7**
Fall River MA ...... 41°43N 71°10W **78 C3**
Fall River WI ...... 43°23N 89°3W **103 E4**
Fall River County ☆
SD ...... 43°10N 103°30W **91 G2**
Fall River Lake KS ... 37°39N 96°4W **74 D7**
Fall River Mills CA ... 41°3N 121°28W **64 D5**
Fallasbee CA ...... 33°23N 117°15W **65 K9**
Fallis OK ...... 35°45N 97°7W **93 C6**

Fallon MT ...... 46°50N 105°8W **83 D12**
Fallon NV ...... 39°28N 118°47W **85 C2**
Fallon County ☆
MT ...... 46°20N 104°30W **83 D13**
Fallon Indian Reservation
NV ...... 39°25N 118°45W **85 C2**
Fallon N.A.S. NV ... 39°27N 118°44W **85 C2**
Falls Church VA ...... 38°53N 77°12W **119 B2**
Falls City NE ...... 40°3N 95°36W **84 D10**
Falls City OR ...... 44°52N 123°26W **94 C2**
Falls City TX ...... 28°59N 98°1W **99 J9**
Falls County ☆ TX ... 31°18N 96°54W **99 F11**
Falls Creek PA ...... 41°9N 78°48W **95 C4**
Falls L. NC ...... 35°57N 78°35W **90 C7**
Fallsburg KY ...... 38°11N 82°40W **97 B10**
Fallstaff MD ...... 39°22N 76°42W **107 A1**
Fallston MD ...... 39°31N 76°25W **77 A4**
Falmouth IL ...... 30°21N 83°8W **67 A5**
Falmouth KY ...... 38°41N 84°20W **97 B8**
Falmouth ME ...... 43°44N 70°14W **76 E3**
Falmouth MA ...... 41°33N 70°37W **78 C4**
Falmouth MI ...... 44°15N 85°5W **79 E6**
Falmouth VA ...... 38°20N 77°28W **102 C7**
Faloma OR ...... 45°36N 122°40W **116 A2**
False Pass AK ...... 54°51N 163°25W **61 J7**
Fancy Farm KY ...... 36°48N 88°47W **96 D4**
Far Rockaway NY ... 40°36N 73°45W **114 C4**
Farallon de Medinilla
N. Marianas ...... 16°1N 146°4E **105 a**
Farallon de Pajaros
N. Marianas ...... 20°32N 144°54E **105 a**
Farallon Islands Nat. Wildlife
Refuge CA ...... 37°44N 123°2W **64 F3**
Farbach-Werner Nature Preserve
OH ...... 39°14N 84°35W **107 A1**
Farewell AK ...... 62°31N 153°54W **61 E9**
Fargo GA ...... 30°41N 82°34W **68 F4**
Fargo ND ...... 46°53N 96°48W **91 D9**
Fargo OK ...... 36°22N 99°37W **93 B4**
Faribault MN ...... 44°18N 93°16W **80 F5**
Faribault County ☆
MN ...... 43°45N 94°0W **80 G5**
Farina IL ...... 38°50N 88°46W **71 E5**
Farley IA ...... 42°27N 91°0W **73 C7**
Farmer City IL ...... 40°15N 88°39W **71 C5**
Farmers Branch TX 32°55N 96°53W **109 A4**
Farmersburg IN ...... 39°15N 87°23W **72 D3**
Farmersville CA ...... 36°18N 119°12W **65 G7**
Farmersville IL ...... 39°27N 89°39W **71 D4**
Farmersville TX ...... 33°10N 96°22W **99 D11**
Farmingdale NJ ...... 40°12N 74°10W **87 B2**
Farmington AR ...... 36°3N 94°15W **63 B1**
Farmington DE ...... 38°52N 75°35W **77 B5**
Farmington IA ...... 40°38N 91°44W **73 E7**
Farmington IL ...... 40°42N 90°0W **71 C3**
Farmington ME ...... 44°40N 70°9W **76 D3**
Farmington MN ...... 44°38N 93°8W **80 F5**
Farmington MO ...... 37°47N 90°25W **82 D6**
Farmington MT ...... 47°53N 112°10W **83 C5**
Farmington NH ...... 43°24N 71°4W **86 C3**
Farmington NM ...... 36°44N 108°12W **88 A2**
Farmington UT ...... 40°59N 111°53W **100 C4**
Farmington WA ...... 47°5N 117°3W **101 C8**
Farmington → CT ... 41°51N 72°38W **78 C2**
Farmland IN ...... 40°11N 85°8W **72 C5**
Farmville NC ...... 35°36N 77°35W **90 C8**
Farmville VA ...... 37°18N 78°24W **102 D6**
Farnam NE ...... 40°42N 100°13W **84 D5**
Farner TN ...... 35°9N 84°19W **97 E8**
Farnham VA ...... 37°53N 76°38W **77 C4**
Farnsworth TX ...... 36°19N 100°58W **98 A7**
Farragut IA ...... 40°43N 95°29W **73 E3**
Farragut TN ...... 35°53N 84°9W **97 E8**
Farrar Pond MA ...... 42°24N 71°21W **106 A1**
Farrell PA ...... 41°13N 80°30W **95 C2**
Farson WY ...... 42°7N 109°26W **100 B9**
Farwell MI ...... 43°50N 84°52W **79 F7**
Farwell MN ...... 45°45N 95°37W **80 E3**
Farwell NE ...... 41°13N 98°38W **84 C7**
Farwell TX ...... 34°23N 103°2W **98 C4**
Father Marquette Nat. Memorial
MI ...... 45°55N 84°46W **79 D7**
Faucett MO ...... 39°36N 94°48W **82 B2**
Faulk County ☆ SD ... 45°0N 99°0W **91 E6**
Faulkner County ☆
AR ...... 35°10N 92°16W **63 C3**
Faulkton SD ...... 45°2N 99°8W **91 E6**
Fauquier County ☆
VA ...... 38°43N 77°48W **102 C7**
Faust UT ...... 40°11N 112°24W **100 C3**
Fawn Grove PA ...... 39°44N 76°27W **77 A4**
Faxon OK ...... 34°28N 98°35W **93 D5**
Fay OK ...... 35°49N 98°39W **93 C5**
Fayette AL ...... 33°41N 87°50W **60 C3**
Fayette IA ...... 42°51N 91°48W **73 C7**
Fayette MO ...... 39°9N 92°41W **82 C4**
Fayette MS ...... 31°43N 91°4W **81 E2**
Fayette NY ...... 42°49N 76°49W **89 C4**
Fayette OH ...... 41°40N 84°20W **92 B2**
Fayette UT ...... 39°14N 111°51W **100 D4**
Fayette County ☆
AL ...... 33°41N 87°50W **60 C3**
Fayette County ☆
GA ...... 33°25N 84°30W **68 C2**
Fayette County ☆ IL ... 39°0N 89°0W **71 E4**
Fayette County ☆ IN 39°35N 85°10W **72 D5**
Fayette County ☆ IA ... 42°50N 91°50W **73 C7**
Fayette County ☆ KY 38°0N 84°30W **97 B8**
Fayette County ☆
OH ...... 39°32N 83°26W **92 D3**
Fayette County ☆ PA 40°0N 79°40W **95 E3**
Fayette County ☆ TN 35°15N 89°21W **96 E3**
Fayette County ☆
TX ...... 29°54N 96°52W **99 H11**
Fayetteville AR ...... 36°4N 94°10W **63 B1**
Fayetteville GA ...... 33°27N 84°27W **68 C2**
Fayetteville NC ...... 35°3N 78°53W **90 C7**
Fayetteville NY ...... 43°3N 76°0W **89 B5**
Fayetteville TN ...... 35°9N 86°34W **96 E6**
Fayetteville TX ...... 29°54N 96°41W **99 H11**
Fayetteville WV ...... 38°3N 81°6W **102 C3**
Fear, C. NC ...... 33°50N 77°58W **90 E8**
Feather → CA ...... 38°47N 121°36W **64 E5**
Feather Falls CA ...... 39°36N 121°16W **64 E5**
Featherville ID ...... 43°37N 115°15W **70 F3**
Federal WY ...... 41°16N 105°17W **104 E7**
Federal Dam MN ... 47°15N 94°14W **80 D4**
Federal Heights
CO ...... 39°51N 104°59W **109 A1**
Federal Way WA ... 47°18N 122°19W **101 C3**
Federalsburg MD ... 38°42N 75°47W **77 B5**
Feeding Hills MA ... 42°4N 72°41W **78 B2**
Felda FL ...... 26°34N 81°26W **67 E7**
Felicity OH ...... 38°51N 84°6W **92 E1**
Felix → NM ...... 33°5N 104°25W **88 D6**
Fellsmere FL ...... 27°46N 80°36W **67 D8**
Felsenthal Nat. Wildlife Refuge
AR ...... 33°8N 92°8W **63 D3**
Felt ID ...... 43°52N 111°11W **70 F7**

Felt OK ...... 36°34N 102°48W **93 B1**
Felton DE ...... 39°1N 75°35W **77 A5**
Felton MN ...... 47°5N 96°30W **80 C2**
Felton PA ...... 39°51N 76°34W **95 E6**
Fence Lake NM ...... 34°40N 108°40W **88 C2**
Fenn ID ...... 45°58N 116°16W **70 D2**
Fennimore WI ...... 42°59N 90°39W **103 F3**
Fenton IA ...... 43°13N 94°26W **73 B4**
Fenton LA ...... 30°22N 92°55W **75 D3**
Fenton MI ...... 42°48N 83°42W **79 G8**
Fenton MO ...... 38°31N 90°26W **117 C2**
Fenwood WI ...... 44°52N 90°1W **103 D3**
Ferdinand ID ...... 46°9N 116°24W **70 C2**
Ferdinand IN ...... 38°14N 86°52W **72 E4**
Fergus County ☆
MT ...... 47°30N 109°10W **83 C8**
Fergus Falls MN ...... 46°17N 96°4W **80 D2**
Ferguson KY ...... 37°3N 84°36W **97 C8**
Ferguson MO ...... 38°44N 90°18W **117 A2**
Fern, Pt. CA ...... 33°42N 118°17W **111 D3**
Fern Creek KY ...... 38°9N 85°36W **97 B7**
Fern Ridge L. OR ... 44°7N 123°18W **94 C2**
Fernandina Beach
FL ...... 30°40N 81°27W **67 A7**
Ferndale CA ...... 40°35N 124°16W **64 C2**
Ferndale MD ...... 39°10N 76°38W **107 B2**
Ferndale MI ...... 42°27N 83°8W **108 A2**
Ferndale WA ...... 48°51N 122°36W **101 B3**
Fernley NV ...... 39°36N 119°15W **85 C1**
Fernwood ID ...... 47°7N 116°24W **70 B2**
Fernwood MS ...... 31°11N 90°27W **81 E3**
Fernwood NY ...... 43°16N 73°40W **89 B7**
Ferriday LA ...... 31°38N 91°33W **75 C4**
Ferris IL ...... 40°28N 91°10W **71 C2**
Ferris TX ...... 32°32N 96°40W **99 E11**
Ferrisburg VT ...... 44°12N 73°15W **86 B1**
Ferron UT ...... 39°5N 111°8W **100 D4**
Ferrum VA ...... 36°55N 80°1W **102 E4**
Ferry → WA ...... 48°30N 118°30W **101 B7**
Ferry Pass FL ...... 30°31N 87°13W **67 A1**
Ferrysburg MI ...... 43°5N 86°13W **79 F5**
Ferryville WI ...... 43°21N 91°6W **103 E2**
Fertile IA ...... 43°16N 93°25W **73 B5**
Fertile MN ...... 47°32N 96°17W **80 C2**
Fessenden ND ...... 47°39N 99°38W **91 C6**
Festus MO ...... 38°13N 90°24W **82 C6**
Field KY ...... 36°54N 83°36W **97 D9**
Field Museum of Natural History
IL ...... 41°51N 87°37W **108 B3**
Fielddale VA ...... 36°42N 79°56W **102 E5**
Fielding UT ...... 41°49N 112°7W **100 B3**
Fieldon IL ...... 39°7N 90°30W **71 D3**
Fields LA ...... 30°32N 93°35W **75 D2**
Fields Corner MA ... 42°18N 71°3W **106 B3**
Fields Landing CA ... 40°44N 124°13W **64 C2**
Fierro NM ...... 32°45N 108°5W **88 E2**
Fife TX ...... 31°24N 99°2W **99 F8**
Fife Lake MI ...... 44°35N 85°21W **79 E6**
Fifield WI ...... 45°53N 90°25W **103 C3**
Fifer ID ...... 42°34N 114°37W **70 G4**
Fillmore CA ...... 34°24N 118°55W **65 J8**
Fillmore IL ...... 39°7N 89°17W **71 D4**
Fillmore UT ...... 38°58N 112°20W **100 D3**
Fillmore County ☆
MN ...... 43°40N 92°0W **80 G7**
Fillmore County ☆
NE ...... 40°30N 97°40W **84 D8**
Fincastle VA ...... 37°30N 79°53W **102 D5**
Findlay IL ...... 39°31N 88°45W **71 D5**
Findlay OH ...... 41°2N 83°39W **92 B3**
Fine NY ...... 44°15N 75°8W **89 A5**
Fine Arts, Museum of
MA ...... 42°20N 71°5W **106 A3**
Fingal ND ...... 46°46N 97°47W **91 D8**
Finger TN ...... 35°22N 88°36W **96 E4**
Finger Lakes NY ... 42°40N 76°30W **89 C4**
Finger Lakes Nat. Forest
NY ...... 42°31N 76°47W **89 C4**
Finksburg MD ...... 39°30N 76°54W **77 A4**
Finlayson MN ...... 46°12N 92°55W **80 D6**
Finley ND ...... 47°31N 97°50W **91 C8**
Finley OK ...... 34°20N 95°30W **93 D8**
Finney County ☆ KS 38°0N 100°40W **74 C3**
Finneytown OH ...... 39°12N 84°31W **107 A1**
Fire I. NY ...... 40°40N 73°11W **89 E7**
Fire Island Nat. Seashore
NY ...... 40°38N 73°8W **87 B3**
Firebaugh CA ...... 36°52N 120°27W **65 G6**
First Connecticut L.
NH ...... 45°5N 71°15W **86 A3**
Firth ID ...... 43°18N 112°11W **70 F6**
Firth NE ...... 40°33N 96°37W **84 D9**
Fischer TX ...... 29°58N 98°16W **99 H9**
Fish, L. UT ...... 38°33N 111°42W **100 E4**
Fish Creek WI ...... 45°8N 87°13W **103 C6**
Fish Lake MN ...... 45°5N 93°27W **113 A1**
Fish Lake Regional Park
MN ...... 45°5N 93°27W **113 A1**
Fish Lake Res. MN ... 46°57N 92°17W **80 D6**
Fish Pt. MI ...... 43°44N 83°31W **79 F8**
Fish River L. ME ...... 46°50N 68°47W **76 B5**
Fish Springs Nat. Wildlife Range
UT ...... 39°51N 113°22W **100 D2**
Fisheating Cr. → FL ... 26°57N 81°7W **67 E7**
Fisher AR ...... 35°30N 90°58W **63 C5**
Fisher IL ...... 40°19N 88°21W **71 C5**
Fisher LA ...... 31°30N 93°28W **75 C2**
Fisher MN ...... 47°48N 96°48W **80 C2**
Fisher → MT ...... 48°22N 115°19W **83 B2**
Fisher County ☆ TX 32°45N 100°23W **98 E7**
Fishermans Island Nat. Wildlife
Refuge → VA ...... 37°6N 75°57W **102 D9**
Fishers IN ...... 39°57N 86°0W **110 A2**
Fishers I. NY ...... 41°15N 72°0W **78 C4**
Fishers Peak CO ...... 37°6N 104°28W **66 E6**
Fishing Bridge WY ... 44°34N 110°22W **104 B2**
Fishing Creek MD ... 38°20N 76°14W **77 B4**
Fishing Creek NC ... 36°56N 77°31W **90 B7**
Fishkill NY ...... 41°32N 73°54W **87 A3**
Fishlake Nat. Forest
UT ...... 38°40N 112°20W **100 E3**
Fishtrap L. KY ...... 37°25N 82°26W **97 C10**
Fisk MO ...... 36°47N 90°12W **82 E6**
Fiskdale MA ...... 42°7N 72°7W **78 B2**
Fitchburg MA ...... 42°35N 71°48W **78 B3**
Fitchburg WI ...... 42°58N 89°28W **103 F4**
Fittstown OK ...... 34°37N 96°38W **93 D7**
Fitzgerald GA ...... 31°43N 83°15W **68 E3**
Fitzhugh AR ...... 35°22N 91°19W **63 C4**
Fitzhugh OK ...... 34°40N 96°46W **93 D7**
Flagler CO ...... 39°18N 103°4W **66 C7**
Flagler Beach FL ... 29°29N 81°8W **67 B7**
Flagler County ☆ FL 29°30N 81°20W **67 B7**
Flagstaff AZ ...... 35°12N 111°39W **62 B4**
Flagstaff L. ME ...... 45°12N 70°18W **76 C3**
Flagstaff L. OR ...... 42°35N 120°4W **94 E6**
Flambeau → WI ... 45°18N 91°14W **103 C2**
Flaming Gorge Dam
UT ...... 40°55N 109°25W **100 C6**
Flaming Gorge Nat. Recr. Area
WY ...... 41°10N 109°25W **104 E3**
Flaming Gorge Res.
WY ...... 41°10N 109°25W **104 E3**
Flamingo FL ...... 25°8N 80°55W **67 F8**
Flanagan IL ...... 40°53N 88°52W **71 C5**
Flandreau SD ...... 44°3N 96°36W **91 F9**

Flasher ND ...... 46°27N 101°14W **91 D4**
Flat AK ...... 62°28N 158°1W **61 E8**
Flat → MI ...... 42°56N 85°20W **79 G6**
Flat → NC ...... 36°5N 78°49W **90 B7**
Flat Lick KY ...... 36°50N 83°46W **97 D9**
Flat Rock AL ...... 34°46N 85°42W **60 B5**
Flat Rock IL ...... 38°54N 87°40W **71 E6**
Flat Rock MI ...... 42°6N 83°17W **79 G8**
Flat Top Mt. UT ...... 40°22N 112°11W **100 C3**
Flat Tops, The CO ... 39°50N 107°10W **66 C3**
Flat Woods TN ...... 35°29N 87°50W **96 E5**
Flatbush KY ...... 38°39N 73°56W **114 C3**
Flathead → MT ...... 47°22N 114°47W **83 C3**
Flathead County ☆
MT ...... 48°15N 113°30W **83 B4**
Flathead Indian Reservation
MT ...... 47°35N 114°9W **83 C3**
Flathead L. MT ...... 47°51N 114°8W **83 C3**
Flathead Nat. Forest
MT ...... 47°50N 113°18W **83 C4**
Flatonia TX ...... 29°41N 97°7W **99 H10**
Flatrock → IN ...... 39°12N 85°56W **72 D5**
Flattery, C. WA ...... 48°23N 124°29W **101 B1**
Flatwillow Cr. →
MT ...... 46°56N 107°55W **83 D10**
Flatwoods KY ...... 38°31N 82°43W **97 B10**
Flatwoods LA ...... 31°24N 92°52W **75 C3**
Flatwoods WV ...... 38°43N 80°39W **102 C4**
Flaxton ND ...... 48°54N 102°24W **91 B3**
Flaxville MT ...... 48°48N 105°11W **83 B12**
Fleetwood PA ...... 40°27N 75°49W **95 D7**
Fleischmanns NY ... 42°10N 74°32W **89 C6**
Fleming CO ...... 40°41N 102°50W **66 B8**
Fleming County ☆
KY ...... 38°20N 83°40W **97 B9**
Fleming-Neon KY ... 37°12N 82°42W **97 C10**
Flemingsburg KY ... 38°25N 83°45W **97 B9**
Flemington NJ ...... 40°31N 74°52W **87 B2**
Flensburg MN ...... 39°16N 80°8W **102 B4**
Fletcher → Aurora
Fletcher NC ...... 35°43N 104°49W **109 B3**
Fletcher OK ...... 34°50N 98°15W **93 D5**
Fletcher Pond MI ... 45°1N 83°47W **79 D8**
Flint ID ...... 43°1N 83°41W **79 F8**
Flint → GA ...... 34°30N 86°30W **60 B4**
Flint → AL ...... 34°35N 86°56W **60 B4**
Flint Hill VA ...... 38°46N 78°5W **77 B2**
Flint Hills KS ...... 38°0N 96°40W **74 D7**
Flint Pk. CA ...... 34°9N 118°11W **111 B3**
Flintstone MD ...... 39°42N 78°34W **77 A2**
Flippin AR ...... 36°17N 92°36W **63 A3**
Flomaton AL ...... 31°0N 87°16W **60 E3**
Flomot TX ...... 34°14N 100°59W **98 C7**
Floodwood MN ...... 46°56N 92°55W **80 D6**
Flora IL ...... 38°40N 88°29W **71 E5**
Flora IN ...... 40°33N 86°31W **72 C4**
Flora MS ...... 32°33N 90°19W **81 D3**
Flora OR ...... 45°54N 117°19W **94 B8**
Flora Vista NM ...... 36°48N 108°3W **88 A2**
Florahome FL ...... 29°44N 81°54W **67 B7**
Floral City FL ...... 28°45N 82°17W **67 C6**
Floral Park NY ...... 40°43N 73°42W **114 B4**
Florala AL ...... 31°0N 86°20W **60 E4**
Flordell Hills MO ... 38°43N 90°15W **117 A2**
Florence AL ...... 34°48N 87°41W **60 B3**
Florence AZ ...... 33°2N 111°23W **62 D4**
Florence AR ...... 33°6N 93°40W **93 B3**
Florence CO ...... 38°23N 105°8W **66 D5**
Florence KS ...... 38°15N 96°56W **74 C7**
Florence KY ...... 39°0N 84°38W **97 B8**
Florence MS ...... 32°9N 90°8W **81 D3**
Florence MT ...... 46°38N 114°5W **83 D3**
Florence OR ...... 43°58N 124°7W **94 D1**
Florence SC ...... 34°12N 79°46W **90 D6**
Florence TX ...... 30°51N 97°48W **99 G10**
Florence WI ...... 45°56N 88°15W **103 C5**
Florence County ☆ SC 34°0N 79°45W **90 D6**
Florence County ☆
WI ...... 45°55N 88°20W **103 C5**
Florenton TX ...... 29°8N 98°10W **99 H9**
Florey TX ...... 32°27N 102°36W **98 E5**
Florida NY ...... 40°40N 73°11W **89 E7**
Florida
Puerto Rico ... 18°22N 66°34W **105 G16**
Florida NY ...... 41°20N 74°21W **87 A2**
Florida U.S.A. ...... 28°0N 82°0W **67 D7**
Florida, Straits of
U.S.A. ...... 25°0N 80°0W **67 G8**
Florida B. U.S.A. ...... 25°0N 80°45W **67 F8**
Florida City FL ...... 25°27N 80°29W **67 F8**
Florida Keys FL ...... 24°40N 81°0W **67 G7**
Florien LA ...... 31°27N 93°28W **75 C2**
Florin CA ...... 38°30N 121°24W **64 E5**
Florissant MO ...... 38°52N 90°22W **73 E6**
Florissant Fossil Beds Nat.
Monument CO 38°54N 105°17W **66 D5**
Flourtown PA ...... 40°6N 75°12W **116 A1**
Flower Hill NY ...... 40°48N 73°40W **114 B4**
Floyd NM ...... 34°13N 103°36W **88 C7**
Floyd VA ...... 36°55N 80°19W **102 E4**
Floyd → IA ...... 42°29N 96°23W **73 C2**
Floyd County ☆ GA 34°15N 85°10W **68 B1**
Floyd County ☆ IN ... 38°20N 85°55W **72 E5**
Floyd County ☆ IA ... 43°5N 92°45W **73 B6**
Floyd County ☆ KY ... 37°30N 82°45W **97 C10**
Floyd County ☆ TX ... 34°0N 101°15W **98 C6**
Floyd Lamb State Park
NV ...... 36°19N 115°14W **110 A1**
Floydada TX ...... 33°59N 101°20W **98 D6**
Flume, The NH ...... 44°6N 71°41W **86 B3**
Flushing MI ...... 43°4N 83°51W **79 F8**
Flushing NY ...... 40°45N 73°49W **114 B4**
Flushing OH ...... 40°9N 81°4W **92 C5**
Flushing Meadows Corona Park
NY ...... 40°44N 73°50W **114 B3**
Fluvanna County ☆
VA ...... 37°52N 78°16W **102 D6**
Flynn TX ...... 31°9N 96°8W **99 F11**
Foard County ☆ TX ... 33°59N 99°48W **99 D8**
Fogelsville PA ...... 40°35N 75°38W **87 B1**
Folcroft PA ...... 39°53N 75°17W **116 B1**
Foley AL ...... 30°24N 87°41W **60 F3**
Foley MN ...... 45°40N 93°55W **80 E5**
Folkston GA ...... 30°50N 82°0W **68 F4**
Follett TX ...... 36°26N 100°8W **98 A7**
Folly Beach SC ...... 32°39N 79°56W **90 F6**
Folsom CA ...... 38°40N 121°10W **64 E5**
Folsom NM ...... 36°51N 103°55W **88 A7**
Folsom PA ...... 39°53N 75°19W **116 B1**
Folsom L. CA ...... 38°42N 121°9W **64 E5**
Fond du Lac WI ...... 43°47N 88°27W **103 E5**
Fond du Lac County ☆
WI ...... 43°45N 88°30W **103 E5**
Fond du Lac Indian Reservation
MN ...... 46°45N 92°40W **80 D6**
Fonda IA ...... 42°35N 94°51W **73 C4**
Fonda NY ...... 42°57N 74°22W **89 C6**

Fonde KY ...... 36°36N 83°53W **97 D9**
Fontana CA ...... 34°6N 117°26W **65 J9**
Fontana KS ...... 38°25N 94°51W **74 C9**
Fontana, L. NC ...... 35°27N 83°48W **90 C2**
Fontanelle IA ...... 41°17N 94°34W **73 D4**
Fontenelle Res. WY ... 42°1N 110°3W **104 E2**
Foosland IL ...... 40°22N 88°26W **71 C5**
Foote Village
MD ...... 38°46N 77°1W **119 C3**
Ford, L. MI ...... 45°8N 88°10W **79 D4**
Ford City CA ...... 35°9N 119°27W **65 H7**
Ford City PA ...... 40°46N 79°32W **95 D3**
Ford County ☆ IL ... 40°30N 88°10W **71 C5**
Ford County ☆ KS ... 37°45N 100°0W **74 D4**
Ford Dry L. CA ...... 33°37N 114°59W **65 K12**
Ford I. HI ...... 21°22N 157°58W **69 K14**
Ford River MI ...... 45°41N 87°8W **79 D4**
Ford Road MO ...... 37°9N 92°57W **82 D4**
Fordoche LA ...... 30°36N 91°37W **75 D4**
Fords Prairie WA ... 46°44N 122°59W **101 D3**
Fordsville KY ...... 37°38N 86°43W **96 C5**
Fordville ND ...... 48°13N 97°48W **91 B8**
Fordyce AR ...... 33°49N 92°25W **63 D3**
Fordyce NE ...... 42°42N 97°22W **84 B8**
Foreman AR ...... 33°43N 94°24W **63 E1**
Forest IL ...... 32°47N 91°25W **75 E4**
Forest MS ...... 32°22N 89°29W **81 D4**
Forest OH ...... 40°48N 83°31W **92 C3**
Forest VA ...... 37°22N 79°17W **102 D5**
Forest → ND ...... 48°21N 97°9W **91 B8**
Forest Acres SC ...... 34°1N 80°58W **90 D5**
Forest Center MN ... 47°48N 91°19W **80 C7**
Forest City IL ...... 43°16N 93°39W **73 B5**
Forest City NC ...... 35°20N 81°52W **90 C4**
Forest City PA ...... 41°39N 75°28W **95 C7**
Forest County ☆ WI 45°35N 88°45W **103 C5**
Forest Dale VT ...... 43°48N 73°0W **86 C1**
Forest Grove OR ... 45°31N 123°7W **94 B2**
Forest Heights MD ... 38°48N 77°0W **119 C3**
Forest Hill LA ...... 37°45N 122°27W **118 B2**
Forest Hill MD ...... 31°3N 92°32W **75 C3**
Forest Hill MD ...... 39°35N 76°23W **77 A4**
Forest Hill VA ...... 32°40N 97°16W **109 B2**
Forest Hills NY ...... 40°42N 73°51W **114 B3**
Forest Hills NY ...... 40°25N 79°51W **116 B2**
Forest Home AL ...... 31°52N 86°50W **60 E4**
Forest Lake MN ...... 45°17N 92°59W **80 E6**
Forest Park GA ...... 33°37N 84°22W **68 C2**
Forest Park IL ...... 41°51N 87°47W **108 B2**
Forest Park OH ...... 39°17N 84°30W **92 D2**
Forest Park OR ...... 45°34N 122°46W **116 A1**
Forest View IL ...... 41°48N 87°47W **108 C2**
Forestbrook SC ...... 33°43N 78°58W **90 E7**
Forestburg TX ...... 33°33N 97°35W **99 D10**
Foresthill CA ...... 39°1N 120°49W **64 D6**
Forestville CA ...... 38°28N 122°54W **64 E4**
Forestville MD ...... 38°51N 76°52W **119 B4**
Forestville NY ...... 42°28N 79°10W **89 C1**
Forestville WI ...... 44°41N 87°29W **103 D6**
Forgan OK ...... 36°54N 100°32W **93 B3**
Forge Village MA ... 42°37N 71°26W **106 A1**
Fork Union VA ...... 37°46N 78°16W **102 D6**
Forked Deer → TN ... 35°56N 89°35W **96 E3**
Forked River NJ ...... 39°50N 74°12W **87 C2**
Forkland AL ...... 32°39N 87°53W **60 D3**
Forks WA ...... 47°57N 124°23W **101 C1**
Forks of Salmon CA 41°16N 123°19W **64 B3**
Forkville MS ...... 32°28N 89°40W **81 D4**
Forman ND ...... 46°7N 97°38W **91 D8**
Forrest IL ...... 40°45N 88°25W **71 C5**
Forrest MS ...... 32°9N 90°9W **81 D3**
Forrest City AR ...... 35°1N 90°47W **63 C5**
Forrest County ☆ MS 31°10N 89°13W **81 E4**
Forreston IL ...... 42°8N 89°35W **71 A4**
Forsyth GA ...... 33°2N 83°56W **68 C3**
Forsyth IL ...... 39°56N 88°57W **71 D5**
Forsyth MT ...... 46°16N 106°41W **83 D11**
Forsyth County ☆ GA 34°15N 84°5W **68 B2**
Forsyth County ☆
NC ...... 36°10N 80°15W **90 B5**
Fort A.P. Hill Military Res.
VA ...... 38°7N 77°13W **102 C7**
Fort Adams MS ...... 31°5N 91°33W **81 E2**
Fort Ann NY ...... 43°25N 73°29W **86 C1**
Fort Apache Indian Reservation
AZ ...... 33°50N 110°0W **62 D6**
Fort Ashby WV ...... 39°30N 78°46W **77 A2**
Fort Atkinson IA ... 43°9N 91°56W **73 B7**
Fort Atkinson WI ... 42°56N 88°50W **103 F5**
Fort Belknap Agency
MT ...... 48°29N 108°45W **83 B9**
Fort Belknap Indian Reservation
MT ...... 48°20N 108°40W **83 B9**
Fort Bend County ☆
TX ...... 29°34N 95°49W **99 H12**
Fort Benning Military Reservation
GA ...... 32°21N 84°48W **68 D2**
Fort Benton MT ...... 47°49N 110°40W **83 C7**
Fort Berthold Indian Reservation
ND ...... 47°45N 102°15W **91 C3**
Fort Bidwell Indian Reservation
CA ...... 41°52N 120°12W **64 B6**
Fort Bidwell CA ...... 41°52N 120°9W **64 B6**
Fort Bliss Military Reservation
U.S.A. ...... 31°48N 106°25W **88 F4**
Fort Bowie Nat. Historic Site
AZ ...... 32°9N 109°27W **62 E6**
Fort Bragg CA ...... 39°26N 123°48W **64 D3**
Fort Bragg Military Reservation
NC ...... 35°9N 79°0W **90 C6**
Fort Branch IN ...... 38°15N 87°35W **72 E3**
Fort Bridger WY ... 41°19N 110°23W **104 E2**
Fort Calhoun NE ... 41°27N 96°2W **84 C9**
Fort Campbell TN ... 36°38N 87°26W **96 D5**
Fort Caroline Nat. Memorial
FL ...... 30°23N 81°30W **67 A7**
Fort Chaffee AR ...... 35°19N 94°18W **63 C1**
Fort Clatsop Nat. Memorial
U.S.A. ...... 46°8N 123°53W **94 A2**
Fort Cobb OK ...... 35°6N 98°26W **93 C5**
Fort Cobb Res. OK ... 35°10N 98°23W **93 C5**
Fort Coffee OK ...... 35°17N 94°35W **93 C9**
Fort Collins CO ...... 40°35N 105°5W **66 B5**
Fort Craig Nat. Historic Site
NM ...... 33°38N 106°59W **88 D4**
Fort Davis AL ...... 32°15N 85°43W **60 D5**
Fort Davis TX ...... 30°35N 103°54W **98 G4**
Fort Davis Nat. Historic Site
TX ...... 30°35N 103°53W **98 G3**
Fort De Soto FL ...... 27°36N 82°44W **119 D2**
Fort De Soto Park
FL ...... 27°36N 82°44W **119 D2**
Fort Defiance AZ ... 35°45N 109°5W **62 B6**
Fort Deposit AL ...... 31°59N 86°35W **60 E4**
Fort Dick CA ...... 41°52N 124°9W **64 B2**
Fort Donelson Nat. Battlefield
TN ...... 36°29N 87°52W **96 D5**
Fort Drum FL ...... 27°32N 80°48W **67 D8**
Fort Drum Military Reservation
NY ...... 44°10N 75°35W **89 A5**

Fort Duchesne UT ... 40°17N 109°52W **100 C6**
Fort Dupont Park
DC ...... 38°52N 76°56W **119 B4**
Fort Edward NY ...... 43°16N 73°35W **89 B7**
Fort Eustis VA ...... 37°8N 76°34W **102 D8**
Fort Fairfield ME ... 46°46N 67°50W **76 B6**
Fort Foote Village
MD ...... 38°46N 77°1W **119 C3**
Fort Frederica Nat. Monument ○
GA ...... 31°13N 81°23W **68 E5**
Fort Gaines GA ...... 31°36N 85°3W **68 E1**
Fort Garland CO ... 37°26N 105°26W **66 E5**
Fort Gay WV ...... 38°7N 82°35W **97 B10**
Fort Gibson OK ...... 35°48N 95°15W **93 C8**
Fort Gibson L. OK ... 35°52N 95°14W **93 C8**
Fort Gordon Military Reservation
GA ...... 33°25N 82°10W **68 D4**
Fort Hall ID ...... 43°2N 112°26W **70 F6**
Fort Hall Indian Reservation
ID ...... 43°2N 112°5W **70 F6**
Fort Hancock TX ... 31°18N 105°51W **98 F2**
Fort Hill OH ...... 39°7N 84°49W **92 D2**
Fort Hood Military Reservation
TX ...... 31°8N 97°33W **99 F10**
Fort Huachuca AZ ... 31°35N 110°20W **62 F5**
Fort Hunter Liggett
CA ...... 36°0N 121°15W **65 H5**
Fort Irwin CA ...... 35°16N 116°41W **65 H10**
Fort Jackson Military Reservation
SC ...... 34°3N 80°55W **90 D5**
Fort Jennings OH ... 40°54N 84°18W **92 C2**
Fort Jesup LA ...... 31°37N 93°24W **75 C2**
Fort Jones CA ...... 41°36N 122°51W **64 B4**
Fort Kent ME ...... 47°15N 68°36W **76 A5**
Fort Klamath OR ... 42°42N 122°0W **94 E3**
Fort Knox Military Reservation
KY ...... 37°55N 86°5W **96 C6**
Fort Laramie WY ... 42°13N 104°31W **104 D8**
Fort Larned Nat. Historic Site
KS ...... 38°11N 99°13W **74 C4**
Fort Lauderdale FL ... 26°7N 80°8W **112 B3**
Fort Lauderdale Executive ✈
(FXE) FL ...... 26°11N 80°10W **112 A2**
Fort Lauderdale-Hollywood Int. ✈
(FLL) FL ...... 26°4N 80°10W **112 B3**
Fort Lawn SC ...... 34°42N 80°54W **90 D5**
Fort Leavenworth KS 39°21N 94°55W **74 B9**
Fort Lee NJ ...... 40°50N 73°58W **114 A4**
Fort Leonard Wood Military
Reservation MO ... 37°45N 92°10W **82 D4**
Fort Lewis Military Reservation
WA ...... 47°3N 122°35W **101 C3**
Fort Loudon PA ...... 39°54N 77°56W **95 E5**
Fort Loudoun L. TN 35°47N 84°15W **97 E8**
Fort Lupton CO ...... 40°5N 104°49W **66 B6**
Fort McCoy WI ...... 44°0N 90°41W **103 D3**
Fort McDermitt Indian Reservation
OR ...... 41°58N 117°43W **85 A3**
Fort McDowell Indian Reservation
AZ ...... 33°40N 111°50W **62 D4**
Fort Madison IA ... 40°38N 91°27W **73 E7**
Fort Matanzas Nat. Monument ○
U.S.A. ...... 29°43N 81°14W **67 B7**
Fort Meade FL ...... 27°45N 81°48W **67 D7**
Fort Mill SC ...... 35°2N 80°57W **90 C5**
Fort Mitchell AL ... 32°20N 85°1W **60 D5**
Fort Mitchell KY ... 39°3N 84°33W **107 B1**
Fort Mohave Indian Reservation
AZ ...... 34°55N 114°35W **62 C1**
Fort Morgan CO ... 40°15N 103°48W **66 B7**
Fort Myers FL ...... 26°39N 81°52W **67 E7**
Fort Myers Beach FL 26°27N 81°57W **67 E7**
Fort Myers S.W. Florida
Regional ✈ (RSW)
FL ...... 26°32N 81°45W **67 E7**
Fort Myers Shores
FL ...... 26°43N 81°45W **67 E7**
Fort Necessity Nat. Battlefield
PA ...... 39°49N 79°36W **95 E3**
Fort Niobrara Nat. Wildlife
Refuge → NE ...... 42°54N 100°28W **84 B5**
Fort Ogden FL ...... 27°5N 81°57W **67 E7**
Fort Oglethorpe GA ... 34°57N 85°16W **68 B1**
Fort Payne AL ...... 34°26N 85°43W **60 B5**
Fort Peck MT ...... 48°1N 106°27W **83 B11**
Fort Peck Dam MT ... 48°0N 106°26W **83 C11**
Fort Peck Indian Reservation
MT ...... 48°30N 105°30W **83 B12**
Fort Peck L. MT ...... 48°0N 106°26W **83 C11**
Fort Pierce FL ...... 27°27N 80°20W **67 D8**
Fort Pierre SD ...... 44°21N 100°22W **91 F5**
Fort Pierre Nat. Grassland
SD ...... 44°10N 100°12W **91 F5**
Fort Plain NY ...... 42°56N 74°37W **89 C6**
Fort Point National Historic Site
CA ...... 37°48N 122°28W **118 B2**
Fort Polk Military Reservation
LA ...... 31°2N 93°13W **75 C2**
Fort Raleigh Nat. Historic Site
NC ...... 35°56N 75°43W **90 C10**
Fort Randall Dam SD 43°4N 98°34W **91 G7**
Fort Ransom ND ... 46°31N 97°56W **91 D8**
Fort Recovery OH ... 40°25N 84°47W **92 C1**
Fort Riley KS ...... 39°10N 96°42W **74 B7**
Fort Ripley MN ...... 46°10N 94°22W **80 D4**
Fort Robinson NE ... 42°40N 103°28W **84 B2**
Fort Rucker Military Reservation
AL ...... 31°20N 85°43W **60 E5**
Fort Scott KS ...... 37°50N 94°42W **74 D9**
Fort Scott Nat. Historic Site
KS ...... 37°51N 94°42W **74 D9**
Fort Shawnee OH ... 40°42N 84°7W **92 C2**
Fort Sill Military Res.
OK ...... 34°41N 98°30W **93 D5**
Fort Smith AR ...... 35°23N 94°25W **63 C1**
Fort Smith Nat. Historic Site
AR ...... 35°23N 94°26W **63 C1**
Fort Snelling State Park
MN ...... 44°53N 93°10W **113 B2**
Fort Stanton NM ... 33°30N 105°31W **88 D5**
Fort Stewart Military Reservation
GA ...... 31°52N 81°37W **68 E5**
Fort Stockton TX ... 30°53N 102°53W **98 G5**
Fort Sumner NM ... 34°28N 104°15W **88 C6**
Fort Supply OK ...... 36°35N 99°35W **93 B4**
Fort Thomas KY ... 39°5N 84°26W **107 B2**
Fort Thompson SD ... 44°3N 99°26W **91 F6**
Fort Totten Indian Reservation =
Spirit Lake Indian Reservation
ND ...... 47°58N 99°0W **91 C7**
Fort Towson OK ... 34°1N 95°16W **93 D8**
Fort Union Nat. Monument ○
U.S.A. ...... 35°54N 105°1W **88 B5**
Fort Union Trading Post Nat.
Historic Site → ND ... 48°1N 104°1W **91 B1**
Fort Valley GA ...... 32°33N 83°53W **68 D3**
Fort Vancouver Nat. Historic
Site → WA ...... 45°37N 122°39W **101 E3**
Fort Walton Beach
FL ...... 30°25N 86°36W **67 A2**
Fort Washakie WY ... 43°0N 108°53W **104 C4**
Fort Washington MD ... 38°42N 77°3W **77 B4**
Fort Wayne IN ...... 41°4N 85°9W **72 B5**
Fort White FL ...... 29°55N 82°43W **67 B6**
Fort Worth TX ...... 32°45N 97°19W **109 B2**
Fort Worth-Meacham Int. ✈
(FTW) TX ...... 32°49N 97°21W **109 B1**
Fort Wright KY ...... 39°3N 84°32W **107 B1**
Fort Yates ND ...... 46°5N 100°38W **91 D4**
Fort Yukon AK ...... 66°34N 145°16W **61 C11**
Fort Yuma Indian Reservation
CA ...... 32°45N 114°35W **65 L12**

Fortescue NJ . . . . . . 39°12N 75°12W **87 C1**
Fortine MT . . . . . . 48°46N 114°54W **83 B3**
Fortress Mt. WY . . . . 44°20N 109°48W **104 B3**
Fortsonia GA . . . . . 34°1N 82°47W **68 B4**
Fortuna CA . . . . . . 40°36N 124°9W **64 C2**
Fortuna ND . . . . . . 38°34N 92°48W **82 C4**
Fortuna ND . . . . . . 48°55N 103°47W **91 B2**
Fortuna Ledge = Marshall
  AK . . . . . . 61°53N 162°5W **61 F7**
Fortville IN . . . . . . 39°56N 85°51W **72 D5**
Foss OK . . . . . . 35°27N 99°10W **93 C4**
Foss L. OK . . . . . . 35°33N 99°11W **93 C4**
Fossil OR . . . . . . 45°0N 120°9W **94 B5**
Fossil Butte Nat. Monument △
  WY . . . . . . 41°50N 110°27W **104 E2**
Fosston L. OR . . . . 43°19N 120°25W **94 D5**
Fosston MN . . . . . . 47°35N 95°45W **80 C3**
Foster KY . . . . . . 38°48N 84°13W **97 B8**
Foster NE . . . . . . 42°16N 97°40W **84 B8**
Foster OR . . . . . . 44°25N 122°40W **94 C3**
Foster RI . . . . . . 41°47N 71°44W **78 C3**
Foster City MI . . . . 45°58N 87°45W **79 D4**
Foster County ☆ ND . . 47°30N 99°0W **91 C7**
Foster L. OR . . . . . 42°59N 119°15W **94 E6**
Foster Village HI . . . 21°21N 157°55W **69 K14**
Fosters AL . . . . . . 33°6N 87°41W **60 C3**
Fostoria IA . . . . . . 43°15N 95°9W **73 B3**
Fostoria KS . . . . . . 39°26N 96°30W **74 B7**
Fostoria OH . . . . . . 41°10N 83°25W **92 B5**
Fouke AR . . . . . . 33°16N 93°53W **63 E2**
Fountain CO . . . . . 38°41N 104°42W **66 D6**
Fountain FL . . . . . . 30°29N 85°25W **67 A3**
Fountain MI . . . . . . 44°3N 86°11W **79 E5**
Fountain MN . . . . . 43°45N 92°8W **80 G6**
Fountain City IN . . . 39°57N 84°55W **72 D6**
Fountain City WI . . . 44°8N 91°43W **103 D2**
Fountain County ☆ IN . 40°8N 87°15W **72 C3**
Fountain Cr. → CO . . 38°15N 104°36W **66 D6**
Fountain Green
  UT . . . . . . 39°38N 111°38W **100 D4**
Fountain Head MD . . 39°42N 77°42W **77 A3**
Fountain Hill AR . . . 33°21N 91°51W **63 E4**
Fountain Hills AZ . . . 33°37N 111°43W **62 D4**
Fountain Inn SC . . . . 34°42N 82°12W **90 D3**
Fountain Run KY . . . 36°43N 85°56W **97 D7**
Four Corners OR . . . 44°56N 122°58W **94 C3**
Four Corners WY . . . 44°5N 104°8W **104 B8**
Four Corners UT . . . 37°0N 109°3W **100 F6**
Four League B. L . . . 29°20N 91°13W **75 E4**
Four Mountains, Is. of
  AK . . . . . . 53°0N 170°0W **61 K5**
Four Oaks NC . . . . . 35°27N 78°26W **90 C7**
Four Town MN . . . . 48°17N 95°20W **80 B3**
Fourteen Mile Pt. MI . 47°0N 89°10W **79 B4**
Fowlesburg MD . . . . 39°34N 76°50W **77 A4**
Fowler CA . . . . . . 36°38N 119°41W **65 G7**
Fowler CO . . . . . . 38°8N 104°2W **66 D6**
Fowler IN . . . . . . 40°37N 87°19W **72 C3**
Fowler KS . . . . . . 37°23N 100°12W **74 D3**
Fowler MI . . . . . . 43°0N 84°45W **79 F7**
Fowlerton IN . . . . . 40°25N 85°34W **72 C5**
Fowlerton TX . . . . . 28°28N 98°48W **99 J9**
Fowlerville MI . . . . 42°40N 84°4W **79 F7**
Fowlstown GA . . . . . 30°48N 84°33W **68 E2**
Fox CO . . . . . . 38°22N 97°30W **93 D6**
Fox → IL . . . . . . 41°21N 88°50W **71 B5**
Fox → MO . . . . . . 40°17N 91°30W **82 A5**
Fox → WI . . . . . . 44°32N 88°0W **103 D5**
Fox Chapel PA . . . . 40°30N 79°52W **116 A2**
Fox Is. AK . . . . . . 53°0N 168°0W **61 K6**
Fox Lake IL . . . . . . 42°24N 88°11W **71 A5**
Fox Lake WI . . . . . . 43°34N 88°55W **103 E5**
Fox Point WI . . . . . 43°9N 87°54W **112 B2**
Fox Pt. WI . . . . . . 43°10N 87°52W **112 A2**
Foxboro MA . . . . . . 42°4N 71°16W **78 B3**
Foxfield CO . . . . . . 39°35N 104°47W **109 C5**
Foxpark WY . . . . . . 41°5N 106°9W **104 E6**
Foxworth MS . . . . . 31°14N 89°52W **81 E4**
Foyil OK . . . . . . 36°26N 95°31W **93 B8**
Frametown WV . . . . 38°38N 80°52W **102 C4**
Framingham MA . . . . 42°18N 71°24W **106 B1**
Frances OK . . . . . . 34°35N 123°30W **101 D2**
Frances, L. MT . . . . 48°16N 112°13W **83 B5**
Francestown NH . . . . 42°58N 71°48W **86 D3**
Francesville IN . . . . 40°59N 86°53W **72 C4**
Francis OK . . . . . . 34°52N 96°36W **93 D7**
Francis UT . . . . . . 40°37N 111°17W **100 C4**
Francis, L. NH . . . . 45°2N 71°20W **86 A3**
Francis Case, L. SD . . 43°4N 98°34W **91 G7**
Francis Creek WI . . . 44°12N 87°44W **103 D6**
Francis E. Walter Res.
  PA . . . . . . 41°8N 75°44W **87 A1**
Francis Marion Nat. Forest
  SC . . . . . . 33°10N 79°40W **90 E6**
Franconia NH . . . . . 44°14N 71°44W **86 B3**
Franconia VA . . . . . 38°47N 77°7W **119 C3**
Francs Pk. WY . . . . . 43°58N 109°20W **104 C3**
Frank Church River of No Return
  Wilderness ID . . . . 44°41N 114°30W **70 E4**
Frank Lloyd Wright Home
  IL . . . . . . 41°53N 87°47W **108 B2**
Frankenmuth MI . . . 43°20N 83°44W **79 F8**
Frankewing TN . . . . 35°12N 86°51W **96 E6**
Frankford DE . . . . . 38°31N 75°14W **77 B5**
Frankford MO . . . . . 39°29N 91°19W **82 B5**
Frankford WV . . . . . 37°56N 80°23W **102 D4**
Frankfort IN . . . . . . 40°17N 86°31W **72 C4**
Frankfort KS . . . . . 39°42N 96°25W **74 B7**
Frankfort KY . . . . . 38°12N 84°52W **97 B8**
Frankfort ME . . . . . 44°37N 68°53W **76 D5**
Frankfort MI . . . . . 44°38N 86°14W **79 E5**
Frankfort OH . . . . . 39°24N 83°11W **92 D3**
Frankfort SD . . . . . 44°53N 98°18W **91 F7**
Franklin AL . . . . . . 32°41N 109°5W **62 E6**
Franklin GA . . . . . . 33°17N 85°6W **68 C1**
Franklin ID . . . . . . 42°1N 111°48W **70 G7**
Franklin IL . . . . . . 39°37N 90°3W **71 D3**
Franklin IN . . . . . . 39°29N 86°3W **72 D4**
Franklin KS . . . . . . 37°32N 94°42W **74 D9**
Franklin KY . . . . . . 36°43N 86°35W **96 D6**
Franklin LA . . . . . . 29°48N 91°30W **75 E4**
Franklin ME . . . . . . 44°35N 68°14W **76 D5**
Franklin MA . . . . . . 42°5N 71°24W **78 B3**
Franklin MN . . . . . . 44°32N 94°53W **80 F4**
Franklin NC . . . . . . 35°11N 83°23W **90 C2**
Franklin NH . . . . . . 43°27N 71°39W **86 C2**
Franklin NJ . . . . . . 41°7N 74°35W **87 A2**
Franklin NY . . . . . . 42°21N 75°10W **89 C5**
Franklin NE . . . . . . 40°6N 98°57W **84 E7**
Franklin OH . . . . . . 39°34N 84°18W **92 D2**
Franklin PA . . . . . . 41°24N 79°50W **95 C3**
Franklin TN . . . . . . 35°55N 86°52W **96 E6**
Franklin TX . . . . . . 31°2N 96°29W **99 F11**
Franklin VA . . . . . . 36°41N 76°56W **102 E8**
Franklin WV . . . . . . 38°39N 79°20W **102 C5**
Franklin, Pt. AK . . . . 70°55N 158°48W **61 A8**
Franklin County ☆
  AL . . . . . . 34°21N 87°42W **60 B2**
Franklin County ☆
  AR . . . . . . 35°29N 93°50W **63 C2**
Franklin County ☆
  FL . . . . . . 29°50N 84°45W **67 B4**
Franklin County ☆
  GA . . . . . . 34°20N 83°10W **68 B3**
Franklin County ☆
  ID . . . . . . 42°10N 111°50W **70 G7**
Franklin County ☆ IN . 39°25N 85°5W **72 D5**
Franklin County ☆
  IA . . . . . . 42°45N 93°25W **73 C5**
Franklin County ☆
  KS . . . . . . 38°30N 95°15W **74 C8**
Franklin County ☆
  KY . . . . . . 38°15N 84°55W **97 B8**
Franklin County ☆
  ME . . . . . . 45°0N 70°30W **76 D3**
Franklin County ☆
  MA . . . . . . 42°30N 72°35W **78 B2**
Franklin County ☆
  MS . . . . . . 31°28N 90°54W **81 E3**
Franklin County ☆
  MO . . . . . . 38°25N 91°0W **82 C5**
Franklin County ☆ NC . 36°0N 78°20W **90 B7**
Franklin County ☆
  NY . . . . . . 44°30N 74°15W **89 A6**
Franklin County ☆
  NE . . . . . . 40°15N 99°0W **84 D7**
Franklin County ☆ OH . 40°0N 83°4W **92 D3**
Franklin County ☆
  PA . . . . . . 39°56N 77°40W **95 E5**
Franklin County ☆ TN . 35°10N 86°1W **96 E6**
Franklin County ☆
  TX . . . . . . 33°11N 95°13W **99 D12**
Franklin County ☆ VA . 37°15N 79°45W **102 D6**
Franklin County ☆
  VT . . . . . . 44°50N 72°50W **86 B2**
Franklin County ☆
  WA . . . . . . 46°30N 119°0W **101 D7**
Franklin D. Roosevelt L.
  WA . . . . . . 48°18N 118°9W **101 B7**
Franklin Grove IL . . . 41°51N 89°18W **71 B4**
Franklin L. NV . . . . 40°25N 115°22W **85 B5**
Franklin Parish ☆ LA . 32°10N 91°43W **75 B4**
Franklin Park IL . . . . 41°55N 87°52W **108 B1**
Franklin Park MA . . . 42°18N 71°5W **106 B3**
Franklin Park NJ . . . 40°42N 73°40W **114 B4**
Franklin Square NY . . 40°42N 73°40W **114 B4**
Franklin Res. LA . . . 34°5N 118°24W **111 B2**
Franklinton LA . . . . 30°51N 90°9W **75 D5**
Franklinton NC . . . . 36°6N 78°27W **90 B7**
Franklinville NJ . . . . 39°37N 75°5W **87 C1**
Franklinville NY . . . . 42°20N 78°27W **89 C2**
Frankston TX . . . . . 32°3N 95°30W **99 E12**
Frankton IN . . . . . . 40°13N 85°46W **72 C5**
Frankville AL . . . . . 31°39N 88°9W **60 D2**
Frannie WY . . . . . . 44°58N 108°37W **104 B4**
Fraser CO . . . . . . 39°57N 105°49W **66 C5**
Frazee MN . . . . . . 46°44N 95°42W **80 D3**
Frazer MT . . . . . . 48°3N 106°2W **83 B11**
Frazeysburg OH . . . . 40°7N 82°7W **92 C4**
Frazier Park CA . . . . 34°49N 118°56W **65 J8**
Fred TX . . . . . . 30°34N 94°10W **99 G13**
Freda ND . . . . . . 47°8N 88°49W **79 B3**
Frederic MI . . . . . . 44°47N 84°45W **79 E7**
Frederic WI . . . . . . 45°40N 92°28W **103 C1**
Frederica DE . . . . . 39°1N 75°28W **77 A5**
Frederick CO . . . . . 40°6N 104°56W **66 B6**
Frederick MD . . . . . 39°25N 77°25W **77 A3**
Frederick OK . . . . . 34°23N 99°1W **93 D4**
Frederick SD . . . . . 45°50N 98°31W **91 E7**
Frederick County ☆
  MD . . . . . . 39°30N 77°25W **77 A3**
Frederick County ☆
  VA . . . . . . 39°5N 78°13W **102 B6**
Fredericksburg IA . . . 42°58N 92°12W **73 C6**
Fredericksburg TX . . . 30°16N 98°52W **99 G9**
Fredericksburg VA . . . 38°18N 77°28W **102 C7**
Fredericksburg and Spotsylvania
  Nat. Military Park
  VA . . . . . . 38°18N 77°43W **102 C7**
Fredericktown MO . . . 37°34N 90°18W **82 D6**
Fredericktown OH . . . 40°29N 82°33W **92 C4**
Frederika IA . . . . . . 42°53N 92°19W **73 C6**
Frederiksted
  U.S. Virgin Is. L . . . 17°43N 64°53W **105 H18**
Fredonia AZ . . . . . . 36°57N 112°32W **62 A3**
Fredonia KS . . . . . . 37°32N 95°49W **74 D8**
Fredonia ND . . . . . 46°20N 99°6W **91 D6**
Fredonia NY . . . . . . 42°26N 79°20W **89 C1**
Fredonia PA . . . . . . 41°19N 80°16W **95 C2**
Fredrica, L. FL . . . . 28°30N 81°18W **115 A3**
Freeborn County ☆
  MN . . . . . . 43°40N 93°15W **80 G5**
Freeburg IL . . . . . . 38°26N 89°55W **71 E4**
Freeburg MO . . . . . 38°19N 91°56W **82 C5**
Freedom OK . . . . . . 36°46N 99°7W **93 B4**
Freedom Park NC . . . 35°11N 80°50W **107 A1**
Freedom WY . . . . . 42°59N 111°3W **104 D1**
Freehold NJ . . . . . . 40°16N 74°17W **87 B2**
Freeland PA . . . . . . 41°1N 75°54W **95 C7**
Freeman MO . . . . . 38°37N 94°30W **82 C2**
Freeman SD . . . . . . 43°21N 97°26W **91 G8**
Freeman, L. IN . . . . 40°42N 86°45W **72 C4**
Freeman, L. CA . . . . 33°44N 118°9W **111 D4**
Freeport FL . . . . . . 30°30N 86°8W **67 A2**
Freeport IL . . . . . . 42°17N 89°36W **71 A4**
Freeport KS . . . . . . 37°12N 97°51W **74 D6**
Freeport ME . . . . . . 43°50N 70°6W **76 E3**
Freeport MI . . . . . . 42°46N 85°19W **79 G6**
Freeport MN . . . . . 45°40N 94°42W **80 E4**
Freeport NY . . . . . . 40°39N 73°35W **87 B2**
Freeport OH . . . . . . 40°41N 79°41W **95 D3**
Freeport PA . . . . . . 40°41N 79°41W **95 D3**
Freeport TX . . . . . . 28°57N 95°21W **99 J12**
Freer TX . . . . . . 27°53N 98°37W **99 J9**
Freesoil MI . . . . . . 44°7N 86°13W **79 E5**
Freestone County ☆
  TX . . . . . . 31°44N 96°10W **99 F11**
Freeville NY . . . . . . 42°31N 76°21W **89 C4**
Freistatt MO . . . . . 37°1N 93°54W **82 D3**
Fremont CA . . . . . . 37°32N 121°57W **64 F5**
Fremont IA . . . . . . 41°13N 92°26W **73 D6**
Fremont IN . . . . . . 41°44N 84°56W **72 B6**
Fremont KY . . . . . . 36°31N 88°37W **96 D4**
Fremont NE . . . . . . 41°26N 96°30W **84 C9**
Fremont OH . . . . . . 41°21N 83°7W **92 B3**
Fremont UT . . . . . . 38°27N 111°37W **100 E4**
Fremont WI . . . . . . 44°16N 88°52W **103 D5**
Fremont → UT . . . . 38°24N 110°42W **100 E5**
Fremont County ☆
  CO . . . . . . 38°30N 105°30W **66 D5**
Fremont County ☆
  ID . . . . . . 44°15N 111°20W **70 E7**
Fremont County ☆
  IA . . . . . . 40°45N 95°35W **73 E3**
Fremont County ☆
  WY . . . . . . 43°0N 108°30W **104 D4**
Fremont I. UT . . . . . 41°10N 112°21W **100 B3**
Fremont Junction
  UT . . . . . . 38°45N 111°23W **100 E4**
Fremont Nat. Forest
  OR . . . . . . 42°20N 120°50W **94 E5**
French Broad →
  U.S.A. . . . . . . 35°57N 83°51W **97 E9**
French Camp CA . . . 37°53N 121°16W **64 F5**
French Camp MS . . . 33°18N 89°24W **81 C4**
French Creek WV . . . 38°53N 80°18W **102 C4**
French Creek → PA . . 41°24N 79°50W **95 C3**
French Frigate Shoals
  HI . . . . . . 23°45N 166°10W **69 G10**
French Gulch CA . . . 40°42N 122°38W **64 D4**
French Lick IN . . . . 38°33N 86°37W **72 E4**
French Meadows Res.
  CA . . . . . . 39°10N 120°24W **107 A2**
French Park CA . . . . 39°11N 84°25W **108 A4**
French Regional Park
  MN . . . . . . 45°2N 93°26W **113 A1**
French River MN . . . 46°54N 91°54W **80 D7**
French Settlement
  LA . . . . . . 30°18N 90°47W **75 D5**
Frenchboro ME . . . . 44°7N 68°22W **76 D5**

Frenchburg KY . . . . 37°57N 83°38W **97 C9**
Frenchglen OR . . . . 42°50N 118°55W **94 E7**
Frenchman Cr. →
  N. Amer. . . . . . . 48°31N 107°10W **83 B10**
Frenchman Cr. →
  U.S.A. . . . . . . 40°14N 100°50W **84 D5**
Frenchman L. NV . . . 39°54N 120°11W **64 D6**
Frenchman L. NV . . . 36°48N 115°56W **85 F5**
Frenchman NJ . . . . . 40°32N 75°4W **87 B1**
Frenchtown NJ . . . . 40°32N 75°4W **87 B1**
Frenchville ME . . . . 47°17N 68°23W **76 A5**
Fresh Meadows NY . . 40°44N 73°47W **114 B4**
Fresh Pond MA . . . . 42°23N 71°8W **106 A3**
Fresno CA . . . . . . 36°44N 119°47W **65 G7**
Fresno County ☆ CA . 36°40N 120°0W **65 G7**
Fresno Res. MT . . . . 48°36N 109°57W **83 B8**
Frewsburg NY . . . . . 42°3N 79°10W **89 C1**
Friars Point MS . . . . 34°22N 90°38W **81 B3**
Friday Harbor WA . . . 48°32N 123°1W **101 B2**
Fridley MN . . . . . . 45°5N 93°15W **113 A2**
Friend KS . . . . . . 38°16N 100°55W **74 C3**
Friend NE . . . . . . 40°38N 97°17W **84 D8**
Friendly MD . . . . . 38°45N 76°59W **77 B4**
Friendship NY . . . . . 42°12N 78°8W **89 C2**
Friendship TN . . . . . 35°55N 89°14W **96 E3**
Friendship WI . . . . . 43°58N 89°49W **103 E4**
Friendship Hill Nat. Historic Site
  PA . . . . . . 39°47N 79°56W **95 E3**
Friendsville MD . . . . 39°40N 79°24W **77 A1**
Friendsville TN . . . . 35°46N 84°8W **97 E8**
Fries VA . . . . . . 36°43N 80°59W **102 E4**
Friesland WI . . . . . 43°35N 89°4W **103 E4**
Frio → TX . . . . . . 28°26N 98°11W **99 J9**
Frio County ☆ TX . . . 28°54N 99°6W **99 J8**
Frio Draw → TX . . . 34°50N 102°10W **98 C5**
Friona TX . . . . . . 34°38N 102°43W **98 C5**
Frisco CO . . . . . . 39°35N 106°6W **66 C4**
Frisco TX . . . . . . 33°9N 96°49W **99 D11**
Frisco Peak UT . . . . 38°31N 113°17W **100 E2**
Frissell, Mt. CT . . . . 42°3N 73°28W **78 B1**
Froid MT . . . . . . 48°20N 104°30W **83 B12**
Fromberg MT . . . . . 45°24N 108°54W **83 E9**
Front Range CO . . . . 40°25N 105°45W **66 B5**
Front Royal VA . . . . 38°55N 78°12W **77 B2**
Frontenac KS . . . . . 37°27N 94°42W **74 D9**
Frontier WY . . . . . . 41°49N 110°32W **104 E1**
Frontier County ☆
  NE . . . . . . 40°30N 100°30W **84 D5**
Frost MN . . . . . . 43°35N 93°56W **80 G5**
Frost TX . . . . . . 32°5N 96°49W **99 E11**
Frost Place, The NH . . 44°13N 71°45W **86 B3**
Frostburg MD . . . . . 39°39N 78°56W **77 A2**
Frostproof FL . . . . . 27°45N 81°32W **67 D7**
Fruit Cove FL . . . . . 30°7N 81°39W **67 A7**
Fruit Hill OH . . . . . 39°4N 84°21W **108 B3**
Fruita CO . . . . . . 39°9N 108°44W **66 C2**
Fruitdale AL . . . . . . 31°21N 88°25W **60 D2**
Fruitdale SD . . . . . 44°40N 103°42W **91 E2**
Fruitland ID . . . . . . 44°0N 116°55W **70 F2**
Fruitland IA . . . . . . 41°21N 91°8W **73 D7**
Fruitland MD . . . . . 38°19N 75°37W **77 B5**
Fruitland NM . . . . . 36°37N 108°24W **88 C3**
Fruitland UT . . . . . 40°13N 110°50W **100 C5**
Fruitland Park FL . . . 28°51N 81°54W **67 C7**
Fruitport MI . . . . . . 43°7N 86°9W **79 F5**
Fruitvale WA . . . . . 46°37N 120°33W **101 D5**
Fry Canyon UT . . . . 37°38N 110°9W **100 F5**
Fryeburg ME . . . . . 44°1N 70°59W **86 B4**
Fulda MN . . . . . . 43°53N 95°36W **80 G3**
Fulford
  FL = North Miami Beach
  FL . . . . . . 25°55N 80°9W **112 C2**
Fullerton MD . . . . . 39°22N 76°30W **107 A2**
Fullerton CA . . . . . 33°53N 117°56W **65 K9**
Fullerton NE . . . . . 41°22N 97°58W **84 C8**
Fulton AL . . . . . . 31°47N 87°44W **60 E3**
Fulton AR . . . . . . 33°37N 93°49W **63 E2**
Fulton IL . . . . . . 41°52N 90°11W **71 B3**
Fulton KS . . . . . . 38°1N 94°43W **74 C9**
Fulton KY . . . . . . 36°30N 88°53W **96 D4**
Fulton MI . . . . . . 42°10N 85°25W **79 G6**
Fulton MO . . . . . . 38°52N 91°57W **82 C5**
Fulton NY . . . . . . 43°19N 76°25W **89 B4**
Fulton OH . . . . . . 40°28N 82°50W **92 C4**
Fulton SD . . . . . . 43°44N 97°49W **91 G8**
Fulton County ☆ AR . . 36°22N 91°50W **63 B4**
Fulton County ☆ GA . . 33°50N 84°40W **68 C2**
Fulton County ☆ IL . . 40°30N 90°10W **71 C3**
Fulton County ☆ IN . . 41°5N 86°15W **72 B4**
Fulton County ☆ KY . . 36°32N 89°10W **96 D3**
Fulton County ☆ NY . . 43°10N 74°30W **89 B6**
Fulton County ☆ OH . . 41°35N 84°9W **92 B2**
Fulton County ☆ PA . . 39°55N 78°5W **95 E5**
Fultondale AL . . . . . 33°37N 86°48W **60 C4**
Fults IL . . . . . . 38°10N 90°13W **71 E3**
Funk NE . . . . . . 40°28N 99°15W **84 D6**
Funston GA . . . . . . 31°12N 83°52W **68 E3**
Fuquay-Varina NC . . . 35°35N 78°48W **90 C7**
Furman SC . . . . . . 32°41N 81°11W **90 E4**
Furnas County ☆ NE . . 40°15N 100°0W **84 D6**
Futiga Amer. Samoa . . 14°21S 170°45W **105 e**

G

Gabaret I. IL . . . . . 38°42N 90°10W **117 A2**
Gabbettville GA . . . . 32°57N 85°8W **68 D1**
Gabbs NV . . . . . . 38°52N 117°55W **85 D3**
Gabbs Valley NV . . . 38°51N 118°12W **85 D2**
Gabbs Valley Range
  NV . . . . . . 38°34N 118°0W **85 D2**
Gabilan Range CA . . . 36°30N 121°15W **64 G5**
Gabriel Park OR . . . . 45°28N 122°43W **116 B1**
Gackle ND . . . . . . 46°38N 99°9W **91 D6**
Gadsden AL . . . . . . 34°1N 86°1W **60 B4**
Gadsden AZ . . . . . . 32°33N 114°47W **62 E1**
Gadsden TN . . . . . . 35°47N 88°59W **96 E4**
Gadsden County ☆
  FL . . . . . . 30°30N 84°45W **67 A4**
Gadsden Point FL . . . 27°49N 82°28W **119 C4**
Gaffney SC . . . . . . 35°5N 81°39W **90 C4**
Gage OK . . . . . . 36°19N 99°45W **93 B4**
Gage County ☆ NE . . 40°20N 96°45W **84 D9**
Gage Park IL . . . . . 41°47N 87°42W **108 C2**
Gahanna OH . . . . . 40°1N 82°53W **92 C4**
Gail TX . . . . . . 32°46N 101°27W **98 E6**
Gaillard, L. CT . . . . 41°21N 72°46W **78 C2**
Gainesboro TN . . . . 36°21N 85°39W **97 D7**
Gainesville FL . . . . . 29°40N 82°20W **67 B6**
Gainesville GA . . . . 34°18N 83°50W **68 B3**
Gainesville MO . . . . 36°36N 92°26W **82 E4**
Gainesville TX . . . . 33°38N 97°8W **99 D10**
Gaithersburg MD . . . 39°8N 77°12W **77 A3**
Galatia IL . . . . . . 37°51N 88°37W **71 E5**
Galatia KS . . . . . . 38°38N 98°58W **74 C5**
Galax VA . . . . . . 36°40N 80°56W **102 E4**
Galena AK . . . . . . 64°44N 156°56W **61 D8**
Galena IL . . . . . . 42°25N 90°26W **71 A3**
Galena KS . . . . . . 37°4N 94°38W **74 D9**
Galena MD . . . . . . 39°21N 75°53W **77 A5**

Galena MO . . . . . . 36°48N 93°28W **82 E3**
Galena Park TX . . . . 29°44N 95°14W **118 B3**
Galesburg IL . . . . . 40°57N 90°22W **71 C3**
Galesburg KS . . . . . 37°28N 95°21W **74 D8**
Galesburg ND . . . . . 47°16N 97°24W **91 C8**
Galesville MD . . . . . 38°50N 76°33W **77 B4**
Galesville WI . . . . . 44°5N 91°21W **103 D2**
Galeton CO . . . . . . 40°31N 104°35W **66 B6**
Galeton PA . . . . . . 41°44N 77°39W **95 C5**
Galiano MN . . . . . . 48°36N 93°10W **80 B5**
Galiuro Mts. AZ . . . . 32°30N 110°20W **62 E5**
Gallatin MO . . . . . . 39°55N 93°58W **82 B3**
Gallatin TN . . . . . . 36°24N 86°27W **96 D6**
Gallatin TX . . . . . . 31°54N 95°9W **99 F12**
Gallatin County ☆ IL . . 37°45N 88°15W **71 E5**
Gallatin County ☆
  KY . . . . . . 38°45N 84°55W **97 B8**
Gallatin County ☆
  MT . . . . . . 45°55N 111°15W **83 E6**
Gallatin Gateway
  MT . . . . . . 45°35N 111°12W **83 E6**
Gallatin Nat. Forest
  MT . . . . . . 45°15N 111°15W **83 E6**
Gallatin Range MT . . . 44°50N 110°53W **83 F7**
Gallia County ☆ OH . . 38°49N 82°12W **92 E4**
Gallinas → NM . . . . 35°0N 104°54W **88 B6**
Gallinas Mts. NM . . . 34°25N 107°45W **88 C3**
Gallion AL . . . . . . 32°30N 87°43W **60 D3**
Gallipolis OH . . . . . 38°49N 82°12W **92 E4**
Gallitzin PA . . . . . . 40°29N 78°33W **95 D4**
Gallman MS . . . . . . 31°56N 90°23W **81 E3**
Gallo Mts. NM . . . . 34°5N 108°35W **88 C2**
Galloo I. NY . . . . . 43°55N 76°25W **89 B4**
Gallup NM . . . . . . 35°32N 108°45W **88 B2**
Galt CA . . . . . . 38°15N 121°18W **64 E5**
Galt IA . . . . . . 42°42N 93°36W **73 C5**
Galt MO . . . . . . 40°8N 93°23W **82 A3**
Galva IA . . . . . . 41°10N 90°3W **71 B3**
Galva KS . . . . . . 38°23N 97°32W **74 C6**
Galveston IN . . . . . 40°35N 86°11W **72 C4**
Galveston TX . . . . . 29°22N 96°31W **99 H11**
Galveston B. TX . . . . 29°36N 94°50W **99 H13**
Galveston County ☆
  TX . . . . . . 29°28N 95°5W **99 H11**
Galveston I. TX . . . . 29°16N 94°51W **99 H11**
Gamaliel AR . . . . . 36°27N 92°14W **63 B3**
Gamaliel KY . . . . . 36°38N 85°48W **97 D7**
Gambell AK . . . . . . 63°47N 171°45W **61 E5**
Gamber MD . . . . . . 39°28N 76°56W **77 A4**
Ganado AZ . . . . . . 35°43N 109°33W **62 B6**
Ganado TX . . . . . . 29°2N 96°31W **99 H11**
Gandeeville WV . . . . 38°42N 81°25W **102 C3**
Gannett ID . . . . . . 43°22N 114°11W **70 F4**
Gannett Peak WY . . . 43°11N 109°39W **104 C3**
Gannvalley SD . . . . 44°2N 98°59W **91 F7**
Gans OK . . . . . . 35°23N 94°42W **93 C9**
Gantt AL . . . . . . 31°25N 86°29W **60 E4**
Gantt SC . . . . . . 34°48N 82°24W **90 D3**
Gap Mills WV . . . . . 37°34N 80°24W **102 D4**
Garapan N. Marianas . . 15°12N 145°43E **105 c**
Garber IA . . . . . . 42°45N 91°16W **73 C7**
Garber OK . . . . . . 36°26N 97°35W **93 B6**
Garberville CA . . . . 40°6N 123°48W **64 C2**
Garcia CO . . . . . . 37°0N 105°32W **66 E5**
Gardar ND . . . . . . 48°35N 97°53W **91 B8**
Garden MI . . . . . . 45°47N 86°33W **79 D5**
Garden City AL . . . . 34°1N 86°45W **60 B4**
Garden City GA . . . . 32°6N 81°9W **68 D5**
Garden City ID . . . . 43°38N 116°16W **70 F2**
Garden City KS . . . . 37°58N 100°53W **74 D3**
Garden City MO . . . . 38°34N 94°12W **82 C2**
Garden City NY . . . . 40°43N 73°38W **114 B5**
Garden City SC . . . . 33°36N 79°1W **90 E6**
Garden City SD . . . . 44°57N 97°35W **91 F8**
Garden City TX . . . . 31°52N 101°29W **98 F6**
Garden City UT . . . . 41°57N 111°24W **100 B4**
Garden County ☆
  NE . . . . . . 41°30N 102°15W **84 C3**
Garden District LA . . . 29°56N 90°5W **113 C2**
Garden Grove CA . . . 33°47N 117°55W **65 K9**
Garden Grove IA . . . 40°50N 93°36W **73 E5**
Garden Home OR . . . 45°27N 122°45W **116 B1**
Garden I. MI . . . . . 45°49N 85°30W **79 D6**
Garden Island B. LA . . 29°0N 89°0W **75 F7**
Garden Lakes GA . . . 34°14N 85°13W **68 B1**
Garden Peninsula MI . . 45°42N 86°38W **79 D5**
Garden Plain KS . . . . 37°40N 97°41W **74 D6**
Garden Reach NY . . . 39°34N 85°17W **68 B1**
Garden Valley ID . . . 44°6N 115°57W **70 E3**
Garden View PA . . . . 41°15N 77°2W **95 C5**
Gardena CA . . . . . . 33°53N 118°18W **111 C3**
Gardendale AL . . . . 33°39N 86°49W **60 C4**
Gardendale TX . . . . 29°28N 98°21W **117 A3**
Gardenville MD . . . . 39°19N 76°33W **107 B2**
Gardi GA . . . . . . 31°32N 81°48W **68 D4**
Gardiner ME . . . . . 44°14N 69°47W **76 D4**
Gardiner MT . . . . . 45°2N 110°22W **83 E7**
Gardiners B. NY . . . . 41°5N 72°5W **78 C2**
Gardiners I. NY . . . . 41°6N 72°6W **78 C2**
Gardner CO . . . . . . 37°47N 105°10W **66 E5**
Gardner KS . . . . . . 38°49N 94°56W **74 C9**
Gardner MA . . . . . . 42°34N 71°59W **78 B3**
Gardner ND . . . . . . 46°58N 96°58W **91 C9**
Gardner L. ME . . . . 44°45N 67°20W **76 D6**
Gardner Pinnacles
  HI . . . . . . 25°0N 167°55W **69 F10**
Gardnerville NV . . . . 38°56N 119°45W **85 D1**
Gareloi I. AK . . . . . 51°48N 178°48W **61 K1**
Garfield AR . . . . . . 36°27N 93°58W **63 B2**
Garfield MN . . . . . . 45°56N 95°30W **80 E3**
Garfield NJ . . . . . . 40°52N 74°7W **114 A2**
Garfield NM . . . . . . 32°46N 107°16W **88 E3**
Garfield WA . . . . . . 47°1N 117°9W **101 C8**
Garfield County ☆
  CO . . . . . . 39°30N 108°0W **66 C3**
Garfield County ☆
  MT . . . . . . 47°15N 107°0W **83 C11**
Garfield County ☆ NE . 41°50N 99°0W **84 C7**
Garfield County ☆
  OK . . . . . . 36°20N 97°45W **93 B6**
Garfield County ☆
  UT . . . . . . 37°50N 111°20W **100 F4**
Garfield County ☆
  WA . . . . . . 46°28N 117°36W **101 D8**
Garfield Heights
  OH . . . . . . 41°25N 81°36W **107 B2**
Garfield Mt. MT . . . . 44°31N 112°37W **83 F5**
Garfield Park IL . . . . 41°52N 87°42W **108 B2**
Garfield Park IN . . . . 39°43N 86°8W **110 B2**
Garfield Park Res.
  IN . . . . . . 39°43N 86°8W **110 B2**
Garibaldi OR . . . . . 45°34N 123°55W **94 B2**
Garland AL . . . . . . 31°38N 86°50W **60 E4**
Garland KS . . . . . . 37°44N 94°49W **74 D9**
Garland NC . . . . . . 34°47N 78°24W **90 D7**
Garland TX . . . . . . 32°54N 96°38W **109 A6**
Garland UT . . . . . . 41°45N 112°10W **100 B3**
Garland County ☆
  AR . . . . . . 34°34N 93°10W **63 D2**
Garnavillo IA . . . . . 42°52N 91°14W **73 C7**
Garner IA . . . . . . 43°6N 93°36W **73 B5**
Garner NC . . . . . . 35°43N 78°37W **90 C7**
Garnett KS . . . . . . 38°17N 95°14W **74 C8**

Garrard County ☆
  KY . . . . . . 37°35N 84°30W **97 C8**
Garretson SD . . . . . 43°43N 96°30W **91 G9**
Garrett IN . . . . . . 41°21N 85°8W **72 B5**
Garrett PA . . . . . . 39°52N 79°4W **77 A1**
Garrison
  MD . . . . . . 39°30N 79°20W **77 A1**
Garrison IA . . . . . . 42°9N 92°8W **73 C6**
Garrison KY . . . . . 38°36N 83°10W **119 B3**
Garrison MN . . . . . 46°18N 93°50W **80 D5**
Garrison MT . . . . . 46°31N 112°49W **83 D5**
Garrison ND . . . . . 47°40N 101°25W **91 C4**
Garrison NE . . . . . 41°11N 97°10W **84 C8**
Garrison TX . . . . . . 31°49N 94°30W **99 F13**
Garrison UT . . . . . . 38°59N 87°38W **71 D6**
Garrison Dam ND . . . 47°30N 101°25W **91 C4**
Garrison Res. = Sakakawea, L.
  ND . . . . . . 47°30N 101°25W **91 C4**
Garvanza CA . . . . . 34°6N 118°11W **111 B3**
Garvin OK . . . . . . 33°57N 94°56W **93 E9**
Garvin County ☆
  OK . . . . . . 34°45N 97°20W **93 D6**
Garwood IA . . . . . . 42°6N 92°41W **73 C6**
Gary IN . . . . . . 41°36N 87°20W **72 B3**
Gary MN . . . . . . 47°22N 96°16W **80 C2**
Gary SD . . . . . . 44°48N 96°27W **91 F9**
Gary TX . . . . . . 32°2N 94°22W **99 E13**
Gary WV . . . . . . 37°22N 81°33W **102 D3**
Garysburg NC . . . . . 36°27N 77°33W **90 B8**
Garza County ☆ TX . . 33°12N 101°23W **98 E6**
Gas KS . . . . . . 37°55N 95°20W **74 D8**
Gas City IN . . . . . . 40°29N 85°37W **72 C5**
Gascon NM . . . . . . 35°53N 105°27W **88 B5**
Gasconade → MO . . . 38°40N 91°34W **82 C5**
Gasconade MO . . . . 38°41N 91°33W **82 C5**
Gasconade County ☆
  MO . . . . . . 38°25N 91°30W **82 C5**
Gascoyne ND . . . . . 46°7N 103°5W **91 D2**
Gasparilla I. FL . . . . 26°46N 82°16W **67 E6**
Gasquet CA . . . . . . 41°51N 123°58W **64 B3**
Gassaway WV . . . . . 38°41N 80°47W **102 C4**
Gaston IN . . . . . . 40°19N 85°31W **72 C5**
Gaston OR . . . . . . 45°26N 123°8W **94 B2**
Gaston SC . . . . . . 33°49N 81°5W **90 E4**
Gaston, L. NC . . . . . 36°30N 77°58W **90 B8**
Gaston County ☆ NC . 35°18N 81°12W **90 C4**
Gastonia NC . . . . . 35°16N 81°11W **90 C4**
Gatchellville PA . . . . 39°46N 76°28W **77 A4**
Gate OK . . . . . . 36°51N 100°4W **93 B3**
Gate City VA . . . . . 36°38N 82°35W **102 E2**
Gates NY . . . . . . 43°9N 77°42W **89 B3**
Gates OR . . . . . . 44°45N 122°25W **94 C3**
Gates TN . . . . . . 35°50N 89°24W **96 E3**
Gates, L. ME . . . . . 45°55N 69°3W **76 C4**
Gates County ☆ NC . . 36°25N 76°45W **90 B9**
Gates of the Arctic Nat. Park and
  Preserve AK . . . . 67°45N 153°15W **61 C9**
Gatesville NC . . . . . 36°24N 76°45W **90 B9**
Gatesville TX . . . . . 31°26N 97°45W **99 F10**
Gateway CO . . . . . 38°41N 108°59W **66 D2**
Gateway Nat. Recr. Area △
  NJ . . . . . . 40°26N 74°0W **87 B3**
Gateway Nat. Recr. Area △
  NY . . . . . . 40°38N 73°51W **114 C3**
Gateway Park TX . . . 32°43N 96°42W **109 B2**
Gatliff KY . . . . . . 36°41N 84°1W **97 D8**
Gatlinburg TN . . . . . 35°43N 83°31W **97 E9**
Gato CO . . . . . . 37°3N 107°12W **66 E3**
Gauley → WV . . . . 38°10N 81°12W **102 C3**
Gauley Bridge WV . . . 38°10N 81°12W **102 C3**
Gauley River Nat. Recr. Area △
  WV . . . . . . 38°13N 81°0W **102 C4**
Gautier MS . . . . . . 30°23N 88°37W **81 F5**
Gavilan NM . . . . . . 36°24N 107°2W **88 A3**
Gaviota CA . . . . . . 34°29N 120°13W **65 J6**
Gay CA . . . . . . 34°39N 120°13W **65 J6**
Gay GA . . . . . . 33°6N 84°33W **68 C2**
Gaylord KS . . . . . . 39°39N 98°51W **74 B5**
Gaylord MI . . . . . . 45°2N 84°41W **79 D7**
Gaylord MN . . . . . . 44°33N 94°13W **80 F4**
Gaylordsville CT . . . . 41°39N 73°29W **78 C1**
Gayville SD . . . . . . 42°53N 97°10W **91 H8**
Gazelle CA . . . . . . 41°31N 122°31W **64 B4**
Gearhart OR . . . . . 46°1N 123°55W **94 A2**
Gearhart Mt. OR . . . 42°30N 120°53W **94 E5**
Geary OK . . . . . . 35°38N 98°19W **93 C5**
Geary County ☆ KS . . 39°0N 96°45W **74 C7**
Geauga County ☆
  OH . . . . . . 41°35N 81°12W **92 B5**
Geddes SD . . . . . . 43°15N 98°42W **91 G7**
Geiger AL . . . . . . 32°52N 88°18W **60 D2**
Geistown PA . . . . . 40°18N 78°52W **95 D4**
Gem KS . . . . . . 39°26N 100°54W **74 B3**
Gem County ☆ ID . . . 44°0N 116°25W **70 E2**
Gem Lake MN . . . . . 45°3N 93°2W **113 A3**
Gene Autry OK . . . . 34°16N 97°3W **93 D6**
General Dewitt Spain ✈
  TN . . . . . . 35°12N 90°3W **112 A1**
General Mitchell Int., Milwaukee
  (MKE) WI . . . . 42°57N 87°54W **112 C2**
Genesee ID . . . . . . 46°33N 116°56W **70 C2**
Genesee → NY . . . . 43°16N 77°36W **89 B3**
Genesee County ☆ MI . 43°0N 83°40W **79 F8**
Genesee County ☆
  NY . . . . . . 43°0N 78°10W **89 B2**
Geneseo KS . . . . . . 38°31N 98°10W **74 C5**
Geneseo NY . . . . . . 42°48N 77°49W **89 C3**
Geneva AL . . . . . . 31°2N 85°52W **60 E5**
Geneva GA . . . . . . 32°35N 84°33W **68 D2**
Geneva IL . . . . . . 41°53N 88°18W **71 B5**
Geneva IN . . . . . . 40°36N 84°58W **72 C6**
Geneva MN . . . . . . 43°49N 93°16W **80 G5**
Geneva NE . . . . . . 40°32N 97°36W **84 D8**
Geneva NY . . . . . . 42°52N 76°59W **89 C4**
Geneva OH . . . . . . 41°48N 80°57W **92 B6**
Geneva County ☆ AL . 31°6N 85°42W **60 E5**
Genoa CO . . . . . . 39°17N 103°30W **66 C7**
Genoa IL . . . . . . 42°6N 88°42W **71 A5**
Genoa NE . . . . . . 41°27N 97°44W **84 C8**
Genoa OH . . . . . . 41°31N 83°22W **92 B3**
Genoa WV . . . . . . 38°3N 82°11W **102 C2**
Genoa City WI . . . . 42°30N 88°20W **103 F5**
Genola UT . . . . . . 39°59N 111°55W **100 D4**
Gentry AR . . . . . . 36°16N 94°29W **63 B1**
Gentry MO . . . . . . 40°20N 94°25W **82 A2**
Gentry County ☆
  MO . . . . . . 40°10N 94°25W **82 A2**
Geographic Center of the 48
  Contiguous States
  KS . . . . . . 39°50N 98°35W **74 B5**
Geographical Center of North
  America ND . . . . 48°21N 99°59W **91 B6**
Geographical Center of the 50
  United States SD . . 44°58N 103°46W **91 F2**
George WA . . . . . . 47°5N 119°53W **101 C6**
George, L. FL . . . . . 29°17N 81°36W **67 B7**
George, L. MI . . . . . 29°17N 81°36W **79 C7**
George, L. NY . . . . . 43°37N 73°33W **86 C1**
George Bush Intercontinental,
  Houston ✈ (IAH)
  TX . . . . . . 29°59N 95°20W **99 H12**
George Rogers Clark Nat.
  Memorial △ IN . . . 38°41N 87°32W **72 E3**
George Washington Birthplace Nat.
  Monument → VA . . 38°12N 76°56W **102 C8**
George Washington Bridge
  NY . . . . . . 40°51N 73°57W **114 A3**

George Washington Carter Nat.
  Monument → MO . . 36°59N 94°21W **82 E2**
George Washington Nat. Forest
  U.S.A. . . . . . . 38°15N 79°30W **77 B2**
George West TX . . . . 28°20N 98°7W **99 J9**
Georges I. MA . . . . 42°19N 70°55W **106 B4**
Georgetown CA . . . . 38°54N 120°50W **64 E6**
Georgetown CO . . . . 39°42N 105°42W **66 C5**
Georgetown DC . . . . 38°54N 77°3W **119 B3**
Georgetown DE . . . . 38°41N 75°23W **77 B5**
Georgetown FL . . . . 29°23N 81°38W **67 B7**
Georgetown GA . . . . 31°53N 85°6W **68 E1**
Georgetown IL . . . . 39°59N 87°38W **71 D6**
Georgetown KY . . . . 38°13N 84°33W **97 B8**
Georgetown LA . . . . 31°46N 92°23W **75 C3**
Georgetown MS . . . . 31°52N 90°10W **81 E3**
Georgetown OH . . . . 38°52N 83°54W **92 E3**
Georgetown SC . . . . 33°23N 79°17W **90 E6**
Georgetown TX . . . . 30°38N 97°41W **99 G10**
Georgetown County ☆
  SC . . . . . . 33°30N 79°15W **90 E6**
Georgia, Str. of
  N. Amer. . . . . . . 49°25N 124°0W **101 A2**
Georgia Center VT . . . 44°42N 73°9W **86 B1**
Georgia Dome GA . . . 33°45N 84°23W **106 B2**
Georgiana AL . . . . . 31°38N 86°44W **60 E4**
Gerald MO . . . . . . 38°24N 91°20W **82 C5**
Geraldine MT . . . . . 47°36N 110°16W **83 C7**
Gerber CA . . . . . . 40°4N 122°9W **64 C4**
Gerber Res. OR . . . . 42°12N 121°8W **94 E4**
Gerdine, Mt. AK . . . . 61°35N 152°27W **61 F9**
Gerlach NV . . . . . . 40°39N 119°21W **85 B1**
Germantown IL . . . . 38°33N 89°32W **71 E4**
Germantown MD . . . 39°10N 77°16W **77 A3**
Germantown OH . . . . 39°38N 84°22W **92 D2**
Germantown TN . . . . 35°5N 89°49W **96 E3**
Germfask MI . . . . . 46°15N 85°56W **79 C6**
Geronimo OK . . . . . 34°29N 98°23W **93 D5**
Gerty OK . . . . . . 34°50N 96°17W **93 D7**
Gervais, L. MN . . . . 45°1N 93°4W **113 A3**
Getty Center, The
  CA . . . . . . 34°4N 118°29W **111 B2**
Gettysburg PA . . . . 39°50N 77°14W **77 A3**
Gettysburg Nat. Military Park
  PA . . . . . . 39°49N 77°13W **95 E5**
Geuda Springs KS . . . 37°7N 97°9W **74 D6**
Geyser MT . . . . . . 47°16N 110°30W **83 C7**
Geyserville CA . . . . 38°42N 122°54W **64 E3**
Ghent KY . . . . . . 38°44N 85°4W **97 B7**
Ghent MN . . . . . . 44°31N 95°54W **80 F3**
Ghent NY . . . . . . 42°20N 73°37W **78 B1**
Ghent WV . . . . . . 37°37N 81°7W **102 D3**
Giant Sequoia Nat. Monument △
  CA . . . . . . 36°10N 118°35W **65 G8**
Giants Stadium NJ . . . 40°48N 74°5W **114 B2**
Gibbon MN . . . . . . 40°45N 98°51W **84 D7**
Gibbon NE . . . . . . 40°45N 98°51W **84 D7**
Gibbonsville ID . . . . 45°33N 113°56W **70 D5**
Gibbstown NJ . . . . . 39°50N 75°18W **87 C1**
Gibsland LA . . . . . 32°33N 93°3W **75 B2**
Gibson GA . . . . . . 33°14N 82°36W **68 C4**
Gibson LA . . . . . . 29°41N 90°59W **75 E5**
Gibson County ☆ IN . . 38°20N 87°34W **72 E3**
Gibson County ☆ TN . . 36°0N 89°0W **96 D4**
Gibsonburg OH . . . . 41°23N 83°19W **92 B3**
Gibsonton FL . . . . . 27°51N 82°22W **119 C3**
Giddings TX . . . . . 30°11N 96°56W **99 G11**
Gideon MO . . . . . . 36°27N 89°55W **82 E7**
Gifford FL . . . . . . 27°40N 80°25W **67 D8**
Gifford WA . . . . . . 48°17N 118°8W **101 B7**
Gifford Pinchot Nat. Forest
  WA . . . . . . 46°15N 121°55W **101 D4**
Gig Harbor WA . . . . 47°19N 122°34W **118 C2**
Gila → AZ . . . . . . 32°58N 108°38W **62 E6**
Gila Bend AZ . . . . . 32°57N 112°43W **62 E3**
Gila Bend Indian Reservation
  AZ . . . . . . 33°0N 112°30W **62 D3**
Gila Bend Mts. AZ . . . 33°10N 113°0W **62 D2**
Gila Cliff Dwellings Nat.
  Monument △ NM . . 33°12N 108°16W **88 D2**
Gila County ☆ AZ . . . 33°30N 110°45W **62 D5**
Gila Mts. AZ . . . . . 33°10N 109°0W **62 D6**
Gila Nat. Forest
  NM . . . . . . 33°30N 108°30W **88 D2**
Gila River Indian Reservation
  AZ . . . . . . 33°15N 112°0W **62 D4**
Gilbert IA . . . . . . 33°21N 111°47W **62 D4**
Gilbert IA . . . . . . 42°7N 93°39W **73 C5**
Gilbert LA . . . . . . 32°2N 91°39W **75 B4**
Gilbert MN . . . . . . 47°29N 92°28W **80 C6**
Gilbert WV . . . . . . 37°37N 81°52W **102 D3**
Gilbert WV . . . . . . 46°25N 121°25W **101 D4**
Gilbertown AL . . . . 31°53N 88°19W **60 E2**
Gilbertville MA . . . . 42°19N 72°12W **78 B2**
Gilboa OH . . . . . . 41°9N 83°55W **92 B3**
Gilby ND . . . . . . 48°3N 97°28W **91 B8**
Gilchrist OR . . . . . 43°29N 121°41W **94 D4**
Gilchrist TX . . . . . . 29°31N 94°29W **99 H13**
Gilchrist County ☆
  FL . . . . . . 29°45N 82°45W **67 B6**
Gilcrest CO . . . . . . 40°17N 104°47W **66 B6**
Gildford MT . . . . . 48°34N 110°18W **83 B7**
Gilead NE . . . . . . 40°9N 97°25W **84 E8**
Gilead NE . . . . . . 40°9N 97°25W **84 E8**
Giles County ☆ TN . . . 35°10N 87°0W **96 E6**
Gilford NH . . . . . . 43°33N 71°24W **86 C3**
Gilford Park NJ . . . . 39°58N 74°8W **87 C2**
Gillespie IL . . . . . . 39°8N 89°49W **71 D4**
Gillespie County ☆
  TX . . . . . . 30°16N 98°52W **99 G9**
Gillett AR . . . . . . 34°7N 91°23W **63 D4**
Gillett WI . . . . . . 44°54N 88°19W **103 D5**
Gillett Grove IA . . . . 43°1N 95°2W **73 B3**
Gillette WY . . . . . . 44°18N 105°30W **104 B7**
Gillham AR . . . . . . 34°10N 94°19W **63 D1**
Gilliam LA . . . . . . 32°50N 93°51W **75 B2**
Gilliam County ☆
  OR . . . . . . 46°50N 120°10W **94 B4**
Gillis LA . . . . . . 30°22N 93°12W **75 D2**
Gillis Range NV . . . . 38°42N 118°21W **85 D2**
Gillsville GA . . . . . 34°18N 83°38W **68 B3**
Gilman CO . . . . . . 39°32N 106°24W **66 C4**
Gilman IL . . . . . . 40°46N 88°0W **71 C6**
Gilman IA . . . . . . 41°53N 92°47W **73 D6**
Gilman WI . . . . . . 45°10N 90°47W **103 C3**
Gilman City MO . . . . 40°8N 93°53W **82 A3**
Gilmanton NH . . . . . 43°25N 71°25W **86 C3**
Gilmer TX . . . . . . 32°44N 94°57W **99 E13**
Gilmer County ☆ GA . . 34°40N 84°30W **68 B2**
Gilmer County ☆
  WV . . . . . . 38°56N 80°50W **102 C4**
Gilmore AR . . . . . . 35°25N 90°17W **63 C5**
Gilpin County ☆
  CO . . . . . . 39°50N 105°40W **66 C5**
Gilroy CA . . . . . . 37°1N 121°34W **64 F5**
Gilsum NH . . . . . . 43°3N 72°16W **86 C2**
Giltner NE . . . . . . 40°47N 98°9W **84 D7**
Girard GA . . . . . . 33°3N 81°43W **68 C4**
Girard IL . . . . . . 39°27N 89°47W **71 D4**
Girard KS . . . . . . 37°31N 94°51W **74 D9**

Girard OH . . . . 41°9N 80°42W **92 B6**
Girard PA . . . . 42°0N 80°19W **95 C2**
Girard TX . . . . 33°22N 100°40W **98 F5**
Girdletree MD . . . . . 38°6N 75°24W **77 B5**
Girvin TX . . . . 31°5N 102°24W **98 F5**
Glacier WA . . . . . 48°53N 121°57W **101 B4**
Glacier Bay AK . . . 58°40N 136°0W **61 G14**
Glacier Bay Nat. Park and
  Preserve △ AK . 58°45N 136°30W **61 G13**
Glacier County ☆
  MT . . . . 48°50N 112°50W **83 B5**
Glacier Nat. Park △
  MT . . . . 48°42N 113°48W **83 B4**
Glacier Peak WA . . 48°7N 121°7W **101 B4**
Glad Valley SD . . . 45°24N 101°47W **91 E4**
Gladbrook IA . . . . . 42°11N 92°43W **73 C6**
Glade KS . . . . 39°41N 99°19W **74 B4**
Glade Spring VA . . 36°47N 81°47W **102 E3**
Glades County ☆ FL 26°50N 81°15W **67 E7**
Gladewater TX . . . . 32°33N 94°56W **99 E13**
Gladstone MI . . . . . 45°51N 87°1W **79 D4**
Gladstone MO . . . . 39°13N 94°35W **82 B2**
Gladstone ND . . . . 46°52N 102°34W **91 D3**
Gladstone NJ . . . . . 40°43N 74°40W **87 B2**
Gladstone NM . . . . 36°18N 103°58W **88 A7**
Gladstone OR . . . . 45°22N 122°35W **116 B2**
Gladwin MI . . . . 43°59N 84°29W **79 F7**
Gladwin County ☆ MI 44°0N 84°25W **79 F7**
Gladwyne PA . . . . . 40°2N 75°16W **116 A1**
Glady WV . . . . 38°48N 79°43W **102 C5**
Glady VA . . . . 37°10N 79°4W **102 D5**
Glamis CA . . . . 32°55N 115°5W **65 L11**
Glasco KS . . . . 39°22N 97°50W **74 B6**
Glascock County ☆
  GA . . . . 33°15N 82°40W **68 C4**
Glasford IL . . . . 40°34N 89°49W **71 C4**
Glasgow DE . . . . . . 39°38N 75°45W **77 A5**
Glasgow KY . . . . . . 37°0N 85°55W **97 C7**
Glasgow MO . . . . . 39°14N 92°51W **82 B4**
Glasgow MT . . . . . 48°12N 106°38W **83 B11**
Glasgow VA . . . . . 37°38N 79°27W **102 D5**
Glasgow Junction = Park City
  KY . . . . 37°6N 86°3W **96 C6**
Glasgow Village
  MO . . . . 38°45N 90°11W **117 A2**
Glassboro NJ . . . . 39°42N 75°7W **87 C1**
Glasscock County ☆
  TX . . . . 31°52N 101°29W **98 F6**
Glassmanor MD . . . 38°49N 77°0W **119 C4**
Glassport PA . . . . . 40°19N 79°53W **116 C2**
Glastonbury CT . . . 41°43N 72°37W **78 C2**
Glazier TX . . . . 36°1N 100°16W **98 A7**
Gleason TN . . . . . . 36°13N 88°37W **96 D4**
Gleason Lake MN . . 44°58N 93°29W **113 B1**
Glen MT . . . . 45°28N 112°43W **83 E5**
Glen NH . . . . 44°7N 71°11W **86 B3**
Glen Allan MS . . . . 33°2N 91°2W **81 C1**
Glen Alpine NC . . . 35°44N 81°47W **90 C4**
Glen Burnie MD . . . 39°10N 76°37W **77 A4**
Glen Campbell PA . . 40°49N 78°50W **95 C4**
Glen Canyon UT . . 37°30N 110°40W **100 F5**
Glen Canyon Dam
  AZ . . . . 36°57N 111°29W **62 A4**
Glen Canyon Nat. Recr. Area △
  UT . . . . 37°15N 111°0W **100 F5**
Glen Cove NY . . . . 40°51N 73°38W **114 A3**
Glen Dean KY . . . . 37°39N 86°52W **96 C6**
Glen Elder KS . . . . 39°30N 98°18W **74 B5**
Glen Flora TX . . . . 29°21N 96°12W **99 H11**
Glen Head NY . . . . 40°50N 73°37W **114 A3**
Glen L. MI . . . . 44°52N 85°59W **79 E6**
Glen Lake MN . . . . 44°54N 93°29W **113 B1**
Glen Lyon PA . . . . . 41°10N 76°5W **95 C6**
Glen Mar Park MD . 38°57N 77°7W **119 B3**
Glen Martin Nat. Wildlife
  Refuge △ MD . . 38°0N 76°0W **77 C5**
Glen Oaks NY . . . . 40°44N 73°42W **114 B4**
Glen Raven NC . . . 36°31N 79°29W **90 B6**
Glen Ridge NJ . . . . 40°48N 74°12W **114 B1**
Glen Rock PA . . . . 39°48N 76°44W **77 A4**
Glen Rose TX . . . . 32°14N 97°45W **99 E10**
Glen Ullin ND . . . . 46°49N 101°50W **91 D3**
Glenallen MO . . . . 37°19N 90°2W **82 D6**
Glenarden MD . . . . 38°56N 76°51W **119 B4**
Glenburn ND . . . . . 48°31N 101°13W **91 B4**
Glencliff NH . . . . . . 43°57N 71°53W **86 C3**
Glencoe AL . . . . . . 33°57N 85°56W **60 C5**
Glencoe KY . . . . . . 38°43N 84°49W **97 B8**
Glencoe MN . . . . . 44°46N 94°9W **80 F4**
Glencoe OK . . . . . . 36°14N 96°56W **93 B7**
Glendale AZ . . . . . . 33°32N 112°11W **116 B1**
Glendale CA . . . . . 34°9N 118°15W **111 B3**
Glendale CO . . . . . 39°42N 104°55W **109 B2**
Glendale FL . . . . . . 30°52N 86°7W **67 A2**
Glendale KY . . . . . 37°36N 85°54W **97 C7**
Glendale MO . . . . . 38°35N 90°22W **117 B3**
Glendale NV . . . . . 36°40N 114°34W **85 F6**
Glendale OR . . . . . 42°44N 123°26W **94 E2**
Glendale PA . . . . . . 40°23N 80°5W **116 B1**
Glendale UT . . . . . 37°19N 112°36W **100 F3**
Glendale WI . . . . . . 43°8N 87°56W **112 B2**
Glendale L. PA . . . . 40°42N 78°32W **95 C4**
Glendevey CO . . . . 40°48N 105°56W **66 B5**
Glendive MT . . . . . 47°7N 104°43W **83 C13**
Glendo WY . . . . . . 42°30N 105°2W **104 D8**
Glendo Res. WY . . . 42°29N 104°57W **104 D8**
Glendora MS . . . . . 33°50N 90°18W **81 C3**
Glendora NJ . . . . . 39°50N 75°4W **87 C1**
Glenfield ND . . . . . 47°27N 98°34W **91 C7**
Glenfield NY . . . . . . 43°43N 75°24W **89 B5**
Glenham SD . . . . . 45°32N 100°16W **91 E6**
Glenmont OH . . . . . 40°31N 82°6W **92 C4**
Glenmora LA . . . . . 30°59N 92°35W **75 D3**
Glenn CA . . . . 39°31N 122°1W **64 D4**
Glenn MI . . . . 42°31N 86°14W **79 G5**
Glenn County ☆
  CA . . . . 39°40N 122°20W **64 D4**
Glennallen AK . . . . 62°7N 145°33W **61 E11**
Glenns Ferry ID . . . 42°57N 115°18W **70 G3**
Glennville GA . . . . . 31°56N 81°56W **68 E5**
Glenolden PA . . . . . 39°54N 75°17W **116 B3**
Glenwood IA . . . . . 41°3N 95°45W **73 D2**
Glenpool OK . . . . . 35°58N 96°1W **93 C7**
Glenrock WY . . . . . 42°52N 105°52W **104 D7**
Glens Falls NY . . . . 43°19N 73°39W **89 B6**
Glenshaw PA . . . . . 40°31N 79°58W **116 A2**
Glenside PA . . . . . . 40°6N 75°9W **116 A2**
Glenview IL . . . . . . 42°3N 87°48W **108 A2**
Glenview Countryside
  IL . . . . 42°3N 87°49W **108 A2**
Glenville MN . . . . . 43°34N 93°17W **80 G5**
Glenville NE . . . . . . 40°30N 98°14W **84 D7**
Glenville WV . . . . . 38°56N 80°50W **102 C4**
Glenwood AL . . . . . 31°40N 86°10W **60 E4**
Glenwood AR . . . . 34°20N 93°33W **63 D2**
Glenwood GA . . . . 32°11N 82°40W **68 D4**
Glenwood HI . . . . . 19°29N 155°9W **69 M6**
Glenwood IL . . . . . 41°33N 87°37W **71 B6**
Glenwood IN . . . . . 39°37N 85°18W **72 D3**
Glenwood MN . . . . 45°39N 95°23W **80 E3**
Glenwood NM . . . . 33°19N 108°53W **88 D2**
Glenwood OR . . . . 45°39N 123°16W **94 B2**
Glenwood UT . . . . 38°46N 111°59W **100 E4**
Glenwood WA . . . . 46°1N 121°17W **101 D4**
Glenwood City WI . 45°4N 92°10W **103 C1**
Glenwood Landing
  NY . . . . 40°49N 73°38W **114 A3**
Glenwood Springs
  CO . . . . 39°33N 107°19W **66 C3**
Glidden IA . . . . 42°4N 94°44W **73 C4**

Glide OR . . . . 43°18N 123°6W **94 D2**
Globe AZ . . . . 33°24N 110°47W **62 D5**
Glorieta NM . . . . . 35°35N 105°46W **88 B5**
Gloster MS . . . . . . 31°12N 91°1W **81 E2**
Gloucester MA . . . . 42°37N 70°40W **78 B4**
Gloucester VA . . . . 37°25N 76°32W **102 D8**
Gloucester City NJ . 39°53N 75°7W **116 B2**
Gloucester County ☆
  NJ . . . . 39°40N 75°15W **87 C1**
Gloucester County ☆
  VA . . . . 37°25N 76°32W **102 D8**
Gloucester Point
  VA . . . . 37°15N 76°30W **102 D8**
Glover MO . . . . 37°29N 90°42W **82 D6**
Glover VT . . . . 44°42N 72°12W **86 B2**
Gloversville NY . . . 43°3N 74°21W **89 B5**
Gloverville = Warrenville
  SC . . . . 33°33N 81°48W **90 E4**
Glynn County ☆ GA 31°10N 81°30W **68 E5**
Gnadenhutten OH . . 40°22N 81°26W **92 C5**
Gobernador NM . . . 36°43N 107°21W **88 A3**
Gobles MI . . . . 42°22N 85°53W **79 G6**
Godfrey IL . . . . 38°58N 90°11W **71 E3**
Godfrey GA . . . . . . 33°27N 83°30W **68 C3**
Goehner NE . . . . . . 40°50N 97°13W **84 D8**
Goessel KS . . . . . . 38°15N 97°21W **74 C6**
Goetzville MI . . . . . 46°3N 84°5W **79 C7**
Goff KS . . . . 39°40N 95°56W **74 B8**
Goff Cr. → OK . . . 36°43N 101°29W **93 B2**
Goffs CA . . . . 34°55N 115°4W **65 J11**
Goffstown NH . . . . 43°1N 71°36W **86 C3**
Gogebic, L. MI . . . . 46°30N 89°35W **79 C2**
Gogebic County ☆
  MI . . . . 46°25N 89°45W **79 C2**
Gogebic Range MI . 46°40N 89°40W **79 C2**
Gogebic Range
  WA . . . . 47°51N 121°42W **101 C4**
Golconda IL . . . . . . 37°22N 88°29W **71 F5**
Golconda NV . . . . . 40°58N 117°30W **85 B3**
Gold Beach OR . . . 42°25N 124°25W **94 E1**
Gold Coast IL . . . . 41°54N 87°37W **108 B3**
Gold Creek AK . . . . 62°46N 149°41W **61 E10**
Gold Hill OR . . . . . 42°26N 123°3W **94 E2**
Gold Point NV . . . . 37°21N 117°22W **85 E3**
Goldcreek MT . . . . 46°35N 112°55W **83 D5**
Golden IL . . . . 40°7N 91°1W **71 C2**
Golden MO . . . . . . 36°31N 93°39W **82 E3**
Golden NM . . . . . . 35°16N 106°13W **88 B4**
Golden OK . . . . . . 34°2N 94°54W **93 D9**
Golden Beach FL . . 25°57N 80°7W **112 C3**
Golden City MO . . . 37°24N 94°5W **82 D2**
Golden Gate CA . . . 37°48N 122°29W **118 B2**
Golden Gate FL . . . 26°11N 81°42W **67 E7**
Golden Gate IL . . . 38°22N 88°12W **71 E5**
Golden Gate Bridge
  CA . . . . 37°49N 122°28W **118 B2**
Golden Gate Park
  CA . . . . 37°46N 122°28W **118 B2**
Golden Meadow LA 29°24N 90°16W **75 E6**
Golden Spike Nat. Historic Site △
  U.S.A. . . . . 41°37N 112°33W **100 B3**
Golden Valley MN . 44°59N 93°21W **113 B1**
Golden Valley ND . 47°17N 102°4W **91 C3**
Golden Valley County ☆
  MT . . . . 46°30N 109°15W **83 D8**
Golden Valley County ☆
  ND . . . . 47°0N 103°58W **91 D2**
Goldfield IA . . . . . . 42°44N 93°55W **73 C5**
Goldfield NV . . . . . 37°42N 117°14W **85 E3**
Goldonna LA . . . . . 32°1N 92°54W **75 B3**
Goldsboro NC . . . . 39°2N 75°47W **77 A5**
Goldsboro NC . . . . 35°23N 77°59W **90 C8**
Goldsmith TX . . . . 31°59N 102°37W **98 F5**
Goldston NC . . . . . 35°36N 79°20W **90 C6**
Goldthwaite TX . . . 31°27N 98°34W **99 F9**
Goleta CA . . . . 34°27N 119°50W **65 J7**
Golf Manor OH . . . 39°11N 84°26W **107 A2**
Goliad TX . . . . 28°40N 97°23W **99 J10**
Goliad County ☆ TX 28°45N 97°25W **99 J10**
Golovin AK . . . . . . 64°33N 163°2W **61 D7**
Goltry OK . . . . 36°32N 98°9W **93 B5**
Golva ND . . . . 46°44N 103°59W **91 D2**
Gonvick MN . . . . . 47°44N 95°31W **80 C3**
Gonzales CA . . . . . 36°30N 121°26W **64 G5**
Gonzales LA . . . . . 30°14N 90°55W **75 D5**
Gonzales TX . . . . . 29°30N 97°27W **99 H10**
Gonzales County ☆
  TX . . . . 29°26N 97°32W **99 H10**
Gonzalez FL . . . . . 30°35N 87°17W **67 A1**
Goochland VA . . . . 37°41N 77°53W **102 D7**
Goochland County ☆
  VA . . . . 37°41N 77°53W **102 D7**
Good Hope IL . . . . 40°34N 90°41W **71 C3**
Good Thunder MN . 44°0N 94°4W **80 F4**
Goodell IA . . . . 42°55N 93°37W **73 C5**
Goodfellow Air Force Base
  TX . . . . 31°25N 100°25W **98 F7**
Goodhue MN . . . . . 44°24N 92°37W **80 F6**
Goodhue County ☆
  MN . . . . 44°25N 92°45W **80 F6**
Gooding ID . . . . . . 42°56N 114°43W **70 G4**
Gooding County ☆ ID 43°0N 115°0W **70 F7**
Goodland IN . . . . . 40°46N 87°18W **72 C3**
Goodland KS . . . . . 39°21N 101°43W **74 B2**
Goodlett TX . . . . . . 34°20N 99°53W **99 C8**
Goodlettsville TN . . 36°19N 86°43W **96 D6**
Goodman MS . . . . 32°58N 89°55W **81 D4**
Goodman MO . . . . 36°44N 94°25W **82 E2**
Goodman WI . . . . . 45°38N 88°21W **103 C5**
Goodman Hill MA . . 42°21N 71°23W **106 A1**
Goodnews Bay AK . 59°7N 161°35W **61 G7**
Goodnight TX . . . . 35°2N 101°11W **98 B6**
Goodrich ND . . . . . 47°29N 100°8W **91 C5**
Goodrich TX . . . . . 30°36N 94°57W **99 G13**
Goodridge MN . . . . 48°9N 95°48W **80 B3**
Goodsprings NV . . . 35°49N 115°27W **85 G5**
Goodwater AL . . . . 33°4N 86°3W **60 D4**
Goodwater MS . . . . 36°36N 101°38W **93 B2**
Goodyear AZ . . . . . 33°26N 112°21W **62 D3**
Goodwell OK . . . . . 36°35N 101°38W **93 B2**
Goose Cr. → MI . . 46°33N 86°40W **79 C5**
Goose Creek SC . . . 32°59N 80°2W **90 F5**
Goose L. CA . . . . . 41°56N 120°26W **64 B6**
Gooseberry Cr. →
  WY . . . . 43°55N 108°3W **104 C4**
Gorda, Punta CA . . 40°16N 124°22W **64 C2**
Gordo AL . . . . 33°19N 87°54W **60 C3**
Gordon GA . . . . . . 32°54N 83°20W **68 D3**
Gordon NE . . . . . . 42°48N 102°12W **84 B3**
Gordon OH . . . . . . 39°56N 84°31W **92 D2**
Gordon TX . . . . . . 32°33N 98°22W **99 E9**
Gordon WI . . . . . . 46°15N 91°48W **103 B2**
Gordon County ☆
  GA . . . . 34°30N 84°50W **68 B2**
Gordon Cr. → NE . 42°49N 100°40W **84 B5**
Gordonsville TN . . . 36°10N 85°56W **97 D7**
Gordonsville VA . . . 38°9N 78°11W **102 C6**
Gordonville MO . . . 37°19N 89°41W **82 D6**
Gore OK . . . . 35°31N 95°7W **93 C8**
Gore TX . . . . 33°48N 96°51W **99 D11**
Gore Mt. VT . . . . . 44°55N 71°48W **86 B3**
Gore Range CO . . . 39°50N 106°25W **66 C4**
Goree TX . . . . 33°28N 99°31W **99 D8**
Gorham IL . . . . 37°43N 89°29W **71 F4**
Gorham KS . . . . . . 38°53N 99°1W **74 C4**
Gorham ME . . . . . . 43°41N 70°26W **76 E3**
Gorham NH . . . . . . 44°23N 71°10W **86 B3**
Gorman NC . . . . . . 36°2N 78°49W **90 B7**

Gorman TX . . . . . . 32°12N 98°41W **99 E9**
Gortner MD . . . . . . 39°20N 79°24W **77 A1**
Gorum LA . . . . 31°26N 92°56W **75 C3**
Grand Portage MN . 47°58N 89°41W **80 C9**
Grand Portage Indian Reservation
  MN . . . . 47°55N 89°50W **80 C9**
Grand Prairie TX . . 32°44N 96°59W **109 B3**
Grand Rapids = Wisconsin Rapids
  WI . . . . 44°23N 89°49W **103 D4**
Grand Rapids MI . . 42°58N 85°40W **79 G6**
Grand Rapids MN . . 47°14N 93°31W **80 C5**
Grand Rapids OH . . 41°25N 83°52W **92 B3**
Grand Rapids ✈ (GRR)
  MI . . . . 42°53N 85°31W **79 G6**
Grand Ridge FL . . . 30°43N 85°1W **67 A3**
Grand Ridge IL . . . . 41°14N 88°50W **71 B5**
Grand River IA . . . . 40°49N 93°58W **73 E5**
Grand River Nat. Grassland
  SD . . . . 45°47N 102°30W **91 E3**
Grand Rivers KY . . 37°1N 88°14W **96 C4**
Grand Ronde OR . . 45°4N 123°37W **94 B2**
Gosnell AR . . . . . . 35°58N 89°58W **63 C6**
Gospel Hump Wilderness
  ID . . . . 45°34N 115°46W **70 D3**
Gospel County ☆
  NE . . . . 40°30N 99°50W **84 D6**
Gosport IN . . . . 39°21N 86°40W **72 D4**
Gossville NH . . . . . 43°12N 71°22W **86 C3**
Gotebo OK . . . . . . 35°4N 98°53W **93 C5**
Gotha FL . . . . 28°31N 81°31W **115 A1**
Gotham WI . . . . . . 43°13N 90°18W **103 E3**
Gothenburg NE . . . 40°56N 100°10W **84 D5**
Gough GA . . . . 33°6N 82°14W **68 C4**
Gould AR . . . . 33°59N 91°34W **63 E4**
Gould OK . . . . 34°40N 99°47W **93 D4**
Goulds FL . . . . 25°33N 80°23W **67 F8**
Gouverneur NY . . . 44°20N 75°28W **89 A5**
Gove KS . . . . 38°58N 100°29W **74 C3**
Gove County ☆ KS 38°50N 100°30W **74 C3**
Governors I. NY . . . 40°41N 74°1W **114 B2**
Govons MD . . . . . . 39°23N 76°36W **107 A2**
Gowanda NY . . . . . 42°28N 78°56W **89 C2**
Gower MO . . . . 39°37N 94°36W **82 B2**
Gowrie IA . . . . 42°17N 94°17W **73 C4**
Grace ID . . . . 42°35N 111°44W **70 G7**
Graceland TN . . . . 35°3N 90°1W **96 E2**
Gracemont OK . . . . 35°11N 98°16W **93 C5**
Graceville FL . . . . . 30°58N 85°31W **67 A3**
Graceville MN . . . . 45°34N 96°26W **80 E2**
Gracey KY . . . . 36°53N 87°40W **96 D5**
Grady AL . . . . 31°59N 86°33W **60 E4**
Grady AR . . . . 34°5N 91°42W **63 D4**
Grady NM . . . . 34°49N 103°19W **88 C7**
Grady County ☆ GA 30°50N 84°10W **68 F2**
Grady County ☆ OK 35°0N 97°50W **93 C7**
Gradyville KY . . . . 37°4N 85°29W **97 C7**
Graettinger IA . . . . 43°14N 94°45W **73 B4**
Graford TX . . . . . . 32°56N 98°14W **99 E9**
Grafton IL . . . . 38°58N 90°26W **71 E3**
Grafton IA . . . . 43°20N 93°4W **73 B5**
Grafton MA . . . . . . 42°12N 71°41W **78 B3**
Grafton ND . . . . . . 48°25N 97°25W **91 B8**
Grafton NH . . . . . . 43°34N 71°57W **86 C3**
Grafton NY . . . . . . 42°46N 73°27W **78 B1**
Grafton OH . . . . . . 41°16N 82°4W **92 B4**
Grafton VT . . . . . . 43°10N 72°37W **86 C2**
Grafton WV . . . . . . 39°21N 80°2W **102 B4**
Grafton WI . . . . 43°19N 87°57W **103 E6**
Grafton County ☆
  NH . . . . 43°50N 71°45W **86 C3**
Graham GA . . . . . . 31°50N 82°30W **68 D4**
Graham NC . . . . . . 36°5N 79°25W **90 C2**
Graham TX . . . . . . 33°6N 98°35W **99 D9**
Graham, Mt. AZ . . . 32°42N 109°52W **62 E6**
Graham County ☆ AZ 33°0N 110°0W **62 E6**
Graham County ☆
  KS . . . . 39°20N 99°45W **74 B4**
Graham County ☆
  NC . . . . 35°20N 83°50W **90 C2**
Graham L. ME . . . . 44°39N 68°24W **76 D5**
Grain Valley MO . . . 39°1N 94°12W **82 B2**
Grainger County ☆
  TN . . . . 36°17N 83°31W **97 D9**
Gramalia OK . . . . . 36°57N 96°39W **93 B7**
Grambling LA . . . . 32°32N 92°43W **75 B3**
Gramercy LA . . . . . 30°4N 90°42W **75 D5**
Grampian PA . . . . . 40°58N 78°37W **95 C4**
Granada CO . . . . . 38°4N 102°19W **66 D8**
Granada MN . . . . . 43°42N 94°21W **80 G4**
Granbury TX . . . . . 32°27N 97°47W **99 E10**
Granbury, L TX . . . 32°36N 97°42W **99 E10**
Granby CO . . . . . . 40°5N 105°56W **66 B5**
Granby CT . . . . 41°57N 72°47W **78 C2**
Granby MO . . . . . . 36°55N 94°15W **82 E2**
Granby, L. CO . . . . 40°9N 105°52W **66 B5**
Grand → MI . . . . . 43°4N 86°15W **79 F5**
Grand → MO . . . . 39°23N 93°7W **82 B3**
Grand → OH . . . . 41°44N 81°17W **92 A5**
Grand → SD . . . . . 45°40N 100°45W **91 E5**
Grand Bay AL . . . . 30°29N 88°21W **60 F2**
Grand Blanc MI . . . 42°56N 83°38W **79 G8**
Grand Cane LA . . . 32°5N 93°49W **75 B2**
Grand Canyon AZ . . 36°3N 112°9W **62 A3**
Grand Canyon Nat. Park △
  AZ . . . . 36°15N 112°30W **62 A3**
Grand Canyon-Parashant Nat.
  Monument △ AZ 36°30N 113°45W **62 A2**
Grand Chenier LA . 29°46N 92°58W **75 E3**
Grand Coteau LA . . 30°25N 92°3W **75 D3**
Grand Coulee WA . 47°57N 119°0W **101 C6**
Grand Coulee Dam
  WA . . . . 47°57N 118°59W **101 C7**
Grand County ☆
  CO . . . . 40°10N 106°15W **66 B4**
Grand County ☆
  UT . . . . 39°0N 109°30W **100 D6**
Grand Forks ND . . . 47°55N 97°3W **91 C8**
Grand Forks County ☆
  ND . . . . 47°55N 97°22W **91 C8**
Grand Haven MI . . . 43°4N 86°13W **79 F5**
Grand L. LA . . . . . 29°10N 90°0W **75 E6**
Grand L. MI . . . . . . 45°18N 83°30W **79 D8**
Grand L. OH . . . . . 40°32N 84°25W **92 C2**
Grand Lake CO . . . 40°15N 105°49W **66 B5**
Grand Lake LA . . . . 30°2N 93°17W **75 D2**
Grand Lake Matagamon
  ME . . . . 46°12N 68°47W **76 B5**
Grand Lake Seboeis
  ME . . . . 45°46N 68°25W **76 C5**
Grand Ledge MI . . . 42°45N 84°45W **79 G7**
Grand Manan Channel
  ME . . . . 44°40N 67°0W **76 D7**
Grand Marais MN . . 47°45N 90°25W **80 C8**
Grand Meadow MN . 43°42N 92°34W **80 G6**
Grand Mesa CO . . . 39°0N 108°15W **66 C3**
Grand Mesa Nat. Forest
  CO . . . . 39°20N 107°50W **66 C3**

Grand Rounde →
  U.S.A. . . . . 46°5N 117°0W **101 D8**
Grand Saline TX . . . 32°41N 95°43W **99 E12**
Grand Staircase-Escalante Nat.
  Monument △ UT 37°25N 111°33W **100 F4**
Grand Teton WY . . 43°54N 110°50W **104 C2**
Grand Teton Nat. Park △
  WY . . . . 43°50N 110°50W **104 C2**
Grand Traverse B. MI 45°5N 85°35W **79 D6**
Grand Traverse County ☆
  MI . . . . 44°40N 85°35W **79 E6**
Grand Traverse Indian Reservation
  MI . . . . 45°4N 85°40W **79 D6**
Grand View ID . . . . 42°59N 116°6W **70 G2**
Grand Wash Cliffs
  AZ . . . . 36°0N 113°50W **62 A2**
Grande, Rio →
  N. Amer. . . . . . 25°58N 97°9W **98 M10**
Grande Ronde →
  OR . . . . 45°56N 116°59W **94 A9**
Grande Ronde Indian Reservation
  OR . . . . 45°8N 123°40W **94 B2**
Grandfalls TX . . . . 31°20N 102°51W **98 F5**
Grandfield OK . . . . 34°14N 98°41W **93 D5**
Grandin MO . . . . . 36°50N 90°50W **82 E6**
Grandin ND . . . . . . 47°14N 97°0W **91 C9**
Grandjean ID . . . . . 44°9N 115°10W **70 E3**
Grandview IN . . . . . 41°16N 91°11W **73 D7**
Grandview MO . . . . 38°53N 94°32W **82 C2**
Grandview TX . . . . 32°16N 97°11W **99 E10**
Grandview WA . . . 46°15N 119°54W **101 D6**
Grandview Peak
  UT . . . . 40°51N 111°45W **117 A3**
Granger IN . . . . . . 41°45N 86°7W **72 B4**
Granger IA . . . . 30°43N 97°26W **99 G10**
Granger WA . . . . . 46°21N 120°11W **101 D5**
Granger WY . . . . . 41°35N 109°58W **104 E3**
Grangeville ID . . . . 45°56N 116°7W **70 D2**
Granite CO . . . . . . 39°3N 106°16W **66 C4**
Granite OK . . . . . . 34°58N 99°23W **93 D4**
Granite OR . . . . . . 44°49N 118°25W **94 C7**
Granite UT . . . . . . 40°34N 111°48W **117 C3**
Granite City IL . . . . 38°42N 90°8W **117 A3**
Granite County ☆
  MT . . . . 46°25N 113°30W **83 D4**
Granite Falls MN . . 44°49N 95°33W **80 F3**
Granite Falls NC . . 35°48N 81°26W **90 C4**
Granite Falls WA . . 48°5N 121°58W **101 B4**
Granite Mts. AZ . . . 32°20N 113°20W **62 E2**
Granite Pass WY . . 44°38N 107°30W **104 B5**
Granite Pk. MT . . . 45°10N 109°48W **83 E8**
Granite Pt. MI . . . . 46°47N 87°36W **79 C4**
Granite Quarry NC . 35°37N 80°26W **90 C5**
Granite Range NV . 40°5N 119°25W **85 B4**
Granite Springs Valley
  NV . . . . 40°9N 118°57W **85 B2**
Graniteville SC . . . . 33°34N 81°49W **90 E4**
Graniteville VT . . . . 44°8N 72°29W **86 B2**
Grannis AR . . . . . . 34°14N 94°20W **63 D1**
Grano ND . . . . 48°37N 101°35W **91 B4**
Grant CO . . . . 39°28N 105°40W **66 C5**
Grant FL . . . . 27°56N 80°32W **67 D8**
Grant IA . . . . 41°9N 94°59W **73 D4**
Grant LA . . . . 43°20N 85°51W **79 F6**
Grant MN . . . . 45°5N 92°54W **113 A4**
Grant MT . . . . 45°1N 113°4W **83 E4**
Grant NE . . . . 40°50N 101°43W **84 D4**
Grant OK . . . . 33°57N 95°31W **93 E8**
Grant, Mt. NV . . . . 38°34N 118°48W **85 D2**
Grant City MO . . . . 40°29N 94°25W **82 A2**
Grant County ☆ IN . 40°30N 85°40W **72 C5**
Grant County ☆ KS . 37°35N 101°15W **74 D2**
Grant County ☆ KY . 38°35N 84°35W **97 B8**
Grant County ☆ MN . 45°55N 96°0W **80 E2**
Grant County ☆
  ND . . . . 46°30N 101°30W **91 D4**
Grant County ☆ NM 32°30N 108°30W **88 E2**
Grant County ☆ NE 41°50N 101°45W **84 C4**
Grant County ☆ OR 44°30N 119°0W **94 C7**
Grant County ☆ SD . 45°0N 96°45W **91 E8**
Grant County ☆ WV . 39°4N 79°4W **102 B5**
Grant County ☆
  WA . . . . 47°10N 119°30W **101 C6**
Grant Parish ☆ LA . 31°32N 92°25W **75 C3**
Grant Park IL . . . . . 41°14N 87°39W **71 B6**
Grant Park IL . . . . . 41°52N 87°37W **108 B3**
Grants NM . . . . . . 35°9N 107°52W **88 B3**
Grants Pass OR . . . 42°26N 123°19W **94 E2**
Grantsburg WI . . . 45°47N 92°41W **103 C1**
Grantsdale MT . . . . 46°12N 114°9W **83 D3**
Grantsville UT . . . . 40°36N 112°28W **100 C3**
Grantsville WV . . . 38°55N 81°6W **102 C3**
Grantville GA . . . . . 33°14N 84°50W **68 C2**
Granville IL . . . . . . 41°16N 89°14W **71 B4**
Granville MA . . . . . 42°4N 72°52W **78 B2**
Granville NY . . . . . 43°24N 73°16W **86 C1**
Granville OH . . . . . 40°4N 82°31W **92 C4**
Granville VT . . . . . 43°58N 72°51W **86 C2**
Granville County ☆
  NC . . . . 36°20N 78°40W **90 B7**
Grape L. ME . . . . . 42°16N 70°55W **106 B4**
Grapeland TX . . . . 31°30N 95°29W **99 F12**
Grapevine TX . . . . 32°56N 97°4W **109 A3**
Grapevine Recr. Area
  TX . . . . 32°58N 97°3W **109 A3**
Grasmere ID . . . . . 42°23N 115°53W **70 G3**
Grass Valley CA . . . 39°13N 121°4W **64 D5**
Grass Valley OR . . . 45°22N 120°47W **94 B5**
Grasston MN . . . . . 45°48N 93°9W **80 E5**
Grassy Bay NY . . . 40°38N 73°48W **114 C4**
Grassy Butte ND . . 47°24N 103°15W **91 C2**

Gratiot WI . . . . 42°35N 90°1W **103 F3**
Gratiot County ☆ MI 43°15N 84°40W **79 F7**
Gratz KY . . . . 38°28N 84°57W **97 B8**
Gravelly AR . . . . . . 34°53N 93°41W **63 D2**
Gravette AR . . . . . . 36°25N 94°27W **63 B1**
Gravina IA . . . . 40°46N 94°45W **73 E4**
Gravois Mills MO . . 38°19N 92°49W **82 C4**
Gray GA . . . . 33°1N 83°32W **68 C3**
Gray IA . . . . 41°49N 94°59W **73 D4**
Gray KY . . . . 36°57N 84°0W **97 D9**
Gray ME . . . . 43°53N 70°20W **76 E3**
Gray TN . . . . 36°26N 82°29W **97 D10**
Gray County ☆ KS . 37°40N 100°20W **74 D3**
Gray County ☆ TX . 35°26N 100°48W **98 B7**
Gray Court SC . . . . 34°36N 82°7W **90 D3**
Gray Hawk KY . . . 37°24N 83°56W **97 C9**
Gray Summit MO . . 38°29N 90°49W **82 C6**
Grayling MI . . . . . . 44°40N 84°43W **79 E7**
Grayling AK . . . . . . 62°57N 160°3W **61 E7**
Grays Harbor WA . . 46°59N 124°1W **101 D1**
Grays Harbor County ☆
  WA . . . . 47°15N 123°45W **101 C2**
Grays L. ID . . . . . . 43°4N 111°26W **70 F7**
Grays Lake Nat. Wildlife Refuge △
  ID . . . . 43°4N 111°23W **70 F7**
Grayslake IL . . . . . 42°21N 88°2W **71 A5**
Grayson GA . . . . . . 33°20N 82°57W **97 B10**
Grayson KY . . . . . . 38°20N 82°57W **97 B10**
Grayson OK . . . . . . 35°32N 95°51W **93 C8**
Grayson County ☆
  KY . . . . 37°25N 86°20W **96 C6**
Grayson County ☆
  TX . . . . 33°38N 96°36W **99 D11**
Grayson County ☆
  VA . . . . 36°40N 81°10W **102 E3**
Grayson L. KY . . . . 38°15N 82°59W **97 B10**
Grayson Valley AL . 33°39N 86°38W **60 C4**
Graysville TN . . . . . 35°27N 85°8W **97 E7**
Grayville IL . . . . . . 38°16N 88°0W **71 E5**
Great B. NH . . . . . 43°5N 70°53W **86 C4**
Great Barrington MA 42°12N 73°22W **78 B1**
Great Basin NV . . . 40°0N 117°0W **85 C4**
Great Basin Nat. Park △
  NV . . . . 38°56N 114°15W **85 D6**
Great Bay NJ . . . . . 39°30N 74°25W **87 C2**
Great Bend KS . . . . 38°22N 98°46W **74 C5**
Great Bend ND . . . 46°9N 96°48W **91 D9**
Great Bend PA . . . . 41°58N 75°45W **95 C7**
Great Camanoe
  Br. Virgin Is. . . . 18°30N 64°35W **105 G18**
Great Dismal Swamp Nat. Wildlife
  Refuge △ VA . . 36°35N 76°28W **115 B1**
Great Divide Basin
  WY . . . . 42°0N 108°0W **104 D5**
Great Egg Harbor →
  NJ . . . . 39°18N 74°40W **87 C2**
Great Falls MT . . . . 47°30N 111°17W **83 C6**
Great Falls SC . . . . 34°34N 80°54W **90 D5**
Great Falls VA . . . . 38°59N 77°17W **119 B2**
Great Falls Park
  MD . . . . 38°59N 77°14W **119 B2**
Great Harbor
  Bah. NY . . . . . . 40°33N 74°9W **114 C2**
Great Kills Park NY . 40°32N 74°7W **114 C2**
Great Kills Park NY . 40°32N 74°7W **114 C2**
Great Lakes N. Amer. 46°0N 84°0W **53 A10**
Great Meadows Nat. Wildlife
  Refuge △ MA . . 42°28N 71°19W **106 A1**
Great Miami → OH . 39°7N 84°49W **107 B2**
Great Mills MD . . . 38°14N 76°30W **77 B4**
Great Neck NY . . . 40°47N 73°44W **114 B4**
Great Peconic B. NY 40°57N 72°30W **78 D2**
Great Pee Dee → SC 33°21N 79°10W **90 E6**
Great Plains N. Amer. 47°0N 105°0W **52 A6**
Great Plains Res.
  CO . . . . 38°15N 102°43W **66 D8**
Great Pond ME . . . 44°57N 68°19W **76 D5**
Great Pt. MA . . . . . 41°24N 70°4W **78 C4**
Great Quittacas Pond
  MA . . . . 41°48N 70°54W **78 C4**
Great River Nat. Wildlife Refuge △
  IL . . . . 39°27N 90°58W **71 D3**
Great Sacandaga L.
  NY . . . . 43°6N 74°16W **89 B6**
Great Salt L. UT . . 41°15N 112°40W **100 B3**
Great Salt Lake Desert
  UT . . . . 40°50N 113°30W **100 C2**
Great Salt Plains L.
  OK . . . . 36°45N 98°8W **93 B5**
Great Sand Dunes Nat.
  Monument △ CO 37°48N 105°45W **66 E5**
Great Sandy Desert
  OR . . . . 43°35N 120°15W **94 D5**
Great Sitkin I. AK . . 52°3N 176°6W **61 K3**
Great Smoky Mountains Nat.
  Park △ TN . . . . 35°40N 83°40W **97 E9**
Great Smoky Mts.
  TN . . . . 35°40N 83°40W **97 E9**
Great South Bay NY 40°40N 73°15W **87 B3**
Great Wass I. ME . . 44°29N 67°36W **76 D6**
Great Western Forum
  CA . . . . 33°57N 118°20W **111 C2**
Great White Heron Nat. Wildlife
  Refuge △ FL . . 24°45N 81°10W **67 G7**
Greater Buffalo Int. ✈ (BUF)
  NY . . . . 42°56N 78°44W **89 C2**
Greece NY . . . . . . 43°13N 77°41W **89 B3**
Greeley CO . . . . . . 40°25N 104°42W **66 B6**
Greeley IA . . . . 42°35N 91°21W **73 C7**
Greeley KS . . . . . . 38°22N 95°8W **74 C8**
Greeley NE . . . . . . 41°33N 98°32W **84 C7**
Greeley County ☆
  KS . . . . 38°30N 101°45W **74 C2**
Greeley County ☆
  NE . . . . 41°30N 98°30W **84 C7**
Green KS . . . . 39°26N 97°0W **74 B6**
Green OH . . . . 40°57N 81°29W **92 C5**
Green → IL . . . . . 41°28N 90°23W **71 B3**
Green → KY . . . . 37°54N 87°30W **96 C5**
Green → ND . . . . 46°52N 102°35W **91 D3**
Green → UT . . . . 38°11N 109°53W **100 E6**
Green → WA . . . . 47°28N 122°15W **101 C3**
Green Acres VA . . . 36°54N 76°24W **115 A3**
Green B. WI . . . . . 45°0N 87°30W **103 D6**
Green Bank NJ . . . 39°37N 74°34W **87 C2**
Green Bank WV . . . 38°25N 79°50W **102 C5**
Green Bay WI . . . . 44°31N 88°0W **103 D6**
Green Camp OH . . . 40°32N 83°13W **92 C3**
Green City MO . . . . 40°16N 92°57W **82 A4**
Green County ☆ KY . 37°15N 85°35W **97 C7**
Green County ☆ WI 42°45N 89°40W **103 F4**
Green Cove Springs
  FL . . . . 29°59N 81°42W **67 B7**
Green Creek NJ . . . 39°3N 74°54W **87 C2**
Green Forest AR . . . 36°20N 93°26W **63 B2**
Green Isle MN . . . . 44°41N 94°0W **80 F4**
Green L. MN . . . . . 45°15N 94°54W **80 E4**
Green Lake WI . . . 43°51N 88°58W **103 E5**
Green Lake County ☆
  WI . . . . 43°45N 89°0W **103 E5**
Green Mountain Nat. Forest
  VT . . . . 43°45N 72°54W **86 C2**
Green Mts. VT . . . . 43°45N 72°45W **86 C2**
Green Peter L. OR . 44°26N 122°37W **94 C3**
Green Ridge MO . . 38°37N 93°25W **82 C3**

Green Ridge State Forest
  MD . . . . 39°36N 78°30W **77 A2**
Green River UT . . . 38°59N 110°10W **100 E5**
Green River WY . . . 41°32N 109°28W **104 E3**
Green River L. KY . 37°15N 85°15W **97 C7**
Green River, L. KY . 37°15N 85°15W **97 C7**
Green Spring WV . . 39°32N 78°37W **102 B4**
Greene NY . . . . . . 40°58N 73°54W **114 B3**
Green Swamp FL . . 28°12N 81°46W **67 C7**
Green Swamp NC . . 34°15N 78°20W **90 D7**
Green Tree PA . . . . 40°24N 80°2W **116 B1**
Green Valley IL . . . 40°24N 89°38W **71 C4**
Green Valley MD . . 39°19N 77°18W **77 A3**
Greenacres CA . . . 35°23N 119°7W **65 H7**
Greenback TN . . . . 35°40N 84°10W **97 E8**
Greenbelt MD . . . . 38°58N 76°53W **119 A4**
Greenbrier TN . . . . 36°26N 86°48W **96 D6**
Greenbrier County ☆
  WV . . . . 37°56N 80°23W **102 D4**
Greenbush MN . . . 48°42N 96°11W **80 B2**
Greenbush WI . . . . 43°38N 86°52W **72 D4**
Greencastle IN . . . . 39°38N 86°52W **72 D4**
Greencastle PA . . . 39°47N 77°44W **77 A3**
Greendale IN . . . . . 39°7N 84°52W **72 D6**
Greendale WI . . . . 42°56N 87°59W **112 C2**
Greendale MO . . . . 38°41N 90°18W **117 A2**
Greene IA . . . . 42°54N 92°48W **73 C6**
Greene ME . . . . . . 44°12N 70°8W **76 D3**
Greene NY . . . . . . 42°20N 75°46W **89 C5**
Greene County ☆
  AL . . . . 32°50N 87°53W **60 D3**
Greene County ☆ AR 36°3N 90°29W **63 B5**
Greene County ☆ GA 33°30N 83°5W **68 C3**
Greene County ☆ IL 39°20N 90°20W **71 D3**
Greene County ☆ IN . 39°0N 87°0W **72 D4**
Greene County ☆ IA 42°0N 94°22W **73 C4**
Greene County ☆
  MS . . . . 31°10N 88°45W **81 E5**
Greene County ☆
  MO . . . . 37°15N 93°20W **82 D3**
Greene County ☆
  NC . . . . 35°30N 77°40W **90 C8**
Greene County ☆ NY 42°20N 74°0W **89 C7**
Greene County ☆
  OH . . . . 39°40N 83°56W **92 D3**
Greene County ☆ PA 39°55N 80°5W **95 E2**
Greene County ☆
  TN . . . . 36°10N 82°50W **97 D10**
Greene County ☆
  VA . . . . 38°18N 78°26W **102 C6**
Greeneville TN . . . . 36°10N 82°50W **97 D10**
Greenfield IN . . . . . 39°21N 90°12W **71 D3**
Greenfield IN . . . . . 39°47N 85°46W **72 D5**
Greenfield IA . . . . . 41°18N 94°28W **73 D4**
Greenfield MA . . . . 42°35N 72°36W **78 B2**
Greenfield MO . . . . 37°25N 93°51W **82 D2**
Greenfield NH . . . . 42°55N 71°51W **86 D3**
Greenfield OH . . . . 39°21N 83°23W **92 D3**
Greenfield TN . . . . 36°9N 88°48W **96 D4**
Greenfield WI . . . . 42°57N 88°0W **112 C2**
Greenfield Park WI . 43°0N 88°1W **112 B1**
Greenhorn AR . . . . 44°42N 118°29W **94 C7**
Greenhorn Mts. CA . 35°51N 118°34W **65 H8**
Greenland AR . . . . 46°47N 89°6W **79 C2**
Greenland NH . . . . 43°4N 70°50W **86 C4**
Greenleaf KS . . . . . 39°44N 96°59W **74 B7**
Greenlee County ☆
  AZ . . . . 33°0N 109°15W **62 D6**
Greenough MT . . . . 46°55N 113°5W **83 D4**
Greenport NY . . . . 41°6N 72°22W **78 C2**
Greensboro AL . . . 32°42N 87°36W **60 D3**
Greensboro FL . . . . 30°34N 84°45W **67 A4**
Greensboro GA . . . 33°35N 83°11W **68 C3**
Greensboro MD . . . 38°58N 75°48W **77 B5**
Greensboro NC . . . 36°4N 79°48W **90 B6**
Greensboro VT . . . 44°36N 72°18W **86 B2**
Greensboro-High Point ✈
  NC . . . . 36°5N 79°56W **90 B6**
Greensburg IN . . . . 39°20N 85°29W **72 D5**
Greensburg KS . . . 37°16N 85°30W **97 C7**
Greensburg LA . . . 30°50N 90°40W **75 D5**
Greensburg PA . . . 40°18N 79°33W **95 D3**
Greenville County ☆
  VA . . . . 36°42N 77°32W **102 E7**
Greentown IN . . . . 40°29N 85°58W **72 C5**
Greenup IL . . . . . . 39°15N 88°10W **71 D5**
Greenup KY . . . . . 38°35N 82°50W **97 B10**
Greenup County ☆
  KY . . . . 38°30N 83°0W **97 B9**
Greenview CA . . . . 41°25N 89°44W **71 C4**
Greenview IL . . . . . 40°5N 89°44W **71 C4**
Greenville AL . . . . . 31°50N 86°38W **60 E4**
Greenville FL . . . . . 30°28N 83°15W **67 A5**
Greenville GA . . . . 33°2N 84°43W **68 C2**
Greenville IL . . . . . 38°53N 89°25W **71 E4**
Greenville KY . . . . 37°12N 87°11W **96 C5**
Greenville ME . . . . 45°28N 69°35W **76 C4**
Greenville MI . . . . . 43°11N 85°15W **79 F6**
Greenville MS . . . . 33°24N 91°4W **81 C2**
Greenville MO . . . . 37°8N 90°27W **82 D6**
Greenville NC . . . . 35°37N 77°23W **90 C8**
Greenville NH . . . . 42°46N 71°49W **86 D3**
Greenville OH . . . . 40°6N 84°38W **92 C2**
Greenville PA . . . . . 41°24N 80°23W **95 C2**
Greenville SC . . . . 34°51N 82°24W **90 D3**
Greenville TX . . . . 33°8N 96°7W **99 D11**
Greenville County ☆
  SC . . . . 34°50N 82°25W **90 D3**
Greenville County ☆
  SC . . . . 34°10N 82°55W **90 D3**
Greenville L. U.S.A. 33°25N 74°20W **87 A2**
Greenwald MN . . . . 45°36N 94°52W **80 E4**
Greenway AR . . . . 36°21N 90°13W **63 B5**
Greenwich CT . . . . 41°2N 73°38W **78 C1**
Greenwich NJ . . . . 39°24N 75°21W **87 C1**
Greenwich NY . . . . 43°5N 73°30W **89 B6**
Greenwich OH . . . . 41°2N 82°31W **92 B4**
Greenwich Village
  NY . . . . 40°44N 73°59W **114 B3**
Greenwood AR . . . 35°13N 94°16W **63 C1**
Greenwood DE . . . 38°49N 75°35W **77 B5**
Greenwood FL . . . . 30°52N 85°10W **67 A3**
Greenwood IN . . . . 39°37N 86°7W **72 D4**
Greenwood MS . . . 33°31N 90°11W **81 C3**
Greenwood SC . . . 34°12N 82°10W **90 D3**
Greenwood WI . . . 44°46N 90°36W **103 D3**
Greenwood County ☆
  KS . . . . 37°45N 96°15W **74 D7**
Greenwood County ☆
  SC . . . . 34°10N 82°5W **90 D3**
Greenwood, L. U.S.A. 34°17N 82°4W **90 D3**
Greenwood Village
  CO . . . . 39°37N 104°57W **109 C2**
Greenwood Cemetery
  NY . . . . 40°39N 73°59W **114 C3**
Greer ID . . . . 46°24N 116°11W **70 D2**
Greer MO . . . . 36°46N 91°21W **82 E5**
Greer SC . . . . 34°56N 82°14W **90 D3**
Greer County ☆ OK . 35°0N 99°30W **93 D4**
Greers Ferry AR . . . 35°35N 92°11W **63 C3**
Greers Ferry L. AR . 35°32N 92°10W **63 C3**

Greeson, L. AR..... 34°9N 93°43W 63 D2
Gregg County ☆ TX 32°30N 94°44W 99 E13
Gregory AR..... 35°9N 91°21W 63 E4
Gregory MI..... 42°28N 84°5W 79 G7
Gregory SD..... 43°14N 99°26W 91 G6
Gregory TX..... 27°56N 97°18W 99 K10
Gregory County ☆
SD..... 43°11N 99°18W 91 G6
Grenada CA..... 41°39N 122°31W 64 B4
Grenada MS..... 33°47N 89°49W 81 C4
Grenada County ☆
MS..... 33°47N 89°49W 81 C4
Grenada L. MS..... 33°50N 89°47W 81 C4
Grenola KS..... 37°21N 96°27W 74 D7
Grenora ND..... 48°37N 103°56W 91 B2
Grenville NM..... 36°36N 103°13W 88 A7
Grenville SD..... 45°28N 97°23W 91 E8
Gres, Pt. au MI..... 43°59N 83°41W 79 F8
Gresham NE..... 41°2N 97°24W 84 C8
Gresham OR..... 45°29N 122°25W 116 A2
Gresham Park GA..... 33°43N 84°20W 106 B2
Gressitt VA..... 37°29N 76°43W 102 D8
Gresston GA..... 32°17N 83°15W 68 D3
Gretna LA..... 30°37N 84°40W 67 A4
Gretna LA..... 29°54N 90°3W 113 C2
Gretna NE..... 41°8N 96°15W 84 C9
Gretna VA..... 36°57N 79°22W 102 E5
Gretna City Park LA 29°54N 90°3W 113 C2
Grey Eagle MN..... 45°50N 94°45W 80 E4
Grey Forest TX..... 29°36N 98°40W 117 B1
Greybull WY..... 44°30N 108°3W 104 B4
Greybull → WY..... 44°28N 108°3W 104 B4
Greylock, Mt. MA..... 42°38N 73°10W 78 B1
Greynolds Park FL..... 25°56N 80°9W 112 C3
Greystone CO..... 40°37N 108°41W 66 B2
Gridley CA..... 39°22N 121°42W 64 D5
Gridley IL..... 40°45N 88°53W 71 C5
Gridley KS..... 38°6N 95°53W 74 C8
Griffin GA..... 33°15N 84°16W 68 C2
Griffin IL..... 38°12N 87°55W 72 E3
Griffin, L. FL..... 28°52N 81°51W 67 C7
Griffith Lakes NC..... 35°19N 80°48W 107 A2
Griffith Park CA..... 34°8N 118°17W 111 B3
Griffithsville WV..... 38°14N 81°59W 102 C3
Grifton NC..... 35°23N 77°26W 90 C8
Griggs County ☆ ND 47°34N 98°21W 91 C7
Griggsville IL..... 39°43N 90°43W 71 D3
Grimes IA..... 41°41N 93°47W 73 D5
Grimes County ☆
TX..... 30°29N 95°59W 99 G12
Grimsley TN..... 36°16N 84°59W 97 D8
Grinnell IA..... 41°45N 92°43W 73 D6
Grinnell KS..... 39°6N 100°38W 74 B3
Griswold IA..... 41°14N 95°8W 73 D3
Groesbeck OH..... 39°13N 84°35W 107 A4
Groesbeck TX..... 31°31N 96°32W 99 F11
Groom TX..... 35°12N 101°6W 98 B6
Groom L. NV..... 37°17N 115°48W 65 F5
Gros Ventre Range
WY..... 43°12N 110°22W 104 C2
Gross NE..... 42°57N 98°34W 84 B7
Grosse Point Lighthouse
IL..... 42°2N 87°41W 108 A2
Grosse Pointe MI..... 42°24N 82°56W 79 G9
Grosse Tete LA..... 30°25N 91°26W 75 D4
Groton CT..... 41°21N 72°5W 78 C2
Groton MA..... 42°37N 71°34W 78 B3
Groton NY..... 42°36N 76°22W 89 C4
Groton SD..... 45°27N 98°6W 91 E7
Groton VT..... 44°12N 72°12W 86 B2
Grottoes VA..... 38°16N 78°50W 102 C6
Grouse Creek UT..... 41°42N 113°53W 100 B2
Grouse Creek Mts.
UT..... 41°30N 113°50W 100 B2
Grovania GA..... 32°22N 83°40W 68 D3
Grove OK..... 36°36N 94°46W 93 B9
Grove, The IL..... 42°5N 87°52W 108 A1
Grove, The TX..... 31°16N 97°33W 99 F10
Grove City OH..... 39°53N 83°6W 92 D2
Grove City PA..... 41°10N 80°5W 95 C2
Grove Hall MA..... 42°18N 71°4W 106 B3
Grove Hill AL..... 31°42N 87°47W 60 E3
Grove Park GA..... 33°46N 84°26W 106 B2
Groveland CA..... 37°50N 120°14W 64 F6
Groveland FL..... 28°34N 81°51W 67 C7
Groveland MA..... 42°46N 71°2W 78 B3
Groveport OH..... 39°51N 82°53W 92 D4
Grover CO..... 40°52N 104°14W 66 B6
Grover UT..... 38°14N 111°21W 100 E4
Grover WY..... 42°48N 110°56W 104 D2
Grover Beach CA..... 35°7N 120°37W 65 H6
Grover Hill OH..... 41°1N 84°29W 92 B2
Groves TX..... 29°57N 93°54W 99 H14
Grovespring MO..... 37°24N 92°37W 82 D4
Groveton NH..... 44°36N 71°31W 86 B3
Groveton TX..... 31°4N 95°8W 99 F12
Groveton VA..... 38°46N 77°6W 119 C3
Grovetown GA..... 33°27N 82°12W 68 C4
Growler Mts. AZ..... 32°15N 113°0W 62 E3
Growler Wash →
AZ..... 32°40N 113°30W 62 E2
Gruetli-Leager TN..... 35°22N 85°37W 97 E7
Grulla TX..... 26°16N 98°39W 98 L9
Grundy VA..... 37°17N 82°6W 102 D2
Grundy Center IA..... 42°22N 92°47W 73 C6
Grundy County ☆ IL 41°20N 88°25W 71 B5
Grundy County ☆ IA 42°25N 92°45W 73 C6
Grundy County ☆
MO..... 40°5N 93°30W 82 A3
Grundy County ☆
TN..... 35°26N 85°44W 97 E7
Gruver IA..... 43°24N 94°42W 73 B4
Gruver TX..... 36°16N 101°24W 98 A6
Grygla MN..... 48°18N 95°37W 80 B3
Grymes Hill NY..... 40°36N 74°6W 114 C2
Guadalupe AZ..... 33°22N 111°57W 116 C2
Guadalupe CA..... 34°58N 120°34W 65 E6
Guadalupe → TX..... 28°27N 96°47W 99 J11
Guadalupe County ☆
NM..... 35°0N 104°45W 88 C6
Guadalupe County ☆
TX..... 29°34N 97°58W 99 H10
Guadalupe Mountains Nat. Park ☆
TX..... 31°40N 104°30W 98 F3
Guadalupe Mts. NM. 32°15N 105°0W 88 E6
Guadalupe Peak TX 31°50N 104°52W 98 F3
Guadalupita NM..... 36°8N 105°14W 88 A5
Gualala CA..... 38°46N 123°32W 64 E3
Guam ☑ Pac. Oc..... 13°27N 144°45E 105 b
Guam I.
Br. Virgin Is. ..... 18°30N 64°30W 105 G18
Guanica
Puerto Rico..... 17°58N 66°55W 105 H16
Guano L. OR..... 42°11N 119°32W 94 E6
Guayama
Puerto Rico..... 17°59N 66°7W 105 H16
Guayanilla
Puerto Rico..... 18°1N 66°47W 105 G16
Guaynabo
Puerto Rico..... 18°22N 66°7W 105 G16
Guerneville CA..... 38°30N 123°0W 64 E3
Guernsey IA..... 41°39N 92°21W 73 D6
Guernsey WY..... 42°16N 104°45W 104 D8
Guernsey County ☆
OH..... 40°2N 81°55W 92 C5
Guernsey Res. WY..... 42°19N 104°46W 104 D8
Guerra TX..... 26°53N 98°34W 98 L9
Gueydan LA..... 30°2N 92°31W 75 D3
Guffey CO..... 38°45N 105°31W 66 D5
Guffy Peak WY..... 43°29N 107°54W 104 C5
Guguan N Marianas 17°18N 145°51E 105 a
Guide Rock NE..... 40°4N 98°20W 84 D7
Guildhall VT..... 44°34N 71°34W 86 B3

Guilford CT..... 41°17N 72°41W 78 C2
Guilford ME..... 45°10N 69°23W 76 C4
Guilford County ☆
NC..... 36°10N 79°45W 90 B6
Guin AL..... 33°58N 87°55W 60 C3
Guinda CA..... 38°50N 122°12W 64 E4
Guion AR..... 35°56N 91°57W 63 E4
Gulf Breeze FL..... 30°21N 87°9W 67 E2
Gulf City FL..... 27°42N 82°27W 119 C4
Gulf County ☆ FL..... 29°50N 85°15W 67 B3
Gulf Hammock FL..... 29°15N 82°43W 67 B6
Gulf Islands Nat. Seashore →
AL..... 30°10N 87°10W 67 A1
Gulf Shores AL..... 30°17N 87°41W 60 F3
Gulfport FL..... 27°44N 82°42W 119 C2
Gulfport MS..... 30°22N 89°6W 81 F4
Gulkana AK..... 62°16N 145°23W 61 E11
Gull L. MN..... 46°25N 94°21W 80 D4
Gullivan B. FL..... 25°45N 81°40W 67 F7
Gully MN..... 47°46N 95°37W 80 C3
Gumbro DE..... 38°28N 75°22W 77 B5
Gun L. MI..... 42°36N 85°31W 79 G6
Gunnison CO..... 38°33N 106°56W 66 D4
Gunnison MS..... 33°57N 90°57W 81 C3
Gunnison UT..... 39°9N 111°49W 100 D4
Gunnison → CO..... 39°4N 108°35W 66 C2
Gunnison, Mt. CO..... 38°49N 107°23W 66 D3
Gunnison County ☆
CO..... 38°40N 107°0W 66 D4
Gunnison Nat. Forest
CO..... 38°30N 107°0W 66 D4
Gunpowder → MD..... 39°20N 76°20W 77 A4
Guntersville AL..... 34°21N 86°18W 60 B4
Guntersville L. AL..... 34°25N 86°23W 60 B4
Guntown MS..... 34°27N 88°40W 81 B5
Gurabo
Puerto Rico..... 18°16N 65°58W 105 G17
Gurdon AR..... 33°55N 93°9W 63 E2
Gurley AL..... 34°42N 86°23W 60 B4
Gurley NE..... 41°19N 102°58W 84 C3
Gurnee IL..... 42°22N 87°55W 71 A6
Gurnet Point MA..... 42°1N 70°34W 78 B4
Gustavus AK..... 58°25N 135°44W 61 G14
Gustine CA..... 37°16N 121°0W 64 F5
Gustine TX..... 31°51N 98°24W 99 F9
Guthrie KY..... 36°39N 87°10W 96 D5
Guthrie TX..... 33°37N 100°19W 98 D7
Guthrie Center IA..... 41°41N 94°30W 73 D4
Guthrie County ☆ IA 41°40N 94°30W 73 D4
Guttenberg IA..... 42°47N 91°6W 73 C7
Guttenberg NJ..... 40°48N 74°0W 114 B2
Guyandotte → WV 38°26N 82°23W 102 C2
Guymon OK..... 36°41N 101°29W 93 B2
Guyot, Mt. TN..... 35°42N 83°15W 97 E9
Guyton GA..... 32°20N 81°24W 68 D5
Gwinn MI..... 46°19N 87°27W 79 C4
Gwinner ND..... 46°11N 97°40W 91 D8
Gwinnett County ☆ GA 34°0N 84°0W 68 C2
Gwynns Falls Park
MD..... 39°18N 76°41W 107 B1
Gypsum CO..... 39°39N 106°57W 66 C4
Gypsum KS..... 38°42N 97°26W 74 C6

H

H. Neely Henry L. AL 33°55N 86°2W 60 C4
Haakon County ☆
SD..... 44°25N 101°35W 91 F4
Habersham GA..... 34°36N 83°34W 68 B3
Habersham County ☆
GA..... 34°40N 83°40W 68 B3
Hachita NM..... 31°55N 108°19W 88 F2
Hackberry AZ..... 35°22N 113°44W 62 C2
Hackberry LA..... 30°0N 93°17W 75 D2
Hackensack MN..... 46°56N 94°31W 80 D4
Hackensack NJ..... 40°52N 74°4W 114 A2
Hackensack → NJ..... 40°42N 74°7W 114 B2
Hackett AR..... 35°11N 94°25W 63 C1
Hackettstown NJ..... 40°51N 74°50W 87 B2
Hackleburg AL..... 34°17N 87°50W 60 B3
Hadar NE..... 42°6N 97°27W 84 B8
Haddam KS..... 39°52N 97°18W 74 B6
Haddock GA..... 33°2N 83°26W 68 C3
Haddon Heights NJ..... 39°52N 75°3W 116 B2
Hadlyme CT..... 41°25N 72°25W 78 C2
Ha'ena HI..... 22°14N 159°34W 69 A2
Hagemeister I. AK..... 58°39N 160°54W 61 G7
Hagerman ID..... 42°49N 114°54W 70 G4
Hagerman NM..... 33°7N 104°20W 88 D6
Hagerman Fossil Beds Nat.
Monument →
U.S.A..... 42°48N 114°57W 70 G4
Hagerman Nat. Wildlife Refuge →
TX..... 33°45N 96°47W 99 D11
Hagerstown IN..... 39°55N 85°10W 72 D5
Hagerstown MD..... 39°39N 77°43W 77 A3
Hague ND..... 46°2N 99°59W 91 D6
Hague NY..... 43°45N 73°30W 86 C1
Hague SD..... 38°4N 76°39W 102 C8
Hahira GA..... 30°59N 83°22W 68 F3
Hahnville LA..... 29°59N 90°25W 75 E5
Haight-Ashbury
CA..... 37°46N 122°26W 118 B2
Haigler NE..... 40°1N 101°56W 84 D4
Haiku-Pauwela HI..... 20°56N 156°19W 69 C5
Hailey ID..... 43°31N 114°19W 70 F4
Haileyville OK..... 34°51N 95°35W 93 C8
Haines OR..... 44°55N 117°56W 94 C8
Haines AK..... 59°15N 135°30W 61 G14
Haines City FL..... 28°7N 81°38W 67 C7
Hainesport NJ..... 39°59N 74°50W 116 B2
Haiwee Res. CA..... 36°8N 117°57W 65 G9
Hālawa, C. HI..... 21°10N 156°42W 69 B5
Hālawa Heights HI 21°23N 157°55W 69 K14
Halbur IA..... 42°0N 94°59W 73 D4
Haldeman KY..... 38°15N 83°19W 97 B9
Hale CO..... 39°38N 102°9W 66 C8
Hale Center TX..... 34°4N 101°51W 98 C6
Hale County ☆ AL..... 32°42N 87°36W 60 D3
Hale County ☆ TX..... 34°0N 101°55W 98 C6
Haleakalā Nat. Park △
HI..... 20°40N 156°15W 69 C5
Haledon NJ..... 40°56N 74°11W 114 A1
Hale'iwa HI..... 21°36N 158°6W 69 J13
Hales Corners WI..... 42°56N 88°2W 112 C1
Halethorpe MD..... 39°14N 76°40W 107 B1
Haley ND..... 45°58N 103°7W 91 E2
Haleyville AL..... 34°14N 87°37W 60 B3
Haleyville NJ..... 39°17N 75°2W 87 C1
Half Moon NC..... 34°50N 77°28W 90 C8
Half Way MO..... 37°37N 93°15W 82 D3
Halfmoon Landing
GA..... 31°42N 81°16W 68 E5
Halfway OR..... 44°53N 117°7W 94 C8
Halfway Springs FL..... 30°5N 83°40W 67 A5
Hana Fork → WY 41°35N 109°7W 104 E3
Halibut MC..... 36°20N 77°33W 90 B8
Halifax VA..... 36°20N 78°56W 102 D6
Halifax County ☆ NC 36°15N 77°40W 90 B8
Halifax County ☆ VA 36°55N 79°0W 102 E6
Halkett, C. AK..... 70°48N 152°11W 61 A9
Hall MT..... 46°35N 113°12W 83 D4
Hall Park OK..... 35°14N 97°24W 93 C6
Hall Summit LA..... 32°11N 93°18W 75 B2

Hallam NE..... 40°32N 96°47W 84 D9
Hallandale FL..... 25°58N 80°8W 112 C3
Hallandale Beach FL..... 25°59N 115°27W 85 B5
Hallett OK..... 36°19N 96°35W 93 B7
Halletsville TX..... 29°27N 96°57W 99 H11
Halliday ND..... 47°21N 102°20W 91 C3
Halligan Res. CO..... 40°53N 105°20W 66 B5
Hallock MN..... 48°47N 96°57W 80 B2
Hallowell KS..... 37°10N 95°0W 74 D9
Hallowell ME..... 44°17N 69°47W 76 D4
Halls GA..... 34°18N 84°56W 68 B2
Halls TN..... 35°53N 89°24W 96 D3
Halls Summit KS..... 38°21N 95°41W 74 C8
Hallstead PA..... 41°58N 75°45W 95 C7
Hallsville TX..... 32°30N 94°35W 99 E13
Halltown MO..... 37°12N 93°38W 82 D3
Hallwood VA..... 37°53N 75°36W 77 C5
Halma MN..... 48°40N 96°36W 80 B2
Halsey NE..... 41°54N 100°16W 84 C5
Halsey OR..... 44°23N 123°7W 94 C2
Halstad MN..... 47°21N 96°50W 80 C2
Halstead KS..... 38°0N 97°31W 74 D6
Haltom City TX..... 32°47N 97°16W 109 B2
Hamberg ND..... 47°46N 99°31W 91 C6
Hamblen County ☆
TN..... 36°13N 83°18W 97 D9
Hambleton WV..... 39°5N 79°39W 102 B5
Hamburg AR..... 33°14N 91°48W 63 E4
Hamburg CT..... 41°23N 72°21W 78 C2
Hamburg IL..... 39°14N 90°43W 71 D3
Hamburg IA..... 40°36N 95°39W 73 E3
Hamburg MN..... 44°44N 93°58W 80 F5
Hamburg NJ..... 41°9N 74°35W 87 A2
Hamburg NY..... 42°43N 78°50W 89 C2
Hamburg PA..... 40°33N 75°59W 95 D7
Hamden CT..... 41°23N 72°54W 78 C2
Hamer ID..... 43°56N 112°12W 70 F6
Hamersville OH..... 38°55N 83°59W 92 E3
Hamilton AL..... 34°9N 87°59W 60 B3
Hamilton AK..... 62°54N 163°53W 61 E7
Hamilton MD..... 39°21N 76°33W 107 A2
Hamilton CO..... 40°22N 107°37W 66 B3
Hamilton GA..... 32°45N 84°53W 68 D2
Hamilton IL..... 40°24N 91°21W 71 C2
Hamilton KS..... 37°59N 96°10W 74 D7
Hamilton MA..... 42°38N 70°51W 78 B4
Hamilton MO..... 39°45N 94°0W 82 B2
Hamilton MT..... 46°15N 114°10W 83 D3
Hamilton ND..... 48°48N 97°24W 91 B8
Hamilton NY..... 42°50N 75°33W 89 C5
Hamilton OH..... 39°24N 84°34W 92 D2
Hamilton TX..... 31°42N 98°7W 99 F9
Hamilton, L. AR..... 34°26N 93°2W 63 D2
Hamilton City CA..... 39°45N 122°1W 64 D4
Hamilton County ☆
FL..... 30°30N 83°0W 67 A6
Hamilton County ☆
IL..... 38°5N 88°30W 71 E5
Hamilton County ☆ IN 40°5N 86°5W 72 C4
Hamilton County ☆
IA..... 42°20N 93°40W 73 C5
Hamilton County ☆
KS..... 38°0N 101°45W 74 D2
Hamilton County ☆
NE..... 40°45N 98°0W 84 D8
Hamilton County ☆
OH..... 39°13N 84°33W 92 D2
Hamilton County ☆
TN..... 35°17N 85°10W 97 E7
Hamilton County ☆
TX..... 31°40N 98°8W 99 F9
Hamilton Dome
WY..... 43°46N 108°35W 104 C4
Hamlet, N. MY..... 43°25N 74°22W 89 B6
Hamler OH..... 41°14N 84°2W 92 B2
Hamlet IN..... 41°23N 86°35W 72 B4
Hamlet NC..... 34°53N 79°42W 90 D6
Hamlet NE..... 40°23N 101°14W 84 D4
Hamlin PA..... 41°24N 75°24W 87 A1
Hamlin TX..... 32°53N 100°8W 98 E7
Hamlin WV..... 38°17N 82°6W 102 C2
Hamlin County ☆ SD 44°40N 97°13W 91 F8
Hamlin, L. MI..... 44°2N 86°24W 79 E4
Hamlin Valley Wash →
U.S.A..... 38°42N 114°4W 100 E1
Hammel Arverne
NY..... 40°36N 73°48W 114 C4
Hammett ID..... 42°57N 115°28W 70 G3
Hammon OK..... 35°38N 99°23W 93 C4
Hammond IL..... 39°48N 88°36W 71 D5
Hammond IN..... 41°38N 87°30W 72 B3
Hammond LA..... 30°30N 90°28W 75 D5
Hammond MN..... 44°13N 92°23W 80 F6
Hammond NY..... 44°27N 75°42W 89 A5
Hammond WI..... 44°58N 92°26W 80 E2
Hammondsport NY..... 42°25N 77°13W 89 C3
Hammonton NJ..... 39°39N 74°48W 87 C2
Hampden CO..... 39°39N 104°52W 109 C2
Hampden ME..... 44°44N 68°51W 76 D5
Hampden ND..... 48°32N 98°40W 91 B7
Hampden County ☆
MA..... 42°10N 72°35W 78 B2
Hampden Sydney
VA..... 37°14N 78°28W 102 D6
Hampshire IL..... 42°6N 88°32W 71 A5
Hampshire TN..... 35°36N 87°18W 96 E5
Hampshire County ☆
MA..... 42°15N 72°35W 78 B2
Hampshire County ☆
WV..... 39°18N 78°38W 102 B6
Hampstead MD..... 39°37N 76°51W 77 A4
Hampstead NC..... 34°22N 77°44W 90 D8
Hampton NH..... 42°57N 71°10W 86 D3
Hampton AR..... 33°32N 92°28W 63 E3
Hampton MD..... 39°25N 76°35W 107 A2
Hampton CT..... 41°47N 72°3W 78 C2
Hampton FL..... 29°52N 82°8W 67 B6
Hampton GA..... 33°23N 84°17W 68 C2
Hampton IA..... 42°45N 93°13W 73 C5
Hampton NH..... 42°57N 70°58W 86 D3
Hampton SC..... 32°52N 81°7W 90 E6
Hampton VA..... 37°2N 76°21W 102 D8
Hampton Bays NY..... 40°52N 72°31W 87 B4
Hampton County ☆
SC..... 32°50N 81°10W 90 E6
Hampton Roads VA 36°57N 76°21W 115 A1
Hampton Springs FL..... 30°5N 83°40W 67 A5
Hams Fork → WY 41°35N 109°7W 104 E3
Hamtramck MI..... 42°23N 83°2W 109 A2
Hana HI..... 20°45N 155°59W 69 C6
Hanahan SC..... 32°55N 79°0W 90 E6
Hanaford IL..... 37°57N 88°50W 71 F5
Hanalei HI..... 22°12N 159°30W 69 A2
Hanamaulu HI..... 21°59N 159°22W 69 B2
Hanapēpē HI..... 21°55N 159°35W 69 B2
Hanamana B. HI..... 21°15N 157°40W 69 K14
Hanceville AL..... 34°4N 86°46W 60 B4
Hancock MD..... 39°42N 78°11W 77 A2

Hancock MI..... 47°8N 88°35W 79 B3
Hancock MN..... 45°30N 95°48W 80 E3
Hancock NY..... 41°57N 75°17W 89 D6
Hancock TX..... 43°56N 72°51W 86 C2
Hancock WI..... 44°8N 89°31W 103 D4
Hancock, Mt. WY..... 44°9N 110°25W 104 B2
Hancock County ☆
GA..... 33°20N 83°0W 68 C4
Hancock County ☆
IL..... 40°25N 91°10W 71 C2
Hancock County ☆ IA 43°5N 93°45W 73 B5
Hancock County ☆
KY..... 37°50N 86°45W 96 C6
Hancock County ☆
ME..... 44°40N 68°30W 76 D5
Hancock County ☆
MS..... 30°17N 89°23W 81 F4
Hancock County ☆
OH..... 41°2N 83°39W 92 B3
Hancock County ☆
TN..... 36°32N 83°13W 97 D9
Hancock County ☆
WV..... 40°30N 80°35W 102 A4
Hancocks Bridge NJ. 39°31N 75°28W 87 C1
Hand County ☆ SD. 44°31N 98°59W 91 F7
Hanford CA..... 36°20N 119°39W 65 G7
Hanford WA..... 46°37N 119°19W 101 D6
Hanford Reach Nat. Monument →
U.S.A..... 46°40N 119°30W 101 D6
Hanford Site, U.S. Dept. of Energy
WA..... 46°35N 119°23W 101 D6
Hangman Cr. →
WA..... 47°40N 117°27W 101 C8
Hankinson ND..... 46°4N 96°54W 91 D8
Hanksville UT..... 38°22N 110°43W 100 E5
Hanley Falls MN..... 44°42N 95°37W 80 F3
Hanley Hills MO..... 38°41N 90°19W 117 A2
Hanna LA..... 31°25N 86°47W 72 B4
Hanna WY..... 41°52N 106°34W 104 E6
Hanna City IL..... 40°42N 89°48W 71 C4
Hannaford ND..... 47°19N 98°11W 91 C7
Hannah ND..... 48°58N 98°42W 91 B7
Hannahville Indian Reservation
MI..... 45°43N 87°25W 79 D4
Hannibal MO..... 39°42N 91°22W 82 B5
Hannibal NY..... 43°19N 76°35W 89 B4
Hanover ND..... 47°7N 101°26W 91 C4
Hanover MD..... 39°11N 76°43W 107 B1
Hanover IL..... 42°15N 90°17W 71 A3
Hanover IN..... 38°43N 85°28W 72 E5
Hanover KS..... 39°54N 96°53W 74 B7
Hanover ME..... 44°30N 70°42W 86 B4
Hanover MA..... 42°7N 70°49W 78 B4
Hanover MI..... 42°6N 84°33W 79 G7
Hanover MN..... 45°10N 93°40W 80 E5
Hanover NH..... 43°42N 72°17W 86 C2
Hanover NM..... 32°48N 108°5W 88 E2
Hanover OH..... 40°4N 82°16W 92 C4
Hanover PA..... 39°48N 76°59W 77 A4
Hanover VA..... 37°46N 77°22W 102 D7
Hanover County ☆
VA..... 37°46N 77°29W 102 D7
Hanoverton OH..... 40°45N 80°56W 92 C5
Hans Lollik I.
U.S. Virgin Is...... 18°24N 64°53W 105 G18
Hansboro ND..... 48°57N 99°23W 91 B6
Hansen ID..... 42°32N 114°18W 70 G4
Hansford County ☆
TX..... 36°10N 101°30W 98 A6
Hanska MN..... 44°9N 94°30W 80 F4
Hanson FL..... 30°34N 83°21W 67 A5
Hanson KY..... 37°25N 87°29W 96 C5
Hanson County ☆
SD..... 43°39N 97°43W 91 G8
Hapeville GA..... 33°39N 84°24W 106 C2
Happy TX..... 34°45N 101°52W 98 C6
Happy Camp CA..... 41°48N 123°23W 64 B3
Happy Jack AZ..... 34°45N 111°24W 62 D4
Happy Valley OR..... 45°26N 122°31W 116 B2
Haralson LA..... 29°56N 90°12W 113 C1
Haralson GA..... 33°14N 84°34W 68 C2
Haralson County ☆
GA..... 33°45N 85°10W 68 C1
Harbeson DE..... 38°43N 75°17W 77 B5
Harbor, L. CA..... 33°47N 118°17W 111 D3
Harbor Beach MI..... 43°51N 82°39W 79 F9
Harbor Bluffs FL..... 24°54N 87°49W 119 B2
Harbor Hills NY..... 40°47N 73°44W 114 B4
Harbor Springs MI..... 45°26N 85°0W 79 D7
Harborcreek PA..... 42°10N 79°57W 95 B3
Harbour OR..... 42°3N 124°1W 94 E1
Harbor Heights FL..... 26°59N 82°0W 67 E7
Harcourt IA..... 42°16N 94°11W 73 C4
Harcuvar Mts. AZ..... 34°0N 113°30W 62 D2
Hardee County ☆ FL 27°30N 81°45W 67 D7
Hardeeville SC..... 32°17N 81°5W 90 F4
Hardeman County ☆
TN..... 35°12N 88°50W 96 E4
Hardeman County ☆
TX..... 34°20N 99°50W 98 C8
Hardesty OK..... 36°37N 101°12W 93 B2
Hardin IL..... 39°10N 90°37W 71 D3
Hardin KY..... 36°46N 88°18W 96 D4
Hardin MO..... 39°16N 93°50W 82 B3
Hardin MT..... 45°44N 107°37W 83 E10
Hardin TX..... 30°9N 94°44W 99 G13
Hardin County ☆ IL 37°30N 88°15W 71 F5
Hardin County ☆ IA 42°25N 93°15W 73 C5
Hardin County ☆ KY. 37°40N 86°0W 96 C6
Hardin County ☆
OH..... 40°42N 83°47W 92 C3
Hardin County ☆ TN 35°14N 88°15W 96 E4
Hardin County ☆
TX..... 30°22N 94°19W 99 G13
Harding MN..... 46°7N 94°2W 80 D4
Harding, L. AL..... 32°40N 85°5W 60 D5
Harding County ☆
NM..... 35°52N 103°50W 88 B6
Harding County ☆
SD..... 45°30N 103°30W 91 E2
Hardinsburg IN..... 38°28N 86°17W 72 E4
Hardinsburg KY..... 37°47N 86°28W 96 C6
Hardman OR..... 45°10N 119°41W 94 D6
Hardtner KS..... 37°1N 98°39W 74 D5
Hardwick GA..... 33°4N 83°14W 68 C3
Hardwick MN..... 43°47N 96°12W 80 G2
Hardwick VT..... 44°30N 72°22W 86 B2
Hardy AR..... 36°19N 91°29W 63 E5
Hardy MT..... 47°12N 111°47W 83 C6
Hardy County ☆ WV 39°0N 78°50W 102 C6
Hardy Dam Pond MI. 43°26N 85°31W 79 F6
Hartley TX..... 35°53N 102°24W 98 B5 (Hardy...)
Harford County ☆
MD..... 39°35N 76°25W 77 A4
Hargill TX..... 26°26N 98°5W 98 L9
Harker Heights TX. 31°5N 97°40W 99 F10
Harkers Island NC..... 34°42N 76°33W 90 D9
Harlan IA..... 41°39N 95°19W 73 D3
Harlan KY..... 36°51N 83°19W 97 D9
Harlan County ☆ KY 36°51N 83°19W 97 D9
Harlan County ☆ NE 40°15N 99°30W 84 D6

Harlan County Lake
NE..... 40°4N 99°13W 84 D6
Harlem FL..... 26°44N 80°57W 67 E8
Harlem GA..... 33°25N 82°19W 68 C4
Harlem MT..... 48°32N 108°47W 83 B9
Harlem NY..... 40°48N 73°56W 114 B3
Harleyville SC..... 39°43N 74°11W 90 E6
Harlingen TX..... 26°12N 97°42W 98 L10
Harlowton MT..... 46°26N 109°50W 83 D8
Harmon IL..... 41°43N 89°33W 71 B4
Harmon County ☆
OK..... 34°45N 99°50W 93 D4
Harmony ME..... 44°58N 69°33W 76 D4
Harmony MN..... 43°33N 92°1W 80 G6
Harned KY..... 37°50N 86°30W 96 C6
Harnett County ☆
NC..... 35°20N 78°50W 90 C7
Harney IL..... 39°44N 77°13W 77 A3
Harney ND..... 47°47N 99°56W 91 C6
Harney Basin OR..... 43°30N 119°30W 94 D6
Harney County ☆ OR 43°0N 119°0W 94 D6
Harney L. OR..... 43°14N 119°8W 94 D6
Harney Peak SD..... 43°52N 103°32W 91 G2
Harold FL..... 30°40N 86°53W 67 A2
Harper = Costa Mesa
CA..... 33°38N 117°55W 65 K9
Harper IA..... 41°22N 92°3W 73 D6
Harper KS..... 37°17N 98°1W 74 D5
Harper OR..... 43°52N 117°37W 94 D8
Harper, Mt. AK..... 64°14N 143°51W 61 D12
Harper, L. CA..... 35°15N 98°0W 74 D5
Harper County ☆
KS..... 37°15N 98°0W 74 D5
Harper County ☆
OK..... 36°50N 99°40W 93 B4
Harper L. CA..... 35°2N 117°17W 65 H9
Harpers Ferry IA..... 43°12N 91°9W 73 B7
Harpers Ferry WV..... 39°20N 77°44W 77 A3
Harpers Ferry Nat. Historical
Park → WV..... 39°19N 77°45W 102 B7
Harpersville AL..... 33°21N 86°26W 60 C4
Harquahala Mts. AZ 33°45N 113°20W 62 D2
Harrah WA..... 46°24N 120°33W 101 D5
Harrah OK..... 35°29N 97°10W 93 C6
Harrells NC..... 34°45N 78°12W 90 D7
Harriet, L. MN..... 44°55N 93°18W 113 B2
Harriman State Park
NY..... 41°13N 74°5W 89 D6
Harrington ME..... 38°56N 75°35W 89 D8
Harrington DE..... 44°37N 67°49W 76 D6
Harrington WA..... 47°29N 118°15W 101 C7
Harrington Park NJ 40°59N 73°59W 114 A3
Harris MN..... 45°35N 92°58W 80 E6
Harris OK..... 40°18N 93°21W 93 E9
Harris MO..... 40°18N 93°21W 82 A3
Harris County ☆ GA 32°40N 84°55W 68 D2
Harris County ☆
TX..... 29°46N 95°22W 99 H12
Harrisburg AR..... 35°34N 90°43W 63 C5
Harrisburg IL..... 37°44N 88°32W 71 F5
Harrisburg MO..... 39°9N 92°28W 82 B4
Harrisburg NE..... 41°33N 103°44W 84 C2
Harrisburg OR..... 44°16N 123°10W 94 C2
Harrisburg PA..... 40°16N 76°53W 95 D6
Harrison AR..... 36°14N 93°7W 63 B2
Harrison ID..... 47°27N 116°47W 70 B2
Harrison MI..... 44°1N 84°48W 79 E7
Harrison MT..... 45°42N 111°47W 83 E6
Harrison NE..... 42°41N 103°53W 84 B2
Harrison NY..... 40°58N 73°43W 114 B4
Harrison OH..... 39°16N 84°49W 92 D2
Harrison TN..... 35°2N 85°8W 97 E7
Harrison Bay AK..... 70°40N 151°0W 61 A10
Harrison County ☆
IN..... 38°10N 86°10W 72 E4
Harrison County ☆
KY..... 38°25N 84°20W 97 B8
Harrison County ☆
MS..... 30°30N 89°7W 81 F4
Harrison County ☆
MO..... 40°20N 94°0W 82 A2
Harrison County ☆
OH..... 40°18N 81°11W 92 C5
Harrison County ☆
TX..... 32°33N 94°23W 99 E13
Harrison County ☆
WV..... 39°17N 80°30W 102 B4
Harrisonburg LA..... 31°46N 91°49W 75 C4
Harrisonburg VA..... 38°27N 78°52W 102 C6
Harrisonville MO..... 38°39N 94°21W 82 C2
Harriston MS..... 31°44N 91°2W 81 E2
Harrisville MI..... 44°39N 83°17W 79 E8
Harrisville MS..... 32°2N 90°11W 81 D3
Harrisville NY..... 44°9N 75°19W 89 A5
Harrisville RI..... 41°58N 71°41W 78 C3
Harrisville WV..... 39°13N 81°3W 102 B3
Harrod OH..... 40°43N 83°56W 92 C3
Harrodsburg KY..... 37°46N 84°51W 97 C8
Harrogate TN..... 36°35N 83°40W 97 D9
Harrold SD..... 44°31N 99°44W 91 F6
Harry S. Moss Park
TX..... 32°53N 96°44W 109 A5
Harry S. Truman Res.
MO..... 38°16N 93°24W 82 C3
Harry Strunk L. NE 40°23N 100°13W 84 D5
Hart MI..... 43°42N 86°22W 79 F5
Hart TX..... 34°23N 102°7W 98 C5
Hart County ☆ GA..... 34°15N 83°0W 68 B4
Hart County ☆ KY..... 37°20N 85°50W 97 C7
Hart Island NY..... 40°51N 73°46W 114 A4
Hart, L. OR..... 42°23N 119°51W 94 E6
Hart Mt. OR..... 42°23N 119°53W 94 E6
Hartfield VA..... 37°33N 76°27W 102 D8
Hartford AR..... 35°1N 94°23W 63 C1
Hartford CT..... 41°46N 72°41W 78 C2
Hartford IA..... 41°27N 93°24W 73 D5
Hartford KY..... 37°27N 86°55W 96 C6
Hartford MI..... 42°12N 86°10W 79 G5
Hartford NY..... 43°22N 73°24W 86 C1
Hartford SD..... 43°38N 96°57W 91 G9
Hartford VT..... 43°40N 72°21W 86 C2
Hartford WI..... 43°19N 88°22W 103 E5
Hartford Bradley Int. ✈ (BDL,)
CT..... 41°45N 72°45W 78 C2
Hartford City IN..... 40°27N 85°22W 72 C5
Hartington NE..... 42°53N 96°44W 91 H8
Hartland ME..... 44°53N 69°27W 76 D4
Hartland VT..... 43°32N 72°24W 86 C2
Hartland WI..... 43°6N 88°21W 103 E5
Hartley IA..... 43°11N 95°29W 73 B3
Hartley TX..... 35°53N 102°24W 98 B4
Hartley County ☆
TX..... 35°50N 102°30W 98 B5
Hartline WA..... 47°41N 119°6W 101 C6
Hartly DE..... 39°10N 75°43W 77 A5
Hartman CO..... 38°7N 102°13W 66 D8
Hartsburg MO..... 38°42N 92°19W 82 C4
Hartselle AL..... 34°27N 86°56W 60 B4

Hartsfield-Atlanta Int. ✈ (ATL)
GA..... 33°38N 84°26W 106 C2
Hartshorne OK..... 34°51N 95°34W 93 C8
Hartsville SC..... 34°23N 80°4W 90 D5
Hartsville TN..... 36°24N 86°9W 96 D6
Hartville MO..... 37°15N 92°31W 82 D4
Hartville OH..... 40°58N 81°20W 92 C5
Hartville WY..... 42°20N 104°44W 104 D8
Hartwell GA..... 34°21N 82°56W 68 B4
Hartwell L. SC..... 34°21N 82°49W 90 D3
Hartwick IA..... 41°47N 92°21W 73 D6
Harvard ID..... 46°55N 116°44W 70 C2
Harvard IL..... 39°32N 87°4W 71 B6
Harvard, Mt. CO..... 38°56N 106°19W 66 D4
Harvard University
MA..... 42°22N 71°7W 106 A3
Harvey IL..... 41°36N 87°50W 71 B6
Harvey LA..... 29°54N 90°4W 113 C2
Harvey ND..... 47°47N 99°56W 91 C6
Harvey Cedars NJ..... 39°43N 74°11W 87 C3
Harvey County ☆ KS. 38°0N 97°30W 74 C6
Harveys Lake PA..... 41°23N 76°1W 95 C6
Harveyville KS..... 38°47N 95°58W 74 C8
Harwich MA..... 41°41N 70°5W 78 C4
Harwinton CT..... 41°46N 73°4W 78 C1
Harwood MO..... 37°57N 94°9W 82 D2
Harwood TX..... 29°40N 97°30W 99 H10
Harwood Heights
IL..... 41°57N 87°46W 108 B2
Harwood Park MD..... 39°11N 76°44W 107 B1
Hasbrouck Heights
NJ..... 40°51N 74°6W 114 A2
Haskell AR..... 34°30N 92°38W 63 D3
Haskell OK..... 35°50N 95°40W 93 C8
Haskell TX..... 33°10N 99°44W 99 D8
Haskell County ☆
KS..... 37°33N 100°45W 74 D3
Haskell County ☆
OK..... 35°10N 95°10W 93 C8
Haskell County ☆
TX..... 33°12N 99°45W 99 D8
Haskins OH..... 41°28N 83°42W 92 B3
Haslet TX..... 32°59N 97°21W 99 E10
Hassayampa → AZ 33°19N 112°42W 62 D3
Hastings FL..... 29°43N 81°31W 67 B7
Hastings IA..... 41°1N 95°30W 73 D3
Hastings MI..... 42°39N 85°17W 79 G6
Hastings MN..... 44°44N 92°51W 80 F6
Hastings NE..... 40°35N 98°23W 84 D7
Hastings OK..... 34°14N 98°73W 93 D5
Hasty CO..... 38°7N 102°58W 66 D8
Haswell CO..... 38°27N 103°10W 66 D7
Hat Cr. → SD..... 43°15N 103°37W 91 G2
Hatch UT..... 37°39N 112°26W 100 F3
Hatch Wash → UT 38°35N 109°35W 100 E6
Hatchet Cr. → AL..... 32°51N 86°27W 60 D4
Hatchie → TN..... 35°35N 89°53W 96 E3
Hatchie Nat. Wildlife Refuge →
TN..... 35°30N 89°13W 96 E3
Hatchineha, L. FL..... 28°2N 81°25W 67 C7
Hatfield AR..... 34°29N 94°23W 63 D1
Hatfield IN..... 37°54N 87°14W 72 F3
Hatfield MA..... 42°22N 72°36W 78 B2
Hatfield MN..... 43°58N 96°12W 80 G2
Hatfield PA..... 40°17N 75°18W 87 B1
Hatillo Puerto Rico..... 18°29N 66°49W 105 G16
Hatteras NC..... 35°13N 75°42W 90 C10
Hatteras, C. NC..... 35°14N 75°32W 90 C10
Hatteras I. NC..... 35°30N 75°28W 90 C10
Hattiesburg MS..... 31°20N 89°17W 81 E4
Hattieville AR..... 35°17N 92°47W 63 C3
Hatton AL..... 34°34N 87°25W 60 B3
Hatton ND..... 47°38N 97°27W 91 C8
Hatton WA..... 46°47N 118°50W 101 D7
Haubstadt IN..... 38°12N 87°35W 72 E3
Haugen WI..... 45°37N 91°46W 103 C2
Haughton LA..... 32°32N 93°34W 75 B2
Hauser OR..... 43°30N 124°13W 94 D1
Haut, L. au ME..... 44°3N 68°15W 76 D5
Hau'ula HI..... 21°37N 157°55W 69 J14
Havana AR..... 35°7N 93°32W 63 C2
Havana IL..... 40°18N 90°4W 71 C3
Havana ND..... 45°57N 97°37W 91 E8
Havana, L. AZ..... 34°13N 114°8W 62 D1
Havasu Cr. → AZ. 36°19N 112°46W 62 A3
Havasupai Indian Reservation
AZ..... 36°15N 112°35W 62 A3
Havelock NC..... 34°53N 76°54W 90 D9
Havelock IA..... 42°44N 94°42W 73 C4
Haven KS..... 37°54N 97°47W 74 D6
Havensville KS..... 39°31N 96°5W 74 B7
Haverford PA..... 40°0N 75°17W 116 A1
Haverhill FL..... 26°42N 80°7W 67 E8
Haverhill MA..... 42°47N 71°5W 78 B3
Haverhill NH..... 44°2N 72°4W 86 B2
Haverstraw NY..... 41°12N 73°58W 87 A3
Havertown PA..... 39°58N 75°18W 116 B1
Haviland KS..... 37°37N 99°6W 74 D4
Havre de Grace MD. 39°33N 76°6W 77 A4
Haw → NC..... 35°36N 79°3W 90 C6
Haw Knob NC..... 35°19N 84°2W 90 C1
Hawai'i ☐ HI..... 19°30N 155°30W 69 C6
Hawai'i County ☆
HI..... 19°30N 155°30W 69 C6
Hawai'i Volcanoes Nat. Park △
HI..... 19°25N 155°18W 69 D6
Hawaiian Gardens
CA..... 33°49N 118°4W 111 D4
Hawaiian Is.
Pac. Oc..... 20°30N 156°0W 69 G12
Hawarden IA..... 43°0N 96°29W 73 B2
Hawesville KY..... 37°54N 86°45W 96 C6
Hawi HI..... 20°14N 155°50W 69 C6
Hawk Point MO..... 38°58N 91°8W 82 C5
Hawk Springs WY..... 41°47N 104°16W 104 E8
Hawkeye IA..... 42°56N 91°57W 73 C7
Hawkins WI..... 45°31N 90°43W 103 C3
Hawkins County ☆
TN..... 36°24N 83°1W 97 D9
Hawkinsville GA..... 32°17N 83°28W 68 D3
Hawks MI..... 45°18N 83°53W 79 D8
Hawksbill VA..... 38°34N 78°27W 102 C6
Hawksbill Mt. NC..... 35°55N 81°53W 90 B4
Hawley MN..... 46°53N 96°19W 80 D2
Hawley TX..... 32°36N 99°49W 99 E8
Haworth OK..... 33°51N 94°39W 93 E9
Hawthorne FL..... 29°36N 82°5W 67 B6
Hawthorne NJ..... 40°57N 74°9W 114 A1
Hawthorne NV..... 38°32N 118°38W 85 D2
Hawthorne Army Depot
NV..... 38°29N 118°35W 85 D2
Hawthorne Racecourse
IL..... 41°49N 87°44W 108 C2
Haxtun CO..... 40°39N 102°38W 66 B8
Hay WI..... 44°37N 90°54W 103 D3
Hay → WI..... 44°59N 91°51W 103 D2
Hay Springs NE..... 42°41N 102°41W 84 B3
Hayden AL..... 33°53N 86°45W 60 C4
Hayden CO..... 40°30N 107°16W 66 B3
Hayden ID..... 47°46N 116°47W 70 B2
Hayden IN..... 38°55N 85°45W 72 E5
Hayden Peak ID..... 42°59N 116°40W 70 G2

Hayes *LA* .... 30°7N 92°55W 75 D3
Hayes *SD* .... 44°23N 101°1W 91 F4
Hayes, Mt. *AK* ... 63°37N 146°43W 61 E11
Hayes Center *NE* . 40°31N 101°1W 84 D4
Hayes County ☆ *NE* 40°30N 101°1W 84 D4
Hayesville *IA* .... 41°16N 92°15W 73 D6
Hayesville *NC* .... 35°3N 83°49W 90 C2
Hayesville *OR* .... 44°59N 122°59W 94 C3
Hayfield *MN* ..... 43°53N 92°51W 80 G6
Hayfork *CA* ...... 40°33N 123°11W 64 C3
Haylow *GA* ...... 30°50N 82°54W 68 F4
Haymarket *VA* .... 38°49N 77°38W 77 B3
Haynes *AR* ...... 34°54N 90°47W 63 D5
Haynes *ND* ...... 45°59N 102°28W 91 E3
Haynesville *LA* ... 32°58N 93°8W 75 B2
Haynesville *ME* ... 45°50N 67°59W 76 C6
Haynesville *VA* ... 37°57N 76°40W 77 C4
Hayneville *AL* .... 32°11N 86°35W 60 D4
Hayneville *GA* .... 32°23N 83°37W 68 D3
Hays *KS* .... 38°53N 99°20W 74 C4
Hays Canyon Ra.
  NV .... 41°25N 119°53W 85 A1
Hays County ☆ *TX* 29°59N 97°53W 99 H10
Haysi *VA* .... 37°12N 82°18W 102 D2
Haystack Peak *UT* 38°50N 113°55W 100 D2
Haysville *KS* ..... 37°34N 97°21W 74 D6
Hayti *MO* .... 36°14N 89°44W 82 E7
Hayti *SD* .... 44°40N 97°13W 91 F8
Hayward *CA* ..... 37°40N 122°4W 118 B4
Hayward *MN* ..... 43°39N 93°15W 80 G5
Hayward *WI* ..... 46°1N 91°29W 103 B2
Hayward Fault *CA* 37°46N 122°10W 118 B3
Hayward Municipal ✈ (HWD)
  CA .... 37°39N 122°7W 118 C4
Haywood County ☆
  NC .... 35°30N 83°0W 90 C3
Haywood County ☆
  TN .... 35°36N 89°16W 96 B3
Hazard *KY* ...... 37°15N 83°12W 97 C9
Hazard *NE* ...... 41°6N 99°9W 84 C6
Hazardville *CT* ... 41°59N 72°32W 78 C2
Hazel *KY* .... 36°30N 88°20W 96 D4
Hazel *SD* .... 44°46N 97°23W 91 F8
Hazel → *VA* ..... 38°33N 77°51W 102 C7
Hazel Green *AL* ... 34°56N 86°34W 60 B4
Hazel Green *WI* ... 42°32N 90°26W 103 F3
Hazel Park *MI* .... 42°27N 83°6W 109 A2
Hazel Run *MN* .... 44°45N 95°43W 80 F3
Hazelton *ID* ..... 42°36N 114°8W 70 G4
Hazelton *KS* ..... 37°5N 98°24W 74 D5
Hazelton *ND* ..... 46°29N 100°17W 91 D5
Hazelton Peak *WY* 44°6N 107°3W 104 B5
Hazelwood *MO* ... 38°46N 90°22W 117 A1
Hazen *AR* .... 34°47N 91°35W 63 D4
Hazen *ND* .... 47°18N 101°38W 91 C4
Hazen *NV* .... 39°34N 119°3W 85 C1
Hazlehurst *GA* ... 31°52N 82°36W 68 E4
Hazlehurst *MS* ... 31°52N 90°24W 81 E3
Hazlet *NJ* .... 40°25N 74°12W 87 B2
Hazleton *IN* ..... 38°29N 87°33W 72 E3
Hazleton *IA* ..... 42°37N 91°54W 73 C7
Hazleton *PA* ..... 40°57N 75°59W 95 D7
Hazlettville *DE* ... 39°7N 75°37W 119 D2
He Devil *ID* ..... 45°21N 116°33W 70 D2
Headland *AL* ..... 31°21N 85°21W 60 E6
Headquarters *ID* .. 46°38N 115°48W 70 C3
Headrick *OK* ..... 34°38N 99°9W 93 D4
Healdsburg *CA* ... 38°37N 122°52W 64 D3
Healdton *OK* ..... 34°14N 97°29W 93 D6
Healdville *VT* .... 43°25N 72°47W 78 C2
Healy *AK* .... 63°52N 148°58W 61 E10
Healy *KS* .... 38°36N 100°37W 74 C3
Heard County ☆ *GA* 33°15N 85°0W 68 C1
Heard Pond *MA* ... 42°20N 71°23W 106 A1
Hearne *TX* ...... 30°53N 96°36W 99 G11
Heart → *ND* ..... 46°46N 100°50W 91 D5
Heart L. *WY* ..... 44°16N 110°29W 104 B2
Heartwell *NE* .... 40°34N 98°47W 84 D7
Heartwell Park L. *CA* 33°49N 118°11W 115 D2
Heath Springs *SC* . 34°36N 80°40W 90 D5
Heathsville *VA* ... 37°55N 76°29W 77 C4
Heavener *OK* ..... 34°53N 94°36W 93 D9
Hebbardsville *KY* . 37°47N 87°33W 96 C7
Hebbronville *TX* .. 27°18N 98°41W 98 K9
Heber *AZ* .... 34°26N 110°36W 62 C5
Heber *CA* .... 32°44N 115°32W 65 L11
Heber City *UT* ... 40°31N 111°25W 100 C4
Heber Springs *AR* 35°30N 92°2W 63 C4
Hebgen L. *MT* .... 44°52N 111°20W 83 F6
Hebo *OR* .... 45°14N 123°52W 94 B2
Hebron *CT* ...... 41°39N 72°22W 78 C2
Hebron *IL* ...... 42°28N 88°26W 71 A5
Hebron *IN* ...... 41°19N 87°12W 72 B3
Hebron *MD* ...... 38°25N 75°41W 77 B5
Hebron *ND* ...... 46°54N 102°3W 91 D3
Hebron *NE* ...... 40°10N 97°35W 84 D8
Hebron *NH* ...... 43°42N 71°48W 86 C3
Hebron *TX* ...... 33°2N 96°52W 99 D11
Hecla *SD* .... 45°53N 98°9W 91 E7
Hector *AR* ...... 35°28N 92°59W 63 C3
Hector *MN* ...... 44°45N 94°43W 80 F4
Hedgesville *WV* ... 39°31N 77°58W 77 A3
Hedley *TX* ...... 34°52N 100°39W 98 C7
Hedrick *IA* ...... 41°11N 92°19W 73 D6
Hedwig Village *TX* 29°46N 95°31W 110 B1
He'eia *HI* ...... 21°25N 157°48W 69 K14
Heflin *AL* ...... 33°39N 85°35W 60 C5
Heiberger *AL* .... 32°46N 87°17W 60 D3
Heidelberg *MN* ... 44°30N 93°38W 80 F5
Heidelberg *MS* ... 31°53N 88°59W 81 E5
Heidelberg *PA* ... 40°23N 80°5W 116 B1
Heidrick *KY* ..... 36°53N 83°54W 97 D9
Heizer *KS* ...... 38°25N 98°53W 74 C5
Helemano → *HI* .. 21°35N 158°7W 69 J13
Helen *GA* .... 34°42N 83°44W 68 B3
Helen *MD* .... 38°22N 76°42W 77 B4
Helena *AL* ...... 33°18N 86°51W 60 C4
Helena *AR* ...... 34°32N 90°36W 63 D5
Helena *CA* ...... 40°47N 123°8W 64 C3
Helena *GA* ...... 32°5N 82°55W 68 D4
Helena *MT* ...... 46°36N 112°2W 83 D5
Helena *OK* ...... 36°33N 98°16W 93 B5
Helena Nat. Forest
  MT .... 46°40N 111°30W 83 D6
Heliotrope Mt. *UT* 39°7N 111°27W 100 D4
Helix *OR* .... 45°51N 118°39W 94 B7
Hell Cr. → *CO* .. 39°30N 102°30W 66 C8
Hellertown *PA* ... 40°35N 75°21W 87 B1
Hells Canyon *OR* . 45°10N 116°50W 94 B9
Hells Canyon Nat. Recr. Area →
  OR .... 45°30N 117°40W 94 B8
Helmville *MT* .... 46°52N 112°58W 83 D5
Helotes *TX* ..... 29°34N 98°41W 111 D3
Helper *UT* ...... 39°41N 110°51W 100 D5
Helton *KY* ...... 36°58N 83°49W 97 D9
Hematite *MO* .... 38°12N 90°29W 82 C6
Hemet *CA* ...... 33°45N 116°58W 65 K10
Hemingford *NE* ... 42°19N 103°4W 84 B2
Hemingway *SC* ... 33°45N 79°27W 90 D7
Hemphill *TX* .... 31°20N 93°51W 99 F14
Hemphill County ☆
  TX .... 35°55N 100°15W 98 B7
Hempstead *NY* ... 40°42N 73°37W 114 B5
Hempstead *TX* ... 30°6N 96°5W 99 G11
Hempstead County ☆
  AR .... 33°40N 93°36W 63 D2
Hempstead Harbor
  NY .... 40°42N 73°39W 114 A5
Henagar *AL* ..... 34°38N 85°46W 60 B5
Henderson *CA* ... 32°21N 83°47W 68 D3
Henderson *IA* ... 41°8N 95°26W 73 D3

Henderson *KY* .... 37°50N 87°35W 96 C5
Henderson *MD* ... 39°6N 75°47W 77 A5
Henderson *NC* .... 36°20N 78°25W 90 B7
Henderson *NE* .... 40°47N 97°49W 84 D8
Henderson *NV* .... 36°2N 114°58W 110 D2
Henderson *TN* .... 35°26N 88°38W 96 B4
Henderson *TX* .... 32°9N 94°48W 99 E13
Henderson County ☆
  IL .... 40°50N 90°55W 71 C3
Henderson County ☆
  KY .... 37°45N 87°35W 96 C6
Henderson County ☆
  NC .... 35°15N 82°30W 90 C3
Henderson County ☆
  TN .... 35°39N 88°24W 96 B4
Henderson County ☆
  TX .... 32°12N 95°51W 99 E12
Henderson Executive ✈
  NV .... 35°59N 115°8W 110 D2
Hendersonville *NC* 35°19N 82°28W 90 C3
Hendersonville *TN*. 36°18N 86°37W 96 A6
Hendley *NE* ..... 40°8N 99°58W 84 D6
Hendricks *MN* ... 44°30N 96°25W 80 F2
Hendricks County ☆
  IN .... 39°45N 86°30W 72 D4
Hendrum *MN* .... 47°16N 96°49W 80 C2
Henefer *UT* ..... 41°1N 111°30W 100 B4
Henlopen, C. *DE*. 38°48N 75°6W 77 B5
Hennepin *IL* ..... 41°15N 89°21W 71 B4
Hennepin *OK* .... 34°31N 97°21W 93 D6
Hennepin Canal *IL* 41°29N 90°12W 71 B3
Hennepin County ☆
  MN .... 45°0N 93°30W 80 E5
Henniker *NH* .... 43°11N 71°50W 86 D3
Henning *IL* ..... 40°18N 87°42W 71 C6
Henning *MN* .... 46°19N 95°27W 80 D3
Henning *TN* ..... 35°41N 89°34W 96 B3
Henrico County ☆
  VA .... 37°33N 77°20W 102 D7
Henrietta *NC* .... 35°15N 81°48W 90 C4
Henrietta *NY* .... 43°4N 77°37W 89 D3
Henrietta *TX* .... 33°49N 98°12W 99 D9
Henriette *MN* .... 45°53N 93°7W 80 E5
Henrieville *UT* ... 37°30N 112°0W 100 F4
Henry *IL* .... 41°7N 89°22W 71 B4
Henry *NE* ...... 41°58N 104°4W 84 C1
Henry *SD* ...... 44°53N 97°28W 91 F8
Henry C. *VA* .... 36°56N 76°1W 102 E8
Henry County ☆ *AL* 31°34N 85°15W 60 E6
Henry County ☆ *GA* 33°25N 84°5W 68 C2
Henry County ☆ *IL* 41°20N 90°7W 71 B3
Henry County ☆ *IN* 39°55N 85°25W 72 D5
Henry County ☆ *IA* 41°0N 91°30W 73 D7
Henry County ☆ *KY* 38°25N 85°10W 97 B7
Henry County ☆ *MO* 38°25N 93°45W 82 C3
Henry County ☆ *OH* 41°19N 84°2W 92 B2
Henry County ☆ *TN* 36°18N 88°19W 96 A4
Henry County ☆
  VA .... 36°50N 79°56W 102 E5
Henry Mts. *UT* ... 38°0N 110°50W 100 E5
Henryetta *OK* .... 35°27N 95°59W 93 C8
Henrys Fork → *ID* 43°57N 111°45W 70 F7
Henrys Lake *ID* .. 44°36N 111°21W 70 E7
Henshaw *KY* ..... 37°37N 88°3W 96 C4
Henshaw, L. *CA*.. 33°15N 116°45W 65 K10
Hensler *ND* ..... 47°16N 101°5W 91 C4
Henson Cr. → *MD* 38°47N 76°58W 119 C4
Hepburn *IA* ..... 40°51N 95°1W 73 E3
Hephzibah *GA* ... 33°19N 82°6W 68 D5
Hepler *KS* ...... 37°40N 94°58W 74 D9
Heppner *OR* ..... 45°21N 119°33W 94 B6
Herbert Hoover Nat. Historic
  Site → *IA* .... 41°40N 91°21W 73 D7
Herbert I. *AK* .... 52°45N 170°7W 61 K5
Herbes, Point aux
  LA .... 29°56N 90°10W 113 B3
Herculaneum *MO*. 38°16N 90°23W 82 C6
Hereford *AZ* .... 31°26N 110°6W 62 F5
Hereford *CO* .... 40°57N 104°18W 66 B6
Hereford *MD* .... 39°35N 76°40W 77 A4
Hereford *TX* .... 34°49N 102°24W 98 C5
Herington *KS* .... 38°40N 96°57W 74 C7
Herkimer *KS* .... 39°54N 96°43W 74 B7
Herkimer *NY* .... 43°0N 74°59W 89 C6
Herkimer County ☆
  NY .... 43°0N 75°0W 89 B6
Herman *MN* ..... 45°49N 96°9W 80 E2
Herman *NE* ..... 41°40N 96°13W 84 C9
Hermansville *MI*.. 45°42N 87°36W 79 D4
Hermantown *MN*.. 46°50N 92°15W 80 D6
Hermanville *MS*.. 31°58N 90°50W 81 E3
Hermiston *OR* .... 45°51N 119°17W 94 B6
Hermitage *AR* .... 33°27N 92°10W 63 D3
Hermitage *MO* ... 37°56N 93°19W 82 D3
Hermitage *PA* .... 41°14N 80°27W 95 C2
Hermleigh *TX* ... 32°38N 100°46W 98 E7
Hermon *NY* ..... 44°28N 75°14W 89 A5
Hermosa *SD* .... 43°50N 103°12W 91 G2
Hermosa Beach
  CA .... 33°51N 118°23W 111 C2
Hernando *FL* .... 28°54N 82°23W 67 C6
Hernando *MS* .... 34°50N 90°0W 81 B3
Hernando County ☆
  FL .... 28°35N 82°30W 67 C6
Herndon *KS* ..... 39°55N 100°47W 74 B3
Herndon *PA* ..... 40°43N 76°51W 95 D6
Herndon *VA* ..... 38°58N 77°23W 102 C7
Herod *GA* ...... 31°42N 84°26W 68 E2
Heron *IA* ...... 48°3N 115°57W 83 B2
Heron L. *NM* .... 36°41N 106°43W 88 A4
Heron Lake *MN*.. 43°48N 95°19W 80 G3
Herreid *SD* ..... 45°50N 100°4W 91 E5
Herrick *SD* ..... 43°7N 99°11W 91 G6
Herriman *UT* .... 40°30N 112°1W 117 C1
Herrin *IL* ...... 37°48N 89°2W 71 F5
Herring Run Park
  MD .... 39°19N 76°33W 107 B2
Herrington L. *KY*. 37°45N 84°44W 97 C8
Herscher *IL* ..... 41°3N 88°6W 71 B5
Hersey *MI* ...... 43°51N 85°27W 79 F6
Hershey *NE* ..... 41°10N 101°0W 84 C5
Hershey *PA* ..... 40°17N 76°39W 95 D6
Hershey Park *PA*. 40°17N 76°39W 95 D6
Hertford *NC* .... 36°12N 76°28W 90 B8
Hertford County ☆
  NC .... 36°20N 77°0W 90 B7
Hesperia *CA* .... 34°25N 117°18W 65 J9
Hesperia *MI* .... 43°34N 86°3W 79 F5
Hesperus *CO* .... 37°17N 108°2W 66 E2
Hessel *MI* ...... 46°0N 84°26W 79 C7
Hessmer *LA* ..... 31°3N 92°7W 75 D3
Hesston *KS* ..... 38°8N 97°26W 74 C6
Hetch Hetchy Aqueduct
  CA .... 37°57N 119°47W 64 F7
Hetch Hetchy Res.
  CA .... 37°57N 119°47W 64 F7
Hettinger *ND* .... 46°0N 102°42W 91 D3
Hettinger County ☆
  ND .... 46°25N 102°30W 91 D3
Heuvelton *NY* ... 44°37N 75°25W 89 A5
Hewins *KS* ..... 37°3N 96°25W 74 D7
Hewitt *MN* ..... 46°19N 95°5W 80 D3
Hewitt *TX* ...... 31°28N 97°12W 99 F10
Hewlett Neck *NY*. 40°37N 73°41W 114 C4
Hext *TX* .... 30°52N 99°33W 99 G8
Heyburn *ID* ..... 42°34N 113°46W 70 G5
Heyburn L. *OK*... 35°57N 96°18W 93 C7

Heyworth *IL* ..... 40°19N 88°59W 71 C5
Hialeah *FL* ..... 25°51N 80°16W 112 C1
Hiattville *KS* .... 37°43N 94°52W 74 D9
Hiawassa, L. *FL*.. 28°33N 81°28W 115 A2
Hiawassee *GA* ... 34°58N 83°46W 68 B3
Hiawatha *IA* .... 42°2N 91°41W 73 C7
Hiawatha *KS* .... 39°51N 95°32W 74 B8
Hiawatha *UT* .... 39°29N 111°1W 100 D4
Hiawatha Nat. Forest
  MI .... 46°15N 86°40W 79 C5
Hibbing *MN* ..... 47°25N 92°56W 80 C6
Hickam Air Force Base
  HI .... 21°20N 157°56W 69 K14
Hickam Housing
  HI .... 21°21N 157°57W 69 K14
Hickman *DE* ..... 38°50N 75°42W 77 B5
Hickman *KY* ..... 36°34N 89°11W 96 D3
Hickman *NE* ..... 40°37N 96°38W 84 D9
Hickman County ☆
  KY .... 36°40N 89°0W 96 D4
Hickman County ☆
  TN .... 35°47N 87°28W 96 E5
Hickok *KS* ...... 37°34N 101°14W 74 D2
Hickory *KY* ..... 36°48N 88°40W 96 D4
Hickory *MS* ..... 32°19N 89°2W 81 D4
Hickory *NC* ..... 35°44N 81°21W 90 C4
Hickory County ☆ *FL* 26°30N 81°20W 93 D7
Hickory, L. *NC*.. 35°49N 81°12W 90 C4
Hickory County ☆
  MO .... 37°55N 93°15W 82 D3
Hickory Flat *MS*. 34°37N 89°11W 81 B4
Hickory Hills *IL*.. 41°43N 87°49W 108 C2
Hickory Plains *AR* 34°59N 91°44W 63 C4
Hickory Ridge *AR* 35°24N 90°58W 63 C5
Hickory Run State Park
  PA .... 41°2N 75°41W 95 C7
Hickory Valley *TN* 35°9N 89°8W 96 B3
Hickory Withe *TN* 35°14N 89°33W 96 B3
Hicksville *NY* .... 40°46N 73°32W 87 B3
Hicksville *OH* .... 41°18N 84°46W 92 B2
Hico *CA* .... 31°59N 98°2W 99 99
Hidalgo *IL* ..... 39°9N 88°9W 71 D5
Hidalgo *TX* ..... 26°6N 98°16W 98 L9
Hidalgo County ☆
  NM .... 32°0N 108°45W 88 F2
Hidalgo County ☆
  TX .... 26°25N 98°18W 98 L9
Hidden Falls-Crosby Farm
  Regional Park →
  MN .... 44°54N 93°9W 113 B3
Higbee *MO* ..... 39°19N 92°31W 82 B4
Higgins *TX* ..... 36°7N 100°2W 98 A7
Higgins L. *MI*.... 44°29N 84°43W 79 E7
Higginsport *OH*.. 38°47N 83°58W 92 E3
Higginsville *MO*.. 39°4N 93°43W 82 B3
High Bridge *NJ*.. 40°40N 74°54W 87 B2
High Desert *CA*.. 34°40N 116°30W 65 J10
High Island *TX*... 29°34N 94°24W 99 H13
High Point *NJ*... 41°19N 74°40W 87 A2
High Point *FL*.... 27°54N 82°42W 119 B2
High Pt. *NJ*..... 41°19N 74°40W 87 A2
High Pt. *WY*.... 41°37N 107°43W 104 E5
High Rock L. *NC*. 35°36N 80°14W 90 C5
High Rock L. *NV*. 41°17N 119°17W 85 A1
High Rolls *NM*... 32°57N 105°50W 88 E5
High Springs *FL*.. 29°50N 82°36W 67 B6
Hightstown *NJ*... 40°16N 74°31W 87 B2
Highland *CA*.... 34°8N 117°13W 115 A10
Highland *IL*..... 38°44N 89°41W 71 E4
Highland *IN*..... 41°33N 87°28W 72 B3
Highland *KS*.... 39°52N 95°16W 74 B8
Highland *NY*.... 41°43N 73°58W 89 B7
Highland *WI*.... 43°5N 90°22W 103 E3
Highland Beach *MD* 38°56N 76°28W 77 B4
Highland City *FL*. 27°58N 81°53W 67 D7
Highland County ☆
  OH .... 39°12N 83°37W 92 D3
Highland County ☆
  VA .... 38°25N 79°35W 102 C5
Highland Falls *NY* 41°22N 73°58W 87 A3
Highland Heights *KY* 39°1N 84°27W 107 B2
Highland Heights
  TX .... 29°51N 95°25W 110 A2
Highland Hills *IL*.. 41°51N 88°1W 71 B5
Highland Home *AL* 31°57N 86°19W 60 E4
Highland Lakes *NJ* 41°11N 74°28W 87 A2
Highland Mills *GA* 33°17N 84°17W 68 C2
Highland Park *CA* 34°8N 118°13W 111 B3
Highland Park *IL*. 42°11N 87°48W 71 A6
Highland Park *MI* 42°24N 83°5W 109 A2
Highland Park *TX* 32°50N 96°47W 109 B5
Highland Springs
  VA .... 37°33N 77°20W 102 D7
Highland View *FL* 29°50N 85°19W 67 A3
Highlands = Fort Thomas
  KY .... 39°4N 84°26W 107 B2
Highlands *NC* .... 35°3N 83°12W 90 C2
Highlands *NJ* .... 40°24N 73°59W 87 B3
Highlands *TX* .... 29°49N 95°3W 110 A3
Highlands County ☆
  FL .... 27°20N 81°20W 67 D7
Highlands Ranch
  CO .... 39°33N 104°58W 109 C2
Highlandtown *MD* 39°17N 76°34W 107 B2
Highmore *SD* .... 44°31N 99°27W 91 F6
Hightstown *NJ*... 40°16N 74°31W 87 B2
Highway City *CA*. 36°49N 119°50W 65 G7
Highwood Mts. *MT* 47°30N 110°30W 83 C7
Higuero, Pta.
  Puerto Rico ... 18°22N 67°16W 105 G15
Hiko *NV* .... 37°32N 115°14W 85 E5
Hiland *WY* ...... 43°7N 107°21W 104 E8
Hildale *UT* ..... 37°0N 112°58W 100 F3
Hildreth *NE* ..... 40°20N 99°3W 84 D6
Hilgard *OR* ..... 45°21N 118°14W 94 B7
Hill City *ID* ..... 43°18N 115°3W 70 F3
Hill City *KS* .... 39°22N 99°51W 74 B4
Hill City *MN* .... 46°59N 93°36W 80 D5
Hill City *SD* .... 43°56N 103°35W 91 G2
Hill Country Village
  TX .... 29°34N 98°29W 111 D3
Hill County ☆ *MT* 48°40N 110°0W 83 B7
Hill County ☆ *TX*. 32°1N 97°8W 99 E10
Hill Cr. → *UT*... 39°55N 109°40W 100 D6
Hill-Stead Museum
  CT .... 41°43N 72°49W 78 C2
Hillcrest Heights
  MD .... 38°49N 76°57W 119 C4
Hilliard *FL* ..... 30°41N 81°55W 67 A7
Hilliard *OH* ..... 40°2N 83°10W 92 C3
Hilliards *PA* ..... 41°5N 79°50W 95 C3
Hillister *TX* ..... 30°40N 94°23W 99 G13
Hillman *MI* ..... 45°4N 83°54W 79 D8
Hillman *MO* ..... 37°53N 91°32W 82 D5
Hillrose *CO* ..... 40°20N 103°31W 66 B7
Hills *IA* .... 41°33N 91°32W 73 D7
Hills *MN* ...... 43°32N 96°21W 80 G2
Hills Creek L. *OR* 43°43N 122°26W 94 C3
Hillsboro = Deerfield Beach
  FL .... 26°19N 80°6W 67 E8
Hillsboro *GA* .... 33°11N 83°38W 68 C3
Hillsboro *IL* .... 39°9N 89°29W 71 D4
Hillsboro *IN* .... 40°6N 87°8W 72 C3
Hillsboro *MD* .... 38°55N 75°50W 77 B5
Hillsboro *MO* .... 38°14N 90°34W 82 C6
Hillsboro *ND* .... 47°26N 97°3W 91 C8
Hillsboro *NH* .... 43°7N 71°54W 86 C3
Hillsboro *OH* .... 39°12N 83°37W 92 D3
Hillsboro *TX* .... 32°1N 97°8W 99 E10

Hillsboro *VA* .... 39°12N 77°43W 77 A3
Hillsboro *WV* .... 38°8N 80°13W 102 C4
Hillsboro *WI* .... 43°39N 90°21W 103 E3
Hillsboro Canal *FL* 26°30N 80°15W 67 E8
Hillsborough *NC*. 36°5N 79°7W 90 B6
Hillsborough *NH*. 43°7N 71°54W 86 C3
Hillsborough Bay
  FL .... 27°50N 82°26W 119 B4
Hillsborough County ☆
  FL .... 27°50N 82°20W 67 D6
Hillsborough County ☆
  NH .... 42°50N 71°45W 86 D3
Hillsborough Upper Village
  NH .... 43°9N 71°58W 86 C3
Hillsdale *IL* ..... 41°37N 90°11W 71 B3
Hillsdale *KS* .... 38°40N 94°51W 74 C9
Hillsdale *MI* .... 41°56N 84°38W 79 H7
Hillsdale *MO* .... 38°41N 90°17W 117 A2
Hillsdale *NY* .... 42°11N 73°32W 78 B1
Hillsdale *OK* .... 36°34N 97°59W 93 B6
Hillsdale County ☆
  MI .... 41°50N 84°40W 79 H7
Hillside = Belle Glade
  FL .... 26°41N 80°40W 67 E8
Hillside *IL* ..... 41°52N 87°54W 108 B2
Hillside *NJ* ..... 40°42N 74°13W 114 B1
Hillside *NY* ..... 40°42N 73°47W 114 B4
Hillside Manor *NY* 40°45N 73°40W 114 B4
Hillsmere Shores *MD* 38°56N 76°32W 77 B4
Hillsville *VA* .... 36°46N 80°44W 102 E4
Hilltonia *GA* .... 32°53N 81°40W 68 D5
Hilltop *MN* ..... 45°3N 93°14W 113 A2
Hillview *KY* ..... 38°5N 85°49W 97 B7
Hillwood *VA* .... 38°52N 77°9W 119 B3
Hilo *HI* .... 19°44N 155°5W 69 D6
Hilo → (ITO) *HI*. 19°43N 155°2W 69 D6
Hilo B. *HI* ..... 19°45N 155°5W 69 D6
Hilshire Village *TX* 29°47N 95°29W 110 B2
Hilt *CA* .... 41°50N 122°37W 64 B4
Hilton *NY* ...... 43°17N 77°48W 89 B3
Hilton Head Island
  SC .... 32°13N 80°45W 90 F5
Hinckley *IL* ..... 41°46N 88°38W 71 B5
Hinckley *MN* .... 46°1N 92°56W 80 D6
Hinckley *UT* .... 39°20N 112°40W 100 D3
Hinckley Res. *NY* 43°19N 75°7W 89 B5
Hindman *KY* .... 37°20N 82°59W 97 C10
Hinds County ☆ *MS* 32°16N 90°25W 81 D3
Hindsboro *IL* .... 39°41N 88°8W 71 D5
Hines *FL* ...... 29°45N 83°14W 67 B5
Hines *OR* ...... 43°34N 119°5W 94 D6
Hinesburg *VT* ... 44°18N 73°6W 86 B1
Hinesville *GA* ... 31°51N 81°36W 68 E5
Hingham *MT* .... 48°33N 110°25W 83 B7
Hingham *MA* .... 42°14N 70°54W 106 B4
Hingham B. *MA*.. 42°17N 70°56W 106 B4
Hingham Harbor
  MA .... 42°15N 70°53W 106 B4
Hinsdale *IL* ..... 41°48N 87°56W 108 C2
Hinsdale *MA* .... 42°26N 73°8W 78 B1
Hinsdale *MT* .... 48°24N 107°5W 83 B10
Hinsdale *NH* .... 42°47N 72°29W 86 D2
Hinsdale County ☆
  CO .... 37°50N 107°20W 66 E3
Hinson *FL* ...... 30°39N 84°25W 67 A4
Hinton *IA* ...... 42°38N 96°18W 73 C2
Hinton *OK* ...... 35°28N 98°21W 93 C5
Hinton *WV* ...... 37°40N 80°54W 102 D4
Hiram *GA* ...... 33°52N 84°46W 68 C1
Hiram *OH* ...... 41°19N 81°9W 92 B5
History Center *GA* 33°45N 84°22W 106 B2
Hitchcock *OK* ... 35°58N 98°21W 93 C5
Hitchcock *SD* ... 44°38N 98°25W 91 F7
Hitchcock *TX* ... 29°21N 95°1W 99 H12
Hitchcock County ☆
  NE .... 40°15N 101°0W 84 D4
Hitchita *OK* .... 35°31N 95°44W 93 C8
Hitterdal *MN* .... 46°59N 96°16W 80 D2
Hiwassee *VA* .... 36°58N 80°43W 102 E4
Hiwasse *AR* .... 36°36N 94°22W 63 B1
Hiwassee → *TN*. 35°19N 84°47W 97 E8
Hiwassee L. *NC*.. 35°21N 83°58W 90 C2
Hixton *WI* ..... 44°23N 91°1W 103 D2
Hoback Junction
  WY .... 43°19N 110°44W 104 C2
Hoback Pk. *WY*.. 43°5N 110°34W 104 C2
Hobart *IN* ...... 41°32N 87°15W 72 B3
Hobart *NY* ...... 42°22N 74°40W 89 C6
Hobart *OK* ...... 35°1N 99°6W 93 C4
Hobbs *NM* ...... 32°42N 103°8W 88 E7
Hobe Sound *FL*.. 27°4N 80°8W 67 D8
Hoberg *MO* ..... 37°4N 93°51W 82 D3
Hoboken *GA* .... 31°11N 82°8W 68 E4
Hoboken *NJ* .... 40°44N 74°3W 114 B2
Hobson *MT* ..... 47°0N 109°52W 83 C8
Hochheim *TX* ... 29°19N 97°17W 99 H11
Hockessin *DE* ... 39°47N 75°42W 77 A5
Hocking *OH* .... 39°12N 81°45W 92 D5
Hocking County ☆
  OH .... 39°32N 82°25W 92 D4
Hockley = Levelland
  TX .... 33°35N 102°23W 98 D5
Hockley County ☆
  TX .... 33°35N 102°23W 98 D5
Hodge *LA* ...... 32°17N 92°43W 75 B3
Hodgeman County ☆
  KS .... 38°0N 100°0W 74 C4
Hodgenville *KY*.. 37°34N 85°44W 97 C7
Hodges *SC* ..... 34°17N 82°10W 90 D3
Hodgkins *IL* .... 41°46N 87°53W 108 C2
Hoehne *CO* ..... 37°17N 104°23W 66 E6
Hoffman *IL* ..... 38°32N 89°16W 71 E4
Hoffman *MN* .... 45°50N 95°48W 80 E3
Hoffman *OK* .... 35°29N 95°51W 93 C8
Hoffman *NC* .... 35°47N 79°33W 90 C6
Hoffman I. *NY*... 40°35N 74°3W 114 C2
Hog I. *MI* ...... 45°48N 85°22W 79 C6
Hog I. *VA* ...... 37°26N 75°42W 102 D9
Hogansville *GA*.. 33°10N 84°55W 68 C2
Hogback Mt. *MT*. 44°54N 112°7W 83 F5
Hogback Mt. *ND*. 44°44N 103°42W 84 C2
Hogeland *MT* ... 48°51N 108°40W 83 B9
Hogup Mts. *UT*.. 41°30N 113°7W 100 B2
Hoh Indian Reservation
  WA .... 47°44N 124°25W 101 C1
Hohenwald *TN*... 35°33N 87°33W 96 E5
Hohokam Pima Nat. Monument △
  AZ .... 33°11N 111°56W 62 D4
Hoisington *KS*... 38°31N 98°47W 74 C5
Hoke County ☆ *NC* 35°0N 79°15W 90 C6
Holbrook *AZ* .... 34°54N 110°10W 62 C5
Holbrook *ID* .... 42°10N 112°39W 70 G6
Holbrook *MA* .... 42°9N 71°1W 78 B3
Holbrook *NY* .... 40°49N 73°5W 87 B3
Holbrook *NE* .... 40°18N 100°1W 84 D5
Holcomb *KS* .... 37°59N 100°59W 74 D3
Holcomb *MS* .... 33°46N 89°59W 81 C4
Holcomb *MO* .... 36°54N 90°2W 82 E6
Holcombe *WI* ... 45°14N 91°10W 103 C2
Holden *MA* ..... 42°21N 71°52W 78 B3
Holden *MO* ..... 38°43N 94°1W 82 C3
Holden *UT* ..... 39°6N 112°16W 100 D3
Holden, L. *FL*... 28°30N 81°23W 115 B2
Holden Beach *NC* 33°55N 78°15W 90 E7
Holdenville *OK*.. 35°5N 96°24W 93 C7
Holder *FL* ...... 28°58N 82°25W 67 C6
Holderness *NH*.. 43°43N 71°37W 86 C3
Holdingford *MN*. 45°44N 94°28W 80 E4
Holdrege *NE* .... 40°26N 99°23W 84 D6
Holgate *OH* .... 41°15N 84°8W 92 B2

Holgate *OH* ..... 41°15N 84°8W 92 B2
Holladay *UT* .... 40°40N 111°49W 117 C3
Holladay *TN* .... 35°52N 88°9W 96 B4
Holland *AR* ..... 35°10N 92°16W 63 C3
Holland *GA* ..... 34°21N 85°22W 68 B1
Holland *IA* ..... 42°24N 92°48W 73 C6
Holland *MI* ..... 42°47N 86°7W 79 G5
Holland *MN* ..... 44°6N 96°11W 80 F2
Holland *MO* ..... 36°3N 89°52W 82 E7
Holland *TX* ..... 30°53N 97°24W 99 G10
Holland Patent *NY* 43°15N 75°15W 89 B5
Hollandale *MS*... 33°10N 90°51W 81 C3
Hollandale *WI*... 42°53N 89°56W 103 F3
Hollenberg *KS*... 39°58N 96°59W 74 B7
Holley *FL* ...... 30°27N 86°54W 67 A2
Holley *NY* ...... 43°14N 78°2W 89 B2
Holliday *TX* .... 33°49N 98°42W 99 D9
Hollidaysburg *PA* 40°26N 78°24W 95 D4
Hollins *VA* ..... 37°20N 79°57W 102 D5
Hollis *AR* ...... 34°52N 93°7W 63 D2
Hollis *KS* ...... 39°38N 97°34W 74 B6
Hollis *NH* ...... 42°45N 71°36W 86 D3
Hollis *OK* ...... 34°41N 99°55W 93 D4
Hollister *CA* .... 36°51N 121°24W 64 G5
Hollister *ID* .... 42°21N 114°35W 70 G4
Hollister *MO* ... 36°38N 93°12W 82 E3
Hollister *OK* .... 34°21N 98°52W 93 D5
Holliston *MA* .... 42°12N 71°26W 78 B3
Holloman Air Force Base
  NM .... 32°50N 106°4W 88 E4
Hollow Rock *TN*. 36°2N 88°16W 96 A4
Holloway *MN* ... 45°15N 95°55W 80 E3
Holloway *CO* .... 38°3N 102°7W 66 D8
Holly *CO* ...... 38°3N 102°7W 66 D8
Holly Bluff *MS*.. 32°49N 90°43W 81 D3
Holly Grove *AR*.. 34°36N 91°12W 63 D4
Holly Hill *FL* .... 29°16N 81°3W 67 B7
Holly Hill *SC* ... 33°19N 80°25W 90 E5
Holly Pond *AL* ... 34°10N 86°37W 60 B4
Holly Ridge *NC*.. 34°30N 77°33W 90 D8
Holly Springs *GA* 34°10N 84°30W 68 B2
Holly Springs *MS* 34°46N 89°27W 81 B4
Holly Springs *NC* 35°39N 78°50W 90 C7
Holly Springs Nat. Forest
  MS .... 34°44N 89°8W 81 B4
Hollywood *AL* ... 34°44N 85°59W 60 B5
Hollywood *CA* ... 34°5N 118°19W 111 B3
Hollywood *FL* .... 26°0N 80°8W 112 B3
Hollywood *MD* ... 38°21N 76°34W 77 B4
Hollywood *SC* ... 32°44N 80°15W 90 F5
Hollywood Bowl
  CA .... 34°7N 118°20W 111 B2
Hollywood-Burbank ✈ (BUR)
  CA .... 34°12N 118°22W 111 A3
Hollywood Lake *CA* 34°5N 118°20W 111 B3
Hollywood Park *TX* 29°36N 98°29W 111 C3
Holman *NM* .... 36°2N 105°23W 88 A5
Holman Field = St. Paul
  Downtown ✈ *MN* 44°56N 93°3W 113 B3
Holmen *WI* ..... 43°58N 91°15W 103 E2
Holmes Beach *FL* 27°31N 82°43W 67 D6
Holmes County ☆
  FL .... 30°50N 85°45W 67 A3
Holmes County ☆ *MS* 33°7N 90°3W 81 C3
Holmes County ☆
  OH .... 40°33N 81°55W 92 C5
Holmes Cr. → *FL* 30°30N 85°50W 67 A3
Holmes Run Acres
  VA .... 38°51N 77°13W 119 B2
Holmesville *OH*.. 40°38N 81°56W 92 C5
Holopaw *FL* .... 28°8N 81°5W 67 C7
Holstein *IA* ..... 42°29N 95°33W 73 C3
Holstein *NE* .... 40°28N 98°39W 84 D7
Holston → *TN*.. 35°58N 83°51W 97 E9
Holt *AL* .... 33°14N 87°29W 60 C3
Holt *FL* .... 30°43N 86°45W 67 A2
Holt *MN* ...... 48°18N 96°11W 80 B2
Holt *MO* ...... 39°27N 94°21W 82 B2
Holt County ☆ *NE* 42°30N 98°45W 84 B7
Holt County ☆ *MO* 40°5N 95°12W 82 A2
Holton *IN* ..... 39°5N 85°23W 72 D5
Holton *KS* ..... 39°28N 95°44W 74 B8
Holts Summit *MO* 38°38N 92°7W 82 C4
Holtville *CA* .... 32°49N 115°23W 65 L11
Holualoa *HI* .... 19°37N 155°57W 69 D6
Holy Cross *AK*.. 62°12N 159°46W 61 E8
Holyoke *CO* .... 40°35N 102°18W 66 B8
Holyoke *MA* .... 42°12N 72°37W 78 B2
Holyrood *KS* .... 38°35N 98°25W 74 C5
Homasote *NJ* ... 40°11N 74°42W 87 B2
Homedale *ID* ... 43°37N 116°56W 70 F2
Homeland *GA* ... 30°51N 82°1W 68 F4
Homeland Park *SC* 34°28N 82°40W 90 D3
Homer *AK* ..... 59°39N 151°33W 61 F9
Homer *GA* ..... 34°20N 83°30W 68 B3
Homer *LA* ..... 32°48N 93°4W 75 B2
Homer *MI* ..... 42°9N 84°49W 79 G7
Homer *NY* ..... 42°38N 76°11W 89 C4
Homer City *PA*.. 40°32N 79°10W 95 D3
Homer Youngs Pk.
  MT .... 45°19N 113°41W 83 E4
Homerville *GA*.. 31°2N 82°45W 68 E4
Homestead *FL*... 25°28N 80°29W 67 F8
Homestead *PA*... 40°24N 79°54W 116 B2
Homestead Nat. Monument of
  America *NE* ... 40°17N 96°50W 84 D9
Hometown *IL* ... 41°44N 87°42W 108 C2
Homewood *AL*... 33°29N 86°47W 60 C4
Homewood *IL*... 41°34N 87°40W 71 B6
Hominy *OK* .... 36°25N 96°24W 93 B7
Homochitto Nat. Forest
  MS .... 31°15N 90°45W 81 E3
Homosassa Springs
  FL .... 28°48N 82°35W 67 C6
Hon *AR* .... 34°47N 94°11W 63 D1
Honaker *VA* .... 37°1N 81°59W 102 D3
Honaunau *HI* ... 19°26N 155°55W 69 D6
Hondo *NM* ..... 33°24N 105°16W 88 D5
Hondo *TX* ..... 29°21N 99°9W 99 H8
Hondo, Rio → *CA* 34°2N 118°15W 111 B4
Honea Path *SC*.. 34°27N 82°24W 90 D3
Honesdale *PA*... 41°34N 75°16W 95 C7
Honey Brook *PA*. 40°6N 75°55W 95 D7
Honey Grove *TX* 33°35N 95°55W 99 D12
Honey Island *TX* 30°24N 94°25W 99 G13
Honey L. *CA*.... 40°15N 120°19W 64 C6
Honeoye *NY* .... 42°47N 77°31W 89 C3
Honeoye Falls *NY* 42°57N 77°35W 89 C3
Honeyville *UT*... 41°38N 112°5W 100 B3
Honga *MD* ..... 38°16N 76°14W 77 B4
Honga → *MD*... 38°16N 76°12W 77 B4
Honokaa *HI* .... 20°5N 155°28W 69 C6
Honokahua *HI*... 21°0N 156°40W 69 B5
Honokohau *HI*... 21°2N 159°46W 69 A2
Honolulu *HI* .... 21°19N 157°52W 69 K14
Honolulu District ☆
  HI .... 21°19N 157°46W 69 K14
Honolulu Int. ✈ (HNL)
  HI .... 21°19N 157°55W 69 K14
Honolulu Watershed Forest
  Reserve *HI* ... 21°21N 157°48W 69 K14

Honomu *HI* ..... 19°52N 155°7W 69 D6
Honor *MI* ...... 44°40N 86°1W 79 E5
Honouliuli *HI* ... 21°22N 158°2W 69 K13
Honouliuli Forest Reserve
  HI .... 21°25N 158°4W 69 K13
Honu'apo B. *HI*.. 19°5N 155°33W 69 D6
Hood, Mt. *OR*... 45°23N 121°42W 94 B4
Hood Canal *WA*. 47°35N 123°0W 101 C2
Hood County ☆ *TX* 32°27N 97°47W 99 E10
Hood River *OR*.. 45°43N 121°31W 94 B4
Hood River County ☆
  OR .... 45°30N 121°20W 94 B4
Hoodsport *WA*... 47°24N 123°9W 101 C2
Hooker *OK* ..... 36°52N 101°13W 93 B2
Hooker County ☆
  NE .... 41°50N 101°0W 84 C4
Hooksett *NH* .... 43°5N 71°30W 86 D3
Ho'olehua *HI* ... 21°10N 157°5W 69 B4
Hoonah *AK* ..... 58°7N 135°27W 61 G14
Hoopa *CA* ..... 41°3N 123°41W 64 B3
Hoopa Valley Indian Reservation
  CA .... 41°10N 123°45W 64 B3
Hooper *CO* ..... 37°45N 105°53W 66 E5
Hooper *NE* ..... 41°37N 96°33W 84 C9
Hooper *WA* ..... 46°45N 118°9W 101 D7
Hooper Bay *AK*.. 61°32N 166°6W 61 F6
Hooper Str. *MD*. 38°15N 76°5W 77 B4
Hoopersville *MD*. 38°16N 76°10W 77 B4
Hoopeston *IL* ... 40°28N 87°40W 71 C6
Hoople *ND* ..... 48°32N 97°38W 91 B8
Hoosac Range U.S.A. 42°45N 73°2W 78 B1
Hoosic → *NY*... 42°56N 73°30W 78 B1
Hoosick Falls *NY* 42°54N 73°21W 78 B1
Hoosier Nat. Forest
  IN .... 38°30N 86°35W 72 E4
Hoover *AL* ..... 33°24N 86°49W 60 C4
Hoover Dam U.S.A. 36°1N 114°44W 62 A1
Hoover Res. *OH*.. 40°7N 82°53W 92 C4
Hooversville *PA*. 40°9N 78°55W 95 D4
Hop Bottom *PA*.. 41°42N 75°46W 95 C7
Hopatcong *NJ*... 40°55N 74°40W 87 B2
Hopatcong, L. *NJ* 40°55N 74°37W 87 B2
Hope *AZ* ...... 33°43N 113°42W 62 D2
Hope *AK* ...... 60°54N 149°38W 61 F10
Hope *IN* ...... 39°18N 85°46W 72 D5
Hope *KS* ...... 38°41N 97°5W 74 C6
Hope *ND* ...... 47°19N 97°43W 91 C8
Hope *NM* ...... 32°49N 104°44W 88 E6
Hope, Pt. *AK*... 68°21N 166°47W 61 B6
Hope Mills *NC*.. 34°59N 78°57W 90 D7
Hope Valley *RI*.. 41°30N 71°43W 78 C3
Hopedale *IL* .... 40°26N 89°25W 71 C4
Hopedale *MA* ... 42°8N 71°33W 78 B3
Hopelawn *NJ* ... 40°31N 74°17W 114 C1
Hopeton *OK* .... 36°41N 98°40W 93 B5
Hopewell *TN* ... 35°14N 84°53W 97 E8
Hopewell *VA* .... 37°18N 77°17W 102 D7
Hopewell Culture Nat. Historical
  Park △ *OH* ... 39°17N 82°55W 92 D4
Hopewell Furnace Nat. Historical
  Park △ *PA* ... 40°12N 75°47W 95 D7
Hopi Indian Reservation
  AZ .... 35°45N 110°30W 62 B5
Hopkins *MI* .... 42°37N 85°46W 79 G6
Hopkins *MN* .... 44°55N 93°23W 113 B1
Hopkins *MO* .... 40°33N 94°49W 82 A2
Hopkins County ☆
  KY .... 37°20N 87°30W 96 C5
Hopkins County ☆
  TX .... 33°8N 95°36W 99 D12
Hopkinsville *KY*. 36°52N 87°29W 96 D5
Hopkinton *IA* ... 42°21N 91°15W 73 C7
Hopkinton *MA* ... 42°14N 71°31W 78 B3
Hopkinton *NH* ... 43°12N 71°41W 86 C3
Hopkinton *RI* ... 41°28N 71°48W 78 C3
Hoquiam *WA* ... 46°59N 123°53W 101 D2
Horace *KS* ..... 38°29N 101°47W 74 C2
Horace *ND* ..... 46°45N 96°54W 91 D9
Horatio *AR* ..... 33°56N 94°21W 63 D1
Hordville *NE* .... 41°5N 97°53W 84 C8
Horicon *WI* .... 43°26N 88°38W 103 D5
Horicon Nat. Wildlife Refuge △
  WI .... 43°35N 88°38W 103 E5
Hormigueros
  Puerto Rico .. 18°8N 67°8W 105 G15
Horn L. *MS* .... 30°14N 88°39W 81 F5
Horn Lake *MS*.. 34°58N 90°2W 81 B3
Hornbeak *TN*... 36°20N 89°18W 96 D3
Hornbeck *LA* ... 31°20N 93°24W 75 C2
Hornbrook *CA*... 41°55N 122°33W 64 B4
Hornell *NY* ..... 42°20N 77°40W 89 C3
Hornersville *MO*. 36°2N 90°7W 82 E6
Hornitos *CA* .... 37°30N 120°14W 64 F6
Hornsby *TN* .... 35°14N 88°50W 96 B4
Horry County ☆ *SC* 35°0N 79°0W 90 E7
Horse → *CO*... 38°5N 103°19W 66 D7
Horse Cave *KY*.. 37°11N 85°55W 97 C7
Horse Cr. → *NE* 41°57N 103°58W 84 C2
Horse Cr. → *WY* 41°57N 103°58W 104 E7
Horse Creek *WY* 41°25N 105°11W 104 E7
Horse Creek Res.
  CO .... 38°10N 103°24W 66 D7
Horse Heaven Hills
  WA .... 46°3N 119°30W 101 D6
Horse L. *CA* .... 40°40N 120°31W 64 C6
Horse Pasture *VA* 36°39N 79°57W 102 E5
Horseheads L. *ND* 47°3N 99°47W 91 C6
Horseheads *NY*. 42°10N 76°49W 89 C4
Horsehoe Bend *AR* 36°14N 91°46W 63 B4
Horseshoe Bend Nat. Military
  Park △ *AL* ... 32°59N 85°44W 60 D5
Horseshoe Lake State Park
  IL .... 38°41N 90°5W 117 A3
Horseshoe Res. *AZ* 33°59N 111°42W 62 C4
Horseshoe L. *IL*. 37°9N 89°21W 71 G5
Horton *KS* ..... 39°40N 95°32W 74 B8
Hortonville *WI*.. 44°20N 88°38W 103 D5
Hosford *FL* .... 30°23N 84°48W 67 A4
Hoskins *NE* .... 42°7N 97°18W 84 C8
Hoskinston *KY*.. 37°5N 83°24W 97 D9
Hosmer *SD* .... 45°34N 99°28W 91 E6
Hospers *IA* .... 43°5N 95°54W 73 B3
Hot Creek Range
  NV .... 38°40N 116°20W 85 D4
Hot Spring County ☆
  AR .... 34°14N 92°55W 63 D3
Hot Springs = Truth or
  Consequences *NM* 33°8N 107°15W 88 D3
Hot Springs *AR*. 34°31N 93°3W 63 D2
Hot Springs *MT*. 47°37N 114°40W 83 C3
Hot Springs *SD*. 43°26N 103°29W 91 G2
Hot Springs *VA*. 37°59N 79°50W 102 D5
Hot Springs County ☆
  WY .... 43°55N 108°30W 104 C4
Hot Springs Nat. Park △
  AR .... 34°31N 93°3W 63 D2
Hot Springs Village
  AR .... 34°40N 93°0W 63 D3
Hot Sulphur Springs
  CO .... 40°4N 106°6W 66 B4
Hotchkiss *CO* ... 38°48N 107°43W 66 D3
Hotevilla *AZ* .... 35°56N 110°10W 62 B5
Houck *AZ* ..... 35°18N 109°12W 62 B6
Houghs Neck *MA* 42°15N 70°57W 106 B4

Houghton *MI* . . . . 47°7N 88°34W **79** B3
Houghton *NY* . . . . . . 42°25N 78°10W **89** C2
Houghton County ☆
   MI . . . . 47°0N 88°45W **79** C3
Houghton L. *MI* . . . . 44°21N 84°44W **79** E7
Houghton Lake *MI* . . 44°18N 84°45W **79** E7
Houlton *ME* . . . . . . 46°8N 67°51W **76** B6
Houma *LA* . . . . . . 29°36N 90°43W **75** E5
Housatonic *MA* . . . . 42°16N 73°22W **78** B1
Housatonic ➛ *CT* . . 41°10N 73°7W **78** C1
House *NM* . . . . . . 34°39N 103°54W **88** C7
House Range *UT* . 39°30N 113°20W **100** D2
Houston *AR* . . . . . . 35°2N 92°42W **63** C3
Houston *FL* . . . . . . 30°15N 82°54W **67** A6
Houston *MN* . . . . . 43°46N 91°34W **80** G7
Houston *MS* . . . . . 33°54N 89°0W **81** C4
Houston *MO* . . . . . 37°22N 91°58W **82** D5
Houston *TX* . . . . . . 29°45N 95°21W **110** B2
Houston, L. ➛ *LA* . . 30°16N 93°13W **75** D2
Houston, L. *TX* . . . . 29°55N 95°8W **99** H12
Houston County ☆
   AL . . . . 31°11N 85°14W **60** E5
Houston County ☆
   GA . . . . 32°20N 83°45W **68** D3
Houston County ☆
   MN . . . . 43°35N 91°30W **80** G7
Houston County ☆
   TN . . . . 36°19N 87°42W **96** D5
Houston County L.
   TX . . . . 31°25N 95°35W **99** F12
Houston George Bush
   Intercontinental ✕ (IAH)
   TX . . . . 29°59N 95°20W **99** H12
Houston William P. Hobby ✕
   (HOU) *TX* . . . . 29°38N 95°16W **110** C3
Houstonia *MO* . . . . 38°54N 93°22W **82** E3
Hoven *SD* . . . . . . 45°15N 99°47W **91** E6
Hovenweep Nat. Monument △
   CO . . . . 37°20N 109°0W **66** E2
Howard *MN* . . . . . 47°51N 89°58W **80** C2
Howard *CO* . . . . . . 38°27N 105°50W **66** D5
Howard *GA* . . . . . 32°36N 84°23W **68** D2
Howard *KS* . . . . . 37°28N 96°16W **74** D7
Howard *PA* . . . . . . 41°1N 77°40W **95** C5
Howard *SD* . . . . . . 44°1N 97°32W **91** F8
Howard *WI* . . . . . 44°33N 88°4W **103** D5
Howard Beach *NY* . 40°39N 73°50W **114** C3
Howard City *MI* . . 43°24N 85°28W **79** F6
Howard County ☆ *AR* . 34°7N 94°1W **63** D1
Howard County ☆ *IN* 40°30N 86°10W **72** C4
Howard County ☆ *IA* 43°20N 92°30W **73** D5
Howard County ☆
   MD . . . . 39°15N 77°0W **77** A4
Howard County ☆
   MO . . . . 39°10N 92°40W **82** B4
Howard County ☆
   NE . . . . 41°15N 98°30W **84** C7
Howard County ☆
   TX . . . . 32°15N 101°28W **98** E6
Howard Draw ➛
   TX . . . . 30°10N 101°35W **98** G6
Howard Hanson Res.
   WA . . . . . . 47°17N 121°47W **101** C4
Howard Lake *MN* . . 45°4N 94°4W **80** C4
Howard Prairie L.
   OR . . . . 42°13N 122°22W **94** E3
Howe *ID* . . . . 43°48N 113°0W **70** E5
Howe *IN* . . . . 41°43N 85°25W **72** B5
Howe *OK* . . . . . . 34°57N 94°38W **93** D9
Howe *TX* . . . . 33°30N 96°37W **99** D11
Howell *MI* . . . . . . 42°36N 83°56W **79** G8
Howell *UT* . . . . . 41°48N 112°27W **100** B3
Howell County ☆
   MO . . . . 36°45N 91°50W **82** E5
Howells *NE* . . . . . 41°44N 97°0W **84** C9
Howes *SD* . . . . . 44°37N 102°3W **91** F3
Howes Mill *MO* . . . 37°39N 91°16W **82** D5
Howland *ME* . . . . 45°14N 68°40W **76** C5
Howland L. Pac. Oc. 0°48N 176°38W **105** G8
Hoxie *AR* . . . . . . 36°3N 90°59W **63** B5
Hoxie *KS* . . . . . . 39°21N 100°26W **74** B3
Hoyleton *IL* . . . . . 38°27N 89°16W **71** E4
Hoyt *CO* . . . . 40°1N 104°5W **66** B6
Hoyt *KS* . . . . . . 39°15N 95°43W **74** B8
Hoyt Lakes *MN* . . 47°32N 92°8W **80** C6
Huachuca City *AZ* . 31°34N 110°21W **62** F5
Hualalai *HI* . . . . 19°42N 155°52W **69** D6
Hualapai Indian Reservation
   AZ . . . . 35°45N 113°20W **62** C1
Hualapai Mts. *AZ* . 34°45N 113°45W **62** C2
Hualapai Peak *AZ* . 35°5N 113°54W **62** C2
Hubbard *IA* . . . . . 42°18N 93°18W **73** C5
Hubbard *NE* . . . . . 42°23N 96°36W **84** B9
Hubbard *OH* . . . . 41°9N 80°34W **92** B6
Hubbard *OR* . . . . 45°11N 122°48W **94** B3
Hubbard *TX* . . . . 31°51N 96°48W **99** F11
Hubbard, Mt.
   N. Amer. . . . . 60°19N 139°4W **61** F13
Hubbard County ☆
   MN . . . . 47°10N 94°50W **80** C4
Hubbard Creek L.
   TX . . . . 32°50N 98°58W **99** E9
Hubbard L. *MI* . . 44°48N 83°34W **79** E8
Hubbardston *MA* . 42°28N 72°0W **78** B3
Hubbardston *VT* . 43°42N 73°12W **86** C1
Hubbell *MI* . . . . . 47°11N 88°26W **79** B3
Hubbell *NE* . . . . 40°1N 97°29W **84** D8
Hubbell Trading Post Nat. Historic
   Site △ *AZ* . . . 35°43N 109°33W **62** B6
Huber Heights *OH* . 39°50N 84°5W **92** D3
Huddy *KY* . . . . . 37°36N 82°17W **97** C10
Hudson *CO* . . . . 40°4N 104°39W **66** B6
Hudson *FL* . . . . . 28°22N 82°42W **67** C6
Hudson *IA* . . . . . 42°24N 92°28W **73** C6
Hudson *KS* . . . . 38°6N 98°40W **74** C5
Hudson *ME* . . . . 45°0N 68°53W **76** C5
Hudson *MI* . . . . 41°51N 84°21W **79** H7
Hudson *MD* . . . . 38°36N 76°15W **77** B4
Hudson *NC* . . . . 35°51N 81°30W **90** B5
Hudson *NH* . . . . 42°46N 71°26W **86** E3
Hudson *NY* . . . . 42°15N 73°46W **89** C7
Hudson *OH* . . . . 41°14N 81°26W **92** B5
Hudson *SD* . . . . 43°8N 96°28W **91** G9
Hudson *WI* . . . . 44°58N 92°45W **103** D1
Hudson ➛ *NY* . . 40°42N 74°2W **89** E6
Hudson, L. *OK* . . 36°14N 95°11W **93** B8
Hudson County ☆ *NJ* 40°45N 74°5W **87** B2
Hudson Falls *NY* . 43°18N 73°35W **89** C7
Hudsonville *MI* . . 42°52N 85°52W **79** G6
Hudspeth County ☆
   TX . . . . . . 31°30N 105°30W **98** F2
Hueco Mts. *TX* . . 31°53N 105°58W **98** F2
Hueneme = Port Hueneme
   CA . . . . 34°7N 119°12W **65** J7
Huerfano ➛ *CO* . 38°14N 104°15W **66** D6
Huerfano County ☆
   CO . . . . 37°40N 104°50W **66** E6
Hueytown *AL* . . . 33°27N 86°59W **60** C4
Huffman *TX* . . . . 30°1N 95°6W **99** G12
Hugh Butler L. *NE* 40°21N 100°39W **84** D5
Hugh Taylor Birch State Recr.
   Area △ *FL* . . 26°8N 80°6W **112** B3
Hughes *AK* . . . . 66°3N 154°15W **61** C9
Hughes County ☆ *OK* 35°0N 96°15W **93** C7
Hughes County ☆ *SD* 44°30N 100°0W **91** F5
Hughes Springs *TX* 33°0N 94°38W **99** E13
Hughesville *MD* . 38°32N 76°47W **77** B4
Hughesville *MO* . 38°50N 93°18W **82** C3

Hughesville *PA* . . 41°14N 76°44W **95** C5
Hughson *CA* . . . 37°36N 120°52W **64** F6
Hugo *CO* . . . . . 39°8N 103°28W **66** C7
Hugo *OK* . . . . . 34°1N 95°31W **93** D8
Hugoton *KS* . . . 37°11N 101°21W **74** D2
Huguenot *NY* . . . 41°28N 74°11W **114** C1
Huguenot Park *NY* 40°33N 74°11W **114** C1
Hulah L. *OK* . . . 36°56N 96°5W **93** B7
Hulbert *MI* . . . . 46°21N 85°9W **79** C6
Hulbert *OK* . . . . 35°56N 95°9W **93** C8
Huletts Landing *NY* 43°38N 73°30W **86** C1
Hulett *WY* . . . . 44°41N 104°36W **104** B8
Hull *FL* . . . . 27°7N 81°56W **67** D7
Hull *IL* . . . . 39°43N 91°13W **71** D2
Hull *IA* . . . . 43°11N 96°8W **73** B2
Hull *MA* . . . . . 42°18N 70°54W **106** B4
Humacao
   Puerto Rico . 18°9N 65°50W **105** G17
Humansville *MO* . 37°48N 93°35W **82** D3
Humble *TX* . . . . 30°0N 95°18W **99** H12
Humble City *NM* . 32°47N 103°19W **88** D7
Humboldt *AZ* . . . 34°30N 112°14W **62** C3
Humboldt *IL* . . . 39°36N 88°19W **71** D5
Humboldt *IA* . . . 42°44N 94°13W **73** C4
Humboldt *KS* . . . 37°49N 95°26W **74** D8
Humboldt *NE* . . . 40°10N 95°57W **84** D10
Humboldt *SD* . . . 43°39N 97°5W **91** G8
Humboldt *TN* . . . 35°50N 88°55W **96** E4
Humboldt ➛ *NV* . 39°59N 118°36W **85** C2
Humboldt B. *CA* . 40°45N 124°10W **64** C2
Humboldt County ☆
   CA . . . . . . 40°50N 124°0W **64** C3
Humboldt County ☆
   IA . . . . 42°50N 94°10W **73** C4
Humboldt County ☆
   NV . . . . . . 41°20N 118°10W **85** A2
Humboldt Nat. Forest
   NV . . . . . 41°45N 115°30W **85** A5
Humboldt Park *IL* 41°54N 87°42W **108** B2
Humboldt Peak *CO* 37°59N 105°33W **66** D5
Humboldt Range
   NV . . . . . 40°20N 118°0W **85** B2
Humboldt Redwoods State Park △
   CA . . . . . 40°19N 123°59W **64** C3
Humboldt Salt Marsh
   NV . . . . . 39°50N 117°55W **85** D3
Humboldt Sink *NV* 40°1N 118°38W **85** B2
Humboldt-Toiyabe Nat. Forest
   NV . . . . . 40°30N 117°0W **85** D4
Hume *MO* . . . . 38°6N 94°34W **82** C2
Hume *VA* . . . . 38°50N 78°0W **77** B3
Humeston *IA* . . 40°52N 93°30W **73** E5
Humnoke *AR* . . 34°25N 91°43W **63** D4
Humphrey *AR* . . 34°25N 91°43W **63** D4
Humphrey *ID* . . 44°29N 112°14W **70** E6
Humphrey *NE* . . 41°42N 97°29W **84** C8
Humphreys *OK* . 34°33N 99°14W **93** D6
Humphreys, Mt. *CA* 37°17N 118°40W **65** F8
Humphreys County ☆
   MS . . . . . 33°6N 90°30W **81** C3
Humphreys County ☆
   TN . . . . . 36°5N 87°48W **96** D5
Humphreys Peak
   AZ . . . . . 35°21N 111°41W **62** B4
Hundred *WV* . . 39°41N 80°28W **102** B4
Hungry Horse *MT* 48°23N 114°4W **83** B3
Hungry Horse Res.
   MT . . . . 48°21N 114°1W **83** B3
Hunnewell *KS* . 37°1N 97°25W **74** D7
Hunnewell *MO* . 39°40N 91°52W **82** B5
Hunt *TX* . . . . 30°4N 99°20W **99** G8
Hunt County ☆ *TX* 33°8N 96°7W **99** E11
Hunt Mt. *WY* . 44°55N 107°59W **104** B5
Hunter *ND* . . 47°12N 97°13W **91** C8
Hunter *OK* . . 36°34N 97°40W **93** B6
Hunters Creek Village
   TX . . . . 29°46N 95°30W **110** B2
Hunters Pt. *CA* . 37°43N 122°21W **118** B2
Hunters Valley *VA* 38°54N 77°17W **119** B2
Hunterstown *PA* 39°53N 77°0W **95** D4
Huntersville *NC* 35°25N 80°51W **90** C5
Huntertown *IN* 41°14N 85°10W **72** B5
Huntingdon *PA* 40°30N 78°1W **95** D4
Huntingdon *TN* 36°0N 88°26W **96** E4
Huntingdon County ☆
   PA . . . . 40°15N 78°0W **95** D5
Huntington = Shelton
   CT . . . . 41°19N 73°5W **78** C1
Huntington *AR* 35°5N 94°16W **63** C1
Huntington *IN* 40°53N 85°30W **72** C5
Huntington *MA* 42°14N 72°53W **78** B2
Huntington *NY* 40°52N 73°26W **78** D1
Huntington *OR* 44°21N 117°16W **94** C8
Huntington *TX* 31°17N 94°34W **99** F13
Huntington *UT* 39°20N 110°58W **100** D5
Huntington *VA* 38°47N 77°4W **119** C3
Huntington *VT* 44°18N 72°59W **86** C2
Huntington *WV* 38°25N 82°27W **102** C2
Huntington ➛ *NV* 40°37N 115°43W **85** B5
Huntington ➛ *UT* 39°7N 110°55W **100** D5
Huntington Beach
   CA . . . . 33°40N 118°0W **65** K8
Huntington County ☆
   IN . . . . 40°50N 85°30W **72** C5
Huntington Park
   CA . . . . 33°58N 118°13W **111** C3
Huntington Station
   NY . . . . 40°51N 73°25W **87** B3
Huntington Woods
   MI . . . . 42°28N 83°10W **109** A1
Huntland *MD* . 38°37N 76°37W **77** A4
Huntland *TN* . 35°3N 86°16W **96** E6
Huntley *IL* . . 42°10N 88°26W **71** A5
Huntley *MT* . 45°54N 108°19W **83** D9
Hunts Point *WA* 47°38N 122°13W **118** C4
Huntsville *AL* 34°44N 86°35W **60** B4
Huntsville *AR* 36°5N 93°44W **63** B2
Huntsville *KY* 37°10N 86°53W **96** C6
Huntsville *MO* 39°26N 92°33W **82** B4
Huntsville *OH* 40°26N 83°48W **92** C3
Huntsville *TN* 36°25N 84°29W **97** D8
Huntsville *TX* 30°43N 95°33W **99** G12
Huntsville *UT* 41°16N 111°46W **100** B4
Hurdsfield *ND* 47°26N 99°55W **91** C6
Hurley *MS* . 30°40N 88°30W **81** F5
Hurley *MO* 36°56N 93°30W **82** E3
Hurley *NM* 32°42N 108°8W **88** E2
Hurley *NY* 41°55N 74°4W **89** D6
Hurley *SD* 43°17N 97°5W **91** G8
Hurley *WI* 46°27N 90°11W **103** B3
Hurlock *MD* 38°37N 75°52W **77** B5
Huron *CA* 36°12N 120°6W **65** G6
Huron *IN* 38°44N 86°40W **72** E4
Huron *OH* 41°24N 82°33W **92** B4
Huron *SD* 44°22N 98°13W **91** F7
Huron ➛ *MI* 42°2N 83°11W **79** G8
Huron, L. *MI* 44°30N 82°40W **79** E9
Huron Bay *MI* 46°54N 88°13W **79** C4
Huron Beach *MI* 45°30N 84°6W **79** D7
Huron County ☆ *MI* 43°50N 83°0W **79** F9
Huron County ☆ *OH* 41°15N 82°37W **92** B4
Huron Mts. *MI* 46°50N 88°0W **79** C4
Huron Nat. Forest *MI* 44°30N 84°0W **79** E8

Huron Potawatomi Indian
   Reservation *MI* . 42°55N 85°16W **79** G6
Hurricane *UT* . . 37°11N 113°17W **100** F2
Hurricane *WV* . 38°26N 82°1W **102** C2
Hurricane Cliffs *AZ* 36°45N 113°20W **62** A2
Hurricane L. *ND* 48°26N 99°31W **91** B6
Hurst *TX* . . . . 32°49N 97°11W **109** B3
Hurt *VA* . . . . 37°6N 79°18W **102** D5
Hurtsboro *AL* . 32°15N 85°25W **60** D5
Huslia *AK* . . . 65°41N 156°24W **61** C8
Hustisford *WI* . 43°21N 88°36W **103** E5
Hustle *VA* . . . 38°3N 77°4W **77** B3
Hustonville *KY* . 37°28N 84°49W **97** C8
Husum *WA* . . 45°48N 121°29W **101** A4
Hutch Mt. *AZ* . 34°47N 111°22W **62** C4
Hutchins *TX* . . 32°38N 96°42W **109** C5
Hutchinson *KS* . 38°5N 97°56W **74** C6
Hutchinson *MN* 44°54N 94°22W **80** F4
Hutchinson County ☆
   SD . . . . . 43°25N 97°48W **91** G8
Hutchinson County ☆
   TX . . . . . 35°50N 101°30W **98** B6
Hutsonville *IL* 39°7N 87°40W **71** D6
Huttig *AR* . . . 33°2N 92°11W **63** E3
Hutto *TX* . . . 30°33N 97°33W **99** G10
Hutton *ID* . . . 39°25N 79°28W **77** A1
Huttonsville *WV* 38°43N 79°59W **102** C5
Huxford *AL* . . 31°13N 87°28W **60** E3
Huxley *IA* . . 41°54N 93°36W **73** D5
Huyett *MD* . . 39°40N 77°20W **77** A3
Hyak *WA* . . 47°24N 121°24W **101** C4
Hyannis *MA* 41°39N 70°17W **78** C4
Hyannis *NE* 42°0N 101°46W **84** C4
Hyattsville *MD* 38°57N 76°57W **119** B4
Hyattsville *WY* 44°15N 107°36W **104** B5
Hybart *AL* . 31°50N 87°23W **60** D3
Hyco L. *NC* 36°31N 79°3W **90** A6
Hydaburg *AK* 55°15N 132°50W **61** J14
Hyde *VA* . . 45°30N 76°20W **90** C9
Hyde County ☆ *SD* 44°31N 99°27W **91** F6
Hyde Park *ID* 41°47N 87°55W **108** C3
Hyde Park *MA* 42°15N 71°7W **106** B3
Hyde Park *NY* 41°47N 73°56W **89** D7
Hyde Park *VT* 44°36N 72°37W **86** B2
Hyden *KY* . 37°10N 83°22W **97** C9
Hydes *MD* 39°30N 76°29W **77** A4
Hydro *OK* 35°33N 98°39W **93** C5
Hygiene *CO* 40°11N 105°11W **66** B5
Hymera *IN* 39°11N 87°18W **72** D3
Hyndman *PA* 39°49N 78°43W **77** A2
Hyndman Peak *ID* 43°45N 114°8W **70** F4
Hyrum *UT* 41°38N 111°51W **100** B4
Hysham *MT* 46°18N 107°14W **83** D10

I

Iaeger *WV* . . 37°28N 81°49W **102** D3
Iamonia L. *FL* 30°38N 84°14W **67** A4
Iatan *MO* . . 39°29N 94°59W **82** B2
Iatt L. *LA* . 31°35N 92°40W **75** C3
Ibapah *UT* . 40°2N 113°59W **100** C2
Ibapah Pk. *UT* 40°2N 113°53W **100** C2
Iberia *MO* . 38°5N 92°18W **82** C4
Iberia Parish ☆ *LA* 30°1N 91°49W **75** D4
Iberville Parish ☆
   LA . . . . 30°17N 91°14W **75** D4
Icard *NC* . 35°44N 81°28W **90** C4
Ice Harbor Dam
   WA . . . 46°15N 118°53W **101** D7
Icy C. *AK* . 70°20N 161°52W **61** A7
Ida *MI* . . 41°55N 83°34W **79** H8
Ida County ☆ *IA* 42°25N 95°30W **73** C3
Ida Grove *IA* 42°21N 95°28W **73** C3
Idabel *OK* 33°54N 94°50W **93** E9
Idaho □ *U.S.A.* 45°0N 115°0W **70** D4
Idaho City *ID* 43°50N 115°50W **70** F4
Idaho Falls *ID* 43°30N 112°2W **70** F6
Idaho Nat. Engineering Laboratory
   ID . . . 43°38N 112°45W **70** F6
Idaho Springs *CO* 39°45N 105°31W **66** C5
Idalia *CO* 39°43N 102°18W **66** C8
Idalou *TX* 33°40N 101°41W **98** D4
Idana *KS* 39°38N 96°57W **74** B6
Idanha *OR* 44°42N 122°5W **94** C3
Ideal *GA* 32°22N 84°11W **68** D2
Ideal *SD* 43°33N 99°54W **91** G6
Ideal *AL* 34°43N 85°41W **60** B5
Idlewild *NC* 35°11N 80°44W **107** A2
Idria *CA* 36°25N 120°41W **65** G6
Iguacu *AK* 59°20N 155°55W **61** G9
Ignacio *CO* 37°7N 107°38W **66** E3
Ihlen *MN* 43°55N 96°22W **80** G2
Ilinamna *AK* 59°45N 154°54W **61** G9
Ilinamna L. *AK* 59°30N 155°0W **61** G9
Iliff *CO* 40°45N 103°4W **66** B7
Ilio Pt. *HI* 21°13N 157°16W **69** L7
Ilion *NY* 43°1N 75°2W **89** B5
Illinois □ *U.S.A.* 40°15N 89°30W **71** C4
Illinois ➛ *IL* 38°58N 90°28W **71** E3
Illinois ➛ *OK* 35°30N 95°5W **93** C8
Illinois ➛ *OR* 42°18N 124°3W **94** E1
Illinois at Chicago, University of
   IL . . . . 41°52N 87°38W **108** B3
Illinois Institute of Technology
   IL . . . . 41°50N 87°37W **108** B3
Illiopolis *IL* 39°51N 89°14W **71** D4
Illmo = Scott City *MO* 37°14N 89°31W **82** E8
Ilwaco *WA* 46°19N 124°3W **101** D1
Imbler *OR* 45°28N 117°58W **94** B8
Imboden *AR* 36°12N 91°11W **63** B4
Imlay *NV* 40°40N 118°9W **85** B2
Imlay City *MI* 43°2N 83°5W **79** F8
Immokalee *FL* 26°25N 81°25W **67** E7
Imnaha *OR* 45°34N 116°46W **94** B9
Imnaha ➛ *OR* 45°49N 116°46W **94** B9
Imogene *IA* 40°51N 95°26W **73** E3
Imperial *CA* 32°51N 115°34W **65** L11
Imperial *NE* 40°31N 101°39W **84** D4
Imperial Beach *CA* 32°35N 117°6W **117** C2
Imperial County ☆
   CA . . . . 33°0N 115°0W **65** K11
Imperial Dam *AZ* 32°55N 114°25W **62** E1
Imperial Res. *AZ* 32°53N 114°28W **62** E1
Imperial Valley *CA* 33°0N 115°30W **65** L11
Ina *IL* . . . 38°9N 88°54W **71** E5
Inarajan *Guam* 13°16N 144°45E **105 b**
Incelium *WA* 48°18N 118°12W **101** B7
Incline Village *NV* 39°10N 119°58W **85** C1
Independence *CA* 36°48N 118°12W **65** G8
Independence *IA* 42°28N 91°54W **73** C7
Independence *KS* 37°14N 95°42W **74** D8
Independence *KY* 38°57N 84°33W **97** B8
Independence *LA* 30°38N 90°30W **75** D5
Independence *MS* 34°42N 89°49W **81** B4
Independence *MO* 39°6N 94°25W **82** B2
Independence *OH* 41°22N 81°38W **107** B2
Independence *OR* 44°51N 123°11W **94** C2
Independence *VA* 36°37N 81°8W **102** D3
Independence *WI* 44°21N 91°24W **103** D2
Independence County ☆
   AR . . . . 35°46N 91°39W **63** C4
Independence Cr. ➛
   TX . . . 30°27N 101°44W **98** G6
Independence Mts.
   NV . . . 41°20N 116°0W **85** A4
Independence Pass
   CO . . . 39°7N 106°33W **66** C4

Indiahoma *OK* 34°37N 98°45W **93** D5
Indialantic *FL* 28°6N 80°34W **67** C8
Indian Cr. ➛ *MO* 42°59N 90°34W **80** H3
Indian Cr. ➛ *TX* 34°39N 103°19W **91** F2
Indian Creek Village
   FL . . . 25°52N 80°8W **112** C3
Indian Harbour Beach
   FL . . . 28°10N 80°35W **67** C8
Indian Head *MD* 38°38N 77°12W **77** B3
Indian Heights *IN* 40°26N 86°10W **72** C4
Indian L. *MI* 45°59N 86°20W **79** D5
Indian L. *NY* 43°47N 74°19W **89** B6
Indian L. *OH* 40°30N 83°53W **92** C3
Indian L. *WI* 43°47N 74°16W **89** B6
Indian Mills *NJ* 39°48N 74°46W **87** C2
Indian Mounds Park
   MN . . . 44°56N 93°3W **113** B3
Indian Peak *UT* 38°16N 113°53W **100** E2
Indian Peak Range = Needle Range
   UT . . . 38°25N 113°55W **100** E2
Indian River *MI* 45°25N 84°37W **79** D7
Indian River Bay *DE* 38°36N 75°4W **77** B5
Indian River County ☆
   FL . . . 27°40N 80°45W **67** D8
Indian River Park
   VA . . . 36°48N 76°13W **115** B2
Indian River Shores
   FL . . . 27°43N 80°23W **67** D8
Indian Rock WA. 45°59N 120°49W **101** D5
Indian Rocks Beach
   FL . . . 27°52N 82°51W **119** B1
Indian Shores *FL* 27°51N 82°50W **119** B1
Indian Springs *NV* 36°35N 115°40W **85** F5
Indian Township Indian
   Reservation *ME* 45°18N 67°34W **76** C6
Indian Trail *NC* 35°5N 80°40W **90** C5
Indian Valley *ID* 44°33N 116°26W **70** E2
Indian Valley Res.
   CA . . . 39°5N 122°32W **64** D4
Indian Village *KS* 37°5N 95°38W **74** D8
Indiana *IN* 40°37N 79°9W **95** D3
Indiana *PA* 40°37N 79°9W **95** D3
Indiana □ *U.S.A.* 40°0N 86°0W **72** C5
Indiana County ☆ *PA* 40°45N 79°0W **95** D3
Indiana Dunes Nat. Lakeshore △
   IN . . . 41°40N 87°0W **72** B3
Indiana Motor Speedway
   IN . . . 39°48N 86°14W **72** D4
Indianapolis *IN* 39°46N 86°9W **108** D2
Indianapolis Int. ✕ (IND)
   IN . . . 39°43N 86°17W **110** B1
Indianola *IA* 41°22N 93°34W **73** D5
Indianola *MS* 33°27N 90°39W **81** C3
Indianola *NE* 40°14N 100°25W **84** D5
Indianola *OK* 35°10N 95°46W **93** C8
Indianola *WA* 47°44N 122°31W **118** B2
Indiantown *FL* 27°1N 80°28W **67** D8
Indio *CA* 33°43N 116°13W **65** K10
Industry *IL* 40°20N 90°36W **71** C3
Industry *KS* 39°0N 97°10W **74** B6
Industry *TX* 29°58N 96°30W **99** H11
Inez *KY* 37°52N 82°32W **97** C10
Ingalls *AR* 33°23N 92°9W **63** E3
Ingalls *KS* 37°50N 100°27W **74** D3
Ingham County ☆
   MI . . . 42°35N 84°30W **79** G7
Ingleside *MD* 39°6N 75°53W **77** A5
Ingleside *TX* 27°53N 97°13W **99** K10
Inglewood *CA* 33°58N 118°21W **111** C3
Inglis *FL* 29°2N 82°40W **67** B6
Ingomar *MT* 46°35N 107°23W **83** D10
Ingram *TX* 30°5N 99°14W **99** G8
Ingram *WV* 45°31N 90°49W **103** C3
Inkom *ID* 42°48N 112°15W **70** G6
Inkster *MI* 48°9N 97°39W **91** B8
Inland L. *MI* 42°30N 86°30W **79** G6
Inland L. *AK* 64°30N 74°48W **89** B6
Inlet *NY* 43°45N 74°48W **89** B6
Inman *KS* 38°14N 97°47W **74** C6
Inman *NE* 42°23N 98°32W **84** B7
Inman *SC* 35°2N 82°5W **90** C3
Innoko Nat. Wildlife Refuge ◯
   AK . . . 63°20N 158°25W **61** E8
Inola *OK* 36°9N 95°31W **93** B8
Intercession City *FL* 28°16N 81°31W **67** C7
Interior *SD* 43°44N 101°59W **91** G4
Interlachen *FL* 29°37N 81°53W **67** B7
Interlaken *NY* 42°37N 76°44W **89** C4
International Falls
   MN . . . 48°36N 93°25W **80** B5
International Peace Garden
   ND . . . 49°0N 100°4W **91** B5
Intervale *NH* 44°6N 71°8W **86** B3
Intracoastal City *LA* 29°47N 92°8W **75** E3
Inver Grove Heights
   MN . . . 44°51N 93°1W **80** F5
Inverness *MT* 48°34N 111°9W **83** B7
Inverness *MD* 39°22N 76°29W **107** B3
Inverness *FL* 28°50N 82°20W **67** C6
Inverness *MS* 33°21N 90°35W **81** C3
Inwood *IA* 43°19N 96°26W **73** B2
Inwood *NY* 40°37N 73°44W **114** C4
Inwood *WV* 39°21N 78°2W **77** A2
Inyan Kara Mt.
   WY . . . 44°13N 104°28W **104** B8
Inyo County ☆ *CA* 36°30N 117°40W **65** G9
Inyo L. *CA* 36°40N 118°0W **65** G9
Inyo Nat. Forest
   U.S.A. . 37°18N 118°15W **65** F8
Inyokern *CA* 35°39N 117°49W **65** H9
Iola *KS* 38°50N 88°38W **71** L5
Iola *TX* 30°45N 95°24W **74** D8
Iola *WI* 44°30N 89°8W **103** D4
Iolani Palace *HI* 21°18N 157°51W **69** K14
Iona *ID* 43°32N 111°56W **70** F7
Iona *MN* 43°55N 95°47W **80** G3
Iona *SD* 43°30N 99°26W **91** G6
Iona *OR* 45°20N 119°50W **94** E6
Iona *WA* 48°45N 117°25W **101** B8
Ionia *IA* 43°2N 92°27W **73** B6
Ionia *KS* 39°40N 98°21W **74** B6
Ionia *MI* 42°59N 85°4W **79** G6
Ionia *MO* 38°30N 93°19W **82** C3
Ionia County ☆ *MI* 42°55N 85°5W **79** G6
Iosco County ☆ *MI* 44°20N 83°30W **79** E8
Iota *LA* 30°14N 92°3W **75** D2
Iowa □ *U.S.A.* 42°18N 93°30W **73** C5
Iowa ➛ *IA* 41°10N 91°1W **73** D7
Iowa City *IA* 41°40N 91°32W **73** D7
Iowa County ☆ *IA* 41°40N 92°0W **73** D6
Iowa County ☆ *WI* 43°0N 90°10W **103** F3
Iowa Falls *IA* 42°31N 93°16W **73** C5
Iowa Indian Reservation
   KS . . . 39°55N 95°25W **74** B9
Iowa Park *TX* 33°57N 98°40W **99** D9
Ipava *IL* 40°20N 90°19W **71** C3
Ipswich *MA* 42°41N 70°50W **78** B4
Ipswich *SD* 45°27N 99°2W **91** E6
Ipswich B. *MA* 42°35N 101°0W **98** E4
Ira *TX* 32°35N 101°0W **98** E4
Iraan *TX* 30°55N 101°54W **98** G6
Irasburg *VT* 44°18N 72°31W **86** B1
Iredell *TX* 31°59N 97°52W **99** F10
Iredell County ☆ *NC* 35°45N 80°50W **90** C5
Irene *SD* 43°5N 97°9W **91** G8
Ireton *IA* 42°58N 96°19W **73** C2
Irion County ☆ *TX* 31°15N 100°59W **98** F7
Irish, Mt. *NV* 37°39N 115°24W **85** E5

Irma, L. *FL* 28°35N 81°16W **115** A3
Irmo *SC* 34°5N 81°11W **90** D4
Iron Belt *WI* 46°24N 90°19W **103** B3
Iron City *GA* 31°1N 84°49W **68** E2
Iron City *TN* 35°1N 87°35W **96** E5
Iron County ☆ *MI* 46°15N 88°35W **79** C3
Iron County ☆ *MO* 37°33N 90°38W **82** D6
Iron County ☆ *UT* 37°50N 113°20W **100** F2
Iron County ☆ *WI* 46°15N 90°10W **103** B3
Iron Gate *VA* 37°48N 79°48W **102** D5
Iron Junction *MN* 47°25N 92°36W **80** C6
Iron Mountain *MI* 45°49N 88°4W **79** C3
Iron Mountain *MO* 37°42N 90°39W **82** D6
Iron Mountain *WY* 41°37N 105°13W **104** E7
Iron Mts. *VA* 36°40N 81°45W **102** E3
Iron Nation *SD* 44°10N 99°31W **91** F6
Iron Ridge *WI* 43°24N 88°32W **103** E5
Iron River *MI* 46°6N 88°39W **79** C3
Iron River *WI* 46°34N 91°24W **103** B2
Irondale *AL* 33°32N 86°42W **60** C4
Irondale *MO* 37°50N 90°41W **82** D6
Irondale *OH* 40°34N 80°44W **92** C6
Irondequoit *NY* 43°13N 77°32W **89** B4
Ironside *MD* 38°30N 77°12W **77** B3
Ironton *MN* 46°28N 93°59W **80** D5
Ironton *MO* 37°36N 90°38W **82** D6
Ironton *OH* 38°32N 82°41W **92** E4
Ironwood *MI* 46°27N 90°9W **79** C1
Ironwood Forest Nat. Monument △
   U.S.A. . 32°32N 111°28W **62** E4
Iroquois *IL* 40°50N 87°35W **72** C3
Iroquois *SD* 44°22N 97°51W **91** F8
Iroquois ➛ *IN* 41°5N 87°49W **72** C3
Iroquois County ☆
   IL . . . 40°45N 87°50W **71** C6
Iroquois Nat. Wildlife Refuge ◯
   NY . . . 43°7N 78°21W **89** B2
Iroquois Point *HI* 21°19N 157°58W **69** K14
Irrigon *OR* 45°54N 119°30W **94** B6
Irvine *KY* 37°42N 83°58W **97** C9
Irvine *CA* 33°41N 117°46W **65** K9
Irving *TX* 32°48N 96°56W **109** B4
Irving Park *IL* 41°57N 87°42W **108** B2
Irvington *IL* 38°26N 89°10W **71** E4
Irvington *NJ* 40°43N 74°14W **114** B1
Irvington *NY* 41°4N 73°52W **114** B2
Irvona *PA* 40°46N 78°33W **95** D3
Irwin *IA* 41°47N 95°12W **73** D3
Irwin County ☆ *GA* 31°40N 83°15W **68** E3
Irwinton *GA* 32°49N 83°10W **68** D3
Irwinville *GA* 31°39N 83°23W **68** E3
Isabel *KS* 37°28N 98°33W **74** D5
Isabel *SD* 45°24N 101°26W **91** E4
Isabel Segunda
   Puerto Rico 18°9N 65°27W **105** G17
Isabela *Puerto Rico* 18°30N 67°2W **105** G15
Isabella *MI* 43°40N 84°50W **79** F7
Isabella Indian Reservation
   MI . . . 43°30N 84°42W **79** F7
Isabella L. *CA* 35°39N 118°28W **65** H8
Isabelle, Pt. *MI* 47°21N 87°56W **79** B4
Isanti *MN* 45°29N 93°15W **80** E5
Isanti County ☆ *MN* 45°30N 93°15W **80** E5
Ishpeming *MI* 46°29N 87°40W **79** C4
Isla Vista *CA* 34°25N 119°53W **65** J7
Islamorada *FL* 24°56N 80°37W **67** G8
Island Beach *NJ* 39°50N 74°5W **87** C2
Island Beach State Park △
   NJ . . . 39°51N 74°5W **87** C2
Island Channel *NY* 40°36N 73°53W **114** C3
Island City *OR* 45°20N 118°3W **94** B7
Island County ☆
   WA . . . 48°10N 122°35W **101** B3
Island Creek *MD* 38°27N 76°35W **77** A7
Island Falls *ME* 46°1N 68°16W **76** B5
Island Heights *NJ* 39°57N 74°9W **87** C2
Island Lake Res. *MN* 47°0N 92°14W **80** C6
Island Park *ID* 44°24N 111°19W **70** E7
Island Park *NY* 40°36N 73°39W **114** C4
Island Park Res. *ID* 44°25N 111°24W **70** E7
Island Pond *VT* 44°49N 71°53W **86** B3
Isle *MN* 46°8N 93°28W **80** D5
Isle La Motte *VT* 44°52N 73°18W **86** B1
Isle of Hope *GA* 31°58N 81°5W **68** D5
Isle of Palms *SC* 32°47N 79°48W **90** F6
Isle of Wight *VA* 36°54N 76°43W **102** E8
Isle of Wight Bay *MD* 38°22N 75°6W **77** B5
Isle of Wight County ☆
   VA . . . 36°54N 76°43W **102** E8
Isle Royale Nat. Park △
   MI . . . 48°0N 88°55W **79** A3
Islesboro I. *ME* 44°19N 68°54W **76** C5
Isleta Indian Reservation
   NM . . . 34°55N 106°45W **88** C4
Isleton *CA* 38°10N 121°37W **64** E5
Ismay *MT* 46°30N 104°48W **83** D13
Isola *MS* 33°16N 90°35W **81** C3
Israel ➛ *NH* 44°29N 71°35W **86** B3
Issaquah *WA* 47°32N 122°2W **101** C3
Issaquena County ☆
   MS . . . 32°54N 91°3W **81** D2
Issue *MD* 38°16N 76°53W **77** B4
Isto, Mt. *AK* 69°12N 143°48W **61** B11
Istokpoga, L. *FL* 27°23N 81°17W **67** D7
Itasca *TX* 32°11N 96°53W **99** F11
Itasca *IL* 42°10N 88°1W **108** B1
Itasca County ☆ *MN* 47°25N 93°25W **80** C5
Itasca State Park △
   MN . . . 47°12N 95°12W **80** C3
Itawamba County ☆
   MS . . . 34°16N 88°25W **81** B5
Ithaca *MI* 43°18N 84°36W **79** F7
Ithaca *NY* 42°27N 76°30W **89** C4
Ithaca *NE* 41°10N 96°33W **84** C9
Itikikik ➛ *AK* 70°9N 150°56W **61** A10
Itta Bena *MS* 33°30N 90°20W **81** C3
Iuka *KS* 37°44N 98°44W **74** D5
Iuka *MS* 34°49N 88°12W **81** B5
Iva *SC* 34°19N 82°40W **90** D3
Ivan *AR* 33°56N 92°42W **63** E3
Ivanhoe *CA* 36°23N 119°13W **65** G7
Ivanhoe *MN* 44°28N 96°15W **80** F2
Ivanhoe *NC* 34°23N 78°15W **90** D7
Ivanhoe *TX* 33°53N 96°7W **99** D11
Ivanof Bay *AK* 55°54N 159°29W **61** J8
Ivesdale *IL* 39°55N 88°27W **71** D5
Ivins *UT* 37°10N 113°41W **100** F2
Ivor *VA* 36°54N 76°54W **102** E8
Ivydale *WV* 38°32N 81°2W **102** C3
Izard County ☆ *AR* 36°5N 91°54W **63** B4
Izembek Nat. Wildlife Refuge ◯
   AK . . . 55°15N 162°45W **61** J7

J

Jacks Fork ➛ *MO* 37°12N 91°18W **82** D5
Jacksboro *TN* 36°20N 84°11W **97** D8
Jacksboro *TX* 33°13N 98°10W **99** D9
Jackson *AL* 31°31N 87°53W **60** E3
Jackson *CA* 38°21N 120°46W **64** E6
Jackson *GA* 33°20N 83°57W **68** C3
Jackson *KY* 37°33N 83°23W **97** C9
Jackson *LA* 30°50N 91°13W **75** D4
Jackson *MI* 42°15N 84°24W **79** G7
Jackson *MN* 43°37N 95°1W **80** G3
Jackson *MS* 32°18N 90°12W **81** C3
Jackson *MO* 37°23N 89°40W **82** D7
Jackson *MT* 45°23N 113°23W **83** D5
Jackson *NC* 36°23N 77°25W **90** A8
Jackson *NH* 44°10N 71°11W **86** B3
Jackson *OH* 40°6N 77°24W **92** E4
Jackson *SC* 33°20N 81°47W **90** E4
Jackson *TN* 35°37N 88°49W **96** E4
Jackson *WI* 43°19N 88°10W **103** E5
Jackson *WY* 43°29N 110°46W **104** C2
Jackson ➛ *AL* 34°40N 86°2W **60** B4
Jackson County ☆ *AR* 35°37N 91°16W **63** C4
Jackson County ☆
   CO . . . 40°45N 106°20W **66** B4
Jackson County ☆
   FL . . . 30°45N 85°15W **67** A3
Jackson County ☆
   GA . . . 34°10N 83°30W **68** B3
Jackson County ☆ *IL* 37°45N 89°25W **71** F4
Jackson County ☆ *IN* 38°55N 86°0W **72** E4
Jackson County ☆ *IA* 42°10N 90°33W **73** C8
Jackson County ☆
   KS . . . 39°25N 95°45W **74** B8
Jackson County ☆ *KY* 37°25N 84°0W **97** C8
Jackson County ☆
   MI . . . 42°15N 84°30W **79** G7
Jackson County ☆
   MN . . . 43°40N 95°10W **80** G3
Jackson County ☆
   MS . . . 30°32N 88°42W **81** F5
Jackson County ☆
   MO . . . 39°0N 94°20W **82** C2
Jackson County ☆
   NC . . . 35°20N 83°10W **90** C2
Jackson County ☆ *OH* 39°3N 82°39W **92** D4
Jackson County ☆
   OK . . . 34°30N 99°20W **93** D5
Jackson County ☆
   OR . . . 42°20N 122°45W **94** E3
Jackson County ☆
   SD . . . 43°45N 101°45W **91** G4
Jackson County ☆
   TN . . . 36°21N 85°39W **97** D7
Jackson County ☆
   TX . . . 28°59N 96°39W **99** J11
Jackson County ☆
   WV . . . 38°49N 81°43W **102** C3
Jackson County ☆
   WI . . . 44°20N 90°45W **103** D3
Jackson Heights *NY* 40°44N 73°53W **114** B3
Jackson Hole *WY* 43°36N 110°51W **104** C2
Jackson Junction *IA* 43°7N 92°0W **73** B6
Jackson L. *GA* 33°19N 83°50W **68** C3
Jackson Mts. *NV* 41°15N 118°30W **85** A2
Jackson Parish ☆ *LA* 32°16N 92°33W **75** B3
Jackson Park *IL* 41°46N 87°34W **108** C3
Jackson Res. *CO* 40°25N 104°5W **66** B6
Jacksonville *AL* 33°49N 85°46W **60** C5
Jacksonville *AR* 34°52N 92°7W **63** D3
Jacksonville *FL* 30°20N 81°39W **67** A7
Jacksonville *IL* 39°44N 90°14W **71** D3
Jacksonville *NC* 34°45N 77°26W **90** D8
Jacksonville *OH* 39°29N 82°52W **92** D4
Jacksonville *TX* 31°58N 95°17W **99** F12
Jacksonville *VT* 42°47N 72°49W **86** E1
Jacksonville Beach
   FL . . . 30°17N 81°24W **67** A7
Jacksonville Int. ✕ (JAX)
   FL . . . 30°30N 81°41W **67** A7
Jacob Lake *AZ* 36°43N 112°13W **62** A3
Jacobacy *MD* 39°33N 77°33W **77** A4
Jacobus *PA* 39°52N 76°42W **77** A4
Jacumba *CA* 32°37N 116°11W **65** L10
Jaffrey *NH* 42°49N 72°2W **86** D2
Jakin *GA* 31°6N 84°59W **68** E2
Jal *NM* 32°7N 103°12W **88** E7
Jalalhai Pt. *Guam* 13°18N 144°46E **105 b**
Jamaica *VT* 43°5N 94°18W **73** D4
Jamaica B. *NY* 40°36N 73°51W **114** C3
Jamaica Plain *MA* 42°18N 71°6W **106** B3
James ➛ *MO* 32°58N 83°29W **68** D3
James ➛ *SD* 42°45N 93°30W **91** H8
James, L. *NC* 35°44N 81°54W **90** C4
James City County ☆
   VA . . . 37°16N 76°40W **102** D8
Jamesburg *NJ* 40°21N 74°27W **87** B2
Jamestown *CA* 37°57N 120°25W **64** F6
Jamestown *IN* 39°56N 86°38W **72** D4
Jamestown *KS* 39°36N 97°52W **74** B6
Jamestown *KY* 36°59N 85°4W **97** D7
Jamestown *LA* 32°21N 93°13W **75** B2
Jamestown *NY* 42°6N 79°14W **95** B2
Jamestown *ND* 46°54N 98°42W **91** C7
Jamestown *OH* 39°39N 83°44W **92** D3
Jamestown *PA* 41°29N 80°27W **95** C2
Jamestown *RI* 41°30N 71°22W **78** C3
Jamestown *TN* 36°26N 84°56W **97** D8
Jamestown *VA* 37°12N 76°46W **102** D8
Jamestown Res. *ND* 46°56N 98°43W **91** C7
Jamesville *NC* 35°49N 76°54W **90** C9
Jamul *CA* 44°11N 117°26W **94** C8
Jane *MO* 36°35N 94°1W **63** B1
Jane Lew *WV* 39°6N 80°25W **102** C4
James I. *DE* 38°0N 75°51W **77** C5
Janesville *IA* 42°39N 92°28W **73** C6
Janesville *MN* 44°7N 93°42W **80** F5
Janesville *WI* 42°41N 89°1W **103** F4
Jansen *CO* 37°9N 104°32W **66** E6
Jansen *NE* 40°11N 97°56W **84** D8
Jaroles *NM* . 34°52N 106°46W **88** C4
Jarbidge *NV* 41°52N 115°26W **85** A5
Jarbidge ➛ *ID* 42°20N 115°39W **70** G3
Jarboesville = Lexington Park
   MD . . . 38°16N 76°27W **77** B4
Jarratt *VA* 36°49N 77°28W **102** E7
Jarrettsville *MD* 39°36N 76°29W **77** A4
Jarvis I. Pac. Oc. 0°15S 160°5W **105** E7
Jasonville *IN* 39°10N 87°12W **72** D3
Jasper *AL* 33°50N 87°17W **60** C3
Jasper *AR* 36°1N 93°11W **63** B2
Jasper *FL* 30°31N 82°57W **67** A6
Jasper *GA* 34°28N 84°26W **68** B2
Jasper *IN* 38°24N 86°56W **72** E4
Jasper *MN* 43°51N 96°24W **80** G2
Jasper *MO* 37°20N 94°18W **82** D2
Jasper *TN* 35°5N 85°38W **96** E6
Jasper *TX* 30°56N 94°1W **99** G13

Jasper County ☆ GA   33°20N 83°45W   68 C3
Jasper County ☆ IL   39°00N 88°10W   71 E5
Jasper County ☆ IN   41°00N 87°5W   72 B3
Jasper County ☆ IA   41°40N 93°0W   73 D5
Jasper County ☆ MS   32°2N 89°22W   81 D4
Jasper County ☆ MO   37°10N 94°20W   82 D2
Jasper County ☆ SC   32°30N 81°0W   90 F4
Jasper County ☆
   TX   30°40N 93°54W   99 G14
Java SD   45°30N 99°53W   91 E6
Java VA   36°50N 79°14W   102 E5
Jay FL   30°57N 87°9W   67 A1
Jay ME   44°30N 70°13W   76 D3
Jay NY   44°20N 73°45W   89 A7
Jay OK   36°25N 94°48W   93 B9
Jay County ☆ IN   40°25N 85°0W   72 C6
Jay Em WY   42°28N 104°22W   104 D8
Jay Peak VT   44°55N 72°32W   86 B2
Jaype ID   46°32N 115°50W   70 C3
Jayton TX   33°15N 100°34W   98 D7
Jean NV   35°47N 115°20W   85 G5
Jean TX   33°18N 98°37W   99 D9
Jean Lafitte Nat. Historical Park ○
   LA   29°51N 90°9W   113 D2
Jeanerette LA   29°55N 91°40W   113 D2
Jeanetta TX   29°43N 95°31W   110 B1
Jeff Davis County ☆
   GA   31°50N 82°45W   68 E4
Jeff Davis County ☆
   TX   30°55N 104°5W   98 G3
Jeffers MN   44°3N 95°12W   80 F3
Jefferson CO   39°23N 105°48W   66 C5
Jefferson GA   34°7N 83°35W   68 B3
Jefferson IA   42°1N 94°23W   73 C4
Jefferson LA   59°57N 90°9W   113 C2
Jefferson ME   44°13N 69°27W   76 D4
Jefferson MD   39°22N 77°32W   77 A3
Jefferson NC   36°25N 81°28W   90 B4
Jefferson OH   41°44N 80°46W   92 B6
Jefferson OK   36°43N 97°48W   93 B6
Jefferson OR   44°43N 123°1W   94 C2
Jefferson SC   34°39N 80°23W   90 C6
Jefferson SD   42°36N 96°34W   91 H9
Jefferson TX   32°46N 94°21W   99 E13
Jefferson WI   43°0N 88°48W   103 E5
Jefferson, ← MT   45°56N 111°31W   83 D6
Jefferson, Mt. NV   38°47N 116°56W   85 D4
Jefferson, Mt. OR   44°41N 121°48W   94 C4
Jefferson City MO   38°34N 92°10W   82 C4
Jefferson City TN   36°7N 83°30W   97 D9
Jefferson County ☆
   AL   33°31N 86°48W   60 C4
Jefferson County ☆
   AR   34°13N 92°1W   63 D3
Jefferson County ☆
   CO   39°40N 105°15W   66 C5
Jefferson County ☆
   FL   30°20N 84°0W   67 A5
Jefferson County ☆
   GA   33°10N 82°25W   68 C4
Jefferson County ☆
   ID   43°50N 112°20W   70 F6
Jefferson County ☆
   IL   38°20N 88°55W   71 E5
Jefferson County ☆
   IN   38°40N 85°25W   72 E5
Jefferson County ☆ IA   41°00N 92°0W   73 D7
Jefferson County ☆
   KS   39°15N 95°30W   74 B8
Jefferson County ☆
   KY   38°10N 85°40W   97 B7
Jefferson County ☆
   MS   31°43N 91°4W   81 E2
Jefferson County ☆
   MO   38°15N 90°30W   82 C6
Jefferson County ☆
   MT   46°8N 112°0W   83 D6
Jefferson County ☆ NY   44°0N 76°0W   89 A4
Jefferson County ☆
   NE   40°15N 97°10W   84 D8
Jefferson County ☆
   OH   40°25N 80°54W   92 C6
Jefferson County ☆
   OK   34°10N 97°50W   93 D6
Jefferson County ☆
   OR   44°40N 121°10W   94 C4
Jefferson County ☆ PA   41°5N 79°0W   95 C4
Jefferson County ☆
   TN   36°7N 83°30W   97 D9
Jefferson County ☆
   TX   29°55N 94°15W   99 H13
Jefferson County ☆
   WV   39°17N 77°52W   102 B7
Jefferson County ☆
   WA   47°50N 123°45W   101 C2
Jefferson County ☆
   WI   43°0N 88°45W   103 F5
Jefferson Davis County ☆
   MS   31°36N 89°52W   81 E4
Jefferson Davis Parish ☆
   LA   30°14N 92°49W   75 D3
Jefferson Nat. Forest
   VA   37°10N 81°15W   102 C2
Jefferson Parish ☆ LA   29°44N 90°8W   75 E5
Jefferson Park IL   41°58N 87°46W   108 B2
Jefferson Valley NY   41°20N 73°47W   87 A3
Jeffersonton VA   38°38N 77°55W   102 C7
Jeffersontown KY   38°12N 85°35W   97 B7
Jeffersonville GA   32°41N 83°35W   68 D3
Jeffersonville IN   38°17N 85°44W   72 E5
Jeffersonville KY   37°59N 83°51W   97 C9
Jeffersonville OH   39°39N 83°34W   92 D3
Jeffersonville VT   44°40N 72°50W   86 B2
Jeffrey City WY   42°30N 107°49W   104 D5
Jeffrey Res. NE   40°58N 100°24W   84 D5
Jekyll I. GA   31°4N 81°25W   68 E5
Jellico TN   36°33N 84°8W   97 D8
Jemez Indian Reservation
   NM   35°40N 106°50W   88 B4
Jemez Mts. NM   35°45N 106°30W   88 B4
Jemez Pueblo NM   35°37N 106°44W   88 B4
Jemez Springs NM   35°46N 106°40W   88 B4
Jenison AL   29°40N 83°22W   67 B5
Jena LA   29°40N 83°22W   67 B5
Jenison MI   42°54N 85°47W   79 G6
Jenkins KY   37°10N 82°38W   97 C10
Jenkins MN   46°39N 94°20W   80 D4
Jenkins NJ   40°20N 74°24W   87 C2
Jenkins County ☆ GA   32°45N 82°0W   68 D5
Jenkintown PA   40°5N 75°7W   116 A2
Jenks OK   36°1N 95°58W   93 B8
Jenner CA   38°27N 123°7W   64 E3
Jennings FL   30°36N 83°6W   67 A5
Jennings KS   39°41N 100°18W   74 B3
Jennings LA   30°13N 92°40W   75 D3
Jennings MO   38°43N 90°15W   117 A2
Jennings OK   36°11N 96°34W   93 B7
Jennings County ☆ IN   39°00N 85°40W   72 D5
Jennings Lodge
   OR   45°23N 122°36W   116 B2
Jensen UT   40°20N 109°20W   100 C6
Jensen Beach FL   27°15N 80°14W   67 D8
Jerauld County ☆ SD   44°0N 98°45W   91 F7
Jeremy Point RI   41°58N 69°58W   76 C4
Jerico Springs MO   37°37N 94°1W   82 D2
Jerimoth Hill RI   41°51N 71°47W   78 C3
Jermyn PA   41°32N 75°33W   87 A1
Jermyn TX   33°16N 98°23W   99 D9
Jerome AZ   34°45N 112°7W   62 C3
Jerome AR   33°23N 91°28W   63 E4
Jerome ID   42°44N 114°31W   70 G4

Jerome County ☆
   ID   42°42N 114°15W   70 G4
Jerry City OH   41°15N 83°36W   92 B3
Jersey AR   33°26N 92°19W   63 E3
Jersey GA   33°43N 83°47W   68 C3
Jersey City NJ   40°42N 74°4W   114 B2
Jersey Village TX   29°53N 95°33W   110 A1
Jerseyville IL   39°7N 90°20W   71 D3
Jersey Shore PA   41°12N 77°15W   95 C5
Jessamine, L. FL   28°28N 81°23W   115 B2
Jessamine County ☆
   KY   37°50N 84°35W   97 C8
Jessieville AR   34°42N 93°4W   63 D2
Jessup MD   39°9N 76°46W   77 A4
Jesup GA   31°36N 81°53W   68 E5
Jesup IA   42°29N 92°4W   73 C6
Jesup, L. FL   28°43N 81°14W   67 C7
Jet OK   36°40N 98°11W   93 B5
Jetmore KS   38°4N 99°54W   74 C4
Jewel Cave Nat. Monument ○
   SD   43°45N 103°48W   91 G2
Jewell IA   42°18N 93°39W   73 C5
Jewell KS   39°40N 98°10W   74 B5
Jewell Ridge VA   37°11N 81°47W   102 C3
Jewett IL   39°13N 88°15W   71 D5
Jewett OH   40°22N 81°2W   92 C5
Jewett TX   31°22N 96°9W   99 F11
Jewett City CT   41°36N 71°59W   78 C3
Jicarilla Indian Reservation
   NM   36°45N 107°0W   88 A4
Jigger LA   32°2N 91°45W   75 B4
Jiggs NV   40°26N 115°40W   85 B5
Jim Hogg County ☆
   TX   27°0N 98°45W   98 K9
Jim Thorpe PA   40°52N 75°44W   87 A1
Jim Wells County ☆
   TX   28°0N 98°0W   99 K9
Jimmy Carter Nat. Historic Site ○
   GA   32°2N 84°25W   68 D2
Jo Daviess County ☆
   IL   42°20N 90°10W   71 A3
Joanna SC   34°25N 81°49W   90 C4
Joaquin TX   31°58N 94°3W   99 F13
Joaquin Miller Park
   CA   37°48N 122°10W   118 B3
Jocassee, L. SC   34°58N 82°56W   90 B3
Joe Pool Lake TX   32°38N 96°59W   109 C4
Joes CO   39°39N 102°41W   66 C8
Johanna, L. MN   45°2N 93°10W   113 A2
Johannesburg CA   35°22N 117°38W   65 H9
Juan C. Stennis Space Center
   MS   30°23N 89°37W   81 F4
John D. Rockefeller Jr. Memorial Parkway ☆   44°5N 110°44W   104 B2
John Day WY   44°25N 118°57W   94 D7
John Day ← OR   45°44N 120°39W   94 B5
John Day Dam WA   45°43N 120°41W   101 E5
John Day Fossil Beds Nat. Monument ○   44°33N 119°38W   58 D3
John Day Fossil Beds Nat. Monument Clarno ○
   OR   44°55N 120°28W   94 C5
John Day Fossil Beds Nat. Monument Painted Hills ○
   OR   44°39N 120°15W   94 C5
John Day Fossil Beds Nat. Monument Sheep Rock ○
   OR   44°33N 119°30W   94 C6
John Dickinson Plantation
   DE   39°10N 75°31W   77 A5
John F. Kennedy Nat. Historic Site ○ MA   42°20N 71°7W   106 A3
John F. Kennedy Space Center
   U.S.A.   28°40N 80°42W   67 C8
John H. Kerr Res.
   NC   36°36N 78°18W   90 B7
John Heinz Nat. Wildlife Refuge ○
   PA   39°53N 75°17W   116 B1
John McLaren Park
   CA   37°43N 122°24W   118 C2
John Martin Res. CO   38°4N 102°56W   66 D8
John Redmond Res.
   KS   38°14N 95°46W   74 C8
John W. Flanagan Res.
   VA   37°15N 82°22W   102 D2
John Wayne, Santa Ana ✈ (SNA)
   CA   33°41N 117°52W   65 K9
Johns I. SC   32°47N 80°7W   90 F5
Johnson NE   40°25N 96°0W   84 D10
Johnson VT   44°38N 72°41W   86 B2
Johnson City KS   37°34N 101°45W   74 D2
Johnson City NY   42°7N 75°58W   89 C5
Johnson City TN   36°19N 82°21W   97 D10
Johnson City TX   30°17N 98°25W   99 G9
Johnson County ☆
   AR   35°28N 93°28W   63 C2
Johnson County ☆
   GA   32°42N 82°40W   68 D4
Johnson County ☆ IL   37°30N 88°50W   71 F5
Johnson County ☆ IN   39°30N 86°5W   72 D4
Johnson County ☆
   IA   41°40N 91°35W   73 D7
Johnson County ☆
   KS   38°45N 94°45W   74 C9
Johnson County ☆
   KY   37°50N 82°50W   97 C10
Johnson County ☆
   MO   38°45N 93°45W   82 C3
Johnson County ☆
   NE   40°20N 96°15W   84 D9
Johnson County ☆
   TN   36°29N 81°48W   97 D11
Johnson County ☆
   TX   32°21N 97°23W   99 E10
Johnson County ☆
   WY   44°0N 106°35W   104 B6
Johnson Draw → TX   30°8N 101°7W   98 G6
Johnson L. NE   40°42N 99°49W   84 D6
Johnsonburg NJ   40°58N 74°53W   87 B2
Johnsonburg PA   41°29N 78°41W   95 C4
Johnsondale CA   35°58N 118°32W   65 H8
Johnson's Shut-Ins State Park ○
   MO   37°32N 90°51W   82 D6
Johnsonville SC   33°49N 79°27W   90 D6
Johnston IA   41°40N 93°42W   73 D5
Johnston RI   41°50N 71°30W   78 C3
Johnston SC   33°50N 81°48W   90 D4
Johnston City IL   37°49N 88°56W   71 F5
Johnston County ☆
   NC   35°30N 78°20W   90 C7
Johnston County ☆
   OK   34°20N 96°40W   93 D7
Johnston I. Pac. Oc.   16°45N 169°30W   105 C6
Johnstown CO   40°20N 104°54W   66 B6
Johnstown NY   43°0N 74°22W   89 B6
Johnstown OH   40°9N 82°41W   92 C4
Johnstown PA   40°20N 78°55W   95 D4
Johnstown Flood Nat. Memorial ○
   PA   40°20N 78°55W   95 D4

Kalaoa HI   19°43N 155°58W   69 D6
Kalaupapa HI   21°12N 156°59W   69 B5
Kalaupapa Nat. Historical Park ○
   U.S.A.   21°10N 156°59W   69 B5
Kalawao County ☆
   HI   21°11N 156°58W   69 B5
Kaleva MI   44°22N 86°1W   79 E5
Kalida OH   40°59N 84°12W   92 C2
Kalihi HI   21°20N 157°53W   69 K14
Kalihi Valley HI   21°20N 157°52W   69 K14
Kalispell MT   48°12N 114°19W   83 B3
Kalispel Indian Reservation
   WA   48°23N 117°17W   101 B8
Kalispell MT   48°12N 114°19W   83 B3
Kalkaska MI   44°44N 85°11W   79 E6
Kalkaska County ☆
   MI   44°45N 85°5W   79 E6
Kalohi Channel HI   21°0N 157°0W   69 C5
Kaloko-Honokōhau Nat. Historical Park ○ U.S.A.   19°40N 156°1W   69 D5
Kalona IA   41°29N 91°43W   73 D7
Kaltag AK   64°20N 158°43W   61 D8
Kalskag AK   38°4N 100°18W   74 C3
Kamakou HI   21°7N 156°52W   69 B5
Kamalō HI   21°3N 156°52W   69 B5
Kamananui → HI   21°38N 158°4W   69 J13
Kamas UT   40°38N 111°17W   100 C4
Kamela OR   45°26N 118°24W   94 B7
Kamiah ID   46°14N 116°2W   70 C2
Kamishak Bay AK   59°15N 153°45W   61 G9
Kamloops IL   39°18N 90°37W   71 D3
Kamo'oloa → HI   21°34N 158°7W   69 J13
Kampsville IL   39°18N 90°37W   71 D3
Kamrar IA   42°24N 93°44W   73 C5
Kanab UT   37°3N 112°32W   100 F3
Kanab Cr. → AZ   36°24N 112°38W   62 A3
Kanabec County ☆
   MN   45°55N 93°20W   80 E5
Kanaga I. AK   51°45N 177°22W   61 L3
Kanakanak AK   59°0N 158°32W   61 G8
Kanarraville UT   37°32N 113°11W   100 F2
Kanawha IA   42°56N 93°48W   73 C5
Kanawha → WV   38°50N 82°9W   102 C3
Kanawha County ☆
   WV   38°21N 81°38W   102 C3
Kandiyohi County ☆
   MN   45°10N 95°0W   80 E4
Kane IL   39°11N 90°21W   71 D3
Kane PA   41°40N 78°49W   95 C4
Kane County ☆ IL   41°50N 88°25W   71 B5
Kane County ☆ UT   37°15N 112°0W   100 F3
Kaneilio Pt. HI   21°27N 158°12W   69 K13
Kāne'ohe HI   21°25N 157°48W   69 K14
Kāne'ohe B. HI   21°30N 157°50W   69 K14
Kaneohe Marine Corps Air Station
   HI   21°25N 157°46W   69 K14
Kaniksu Nat. Forest
   ID   48°50N 116°30W   70 A2
Kanisku Nat. Forest
   ID   48°50N 116°30W   70 A2
Kankakee IL   41°7N 87°52W   71 B6
Kankakee → IL   41°23N 88°15W   71 B5
Kankakee County ☆
   IL   41°10N 87°50W   71 B6
Kannapolis NC   35°30N 80°37W   90 C5
Kanopolis KS   38°43N 98°9W   74 C5
Kanopolis Lake KS   38°37N 97°58W   74 C6
Kanorado CO   39°20N 102°2W   74 B1
Kanosh UT   38°48N 112°26W   100 E3
Kansas IL   39°33N 87°56W   71 D6
Kansas OK   36°12N 94°48W   93 B9
Kansas → U.S.A.   38°30N 99°0W   74 C5
Kansas → KS   39°7N 94°37W   74 B9
Kansas City KS   39°7N 94°38W   74 B9
Kansas City MO   39°6N 94°35W   82 B2
Kansas City Int. ✈ (MCI)
   MO   39°18N 94°43W   82 B2
Kantishna AK   63°31N 150°57W   61 E9
Kantishna → AK   64°45N 149°58W   61 D10
Kanuti Nat. Wildlife Refuge ○
   AK   66°25N 151°50W   61 C10
Kapaa HI   22°5N 159°19W   69 A2
Kapahulu HI   21°16N 157°49W   69 K14
Kapapa I. HI   21°29N 157°48W   69 K14
Kapina LA   30°0N 92°17W   75 E3
Kapoho HI   19°30N 154°50W   69 D7
Kapowsin WA   46°59N 122°13W   101 D3
Karlsruhe ND   48°6N 100°37W   91 D5
Karlstad MN   48°35N 96°31W   80 B2
Karluk AK   57°34N 154°28W   61 H9
Karnak IL   37°18N 88°58W   71 F5
Karnes County ☆
   TX   28°49N 97°51W   99 J10
Kasaan AK   55°32N 132°24W   61 J15
Kasilof AK   60°23N 151°18W   61 F10
Kaskaskia → IL   37°58N 89°57W   71 F4
Kasson MN   44°2N 92°45W   80 F6
Katahdin, Mt. ME   45°54N 68°56W   76 C5
Katalla AK   60°12N 144°31W   61 F11
Kathleen FL   28°7N 82°2W   67 C6
Kathryn ND   46°41N 97°58W   91 D8
Katmai Nat. Park and Preserve ○
   AK   58°20N 155°0W   61 G9
Katy TX   29°57N 99°49W   99 H12
Ka'ula HI   21°31N 160°33W   69 B1
Kau'a'i Desert HI   19°21N 155°19W   69 D6
Kaua'i HI   22°3N 159°30W   69 A2
Kaua'i Channel HI   21°45N 158°50W   69 B3
Kauai Island Lihue Municipal ✈ (LIH)   21°58N 159°20W   69 A2
Kaukauna WI   44°17N 88°17W   103 D5
Kaufman TX   32°35N 96°20W   99 E11
Kaufman County ☆
   TX   32°35N 96°20W   99 E11
Kauhola Pt. HI   20°15N 155°47W   69 C6
Kaukauna WI   44°17N 88°17W   103 D5
Kaukonahua → HI   21°35N 158°7W   69 J13
Ka'ula HI   21°40N 160°33W   69 B1
Kaulakahi Channel
   HI   22°0N 159°50W   69 B2
Kaumalapau HI   20°47N 156°59W   69 C5
Kaunā Pt. HI   19°2N 155°53W   69 D6
Kaunakakai HI   21°6N 157°1W   69 B4
Kaupō HI   20°38N 156°8W   69 C5
Kaw City OK   36°46N 96°50W   93 B7
Kaw L. OK   36°20N 96°50W   93 B7
Kawaihae B. HI   20°0N 155°50W   69 C6
Kawaikini HI   22°5N 159°29W   69 A2
Kawailoa HI   21°37N 158°5W   69 J13
Kawailoa Beach HI   21°37N 158°5W   69 J13
Kawailoa Forest Reserve
   HI   21°37N 158°0W   69 J14
Kaweah, L. CA   36°28N 118°52W   65 J8
Kawela HI   21°42N 158°1W   69 J13
Kawela B. HI   21°42N 158°1W   69 J13
Kay County ☆ OK   36°50N 97°9W   93 B6
Kaycee WY   43°43N 106°38W   104 C6
Kayenta AZ   36°44N 110°15W   62 A5
Kaylor SD   43°11N 97°50W   91 G8
Kaysville UT   41°2N 111°56W   100 B4
Kea'au HI   19°37N 155°2W   69 D7
Keahole Pt. HI   19°44N 156°4W   69 D5
Kealaikahiki Channel
   HI   20°35N 156°50W   69 C5
Kealakekua HI   19°31N 155°55W   69 D6
Keams Canyon AZ   35°49N 110°12W   62 B5
Keansburg NJ   40°27N 74°8W   87 B2
Kearny MO   39°22N 94°22W   82 B2
Kearney NE   40°42N 99°5W   84 D6

Kearney County ☆
   NE   40°30N 99°0W   84 D7
Kearneysville WV   39°23N 77°53W   77 A3
Kearns UT   40°39N 111°59W   117 C1
Kearny AZ   33°3N 110°55W   62 D5
Kearny NJ   40°46N 74°8W   114 B2
Kearny County ☆ KS   38°0N 101°15W   74 C2
Kearsarge OR   44°53N 117°53W   94 B8
Keating OR   44°53N 117°53W   94 B8
Keawakapu HI   20°43N 156°27W   69 C5
Keddie CA   40°1N 120°58W   64 C6
Keedysville MD   39°29N 77°40W   77 A3
Keefeton OK   35°36N 95°21W   93 C8
Ke'ehi Lagoon HI   21°20N 157°54W   69 K14
Keene NH   42°56N 72°17W   86 D2
Keene TX   32°24N 97°20W   99 E10
Keenesburg CO   40°7N 104°31W   66 B6
Keeseville NY   44°29N 73°30W   86 B1
Keewatin MN   47°24N 93°5W   80 C5
Kehena HI   21°20N 154°55W   69 D7
Keikwaha Pt. HI   19°31N 155°58W   69 D6
Keiser AR   35°40N 90°6W   63 C5
Keithsburg IL   41°6N 90°56W   71 B3
Keizer OR   44°57N 123°1W   94 C2
Kekaha HI   21°58N 159°43W   69 B2
Kelberg TX   32°42N 96°36W   109 B6
Kell IL   38°30N 88°54W   71 E5
Keller TX   32°56N 97°15W   109 A4
Keller WA   48°5N 118°41W   101 B7
Kellerton IA   40°43N 94°3W   73 E4
Kelleys I. OH   41°36N 82°42W   92 B4
Kelliher MN   47°57N 94°27W   80 C4
Kellogg ID   47°32N 116°7W   70 B2
Kellogg MN   44°18N 91°59W   80 F7
Kellyville OK   35°57N 96°13W   93 C7
Kelseyville CA   38°59N 122°50W   64 D4
Kelso WA   46°9N 122°54W   101 D3
Kemah TX   29°33N 95°1W   99 H12
Kemblesville PA   39°45N 75°50W   77 A5
Kemmerer WY   41°48N 110°32W   104 E2
Kemp OK   33°46N 96°21W   93 E7
Kemp, L. TX   33°26N 99°9W   99 D8
Kemper County ☆
   MS   32°46N 88°39W   81 D5
Kempton IL   40°56N 88°14W   71 C5
Kempton IN   40°17N 86°14W   72 C4
Kemptown MD   39°20N 77°13W   77 A3
Kenai AK   60°25N 151°15W   61 F10
Kenai Mts. AK   60°0N 150°0W   61 G10
Kenai Nat. Wildlife Refuge ○
   AK   59°40N 149°50W   61 G10
Kenai Peninsula ☆
   AK   60°25N 151°15W   61 F10
Kenansville FL   27°53N 80°59W   67 D8
Kenansville NC   34°58N 77°58W   90 D7
Kenbridge VA   36°58N 78°8W   102 E6
Kendall FL   25°40N 80°19W   112 D1
Kendall KS   37°56N 101°33W   74 D2
Kendall WI   43°48N 90°21W   103 E3
Kendall County ☆ IL   41°35N 88°25W   71 B5
Kendall County ☆
   TX   29°57N 98°48W   99 H9
Kendall Green MA   42°22N 71°16W   106 A2
Kendall Park NJ   40°24N 74°34W   87 B2
Kendallville IN   41°27N 85°16W   72 B5
Kendleton TX   29°26N 96°0W   99 H12
Kendrick ID   46°37N 116°39W   70 C2
Kendrick OK   35°47N 96°46W   93 C7
Kenedy TX   28°49N 97°51W   99 J10
Kenedy County ☆
   TX   27°0N 97°40W   98 K10
Kenefick TX   34°0N 96°22W   93 E7
Kenefick NE   30°7N 94°52W   99 G13
Kenesaw NE   40°37N 98°39W   84 D7
Kenhorst PA   40°19N 75°57W   77 A5
Kenilworth IL   42°5N 87°43W   108 A2
Kenly NC   35°36N 78°7W   90 C7
Kenmare ND   48°41N 102°5W   91 B3
Kenmore NY   42°58N 78°52W   89 C2
Kenmore WA   47°45N 122°14W   118 B4
Kenna NM   33°51N 103°46W   88 D7
Kennady WA   46°59N 95°8W   101 C4
Kennan WI   45°32N 90°35W   103 D4
Kennard NE   41°28N 96°12W   84 D7
Kennard TX   31°22N 95°11W   99 F12
Kennebago, L. ME   45°4N 70°44W   86 A4
Kennebec SD   43°54N 99°52W   91 G6
Kennebec → ME   43°45N 69°46W   76 E4
Kennebec County ☆
   ME   44°20N 69°46W   76 D4
Kennebunk ME   43°23N 70°33W   76 E3
Kennebunkport ME   43°21N 70°28W   76 E3
Kennedale TX   32°38N 97°13W   109 C4
Kennedy MN   48°39N 96°54W   80 B2
Kennedy, C. = Canaveral, C.
   FL   28°27N 80°32W   67 C8
Kennedy Entrance
   AK   59°1N 152°0W   61 G10
Kennedy Space Center
   U.S.A.   28°40N 80°42W   67 C8
Kennedyville MD   39°18N 75°58W   77 A5
Kenner LA   29°59N 90°14W   113 B1
Kennesaw GA   34°1N 84°37W   68 B2
Kennett MO   36°14N 90°3W   82 F6
Kennett Square PA   39°51N 75°43W   77 A5
Kennewick WA   46°12N 119°7W   101 D5
Kenney IL   40°6N 89°5W   71 C4
Keno OR   42°8N 121°56W   94 E4
Kenosha WI   42°35N 87°49W   103 F6
Kenosha County ☆
   WI   42°35N 87°50W   103 E5
Kenova WV   38°24N 82°35W   102 C2
Kensal ND   47°18N 98°44W   91 C7
Kensett AR   35°14N 91°40W   63 C4
Kensington CT   41°21N 93°13W   78 B5
Kensington KS   39°46N 99°2W   74 B4
Kensington MN   45°47N 95°42W   80 E3
Kensington NY   40°38N 73°57W   114 C3
Kent CT   41°44N 73°29W   78 C1
Kent IL   42°5N 89°53W   71 A4
Kent MN   46°26N 96°41W   80 D2
Kent OH   41°9N 81°22W   92 B5
Kent WA   47°23N 122°14W   118 C4
Kent City MI   43°13N 85°45W   79 F6
Kent County ☆ DE   39°5N 75°30W   77 A5
Kent County ☆ MD   39°15N 76°10W   77 A4
Kent County ☆ MI   43°0N 85°35W   79 F6
Kent County ☆ RI   41°35N 71°35W   78 C3
Kent County ☆ TX   33°10N 100°50W   98 D7
Kent I. MD   38°52N 76°18W   77 B4
Kent Village MD   38°55N 76°53W   119 B8
Kentland IN   40°46N 87°27W   72 C3

Kentmore Park MD   39°22N 75°58W   77 A5
Kenton DE   39°14N 75°40W   77 A5
Kenton MI   46°28N 88°54W   79 C3
Kenton OH   40°39N 83°37W   92 C3
Kenton OK   36°54N 102°58W   93 B1
Kenton TN   36°12N 89°1W   96 D3
Kenton County ☆
   KY   38°55N 84°32W   97 B8
Kenvale KY   39°3N 84°31W   107 B1
Kenton NY   36°54N 102°58W   93 B1
Kentucky ☆ U.S.A.   37°0N 84°0W   97 C8
Kentucky → KY   38°41N 85°11W   97 B7
Kentwood MD   42°52N 85°39W   79 G6
Kenwood MD   39°0N 76°30W   107 B2
Kenwood MD   39°12N 84°24W   107 A2
Kenyon MN   44°16N 92°59W   80 F6
Keo AR   34°36N 92°1W   63 D3
Keokuk IA   40°24N 91°24W   73 E7
Keokuk County ☆
   IA   41°20N 92°10W   73 D6
Keosauqua IA   40°44N 91°58W   73 E7
Keota CO   40°42N 104°5W   66 B6
Keota IA   41°22N 91°57W   73 D7
Keota OK   35°15N 94°55W   93 C9
Kepuhi Pt. HI   21°29N 158°14W   69 K13
Kerby OR   42°12N 123°39W   94 E2
Kerens TX   32°8N 96°14W   99 E11
Kerhonkson MN   45°12N 95°19W   80 E3
Kerman CA   36°43N 120°4W   65 G6
Kermit TX   31°52N 103°6W   98 F4
Kermit WV   37°50N 82°24W   102 D2
Kern County ☆ CA   35°20N 118°30W   65 H8
Kern Park WI   43°5N 87°57W   112 B2
Kernersville NC   36°7N 80°5W   90 B5
Kernville CA   35°45N 118°26W   65 H8
Kerr County ☆ TX   30°0N 99°21W   99 G8
Kerrick TX   36°30N 102°15W   98 A5
Kerrville TX   30°3N 99°8W   99 G8
Kersey CO   40°23N 104°34W   66 B6
Kershaw SC   34°33N 80°35W   90 D5
Kershaw County ☆
   SC   34°30N 80°40W   90 D5
Keshena WI   44°53N 88°39W   103 D5
Ketchikan AK   55°21N 131°39W   61 J15
Ketchikan Gateway ☆
   AK   55°30N 131°25W   61 J15
Ketchum ID   43°41N 114°22W   70 F4
Ketchum OK   36°32N 95°1W   93 B8
Kettering MD   38°53N 76°49W   119 B5
Kettering OH   39°41N 84°10W   92 D2
Kettle, ← MN   45°52N 92°59W   80 E6
Kettle Cr. → PA   41°18N 77°51W   95 C5
Kettle Falls WA   48°37N 118°3W   101 B7
Kettle River MN   46°29N 92°53W   80 D6
Kettle River Range
   WA   48°30N 118°40W   101 B7
Kettleman City CA   36°1N 119°58W   65 G7
Keuka L. NY   42°30N 77°9W   89 C5
Kevil KY   37°5N 88°53W   96 D3
Kevin MT   48°45N 111°58W   83 B6
Kewanee IL   41°14N 89°56W   71 B4
Kewanna IN   41°1N 86°25W   72 B4
Kewaskum WI   43°31N 88°14W   103 E5
Kewaunee WI   44°27N 87°31W   103 D6
Kewaunee County ☆
   WI   44°20N 87°35W   103 D6
Keweenaw B. MI   47°0N 88°15W   79 B3
Keweenaw County ☆
   MI   47°20N 88°5W   79 B3
Keweenaw Nat. Historical Park ○
   MI   47°15N 88°33W   79 B3
Keweenaw Pen. MI   47°15N 88°15W   79 B3
Keweenaw Pt. MI   47°25N 87°43W   79 B4
Key TX   32°44N 100°43W   98 E6
Key Biscayne FL   25°41N 80°9W   112 D3
Key Colony Beach
   FL   24°45N 80°57W   67 G8
Key Largo FL   25°5N 80°27W   67 F8
Key West FL   24°33N 81°48W   67 G7
Key West Nat. Wildlife Refuge ○
   FL   24°33N 82°22W   67 G6
Keya Paha → NE   42°54N 99°0W   84 B6
Keya Paha County ☆
   NE   42°50N 99°40W   84 B6
Keyapaha SD   43°7N 100°8W   91 G5
Keyes OK   36°49N 102°15W   98 A5
Keyesport IL   38°45N 89°17W   71 E4
Keyhole Reservoir
   WY   44°21N 104°51W   104 B8
Keymar MD   39°38N 77°16W   77 A3
Keyport NJ   40°26N 74°12W   87 B2
Keyport WA   47°42N 122°37W   118 B2
Keystone IA   42°0N 92°12W   73 D6
Keystone NE   41°13N 101°35W   84 C4
Keystone SD   43°54N 103°25W   91 G2
Keystone Heights FL   29°47N 82°2W   67 B6
Keystone Peak AZ   31°53N 111°13W   62 F4
Keysville GA   33°14N 82°14W   68 C4
Keysville MO   39°22N 78°29W   102 D6
Keytesville MO   39°26N 92°56W   82 B4
Kezar Falls ME   43°48N 70°53W   86 C4
Kiamichi → OK   34°38N 94°35W   93 D9
Kiamichi Mt. OK   34°37N 95°8W   93 D9
Kiana AK   66°58N 160°26W   61 C7
Kiawah Island SC   32°36N 80°5W   90 F5
Kickapoo → WI   43°5N 90°53W   103 E3
Kickapoo, L. TX   33°40N 98°47W   99 D9
Kickapoo Indian Reservation
   KS   39°40N 95°50W   74 B8
Kidder MO   39°47N 94°6W   82 B2
Kidder County ☆ ND   47°0N 99°50W   91 C6
Kiel WI   43°55N 88°2W   103 E5
Kiefer OK   35°57N 96°4W   93 C7
Kiel WI   43°55N 88°2W   103 E5
Kiester MN   43°32N 93°43W   80 G5
Kihei HI   20°47N 156°28W   69 C5
Kiholo B. HI   19°50N 155°55W   69 D6
Kijik AK   60°20N 154°20W   61 F9
Kila MT   48°7N 114°27W   83 B3
Kilauea HI   22°13N 159°25W   69 A2
Kilauea Caldera HI   19°25N 155°17W   69 D6
Kilbourne IL   40°9N 90°1W   71 C3
Kilbourne LA   33°0N 91°20W   75 B4
Kilbuck Mts. AK   60°30N 159°53W   61 F8
Kildare GA   32°32N 81°27W   68 D5
Kildare OK   36°48N 97°3W   93 B6
Kilgore ID   44°24N 111°54W   70 E7
Kilgore NE   42°56N 100°57W   84 B5
Kilgore TX   32°23N 94°53W   99 E13
Kilkenny MN   44°19N 93°34W   80 F5
Kill Devil Hills NC   36°1N 75°39W   90 B10
Kill Van Kull → NY   40°39N 74°5W   114 C2
Killbuck OH   40°30N 81°59W   92 C5
Killdeer ND   47°22N 102°45W   91 C3
Killeen TX   31°7N 97°44W   99 F10
Killen AL   34°52N 87°32W   60 B3
Killingly CT   41°50N 71°55W   78 C2
Killington Pk. VT   43°36N 72°49W   86 C2
Killingworth CT   41°21N 72°30W   78 C2
Kilmarnock VA   37°43N 76°23W   77 C4
Kilmichael MS   33°27N 89°34W   81 C4
Kim CO   37°15N 103°21W   66 E7
Kimball MN   45°14N 103°40W   80 E4
Kimball NE   41°14N 103°40W   84 C2
Kimball SD   43°45N 98°57W   91 G7
Kimball TN   37°26N 81°30W   102 D4

Kimball County ☆
  NE.......... 41°15N 103°40W 84 C2
Kimballton IA.... 41°38N 95°4W 73 D3
Kimberling City MO 36°38N 93°27W 82 E3
Kimberly ID.... 42°32N 114°22W 70 G4
Kimberly OR.... 44°46N 119°39W 94 C6
Kimble County ☆
  TX.......... 30°29N 99°46W 99 G4
Kimbolton OH.... 40°9N 81°34W 92 C5
Kimbrough AL.... 32°2N 87°34W 60 D3
Kinard FL.... 30°16N 85°15W 67 A3
Kincaid IL.... 39°35N 89°25W 71 D4
Kincaid KS.... 38°5N 95°9W 74 D8
Kinchafoonee Cr. →
  GA.......... 31°38N 84°10W 68 E2
Kinde MI.... 43°56N 83°0W 79 F9
Kinder LA.... 30°29N 92°51W 75 D3
Kinderhook NY.... 42°24N 73°42W 78 B4
Kindred ND.... 46°39N 97°1W 91 D8
King FL.... 36°17N 80°22W 90 B5
King and Queen County ☆
  VA.......... 37°40N 76°53W 102 D8
King and Queen Court House
  VA.......... 37°40N 76°53W 77 C4
King City CA.... 36°13N 121°8W 65 G5
King City MO.... 40°3N 94°31W 82 A2
King City TX.... 33°37N 100°19W 98 D7
King County ☆
  WA.......... 47°25N 121°40W 101 C4
King County Int. ✕ (BFI)
  WA.......... 47°27N 122°18W 118 C4
King Cove AK.... 55°3N 162°19W 61 J7
King George VA.... 38°16N 77°11W 77 B3
King George County ☆
  VA.......... 38°16N 77°11W 102 C7
King of Prussia PA.... 40°5N 75°23W 87 B1
King Range Nat. Conservation
  Area ◌ CA.... 40°4N 124°8W 64 C2
King Salmon AK.... 58°42N 156°40W 61 G8
King William VA.... 37°41N 77°1W 102 D7
King William County ☆
  VA.......... 37°41N 77°1W 102 D7
Kingfield ME.... 44°58N 70°9W 76 D3
Kingfisher OK.... 35°52N 97°56W 93 C6
Kingfisher County ☆
  OK.......... 36°0N 98°0W 93 C6
Kingman AZ.... 35°12N 114°4W 62 B1
Kingman KS.... 37°39N 98°7W 74 D5
Kingman County ☆
  KS.......... 37°30N 98°0W 74 D5
Kings → AR.... 36°30N 93°35W 63 B2
Kings → CA.... 36°3N 119°50W 65 G7
Kings → NV.... 41°31N 118°8W 85 A2
Kings Canyon Nat. Park △
  CA.......... 36°50N 118°40W 65 G8
Kings County ☆ CA.... 36°0N 119°50W 65 G7
Kings County ☆ NY.... 40°37N 73°55W 89 E7
Kings Mountain NC.... 35°15N 81°20W 90 G4
Kings Park NY.... 40°53N 73°14W 114 B4
Kings Park West VA.... 38°48N 77°18W 119 C12
Kings Peak UT.... 40°46N 110°23W 104 D5
Kings Valley OR.... 44°42N 123°26W 94 C2
Kingsburg CA.... 36°31N 119°33W 65 G7
Kingsbury NY.... 43°22N 73°32W 86 C1
Kingsbury County ☆
  SD.......... 44°23N 97°33W 91 F8
Kingsdown KS.... 37°32N 99°46W 74 D4
Kingsford MI.... 45°48N 88°4W 79 D3
Kingsford Heights IN 41°29N 86°42W 72 B4
Kingsland AR.... 33°52N 92°18W 63 E3
Kingsland GA.... 30°48N 81°41W 68 F6
Kingsland TX.... 30°40N 98°26W 99 G9
Kingsley IA.... 42°35N 95°58W 73 C5
Kingsley MI.... 44°35N 85°32W 79 E6
Kingsmill TX.... 35°29N 101°4W 98 B6
Kingsport TN.... 36°33N 82°33W 97 D10
Kingston → AR.... 36°3N 93°35W 63 B2
Kingston GA.... 34°14N 84°57W 68 C2
Kingston IL.... 42°6N 88°46W 71 A5
Kingston KY.... 37°39N 84°15W 97 C8
Kingston MA.... 42°0N 70°43W 78 B4
Kingston MD.... 38°5N 75°46W 77 B5
Kingston MI.... 43°25N 83°11W 79 F8
Kingston MN.... 45°12N 94°19W 80 E4
Kingston MO.... 39°39N 94°2W 82 A2
Kingston NH.... 42°56N 71°3W 86 D3
Kingston NM.... 32°55N 107°42W 88 E3
Kingston NY.... 41°56N 73°59W 89 D7
Kingston OH.... 39°28N 82°55W 92 D4
Kingston OK.... 33°59N 96°45W 93 E7
Kingston PA.... 41°16N 75°54W 95 C7
Kingston RI.... 41°29N 71°30W 78 C3
Kingston TN.... 35°52N 84°31W 97 E8
Kingston UT.... 38°13N 112°11W 100 E3
Kingston WA.... 47°47N 122°30W 118 B3
Kingston WI.... 43°42N 89°8W 103 E4
Kingston Pk. CA.... 35°44N 115°55W 65 H11
Kingston Springs TN.. 36°6N 87°7W 96 D5
Kingstree SC.... 33°40N 79°50W 90 E6
Kingsville MD.... 39°27N 76°25W 77 A4
Kingsville OH.... 38°45N 94°4W 82 C2
Kingsville TX.... 27°31N 97°52W 98 K10
Kingwood TX.... 30°2N 95°16W 99 G12
Kingwood WV.... 39°28N 79°41W 102 B5
Kinkaid L. IL.... 37°40N 89°25W 71 F4
Kinloch MO.... 38°44N 90°19W 117 A2
Kinmundy IL.... 38°46N 88°51W 71 E5
Kinnear WY.... 43°9N 108°41W 104 C4
Kinnelon NJ.... 40°58N 74°22W 87 B2
Kinney County ☆
  TX.......... 29°19N 100°25W 98 H7
Kinsale VA.... 38°2N 76°35W 77 B4
Kinsley KS.... 37°55N 99°25W 74 D4
Kinston AL.... 31°13N 86°10W 60 E4
Kinston NC.... 35°16N 77°35W 90 C8
Kinta OK.... 35°8N 95°14W 93 C8
Kinzua OR.... 44°59N 120°3W 94 C5
Kiowa CO.... 39°21N 104°28W 66 C6
Kiowa KS.... 37°1N 98°29W 74 D5
Kiowa OK.... 34°43N 95°54W 93 D8
Kiowa County ☆ CO.. 38°25N 102°50W 66 D8
Kiowa County ☆ KS.. 37°30N 99°15W 74 D4
Kiowa County ☆ OK.. 35°0N 99°0W 93 D5
Kiowa Cr. → CO.... 40°20N 104°5W 66 B6
Kiowa Cr. → OK.... 36°46N 99°55W 93 B4
Kipapa → HI.... 21°24N 158°1W 69 G13
Kipnuk AK.... 59°56N 164°3W 61 G6
Kipp KS.... 38°47N 97°27W 74 C6
Kiptopeke VA.... 37°8N 75°58W 102 D9
Kirby TX.... 29°27N 98°23W 117 C3
Kirby WY.... 43°48N 108°11W 104 C4
Kirbyville TX.... 30°40N 93°54W 99 G14
Kirk CO.... 39°37N 102°36W 66 C8
Kirk OR.... 42°45N 121°43W 94 D4
Kirkland AZ.... 34°25N 112°43W 62 C3
Kirkland IL.... 42°6N 88°51W 71 A5
Kirkland TX.... 34°23N 100°4W 98 C7
Kirkland WA.... 47°40N 122°12W 118 B4
Kirkland Junction
  AZ.......... 34°22N 112°40W 62 C3
Kirklin IN.... 40°12N 86°22W 72 C4
Kirkman IA.... 41°44N 95°16W 73 D3
Kirkmansville KY.... 37°1N 87°15W 96 C4
Kirksey KY.... 36°42N 88°24W 96 D4
Kirksville MO.... 40°12N 92°35W 82 A4
Kirkwood DE.... 39°34N 75°42W 77 A5
Kirkwood IL.... 40°52N 90°45W 71 C3
Kirkwood MO.... 38°35N 90°24W 82 C6
Kirkwood PA.... 39°51N 76°5W 77 A4
Kiron IA.... 42°12N 95°20W 73 C3

Kirtland NM.... 36°44N 108°21W 88 A2
Kirwin KS.... 39°40N 99°7W 74 B4
Kirwin Res. KS.... 39°40N 99°8W 74 B4
Kiryas Joel NY.... 41°21N 74°10W 87 A2
Kisatchie LA.... 31°25N 93°10W 75 C2
Kisatchie Nat. Forest
  LA.......... 31°45N 92°30W 75 C3
Kiska I. AK.... 51°59N 177°30E 61 L2
Kismet KS.... 37°12N 100°42W 74 D3
Kissena Park NY.... 40°44N 73°48W 114 B4
Kissimmee FL.... 28°18N 81°24W 67 C7
Kissimmee → FL.... 27°9N 80°52W 67 D8
Kissimmee, L. FL.... 27°55N 81°17W 67 C7
Kit Carson CO.... 38°46N 102°48W 66 D8
Kit Carson County ☆
  CO.......... 39°15N 102°30W 66 C8
Kitsap County ☆
  WA.......... 47°30N 122°45W 101 C3
Kittanning PA.... 40°49N 79°31W 95 D3
Kittatinny Mt. NJ.... 41°19N 74°39W 87 A2
Kittery ME.... 43°5N 70°45W 86 C4
Kittitas WA.... 46°59N 120°25W 101 D5
Kittitas County ☆
  WA.......... 47°0N 120°30W 101 C5
Kitts Hummock DE.. 39°8N 75°25W 77 A3
Kittson County ☆
  MN.......... 48°50N 96°50W 80 B2
Kitzmiller MD.... 39°23N 79°10W 77 A1
Kivalina AK.... 67°44N 164°33W 61 C6
Klamath CA.... 41°32N 124°2W 64 B1
Klamath → CA.... 41°33N 124°5W 64 B2
Klamath County ☆
  OR.......... 42°40N 121°40W 94 E4
Klamath Falls OR.... 42°13N 121°46W 94 E4
Klamath Marsh OR.... 43°0N 121°40W 94 E4
Klamath Mts. AK.... 62°30N 156°0W 61 E9
Klamath Nat. Forest
  CA.......... 41°30N 123°20W 64 B3
Klamath River CA.... 41°52N 122°50W 64 B4
Klawock AK.... 55°33N 133°6W 61 J14
Kleberg County ☆
  TX.......... 27°31N 97°52W 98 K10
Klein MT.... 46°24N 108°33W 83 D9
Klemme IA.... 43°1N 93°36W 73 B5
Kletzsch Park WI.... 43°8N 87°55W 112 B2
Klickitat WA.... 45°49N 121°9W 101 E4
Klickitat → WA.... 45°41N 121°17W 101 E4
Klickitat County ☆
  WA.......... 45°55N 120°30W 101 E5
Klondike Goldrush Nat. Historical
  Park ◌ U.S.A. 59°27N 135°19W 61 G14
Klukwan AK.... 59°24N 135°54W 61 G14
Knapp WI.... 44°57N 92°5W 103 D1
Kneeland CA.... 40°45N 123°54W 64 C2
Knierim IA.... 42°27N 94°27W 73 C4
Knife → ND.... 47°17N 101°20W 91 C4
Knife River MN.... 46°57N 91°47W 80 D7
Knife River Indian Village Nat.
  Historic Site ◌
  ND.......... 47°20N 101°23W 91 C4
Knight L. AK.... 60°21N 147°45W 61 F11
Knightdale NC.... 35°47N 78°29W 90 C7
Knights Landing CA 38°48N 121°43W 64 E5
Knightstown IN.... 39°48N 85°32W 72 D5
Knob Lick KY.... 37°5N 85°42W 97 C7
Knob Lick MO.... 37°41N 90°22W 82 D6
Knob Noster MO.... 38°46N 93°33W 82 C3
Knobel AR.... 36°19N 90°36W 63 B5
Knott County ☆ KY.... 37°20N 83°0W 97 C10
Knowland State Arboretum and
  Park ◌ CA.... 37°45N 122°7W 118 B4
Knowles OK.... 36°53N 100°12W 93 B3
Knox IN.... 41°18N 86°37W 72 B4
Knox PA.... 41°14N 79°32W 95 C3
Knox City MO.... 40°9N 92°1W 82 A4
Knox City TX.... 33°25N 99°49W 98 D8
Knox County ☆ IL.... 40°55N 90°10W 71 C3
Knox County ☆ IN.... 38°40N 87°25W 72 E3
Knox County ☆ KY.... 36°55N 83°50W 97 D9
Knox County ☆ ME.... 44°5N 69°5W 76 D4
Knox County ☆ MO.. 40°10N 92°10W 82 A4
Knox County ☆ NE.. 42°40N 97°50W 84 B8
Knox County ☆ OH.. 40°23N 82°29W 92 C4
Knox County ☆ TN.. 36°0N 84°0W 97 D9
Knox County ☆ TX.. 33°35N 99°48W 98 D8
Knoxville GA.... 32°47N 83°59W 68 D3
Knoxville IA.... 41°19N 93°6W 73 D5
Knoxville IL.... 40°55N 90°17W 71 C3
Knoxville PA.... 41°57N 77°27W 95 C5
Knoxville TN.... 35°58N 83°55W 97 E9
Knoxville McGhee Tyson ✕ (TYS)
  TN.......... 35°49N 83°59W 97 E9
Kobuk AK.... 66°55N 156°52W 61 C8
Kobuk → AK.... 66°54N 160°38W 61 C7
Kobuk Valley Nat. Park △
  AK.......... 67°0N 160°0W 61 C7
Kodiak AK.... 57°47N 152°24W 61 H9
Kodiak I. AK.... 57°30N 152°45W 61 H9
Kodiak Island ☆
  AK.......... 57°20N 153°20W 61 H9
Koehn Dry L. CA.... 35°20N 117°53W 65 H9
Kofa Mts. AZ.... 33°15N 113°40W 62 D2
Kofa Nat. Wildlife Refuge ◌
  AZ.......... 33°15N 113°50W 62 D2
Kohala Forest Reserve
  HI.......... 20°9N 155°4W 69 C6
Kohala Mts. HI.... 20°5N 155°43W 69 C6
Kohler WI.... 43°44N 87°47W 103 E6
Kohlman Lake MN.. 45°1N 93°3W 113 A3
Kōke'e State Park ◌
  HI.......... 22°6N 159°40W 69 A2
Koko Head HI.... 21°16N 157°43W 69 K14
Kokomo IN.... 40°29N 86°8W 72 C4
Kokomo MS.... 31°12N 90°0W 81 E3
Koliganek AK.... 59°48N 157°25W 61 G8
Koloa HI.... 21°55N 159°28W 69 B2
Komatke AZ.... 33°17N 112°10W 116 D2
Kona ✕ (KOA) HI.. 19°44N 156°3W 69 D5
Konahuanui HI.... 21°21N 157°47W 69 K14
Konawa OK.... 34°58N 96°45W 93 D7
Koochiching County ☆
  MN.......... 48°15N 93°50W 80 B5
Ko'olau Range HI.. 21°35N 157°50W 69 J14
Ko'olauloa District
  HI.......... 21°35N 157°55W 69 J14
Ko'olaupoko District
  HI.......... 21°25N 157°50W 69 K14
Koosharem UT.... 38°31N 111°53W 100 E4
Kooskia ID.... 46°9N 115°59W 70 C3
Kootenai → ID.... 49°0N 116°30W 70 A2
Kootenai County ☆
  ID.......... 47°45N 116°30W 70 B2
Kootenai Nat. Forest
  MT.......... 48°30N 115°40W 83 B2
Kopperston WV.... 37°45N 81°35W 102 D3
Korona FL.... 29°25N 81°12W 67 B7
Kosciusko MS.... 33°4N 89°35W 81 C4
Kosciusko County ☆
  IN.......... 41°15N 85°50W 72 B5
Koshkonong MO.... 36°36N 91°39W 82 E5
Koshkonong L. WI.. 42°53N 88°58W 103 F5
Kosse TX.... 31°18N 96°38W 99 F11
Kossuth MS.... 34°56N 88°41W 81 B5
Kossuth County ☆ IA 43°15N 94°10W 73 B4
Kotlik AK.... 63°2N 163°33W 61 E6
Kotzebue AK.... 66°53N 162°39W 61 C7
Kotzebue Sound AK.. 66°20N 163°0W 61 C6
Kouts IN.... 41°19N 87°2W 72 B3
Kountze TX.... 30°22N 94°19W 99 G13
Koyuk AK.... 64°56N 161°9W 61 D7
Koyuk → AK.... 64°55N 161°9W 61 D7
Koyukuk AK.... 64°56N 157°30W 61 D8
Koyukuk → AK.... 64°55N 157°32W 61 D8

Koyukuk Nat. Wildlife Refuge ◌
  AK.......... 65°35N 156°30W 61 D8
Kramer ND.... 48°42N 100°43W 91 B5
Kranzburg SD.... 44°54N 96°55W 91 F8
Krebs OK.... 34°56N 95°43W 93 D8
Kremlin MT.... 48°33N 110°5W 83 B7
Kremmling CO.... 40°4N 106°24W 66 B4
Kress TX.... 34°22N 101°45W 98 C6
Krotz Springs LA.... 30°32N 91°45W 75 D4
Krum TX.... 33°16N 97°14W 99 D10
Krusenstern, C. AK 67°8N 163°45W 61 C7
Ku Tree Res. HI.... 21°30N 157°59W 69 J14
Kualapu'u HI.... 21°9N 157°2W 69 H5
Kualoa Pt. HI.... 21°31N 157°50W 69 J14
Kuapā Pond HI.... 21°17N 157°43W 69 K14
Kuehn MT.... 45°49N 107°5W 83 E10
Kuiu I. AK.... 57°45N 134°10W 61 H14
Kukuihaele HI.... 20°5N 155°35W 69 C6
Kulm ND.... 46°18N 98°57W 91 D7
Kumukahi, C. HI.... 19°31N 154°49W 69 D7
Kuna ID.... 43°30N 116°25W 70 F2
Kunkletown PA.... 40°51N 75°27W 87 B1
Kūpikipiki'o Pt. HI 21°15N 157°47W 69 K14
Kupreanof I. AK.... 56°50N 133°30W 61 H14
Kure I. HI.... 28°25N 178°25W 69 F8
Kurthwood LA.... 31°20N 93°10W 75 C2
Kurtistown HI.... 19°36N 155°4W 69 D6
Kuskokwim → AK.. 60°5N 162°25W 61 F7
Kuskokwim B. AK.. 59°45N 162°25W 61 G7
Kuskokwim Mts. AK 62°30N 156°0W 61 E9
Kuttawa KY.... 37°4N 88°7W 96 C3
Kutztown PA.... 40°31N 75°47W 87 B1
Kuzitrin → AK.... 65°10N 165°25W 61 D6
Kvichak B. AK.... 58°48N 157°30W 61 G8
Kwethluk AK.... 60°49N 161°26W 61 F7
Kwigillingok AK.... 59°51N 163°8W 61 G7
Kyburz CA.... 38°47N 120°18W 64 E6
Kykotsmovi Village
  AZ.......... 35°52N 110°37W 62 B5
Kyle SD.... 43°26N 102°10W 91 G3
Kyle TX.... 29°59N 97°53W 99 H10

L

La Barge WY.... 42°16N 110°12W 104 D2
La Belle FL.... 26°46N 81°26W 67 E7
La Belle MO.... 40°7N 91°55W 82 A5
La Canada Flintridge
  CA.......... 34°11N 118°11W 111 A2
La Center KY.... 37°4N 88°58W 96 C4
La Center WA.... 45°52N 122°40W 101 E3
La Cienega NM.... 35°34N 106°4W 88 B4
La Conner WA.... 48°23N 122°30W 101 B3
La Crescent MN.... 43°50N 91°18W 80 G7
La Crescenta CA.... 34°14N 118°14W 111 A2
La Crosse FL.... 29°51N 82°24W 67 B6
La Crosse KS.... 38°32N 99°18W 74 C4
La Crosse VA.... 36°42N 78°6W 102 E6
La Crosse WI.... 43°48N 91°15W 103 E2
La Crosse County ☆
  WI.......... 44°0N 91°0W 103 E2
La Cygne KS.... 38°21N 94°46W 74 C9
La Cygne, L. KS.... 38°20N 94°39W 74 C9
La Fayette GA.... 34°42N 85°17W 68 B1
La Fayette KY.... 36°40N 87°40W 96 D5
La Follette TN.... 36°23N 84°7W 97 D8
La Fontaine IN.... 40°40N 85°43W 72 C5
La Garita CO.... 37°50N 106°15W 66 E4
La Grande OR.... 45°20N 118°5W 94 B7
La Grange AR.... 34°39N 90°44W 63 D5
La Grange GA.... 33°2N 85°2W 68 D1
La Grange IN.... 41°48N 85°23W 72 B5
La Grange KY.... 38°24N 85°23W 97 B7
La Grange MO.... 40°3N 91°29W 82 A5
La Grange NC.... 35°19N 77°47W 90 C8
La Grange TN.... 35°3N 89°16W 96 E2
La Grange TX.... 29°54N 96°52W 99 H11
La Grange WY.... 41°38N 104°10W 104 D8
La Grange Park IL.. 41°49N 87°51W 108 C1
La Guardia, New York ✕ (LGA)
  NY.......... 40°46N 73°52W 114 B4
La Harpe IL.... 40°35N 90°58W 71 C3
La Harpe KS.... 37°55N 95°18W 74 D8
La Jara CO.... 37°16N 105°58W 66 E5
La Jara NM.... 36°33N 106°44W 88 A4
La Jolla CA.... 32°50N 117°16W 117 A1
La Jolla Indian Reservation
  CA.......... 33°16N 116°52W 65 K10
La Joya NM.... 34°21N 106°51W 88 C4
La Joya TX.... 26°14N 98°27W 98 L9
La Junta CO.... 37°59N 103°33W 66 E7
La Luz NM.... 32°59N 105°57W 88 E5
La Madera NM.... 36°23N 106°3W 88 A4
La Marque TX.... 29°23N 94°58W 99 H13
La Mesa CA.... 32°46N 117°1W 117 B3
La Mesa NM.... 32°16N 106°42W 88 F4
La Mesilla NM.... 32°16N 106°48W 88 E4
La Moille IL.... 41°32N 89°17W 71 B4
La Moine → IL.... 39°59N 90°31W 71 D3
La Monte MO.... 38°46N 93°26W 82 C3
La Moure ND.... 46°21N 98°18W 91 D7
La Moure County ☆
  ND.......... 46°23N 98°29W 91 D7
La Palma AZ.... 32°53N 111°31W 62 D4
La Paz ☆ AZ.... 33°55N 113°53W 62 D2
La Pine OR.... 43°40N 121°30W 94 D4
La Plant SD.... 45°9N 100°39W 91 E5
La Plata MD.... 38°32N 76°59W 77 B4
La Plata MO.... 40°2N 92°29W 82 A4
La Plata NM.... 36°56N 108°12W 88 A2
La Plata County ☆
  CO.......... 37°15N 107°50W 66 E3
La Porte TX.... 29°40N 95°1W 99 H12
La Porte City IA.... 42°19N 92°12W 73 C6
La Pryor TX.... 28°57N 99°51W 98 J8
La Puente NM.... 36°42N 106°36W 88 A4
La Push WA.... 47°55N 124°38W 101 C1
La Rue OH.... 40°35N 83°23W 92 C3
La Sal UT.... 38°19N 109°14W 100 E6
La Sal Mts. UT.... 38°30N 109°10W 100 E6
La Salle CO.... 40°21N 104°42W 66 B6
La Salle IL.... 41°20N 89°6W 71 B4
La Salle County ☆ IL 41°25N 88°50W 71 B5
La Salle County ☆
  TX.......... 28°26N 99°14W 99 J8
La Salle Parish ☆ LA 31°41N 92°8W 75 C3
La Union NM.... 31°57N 106°40W 88 F4
La Vale MD.... 39°40N 78°48W 77 A2
La Vale WI.... 43°35N 90°8W 103 E3
La Vergne TN.... 36°1N 86°35W 96 D6
La Verkin UT.... 37°12N 113°16W 100 F2
La Veta CO.... 37°31N 105°0W 66 E6
Lā'au Pt. HI.... 21°6N 157°19W 69 B4
Labadieville LA.... 29°50N 90°57W 75 E5
Labette KS.... 37°14N 95°11W 74 D8
Labette County ☆
  KS.......... 37°15N 95°15W 74 D8
Lac Courte Oreilles Indian
  Reservation WI.. 45°50N 91°15W 103 C2
Lac du Flambeau WI 45°58N 89°53W 103 C4
Lac du Flambeau Indian
  Reservation WI.. 46°0N 89°50W 103 B4

Lac qui Parle County ☆
  MN.......... 44°55N 96°0W 80 F2
Lac Vieux Desert Indian
  Reservation MI.. 46°10N 89°9W 79 C2
Lacassine, Bayou →
  LA.......... 30°19N 92°53W 75 D3
Lacey WA.... 47°7N 122°49W 101 C3
Lacey Spring VA.... 38°32N 78°46W 102 C6
Lachine MI.... 45°4N 83°43W 79 D8
Lackawanna NY.... 42°50N 78°50W 89 C2
Lackawanna → PA.. 41°20N 75°48W 87 A1
Lackawanna County ☆
  PA.......... 41°30N 75°30W 95 C7
Lackawaxen → PA.. 41°29N 74°59W 87 A1
Lackland City TX.. 29°23N 98°38W 117 C2
Laclede County ☆
  MO.......... 37°40N 92°35W 82 D4
Lacombe LA.... 30°19N 89°56W 75 E6
Lacon IL.... 41°2N 89°24W 71 B4
Lacona NY.... 43°39N 76°10W 89 B4
Laconia IN.... 38°2N 86°5W 72 F4
Laconia NH.... 43°32N 71°28W 86 C3
Lacoochee FL.... 28°28N 82°11W 67 C6
Lacreek L. SD.... 43°7N 101°33W 91 G4
Ladd IL.... 41°23N 89°13W 71 B4
Ladder Cr. → KS.. 38°45N 100°52W 74 C3
Laddonia MO.... 39°15N 91°39W 82 B5
Ladelle AR.... 33°45N 91°48W 63 E4
Ladera Heights CA 33°59N 118°22W 111 C2
Ladonia TX.... 33°26N 95°57W 99 D12
Ladonia AL.... 32°22N 85°1W 60 D6
Ladson SC.... 32°59N 80°6W 90 F5
Ladue MO.... 38°38N 90°22W 117 B1
Lady Lake FL.... 28°55N 81°55W 67 C7
Ladysmith WI.... 45°28N 91°12W 103 C2
Lae 'o Kākā HI.... 20°31N 156°33W 69 C9
Lae 'o Kealaikahiki
  HI.......... 20°32N 156°42W 69 C5
Lafayette AL.... 32°54N 85°24W 60 D6
Lafayette CA.... 37°53N 122°7W 118 B4
Lafayette CO.... 39°58N 105°12W 66 B5
Lafayette IN.... 40°25N 86°54W 72 C3
Lafayette LA.... 30°14N 92°1W 75 D3
Lafayette MN.... 44°27N 94°24W 80 F4
Lafayette OH.... 40°46N 83°57W 92 C3
Lafayette OR.... 45°15N 123°7W 94 B2
Lafayette County ☆
  AR.......... 33°22N 93°43W 63 E2
Lafayette County ☆ FL 30°0N 83°0W 67 B5
Lafayette County ☆
  MO.......... 39°4N 93°45W 82 B3
Lafayette County ☆
  MS.......... 34°22N 89°31W 81 B4
Lafayette County ☆
  WI.......... 42°35N 90°10W 103 F3
Lafayette Hill PA.. 40°4N 75°15W 116 A1
Lafayette Parish ☆
  LA.......... 30°14N 92°1W 75 D3
Lafayette Res. CA.. 37°53N 122°8W 118 A4
Lafitte LA.... 29°40N 90°6W 75 E5
Lafontaine KS.... 37°24N 95°51W 74 D8
Lafourche, Bayou →
  LA.......... 29°5N 90°14W 75 E5
Lafourche Parish ☆
  LA.......... 29°30N 90°15W 75 E5
Lagrange IN.... 41°39N 85°25W 72 B5
Lagrange ME.... 45°11N 68°54W 76 C5
Lagrange OH.... 41°14N 82°7W 92 B4
Lagrange County ☆
  IN.......... 41°35N 85°25W 72 B5
Laguna NM.... 35°2N 107°25W 88 B3
Laguna Atascosa Nat. Wildlife
  Refuge ◌ TX.... 26°17N 97°23W 99 L10
Laguna Beach CA.. 33°33N 117°47W 65 K9
Laguna Beach FL.. 30°14N 85°55W 67 A3
Laguna Indian Reservation
  NM.......... 35°0N 107°20W 88 C3
Laguna Mts. CA.... 33°0N 116°40W 65 K10
Lahaina HI.... 20°53N 156°41W 69 C5
Lahaina Pt. HI.... 21°28N 158°13W 69 K13
Lahoma OK.... 36°23N 98°5W 93 B5
Lahontan Res. NV.. 39°28N 119°4W 85 D1
Lā'ie HI.... 21°39N 157°56W 69 J14
Laingsburg MI.... 42°54N 84°21W 79 G7
Lair KY.... 38°20N 84°18W 97 B8
Lajitas TX.... 29°16N 103°46W 98 H4
Lake MS.... 32°21N 89°20W 81 D4
Lake WY.... 44°33N 110°24W 104 B2
Lake Alfred FL.... 28°6N 81°44W 67 C7
Lake Andes SD.... 43°9N 98°32W 91 G7
Lake Ann MI.... 44°43N 85°51W 79 E6
Lake Arthur LA.... 30°5N 92°41W 75 D3
Lake Arthur NM.... 33°0N 104°22W 88 E6
Lake Benton MN.... 44°15N 96°17W 80 F2
Lake Bird FL.... 30°14N 83°37W 67 A5
Lake Bronson MN.. 48°44N 96°40W 80 B2
Lake Buena Vista
  FL.......... 28°23N 81°32W 115 B1
Lake Butler FL.... 30°1N 82°21W 67 A6
Lake Cain Hill FL.. 28°29N 81°28W 115 B2
Lake Carmel NY.... 41°28N 73°40W 87 A3
Lake Charles LA.... 30°14N 93°13W 75 D2
Lake Chelan Nat. Recr. Area ◌
  WA.......... 48°25N 120°32W 101 B5
Lake City AR.... 35°49N 90°26W 63 C5
Lake City CA.... 41°39N 120°13W 64 B6
Lake City CO.... 38°2N 107°19W 66 D3
Lake City FL.... 30°11N 82°38W 67 A6
Lake City IA.... 42°16N 94°44W 73 C4
Lake City KS.... 37°22N 98°49W 74 D5
Lake City MI.... 44°20N 85°13W 79 E6
Lake City MN.... 44°27N 92°16W 80 F6
Lake City PA.... 42°1N 80°21W 95 B2
Lake City SC.... 33°52N 79°45W 90 E6
Lake City TN.... 36°13N 84°9W 97 D8
Lake Clark Nat. Park and
  Preserve △ AK.. 61°0N 154°0W 61 F9
Lake Clear NY.... 44°22N 74°14W 89 A6
Lake County ☆ CA.. 39°5N 122°45W 64 D4
Lake County ☆ CO.. 39°10N 106°20W 66 C4
Lake County ☆ FL.. 28°45N 81°45W 67 C7
Lake County ☆ IL.. 42°25N 87°55W 72 A5
Lake County ☆ IN.. 41°25N 87°25W 72 B3
Lake County ☆ MI.. 44°0N 85°45W 79 E6
Lake County ☆ MN.. 47°40N 91°30W 80 C7
Lake County ☆ MT.. 47°40N 114°10W 83 C3
Lake County ☆ OH.. 41°45N 81°15W 92 B5
Lake County ☆ OR.. 42°45N 120°30W 94 E5
Lake County ☆ SD.. 44°0N 97°10W 91 F8
Lake County ☆ TN.. 36°23N 89°29W 96 D3
Lake Crystal MN.... 44°6N 94°13W 80 F4
Lake Delton WI.... 43°36N 89°47W 103 E4
Lake Elmo MN.... 44°59N 92°53W 113 B4
Lake Elmo Regional Park
  MN.......... 44°59N 92°55W 113 B4
Lake Elsinore CA.. 33°38N 117°20W 65 K9
Lake Fairfax Park
  VA.......... 38°57N 77°19W 119 B2
Lake Forest IL.... 42°15N 87°50W 72 A6
Lake Forest Park
  WA.......... 47°45N 122°16W 118 B4
Lake Fork ID.... 44°58N 116°7W 70 E2
Lake Fork → UT.... 40°13N 110°7W 100 D5
Lake Geneva WI.... 42°36N 88°26W 103 F5
Lake George CO.... 38°59N 105°22W 66 C5

Lake George MN.... 47°12N 94°59W 80 C4
Lake George NY.... 43°26N 73°43W 89 B7
Lake Hamilton AR.. 34°25N 93°6W 63 D2
Lake Harbor FL.... 26°42N 80°48W 67 E8
Lake Havasu City
  AZ.......... 34°27N 114°22W 62 C1
Lake Helen FL.... 28°59N 81°14W 67 C7
Lake Hughes CA.... 34°41N 118°26W 65 J8
Lake Isabella CA.. 35°38N 118°28W 65 H8
Lake Jackson TX.. 29°3N 95°27W 99 H12
Lake Lenore Caves
  WA.......... 47°28N 119°31W 101 C6
Lake Lillian MN.... 44°57N 94°52W 80 F4
Lake Linden MI.... 47°12N 88°25W 79 B3
Lake Lure NC.... 35°26N 82°13W 90 C3
Lake Luzerne NY.. 43°19N 73°50W 89 B7
Lake Mary FL.... 28°46N 81°19W 67 C7
Lake Mason Nat. Wildlife
  Refuge ◌ MT.... 46°38N 108°44W 83 D9
Lake Mead NV.... 36°1N 114°44W 85 F6
Lake Mead Nat. Recr. Area ◌
  AZ.......... 36°30N 114°22W 62 A1
Lake Meredith Nat. Recr. Area ◌
  TX.......... 35°50N 101°50W 98 B6
Lake Mills IA.... 43°25N 93°32W 73 B5
Lake Mills WI.... 43°5N 88°55W 103 E5
Lake Mohawk NJ.. 41°1N 74°39W 87 A2
Lake Montezuma
  AZ.......... 34°38N 111°47W 62 C4
Lake Murray UT.... 40°39N 111°52W 117 B2
Lake Nebagamon WI 46°31N 91°42W 103 B2
Lake Norden SD.... 44°35N 97°13W 91 F8
Lake Odessa MI.... 42°47N 85°8W 79 G6
Lake of the Woods County ☆
  MN.......... 48°40N 94°50W 80 B4
Lake Ophelia Nat. Wildlife
  Refuge ◌ LA.... 31°15N 91°55W 75 C4
Lake Orion MI.... 42°47N 83°14W 79 G8
Lake Oswego OR.. 45°25N 122°40W 116 B1
Lake Ozark MO.... 38°12N 92°38W 82 C4
Lake Park GA.... 30°42N 83°11W 68 F3
Lake Park IA.... 43°27N 95°19W 73 B3
Lake Park MN.... 46°53N 96°6W 80 D2
Lake Placid FL.... 27°18N 81°22W 67 D7
Lake Placid NY.... 44°17N 73°59W 89 A7
Lake Pleasant NY.. 43°28N 74°25W 89 B6
Lake Preston SD.... 44°22N 97°23W 91 F8
Lake Providence LA 32°48N 91°10W 75 B4
Lake Range NV.... 40°10N 119°20W 85 B1
Lake Roosevelt Nat. Recr. Area ◌
  WA.......... 48°5N 118°14W 101 B7
Lake Seminole Park
  FL.......... 27°51N 82°46W 119 B2
Lake Shore MD.... 39°7N 76°29W 77 A4
Lake Stevens WA.. 48°1N 122°4W 101 B4
Lake Success NY.. 40°47N 73°43W 114 B4
Lake Traverse Indian Reservation
  ND.......... 46°0N 97°10W 91 E8
Lake Valley NV.... 38°20N 114°30W 85 D6
Lake View AR.... 34°27N 90°48W 63 D5
Lake View IA.... 42°18N 95°3W 73 C3
Lake View NY.... 42°43N 78°56W 89 C2
Lake View SC.... 34°21N 79°10W 90 D6
Lake Villa IL.... 42°25N 88°5W 71 A5
Lake Village AR.... 33°20N 91°17W 63 E4
Lake Wales FL.... 27°54N 81°35W 67 D7
Lake Wilson MN.... 43°59N 95°57W 80 G3
Lake Worth FL.... 26°37N 80°3W 67 E8
Lakecreek OR.... 42°26N 122°37W 94 E3
Lakefield MN.... 43°41N 95°10W 80 G3
Lakefront State Park ◌
  OH.......... 41°32N 81°39W 107 A2
Lakehurst NJ.... 40°1N 74°19W 87 B2
Lakeland GA.... 31°3N 83°4W 68 E3
Lakeland TN.... 35°14N 89°44W 96 E3
Lakemont GA.... 34°47N 83°25W 68 B3
Lakemont PA.... 40°28N 78°24W 95 D4
Lakeport CA.... 39°3N 122°55W 64 D4
Lakeport MI.... 43°7N 82°30W 79 F9
Lakeshore CA.... 37°15N 119°12W 65 F7
Lakeshore MS.... 30°17N 89°27W 81 F4
Lakeside CA.... 32°52N 116°55W 65 L10
Lakeside CO.... 39°46N 105°3W 106 A1
Lakeside MT.... 48°1N 114°14W 83 B3
Lakeside NE.... 42°3N 102°26W 84 B3
Lakeside OH.... 41°33N 82°45W 92 B4
Lakeside TX.... 34°40N 100°42W 98 C7
Lakeside UT.... 41°13N 112°52W 100 B3
Lakeside VA.... 37°37N 77°28W 102 D7
Lakeside Park KY.. 39°2N 84°34W 107 B1
Laketon IN.... 41°1N 85°41W 72 B5
Laketown UT.... 41°49N 111°19W 100 B4
Lakeview IL.... 41°56N 87°38W 108 B2
Lakeview MI.... 43°27N 85°17W 79 F6
Lakeview MT.... 44°36N 111°49W 83 F6
Lakeview OH.... 40°29N 83°56W 92 C3
Lakeview OR.... 42°11N 120°21W 94 E5
Lakeview TX.... 34°40N 100°42W 98 C7
Lakeville CT.... 41°58N 73°26W 78 C1
Lakeville IN.... 41°31N 86°16W 72 B4
Lakeville MA.... 41°50N 70°56W 78 C4
Lakeville MN.... 44°39N 93°14W 113 C2
Lakeville NY.... 42°49N 77°42W 89 C4
Lakewood CA.... 33°51N 118°8W 111 D3
Lakewood CO.... 39°42N 105°4W 106 B1
Lakewood NJ.... 40°6N 74°13W 87 B2
Lakewood NM.... 32°38N 104°23W 88 E6
Lakewood NY.... 42°6N 79°19W 95 B3
Lakewood OH.... 41°28N 81°47W 107 B1
Lakewood WA.... 48°9N 122°13W 101 B3
Lakewood Park GA.. 33°43N 84°24W 110 C3
Lakin KS.... 37°57N 101°15W 74 D2
Lakota IA.... 43°23N 94°6W 73 B4
Lakota ND.... 48°2N 98°21W 91 B7
Lamar AR.... 35°27N 93°23W 63 C2
Lamar CO.... 38°5N 102°37W 66 D8
Lamar MO.... 37°30N 94°16W 82 D2
Lamar MS.... 34°55N 89°19W 81 B4
Lamar NE.... 40°34N 101°57W 84 D3
Lamar SC.... 34°10N 80°4W 90 D5
Lamar County ☆ AL 33°45N 88°7W 60 C2
Lamar County ☆ GA 33°5N 84°8W 68 D2
Lamar County ☆ MS 31°9N 89°28W 81 E4
Lamar County ☆
  TX.......... 33°40N 95°33W 99 D12
Lamb County ☆ TX 34°0N 102°15W 98 C6
Lambert MS.... 34°12N 90°17W 81 B3
Lambert MT.... 47°41N 104°37W 83 C13
Lambert-St. Louis Int. ✕ (STL)
  MO.......... 38°45N 90°23W 117 A1
Lamberton MN.... 44°14N 95°16W 80 F3
Lambertville MI.... 41°45N 83°37W 79 H8
Lambertville NJ.... 40°22N 74°57W 87 B2
Lame Deer MT.... 45°37N 106°40W 83 E11
Lamesa TX.... 32°44N 101°58W 98 D5
Lamine → MO.... 38°59N 92°51W 82 C4
Lamlam, Mt. Guam. 13°22N 144°41E 105 b
Lamoille NV.... 40°44N 115°29W 85 B5
Lamoille County ☆
  VT.......... 44°38N 72°40W 86 B1
Lamona WA.... 47°22N 118°29W 101 C7
Lamoni IA.... 40°37N 93°56W 73 E5
Lamont CA.... 35°15N 118°55W 65 H8
Lamont FL.... 30°23N 83°49W 67 A5
Lamont IA.... 42°36N 91°39W 73 C6
Lamont MS.... 33°32N 91°5W 81 B2

Lamont OK.... 36°42N 97°30W 93 B6
Lamont WA.... 47°12N 117°54W 101 C8
Lamont WY.... 42°13N 107°29W 104 D5
Lampasas TX.... 31°4N 98°11W 99 F9
Lampasas → TX.... 30°59N 97°24W 99 G10
Lampasas County ☆
  TX.......... 31°5N 98°10W 99 F9
Lamy NM.... 35°29N 105°53W 88 B5
Lanagan MO.... 36°37N 94°26W 82 E2
Lāna'i HI.... 20°50N 156°55W 69 C5
Lāna'i City HI.... 20°50N 156°55W 69 C5
Lāna'ihale HI.... 20°49N 156°53W 69 C5
Lanark IL.... 42°6N 89°50W 71 A4
Lanark Village FL.. 29°53N 84°36W 67 B4
Lancaster CA.... 34°42N 118°8W 65 J8
Lancaster KY.... 37°37N 84°35W 97 C8
Lancaster MN.... 48°52N 96°48W 80 B2
Lancaster MO.... 40°31N 92°32W 82 A4
Lancaster NH.... 44°29N 71°34W 86 B3
Lancaster NY.... 42°54N 78°40W 89 C2
Lancaster OH.... 39°43N 82°36W 92 D4
Lancaster PA.... 40°2N 76°19W 95 D6
Lancaster SC.... 34°43N 80°46W 90 D5
Lancaster TX.... 32°35N 96°45W 99 D11
Lancaster VA.... 37°46N 76°28W 77 C4
Lancaster WI.... 42°51N 90°43W 103 F3
Lancaster County ☆
  NE.......... 40°45N 96°45W 84 D9
Lancaster County ☆
  PA.......... 40°0N 76°15W 95 E6
Lancaster County ☆
  SC.......... 34°40N 80°40W 90 D5
Lancaster County ☆
  VA.......... 37°45N 76°30W 102 D8
Lance Creek WY.... 43°2N 104°39W 104 C8
Land Between the Lakes Nat. Recr.
  Area ◌ U.S.A... 36°25N 88°0W 96 D4
Land O'Lakes FL.. 28°13N 82°27W 67 C6
Landa ND.... 48°54N 100°55W 91 B5
Landenburg PA.... 39°47N 75°46W 77 A5
Lander WY.... 42°50N 108°44W 104 D4
Landfall MN.... 44°57N 92°58W 113 B4
Landis NC.... 35°33N 80°37W 90 C5
Lando SC.... 34°46N 81°1W 90 D4
Landover Hills MD.. 38°56N 76°54W 119 B4
Landrum SC.... 35°11N 82°11W 90 C3
Lane SC.... 33°32N 79°53W 90 E6
Lane SD.... 44°4N 98°26W 91 F7
Lane County ☆ KS.. 38°30N 100°30W 74 C3
Lane County ☆ OR.. 44°0N 123°0W 94 D2
Lanesboro MN.... 43°43N 91°58W 80 G7
Lanesborough MA.. 42°31N 73°14W 78 B1
Lanett AL.... 32°52N 85°12W 60 D6
Langdon KS.... 37°51N 98°19W 74 D5
Langdon ND.... 48°45N 98°22W 91 B7
Langford SD.... 45°36N 97°50W 91 E8
Langhorne PA.... 40°10N 74°55W 87 B2
Langlade County ☆
  WI.......... 45°15N 89°10W 103 C4
Langley AR.... 34°19N 93°51W 63 D2
Langley OK.... 36°28N 95°3W 93 B8
Langley VA.... 38°57N 77°11W 119 B2
Langley WA.... 48°2N 122°24W 101 B3
Langley Park MD.. 38°59N 76°58W 119 B4
Langlois OR.... 42°56N 124°27W 94 E1
Langston OK.... 35°56N 97°15W 93 C6
L'Anguille → AR.. 34°44N 90°40W 63 D5
Lanham MD.... 38°59N 76°51W 119 B4
Lanier County ☆ GA 31°0N 83°5W 68 E3
Lankin ND.... 48°19N 97°55W 91 B8
Lansdale PA.... 40°14N 75°17W 87 B1
Lansdowne MD.... 39°14N 76°39W 107 B2
Lansdowne PA.... 39°56N 75°16W 116 B1
L'Anse MI.... 46°45N 88°27W 79 C3
L'Anse Indian Reservation
  MI.......... 46°45N 88°26W 79 C3
Lansford ND.... 48°38N 101°23W 91 B4
Lansford PA.... 40°50N 75°53W 87 B1
Lansing IA.... 43°22N 91°13W 73 B7
Lansing KS.... 39°15N 94°54W 74 B9
Lansing MI.... 42°44N 84°33W 79 G7
Lantana FL.... 26°35N 80°3W 67 E8
Laona WI.... 45°34N 88°40W 103 C5
Lapeer MI.... 43°3N 83°19W 79 F8
Lapeer County ☆ MI 43°5N 83°15W 79 F8
Lapel IN.... 40°4N 85°51W 72 C5
Laplace LA.... 30°4N 90°29W 75 D5
LaPorte IN.... 41°36N 86°43W 72 B4
Laporte MN.... 47°13N 94°45W 80 C4
Laporte PA.... 41°25N 76°30W 95 C6
LaPorte County ☆ IN 41°30N 86°45W 72 B4
Lappans MD.... 39°33N 77°43W 77 A3
Lapwai ID.... 46°24N 116°48W 70 C2
Laramie WY.... 41°19N 105°35W 104 E7
Laramie → WY.... 42°13N 104°33W 104 D8
Laramie County ☆
  WY.......... 41°15N 104°40W 104 E8
Laramie Mts. WY.. 42°0N 105°30W 104 E7
Laramie Pk. WY.... 42°17N 105°27W 104 D7
Larchmont NY.... 40°55N 73°45W 114 A4
Larchwood IA.... 43°27N 96°26W 73 B2
Lardo ID.... 44°55N 116°8W 70 E2
Laredo MO.... 40°2N 93°27W 82 A3
Laredo TX.... 27°34N 99°29W 98 K8
Lares Puerto Rico.. 18°18N 66°53W 105 G16
Larga, Laguna TX 27°30N 97°25W 98 K10
Largo, Key FL.... 25°15N 80°15W 67 F8
Largo Cr. → NM.. 36°30N 108°51W 88 C2
Larimer County ☆
  CO.......... 40°40N 105°20W 66 B5
Larimore ND.... 47°54N 97°37W 91 C8
Lark ND.... 46°27N 101°24W 91 D4
Lark TX.... 35°13N 101°25W 98 C6
Lark UT.... 40°32N 112°6W 100 C3
Larkins = South Miami
  FL.......... 25°42N 80°17W 112 D1
Larkspur CO.... 39°14N 104°53W 66 C6
Larned KS.... 38°11N 99°6W 74 C4
Larose LA.... 29°34N 90°23W 75 E5
Larrabee IA.... 42°52N 95°33W 73 C3
Larsen Bay AK.... 57°32N 153°59W 61 H9
Larson ND.... 48°53N 102°52W 91 B3
Larue County ☆ KY 37°30N 85°40W 97 C7
Las Animas CO.... 38°4N 103°13W 66 D7
Las Animas County ☆
  CO.......... 37°15N 104°0W 66 E7
Las Cruces NM.... 32°19N 106°47W 88 E4
Las Lomas CA.... 38°41N 123°8W 64 E3
Las Nutrias NM.... 34°34N 106°46W 88 C4
Las Piedras
  Puerto Rico.. 18°11N 65°52W 105 G17
Las Trampas Regional Park
  CA.......... 37°48N 122°2W 118 B4
Las Trampas Ridge
  CA.......... 37°48N 122°1W 118 A4
Las Vegas NM.... 35°36N 105°13W 88 B5
Las Vegas NV.... 36°10N 115°8W 110 D2
Las Vegas Bay NV.. 36°7N 114°51W 110 C3
Las Vegas McCarran Int. ✕ (LAS)
  NV.......... 36°5N 115°9W 110 C2
Las Vegas-Dunes Recreation Lands
  NV.......... 36°15N 114°55W 110 B3
LaSalle Street Station
  IL.......... 41°52N 87°37W 108 B3

Lassen County ☆ CA ...... 40°45N 120°30W **64 C6**
Lassen Nat. Forest CA ...... 40°30N 121°15W **64 C5**
Lassen Pk. CA ...... 40°29N 121°30W **64 C5**
Lassen Volcanic Nat. Park and Wilderness △ CA 40°30N 121°20W **64 C5**
Last Chance CO ...... 39°44N 103°36W **66 C7**
Last Chance Cr. ➤ UT ...... 38°38N 111°21W **100 E4**
Last Chance Range CA ...... 36°55N 117°36W **65 G9**
Lastrup MN ...... 46°2N 94°4W **80 D4**
Lata Mt. Amer. Samoa ...... 14°14S 169°27W **105 f**
Latah County ☆ ID 46°45N 116°50W **70 C2**
Latham ID ...... 39°58N 89°58W **71 D4**
Latham KS ...... 37°32N 96°38W **74 D7**
Lathrop CA ...... 37°49N 121°16W **64 F5**
Lathrop MO ...... 39°33N 94°20W **82 B2**
Lathrop Village MI 42°29N 83°13W **109 A1**
Latimer IA ...... 42°46N 93°22W **73 C5**
Latimer KS ...... 38°44N 96°51W **74 C7**
Latimer County ☆ OK ...... 34°50N 95°10W **93 D8**
Laton CA ...... 36°26N 119°41W **65 G7**
Latrobe PA ...... 40°19N 79°23W **95 D3**
Latta SC ...... 34°21N 79°26W **90 D6**
Lauderdale MN ...... 44°59N 93°12W **113 B2**
Lauderdale MS ...... 32°31N 88°31W **81 D5**
Lauderdale County ☆ AL ...... 34°56N 87°46W **60 B3**
Lauderdale County ☆ MS ...... 32°22N 88°42W **81 D5**
Lauderdale County ☆ TN ...... 35°45N 89°23W **96 E3**
Lauderdale Lakes FL 26°9N 80°12W **112 B1**
Lauderhill FL ...... 26°8N 80°12W **112 B2**
Laughing Fish Pt. MI . 46°32N 87°1W **79 C4**
Laughlin NV ...... 35°10N 114°34W **85 G6**
Laughlin Pk. NM . . 36°40N 104°10W **88 A6**
Laulau, Bahia N. Marianas ...... 15°8N 145°45E **105 c**
Laura OH ...... 39°59N 84°22W **92 D2**
Laurel DE ...... 38°33N 75°34W **77 B5**
Laurel FL ...... 27°8N 82°27W **67 D6**
Laurel IN ...... 39°30N 85°11W **72 D5**
Laurel IA ...... 41°53N 92°55W **73 C4**
Laurel MD ...... 39°6N 76°51W **77 A4**
Laurel MS ...... 31°41N 89°8W **81 E4**
Laurel MT ...... 45°40N 108°46W **83 E9**
Laurel NE ...... 42°26N 97°6W **84 B8**
Laurel Bay SC ...... 32°27N 80°42W **90 F5**
Laurel County ☆ KY . 37°5N 84°10W **97 C8**
Laurel Hill PA ...... 40°14N 79°6W **95 D3**
Laurel River L. KY . 36°57N 84°10W **97 D8**
Laureldale NJ ...... 39°30N 74°41W **87 C2**
Laureldale PA ...... 40°23N 75°55W **95 D7**
Laurelton NY ...... 40°40N 73°45W **114 B4**
Laurelville OH ...... 39°28N 82°44W **92 D4**
Laurence G. Hanscom Field MA ...... 42°28N 71°16W **106 A2**
Laurens IA ...... 42°51N 94°52W **73 C4**
Laurens SC ...... 34°30N 82°1W **90 D3**
Laurens County ☆ GA ...... 32°30N 83°0W **68 D4**
Laurens County ☆ SC 34°30N 82°0W **90 D4**
Laurie MO ...... 38°12N 92°50W **82 C4**
Laurinburg NC ...... 34°47N 79°28W **90 D6**
Laurium MI ...... 47°14N 88°27W **79 C3**
Lava Beds Nat. Monument △ CA ...... 41°40N 121°30W **64 B5**
Lava Hot Springs ID 42°37N 112°1W **70 G6**
Lavaca AR ...... 35°20N 94°10W **63 C1**
Lavaca ➤ CA ...... 28°41N 96°35W **99 J11**
Lavaca County ☆ TX ...... 29°27N 96°57W **99 H11**
Lavalette NJ ...... 39°58N 74°4W **87 C2**
Lavaca AZ ...... 33°21N 112°12W **116 C1**
Laverne OK ...... 36°43N 99°54W **93 B4**
Lavic L. CA ...... 34°40N 116°21W **65 J10**
Lavina MT ...... 46°18N 108°56W **83 D9**
Lavon L. TX ...... 33°2N 96°4W **99 D11**
Lavonia GA ...... 34°26N 83°6W **68 B3**
Lawen OR ...... 43°27N 118°48W **94 D7**
Lawler IA ...... 43°4N 92°9W **73 B6**
Lawn TX ...... 32°8N 99°45W **99 E8**
Lawndale CA 33°53N 118°21W **111 C2**
Lawndale FL ...... 41°50N 87°42W **108 B5**
Lawndale L. FL ...... 28°33N 81°26W **115 A2**
Lawrence IN ...... 39°50N 86°2W **72 D4**
Lawrence KS ...... 38°58N 95°14W **74 C8**
Lawrence MA ...... 42°43N 71°10W **78 B3**
Lawrence MI ...... 42°13N 86°3W **79 G5**
Lawrence NY ...... 40°36N 73°43W **114 C5**
Lawrence NE ...... 40°18N 98°16W **84 D7**
Lawrence County ☆ AL ...... 34°29N 87°18W **60 B3**
Lawrence County ☆ AR ...... 36°0N 91°0W **63 B4**
Lawrence County ☆ IL ...... 38°45N 87°45W **71 E6**
Lawrence County ☆ IN ...... 38°50N 86°30W **72 E4**
Lawrence County ☆ KY ...... 38°5N 82°45W **97 B10**
Lawrence County ☆ MS ...... 31°33N 90°7W **81 E3**
Lawrence County ☆ MO ...... 37°10N 93°50W **82 D3**
Lawrence County ☆ OH ...... 38°32N 82°41W **92 E4**
Lawrence County ☆ PA ...... 41°0N 80°15W **95 D2**
Lawrence County ☆ SD ...... 44°23N 103°44W **91 F2**
Lawrence County ☆ TN ...... 35°14N 87°20W **96 E5**
Lawrence Creek OK . 36°5N 96°26W **93 B7**
Lawrence J. Timmerman ✈ (MWC) WI ...... 43°6N 88°2W **112 B1**
Lawrenceburg IN ...... 39°6N 84°52W **72 D6**
Lawrenceburg KY ...... 38°2N 84°54W **97 B8**
Lawrenceville GA ...... 33°57N 83°59W **68 C3**
Lawrenceville IL ...... 38°44N 87°41W **71 E6**
Lawrenceville NJ ...... 40°18N 74°44W **87 B2**
Lawrenceville PA ...... 41°59N 77°8W **95 C5**
Lawrenceville VA ...... 36°46N 77°51W **102 E7**
Lawson MO ...... 39°26N 94°12W **82 B2**
Lawtey FL ...... 30°3N 82°5W **67 A6**
Lawton MI ...... 42°10N 85°50W **79 G6**
Lawton ND ...... 48°18N 98°22W **91 B7**
Lawton OK ...... 34°37N 98°25W **93 D5**
Lay CO ...... 40°32N 107°53W **66 B4**
Laysan I. HI ...... 25°50N 171°50W **69 E9**
Layton FL ...... 24°50N 80°47W **67 G8**
Layton NJ ...... 41°13N 74°50W **87 A2**
Layton UT ...... 41°4N 111°58W **100 B4**
Laytonsville MD ...... 39°13N 77°9W **77 A3**
Laytonville CA ...... 39°41N 123°29W **64 D3**
Lazear CO ...... 38°47N 107°47W **66 D3**
Le Center MN ...... 44°23N 93°44W **80 F5**
Le Claire IA ...... 41°36N 90°21W **73 C8**
Le Flore County ☆ OK ...... 35°0N 94°45W **93 D9**
Le Grand CA ...... 37°14N 120°15W **64 F6**
Le Grand IA ...... 42°0N 92°47W **73 C6**
Le Loup KS ...... 38°35N 95°13W **74 C8**
Le Mars IA ...... 42°47N 96°10W **73 C2**
Le Moyen LA ...... 30°48N 92°4W **75 D3**
Le Raysville PA ...... 41°51N 76°11W **95 C6**

Le Roy IL ...... 40°21N 88°46W **71 C5**
Le Roy KS ...... 38°5N 95°38W **74 C8**
Le Roy MI ...... 44°2N 85°27W **79 E6**
Le Roy MN ...... 43°31N 92°30W **80 G6**
Le Roy NY ...... 42°58N 78°0W **89 C2**
Le Roy PA ...... 41°41N 76°43W **95 C6**
Le Sueur MN ...... 44°28N 93°55W **80 F5**
Le Sueur County ☆ MN ...... 44°20N 93°45W **80 F5**
Lea County ☆ NM . 32°50N 103°30W **88 E7**
Leachville AR ...... 35°56N 90°16W **63 C5**
Lead SD ...... 44°21N 103°46W **91 F2**
Lead Hill AR ...... 36°25N 92°55W **63 B3**
Lead Hill MO ...... 37°6N 92°38W **82 D4**
Leadbetter Pt. WA . 46°39N 124°3W **101 D1**
Leadore ID ...... 44°41N 113°21W **70 E5**
Leadville CO ...... 39°15N 106°18W **66 C4**
Leadwood MO ...... 37°52N 90°36W **82 D6**
Leaf ➤ MS ...... 30°59N 88°44W **81 F5**
League City TX ...... 29°31N 95°6W **99 H12**
Leakey TX ...... 29°44N 99°46W **99 H8**
Leakesville MS ...... 31°9N 88°33W **81 E5**
Leaksville = Eden NC ...... 36°29N 79°53W **90 B6**
Lealman FL ...... 27°49N 82°40W **119 C3**
Leamington UT . 39°32N 112°17W **100 D3**
Leary GA ...... 31°29N 84°31W **68 E2**
Leasburg MO ...... 38°5N 91°18W **82 C5**
Leatherwood KY ...... 37°2N 83°11W **97 C9**
Leavenworth IN ...... 38°12N 86°21W **72 E4**
Leavenworth KS ...... 39°19N 94°55W **74 B9**
Leavenworth WA . 47°36N 120°40W **101 C5**
Leavenworth County ☆ KS ...... 39°15N 95°0W **74 B9**
Leavittsburg OH ...... 41°14N 80°53W **92 B6**
Leawood KS ...... 38°58N 94°37W **74 C9**
Lebam WA ...... 46°34N 123°33W **101 D2**
Lebanon CT ...... 41°38N 72°13W **78 C2**
Lebanon IN ...... 40°3N 86°28W **72 C4**
Lebanon KS ...... 39°49N 98°33W **74 B5**
Lebanon KY ...... 37°34N 85°15W **97 C7**
Lebanon MO ...... 37°41N 92°40W **82 D4**
Lebanon NH ...... 43°39N 72°15W **86 C2**
Lebanon NE ...... 40°3N 100°17W **84 D5**
Lebanon OH ...... 39°26N 84°13W **92 D2**
Lebanon OK ...... 33°59N 96°55W **93 E7**
Lebanon OR ...... 44°32N 122°55W **94 C3**
Lebanon PA ...... 40°20N 76°26W **95 D6**
Lebanon SD ...... 45°4N 99°46W **91 E6**
Lebanon TN ...... 36°12N 86°18W **96 D6**
Lebanon VA ...... 36°54N 82°5W **102 E2**
Lebanon County ☆ PA ...... 40°20N 76°25W **95 D6**
Lebanon Junction KY ...... 37°50N 85°44W **97 C7**
Lebanon State Forest NJ ...... 39°53N 74°30W **87 C2**
Lebanon Station FL . 29°10N 82°37W **67 B6**
Lebec CA ...... 34°51N 118°52W **65 J8**
Lebo KS ...... 38°25N 95°51W **74 C8**
Lecompte LA ...... 31°6N 92°24W **75 C3**
Lecompton KS ...... 39°3N 95°24W **74 C8**
Ledyard IA ...... 43°25N 94°10W **73 B4**
Lee FL ...... 30°25N 83°18W **67 A5**
Lee IL ...... 41°48N 88°56W **71 B5**
Lee ME ...... 45°22N 68°17W **76 C5**
Lee MA ...... 42°19N 73°15W **78 B1**
Lee NV ...... 40°34N 115°36W **85 B8**
Lee City KY ...... 37°44N 83°20W **97 C9**
Lee County ☆ AL ...... 32°36N 85°22W **60 D5**
Lee County ☆ AR ...... 34°46N 90°46W **63 D5**
Lee County ☆ FL ...... 26°30N 81°45W **67 E7**
Lee County ☆ GA ...... 31°45N 84°5W **68 E2**
Lee County ☆ IL ...... 41°45N 89°15W **71 B5**
Lee County ☆ IA ...... 40°40N 91°30W **73 E7**
Lee County ☆ KY ...... 37°35N 83°43W **97 C9**
Lee County ☆ MS ...... 34°16N 88°43W **81 B5**
Lee County ☆ NC ...... 35°30N 79°10W **90 C6**
Lee County ☆ SC ...... 34°10N 80°15W **90 D5**
Lee County ☆ TX . 30°17N 96°58W **99 G11**
Lee County ☆ VA . 36°45N 83°0W **102 E1**
Lee Vining CA ...... 37°58N 119°7W **64 F7**
Lee's Creek L. MN . 47°10N 94°24W **80 C4**
Leech Lake Indian Reservation MN ...... 47°20N 94°10W **80 C4**
Leedey OK ...... 35°52N 99°21W **93 C4**
Leeds AL ...... 33°33N 86°33W **60 C4**
Leeds ND ...... 48°18N 99°27W **91 B6**
Leeds UT ...... 37°14N 113°22W **100 F2**
Leektown NJ ...... 39°38N 74°26W **87 C2**
Leelanau County ☆ MI ...... 44°55N 85°50W **79 E6**
Lee's Summit MO . 38°55N 94°23W **82 C2**
Leesburg FL ...... 28°49N 81°53W **67 C7**
Leesburg GA ...... 31°44N 84°10W **68 E2**
Leesburg NJ ...... 39°15N 74°59W **87 C2**
Leesburg VA ...... 39°7N 77°34W **77 A3**
Leesport PA ...... 40°27N 75°58W **95 D7**
Leesville LA ...... 31°8N 93°16W **75 C2**
Leesville SC ...... 33°55N 81°31W **90 D3**
Leesville, L. VA ...... 37°3N 79°25W **102 D5**
Leeton MO ...... 38°35N 93°42W **82 C3**
Leetonia MN ...... 47°26N 92°59W **80 C6**
Leeville LA ...... 29°15N 90°12W **75 E5**
Leewood WV ...... 38°4N 81°27W **102 C4**
Leflore OK ...... 34°54N 94°59W **93 D9**
Leflore County ☆ MS 33°30N 90°20W **81 B3**
Lefors TX ...... 35°26N 100°48W **98 B7**
Leggett CA ...... 39°52N 123°43W **64 D3**
Leggett TX ...... 30°49N 94°52W **99 G13**
Lehi UT ...... 40°24N 111°51W **100 C4**
Lehigh IA ...... 42°22N 94°3W **73 C4**
Lehigh KS ...... 38°22N 97°18W **74 C6**
Lehigh OK ...... 34°28N 96°13W **93 D7**
Lehigh ➤ PA ...... 40°41N 75°12W **87 B1**
Lehigh Acres FL ...... 26°36N 81°39W **67 E7**
Lehighton PA ...... 40°50N 75°43W **87 B1**
Lehr ND ...... 46°17N 99°21W **91 C6**
Lehua I. HI ...... 22°1N 160°6W **69 A1**
Leicester MA ...... 42°15N 71°55W **78 B3**
Leicester VT ...... 43°50N 73°8W **86 C1**
Leicester, Mt. WY . 43°44N 110°24W **104 C2**
Leigh NE ...... 41°42N 97°14W **84 C8**
Leighton AL ...... 34°42N 87°32W **60 B3**
Leighton IA ...... 41°20N 92°47W **73 D6**
Leipsic DE ...... 39°14N 75°31W **77 A5**
Leipsic OH ...... 41°6N 83°59W **92 B3**
Leisure City FL ...... 25°30N 80°26W **67 F8**
Leitchfield KY ...... 37°29N 86°18W **96 C5**
Leiter WY ...... 44°43N 106°16W **104 B6**
Leitersburg MD ...... 39°32N 77°37W **77 A3**
Leith ND ...... 46°22N 101°38W **91 D4**
Lela TX ...... 35°14N 100°21W **98 B7**
Leland IL ...... 41°37N 88°48W **71 B5**
Leland MI ...... 45°1N 85°45W **79 D6**
Leland MS ...... 33°24N 90°54W **81 C2**
Leland NC ...... 34°15N 78°3W **90 D7**
Lelia Lake TX ...... 34°53N 100°46W **98 C7**
Lemhi ➤ ID ...... 44°52N 113°38W **70 E5**
Lemhi ID ...... 45°12N 113°53W **70 E5**
Lemhi County ☆ ID . 44°0N 113°0W **70 E4**
Lemhi Ra. ID ...... 44°0N 113°0W **70 E4**
Lemington VT ...... 44°51N 71°36W **86 B3**
Lemitar NM ...... 34°10N 106°55W **88 C4**

Lemmon SD ...... 45°57N 102°10W **91 E3**
Lemon L. TX . 32°41N 96°44W **109 B5**
Lemon Grove CA . 32°44N 117°1W **117 B2**
Lemont PA ...... 40°48N 77°49W **95 D5**
Lemoore CA ...... 36°18N 119°46W **65 G7**
Lemoyne NE ...... 41°17N 101°49W **84 C4**
Lempster NH ...... 43°15N 72°12W **86 C2**
Lena IL ...... 42°23N 89°49W **71 A4**
Lena MS ...... 32°36N 89°36W **81 D4**
Lena, Mt. UT ...... 40°50N 109°20W **100 C6**
Lenapah OK ...... 36°51N 95°38W **93 B8**
Lenawee County ☆ MI ...... 41°50N 84°5W **79 H7**
Lenexa KS ...... 38°57N 94°44W **74 C9**
Lennep MT ...... 46°25N 110°33W **83 D7**
Lennox CA ...... 33°56N 118°20W **111 C2**
Lennox SD ...... 43°21N 96°53W **91 G9**
Lenoir NC ...... 35°55N 81°32W **90 C4**
Lenoir City TN ...... 35°48N 84°16W **97 C8**
Lenoir County ☆ NC 35°10N 77°40W **90 C8**
Lenora KS ...... 39°37N 100°0W **74 B3**
Lenore ID ...... 46°31N 116°37W **70 C2**
Lenox GA ...... 31°16N 83°28W **68 E3**
Lenox IA ...... 40°53N 94°34W **73 E4**
Lenox MA ...... 42°22N 73°17W **78 B1**
Lenox MO ...... 37°39N 91°46W **82 D5**
Lenwood CA ...... 34°53N 117°7W **65 J9**
Leo-Cedarville IN ...... 41°13N 85°1W **72 B5**
Leola AR ...... 34°10N 92°35W **63 D3**
Leola SD ...... 45°43N 98°56W **91 E7**
Leoma TN ...... 35°10N 87°21W **96 E5**
Leominster MA ...... 42°32N 71°46W **78 B3**
Leon IA ...... 40°44N 93°45W **73 E5**
Leon KS ...... 37°42N 96°46W **74 D7**
Leon OK ...... 33°53N 97°26W **93 E6**
Leon County ☆ FL . 30°30N 84°15W **67 A4**
Leon County ☆ TX . 31°16N 95°59W **99 F12**
Leon Valley TX . 29°29N 98°39W **117 B2**
Leona KS ...... 39°47N 95°19W **74 B8**
Leona TX ...... 31°9N 95°58W **99 F12**
Leonard MN ...... 46°39N 97°15W **91 D8**
Leonard MN ...... 47°39N 95°16W **80 C3**
Leonard TX ...... 33°23N 96°15W **99 D11**
Leonardtown MD ...... 38°17N 76°38W **77 B4**
Leonardville KS ...... 39°22N 96°51W **74 B7**
Leone Amer. Samoa . 14°23S 170°48W **105 e**
Leonia FL ...... 30°55N 86°1W **67 A2**
Leonia NJ ...... 40°52N 73°59W **114 A3**
Leoti KS ...... 38°29N 101°21W **74 C2**
Lepanto AR ...... 35°37N 90°20W **63 C5**
Leroux Wash ➤ AZ 34°50N 110°10W **62 C5**
Lesage WV ...... 38°30N 82°18W **102 C2**
Leslie GA ...... 31°57N 84°5W **68 E2**
Leslie ID ...... 43°52N 113°28W **70 F5**
Leslie MI ...... 42°27N 84°25W **79 G7**
Leslie SC ...... 34°53N 80°57W **90 D5**
Lester WV ...... 37°44N 81°18W **102 D3**
Lestershire = Johnson City
Lesterville SD ...... 43°2N 97°35W **91 G8**
Letart Falls OH ...... 38°54N 81°56W **92 E5**
Letcher SD ...... 43°54N 98°8W **91 F7**
Letcher County ☆ KY ...... 37°5N 82°55W **97 C10**
Letchworth State Park △ NY ...... 42°37N 78°0W **89 C2**
Letha ID ...... 43°54N 116°39W **70 F2**
Letohatchee AL ...... 32°8N 86°29W **60 D4**
Letterkenny Army Depot PA ...... 40°2N 77°37W **95 D5**
Letts IA ...... 41°20N 91°14W **73 D7**
Leucadia CA ...... 33°4N 117°18W **65 K9**
Leupp Corner AZ . 35°17N 110°52W **62 C4**
Leusoalii Amer. Samoa . 14°14S 169°25W **105 f**
Levan UT . 39°33N 111°52W **100 D4**
Leveaux Mt. MN . 47°37N 90°48W **80 C8**
Levelland TX ...... 33°35N 102°23W **98 D3**
Levelock AK ...... 59°7N 156°51W **61 G8**
Levering MI ...... 45°38N 84°47W **79 D7**
Levisa Fork ➤ KY . 38°8N 82°37W **97 B10**
Levittown NY ...... 40°44N 73°31W **87 B3**
Levittown PA ...... 40°9N 74°51W **87 B2**
Levy ➤ WA ...... 36°5N 104°41W **88 A6**
Levy County ☆ FL . 29°15N 82°45W **67 B6**
Lewellen NE ...... 41°20N 102°9W **84 C3**
Lewes DE ...... 38°46N 75°9W **77 B5**
Lewis IA ...... 41°18N 95°5W **73 D3**
Lewis KS ...... 37°56N 99°15W **74 D4**
Lewis NY ...... 44°17N 73°34W **86 B1**
Lewis ➤ WA ...... 45°51N 122°48W **101 E3**
Lewis, Mt. NV . 40°24N 116°52W **85 B4**
Lewis and Clark County ☆ MT ...... 47°25N 112°35W **83 C5**
Lewis and Clark L. U.S.A. ...... 42°52N 97°48W **84 B8**
Lewis and Clark Nat. Forest MT ...... 47°12N 112°55W **83 C5**
Lewis and Clark Nat. Historic Trail ✈ U.S.A. . . . . 43°30N 99°20W **91 G6**
Lewis County ☆ ID . 46°15N 116°29W **70 C2**
Lewis County ☆ KY . 38°30N 83°25W **97 B9**
Lewis County ☆ MO . 40°5N 91°40W **82 A5**
Lewis County ☆ NY . 43°45N 75°30W **89 B5**
Lewis County ☆ TN . 35°33N 87°33W **96 E4**
Lewis County ☆ WV . 39°2N 80°28W **102 B4**
Lewis County ☆ WA ...... 46°30N 122°0W **101 D3**
Lewis, L. WY ...... 44°11N 110°38W **104 C2**
Lewis Range MT . 48°5N 113°5W **83 B4**
Lewis Run PA ...... 41°52N 78°40W **95 C4**
Lewis Smith L. AL ...... 33°56N 87°6W **60 C3**
Lewisburg KY ...... 36°59N 86°57W **96 D6**
Lewisburg OH ...... 39°51N 84°33W **92 D2**
Lewisburg PA ...... 40°58N 76°54W **95 D6**
Lewisburg TN ...... 35°27N 86°48W **96 E5**
Lewisburg WV ...... 37°48N 80°27W **102 D4**
Lewisdale MD ...... 38°58N 76°59W **119 B4**
Lewisetta VA ...... 38°0N 76°28W **77 B4**
Lewisport KY ...... 37°56N 86°54W **96 C6**
Lewiston CA ...... 40°43N 122°48W **64 C4**
Lewiston ID ...... 46°25N 117°1W **70 C1**
Lewiston ME ...... 44°6N 70°13W **76 D3**
Lewiston MN ...... 44°53N 84°18W **79 E7**
Lewiston MT ...... 46°58N 112°41W **83 D5**
Lewiston ND ...... 46°45N 100°44W **91 D5**
Lewiston NE ...... 40°14N 96°25W **84 D9**
Lewiston NY ...... 43°11N 79°3W **89 B2**
Lewiston UT ...... 41°59N 111°51W **100 B4**
Lewiston Woodville NC ...... 36°7N 77°11W **90 B8**
Lewistown IL ...... 40°24N 90°9W **71 C4**
Lewistown MD ...... 39°32N 77°25W **77 A3**
Lewistown MO ...... 40°5N 91°49W **82 A5**
Lewistown MT . 47°4N 109°26W **83 C8**
Lewistown PA ...... 40°36N 77°34W **95 D5**
Lexington GA ...... 33°52N 83°7W **68 C3**
Lexington IL ...... 40°39N 88°47W **71 C5**
Lexington KY ...... 38°3N 84°30W **97 B8**
Lexington MA ...... 42°26N 71°14W **106 A2**
Lexington MI ...... 43°16N 82°32W **79 F9**

Lexington MS ...... 33°7N 90°3W **81 C3**
Lexington MO ...... 39°11N 93°52W **82 B3**
Lexington NC ...... 35°49N 80°15W **90 C5**
Lexington NE ...... 40°47N 99°45W **84 D6**
Lexington OH ...... 40°41N 82°35W **92 C4**
Lexington OK ...... 35°1N 97°20W **93 C6**
Lexington OR ...... 45°27N 119°42W **94 B6**
Lexington SC ...... 33°59N 81°11W **90 E4**
Lexington TN ...... 35°39N 88°24W **96 E4**
Lexington TX ...... 30°25N 97°1W **99 G10**
Lexington VA ...... 37°47N 79°27W **102 D5**
Lexington WA . 46°11N 122°54W **101 D3**
Lexington Blue Grass KY ...... 37°43N 84°14W **97 C8**
Lexington County ☆ SC ...... 33°56N 81°20W **90 D4**
Lexington Park MD . 38°16N 76°27W **77 B4**
Libby MT ...... 48°23N 115°33W **83 B2**
Libby Dam MT . 48°24N 115°19W **83 B2**
Liberal KS ...... 37°3N 100°55W **74 D3**
Liberal MO ...... 37°34N 94°31W **82 D2**
Liberty IL ...... 39°53N 91°6W **71 C2**
Liberty IN ...... 39°38N 84°56W **72 D6**
Liberty KS ...... 37°9N 95°36W **74 D8**
Liberty KY ...... 37°19N 84°56W **97 C8**
Liberty ME ...... 44°24N 69°18W **76 D4**
Liberty MS ...... 31°10N 90°49W **81 E3**
Liberty MO ...... 39°15N 94°25W **82 B2**
Liberty NY ...... 41°48N 74°45W **89 D6**
Liberty NC ...... 35°51N 79°34W **90 C6**
Liberty PA ...... 41°34N 77°6W **95 C5**
Liberty SC ...... 34°48N 82°42W **90 D3**
Liberty TN ...... 36°1N 85°58W **97 D7**
Liberty TX ...... 30°3N 94°48W **99 G13**
Liberty Center OH . 41°27N 84°1W **92 B2**
Liberty County ☆ FL . 30°15N 85°0W **67 A4**
Liberty County ☆ GA ...... 31°55N 81°30W **68 E5**
Liberty County ☆ MT ...... 48°40N 111°0W **83 B7**
Liberty County ☆ TX ...... 30°7N 94°52W **99 G13**
Liberty Hill TX ...... 30°40N 97°55W **99 G10**
Liberty I. NY ...... 40°41N 74°2W **114 B2**
Liberty-Newark ✈ (EWR) NJ ...... 40°42N 74°10W **114 B1**
Liberty Res. MD ...... 39°23N 76°54W **77 A4**
Liberty State Park △ NJ ...... 40°42N 74°2W **114 B2**
Libertytown MD ...... 39°30N 77°15W **77 A3**
Libertyville IL ...... 42°18N 87°57W **71 A6**
Libertyville IA ...... 40°57N 92°3W **73 E6**
Licking MO ...... 37°30N 91°54W **82 D5**
Licking ➤ KY . 40°3N 82°23W **92 C4**
Lida NV ...... 37°28N 117°30W **85 E3**
Lidderdale IA ...... 42°8N 94°47W **73 C4**
Lidgerwood ND ...... 46°5N 97°9W **91 D8**
Lido Beach NY ...... 40°35N 73°39W **114 C5**
Lighthouse Point FL . 26°15N 80°7W **67 E8**
Lighthouse Pt. FL . 29°54N 84°21W **67 B4**
Lightning Cr. ➤ WY ...... 43°11N 104°44W **104 C8**
Lignite ND ...... 48°53N 102°34W **91 B3**
Lignum VA ...... 38°25N 77°50W **102 C7**
Ligonier IN ...... 41°28N 85°35W **72 B5**
Lihue HI ...... 21°59N 159°23W **69 B2**
Likely CA ...... 41°14N 120°30W **64 B6**
Lillie LA ...... 32°56N 92°39W **75 B3**
Lillian LA ...... 30°36N 89°37W **82 E4**
Lilly PA ...... 40°26N 78°37W **95 D4**
Lily SD ...... 45°11N 97°41W **91 E8**
Lilydale MN ...... 44°54N 93°7W **113 B3**
Lilydale MN ...... 44°11N 91°23W **73 C2**
Lima MT ...... 44°38N 112°36W **83 F5**
Lima NY ...... 42°55N 77°37W **89 C3**
Lima OH ...... 40°44N 84°6W **92 C2**
Lima OH ...... 39°31N 90°11W **71 C2**
Lime Ridge WI ...... 43°28N 90°9W **103 E3**
Lime Springs IA ...... 43°27N 92°17W **73 B6**
Lime Village AK ...... 61°21N 155°28W **61 F9**
Limerick ME ...... 43°41N 70°48W **86 C4**
Limestone FL ...... 27°22N 81°54W **67 D7**
Limestone ME ...... 46°55N 67°50W **76 B6**
Limestone L. TX . 42°22N 78°38W **89 C2**
Limestone County ☆ AL ...... 34°48N 86°58W **60 B4**
Limestone County ☆ TX ...... 31°39N 96°31W **99 F11**
Limestone Hill = Lackawanna NY ...... 42°50N 78°50W **89 C2**
Lincoln CA ...... 38°54N 121°17W **64 E5**
Lincoln DE ...... 38°52N 75°25W **77 B5**
Lincoln IL ...... 40°9N 89°22W **71 C4**
Lincoln KS ...... 39°3N 98°9W **74 B5**
Lincoln ME ...... 45°22N 68°30W **76 C5**
Lincoln MA ...... 42°25N 71°18W **106 A2**
Lincoln MT ...... 46°58N 112°41W **83 D5**
Lincoln ND ...... 46°45N 100°44W **91 D5**
Lincoln NE ...... 40°49N 96°41W **84 D9**
Lincoln NH ...... 44°3N 71°40W **86 B3**
Lincoln City OR ...... 44°57N 124°1W **94 C1**
Lincoln County ☆ AR ...... 33°56N 91°51W **63 E4**
Lincoln County ☆ CO ...... 39°0N 103°20W **66 D7**
Lincoln County ☆ GA ...... 33°45N 82°20W **68 C4**
Lincoln County ☆ ID . 43°0N 114°0W **70 G4**
Lincoln County ☆ KS . 39°0N 98°10W **74 B5**
Lincoln County ☆ KY . 37°25N 84°40W **97 C8**
Lincoln County ☆ ME 44°0N 69°30W **76 D4**
Lincoln County ☆ MN ...... 44°24N 96°10W **80 F2**
Lincoln County ☆ MS ...... 31°35N 90°26W **81 E3**
Lincoln County ☆ MO . 39°0N 91°0W **82 B5**
Lincoln County ☆ MT ...... 48°45N 115°30W **83 B2**
Lincoln County ☆ NV ...... 37°20N 115°0W **85 E6**
Lincoln County ☆ NM ...... 33°40N 105°30W **88 D4**
Lincoln County ☆ NE . 41°0N 101°0W **84 C4**

Lincoln County ☆ SD ...... 43°21N 96°53W **91 G9**
Lincoln County ☆ TN . 35°9N 86°34W **96 E6**
Lincoln County ☆ WV ...... 38°14N 81°59W **102 C3**
Lincoln County ☆ WA ...... 47°45N 118°30W **101 C7**
Lincoln County ☆ WI ...... 45°20N 89°45W **103 C4**
Lincoln County ☆ WY ...... 42°0N 110°30W **104 D2**
Lincoln Creek Parkway WI ...... 43°6N 87°56W **112 B2**
Lincoln Heights OH 39°14N 84°27W **107 A2**
Lincoln Memorial DC ...... 38°52N 77°4W **119 B3**
Lincoln Nat. Forest NM ...... 32°45N 105°40W **88 E5**
Lincoln Park ☆ LA 32°32N 92°38W **75 B3**
Lincoln Park CO . 38°25N 105°10W **66 D5**
Lincoln Park GA . 32°52N 84°20W **68 D2**
Lincoln Park IL . 41°57N 87°38W **108 B3**
Lincoln Park MI . 42°15N 83°11W **79 G8**
Lincoln Park NJ ...... 40°55N 74°18W **114 A1**
Lincoln Park WI . 43°5N 87°53W **112 B2**
Lincoln Park Zoo IL 41°55N 87°38W **108 B3**
Lincolnton GA ...... 33°48N 82°29W **68 C4**
Lincolnton NC ...... 35°29N 81°16W **90 C4**
Lincolnville ME ...... 44°17N 69°1W **76 D4**
Lincolnwood IL ...... 42°1N 87°43W **108 A2**
Lind WA ...... 46°58N 118°37W **101 D7**
Linda CA ...... 39°8N 121°34W **64 D5**
Lindale GA ...... 34°11N 85°11W **68 B1**
Lindale TX ...... 32°31N 95°25W **99 E12**
Linden = Gladstone MO ...... 39°13N 94°35W **82 B2**
Linden AL ...... 32°18N 87°48W **60 D3**
Linden IN ...... 40°11N 86°54W **72 C4**
Linden IA ...... 41°39N 94°16W **73 D4**
Linden MI ...... 42°49N 83°47W **79 G8**
Linden TN ...... 35°37N 87°50W **96 E4**
Linden TX ...... 33°1N 94°22W **99 D13**
Linden WI ...... 42°55N 90°16W **103 F3**
Lindenhurst NY ...... 40°41N 73°23W **87 B3**
Lindenwold NJ ...... 39°49N 74°59W **87 C2**
Lindley NY ...... 42°1N 77°8W **95 C6**
Lindon UT ...... 40°21N 111°43W **100 C4**
Lindsay CA ...... 36°12N 119°5W **65 G7**
Lindsay MT ...... 41°42N 97°42W **84 C8**
Lindsay OK ...... 34°50N 97°38W **93 D6**
Lindsborg KS ...... 38°35N 97°40W **74 C6**
Lindy NE ...... 42°44N 97°44W **84 B8**
Lineville AL ...... 33°19N 85°45W **60 C5**
Lineville IA ...... 40°35N 93°32W **73 E5**
Lingle WY ...... 42°8N 104°21W **104 D8**
Linglestown PA ...... 40°20N 76°47W **95 D6**
Linn KS ...... 39°41N 97°5W **74 B6**
Linn MO ...... 38°29N 91°51W **82 C5**
Linn TX ...... 26°34N 98°7W **98 L9**
Linn County ☆ IA . 42°5N 91°35W **73 C7**
Linn County ☆ KS . 38°15N 94°45W **74 C9**
Linn County ☆ MO . 39°50N 93°0W **82 B4**
Linn County ☆ OR . 44°30N 122°20W **94 C3**
Linn Grove IA ...... 42°53N 95°15W **73 C3**
Linn Valley KS ...... 38°22N 94°41W **74 C9**
Linndale OH ...... 41°26N 81°46W **107 B1**
Linneus ME ...... 46°23N 67°52W **76 B6**
Linneus MO ...... 39°53N 93°11W **82 B3**
Lino Lakes MN . 45°12N 93°6W **80 E5**
Linthicum MD ...... 39°12N 76°39W **107 B1**
Linton IN ...... 39°2N 87°10W **72 D3**
Linton ND ...... 46°16N 100°14W **91 D5**
Linwood KS ...... 39°0N 95°2W **74 C8**
Linwood NJ ...... 39°21N 74°34W **87 C2**
Linwood NE ...... 41°25N 96°56W **84 C9**
Lipscomb TX ...... 36°14N 100°16W **98 A7**
Lipscomb County ☆ TX ...... 36°15N 100°15W **98 A7**
Liquillo, Sierra de Puerto Rico . 18°20N 65°47W **105 G17**
Lisbon IL ...... 41°29N 88°29W **71 B5**
Lisbon ME ...... 44°2N 70°6W **76 D3**
Lisbon ND ...... 46°27N 97°41W **91 D8**
Lisbon NH ...... 44°13N 71°55W **86 B3**
Lisbon NY ...... 44°44N 75°19W **89 A5**
Lisbon OH ...... 40°46N 80°46W **92 C6**
Lisbon Falls ME ...... 44°0N 70°4W **76 D3**
Lisco NE ...... 41°30N 102°37W **84 C3**
Lisianski I. HI ...... 26°2N 174°0W **69 E9**
Lisman AL ...... 32°10N 88°15W **60 D2**
Lisle IL ...... 41°48N 88°4W **108 C1**
Litchfield CT ...... 41°45N 73°11W **78 C1**
Litchfield IL ...... 39°11N 89°39W **71 D4**
Litchfield MN ...... 45°8N 94°32W **80 E4**
Litchfield County ☆ CT ...... 41°40N 73°15W **78 C1**
Litchville ND ...... 46°39N 98°12W **91 D7**
Lititz PA ...... 40°9N 76°18W **95 D6**
Little ➤ LA ...... 31°43N 92°0W **75 C3**
Little PA ...... 40°9N 76°18W **95 D6**
Little ➤ GA ...... 30°46N 83°50W **68 F3**
Little ➤ KY ...... 36°51N 87°58W **96 D5**
Little ➤ LA ...... 31°40N 92°20W **75 C3**
Little ➤ NC ...... 35°18N 78°42W **90 C7**
Little ➤ TN ...... 35°53N 83°59W **97 C8**
Little ➤ TX ...... 30°51N 96°41W **99 G11**
Little America WY . 41°33N 109°52W **104 E3**
Little Arkansas ➤ KS ...... 37°41N 97°21W **74 D6**
Little Beaver Cr. ➤ U.S.A. ...... 39°49N 101°2W **74 B2**
Little Belt Mts. MT. 46°40N 110°45W **83 D7**
Little Bighorn ➤ MT ...... 45°0N 107°34W **104 A5**
Little Bighorn Battlefield Nat. Monument ◌ MT ...... 45°34N 107°25W **83 E10**
Little Black ➤ AR . 36°29N 90°49W **63 B5**
Little Blue ➤ KS . 39°42N 96°41W **74 B7**
Little Calumet ➤ AZ ...... 36°12N 111°48W **62 A4**
Little Creek DE . 39°10N 75°26W **77 A5**
Little Creek Naval Amphibious Base VA ...... 36°54N 76°9W **115 A3**
Little Diomede I. AK ...... 65°45N 168°56W **61 D7**
Little Dry Creek MT ...... 47°21N 106°22W **83 C11**
Little Eagle SD . 45°58N 100°49W **91 E5**
Little Egg Harbor NJ ...... 39°35N 74°18W **87 C2**
Little Falls MN ...... 45°59N 94°22W **80 E4**
Little Falls NY ...... 43°3N 74°51W **89 B6**

Little Ferry NJ ...... 40°50N 74°2W **114 A2**
Little Fork ➤ MN . 48°31N 93°35W **80 B5**
Little Goose Dam WA ...... 46°35N 118°1W **101 D7**
Little Haiti FL ...... 25°50N 80°11W **112 C2**
Little Havana FL . 25°47N 80°15W **112 D1**
Little Haw Cr. ➤ FL 29°23N 81°24W **67 B7**
Little Humboldt ➤ NV ...... 41°1N 117°43W **85 A4**
Little Kanawha ➤ WV ...... 39°16N 81°34W **102 B3**
Little Lake CA ...... 35°56N 117°55W **65 H9**
Little Lost ➤ ID . 43°46N 112°58W **70 F6**
Little Medicine Bow ➤ WY ...... 41°58N 106°17W **104 E6**
Little Menomonee River Parkway WI ...... 43°4N 88°2W **112 B1**
Little Miami ➤ IL . . 39°9N 84°27W **107 A2**
Little Missouri ➤ AR ...... 33°49N 92°54W **63 E3**
Little Missouri ➤ ND ...... 47°36N 102°25W **91 C3**
Little Missouri Badlands ND ...... 47°5N 103°45W **91 C2**
Little Muddy ➤ ND 48°11N 103°36W **91 B2**
Little Neck NY ...... 40°45N 73°44W **114 B4**
Little Pee Dee ➤ SC 34°5N 79°24W **90 E6**
Little Powder ➤ MT ...... 45°28N 105°20W **83 E12**
Little Red ➤ AR . 35°11N 91°27W **63 C4**
Little Red School House Nature Center IL . 41°42N 87°51W **108 C1**
Little River KS ...... 38°24N 98°1W **74 C5**
Little River Canyon Nat. Preserve ✈ AL . 34°25N 85°37W **60 B5**
Little River County ☆ AR ...... 33°40N 94°8W **63 E1**
Little River Indian Reservation MI ...... 44°16N 86°15W **79 E5**
Little Rock AR . 34°45N 92°17W **63 D3**
Little Rock Air Force Base AR ...... 34°54N 92°9W **63 D3**
Little Rocky Mts. MT ...... 47°55N 108°30W **83 C9**
Little Sable Pt. MI . 43°38N 86°33W **79 F5**
Little Salt L. UT . 37°35N 112°53W **100 F3**
Little Sioux ➤ IA . 41°49N 96°4W **73 D2**
Little Sitkin I. AK . 51°57N 178°31E **61 L2**
Little Snake ➤ U.S.A. . 40°27N 108°26W **66 B2**
Little Tallapoosa ➤ U.S.A. ...... 33°19N 85°34W **60 C5**
Little Tennessee ➤ TN ...... 35°47N 84°16W **97 C8**
Little Traverse B. MI 45°25N 85°0W **79 D7**
Little Traverse Bay Indian Reservation MI . 45°20N 84°58W **79 D7**
Little Valley NY . 42°15N 78°48W **89 C3**
Little Wabash ➤ IL . 37°55N 88°5W **71 F5**
Little White ➤ SD . 43°40N 100°40W **91 G5**
Little Wood ➤ ID . 42°57N 114°21W **70 G4**
Little York IL ...... 41°1N 90°45W **71 B3**
Little York NJ ...... 38°42N 85°54W **72 E5**
Littlefield AZ ...... 36°53N 113°56W **62 A2**
Littlefield TX ...... 33°55N 102°20W **98 D5**
Littlefork MN ...... 48°24N 93°34W **80 B5**
Littlerock CA ...... 34°31N 117°59W **65 J9**
Littlerock WA . 46°54N 123°1W **101 D2**
Littleton CO . 39°36N 105°0W **109 C1**
Littleton IL ...... 40°14N 90°37W **71 C3**
Littleton ME ...... 46°14N 67°51W **76 B6**
Littleton NC ...... 36°26N 77°54W **90 B8**
Littleton NH ...... 44°18N 71°46W **86 B3**
Littleton WV ...... 39°42N 80°32W **102 B4**
Littleton Common MA ...... 42°33N 71°28W **78 B3**
Littleville AL ...... 34°36N 87°41W **60 B3**
Live Oak CA ...... 39°17N 121°40W **64 D5**
Live Oak FL ...... 30°18N 82°59W **67 A6**
Live Oak TX . 29°33N 98°20W **117 B3**
Live Oak County ☆ TX ...... 28°20N 98°7W **99 J9**
Livengood AK . 65°32N 148°33W **61 D10**
Livermore CA ...... 37°41N 121°47W **64 F5**
Livermore IA ...... 42°52N 94°11W **73 C4**
Livermore KY ...... 37°29N 87°8W **96 C5**
Livermore, Mt. TX . 30°38N 104°11W **98 G3**
Livermore Falls ME . 44°29N 70°11W **76 D3**
Liverpool NY ...... 43°6N 76°13W **89 B4**
Liverpool PA ...... 40°34N 76°59W **95 D6**
Livingston AL ...... 32°35N 88°11W **60 D2**
Livingston CA . 37°23N 120°43W **64 F6**
Livingston IL ...... 38°58N 89°46W **71 D4**
Livingston KY ...... 37°17N 84°13W **97 C8**
Livingston LA ...... 30°30N 90°45W **75 D5**
Livingston MT . 45°40N 110°34W **83 E7**
Livingston TN ...... 36°23N 85°19W **97 D7**
Livingston TX ...... 30°43N 94°56W **99 G13**
Livingston County ☆ IL ...... 40°55N 88°50W **71 C5**
Livingston County ☆ KY ...... 37°10N 88°20W **96 C3**
Livingston County ☆ MI ...... 42°35N 83°55W **79 G8**
Livingston County ☆ MO ...... 39°50N 93°30W **82 B3**
Livingston County ☆ NY ...... 42°40N 77°45W **89 C3**
Livingston Manor NY ...... 41°54N 74°50W **89 D6**
Livingston Parish ☆ LA ...... 30°30N 90°45W **75 D5**
Livonia IN ...... 38°33N 86°17W **72 E4**
Livonia LA ...... 30°34N 91°33W **75 D4**
Livonia MI ...... 42°23N 83°23W **79 G8**
Livonia NY ...... 42°49N 77°40W **89 C3**
Lizard Cr. ➤ IA . 42°30N 94°14W **73 C4**
Lizella GA ...... 32°48N 83°49W **68 D3**
Lizemores WV ...... 38°20N 81°11W **102 C3**
Llano TX ...... 30°45N 98°41W **99 G9**
Llano ➤ TX ...... 30°39N 98°26W **99 G9**
Llano County ☆ TX . 30°45N 98°35W **99 G9**
Llano Estacado TX . 33°30N 103°0W **98 D5**
Lloyds MD ...... 38°36N 76°12W **77 B4**
Loa UT ...... 38°24N 111°39W **100 E4**
Loami IL ...... 39°40N 89°51W **71 D4**
Lobelville TN ...... 35°46N 87°47W **96 E5**
Lobos, Pt. CA . 37°46N 122°30W **118 B1**
Loch Raven MD ...... 39°26N 76°32W **107 A1**
Lochbuie CO ...... 40°0N 104°43W **66 C6**
Lochearn MD ...... 39°20N 76°42W **107 A1**
Lochloosa L. FL . 29°30N 82°7W **67 B6**
Lock Haven PA . 41°8N 77°28W **95 C5**
Lock Springs MO . 39°51N 93°47W **82 B3**
Lockeford CA . 38°10N 121°9W **64 E5**
Lockesburg AR ...... 33°58N 94°10W **63 E1**
Lockhart TX ...... 29°53N 97°40W **99 H10**
Lockington OH ...... 40°12N 84°14W **92 C2**
Lockland OH ...... 39°14N 84°27W **107 A2**
Lockney TX ...... 34°7N 101°27W **98 C6**
Lockport IL ...... 41°35N 88°3W **71 B5**
Lockport LA ...... 29°39N 90°32W **75 E5**
Lockport NY ...... 43°10N 78°42W **89 B2**
Lockridge IA ...... 40°59N 91°45W **73 E7**

Lockwood MO . . . . . . 37°23N 93°57W **82 D3**
Loco IL . . . . 34°19N 97°41W **93 D6**
Locust Cr. → MO . . . 39°40N 93°17W **82 B3**
Locust Fork ← AL . . . 33°33N 87°11W **60 C3**
Locust Grove CA . . . . 33°21N 84°7W **67 C7**
Locust Grove OK . . . . 36°12N 95°10W **93 B8**
Locust Manor NY . . . 40°41N 73°46W **114 B4**
Locust Valley NY . . . 40°52N 73°35W **114 A5**
Loda IL . . . . 40°31N 88°4W **71 C5**
Lodge Grass MT . . . 45°19N 107°22W **83 E10**
Lodgepole NE . . . . . 41°9N 102°38W **84 C3**
Lodgepole SD . . . . . 45°48N 102°40W **91 E3**
Lodgepole → NE . . . . 41°2N 102°10W **84 C3**
Lodgepole Cr. →
 U.S.A. . . . . . . 40°57N 102°32W **84 B5**
Lodi CA . . . . 38°8N 121°16W **64 E5**
Lodi NJ . . . . 40°52N 74°5W **114 A2**
Lodi OH . . . . 41°2N 82°1W **92 B4**
Lodi WI . . . . 43°19N 89°32W **103 E4**
Lofall WA . . . . . . 47°48N 122°39W **118 B2**
Log Lane Village
 CO . . . . 40°17N 103°51W **66 B7**
Logan IA . . . . . . 41°39N 95°47W **73 D3**
Logan KS . . . . . . 39°40N 99°34W **74 B4**
Logan NM . . . . . . 35°22N 103°25W **88 B7**
Logan OH . . . . . . 39°32N 82°25W **92 D4**
Logan WV . . . . . . 37°51N 81°59W **92 D2**
Logan UT . . . . . . 41°44N 111°50W **100 D4**
Logan County ☆ AR . . 35°18N 93°44W **63 C2**
Logan County ☆ CO . . 40°45N 103°0W **66 B7**
Logan County ☆ IL . . . 41°10N 89°20W **71 C4**
Logan County ☆ KS . . 39°0N 101°0W **74 C2**
Logan County ☆ KY . . 36°50N 86°50W **96 D6**
Logan County ☆ ND . . 46°28N 99°25W **91 D6**
Logan County ☆
 NE . . . . 41°30N 100°30W **84 C5**
Logan County ☆ OH . . 40°22N 83°46W **92 C3**
Logan County ☆ OK . . 36°0N 97°30W **93 C6**
Logan County ☆ WV . . 37°58N 82°0W **102 D3**
Logan Cr. → NE . . . . 41°36N 96°30W **84 C9**
Logan Int., Boston ✈ (BOS)
 MA . . . . 42°22N 71°1W **106 A3**
Logan Martin L. AL . . 33°26N 86°20W **60 C4**
Logan Square IL . . . . 41°55N 87°42W **108 B2**
Logandale NV . . . . . 36°36N 114°29W **85 F6**
Logansport IN . . . . 40°45N 86°22W **72 C4**
Logansport LA . . . . 31°58N 94°0W **75 C2**
Loganton PA . . . . . 41°2N 77°19W **95 C5**
Loganville WI . . . . 43°29N 90°23W **103 E3**
Lohrville IA . . . . . 42°17N 94°33W **73 C4**
Lois TX . . . . 29°49N 95°30W **118 A1**
Lola KY . . . . 37°19N 88°18W **96 C4**
Lola, Mt. CA . . . . . 39°26N 120°22W **64 D4**
Loleta CA . . . . . . 40°38N 124°13W **64 C2**
Lolita TX . . . . . . 28°50N 96°33W **99 J11**
Lolo MT . . . . 46°45N 114°5W **83 D3**
Lolo Hot Springs
 MT . . . . 46°44N 114°32W **83 D3**
Lolo Nat. Forest MT . . 47°8N 114°40W **83 C3**
Lolo Pass U.S.A. . . . 46°38N 114°35W **70 C4**
Lolo Peak MT . . . . . 46°41N 114°14W **83 D3**
Loma CO . . . . 39°12N 108°49W **66 C2**
Loma MT . . . . 47°56N 110°30W **83 C7**
Loma ND . . . . . . 48°38N 98°32W **91 B7**
Loma, Pt. CA . . . . . 32°42N 117°14W **117 C1**
Loma Prieta CA . . . . 37°6N 121°50W **64 F4**
Loman MN . . . . . . 48°31N 93°49W **80 B5**
Lomax IL . . . . . . 40°41N 91°4W **71 C2**
Lometa TX . . . . . . 31°13N 98°24W **99 F9**
Lomita CA . . . . . . 33°47N 118°18W **111 D3**
Lompoc CA . . . . . 34°38N 120°28W **65 J6**
Lonaconing MD . . . . 39°34N 78°59W **77 A2**
London AR . . . . . . 35°20N 93°15W **63 C3**
London KY . . . . . . 37°8N 84°5W **97 C8**
London OH . . . . . . 39°53N 83°27W **92 D3**
London Mills IL . . . . 40°43N 90°11W **71 C3**
Londonderry NH . . . 42°52N 71°22W **86 D3**
Londonderry OH . . . 39°16N 82°48W **92 D3**
Londonderry VT . . . . 43°14N 72°48W **86 C2**
Londontowne MD . . . 38°55N 76°33W **77 A4**
Lone Grove OK . . . . 34°11N 97°14W **93 D6**
Lone Mountain TN . . . 36°24N 83°35W **97 B9**
Lone Mt. SD . . . . . 45°23N 103°44W **91 E2**
Lone Oak KY . . . . . 37°2N 88°40W **96 C4**
Lone Oak TX . . . . . 33°0N 95°57W **99 E12**
Lone Peak UT . . . . . 40°31N 111°45W **117 C3**
Lone Peak Wilderness
 UT . . . . 40°30N 111°42W **117 C3**
Lone Pine CA . . . . . 36°36N 118°4W **65 G8**
Lone Star TX . . . . . 32°55N 94°43W **99 E13**
Lone Tree IA . . . . . 41°29N 91°26W **73 D7**
Lone Wolf OK . . . . . 34°59N 99°15W **93 D4**
Lonejack MO . . . . . 38°52N 94°10W **82 C2**
Lonepine MT . . . . . 47°42N 114°38W **83 C3**
Lonerock OR . . . . . 45°5N 119°53W **94 B6**
Long B. SC . . . . . . 33°35N 78°45W **90 E7**
Long Beach CA . . . . 33°46N 118°11W **111 D3**
Long Beach MS . . . . 30°21N 89°9W **81 F4**
Long Beach NY . . . . 40°35N 73°39W **114 C5**
Long Beach WA . . . . 46°21N 124°3W **101 D1**
Long Beach Harbor
 CA . . . . 33°44N 118°13W **111 D3**
Long Beach I. NJ . . . 39°42N 74°6W **87 C2**
Long Beach Municipal ✈ (LGB)
 CA . . . . 33°48N 118°9W **111 D3**
Long Branch NJ . . . . 40°18N 74°0W **87 B3**
Long Branch L. MO . . 39°50N 92°30W **82 B4**
Long Brook → VA . . . 38°49N 77°15W **119 C2**
Long County ☆ GA . . 31°45N 81°45W **68 E5**
Long Creek OR . . . . 44°43N 119°6W **94 C6**
Long I. MA . . . . . . 42°19N 70°59W **106 B4**
Long I. NY . . . . . . 40°45N 73°30W **87 B3**
Long Island KS . . . . 39°57N 99°32W **74 B4**
Long Island City NY 40°45N 73°56W **114 B3**
Long Island Sd. NY . . 41°10N 73°0W **78 C2**
Long L. IL . . . . . . 47°13N 68°15W **76 A5**
Long L. ME . . . . . . 46°43N 69°23W **76 B4**
Long L. MI . . . . . . 44°2N 70°39W **86 B4**
Long L. MI . . . . . . 45°13N 83°29W **79 D8**
Long L. ND . . . . . . 46°44N 100°6W **91 D5**
Long L. NY . . . . . . 44°1N 74°24W **89 A6**
Long L. WI . . . . . . 47°50N 117°51W **101 C8**
Long L. WI . . . . . . 45°45N 91°45W **103 C2**
Long Lake NY . . . . . 43°58N 74°25W **89 B6**
Long Lake WI . . . . . 46°45N 122°35W **118 D2**
Long Lake Regional Park ☆
 MN . . . . 45°39N 93°11W **113 A2**
Long Mt. MO . . . . . 36°43N 92°31W **82 E4**
Long Pine NE . . . . . 42°32N 99°42W **84 B6**
Long Point IL . . . . . 41°0N 88°54W **71 B5**
Long Pond MA . . . . 41°48N 70°56W **78 C4**
Long Prairie MN . . . . 45°58N 94°52W **80 E4**
Long Prairie → MN . . 46°20N 94°36W **80 D4**
Long Pt. MN . . . . . 48°59N 94°39W **80 B4**
Long Ridge KY . . . . 38°35N 84°49W **97 B8**
Long Valley SD . . . . 43°28N 101°29W **91 G4**
Longboat Key FL . . . 27°23N 82°39W **67 D6**
Longbranch WA . . . . 47°13N 122°46W **101 C3**
Longdale OK . . . . . 36°8N 98°33W **93 B5**
Longford KS . . . . . 39°10N 97°20W **74 C6**
Longjohn Slough IL . . 41°42N 87°52W **108 C1**
Longmeadow MA . . . 42°3N 72°34W **78 B2**
Longmont CO . . . . . 40°10N 105°6W **66 B6**
Longridge MD . . . . . 38°16N 75°37W **77 B5**
Longs Pk. CO . . . . . 40°15N 105°37W **66 B6**
Longstreet LA . . . . . 32°6N 93°57W **75 B2**
Longtown MO . . . . . 37°23N 96°5W **78 D7**
Longtown IL . . . . . 39°53N 88°47W **71 D6**
Longview TX . . . . . 32°30N 94°44W **99 E13**
Longview WA . . . . . 46°8N 122°57W **101 D3**
Longville LA . . . . . 30°36N 93°14W **75 D2**

Longville MN . . . . . 46°59N 94°13W **80 D4**
Longwood FL . . . . . 28°42N 81°21W **67 C7**
Longwoods MD . . . . 38°52N 76°5W **77 B4**
Lonoke AR . . . . . . 34°47N 91°54W **63 D4**
Lonoke County ☆
 AR . . . . 34°47N 91°54W **63 D4**
Lonsdale MN . . . . . 44°29N 93°26W **80 F5**
Loogootee IN . . . . . 38°41N 86°55W **72 E4**
Looking Glass → MI 42°52N 84°54W **79 G7**
Lookout CA . . . . . . 41°13N 121°9W **64 B5**
Lookout, C. NC . . . . 34°35N 76°32W **90 D9**
Lookout, C. OR . . . . 45°20N 124°1W **94 B1**
Lookout, Pt. MI . . . . 44°3N 83°35W **79 E8**
Lookout Mountain
 TN . . . . 34°59N 85°21W **97 F7**
Lookout Mt. AL . . . . 34°20N 85°45W **60 B5**
Lookout Mt. ID . . . . 47°5N 115°58W **70 B3**
Lookout Mt. NM . . . . 35°13N 108°13W **88 B2**
Lookout Mt. OR . . . . 44°18N 117°38W **101 B8**
Lookout Pass U.S.A. . . 47°27N 115°42W **70 C3**
Lookout Point Res.
 OR . . . . 43°55N 122°45W **94 D3**
Loomis CA . . . . . . 40°29N 99°31W **84 D6**
Loomis WA . . . . . . 48°49N 119°38W **101 B6**
Loon L. ME . . . . . . 46°8N 69°36W **76 B4**
Loon Lake WA . . . . 48°4N 117°38W **101 B8**
Loosahatchie Bar TN 35°11N 90°4W **112 A1**
Lopez I. WA . . . . . . 48°29N 122°54W **101 B3**
Lopez Pt. CA . . . . . 36°1N 121°34W **65 G5**
Lorain OH . . . . . . 41°28N 82°11W **92 B4**
Lorain County ☆ OH . 41°14N 82°7W **92 B4**
Loraine IL . . . . . . 40°9N 91°13W **71 C2**
Loraine TX . . . . . . 32°25N 100°43W **98 E7**
Lords Valley PA . . . . 41°22N 75°4W **87 A1**
Lordsburg NM . . . . . 32°21N 108°43W **88 E2**
Lore City OH . . . . . 39°59N 81°28W **92 D5**
Loreauville LA . . . . . 30°3N 91°44W **75 D4**
Lorenzo ID . . . . . . 43°44N 111°52W **70 F7**
Lorenzo TX . . . . . . 33°40N 101°32W **98 D6**
Loretta KS . . . . . . 38°39N 99°12W **74 C4**
Loretto KY . . . . . . 37°38N 85°24W **97 C7**
Loretto TN . . . . . . 35°5N 87°26W **96 E5**
Loretto VA . . . . . . 38°5N 77°3W **77 B3**
Lorimor IA . . . . . . 41°8N 94°3W **73 D4**
Loris SC . . . . 34°4N 78°53W **90 D7**
Lorman MS . . . . . . 31°49N 91°3W **81 E2**
Lorraine = Baker
 MT . . . . 46°22N 104°17W **83 D13**
Lorraine KS . . . . . . 38°34N 98°19W **74 C5**
Lorton NE . . . . . . 40°35N 96°1W **84 D9**
Lorton VA . . . . . . 38°42N 77°14W **77 B3**
Los Alamitos CA . . . 33°48N 118°4W **111 D4**
Los Alamos CA . . . . 34°44N 120°17W **65 J6**
Los Alamos NM . . . . 35°53N 106°19W **88 B4**
Los Alamos County ☆
 NM . . . . 35°55N 106°15W **88 B4**
Los Angeles →
 CA . . . . 33°47N 118°12W **111 D3**
Los Angeles Aqueduct
 CA . . . . 35°22N 118°5W **65 H8**
Los Angeles County ☆
 CA . . . . 34°20N 118°10W **65 J8**
Los Angeles Harbor
 CA . . . . 33°42N 118°16W **111 D3**
Los Angeles Int. ✈ (LAX)
 CA . . . . 33°57N 118°25W **111 C2**
Los Banos CA . . . . 37°4N 120°51W **64 F6**
Los Chaves NM . . . . 34°45N 106°44W **88 C4**
Los Coyotes Indian Reservation
 CA . . . . 33°17N 116°33W **65 K10**
Los Fresnos TX . . . . 26°4N 97°29W **98 L10**
Los Gatos CA . . . . . 37°14N 121°59W **64 F5**
Los Lunas NM . . . . 34°48N 106°44W **88 C4**
Los Molinos CA . . . . 40°1N 122°6W **64 C4**
Los Montoyas NM . . . 35°25N 105°12W **88 B5**
Los Nietos CA . . . . . 33°57N 118°4W **111 C4**
Los Olivos CA . . . . . 34°40N 120°7W **65 J6**
Los Olmos Cr. →
 TX . . . . 27°16N 97°44W **99 K10**
Los Osos CA . . . . . 35°19N 120°50W **65 H6**
Los Padillas NM . . . . 34°58N 106°42W **88 C4**
Los Padres National Forest
 CA . . . . 36°4N 121°43W **65 G5**
Los Pinos → CO . . . 36°56N 107°36W **66 F3**
Los Ranchos de Albuquerque
 NM . . . . 35°10N 106°39W **88 B4**
Losantville IN . . . . . 40°2N 85°11W **72 C5**
Lost → IN . . . . . . 38°33N 86°49W **72 E4**
Lost → OR . . . . . . 41°56N 121°30W **94 F4**
Lost → WY . . . . . . 39°4N 78°39W **102 B6**
Lost Brook Preserve
 NJ . . . . 40°56N 73°56W **114 A3**
Lost City WV . . . . . 38°56N 78°54W **102 C6**
Lost Creek WV . . . . 39°10N 80°21W **102 B4**
Lost Hills CA . . . . . 35°37N 119°41W **65 H7**
Lost Nation IA . . . . . 41°58N 90°49W **73 D8**
Lost Peak UT . . . . . 37°29N 113°55W **100 F2**
Lost River ID . . . . . 43°41N 113°22W **70 F5**
Lost River Range ID . . 43°45N 113°25W **70 E5**
Lost Springs KS . . . . 38°34N 96°58W **74 C7**
Lost Springs WY . . . 42°46N 104°56W **104 D8**
Lost Trail Pass
 U.S.A. . . . . . . 45°42N 113°57W **70 D5**
Lostine OR . . . . . . 45°29N 117°26W **94 B8**
Lostwood ND . . . . . 48°29N 102°25W **91 B3**
Lostwood Nat. Wildlife Reserve ☆
 ND . . . . 48°30N 102°30W **91 B3**
Lothair MT . . . . . . 48°28N 111°14W **83 B6**
Lott TX . . . . 31°12N 97°2W **99 F10**
Lottsburg VA . . . . . 37°58N 76°31W **77 C4**
Loudon NH . . . . . . 43°16N 71°27W **86 C3**
Loudon TN . . . . . . 35°45N 84°20W **97 E8**
Loudon County ☆
 TN . . . . 35°45N 84°20W **97 E8**
Loudonville OH . . . . 40°38N 82°14W **92 C4**
Loudoun County ☆
 VA . . . . 39°5N 77°30W **102 B7**
Loughman FL . . . . . 28°14N 81°34W **67 C7**
Louin MS . . . . 32°4N 89°16W **81 D4**
Louis Armstrong New Orleans
 Int. ✈ (MSY) LA . 30°0N 90°15W **113 C1**
Louisa KY . . . . . . 38°7N 82°36W **97 B10**
Louisa VA . . . . . . 38°1N 78°0W **102 C7**
Louisa County ☆ IA 41°15N 91°15W **73 D7**
Louisa County ☆ VA . 38°1N 78°0W **102 D7**
Louisburg KS . . . . . 38°37N 94°41W **74 C9**
Louisburg MN . . . . . 45°10N 96°10W **80 E2**
Louisburg MO . . . . . 37°46N 93°8W **82 D3**
Louisburg NC . . . . . 36°6N 78°18W **90 B7**
Louise TX . . . . . . 32°59N 90°31W **99 H11**
Louise, L. TX . . . . . 29°6N 96°24W **99 H11**
Louise, L. TX . . . . . 36°25N 109°15W **62 A6**
Louisiana MO . . . . . 39°27N 91°3W **82 B5**
Lukeville AZ . . . . . 31°53N 112°49W **62 F4**
Louisiana □ U.S.A. . . 30°50N 92°0W **75 D3**
Louisville AL . . . . . 31°47N 85°33W **60 C5**
Louisville CO . . . . . 39°59N 105°8W **66 C5**
Louisville IL . . . . . 38°46N 88°30W **71 E5**
Louisville KY . . . . . 38°15N 85°46W **97 B7**
Louisville NE . . . . . 41°0N 96°10W **84 D9**
Louisville OH . . . . . 40°50N 81°17W **92 C5**
Louisville Int. ✈ (SDF)
 KY . . . . 38°10N 85°44W **97 B7**
Loup → NE . . . . . . 41°17N 98°23W **84 C7**
Loup City NE . . . . . 41°17N 98°58W **84 C7**
Loup County ☆ NE . . 41°50N 99°30W **84 C6**
Loutre, Bayou → LA 32°41N 92°8W **75 B3**
Louvale GA . . . . . . 32°11N 84°54W **68 D2**
Louviers CO . . . . . . 39°28N 105°1W **66 C5**

Love County ☆ OK . . 34°0N 97°15W **93 E6**
Love Point MD . . . . 39°2N 76°19W **77 A4**
Lovelady TX . . . . . 31°8N 95°27W **99 F12**
Loveland CO . . . . . 40°24N 105°5W **66 B5**
Loveland OH . . . . . 39°16N 84°16W **92 D2**
Lovell WY . . . . . . 44°50N 108°24W **104 B4**
Lovelock NV . . . . . 40°11N 118°28W **85 E3**
Loves Park IL . . . . . 42°19N 89°3W **71 A4**
Lovett GA . . . . 32°38N 82°46W **68 D4**
Loving NM . . . . . . 32°17N 104°6W **88 E6**
Loving County ☆
 TX . . . . 31°42N 103°36W **98 F4**
Lovington IL . . . . . . 37°46N 78°52W **102 D6**
Lovington IL . . . . . . 39°43N 88°38W **71 D5**
Lovington NM . . . . . 32°57N 103°21W **88 E7**
Low Desert OR . . . . 43°27N 120°27W **94 D5**
Lowden IA . . . . . . 41°52N 90°56W **73 D8**
Lowell AR . . . . 36°15N 94°8W **63 B1**
Lowell FL . . . . 29°20N 82°12W **67 B6**
Lowell IN . . . . 46°9N 115°36W **70 C3**
Lowell IN . . . . 41°18N 87°25W **72 B3**
Lowell MA . . . . 42°38N 71°19W **78 B3**
Lowell OR . . . . 43°55N 122°47W **94 D3**
Lowell, L. ID . . . . . 43°35N 116°44W **70 F2**
Lowell → MN . . . . . 40°32N 70°57W **96 L4**
Lower Alkali L. CA . . 41°16N 120°2W **64 B6**
Lower Brule Indian Reservation
 SD . . . . 44°5N 100°0W **91 F6**
Lower Crab Cr. →
 WA . . . . 46°49N 119°55W **101 D6**
Lower Elwha Indian Reservation
 WA . . . . 48°8N 123°33W **101 B2**
Lower Gilmanton
 NH . . . . 43°24N 71°24W **86 C3**
Lower Granite L.
 WA . . . . 46°26N 117°14W **101 D8**
Lower Kalskag AK . . 61°31N 160°22W **61 F7**
Lower Klamath L.
 CA . . . . 41°57N 121°42W **94 F4**
Lower Lake CA . . . . 38°55N 122°37W **64 E4**
Lower Marlboro MD 38°39N 76°41W **77 B4**
Lower Monumental Dam
 WA . . . . 46°34N 118°33W **101 D7**
Lower New York B. = Lower B.
 NY . . . . 40°32N 74°5W **114 C2**
Lower Paia HI . . . . . 20°55N 156°23W **69 C5**
Lower Red L. MN . . . 47°58N 95°0W **80 C4**
Lower Sioux Indian Reservation
 MN . . . . 44°32N 94°59W **80 F4**
Lower Suwannee Nat. Wildlife
 Refuge → FL . . 29°20N 83°8W **67 B5**
Lowes KY . . . . 36°53N 88°46W **96 D4**
Lowes Crossroads
 DE . . . . 38°34N 75°24W **77 B5**
Lowman ID . . . . . . 44°5N 115°37W **70 F3**
Lowmoor VA . . . . . 37°47N 79°53W **102 D5**
Lowndes County ☆
 AL . . . . 32°11N 86°35W **60 C4**
Lowndes County ☆
 GA . . . . 30°50N 83°15W **68 F3**
Lowndes County ☆
 MS . . . . 33°30N 88°25W **81 C5**
Lowndesboro AL . . . 32°17N 86°37W **60 C4**
Lowry MN . . . . 45°42N 95°31W **80 E3**
Lowry SD . . . . 45°20N 99°59W **91 E6**
Lowry City MO . . . . 38°8N 93°44W **82 C3**
Lowville NY . . . . . . 43°47N 75°29W **89 B5**
Loxahatchee → FL . . 26°53N 80°11W **67 D8**
Loxley AL . . . . 30°37N 87°45W **60 E3**
Loyal OK . . . . 44°44N 90°30W **103 D3**
Loyal Valley TX . . . . 30°35N 99°0W **99 G8**
Loyall KY . . . . 36°51N 83°22W **97 D9**
Loyalton CA . . . . . . 39°41N 120°14W **64 D6**
Loyalton SD . . . . . . 45°17N 99°17W **91 E6**
Loyola University IL . . 42°0N 87°39W **108 A2**
Lu Verne IA . . . . . . 42°55N 94°5W **73 C4**
Lua Makiki HI . . . . . 20°33N 156°37W **69 G14**
Lualualei Naval Reserve
 HI . . . . 21°27N 158°6W **69 K13**
Lubbock TX . . . . . . 33°35N 101°51W **98 D6**
Lubbock County ☆
 TX . . . . 33°35N 101°50W **98 D6**
Lubec ME . . . . 44°52N 66°59W **76 D7**
Lublin WI . . . . 45°5N 90°43W **103 C3**
Lucama NC . . . . . . 35°39N 78°0W **90 C7**
Lucas KS . . . . 39°4N 98°32W **74 B5**
Lucas KY . . . . 36°53N 86°2W **96 D6**
Lucas OH . . . . 40°42N 82°25W **92 C4**
Lucas County ☆ IA 41°0N 93°20W **73 E5**
Lucas County ☆ OH 41°33N 83°48W **92 B3**
Lucasville OH . . . . . 38°53N 82°59W **92 E4**
Lucedale MS . . . . . 30°56N 88°35W **81 E5**
Lucerne = Lake Worth
 FL . . . . 26°37N 80°3W **67 D8**
Lucerne CA . . . . . . 39°6N 122°48W **64 D4**
Lucerne CO . . . . . . 40°29N 104°41W **66 B6**
Lucerne WY . . . . . . 43°44N 108°11W **104 C4**
Lucerne L. CA . . . . . 34°31N 116°58W **65 J10**
Lucerne Valley CA . . . 34°27N 116°57W **65 J10**
Lucero, L. NM . . . . . 32°42N 106°27W **88 E4**
Lucile ID . . . . 45°33N 116°18W **70 D2**
Luck WI . . . . 45°35N 92°29W **103 C1**
Luckey OH . . . . . . 41°27N 83°29W **92 B3**
Lucy, L. FL . . . . . . 28°34N 81°29W **115 A2**
Ludden ND . . . . . . 46°1N 98°8W **91 D7**
Ludell KS . . . . 39°52N 100°58W **74 B3**
Ludington MI . . . . . 43°57N 86°27W **79 F6**
Ludlow CA . . . . . . 34°43N 116°10W **65 J10**
Ludlow CO . . . . . . 37°20N 104°35W **66 E6**
Ludlow KY . . . . . . 39°5N 84°32W **107 B1**
Ludlow MS . . . . . . 32°34N 89°43W **81 D4**
Ludlow SD . . . . . . 45°50N 103°23W **91 E2**
Ludowici GA . . . . . 31°43N 81°45W **68 E5**
Lueders TX . . . . . . 32°48N 99°37W **98 E8**
Lufkin TX . . . . 31°21N 94°44W **99 F13**
Lugoff SC . . . . 34°13N 80°40W **90 D5**
Luis Lopez NM . . . . 33°59N 106°53W **88 D4**
Luis Munoz Marin Int., San Juan ✈
 (SJU)
 Puerto Rico . . . 18°26N 66°0W **105 G16**
Lukachukai AZ . . . . 36°25N 109°15W **62 A6**
Luke MD . . . . 39°30N 79°5W **77 A1**
Lukeville AZ . . . . . . 31°53N 112°49W **62 F4**
Lula GA . . . . 34°23N 83°40W **68 B3**
Lula MS . . . . 34°27N 90°29W **81 B3**
Luling TX . . . . 29°41N 97°39W **99 H10**
Lulu FL . . . . 30°7N 82°29W **67 A6**
Luma Amer. Samoa . . 14°16S 169°33W **105 f**
Lumber → MS . . . . 31°33N 89°18W **81 D4**
Lumber City GA . . . . 31°56N 82°41W **68 E4**
Lumberport WV . . . . 39°22N 80°21W **102 B4**
Lumberton MS . . . . 31°0N 89°27W **81 E4**
Lumberton NC . . . . 34°37N 79°0W **90 D7**
Lumberton NM . . . . 36°56N 106°56W **88 A4**
Lumberton TX . . . . . 30°16N 94°12W **99 G13**
Lummi Indian Reservation
 WA . . . . 48°52N 122°42W **101 B3**
Lumpkin GA . . . . . . 32°3N 84°48W **68 D2**
Lumpkin County ☆
 GA . . . . 34°40N 84°0W **68 B3**

Luna NM . . . . 33°49N 108°57W **88 D2**
Luna County ☆ NM 32°15N 107°45W **88 E3**
Luna Pier MI . . . . . 41°48N 83°27W **79 H8**
Lund NV . . . . 38°51N 115°0W **85 D5**
Lund UT . . . . 38°0N 113°26W **100 E2**
Luning NV . . . . . . 38°30N 118°11W **85 D3**
Lunenburg VA . . . . 36°58N 78°16W **102 E6**
Lunenburg VT . . . . . 44°26N 71°42W **86 B3**
Lunenburg County ☆
 VA . . . . 36°58N 78°16W **102 E6**
Lupton AZ . . . . . . 35°21N 109°4W **62 B6**
Lupus MO . . . . . . 38°51N 92°27W **82 C4**
Luquillo
 Puerto Rico . . . 18°23N 65°43W **105 G17**
Luray KS . . . . 39°7N 98°41W **74 B5**
Luray VA . . . . 40°27N 91°53W **82 A5**
Luray VA . . . . 38°40N 78°28W **77 B2**
Lusby MD . . . . 38°22N 76°26W **77 B4**
Lushton NE . . . . . . 40°43N 97°44W **84 D8**
Lusk WY . . . . 42°46N 104°27W **104 D8**
Lutcher LA . . . . . . 30°2N 90°42W **75 D5**
Luther IA . . . . 41°58N 93°49W **73 D5**
Luther MI . . . . 44°2N 85°41W **79 E6**
Luther OK . . . . 35°40N 97°12W **93 C6**
Luthersville GA . . . . 33°13N 84°45W **68 C2**
Lutherville-Timonium
 MD . . . . 39°25N 76°38W **107 A2**
Lutie TX . . . . 35°1N 100°13W **98 B7**
Lutsen MN . . . . . . 47°39N 90°41W **80 C8**
Luttrell TN . . . . . . 36°12N 83°45W **97 D9**
Lutts TN . . . . 35°9N 87°56W **96 E5**
Lutz FL . . . . 28°9N 82°28W **67 C6**
Luverne AL . . . . . . 31°43N 86°16W **60 D4**
Luverne MN . . . . . . 43°39N 96°13W **80 G2**
Luverne ND . . . . . . 47°16N 97°55W **91 C8**
Luxapallila Cr. →
 U.S.A. . . . . . . 33°27N 88°26W **81 C6**
Luxemburg IA . . . . 42°36N 91°5W **73 C7**
Luxemburg WI . . . . 44°33N 87°42W **103 D6**
Luxora AR . . . . . . 35°45N 89°56W **63 C6**
Luzerne County ☆ PA 41°10N 76°0W **95 C7**
Lycan CO . . . . 37°33N 102°12W **66 E8**
Lycoming County ☆
 PA . . . . 41°20N 77°0W **95 C5**
Lyells VA . . . . 38°0N 76°44W **77 C4**
Lyerly GA . . . . 34°24N 85°24W **68 B1**
Lyford TX . . . . 26°25N 97°48W **98 L10**
Lykens PA . . . . 40°34N 76°42W **95 D6**
Lyle MN . . . . 43°30N 92°57W **80 G6**
Lyles TN . . . . 35°55N 87°21W **96 E5**
Lyman SC . . . . 34°57N 82°8W **90 D3**
Lyman UT . . . . 38°24N 111°35W **100 E4**
Lyman WY . . . . . . 41°20N 110°18W **104 E2**
Lyman County ☆ SD . 44°0N 100°0W **91 G6**
Lyman L. AZ . . . . . 34°21N 109°23W **62 C6**
Lyme NH . . . . 43°48N 72°12W **86 C2**
Lyme L. AZ . . . . . . 34°21N 109°23W **62 C6**
Lynbrook NY . . . . . 40°39N 73°40W **114 C4**
Lynch KY . . . . 36°58N 82°54W **97 D10**
Lynch NE . . . . 42°50N 98°28W **84 B7**
Lynchburg OH . . . . 39°15N 83°48W **92 D3**
Lynchburg SC . . . . . 34°3N 80°4W **90 D5**
Lynchburg TN . . . . . 35°17N 86°22W **96 E6**
Lynchburg VA . . . . . 37°25N 79°9W **102 D5**
Lynches → SC . . . . 33°50N 79°20W **90 E6**
Lynd MN . . . . 44°23N 95°54W **80 F3**
Lynden WA . . . . . . 48°57N 122°27W **101 B3**
Lyndhurst NJ . . . . . 40°49N 74°7W **114 B2**
Lyndon IL . . . . 41°43N 89°56W **71 B4**
Lyndon KS . . . . . . 38°36N 95°41W **74 C8**
Lyndon VT . . . . . . 44°31N 72°1W **86 B2**
Lyndon B. Johnson, L.
 TX . . . . 30°35N 98°25W **99 G9**
Lyndon B. Johnson Nat. Grassland
 TX . . . . 33°33N 97°37W **99 D10**
Lyndon B. Johnson Nat. Historical
 Park → TX . . . 30°15N 98°25W **99 G9**
Lyndon Station WI . . 43°43N 89°54W **103 E4**
Lyndonville NY . . . . 43°20N 78°23W **89 B2**
Lyndonville VT . . . . 44°34N 72°1W **86 B2**
Lynhurst IN . . . . . . 39°46N 86°14W **110 B1**
Lynn AL . . . . 34°3N 87°33W **60 B3**
Lynn IN . . . . 40°3N 84°56W **72 C6**
Lynn MA . . . . 42°28N 70°57W **106 A4**
Lynn WI . . . . 41°53N 113°45W **100 B2**
Lynn County ☆ TX 33°10N 101°48W **98 D6**
Lynn Harbor MA . . . 42°26N 70°56W **106 A4**
Lynn Haven FL . . . . 30°15N 85°39W **67 A3**
Lynn Woods Res.
 MA . . . . 42°29N 70°59W **106 A4**
Lynndyl UT . . . . . . 39°31N 112°20W **100 D3**
Lynne FL . . . . 29°12N 81°55W **67 B7**
Lynnfield MA . . . . . 42°32N 71°3W **78 B3**
Lynnville IN . . . . . . 38°12N 87°18W **72 E3**
Lynnville KY . . . . . . 36°34N 88°34W **96 D4**
Lynnville TN . . . . . . 35°23N 87°0W **96 E5**
Lynnwood WA . . . . 47°49N 122°18W **118 A3**
Lynwood CA . . . . . 33°55N 118°12W **111 C3**
Lynxville WI . . . . . . 43°15N 91°12W **103 E2**
Lyon County ☆ IA . . 43°20N 96°10W **73 B2**
Lyon County ☆ KS . . 38°30N 96°10W **74 C7**
Lyon County ☆ KY . . 37°0N 88°0W **96 D4**
Lyon County ☆ MN 44°23N 95°50W **80 F3**
Lyon County ☆ NV 38°45N 119°10W **85 D1**
Lyon Mountain NY . . 44°43N 73°55W **89 A7**
Lyons CO . . . . 40°14N 105°16W **66 B5**
Lyons GA . . . . 32°12N 82°19W **68 D4**
Lyons KS . . . . 38°21N 98°12W **74 C5**
Lyons NE . . . . 41°56N 96°28W **84 C9**
Lyons NY . . . . 43°5N 77°0W **89 C4**
Lyons Falls NY . . . . 43°37N 75°22W **89 B5**
Lysite WY . . . . 43°16N 107°41W **104 C5**
Lytle TX . . . . 29°14N 98°48W **99 H9**
Lytton IA . . . . 42°25N 94°51W **73 C4**

M

Mabank TX . . . . . . 32°22N 96°6W **99 E11**
Mabel MN . . . . . . 43°32N 91°46W **80 G7**
Mabel, L. FL . . . . . 28°25N 81°32W **115 B1**
Maben WV . . . . . . 37°38N 81°23W **102 D3**
Mableton GA . . . . . 33°49N 84°35W **68 C2**
Mabton WA . . . . . . 46°13N 120°0W **101 D5**
McAdoo PA . . . . . . 40°55N 75°59W **95 D7**
McAlester OK . . . . . 34°56N 95°46W **93 D8**
McAlister NM . . . . . 34°51N 103°48W **88 C6**
McAllen TX . . . . . . 26°12N 98°14W **98 L9**
McAllister Park TX . . 29°33N 98°23W **117 B3**
McAlpin FL . . . . . . 30°8N 82°57W **67 A6**
McAlpine Creek County Park
 NC . . . . 35°9N 80°44W **107 B2**
McArthur CA . . . . . 41°3N 121°24W **64 B5**
McArthur OH . . . . . 39°15N 82°29W **92 D4**
MacArthur Park CA 34°3N 118°16W **111 B3**
McBain MI . . . . . . 44°12N 85°13W **79 E6**
McBee SC . . . . 34°28N 80°15W **90 D5**
McBride MO . . . . . . 37°50N 89°50W **82 D7**
McBride MI . . . . . . 43°14N 85°2W **79 F6**
McBrides MI . . . . . . 43°21N 85°2W **79 F6**
McCall ID . . . . 44°55N 116°6W **70 E2**
McCall Creek MS . . . 31°31N 90°42W **81 E3**
McCallsburg IA . . . . 42°10N 93°23W **73 C5**
McCamey TX . . . . . 31°8N 102°14W **98 F5**
Mackinac, Straits of
 MI . . . . 45°50N 84°40W **79 D7**

McCammon ID . . . . 42°39N 112°12W **70 G6**
McCandless PA . . . . 40°30N 80°4W **95 D2**
McCarran Int., Las Vegas ✈ (LAS)
 NV . . . . 36°5N 115°9W **110 C2**
McCarthy AK . . . . . 61°26N 142°56W **61 F12**
McCarty Park WI . . . 42°59N 88°0W **112 C1**
McCartys NM . . . . . 35°4N 107°41W **88 C3**
McCaysville GA . . . . 34°59N 84°23W **68 B2**
McClain County ☆
 OK . . . . 35°0N 97°30W **93 D6**
McClave CO . . . . . 38°2N 102°51W **66 D8**
McCleary WA . . . . . 47°3N 123°16W **101 C2**
McClelland IA . . . . . 41°20N 95°41W **73 D3**
McClellanville SC . . . 33°5N 79°28W **90 E6**
Macclenny FL . . . . . 30°17N 82°7W **67 A6**
McCloud CA . . . . . 41°15N 122°8W **64 B4**
McCloud → CA . . . . 40°42N 122°21W **64 C4**
McClure PA . . . . . . 40°42N 77°19W **95 D5**
McClure VA . . . . . . 37°6N 82°23W **102 D2**
McClure, L. CA . . . . 37°35N 120°16W **64 F6**
McClusky ND . . . . . 47°29N 100°27W **91 C5**
McColl SC . . . . 34°40N 79°33W **90 D6**
McComb MS . . . . . 31°15N 90°27W **81 E3**
McComb OH . . . . . 41°7N 83°48W **92 B3**
McCone County ☆
 MT . . . . 47°40N 105°50W **83 C12**
McConnell Air Force Base
 KS . . . . 37°40N 97°16W **74 D6**
McConnellsburg PA . . 39°56N 77°59W **95 E5**
McConnelsville OH . . 39°39N 81°51W **92 D5**
McCook IL . . . . 41°47N 87°49W **108 C2**
McCook NE . . . . . . 40°12N 100°38W **84 D5**
McCook County ☆
 SD . . . . 43°44N 97°23W **91 G8**
McCool MS . . . . . . 33°12N 89°21W **81 C4**
McCool Junction NE . 40°44N 97°36W **84 D8**
McCormick SC . . . . 33°55N 82°17W **90 D3**
McCormick County ☆
 SC . . . . 33°50N 82°15W **90 D3**
McCoy CO . . . . . . 39°55N 106°44W **66 C4**
McCracken KS . . . . 38°36N 99°34W **74 C4**
McCracken County ☆
 KY . . . . 37°5N 88°45W **96 C4**
McCreary County ☆
 KY . . . . 36°45N 84°30W **97 D8**
McCrory AR . . . . . . 35°16N 91°12W **63 C4**
McCulloch County ☆
 TX . . . . 31°9N 99°20W **99 F8**
McCullough Ra. NV . . 35°45N 115°5W **85 G5**
McCune KS . . . . . . 37°21N 95°1W **74 D8**
McCurtain OK . . . . . 35°9N 94°58W **93 D9**
McCurtain County ☆
 OK . . . . 34°10N 94°45W **93 D9**
McDade TX . . . . . . 30°17N 97°14W **99 G10**
McDavid FL . . . . . . 30°52N 87°19W **67 A1**
McDermitt NV . . . . . 41°59N 117°43W **85 A3**
McDonald KS . . . . . 39°47N 101°22W **74 B2**
McDonald NM . . . . . 33°9N 103°19W **88 D7**
McDonald, L. MT . . . 48°35N 113°56W **83 B4**
McDonald County ☆
 MO . . . . 36°40N 94°20W **82 E2**
McDonough GA . . . . 33°27N 84°9W **68 C2**
McDonough County ☆
 IL . . . . 40°30N 90°40W **71 C3**
McDougal AR . . . . . 36°26N 90°23W **63 B5**
McDougall, Mt.
 WY . . . . 42°54N 110°36W **104 D2**
McDowell VA . . . . . 38°20N 79°29W **102 C5**
McDowell County ☆
 NC . . . . 35°40N 82°0W **90 C4**
McDowell County ☆
 WV . . . . 37°20N 81°33W **102 D3**
McDuffie County ☆
 GA . . . . 33°30N 82°25W **68 C4**
Macedonia IL . . . . . 38°3N 88°42W **71 E5**
Macedonia IL . . . . . 41°12N 95°25W **73 D3**
Macedonia OH . . . . 41°19N 81°31W **92 B5**
Maceo KY . . . . 37°51N 87°0W **96 C6**
McEwen TN . . . . . . 36°7N 87°38W **96 D5**
McFadden WY . . . . 41°39N 106°8W **104 E6**
McFaddin Nat. Wildlife Refuge
 TX . . . . 29°39N 94°3W **99 H13**
McFall MO . . . . . . 40°7N 94°13W **82 A2**
McFarland CA . . . . . 35°41N 119°14W **65 H7**
McFarland KS . . . . . 39°3N 96°14W **74 B7**
McFarland WI . . . . . 43°1N 89°17W **103 E4**
McGee Creek L. OK . . 34°22N 95°38W **93 D8**
McGehee AR . . . . . 33°38N 91°24W **63 E4**
McGhee Tyson, Knoxville ✈ (TYS)
 TN . . . . 35°49N 83°59W **97 E9**
McGill NV . . . . 39°23N 114°47W **85 C6**
McGrath AK . . . . . . 62°58N 155°36W **61 E9**
McGraw NY . . . . . . 42°36N 76°8W **89 C4**
McGregor IA . . . . . 43°1N 91°11W **73 B7**
McGregor ND . . . . . 48°36N 102°56W **91 B3**
McGregor TX . . . . . 31°27N 97°24W **99 F10**
McGrew NE . . . . . . 41°45N 103°25W **84 C2**
McGuffey OH . . . . . 40°42N 83°47W **92 C3**
McHenry IL . . . . . . 42°21N 88°16W **71 A5**
McHenry MS . . . . . 30°43N 89°9W **81 E4**
McHenry ND . . . . . 47°35N 98°35W **91 C7**
McHenry County ☆
 IL . . . . 42°20N 88°25W **71 A5**
McHenry County ☆
 ND . . . . 48°20N 100°45W **91 B5**
Machesney Park IL . . 42°21N 89°2W **71 A4**
Machias ME . . . . . . 44°43N 67°28W **76 D6**
Machias NY . . . . . . 42°25N 78°30W **89 C2**
Machias → ME . . . . 44°43N 67°22W **76 D6**
McIntire IA . . . . . . 43°26N 92°36W **73 B6**
McIntosh FL . . . . . . 31°16N 88°2W **60 E2**
McIntosh MN . . . . . 47°38N 95°53W **80 C3**
McIntosh NM . . . . . 34°52N 106°3W **88 C4**
McIntosh SD . . . . . 45°55N 101°21W **91 E4**
McIntosh County ☆
 GA . . . . 31°30N 81°20W **68 E5**
McIntosh County ☆
 ND . . . . 46°2N 99°20W **91 D6**
McIntyre GA . . . . . . 32°51N 83°12W **68 D3**
Mack CO . . . . 39°13N 108°52W **66 C2**
Mackay ID . . . . . . 43°55N 113°37W **70 F5**
McKean County ☆
 PA . . . . 41°50N 78°45W **95 C4**
McKee KY . . . . 37°25N 84°0W **97 C9**
McKee City NJ . . . . 39°27N 74°38W **87 C2**
McKees Rocks PA . . . 40°28N 80°3W **116 B1**
McKenney VA . . . . . 36°59N 77°43W **102 E7**
McKenzie AL . . . . . 31°33N 86°43W **60 D4**
Mackenzie MI . . . . . 42°18N 83°9W **109 A1**
Mackenzie ND . . . . 46°50N 100°25W **91 D5**
McKenzie TN . . . . . 36°8N 88°31W **96 D4**
Mackenzie → OR . . . 44°7N 123°6W **94 C2**
McKenzie Bridge
 OR . . . . 44°11N 122°10W **94 C3**
McKenzie County ☆
 ND . . . . 47°45N 103°30W **91 C2**
Mackinac, Straits of
 MI . . . . 45°50N 84°40W **79 D7**

Mackinac County ☆ MI 46°5N 85°0W **79 D6**
Mackinac Island MI . . 45°51N 84°37W **79 D7**
Mackinaw IL . . . . . . 40°32N 89°21W **71 C4**
Mackinaw → IL . . . . 40°33N 89°44W **71 C4**
Mackinaw City MI . . . 45°47N 84°44W **79 D7**
McKinley, Mt. AK . . . 63°4N 151°0W **61 E10**
McKinley County ☆
 NM . . . . 35°30N 108°0W **88 B2**
McKinley Park AK . . . 63°43N 148°55W **61 E10**
McKinleyville CA . . . 40°57N 124°6W **64 C2**
McKinney TX . . . . . 33°12N 96°37W **99 D11**
McKinnon GA . . . . . 31°25N 81°56W **68 E5**
Macksburg IA . . . . . 41°13N 94°11W **73 D4**
Macksville KS . . . . . 37°58N 98°58W **74 D5**
McLain MS . . . . . . 31°7N 88°50W **81 E5**
McLaughlin SD . . . . 45°49N 100°49W **91 E5**
McLaurin MS . . . . . 31°10N 89°13W **81 E4**
McLean IL . . . . 40°19N 89°10W **71 C4**
McLean NE . . . . . . 42°23N 97°28W **84 B8**
McLean VA . . . . . . 38°56N 77°10W **119 B2**
McLean County ☆ IL 40°30N 88°50W **71 C5**
McLean County ☆
 KY . . . . 37°30N 87°15W **96 C5**
McLean County ☆
 ND . . . . 47°30N 101°0W **91 C4**
McLeansboro IL . . . . 38°6N 88°32W **71 E5**
McLellan Res. CO . . . 39°34N 105°1W **109 C17**
McLennan County ☆
 TX . . . . 31°33N 97°9W **99 F10**
McLeod ND . . . . . . 46°24N 97°18W **91 D8**
McLeod County ☆
 MN . . . . 44°50N 94°15W **80 F4**
McLoud OK . . . . . . 35°26N 97°6W **93 C6**
McLoughlin, Mt.
 OR . . . . 42°27N 122°19W **94 E3**
McLouth KS . . . . . . 39°12N 95°13W **74 B8**
McMichael Cr. →
 PA . . . . 40°59N 75°11W **87 B1**
McMinn County ☆
 TN . . . . 35°25N 84°37W **97 E8**
McMinnville OR . . . . 45°13N 123°12W **94 B2**
McMinnville TN . . . . 35°41N 85°46W **97 E7**
McMullen County ☆
 TX . . . . 28°28N 98°33W **99 J9**
McMurray WA . . . . 48°18N 122°14W **101 B3**
McNab AR . . . . . . 33°40N 93°50W **63 E2**
McNairy County ☆
 TN . . . . 35°10N 88°36W **96 E4**
McNary AZ . . . . . . 34°4N 109°51W **62 C6**
McNary TX . . . . . . 31°15N 105°48W **98 F2**
McNeal AR . . . . . . 31°36N 109°40W **62 F6**
McNeil AR . . . . 33°21N 93°13W **63 E2**
McNeill MS . . . . . . 30°40N 89°38W **81 E4**
Macomb IL . . . . . . 40°27N 90°40W **71 C3**
Macomb OK . . . . . . 35°10N 97°0W **93 C6**
Macomb County ☆
 MI . . . . 42°40N 83°0W **79 G9**
Macon GA . . . . 32°51N 83°38W **68 D3**
Macon IL . . . . 39°43N 89°0W **71 D5**
Macon MS . . . . 33°7N 88°34W **81 C5**
Macon MO . . . . . . 39°44N 92°28W **82 B4**
Macon, Bayou → LA 31°55N 91°33W **75 C4**
Macon County ☆ AL 32°25N 85°42W **60 D5**
Macon County ☆ GA . 32°20N 84°0W **68 D2**
Macon County ☆
 MO . . . . 39°50N 92°30W **82 B4**
Macon County ☆ NC . 35°8N 83°30W **90 C2**
Macon County ☆ TN . 36°31N 86°2W **96 D6**
Macoupin County ☆
 IL . . . . 39°20N 89°55W **71 D4**
McPherson KS . . . . 38°22N 97°40W **74 C6**
McPherson County ☆
 KS . . . . 38°20N 97°40W **74 C6**
McPherson County ☆
 NE . . . . 41°30N 101°0W **84 C4**
McPherson County ☆
 SD . . . . 45°46N 99°0W **91 E6**
McQuady KY . . . . . 37°42N 86°31W **96 C6**
McRae AR . . . . 35°7N 91°49W **63 C4**
McRae GA . . . . 32°4N 82°54W **68 D4**
McRoberts KY . . . . . 37°12N 82°40W **97 C10**
McSherrystown PA . . 39°48N 77°1W **77 A3**
Macungie PA . . . . . 40°31N 75°33W **87 B1**
McVeigh KY . . . . . . 37°33N 82°15W **97 C10**
McVeytown PA . . . . 40°30N 77°45W **95 D5**
McVille ND . . . . . . 47°46N 98°11W **91 C7**
Macwahoc ME . . . . 45°38N 68°16W **76 C5**
McWilliams AL . . . . 31°50N 87°6W **60 D3**
Macy NE . . . . 42°7N 96°21W **84 B9**
Mad → CA . . . . . . 40°57N 124°7W **64 C2**
Mad → OH . . . . . . 39°46N 84°12W **92 D2**
Mad → VT . . . . . . 44°18N 72°41W **86 B2**
Mad River Glen VT . . 44°12N 72°55W **86 B2**
Madawaska ME . . . . 47°21N 68°20W **76 A6**
Maddock ND . . . . . 47°58N 99°32W **91 C6**
Maddox MD . . . . . . 38°23N 76°46W **77 B4**
Madeira OH . . . . . . 39°11N 84°21W **107 A2**
Madeira Beach FL . . . 27°47N 82°47W **119 C2**
Madelia MN . . . . . . 44°3N 94°25W **80 F4**
Madeline CA . . . . . 41°3N 120°28W **64 B6**
Madeline I. WI . . . . 46°49N 90°42W **103 B3**
Madera CA . . . . . . 36°57N 120°3W **64 F6**
Madera County ☆
 CA . . . . 37°5N 119°35W **64 F7**
Madill OK . . . . 34°6N 96°46W **93 D7**
Madison AL . . . . . . 34°42N 86°45W **60 B4**
Madison AR . . . . . . 35°1N 90°43W **63 C5**
Madison FL . . . . . . 30°28N 83°25W **67 A5**
Madison GA . . . . . . 33°36N 83°28W **68 C3**
Madison IL . . . . . . 38°40N 90°9W **117 A3**
Madison IN . . . . . . 44°43N 97°23W **72 F5**
Madison ME . . . . . . 44°48N 69°53W **76 D4**
Madison MN . . . . . . 38°30N 76°13W **77 A4**
Madison MN . . . . . . 45°1N 96°11W **80 E2**
Madison MO . . . . . . 39°28N 92°13W **82 B4**
Madison NC . . . . . . 36°23N 79°58W **90 B6**
Madison NE . . . . . . 41°46N 97°27W **84 C8**
Madison OH . . . . . . 41°46N 81°3W **92 B5**
Madison SD . . . . . . 44°0N 97°7W **91 F8**
Madison VA . . . . . . 38°23N 78°15W **102 C6**
Madison WI . . . . . . 43°4N 89°24W **103 E4**
Madison → MT . . . . 45°56N 111°31W **83 E6**
Madison County ☆
 AL . . . . 34°44N 86°33W **60 B4**
Madison County ☆
 AR . . . . 36°5N 93°44W **63 B2**
Madison County ☆
 FL . . . . 30°30N 83°30W **67 A5**
Madison County ☆
 GA . . . . 34°10N 83°10W **68 B3**
Madison County ☆
 ID . . . . 43°55N 111°50W **70 F7**
Madison County ☆
 IL . . . . 38°50N 89°55W **71 E4**
Madison County ☆
 IN . . . . 40°10N 85°40W **72 C5**
Madison County ☆
 KY . . . . 37°40N 84°20W **97 C8**
Madison County ☆
 MS . . . . 32°37N 90°2W **81 D3**

Madison County ☆
  MO . . . . 37°30N 90°20W **82 D6**
Madison County ☆
  MT . . . . 45°12N 112°0W **83 E6**
Madison County ☆
  NC . . . . 35°50N 82°50W **90 C3**
Madison County ☆
  NY . . . . 43°0N 75°45W **89 C5**
Madison County ☆
  NE . . . . 41°50N 97°30W **84 C8**
Madison County ☆
  OH . . . . 39°53N 83°27W **92 D3**
Madison County ☆
  TN . . . . . . 35°37N 88°49W **96 E4**
Madison County ☆
  TX . . . . . . 31°0N 96°0W **99 G12**
Madison County ☆
  VA . . . . . . 38°23N 78°15W **102 C6**
Madison Heights VA 37°25N 79°8W **102 D5**
Madison Lake MN . . 44°12N 93°49W **80 F5**
Madison Mills OH . . 39°39N 83°20W **92 D3**
Madison Parish ☆
  LA . . . . 32°25N 91°11W **75 B4**
Madisonville KY . . 37°20N 87°30W **96 C5**
Madisonville LA . . 30°24N 90°10W **75 D5**
Madisonville TN . . 35°31N 84°22W **97 E8**
Madisonville TX . . 30°57N 95°55W **99 G12**
Madras OR . . . . . 44°38N 121°8W **94 C4**
Madre, L. TX . . . 25°15N 97°30W **98 L10**
Madrid IA . . . . 31°52N 93°49W **73 D5**
Madrid AL . . . . . 31°22N 85°24W **60 E5**
Madrid NM . . . . 35°24N 106°9W **88 B4**
Madrid NY . . . . 44°45N 75°8W **89 A5**
Madrid NE . . . . 40°51N 101°33W **84 D4**
Maeser UT . . . 40°28N 109°35W **100 C6**
Maeystown IL . . . 38°13N 90°14W **71 E3**
Magazine AR . . . 35°9N 93°48W **63 C2**
Magazine Mt. AR . 35°10N 93°41W **63 C2**
Magdalena NM . . 34°7N 107°15W **88 C3**
Magdalena Mts. NM 33°45N 107°15W **88 D3**
Magee MS . . . . 31°52N 89°44W **81 E4**
Maggiore, L. FL . . 27°44N 82°39W **119 C3**
Magic Res. ID . . 43°15N 114°22W **70 F4**
Magna UT . . . . 40°42N 112°6W **100 C4**
Magnet NE . . . 42°27N 97°28W **84 B8**
Magnolia AR . . . 33°16N 93°14W **63 D2**
Magnolia DE . . . 39°4N 75°29W **77 A5**
Magnolia IA . . . 41°42N 95°52W **73 D3**
Magnolia KY . . . 37°27N 85°45W **97 C7**
Magnolia MS . . . 31°9N 90°28W **81 E3**
Magnolia NC . . 34°54N 78°3W **90 D7**
Magnolia OH . . 40°39N 81°18W **92 C5**
Magnolia TX . . 30°13N 95°45W **99 G12**
Magoffin County ☆
  KY . . . . 37°45N 83°5W **97 C9**
Mahaffey PA . . . 40°53N 78°44W **95 D4**
Mahanoy City PA . 40°49N 76°9W **95 D6**
Mahaska KS . . . 39°59N 97°20W **74 B6**
Mahaska County ☆
  IA . . . . 41°20N 92°40W **73 D6**
Mahnomen MN . . 47°19N 95°58W **80 C3**
Mahnomen County ☆
  MN . . . . . . 47°20N 95°45W **80 C3**
Mahogany Mts. OR 43°14N 117°15W **94 D8**
Mahomet IL . . . 40°12N 88°24W **71 C5**
Mahoning County ☆
  OH . . . . . . 41°6N 80°48W **92 B6**
Mahopac NY . . . 41°22N 73°44W **87 A3**
Mahtomedi MN . . 45°3N 92°57W **113 A4**
Mahtowa MN . . 46°34N 92°38W **80 D6**
Maiden NC . . . . 35°35N 81°13W **90 C4**
Maiden Rock WI . 44°34N 92°18W **103 E1**
Māʻili HI . . . . . 21°25N 158°11W **69 K13**
Māʻili Pt. HI . . 21°24N 158°11W **69 K13**
Main Pass LA . . 29°15N 89°14W **75 E6**
Maine ☐ U.S.A. . 45°20N 69°0W **76 C5**
Maitland MD . . . 40°12N 95°5W **82 A1**
Major County ☆ OK 36°15N 98°30W **93 B5**
Majors Place NV . 39°2N 114°35W **85 C6**
Makah Indian Reservation
  WA . . . . . 48°23N 124°29W **101 B1**
Mākaha HI . . . 21°29N 158°13W **69 K13**
Makahoa Pt. HI . 21°41N 157°56W **69 J14**
Makahuena Pt. HI 21°52N 159°27W **69 B2**
Makakilo City HI . 21°21N 158°5W **69 K13**
Makanda IL . . . 37°37N 89°13W **71 E4**
Makapuʻu Pt. HI . 21°19N 157°39W **69 K14**
Makawao HI . . . 20°52N 156°17W **69 C5**
Makoti ND . . . . 47°58N 101°48W **91 C4**
Mākua HI . . . . 21°32N 158°13W **69 J13**
Mākua Keaʻau Forest Reserve
  HI . . . . . . 21°30N 158°12W **69 J13**
Makua Military Reservation
  HI . . . . . . 21°32N 158°14W **69 J13**
Makushin Volcano
  AK . . . . . 53°53N 166°55W **61 K6**
Malabar FL . . . 28°0N 80°34W **67 D8**
Malad City ID . . 42°12N 112°15W **70 G6**
Malae Pt. HI . . . 20°7N 155°53W **69 C6**
Malaga NM . . . 32°14N 104°4W **88 E6**
Malaga OH . . . 39°51N 81°9W **92 D5**
Malakoff TX . . . 32°10N 96°1W **99 F11**
Malaspina Glacier
  AK . . . . 59°50N 140°30W **61 G12**
Malcolm NE . . . 40°54N 96°52W **84 D9**
Malcom IA . . . 41°43N 92°33W **73 D6**
Malden IL . . . . 41°25N 89°22W **71 B4**
Malden MA . . . 42°26N 71°3W **106 A3**
Malden MO . . . 36°34N 89°57W **82 G8**
Malheur → OR . 44°4N 116°59W **94 C9**
Malheur County ☆
  OR . . . . . 43°15N 117°45W **94 D8**
Malheur L. OR . . 43°20N 118°48W **94 D7**
Malheur Nat. Forest
  OR . . . . 44°10N 119°15W **94 C6**
Malin OR . . . 42°1N 121°24W **94 E4**
Malinta OH . . . 41°19N 84°2W **92 B2**
Maljamar NM . . 32°51N 103°46W **88 E7**
Mallard IA . . . 42°56N 94°41W **73 C4**
Malmo NE . . . 41°16N 96°43W **84 C9**
Malmstrom Air Force Base
  MT . . . . 47°30N 111°11W **83 C6**
Malone FL . . . 30°57N 85°10W **67 A3**
Malone NY . . . 44°51N 74°18W **89 A6**
Maloney, L. KY . 37°32N 87°2W **96 C5**
Maloney, L. NE . 41°3N 100°48W **84 C5**
Malott WA . . . 48°17N 119°42W **101 B6**
Maloy IA . . . . 40°49N 94°25W **73 E4**
Malpais, The NM . 33°43N 105°56W **88 D5**
Malta ID . . . . 42°18N 113°22W **70 G5**
Malta IL . . . . 41°56N 88°52W **71 B5**
Malta MT . . . 48°21N 107°52W **83 B10**
Malta Bend MO . 39°12N 93°22W **82 B4**
Maltby WA . . . 47°48N 122°6W **118 B5**
Malvern AR . . . 34°22N 92°49W **63 D3**
Malvern IA . . . 41°0N 95°35W **73 E3**
Malvern OH . . 40°42N 81°11W **92 C5**
Malvern PA . . . 40°2N 75°31W **96 A4**
Malverne NY . . 40°40N 73°40W **114 B4**
Māmala B. HI . . 21°17N 157°56W **69 K14**
Mamaroneck NY . 40°57N 73°44W **87 B3**
Mamaroneck Harbor
  NY . . . . 40°56N 73°42W **114 A4**
Mammoth AZ . . 32°43N 110°39W **62 E5**
Mammoth Cave Nat. Park △
  KY . . . . . 37°8N 86°13W **96 C6**
Mammoth Hot Springs
  WY . . . . 44°59N 110°42W **104 B2**
Mammoth Lakes CA 37°39N 118°59W **64 F5**
Mammoth Pool Res.
  CA . . . . 37°20N 119°19W **64 F7**
Mammoth Spring AR 36°30N 91°33W **63 B4**

Mamou LA . . . 30°38N 92°25W **75 D3**
Man WV . . . . 37°45N 81°53W **102 D3**
Mana HI . . . . 22°2N 159°47W **69 A2**
Manahawkin NJ . 39°42N 74°16W **87 C2**
Manalapan NJ . . 40°15N 74°24W **87 B2**
Mānana I. HI . . 21°20N 157°40W **69 K14**
Manasquan NJ . . 40°8N 74°2W **87 B2**
Manasquan → NJ . 40°6N 74°2W **87 B2**
Manassas CO . . 37°11N 105°56W **66 E5**
Manassas VA . . 38°45N 77°29W **77 B3**
Manassas Park VA . 38°47N 77°28W **77 B3**
Manatee County ☆
  FL . . . . . . 27°30N 82°30W **67 D6**
Manatí
  Puerto Rico . . 18°26N 66°29W **105 G16**
Manawa WI . . . 44°28N 88°55W **103 D5**
Mancelona MI . . 44°54N 85°4W **79 E6**
Manchester CA . 38°58N 123°41W **64 E3**
Manchester GA . 32°51N 84°37W **68 D2**
Manchester IA . . 42°29N 91°27W **73 C7**
Manchester KS . 39°6N 97°19W **74 B6**
Manchester KY . 37°9N 83°46W **97 C9**
Manchester MD . 39°40N 76°53W **77 A4**
Manchester MI . 42°9N 84°2W **79 G7**
Manchester NH . 42°59N 71°28W **86 D3**
Manchester OH . 38°41N 83°36W **92 E3**
Manchester OK . 36°59N 98°2W **93 C5**
Manchester TN . 35°29N 86°5W **96 E6**
Manchester WA . 47°33N 122°32W **118 C2**
Manchester-by-the-Sea
  MA . . . . 42°35N 70°46W **78 B4**
Manchester Center VT 43°10N 73°4W **86 C1**
Mancos CO . . . 37°21N 108°18W **66 E2**
Mandan ND . . . 46°50N 100°54W **91 D5**
Mandaree ND . . 47°43N 102°41W **91 C3**
Manderson WY . 44°16N 107°58W **104 B5**
Mandeville LA . . 30°22N 90°4W **75 D5**
Mangham LA . . 32°19N 91°47W **75 B4**
Mango FL . . . . 27°59N 82°18W **67 D6**
Mangohick VA . . 37°49N 77°16W **77 C3**
Mangum OK . . 34°53N 99°30W **93 C4**
Manhasset NY . . 40°47N 73°42W **114 B4**
Manhasset Bay NY 40°49N 73°43W **114 A4**
Manhasset Hills NY 40°45N 73°40W **114 B3**
Manhattan KS . . 39°11N 96°35W **74 B7**
Manhattan MT . . 45°51N 111°20W **83 E6**
Manhattan NV . . 40°48N 73°57W **114 B3**
Manhattan NV . . 38°32N 117°4W **85 D3**
Manhattan Beach
  CA . . . . . 33°53N 118°24W **111 C2**
Manhattan Beach
  NY . . . . . 40°34N 73°56W **114 C3**
Manifest LA . . . 31°43N 91°58W **75 C4**
Manila AR . . . 35°53N 90°10W **63 C5**
Manila UT . . . . 40°59N 109°43W **100 C6**
Manila KS . . . . 38°13N 95°14W **73 D8**
Manilla IA . . . . 41°53N 95°14W **73 D3**
Manistee MI . . . 44°15N 86°19W **79 E5**
Manistee → MI . . 44°15N 86°21W **79 E5**
Manistee Nat. Forest
  MI . . . . . . 44°20N 86°10W **79 E5**
Manistique MI . . 45°57N 86°15W **79 D5**
Manistique L. MI . 46°15N 85°46W **79 C6**
Manito IL . . . . 40°26N 89°47W **71 C4**
Manitou Beach MI 41°58N 84°19W **79 G7**
Manitou I. MI . . 47°25N 87°37W **79 B4**
Manitou Is. MI . . 45°8N 86°0W **54 C2**
Manitou Springs
  CO . . . . . 38°52N 104°55W **66 D6**
Manitowish WI . 46°8N 90°0W **103 B3**
Manitowish Waters
  WI . . . . . 46°9N 89°53W **103 B4**
Manitowoc WI . 44°5N 87°40W **103 D6**
Manitowoc County ☆
  WI . . . . . 44°10N 87°50W **103 D6**
Mankato KS . . 39°47N 98°13W **74 B5**
Mankato MN . . 44°10N 94°0W **80 F4**
Manley NE . . . 40°55N 96°10W **84 D9**
Manley Hot Springs
  AK . . . . . 65°0N 150°38W **61 D10**
Manlius IL . . . . 41°27N 89°40W **71 B4**
Manlius NY . . . 43°0N 75°59W **89 C5**
Manly IA . . . . 43°17N 93°12W **73 B5**
Manly L. TX . . . 28°32N 81°35W **115 A2**
Mannford OK . . 36°8N 96°24W **93 B7**
Manning AR . . . 34°1N 92°48W **63 D3**
Manning ND . . 47°14N 102°46W **91 C3**
Manning SC . . . 33°42N 80°13W **90 E5**
Mannington WV . 39°32N 80°21W **102 B4**
Mann's Chinese Theatre
  CA . . . . 34°6N 118°20W **111 B2**
Manns Harbor NC 35°53N 75°46W **90 C10**
Mannsville NY . . 43°43N 76°4W **89 B4**
Mannsville OK . . 34°11N 96°53W **93 D7**
Manokin MD . . . 38°5N 75°55W **77 B5**
Manokotak AK . . 58°58N 159°3W **61 G8**
Manorhaven NY . 40°50N 73°42W **114 A4**
Mansfield AR . . . 35°4N 94°15W **63 C1**
Mansfield CT . . . 41°46N 72°14W **78 C2**
Mansfield GA . . . 33°31N 83°44W **68 C3**
Mansfield IL . . . 40°13N 88°31W **71 C5**
Mansfield LA . . . 32°2N 93°43W **75 B3**
Mansfield MO . . . 37°6N 92°35W **82 D4**
Mansfield OH . . . 40°45N 82°31W **92 C4**
Mansfield PA . . . 41°48N 77°5W **95 C5**
Mansfield SD . . . 45°15N 98°34W **91 E7**
Mansfield TN . . . 36°11N 88°17W **96 D4**
Mansfield TX . . . 32°33N 97°8W **109 C3**
Mansfield WA . . . 47°49N 119°38W **101 C6**
Mansfield, Mt. VT . 44°33N 72°49W **86 B2**
Mansfield Hollow L.
  CT . . . . . 41°45N 72°11W **78 C2**
Manson IA . . . . 42°32N 94°32W **73 C4**
Manson WA . . . 47°53N 120°9W **101 C5**
Mansura LA . . . 31°4N 92°3W **75 C3**
Mantador ND . . 46°10N 96°59W **91 D9**
Mantee MS . . . 33°43N 89°3W **81 C4**
Manteca CA . . . 37°48N 121°13W **64 F5**
Manteno IL . . . 41°15N 87°50W **71 B6**
Manteo NC . . . 35°55N 75°40W **90 C10**
Manter KS . . . 37°31N 101°53W **74 D2**
Manti UT . . . . 39°16N 111°38W **100 D4**
Manti-la Sal Nat. Forest
  UT . . . . 37°50N 109°50W **100 F6**
Mantoloking NJ . 40°4N 74°4W **87 B2**
Manton MI . . . . 44°25N 85°24W **79 E6**
Mantorville MN . 44°5N 92°45W **80 F6**
Mantua NJ . . . 39°47N 75°12W **97 A2**
Mantua OH . . . 41°17N 81°14W **92 B5**
Mantua UT . . . 41°30N 111°57W **100 B4**
Manu'a Is.
  Amer. Samoa . 14°13S 169°35W **105 f**
Manuelito NM . . 35°24N 109°0W **88 B2**
Manvel ND . . . 48°5N 97°11W **91 B8**
Manvel TX . . . 29°28N 95°21W **99 H12**
Manville NJ . . . 40°33N 74°35W **87 B2**
Manville WY . . . 42°59N 104°58W **104 D8**
Many LA . . . . 31°34N 93°29W **75 C2**
Many Farms AZ . 36°21N 109°37W **62 A6**
Manzanar Nat. Historic Site
  CA . . . . 36°44N 118°8W **65 G8**
Manzanita OR . . 45°43N 123°56W **94 B2**
Manzanita Indian Reservation
  CA . . . . 32°45N 116°20W **65 L10**
Manzano Mts. NM 34°40N 106°20W **88 C4**
Manzanola CO . . 38°6N 103°52W **66 D7**
Maple → IA . . . 42°2N 96°13W **73 C3**
Maple → MI . . . 42°59N 84°57W **79 G7**

Maple → ND . . . 46°56N 96°55W **91 D9**
Maple → SD . . . 45°48N 98°38W **91 E7**
Maple Falls WA . 48°56N 122°5W **101 B3**
Maple Heights OH 41°24N 81°33W **107 B2**
Maple Hill KS . . 39°5N 96°2W **74 B7**
Maple Rapids MI . 43°6N 84°42W **79 F7**
Maple Shade NJ . 39°57N 74°58W **87 C2**
Maplecrest NY . . 42°17N 74°9W **87 A1**
Maplesville AL . . 32°47N 86°52W **60 D4**
Mapleton IA . . . 42°10N 95°47W **73 C3**
Mapleton KS . . . 38°1N 94°53W **74 C9**
Mapleton MN . . 43°56N 93°57W **80 F4**
Mapleton ND . . 46°53N 97°3W **91 D8**
Mapleton OR . . 44°2N 123°52W **94 C2**
Mapleton UT . . 40°8N 111°35W **100 C4**
Maplewood MN . 44°59N 93°1W **113 A3**
Maplewood MO . 38°36N 90°19W **117 B1**
Maplewood NJ . . 40°44N 74°16W **114 B1**
Maquoketa IA . . 42°4N 90°40W **73 C8**
Maquoketa → IA . 42°11N 90°19W **73 C8**
Maquon IL . . . . 40°48N 90°10W **71 C3**
Mar-Mac NC . . 35°20N 78°3W **90 D7**
Marais des Cygnes
  U.S.A. . . . 38°31N 94°17W **74 C9**
Marana AZ . . . . 32°27N 111°13W **62 E4**
Marathon FL . . . 24°43N 81°5W **67 G7**
Marathon IA . . . 42°52N 94°59W **73 C4**
Marathon NY . . 42°27N 76°2W **89 C4**
Marathon TX . . 30°12N 103°15W **98 G4**
Marathon WI . . 44°56N 89°50W **103 D4**
Marathon County ☆
  WI . . . . . 44°50N 89°45W **103 D4**
Maravillas → TX . 29°34N 102°47W **98 H5**
Marble AR . . . . 36°8N 93°35W **63 B2**
Marble MN . . . 47°20N 107°12W **66 C3**
Marble Canyon AZ 36°49N 111°38W **62 A3**
Marble City OK . 35°35N 94°49W **93 C9**
Marble Falls TX . 30°35N 98°16W **99 G9**
Marble Hill MO . 37°18N 89°58W **82 D7**
Marble Rock IA . 42°58N 92°52W **73 C6**
Marblehead MA . 42°29N 70°51W **106 A4**
Marblehead OH . 41°32N 82°44W **92 B4**
Marbleton WY . . 42°34N 110°7W **104 D2**
Marbury MD . . . 38°35N 77°10W **77 B3**
Marbury NC . . . 39°0N 80°26W **102 C4**
Marbury WV . . . 38°13N 80°6W **102 C4**
Marcellus MI . . 42°2N 85°49W **79 G6**
Marcellus NY . . 42°59N 76°20W **89 C4**
Marcellus WA . . 47°14N 118°24W **101 C7**
Marco Island FL . 25°58N 81°44W **67 F7**
Marcola OR . . . 44°10N 122°52W **94 C3**
Marcus IA . . . . 42°50N 95°48W **73 C3**
Marcus WA . . . 48°40N 118°4W **101 B7**
Marcus Baker, Mt.
  AK . . . . . 61°26N 147°45W **61 F11**
Marcy, Mt. NY . . 44°7N 73°56W **89 A7**
Mardela Springs MD 38°28N 75°45W **77 B5**
Marengo IL . . . . 42°15N 88°37W **71 A5**
Marengo IA . . . 41°48N 92°4W **73 D6**
Marengo OH . . . 40°24N 82°49W **92 C4**
Marengo WA . . . 47°1N 118°12W **101 C7**
Marengo County ☆
  AL . . . . . 32°18N 87°48W **60 D3**
Marenisco MI . . 46°23N 89°45W **79 C2**
Marfa TX . . . . 30°19N 104°1W **98 G3**
Margaretville NY . 42°9N 74°39W **89 C6**
Margate FL . . . 26°15N 80°12W **67 E8**
Margate City NJ . 39°20N 74°30W **87 C3**
Marian, L. FL . . 27°53N 81°6W **67 D7**
Mariana Islands
  Pac. Oc. . . 17°0N 145°0E **105 a**
Mariana Trench
  Pac. Oc. . . 13°0N 145°0E **105 a**
Marianna AR . . 34°46N 90°46W **63 C5**
Marianna FL . . . 30°46N 85°14W **67 A3**
Marianna PA . . . 40°2N 80°6W **95 D2**
Marias → MT . . 47°56N 110°30W **83 C7**
Maricao
  Puerto Rico . 18°11N 66°59W **105 G16**
Maricopa AZ . . . 33°4N 112°3W **62 D3**
Maricopa CA . . . 35°4N 119°24W **65 H7**
Maricopa County ☆
  AZ . . . . . 33°15N 112°30W **62 D3**
Maricopa Indian Reservation
  AZ . . . . . 33°12N 112°1W **62 E3**
Maricopa Mts. AZ 33°0N 112°30W **62 D3**
Maricopa Village
  AZ . . . . . 33°22N 112°14W **116 C1**
Marienthal KS . . 38°29N 101°13W **74 C3**
Marienville PA . . 41°28N 79°8W **95 C3**
Maries → MO . . 38°30N 92°1W **82 C4**
Maries County ☆
  MO . . . . . 38°10N 91°55W **82 C5**
Marietta GA . . . 33°57N 84°33W **68 C2**
Marietta MS . . . 34°30N 88°28W **81 B5**
Marietta OH . . . 39°25N 81°27W **92 D5**
Marietta OK . . . 33°56N 97°7W **93 E6**
Marietta PA . . . 40°3N 76°33W **95 D6**
Marietta WA . . . 48°47N 122°35W **101 B3**
Marin CA . . . . 37°52N 122°30W **118 A1**
Marin County ☆ CA 38°5N 122°45W **64 E4**
Marin Pen. CA . . 37°50N 122°30W **118 A1**
Marina CA . . . . 36°41N 121°48W **64 G5**
Marina del Rey CA 33°58N 118°27W **111 C2**
Marine IL . . . . 38°47N 89°47W **71 E4**
Marine on St. Croix
  MN . . . . 45°12N 92°46W **80 E6**
Marine Park NY . 40°36N 73°55W **114 C3**
Marineland FL . . 29°40N 81°13W **67 B8**
Mariners Harbor NY 40°38N 74°9W **114 C2**
Marinette WI . . . 45°6N 87°38W **103 C6**
Marinette County ☆
  WI . . . . . 45°25N 88°10W **103 C5**
Maringouin LA . . 30°29N 91°31W **75 D4**
Marion AL . . . . 32°38N 87°19W **60 D3**
Marion AR . . . . 35°13N 90°12W **63 C5**
Marion IL . . . . 37°44N 88°56W **71 E5**
Marion ID . . . . 42°17N 113°55W **70 G5**
Marion IN . . . . 40°32N 85°40W **72 C3**
Marion IA . . . . 42°2N 91°36W **73 C7**
Marion KS . . . . 38°21N 97°1W **74 C6**
Marion KY . . . . 37°20N 88°5W **96 C4**
Marion LA . . . . 32°54N 92°15W **75 B3**
Marion MA . . . . 41°42N 70°46W **78 C4**
Marion MI . . . . 44°6N 85°9W **79 E6**
Marion MT . . . . 48°6N 114°40W **83 B3**
Marion NC . . . . 35°41N 82°1W **90 C3**
Marion ND . . . . 46°37N 98°20W **91 D7**
Marion OH . . . . 40°35N 83°8W **92 C3**
Marion SC . . . . 34°11N 79°24W **90 D6**
Marion SD . . . . 43°25N 97°16W **91 G8**
Marion VA . . . . 36°50N 81°31W **102 E3**
Marion WI . . . . 44°39N 88°54W **103 D5**
Marion, L. SC . . 33°28N 80°10W **90 E5**
Marion County ☆ AL 34°9N 87°54W **60 B3**
Marion County ☆ FL 29°10N 82°0W **67 C7**
Marion County ☆ GA 32°22N 84°35W **68 D2**
Marion County ☆ IL 38°40N 88°55W **71 D5**
Marion County ☆ IN 39°45N 86°10W **72 D4**
Marion County ☆ IA 41°20N 93°0W **73 D5**
Marion County ☆ KS 38°20N 97°0W **74 C6**
Marion County ☆ KY 37°35N 85°20W **97 C7**
Marion County ☆ MS 31°15N 89°50W **81 E4**
Marion County ☆
  OH . . . . . 40°35N 83°8W **92 C3**
Marion County ☆ OR 44°50N 122°50W **94 C3**
Marion County ☆ SC 34°10N 79°20W **90 D6**
Marion County ☆ TN 35°5N 85°38W **97 E7**
Marion County ☆
  TX . . . . . 32°46N 94°21W **99 E13**
Marion County ☆
  WV . . . . . 39°30N 80°9W **102 B4**
Marion Junction AL 32°26N 87°14W **60 D3**
Marion Lake KS . 38°22N 97°5W **74 C6**
Marionville MO . 37°0N 93°38W **82 E3**
Mariposa CA . . . 37°29N 119°58W **64 F7**
Mariposa County ☆
  CA . . . . . 37°30N 120°0W **64 F7**
Marissa IL . . . . 38°15N 89°45W **71 E4**
Marked Tree AR . 35°32N 90°25W **63 C5**
Markesan WI . . 43°42N 88°59W **103 E5**
Markham TX . . 28°58N 96°4W **99 J11**
Markle IN . . . . 40°50N 85°20W **72 C3**
Markleeville CA . 38°42N 119°47W **64 E7**
Markleysburg PA . 39°44N 79°27W **95 E3**
Marks MS . . . . 34°16N 90°16W **81 B3**
Marks Butte CO . 40°53N 102°23W **66 B8**
Marksville LA . . 31°8N 92°4W **75 C3**
Marland OK . . . 36°34N 97°9W **93 B6**
Marlboro NJ . . . 40°19N 74°15W **87 B2**
Marlboro NY . . 41°36N 73°59W **89 D7**
Marlboro County ☆
  SC . . . . . 34°40N 79°40W **90 D6**
Marlborough CT . 41°38N 72°27W **78 C2**
Marlborough MA . 42°21N 71°33W **78 B3**
Marlborough MO . 30°34N 90°20W **117 B1**
Marlborough NH . 42°54N 72°13W **86 D2**
Marlette MI . . . 43°20N 83°5W **79 F8**
Marlin TX . . . . 31°18N 96°54W **99 F11**
Marlin WA . . . . 47°25N 118°59W **101 C7**
Marlinton WV . . 38°13N 80°6W **102 C4**
Marlow GA . . . 32°16N 81°23W **68 D5**
Marlow NH . . . 43°9N 72°12W **86 C2**
Marlow OK . . . 34°39N 97°58W **93 D6**
Marlton NJ . . . 39°54N 74°55W **87 C2**
Marmaduke AR . 36°11N 90°23W **63 B5**
Marmarth ND . . 46°18N 103°54W **91 D2**
Marmora NJ . . . 39°16N 74°39W **87 C2**
Maro Reef HI . . 25°25N 170°35W **69 F9**
Marion IL . . . . 40°24N 88°57W **71 C5**
Marott Park IN . 39°53N 86°8W **110 A2**
Marquand MO . . 37°25N 90°6W **82 D6**
Marquesas Keys FL 24°35N 82°10W **67 G6**
Marquette IA . . . 43°3N 91°11W **73 B7**
Marquette KS . . 38°33N 97°50W **74 C6**
Marquette MI . . 46°33N 87°24W **79 C4**
Marquette NE . . 41°0N 98°1W **84 D7**
Marquette County ☆
  WI . . . . . 43°50N 89°25W **103 E4**
Marquette I. MI . 45°58N 84°24W **79 D7**
Marquette Park IL . 41°46N 87°42W **108 C2**
Marquez TX . . . 31°14N 96°15W **99 F11**
Marrowbone KY . 36°50N 85°30W **97 D7**
Mars Hill ME . . 46°31N 67°52W **76 B6**
Mars Hill NC . . . 35°50N 82°33W **90 C3**
Marseilles IL . . . 41°20N 88°43W **71 B5**
Marseilles OH . . 40°42N 83°24W **92 C3**
Marshall AK . . . 61°53N 162°5W **61 F7**
Marshall AR . . . 35°55N 92°38W **63 C3**
Marshall IL . . . . 39°23N 87°42W **71 D6**
Marshall IN . . . 39°51N 87°11W **72 D2**
Marshall MI . . . 42°16N 84°58W **79 G7**
Marshall MN . . . 44°27N 95°47W **80 F3**
Marshall MO . . . 39°7N 93°12W **82 B3**
Marshall NC . . . 35°48N 82°41W **90 C3**
Marshall OK . . . 36°9N 97°38W **93 B6**
Marshall TX . . . 32°33N 94°23W **99 E13**
Marshall VA . . . 38°52N 77°51W **77 B3**
Marshall County ☆
  AL . . . . . 34°21N 86°18W **60 B4**
Marshall County ☆ IL 41°0N 89°20W **71 B4**
Marshall County ☆
  IN . . . . . 41°20N 86°15W **72 B3**
Marshall County ☆ IA 42°0N 93°0W **73 D5**
Marshall County ☆
  KS . . . . . 39°45N 96°30W **74 B7**
Marshall County ☆
  KY . . . . . 36°55N 88°20W **96 D4**
Marshall County ☆
  MN . . . . . 48°15N 96°15W **80 B2**
Marshall County ☆
  MS . . . . . 34°46N 89°27W **81 B4**
Marshall County ☆
  OK . . . . . 34°0N 96°50W **93 D7**
Marshall County ☆
  SD . . . . . 45°48N 97°45W **91 E8**
Marshall County ☆
  TN . . . . . 35°27N 86°48W **96 E6**
Marshall County ☆
  WV . . . . . 39°50N 80°34W **102 B4**
Marshallberg NC . 34°44N 76°31W **90 D9**
Marshallton DE . 39°44N 75°39W **77 A5**
Marshalltown IA . 42°3N 92°55W **73 C6**
Marshallville OH . 40°54N 81°44W **92 C5**
Marshfield = Coos Bay
  OR . . . . . 43°22N 124°13W **94 D1**
Marshfield MO . . 37°15N 92°54W **82 D4**
Marshfield VT . . 44°20N 72°20W **86 B2**
Marshfield WI . . 44°40N 90°10W **103 D3**
Marshfield Hills MA 42°9N 70°44W **78 B4**
Marshville NC . . 35°0N 80°22W **90 C5**
Marshyhope → MD 38°33N 75°48W **77 B5**
Marsing ID . . . . 43°33N 116°48W **70 F2**
Marston MO . . . 36°31N 89°37W **82 E7**
Marston L. CO . . 39°38N 105°3W **109 C1**
Mart TX . . . . . 31°33N 96°50W **99 F11**
Martelle IA . . . . 42°1N 91°22W **73 C7**
Martell NE . . . . 40°42N 96°45W **84 D8**
Martha L. WA . . 47°50N 122°14W **118 A4**
Martha's Vineyard
  MA . . . . 41°25N 70°40W **78 C4**
Marthasville MO . 38°38N 91°4W **82 C5**
Marthaville LA . . 31°44N 93°24W **75 C2**
Martin KY . . . . 37°34N 82°45W **97 C10**
Martin MI . . . . 42°32N 85°38W **79 G6**
Martin SD . . . . 43°11N 101°44W **91 G4**
Martin TN . . . . 36°21N 88°51W **96 D4**
Martin County ☆ FL 27°10N 80°20W **67 E8**
Martin County ☆ IN 38°40N 86°50W **72 E4**
Martin County ☆
  KY . . . . . 37°45N 82°30W **97 C10**
Martin County ☆
  MN . . . . . 43°40N 94°30W **80 G4**
Martin County ☆ NC 35°50N 77°5W **90 C8**
Martin County ☆ TX 32°18N 101°58W **98 E6**
Martin County ☆
  MO . . . . .
Martin L. AL . . . 32°41N 85°55W **60 D5**

Martin Luther King Nat. Historic
  Site → GA . . 33°45N 84°22W **106 B2**
Martin Pk. AK . . 70°8N 143°16W **61 A12**
Martin Van Buren Nat. Historic
  Site → NY . . 42°22N 73°42W **89 C7**
Martinez CA . . . 38°1N 122°8W **64 E4**
Martinez GA . . . 33°31N 82°55W **68 C4**
Martino MD . . . 39°10N 77°28W **77 A3**
Martins Ferry OH 40°6N 80°44W **92 C6**
Martinsburg MO . 39°6N 91°39W **82 B5**
Martinsburg NE . 42°30N 96°50W **84 B9**
Martinsburg PA . 40°19N 78°20W **95 D4**
Martinsburg WV . 39°27N 77°58W **77 A3**
Martinsdale MT . 46°28N 110°18W **83 D7**
Martinsville IL . . 39°20N 87°53W **71 D6**
Martinsville IN . . 39°26N 86°25W **72 D4**
Martinsville VA . 36°41N 79°52W **102 E5**
Martinton IL . . . 40°55N 87°44W **71 C6**
Marvel CO . . . . 37°7N 108°8W **66 E2**
Marvel AR . . . . 34°33N 90°55W **63 D5**
Marvin SD . . . . 45°16N 96°55W **91 E9**
Marvine, L. CA . . 37°22N 122°28W **118 D3**
Marwayne Can . . 43°48N 90°5W **103 E3**
Mary S. Young State Park →
  OR . . . . . 45°22N 122°37W **116 B2**
Maryd MD . . . . 39°7N 75°45W **77 A5**
Maryhill WA . . . 45°41N 120°49W **101 E5**
Maryland ☐ U.S.A. 39°0N 76°30W **77 A4**
Maryland City MD 39°6N 76°50W **77 A4**
Maryland Line MD 39°43N 76°40W **77 A4**
Maryland Point MD 38°22N 77°14W **77 B3**
Maryneal TX . . . 32°14N 100°27W **98 E7**
Marys → NV . . . 41°14N 114°0W **85 A5**
Marys Corner WA 46°33N 122°49W **101 D3**
Marys Pk. OR . . 44°30N 123°33W **94 C2**
Marysvale UT . . 38°27N 112°14W **100 E3**
Marysville CA . . 39°9N 121°35W **64 D5**
Marysville KS . . 39°51N 96°39W **74 B7**
Marysville MI . . 42°54N 82°29W **79 G9**
Marysville OH . . 40°14N 83°22W **92 C3**
Marysville PA . . 40°21N 76°56W **95 D6**
Marysville WA . . 48°3N 122°11W **101 B3**
Maryvale AZ . . . 33°30N 112°10W **116 C1**
Maryville MO . . 40°21N 94°52W **82 A2**
Maryville TN . . 35°46N 83°58W **97 E9**
Masalog Pt.
  N. Marianas . . 15°1N 145°40E **105 c**
Masardis ME . . 46°30N 68°22W **76 B6**
Masarykytown FL 28°27N 82°27W **67 C6**
Mascot TN . . . . 36°4N 83°45W **97 D9**
Mascot TX . . . . 29°38N 99°48W **71 E4**
Mascoutah IL . . 38°29N 89°48W **71 E4**
Masham MA . . . 42°28N 71°11W **106 A3**
Mashantucket Pequot Indian
  Reservation CT 41°27N 71°58W **78 C3**
Mashpee MA . . . 41°39N 70°29W **78 C4**
Maskell NE . . . 42°41N 96°59W **84 B9**
Mason IL . . . . 38°57N 88°38W **71 E5**
Mason MI . . . . 42°35N 84°27W **79 G7**
Mason NH . . . . 42°44N 71°47W **86 D3**
Mason OH . . . . 39°22N 84°19W **92 D2**
Mason TN . . . . 35°25N 89°32W **96 A3**
Mason TX . . . . 30°45N 99°14W **99 G8**
Mason WV . . . . 39°1N 82°2W **102 B2**
Mason WI . . . . 46°26N 91°4W **103 B2**
Mason City IL . . 40°12N 89°42W **71 C4**
Mason City IA . . 43°9N 93°12W **73 B5**
Mason City NE . . 41°13N 99°18W **84 C6**
Mason County ☆ IL 40°10N 90°0W **71 C4**
Mason County ☆
  KY . . . . . 38°35N 83°50W **97 B9**
Mason County ☆
  MI . . . . . 44°0N 86°15W **79 F5**
Mason County ☆
  TX . . . . . 30°45N 99°15W **99 G8**
Mason County ☆
  WA . . . . . 47°20N 123°10W **101 C2**
Masonboro NC . 34°11N 77°51W **90 D8**
Masontown PA . . 39°33N 79°54W **95 E3**
Masontown WV . 39°33N 79°48W **102 B5**
Masonville IA . . 42°29N 91°36W **73 C7**
Maspeth NY . . . 40°43N 73°55W **114 B3**
Mass City MI . . 46°46N 89°5W **79 C2**
Massabesic L. NH 43°0N 71°23W **86 C3**
Massac County ☆ IL 37°15N 88°45W **71 F5**
Massachusetts ☐
  U.S.A. . . . 42°30N 72°0W **78 B2**
Massachusetts B.
  MA . . . . 42°25N 70°50W **106 A4**
Massachusetts Inst. of Tech.
  MA . . . . 42°21N 71°5W **106 A3**
Massacre L. NV . 41°39N 119°36W **85 A1**
Massapequa NY . 40°41N 73°29W **87 B3**
Massena IA . . . 41°15N 94°46W **73 D4**
Massena NY . . . 44°56N 74°54W **89 A6**
Massey MD . . . 39°18N 75°49W **77 A5**
Massillon OH . . 40°48N 81°32W **92 C5**
Mastens Corner DE 38°57N 75°37W **77 A5**
Masters CO . . . 40°18N 104°15W **66 B6**
Mastic NY . . . . 40°47N 72°54W **89 E8**
Matador TX . . . 34°1N 100°49W **98 C7**
Matagorda TX . . 28°42N 95°58W **99 J12**
Matagorda B. TX . 28°40N 96°12W **99 J12**
Matagorda County ☆
  TX . . . . . 29°0N 96°0W **99 J12**
Matagorda I. TX . 28°15N 96°30W **99 J11**
Matagorda Peninsula
  TX . . . . . 28°38N 96°0W **99 J12**
Matanuska-Susitna ☆
  AK . . . . . 62°30N 150°0W **61 E10**
Matatula, C.
  Amer. Samoa . 14°15S 170°33W **105 e**
Matawan NJ . . . 40°25N 74°14W **87 B2**
Matewan WV . . 37°37N 82°10W **102 D2**
Matfield Green KS 38°9N 96°33W **74 C7**
Matheson CO . . 39°10N 103°59W **66 C7**
Matheny MP . . . 32°40N 100°42W **98 E6**
Mathews, L. CA . 33°51N 117°27W **65 K9**
Mathews County ☆
  VA . . . . . 37°26N 76°19W **102 D8**
Mathias WV . . . 38°53N 78°52W **102 C6**
Mathis TX . . . . 28°6N 97°50W **99 J10**
Mathiston MS . . 33°32N 89°7W **81 C4**
Matinicus ME . . 43°52N 68°54W **76 E5**
Matinicus I. ME . 43°52N 68°54W **76 E5**
Matlock IA . . . . 43°15N 95°56W **73 B3**
Matoaka WV . . . 37°25N 81°15W **102 D3**
Matooka WV . . . 37°25N 81°15W **102 D3**
Mattamuskeet, L. NC 35°30N 76°12W **90 C9**
Mattapan MA . . . 42°16N 71°6W **106 B3**
Mattapoisett MA . 41°40N 70°49W **78 C4**
Mattapoint MA . . 41°40N 70°49W **78 C4**
Mattawamkeag ME 45°32N 68°21W **76 C5**
Mattawoman → MD 38°32N 77°0W **77 B3**
Matterhorn NV . . 41°49N 115°23W **85 A5**
Matthews IN . . . 40°23N 85°30W **72 C3**
Matthews MO . . 36°46N 89°35W **82 E7**
Matthews NC . . . 35°7N 80°43W **107 B2**
Matthews Pk. AZ . 36°20N 109°8W **62 A6**
Mattituck NY . . 40°59N 72°32W **78 D2**
Mattoon IL . . . . 39°29N 88°23W **71 D5**
Mattoon WI . . . 44°58N 89°2W **103 D4**
Mattson MS . . . 34°6N 90°31W **81 B3**
Mattydale NY . . 43°6N 76°9W **89 C5**
Matuteja MS . . . 34°51N 92°29W **63 D3**
Maud OK . . . . . 35°8N 96°46W **93 C7**
Maud TX . . . . . 33°20N 94°21W **99 D13**
Mauckport IN . . 38°4N 86°12W **72 E4**
Maug Is. N. Marianas 20°1N 145°13E **105 a**
Mauldin SC . . . 34°47N 82°19W **90 D3**
Maumee OH . . . 41°34N 83°39W **92 B3**
Maumee → OH . 41°42N 83°28W **92 B3**
Maumelle AR . . 34°52N 92°24W **63 D3**
Maumelle, L. AR . 34°51N 92°29W **63 D3**

Mauna Kea HI . . 19°50N 155°28W **69 D6**
Mauna Kea Forest Reserve
  HI . . . . . 19°52N 155°26W **69 D6**
Mauna Loa HI . . 19°30N 155°35W **69 D6**
Mauna Loa Forest Reserve
  HI . . . . . 19°35N 155°33W **69 D6**
Maunabo
  Puerto Rico . . 18°1N 65°54W **105 G17**
Maunaloa HI . . . 21°8N 157°13W **69 B4**
Maunalua B. HI . 21°15N 157°45W **69 K14**
Maunie IL . . . . 38°2N 88°3W **71 E5**
Maupin OR . . . 45°11N 121°5W **94 B4**
Maurepas, L. LA . 30°15N 90°30W **75 D5**
Maurice LA . . . 30°7N 92°7W **75 D3**
Maurice → NJ . . 39°13N 75°2W **87 C1**
Mauriceville TX . 30°12N 93°52W **99 G14**
Maurine SD . . . 45°1N 102°35W **91 E3**
Maury → TX . . 37°50N 79°25W **102 D5**
Maury County ☆ TN 35°37N 87°2W **96 E5**
Maury Island WA . 47°22N 122°23W **118 D3**
Maverick County ☆
  TX . . . . . 28°55N 100°8W **98 J7**
Max ND . . . . . 47°49N 101°18W **91 C4**
Maxbass ND . . . 48°43N 101°9W **91 B4**
Maxeys GA . . . 33°45N 83°11W **68 C3**
Maxinkuckee, L. IN 41°12N 86°24W **72 B4**
Maxton NC . . . 34°44N 79°21W **90 D6**
Maxville MT . . . 46°28N 113°14W **83 D4**
Maxville NC . . . 39°17N 122°11W **64 D4**
Maxwell CA . . . 39°17N 122°11W **64 D4**
Maxwell IA . . . 41°53N 93°24W **73 D5**
Maxwell NM . . . 36°32N 104°33W **88 A6**
Maxwell NE . . . 41°5N 100°31W **84 C5**
May ID . . . . . . 44°36N 113°55W **70 E5**
May OK . . . . . 36°37N 99°45W **93 B4**
May, C. NJ . . . 38°56N 74°58W **87 D2**
May Mt. ID . . . 44°41N 113°55W **70 E5**
Mayagüez
  Puerto Rico . 18°12N 67°9W **105 G15**
Maybell CO . . . 40°31N 108°5W **66 B2**
Maybury WV . . 37°22N 81°22W **102 D3**
Maybrook NY . . 41°29N 74°13W **87 A2**
Mayer AZ . . . . 34°24N 112°14W **62 C3**
Mayersville MS . 32°54N 91°3W **81 D2**
Mayes County ☆ OK 36°15N 95°15W **93 B8**
Mayesville SC . . 34°0N 80°12W **90 D5**
Mayetta KS . . . 39°20N 95°43W **74 B8**
Mayetta NJ . . . 39°40N 74°18W **87 C2**
Mayfair TX . . . 29°41N 95°19W **110 B3**
Mayfield GA . . . 33°21N 82°48W **68 C4**
Mayfield IL . . . 43°25N 115°54W **70 F3**
Mayfield KS . . . 37°16N 97°33W **74 D6**
Mayfield KY . . . 36°44N 88°38W **96 D4**
Mayfield UT . . . 39°7N 111°43W **100 D4**
Mayflower AR . . 34°57N 92°26W **63 D3**
Maysan NE . . . 42°53N 105°29W **88 E5**
Mason IL . . . . 42°35N 88°38W **71 E5**
Mason MI . . . . 42°35N 84°27W **79 G7**
Maynard IA . . . 42°47N 91°53W **73 C7**
Maynard MA . . . 42°26N 71°27W **78 B3**
Maynard MN . . 44°54N 95°28W **80 F3**
Maynardville TN . 36°15N 83°48W **97 D9**
Mayo FL . . . . . 30°3N 83°10W **67 A5**
Mayo SC . . . . 35°5N 81°52W **90 C4**
Mayo Res. NC . . 36°35N 79°5W **90 B6**
Maysworth WY . 43°50N 106°47W **104 C6**
Mayport Naval Station
  FL . . . . . 30°24N 81°25W **67 A7**
Mays Lick KY . . 38°31N 83°50W **97 B9**
Maysville GA . . 34°15N 83°34W **68 B3**
Maysville KY . . 38°39N 83°46W **97 B9**
Maysville MO . . 39°54N 94°22W **82 B3**
Maysville OK . . 34°49N 97°24W **93 D6**
Maysville WV . . 39°7N 79°10W **77 A1**
Mayville MI . . . 43°20N 83°21W **79 F8**
Mayville ND . . 47°30N 97°20W **91 C8**
Mayville NY . . . 42°15N 79°30W **89 C1**
Mayville WI . . . 43°30N 88°33W **103 E5**
Maywood CA . . 33°58N 118°12W **111 C3**
Maywood IL . . 41°52N 87°51W **108 B1**
Maywood MO . . 39°54N 91°42W **82 B5**
Maywood NJ . . 40°53N 74°3W **114 A2**
Maywood NE . . 40°38N 100°37W **84 D5**
Maywood Park OR 45°33N 122°33W **116 A2**
Maywood Park Race Track
  IL . . . . . 41°54N 87°50W **108 B1**
Maza ND . . . . . 48°22N 99°12W **91 B6**
Mazama WA . . 48°36N 120°24W **101 B5**
Mazatzal Mts. AZ 34°0N 111°30W **62 D4**
Mazie KY . . . . 38°2N 82°58W **97 B10**
Mazie OK . . . . 36°6N 95°22W **93 B8**
Mazomanie WI . 43°11N 89°48W **103 E4**
Mazon IL . . . . 41°14N 88°25W **71 B5**
Meacham OR . . 45°31N 118°25W **94 B7**
Mead NE . . . . 41°14N 96°29W **84 C9**
Mead OK . . . . 34°0N 96°31W **93 E7**
Mead, L. U.S.A. . 36°1N 114°44W **62 A1**
Mead = Atqasuk →
  AK . . . . . 70°52N 155°7W **61 A9**
Meade KS . . . . 37°17N 100°20W **74 D3**
Meade County ☆
  KY . . . . . 37°55N 86°10W **96 C6**
Meade County ☆
  SD . . . . . 44°30N 102°30W **91 F3**
Meade River = Atqasuk
  AK . . . . . 70°28N 157°24W **61 A8**
Meadow SD . . . 45°32N 102°13W **91 E3**
Meadow TX . . . 33°20N 102°12W **98 D5**
Meadow UT . . . 38°53N 112°24W **100 E3**
Meadow → WV . 38°10N 80°57W **102 D4**
Meadow Bridge WV 37°52N 80°51W **102 D4**
Meadow Brook Park
  MN . . . . 44°55N 93°21W **113 B1**
Meadow Grove NE 42°2N 97°44W **84 B8**
Meadow Lake NY 40°44N 73°50W **114 B3**
Meadow Park MN . 44°57N 93°26W **113 B1**
Meadow Valley Wash →
  NV . . . . 36°40N 114°34W **85 F6**
Meadow Vista CA 39°0N 121°1W **64 D5**
Meadowbrook WY 42°33N 104°42W **104 D8**
Meadowlands MN 47°4N 92°44W **80 D6**
Meadows NH . . 44°21N 71°28W **86 B3**
Meadowview VA . 36°46N 81°52W **102 E2**
Meadville MS . . 31°28N 90°54W **81 E3**
Meadville PA . . 41°39N 80°9W **95 C2**
Meagher County ☆
  MT . . . . . 46°40N 111°0W **83 D6**
Meansville GA . . 33°3N 84°18W **68 D2**
Meares, C. OR . . 45°37N 124°0W **58 D2**
Mears Corner VA . 36°46N 76°11W **115 B2**
Mebane NC . . . 36°6N 79°16W **90 B6**
Mecca CA . . . . 33°34N 116°5W **65 K10**
Mechanic Falls ME 44°7N 70°24W **76 D3**
Mechanicsburg IL . 39°48N 89°24W **71 D4**
Mechanicsburg OH 40°4N 83°33W **92 C3**
Mechanicsburg PA 40°13N 77°1W **95 D6**
Mechanicsville IA . 41°54N 91°16W **73 D7**
Mechanicsville VA 37°36N 77°22W **102 D7**
Mechanicville NY 42°54N 73°41W **78 B1**
Mecklenburg County ☆
  NC . . . . . 35°10N 80°50W **90 C5**
Mecklenburg County ☆
  VA . . . . . 36°55N 78°20W **102 E6**
Meckling SD . . . 42°51N 97°4W **91 H8**

Mecosta *MI* . . . 43°37N 85°14W **79 F6**
Mecosta County ☆
  MI . . . . . . 43°35N 85°20W **79 F6**
Medanales *NM* . . 36°11N 106°11W **88 A4**
Medart *FL* . . . . 30°5N 84°23W **67 A4**
Medaryville *IN* . . 41°5N 86°55W **72 B4**
Medfield *MA* . . . 42°11N 71°18W **78 B3**
Medford *MN* . . . 44°11N 93°15W **80 F5**
Medford *NJ* . . . . 39°54N 74°50W **87 C2**
Medford *NY* . . . . 40°49N 73°0W **87 B3**
Medford *OK* . . . 36°48N 97°44W **93 B6**
Medford *OR* . . . 42°19N 122°52W **94 E3**
Medford *WI* . . . 45°9N 90°20W **103 C3**
Medford Lakes *NJ* 39°52N 74°48W **87 C2**
Media *PA* . . . . . 39°55N 75°23W **87 C1**
Mediapolis *IA* . . . 41°0N 91°10W **73 E7**
Medical Lake *WA* . 47°34N 117°41W **101 C8**
Medicine Bow →
  WY . . . . . . 42°0N 106°40W **104 D6**
Medicine Bow *WY* 41°54N 106°12W **104 E6**
Medicine Bow Mts.
  U.S.A. . . . . 40°40N 106°0W **66 B5**
Medicine Bow Nat. Forest
  WY . . . . . . 42°20N 105°38W **104 D7**
Medicine Bow Pk.
  WY . . . . . . 41°21N 106°19W **58 F10**
Medicine Cr. → *MO* 39°43N 93°24W **82 B3**
Medicine Cr. → *NE* 40°17N 100°10W **84 D5**
Medicine L. *MN* . 45°0N 93°25W **113 A1**
Medicine L. *MT* . 48°28N 104°24W **83 B13**
Medicine Lake *MN* 44°59N 93°24W **113 A1**
Medicine Lake *MT* 48°30N 104°30W **83 B13**
Medicine Lodge *KS* 37°17N 98°35W **74 D5**
Medicine Lodge →
  KS . . . . . . 36°49N 98°20W **74 E5**
Medicine Park *OK* 34°44N 98°30W **93 D5**
Medina *ND* . . . 46°54N 99°18W **91 D6**
Medina *NY* . . . 43°13N 78°23W **89 B2**
Medina *OH* . . . 41°8N 81°52W **92 B5**
Medina *TX* . . . 35°48N 88°46W **96 E4**
Medina → *TX* . . 29°16N 98°29W **99 H9**
Medina County ☆ *OH* 41°8N 81°52W **92 B5**
Medina County ☆ *TX* 29°21N 99°9W **99 H8**
Medina L. *TX* . . 29°32N 98°56W **99 H9**
Medora *IL* . . . . 39°11N 90°9W **71 D3**
Medora *IN* . . . . 38°49N 86°10W **72 F4**
Medora *ND* . . . 46°55N 103°31W **91 D2**
Medway *MA* . . . 42°8N 71°24W **78 B3**
Meeker *CO* . . . 40°2N 107°55W **66 B3**
Meeker *OK* . . . 35°30N 96°54W **93 C7**
Meeker County ☆
  MN . . . . . . 45°10N 94°30W **80 E4**
Meeks Bay *CA* . . 39°2N 120°8W **64 D6**
Meeteetse *WY* . . 44°9N 108°52W **104 B4**
Megargel *TX* . . 33°27N 98°56W **99 D9**
Meherrin → *VA* . 36°26N 76°57W **102 E8**
Mehlville *MO* . . 38°31N 90°19W **82 C6**
Meigs *GA* . . . . 31°4N 84°5W **68 E2**
Meigs County ☆ *OH* 39°3N 82°8W **92 D4**
Meigs County ☆ *TN* 35°31N 84°47W **97 E8**
Meiss L. *CA* . . . 41°52N 122°4W **64 B4**
Mekinock *ND* . . 48°1N 97°22W **91 B8**
Mekoryuk *AK* . . 60°23N 166°11W **61 F7**
Melba *ID* . . . . 43°23N 116°32W **70 F2**
Melber *KY* . . . 36°49N 88°39W **96 F2**
Melbourne *AR* . . 35°57N 91°54W **63 B4**
Melbourne *FL* . . 28°5N 80°37W **67 C8**
Melbourne *IA* . . 41°57N 93°6W **73 D5**
Melbourne *KY* . . 39°1N 84°21W **107 B2**
Melcher-Dallas *IA* . 41°13N 93°15W **73 D5**
Melfa *VA* . . . . 37°39N 75°45W **102 D9**
Melissa *TX* . . . 33°17N 96°34W **99 D11**
Melitota *MD* . . . 39°16N 76°9W **77 A4**
Mellen *WI* . . . . 46°20N 90°40W **103 B3**
Mellette *SD* . . . 45°9N 98°30W **91 E7**
Mellette County ☆
  SD . . . . . . 43°35N 101°0W **91 G5**
Mellott *IN* . . . . 40°10N 87°9W **72 C3**
Mellwood *AR* . . 34°12N 90°56W **63 D5**
Melrose *IA* . . . . 40°59N 93°3W **73 E5**
Melrose *MA* . . . 42°27N 71°2W **106 A3**
Melrose *MN* . . . 45°40N 94°49W **80 E4**
Melrose *MT* . . . 45°38N 112°41W **83 D5**
Melrose *NM* . . . 34°26N 103°38W **88 C7**
Melrose *NY* . . . 40°49N 73°55W **114 B3**
Melrose *WI* . . . 44°8N 91°1W **103 D2**
Melrose Park *FL* . 26°6N 80°11W **112 B3**
Melrose Park *IL* . 41°53N 87°50W **108 B1**
Melrose Park *PA* . 40°3N 75°7W **116 A2**
Melstone *MT* . . 46°36N 107°52W **83 D10**
Melstrand *MI* . . 46°28N 86°25W **79 C5**
Melton Hill L. *TN* . 35°53N 84°18W **97 E8**
Melvern *KS* . . . 38°30N 95°38W **74 C8**
Melvern Lake *KS* . 38°30N 95°38W **74 C8**
Melville *LA* . . . 30°42N 91°45W **75 D4**
Melvin *AL* . . . . 31°55N 88°27W **60 E2**
Melvin *IL* . . . . 40°34N 88°15W **71 C5**
Melvin *KY* . . . 37°22N 82°39W **97 D11**
Melvin *TX* . . . 31°12N 99°35W **99 F8**
Melvin Village *NH* 43°42N 71°28W **86 C3**
Melvina *WI* . . . 43°48N 90°47W **103 E3**
Melvindale *MI* . . 42°17N 83°10W **109 B11**
Memorial Park *TX* . 29°45N 95°26W **110 B2**
Memphis *FL* . . . 27°32N 82°34W **67 D6**
Memphis *MI* . . . 42°54N 82°46W **79 G9**
Memphis *MO* . . 40°28N 92°10W **82 A4**
Memphis *NE* . . 41°6N 96°26W **84 C9**
Memphis *TN* . . 35°8N 90°2W **112 B1**
Memphis *TX* . . 34°44N 100°33W **98 C7**
Memphis Int. ✈ (MEM)
  TN . . . . . . 35°3N 89°59W **112 B2**
Memphrémagog, L.
  N. Amer. . . . 45°2N 72°17W **86 A2**
Mena *AR* . . . . 34°35N 94°15W **63 D1**
Menahga *MN* . . 46°45N 95°6W **80 D3**
Menan *ID* . . . . 43°43N 111°59W **70 F7**
Menard *MT* . . . 45°59N 111°10W **83 E6**
Menard *TX* . . . 30°55N 99°47W **99 G8**
Menard County ☆
  TX . . . . . . 30°55N 99°45W **99 G8**
Menasha *WI* . . 44°13N 88°26W **103 D5**
Mendenhall *MS* . 31°58N 89°52W **81 E4**
Mendenhall, C. *AK* 59°45N 166°10W **61 G6**
Mendham *NJ* . . 40°47N 74°36W **87 B2**
Mendocino *CA* . 39°19N 123°48W **64 D3**
Mendocino, C. *CA* 40°26N 124°25W **64 C2**
Mendocino County ☆
  CA . . . . . . 39°20N 123°20W **64 D3**
Mendocino Nat. Forest
  CA . . . . . . 39°45N 122°50W **64 D4**
Mendon *IL* . . . 40°5N 91°16W **71 C2**
Mendon *MI* . . . 42°0N 85°27W **79 G6**
Mendon *MO* . . . 39°36N 93°8W **82 B3**
Mendon *OH* . . . 40°40N 84°31W **92 C2**
Mendon *VT* . . . 43°40N 72°54W **86 C2**
Mendota *CA* . . . 36°45N 120°23W **65 G6**
Mendota *IL* . . . 41°33N 89°7W **71 B4**
Mendota *MN* . . 44°53N 93°9W **113 D3**
Mendota, L. *WI* . 43°7N 89°25W **103 E4**
Mendota Heights *MN* 44°53N 93°10W **113 D3**
Menifee County ☆
  KY . . . . . . 37°55N 83°35W **97 C9**
Menlo *GA* . . . . 34°29N 85°29W **68 C1**
Menlo *IA* . . . . 41°31N 94°24W **73 D4**
Menlo *KS* . . . . 39°21N 100°43W **74 B3**
Menlo *WA* . . . . 46°38N 123°39W **101 D2**
Menlo Park *CA* . 37°27N 122°12W **118 D3**
Menlo Park Terrace
  NJ . . . . . . 40°33N 74°19W **114 C1**
Menno *SD* . . . . 43°14N 97°34W **91 G8**

Meno *OK* . . . . 36°23N 98°11W **93 B5**
Menominee *MI* . 45°6N 87°37W **79 D4**
Menominee → *U.S.A.* 45°6N 87°35W **79 D4**
Menominee County ☆
  MI . . . . . . 45°30N 87°40W **79 D4**
Menominee County ☆
  WI . . . . . . 45°0N 88°45W **103 C5**
Menominee Ind. Reservation
  WI . . . . . . 45°0N 88°45W **103 C5**
Menominee Ra. *MI* 46°0N 88°10W **79 D3**
Menomonee Falls *WI* 43°10N 88°7W **112 B1**
Menomonie *WI* . 44°53N 91°55W **103 D2**
Mentasta Lake *AK* 62°55N 143°45W **61 E12**
Mentone *IN* . . . 41°10N 86°2W **72 B4**
Mentone *TX* . . . 31°42N 103°36W **98 F4**
Mentor *MN* . . . 47°42N 96°9W **80 C2**
Mentor *OH* . . . 41°40N 81°21W **92 B5**
Mentor-on-the-Lake
  OH . . . . . . 41°43N 81°22W **92 B5**
Mequon *WI* . . . 43°14N 87°59W **103 E6**
Mer Rouge *LA* . 32°47N 91°48W **75 B4**
Meramec → *MO* 38°24N 90°21W **82 C6**
Meramec State Park
  MO . . . . . . 38°13N 91°5W **82 C5**
Meraux *LA* . . . 29°55N 89°56W **113 C3**
Merced *CA* . . . 37°18N 120°29W **64 F6**
Merced, L. *CA* . 37°43N 122°29W **118 B2**
Merced County ☆
  CA . . . . . . 37°15N 120°30W **64 F6**
Mercedes *TX* . . 26°9N 97°55W **98 L10**
Mercer *ME* . . . 44°41N 69°56W **76 D4**
Mercer *MO* . . . 40°31N 93°32W **82 A3**
Mercer *PA* . . . 41°14N 80°15W **95 C2**
Mercer *TN* . . . 35°29N 89°2W **96 E3**
Mercer *WI* . . . 46°10N 90°4W **103 B3**
Mercer County ☆ *IL* 41°0N 90°40W **71 B3**
Mercer County ☆ *KY* 37°50N 84°50W **97 C8**
Mercer County ☆
  MO . . . . . . 40°25N 93°30W **82 A3**
Mercer County ☆ *NJ* 40°15N 74°40W **87 B2**
Mercer County ☆
  OH . . . . . . 40°33N 84°35W **92 C2**
Mercer County ☆ *PA* 41°15N 80°15W **95 C2**
Mercer County ☆
  WV . . . . . . 37°22N 81°6W **102 D3**
Mercer Island *WA* 47°34N 122°13W **118 C4**
Mercersburg *PA* . 39°50N 77°55W **95 D4**
Mercerville *NJ* . 40°14N 74°41W **87 B2**
Merchantville *NJ* . 39°56N 75°4W **116 B2**
Mercury *NV* . . . 36°40N 115°59W **85 F5**
Mercury *TX* . . . 31°28N 99°9W **99 F8**
Meredith *CO* . . 39°22N 106°44W **66 C4**
Meredith, L. *CO* . 38°12N 103°43W **66 D6**
Meredith, L. *TX* . 35°43N 101°33W **98 B6**
Meredosia *IL* . . 39°50N 90°34W **71 D3**
Meredosia Nat. Wildlife Refuge
  IL . . . . . . 39°53N 90°34W **71 D3**
Meriden *CT* . . . 41°32N 72°48W **78 C2**
Meriden *IA* . . . 42°48N 95°38W **73 C3**
Meriden *KS* . . . 39°11N 95°34W **74 B8**
Meriden *NH* . . . 43°36N 72°16W **86 C2**
Meriden *WY* . . 41°33N 104°19W **104 E8**
Meridian *GA* . . 31°27N 81°23W **68 E5**
Meridian *ID* . . . 43°37N 116°24W **70 F2**
Meridian *MS* . . 32°22N 88°42W **81 D5**
Meridian *OK* . . 35°48N 97°15W **93 C6**
Meridian *TX* . . 31°56N 97°39W **99 F10**
Meridian Hills *IN* 39°53N 86°9W **110 A2**
Meridian Naval Air Sta.
  MS . . . . . . 32°35N 88°33W **81 C5**
Merigold *MS* . . 33°50N 90°43W **81 C3**
Meriwether County ☆
  GA . . . . . . 33°0N 84°40W **68 C2**
Meriton *Guam* . 13°16N 144°40E **105 b**
Merkel *TX* . . . 32°28N 100°1W **99 E7**
Merlin *OR* . . . 42°31N 123°25W **94 E2**
Mermentau *LA* . 30°11N 92°35W **75 D3**
Merna *NE* . . . 41°29N 99°46W **84 C6**
Merrick *NY* . . . 40°40N 73°33W **87 B3**
Merrick County ☆ *NE* 41°15N 98°0W **84 C7**
Merricourt *ND* . 46°12N 98°46W **91 D7**
Merrill *IA* . . . 42°43N 96°15W **73 C2**
Merrill *MI* . . . 43°25N 84°20W **79 F7**
Merrill *MS* . . . 30°59N 88°43W **81 F5**
Merrill *OR* . . . 42°1N 121°36W **94 E4**
Merrill *WI* . . . 45°11N 89°41W **103 C4**
Merrillan *WI* . . 44°27N 90°50W **103 D3**
Merrillville *IN* . 41°29N 87°20W **72 B3**
Merrimac *MA* . . 42°49N 71°0W **78 B3**
Merrimac *WI* . . 43°22N 89°37W **103 E4**
Merrimack *NH* . 42°52N 71°30W **86 D3**
Merrimack → *MA* . 42°49N 70°49W **86 D4**
Merrimack County ☆
  NH . . . . . . 43°15N 71°45W **86 C3**
Merriman *NE* . . 42°55N 101°42W **84 B4**
Merrionette Park *IL* 41°41N 87°40W **108 C2**
Merritt *WA* . . . 47°47N 120°50W **101 C5**
Merritt, L. *CA* . 37°48N 122°15W **118 B3**
Merritt Island *FL* 28°21N 80°42W **67 C8**
Merritt Island Nat. Wildlife
  Refuge *FL* . . 28°40N 80°42W **67 C8**
Merritt Res. *NE* . 42°38N 100°53W **84 B5**
Merryville *LA* . . 30°45N 93°33W **75 D2**
Mershon *GA* . . 31°29N 82°13W **68 E4**
Mertzon *TX* . . . 31°16N 100°49W **98 F7**
Mesa *AZ* . . . . 33°25N 111°50W **62 D4**
Mesa *CO* . . . . 39°10N 108°8W **66 C2**
Mesa *ID* . . . . 44°38N 116°27W **70 E2**
Mesa *WA* . . . . 46°35N 119°0W **101 D6**
Mesa County ☆ *CO* 39°0N 108°30W **66 C2**
Mesa Verde Nat. Park △
  CO . . . . . . 37°11N 108°29W **66 E2**
Mesabi Iron Range
  MN . . . . . . 47°40N 92°45W **80 C6**
Mescalero *NM* . 33°9N 105°46W **88 D5**
Mescalero Apache Indian
  Reservation *NM* 33°12N 105°40W **88 D5**
Meservey *IA* . . 42°55N 93°29W **73 C5**
Mesick *MI* . . . 44°24N 85°43W **79 E6**
Mesita *CO* . . . 37°6N 105°36W **66 E5**
Mesquite *NM* . . 32°10N 106°42W **88 E4**
Mesquite *NV* . . 36°48N 114°4W **85 F7**
Mesquite *TX* . . 32°46N 96°36W **99 E11**
Mesquite L. *CA* . 35°43N 115°35W **65 H11**
Meta *MO* . . . . 38°19N 92°10W **82 C4**
Metairie *LA* . . . 29°59N 90°9W **113 C2**
Metaline *WA* . . 48°51N 117°23W **101 B8**
Metaline Falls *WA* 48°52N 117°22W **101 B8**
Metamora *IL* . . 40°47N 89°22W **71 C4**
Metamora *MI* . . 42°57N 83°17W **79 G8**
Metamora *PA* . . 42°57N 83°17W **87 A2**
Metcalf *GA* . . . 30°43N 83°59W **68 F3**
Metcalf *IL* . . . 39°48N 87°48W **72 D3**
Metcalfe County ☆
  KY . . . . . . 37°0N 85°40W **97 D7**
Methow *OR* . . . 48°0N 120°0W **101 B6**
Methow → *WA* . 48°5N 119°55W **101 B6**
Metlakatla *AK* . . 55°8N 131°35W **61 J15**
Metolius *OR* . . 44°35N 121°11W **94 C4**
Metropolis *IL* . . 37°9N 88°44W **71 F5**
Metter *GA* . . . 32°24N 82°3W **68 D4**
Metuchen *NJ* . . 40°32N 74°22W **87 B2**
Metz *ND* . . . . 47°59N 94°27W **82 D2**
Metzger *OR* . . 45°26N 122°45W **116 B1**

Mexia *TX* . . . 31°41N 96°29W **99 F11**
Mexican Hat *UT* . 37°9N 109°52W **100 F6**
Mexican Springs
  NM . . . . . . 35°47N 108°50W **88 B2**
Mexican Water *AZ* . 36°57N 109°32W **62 A6**
Mexico *IN* . . . 40°49N 86°7W **72 C4**
Mexico *ME* . . . 44°34N 70°33W **76 D3**
Mexico *MO* . . . 39°10N 91°53W **82 B5**
Mexico *NY* . . . 43°28N 76°14W **89 B4**
Mexico B. *NY* . . 43°35N 76°20W **89 B4**
Mexico Beach *FL* . 29°57N 85°25W **67 B2**
Meyerland *TX* . . 29°41N 95°28W **110 B2**
Meyers Chuck *AK* 55°45N 132°15W **61 J14**
Meyersdale *PA* . 39°49N 79°2W **77 A1**
Miami *AZ* . . . . 33°24N 110°52W **62 D5**
Miami *FL* . . . . 25°46N 80°11W **112 D1**
Miami *MO* . . . 39°19N 93°14W **82 B3**
Miami *OK* . . . 36°53N 94°53W **93 B9**
Miami *TX* . . . 35°42N 100°38W **98 B6**
Miami → *FL* . . 25°46N 80°11W **112 D1**
Miami County ☆ *IN* 40°45N 86°0W **72 C4**
Miami County ☆ *KS* 38°30N 94°45W **74 C9**
Miami County ☆ *OH* 40°9N 84°15W **92 C2**
Miami-Dade County ☆
  FL . . . . . . 25°30N 80°30W **67 F8**
Miami Beach *FL* . 25°48N 80°17W **112 D1**
Miami Canal *FL* . 26°30N 80°45W **67 E8**
Miami Int. ✈ (MIA)
  FL . . . . . . 25°48N 80°17W **112 D1**
Miami Lakes *FL* . 25°54N 80°19W **112 C1**
Miami Shores *FL* 25°51N 80°11W **112 C2**
Miami Springs *FL* 25°49N 80°17W **112 D1**
Miamisburg *OH* . 39°38N 84°17W **92 D2**
Micanopy *FL* . . 29°30N 82°17W **67 B6**
Micco *FL* . . . . 27°53N 80°30W **67 D8**
Miccosukee *FL* . 30°36N 84°3W **67 A4**
Miccosukee, L. *FL* 30°33N 83°53W **67 A5**
Miccosukee Indian Reservation
  FL . . . . . . 25°46N 80°46W **67 F8**
Michigamme, L. *MI* 46°32N 88°5W **79 C3**
Michigamme Res. *MI* 46°10N 88°10W **79 C3**
Michigan *ND* . . 48°1N 98°7W **91 B7**
Michigan □ *U.S.A.* 44°0N 85°0W **79 F5**
Michigan, L. *MI* . 44°0N 87°0W **79 F4**
Michigan Center *MI* 42°14N 84°20W **79 G7**
Michigan City *IN* 41°43N 86°54W **72 B4**
Michigan I. *WI* . 46°53N 90°29W **103 B3**
Michigan Islands Nat. Wildlife
  Refuge *MI* . . 44°52N 85°50W **79 E6**
Michigantown *IN* 40°20N 86°24W **72 C4**
Middle → *MN* . 40°20N 97°5W **80 B1**
Middle Alkali L. *CA* 41°27N 120°5W **64 B6**
Middle Bass I. *OH* 41°41N 82°48W **92 B4**
Middle Bay *NY* . 40°37N 73°36W **114 C5**
Middle Branch
  MD . . . . . . 39°15N 76°37W **107 B2**
Middle Concho →
  TX . . . . . . 31°27N 100°25W **98 F7**
Middle Falls *NY* . 43°6N 73°32W **86 C1**
Middle Fork Feather →
  CA . . . . . . 38°33N 121°30W **64 E5**
Middle Fork Forked Deer →
  TN . . . . . . 36°1N 89°13W **96 D3**
Middle Fork John Day →
  OR . . . . . . 44°45N 119°38W **94 C6**
Middle Fork Powder →
  WY . . . . . . 43°42N 106°34W **104 C6**
Middle Fork Sappa Cr. →
  KS . . . . . . 40°0N 100°51W **74 B3**
Middle Granville *NY* 43°26N 73°17W **86 C1**
Middle Island *NY* 40°53N 72°56W **78 D2**
Middle Loup → *NE* 41°17N 98°24W **84 C7**
Middle Pease → *TX* 34°15N 100°7W **98 C7**
Middle Point *OH* 40°51N 84°27W **92 C2**
Middle River *MD* 39°20N 76°27W **77 A4**
Middle River → *MN* 48°26N 96°10W **80 B2**
Middle Valley *TN* 35°12N 85°11W **97 E7**
Middle Village *NY* 40°43N 73°52W **114 B3**
Middleboro *MA* . 41°54N 70°55W **78 C4**
Middlebourne *WV* 39°30N 80°54W **102 B4**
Middleburg *FL* . 30°4N 81°52W **67 A7**
Middleburg *PA* . 40°47N 77°3W **95 D5**
Middleburg *VA* . 38°58N 77°44W **77 B3**
Middleburg Heights
  OH . . . . . . 41°22N 81°48W **107 B1**
Middleburgh *NY* 42°36N 74°20W **89 C6**
Middlebury *CT* . 41°32N 73°7W **78 C1**
Middlebury *IN* . 41°41N 85°42W **72 B5**
Middlebury *VT* . 44°1N 73°10W **86 B1**
Middlefield *MA* . 42°20N 73°2W **78 B1**
Middlefield *OH* . 41°28N 81°5W **92 B5**
Middlegate *NV* . 39°17N 118°2W **85 C2**
Middleport *NY* . 43°13N 78°29W **89 B2**
Middleport *OH* . 39°0N 82°3W **92 D4**
Middlesboro *KY* . 36°36N 83°43W **97 D9**
Middlesex *NC* . . 35°47N 78°12W **90 C7**
Middlesex County ☆
  CT . . . . . . 41°25N 72°30W **78 C2**
Middlesex County ☆
  MA . . . . . . 42°30N 71°20W **78 B3**
Middlesex County ☆
  NJ . . . . . . 40°30N 74°25W **87 B2**
Middlesex County ☆
  VA . . . . . . 37°36N 76°36W **102 D8**
Middlesex Fells Reservation
  MA . . . . . . 42°27N 71°6W **106 A3**
Middleton *ID* . . 43°42N 116°37W **70 F2**
Middleton *MA* . 42°36N 71°1W **78 B3**
Middleton *TN* . . 35°4N 88°53W **96 E4**
Middleton *WI* . . 43°6N 89°30W **103 E4**
Middleton I. *AK* . 59°26N 146°20W **61 G11**
Middletown *CA* . 38°45N 122°37W **64 E4**
Middletown *CT* . 41°34N 72°39W **78 C2**
Middletown *DE* . 39°27N 75°43W **77 A5**
Middletown *IL* . 40°11N 89°35W **71 C4**
Middletown *IN* . 40°3N 85°32W **72 C5**
Middletown *MD* 39°27N 77°33W **77 A3**
Middletown *MO* 39°8N 91°25W **82 B5**
Middletown *NJ* . 40°24N 74°8W **87 B3**
Middletown *NY* . 41°27N 74°25W **87 A2**
Middletown *OH* . 39°31N 84°24W **92 D2**
Middletown *PA* . 40°12N 76°44W **95 D6**
Middletown *RI* . 41°32N 71°17W **78 C3**
Middletown *VA* . 39°2N 78°17W **77 A2**
Middletown Springs
  VT . . . . . . 43°28N 73°8W **86 C1**
Middleville *MI* . 42°43N 85°28W **79 G6**
Middleville *NY* . 43°8N 74°58W **89 C6**
Midfield *TX* . . . 28°59N 96°2W **99 H11**
Midland *MD* . . 39°36N 78°56W **77 A2**
Midland *MI* . . . 43°37N 84°14W **79 F7**
Midland *OR* . . 42°8N 121°49W **94 E4**
Midland *TX* . . 32°0N 102°3W **98 F5**
Midland Beach *NY* . 40°34N 74°6W **114 C2**
Midland City *AL* . 31°19N 85°30W **60 E5**
Midland County ☆
  MI . . . . . . 43°35N 84°20W **79 F7**
Midlothian *IL* . . 41°37N 87°43W **108 C2**
Midlothian *TX* . 32°30N 97°0W **99 E11**
Midlothian *VA* . 37°30N 77°28W **102 D7**
Midnight *MS* . . 33°3N 90°35W **81 C3**
Midvale *ID* . . . 44°28N 116°44W **70 E2**
Midvale *OH* . . 40°26N 81°22W **92 C5**
Midville *GA* . . 32°49N 82°14W **68 D4**
Midway *FL* . . . 30°30N 84°27W **67 A4**

Midway *GA* . . . 31°48N 81°26W **68 E5**
Midway *KY* . . . 38°9N 84°41W **97 B8**
Midway *TX* . . . 31°2N 95°45W **99 F12**
Midway *UT* . . . 40°31N 111°28W **100 C4**
Midwest *WY* . . 43°25N 106°16W **104 C6**
Midwest City *OK* 35°27N 97°24W **93 C6**
Midwood *NC* . . 35°13N 80°48W **107 A2**
Miesville *MN* . . 44°36N 92°49W **80 F6**
Mifflin *OH* . . . 40°46N 82°22W **92 C4**
Mifflin County ☆ *PA* 40°45N 77°45W **95 D5**
Mifflinburg *PA* . 40°55N 77°3W **95 D5**
Mifflintown *PA* . 40°34N 77°24W **95 D5**
Mikado *MI* . . . 44°36N 83°20W **79 E8**
Mikalo *OR* . . . 45°28N 120°14W **94 B5**
Milaca *MN* . . . 45°45N 93°39W **80 E5**
Milam County ☆ *TX* 31°26N 93°51W **99 F14**
Milan *GA* . . . . 32°1N 83°4W **68 D3**
Milan *IL* . . . . 41°27N 90°34W **71 B3**
Milan *IN* . . . . 39°7N 85°8W **72 D5**
Milan *MI* . . . . 42°5N 83°41W **79 G8**
Milan *MN* . . . 45°7N 95°55W **80 E3**
Milan *MO* . . . 40°12N 93°7W **82 A3**
Milan *NH* . . . . 44°36N 71°11W **86 B3**
Milan *NM* . . . . 35°9N 107°54W **88 B3**
Milan *OH* . . . . 41°18N 82°37W **92 B4**
Milan *TN* . . . . 35°55N 88°46W **96 E4**
Milan *WA* . . . . 47°58N 117°20W **101 C8**
Milan Arsenal *TN* 35°52N 88°43W **96 E4**
Milano *TX* . . . 30°43N 96°52W **99 G11**
Milbank *SD* . . . 45°13N 96°38W **91 E9**
Milbridge *ME* . . 44°32N 67°53W **76 D6**
Milburn *OK* . . . 34°13N 96°34W **93 D6**
Milburn *WV* . . 34°14N 96°59W **93 D7**
Mildred *KS* . . . 38°0N 95°7W **74 C9**
Mildred *MT* . . . 46°39N 105°18W **83 D12**
Miles *TX* . . . . 31°36N 100°11W **98 F7**
Miles *WA* . . . . 47°55N 118°8W **101 C7**
Miles City *MT* . 46°25N 105°51W **83 D12**
Milesburg *PA* . . 40°57N 77°47W **95 D5**
Milford *CA* . . . 40°10N 120°22W **64 C6**
Milford *CT* . . . 41°14N 73°3W **78 C1**
Milford *DE* . . . 38°55N 75°26W **77 B5**
Milford *GA* . . . 31°23N 84°33W **68 E2**
Milford *IL* . . . . 40°38N 87°42W **71 C6**
Milford *IA* . . . . 43°20N 95°9W **73 B3**
Milford *KS* . . . 39°10N 96°55W **74 B7**
Milford *MA* . . . 42°8N 71°31W **78 B3**
Milford *ME* . . . 44°57N 68°39W **76 D5**
Milford *MI* . . . 42°35N 83°36W **79 G8**
Milford *NE* . . . 40°47N 97°3W **84 C8**
Milford *NH* . . . 42°50N 71°39W **86 D3**
Milford *NJ* . . . 40°34N 75°6W **87 B1**
Milford *NV* . . . 38°57N 119°46W **85 D1**
Milford *OH* . . . 39°10N 84°18W **107 B3**
Milford *PA* . . . 41°19N 74°48W **87 A2**
Milford *TX* . . . 32°8N 96°57W **99 E11**
Milford *UT* . . . 38°24N 113°1W **100 E2**
Milford Center *OH* 40°11N 83°26W **92 C3**
Milford Lakes *KS* 39°5N 96°54W **74 B7**
Milford Square *PA* 40°26N 75°23W **87 B1**
Mililani Town *HI* 21°28N 158°1W **69 K13**
Mill → *AZ* . . . 43°2N 82°35W **79 F9**
Mill City *NV* . . 40°41N 118°4W **85 B2**
Mill City *OR* . . 44°45N 122°29W **94 C3**
Mill Creek *WA* . 47°51N 122°12W **118 A4**
Mill Creek → *IN* 39°55N 84°42W **107 B4**
Mill Hall *PA* . . 41°6N 77°29W **95 C5**
Mill Shoals *IL* . 38°15N 88°21W **71 E5**
Mill Stream Run Reservation
  OH . . . . . . 41°19N 81°48W **107 C1**
Milladore *WI* . . 44°36N 89°51W **103 D4**
Millard *MO* . . . 40°7N 92°33W **82 A4**
Millard County ☆
  UT . . . . . . 39°0N 113°0W **100 D3**
Millboro *SD* . . . 43°25N 100°48W **91 G6**
Millboro *VA* . . 37°57N 79°25W **102 D5**
Millbrae *CA* . . 37°36N 122°24W **118 C2**
Millbrook *AL* . . 32°29N 86°22W **60 D4**
Millbrook *NY* . . 41°47N 73°42W **89 D7**
Millbury *MA* . . 42°11N 71°46W **78 B3**
Millcreek *UT* . . 40°41N 111°52W **117 B2**
Mille Lacs County ☆
  MN . . . . . . 45°50N 93°45W **80 E5**
Mille Lacs Indian Reservation
  MN . . . . . . 46°15N 93°39W **80 D5**
Milledgeville *GA* 33°5N 83°14W **68 C3**
Milledgeville *IL* . 41°58N 89°46W **71 B4**
Milledgeville *TN* 35°22N 88°22W **96 E4**
Millen *GA* . . . 32°48N 81°57W **68 D5**
Miller *MO* . . . 37°13N 93°50W **82 D3**
Miller *SD* . . . . 44°31N 98°59W **91 F7**
Miller County ☆ *AR* 33°19N 93°58W **63 E2**
Miller County ☆ *GA* 31°10N 84°45W **68 E2**
Miller County ☆ *MO* 38°15N 92°25W **82 C4**
Miller Meadow *IL* 41°51N 87°49W **108 B2**
Millers → *AZ* . 33°30N 93°20W **88 C4**
Millers Creek Res.
  TX . . . . . . 33°35N 99°20W **99 D8**
Millers Falls *MA* 42°35N 72°30W **78 B2**
Millers Ferry *AL* 32°6N 87°22W **60 D3**
Millers Tavern *VA* 37°50N 76°54W **77 C4**
Millersburg *IN* . 41°32N 85°42W **72 B5**
Millersburg *KY* . 38°18N 84°9W **97 B8**
Millersburg *OH* . 40°33N 81°55W **92 C5**
Millersburg *PA* . 40°32N 76°58W **95 D6**
Millersport *OH* . 39°54N 82°32W **92 C4**
Millersville *MD* . 39°4N 76°39W **77 A4**
Millersville *PA* . 40°0N 76°21W **95 E6**
Millerton *IA* . . 40°51N 93°18W **73 E5**
Millerton *NY* . . 41°57N 73°31W **78 C1**
Millerton *OK* . . 33°59N 95°1W **93 E8**
Millett *TX* . . . 28°35N 99°12W **99 H8**
Millheim *PA* . . 40°54N 77°29W **95 D5**
Milligan *FL* . . . 30°45N 86°38W **67 A2**
Milligan *NE* . . 40°30N 97°23W **84 D8**
Milliken *CO* . . 40°20N 104°55W **66 B6**
Millington *MD* . 39°16N 75°50W **77 A5**
Millington *TN* . . 35°17N 89°53W **96 E3**
Millinocket *ME* . 45°39N 68°43W **76 C5**
Millinocket, L. *ME* 45°46N 68°48W **76 C5**
Millis *MA* . . . . 42°10N 71°22W **78 B3**
Millport *AL* . . . 33°34N 88°5W **60 C2**
Millry *AL* . . . . 31°38N 88°19W **60 E2**
Mills *WY* . . . . 42°50N 106°22W **104 D6**
Mills County ☆ *IA* 41°0N 95°35W **73 D3**
Mills County ☆ *TX* 31°27N 98°34W **99 F9**
Millsap *TX* . . . 32°45N 98°1W **99 E9**
Millsboro *DE* . . 38°36N 75°18W **77 B5**
Millstadt *IL* . . . 38°28N 90°6W **71 E3**
Millstone → *NJ* . 40°27N 74°38W **87 B2**
Milltown *IN* . . 38°21N 86°17W **72 E4**
Milltown *MT* . . 46°52N 113°54W **83 C4**
Milltown *NJ* . . 40°27N 74°27W **87 B2**
Milltown *SD* . . 43°25N 97°48W **91 G8**
Milltown *WI* . . 45°31N 92°30W **103 C1**
Millvale *PA* . . . 40°28N 79°58W **116 B2**
Millville *DE* . . . 38°33N 75°6W **77 B5**
Millville *IA* . . . 42°42N 91°5W **73 C7**
Millville *KY* . . 38°8N 84°49W **97 B8**

Millville *NJ* . . . 39°24N 75°2W **87 C1**
Millville *PA* . . . 41°7N 76°32W **95 C6**
Millwood *GA* . . 31°16N 82°40W **68 E4**
Millwood *MD* . 38°34N 78°2W **77 B3**
Millwood *WA* . 47°41N 117°17W **101 C8**
Millwood L. *AR* 33°42N 93°58W **63 E2**
Millwood Lake *AR* 33°42N 93°58W **63 E2**
Milmay *NJ* . . . 39°26N 74°52W **87 C2**
Milner *CO* . . . 40°29N 107°1W **66 B3**
Milnesand *NM* . 33°39N 103°20W **88 D7**
Milnor *ND* . . . 46°16N 97°27W **91 D8**
Milo *IA* . . . . . 41°17N 93°27W **73 D5**
Milo *ME* . . . . 45°15N 68°59W **76 C5**
Milo *MO* . . . . 37°45N 94°18W **82 D2**
Miloli'i *HI* . . . 19°11N 155°55W **69 D6**
Milpitas *CA* . . 37°26N 121°55W **64 F5**
Milroy *IN* . . . 39°30N 85°28W **72 D5**
Milroy *MN* . . . 44°25N 95°33W **80 F3**
Milroy *PA* . . . 40°43N 77°35W **95 D5**
Milton *DE* . . . 38°47N 75°19W **77 B5**
Milton *FL* . . . 30°38N 87°3W **67 A1**
Milton *IL* . . . . 39°34N 90°39W **71 D3**
Milton *IA* . . . . 40°41N 92°10W **73 E6**
Milton *KY* . . . 38°43N 85°22W **97 B7**
Milton *MA* . . . 42°14N 71°2W **106 B3**
Milton *NH* . . . 43°25N 70°59W **86 C4**
Milton *ND* . . . 48°38N 98°3W **91 B7**
Milton *NY* . . . 41°1N 76°51W **95 C6**
Milton *VT* . . . 44°38N 73°7W **86 B1**
Milton *WI* . . . 42°47N 88°56W **103 E5**
Milton-Freewater
  OR . . . . . . 45°56N 118°23W **94 B7**
Miltona *MN* . . 46°3N 95°18W **80 D3**
Miltonvale *KS* . 39°21N 97°27W **74 B6**
Milwaukee → *WI* 43°2N 87°54W **112 B2**
Milwaukee *WI* . 43°2N 87°54W **112 B2**
Milwaukee County ☆
  WI . . . . . . 43°0N 88°0W **103 E6**
Milwaukee General Mitchell Int.
  (MKE) *WI* . . 42°57N 87°54W **112 C2**
Milwaukie *OR* . 45°26N 122°38W **116 B2**
Mimbres *NM* . . 32°51N 107°59W **88 D3**
Mimbres Mts. *NM* . 32°50N 107°45W **88 D3**
Mims *FL* . . . . 28°40N 80°51W **67 C8**
Mina *NV* . . . . 38°24N 118°7W **85 D2**
Minam *OR* . . . 45°38N 117°43W **94 B7**
Minatare *NE* . . 41°49N 103°30W **84 C2**
Minburn *IA* . . 41°45N 94°2W **73 D4**
Minco *OK* . . . 35°19N 97°57W **93 C6**
Minden *LA* . . . 32°37N 93°17W **75 B2**
Minden *NE* . . . 40°30N 98°57W **84 D7**
Minden *NV* . . . 38°57N 119°46W **85 D1**
Minden City *MI* 43°40N 82°47W **79 F9**
Mindenmines *MO* 37°28N 94°35W **82 D2**
Minebank Run →
  MD . . . . . . 39°25N 76°32W **107 A2**
Mineola *NY* . . 40°44N 73°38W **114 B5**
Mineola *TX* . . 32°40N 95°29W **99 E12**
Mineola *KS* . . 37°25N 100°25W **74 D3**
Miner *MO* . . . 36°53N 89°32W **82 E7**
Miner County ☆ *SD* 44°1N 97°36W **91 F8**
Mineral *CA* . . 40°21N 121°36W **64 C5**
Mineral *IL* . . . 41°23N 89°49W **71 B4**
Mineral *WA* . . 46°43N 122°11W **101 D3**
Mineral County ☆
  CO . . . . . . 37°40N 106°50W **66 E4**
Mineral County ☆ *MT* 47°4N 115°0W **83 C3**
Mineral County ☆
  NV . . . . . . 38°30N 118°30W **85 D3**
Mineral County ☆
  WV . . . . . . 39°21N 79°0W **102 B6**
Mineral Mts. *UT* . 38°30N 112°45W **100 E3**
Mineral Point *WI* 42°52N 90°11W **103 F3**
Mineral Springs *AR* 33°53N 93°55W **63 E2**
Mineral Wells *TX* 32°48N 98°7W **99 E9**
Minersville *OH* . 40°41N 76°16W **95 D6**
Minersville *UT* . 38°13N 112°56W **100 E2**
Minerva *NY* . . 43°47N 73°59W **89 B7**
Minerva *OH* . . 40°44N 81°6W **92 C5**
Mineville *NY* . . 44°6N 73°31W **86 B1**
Mingo County ☆
  WV . . . . . . 37°43N 82°11W **102 D2**
Mingo Junction *OH* 40°19N 80°37W **92 C6**
Minidoka *ID* . . 42°45N 113°29W **70 G5**
Minidoka County ☆
  ID . . . . . . 42°45N 113°39W **70 G5**
Minidoka Nat. Wildlife Refuge
  ID . . . . . . 42°48N 113°21W **70 G5**
Minier *IL* . . . . 40°26N 89°19W **71 C4**
Minneapolis *MN* 44°57N 93°16W **113 B2**
Minneapolis Crystal ✈ (MIC)
  MN . . . . . . 45°3N 93°23W **113 A1**
Minneapolis-St. Paul Int. ✈ (MSP)
  MN . . . . . . 44°53N 93°13W **113 B2**
Minnehaha County ☆
  SD . . . . . . 43°40N 96°49W **91 G9**
Minnehaha Regional Park
  MN . . . . . . 44°55N 93°12W **113 B2**
Minneola *KS* . . 37°26N 100°1W **74 D3**
Minneota *MN* . 44°34N 95°59W **80 F3**
Minnesota □ *U.S.A.* 46°0N 94°15W **80 D4**
Minnesota → *MN* 44°54N 93°9W **80 F5**
Minnesota City *MN* 44°6N 91°46W **80 F7**
Minnesota Lake *MN* 43°51N 93°50W **80 F5**
Minnetex *TX* . . 29°31N 95°21W **110 C2**
Minnetonka *MN* 44°55N 93°28W **113 B1**
Minnetonka, L. *MN* 44°55N 93°38W **113 B1**
Minnewaukan *ND* 48°4N 99°15W **91 B6**
Minong *WI* . . . 46°6N 91°49W **103 B2**
Minonk *IL* . . . 40°54N 89°2W **71 C4**
Minooka *IL* . . . 41°27N 88°16W **71 B5**
Minor Hill *TN* . 35°4N 87°9W **96 E5**
Minot *ND* . . . 48°14N 101°18W **91 B4**
Minot *ME* . . . 44°7N 70°18W **76 D3**
Minster *OH* . . 40°24N 84°23W **92 C2**
Mint Hill *NC* . . 35°9N 80°39W **90 C5**
Minter City *MS* 33°45N 90°19W **81 C3**
Minto *AK* . . . 64°53N 149°11W **61 D10**
Minto *ND* . . . 48°17N 97°22W **91 B8**
Minturn *CO* . . 39°35N 106°26W **66 C4**
Minute Man Nat. Historic Park ⌂
  MA . . . . . . 42°27N 71°16W **106 A2**
Minuteman Missile Nat. Historic
  Site → *SD* . . 43°55N 102°8W **91 G3**
Mio *MI* . . . . . 44°39N 84°8W **79 E7**
Miramar *FL* . . 25°59N 80°13W **112 C1**
Mirando City *TX* 27°26N 99°0W **98 K9**
Mishawaka *IN* . 41°40N 86°11W **72 B4**
Mishicot *WI* . . 44°14N 87°39W **103 D6**
Misquah Hills *MN* 47°50N 90°30W **80 C8**
Misquamicut *RI* 41°20N 71°49W **78 C3**
Missaukee County ☆
  MI . . . . . . 44°20N 85°0W **79 E6**
Mission *CA* . . . 37°44N 122°25W **118 B2**
Mission *KS* . . 39°1N 94°39W **111 B3**
Mission *SD* . . 43°18N 100°39W **91 G5**
Mission *TX* . . 26°13N 98°20W **98 L9**
Mission Bay Park
  CA . . . . . . 32°46N 117°13W **117 B1**
Mission Dolores
  CA . . . . . . 37°45N 122°25W **118 B2**
Mission Mt. *OK* 36°... **93 ...**
Mission Ridge *SD* 44°42N 100°47W **91 F5**
Mission Trails Regional Park
  CA . . . . . . 32°47N 117°2W **117 A2**
Mission Viejo *CA* 33°36N 117°40W **65 K9**
Missisquoi → *VT* 45°0N 73°8W **86 B1**

Missisquoi, B. *N. Amer.* 45°2N 73°9W **86 A1**
Missisquoi B. *VT.* 41°7N 76°32W **86 A1**
Missisquoi Nat. Wildlife Refuge
  VT . . . . . . 44°57N 73°10W **86 B1**
Mississinewa L. *IN* 40°42N 85°52W **72 C5**
Mississippi □ *U.S.A.* 33°0N 90°0W **81 D4**
Mississippi → *LA* 29°9N 89°15W **75 E6**
Mississippi Choctaw Indian
  Reservation *MS* 32°48N 89°7W **81 D4**
Mississippi County ☆
  AR. . . . . . . 35°45N 90°5W **63 C5**
Mississippi County ☆
  MO . . . . . . 36°50N 89°15W **82 E7**
Mississippi River Delta
  LA . . . . . . 29°10N 89°15W **75 E6**
Mississippi Sd. *MS* 30°20N 89°0W **81 F5**
Missoula *MT* . . 46°52N 114°1W **83 C4**
Missoula County ☆
  MT . . . . . . 47°4N 114°0W **83 C4**
Missouri □ *U.S.A.* 38°25N 92°30W **82 C4**
Missouri → *MO* 38°49N 90°7W **82 C6**
Missouri Buttes
  WY . . . . . . 44°37N 104°47W **104 B8**
Missouri City *MO* 39°14N 94°18W **82 B2**
Missouri City *TX* 29°37N 95°32W **110 C1**
Missouri Nat. Scenic River ⌂
  U.S.A. . . . . 42°48N 97°25W **84 B8**
Missouri Valley *IA* 41°34N 95°53W **73 D3**
Misty Fjords Nat. Monument ⌂
  AK . . . . . . 55°40N 130°40W **61 J15**
Mitchell *GA* . . 33°13N 82°42W **68 C4**
Mitchell *IN* . . 38°44N 86°28W **72 E4**
Mitchell *IA* . . 43°19N 92°52W **73 B5**
Mitchell *NE* . . 41°57N 103°49W **84 C2**
Mitchell *SD* . . 43°43N 98°2W **91 G7**
Mitchell, L. *MI* . 44°15N 85°35W **79 E6**
Mitchell, Mt. *NC* 35°46N 82°16W **90 C3**
Mitchell County ☆
  GA . . . . . . 31°15N 84°10W **68 E2**
Mitchell County ☆
  IA . . . . . . 43°20N 92°45W **73 B6**
Mitchell County ☆
  KS . . . . . . 39°30N 98°10W **74 B5**
Mitchell County ☆ *NC* 36°5N 82°10W **90 B3**
Mitchell County ☆
  TX . . . . . . 32°24N 100°52W **98 E7**
Mitchell L. *AL* . 32°48N 86°27W **60 D4**
Mitchell Lake *TX* . 29°16N 98°27W **117 D3**
Mitchell Museum of the American
  Indian *IL* . . 42°4N 87°43W **108 A2**
Mitchellsburg *KY* 37°36N 84°57W **97 C8**
Mitchellville *IA* . 41°40N 93°22W **73 D5**
Mize *MS* . . . . 31°52N 89°33W **81 E4**
Mizpah *MN* . . 47°55N 94°12W **80 C4**
Mizpah *MT* . . 46°14N 105°16W **83 D12**
Moab *UT* . . . 38°35N 109°33W **100 E6**
Moapa *NV* . . . 36°40N 114°37W **85 F6**
Moapa River Indian Reservation
  NV . . . . . . 36°36N 114°45W **85 F6**
Mobeetie *TX* . . 35°31N 100°26W **98 B7**
Moberly *MO* . . 39°25N 92°26W **82 B4**
Mobile *AL* . . . 30°41N 88°3W **60 F2**
Mobile *AZ* . . . 33°3N 112°16W **62 D3**
Mobile → *AL* . 30°30N 88°2W **60 F2**
Mobile B. *AL* . . 30°30N 88°0W **60 F3**
Mobile County ☆ *AL* 30°50N 88°15W **60 F2**
Mobridge *SD* . . 45°32N 100°26W **91 E5**
Moca *Puerto Rico* 18°24N 67°10W **105 G15**
Moccasin *AZ* . . 36°55N 112°46W **62 A3**
Moccasin Gap *VA* 36°38N 82°33W **102 D2**
Mocksville *NC* . 35°54N 80°34W **90 C5**
Moclips *WA* . . 47°14N 124°13W **101 C1**
Model *CO* . . . 37°22N 104°15W **66 E6**
Modena *UT* . . . 37°48N 113°56W **100 F2**
Modesto *CA* . . 37°39N 121°0W **64 F5**
Modoc *GA* . . . 33°36N 82°13W **68 C4**
Modoc County ☆
  CA . . . . . . 41°30N 120°50W **64 B6**
Modoc Nat. Forest
  CA . . . . . . 41°30N 121°0W **64 B6**
Modoc Point *OR* 42°27N 121°52W **94 E4**
Moenkopi *AZ* . 36°7N 111°13W **62 A4**
Moenkopi Wash →
  AZ . . . . . . 35°50N 111°0W **62 B4**
Moffat County ☆
  CO . . . . . . 40°45N 108°10W **66 B2**
Mogollon Mts. *NM* 33°20N 108°40W **88 D2**
Mogollon Plateau *AZ* 34°30N 111°0W **62 C5**
Mogollon Rim *AZ* 34°10N 110°50W **62 C5**
Mohall *ND* . . . 48°46N 101°31W **91 B4**
Mohave County ☆ *AZ* 35°35N 114°0W **62 C1**
Mohave Mts. *AZ* 34°35N 114°10W **62 C1**
Mohawk *NY* . . 43°0N 75°0W **89 C6**
Mohawk → *NY* . 42°47N 73°42W **89 C7**
Mohawk Mts. *AZ* 32°30N 113°35W **62 E2**
Mohawksin, L. *WI* 45°26N 89°43W **103 C4**
Mohican → *OH* . 40°22N 82°16W **92 C4**
Mohican, C. *AK* 60°12N 167°25W **61 F6**
Mohon Pk. *AZ* . 34°57N 113°9W **62 C2**
Mojave *CA* . . . 35°3N 118°10W **65 H8**
Mojave → *CA* . 35°6N 116°4W **65 H10**
Mojave Desert *CA* 35°0N 116°30W **65 H10**
Mojave Nat. Preserve ⌂
  U.S.A. . . . . 35°7N 115°32W **65 H11**
Mokane *MO* . . 38°41N 91°53W **82 C4**
Mokapu Peninsula
  HI . . . . . . 21°27N 157°45W **69 K14**
Mokelumne → *CA* 38°13N 121°28W **64 E5**
Mokelumne Hill *CA* 38°18N 120°43W **64 E5**
Mokōlea Rock *HI* 21°27N 157°44W **69 K14**
Mokuaula I. *HI* . 21°24N 157°42W **69 K14**
Mokulua Is. *HI* . 21°28N 157°42W **69 K14**
Mokumanu I. *HI* 21°32N 157°43W **69 K14**
Molalla *OR* . . . 45°9N 122°35W **94 B3**
Molena *GA* . . . 33°1N 84°30W **68 C2**
Mōli'i Pond *HI* . 21°29N 157°50W **69 J14**
Molina *CO* . . . 39°11N 108°4W **66 C2**
Moline *IL* . . . . 41°30N 90°31W **71 B3**
Moline *KS* . . . 37°22N 96°18W **74 D7**
Moline Acres *MO* 38°45N 90°15W **117 A2**
Molino *FL* . . . 30°43N 87°20W **67 A1**
Moloka'i *HI* . . 21°8N 157°0W **69 L8**
Molokini I. *HI* . 20°38N 156°30W **69 C5**
Molybdenite Mt.
  WA . . . . . . 48°42N 117°15W **101 B8**
Momence *IL* . . 41°10N 87°40W **71 B6**
Mona *UT* . . . . 39°49N 111°51W **100 D4**
Monadnock, Mt. *NH* 42°52N 72°7W **86 D2**
Monahans *TX* . 31°36N 102°54W **98 F5**
Monango *ND* . . 46°10N 98°36W **91 D7**
Monarch *SC* . . 34°43N 81°36W **90 D4**
Monarch Pass *CO* 38°30N 106°20W **66 D4**
Moncks Corner *SC* 33°12N 80°1W **90 E5**
Mondamin *IA* . . 41°42N 96°1W **73 D2**
Mondovi *WI* . . 44°34N 91°40W **103 D2**
Monero *NM* . . 36°56N 106°49W **88 A4**
Monessen *PA* . . 40°9N 79°54W **95 D3**
Moneta *VA* . . . 37°9N 79°37W **102 D5**
Moneta *WY* . . 43°9N 107°43W **104 C5**
Monett *MO* . . 36°55N 93°55W **82 E3**
Monette *AR* . . 35°53N 90°21W **63 C5**
Monfort Heights
  OH . . . . . . 39°11N 84°35W **107 A1**

Moniteau County ☆
   MO. . . . . 38°35N 92°35W **82 C4**
Monitor *WA*. . . . . . 47°29N 120°25W **101 C5**
Monitor Range *NV*. . 38°40N 116°40W **85 D4**
Monkstown *TX*. . . . 33°48N 95°56W **99 D12**
Monkton *MD*. . . . . 39°35N 76°37W **77 A4**
Monmouth *IL*. . . . . 40°55N 90°39W **71 C3**
Monmouth *OR*. . . . 44°51N 123°14W **94 C2**
Monmouth County ☆
   NJ. . . . . 40°15N 74°15W **87 B2**
Monmouth Junction
   NJ. . . . . 40°23N 74°33W **87 B2**
Mono County ☆ *CA*. . 38°0N 119°0W **64 E7**
Mono L. *CA*. . . . . 38°1N 119°1W **64 E7**
Monocacy → *MD*. . . 39°13N 77°27W **77 A3**
Monolith *CA*. . . . . 35°7N 118°22W **65 H8**
Monomoy I. *MA*. . . 41°36N 69°59W **78 C5**
Monomoy Nat. Wildlife Refuge △
   MA. . . . . 41°29N 69°58W **78 C5**
Monomoy Point *MA*. . 41°33N 70°2W **78 C4**
Monon *IN*. . . . . . . 40°52N 86°53W **72 C4**
Monona *IA*. . . . . . 43°3N 91°23W **73 B7**
Monona *WI*. . . . . . 43°4N 89°20W **103 E4**
Monona County ☆ *IA*. 42°0N 96°0W **73 D3**
Monongah *WV*. . . . 39°28N 80°13W **102 B4**
Monongah *CA*. . . . . 40°12N 79°56W **95 D3**
Monongahela *PA*. . . 40°12N 79°56W **95 D3**
Monongahela → *WV*. . 40°27N 80°1W **95 D2**
Monongahela Nat. Forest
   WV. . . . . 38°30N 79°57W **102 C5**
Monongalia County ☆
   WV. . . . . 39°39N 80°1W **102 B4**
Monowi *NE*. . . . . . 42°50N 98°20W **84 B7**
Monroe *AR*. . . . . . 34°44N 91°6W **63 D4**
Monroe *GA*. . . . . . 33°47N 83°43W **68 C3**
Monroe *IN*. . . . . . 40°45N 84°56W **72 C6**
Monroe *IA*. . . . . . 41°31N 93°6W **73 D5**
Monroe *LA*. . . . . . 32°30N 92°7W **75 B3**
Monroe *MI*. . . . . . 41°55N 83°24W **79 H8**
Monroe *NC*. . . . . . 34°59N 80°33W **90 D5**
Monroe *NY*. . . . . . 41°20N 74°11W **87 A2**
Monroe *NE*. . . . . . 41°28N 97°36W **84 C8**
Monroe *OH*. . . . . . 39°27N 84°22W **92 D2**
Monroe *OK*. . . . . . 34°59N 94°30W **93 D9**
Monroe *OR*. . . . . . 44°19N 123°18W **94 C2**
Monroe *SD*. . . . . . 43°28N 97°12W **91 G8**
Monroe *UT*. . . . . . 38°38N 112°7W **100 D3**
Monroe *VA*. . . . . . 37°30N 79°8W **102 D5**
Monroe *WA*. . . . . . 47°51N 121°58W **101 C4**
Monroe *WI*. . . . . . 42°36N 89°38W **103 F4**
Monroe, L. *FL*. . . . 28°50N 81°19W **67 C7**
Monroe City *MO*. . . 39°39N 91°44W **82 B5**
Monroe County ☆
   AL. . . . . 31°31N 87°20W **60 E3**
Monroe County ☆
   AR. . . . . 34°42N 91°19W **63 D4**
Monroe County ☆ *FL*. 25°30N 81°0W **67 F7**
Monroe County ☆ *GA*. 33°0N 83°55W **68 C3**
Monroe County ☆ *IL*. 38°15N 90°10W **71 E3**
Monroe County ☆
   IN. . . . . 39°10N 86°30W **72 D4**
Monroe County ☆ *IA*. 41°0N 92°50W **73 E6**
Monroe County ☆
   KY. . . . . 36°45N 85°45W **97 D7**
Monroe County ☆
   MI. . . . . 41°50N 83°35W **79 H8**
Monroe County ☆
   MS. . . . . 33°49N 88°33W **81 C5**
Monroe County ☆
   MO. . . . . 39°30N 92°0W **82 B5**
Monroe County ☆
   NY. . . . . 43°10N 77°40W **89 B3**
Monroe County ☆
   OH. . . . . 39°46N 81°7W **92 D5**
Monroe County ☆ *PA*. 41°0N 75°15W **95 D7**
Monroe County ☆
   TN. . . . . 35°31N 84°22W **97 E8**
Monroe County ☆
   WV. . . . . 37°36N 80°33W **102 D4**
Monroe County ☆
   WI. . . . . 43°50N 90°40W **103 E3**
Monroe L. *IN*. . . . . 39°1N 86°31W **72 D4**
Monroeton *PA*. . . . 41°43N 76°29W **95 C6**
Monroeville *AL*. . . . 31°31N 87°20W **60 E3**
Monroeville *OH*. . . 40°59N 84°52W **79 F8**
Monroeville *OH*. . . 41°15N 82°42W **92 B3**
Monroeville *PA*. . . 40°26N 79°45W **95 D3**
Monrovia *CA*. . . . . 34°9N 118°1W **111 B4**
Monsey *NY*. . . . . . 41°7N 74°4W **87 A2**
Monson *ME*. . . . . . 45°17N 69°30W **76 C4**
Monson *MA*. . . . . . 42°6N 72°19W **78 B2**
Mont Alto *PA*. . . . 39°51N 77°34W **77 A3**
Mont Belvieu *TX*. . 29°51N 94°53W **99 H13**
Mont Ida *KS*. . . . . 38°13N 95°22W **74 C8**
Mont Vernon *NH*. . . 42°50N 71°42W **86 D4**
Montague *CA*. . . . 41°44N 122°32W **64 B4**
Montague *MA*. . . . 42°32N 72°32W **78 B2**
Montague *MI*. . . . . 43°25N 86°22W **79 F5**
Montague *TX*. . . . 33°42N 97°48W **99 D10**
Montague County ☆
   TX. . . . . 33°47N 97°44W **99 D10**
Montague I. *AK*. . . 60°0N 147°30W **61 G11**
Montalba *TX*. . . . . 31°53N 95°44W **99 F12**
Montana □ *U.S.A.*. . . 47°0N 110°0W **83 C7**
Montana City *MT*. . 46°32N 111°56W **83 D6**
Montank Pt. *NY*. . . 41°4N 71°57W **78 C3**
Montauk Pt. *NY*. . . 41°4N 71°51W **78 C3**
Montbello *CO*. . . . 39°47N 104°49W **109 B3**
Montcalm County ☆
   MI. . . . . 43°15N 85°10W **79 F6**
Montclair *NJ*. . . . . 40°49N 74°12W **114 B1**
Monte Vista *CO*. . . 37°35N 106°9W **66 E4**
Monteagle *TN*. . . . 35°15N 85°50W **97 E7**
Montebello *CA*. . . 34°1N 118°8W **111 B4**
Montecito *CA*. . . . 34°26N 119°40W **65 J7**
Montegut *LA*. . . . . 29°28N 90°33W **75 B5**
Montello *NV*. . . . . 41°16N 114°12W **85 A6**
Montello *WI*. . . . . 43°48N 89°20W **103 E4**
Monterey *CA*. . . . 36°37N 121°55W **64 G5**
Monterey *IN*. . . . . 41°11N 86°30W **72 B4**
Monterey *KY*. . . . 38°25N 84°52W **97 B8**
Monterey *MA*. . . . 42°11N 73°13W **78 B1**
Monterey *TN*. . . . 36°9N 85°16W **97 D7**
Monterey *VA*. . . . 38°25N 79°35W **102 C5**
Monterey B. *CA*. . . 36°45N 122°0W **64 G5**
Monterey County ☆
   CA. . . . . 36°15N 121°0W **64 G5**
Monterey Park *CA*. . 34°3N 118°7W **111 B4**
Montesano *WA*. . . 46°59N 123°36W **101 D2**
Montevallo *AL*. . . 33°6N 86°52W **60 C4**
Montevideo *MN*. . . 44°57N 95°43W **80 F3**
Monteview *ID*. . . . 43°56N 112°32W **70 F6**
Montezuma *GA*. . . 32°18N 84°0W **68 D2**
Montezuma *IN*. . . 39°48N 87°22W **72 D3**
Montezuma *IA*. . . . 41°35N 92°32W **73 D6**
Montezuma *KS*. . . 37°36N 100°27W **74 D3**
Montezuma Castle Nat.
   Monument △ *AZ*. . 34°39N 111°45W **62 C4**
Montezuma County ☆
   CO. . . . . 37°20N 108°30W **66 E2**
Montezuma Cr. →
   UT. . . . . 37°17N 109°20W **100 F6**
Montezuma Creek
   UT. . . . . 37°16N 109°19W **100 F6**
Montfort *WI*. . . . . 42°58N 90°26W **103 F3**
Montgomery *AL*. . . 32°23N 86°19W **60 D4**
Montgomery *LA*. . . 31°40N 92°53W **75 B3**
Montgomery *MN*. . . 44°26N 93°35W **80 F5**
Montgomery *NY*. . . 41°32N 74°14W **87 A2**
Montgomery *PA*. . . 41°10N 76°53W **95 C6**
Montgomery *WV*. . . 38°11N 81°19W **102 C3**
Montgomery Center
   VT. . . . . 44°53N 73°40W **86 B1**

Montgomery City
   MO. . . . . 38°59N 91°30W **82 C5**
Montgomery County ☆
   AL. . . . . 32°15N 86°18W **60 D4**
Montgomery County ☆
   AR. . . . . 34°34N 93°38W **63 D2**
Montgomery County ☆
   GA. . . . . 32°15N 82°35W **68 D4**
Montgomery County ☆
   IL. . . . . 39°10N 89°30W **71 D4**
Montgomery County ☆
   IN. . . . . 40°5N 86°55W **72 C4**
Montgomery County ☆
   IA. . . . . 41°0N 95°10W **73 D3**
Montgomery County ☆
   KS. . . . . 37°15N 95°45W **74 D8**
Montgomery County ☆
   KY. . . . . 38°0N 83°55W **97 B9**
Montgomery County ☆
   MD. . . . . 39°15N 77°15W **77 A3**
Montgomery County ☆
   MS. . . . . 33°29N 89°44W **81 C4**
Montgomery County ☆
   MO. . . . . 38°55N 91°30W **82 C5**
Montgomery County ☆
   NC. . . . . 35°20N 79°50W **90 C6**
Montgomery County ☆
   NY. . . . . 42°50N 74°30W **89 C6**
Montgomery County ☆
   OH. . . . . 39°45N 84°12W **92 D2**
Montgomery County ☆
   PA. . . . . 40°10N 75°10W **95 D7**
Montgomery County ☆
   TN. . . . . 36°32N 87°21W **96 D5**
Montgomery County ☆
   TX. . . . . 30°19N 95°27W **99 G12**
Montgomery County ☆
   VA. . . . . 37°8N 80°25W **102 D4**
Montgomery Field
   CA. . . . . 32°48N 117°8W **117 B2**
Montgomery Pass
   NV. . . . . 37°58N 118°20W **85 E2**
Montgomery Village
   MD. . . . . 39°12N 77°13W **77 A3**
Monticello *AR*. . . . 33°38N 91°47W **63 E4**
Monticello *FL*. . . . 30°33N 83°52W **67 A5**
Monticello *IL*. . . . . 40°1N 88°34W **71 C5**
Monticello *IA*. . . . . 42°15N 91°12W **73 C7**
Monticello *KY*. . . . 36°50N 84°51W **97 D8**
Monticello *MN*. . . . 45°18N 93°48W **80 E5**
Monticello *MS*. . . . 31°33N 90°7W **81 A5**
Monticello *MO*. . . . 40°7N 91°43W **82 A5**
Monticello *NM*. . . . 33°24N 107°27W **88 D3**
Monticello *NY*. . . . 41°39N 74°42W **89 D6**
Monticello *UT*. . . . 37°52N 109°21W **100 F6**
Monticello *WI*. . . . 42°45N 89°36W **103 F4**
Montmorency County ☆
   MI. . . . . 45°0N 84°10W **79 D7**
Montour *IA*. . . . . . 41°59N 92°43W **73 D6**
Montour County ☆
   PA. . . . . 41°0N 76°40W **95 D6**
Montour Falls *NY*. . 42°21N 76°51W **89 C4**
Montoursville *PA*. . 41°15N 76°55W **95 C6**
Montoya *NM*. . . . 35°6N 104°48W **88 B6**
Montpelier *IN*. . . . 40°33N 85°17W **72 C5**
Montpelier *MS*. . . . 33°43N 88°57W **81 C5**
Montpelier *ND*. . . . 46°42N 98°35W **91 D7**
Montpelier *OH*. . . . 41°35N 84°37W **92 B2**
Montpelier *VA*. . . . 37°49N 77°41W **102 D7**
Montpelier *VT*. . . . 44°16N 72°35W **86 B2**
Montreat *NC*. . . . . 35°39N 82°15W **90 C3**
Montrose *AR*. . . . . 33°18N 91°30W **63 E4**
Montrose *CA*. . . . . 34°12N 118°13W **111 A4**
Montrose *CO*. . . . 38°29N 107°53W **66 D3**
Montrose *IL*. . . . . 39°10N 88°23W **71 D5**
Montrose *IA*. . . . . 40°31N 91°25W **73 E7**
Montrose *MI*. . . . . 43°11N 83°54W **79 F8**
Montrose *MS*. . . . 32°8N 89°14W **81 C4**
Montrose *PA*. . . . . 41°50N 75°53W **95 C7**
Montrose *SD*. . . . . 43°42N 97°11W **91 G8**
Montrose *WV*. . . . 39°4N 79°49W **102 B5**
Montrose County ☆
   CO. . . . . 38°30N 108°15W **66 D2**
Montross *VA*. . . . . 38°6N 76°50W **77 B4**
Montvale *NJ*. . . . . 37°23N 79°44W **102 D5**
Montville *CT*. . . . . 41°27N 72°8W **78 C2**
Monument *CO*. . . . 39°6N 104°52W **66 C6**
Monument *KS*. . . . 39°6N 101°1W **74 B2**
Monument *OR*. . . . 44°49N 119°25W **94 C6**
Monument Draw →
   TX. . . . . 32°29N 102°20W **98 E5**
Monument Pass *AZ*. . 36°58N 110°5W **62 A5**
Monument Pk. *ID*. . . 42°7N 114°14W **70 G4**
Monument Valley
   UT. . . . . 36°56N 110°5W **62 A5**
Moodus *CT*. . . . . . 41°30N 72°25W **78 C2**
Moody *MO*. . . . . . 33°35N 86°29W **60 C4**
Moody *TX*. . . . . . 31°18N 97°21W **99 F10**
Moody Air Force Base
   GA. . . . . 30°58N 83°12W **68 F3**
Moody County ☆ *SD*. 44°3N 96°36W **91 F9**
Mooers *NY*. . . . . . 44°58N 73°35W **86 B1**
Mooleyville *KY*. . . 37°48N 86°28W **96 B6**
Moomaw, L. *VA*. . . 37°57N 79°57W **102 D5**
Moon L. *CA*. . . . . 41°10N 120°22W **64 B6**
Moon Res. *OR*. . . . 43°24N 119°24W **94 D6**
Moonachie *NJ*. . . . 40°50N 74°2W **114 A2**
Moorcroft *WY*. . . . 44°16N 104°57W **104 B8**
Moore *ID*. . . . . . . 43°44N 113°22W **70 F5**
Moore *MT*. . . . . . 46°59N 109°42W **83 D8**
Moore *OK*. . . . . . 35°20N 97°29W **93 C6**
Moore *TX*. . . . . . 29°3N 99°1W **99 H8**
Moore *UT*. . . . . . 38°58N 111°10W **100 D4**
Moore County ☆
   NC. . . . . 35°25N 79°20W **90 C6**
Moore County ☆ *TN*. 35°17N 86°22W **96 E6**
Moore County ☆
   TX. . . . . 35°55N 101°59W **98 B6**
Moore Haven *FL*. . . 26°50N 81°6W **67 E7**
Moorefield *NE*. . . . 40°41N 100°24W **84 D5**
Moorefield *WV*. . . . 39°4N 78°58W **77 A2**
Mooreland *OK*. . . . 36°26N 99°12W **93 B4**
Moores Creek Nat. Battlefield ○
   NC. . . . . 34°27N 78°7W **90 D7**
Mooresville *IN*. . . . 39°37N 86°22W **72 D4**
Mooresville *NC*. . . 35°35N 80°48W **90 C5**
Mooreton *ND*. . . . 46°16N 96°53W **91 D9**
Moorhead *IA*. . . . . 41°56N 95°53W **73 D3**
Moorhead *MN*. . . . 46°53N 96°45W **80 D2**
Moorhead *MS*. . . . 33°27N 90°30W **81 B3**
Mooringsport *LA*. . 42°26N 94°18W **73 C4**
Moorland *IA*. . . . . 42°26N 94°18W **73 C4**
Moose → *ME*. . . . . 43°39N 110°43W **104 C2**
Moose *WY*. . . . . . 43°39N 110°43W **104 C2**
Moose → *VT*. . . . . 44°24N 72°1W **86 B2**
Moose County ☆
   KS. . . . . 37°50N 100°30W **74 D3**
Moose Lake *MN*. . . 46°45N 101°30W **91 D4**
Moose Pass *AK*. . . 60°29N 149°22W **61 F10**
Moose River *ME*. . . 45°36N 70°16W **76 C3**
Mooselookmeguntic L.
   ME. . . . . 44°55N 70°49W **86 B4**

Moosic *PA*. . . . . . 41°21N 75°44W **87 A1**
Moosilauke, Mt. *NH*. 44°3N 71°40W **86 B3**
Moosup *CT*. . . . . . 41°43N 71°53W **78 C3**
Mora *GA*. . . . . . . 31°25N 82°57W **68 E4**
Mora *MN*. . . . . . . 45°53N 93°18W **80 E5**
Mora *NM*. . . . . . . 35°58N 105°20W **88 B5**
Mora → *NM*. . . . . 35°35N 104°25W **88 B6**
Morada *CA*. . . . . . 38°2N 121°15W **64 E5**
Moraga *CA*. . . . . . 37°50N 122°7W **118 B4**
Morales *TX*. . . . . . 29°8N 96°46W **99 H11**
Moran *KS*. . . . . . . 37°55N 95°10W **74 D8**
Moran *MI*. . . . . . . 46°0N 84°50W **79 C7**
Moran *TX*. . . . . . . 32°33N 99°10W **99 E8**
Moran *WY*. . . . . . 43°50N 110°31W **104 C2**
Moravia *IA*. . . . . . 40°53N 92°49W **73 E5**
Moravia *NY*. . . . . 42°43N 76°25W **89 C4**
Moreau → *SD*. . . . 45°18N 100°43W **91 E5**
Morehead *KY*. . . . 38°11N 83°26W **97 B9**
Morehead City *NC*. . 34°43N 76°43W **90 D8**
Morehouse *MO*. . . . 36°51N 89°41W **82 E7**
Morehouse Parish ☆
   LA. . . . . 32°47N 91°48W **75 B4**
Moreland *GA*. . . . . 33°17N 84°46W **68 C2**
Moreland *KY*. . . . . 37°30N 84°49W **97 C8**
Morenci *AZ*. . . . . . 33°5N 109°22W **62 D6**
Morenci *MI*. . . . . . 41°43N 84°13W **79 H7**
Moreno Valley *CA*. . 33°56N 117°14W **65 K9**
Morevain Falls *NC*. . 36°6N 81°11W **90 B4**
Morgan *GA*. . . . . . 31°32N 84°36W **68 E2**
Morgan *KY*. . . . . . 38°36N 84°24W **97 A8**
Morgan *MN*. . . . . . 44°25N 94°55W **80 F4**
Morgan *UT*. . . . . . 41°2N 111°41W **100 B4**
Morgan, Mt. *CA*. . . 37°31N 118°47W **65 F8**
Morgan City *LA*. . . 29°42N 91°12W **75 E4**
Morgan City *MS*. . . 33°23N 90°21W **81 C3**
Morgan County ☆
   AL. . . . . 34°27N 86°56W **60 B4**
Morgan County ☆
   CO. . . . . 40°15N 103°50W **66 B7**
Morgan County ☆
   GA. . . . . 33°40N 83°25W **68 C3**
Morgan County ☆ *IL*. 39°45N 90°10W **71 D3**
Morgan County ☆ *IN* 39°30N 86°25W **72 D4**
Morgan County ☆
   KY. . . . . 37°55N 83°15W **97 C9**
Morgan County ☆
   MO. . . . . 38°25N 92°50W **82 C4**
Morgan County ☆
   OH. . . . . 39°39N 81°51W **92 D5**
Morgan County ☆ *TN* 36°6N 84°36W **97 D8**
Morgan County ☆
   UT. . . . . 41°10N 111°45W **100 B4**
Morgan County ☆
   WV. . . . . 39°35N 78°16W **102 B6**
Morgan Hill *CA*. . . 37°8N 121°39W **64 G5**
Morgan, L. *NM*. . . . 36°52N 108°41W **88 A2**
Morgan Mill *TX*. . . 32°23N 98°10W **99 E9**
Morgan Park *IL*. . . 41°41N 87°38W **108 C3**
Morganton *GA*. . . . 34°53N 84°15W **68 B2**
Morganton *NC*. . . . 35°45N 81°41W **90 C4**
Morgantown *KY*. . . 37°14N 86°41W **96 C6**
Morgantown *MD*. . . 38°21N 76°58W **77 B4**
Morgantown *MS*. . . 31°18N 88°55W **81 E5**
Morgantown *MS*. . . 31°34N 91°21W **81 A4**
Morgantown *OH*. . . 39°8N 83°12W **92 D3**
Morgantown *WV*. . . 39°38N 79°57W **102 B5**
Morganville *KS*. . . 39°28N 97°12W **74 B6**
Morganza *LA*. . . . . 30°44N 91°36W **75 D4**
Moriah, Mt. *NV*. . . 39°17N 114°12W **85 C6**
Moriarty *NM*. . . . . 34°59N 106°3W **88 C4**
Morland *KS*. . . . . . 39°21N 100°5W **74 B3**
Morley *MI*. . . . . . . 43°29N 85°27W **79 F6**
Morley *MO*. . . . . . 37°3N 89°37W **82 D7**
Mormon L. *AZ*. . . . 34°57N 111°29W **62 C4**
Mormon Lake *AZ*. . 34°55N 111°28W **62 C4**
Mormon Mts. *NV*. . 37°0N 114°0W **85 F6**
Morning Sun *IA*. . . 41°5N 91°15W **73 D7**
Morningside Park
   FL. . . . . 28°26N 81°24W **115 B2**
Moro *AR*. . . . . . . 34°48N 90°59W **63 D5**
Moro *OR*. . . . . . . 45°29N 120°44W **94 B5**
Moro → *AR*. . . . . . 33°17N 92°21W **63 E3**
Morocco *IN*. . . . . . 40°57N 87°27W **72 C3**
Morongo Indian Reservation
   CA. . . . . 33°57N 116°49W **65 K10**
Morongo Valley
   CA. . . . . 34°3N 116°35W **65 K10**
Moroni *UT*. . . . . . 39°32N 111°35W **100 D4**
Morra *OH*. . . . . . . 40°41N 83°13W **92 C3**
Morral *OH*. . . . . . 40°41N 83°13W **92 C3**
Morrill *NE*. . . . . . 41°58N 103°56W **84 C2**
Morrill County ☆ *NE* 41°45N 103°0W **84 C3**
Morrilton *AR*. . . . . 35°9N 92°44W **63 C3**
Morris *CT*. . . . . . . 41°43N 73°15W **78 C1**
Morris *IL*. . . . . . . 41°22N 88°26W **71 B5**
Morris *MN*. . . . . . 45°35N 95°55W **80 E3**
Morris *NY*. . . . . . 42°33N 75°15W **89 C5**
Morris *OK*. . . . . . 35°36N 95°51W **93 C8**
Morris County ☆ *KS* 38°30N 96°40W **74 C7**
Morris County ☆ *NJ* 40°50N 74°30W **87 B2**
Morris County ☆ *TX* 33°2N 94°44W **99 D13**
Morrison *IL*. . . . . . 41°49N 89°58W **71 B4**
Morrison *OK*. . . . . 36°18N 97°1W **93 B6**
Morrison *TN*. . . . . 35°36N 85°55W **97 E7**
Morrison County ☆
   MN. . . . . 46°0N 94°10W **80 E4**
Morrisonville *IL*. . . 39°25N 89°27W **71 D4**
Morristown *AZ*. . . 33°51N 112°37W **62 D3**
Morristown *MN*. . . 44°14N 93°27W **80 F5**
Morristown *NJ*. . . . 40°48N 74°29W **87 B2**
Morristown *NY*. . . 44°35N 75°39W **89 A5**
Morristown *TN*. . . 36°13N 83°18W **97 D9**
Morristown *VT*. . . 44°33N 72°37W **86 B2**
Morris, L. *NY*. . . . 42°44N 77°52W **89 C3**
Morrisville *NC*. . . . 35°49N 78°50W **90 C7**
Morrisville *NY*. . . . 42°53N 75°35W **89 C5**
Morrisville *PA*. . . . 40°13N 74°47W **87 B2**
Morrisville *VT*. . . . 44°34N 72°36W **86 B2**
Morro Bay *CA*. . . . 35°22N 120°51W **65 H6**
Morrow *LA*. . . . . . 30°47N 91°59W **75 D3**
Morrow *OH*. . . . . . 39°21N 84°8W **92 D2**
Morrow County ☆
   OH. . . . . 40°33N 82°50W **92 C4**
Morrow County ☆
   OR. . . . . 45°25N 119°40W **94 B6**
Morrowville *KS*. . . 39°51N 97°10W **74 B6**
Morse *LA*. . . . . . . 30°17N 92°30W **75 D3**
Morse *TX*. . . . . . . 36°4N 101°29W **98 A6**
Morse Bluff *NE*. . . 41°26N 96°46W **84 C8**
Morse *IL*. . . . . . . 40°37N 89°28W **71 C4**
Morton *MN*. . . . . . 44°33N 94°59W **80 F4**
Morton *MS*. . . . . . 32°21N 89°39W **81 D4**
Morton *TX*. . . . . . 33°44N 102°46W **98 D4**
Morton *WA*. . . . . . 46°34N 122°17W **101 D3**
Morton *WY*. . . . . . 43°12N 108°46W **104 C4**
Morton County ☆
   KS. . . . . 37°10N 101°50W **74 D2**
Morton County ☆
   ND. . . . . 46°45N 101°30W **91 D4**
Morton Grove *IL*. . . 42°2N 87°46W **108 A2**
Mortons Gap *KY*. . . 37°14N 87°28W **96 C5**
Morven *GA*. . . . . . 30°57N 83°30W **68 F3**
Morven *NC*. . . . . . 34°52N 80°0W **90 D5**
Morven *VA*. . . . . . 37°58N 78°28W **102 D6**

Mosby *MT*. . . . . . 47°0N 107°52W **83 C11**
Mosca *CO*. . . . . . 37°38N 105°52W **66 E5**
Moscow *ID*. . . . . . 46°44N 117°0W **70 C2**
Moscow *KS*. . . . . . 37°20N 101°12W **74 D2**
Moscow *KY*. . . . . 36°37N 89°2W **96 D3**
Moscow *OH*. . . . . 38°52N 84°14W **92 E2**
Moscow *PA*. . . . . . 41°20N 75°31W **87 A1**
Moscow *TN*. . . . . 35°4N 89°24W **96 E3**
Moscow Mills *MO*. . 38°57N 90°55W **82 C6**
Moselle *MS*. . . . . . 31°30N 89°17W **81 E4**
Mosenthein Island
   PA. . . . . 41°7N 78°22W **95 C4**
Mosheim *TN*. . . . . 36°11N 82°57W **97 D10**
Mosher *SD*. . . . . . 43°28N 100°18W **91 G5**
Mosier *OR*. . . . . . 45°41N 121°24W **94 B4**
Mosinee *WI*. . . . . 44°47N 89°43W **103 D4**
Mosquero *NM*. . . . 35°47N 103°58W **88 B7**
Mosquito Creek L.
   OH. . . . . 41°18N 80°46W **92 B6**
Moss *TN*. . . . . . . 36°36N 85°37W **97 D7**
Moss Bluff *LA*. . . . 30°18N 93°11W **75 D2**
Moss Point *MS*. . . . 30°25N 88°30W **81 F5**
Mossy Head *FL*. . . 30°45N 86°19W **67 A2**
Mossyrock *WA*. . . 46°32N 122°29W **101 D3**
Motley *MN*. . . . . . 46°20N 94°40W **80 D4**
Motley County ☆ *TX* 34°1N 73°49W **114 A4**
Mott *ND*. . . . . . . 46°23N 102°20W **91 D3**
Motters *MD*. . . . . . 39°40N 77°20W **77 A3**
Moulton *AL*. . . . . . 34°29N 87°18W **60 B3**
Moulton *IA*. . . . . . 40°41N 92°41W **73 E6**
Moulton *TX*. . . . . . 29°35N 97°9W **99 H10**
Moultonborough *NH* 43°45N 71°10W **86 C3**
Moultrie *GA*. . . . . 31°11N 83°47W **68 E3**
Moultrie, L. *SC*. . . . 33°20N 80°5W **90 E5**
Moultrie County ☆
   IL. . . . . 39°40N 88°35W **71 D5**
Mount Wolf *PA*. . . . 40°4N 76°43W **95 D6**
Mound Bayou *MS*. . 33°53N 90°44W **81 C3**
Mound City *IL*. . . . 37°5N 89°10W **71 F4**
Mound City *KS*. . . . 38°8N 94°49W **74 C9**
Mound City *MO*. . . 40°7N 95°14W **82 A1**
Mound City *SD*. . . . 45°44N 100°4W **91 E5**
Mound Valley *KS*. . . 37°12N 95°24W **74 D8**
Moundridge *KS*. . . 38°12N 97°31W **74 C6**
Mounds *IL*. . . . . . . 37°7N 89°12W **71 F4**
Mounds *OK*. . . . . . 35°53N 96°4W **93 C7**
Moundsville *WV*. . . 39°55N 80°44W **102 B5**
Moundville *AL*. . . . 33°1N 87°37W **60 C3**
Mount Airy *MD*. . . 39°22N 77°10W **77 A3**
Mount Airy *NC*. . . 36°31N 80°37W **90 B5**
Mount Airy Forest
   OH. . . . . 39°9N 84°34W **107 A2**
Mount Angel *OR*. . 45°4N 122°48W **94 B3**
Mount Auburn *IL*. . 39°46N 89°14W **71 D4**
Mount Ayr *IN*. . . . 40°57N 87°18W **72 C3**
Mount Ayr *IA*. . . . 40°43N 94°14W **73 E4**
Mount Baker Nat. Recr. Area ○
   WA. . . . . 47°44N 121°48W **101 C4**
Mount Baker-Snoqualmie Nat.
   Forest *WA*. . . . 48°10N 121°15W **101 B4**
Mount Bennett Hills
   ID. . . . . 43°13N 115°5W **70 F3**
Mount Blanchard
   OH. . . . . 40°54N 83°34W **92 C3**
Mount Calm *TX*. . . 31°46N 96°53W **99 F11**
Mount Carmel *IL*. . 38°25N 87°46W **71 E6**
Mount Carmel *PA*. . 40°47N 76°26W **95 D6**
Mount Carmel *UT*. . 37°15N 112°40W **100 F3**
Mount Carroll *IL*. . 42°6N 89°59W **71 A4**
Mount Clemens *MI*. 42°35N 82°53W **79 G9**
Mount Desert I. *ME*. 44°21N 68°20W **76 D5**
Mount Dora *FL*. . . 28°48N 81°38W **67 C7**
Mount Dora *NM*. . . 36°13N 103°29W **88 A7**
Mount Eaton *OH*. . 40°42N 81°43W **92 C5**
Mount Echo Park
   OH. . . . . 39°5N 84°33W **107 B1**
Mount Eden *KY*. . . 38°3N 85°9W **97 B7**
Mount Enterprise
   TX. . . . . 31°55N 94°41W **99 F13**
Mount Ephraim *NJ*. 39°52N 75°5W **116 B2**
Mount Erie *IL*. . . . 38°31N 88°14W **71 E5**
Mount Etna *IN*. . . 40°45N 85°34W **72 C5**
Mount Gay *WV*. . . 37°51N 82°1W **102 D2**
Mount Gilead *NC*. . 35°13N 80°0W **90 C6**
Mount Gilead *OH*. . 40°33N 82°50W **92 C4**
Mount Greenwood
   IL. . . . . 41°42N 87°42W **108 C2**
Mount Healthy *OH*. 39°14N 84°32W **107 A1**
Mount Holly *NC*. . . 35°18N 81°1W **90 C4**
Mount Holly *NJ*. . . 39°59N 74°47W **87 C2**
Mount Holly Springs
   PA. . . . . 40°7N 77°12W **95 D5**
Mount Hood Memorial Park
   MA. . . . . 42°26N 71°1W **106 A3**
Mount Hood Nat. Forest
   OR. . . . . 45°15N 122°0W **94 B4**
Mount Hope *KS*. . . 37°52N 97°40W **74 D6**
Mount Hope *WV*. . . 37°54N 81°10W **102 D3**
Mount Horeb *WI*. . . 43°1N 89°44W **103 E4**
Mount Ida *AR*. . . . 34°34N 93°38W **63 D2**
Mount Jackson *VA*. 38°45N 78°39W **77 B2**
Mount Jewett *PA*. . 41°44N 78°39W **95 C4**
Mount Joy *PA*. . . . 40°7N 76°30W **95 D6**
Mount Juliet *TN*. . . 36°12N 86°31W **96 D6**
Mount Ka'ala Nat. Area Reserve ○
   HI. . . . . 21°31N 158°9W **69 J13**
Mount Kisco *NY*. . . 41°12N 73°44W **87 A3**
Mount Laguna *CA*. . 32°52N 116°25W **65 L10**
Mount Lebanon *PA*. 40°23N 80°2W **116 B1**
Mount Liberty *OH*. . 40°21N 82°38W **92 C4**
Mount McGuire *ID*. 45°10N 114°36W **70 D4**
Mount McKinley = Denali Nat.
   Park and Preserve △
   AK. . . . . 63°30N 152°0W **61 E10**
Mount Moriah *MO*. . 40°20N 93°48W **82 A3**
Mount Morris *IL*. . 42°3N 89°26W **71 A4**
Mount Morris *MI*. . 43°7N 83°42W **79 F8**
Mount Morris L. *NY* 42°44N 77°52W **89 C3**
Mount Nebo *PA*. . . 39°53N 76°20W **77 A4**
Mount Olive *IL*. . . 39°4N 89°44W **71 D4**
Mount Olive *MS*. . . 31°46N 89°39W **81 E4**
Mount Olive *NC*. . . 35°12N 78°4W **90 C7**
Mount Olivet *KY*. . 38°32N 84°2W **97 B8**
Mount Olympus
   UT. . . . . 40°41N 111°47W **117 B3**
Mount Olympus Wilderness
   WA. . . . . 47°48N 123°30W **101 C2**
Mount Orab *OH*. . . 39°2N 83°55W **92 D3**
Mount Pleasant *AR*. 35°58N 91°45W **63 C4**
Mount Pleasant *IA*. 40°58N 91°33W **73 E7**
Mount Pleasant *MI*. 43°36N 84°46W **79 F7**
Mount Pleasant *MS*. 34°56N 89°31W **81 B4**
Mount Pleasant *NC*. 35°24N 80°26W **90 C5**
Mount Pleasant *PA*. 40°9N 79°33W **95 D3**
Mount Pleasant *SC*. 32°47N 79°52W **90 F6**
Mount Pleasant *TN*. 35°32N 87°12W **96 E5**
Mount Pleasant *TX*. 33°9N 94°58W **99 D13**
Mount Pleasant
   UT. . . . . 39°33N 111°27W **100 D4**
Mount Pocono *PA*. . 41°7N 75°22W **87 A1**
Mount Prospect *IL*. 42°4N 87°56W **71 A6**
Mount Pulaski *IL*. . 40°1N 89°17W **71 C4**
Mount Rainier *MD*. 38°56N 76°57W **119 B4**
Mount Rainier Nat. Park ○
   WA. . . . . 46°52N 121°50W **101 D4**
Mount Rushmore Nat. Memorial △
   SD. . . . . 43°53N 103°27W **91 G2**

Mount St. Helens Nat. Volcanic
   Monument ○
   WA. . . . . 46°14N 122°11W **101 D3**
Mount Savage *MD*. . 39°42N 78°53W **77 A2**
Mount Shasta *CA*. . 41°19N 122°19W **64 B4**
Mount Snow Resort
   VT. . . . . 42°58N 72°54W **86 D2**
Mount Solon *VA*. . . 38°21N 79°5W **102 C5**
Mount Sterling *IL*. . 39°59N 90°45W **71 D3**
Mount Sterling *KY*. 38°4N 83°56W **97 B9**
Mount Sterling *OH*. 39°43N 83°16W **92 D3**
Mount Storm *WV*. . 39°17N 79°15W **77 A1**
Mount Storm L. *WV* 39°13N 79°16W **77 A1**
Mount Summit *IN*. . 40°0N 85°22W **72 C5**
Mount Sunapee *NH*. 43°19N 72°6W **86 C2**
Mount Tabor Park
   OR. . . . . 45°30N 122°35W **116 A2**
Mount Union *IA*. . . 41°3N 91°23W **73 D7**
Mount Union *PA*. . . 40°23N 77°53W **95 D5**
Mount Vernon *AL*. . 31°5N 88°1W **60 E2**
Mount Vernon *GA*. . 32°11N 82°36W **68 D4**
Mount Vernon *IL*. . 38°19N 88°55W **71 E5**
Mount Vernon *IN*. . 37°56N 87°54W **72 F3**
Mount Vernon *IA*. . 41°55N 91°23W **73 D7**
Mount Vernon *KY*. . 37°21N 84°21W **97 C8**
Mount Vernon *MO*. 37°6N 93°49W **82 D3**
Mount Vernon *NY*. 40°54N 73°49W **114 A4**
Mount Vernon *OH*. 40°23N 82°29W **92 C4**
Mount Vernon *SD*. 43°43N 98°16W **91 G7**
Mount Vernon *TN*. 35°25N 84°22W **97 E8**
Mount Vernon *TX*. 33°11N 95°13W **99 D12**
Mount Vernon *WA*. 48°25N 122°20W **101 B3**
Mount Washington
   KY. . . . . 39°5N 84°22W **107 B2**
Mount Washington Cog Railway
   NH. . . . . 44°17N 71°21W **86 B3**
Mount Zion *IL*. . . . 39°46N 88°53W **71 D5**
Mountain *ND*. . . . . 48°41N 97°52W **91 B8**
Mountain *WI*. . . . . 45°12N 88°28W **103 C5**
Mountain Brook *AL*. 33°30N 86°45W **60 C4**
Mountain City *GA*. . 34°55N 83°23W **68 B3**
Mountain City *NV*. . 41°50N 115°58W **85 A5**
Mountain City *TN*. . 36°29N 81°48W **97 D11**
Mountain Creek *AL*. 32°43N 86°29W **60 D4**
Mountain Creek Lake Park
   TX. . . . . 32°43N 96°56W **109 B4**
Mountain Grove *MO*. 37°8N 92°16W **82 D4**
Mountain Home *AR*. 36°20N 92°23W **63 B3**
Mountain Home *ID*. 43°8N 115°41W **70 F3**
Mountain Home *NC*. 35°23N 82°30W **90 C3**
Mountain Home *TX*. 30°10N 99°22W **99 G8**
Mountain Home Air Force Base
   ID. . . . . 43°3N 115°51W **70 F3**
Mountain Iron *MN*. 47°32N 92°37W **80 C6**
Mountain Lake *MN*. 43°57N 94°56W **80 G4**
Mountain Lake Park
   MD. . . . . 39°24N 79°23W **77 A1**
Mountain Meadows Res.
   CA. . . . . 40°17N 120°49W **64 C6**
Mountain Park *OK*. 34°42N 98°57W **93 D5**
Mountain Pine *AR*. 34°34N 93°10W **63 D2**
Mountain View *AR*. 35°52N 92°7W **63 C3**
Mountain View *CA*. 37°23N 122°5W **64 F4**
Mountain View *HI*. 19°33N 155°7W **69 D6**
Mountain View *MO*. 36°59N 91°47W **82 D5**
Mountain View *NJ*. 40°55N 74°15W **114 A1**
Mountain View *OK*. 35°5N 98°45W **93 C5**
Mountain View
   WY. . . . . 41°16N 110°20W **104 E2**
Mountain Village *AK* 62°5N 163°43W **61 E7**
Mountainair *NM*. . . 34°31N 106°15W **88 C4**
Mountainaire *AZ*. . 35°9N 111°40W **62 B4**
Mountainburg *AR*. . 35°38N 94°10W **63 C1**
Mountlake Terrace
   WA. . . . . 47°47N 122°18W **118 B3**
Mountrail County ☆
   ND. . . . . 48°10N 102°30W **91 B3**
Mousie *KY*. . . . . . 37°25N 82°53W **97 C10**
Moville *IA*. . . . . . 42°29N 96°4W **73 C2**
Moweaqua *IL*. . . . . 39°38N 89°1W **71 D4**
Mower County ☆
   MN. . . . . 43°40N 92°45W **80 G6**
Mowrystown *OH*. . 39°2N 83°45W **92 D3**
Moxee City *WA*. . . 46°33N 120°23W **101 D5**
Moxox *OK*. . . . . . 34°19N 95°30W **93 D8**
Moyie Springs *ID*. . 48°44N 116°11W **70 A2**
Moylie *ID*. . . . . . . 48°43N 116°11W **70 A2**
Muckalee Cr. → *GA*. 31°38N 84°9W **68 E2**
Mud → *KY*. . . . . . 37°13N 86°54W **96 C6**
Mud Butte *SD*. . . . 45°0N 102°54W **91 F3**
Mud Cr. → *OK*. . . . 33°55N 97°28W **93 E6**
Mud Cr. → *SD*. . . . 43°55N 99°28W **91 G6**
Mud L. *FL*. . . . . . . 28°23N 81°17W **115 B3**
Mud L. *MN*. . . . . . 37°52N 117°4W **85 E3**
Mud Lake Res. *SD*. 45°47N 98°15W **91 E7**
Muddy → *NV*. . . . . 36°31N 114°24W **85 F6**
Muddy Boggy Cr. →
   OK. . . . . 34°3N 95°47W **93 D8**
Muddy Cr. → *UT*. . 38°24N 110°42W **100 E4**
Muddy Cr. → *WY* 41°35N 109°58W **104 E3**
Muddy Creek Res.
   CO. . . . . 37°45N 103°15W **66 E7**
Muddy Gap *WY*. . . 42°22N 107°28W **104 D5**
Muddy Mts. *NV*. . . 36°24N 114°39W **85 F6**
Muenster *TX*. . . . . 33°39N 97°23W **99 D10**
Muhlenberg County ☆
   KY. . . . . 37°10N 87°10W **96 C5**
Muir *MI*. . . . . 43°0N 84°56W **79 G7**
Muir Beach *CA*. . . 37°51N 122°34W **118 A1**
Muir Woods Nat. Monument ○
   CA. . . . . 37°55N 122°35W **118 A1**
Mukilteo *WA*. . . . . 47°57N 122°18W **101 C1**
Mukwonago *WI*. . . 42°52N 88°20W **103 F5**
Mulberry *AR*. . . . . 35°30N 94°3W **63 C1**
Mulberry *FL*. . . . . 27°54N 81°59W **67 D7**
Mulberry *IN*. . . . . 40°21N 86°40W **72 C4**
Mulberry *NC*. . . . . 36°14N 81°11W **90 B4**
Mulberry Fork →
   AL. . . . . 33°33N 87°11W **60 C3**
Mulberry Grove *IL*. 38°56N 89°16W **71 E4**
Mulchatna → *AK*. . 59°40N 157°7W **61 G8**
Muldraugh *KY*. . . . 37°56N 85°59W **97 B7**
Muldrow *OK*. . . . . 35°24N 94°36W **93 C9**
Mule Creek *NM*. . . 33°7N 108°57W **88 D2**
Mule Creek Junction
   WY. . . . . 43°23N 104°13W **104 C8**
Muleshoe *TX*. . . . . 34°13N 102°43W **98 D5**
Muleshoe Nat. Wildlife Refuge △
   TX. . . . . 33°58N 102°44W **98 D5**
Mulford Gardens
   CA. . . . . 37°42N 122°10W **118 B3**
Mulhall *OK*. . . . . . 35°55N 97°24W **93 C6**
Mullan *ID*. . . . . . . 47°28N 115°48W **70 B3**
Mullen *NE*. . . . . . 42°3N 101°1W **84 B4**
Mullett Lake *MI*. . . 45°31N 84°31W **79 D7**
Mullett L. *MI*. . . . . 45°31N 84°31W **79 D7**
Mullica → *NJ*. . . . 39°33N 74°25W **87 C2**
Mullins *SC*. . . . . . 34°12N 79°15W **90 D6**
Mullinville *KS*. . . . 37°35N 99°29W **74 D4**
Multnomah County ☆
   OR. . . . . 45°30N 122°10W **94 B3**

Mulvane *KS*. . . . . 37°29N 97°15W **74 D6**
Muncie *IN*. . . . . . . 40°12N 85°23W **72 C5**
Muncy *PA*. . . . . . . 41°12N 76°47W **95 C6**
Mundelein *IL*. . . . . 42°16N 88°0W **71 A5**
Munden *KS*. . . . . . 39°55N 97°32W **74 B6**
Munford *TN*. . . . . 35°27N 89°49W **96 E3**
Munfordville *KY*. . . 37°16N 85°54W **97 C7**
Munhall *PA*. . . . . . 40°23N 79°54W **116 B2**
Munich *ND*. . . . . . 48°40N 98°50W **91 B7**
Municipal Park *MN*. 44°52N 93°22W **113 B1**
Munising *MI*. . . . . 46°25N 86°40W **79 C5**
Munnerlyn *GA*. . . . 38°49N 99°16W **74 C4**
Munnsville *NY*. . . . 42°59N 75°35W **89 C5**
Munson *FL*. . . . . . 30°52N 86°52W **67 A2**
Munsungan L. *ME*. . 46°22N 69°0W **76 B5**
Murdo *SD*. . . . . . . 43°53N 100°43W **91 G5**
Murdock *IL*. . . . . . 39°37N 97°56W **74 D6**
Murdock *MN*. . . . . 45°13N 95°24W **80 E3**
Murdock Peak *UT*. . 40°41N 111°36W **117 B4**
Murfreesboro *AR*. . 34°4N 93°41W **63 D2**
Murfreesboro *NC*. . 36°27N 77°6W **90 B8**
Murfreesboro *TN*. . 35°51N 86°24W **96 E6**
Murphy *ID*. . . . . . 43°13N 116°33W **70 F2**
Murphy *MO*. . . . . 38°29N 90°29W **82 C6**
Murphy *NC*. . . . . . 35°5N 84°2W **90 C1**
Murphy's Station = Sunnyvale
   CA. . . . . 37°23N 122°2W **64 F4**
Murphysboro *IL*. . . 37°46N 89°20W **71 F4**
Murray *IA*. . . . . . . 41°3N 93°57W **73 D5**
Murray *KY*. . . . . . 36°37N 88°19W **96 D4**
Murray *UT*. . . . . . 40°40N 111°53W **117 C2**
Murray, L. *OK*. . . . 34°2N 97°3W **93 D6**
Murray, L. *SC*. . . . 34°3N 81°13W **90 D4**
Murray City *OH*. . . 39°29N 82°9W **92 D4**
Murray County ☆
   GA. . . . . 34°50N 84°45W **68 B2**
Murray County ☆ *MN* 44°0N 95°45W **80 F3**
Murray County ☆ *OK* 34°30N 97°0W **93 D6**
Murrayville *IL*. . . . 39°35N 90°15W **71 D3**
Murrells Inlet *SC*. . 33°33N 79°2W **90 E6**
Murtaugh *ID*. . . . . 42°30N 114°10W **70 G4**
Murvaul L. *TX*. . . . 32°2N 94°29W **99 E13**
Muscatatuck → *IN*. 38°50N 85°50W **72 E5**
Muscatatuck Nat. Wildlife
   Refuge △ *IN*. . . 38°56N 85°49W **72 E5**
Muscatine *IA*. . . . . 41°25N 91°3W **73 D7**
Muscatine County ☆
   IA. . . . . 41°30N 91°0W **73 D7**
Muscle Shoals *AL*. . 34°45N 87°40W **60 B3**
Muscoda *WI*. . . . . 43°11N 90°27W **103 E3**
Muscogee County ☆
   GA. . . . . 32°30N 84°58W **68 D2**
Muscotcong → *NJ*. 40°36N 75°11W **87 B1**
Muscotah *KS*. . . . . 39°33N 95°31W **74 B8**
Musella *GA*. . . . . . 32°48N 84°2W **68 D2**
Muskeg B. *MN*. . . . 48°55N 95°10W **80 B3**
Muskeget Channel
   MA. . . . . 41°25N 70°25W **78 C4**
Muskego *WI*. . . . . 42°55N 88°8W **103 F5**
Muskegon *MI*. . . . 43°14N 86°16W **79 F5**
Muskegon → *MI*. . 43°14N 86°21W **79 F5**
Muskegon County ☆
   MI. . . . . 43°15N 86°15W **79 F5**
Muskegon Heights
   MI. . . . . 43°12N 86°16W **79 F5**
Muskingum → *OH*. 39°30N 81°59W **92 C4**
Muskingum County ☆
   OH. . . . . 39°56N 82°1W **92 D4**
Muskogee *OK*. . . . 35°45N 95°22W **93 C8**
Muskogee County ☆
   OK. . . . . 35°35N 95°25W **93 C8**
Muskrat Cr. → *WY*. 43°9N 108°12W **104 C4**
Mussel Fork → *MO*. 39°26N 92°57W **82 B4**
Musselshell → *MT*. 47°21N 107°57W **83 C10**
Musselshell County ☆
   MT. . . . . 46°35N 108°30W **83 D9**
Mustang *OK*. . . . . 35°23N 97°44W **93 C6**
Mustang Draw →
   TX. . . . . 31°58N 102°40W **98 F5**
Mustang I. *TX*. . . . 27°52N 97°9W **99 K10**
Mustinka → *MN*. . . 45°45N 96°38W **80 E2**
Mutual *ID*. . . . . . . 40°5N 83°38W **92 C3**
Mutual *OK*. . . . . . 36°14N 99°9W **93 B4**
Muzon, C. *AK*. . . . 54°40N 132°42W **61 J14**
Myakka → *FL*. . . . 26°56N 82°11W **67 E6**
Myakka City *FL*. . . 27°21N 82°10W **67 D6**
Myerstown *PA*. . . . 40°22N 76°19W **95 D6**
Mylo *ND*. . . . . . . 48°38N 99°37W **91 B6**
Myrick *MS*. . . . . . 34°34N 89°7W **81 E4**
Myrtle *MS*. . . . . . 36°31N 91°16W **82 E5**
Myrtle *WV*. . . . . . 37°46N 82°12W **102 D2**
Myrtle Beach *SC*. . 33°42N 78°53W **90 E7**
Myrtle Creek *FL*. . . 30°23N 87°17W **67 A1**
Myrtle Creek *OR*. . 43°1N 123°17W **94 D2**
Myrtle Grove *NC*. . 34°7N 77°53W **90 D8**
Myrtle Point *OR*. . 43°4N 124°8W **94 D1**
Myrtlewood *AL*. . . 32°16N 87°57W **60 D3**
Mystic *CT*. . . . . . 41°21N 71°58W **78 C3**
Mystic *IA*. . . . . . . 40°47N 92°57W **73 E6**
Mystic Island *NJ*. . 39°34N 74°22W **87 C2**
Mystic Seaport *CT*. 41°21N 71°58W **78 C3**
Myton *UT*. . . . . . . 40°12N 110°4W **100 C5**

N

N.A.S.A. Michoud Facility
   LA. . . . . 30°1N 89°55W **113 B3**
N.A.S.A. Space Center = John C.
   Stennis Space Center
   MS. . . . . 30°23N 89°37W **81 F4**
N.A.S.A. Wallops I.
   VA. . . . . 37°52N 75°30W **102 D9**
Nā'ālehu *HI*. . . . . . 19°4N 155°35W **69 D4**
Nabesna *AK*. . . . . 62°22N 143°0W **61 E12**
Naches *WA*. . . . . . 46°44N 120°31W **101 D5**
Naches → *WA*. . . . 46°38N 120°31W **101 D5**
Nacimiento, L. *CA*. 35°46N 120°53W **65 H6**
Naco *AZ*. . . . . . . 31°21N 109°57W **62 E6**
Nacogdoches *TX*. . 31°36N 94°39W **99 F13**
Nacogdoches County ☆
   TX. . . . . 31°35N 94°40W **99 F13**
Nadeau *MI*. . . . . . 45°39N 87°37W **79 D4**
Naftan Pt. *N. Marianas* 15°5N 145°45E **105 c**
Nagai I. *AK*. . . . . . 55°5N 160°0W **61 J8**
Nageezi *NM*. . . . . 36°16N 107°45W **88 A4**
Nags Head *NC*. . . . 35°57N 75°38W **90 C10**
Naguabo
   Puerto Rico. . . . 18°13N 65°44W **105 G17**
Nahant *MA*. . . . . . 42°25N 70°54W **106 A4**
Nahant B. *MA*. . . . 42°26N 70°54W **106 A4**
Nahant Harbor *MA*. 42°25N 70°56W **106 A4**
Nahma *MI*. . . . . . 45°50N 86°40W **79 D5**
Nahunta *GA*. . . . . 31°12N 81°59W **68 E5**
Nain *LA*. . . . . 39°14N 78°12W **77 A1**
Nairn *LA*. . . . . . . 29°26N 89°37W **75 E6**
Nakalele Pt. *HI*. . . 21°2N 156°35W **69 B5**
Naknek *AK*. . . . . . 58°44N 157°1W **61 G8**
Nallen *WV*. . . . . . 38°2N 80°53W **102 C4**
Nambe Indian Reservation
   NM. . . . . 35°52N 105°52W **88 B5**
Namekagon → *WI*. 45°5N 92°50W **80 D6**
Nampa *ID*. . . . . . . 43°34N 116°34W **70 F2**
Nānākuli *HI*. . . . . 21°24N 158°9W **69 K13**
Nance County ☆ *NE* 41°25N 98°0W **84 C8**
Nancy *KY*. . . . . . . 37°4N 84°45W **97 C8**

Nanjemoy MD ..... 38°27N 77°13W 77 B3
Nantahala Nat. Forest NC ...... 35°15N 83°30W 90 C2
Nantasket Beach MA ...... 42°16N 70°52W 106 B4
Nanticoke MD .. 38°16N 75°54W 77 B5
Nanticoke PA .... 41°12N 76°0W 95 C6
Nanticoke → MD .. 38°16N 75°56W 77 C5
Nantucket MA .... 41°17N 70°6W 78 C4
Nantucket County ☆ MA .... 41°15N 70°5W 78 C4
Nantucket Harbor MA 41°17N 70°5W 78 C4
Nantucket I. MA .. 41°16N 70°5W 78 C4
Nantucket Sd. MA .. 41°18N 70°15W 78 C4
Nanty Glo PA .... 40°28N 78°50W 95 D4
Naomi Peak UT .. 41°55N 111°41W 100 B4
Napa CA ...... 38°18N 122°17W 64 E4
Napa County ☆ CA 38°30N 122°20W 64 E4
Napaimiut AK .... 61°33N 158°42W 61 F8
Napakiak AK .... 60°42N 161°57W 61 F7
Napali Coast HI .. 22°11N 159°39W 69 A2
Napaskiak A .... 60°43N 161°55W 61 F7
Napavine WA .... 46°35N 122°54W 101 D3
Naper NE ...... 42°58N 99°6W 84 B6
Naperville IL .... 41°46N 88°9W 71 B5
Napili-Honokowai HI ...... 20°58N 156°39W 69 C3
Naples FL ...... 26°8N 81°48W 67 E7
Naples ID ...... 48°34N 116°24W 70 A2
Naples NY .... 42°37N 77°24W 89 C3
Naples TX .... 33°12N 94°41W 99 C13
Naples UT .... 40°26N 109°30W 100 C6
Naples Park FL .. 26°17N 81°46W 67 E7
Napoleon IN .... 39°12N 85°20W 72 D5
Napoleon ND .... 46°30N 99°46W 91 D6
Napoleon OH .... 41°23N 84°8W 92 B2
Napoleon NE .... 40°5N 99°9W 84 D6
Nappanee IN .... 41°27N 86°0W 72 B5
Nara Visa NM .... 35°37N 103°6W 98 B7
Narberth PA .... 40°0N 75°13W 116 A1
Nardin OK .... 36°47N 97°27W 93 B6
Narka KS .... 39°58N 97°25W 74 B6
Narragansett Bay RI. 41°36N 71°19W 78 C3
Narragansett Pier RI 41°26N 71°12W 78 C3
Narrows ...... 37°20N 80°49W 102 E4
Narrows, The N .. 40°37N 74°3W 114 C2
Naruna VA ...... 37°6N 79°9W 102 D6
Naschitti NM .... 36°4N 108°41W 88 A2
Naselle WA ...... 46°22N 123°49W 101 D2
Nash OK .... 36°40N 98°3W 93 B5
Nash County ☆ NC .. 36°0N 78°0W 90 B8
Nash Stream Forest NH ...... 44°42N 71°25W 86 B3
Nashawena I. MA .. 41°26N 70°53W 78 C4
Nashoba OK .... 34°29N 95°13W 93 D8
Nashua IA .... 42°57N 92°32W 73 C6
Nashua MN .... 46°2N 96°19W 80 D2
Nashua MT .... 48°8N 106°22W 83 B11
Nashua NH .... 42°45N 71°28W 86 D3
Nashville AR .... 33°57N 93°51W 63 E2
Nashville GA .... 31°12N 83°15W 68 E3
Nashville IL .... 38°21N 89°23W 71 E4
Nashville IN .... 39°12N 86°15W 72 D4
Nashville KS .... 37°26N 98°25W 74 C5
Nashville MI .... 42°36N 85°5W 79 G6
Nashville MO .... 37°23N 94°30W 82 D2
Nashville NC .... 35°58N 77°58W 90 C8
Nashville OH .... 40°36N 82°7W 92 C4
Nashville TN .... 36°10N 86°47W 96 D6
Nashville ✈ (BNA) TN ...... 36°7N 86°41W 96 D6
Nashwauk MN .... 47°23N 93°10W 80 C5
Nassau MN .... 45°4N 96°26W 80 B2
Nassau NY .... 42°31N 73°37W 78 B1
Nassau County ☆ FL 30°40N 81°45W 67 A7
Nassau County ☆ NY 40°45N 73°10W 89 E7
Nassawadox VA .. 37°28N 75°52W 102 D9
Natalbany LA .... 30°20N 90°30W 75 D3
Natalia TX .... 29°11N 98°50W 99 H9
Natchez Nat. Historical Park ○ MS .... 31°30N 91°23W 81 E2
Natchez LA .... 31°41N 93°3W 75 C2
Natchez MS .... 31°34N 91°24W 81 E2
Natchez Trace Parkway U.S.A. .... 31°37N 91°16W 81 D3
Natchez Trace State Park ○ TN ...... 35°47N 88°17W 96 E4
Natchitoches LA .. 31°46N 93°5W 75 C2
Natchitoches Parish ☆ LA .... 31°41N 93°3W 75 C2
Nathrop CO .... 38°45N 106°5W 66 D4
Natick MA .... 42°16N 71°19W 106 B2
National Arboretum DC .... 38°54N 76°59W 119 B3
National Bison Range ○ MT .... 47°20N 114°14W 83 C3
National City CA .. 32°40N 117°5W 117 B2
National Elk Refuge ○ WY .... 43°38N 110°35W 104 C2
National Key Deer Refuge ○ FL .... 24°43N 81°30W 67 G7
National Zoological Park ○ DC .... 38°55N 77°4W 119 B3
Natoma KS .... 39°11N 99°2W 74 B4
Natrona WY .... 43°2N 104°49W 104 C8
Natrona County ☆ WY .... 43°0N 107°0W 104 D6
Natrona Heights PA. 40°37N 79°43W 95 D3
Natural Bridge AL .. 34°6N 87°36W 60 B3
Natural Bridge VA .. 37°38N 79°33W 102 D5
Natural Bridges Nat. UT .... 37°36N 110°0W 100 F5
Naturita CO .... 38°14N 108°34W 66 D2
Naubinway MI .... 46°6N 85°27W 79 C6
Naugatuck IN .... 41°30N 73°3W 78 C1
Naugatuck → CT .. 41°18N 73°7W 78 C1
Nauvoo AL .... 33°59N 87°29W 60 B3
Nauvoo IL .... 40°33N 91°23W 71 C2
Navajo AZ .... 35°7N 109°32W 62 B6
Navajo NM .... 35°54N 109°2W 88 B1
Navajo Co. → AZ .. 36°59N 111°24W 62 A4
Navajo County ☆ AZ 36°0N 110°20W 62 B5
Navajo Indian Reservation AZ .... 36°0N 110°0W 62 B6
Navajo Mt. UT .... 37°2N 110°52W 100 F5
Navajo Nat. Monument ○ AZ .... 36°41N 110°32W 62 A5
Navajo Res. NM .. 36°48N 107°36W 88 A3
Navarre FL .... 30°24N 86°52W 67 A2
Navarre OH .... 40°43N 81°31W 78 C4
Navarro → CA .... 39°11N 123°45W 64 D3
Navarro County ☆ TX .... 32°6N 96°28W 99 E11
Navarro Mills L. TX .. 31°57N 96°42W 99 F11
Navasota TX .... 30°23N 96°5W 99 G11
Navasota → TX .... 30°21N 96°10W 99 G11
Navidad → TX .... 28°50N 96°35W 99 J11
Navy Pier IL .... 41°53N 87°36W 108 B3
Naylor MO .... 36°34N 90°36W 82 E6
Nazareth PA .... 40°44N 75°19W 87 B2
Nazareth TX .... 34°33N 102°6W 98 C5
Neah Bay WA .... 48°22N 124°37W 101 B1
Neal MO .... 37°50N 96°5W 74 D7
Neal Smith Nat. Wildlife Refuge ○ IA .... 41°35N 93°15W 73 D5
Near Is. AK .... 52°30N 174°0E 61 K1
Nebo LA .... 31°35N 92°9W 75 C3
Nebo, Mt. UT .... 39°49N 111°46W 100 D4
Nebraska □ U.S.A. 41°30N 99°30W 84 C6

Nebraska City NE .. 40°41N 95°52W 84 D10
Nebraska Nat. Forest NE ...... 42°45N 103°10W 84 B2
Necedah WI .... 44°2N 90°4W 103 D3
Necedah Nat. Wildlife Refuge ○ WI .... 44°9N 90°11W 103 D3
Neche ND .... 48°59N 97°33W 91 B8
Neches → TX .... 29°58N 93°51W 99 H14
Necker I. HI .... 23°35N 164°42W 69 G11
Nederland CO .... 39°58N 105°31W 66 C5
Nederland TX .... 29°59N 94°0W 99 H12
Needham MA .... 41°27N 71°14W 106 B2
Needham Heights MA .... 42°17N 71°14W 106 B2
Needle Range UT .. 38°25N 113°55W 100 E2
Needles CA .... 34°51N 114°37W 65 J12
Needmore GA .... 30°41N 82°43W 68 F4
Needmore PA .... 39°51N 78°9W 77 A2
Needmore TX .... 34°2N 102°45W 98 C5
Needville TX .... 29°24N 95°50W 99 H12
Neely MS .... 31°10N 88°45W 81 E5
Neelyville MO .... 36°34N 90°30W 82 E6
Neenah WI .... 44°11N 88°28W 103 D5
Negaunee MI .... 46°30N 87°36W 79 C4
Negreet LA .... 31°28N 93°35W 75 C2
Nehalem OR .... 45°43N 123°54W 94 B2
Nehalem → OR .. 45°40N 123°56W 94 B2
Nehawka NE .... 40°50N 95°59W 84 D10
Neihart MT .... 46°56N 110°44W 83 D7
Neillsville WI .... 44°34N 90°36W 103 D3
Nekoma KS .... 38°28N 99°27W 74 C4
Nekoma ND .... 48°35N 98°22W 91 B7
Nekoosa WI .... 44°19N 89°54W 103 D4
Neligh NE .... 42°8N 98°2W 84 B7
Nellis Air Force Base NV .... 36°14N 115°2W 110 B2
Nellis Air Force Range Complex NV .... 37°15N 116°30W 85 E4
Nelson AZ .... 35°31N 113°19W 62 B2
Nelson MO .... 38°59N 93°3W 82 C3
Nelson NE .... 40°12N 98°4W 84 D7
Nelson NV .... 35°42N 114°49W 85 G6
Nelson WI .... 44°25N 92°0W 103 D2
Nelson County ☆ KY. 37°50N 85°30W 97 C7
Nelson County ☆ ND. 48°0N 98°5W 91 C7
Nelson County ☆ VA .... 37°50N 78°52W 102 D6
Nelson Res. MT .. 48°32N 107°31W 83 B10
Nelsonville OH .. 39°28N 82°13W 92 D4
Nemah WA .... 46°31N 123°53W 101 D2
Nemaha IA .... 42°31N 95°6W 73 C3
Nemaha NE .... 40°20N 95°41W 84 D10
Nemaha County ☆ KS 39°45N 96°0W 74 B8
Nemaha County ☆ NE .... 40°20N 95°45W 84 D10
Nenana AK .... 64°34N 149°5W 61 D10
Nenzel NE .... 42°56N 101°6W 84 B4
Neodesha KS .... 37°25N 95°41W 74 D8
Neoga IL .... 39°19N 88°27W 71 D5
Neola IA .... 41°27N 95°37W 73 D3
Neola UT .... 40°26N 110°2W 100 C5
Neopit WI .... 44°59N 88°50W 103 D5
Neosho MO .... 36°52N 94°22W 82 E2
Neosho → OK .... 36°48N 95°18W 93 B8
Neosho County ☆ KS .... 37°30N 95°15W 74 D8
Neosho Falls KS .. 37°59N 95°33W 74 D8
Neosho Rapids KS .. 38°22N 95°54W 74 C8
Neppel = Moses Lake WA .... 47°8N 119°17W 101 C6
Neptune NJ .... 40°13N 74°2W 87 B2
Neptune Beach FL .. 30°19N 81°24W 67 A7
Nerstrand MN .... 44°20N 93°4W 80 F5
Nesbit MS .... 34°53N 90°1W 81 C2
Neshaminy Cr. → PA 40°8N 74°53W 116 A5
Neshanic WI .... 43°58N 89°13W 103 E4
Neshkoro WI .... 32°37N 89°8W 81 D4
Neshoba County ☆ MS .... 32°46N 89°7W 81 D4
Nesquehoning PA .. 40°52N 75°48W 87 B2
Ness City KS .... 38°27N 99°54W 74 C4
Ness County ☆ KS .. 38°30N 100°0W 74 C4
Netarts OR .... 45°26N 123°57W 94 B2
Netawaka KS .... 39°36N 95°43W 74 B8
Netcong NJ .... 40°54N 74°42W 87 B2
Nett L. MN .... 48°7N 93°7W 80 B5
Nettleton MS .... 34°5N 88°37W 81 B5
Nettleton TX .... 34°23N 88°45W 103 D5
Neuville TX .... 31°41N 94°9W 99 F13
Nevada IA .... 42°1N 93°27W 73 C5
Nevada MO .... 37°51N 94°22W 82 D2
Nevada □ U.S.A. .. 39°0N 117°0W 85 C4
Nevada City CA .. 39°16N 121°1W 64 D5
Nevada County ☆ AR .... 33°36N 93°17W 63 E2
Nevada County ☆ CA .... 39°15N 121°0W 64 D6
Neversink → NY .. 41°21N 74°42W 89 D6
Neversink Res. NY .. 41°48N 74°42W 89 D6
Nevis MS .... 46°58N 94°51W 80 D4
New → FL .... 29°50N 84°40W 67 B4
New → NC .... 34°32N 77°20W 90 D8
New → TN .... 36°25N 84°37W 97 D8
New → WV .... 38°10N 81°12W 102 C3
New Albany IN .... 38°18N 85°49W 72 E5
New Albany KS .... 37°34N 95°56W 74 D8
New Albany MS .... 34°29N 89°0W 81 B5
New Albany PA .... 41°36N 76°27W 95 C6
New Albin IA .... 43°30N 91°17W 73 B7
New Alluwe OK .... 36°37N 95°29W 93 B8
New Almelo KS .... 39°36N 100°7W 74 B3
New Athens IL .... 38°19N 89°53W 71 E4
New Athens OH .... 40°11N 81°0W 92 C5
New Auburn WI .... 45°12N 91°33W 103 C2
New Augusta MS .... 31°12N 89°2W 81 E4
New Baden IL .... 38°32N 89°42W 71 E4
New Baltimore MI .. 42°41N 82°44W 79 G9
New Baltimore PA .. 39°59N 78°46W 95 E4
New Barbadoes = Hackensack NJ .... 40°52N 74°4W 114 A2
New Bavaria OH .. 41°12N 84°10W 92 B2
New Bedford MA .. 41°38N 70°56W 78 C4
New Berlin = North Canton OH .... 40°53N 81°24W 92 C5
New Berlin IL .... 39°44N 89°55W 71 C4
New Berlin NY .... 42°37N 75°20W 89 C5
New Berlin WI .... 42°59N 88°6W 103 F5
New Bern NC .... 35°7N 77°3W 90 C8
New Bethlehem PA .. 41°0N 79°20W 95 D3
New Bloomfield MO .. 38°43N 92°5W 82 C4
New Bloomfield PA .. 40°25N 77°11W 95 D5
New Boston IL .... 41°10N 91°0W 71 B3
New Boston NH .... 42°58N 71°41W 86 D3
New Boston OH .... 38°45N 82°56W 92 E4
New Boston TX .... 33°28N 94°25W 99 D13
New Braunfels TX .. 29°42N 98°8W 99 H9
New Bremen OH .. 40°26N 84°23W 92 C2
New Brighton MN .. 45°3N 93°12W 113 A2
New Brighton NY .. 40°38N 74°5W 114 C2
New Britain CT .... 41°40N 72°47W 78 C1
New Brockland = West Columbia SC .... 33°59N 81°4W 90 E4
New Brockton AL .. 31°23N 85°56W 60 E5
New Brunswick NJ .. 40°30N 74°27W 87 B2
New Buffalo MI .... 41°47N 86°45W 79 H5
New Bullards Bar Dam CA .... 39°24N 121°8W 64 D5

New Cambria KS .. 38°53N 97°30W 74 C6
New Canaan CT .. 41°9N 73°30W 78 C1
New Carlisle OH .. 39°56N 84°2W 92 D2
New Carrollton MD 38°58N 76°53W 119 B4
New Castle CO .... 39°34N 107°32W 66 C3
New Castle DE .... 39°40N 75°34W 77 A5
New Castle IN .... 39°55N 85°22W 72 D5
New Castle KY .... 38°26N 85°10W 97 B7
New Castle PA .... 41°0N 80°21W 95 D2
New Castle TX .... 33°30N 87°7W 102 D4
New Castle County ☆ DE .... 39°30N 75°40W 77 A5
New Church VA .... 37°59N 75°32W 77 C5
New City NY .... 41°9N 73°59W 87 A3
New Concord KY .. 36°33N 88°9W 96 D4
New Concord OH .. 39°59N 81°44W 92 C5
New Cumberland WV .... 40°30N 80°36W 102 A4
New Deal TX .... 33°44N 101°50W 98 D6
New Don Pedro Res. CA .... 37°43N 120°24W 64 F6
New Dorp NY .... 40°34N 74°7W 114 C2
New Dorp Beach NY 40°33N 74°6W 114 C2
New Edinburg AR .. 33°46N 92°14W 63 E3
New Effington SD .. 45°51N 96°55W 91 C7
New Egypt NJ .... 40°4N 74°32W 87 B2
New Ellenton SC .. 33°28N 81°41W 90 E4
New England U.S.A. 35°0N 115°20W 65 H11
New England ND .. 46°32N 102°52W 91 D3
New Era MI .... 43°34N 86°21W 79 F5
New Fairfield CT .. 41°27N 73°14W 78 C1
New Florence MO .. 38°55N 91°27W 82 C5
New Florence PA .. 40°23N 79°5W 95 D3
New Fork Lakes WY .... 43°6N 109°57W 104 C3
New Franklin MO .. 39°1N 92°44W 82 B4
New Freedom PA .. 39°44N 76°42W 77 A4
New Glarus WI .... 42°49N 89°38W 103 F4
New Hampshire □ U.S.A... 44°0N 71°30W 86 C3
New Hampton IA .. 43°3N 92°19W 73 B6
New Hampton MO .. 40°16N 94°12W 82 A2
New Hampton NH .. 43°36N 71°39W 86 C3
New Hanover County ☆ NC .... 34°15N 77°50W 90 D8
New Harmony IN .. 38°8N 87°56W 72 E3
New Harmony UT .. 37°29N 113°19W 100 F2
New Hartford CT .. 41°53N 72°59W 78 C1
New Hartford IA .. 42°34N 92°37W 73 C6
New Hartford NY .. 43°4N 75°18W 89 C5
New Haven CT .... 41°18N 72°55W 78 C2
New Haven IL .... 37°55N 88°8W 71 F5
New Haven IN .... 41°4N 85°1W 72 B5
New Haven KY .... 37°40N 85°36W 97 C7
New Haven MI .... 42°44N 82°48W 79 G9
New Haven MO .... 38°37N 91°13W 82 C5
New Haven NY .... 43°29N 76°19W 89 B4
New Haven WV .... 38°59N 81°58W 102 C3
New Haven County ☆ CT .... 41°25N 72°50W 78 C2
New Hebron MS .. 31°44N 89°59W 81 E4
New Hogan L. CA .. 38°9N 120°49W 64 E6
New Holland OH .. 39°33N 83°15W 92 D3
New Holland PA .. 40°6N 76°5W 95 D6
New Holstein WI .. 43°57N 88°6W 103 E5
New Hope AL .... 34°32N 86°24W 60 B4
New Hope MN .... 45°2N 93°23W 113 A1
New Hope PA .... 40°22N 74°57W 87 B2
New Hyde Park NY 40°44N 73°41W 114 B4
New Iberia LA .... 30°1N 91°49W 75 D4
New Ipswich NH .. 42°46N 71°51W 86 D3
New Jersey □ U.S.A. 40°0N 74°30W 87 B2
New Johnsonville TN. 36°1N 87°58W 96 D5
New Kensington PA. 40°34N 79°46W 95 D3
New Kent VA .... 37°31N 76°59W 102 D8
New Kent County ☆ VA .... 37°31N 76°59W 102 D8
New L. NC .... 35°39N 76°22W 90 C9
New Leipzig ND .. 46°22N 101°57W 91 D4
New Lexington OH. 39°43N 82°13W 92 D4
New Lisbon WI .... 43°53N 90°10W 103 E3
New Llano LA .... 31°7N 93°16W 75 C2
New London CT .. 41°22N 72°6W 78 C2
New London IA .. 40°55N 91°24W 73 E7
New London MD .. 39°25N 77°16W 77 A3
New London MN .. 45°18N 94°56W 80 E4
New London OH .. 41°5N 82°24W 92 B4
New London WI .. 44°23N 88°45W 103 D5
New London County ☆ CT .... 41°30N 72°15W 78 C2
New Madison OH .. 39°58N 84°43W 92 D2
New Madrid MO .. 36°36N 89°32W 82 E7
New Madrid County ☆ MO .... 36°40N 89°35W 82 E7
New Market AL .... 34°55N 86°26W 60 B4
New Market IN .... 39°57N 86°55W 72 D4
New Market IA .... 40°44N 94°54W 73 E4
New Market MD .. 39°23N 77°16W 77 A3
New Market TN .... 36°6N 83°33W 97 D9
New Market VA .. 38°39N 78°40W 102 C6
New Marlborough MA 42°7N 73°14W 78 B1
New Martinsville WV .... 39°39N 80°52W 102 B4
New Matamoras OH. 39°31N 81°4W 102 C3
New Meadows ID .. 44°58N 116°18W 70 E2
New Melle MO .... 38°43N 90°53W 82 C5
New Melones L. CA. 37°57N 120°32W 64 F6
New Melones Dam CA .... 37°57N 120°31W 64 F6
New Mexico □ U.S.A... 34°30N 106°0W 88 C5
New Miami OH .... 39°26N 84°32W 92 D2
New Milford CT .. 41°35N 73°25W 78 C1
New Milford PA .. 41°52N 75°44W 95 C7
New Munich MN .. 45°38N 94°43W 80 E4
New Orleans LA .. 29°58N 90°4W 113 C2
New Orleans Int. ✈ (MSY) LA .... 30°0N 90°15W 113 C1
New Oxford PA .... 39°52N 77°4W 77 A3
New Paltz NY .... 41°45N 74°5W 89 D6
New Paris IN .... 41°30N 85°50W 72 B5
New Paris OH .... 39°51N 84°48W 92 D2
New Pekin IN .... 38°30N 86°0W 97 C5
New Philadelphia OH .... 40°30N 81°27W 92 C5
New Pine Creek OR. 42°0N 120°18W 94 E5
New Plymouth ID .. 43°58N 116°49W 70 F2
New Point VA .... 37°21N 76°17W 102 D8
New Port Richey FL. 28°16N 82°43W 67 C6
New Prague MN .. 44°32N 93°35W 80 F5
New Preston CT .. 41°40N 73°20W 78 C1
New Princeton OR. 43°15N 118°35W 94 D7
New Providence NJ. 40°42N 74°24W 87 B2
New Raymer CO .. 40°36N 103°51W 66 B7
New Richland MN .. 43°54N 93°30W 80 G5
New Richmond IN .. 40°12N 86°55W 72 C4
New Richmond OH. 38°57N 84°17W 92 E2
New Richmond WI .. 45°7N 92°32W 103 C1
New Riegel OH .... 41°4N 83°19W 92 B3
New River AZ .... 33°55N 112°8W 62 C4
New River FL .... 26°6N 80°6W 112 B3
New River → FL .. 26°6N 80°6W 112 B3
New River Gorge Nat. River ○ WV .... 38°5N 81°5W 102 D3
New Roads LA .... 30°42N 91°26W 75 D3
New Rochelle NY .. 40°55N 73°46W 114 A4
New Ross IN .... 40°7N 86°35W 72 C4
New Salem MA .... 42°30N 72°20W 78 B2
New Salem ND .... 46°51N 101°25W 91 D4
New Sharon IA .... 41°28N 92°39W 73 D6
New Smyrna Beach FL .... 29°1N 80°56W 67 B8

New Springville NY. 40°35N 74°9W 114 C2
New Straitsville OH. 39°35N 82°14W 92 D4
New Stuyahok AK .. 59°29N 157°20W 61 C8
New Tazewell TN .. 36°27N 83°36W 97 D9
New Town ND .... 47°59N 102°30W 91 C3
New Tripoli PA .... 40°41N 75°45W 87 B1
New Tulsa OK .... 36°9N 95°48W 93 B8
New Ulm MN .... 44°19N 94°28W 80 F4
New Underwood SD 44°6N 102°50W 91 F3
New Utrecht NY .. 40°36N 73°59W 114 C3
New Vienna IA .... 42°33N 91°7W 73 C7
New Vienna OH .. 39°19N 83°42W 92 D3
New Vineyard ME .. 44°48N 70°7W 86 B2
New Virginia IA .. 41°11N 93°44W 73 D5
New Washington OH 40°58N 82°51W 92 C4
New Waverly TX .. 30°32N 95°29W 99 G12
New Whiteland IN .. 39°33N 86°5W 72 D4
New Windsor MD .. 39°34N 77°9W 77 A3
New Windsor NY .. 41°29N 74°1W 87 A2
New York □ U.S.A... 43°0N 75°0W 89 B5
New York NY .... 43°0N 75°0W 89 B5
New York Mts. CA .. 35°0N 115°20W 65 H11
New York Mills MN. 46°31N 95°22W 80 D3
New York J.F. Kennedy Int. ✈ (JFK) NY.. 40°38N 73°47W 114 C4
New York La Guardia ✈ (LGA) NY .... 40°46N 73°52W 114 B3
Newald WI .... 45°46N 88°30W 103 C5
Newark DE .... 39°41N 75°46W 77 A5
Newark CA .... 37°32N 122°2W 64 F4
Newark IL .... 41°32N 88°35W 71 B5
Newark MD .... 38°15N 75°17W 77 B5
Newark MO .... 40°0N 92°0W 82 B4
Newark NY .... 43°3N 77°6W 89 B3
Newark OH .... 40°3N 82°24W 92 C4
Newark TX .... 33°0N 97°29W 99 D10
Newark Valley NY .. 42°14N 76°11W 89 C4
Newaygo MI .... 43°25N 85°48W 79 F6
Newaygo County ☆ MI .... 43°20N 84°0W 79 F6
Newberg OR .... 45°18N 122°58W 94 B3
Newbern AL .... 32°36N 87°32W 60 D3
Newbern TN .... 36°7N 89°16W 96 D3
Newberry FL .... 29°39N 82°37W 67 B6
Newberry IN .... 38°55N 87°1W 72 E3
Newberry MI .... 46°21N 85°30W 79 C6
Newberry SC .... 34°17N 81°37W 90 D4
Newberry County ☆ SC .... 34°17N 81°37W 90 D4
Newberry Nat. Volcanic Monument ○ OR 43°43N 121°14W 94 D4
Newberry Springs CA .... 34°50N 116°41W 65 J10
Newburg MD .... 38°22N 76°37W 77 B4
Newburg ND .... 48°43N 100°55W 91 B5
Newburg PA .... 40°8N 77°33W 95 D5
Newburg WV .... 39°23N 79°51W 102 B5
Newburgh IN .... 37°57N 87°24W 72 E3
Newburgh NY .... 41°30N 74°1W 87 A2
Newburgh Heights OH .... 41°27N 81°39W 107 B3
Newbury NH .... 43°19N 72°3W 86 C2
Newbury VT .... 44°5N 72°4W 86 B1
Newburyport MA .. 42°49N 70°53W 78 B4
Newcastle ME .... 44°2N 69°32W 76 D2
Newcastle CA .... 38°53N 121°8W 64 E5
Newcastle NE .... 42°39N 96°53W 84 B9
Newcastle OK .... 35°15N 97°36W 93 C6
Newcastle TX .... 33°12N 98°44W 99 D9
Newcastle WY .... 43°50N 104°11W 104 C8
Newcomb MD .... 38°45N 76°12W 77 B4
Newcomb NM .... 36°17N 108°42W 88 A2
Newcomb NY .... 43°58N 74°10W 89 B6
Newcomerstown OH 40°16N 81°36W 92 C5
Newell SD .... 44°43N 103°25W 91 E2
Newell WV .... 40°37N 80°36W 102 A4
Newellton LA .... 32°4N 91°14W 75 B4
Newenham, C. AK .. 58°39N 162°11W 61 G7
Newfane VT .... 42°59N 72°39W 86 D2
Newfield NY .... 42°23N 76°35W 89 C4
Newfolden MN .... 48°21N 96°20W 80 B2
Newfound L. NH .. 43°40N 71°47W 86 C3
Newfoundland PA .. 41°18N 75°19W 87 A1
Newfoundland Evaporation Basin UT .... 40°50N 113°20W 100 C2
Newfoundland Mts. UT .... 41°10N 113°20W 100 B2
Newhalem WA .... 48°40N 121°15W 101 B4
Newhalen AK .... 59°43N 154°54W 61 G9
Newhall IA .... 41°59N 91°59W 73 D7
Newington CT .... 41°42N 72°45W 78 C2
Newington GA .... 32°35N 81°30W 68 D5
Newkirk NM .... 35°4N 104°16W 88 B6
Newkirk OK .... 36°53N 97°3W 93 B6
Newland NC .... 36°5N 81°56W 90 B4
Newman CA .... 37°19N 121°1W 64 F5
Newman Grove NE .. 41°45N 97°47W 84 C8
Newman IL .... 39°48N 87°59W 71 D6
Newman L. WA .. 47°59N 117°3W 101 C8
Newmanstown PA .. 40°21N 76°12W 95 D6
Newman GA.... 33°23N 84°48W 68 C2
Newport AR .... 35°37N 91°16W 63 C4
Newport DE .... 39°43N 75°37W 77 A5
Newport IN .... 39°53N 87°25W 72 D3
Newport KY .... 39°5N 84°29W 107 B2
Newport ME .... 44°50N 69°17W 76 D2
Newport MN .... 44°52N 92°59W 113 B4
Newport NC .... 34°48N 76°52W 90 D8
Newport NH .... 43°22N 72°10W 86 C2
Newport NY .... 43°11N 75°1W 89 C5
Newport OR .... 44°39N 124°3W 94 C1
Newport PA .... 40°29N 77°8W 95 D5
Newport RI .... 41°30N 71°17W 78 C3
Newport TN .... 35°58N 83°11W 97 E9
Newport VT .... 44°56N 72°13W 86 B1
Newport VA .... 37°18N 80°30W 102 D4
Newport WA .... 48°11N 117°3W 101 B8
Newport Beach CA. 33°37N 117°56W 65 K9
Newport County ☆ RI .... 41°30N 71°20W 78 C3
Newport News VA .. 36°58N 76°25W 115 A1
Newsom TX .... 32°6N 94°34W 99 E13
Newsoms VA .... 36°36N 77°6W 102 E7
Newton GA .... 31°19N 84°20W 68 E2
Newton IL .... 38°59N 88°10W 71 E5
Newton IA .... 41°42N 93°3W 73 D5
Newton KS .... 38°3N 97°21W 74 C6
Newton MS .... 32°19N 89°10W 81 D4
Newton NJ .... 41°3N 74°45W 87 A2
Newton NC .... 35°40N 81°13W 90 C4
Newton TX .... 30°51N 93°46W 99 G14
Newton UT .... 41°52N 112°0W 100 B4
Newton County ☆ AR .... 35°58N 93°13W 63 C2
Newton County ☆ GA .... 33°35N 83°51W 68 C3
Newton County ☆ IN. 41°0N 87°25W 72 B3
Newton County ☆ MS 32°26N 89°7W 81 D4

Newton County ☆ MO .... 36°55N 94°20W 82 E2
Newton County ☆ TX .... 30°32N 93°49W 99 G14
Newton Falls NY .. 44°13N 74°59W 89 A6
Newton Falls OH .. 41°11N 80°59W 92 B6
Newtok AK .... 60°56N 164°38W 61 F6
Newtonia MO .... 36°53N 94°11W 82 E2
Newtonville AL .... 33°33N 87°48W 60 C3
Newtonville NY .... 42°20N 71°11W 106 A2
Newtown CT .... 41°25N 73°19W 78 C1
Newtown MO .... 40°22N 93°20W 82 A3
Newtown OH .... 39°7N 84°22W 107 B2
Newtown PA .... 40°14N 74°57W 87 B2
Newville AL .... 31°25N 85°49W 60 E5
Newville PA .... 40°10N 77°24W 95 D5
Ney OH .... 41°23N 84°32W 92 B2
Nez Perce County ☆ ID .... 46°10N 116°55W 70 C2
Nez Perce Indian Reservation ID .... 46°15N 116°30W 70 C2
Nezperce ID .... 46°14N 116°14W 70 C2
Nezperce Nat. Forest ID .... 45°50N 115°20W 70 D3
Nezpique, Bayou → LA .... 30°11N 92°34W 75 D3
Niagara ND .... 48°0N 97°54W 91 C8
Niagara WI .... 45°46N 88°0W 103 C5
Niagara NY .... 43°16N 79°4W 89 B1
Niagara County ☆ NY .... 43°15N 78°45W 89 B2
Niagara Falls NY .. 43°5N 79°4W 89 B1
Niangua MO .... 37°23N 92°50W 82 D4
Niangua → MO .. 38°58N 92°48W 82 C4
Niantic CT .... 41°20N 72°11W 78 C2
Niarada MT .... 47°49N 114°36W 83 C3
Nicatous L. ME .. 45°5N 68°9W 76 C5
Nice CA .... 39°7N 122°51W 64 D4
Niceville FL .... 30°31N 86°30W 67 A2
Nicholas County ☆ KY .... 38°20N 84°0W 97 B9
Nicholas County ☆ WV .... 38°17N 80°51W 102 C4
Nicholasville KY .. 37°53N 84°34W 97 C8
Nicholls GA .... 31°31N 82°38W 68 E4
Nichols IA .... 41°29N 91°19W 73 D7
Nichols NY .... 42°1N 76°22W 89 C4
Nichols SC .... 34°14N 79°9W 90 D6
Nicholson MS .... 30°29N 89°43W 81 F4
Nicholson PA .... 41°37N 75°47W 95 C7
Nickel Creek TX .. 31°55N 104°45W 98 F3
Nickerson KS .... 38°8N 98°5W 74 C5
Nickerson NE .... 41°32N 96°28W 84 C9
Nicodemus KS .... 39°24N 99°37W 74 B4
Nicolet Nat. Forest WI .... 45°35N 88°45W 103 C5
Nicollet MN .... 44°17N 94°11W 80 F4
Nicollet County ☆ MN .... 44°20N 94°15W 80 F4
Nielsville MN .... 47°32N 96°49W 80 C2
Nighthawk WA .... 48°58N 119°38W 101 B6
Nightmute AK .... 60°29N 164°44W 61 F6
Nihoa HI .... 23°6N 161°58W 69 G11
Niihau HI .... 21°54N 160°9W 69 B1
Nikep MD .... 39°32N 79°1W 77 A3
Nikiski AK .... 61°41N 151°18W 61 F10
Nikolai AK .... 63°1N 154°23W 61 F9
Nikolski AK .... 52°56N 168°52W 61 K5
Niland CA .... 33°14N 115°31W 65 K11
Niles IL .... 42°1N 87°48W 108 A2
Niles KS .... 38°59N 97°28W 74 C6
Niles MI .... 41°50N 86°15W 79 H5
Niles OH .... 41°11N 80°46W 92 B6
Niles Center = Skokie IL .... 42°1N 87°43W 108 A2
Nimrod MO .... 37°59N 92°44W 82 D4
Nimrod L. AR .... 34°57N 93°10W 63 D2
Ninaview CO .... 37°36N 103°17W 66 D7
Nine Mile Cr. → WI .... 39°50N 109°53W 100 C6
Ninety Six SC .... 34°11N 82°1W 90 D3
Ninety Six Nat. Historical Site ○ SC .... 34°11N 82°1W 90 D3
Ninini Pt. HI .... 21°58N 159°20W 69 B2
Ninnekah OK .... 34°57N 97°56W 93 D6
Ninnescah → KS .. 37°20N 97°10W 74 D6
Niobrara NE .... 42°45N 98°2W 84 B7
Niobrara → NE .. 42°46N 98°3W 84 B7
Niobrara County ☆ WY .... 43°0N 104°25W 104 C8
Niobrara Nat. Scenic River ○ NE .... 42°48N 98°7W 84 B7
Niota TN .... 35°31N 84°33W 97 E8
Nipomo CA .... 35°3N 120°29W 65 J5
Nipton CA .... 35°28N 115°16W 65 H11
Nisland SD .... 44°40N 103°33W 91 E2
Nisqually WA .... 47°7N 122°42W 101 C3
Nisqually → WA .. 47°7N 122°42W 101 C3
Niswa MN .... 46°31N 94°17W 80 D4
Nisula MI .... 46°46N 88°48W 79 C3
Nitro WV .... 38°25N 81°51W 102 C3
Nitta Yuma MS .... 33°2N 90°51W 81 C3
Niu Valley HI .... 21°19N 157°44W 69 K14
Niverville NY .... 42°26N 73°40W 78 B1
Niwot CO .... 40°6N 105°10W 66 B5
Nixa MO .... 37°3N 93°18W 82 D3
Nixon TX .... 29°16N 97°46W 99 H10
Noank CT .... 41°19N 71°59W 78 C2
Noatak AK .... 67°34N 162°58W 61 C7
Noatak Nat. Preserve ○ AK .... 68°0N 160°0W 61 B8
Noble IL .... 38°42N 88°14W 71 E5
Noble LA .... 31°41N 93°41W 75 C2
Noble OK .... 35°8N 97°24W 93 C6
Noble County ☆ IN. 41°25N 85°25W 72 B5
Noble County ☆ OH 39°45N 81°31W 92 D5
Noble County ☆ OK 36°20N 97°10W 93 B6
Nobles County ☆ MN .... 43°45N 95°45W 80 G3
Noblesville IN .... 40°3N 86°1W 72 C4
Nocatee FL .... 27°10N 81°53W 67 D7
Nockamixon Lake PA .... 40°28N 75°11W 87 B1
Nocona TX .... 33°47N 97°44W 99 D10
Nodaway IA .... 40°57N 94°54W 73 E4
Nodaway → MO .. 39°54N 94°58W 82 B2
Nodaway County ☆ MO .... 40°20N 94°53W 82 A2
Node WY .... 42°43N 104°18W 104 D8
Noel MO .... 36°33N 94°29W 82 E2
Nogal NM .... 33°33N 105°42W 88 D5
Nogales AZ .... 31°21N 110°56W 62 F5
Nohili Pt. HI .... 22°1N 159°47W 69 A2
Nokesville VA .... 38°42N 77°35W 77 B3
Nokomis IL .... 39°18N 89°18W 71 D4
Nokomis FL .... 27°7N 82°27W 67 D6
Nokomis, L. MN .. 44°54N 93°14W 113 B2
Nokomis-Hiawatha Park MN .... 44°55N 93°15W 113 B2
Nolan County ☆ TX 32°28N 100°25W 98 E7
Nolensville TN .... 35°57N 86°40W 96 D6
Nolichucky → TN .. 36°5N 83°14W 97 D9
Nolin L. KY .... 37°17N 86°15W 97 C6
Nolin River L. KY .. 37°16N 86°13W 97 C6
Noma FL .... 30°59N 85°37W 67 A3
Nomans Land MA .. 41°15N 70°49W 78 C4
Nomans Land Nat. Wildlife Refuge ○ MA .... 41°15N 70°49W 78 C4
Nome AK .... 64°30N 165°25W 61 D6

Nome ND .... 46°41N 97°49W 91 D8
Nome TX .... 30°2N 94°25W 99 G13
Nome, C. AK .... 64°50N 163°45W 61 D7
Nona, L. FL .... 28°24N 81°16W 115 B3
Nondalton AK .... 60°0N 154°51W 61 F9
Nooksack WA .... 48°56N 122°19W 101 B3
Noonan ND .... 48°54N 103°1W 91 B2
Noorvik AK .... 66°50N 161°3W 61 C7
Nopah Range CA .. 36°10N 116°10W 65 G10
Nora IL .... 39°54N 86°8W 110 A2
Nora NE .... 40°10N 97°58W 84 D8
Nora Springs IA .. 43°9N 93°0W 73 B6
Norborne MO .... 39°18N 93°40W 82 B3
Norcatur KS .... 39°50N 100°11W 74 B3
Norco CA .... 33°56N 117°33W 65 K9
Norcross GA .... 33°56N 84°13W 68 B2
Norcross MN .... 45°52N 96°12W 80 D2
Nordheim TX .... 28°55N 97°37W 99 J10
Nordman ID .... 48°38N 116°57W 70 A2
Norfolk NY .... 44°59N 75°1W 89 A5
Norfolk NE .... 42°2N 97°25W 84 B8
Norfolk VA .... 36°51N 76°17W 115 A3
Norfolk County ☆ MA .... 42°10N 71°20W 78 C4
Norfolk Int. ✈ (ORF) VA .... 36°54N 76°12W 115 A2
Norfork AR .... 36°13N 92°17W 63 B3
Norfork L. AR .... 36°15N 92°14W 63 B3
Norge OK .... 34°59N 98°0W 93 D6
Norias TX .... 26°47N 97°47W 98 L10
Norlina NC .... 36°27N 78°12W 90 B7
Normal IL .... 40°31N 88°59W 71 C5
Norman AR .... 34°27N 93°41W 63 D2
Norman NE .... 40°29N 98°48W 84 D7
Norman OK .... 35°13N 97°26W 93 C6
Norman, L. NC .... 35°26N 80°57W 90 C5
Norman County ☆ MN .... 47°20N 96°30W 80 C2
Norman Park GA .... 31°16N 83°41W 68 E3
Normandy MO .... 38°43N 90°17W 117 A2
Normandy L. TN .. 35°28N 86°15W 96 E6
Normandy Park WA .... 47°26N 122°20W 118 B3
Normangee TX .... 31°2N 96°7W 99 F11
Norphlet AR .... 33°19N 92°40W 63 E3
Norridge IL .... 41°57N 87°49W 108 B2
Norridgewock ME .. 44°43N 69°47W 76 D4
Norris MT .... 45°34N 111°41W 83 E6
Norris SD .... 43°28N 101°12W 91 G4
Norris TN .... 36°12N 84°4W 97 D8
Norris City IL .... 37°59N 88°20W 71 F5
Norristown PA .... 40°7N 75°21W 87 B1
North → MA .... 42°25N 72°44W 78 B2
North → WV .... 39°25N 78°23W 77 A2
North Adams MA .. 42°42N 73°7W 78 B1
North Adams MI .. 41°58N 84°32W 79 H7
North Amherst MA. 42°25N 72°31W 78 B2
North Andover MA. 42°42N 71°8W 78 B3
North Anna → VA. 37°48N 77°22W 102 D7
North Arlington NJ. 40°47N 74°7W 114 B2
North Atlanta GA .. 33°52N 84°21W 68 C2
North Attleboro MA 41°59N 71°20W 78 C3
North Augusta SC .. 33°30N 81°59W 90 E4
North Baltimore OH 41°11N 83°41W 92 B3
North Bass I. OH .. 41°40N 82°56W 92 B4
North Bay Village FL 25°50N 80°9W 112 C3
North Beach MD .. 38°43N 76°32W 77 B4
North Beach Peninsula WA .... 46°30N 124°2W 101 D1
North Bend NE .... 41°28N 96°47W 84 C9
North Bend OR .... 43°24N 124°14W 94 D1
North Bend WA .... 47°30N 121°47W 101 C4
North Bennington VT .... 42°56N 73°15W 86 D1
North Bergen NJ .. 40°48N 74°0W 114 B2
North Berwick ME. 43°18N 70°44W 86 C4
North Bonneville WA .... 45°39N 121°59W 101 E4
North Braddock PA 40°23N 79°50W 116 B2
North Branch MI .. 43°14N 83°12W 79 F8
North Branch MN .. 45°31N 92°59W 80 E6
North Branch Chicago River → IL .... 41°53N 87°42W 108 B2
North Branch Elkhorn → NE .... 41°59N 97°23W 84 C8
North Branch Potomac → U.S.A... 39°32N 78°35W 77 A2
North Branford CT. 41°22N 72°46W 78 C2
North Brookfield MA 42°16N 72°5W 78 B2
North Brunswick NJ 40°28N 74°28W 87 B2
North Buena Vista IA .... 42°41N 90°58W 73 C8
North Butte WY .. 43°10N 105°35W 104 C7
North Caldwell NJ. 40°51N 74°15W 114 A1
North Canadian → OK .... 35°22N 95°37W 93 C8
North Canton OH .. 40°53N 81°24W 92 C5
North Cape May NJ 38°59N 74°57W 87 D2
North Carolina □ U.S.A... 35°30N 80°0W 90 C6
North Cascades Nat. Park ○ WA .... 48°45N 121°10W 101 B4
North Charleston NH 43°18N 72°24W 86 C2
North Charleston SC 32°53N 79°58W 90 F6
North Chelmsford MA .... 42°38N 71°23W 78 B3
North Chicago IL .. 42°19N 87°51W 71 A6
North Chichester NH 43°15N 71°12W 86 C3
North Cohasset MA 42°15N 70°50W 106 B4
North College Hill OH .... 39°13N 84°33W 107 A1
North Collins NY .. 42°36N 78°56W 89 C2
North Concho → TX .... 31°27N 100°25W 98 F7
North Conway NH. 44°3N 71°8W 86 B3
North Creek NY .. 43°42N 73°59W 89 B7
North Crossett AR. 33°10N 91°56W 63 E4
North Crows Nest IN 39°51N 86°9W 110 A1
North Dakota □ U.S.A... 47°30N 100°15W 91 C5
North Dartmouth MA .... 41°36N 70°59W 78 C4
North Decatur GA. 33°48N 84°17W 106 B3
North Dighton MA. 41°50N 71°9W 78 C3
North Druid Hills GA .... 33°49N 84°17W 106 B3
North East PA .... 42°13N 79°50W 95 B3
North East Cape Fear → NC .... 34°11N 77°57W 90 D8
North Eastham MA. 41°52N 69°59W 78 C5
North English IA .. 41°31N 92°6W 73 D6
North Enid OK .... 36°26N 97°52W 93 B6
North Fabius → MO 39°51N 91°37W 82 B5
North Fairfield OH. 41°6N 82°37W 92 B4
North Fork Holston → VA .... 36°33N 82°37W 102 E2
North Fond du Lac WI .... 43°49N 88°29W 103 E5
North Fork ID .... 45°25N 113°59W 70 D5
North Fork, Salt → MO .... 39°26N 91°53W 82 B5
North Fork American → CA .... 38°57N 120°59W 64 E6
North Fork Bad → SD .... 44°2N 101°40W 91 F4

North Fork Cimarron →
  U.S.A. . . . 37°15N 102°9W **74 D1**
North Fork Cuivre →
  MO . . . 39°2N 90°59W **82 B6**
North Fork Edisto →
  SC . . . 33°16N 80°54W **90 E5**
North Fork Feather →
  CA . . . 38°33N 121°30W **64 E5**
North Fork Forked Deer →
  TN . . . 36°0N 89°26W **96 E3**
North Fork Grand →
  SD . . . 45°47N 102°16W **91 E3**
North Fork Humboldt →
  NV . . . 40°56N 115°32W **85 B5**
North Fork John Day →
  OR . . . 44°45N 119°38W **94 C6**
North Fork Kentucky →
  KY . . . 37°35N 83°40W **97 C9**
North Fork Licking →
  KY . . . 38°35N 84°12W **97 B8**
North Fork Moreau →
  SD . . . 45°9N 102°50W **91 E3**
North Fork Red →
  OK . . . 34°24N 99°14W **93 D4**
North Fork Shenandoah →
  VA . . . 38°59N 78°22W **102 C6**
North Fork Shoshone →
  WY . . . 44°29N 109°18W **104 B3**
North Fork Smoky Hill →
  KS . . . 38°54N 101°18W **74 C2**
North Fork Solomon →
  KS . . . 39°28N 98°26W **74 B5**
North Fork South Platte →
  CO . . . 39°25N 105°10W **66 C5**
North Fort Myers FL . . . 26°41N 81°53W **67 E7**
North Fox I. MI . . . 45°29N 85°47W **79 D6**
North Freedom WI . . . 43°28N 89°52W **103 E4**
North Grafton MA . . . 42°14N 71°42W **78 B3**
North Greenfield = West Allis
  WI . . . 43°1N 88°0W **112 B2**
North Grosvenor Dale
  CT . . . 41°59N 71°54W **78 C3**
North Hackensack
  NJ . . . 40°54N 74°2W **114 A2**
North Hampton NH . . . 42°57N 70°48W **86 D4**
North Hartsville SC . . . 34°24N 80°4W **90 D5**
North Haven CT . . . 41°23N 72°52W **78 C2**
North Haven ME . . . 44°8N 68°53W **76 D5**
North Hero VT . . . 44°49N 73°18W **86 B2**
North Highlands CA 38°40N 121°23W **64 E5**
North Hills NY . . . 40°46N 73°40W **114 B5**
North Hollywood
  CA . . . 34°9N 118°22W **111 B2**
North Hoosick NY . . . 42°55N 73°21W **78 B1**
North Houston TX . . . 29°55N 95°30W **110 A2**
North I. SC . . . 33°17N 79°11W **90 E6**
North Java NY . . . 42°41N 78°20W **89 C2**
North Judson IN . . . 41°13N 86°46W **72 B4**
North Kingstown RI . . . 41°33N 71°28W **78 C3**
North Kingsville OH . . . 41°54N 80°42W **92 B6**
North L. TX . . . 32°56N 96°58W **109 A4**
North La Veta Pass
  CO . . . 37°36N 105°13W **66 E5**
North Lake Park
  TX . . . 32°55N 96°58W **109 A4**
North Las Vegas NV 36°11N 115°7W **110 B1**
North Las Vegas × (VGT)
  NV . . . 36°12N 115°11W **110 B1**
North Lewisburg OH 40°13N 83°33W **92 C3**
North Lexington
  MA . . . 42°27N 71°14W **106 A2**
North Liberty IN . . . 41°32N 86°26W **72 B4**
North Liberty IA . . . 41°45N 91°35W **73 C9**
North Little Rock
  AR . . . 34°45N 92°16W **63 D3**
North Logan UT . . . 41°46N 111°48W **100 B4**
North Long Beach
  CA . . . 33°51N 118°11W **111 C3**
North Loon Mt. ID . . . 45°7N 115°52W **70 D3**
North Loup LA . . . 41°30N 98°46W **84 C7**
North Loup → NE . . . 41°17N 98°24W **84 C7**
North Manchester IN . . . 41°0N 85°46W **72 B5**
North Manitou MI . . . 45°7N 86°1W **79 D6**
North Manitou I. MI . . . 45°7N 86°1W **79 D6**
North Mankato MN . . . 44°10N 94°2W **80 F4**
North Miami FL . . . 25°53N 80°11W **112 C2**
North Miami OK . . . 36°55N 94°53W **93 B9**
North Miami Beach
  FL . . . 25°55N 80°9W **112 C2**
North Middletown KY.. 38°9N 84°7W **97 B8**
North Mountain Recreation Area
  AZ . . . 33°35N 112°4W **116 B2**
North Muskegon MI 43°15N 86°17W **79 F5**
North Myrtle Beach
  SC . . . 33°48N 78°42W **90 E7**
North Naples FL . . . 26°12N 81°48W **67 E7**
North New Hyde Park
  NY . . . 40°44N 73°41W **114 B4**
North Oaks MN . . . 45°6N 93°5W **113 A3**
North Ogden UT . . . 41°19N 111°58W **100 B4**
North Olmsted OH.. 41°25N 81°56W **92 B5**
North Palisade CA . . . 37°6N 118°31W **65 F8**
North Pass LA . . . 29°12N 89°2W **75 E6**
North Pease → TX . . . 34°15N 100°7W **98 C7**
North Pelham NY.. 40°54N 73°49W **114 A4**
North Perry OH . . . 41°47N 81°9W **92 B5**
North Perry × FL . . . 26°0N 80°14W **112 B2**
North Plains NM . . . 34°45N 108°0W **88 C2**
North Plains OR . . . 45°37N 123°0W **94 B3**
North Platte → NE.. 41°7N 100°42W **84 C5**
North Platte Nat. Wildlife
  Refuge △ NE . . . 41°56N 103°29W **84 C2**
North Pole AK . . . 64°45N 147°21W **61 D11**
North Port FL . . . 27°3N 82°14W **67 D6**
North Powder OR . . . 45°2N 117°55W **94 B8**
North Prairie WI . . . 42°55N 88°24W **103 F5**
North Providence RI 41°50N 71°25W **78 C3**
North Pt. MI . . . 45°32N 83°16W **79 D8**
North Quincy MA.. 42°16N 71°1W **106 B3**
North Redington Beach
  FL . . . 27°48N 82°49W **119 C2**
North Res. MA . . . 42°31N 70°59W **106 A4**
North Richland Hills
  TX . . . 32°50N 97°13W **109 A2**
North Rim AZ . . . 36°12N 112°3W **62 A3**
North Riverside IL.. 41°50N 87°48W **108 B2**
North Royalton OH 41°18N 81°43W **107 C1**
North St. Paul MN.. 45°1N 92°59W **113 A4**
North Salem IN . . . 39°52N 86°39W **72 D4**
North Salt Lake
  UT . . . 40°50N 111°54W **117 A1**
North Santiam →
  OR . . . 44°41N 123°0W **94 C3**
North Saugus MA.. 42°29N 71°0W **106 A3**
North Schell Peak
  NV . . . 39°25N 114°36W **85 C6**
North Sea NY . . . 40°56N 72°25W **117 D6**
North Shapleigh ME 43°36N 70°53W **76 C3**
North Shore HI . . . 21°39N 158°30W **69 J13**
North Shore Channel →
  IL . . . 41°58N 87°42W **108 B2**
North Sioux City SD 42°32N 96°30W **91 H9**
North Slope ☆ AK.. 69°15N 152°0W **61 B9**
North Springfield PA 41°54N 80°26W **92 B5**
North Springfield
  VA . . . 38°48N 77°11W **119 C2**
North Springfield VT 43°20N 72°32W **86 C2**
North Station MA.. 42°21N 71°4W **106 A3**
North Stratford NH.. 44°45N 71°38W **86 B3**
North Sudbury MA 42°24N 71°24W **106 A1**
North Sulphur →
  TX . . . 33°23N 95°18W **99 D12**

North Sutton NH . . . 43°22N 71°56W **86 C3**
North Syracuse NY . . . 43°8N 76°7W **89 B4**
North Terre Haute
  IN . . . 39°31N 87°22W **72 D3**
North Tonawanda NY 43°2N 78°53W **89 B2**
North Troy VT . . . 45°0N 72°24W **86 B2**
North Truro MA . . . 42°2N 70°5W **78 B4**
North Umpqua →
  OR . . . 43°16N 123°27W **94 D2**
North Valley Stream
  NY . . . 40°41N 73°42W **114 B4**
North Vernon IN . . . 39°0N 85°38W **72 D5**
North Wales PA . . . 40°13N 75°17W **87 B1**
North Washington IA 43°9N 92°25W **73 B6**
North Waterford ME 44°14N 70°46W **86 B4**
North Wichita → TX 33°43N 99°29W **98 D8**
North Wildwood NJ . . . 39°0N 74°48W **87 D2**
North Wilkesboro NC 36°10N 81°9W **90 B4**
North Windham ME 43°50N 70°26W **76 E3**
North Wolf Cr. →
  SD . . . 44°42N 98°46W **91 F7**
North Yakima = Yakima
  WA . . . 46°36N 120°31W **101 B5**
Northampton MA . . . 42°19N 72°38W **78 B2**
Northampton PA . . . 40°41N 75°30W **87 B1**
Northampton County ☆
  NC . . . 36°20N 77°30W **90 B8**
Northampton County ☆
  PA . . . 40°45N 75°25W **87 B1**
Northampton County ☆
  VA . . . 37°15N 75°55W **102 D9**
Northborough MA . . . 42°19N 71°39W **78 B3**
Northbridge MA . . . 42°9N 71°39W **78 B3**
Northbrook OH . . . 39°14N 84°35W **107 A1**
Northeast C. AK . . . 63°18N 168°42W **61 E5**
Northeastern University
  MA . . . 42°20N 71°4W **106 A3**
Northern Cambria
  PA . . . 40°40N 78°47W **95 D4**
Northern Cheyenne Indian
  Reservation MT 45°30N 106°40W **83 E11**
  Pac. Oc. . . . 17°0N 145°0E **105 a**
Northern Virginia Regional Park △
  VA . . . 38°55N 77°6W **119 B3**
Northfield ME . . . 44°52N 67°34W **76 D6**
Northfield MA . . . 42°42N 72°27W **78 B2**
Northfield MN . . . 44°27N 93°9W **80 F5**
Northfield NH . . . 43°26N 71°36W **86 C4**
Northfield NJ . . . 39°22N 74°33W **87 C2**
Northfield VT . . . 44°9N 72°40W **86 B2**
Northford CT . . . 41°24N 72°48W **78 C2**
Northgate ND . . . 48°59N 102°15W **91 B3**
Northglenn CO . . . 39°53N 104°59W **109 A2**
Northlake CA . . . 41°54N 87°53W **108 B1**
Northome MN . . . 47°52N 94°17W **80 D4**
Northport AL . . . 33°14N 87°35W **60 C3**
Northport NY . . . 40°54N 73°21W **78 D1**
Northport NE . . . 41°41N 103°5W **84 C2**
Northport WA . . . 48°55N 117°48W **101 B8**
Northridge CA . . . 34°13N 118°32W **111 A1**
Northridge OH . . . 39°59N 83°46W **92 D3**
Northrop MN . . . 43°44N 94°26W **80 G4**
Northumberland Pa 40°54N 76°48W **95 D6**
Northumberland County ☆
  PA . . . 40°55N 76°50W **95 D6**
Northumberland County ☆
  VA . . . 37°55N 76°29W **102 D8**
Northview MO . . . 37°17N 93°0W **82 D4**
Northville NY . . . 43°13N 74°11W **89 B6**
Northville SD . . . 45°9N 98°35W **91 E7**
Northway AK . . . 62°58N 141°56W **61 E12**
Northway Jct.
  AK . . . 66°50N 161°0W **61 C7**
Northwest Arctic
  AK . . . 66°50N 161°0W **61 C7**
Northwestern Station
  IL . . . 41°52N 87°38W **108 B3**
Northwestern University
  IL . . . 42°3N 87°40W **108 A2**
Northwesterly Park
  IN . . . 39°52N 86°14W **110 A1**
Northwood IA . . . 43°27N 93°13W **73 B5**
Northwood ND . . . 47°44N 97°34W **91 C8**
Northwood NH . . . 43°12N 71°9W **86 C3**
Northwoods MO . . . 38°42N 90°17W **117 A2**
Norton KS . . . 39°50N 99°53W **74 B4**
Norton MA . . . 41°58N 71°11W **78 C3**
Norton VA . . . 36°56N 82°38W **102 E2**
Norton VT . . . 45°0N 71°48W **86 B3**
Norton B. AK . . . 64°45N 161°15W **61 D7**
Norton County ☆ KS 39°45N 99°50W **74 B4**
Norton Pk. ID . . . 43°46N 114°39W **70 F4**
Norton Sd. AK . . . 63°50N 164°0W **61 E7**
Norton Shores MI . . . 43°10N 86°16W **79 F5**
Nortonville KS . . . 39°25N 95°20W **82 B2**
Nortonville KY . . . 37°11N 87°27W **97 C6**
Norumbega Res.
  MA . . . 42°19N 71°17W **106 B2**
Norwalk CA . . . 33°54N 118°4W **111 C4**
Norwalk CT . . . 41°7N 73°22W **78 C1**
Norwalk IA . . . 41°29N 93°41W **73 C5**
Norwalk OH . . . 41°15N 82°37W **92 C4**
Norwalk WI . . . 43°50N 90°37W **103 E3**
Norway IA . . . 41°54N 91°55W **73 D7**
Norway KS . . . 39°42N 97°47W **74 B6**
Norway ME . . . 44°13N 70°32W **76 D3**
Norway MI . . . 45°47N 87°55W **79 D4**
Norwell MA . . . 42°10N 70°48W **78 B4**
Norwich CT . . . 41°31N 72°5W **78 C2**
Norwich KS . . . 37°27N 97°51W **74 D6**
Norwich NY . . . 42°32N 75°32W **89 C5**
Norwich VT . . . 43°43N 72°18W **86 C2**
Norwood CO . . . 38°8N 108°20W **66 C2**
Norwood LA . . . 30°58N 91°6W **75 D4**
Norwood MA . . . 42°11N 71°12W **78 B3**
Norwood MO . . . 37°7N 92°24W **82 D4**
Norwood NC . . . 35°14N 80°7W **90 C5**
Norwood NY . . . 44°45N 75°0W **89 A6**
Norwood PA . . . 39°53N 75°18W **116 B1**
Norwood → WY . . . 44°17N 107°58W **104 B5**
Norwood Park IL . . . 41°59N 87°48W **108 B2**
Norwood-Young America
  MN . . . 44°46N 93°55W **80 F5**
Norwoodville IA . . . 41°39N 93°33W **73 D5**
Notasulga AL . . . 32°34N 85°41W **60 D5**
Notch Peak UT . . . 39°9N 113°25W **100 D2**
Notrees TX . . . 31°55N 102°45W **98 F5**
Nottely L. GA . . . 34°58N 84°5W **68 B2**
Nottingham NH . . . 43°7N 71°6W **86 C4**
Nottingham PA . . . 39°45N 76°1W **77 A4**
Nottoway → VA . . . 36°33N 76°55W **102 E8**
Nottoway County ☆
  VA . . . 37°8N 78°5W **102 D6**
Nottoway Court House
  VA . . . 37°8N 78°5W **102 D6**
Notus ID . . . 43°43N 116°48W **70 F2**
Novato CA . . . 38°6N 122°35W **64 E4**
Novinger MO . . . 40°14N 92°43W **82 A4**
Nowata OK . . . 36°42N 95°38W **93 B8**
Nowata County ☆
  OK . . . 36°50N 95°40W **93 B8**
Nowitna Nat. Wildlife Refuge △
  AK . . . 64°30N 154°16W **61 D9**
Noxapater MS . . . 33°1N 89°1W **81 C5**
Noxon Res. MT . . . 47°57N 115°44W **83 C2**
Noxubee → U.S.A . . . 32°50N 88°10W **60 D2**
Noxubee County ☆
  MS . . . 33°7N 88°34W **81 C5**
Noyes MN . . . 49°0N 97°12W **80 B1**

Nubieber CA . . . 41°6N 121°11W **64 F5**
Nuckolls County ☆
  NE . . . 40°15N 98°0W **84 D8**
Nucla CO . . . 38°16N 108°33W **66 D2**
Nueces → TX . . . 27°51N 97°30W **99 K10**
Nueces County ☆
  TX . . . 27°47N 97°40W **99 K10**
Nulato AK . . . 64°43N 158°6W **61 D8**
Nulhegan → VT . . . 44°45N 71°38W **86 B3**
Numa IA . . . 40°41N 92°59W **73 E6**
Nunda NY . . . 42°35N 77°56W **89 C3**
Nunda SD . . . 44°10N 97°1W **91 F8**
Nunivak I. AK . . . 60°10N 166°30W **61 F6**
Nunn CO . . . 40°42N 104°47W **66 B6**
Nunnelly TN . . . 35°52N 87°28W **96 E5**
Nursery TX . . . 28°56N 97°6W **99 J10**
Nutley NJ . . . 40°49N 74°9W **114 A2**
Nutrioso AZ . . . 33°57N 109°13W **62 D6**
Nu'uuli Amer. Samoa 14°19S 170°42W **105 e**
Nyack NY . . . 41°5N 73°55W **87 A3**
Nye County ☆ NV.. 38°0N 116°40W **85 E4**

O

O.C. Fisher L. TX . . . 31°29N 100°29W **98 F7**
O.H. Ivie Res. TX . . . 31°34N 99°41W **99 F8**
Oacoma SD . . . 43°48N 99°24W **91 G6**
Oahe, L. U.S.A . . . 44°27N 100°24W **91 F5**
Oahe Dam SD . . . 44°27N 100°24W **91 F5**
O'ahu HI . . . 21°28N 157°58W **69 K14**
Oak NE . . . 40°14N 97°54W **84 D8**
Oak Bluffs MA . . . 41°27N 70°34W **78 C4**
Oak City UT . . . 39°22N 112°20W **100 D3**
Oak Cr. → AZ . . . 34°45N 111°55W **62 C4**
Oak Cr. → SD . . . 45°35N 100°30W **91 E5**
Oak Creek CO . . . 40°16N 106°57W **66 B4**
Oak Creek WI . . . 42°52N 87°55W **103 F6**
Oak Grove GA . . . 33°50N 84°18W **106 A3**
Oak Grove KY . . . 36°40N 87°26W **96 D5**
Oak Grove LA . . . 32°52N 91°23W **75 B4**
Oak Grove MO . . . 39°0N 94°8W **82 C3**
Oak Grove OR . . . 45°25N 122°38W **116 B2**
Oak Grove TN . . . 36°25N 82°25W **97 D10**
Oak Grove VA . . . 38°11N 77°0W **77 B4**
Oak Harbor OH . . . 41°30N 83°9W **92 B3**
Oak Harbor WA . . . 48°18N 122°39W **101 B3**
Oak Hill FL . . . 31°55N 80°51W **60 E3**
Oak Hill KS . . . 39°15N 97°21W **74 B6**
Oak Hill MA . . . 42°18N 71°10W **106 B2**
Oak Hill OH . . . 38°54N 82°35W **92 E4**
Oak Hill TN . . . 36°5N 86°47W **96 M6**
Oak Hill WV . . . 37°59N 81°9W **102 D3**
Oak Island ME . . . 44°25N 70°59W **106 A4**
Oak Island NC . . . 33°55N 78°10W **90 E7**
Oak Lawn IL . . . 41°42N 87°45W **108 C2**
Oak Orchard DE . . . 38°36N 75°12W **77 B5**
Oak Park IL . . . 32°22N 87°51W **108 B2**
Oak Park MI . . . 42°27N 83°10W **109 A1**
Oak Ridge LA . . . 32°38N 91°47W **75 B4**
Oak Ridge MO . . . 37°30N 89°44W **82 D7**
Oak Ridge TN . . . 36°1N 84°16W **97 D8**
Oak Vale MS . . . 31°26N 89°58W **81 E4**
Oak Valley KS . . . 37°20N 96°1W **74 D7**
Oak View CA . . . 34°24N 119°18W **65 J7**
Oak View MD . . . 39°1N 76°58W **119 A4**
Oakboro NC . . . 35°7N 75°59W **90 C10**
Oakdale CA . . . 37°46N 120°51W **64 F6**
Oakdale NC . . . 35°18N 80°53W **107 A1**
Oakdale NE . . . 42°4N 97°58W **84 C7**
Oakdale IL . . . 38°16N 89°30W **71 E4**
Oakdale LA . . . 30°49N 92°40W **75 D3**
Oakdale MN . . . 44°57N 92°57W **113 A4**
Oakdale NY . . . 40°44N 97°58W **84 B8**
Oakdale Park MN . . . 45°1N 92°57W **113 A4**
Oakes ND . . . 46°8N 98°6W **91 D7**
Oakesdale WA . . . 47°8N 117°15W **101 C8**
Oakfield GA . . . 31°47N 83°58W **68 E3**
Oakfield NY . . . 43°4N 78°16W **89 B2**
Oakfield WI . . . 43°41N 88°33W **103 E5**
Oakford IL . . . 40°6N 89°58W **71 C4**
Oakgrove AR . . . 36°27N 93°36W **63 B2**
Oakhurst CA . . . 37°19N 119°40W **64 F7**
Oakhurst OK . . . 36°6N 74°1W **87 B2**
Oakland CA . . . 37°49N 122°16W **115 B3**
Oakland MD . . . 39°25N 79°24W **63 L1**
Oakland IA . . . 39°39N 88°2W **71 D5**
Oakland IL . . . 41°19N 95°23W **73 D3**
Oakland KY . . . 36°58N 86°33W **96 D6**
Oakland ME . . . 44°33N 69°43W **76 D4**
Oakland MD . . . 38°53N 76°54W **119 B4**
Oakland MS . . . 34°4N 89°55W **81 B4**
Oakland MO . . . 38°34N 90°24W **117 B1**
Oakland NE . . . 41°50N 96°28W **84 C9**
Oakland OK . . . 43°25N 123°18W **94 D2**
Oakland OR . . . 41°57N 75°37W **95 C7**
Oakland TN . . . 35°14N 89°31W **96 E3**
Oakland City IN . . . 38°20N 87°21W **72 E3**
Oakland County ☆
  MI . . . 42°35N 83°20W **79 G8**
Oakland Gardens
  NY . . . 40°44N 73°44W **114 B4**
Oakland Int. × (OAK)
  CA . . . 37°43N 122°13W **118 B3**
Oakland Park FL . . . 26°10N 80°7W **112 A3**
Oaklawn KS . . . 37°38N 97°18W **74 D6**
Oaklawn MD . . . 38°46N 76°56W **119 C4**
Oakley CA . . . 38°1N 121°43W **64 D2**
Oakley ID . . . 42°15N 113°53W **70 G5**
Oakley KS . . . 39°8N 100°51W **74 B3**
Oakley MI . . . 43°9N 84°10W **79 F7**
Oakley OH . . . 39°9N 84°26W **107 B2**
Oakley UT . . . 40°43N 111°18W **100 C4**
Oaklyn PA . . . 39°54N 79°5W **116 B2**
Oakman GA . . . 33°43N 87°23W **60 C3**
Oakman AL . . . 33°43N 87°23W **60 C3**
Oakmont PA . . . 40°31N 79°50W **116 A4**
Oakridge OR . . . 43°45N 122°28W **94 D3**
Oaks OK . . . 36°10N 94°51W **93 B9**
Oakton KY . . . 36°31N 89°4W **96 D3**
Oakton IN . . . 38°52N 87°27W **72 E3**
Oaktown IN . . . 38°52N 87°27W **72 E3**
Oakville CT . . . 41°36N 73°5W **78 C1**
Oakville LA . . . 41°6N 91°3W **73 D7**
Oakville WA . . . 46°51N 123°14W **101 D2**
Oakwood GA . . . 34°14N 83°53W **60 B6**
Oakwood OH . . . 41°6N 84°23W **92 B2**
Oakwood PA . . . 41°11N 80°23W **92 B6**
Oakwood TX . . . 31°35N 95°51W **99 F12**
Oakwood Beach NY 40°33N 74°7W **114 C2**
Oark AR . . . 35°41N 93°35W **63 C2**
Oasis NV . . . 41°2N 114°9W **85 A6**
Oatman AZ . . . 35°1N 114°19W **62 B1**
Obed → TN . . . 36°5N 84°39W **97 D8**
Oberlin KS . . . 39°49N 100°32W **74 B3**
Oberlin OH . . . 41°18N 82°13W **92 B4**
Oberon ND . . . 47°55N 99°13W **91 C6**
Obert NE . . . 42°42N 96°56W **84 B8**
Obion TN . . . 36°16N 89°12W **96 D3**
Obion → TN . . . 35°55N 89°39W **96 D3**
Obion County ☆ TN 36°20N 89°10W **96 D3**
Oblong IL . . . 39°0N 87°55W **71 D6**
O'Brien FL . . . 30°2N 82°57W **67 A6**

O'Brien OR . . . 42°4N 123°42W **94 E2**
O'Brien TX . . . 33°23N 99°51W **99 D8**
O'Brien County ☆ IA 43°5N 95°35W **73 B3**
O'Bryonville OH . . . 39°8N 84°28W **107 B2**
Obscura, Sierra NM 33°45N 106°25W **88 D4**
Observatorio de Arecibo
  Puerto Rico . . . 18°21N 66°45W **105 G16**
Obsidian ID . . . 44°5N 114°51W **70 E4**
Ocala FL . . . 29°11N 82°8W **67 B6**
Ocate NM . . . 36°11N 105°3W **88 A5**
Ocate → NM . . . 36°0N 104°30W **88 A6**
Occoquan Cr. → VA . . . 38°39N 77°14W **77 B3**
Ocean Beach CT . . . 41°19N 72°5W **117 B1**
Ocean Bluff MA . . . 42°6N 70°39W **78 B4**
Ocean City MD . . . 38°20N 75°5W **77 B6**
Ocean City NJ . . . 39°17N 74°35W **87 C2**
Ocean County ☆ NJ 39°50N 74°15W **87 C2**
Ocean L. WY . . . 43°12N 108°36W **104 C4**
Ocean Park WA . . . 46°30N 124°3W **101 D1**
Ocean Pines MD . . . 38°24N 75°9W **77 B5**
Ocean Springs MS . . . 30°25N 88°50W **93 C6**
Oceana WV . . . 37°42N 81°38W **102 D3**
Oceana County ☆ MI 43°40N 86°20W **79 F5**
Oceano CA . . . 35°6N 120°37W **65 H6**
Oceanport NJ . . . 40°19N 74°3W **87 B2**
Oceanside CA . . . 33°12N 117°23W **65 K9**
Oceanside NY . . . 40°38N 73°37W **114 C5**
Oceanville NJ . . . 39°28N 74°28W **87 C2**
Ochelata OK . . . 36°36N 95°59W **93 B8**
Ocheyedan IA . . . 43°25N 95°32W **73 B3**
Ocheyedan Mound
  IA . . . 43°24N 95°31W **73 B3**
Ochiltree County ☆ TX 36°10N 100°55W **98 A7**
Ochlockonee GA . . . 30°58N 84°3W **68 F2**
Ochlockonee → FL . . . 29°59N 84°26W **67 B4**
Ochoco Mts. OR . . . 44°30N 120°35W **94 C5**
Ochoco Nat. Forest
  OR . . . 44°30N 120°35W **94 C5**
Ochopee FL . . . 25°54N 81°18W **67 F7**
Ocilla GA . . . 31°36N 83°15W **68 E4**
Ocmulgee → GA . . . 31°58N 82°33W **68 E4**
Ocoee FL . . . 28°34N 81°32W **67 C6**
Ocoee → TN . . . 35°12N 84°39W **97 E8**
Ocoee, L. TN . . . 35°6N 84°39W **97 E8**
Ocoee IL . . . 39°17N 89°7W **71 D4**
Oconee → GA . . . 31°58N 82°33W **68 E4**
Oconee, L. GA . . . 33°28N 83°15W **68 C3**
Oconee County ☆
  GA . . . 33°50N 83°25W **68 C3**
Oconee County ☆ SC 34°45N 83°0W **90 D2**
Oconee Nat. Forest
  GA . . . 33°15N 83°45W **68 C3**
Oconomowoc WI . . . 43°7N 88°30W **103 E5**
Oconto NE . . . 41°9N 99°46W **84 C6**
Oconto WI . . . 44°53N 87°52W **103 D6**
Oconto → WI . . . 44°53N 87°52W **103 D6**
Oconto County ☆ WI 45°0N 88°15W **103 D5**
Oconto Falls WI . . . 44°52N 88°9W **103 D5**
Ocracoke NC . . . 35°7N 75°59W **90 C10**
Ocracoke I. NC . . . 35°10N 75°50W **90 C10**
Ocurtia NE . . . 41°21N 97°4W **84 C8**
Odebolt IA . . . 42°19N 95°15W **73 C3**
Odell IL . . . 41°0N 88°31W **71 B5**
Odell NE . . . 40°3N 96°48W **84 D9**
Odell → OR . . . 45°38N 121°32W **94 B4**
Odell TX . . . 34°20N 99°25W **98 C8**
Odem TX . . . 27°57N 97°35W **99 K10**
Oden AR . . . 34°37N 93°42W **63 D2**
Odenton MD . . . 39°5N 76°42W **77 A4**
Odessa DE . . . 39°27N 75°40W **77 A5**
Odessa MO . . . 45°16N 90°20W **80 F6**
Odessa MO . . . 39°0N 93°57W **82 C3**
Odessa TX . . . 31°52N 102°23W **98 F5**
Odessa WA . . . 47°20N 118°41W **101 C7**
Odon IN . . . 38°51N 86°59W **72 E4**
O'Donnell TX . . . 32°58N 101°50W **98 E6**
Odum GA . . . 31°40N 82°2W **68 E4**
Oelrichs SD . . . 43°11N 103°14W **91 G2**
Oelwein IA . . . 42°41N 91°55W **73 C7**
O'Fallon IL . . . 38°49N 90°42W **82 C6**
O'Fallon Park MO . . . 38°40N 90°13W **117 A2**
Offerle KS . . . 37°54N 99°33W **74 D4**
Ofu Amer. Samoa . . . 14°11S 169°41W **105 f**
Ogallah NE . . . 38°59N 99°44W **74 D4**
Ogallala NE . . . 41°8N 101°43W **84 C4**
Ogden → AR . . . 33°38N 94°3W **63 E1**
Ogden IA . . . 42°2N 94°2W **73 C4**
Ogden KS . . . 39°7N 96°43W **74 B7**
Ogden UT . . . 41°13N 111°58W **100 B4**
Ogden Park IL . . . 41°46N 87°39W **108 C2**
Ogdensburg NJ . . . 41°5N 74°36W **87 A2**
Ogdensburg NY . . . 44°42N 75°30W **89 A5**
Ogeechee → GA . . . 31°50N 81°3W **68 E5**
Ogema MN . . . 47°6N 95°56W **80 C3**
Ogema WI . . . 45°28N 90°16W **103 D3**
Ogemaw County ☆
  MI . . . 44°15N 84°10W **79 E7**
Ogilvie MN . . . 45°50N 93°26W **80 E5**
Oglala NE . . . 42°55N 103°45W **84 B2**
Oglala Nat. Grassland
  NE . . . 42°55N 103°45W **84 B2**
Ogle County ☆ IL . . . 42°0N 89°20W **71 A4**
Oglesby IL . . . 41°18N 89°4W **71 B4**
Oglesby TX . . . 31°25N 97°30W **99 F10**
Oglethorpe GA . . . 32°18N 84°4W **68 D2**
Oglethorpe County ☆
  GA . . . 33°50N 83°0W **68 C4**
Ogontz PA . . . 40°5N 75°6W **116 A2**
Ogunquit ME . . . 43°15N 70°36W **86 C4**
O'Hare Int., Chicago × (ORD)
  IL . . . 41°59N 87°55W **108 B1**
Ohatchee AL . . . 33°47N 86°0W **60 C5**
Ohio CO . . . 38°34N 106°37W **66 D4**
Ohio IL . . . 41°34N 89°27W **71 B4**
Ohio → U.S.A . . . 36°59N 89°8W **96 D3**
Ohio ☆ OH . . . 40°15N 82°45W **92 C4**
Ohio City OH . . . 40°46N 84°37W **92 C2**
Ohio City IN . . . 28°35N 80°50W **72 C6**
Ohio County ☆ KY . . . 37°30N 86°50W **96 C6**
Ohio County ☆ WV . . . 40°4N 80°34W **102 A4**
Ohio River Islands Nat. Wildlife
  Refuge △ U.S.A . . . 39°25N 81°12W **102 B3**
Ohiopyle PA . . . 39°52N 79°30W **77 A1**
Ohiopyle State Park △
  PA . . . 39°52N 79°30W **77 A1**
Ohioville PA . . . 40°41N 80°30W **95 D2**
Oil City LA . . . 32°45N 93°58W **75 B2**
Oil City PA . . . 41°26N 79°42W **95 D3**
Oil Springs Indian Reservation
  NY . . . 42°18N 78°18W **89 C2**
Oil Trough AR . . . 35°38N 91°28W **63 C5**
Oildale CA . . . 35°25N 119°1W **65 H7**
Oilmont MT . . . 48°44N 111°51W **83 B6**
Oilton OK . . . 36°5N 96°35W **93 B7**
Ojai CA . . . 34°27N 119°15W **65 J7**
Ojo Caliente NM . . . 36°18N 106°3W **88 A4**
Ojo Feliz NM . . . 36°4N 105°7W **88 A5**
Ojo Sarco NM . . . 36°7N 105°47W **88 A5**
Okaloosa County ☆
  FL . . . 30°40N 86°40W **67 A2**
Okanogan → WA . . . 48°6N 119°44W **101 B6**
Okanogan WA . . . 48°22N 119°35W **101 B6**
Okanogan County ☆
  WA . . . 48°30N 120°0W **101 B6**
Okanogan Nat. Forest
  WA . . . 48°30N 120°10W **101 B5**

Okarche OK . . . 35°44N 97°58W **93 C6**
Okatibbee L. MS . . . 32°35N 88°48W **81 D5**
Okaton SD . . . 43°53N 100°53W **91 G5**
Okay OK . . . 35°51N 95°19W **93 C8**
O'Kean AR . . . 36°10N 90°49W **63 B5**
Okeechobee FL . . . 27°15N 80°50W **67 D8**
Okeechobee, L. FL . . . 27°0N 80°50W **67 E8**
Okeechobee County ☆
  FL . . . 27°30N 81°0W **67 D8**
Okeene OK . . . 36°7N 98°19W **93 B5**
Okefenokee Nat. Wildlife
  Refuge △ GA . . . 30°45N 82°18W **68 F4**
Okefenokee Swamp
  GA . . . 30°40N 82°20W **68 F4**
Okemah OK . . . 35°26N 96°19W **93 C7**
Okemo Mt. VT . . . 43°24N 72°45W **86 C2**
Okemos MI . . . 42°43N 84°26W **79 G7**
Oketo KS . . . 39°58N 96°36W **74 B7**
Oktuskee County ☆
  OK . . . 35°25N 96°15W **93 C7**
Oklahoma □ U.S.A . . . 35°20N 97°30W **93 C6**
Oklahoma City Will Rogers ×
  (OKC) OK . . . 35°24N 97°36W **93 C6**
Oklahoma County ☆
  OK . . . 35°35N 97°20W **93 C6**
Oklaunion TX . . . 34°8N 99°9W **99 C8**
Oklawaha → FL . . . 29°28N 81°41W **67 B7**
Oklawaha, L. FL . . . 29°30N 81°45W **67 B7**
Oklee MN . . . 47°50N 95°51W **80 C3**
Okmulgee OK . . . 35°37N 95°58W **93 C8**
Okmulgee County ☆
  OK . . . 35°40N 96°0W **93 C8**
Okoboji IA . . . 43°23N 95°8W **73 B3**
Okolona AR . . . 34°0N 93°20W **63 E2**
Okolona KY . . . 38°8N 85°41W **97 B7**
Okolona MS . . . 34°0N 88°45W **81 B5**
Oktaha OK . . . 35°35N 95°29W **93 C8**
Oktibbeha County ☆
  MS . . . 33°28N 88°49W **81 C5**
Oktoc MS . . . 33°20N 88°45W **81 C5**
Ola AR . . . 35°2N 93°13W **63 C2**
Ola ID . . . 44°11N 116°18W **70 E2**
Olalla WA . . . 47°25N 122°32W **118 D2**
Olamon ME . . . 45°7N 68°37W **76 C5**
Olancha CA . . . 36°17N 118°1W **65 G8**
Olancha Pk. CA . . . 36°16N 118°7W **65 G8**
Olanta SC . . . 33°56N 79°56W **90 D6**
Olathe CO . . . 38°36N 107°59W **66 D3**
Olathe KS . . . 38°53N 94°49W **74 C9**
Olberg AZ . . . 33°6N 111°41W **62 D4**
Old Bridge NJ . . . 40°25N 74°22W **87 B2**
Old Faithful WY . . . 44°28N 110°50W **104 B2**
Old Field NY . . . 40°58N 73°7W **78 D1**
Old Forge NY . . . 43°43N 74°58W **89 B6**
Old Forge PA . . . 41°22N 75°45W **87 A1**
Old Fort NC . . . 35°38N 82°11W **90 C3**
Old Harbor AK . . . 57°12N 153°18W **61 H9**
Old Harbor MA . . . 42°19N 71°1W **106 B3**
Old Hickory L. TN . . . 36°18N 86°40W **96 D6**
Old Horse Springs
  NM . . . 33°55N 108°14W **88 D2**
Old Lyme CT . . . 41°19N 72°20W **78 C2**
Old Mines MO . . . 38°1N 90°45W **82 C6**
Old Monroe MO . . . 38°56N 90°45W **82 C6**
Old Ocean TX . . . 29°5N 95°45W **99 H12**
Old Orchard Beach
  ME . . . 43°31N 70°23W **76 E3**
Old Saybrook CT . . . 41°18N 72°23W **78 C2**
Old Speck Mt. ME . . . 44°34N 70°57W **76 D3**
Old Tampa Bay FL . . . 27°54N 82°35W **119 B3**
Old Tampa Bay Park
  FL . . . 27°58N 82°35W **119 B3**
Old Tavern VA . . . 38°50N 77°49W **77 B3**
Old Town FL . . . 29°36N 82°59W **67 B6**
Old Town IL . . . 41°54N 87°37W **108 B3**
Old Town ME . . . 44°56N 68°39W **76 D5**
Old Washington OH . . . 40°2N 81°27W **92 C5**
Old Woman Mts. CA 34°20N 115°0W **65 J11**
Olde Providence NC 35°6N 80°47W **107 B2**
Oldenburg IN . . . 39°21N 85°12W **72 D5**
Oldham SD . . . 44°14N 97°19W **91 F8**
Oldham County ☆
  KY . . . 38°25N 85°30W **97 B7**
Oldham County ☆
  TX . . . 35°30N 102°30W **98 B5**
Oldhams VA . . . 38°0N 76°40W **77 B4**
Oldsmar FL . . . 28°2N 82°39W **119 A2**
Oldtown MD . . . 39°33N 78°37W **77 A2**
Olean MO . . . 38°25N 92°32W **82 C4**
Olean NY . . . 42°5N 78°26W **89 C2**
Olentangy → OH . . . 39°58N 83°0W **92 D3**
Oleta River State Rec. Area
  FL . . . 25°56N 80°8W **112 C3**
Olex OR . . . 45°30N 120°11W **94 B5**
Olin IA . . . 42°0N 91°8W **73 C7**
Olive Branch MS . . . 34°57N 89°49W **112 C2**
Olive Hill KY . . . 38°18N 83°10W **97 B9**
Olivehurst CA . . . 39°6N 121°34W **64 D5**
Olivet KS . . . 38°29N 95°45W **74 C8**
Olivet MI . . . 42°27N 84°56W **79 G7**
Olivet SD . . . 43°14N 97°40W **91 G8**
Olivette MO . . . 38°39N 90°22W **117 A1**
Olivia MN . . . 44°47N 94°59W **80 F4**
Olivia, L. FL . . . 28°31N 81°31W **115 A1**
Olla LA . . . 31°54N 92°14W **75 C3**
Ollie IA . . . 41°12N 92°6W **73 D6**
Olmos Basin Park
  TX . . . 29°29N 98°28W **117 B2**
Olmos Park TX . . . 29°28N 98°29W **117 B2**
Olmsted IL . . . 37°11N 89°5W **71 F4**
Olmsted County ☆
  MN . . . 44°0N 92°30W **80 G6**
Olney IL . . . 38°44N 88°5W **71 D5**
Olney MO . . . 39°9N 77°4W **77 A3**
Olney MT . . . 48°33N 114°35W **83 B3**
Olney TX . . . 33°22N 98°45W **99 D9**
Olney Springs CO . . . 38°10N 103°57W **66 D7**
Olosega Amer. Samoa 14°10S 169°37W **105 f**
Olowalu HI . . . 20°49N 156°38W **69 L5**
Olpe KS . . . 38°16N 96°9W **74 C7**
Olsburg KS . . . 39°26N 96°37W **74 B7**
Olton TX . . . 34°11N 102°8W **98 D5**
Olustee FL . . . 30°12N 82°26W **67 A6**
Olustee OK . . . 34°33N 99°25W **93 D4**
Olympia WA . . . 47°3N 122°53W **101 C3**
Olympian Village MO 38°8N 90°27W **82 C6**
Olympic Mts. WA . . . 47°55N 123°45W **101 C2**
Olympic Nat. Forest
  WA . . . 47°25N 123°35W **101 C2**
Olympic Nat. Park △
  WA . . . 48°16N 124°40W **101 B1**
Olympic Stadium = Turner Field
  GA . . . 33°44N 84°23W **106 C3**
Olympus, Mt. WA . . . 47°48N 123°43W **101 C2**
Omaha NE . . . 41°17N 95°58W **84 C10**
Omaha Eppley Airfield × (OMA)
  NE . . . 41°18N 95°53W **84 C10**
Omaha Indian Reservation
  NE . . . 42°10N 96°30W **84 B9**

Omemee ND . . . 48°42N 100°22W **91 B5**
Omer WI . . . 39°30N 78°17W **77 A2**
Ommaney, C. AK . . . 56°10N 134°40W **61 H14**
Ompompanoosuc →
  VT . . . 43°45N 72°14W **86 C2**
Omps WI . . . 39°30N 78°17W **77 A2**
Omro WI . . . 44°2N 88°45W **103 D5**
Ona FL . . . 27°29N 81°55W **67 D7**
Onaga KS . . . 39°29N 96°10W **74 B7**
Onaka SD . . . 45°12N 99°28W **91 E6**
Onalaska WI . . . 43°53N 91°14W **103 E2**
Onamia MN . . . 46°4N 93°40W **80 D5**
Onancock VA . . . 37°43N 75°45W **102 D9**
Onarga IL . . . 40°43N 88°1W **71 C5**
Onawa IA . . . 42°2N 96°6W **84 B9**
Onaway ID . . . 46°56N 116°53W **70 C2**
Onaway MI . . . 45°21N 84°14W **79 D7**
Oneco FL . . . 27°25N 82°33W **67 D6**
Oneida IL . . . 41°4N 90°13W **71 B3**
Oneida IA . . . 42°28N 91°21W **73 C7**
Oneida KS . . . 39°52N 95°56W **74 B8**
Oneida NY . . . 43°6N 75°39W **89 B5**
Oneida TN . . . 36°30N 84°31W **97 D8**
Oneida County ☆
  ID . . . 42°10N 112°30W **70 G6**
Oneida County ☆ NY 43°20N 75°30W **89 B5**
Oneida County ☆
  WI . . . 45°40N 89°35W **103 C4**
Oneida Indian Reservation
  NY . . . 43°1N 75°38W **89 B5**
Oneida Indian Reservation
  WI . . . 44°25N 88°10W **103 D5**
Oneida L. NY . . . 43°12N 75°54W **89 B5**
O'Neill NE . . . 42°27N 98°39W **84 B7**
Onekama MI . . . 44°22N 86°12W **79 E5**
Oneonta AL . . . 33°57N 86°28W **60 C4**
Oneonta NY . . . 42°27N 75°4W **89 C5**
Onida SD . . . 44°42N 100°4W **91 F5**
Onley VA . . . 37°41N 75°43W **102 D9**
Ono CA . . . 40°29N 122°37W **64 C4**
Onondaga County ☆
  NY . . . 43°0N 76°15W **89 B4**
Onondaga Indian Reservation
  NY . . . 42°56N 76°10W **89 C4**
Onset MA . . . 41°45N 70°39W **78 C4**
Onslow IA . . . 42°6N 91°1W **73 C7**
Onslow B. NC . . . 34°20N 77°15W **90 D8**
Onslow County ☆
  NC . . . 34°50N 77°30W **90 D8**
Ontario CA . . . 34°4N 117°39W **65 J9**
Ontario OR . . . 44°2N 116°58W **94 C9**
Ontario WI . . . 43°45N 90°35W **103 E3**
Ontario, L. N. Amer. . . . 43°20N 78°0W **89 B3**
Ontario Int. × (ONT)
  CA . . . 34°3N 117°36W **65 J9**
Ontonagon MI . . . 46°52N 89°19W **79 C2**
Ontonagon County ☆
  MI . . . 46°40N 89°25W **79 C2**
Ontonagon Indian Reservation
  MI . . . 46°29N 89°6W **79 C2**
'O'okala HI . . . 20°1N 155°17W **69 C6**
Oolitic IN . . . 38°54N 86°31W **72 E4**
Oologah OK . . . 36°27N 95°43W **93 B8**
Oologah L. OK . . . 36°26N 95°41W **93 B8**
Oostburg WI . . . 43°38N 87°48W **103 E6**
Opal SD . . . 45°5N 102°20W **91 E3**
Opal WY . . . 41°46N 110°20W **104 E2**
Opelika AL . . . 32°39N 85°23W **60 D5**
Opelousas LA . . . 30°32N 92°5W **75 D3**
Opequon → WV . . . 39°31N 77°52W **77 A3**
Opheim MT . . . 48°51N 106°24W **83 B11**
Ophir AK . . . 63°10N 156°31W **61 E8**
Ophir OR . . . 42°34N 124°23W **94 E1**
Opihikao HI . . . 19°26N 154°53W **69 D7**
Opp AL . . . 31°17N 86°16W **60 E4**
Opportunity MT . . . 46°6N 112°56W **83 D6**
Opportunity WA . . . 47°39N 117°15W **101 C8**
Optima OK . . . 36°46N 101°23W **93 B2**
Optima L. OK . . . 36°40N 101°8W **93 B2**
Optima Nat. Wildlife Refuge △
  OK . . . 36°48N 101°19W **93 B2**
Oquawka IL . . . 40°56N 90°57W **71 C3**
Oquirrh UT . . . 40°35N 112°1W **117 C1**
Oquossoc ME . . . 44°58N 70°46W **86 B4**
Oracle AZ . . . 32°37N 110°46W **62 E5**
Oran MO . . . 37°5N 89°39W **82 D7**
Orange CA . . . 33°47N 117°51W **65 K9**
Orange CT . . . 41°17N 73°2W **78 C1**
Orange MA . . . 42°35N 72°19W **78 B2**
Orange NJ . . . 40°46N 74°13W **114 B1**
Orange TX . . . 30°6N 93°44W **99 G14**
Orange VA . . . 38°15N 78°7W **102 C6**
Orange Beach AL . . . 30°18N 87°34W **60 F3**
Orange Bowl Stadium
  FL . . . 25°46N 80°14W **112 D2**
Orange City FL . . . 28°57N 81°18W **67 C7**
Orange City IA . . . 43°0N 96°4W **73 B2**
Orange County ☆
  CA . . . 33°30N 117°45W **65 K9**
Orange County ☆ FL 28°30N 81°20W **67 C7**
Orange County ☆ NC 36°0N 79°10W **90 B6**
Orange County ☆
  NY . . . 41°20N 74°15W **89 D6**
Orange County ☆
  TX . . . 30°5N 93°52W **99 G14**
Orange County ☆
  VA . . . 38°15N 78°7W **102 C6**
Orange Cove CA . . . 36°38N 119°19W **65 G7**
Orange Grove TX . . . 27°58N 97°56W **99 K10**
Orange L. FL . . . 29°25N 82°13W **67 B6**
Orange Park FL . . . 30°10N 81°42W **67 A7**
Orange Res. NJ . . . 40°46N 74°17W **114 A1**
Orangeburg SC . . . 33°30N 80°52W **90 D5**
Orangeburg County ☆
  SC . . . 33°30N 80°50W **90 D5**
Orangevale CA . . . 38°41N 121°13W **64 E5**
Orangeville IL . . . 42°28N 89°39W **71 A4**
Orangeville PA . . . 41°5N 76°25W **95 C6**
Orangeville UT . . . 39°14N 111°3W **100 D4**
Orbisonia PA . . . 40°15N 77°54W **95 D5**
Orcas I. WA . . . 48°42N 122°56W **101 B3**
Orchard CO . . . 40°20N 104°7W **66 B6**
Orchard ID . . . 43°19N 116°2W **70 F2**
Orchard IA . . . 43°14N 92°47W **73 B6**
Orchard NE . . . 42°20N 98°15W **84 B7**
Orchard City CO . . . 38°49N 107°58W **66 D3**
Orchard Homes MT . . . 46°55N 114°4W **83 D3**
Orchard Mesa CO . . . 39°4N 108°33W **66 C2**
Orchard Park NY . . . 42°46N 78°45W **89 C2**
Orchard Valley WY . . . 41°6N 104°48W **104 E8**
Orchards WA . . . 45°41N 122°33W **101 E3**
Orcutt CA . . . 34°52N 120°27W **65 J6**
Ord NE . . . 41°36N 98°56W **84 C7**
Ord, Mt. TX . . . 30°18N 103°30W **98 G4**
Orderville UT . . . 37°17N 112°38W **100 F3**
Ordway CO . . . 38°13N 103°46W **66 D7**
Ore City TX . . . 32°48N 94°43W **99 E13**
Oreana NV . . . 40°20N 118°19W **85 B2**
Oregon IL . . . 42°1N 89°20W **71 A4**
Oregon MO . . . 39°59N 95°9W **82 B1**
Oregon OH . . . 41°38N 83°29W **92 B3**
Oregon WI . . . 42°56N 89°23W **103 F4**
Oregon □ U.S.A . . . 44°0N 121°0W **94 D4**
Oregon Butte . . . 45°31N 115°40W **70 D3**

Oregon Butte WA.. 46°7N 117°41W 101 D8
Oregon Caves Nat. Monument △
　OR.......... 42°6N 123°24W 94 E2
Oregon City OR .. 45°21N 122°36W 94 B3
Oregon County ☆
　MO.......... 36°40N 91°25W 82 E5
Oregon Dunes Nat. Recr. Area △
　OR....... 43°40N 124°10W 94 D1
Oreland PA...... 40°7N 75°10W 116 A1
Orem UT...... 40°19N 111°42W 100 C4
Organ NE...... 32°26N 106°36W 88 E4
Organ Pipe Cactus Nat.
　Monument △ AZ . 32°0N 112°52W 62 E3
Orick CA...... 41°17N 124°4W 64 B2
Orient IA...... 41°12N 94°25W 73 C4
Orient ME...... 45°49N 67°50W 76 C6
Orient SD...... 44°54N 99°5W 91 F6
Orient WA...... 48°52N 118°12W 101 B7
Orient Heights MA. 42°23N 70°59W 106 A4
Oriental NC...... 35°2N 76°42W 90 C9
Orin WY...... 42°39N 105°12W 104 D7
Orinda CA...... 37°52N 122°10W 118 A3
Orion AL...... 31°58N 86°0W 60 E5
Orion IL...... 41°21N 90°23W 71 B3
Orion OK...... 36°13N 98°47W 93 B5
Oriska ND...... 46°56N 97°47W 91 D8
Oriskany NY...... 43°10N 75°20W 89 B5
Orla TX...... 31°50N 103°55W 98 F4
Orland CA...... 39°45N 122°12W 64 F4
Orland Park IL... 41°38N 87°52W 71 B6
Orlando FL...... 28°32N 81°22W 115 A2
Orlando OK...... 36°9N 97°4W 93 B6
Orlando Executive ✕
　FL........ 28°32N 81°20W 115 A2
Orlando Int. ✕ (MCO)
　FL........ 28°26N 81°19W 115 B3
Orlean VA...... 38°45N 77°58W 77 B3
Orleans CA...... 41°18N 123°32W 64 B3
Orleans IN...... 38°40N 86°27W 72 F4
Orleans IA...... 43°27N 95°6W 73 B3
Orleans MA...... 41°47N 69°59W 78 C5
Orleans NE...... 40°8N 99°27W 84 D6
Orleans VT...... 44°49N 72°12W 78 B3
Orleans County ☆
　NY........ 43°15N 78°10W 89 B2
Orleans County ☆
　VT........ 44°45N 72°15W 86 B2
Orleans Parish ☆ LA . 29°58N 90°4W 75 E5
Orlinda TN...... 36°36N 86°43W 96 D6
Orlovista FL...... 28°32N 81°27W 115 A2
Ormond Beach FL.. 29°17N 81°3W 67 B7
Ormond-by-the-Sea
　FL........ 29°17N 81°3W 67 B7
Ormsby MN...... 43°51N 94°42W 80 G4
Oro Grande CA ... 34°36N 117°20W 65 J9
Oro Valley AZ...... 32°26N 110°58W 62 E5
Orofino ID...... 46°29N 116°15W 70 C2
Orogrande ID..... 45°42N 115°33W 70 D3
Orogrande NM.... 32°24N 106°5W 88 E4
Orono ME...... 44°53N 68°40W 76 D5
Oronoco MN..... 44°10N 92°32W 80 F6
Orote Pen. Guam .. 13°26N 144°38E 105 b
Orovada NV...... 41°34N 117°47W 85 A3
Oroville CA...... 39°31N 121°33W 64 D5
Oroville WA...... 48°56N 119°26W 101 B6
Oroville, L. CA ... 39°33N 121°29W 64 D5
Oroville Dam CA .. 39°33N 121°29W 64 D5
Orpha WY...... 42°51N 105°30W 104 D7
Orr MN...... 48°3N 92°50W 80 B6
Orr OK...... 39°23N 97°32W 93 D6
Orrick MO...... 39°13N 94°7W 82 B2
Orrin ND...... 48°6N 100°10W 91 B5
Orrville AL...... 34°40N 86°59W 60 D4
Orrville OH...... 40°50N 81°46W 92 C5
Orting WA...... 47°6N 122°12W 101 C4
Ortley SD...... 45°20N 97°12W 91 E8
Ortonville MN.... 45°19N 96°27W 80 E2
Orwell OH...... 41°32N 80°52W 92 B5
Osage AR...... 36°11N 93°24W 63 B2
Osage IA...... 43°17N 92°49W 73 B6
Osage OK...... 36°19N 96°4W 93 B7
Osage WY...... 43°59N 104°25W 104 C8
Osage → MO ... 38°36N 91°57W 82 C5
Osage Beach MO .. 38°9N 92°37W 82 C4
Osage City KS... 38°38N 95°50W 74 C8
Osage City MO ... 38°33N 92°2W 82 C4
Osage County ☆ KS. 38°40N 95°40W 74 C8
Osage County ☆ OK 36°40N 96°30W 93 B7
Osage Fork → . 37°46N 92°26W 82 D4
Osage Indian Reservation
　OK....... 36°35N 96°30W 93 B7
Osakis MN...... 45°52N 95°9W 80 E3
Osakis, L. MN.... 45°52N 95°9W 80 E3
Osawatomie KS ... 38°31N 94°57W 74 C9
Osborne KS...... 39°26N 98°42W 74 B5
Osborne County ☆
　KS........ 39°30N 98°45W 74 B5
Osburn ID...... 47°30N 116°0W 70 B2
Osceola AR...... 35°42N 89°58W 63 C6
Osceola IA...... 41°2N 93°46W 73 D5
Osceola MO...... 38°3N 93°42W 82 C3
Osceola NE...... 41°11N 97°33W 84 C8
Osceola WI...... 45°19N 92°42W 103 C1
Osceola County ☆ FL. 28°0N 81°0W 67 C7
Osceola County ☆ IA 43°20N 95°35W 73 B3
Osceola County ☆ MI 44°0N 85°20W 79 F6
Osceola Mills PA .. 40°51N 78°16W 95 D4
Osceola Nat. Forest
　FL........ 30°20N 82°30W 67 A6
Oscoda MI...... 44°26N 83°20W 79 E8
Oscoda County ☆ MI 44°40N 84°10W 79 E7
Oscuro NM...... 33°29N 106°3W 88 D4
Osgood IN...... 39°8N 85°18W 72 D5
Osgood MO...... 40°20N 84°30W 92 C2
Osgood Mts. NV .. 41°10N 117°20W 85 A3
Oshkosh NE...... 41°24N 102°21W 84 C3
Oshkosh WI...... 44°1N 88°33W 103 D5
Osierfield GA..... 31°40N 83°7W 68 E3
Oskaloosa IA...... 41°18N 92°39W 73 D6
Oskaloosa KS..... 39°13N 95°19W 74 B8
Oslo MN...... 48°12N 97°8W 80 B1
Osmond ND...... 48°40N 98°9W 91 B7
Osprey FL...... 27°12N 82°29W 67 C6
Ossabaw I. GA .... 31°50N 81°5W 68 E5
Ossabaw Sd. GA .. 31°50N 81°6W 68 E5
Osseo MI...... 41°53N 84°33W 79 H7
Osseo WI...... 44°35N 91°13W 103 D2
Ossian IN...... 40°53N 85°10W 72 E4
Ossian IA...... 43°9N 91°46W 73 B7
Ossineke MI...... 44°55N 83°26W 79 E8
Ossining NY...... 41°10N 73°55W 87 A3
Ossipee NH...... 43°41N 71°7W 86 C3
Ossipee L. MI.... 44°55N 84°42W 79 E7
Osterville MA..... 41°38N 70°22W 78 C4
Ostrander MN.... 43°37N 92°26W 80 G6
O'Sullivan Dam
　WA........ 46°59N 119°16W 101 C6
Oswegatchie → NY.. 44°42N 75°30W 89 A5
Oswego IL...... 41°41N 88°21W 71 B5
Oswego KS...... 37°10N 95°6W 74 D8
Oswego NY...... 43°27N 76°31W 89 B4
Oswego → NY ... 43°27N 76°30W 89 B4
Oswego, L. OR ... 45°25N 122°40W 116 B1
Oswego County ☆
　NY........ 43°15N 76°10W 89 B4
Osyka MS...... 31°0N 90°28W 81 E3
Otay Mesa CA.... 32°34N 117°3W 117 J12
Otego NY...... 42°42N 75°10W 89 C5

Otero County ☆ CO 38°0N 103°45W 66 E7
Otero County ☆
　NM........ 32°30N 105°45W 88 E5
Othello WA...... 46°50N 119°10W 101 D6
Otho IA...... 42°25N 94°9W 73 C4
Otis CO...... 40°9N 102°58W 66 B8
Otis KS...... 38°32N 99°3W 74 C4
Otisco IN...... 38°32N 85°40W 72 D5
Otisville MI...... 43°10N 83°31W 79 F8
Otisville NY...... 41°28N 74°32W 87 A2
Otoe NE...... 40°43N 96°7W 84 D9
Otoe County ☆ NE. 40°40N 96°0W 84 D9
Otsego MI...... 42°27N 85°42W 79 G6
Otsego County ☆ MI. 45°0N 84°30W 79 E7
Otsego County ☆ NY. 42°40N 75°0W 89 C6
Otsego L. NY ... 42°45N 74°52W 89 C6
Otsego L. MI..... 44°56N 84°40W 79 E7
Ottawa IL...... 41°21N 88°51W 71 B5
Ottawa KS...... 38°37N 95°16W 74 C8
Ottawa OH...... 41°1N 84°3W 92 B2
Ottawa County ☆ KS 39°15N 97°45W 74 B6
Ottawa County ☆ MI 43°0N 86°0W 79 G5
Ottawa County ☆ OH 41°30N 83°0W 92 B3
Ottawa Nat. Forest
　OK........ 36°50N 94°50W 93 B9
Ottawa Nat. Wildlife Refuge △
　OH....... 41°36N 83°13W 92 B3
Otter MT...... 45°12N 106°12W 83 E11
Otter Cr. → IN ... 38°10N 112°2W 100 E2
Otter Cr. → VT ... 44°13N 73°17W 86 B1
Otter Creek FL.... 29°19N 82°46W 67 B6
Otter Creek Res.
　UT........ 38°10N 112°1W 100 E3
Otter Lake IL..... 39°28N 89°56W 71 D4
Otter Lake MI..... 43°13N 83°28W 79 F8
Otter Tail → MN .. 46°16N 96°36W 80 D2
Otter Tail County ☆
　MN........ 46°20N 95°45W 80 D3
Otter Tail L. MN .. 46°24N 95°40W 80 D3
Otterbein IN...... 40°29N 87°6W 72 D3
Ottertail MN...... 46°26N 95°33W 80 D3
Otterville MO..... 38°42N 93°0W 82 C4
Otto WY...... 44°24N 108°16W 104 B4
Ottosen IA...... 42°54N 94°23W 73 C4
Ottumwa IA...... 41°1N 92°25W 73 D6
Otway OH...... 38°52N 83°11W 92 E3
Otwell AR...... 33°51N 92°50W 63 C3
Ouachita → LA .. 31°38N 91°49W 75 C4
Ouachita, L. AR ... 34°34N 93°12W 63 C2
Ouachita County ☆
　AR........ 33°35N 92°50W 63 D3
Ouachita Mts. AR.. 34°30N 94°30W 93 D9
Ouachita Nat. Forest
　AR........ 34°50N 94°50W 93 D9
Ouachita Nat. Forest
　OK........ 34°40N 94°30W 93 D9
Ouachita Parish ☆ LA 32°30N 92°7W 75 B3
Ouray CO...... 38°1N 107°40W 66 D3
Ouray UT...... 40°6N 109°41W 100 C6
Outagamie County ☆
　WI........ 44°20N 88°30W 103 D5
Outer Banks U.S.A. 35°54N 75°28W 90 C10
Outer I. WI...... 47°2N 90°26W 103 A3
Outer Mission
　CA........ 37°43N 122°26W 118 B2
Outer Santa Barbara
　CA........ 33°15N 118°40W 65 K8
Outlook MT...... 48°53N 104°47W 83 B13
Outlook WA...... 46°22N 120°8W 101 D5
Oval Pk. WA ... 48°17N 120°25W 101 B5
Ovando MT...... 47°1N 113°8W 83 C4
Overbrook KS..... 38°47N 95°33W 74 C8
Overflow Nat. Wildlife Refuge △
　AR........ 33°4N 91°41W 63 D4
Overland MO..... 38°42N 90°21W 117 A1
Overland Park KS .. 38°58N 94°40W 74 C9
Overly ND...... 48°41N 100°9W 91 B5
Overton NE...... 40°44N 99°32W 84 D6
Overton NV...... 36°33N 114°27W 85 F6
Overton TX...... 32°16N 94°59W 99 E13
Overton County ☆
　TN........ 36°23N 85°19W 97 D7
Overton Park TN .. 35°8N 89°59W 112 B2
Ovett MS...... 31°29N 89°2W 81 E4
Ovid CO...... 40°58N 102°23W 66 B8
Ovid MI...... 43°1N 84°22W 79 F7
Ovid NY...... 42°41N 76°49W 89 C4
Oviedo FL...... 28°40N 81°13W 67 C7
Owanka SD...... 44°1N 102°35W 91 F3
Owasco L. NY ... 42°50N 76°31W 89 C4
Owasso OK...... 36°16N 95°51W 93 B8
Owasso, L. MN ... 44°59N 93°9W 113 A3
Owatonna MN.... 44°5N 93°14W 80 F5
Owego NY...... 42°6N 76°16W 89 C4
Owen WI...... 44°57N 90°33W 103 D3
Owen County ☆ IN. 39°20N 86°50W 72 D4
Owen County ☆ KY. 38°30N 84°50W 97 B8
Owens → CA .... 36°32N 117°59W 65 G9
Owens L. CA .... 36°26N 117°57W 65 G9
Owensboro KY.... 37°46N 87°7W 96 C5
Owensville IN.... 38°16N 87°41W 72 E3
Owensville MO ... 38°21N 91°30W 82 C5
Owenton KY...... 38°32N 84°50W 97 B8
Owentown VA .... 37°53N 77°6W 77 C3
Owings Mills MD .. 39°25N 76°47W 77 A4
Owingsville KY ... 38°9N 83°46W 97 B9
Owl Creek Mts.
　WY........ 43°40N 108°55W 104 C4
Owls Head ME .... 44°5N 69°4W 76 D4
Owosso MI...... 43°0N 84°10W 79 F7
Owsley County ☆ KY. 37°25N 83°40W 97 C9
Owyhee NV...... 41°57N 116°6W 85 A4
Owyhee → OR ... 43°49N 117°2W 94 D8
Owyhee, L. OR ... 43°38N 117°14W 94 D8
Owyhee County ☆
　ID........ 42°45N 116°0W 70 G2
Owyhee Desert NV. 41°40N 116°50W 85 A4
Owyhee Mts. ID .. 42°45N 116°50W 70 G2
Ox Cr. → ND .... 48°35N 100°8W 91 B5
Oxbow ME...... 46°25N 68°28W 76 B5
Oxford AL...... 33°36N 85°51W 60 C5
Oxford AR...... 36°13N 91°56W 63 B4
Oxford IN...... 40°31N 87°15W 72 C3
Oxford IA...... 41°43N 91°47W 73 D7
Oxford KS...... 37°17N 97°10W 74 D6
Oxford MA...... 42°7N 71°52W 78 B3
Oxford ME...... 44°8N 70°30W 76 D3
Oxford MD...... 38°41N 76°11W 77 C4
Oxford MI...... 42°49N 83°15W 79 F8
Oxford MS...... 34°22N 89°31W 81 B4
Oxford NC...... 36°19N 78°35W 90 B7
Oxford NY...... 42°27N 75°36W 89 C5
Oxford OH...... 39°31N 84°45W 92 D2
Oxford PA...... 39°47N 75°59W 77 A5
Oxford WI...... 43°47N 89°34W 103 E4
Oxford County ☆
　ME........ 44°30N 70°30W 76 D3
Oxford Junction IA. 42°16N 90°57W 73 D8
Oxford Pk. ID .... 42°16N 112°6W 70 G6
Oxnard CA...... 34°12N 119°11W 65 J7
Oxon Hill MD.... 38°48N 76°59W 119 C4
Oyster Bay NY ... 40°52N 73°32W 78 D1
Ozan AR...... 33°51N 93°43W 63 D2

Ozark AL...... 31°28N 85°39W 60 E5
Ozark AR...... 35°29N 93°50W 63 B2
Ozark MO...... 37°1N 93°12W 82 D3
Ozark County ☆ MO 36°40N 92°25W 82 E4
Ozark Folk Center State Park
　AR........ 35°53N 92°7W 63 B3
Ozark Lake AR.... 35°30N 94°10W 63 C1
Ozark Nat. Forest
　AR........ 35°40N 93°20W 63 C2
Ozark Nat. Scenic Riverways
　MO....... 37°20N 91°40W 82 D5
Ozark Plateau MO. 37°20N 91°40W 82 E3
Ozarks, L. of the MO 38°10N 92°38W 82 C4
Ozaukee County ☆
　WI........ 43°20N 88°0W 103 E6
Ozawkie KS...... 39°14N 95°28W 74 B8
Ozette, L. WA .... 48°6N 124°38W 101 B1
Ozette Indian Reservation
　WA....... 48°10N 124°43W 101 B1
Ozona TX...... 30°43N 101°12W 98 G6
Ozone TN...... 35°53N 84°49W 97 D8
Ozone Park NY ... 40°40N 73°50W 114 B3

P

Pa'auilo HI........ 20°2N 155°22W 69 C6
Pablo MT........ 47°36N 114°7W 83 C3
Pace FL......... 30°36N 87°10W 67 A1
Pachuta MS....... 32°2N 88°53W 81 D5
Pacific MO....... 38°29N 90°45W 82 C6
Pacific Beach CA .. 32°47N 117°14W 117 E2
Pacific Beach WA .. 47°13N 124°12W 101 C1
Pacific City = Huntington Beach
Pacific City OR ... 33°40N 118°5W 65 K8
Pacific County ☆
　WA........ 46°30N 123°55W 101 D2
Pacific Grove CA .. 36°38N 121°56W 64 G5
Pacific Heights CA. 37°47N 122°26W 118 B2
Pacific Junction IA. 41°1N 95°48W 73 D3
Pacific Manor CA .. 37°38N 122°12W 118 C2
Pacific Palisades CA 34°2N 118°32W 111 J8
Pacific Palisades
　HI........ 21°25N 157°58W 69 K14
Pacifica CA...... 37°36N 122°30W 118 C2
Packanack Lake NJ. 40°56N 74°13W 114 A1
Packwood WA .... 46°36N 121°40W 101 D4
Pacolet SC...... 34°54N 81°46W 90 D4
Pacolet → SC .... 34°55N 81°56W 90 D4
Paden OK...... 35°30N 96°34W 93 C7
Paden City WV ... 39°36N 80°56W 102 B4
Padre Island Nat. Seashore △
　U.S.A...... 27°0N 97°25W 98 K10
Padroni CO...... 40°47N 103°10W 66 B7
Paducah KY...... 37°5N 88°37W 96 C4
Paducah TX...... 34°1N 100°18W 98 C7
Pagan N. Marianas. 18°7N 145°46E 105 a
Pagai'au HI...... 21°26N 160°5W 69 B1
Page AZ...... 36°57N 111°27W 62 A4
Page ND...... 47°10N 97°34W 91 C8
Page NE...... 42°26N 98°25W 84 B7
Page OK...... 34°45N 94°40W 93 D9
Page County ☆ IA. 40°45N 95°10W 73 E3
Page County ☆ VA. 38°40N 78°28W 102 D6
Pagedale MO..... 38°41N 90°18W 117 A2
Pageland SC...... 34°46N 80°24W 90 D5
Pago B. Guam ... 13°25N 144°47E 105 b
Pago, Amer. Samoa. 14°16S 170°43W 105 e
Pago Pago Harbor
　Amer. Samoa. 14°17S 170°40W 105 e
Pagosa Springs CO. 37°16N 107°1W 66 E3
Paguate NM...... 35°7N 107°23W 88 B3
Pāhala HI...... 19°12N 155°29W 69 D6
Pahaska WY...... 44°30N 109°58W 104 B3
Pāhoa HI...... 19°30N 154°57W 69 D7
Pahokee FL...... 26°50N 80°40W 67 C8
Pahrump NV...... 36°12N 115°59W 85 F5
Pahranagat Ra. NV. 37°15N 115°8W 85 E5
Pahrock Ra. NV... 37°35N 114°58W 85 E6
Pahute Mesa NV .. 37°20N 116°45W 85 E4
Pahvant Range UT. 39°0N 112°5W 100 D3
Paia HI...... 20°54N 156°22W 69 C5
Paige TX...... 30°13N 97°7W 99 G10
Pailolo Channel HI. 21°0N 156°40W 69 C5
Paincourtville LA .. 29°59N 91°3W 75 E4
Painesdale MI .... 47°3N 88°40W 79 B3
Painesville OH.... 41°43N 81°15W 92 B5
Paint Cr. → OH .. 39°15N 83°20W 92 D3
Paint Rock AL .... 34°40N 86°20W 60 B4
Paint Rock TX .... 31°31N 99°55W 99 F8
Paint Rock → TX. 31°30N 99°56W 99 F8
Painted Desert AZ. 36°0N 111°0W 62 B5
Paintsville KY .... 37°49N 82°48W 97 C10
Paisley FL...... 28°59N 81°32W 67 C7
Paisley OR...... 42°42N 120°32W 94 E5
Paiute Indian Reservation
　UT........ 37°10N 113°46W 100 F2
Pajarito NM...... 34°59N 106°42W 88 C3
Pala CA...... 33°22N 117°5W 65 K10
Pala Indian Reservation
　CA........ 33°22N 116°58W 65 K10
Palacios TX...... 28°42N 96°13W 99 J11
Palaoa Pt. HI .... 20°44N 156°58W 69 C5
Palatine IL...... 42°7N 88°3W 71 A5
Palatka FL...... 29°39N 81°38W 67 B7
Palco KS...... 39°15N 99°34W 74 B4
Palen Dry L. CA .. 33°46N 115°13W 65 K11
Palermo CA...... 39°26N 121°33W 64 D5
Palermo ND...... 48°21N 102°14W 91 B3
Palestine AR...... 34°58N 90°54W 63 C5
Palestine IL...... 39°0N 87°37W 71 D6
Palestine OH..... 40°3N 84°45W 92 C2
Palestine TX...... 31°46N 95°38W 99 F12
Palestine, L. TX .. 32°6N 95°27W 99 E12
Palikea HI...... 21°26N 158°6W 69 K13
Palito Blanco TX .. 27°35N 98°11W 98 K9
Palm Bay FL...... 28°2N 80°35W 67 C8
Palm Beach FL.... 26°43N 80°2W 67 C8
Palm Beach County ☆
　FL........ 26°49N 80°8W 67 E8
Palm Beach Gardens
　FL........ 26°41N 80°6W 67 E8
Palm Beach Int. ✕ (PBI)
　FL........ 26°41N 80°6W 67 E8
Palm City CA..... 32°35N 117°5W 117 C2
Palm Coast FL .... 29°35N 81°12W 67 B7
Palm Desert CA .. 33°43N 116°22W 65 K10
Palm Harbor FL .. 28°5N 82°46W 67 C6
Palm Valley FL.... 30°11N 81°23W 67 A7
Palmdale CA...... 34°35N 118°7W 65 J8
Palmer AK...... 61°36N 149°7W 61 F10
Palmer IA...... 42°37N 94°36W 73 C4
Palmer KS...... 39°38N 97°8W 74 B6
Palmer MA...... 42°9N 72°20W 78 B2
Palmer NE...... 41°13N 98°15W 84 C7
Palmer TN...... 35°21N 85°34W 97 D7
Palmer Lake CO .. 39°7N 104°55W 66 C6
Palmer Park MD .. 38°55N 76°52W 119 B4
Palmers Crossing MS 31°16N 89°15W 81 E4

Palmerton PA .... 40°48N 75°37W 87 B1
Palmetto FL...... 27°31N 82°34W 67 C6
Palmetto GA...... 33°31N 84°40W 68 C2
Palmetto LA...... 30°43N 91°55W 75 D4
Palmyra IN...... 38°24N 86°7W 72 E4
Palmyra MO...... 39°48N 91°32W 82 B5
Palmyra NJ...... 40°0N 75°1W 116 B2
Palmyra NE...... 40°42N 96°23W 84 D9
Palmyra NY...... 43°4N 77°14W 89 B4
Palmyra PA...... 40°18N 76°36W 95 D6
Palmyra VA...... 37°52N 78°16W 102 D6
Palmyra Is. Pac. Oc.. 5°52N 162°5W 105 D7
Palo Alto CA...... 37°27N 122°10W 64 F4
Palo Alto County ☆
　IA........ 43°5N 94°40W 73 B4
Palo Duro Cr. → TX 35°0N 101°5W 98 B6
Palo Pinto TX .... 32°46N 98°18W 99 E9
Palo Pinto County ☆
　TX........ 32°45N 98°20W 99 E9
Palo Verde AZ.... 33°21N 112°41W 62 D3
Palo Verde CA .... 33°26N 114°44W 65 K12
Palos Heights IL .. 41°39N 87°47W 108 C2
Palos Hills IL..... 41°42N 87°49W 108 C2
Palos Hills Forest IL 41°40N 87°52W 108 C1
Palos Park IL..... 41°40N 87°50W 108 C1
Palos Verdes, Pt.
　CA........ 33°46N 118°25W 111 J7
Palos Verdes Estates
　CA........ 33°48N 118°23W 111 J2
Palos Verdes Hills
　CA........ 33°44N 118°20W 111 J7
Palouse WA...... 46°55N 117°4W 101 D8
Palouse → WA ... 46°35N 118°13W 101 D7
Pamlico County ☆
　NC........ 35°10N 76°45W 90 C9
Pamlico Sd. NC... 35°20N 76°0W 90 C10
Pampa TX...... 35°32N 100°58W 98 B7
Pamplico SC...... 34°0N 79°34W 90 E6
Pamplin VA...... 37°16N 78°41W 102 D6
Pamunkey → VA .. 37°32N 76°48W 102 D8
Pana IL...... 39°23N 89°5W 71 D4
Panaca NV...... 37°47N 114°23W 85 E6
Panacea FL...... 30°2N 84°23W 67 A4
Panama NE...... 40°36N 96°31W 84 D9
Panama OK...... 35°10N 94°40W 93 C9
Panama City FL .. 30°10N 85°40W 67 A3
Panama City Beach
　FL........ 30°11N 85°48W 67 A3
Panamint Range
　CA........ 36°20N 117°20W 65 G9
Panamint Valley
　CA........ 36°15N 117°20W 65 G9
Pancake Range NV. 38°30N 115°50W 85 D5
Pandora OH...... 40°57N 83°58W 92 C3
Pangburn AR..... 35°26N 91°50W 63 C4
Panguitch UT .... 37°50N 112°26W 100 F3
Panhandle TX .... 35°21N 101°23W 98 B6
Panola AL...... 32°57N 88°16W 60 D2
Panola County ☆ MS 34°40N 89°55W 81 B4
Panola County ☆ TX 32°10N 94°20W 99 E13
Panora IA...... 41°42N 94°22W 73 D4
Panorama City CA. 34°13N 118°26W 111 J8
Panorama Pt. NE .. 41°0N 104°2W 84 C1
Pantego TX...... 32°42N 97°9W 99 b
Panthersville GA .. 33°43N 84°16W 106 B3
Paola KS...... 38°35N 94°53W 74 C9
Paoli CO...... 40°37N 102°28W 66 B8
Paoli IN...... 38°33N 86°28W 72 E4
Paoli OK...... 34°50N 97°15W 93 D6
Paoli PA...... 40°2N 75°24W 116 A3
Paonia CO...... 38°52N 107°36W 66 D3
Pāpā HI...... 19°13N 155°52W 69 D6
Pāpa'aloa HI..... 19°59N 155°13W 69 D6
Pāpa'ikou HI..... 19°47N 155°6W 69 D6
Papawai Pt. HI ... 20°47N 156°32W 69 C5
Papillion NE...... 41°9N 96°3W 84 C9
Papua AK...... 63°7N 163°15W 61 E7
Parachute CO .... 39°27N 108°3W 66 C2
Parade SD...... 45°1N 101°6W 91 E4
Paradise CA...... 39°46N 121°37W 64 D5
Paradise KS...... 39°7N 98°55W 74 B5
Paradise MI...... 46°38N 85°2W 79 C6
Paradise MT...... 47°23N 114°48W 83 C3
Paradise UT...... 41°34N 111°50W 100 B4
Paradise Hill OK .. 35°40N 95°9W 93 C8
Paradise Hills CA. 32°40N 117°3W 117 B2
Paradise Valley AZ 33°31N 111°56W 116 J3
Paradise Valley NV. 41°30N 117°32W 85 A3
Paradise Valley
　WY........ 42°49N 106°32W 104 D6
Paragon IN...... 39°24N 86°34W 72 D4
Paragonah UT .... 37°53N 112°46W 100 F3
Paragould AR .... 36°3N 90°29W 63 B5
Paramount CA.... 33°54N 118°10W 111 J8
Paramount Studios
　CA........ 34°5N 118°19W 111 J8
Paramus NJ...... 40°56N 74°2W 114 A2
Parchment MI .... 42°20N 85°34W 79 G6
Parco = Sinclair WY 41°47N 107°7W 104 E5
Pardee Res. CA ... 38°16N 120°51W 64 F6
Pardeeville WI ... 43°32N 89°18W 103 E4
Parguera
　Puerto Rico. 17°59N 67°3W 105 H15
Paria → AZ .... 36°52N 111°36W 62 A4
Paria Plateau AZ .. 36°50N 111°50W 62 A4
Paris AR...... 35°18N 93°44W 63 C2
Paris ID...... 42°14N 111°24W 70 G7
Paris IL...... 39°36N 87°42W 71 D6
Paris KY...... 38°13N 84°15W 97 B8
Paris ME...... 44°16N 70°30W 76 D3
Paris MO...... 39°29N 92°0W 82 B4
Paris TN...... 36°18N 88°19W 96 D4
Paris TX...... 33°40N 95°33W 99 D12
Parish NY...... 43°25N 76°8W 89 B4
Parishville NY.... 44°38N 74°49W 89 A6
Park KS...... 39°7N 100°22W 74 B3
Park → WA ... 48°28N 97°9W 91 B8
Park City KS...... 37°48N 97°20W 74 D6
Park City MT .... 45°38N 108°55W 83 D9
Park City UT .... 40°39N 111°30W 100 C4
Park County ☆ CO. 39°0N 105°45W 66 C5
Park County ☆ MT. 45°30N 110°30W 83 E7
Park County ☆ WY. 44°30N 109°30W 104 B3
Park Falls WI .... 45°56N 90°27W 103 C3
Park Forest IL.... 41°29N 87°40W 71 B6
Park Hills KY .... 39°4N 84°31W 107 B1
Park Range CO ... 40°41N 106°41W 66 B4
Park Rapids MN .. 46°55N 95°4W 80 D3
Park Ridge IL..... 42°2N 87°51W 108 A1
Park Ridge NJ .... 41°2N 74°2W 114 A2
Park River ND .... 48°24N 97°45W 91 B8
Park Road Park NC 35°8N 80°51W 107 B1
Park View NJ .... 41°42N 90°33W 73 D8
Parkchester NY ... 40°49N 73°51W 114 A3
Parkdale AR...... 33°7N 91°33W 63 E4
Parkdale OH..... 39°8N 84°25W 107 B2
Parker AZ...... 34°9N 114°17W 62 C2
Parker CO...... 39°31N 104°46W 66 C6
Parker ID...... 43°58N 111°46W 70 E7
Parker KS...... 38°18N 95°0W 74 C8
Parker PA...... 41°5N 79°41W 94 E3
Parker SD...... 43°24N 97°8W 91 G8
Parker City IN ... 40°11N 85°12W 72 C5

Parker County ☆
　TX........ 32°46N 97°48W 99 E10
Parker Dam AZ .. 34°18N 114°8W 62 C1
Parker River Nat. Wildlife
　Refuge △ MA. 42°45N 70°49W 78 B4
Parkers Prairie MN. 46°9N 95°20W 80 D3
Parkersburg IL ... 38°36N 88°3W 71 E5
Parkersburg IA ... 42°35N 92°47W 73 C6
Parkersburg WV .. 39°16N 81°34W 102 B3
Parkesburg PA ... 39°58N 75°55W 95 E7
Parkfield CA...... 35°54N 120°26W 65 H6
Parkin AR...... 35°16N 90°34W 63 C5
Parkland WA..... 47°9N 122°26W 101 C3
Parkrose OR...... 38°50N 77°7W 119 B3
Parks AR...... 34°48N 93°58W 63 C1
Parks AZ...... 40°3N 101°44W 62 C4
Parks, L. SD .... 45°1N 95°52W 91 E9
Parksley VA...... 37°47N 75°39W 102 D8
Parksville KY .... 37°34N 84°56W 97 C8
Parkston SD...... 43°24N 97°59W 91 G8
Parkton NC...... 34°54N 78°59W 90 D7
Parkville MD..... 39°22N 76°32W 107 A3
Parkville MO..... 39°12N 94°41W 82 B2
Parkway OR...... 38°31N 121°26W 64 b
Parlier CA...... 36°37N 119°32W 65 G7
Parma ID...... 43°47N 116°57W 70 F2
Parma MI...... 42°16N 84°36W 79 G7
Parma MO...... 36°37N 89°48W 82 E7
Parma OH...... 41°24N 81°43W 107 B1
Parma Heights OH. 41°23N 81°45W 107 B1
Parmelee SD..... 43°19N 101°2W 91 G4
Parmer County ☆
　TX........ 34°38N 102°45W 98 C5
Parnell IA...... 41°35N 92°0W 73 D7
Parnell MO...... 40°26N 94°37W 82 A2
Parol MD...... 38°59N 76°32W 77 B4
Parowan UT...... 37°51N 112°50W 100 F3
Parramore I. VA .. 37°32N 75°39W 102 D7
Parris I. SC...... 32°20N 80°41W 90 F5
Parrish AL...... 33°44N 87°17W 60 C3
Parrish FL...... 27°35N 82°26W 67 D6
Parrott GA...... 31°54N 84°31W 68 E2
Parshall CO...... 40°3N 106°11W 66 B4
Parshall ND...... 47°57N 102°8W 91 C3
Parsippany NJ ... 40°52N 74°26W 87 B2
Parsons KS...... 37°20N 95°16W 74 D8
Parsons TN...... 35°39N 88°8W 96 E4
Parsons WV...... 39°6N 79°41W 102 B5
Parsonsburg MD .. 38°22N 75°28W 77 B5
Partridge KS...... 37°58N 98°5W 74 D5
Pasadena CA..... 34°9N 118°9W 111 J8
Pasadena TX..... 29°43N 95°13W 99 H12
Pasayten →
　N. Amer. .. 49°0N 120°36W 101 A5
Pascagoula MS ... 30°21N 88°33W 81 F5
Pascagoula → MS. 30°23N 88°37W 81 F5
Pasco WA...... 46°14N 119°6W 101 D6
Pasco County ☆ FL. 28°20N 82°30W 67 C6
Pascoag RI...... 41°57N 71°42W 78 C3
Paskenta CA...... 39°53N 122°33W 64 D4
Paso Robles CA .. 35°38N 120°41W 65 H6
Pasquotank County ☆
　NC........ 36°15N 76°10W 90 B9
Pass Christian MS. 30°19N 89°15W 81 F4
Passaconaway NH. 43°59N 71°22W 86 C3
Passadumkeag ME. 45°11N 68°37W 76 C5
Passaic MO...... 38°19N 94°21W 82 C2
Passaic NJ...... 40°51N 74°7W 114 A2
Passaic → NJ .... 40°42N 74°10W 114 B2
Passaic County ☆ NJ 41°0N 74°20W 87 B1
Passumpsic → VT. 44°18N 72°3W 86 B2
Pastol B. AK .... 63°7N 163°15W 61 E7
Pastora Peak AZ .. 36°47N 109°10W 62 A6
Pastura NM...... 34°47N 104°57W 88 C6
Pat Mayse L. TX .. 33°51N 95°33W 99 D12
Patagonia AZ .... 31°33N 110°45W 62 F5
Pataskala OH .... 40°0N 82°40W 92 C4
Patch Grove WI .. 42°56N 90°58W 103 F3
Patchogue NY ... 40°46N 73°1W 87 B3
Pateros WA...... 48°3N 119°54W 101 B6
Paterson WA..... 45°54N 74°9W 114 A2
Paterson NJ...... 40°55N 74°11W 114 A2
Pathfinder Res.
　WY........ 42°28N 106°51W 104 D6
Patillas Puerto Rico. 18°1N 66°1W 105 G16
Patoka IL...... 38°45N 89°5W 71 D4
Patoka IN...... 38°24N 87°35W 72 E3
Patoka → IN .... 38°24N 87°45W 72 E3
Patoka L. IN .... 38°20N 86°40W 72 E4
Paton IA...... 42°10N 94°16W 73 C4
Patricia TX...... 32°32N 101°58W 98 E6
Patrick County ☆
　VA........ 36°55N 80°10W 102 E4
Patsaliga Cr. → AL 31°22N 86°31W 60 E4
Patten ME...... 46°0N 68°38W 76 B5
Patterson CA..... 37°28N 121°8W 64 F5
Patterson GA..... 31°23N 82°8W 68 E4
Patterson LA..... 29°42N 91°18W 75 E4
Patterson MO .... 37°11N 90°33W 82 D6
Patterson NY..... 41°31N 73°36W 78 C1
Patterson, Pt. MI. 45°58N 85°39W 79 D6
Patterson Cr. → WV 39°34N 78°44W 77 A2
Pattison MS...... 31°53N 90°53W 81 E3
Patton = Monroeville
　PA........ 40°26N 79°45W 95 D3
Patton PA...... 40°38N 78°39W 95 D4
Pattonsburg MO .. 40°3N 94°8W 82 A2
Patuxent → MD .. 38°18N 76°25W 77 B4
Patuxent Nat. Wildlife Refuge △
　MD....... 39°6N 76°48W 77 A4
Patuxent River Naval Air Station
　MD....... 38°17N 76°25W 77 B4
Paul ID...... 42°36N 113°47W 70 G5
Paul Smiths NY .. 44°26N 74°15W 89 A6
Paulden AZ...... 34°53N 112°28W 62 C3
Paulding MS...... 32°1N 89°2W 81 D4
Paulding OH..... 41°8N 84°35W 92 B1
Paulding County ☆
　GA........ 34°0N 84°50W 68 C2
Paulding County ☆
　OH........ 41°5N 84°35W 92 B1
Paulina OR...... 44°8N 119°58W 94 D6
Paulina Marsh OR. 43°15N 121°0W 94 D4
Paulins Kill → NJ. 40°55N 75°5W 87 B1
Paullina IA...... 42°59N 95°41W 73 B3
Pauls Valley OK .. 34°44N 97°13W 93 D6
Paulsboro NJ .... 39°50N 75°14W 116 B2
Pauwela HI...... 20°55N 156°19W 69 C5
Pavilion NY...... 42°52N 78°1W 89 C3
Pavillion WY..... 43°15N 108°42W 104 C4
Pavo GA...... 30°58N 83°44W 68 F3
Paw Paw IL...... 41°41N 88°59W 71 B5
Paw Paw MI..... 42°13N 85°53W 79 G6
Paw Paw WV .... 39°32N 78°27W 77 A2
Paw Paw Lake MI. 42°13N 86°16W 79 G5
Pawcatuck CT ... 41°22N 71°50W 78 C3
Pawhuska OK .... 36°40N 96°20W 93 B7
Pawlet VT...... 43°20N 73°12W 86 C1
Pawling NY...... 41°34N 73°36W 78 C1
Pawnee IL...... 39°36N 89°35W 71 D4
Pawnee OK...... 36°20N 96°48W 93 B6
Pawnee → KS ... 38°10N 99°6W 74 C4
Pawnee City NE .. 40°7N 96°9W 84 D9
Pawnee County ☆ KS 38°10N 99°14W 74 C4

Pawnee County ☆
　NE........ 40°10N 96°20W 84 D9
Pawnee County ☆
　OK........ 36°20N 96°50W 93 B7
Pawnee Cr. → CO. 40°34N 103°14W 66 B7
Pawnee Nat. Grassland
　CO........ 40°40N 104°20W 66 B6
Pawnee Rock KS .. 38°16N 99°1W 74 C4
Pawtucket RI..... 41°53N 71°23W 78 C3
Pawtuckaway State Park
　NH........ 43°7N 71°11W 86 C3
Paxico KS...... 39°4N 96°10W 74 B7
Paxson AK...... 63°2N 145°30W 61 E11
Paxton IL...... 40°27N 88°6W 71 C5
Paxton NE...... 41°7N 101°21W 84 C4
Payette ID...... 44°5N 116°56W 70 E2
Payette → ID .... 44°5N 116°55W 70 E2
Payette County ☆ ID 44°0N 116°55W 70 E2
Payette Nat. Forest
　ID........ 45°10N 115°30W 70 D3
Payne OH...... 41°5N 84°44W 92 B1
Payne County ☆ OK 36°5N 97°0W 93 B6
Paynesville MN .. 45°23N 94°43W 80 E4
Payson AZ...... 34°14N 111°20W 62 C4
Payson IL...... 39°49N 91°15W 71 D2
Payson UT...... 40°3N 111°44W 100 C4
Pe Ell WA...... 46°34N 123°18W 101 D2
Pea → AL ...... 31°1N 85°51W 60 E5
Pea Ridge AR.... 36°27N 94°7W 63 B1
Peabody KS...... 38°10N 97°7W 74 C6
Peabody MA..... 42°31N 70°56W 78 B4
Peace → FL .... 26°56N 82°6W 67 E6
Peace Dale RI .... 41°27N 71°30W 78 C3
Peach Creek WV .. 37°53N 81°59W 102 D3
Peach Orchard AR. 36°17N 90°40W 63 B5
Peachtree City GA. 33°25N 84°35W 68 C2
Peale, Mt. UT .... 38°26N 109°14W 100 E6
Pearblossom CA .. 34°30N 117°55W 65 J9
Pearce AZ...... 31°54N 109°49W 62 F6
Pearisburg VA ... 37°20N 80°37W 102 D4
Pearl GA...... 39°28N 90°37W 82 b
Pearl MS...... 32°18N 90°12W 81 D3
Pearl → AL .... 30°11N 89°32W 81 F4
Pearl and Hermes Reef
　HI........ 27°55N 175°45W 69 F8
Pearl City HI..... 21°24N 157°59W 69 K14
Pearl City IL..... 42°16N 89°50W 71 A4
Pearl Harbor HI .. 21°21N 157°57W 69 K14
Pearl Harbor Nat. Wildlife
　Refuge △ HI. 21°23N 157°59W 69 K14
Pearl River LA ... 30°23N 89°45W 75 D6
Pearl River NY ... 41°4N 74°2W 87 A2
Pearl River County ☆
　MS........ 30°40N 89°38W 81 F4
Pearland TX...... 29°33N 95°17W 110 C3
Pearsall TX...... 28°54N 99°6W 99 J8
Pearson GA...... 31°18N 82°51W 68 E4
Pease → TX .... 34°12N 99°39W 98 C7
Pebble Beach CA. 36°34N 121°57W 64 G5
Pecan Island LA .. 29°39N 92°27W 75 E3
Pecatonica IL..... 42°19N 89°22W 71 A4
Pecatonica → IL. 42°26N 89°12W 71 A4
Peck MI...... 43°16N 82°49W 79 F9
Peckerwood L. AR. 34°46N 91°26W 63 C4
Pecos NM...... 35°35N 105°41W 88 B5
Pecos TX...... 31°26N 103°30W 98 F4
Pecos → TX .... 29°42N 101°22W 98 H6
Pecos County ☆ TX 30°53N 102°53W 98 F5
Pecos Nat. Historical Park
　NM........ 35°33N 105°41W 88 B5
Pecos Plains NM .. 33°15N 104°10W 88 D6
Peculiar MO...... 38°43N 94°28W 82 C2
Peddocks I. MA .. 42°17N 70°56W 106 B4
Pedee OR...... 44°48N 123°28W 94 C2
Pedro Bay AK .... 59°47N 154°7W 61 G9
Pee Dee → Great Pee Dee →
　SC........ 33°21N 79°10W 90 E6
Peebles OH...... 38°57N 83°24W 92 E3
Peekskill NY..... 41°17N 73°55W 87 A3
Peerless MT...... 48°47N 105°50W 83 B12
Peetz CO...... 40°58N 103°7W 66 B7
Peever SD...... 45°33N 96°57W 91 E9
Peggs OK...... 36°5N 95°5W 93 B8
Pegram TN...... 36°6N 87°3W 96 D5
Pekin IL...... 40°35N 89°40W 71 C4
Pekin ND...... 47°48N 98°20W 91 C7
Pelahatchie MS .. 32°19N 89°48W 81 D4
Pelham GA...... 31°8N 84°9W 68 E3
Pelham MA...... 42°24N 72°24W 78 B2
Pelham NY...... 40°54N 73°48W 114 A4
Pelham Bay Park
　NY........ 40°51N 73°48W 114 A4
Pelham Manor NY. 40°53N 73°48W 114 A4
Pelican AK...... 57°58N 136°14W 61 H13
Pelican LA...... 31°53N 93°35W 75 C2
Pelican Rapids MN. 46°34N 96°5W 80 D2
Pell City AL...... 33°35N 86°17W 60 C4
Pella IA...... 41°25N 92°55W 73 D6
Pellville KY...... 37°45N 86°49W 96 C5
Pelonicillo Mts. AZ 32°20N 109°20W 62 E6
Pemadumcook L. ME 45°42N 68°57W 76 C5
Pemberton MN ... 44°1N 93°47W 80 F5
Pemberville OH .. 41°25N 83°28W 92 B3
Pembina ND...... 48°58N 97°14W 91 B8
Pembina → ND .. 48°58N 97°14W 91 B8
Pembine WI...... 45°38N 87°59W 103 C6
Pembroke GA .... 32°8N 81°37W 68 D5
Pembroke KY .... 36°47N 87°21W 96 D5
Pembroke MA .... 42°5N 70°48W 78 B4
Pembroke NC .... 34°42N 79°12W 90 D7
Pembroke Pines FL 26°0N 80°13W 112 B1
Pemigewasset → NH. 43°27N 71°40W 86 C3
Pemiscot County ☆
　MO....... 36°10N 89°50W 82 E7
Pen Argyl PA .... 40°52N 75°16W 87 B1
Penacook NH .... 43°15N 71°40W 86 C3
Penalosa KS...... 37°43N 98°19W 74 D5
Peñasco NM...... 36°10N 105°41W 88 A5
Peñasco → NM .. 32°43N 104°17W 88 E5
Pend Oreille → WA 49°4N 117°37W 101 A8
Pend Oreille, L. ID. 48°11N 116°21W 70 A2
Pend Oreille County ☆
　WA....... 48°30N 117°10W 101 B8
Pender NE...... 42°7N 96°43W 84 B9
Pender County ☆ NC 34°30N 78°0W 90 D8
Pendergrass GA .. 34°10N 83°41W 68 B3
Pendleton IN .... 40°0N 85°45W 72 C5
Pendleton OR .... 45°40N 118°47W 94 C7
Pendleton County ☆
　KY........ 38°40N 84°20W 97 B8
Pendleton County ☆
　WV........ 38°40N 79°20W 102 C5
Pendroy MT...... 48°5N 112°19W 83 B5
Penelope TX...... 31°52N 96°56W 99 F11
Penfield PA...... 41°13N 78°35W 95 C4
Penn = Penn Hills
　PA........ 40°28N 79°52W 95 D3
Penn Hills PA .... 40°28N 79°52W 95 D3
Penn Wynne PA .. 39°59N 75°16W 116 B1
Penn Yan NY .... 42°40N 77°3W 89 C4

Pennell, Mt. *UT* .. 37°58N 110°47W **100 F5**
Pennington *AL* ...... 32°13N 88°3W **60 D2**
Pennington *NJ*........ 40°19N 74°48W **87 B2**
Pennington County ☆
MN................ 48°5N 96°0W **80 B3**
Pennington County ☆
SD............... 44°0N 103°0W **91 G2**
Pennington Gap *VA*. 36°46N 83°2W **102 E1**
Pennock *MN*.......... 45°9N 95°10W **80 E3**
Penns Grove *NJ* ..... 39°44N 75°28W **87 C1**
Pennsauken *NJ* ...... 39°58N 75°3W **116 B2**
Pennsboro *WV* ...... 39°17N 80°58W **102 B4**
Pennsburg *PA*....... 40°23N 75°29W **87 B1**
Pennsville *NJ*....... 39°39N 75°31W **87 C1**
Pennsylvania □
U.S.A.............. 40°45N 77°30W **95 D5**
Pennville *IN*......... 40°30N 85°9W **72 C5**
Pennypack Park *PA* .. 40°3N 75°2W **116 A2**
Pennyrile State Forest
KY................ 37°11N 87°33W **96 C5**
Penobscot → *ME*.... 44°30N 68°48W **76 D5**
Penobscot B. *ME* ... 44°35N 68°50W **76 D5**
Penobscot County ☆
ME................. 45°0N 69°0W **76 C5**
Penrose *CO*......... 38°26N 105°1W **66 D5**
Pensacola *FL*........ 30°25N 87°13W **67 A1**
Pensacola *OK* .... 36°28N 95°7W **93 B8**
Pensacola B. *FL* ..... 30°25N 87°5W **67 A1**
Pentagon *VA* .... 38°53N 77°3W **119 B3**
Pentwater *MI* .... 43°47N 86°26W **79 F5**
Penwell *TX* .... 31°45N 102°36W **98 F5**
Peoria *AZ* .... 33°43N 112°14W **116 A1**
Peoria *IL* .... 40°42N 89°36W **71 C4**
Peoria *OK* .... 36°54N 94°41W **93 B9**
Peoria County ☆ *IL*. 40°45N 89°45W **71 C4**
Peoria Heights *IL* ... 40°45N 89°35W **71 C4**
Peotone *IL*.......... 41°20N 87°48W **71 B6**
Pep *NM* .... 33°50N 103°20W **88 D7**
Pepacton Res. *NY*.... 42°5N 74°58W **89 C6**
Pepeekeo *HI* .... 19°51N 155°6W **69 D6**
Pepin *WI* .... 44°27N 92°9W **103 D1**
Pepin County ☆ *WI* 44°30N 92°10W **103 D1**
Pepperell *MA* .... 42°40N 71°35W **78 B3**
Pequannock *NJ*...... 40°57N 74°18W **87 B2**
Pequest → *NJ*....... 40°50N 75°5W **87 B1**
Pequop Mts. *NV* ... 40°45N 114°40W **85 B6**
Pequot Lakes *MN*... 46°36N 94°19W **80 D4**
Peralta *NM* .... 34°50N 106°41W **88 C4**
Perdido *AL* .... 31°0N 87°38W **60 E3**
Perdido → *AL* ...... 30°27N 87°23W **60 F3**
Perdido B. *AL*....... 30°20N 87°30W **60 F3**
Perham *MN*......... 46°36N 95°34W **80 D3**
Peridot *AZ*........ 33°18N 110°28W **62 D5**
Perkasie *PA*......... 40°22N 75°18W **87 B1**
Perkins *GA* .... 32°55N 81°57W **68 D5**
Perkins *OK* .... 35°58N 97°2W **93 C6**
Perkins County ☆
NE.............. 40°45N 101°45W **84 D4**
Perkins County ☆
SD............. 45°30N 102°30W **91 E3**
Perkinston *MS*...... 30°47N 89°8W **81 F4**
Perkiomen → *PA*.... 40°7N 75°28W **87 B1**
Perley *MN* .... 47°11N 96°48W **80 C2**
Perma *MT* .... 47°22N 114°35W **83 C3**
Pernell *OK*.......... 34°34N 97°31W **93 D6**
Perquimans County ☆
NC............... 36°10N 76°30W **90 B9**
Perrin *TX*........... 33°2N 98°4W **99 D9**
Perrine *FL*......... 25°36N 80°21W **67 F8**
Perris *CA* .... 33°47N 117°14W **65 K9**
Perro, L. del *NM*.... 34°41N 105°58W **88 C5**
Perry *AR* .... 35°3N 92°48W **63 C3**
Perry *FL*............ 30°7N 83°35W **67 A5**
Perry *GA* .... 32°28N 83°44W **68 D3**
Perry *IL* .... 39°47N 90°45W **71 D3**
Perry *IA* .... 41°51N 94°6W **73 D4**
Perry *KS*............ 39°5N 95°24W **74 B8**
Perry *ME*.......... 44°58N 67°5W **76 D6**
Perry *MI*............ 42°50N 84°13W **79 G7**
Perry *MO*........... 39°26N 91°40W **82 B5**
Perry *NY* .... 42°43N 78°0W **89 C2**
Perry *OK* .... 36°17N 97°14W **93 B6**
Perry *UT* .... 41°28N 112°2W **100 B3**
Perry County ☆ *AL* . 32°38N 87°19W **60 D3**
Perry County ☆ *AR* . 35°0N 92°48W **63 D3**
Perry County ☆ *IL*... 38°5N 89°20W **71 E4**
Perry County ☆ *IN*.. 38°5N 86°40W **72 E4**
Perry County ☆ *KY*. 37°15N 83°15W **97 C9**
Perry County ☆ *MS*.. 31°12N 89°2W **81 E4**
Perry County ☆ *MO* 37°45N 89°50W **82 D7**
Perry County ☆ *OH*. 39°43N 82°13W **92 D4**
Perry County ☆ *PA* . 40°35N 77°5W **95 D5**
Perry County ☆ *TN* . 35°39N 87°50W **96 E5**
Perry Hall *MD* ...... 39°25N 76°28W **77 A4**
Perry Lake *KS*....... 39°7N 95°26W **74 B8**
Perrydale *OR* ..... 45°3N 123°16W **94 B2**
Perrysburg *OH* ..... 41°34N 83°38W **92 B3**
Perrysville *OH* ..... 40°40N 82°19W **92 C4**
Perrysville *PA*....... 40°32N 80°1W **116 A1**
Perryton *TX* ..... 36°24N 100°48W **98 A7**
Perryville *AK* ..... 55°55N 159°9W **61 J8**
Perryville *AR*....... 35°0N 92°48W **63 C3**
Perryville *KY*....... 37°39N 84°57W **97 C8**
Perryville *MD* ..... 39°34N 76°4W **77 A4**
Perryville *MO* ...... 37°43N 89°52W **82 D7**
Pershing *MI*......... 42°26N 83°3W **109 A2**
Pershing County ☆
NV.............. 40°20N 118°10W **85 B2**
Persia *IA* .... 41°35N 95°33W **73 D3**
Person County ☆ *NC*. 36°15N 79°0W **90 B7**
Perth *KS* .... 37°11N 97°31W **74 D6**
Perth *ND* .... 48°43N 99°28W **91 B6**
Perth Amboy *NJ*.. 40°30N 74°15W **114 C1**
Peru *IL*............ 41°20N 89°8W **71 B4**
Peru *IN*............ 40°45N 86°4W **72 C4**
Peru *KS*............ 37°5N 96°6W **74 D7**
Peru *NY*.......... 44°35N 73°32W **86 B1**
Peru *NE*.......... 40°29N 95°44W **84 D10**
Peru *VT* .... 43°14N 72°54W **86 C2**
Peshtigo *WI*....... 45°3N 87°45W **103 C6**
Peshtigo → *WI*.... 44°58N 87°40W **103 D6**
Pesotum *IL* ...... 39°55N 88°16W **71 D5**
Petal *MS*.......... 31°21N 89°16W **81 E4**
Petaluma *CA*...... 38°14N 122°39W **64 E4**
Petenwell L. *WI* .... 44°4N 90°1W **103 D3**
Peter I.
Br. Virgin Is. ... 18°22N 64°35W **105 G18**
Peter O. Knight ✕
FL............. 27°54N 82°26W **119 B4**
Peterborough *NH*... 42°53N 71°57W **86 D3**
Peterman *AL*...... 31°35N 87°16W **60 E3**
Petersburg *AK* ... 56°48N 132°58W **61 H14**
Petersburg *IL* ...... 40°1N 89°51W **71 C4**
Petersburg *IN* ...... 38°30N 87°17W **72 E3**
Petersburg *MI* ...... 41°54N 83°43W **79 H8**
Petersburg *ND* ...... 48°0N 98°0W **91 C7**
Petersburg *NJ* ...... 39°15N 74°43W **87 C2**
Petersburg *NY*...... 42°44N 73°20W **78 B1**
Petersburg *NE*...... 41°51N 98°5W **84 C7**
Petersburg *OH* .... 40°55N 80°32W **92 C6**
Petersburg *PA*...... 40°34N 78°3W **95 D4**
Petersburg *TN*...... 35°19N 86°38W **96 E6**
Petersburg *TX*.... 33°52N 101°36W **98 D6**
Petersburg *VA*..... 37°14N 77°24W **102 D7**
Petersburg *WV* ...... 39°1N 79°5W **102 B5**
Petersham *MA* ..... 42°29N 72°11W **78 B2**
Peterson *IA* .... 42°55N 95°21W **73 C3**
Peterson *MN* ...... 43°47N 91°50W **80 G7**
Peterson Field, Colorado Springs ✕
(COS) *CO* ..... 38°49N 104°43W **66 D6**
Petestown *WV*.... 37°24N 80°48W **102 D4**
Petersville *KY*...... 38°27N 83°30W **97 B9**
Petit Bois I. *MS*..... 30°12N 88°26W **81 F5**
Petit Jean State Park ⌂
AR.............. 35°7N 92°56W **63 C3**
Petit Manan Pt. *ME* . 44°24N 67°54W **76 D6**
Petoskey *MI* .... 45°22N 84°57W **79 D7**
Petrey *AL* .... 31°51N 86°13W **60 E4**
Petrified Forest Nat. Park △
AZ.............. 35°0N 109°30W **62 B6**
Petroglyph Nat. Monument ⌂
NM.......... 35°10N 106°43W **88 B4**
Petroleum *WV*...... 39°11N 81°16W **102 B3**
Petroleum County ☆
MT............. 47°7N 108°25W **83 C9**
Petrolia *KS* .... 37°45N 95°29W **74 D8**
Petrolia *TX* .... 34°1N 98°14W **99 C9**
Petros *TN*.......... 36°6N 84°27W **97 D8**
Pettibone *ND* ...... 47°7N 99°31W **91 C6**
Pettis County ☆ *MO* 38°40N 93°15W **82 C3**
Pettus *TX*......... 28°37N 97°48W **99 J10**
Pettys Island *NJ* .... 39°57N 75°6W **116 B2**
Pfeifer *KS* .... 38°43N 99°10W **74 C4**
Phalen, L. *MN*...... 44°59N 93°3W **113 B3**
Phalen Park *MN*.... 44°59N 93°3W **113 B3**
Pharr *TX* .... 26°12N 98°11W **98 L9**
Pheba *MS*......... 33°35N 88°57W **81 C5**
Phelps *KY* .... 37°32N 82°9W **97 C10**
Phelps *NY* .... 42°58N 77°3W **89 C3**
Phelps *WI*......... 46°4N 89°5W **103 B4**
Phelps County ☆
MO .... 37°55N 91°45W **82 D5**
Phelps County ☆ *NE* 40°30N 99°30W **84 D6**
Phelps L. *NC*....... 35°46N 76°27W **90 C9**
Phenix *VA* .... 37°5N 78°45W **102 D6**
Phenix City *AL*...... 32°28N 85°0W **60 D5**
Phil Campbell *AL*... 34°21N 87°42W **60 B3**
Philadelphia *MS* ..... 32°46N 89°7W **81 D4**
Philadelphia *NY* .... 44°9N 75°43W **89 A5**
Philadelphia *PA* ..... 39°57N 75°9W **116 B1**
Philadelphia *TN* ..... 35°41N 84°24W **97 E8**
Philadelphia County ☆
PA.............. 39°57N 75°10W **95 E7**
Philadelphia Int. ✕ (PHL)
PA............... 39°51N 75°18W **116 B1**
Philip *SD* .... 44°2N 101°40W **91 F4**
Philip Smith Mts. *AK* 68°0N 148°0W **61 C10**
Philippi *WV* .... 39°9N 80°3W **102 B4**
Philip's L. *OR* ... 45°25N 123°13W **94 B2**
Philipsburg *MT* .. 46°20N 113°18W **83 D4**
Philipsburg *PA* ..... 40°54N 78°13W **95 D4**
Phillips *ME* .... 44°49N 70°21W **76 D3**
Phillips *NE*......... 40°54N 98°13W **84 D7**
Phillips *OK* .... 34°30N 96°12W **93 D7**
Phillips *TX*....... 35°42N 101°22W **98 B6**
Phillips *WI*......... 45°42N 90°24W **103 C3**
Phillips County ☆
AR.............. 34°19N 90°51W **63 D5**
Phillips County ☆
CO .... 40°40N 102°20W **66 B8**
Phillips County ☆ *KS* 39°45N 99°15W **74 B4**
Phillips County ☆
MT .... 48°12N 108°0W **83 B10**
Phillipsburg *GA* ..... 31°25N 83°30W **68 E3**
Phillipsburg *KS*..... 39°45N 99°19W **74 B4**
Phillipsburg *MO*..... 37°33N 92°47W **82 D4**
Phillipsburg *NJ* .... 40°42N 75°12W **87 B1**
Philmont *NY* .... 42°15N 73°39W **89 C7**
Philo *CA* .... 39°4N 123°26W **64 D3**
Philo *IL* .... 40°1N 88°9W **71 C5**
Philomath *GA*...... 33°44N 82°59W **68 C4**
Philomath *OR*..... 44°32N 123°22W **94 C2**
Philpott Res. *VA*.... 36°47N 80°2W **102 E4**
Phippsburg *CO*.... 40°14N 106°57W **66 B4**
Phoenix *AZ* .... 33°26N 112°4W **116 C2**
Phoenix *LA*......... 29°39N 89°56W **75 E6**
Phoenix *NY*........ 43°14N 76°18W **89 B4**
Phoenix *OR*...... 42°16N 122°49W **94 E3**
Phoenix Sky Harbour ✕ (PHX)
AZ............ 33°26N 112°5W **116 C2**
Phoenixville *PA* .... 40°8N 75°31W **87 B1**
Piatt County ☆ *IL* ... 40°0N 88°35W **71 D5**
Picacho *AZ* ...... 32°43N 111°30W **62 E4**
Picacho *NM*...... 33°21N 105°9W **88 D5**
Picacho Pass *AZ*.. 32°40N 111°25W **62 E4**
Picayune *MS* ...... 30°32N 89°41W **81 F4**
Piceance Cr. → *CO*. 40°5N 108°14W **66 B2**
Picher *OK* .... 36°59N 94°50W **93 B9**
Pickaway County ☆
OH .... 39°43N 82°59W **92 D4**
Pickens *AR* .... 33°51N 91°29W **63 E4**
Pickens *MS* .... 32°53N 89°58W **81 D4**
Pickens *OK* .... 34°23N 95°2W **93 D8**
Pickens *SC*........ 34°53N 82°42W **90 D3**
Pickens *WV*....... 38°39N 80°13W **102 C4**
Pickens County ☆ *AL* 33°16N 88°6W **60 C2**
Pickens County ☆
GA .... 34°30N 84°25W **68 B2**
Pickens County ☆ *SC* 34°50N 82°45W **90 D3**
Pickering *MO* ..... 40°27N 94°49W **82 A2**
Pickerington *OH*.... 39°53N 82°45W **92 D4**
Pickett County ☆ *TN*. 36°34N 85°8W **97 D7**
Pickford *MI* .... 46°10N 84°22W **79 C7**
Pickrell *NE* .... 40°23N 96°44W **84 D9**
Pickstown *SD* ..... 43°4N 98°32W **91 G7**
Pickwick L. *AL* ..... 35°4N 88°15W **60 A2**
Pico Rivera *CA*..... 33°59N 118°5W **111 C4**
Pictured Rocks Nat. Lakeshore ⌂
MI.............. 46°30N 86°30W **79 C5**
Picuris Indian Reservation
NM .... 36°12N 105°48W **88 A5**
Pie Town *NM*..... 34°18N 108°9W **88 C2**
Piedmont *AL*...... 33°55N 85°37W **60 C5**
Piedmont *CA*..... 37°49N 122°13W **118 B3**
Piedmont *KS*...... 37°37N 96°22W **74 D7**
Piedmont *MO*...... 37°9N 90°42W **82 D6**
Piedmont *OK*...... 35°39N 97°44W **93 C6**
Piedmont *OR* .... 45°33N 122°40W **116 A1**
Piedmont *SC*...... 34°42N 82°28W **90 D3**
Piedmont *SD*..... 44°14N 103°24W **91 F2**
Piedmont *WV* ..... 39°29N 79°3W **77 A1**
Piedmont L. *OH*... 40°11N 81°13W **92 C5**
Piedmont Nat. Wildlife Refuge ⌂
GA .... 33°8N 83°45W **68 C3**
Piedmont Park *GA*. 33°47N 84°22W **106 B2**
Pierce *CO* .... 40°38N 104°45W **66 B6**
Pierce *ID* .... 46°30N 115°48W **70 C3**
Pierce *NE*........ 42°12N 97°32W **84 B8**
Pierce City *MO*..... 36°57N 94°0W **82 E3**
Pierce County ☆ *GA* 31°20N 82°10W **68 E4**
Pierce County ☆ *ND* 48°22N 99°40W **84 B8**
Pierce County ☆ *NE* 42°10N 97°30W **84 B8**
Pierce County ☆ *WA* 47°0N 122°0W **101 C3**
Pierce County ☆ *WI* 44°45N 92°25W **103 D1**
Pierceton *IN* ...... 41°12N 85°42W **72 B5**
Pierceville *KS* .... 37°53N 100°40W **74 D3**
Piercy *CA*....... 39°59N 123°48W **64 D3**
Pierpont *SD*....... 45°30N 97°50W **91 E8**
Pierre *SD*....... 44°22N 100°21W **91 F5**
Pierre Part *LA*...... 29°58N 91°12W **75 E4**
Pierron *IL* .... 38°47N 89°36W **71 E4**
Pierson *FL*........ 29°14N 81°28W **67 B7**
Pierson *IA* .... 42°33N 95°52W **73 C3**
Pierz *MN* .... 45°59N 94°6W **80 E4**
Pigeon *LA* .... 30°4N 91°17W **75 D4**
Pigeon *MI* .... 43°50N 83°16W **79 F8**
Pigeon → *IN*...... 41°47N 85°49W **72 B5**
Pigeon → *MI*..... 36°2N 83°17W **97 D9**
Pigeon → *TN*...... 36°2N 83°17W **97 D9**
Pigeon Cove *MA* ... 42°41N 70°38W **78 B4**
Pigeon Cr. → *AL*... 31°20N 86°42W **60 E4**
Pigeon Falls *WI* .... 44°26N 91°13W **103 D2**
Pigeon Forge *TN* ... 35°48N 83°33W **97 E9**
Pigg → *VA*......... 37°0N 79°29W **102 E5**
Piggott *AR*........ 36°23N 90°11W **63 B5**
Pigs Eye Lake *MN* .. 44°54N 93°1W **113 B3**
Pike County ☆ *AL* .. 31°48N 85°58W **60 E5**
Pike County ☆ *AR* .. 34°14N 93°45W **63 D2**
Pike County ☆ *GA*... 33°5N 84°20W **68 C2**
Pike County ☆ *IL*... 39°35N 90°50W **71 D3**
Pike County ☆ *IN*... 38°25N 87°10W **72 E3**
Pike County ☆ *KY*. 37°30N 82°25W **97 C10**
Pike County ☆ *MS*.. 31°15N 90°27W **81 E3**
Pike County ☆ *MO* . 39°20N 91°10W **82 B5**
Pike County ☆ *OH*... 39°4N 83°1W **92 D3**
Pike County ☆ *PA* ... 41°20N 75°0W **95 C8**
Pike Nat. Forest *CO* 39°15N 105°20W **66 C5**
Pike Road *AL*....... 32°17N 86°6W **60 D4**
Pikes Peak *CO* ..... 38°50N 105°3W **66 D5**
Pikesville *MD* ...... 39°22N 76°43W **107 A1**
Piketon *OH*........ 39°4N 83°1W **92 D3**
Pikeville *KY* ...... 37°29N 82°31W **97 C10**
Pikeville *NC* ...... 35°30N 77°59W **90 C8**
Pikeville *TN*...... 35°36N 85°11W **97 E7**
Pilger *NE* .... 42°0N 97°3W **84 B8**
Pillager *MN*...... 46°20N 94°28W **80 D4**
Pillsbury *ND* ...... 47°13N 97°48W **91 C8**
Pillsbury, L. *CA* ... 39°25N 122°57W **64 D4**
Pillsbury State Forest
MN............. 46°25N 94°26W **80 D4**
Pillsbury State Park ⌂
NH .... 43°14N 72°6W **86 C2**
Pilot Grove *MO* .... 38°53N 92°55W **82 C4**
Pilot Knob *AR* ..... 35°42N 93°57W **63 C2**
Pilot Knob *KY* ..... 36°50N 86°41W **96 D6**
Pilot Knob *MO* .... 37°40N 90°40W **82 D6**
Pilot Mountain *NC*.. 36°23N 80°28W **90 B5**
Pilot Pk. *NV*...... 41°1N 114°5W **85 A6**
Pilot Pk. *WY* .... 44°58N 109°53W **104 B3**
Pilot Point *AK*.... 57°34N 157°35W **61 H8**
Pilot Point *TX*...... 33°24N 96°58W **99 D11**
Pilot Rock *OR*.... 45°29N 118°50W **94 B7**
Pilot Station *AK*... 61°56N 162°53W **61 F7**
Pima *AZ*.......... 32°54N 109°50W **62 E6**
Pima County ☆ *AZ* . 32°0N 112°0W **62 E4**
Pimmit Hills *VA* ... 38°54N 77°12W **119 B2**
Pinal County ☆ *AZ* . 33°0N 111°15W **62 E4**
Pinaleno Mts. *AZ*.. 32°45N 110°0W **62 E6**
Pinardville *NH* .... 42°59N 71°30W **86 D3**
Pinckard *AL* ..... 31°19N 85°33W **60 E5**
Pinckneyville *IL* ... 38°5N 89°23W **71 E4**
Pinconning *MI*..... 43°51N 83°58W **79 F8**
Pindall *AR*....... 36°4N 92°53W **63 B3**
Pine *AZ* .... 34°23N 111°27W **62 C4**
Pine *OR* .... 44°52N 117°5W **94 C8**
Pine → *MI*....... 43°35N 84°8W **79 F7**
Pine → *MI*....... 44°14N 85°54W **79 E6**
Pine Apple *AL* ..... 31°52N 87°0W **60 E4**
Pine Barrens *NJ* ... 39°30N 74°30W **87 C2**
Pine Bluff *AR* ...... 34°13N 92°1W **63 D3**
Pine Bluff Arsenal *AR* 34°19N 92°6W **63 D3**
Pine Bluffs *WY* .. 41°11N 104°4W **104 E8**
Pine Bush *NY* ..... 41°36N 74°17W **89 D6**
Pine Castle *FL*.... 28°28N 81°22W **115 B2**
Pine City *MN*...... 45°50N 92°59W **80 E6**
Pine City *WA*..... 47°12N 117°31W **101 C8**
Pine County ☆ *MN* . 46°5N 92°50W **80 D6**
Pine Cr. → *NV*.... 40°36N 116°12W **85 B4**
Pine Cr. → *PA*.... 41°10N 77°16W **95 C5**
Pine Creek L. *OK*..... 34°7N 95°5W **93 D8**
Pine Flat L. *CA* ... 36°50N 119°20W **65 G7**
Pine Forest Range
NV............ 41°45N 118°50W **85 A2**
Pine Grove *LA* .... 30°43N 90°45W **75 D5**
Pine Grove *PA* ..... 40°33N 76°23W **95 D6**
Pine Grove *WV*..... 39°34N 80°41W **102 B4**
Pine Haven *WY* ... 44°21N 104°49W **104 B8**
Pine Hill *AL* ...... 31°59N 87°35W **60 E3**
Pine Hills *FL*...... 28°33N 81°27W **115 A2**
Pine Hills *NJ* ...... 39°47N 74°59W **87 C2**
Pine I. *FL*........ 26°36N 82°7W **67 E6**
Pine Island *MN*..... 44°12N 92°39W **80 F6**
Pine Knot *KY* ..... 36°39N 84°26W **97 D8**
Pine Lawn *MO* ..... 38°41N 90°16W **117 A2**
Pine Level *AL*....... 32°4N 86°4W **60 D4**
Pine Level *NC*...... 35°31N 78°14W **90 C7**
Pine Log *GA* ...... 34°21N 84°44W **68 B2**
Pine Mountain *GA*.. 32°49N 84°51W **68 D2**
Pine Mt. *GA* ...... 32°49N 84°50W **68 D2**
Pine Mt. *KY*....... 37°0N 83°45W **97 D9**
Pine Mt. *WY* ..... 41°2N 109°1W **104 E3**
Pine Plains *NY* ..... 42°59N 73°39W **78 B1**
Pine Prairie *LA*..... 30°47N 92°25W **75 D3**
Pine Ridge *SD*..... 43°2N 102°33W **91 G3**
Pine Ridge Indian Reservation
SD............ 43°30N 102°0W **91 G3**
Pine River *MN* .... 46°43N 94°24W **80 D4**
Pine Springs *MN*.... 45°2N 92°57W **113 A4**
Pine Springs *TX* .. 31°54N 104°49W **98 F3**
Pine Valley *UT* ... 38°20N 113°45W **100 E2**
Pinebluff *NC*...... 35°6N 79°28W **90 C6**
Pinecrest *FL* ..... 25°40N 80°18W **112 D1**
Pinedale *CA* ..... 36°50N 119°48W **65 G7**
Pinedale *WY* .... 42°52N 109°52W **104 D3**
Pinehurst *GA* .... 32°12N 83°46W **68 D3**
Pinehurst *ID* .... 45°15N 116°20W **70 D2**
Pinehurst *NC* ..... 35°12N 79°28W **90 C6**
Pineland *TX* ...... 31°15N 93°58W **99 F14**
Pinellas County ☆ *FL* 28°0N 82°45W **67 C6**
Pinellas Nat. Wildlife Refuge ⌂
FL .... 27°39N 82°41W **119 C2**
Pinellas Park *FL* ... 27°50N 82°41W **119 B2**
Pinellas Point *FL* .. 27°42N 82°38W **119 C3**
Pines, Lake O' The
TX............. 32°45N 94°30W **99 E13**
Pinetop-Lakeside *AZ* 34°9N 109°58W **62 C6**
Pinetops *NC*....... 35°46N 77°38W **90 C8**
Pinetta *FL*........ 30°36N 83°21W **67 A5**
Pineview *GA*...... 32°7N 83°30W **68 D3**
Pineville *KY* ..... 36°46N 83°42W **97 D9**
Pineville *LA* ..... 31°19N 92°26W **75 C3**
Pineville *MO*...... 36°36N 94°23W **82 E2**
Pineville *NC* ...... 35°4N 80°53W **107 B1**
Pineville *WV* ..... 37°35N 81°32W **102 D3**
Pinewood *SC*...... 33°44N 80°28W **90 E5**
Pinewood Park *FL*.. 25°52N 80°13W **112 C2**
Piney → *MO*....... 37°54N 92°4W **82 D4**
Piney → *TN*....... 35°49N 87°34W **96 E5**
Piney Buttes *MT*.. 47°35N 106°45W **83 C11**
Piney Green *NC*.... 34°43N 77°19W **90 D8**
Piney Grove *MD*.... 39°42N 78°24W **77 A2**
Piney Point *MD* .... 38°9N 76°31W **77 B4**
Piney Point Village
TX............. 29°45N 95°31W **110 B1**
Piney Pt. *FL*...... 29°46N 83°35W **67 B5**
Piney River *VA*..... 37°42N 79°1W **102 D5**
Piney Run → *VA* .. 38°58N 77°14W **119 B2**
Piney Woods *MS* .... 32°2N 90°0W **81 D3**
Pingree *ND* .... 47°10N 98°55W **91 C7**
Pink *OK*.......... 35°18N 97°6W **93 C6**
Pink Cliffs *UT*..... 37°25N 112°20W **100 F3**
Pink Hill *NC* ...... 35°3N 77°45W **90 C8**
Pinnacle Buttes
WY .... 43°44N 109°57W **104 C3**
Pinnacle Peak *WY* 43°23N 110°32W **104 C2**
Pinnacles Nat. Monument ⌂
CA .... 36°25N 121°12W **65 G5**
Pinola *MS* .... 31°53N 89°58W **81 E4**
Pinon *AZ* .... 36°6N 110°14W **62 A5**
Pinon *NM* ...... 32°37N 105°24W **88 E5**
Pinos, Mt. *CA* ..... 34°49N 119°8W **65 J7**
Pinos Pt. *CA* ..... 36°38N 121°57W **59 H3**
Pinson *AL* .... 33°41N 86°41W **60 C4**
Pinson *TN* .... 35°29N 88°43W **96 E4**
Pinta, Sierra *AZ* .. 32°15N 113°30W **62 E2**
Pintwater Ra. *NV*.. 36°50N 115°34W **85 F5**
Pioche *NV* .... 37°56N 114°27W **85 E6**
Pioneer *IA*....... 42°39N 94°23W **73 C4**
Pioneer *LA* ...... 32°44N 91°26W **75 B4**
Pioneer *OH* .... 41°41N 84°33W **92 B2**
Pioneer *TN* .... 36°25N 84°19W **97 D8**
Pioneer Mts. *ID* ... 43°38N 113°52W **70 F5**
Pioneer Mts. *MT*... 45°29N 112°58W **83 E5**
Pipe Creek *TX* ..... 29°43N 98°56W **99 H9**
Pipe Spring Nat. Monument ⌂
AZ............. 36°50N 112°55W **62 A3**
Pipestem L. *ND* ... 46°57N 98°45W **91 D7**
Pipestone *MN*...... 44°0N 96°19W **80 F2**
Pipestone County ☆
MN .... 44°0N 96°15W **80 F2**
Pipestone Nat. Monument ⌂
MN.............. 43°58N 96°14W **80 G2**
Piqua *KS* .... 37°56N 95°32W **74 D8**
Piqua *OH*.......... 40°9N 84°15W **92 C2**
Pirtleville *AZ*.... 31°21N 109°34W **62 F6**
Piscataquis → *ME* .. 45°15N 68°58W **76 C5**
Piscataquis County ☆
ME .... 46°0N 69°0W **76 C4**
Piscataway *MD*..... 38°42N 76°58W **77 B4**
Piscataway *NJ* ..... 40°34N 74°27W **87 B2**
Pisek *ND* .... 48°19N 97°43W **91 B8**
Pisgah *IA* .... 41°50N 95°55W **73 D3**
Pisgah *MD*........ 38°32N 77°8W **77 B3**
Pisgah, Mt. *NH* .... 44°59N 71°13W **86 B3**
Pisgah Nat. Forest *NC* 35°50N 82°0W **90 C3**
Pisgah State Park ⌂
NH .... 42°50N 72°27W **86 D2**
Pisinimo *AZ* .... 32°2N 112°19W **62 E3**
Pismo Beach *CA*... 35°9N 120°38W **65 H6**
Pistol River *OR*.... 42°17N 124°24W **94 E1**
Pit → *CA*......... 40°47N 122°6W **64 C4**
Pitchfork *WY*...... 44°6N 109°5W **104 B3**
Piti *Guam*........ 13°28N 144°41E **105 b**
Pitkin *CO*....... 38°37N 106°31W **66 D4**
Pitkin *LA*......... 30°56N 92°56W **75 D3**
Pitkin County ☆ *CO* 39°10N 106°50W **66 C4**
Pitman *NJ* .... 39°44N 75°8W **87 C1**
Pitt County ☆ *NC*.. 35°30N 77°20W **90 C8**
Pittock *PA* .... 40°29N 80°5W **116 B1**
Pittsboro *IN*...... 39°52N 86°28W **72 D4**
Pittsboro *MS* ..... 33°56N 89°20W **81 C4**
Pittsboro *NC* ..... 35°43N 79°11W **90 C6**
Pittsburg *CA* .... 38°2N 121°53W **64 E5**
Pittsburg *IL* ...... 37°47N 88°51W **71 F5**
Pittsburg *KS* ...... 37°25N 94°42W **74 D9**
Pittsburg *NH* ...... 45°3N 71°24W **86 A3**
Pittsburg *OK* ...... 34°43N 95°52W **93 D8**
Pittsburg *TX* ...... 33°0N 94°59W **99 D13**
Pittsburg County ☆
OK .... 34°50N 95°50W **93 D8**
Pittsburgh *PA* ..... 40°26N 79°58W **116 B1**
Pittsburgh Int. ✕ (PIT)
PA............. 40°29N 80°14W **95 D2**
Pittsfield *IL* ...... 39°36N 90°49W **71 D3**
Pittsfield *ME* ...... 44°47N 69°23W **76 D4**
Pittsfield *MA* ..... 42°27N 73°15W **78 B1**
Pittsfield *NH* ..... 43°18N 71°20W **86 C3**
Pittsfield *VT* ..... 43°46N 72°48W **86 C2**
Pittsford *VT*...... 43°42N 73°3W **86 C1**
Pittston *PA* ...... 41°19N 75°47W **87 A1**
Pittstown *NJ* ..... 40°36N 74°56W **87 B2**
Pittsview *AL* ..... 32°11N 85°10W **60 D5**
Pittsville *MD* ..... 38°24N 75°52W **77 B5**
Pittsville *MO* ...... 38°50N 94°0W **82 C3**
Pittsville *WI* ...... 44°27N 90°8W **103 D3**
Pittsylvania County ☆
VA .... 36°55N 79°15W **102 E5**
Piumafua Mt.
Amer. Samoa...... 14°11S 169°37W **105 f**
Piute County ☆ *UT* 38°20N 112°10W **100 E3**
Piute Pk. *CA*..... 35°27N 118°23W **65 H8**
Pixley *CA*........ 35°58N 119°18W **65 H7**
Placedo *TX*...... 28°41N 96°50W **99 J11**
Placer County ☆
CA .... 39°10N 120°30W **64 D6**
Placerville *CA*.... 38°44N 120°48W **64 E6**
Placerville *CO*..... 38°1N 108°3W **66 D2**
Placerville *ID* .... 43°57N 115°57W **70 F3**
Placid, L. *FL* ..... 27°15N 81°22W **67 D7**
Placitas *NM*...... 35°18N 106°25W **88 B4**
Plain City *OH* ...... 40°6N 83°16W **92 C3**
Plain City *UT* .... 41°18N 112°6W **100 B3**
Plain Dealing *LA*... 32°54N 93°42W **75 B2**
Plainfield *CT* ..... 41°41N 71°56W **78 C3**
Plainfield *IN* ..... 39°42N 86°24W **72 D4**
Plainfield *IA* ..... 42°51N 92°32W **73 C6**
Plainfield *MA* ..... 42°31N 72°57W **78 B2**
Plainfield *NH* ..... 43°32N 72°21W **86 C2**
Plainfield *NJ* ..... 40°37N 74°25W **87 B2**
Plainfield *VT*...... 44°17N 72°26W **86 B2**
Plainfield *WI* ..... 44°13N 89°30W **103 D4**
Plainfield Heights *MI*. 43°1N 85°37W **79 F6**
Plains *GA*........ 32°2N 84°24W **68 D2**
Plains *KS*...... 37°16N 100°35W **74 D3**
Plains *MT*...... 47°28N 114°53W **83 C3**
Plains *PA* ...... 41°15N 75°37W **95 C7**
Plains *TX*...... 33°11N 102°50W **98 D5**
Plains, The *VA* ..... 38°52N 77°47W **77 B3**
Plainview *AR*...... 34°59N 93°18W **63 D2**
Plainview *MN* ..... 44°10N 92°10W **80 F6**
Plainview *NY*..... 40°46N 73°29W **87 B3**
Plainview *NE*..... 42°21N 97°47W **84 B8**
Plainview *TX* .... 34°11N 101°43W **98 C6**
Plainville *CT* ..... 41°41N 72°51W **78 C2**
Plainville *GA* ..... 34°24N 85°2W **68 B1**
Plainville *IN*...... 38°48N 87°9W **72 E3**
Plainville *KS* ..... 39°14N 99°18W **74 B4**
Plainville *MA* ..... 42°0N 71°20W **78 B3**
Plainwell *MI* ...... 42°27N 85°38W **79 G6**
Plaistow *NH* ...... 42°50N 71°6W **86 D3**
Planada *CA* ..... 37°16N 120°19W **64 F6**
Plandome *NY* ..... 40°48N 73°42W **114 B4**
Plandome Heights
NY............. 40°48N 73°42W **114 B4**
Plankinton *SD*..... 43°43N 98°29W **91 G7**
Plano *IL* .... 41°40N 88°32W **71 B5**
Plano *TX* .... 33°1N 96°42W **99 D11**
Plant City *FL*...... 28°1N 82°7W **67 C6**
Plantation *FL*...... 26°7N 80°14W **112 B2**
Plantersville *AL* .... 32°40N 86°56W **60 D4**
Plantersville *MS* .... 34°12N 88°40W **81 B5**
Plantsite *AZ* ..... 33°2N 109°21W **62 D6**
Plaquemine *LA* .... 30°17N 91°14W **75 D4**
Plaquemines Parish ☆
LA .... 29°29N 89°42W **75 E6**
Platina *CA* ...... 40°22N 122°53W **64 C4**
Platinum *AK* ..... 59°1N 161°49W **61 G7**
Platte *SD* .... 43°23N 98°51W **91 G7**
Platte → *MO*...... 39°16N 94°50W **82 B2**
Platte → *NE* ..... 41°4N 95°53W **84 C10**
Platte Center *NE* .. 41°32N 97°29W **84 C8**
Platte City *MO* .... 39°22N 94°47W **82 B2**
Platte County ☆ *MO* 39°20N 94°45W **82 B2**
Platte County ☆ *NE*. 41°30N 97°30W **84 C8**
Platte County ☆ *WY* 42°0N 105°0W **104 D8**
Platteville *CO* .... 40°13N 104°49W **66 B6**
Platteville *WI*..... 42°44N 90°29W **103 F3**
Plattsburg *MO*..... 39°34N 94°27W **82 B2**
Plattsburgh *NY* ..... 44°42N 73°28W **86 B1**
Plattsmouth *NE* ... 41°1N 95°53W **84 C10**
Playas L. *NM*...... 31°51N 108°35W **88 F2**
Plaza *ND* .... 48°1N 101°58W **91 B4**
Plaza *WA*....... 47°19N 117°23W **101 C8**
Plaza Larga Cr. →
NM............ 35°10N 103°29W **88 B7**
Pleasant, L. *AZ*.... 33°51N 112°16W **62 D3**
Pleasant B. *MA*..... 41°40N 69°57W **78 C5**
Pleasant Dale *NE* ... 40°48N 96°56W **84 D9**
Pleasant Gap *PA* ... 40°52N 77°44W **95 D5**
Pleasant Garden *NC* 35°58N 79°46W **90 C6**
Pleasant Grove *UT* 40°22N 111°44W **100 C4**
Pleasant Hill *CA* .... 37°57N 122°4W **64 F4**
Pleasant Hill *IL*.... 39°27N 90°52W **71 D3**
Pleasant Hill *IA* .... 41°35N 93°31W **73 D5**
Pleasant Hill *LA* .... 31°49N 93°31W **75 C2**
Pleasant Hill *MO* ... 38°47N 94°16W **82 C2**
Pleasant Hill *NM* ... 34°31N 103°4W **88 C7**
Pleasant Hill *OH*.... 40°3N 84°21W **92 C2**
Pleasant Hill *TN*.... 35°59N 85°12W **97 E7**
Pleasant Hill L. *OH* . 40°37N 82°19W **92 C4**
Pleasant Hills *PA* . 40°20N 79°57W **116 C2**
Pleasant Lake *MN*... 45°5N 93°5W **113 A3**
Pleasant Lake *MN* ... 45°30N 94°17W **80 E4**
Pleasant Plains *AR* . 35°33N 91°38W **63 C4**
Pleasant Plains *IL*.... 39°52N 89°55W **71 D4**
Pleasant Point Indian Reservation
ME .... 44°57N 67°3W **76 D6**
Pleasant Prairie *WI*. 42°33N 87°56W **103 F6**
Pleasant Ridge *MI* .. 42°28N 83°8W **109 A2**
Pleasant Site *AL*.... 34°33N 88°4W **60 B2**
Pleasant View *CO*. 37°35N 108°46W **66 E2**
Pleasant View *TN*.... 36°24N 87°2W **96 D5**
Pleasant View *UT*.. 41°19N 112°0W **100 B3**
Pleasant View *WA* 46°29N 118°20W **101 D7**
Pleasanton *IA* ..... 40°35N 93°45W **73 E5**
Pleasanton *KS*...... 38°11N 94°43W **74 C9**
Pleasanton *NM* ... 33°17N 108°53W **88 D2**
Pleasanton *NE* ..... 40°58N 99°5W **84 D6**
Pleasanton *TX*...... 28°58N 98°29W **99 J9**
Pleasants County ☆
WV .... 39°22N 81°12W **102 B3**
Pleasantville *IA*..... 41°23N 93°18W **73 D5**
Pleasantville *NJ*.... 39°24N 74°32W **87 C2**
Pleasantville *NY* .... 41°8N 73°48W **87 A3**
Pleasantville *OH*..... 39°49N 82°32W **92 D4**
Pleasure Ridge Park
KY.............. 38°9N 85°50W **97 B7**
Pleasureville *KY*..... 38°21N 85°7W **97 B7**
Plentywood *MT* ... 48°47N 104°34W **83 B13**
Plevna *KS* .... 37°59N 98°19W **74 D5**
Plevna *MT* .... 46°25N 104°31W **83 D13**
Plimoth Plantation
MA .... 41°56N 70°37W **78 C4**
Plover *IA* .... 42°53N 94°38W **73 C4**
Plover *WI*........ 44°27N 89°32W **103 D4**
Plover → *WI*...... 44°29N 89°35W **103 D4**
Plum *PA*.......... 40°29N 79°47W **95 D3**
Plum City *WI*...... 44°38N 92°11W **103 D1**
Plum Cr. → *SD*.... 44°13N 101°45W **91 F5**
Plum I. *MA* .... 42°45N 70°48W **78 B4**
Plum I. *NY*....... 41°11N 72°12W **78 C2**
Plum Point *MD*..... 38°37N 76°32W **77 B4**
Plum Springs *KY* ... 37°0N 86°20W **96 D6**
Plumas County ☆ *CA* 40°0N 121°0W **64 D5**
Plumas Nat. Forest
CA .... 39°50N 120°40W **64 D6**
Plumerville *AR* ..... 35°10N 92°38W **63 C3**
Plummer *ID*..... 47°20N 116°53W **70 B2**
Plummer *MN*...... 47°55N 96°3W **80 C2**
Plush *OR* .... 42°25N 119°54W **94 E6**
Plymouth *CA*..... 38°29N 120°51W **64 E6**
Plymouth *IL* ...... 40°18N 90°58W **71 C3**
Plymouth *IN* ...... 41°21N 86°19W **72 B4**
Plymouth *IA* ...... 43°15N 93°7W **73 B5**
Plymouth *KS*...... 38°25N 96°20W **74 C7**
Plymouth *MA* ..... 41°57N 70°40W **78 C4**
Plymouth *MN* ..... 45°1N 93°27W **113 A1**
Plymouth *NC*...... 35°52N 76°43W **90 C9**
Plymouth *NH* ..... 43°46N 71°41W **86 C3**
Plymouth *NE*..... 40°18N 96°59W **84 D9**
Plymouth *PA*...... 41°14N 75°57W **95 C7**
Plymouth *UT*..... 41°53N 112°9W **100 B3**
Plymouth *VT*...... 43°34N 72°45W **86 C2**
Plymouth *WI* ..... 43°45N 87°59W **103 E6**
Plymouth Bay *MA* . 41°57N 70°37W **78 C4**
Plymouth County ☆
IA .... 42°45N 96°10W **73 C2**
Plymouth County ☆
MA .... 41°45N 70°45W **78 C4**
Plymouth Creek Park
MN............ 45°1N 93°28W **113 A1**
Plymouth Meeting
PA............. 40°6N 75°16W **116 A1**
Poarch Creek Indian Reservation
AL............. 31°10N 87°35W **60 E3**
Poca *WV* .... 38°28N 81°49W **102 C3**
Pocahontas *AR* .... 36°16N 90°58W **63 B5**
Pocahontas *IL*..... 38°50N 89°33W **71 E4**
Pocahontas *IA*..... 42°44N 94°40W **73 C4**
Pocahontas County ☆
IA .... 42°45N 94°40W **73 C4**
Pocahontas County ☆
WV .... 38°10N 80°2W **102 C4**
Pocasset *MA* ...... 41°41N 70°37W **78 C4**
Pocasset *OK* ...... 35°12N 97°58W **93 C6**
Pocatalico *WV*.... 38°29N 81°40W **102 C3**
Pocatalico → *WV*.. 38°29N 81°49W **102 C3**
Pocatello *ID* ..... 42°52N 112°27W **70 G6**
Pocola *OK* ...... 35°14N 94°29W **93 C9**
Pocomoke → *MD* . 37°58N 75°39W **77 C5**
Pocomoke City *MD* . 38°5N 75°34W **77 B5**
Pocomoke Sd. *VA* .. 37°50N 75°50W **77 C5**
Pocomoke State Forest
MD .... 38°9N 75°32W **77 B5**
Pocono Mts. *PA* ..... 41°7N 75°22W **87 A1**
Pocono Pines *PA* ... 41°6N 75°27W **87 A1**
Pocono Summit *PA* .. 41°7N 75°23W **87 A1**
Poestenkill *NY* ..... 42°41N 73°34W **78 B1**
Pohick Creek →
VA .... 38°48N 77°15W **119 C2**
Pohue B. *HI*...... 19°0N 155°48W **69 E6**
Poinsett, L. *SD* .... 44°34N 97°5W **91 F8**
Poinsett County ☆
AR............ 35°34N 90°43W **63 C5**
Point Arena *CA* ... 38°55N 123°41W **64 E3**
Point au Fer I. *LA* .. 29°18N 91°15W **75 E4**
Point Baker *AK* .. 56°21N 133°37W **61 H14**
Point Blank *TX*..... 30°45N 95°13W **99 G12**
Point Clear *AL* ..... 30°28N 87°55W **60 F3**
Point Comfort *TX* .. 28°41N 96°33W **99 J11**
Point Hope *AK* .... 68°21N 166°47W **61 B6**
Point Lay *AK* .... 69°46N 163°3W **61 B7**
Point Lookout *MD*... 38°5N 76°18W **77 B4**
Point Marion *PA* ... 39°44N 79°54W **95 E3**
Point of Rocks *WY* 41°41N 108°47W **104 E4**
Point Pleasant *NJ*... 40°5N 74°4W **87 B2**
Point Pleasant *WV* .. 38°51N 82°8W **102 C2**
Point Reyes Nat. Seashore ⌂
CA .... 38°10N 122°55W **64 E4**
Point Roberts *WA* . 48°59N 123°4W **101 B2**
Point Vicente Lighthouse
CA .... 33°44N 118°24W **111 D2**
Pointe a la Hache *LA* 29°35N 89°48W **75 E6**
Pointe Aux Pins *MI* . 45°44N 84°29W **79 D7**
Pointe Coupee Parish ☆
LA .... 30°36N 91°37W **75 D4**
Pojoaque *NM* ..... 35°54N 106°1W **88 B4**
Pojoaque Indian Reservation
NM............ 35°54N 106°1W **88 B4**
Pōka'ī B. *HI*..... 21°27N 158°12W **69 K13**
Pokegama L. *MN* ... 47°12N 93°35W **80 D5**
Polacca *AZ* ...... 35°50N 110°23W **62 B5**
Polacca Wash →
AZ............ 35°22N 110°50W **62 B5**
Poland *NY*........ 43°14N 75°4W **89 B5**
Poland *OH*........ 41°1N 80°37W **92 B6**
Pole Mt. *WY* .... 41°14N 105°23W **104 E7**
Polk *NE*.......... 41°5N 97°46W **84 C8**
Polk *OH*......... 40°57N 82°13W **92 C4**
Polk *PA* .... 41°22N 79°56W **95 C3**
Polk City *FL*...... 28°11N 81°49W **67 C7**
Polk City *IA*...... 41°46N 93°43W **73 D5**
Polk County ☆ *AR*.. 34°35N 94°15W **63 D1**
Polk County ☆ *FL* .. 28°0N 81°45W **67 D7**
Polk County ☆ *GA*.. 34°0N 85°10W **68 B1**
Polk County ☆ *IA* .. 41°40N 93°35W **73 D5**
Polk County ☆ *MN* . 47°40N 96°30W **80 C2**
Polk County ☆ *MO* . 37°35N 93°25W **82 D3**
Polk County ☆ *NC*.. 35°15N 82°10W **90 C3**
Polk County ☆ *NE*.. 41°15N 97°40W **84 C8**
Polk County ☆ *OR*. 44°55N 123°20W **94 C2**
Polk County ☆ *TN*.. 35°5N 84°39W **97 E8**
Polk County ☆ *TX*. 30°43N 94°56W **99 G13**
Polk County ☆ *WI* . 45°30N 92°30W **103 C1**
Polkton *NC* ...... 35°1N 80°12W **90 C5**
Polkville *MS* ...... 32°11N 89°42W **81 D4**
Polkville *NC* ..... 35°25N 81°39W **90 C4**
Pollock *ID* ...... 45°19N 116°21W **70 D2**
Pollock *LA* .... 31°32N 92°25W **75 C3**
Pollock *MO* ...... 40°21N 93°5W **82 A3**
Pollock *SD*..... 45°55N 100°17W **91 E5**
Pollock Pines *CA* .. 38°46N 120°34W **64 E6**
Polo *IL*.......... 41°59N 89°35W **71 B4**
Polo *MO* .... 39°33N 94°3W **82 B2**
Polson *MT*...... 47°41N 114°9W **83 C3**
Polvadera *NM* ... 34°12N 106°55W **88 C4**
Polynesian Cultural Center
HI............ 21°38N 157°55W **69 J14**
Pomeroy *IA*...... 42°33N 94°41W **73 C4**
Pomeroy *OH*...... 39°2N 82°2W **92 D4**
Pomeroy *WA*.... 46°28N 117°36W **101 D8**
Pomfret *CT* ...... 41°54N 71°58W **78 C3**
Pomfret *MD* ...... 38°30N 77°2W **77 B3**
Pomme de Terre →
MN............. 45°10N 96°5W **80 E2**
Pomme de Terre →
MO............. 38°11N 93°25W **82 C3**
Pomme de Terre L.
MO............. 37°54N 93°19W **82 D3**
Pomona *CA* ..... 34°4N 117°45W **65 J9**
Pomona *KS* ..... 38°36N 95°27W **74 C8**
Pomona *MD* ..... 39°10N 76°7W **77 A4**
Pomona *MO* ..... 36°52N 91°55W **82 E5**
Pomona *NJ* ...... 39°29N 74°35W **87 C2**
Pomona Lake *KS*... 38°39N 95°34W **74 C8**
Pomona Park *FL* ... 29°30N 81°36W **67 B7**
Pompano Beach *FL*. 26°14N 80°7W **112 A3**
Pompeys Pillar *MT* 45°59N 107°57W **83 E10**
Pompeys Pillar Nat. Monument ⌂
MT............ 46°0N 108°0W **83 D10**
Pompton Lakes *NJ* .. 41°0N 74°17W **87 B2**
Ponca *NE*........ 42°34N 96°43W **84 B9**
Ponca City *OK* ..... 36°42N 97°5W **93 B6**
Ponca Cr. → *NE*.... 42°48N 98°5W **84 B7**
Ponce *Puerto Rico* . 18°1N 66°37W **105 G16**
Ponce de Leon *FL* .. 30°44N 85°56W **67 A3**
Ponce de Leon B. *FL* 25°15N 81°10W **67 F7**
Ponce Inlet *FL* ..... 29°6N 80°56W **67 B8**
Poncha Springs *CO* . 38°31N 106°5W **66 D4**
Ponchatoula *LA* .... 30°26N 90°26W **75 D5**
Pond *CA* .... 35°43N 119°20W **65 H7**
Pond → *KY*....... 37°32N 87°21W **96 C5**
Pond Creek *OK* .... 36°40N 97°48W **93 B6**
Pond Eddy *NY* .... 41°26N 74°49W **87 A2**
Pondera County ☆
MT .... 48°12N 112°30W **83 B5**
Ponderosa *NM* ... 35°40N 106°40W **88 B4**
Pondosa *CA*..... 41°12N 121°41W **64 B5**
Poneto *IN* .... 40°39N 85°13W **72 C5**
Pontchartrain, L. *LA* . 30°5N 90°5W **75 D5**
Ponte Vedra Beach
FL............. 30°15N 81°23W **67 A7**
Pontiac *IL* .... 40°53N 88°38W **71 C5**
Pontiac *MI*....... 42°38N 83°18W **79 G8**
Pontotoc *MS* ...... 34°15N 89°0W **81 B5**
Pontotoc County ☆
MS .... 34°15N 89°0W **81 B5**
Pontotoc County ☆
OK .... 34°45N 96°45W **93 D7**
Poole *KY*........ 37°38N 87°39W **96 C5**
Poole *NE* .... 40°59N 98°58W **84 D7**
Pooler *GA* ...... 32°7N 81°15W **68 D5**
Pooles I. *MD*..... 39°17N 76°16W **77 A4**
Poolesville *MD*.... 39°9N 77°25W **77 A3**
Poorman *AK* .... 64°5N 155°33W **61 D9**
Pope *MS*......... 34°13N 89°57W **81 B4**
Pope County ☆ *AR* . 35°28N 92°59W **63 C3**
Pope County ☆ *IL*... 37°25N 88°35W **71 F5**
Pope County ☆ *MN*. 45°40N 95°25W **80 E3**
Pope Cr. → *IL* .... 41°8N 90°58W **71 B3**
Popejoy *IA*....... 42°36N 93°26W **73 C5**
Popes Creek *MD* ... 38°24N 76°58W **77 B4**
Poplar *MT*..... 48°7N 105°12W **83 B12**
Poplar *WI*....... 46°35N 91°48W **103 B2**
Poplar → *MT*.... 48°5N 105°11W **83 B12**
Poplar Bluff *MO* .... 36°46N 90°24W **82 E6**
Poplar Grove *IL* .... 42°22N 88°49W **71 A5**
Poplar Grove Nat. Cemetery
VA .... 37°10N 77°26W **102 D7**
Poplar Head = Dothan
AL............ 31°13N 85°24W **60 E5**
Poplar Hill *VA* ..... 37°13N 80°44W **102 D4**
Poplar I. *MD*..... 38°46N 76°23W **77 B4**
Poplar Mt. *KY*..... 38°4N 85°34W **97 D7**
Poplar Plains *KY* ... 38°21N 83°41W **97 B9**
Poplarville *MS*.... 30°51N 89°32W **81 F4**
Popo Agie → *WY* . 43°1N 108°21W **104 C4**
Poquetanuck *CT*.... 41°29N 72°3W **78 C2**
Poquonock Bridge
CT............. 41°19N 72°1W **78 C2**
Poquoson *VA* ...... 37°8N 76°24W **102 D8**
Porcupine *SD* .... 43°14N 102°19W **91 G3**
Porcupine → *AK* . 66°34N 145°19W **61 C11**
Porcupine → *MT* .. 48°7N 106°20W **83 B11**
Porcupine Mountains Wilderness
State Park ⌂ *MI* . 46°47N 89°41W **79 C2**
Porcupine Mts. *MI* . 46°47N 89°44W **79 C3**
Porphyry Pk. *MT* . 47°14N 109°18W **83 C8**
Port Alexander
AK .... 56°15N 134°38W **61 H14**
Port Allegany *PA* ... 41°48N 78°17W **95 C4**
Port Allen *LA* ..... 30°27N 91°12W **75 D4**
Port Angeles *WA* . 48°7N 123°27W **101 B2**
Port Aransas *TX*... 27°50N 97°4W **99 K10**
Port Arthur *TX*.... 29°54N 93°56W **99 H14**
Port Austin *MI* ..... 44°3N 83°1W **79 E8**
Port Barre *LA* ..... 30°34N 91°57W **75 D4**
Port Byron *IL* ..... 41°36N 90°20W **71 B3**
Port Charlotte *FL*... 26°59N 82°6W **67 E6**
Port Chester *NY*..... 41°0N 73°40W **89 E7**
Port Clinton *OH* .... 41°31N 82°56W **92 B4**
Port Clyde *ME* ..... 43°56N 69°16W **76 E4**
Port Columbus Int. ✕ (CMH)
OH .... 40°0N 82°53W **92 D4**
Port Edwards *WI* .. 44°21N 89°52W **103 D4**
Port Elizabeth *NJ* .. 39°19N 74°59W **87 C2**
Port Ewen *NY*..... 41°54N 73°59W **89 D7**
Port Fourchon *LA* ... 29°6N 90°11W **75 E5**
Port Gamble *WA* . 47°51N 122°34W **118 A2**
Port Gibson *MS* .... 31°58N 90°59W **81 E3**
Port Hadlock *WA*.. 48°2N 122°45W **101 B3**
Port Heiden *AK*.. 56°55N 158°41W **61 H8**
Port Henry *NY* ..... 44°3N 73°28W **86 B1**
Port Hope *MI* ..... 43°57N 82°43W **79 F9**
Port Hueneme *CA* .. 34°7N 119°12W **65 J7**
Port Huron *MI* .... 42°58N 82°26W **79 G9**
Port Isabel *TX*..... 26°5N 97°12W **98 L10**
Port Jefferson *NY*.... 40°57N 73°3W **78 D1**
Port Jefferson *OH* .... 40°20N 84°6W **92 C2**
Port Jervis *NY*..... 41°22N 74°41W **87 A2**
Port Kent *NY* ..... 44°32N 73°24W **86 B1**
Port Lavaca *TX*.... 28°37N 96°38W **99 J11**
Port Leyden *NY* .... 43°35N 75°21W **89 B5**
Port Lions *AK* ... 57°52N 152°53W **61 H9**
Port Louisa Nat. Wildlife Refuge ⌂
IL .... 41°6N 90°57W **71 B3**
Port Ludlow *WA*.. 47°56N 122°41W **101 C3**
Port Mansfield *TX*. 26°34N 97°26W **98 L10**
Port Mayaca *FL* ... 26°59N 80°36W **67 E8**

Port Moller *AK*.....55°59N 160°34W **61 J7**
Port Neches *TX*.....30°0N 93°59W **99 H14**
Port Newark *NJ*.....40°41N 74°7W **114 B2**
Port Norris *NJ*.....39°15N 75°2W **87 C1**
Port O'Connor *TX*.....28°27N 96°24W **99 J11**
Port of Portland
 OR.....45°34N 122°43W **116 A1**
Port Orange *FL*.....29°9N 80°59W **67 B8**
Port Orchard *WA*.....47°32N 122°38W **118 C2**
Port Orford *OR*.....42°45N 124°30W **94 E1**
Port Penn *DE*.....39°31N 75°35W **77 A5**
Port Reading *NJ*.....40°33N 74°15W **114 C1**
Port Republic *MD*.....38°30N 76°33W **77 B4**
Port Republic *NJ*.....39°31N 74°29W **87 C2**
Port Richey *FL*.....28°16N 82°43W **67 C6**
Port Richmond *NY*.....40°38N 74°7W **114 C2**
Port Royal *SC*.....38°33N 85°5W **97 B7**
Port Royal *SC*.....32°23N 80°42W **90 F5**
Port Royal *VA*.....38°10N 77°12W **77 B3**
Port Royal Sd. *SC*.....32°15N 80°40W **90 F5**
Port St. Joe *FL*.....29°49N 85°18W **67 D3**
Port St. John *FL*.....28°28N 80°47W **67 D8**
Port St. Lucie *FL*.....27°18N 80°21W **67 D8**
Port Salerno *FL*.....27°9N 80°12W **67 D8**
Port Sanilac *MI*.....43°26N 82°33W **79 F9**
Port Sulphur *LA*.....29°29N 89°42W **75 E6**
Port Susan *WA*.....48°5N 122°15W **98 B3**
Port Tobacco *MD*.....38°27N 77°2W **77 B3**
Port Townsend *WA*.....48°7N 122°45W **101 B3**
Port Vincent *LA*.....30°20N 90°51W **75 D5**
Port Vue *PA*.....40°20N 79°52W **116 B2**
Port Washington
 NY.....40°49N 73°41W **114 B4**
Port Washington *OH* 40°20N 81°31W **92 C5**
Port Washington *WI* 43°23N 87°53W **103 E6**
Port Washington North
 NY.....40°50N 73°42W **114 A4**
Port Wentworth *GA*.. 32°9N 81°10W **68 B5**
Port Wing *WI*.....46°47N 91°23W **103 B2**
Portage *ME*.....46°46N 68°29W **76 B3**
Portage *MI*.....42°12N 85°35W **79 G6**
Portage *PA*.....40°23N 78°40W **92 F7**
Portage *UT*.....41°59N 112°14W **100 B3**
Portage *WI*.....47°24N 122°26W **118 C3**
Portage *WI*.....43°33N 89°28W **103 E4**
Portage ➤ *OH*.....41°31N 83°5W **92 B3**
Portage County ☆ *OH* 41°9N 81°15W **92 B5**
Portage County ☆
 WI.....44°25N 89°30W **103 D4**
Portage Park *IL*.....41°56N 87°45W **108 B2**
Portageville *MO*.....36°26N 89°42W **82 E7**
Portal *ND*.....48°59N 102°33W **91 B3**
Portal *AZ*.....31°55N 109°9W **62 F6**
Portal *GA*.....32°33N 81°56W **68 D5**
Portales *NM*.....34°11N 103°20W **88 C7**
Porter *MN*.....44°38N 96°10W **80 F2**
Porter *OK*.....35°52N 95°31W **93 C8**
Porter *WA*.....46°56N 123°18W **101 D2**
Porter, L. *FL*.....28°30N 81°19W **115 A3**
Porter County ☆ *IN*.. 41°25N 87°5W **72 B3**
Porterville *CA*.....36°4N 119°1W **65 G7**
Porterville *MS*.....32°41N 88°28W **81 D5**
Porthill *ID*.....48°59N 116°30W **70 A2**
Portis *KS*.....39°34N 98°41W **74 B5**
Portland *AR*.....33°14N 91°31W **63 E4**
Portland *CT*.....41°34N 72°38W **78 C2**
Portland *IN*.....30°31N 86°12W **67 A2**
Portland *IN*.....40°26N 84°59W **72 C6**
Portland *ME*.....43°39N 70°16W **76 E3**
Portland *MI*.....42°52N 84°54W **79 G7**
Portland *MO*.....38°43N 91°43W **82 C5**
Portland *ND*.....47°30N 97°22W **91 C8**
Portland *OR*.....45°32N 122°37W **116 A1**
Portland *PA*.....40°55N 75°6W **87 B1**
Portland *TN*.....36°35N 86°31W **96 D6**
Portland *TX*.....27°53N 97°20W **99 K10**
Portland Int. ✈ (PDX)
 OR.....45°35N 122°36W **116 A2**
Portneuf ➤ *ID*.....42°58N 112°35W **70 G6**
Portneuf Range *ID*.. 42°50N 112°10W **70 G6**
Portola *CA*.....39°49N 120°28W **64 D6**
Portsmouth *NH*.....43°5N 70°45W **86 C4**
Portsmouth *OH*.....38°44N 82°57W **92 E4**
Portsmouth *RI*.....41°36N 71°15W **78 C3**
Portsmouth *VA*.....36°58N 76°23W **115 A1**
Portville *NY*.....42°3N 78°20W **89 C2**
Porum *OK*.....35°22N 95°16W **93 C8**
Poseyville *IN*.....38°10N 87°47W **72 E3**
Possum Kingdom L.
 TX.....32°52N 98°26W **99 E9**
Post *OR*.....44°10N 120°29W **94 C5**
Post *TX*.....33°12N 101°23W **98 D6**
Post Falls *ID*.....47°43N 116°57W **70 B2**
Poston *AZ*.....34°0N 114°24W **62 C1**
Posts *CA*.....36°14N 121°46W **64 G5**
Postville *IA*.....43°5N 91°34W **73 B7**
Pot Mt. *ID*.....46°44N 115°24W **70 C3**
Potagannissing B. *MI*.. 46°5N 83°50W **79 C8**
Potato *AK*.....46°26N 116°47W **70 C2**
Potawatomi Indian Reservation
 WI.....45°27N 88°35W **103 C5**
Poteau *OK*.....35°3N 94°37W **93 C9**
Poteau ➤ *OK*.....35°23N 94°26W **93 C9**
Poteet *TX*.....29°2N 98°34W **99 H9**
Poth *TX*.....29°4N 98°5W **99 H9**
Potholes Res. *WA*.. 46°59N 119°16W **101 D6**
Potlatch *ID*.....46°55N 116°54W **70 C2**
Potomac *IL*.....40°18N 87°48W **72 C6**
Potomac *MD*.....38°59N 77°13W **119 A2**
Potomac ➤ *MD*.....38°0N 76°23W **77 B4**
Potomac Heights *MD*. 38°36N 77°8W **77 B3**
Potosi *MO*.....37°56N 90°47W **82 D6**
Potrero Hill *CA*.....37°45N 122°23W **118 B2**
Potrero Pt. *CA*.....37°45N 122°22W **118 B2**
Potsdam *NY*.....44°40N 74°59W **89 A6**
Pottawatomie County ☆
 KS.....39°22N 96°15W **74 B7**
Pottawatomie County ☆
 OK.....35°10N 97°0W **93 C7**
Pottawattamie County ☆
 IA.....41°20N 95°30W **73 D4**
Potter *KS*.....39°26N 95°9W **74 B8**
Potter *NE*.....41°13N 103°19W **84 C2**
Potter County ☆ *PA*.. 41°50N 78°0W **89 C5**
Potter County ☆ *SD*.. 45°0N 100°0W **91 D6**
Potter County ☆ *TX* 35°22N 101°50W **98 B6**
Potterville *CA*.....32°13N 84°7W **68 E2**
Potterville *MI*.....42°38N 84°45W **79 G7**
Potts Camp *MS*.....34°38N 89°18W **81 B4**
Pottsboro *TX*.....33°46N 96°40W **99 D11**
Pottstown *PA*.....40°15N 75°39W **87 B5**
Pottsville *PA*.....40°41N 76°12W **87 B4**
Potwin *KS*.....37°56N 97°1W **74 C6**
Poughkeepsie *NY*... 41°42N 73°56W **89 D7**
Poulan *GA*.....31°31N 83°47W **68 E3**
Poulsbo *WA*.....47°44N 122°38W **118 B2**
Poultney *VT*.....43°31N 73°14W **86 C1**
Pound *VA*.....37°8N 82°36W **102 D2**
Pound *WI*.....45°6N 88°2W **103 C5**
Poverty Point Nat. Monument ○
 LA.....32°39N 91°24W **75 B4**
Poway *CA*.....32°58N 117°2W **65 L9**
Powder ➤ *MT*.....46°45N 105°26W **83 D12**
Powder ➤ *OR*.....44°45N 117°3W **94 C7**
Powder Horn Park
 MN.....44°56N 93°15W **113 B2**
Powder River *WY*.... 43°2N 106°59W **104 C6**
Powder River County ☆
 MT.....45°20N 105°40W **83 E12**

Powder River Pass
 WY.....44°9N 107°5W **104 B6**
Powder Springs *GA*.. 33°52N 84°41W **68 C2**
Powderhorn *CO*.....38°17N 107°7W **66 B3**
Powell *ID*.....46°35N 114°43W **70 C4**
Powell *OH*.....40°18N 81°42W **92 C5**
Powell *TN*.....36°2N 84°2W **97 D8**
Powell *WY*.....44°45N 108°46W **104 B4**
Powell, L. *UT*.....36°57N 111°29W **100 G4**
Powell Butte *OR*.....44°15N 121°1W **94 C4**
Powell Butte Park
 OR.....45°29N 122°30W **116 B2**
Powell County ☆ *KY* 37°50N 83°50W **97 C9**
Powell County ☆ *MT*.. 47°0N 113°0W **83 D4**
Powellville *MD*.....38°20N 75°22W **77 B5**
Powers *CA*.....33°26N 82°52W **68 C4**
Powers County ☆ *CO* 38°20N 112°50W **70 G6**
Powers *MI*.....45°41N 87°32W **79 D4**
Powers *OR*.....42°53N 124°4W **94 E1**
Powers Lake *ND*.....48°34N 102°39W **91 B3**
Powersville *MO*.....40°33N 93°15W **82 A4**
Poweshiek County ☆
 IA.....41°40N 92°30W **73 D6**
Powhatan *AR*.....36°5N 91°7W **63 B4**
Powhatan *VA*.....37°32N 77°55W **102 D7**
Powhatan County ☆
 VA.....37°32N 77°55W **102 D7**
Powhatan Point *OH*.. 39°52N 80°49W **92 D6**
Powhattan *KS*.....39°46N 95°38W **74 B8**
Pownal *VT*.....42°46N 73°14W **86 D1**
Poydras *LA*.....29°52N 89°53W **113 C3**
Poygan, L. *WI*.....44°9N 88°50W **103 D5**
Poynette *WI*.....43°24N 89°24W **103 E4**
Prague *NE*.....41°19N 96°49W **84 E8**
Prague *OK*.....35°29N 96°41W **93 C7**
Prairie *MS*.....33°48N 88°40W **81 C5**
Prairie Band of the Potawatomi
 Indian Reservation
 KS.....39°20N 95°52W **74 B8**
Prairie City *IA*.....41°36N 93°14W **73 D5**
Prairie City *OR*.....44°28N 118°43W **94 C7**
Prairie City *SD*.....45°32N 102°49W **91 E3**
Prairie County ☆ *AR* 34°47N 91°35W **63 D4**
Prairie County ☆
 MT.....46°57N 105°30W **83 D12**
Prairie Dog ➤ *KS*.....40°0N 99°10W **74 B3**
Prairie Dog Town Fork Red ➤
 U.S.A......34°34N 99°58W **98 C7**
Prairie du Chien *WI*.. 43°3N 91°9W **103 E2**
Prairie du Rocher *IL*.. 38°5N 90°6W **82 D6**
Prairie du Sac *WI*.....43°17N 89°43W **103 E4**
Prairie Farm *WI*.....45°14N 91°59W **103 C2**
Prairie Grove *AR*.....35°59N 94°19W **63 C1**
Prairie Hill *MO*.....39°31N 92°44W **82 B4**
Prairie Home *MO*.....38°49N 92°35W **82 C4**
Prairie Island Indian Reservation
 MN.....44°39N 92°39W **80 F6**
Prairie View *KS*.....39°50N 99°34W **74 B4**
Prairie View *TX*.....30°6N 95°59W **99 G12**
Prairie Village *KS*.. 38°58N 94°38W **74 C9**
Prairieton *IN*.....37°39N 98°44W **74 D5**
Pratt *KS*.....37°39N 98°44W **74 D5**
Pratt County ☆ *KS*.. 37°35N 98°45W **74 D5**
Prattsville *AL*.....32°28N 86°29W **60 D4**
Prattsburg *NY*.....42°31N 77°29W **89 C4**
Preble *NY*.....42°44N 76°9W **89 C4**
Preble County ☆ *OH* 39°45N 84°38W **92 C2**
Premont *TX*.....27°22N 98°7W **98 K9**
Prentice *WI*.....45°33N 90°17W **103 C3**
Prentiss *MS*.....31°36N 89°52W **81 E4**
Prentiss County ☆
 MS.....34°39N 88°34W **81 B5**
Prescott *AZ*.....34°33N 112°28W **62 C3**
Prescott *AR*.....33°48N 93°23W **63 E2**
Prescott *IA*.....41°1N 94°37W **73 D4**
Prescott *KS*.....38°4N 94°42W **74 C9**
Prescott *OR*.....44°11N 83°56W **79 E8**
Prescott *OR*.....46°3N 122°53W **94 A3**
Prescott *WA*.....46°18N 118°19W **101 D7**
Prescott *WI*.....44°45N 92°48W **103 D1**
Prescott Nat. Forest
 AZ.....34°30N 112°30W **62 C3**
Prescott Valley *AZ*.. 34°40N 112°18W **62 C3**
Presho *SD*.....43°54N 100°3W **91 E5**
Presidential Lakes Estates
 NJ.....39°54N 74°35W **87 C2**
Presidents I. *TN*.....35°6N 90°6W **112 B1**
Presidio *CA*.....37°47N 122°27W **118 B2**
Presidio *TX*.....29°34N 104°22W **98 H3**
Presidio County ☆ *TX* 30°10N 104°0W **98 G3**
Presque I. *PA*.....42°10N 80°6W **98 B2**
Presque Isle *ME*.....46°41N 68°1W **76 B5**
Presque Isle *WI*.....45°18N 83°29W **79 D8**
Presque Isle County ☆
 MI.....45°15N 84°0W **79 D8**
Preston *CT*.....41°33N 72°57W **78 C2**
Preston *GA*.....32°4N 84°32W **68 D2**
Preston *ID*.....42°6N 111°53W **70 G7**
Preston *IA*.....42°3N 90°24W **73 C8**
Preston *KS*.....37°46N 98°33W **74 D5**
Preston *MN*.....43°40N 92°5W **80 G6**
Preston *MD*.....43°40N 92°5W **80 G6**
Preston *MS*.....32°53N 88°50W **81 D5**
Preston *NV*.....38°55N 115°4W **85 D5**
Preston *OK*.....35°43N 95°59W **93 C8**
Preston City *CT*.....41°33N 72°57W **78 C2**
Preston County ☆
 WV.....39°31N 79°48W **102 B5**
Prestonsburg *KY*.....37°40N 82°47W **97 C10**
Pretty Prairie *KS*.....37°47N 98°1W **74 D5**
Prettyboy Res. *MD*.. 39°37N 76°43W **77 A4**
Prewitt *NM*.....35°22N 108°3W **88 B2**
Prewitt Res. *CO*.....40°26N 103°22W **66 B7**
Pribilof Is. *AK*.....57°0N 170°0W **61 H5**
Price *MD*.....39°6N 75°58W **77 A4**
Price *TX*.....32°8N 94°57W **99 E13**
Price *UT*.....39°36N 110°49W **100 D5**
Price County ☆ *WI*.. 45°45N 90°20W **103 C3**
Price Hill *OH*.....39°6N 84°34W **107 B1**
Prichard *AL*.....30°44N 88°5W **60 E2**
Prichard *WV*.....38°15N 82°36W **102 C2**
Priddy *TX*.....31°41N 98°31W **99 F9**
Pride *KY*.....37°34N 87°53W **96 C5**
Priest ➤ *ID*.....48°11N 116°54W **70 A2**
Priest L. *ID*.....48°35N 116°52W **70 A2**
Priest Rapids Dam
 WA.....46°39N 119°54W **101 D6**
Priest River *ID*.....48°11N 116°55W **70 A2**
Prime Hook Nat. Wildlife
 Refuge ○ *DE*.....38°55N 75°18W **77 B5**
Primera *TX*.....26°13N 97°45W **98 L10**
Primghar *IA*.....43°5N 95°38W **73 B3**
Primm *NV*.....35°37N 115°23W **65 L5**
Primrose *NE*.....41°38N 98°14W **84 C7**
Prince Edward County ☆
 VA.....37°15N 78°25W **102 D6**
Prince Frederick *MD*. 38°33N 76°35W **77 B4**
Prince George *VA*.. 37°13N 77°17W **102 D7**
Prince George County ☆
 VA.....37°13N 77°13W **102 D7**
Prince Georges County ☆
 MD.....38°35N 76°50W **77 B4**
Prince of Wales, C.
 AK.....65°36N 168°5W **61 D5**
Prince of Wales I.
 AK.....55°47N 132°50W **61 J14**
Prince of Wales-Outer Ketchikan ☆
 AK.....55°30N 132°30W **61 J15**
Prince William County ☆
 VA.....38°45N 77°29W **102 C7**
Prince William Forest Park ○
 VA.....38°35N 77°24W **102 C7**
Prince William Sd.
 AK.....60°40N 147°0W **61 F11**

Princess Anne *MD*.. 38°12N 75°42W **77 B5**
Princeton *AR*.....33°59N 92°38W **63 E3**
Princeton *IL*.....39°24N 122°1W **64 D4**
Princeton *IL*.....41°23N 89°28W **71 B4**
Princeton *IN*.....38°21N 87°34W **72 E3**
Princeton *IA*.....41°40N 90°20W **73 D8**
Princeton *KS*.....38°29N 95°16W **74 C8**
Princeton *KY*.....37°7N 87°53W **96 C5**
Princeton *ME*.....45°13N 67°34W **76 C6**
Princeton *MN*.....45°34N 93°35W **80 E5**
Princeton *MN*.....42°27N 71°55W **78 B3**
Princeton *MO*.....40°24N 93°35W **82 A3**
Princeton *NJ*.....40°21N 74°39W **87 B2**
Princeton *WV*.....37°22N 81°6W **102 D3**
Princeton *WI*.....43°51N 89°8W **103 E4**
Princeville *HI*.....22°13N 159°29W **69 A2**
Princeville *IL*.....40°56N 89°46W **71 C4**
Prineville *OR*.....44°18N 120°51W **94 C5**
Prineville Res. *OR*.. 44°7N 120°47W **94 C5**
Pringle *SD*.....43°37N 103°36W **91 G2**
Pringle *TX*.....35°57N 101°27W **98 B6**
Prinsburg *MN*.....44°56N 95°11W **80 F3**
Prior Lake *MN*.....44°43N 93°25W **80 F5**
Pritchett *CO*.....37°22N 102°52W **66 E8**
Proctor *MN*.....46°45N 92°14W **80 D6**
Proctor *VT*.....43°40N 73°2W **86 C1**
Proctor *WV*.....39°43N 80°49W **102 B4**
Proctorville *OH*.....38°26N 82°23W **92 E4**
Promise City *IA*.....40°45N 93°9W **73 E5**
Promontory Mts.
 UT.....41°30N 112°30W **100 B3**
Prophetstown *IL*.....41°40N 89°56W **71 B4**
Prospect *CT*.....41°30N 72°59W **78 C2**
Prospect *OH*.....40°27N 83°11W **92 C3**
Prospect *OR*.....42°45N 122°29W **94 E3**
Prospect *PA*.....40°54N 80°3W **92 E5**
Prospect Hill Park
 MA.....42°23N 71°13W **106 A2**
Prospect Park *NJ*.....40°56N 74°10W **114 A1**
Prospect Park *NY*.. 40°39N 73°58W **114 C3**
Prosperity *SC*.....34°12N 81°32W **90 C4**
Prosser *WA*.....46°12N 119°46W **101 D6**
Protection *KS*.....37°12N 99°29W **74 D4**
Protem *MO*.....36°32N 92°51W **82 E4**
Protivin *IA*.....43°13N 92°6W **73 B6**
Providence *KY*.....37°24N 87°46W **96 C5**
Providence *RI*.....41°49N 71°24W **78 C3**
Providence *UT*.....41°43N 111°49W **100 B4**
Providence County ☆
 RI.....41°50N 71°40W **78 C3**
Providence Mts.
 CA.....35°10N 115°15W **65 H11**
Provincetown *MA*.. 42°3N 70°11W **78 B4**
Provo *UT*.....40°14N 111°39W **100 C4**
Prudence I. *RI*.....41°37N 71°19W **78 C3**
Prudhoe Bay *AK*.. 70°18N 148°22W **61 A10**
Prue *OK*.....36°15N 96°15W **93 B7**
Pryor *OK*.....36°19N 95°19W **93 B8**
Pryor Mts. *MT*.....45°15N 108°30W **83 E9**
Puca'una Pt. *HI*.....21°36N 158°6W **69 J13**
Puckaway, L. *WI*.. 43°54N 89°10W **103 E4**
Puckett *MS*.....32°5N 89°47W **81 D4**
Pueblo *CO*.....38°16N 104°37W **66 D6**
Pueblo Colorado Wash ➤
 AZ.....35°5N 110°22W **62 B5**
Pueblo County ☆
 CO.....38°15N 104°30W **66 D6**
Pueblo Mts. *OR*.....42°6N 118°30W **94 E7**
Pueblo West *CO*.....38°20N 104°43W **66 D6**
Puente Hills *CA*.....33°59N 117°55W **111 B4**
Pueo Pt. *HI*.....21°54N 160°4W **69 B1**
Puerca, Pta.
 Puerto Rico.....18°13N 65°36W **105 G17**
Puerco ➤ *AZ*.....34°54N 110°2W **62 C5**
Puerco ➤ *NM*.....34°22N 107°50W **88 C3**
Puerto de Luna *NM* 35°50N 104°37W **88 B6**
Puerto Rico ■
 W. Indies.....18°15N 65°45W **105 G16**
Puget Sound *WA*.. 47°50N 122°30W **118 C3**
Pukalani *HI*.....20°51N 156°20W **69 C5**
Pūko'o *HI*.....21°4N 156°48W **69 B5**
Pulaski *IA*.....37°12N 89°10W **71 F4**
Pulaski *NY*.....43°34N 76°8W **89 B4**
Pulaski *TN*.....35°12N 87°2W **96 E5**
Pulaski *VA*.....37°3N 80°47W **102 D4**
Pulaski *WI*.....44°41N 88°14W **103 D5**
Pulaski County ☆
 AR.....34°45N 92°20W **63 D3**
Pulaski County ☆
 GA.....32°15N 83°30W **68 D3**
Pulaski County ☆ *IL*.. 37°15N 89°5W **71 F4**
Pulaski County ☆ *IN*.. 41°0N 86°40W **72 B4**
Pulaski County ☆ *KY* 37°5N 84°35W **97 C8**
Pulaski County ☆
 MO.....37°50N 92°10W **82 D4**
Pullman *WA*.....46°44N 117°10W **101 D8**
Pullman Historic District
 IL.....41°41N 87°36W **108 C2**
Pumphrey *MD*.....39°13N 76°38W **107 B2**
Pumpkin Creek
 MT.....46°15N 105°45W **83 D12**
Pumpville *TX*.....29°53N 101°45W **98 H6**
Puna Forest Reserve
 HI.....19°26N 154°59W **69 D7**
Punalu'u *HI*.....21°35N 157°53W **69 J14**
Pungo ➤ *NC*.....35°23N 76°30W **90 C9**
Pungo L. *NC*.....35°44N 76°30W **90 C9**
Punta, Cerro de
 Puerto Rico.....18°10N 66°37W **105 G16**
Punta de Agua ➤
 TX.....35°32N 102°27W **98 B5**
Punta Gorda *FL*.....26°56N 82°3W **67 E6**
Punta Rassa *FL*.....26°26N 81°59W **67 E6**
Punxsatawney *PA*.. 40°57N 78°59W **95 D4**
Puolo Pt. *HI*.....21°54N 159°36W **69 B2**
Pūpūkea *HI*.....21°40N 158°3W **69 J13**
Purcell *OK*.....35°1N 97°22W **93 C6**
Purcellville *VA*.....39°8N 77°43W **77 A3**
Purdin *MO*.....39°57N 93°10W **82 B3**
Purdon *TX*.....31°57N 96°37W **99 F11**
Purdum *NE*.....42°5N 100°15W **84 C5**
Purdy *MO*.....36°49N 93°55W **82 E3**
Purdy *OK*.....34°59N 97°35W **93 D6**
Purdy *WA*.....47°23N 122°37W **118 D2**
Purgatoire ➤ *CO*.....38°4N 103°11W **66 D7**
Purgatory Park *MN* 44°53N 93°30W **113 B1**
Purgitsville *WV*.....39°14N 78°55W **77 A2**
Puryear *TN*.....36°27N 88°20W **96 D4**
Pushaw L. *ME*.....44°56N 68°48W **76 D4**
Pushmataha County ☆
 OK.....34°25N 95°20W **93 D8**
Put-in Bay *OH*.....41°39N 82°49W **92 B4**
Putnam *CT*.....41°55N 71°55W **78 C3**
Putnam *TX*.....32°22N 99°12W **99 E8**

Putnam County ☆ *FL* 29°35N 81°45W **67 B7**
Putnam County ☆
 GA.....33°20N 83°15W **68 C3**
Putnam County ☆ *IL* 41°10N 89°15W **71 B4**
Putnam County ☆ *IN* 39°40N 86°50W **72 D4**
Putnam County ☆
 MO.....40°30N 93°0W **82 A4**
Putnam County ☆
 NY.....41°25N 73°45W **89 D7**
Putnam County ☆
 OH.....40°59N 84°12W **92 C2**
Putnam County ☆
 TN.....36°10N 85°30W **97 D7**
Putnam County ☆
 WV.....38°32N 81°54W **102 C3**
Putnam Lake *NY*.. 41°28N 73°33W **78 C1**
Putney *GA*.....31°29N 84°8W **68 E2**
Putney *SD*.....45°34N 98°11W **91 E7**
Putney *VT*.....42°58N 72°31W **86 D2**
Putty Hill *MD*.....39°22N 76°30W **107 A2**
Pu'uanahulu *HI*.....19°49N 155°53W **69 D6**
Pu'uhonua o Hōnaunau Nat.
 Historical Park ○
 HI.....19°25N 155°54W **69 D6**
Pu'uka'aumakua *HI* 21°30N 157°54W **69 J14**
Pu'ukeahiakaho
 HI.....21°23N 157°49W **69 K14**
Pu'ukoholā Heiau Nat. Historic
 Site ○ *HI*.....20°1N 155°49W **69 C6**
Pu'ula'ula *HI*.....20°42N 156°15W **69 C5**
Puunene *HI*.....20°52N 156°23W **69 C5**
Pu'uoke'oke'o *HI* 19°13N 155°44W **69 D6**
Pu'uwai *HI*.....21°54N 160°12W **69 B1**
Puxico *MO*.....36°57N 90°10W **82 E6**
Puyallup *WA*.....47°12N 122°18W **101 C3**
Puyallup Indian Reservation
 WA.....47°14N 122°17W **101 C3**
Pymatuning Res. *OH* 41°30N 80°28W **92 B6**
Pymatuning State Park
 PA.....41°37N 80°24W **95 C2**
Pyote *TX*.....31°32N 103°8W **98 F4**
Pyramid L. *NV*.....40°1N 119°35W **85 B1**
Pyramid Lake Indian Reservation
 NV.....40°0N 119°35W **85 B1**
Pyramid Mts. *NM*.. 32°12N 108°43W **88 E2**
Pyramid Pk. *WY*.. 43°27N 110°28W **104 C2**

Q

Quabbin Res. *MA*.. 42°20N 72°20W **78 B2**
Quail *TX*.....34°55N 100°30W **98 C7**
Quakertown *PA*.....40°26N 75°21W **95 D7**
Quamba *MN*.....45°55N 93°10W **80 E5**
Quanah *TX*.....34°18N 99°44W **98 C8**
Quantico *MD*.....38°23N 75°44W **77 B5**
Quantico U.S.M.C. Base
 VA.....38°30N 77°17W **102 C7**
Quapaw *OK*.....36°58N 94°50W **93 B9**
Quarryville *PA*.....39°54N 76°10W **77 A4**
Quartz Hill *CA*.....34°39N 118°13W **65 J8**
Quartz Mt. *OK*.....34°54N 99°19W **93 D4**
Quartzsite *AZ*.....33°40N 114°13W **62 D1**
Quasqueton *IA*.....42°24N 91°46W **73 C7**
Quay *NM*.....34°56N 103°45W **88 B7**
Quay County ☆ *NM*.. 35°0N 103°30W **88 B7**
Quebradillas
 Puerto Rico.....18°29N 66°56W **105 G16**
Quechee *VT*.....43°40N 72°25W **86 C2**
Queen Anne *MD*.. 38°55N 75°57W **77 B5**
Queen Annes County ☆
 MD.....39°10N 76°0W **77 A5**
Queen City *MO*.....40°25N 92°34W **82 A4**
Queen City *TX*.....33°9N 94°9W **99 D13**
Queen Creek *AZ*.. 33°15N 111°35W **62 D4**
Queens *NY*.....40°44N 73°47W **114 B4**
Queens County ☆
 NY.....40°40N 73°50W **89 E7**
Queens Village *NY*.. 40°43N 73°44W **114 B4**
Queensland *WA*.. 46°31N 83°14W **68 E3**
Queenstown *MD*.. 38°59N 76°9W **77 B4**
Queets *WA*.....47°32N 124°19W **101 C1**
Queets ➤ *WA*.....47°33N 124°21W **101 C1**
Quemado *NM*.....34°20N 108°30W **88 C2**
Quemado *TX*.....28°58N 100°37W **98 J7**
Quenemo *KS*.....38°35N 95°30W **74 C8**
Quentin *MS*.....31°30N 90°45W **81 E3**
Quetico *MN*.....48°32N 91°46W **80 C3**
Quilcene *WA*.....47°49N 122°53W **101 C3**
Quilcene Indian Reservation
 WA.....47°54N 124°37W **101 C1**
Quimby *IA*.....42°38N 95°38W **73 C3**
Quinault *WA*.....47°28N 123°51W **101 C2**
Quinault ➤ *WA*.....47°21N 124°18W **101 C1**
Quinault Indian Reservation
 WA.....47°30N 124°5W **101 C1**
Quinby *SC*.....34°14N 79°44W **90 D6**
Quincy *CA*.....39°56N 120°57W **64 D5**
Quincy *FL*.....30°35N 84°34W **67 A4**
Quincy *IL*.....39°56N 91°23W **71 D2**
Quincy *MA*.....42°15N 71°0W **106 B3**
Quincy *MI*.....41°57N 84°53W **79 H7**
Quincy *OH*.....40°18N 83°58W **92 C3**
Quincy *WA*.....47°14N 119°51W **101 C6**
Quincy B. *MA*.....42°16N 70°59W **106 B4**
Quincy Res. *CO*.. 39°38N 104°46W **66 C6**
Quinebaug *CT*.....42°1N 71°57W **78 B3**
Quinebaug ➤ *CT*.. 41°33N 72°3W **78 C2**
Quinhagak *AK*.....59°45N 161°54W **61 G7**
Quinlan *OK*.....36°27N 99°3W **93 B4**
Quinlan *TX*.....32°55N 96°8W **99 E11**
Quinn ➤ *NV*.....40°53N 119°3W **85 B1**
Quinnesec *MI*.....45°37N 87°59W **103 C5**
Quinter *KS*.....39°4N 100°14W **74 B3**
Quinton *OK*.....35°7N 95°22W **93 C8**
Quinwood *WV*.....38°4N 80°42W **102 C4**
Quitaque *TX*.....34°22N 101°4W **98 C6**
Quitman *AR*.....35°23N 92°13W **63 C3**
Quitman *GA*.....30°47N 83°34W **68 F3**
Quitman *LA*.....32°21N 92°43W **75 B3**
Quitman *MS*.....32°2N 88°44W **81 D5**
Quitman *TX*.....32°48N 95°27W **99 E12**
Quitman County ☆
 GA.....31°50N 85°0W **68 E2**
Quitman County ☆
 MS.....34°12N 90°17W **81 B3**
Quitman Mts. *TX*.. 31°0N 105°16W **98 F2**
Quivira Nat. Wildlife Refuge ○
 KS.....38°11N 98°31W **74 C5**
Qulin *MO*.....36°36N 90°15W **82 E6**
Quonochontaug *RI*.. 41°21N 71°43W **78 C3**

R

R.D. Bailey L. *WV*.. 37°36N 81°49W **102 D3**
Rabbit Cr. ➤ *SD*.. 45°13N 102°10W **91 E3**
Rabbit Ears Pass
 CO.....40°23N 106°37W **66 B3**
Rabun County ☆ *GA* 34°50N 83°30W **68 B3**
Raccoon ➤ *IA*.....41°35N 93°37W **73 D5**
Raccoon Cr. ➤ *OH* 38°54N 82°22W **92 C4**
Raceland *KY*.....38°32N 82°44W **97 B10**
Raceland *LA*.....29°44N 90°36W **75 E5**
Racepond *GA*.....31°1N 82°5W **68 E4**
Rachel *NV*.....37°39N 115°45W **85 E5**
Racine *MN*.....43°46N 92°31W **80 G6**
Racine *OH*.....39°4N 81°55W **92 D5**
Racine ☆ *WI*.....42°44N 87°47W **103 F6**
Racine ☆ *WI*.....42°45N 88°5W **103 F5**
Raco *MI*.....46°23N 84°43W **79 C7**

Radcliff *KY*.....37°51N 85°57W **97 C7**
Rarden *OH*.....38°55N 83°12W **92 E3**
Raritan *NJ*.....40°34N 74°38W **87 B2**
Raritan ➤ *NJ*.....40°29N 74°15W **87 B2**
Raritan Bay *NJ*.. 40°27N 74°15W **87 B2**
Raspberry Pk. *AK*.. 58°10N 152°10W **61 F9**
Rat I. *AK*.....51°48N 178°15E **61 L2**
Rat Islands *AK*.....52°0N 178°0E **61 L2**
Ratcliff *TX*.....31°24N 95°9W **99 F12**
Rathbun *IA*.....40°50N 92°52W **73 E6**
Rathbun L. *IA*.....40°48N 92°53W **73 E5**
Rathdrum *ID*.....47°49N 116°54W **70 B2**
Raton *NM*.....36°54N 104°24W **88 A6**
Raton Pass *U.S.A.*.. 37°0N 104°30W **66 F6**
Rattan *OK*.....34°12N 95°26W **93 D8**
Radcliffe *IA*.....42°20N 93°25W **73 C5**
Rattlesnake ➤
 OR.....42°44N 117°47W **94 E8**
Radcliffe College
 MA.....42°22N 71°7W **106 A2**
Rattlesnake Hills
 WA.....46°31N 120°20W **101 D5**
Radford *VA*.....37°8N 80°34W **102 D4**
Rattlesnake Hills
 WY.....42°45N 107°10W **104 D5**
Radisson *WI*.....45°45N 91°14W **103 C2**
Ravalli *MT*.....47°17N 114°11W **83 C3**
Radium *KS*.....38°12N 98°56W **74 C5**
Ravalli County ☆ *MT* 46°0N 114°20W **83 E3**
Radium Springs *NM* 32°30N 106°55W **88 E4**
Raven ➤ *WA*.....37°5N 81°51W **102 D3**
Radium Springs *NM* 32°30N 106°55W **88 E4**
Ravena *NY*.....42°28N 73°49W **89 C7**
Radnor *OH*.....40°23N 83°9W **92 C3**
Ravendale *CA*.....40°48N 120°22W **64 C6**
Radnor *PA*.....40°3N 75°22W **87 B1**
Ravenel *SC*.....32°46N 80°15W **90 E5**
Raeford *NC*.....34°59N 79°14W **90 C6**
Ravenna *KY*.....37°41N 83°57W **97 C9**
Raft ➤ *ID*.....42°37N 113°15W **70 G5**
Ravenna *MI*.....43°11N 85°56W **79 F5**
Raft River Mts. *UT* 41°55N 113°25W **100 B2**
Ravenna *NE*.....41°1N 98°55W **84 C7**
Ragan *NE*.....40°19N 99°15W **84 D6**
Ravenna *OH*.....41°9N 81°15W **92 B5**
Ragland *AL*.....33°45N 86°9W **60 C4**
Ravenna *TX*.....33°40N 96°15W **99 D7**
Ragley *LA*.....30°30N 93°15W **75 D2**
Ravenswood *WV*.. 38°57N 81°46W **102 C3**
Rago *KS*.....37°36N 98°4W **74 D5**
Ravenwood *MO*.. 40°22N 94°41W **82 A2**
Rahway *NJ*.....40°36N 74°16W **114 C1**
Ravia *SD*.....34°15N 96°45W **93 D7**
Raiford *FL*.....30°4N 82°14W **67 A6**
Rawlins *WY*.....41°47N 107°14W **104 E5**
Railroad Valley *NV* 38°25N 115°40W **85 D5**
Rawlins County ☆
 KS.....39°45N 101°0W **74 B2**
Rainbow Bridge Nat. Monument ○
 U.S.A......37°5N 110°58W **100 F5**
Rawsonville *VT*.. 43°10N 72°50W **86 C2**
Rainbow City *AL*.. 33°57N 86°5W **60 C4**
Ray *MN*.....48°25N 93°13W **80 B5**
Rainbow Plateau *AZ* 36°55N 111°0W **62 A5**
Ray *ND*.....48°21N 103°10W **91 B2**
Rainelle *WV*.....37°58N 80°47W **102 D4**
Ray County ☆ *GA*.. 31°5N 83°11W **68 A3**
Raines *TN*.....35°2N 90°3W **112 B1**
Rayle *GA*.....39°40N 94°0W **82 B3**
Rainier, Mt. *WA*.. 46°52N 121°46W **101 D4**
Rays Mts. *AK*.....66°0N 152°0W **61 D10**
Rainier *OR*.....46°5N 123°0W **94 A2**
Ray Roberts L. *TX* 33°20N 97°2W **99 D10**
Rains County ☆ *TX* 32°52N 95°46W **99 E12**
Rayland *OH*.....40°10N 80°48W **92 C6**
Rainsburg *PA*.....39°54N 78°30W **95 E4**
Raymond *CA*.....37°13N 119°54W **64 F7**
Rainsville *AL*.....34°30N 85°50W **60 B5**
Raymond *GA*.....33°20N 84°43W **68 C2**
Rainy ➤ *MN*.....48°50N 94°42W **80 B4**
Raymond *IL*.....39°19N 89°34W **71 D4**
Rainy L. *MN*.....48°42N 93°10W **80 B4**
Raymond *KS*.....38°17N 98°25W **74 C5**
Raisin ➤ *MI*.....41°54N 83°20W **79 H8**
Raymond *MN*.....45°1N 95°14W **80 E3**
Rake *IA*.....43°35N 93°50W **73 B5**
Raymond *MS*.....32°16N 90°25W **81 D3**
Raleigh *FL*.....29°25N 82°32W **67 B6**
Raymond *NH*.....43°2N 71°11W **86 C3**
Raleigh *MS*.....32°2N 89°31W **81 D4**
Raymond *SD*.....44°55N 97°56W **91 E7**
Raleigh *NC*.....35°47N 78°39W **90 C7**
Raymond *WA*.....46°41N 123°44W **101 D2**
Raleigh *TN*.....35°12N 89°54W **112 A2**
Raymondville *MO*.. 37°20N 91°50W **82 D5**
Raleigh County ☆
 WV.....37°45N 81°10W **102 D3**
Raymondville *TX*.. 26°29N 97°47W **98 L10**
Raleigh-Durham Int. ✈ (RDU)
 NC.....35°52N 78°47W **90 C7**
Raymore *MO*.....38°48N 94°27W **82 C2**
Raleigh Hills *OR*.. 45°28N 122°45W **116 A1**
Raynham Center *MA*. 41°55N 71°3W **78 C3**
Ralls *TX*.....33°41N 101°24W **98 D6**
Raystown Branch ➤
 PA.....40°27N 77°59W **95 D5**
Ralls County ☆ *MO* 39°30N 91°30W **82 B5**
Raystown L. *PA*.. 40°25N 78°5W **95 D4**
Ralston *NE*.....41°7N 96°3W **84 C9**
Raytown *MO*.....39°1N 94°28W **82 B2**
Ralston *OK*.....36°30N 96°44W **93 B7**
Rayville *LA*.....32°29N 91°46W **75 B4**
Rama *NC*.....35°10N 80°46W **107 A2**
Rayville *MO*.....39°21N 94°4W **82 B2**
Ramah *CO*.....39°7N 104°10W **66 C6**
Reach II Recreation Area
 AZ.....33°37N 111°53W **116 A3**
Ramah *NM*.....35°8N 108°29W **88 C2**
Reader *AR*.....33°46N 93°6W **63 E2**
Ramanda *WA*.. 34°10N 117°9W **111 B4**
Reading *KS*.....38°31N 95°58W **74 C8**
Ramer *AL*.....32°3N 86°13W **60 D4**
Reading *MA*.....42°32N 71°6W **78 B3**
Ramer *TN*.....35°4N 88°37W **96 E4**
Reading *MI*.....41°50N 84°45W **79 H7**
Ramon *NM*.....34°14N 104°58W **88 C6**
Reading *OH*.....39°13N 84°26W **107 A2**
Ramona *CA*.....33°2N 116°52W **65 K10**
Reading *PA*.....40°20N 75°56W **95 D7**
Ramona *SD*.....36°36N 97°49W **93 B6**
Readland *AR*.....33°4N 91°13W **63 E4**
Ramona *OK*.....36°32N 95°55W **93 B8**
Readlyn *IA*.....42°42N 92°14W **73 C6**
Ramona *SD*.....44°7N 97°13W **91 F8**
Readsboro *VT*.....42°47N 72°57W **86 D2**
Ramona *TX*.....28°48N 97°58W **99 J10**
Readstown *WI*.....43°27N 90°45W **103 E3**
Rampart *AK*.....65°30N 150°10W **61 D9**
Reagan *TN*.....35°31N 88°21W **96 E4**
Ramsay *MT*.....46°1N 112°42W **83 D5**
Reagan County ☆
 TX.....31°25N 101°34W **98 F5**
Ramseur *NC*.....35°44N 79°39W **90 C6**
Real City *CA*.....29°55N 99°55W **98 H8**
Ramsey *IL*.....39°8N 89°7W **71 D4**
Realitos *TX*.....27°27N 98°32W **98 K9**
Ramsey *MN*.....45°15N 93°27W **80 E5**
Reams, L. *FL*.....28°29N 81°34W **115 B1**
Ramsey *NJ*.....41°4N 74°9W **87 A2**
Reardan *WA*.....47°40N 117°53W **101 C8**
Ramsey County ☆
 MN.....45°0N 93°1W **73 D5**
Reasnor *IA*.....41°35N 93°1W **73 D5**
Ramsey County ☆
 ND.....48°10N 98°50W **91 B7**
Rebecca *GA*.....31°48N 83°29W **68 E3**
Ranchester *WY*.. 44°54N 107°10W **104 B5**
Rector *AR*.....36°16N 90°17W **63 B6**
Rancho Cordova
 CA.....34°10N 117°30W **111 A3**
Red ➤ *KY*.....37°51N 84°5W **97 C8**
Rancho Cucamonga
 CA.....34°10N 117°30W **111 B3**
Red ➤ *TN*.....36°32N 87°22W **96 D5**
Rancho Palos Verdes
 CA.....33°44N 118°23W **111 D2**
Red ➤ *TX*.....31°1N 91°45W **75 C4**
Ranchos de Taos
 NM.....36°22N 105°37W **88 A5**
Red Bird *OK*.....35°54N 95°36W **93 C8**
Rand *WV*.....38°17N 81°34W **102 C3**
Red Bluff *CA*.....40°11N 122°15W **64 C4**
Randalia *IA*.....42°52N 91°53W **73 C7**
Red Bluff Res. *NM* 31°54N 103°55W **88 F7**
Randall *IA*.....42°14N 93°33W **73 C5**
Red Boiling Springs
 TN.....36°32N 85°51W **97 D7**
Randall *KS*.....39°38N 98°3W **74 B5**
Red Bud *IL*.....38°13N 89°59W **71 E4**
Randall *MN*.....46°5N 94°30W **80 E4**
Red Cedar ➤ *WI*.. 44°42N 91°53W **103 D2**
Randall County ☆
 TX.....34°59N 101°55W **98 C6**
Red Cliff *CO*.....39°31N 106°22W **66 C4**
Randallstown *MD* 39°22N 76°48W **77 A4**
Red Cliff Ind. Reservation
 WI.....46°53N 90°47W **103 B3**
Randle *WA*.....46°32N 121°57W **101 D4**
Red Cloud *NE*.....40°5N 98°32W **84 D7**
Randleman *NC*.. 35°49N 79°48W **90 C6**
Red Cr. ➤ *MS*.....30°41N 88°40W **81 F5**
Randlett *UT*.....40°14N 109°48W **100 C6**
Red Devil *AK*.....61°46N 157°19W **61 F8**
Randolph *KS*.....39°26N 96°46W **74 B7**
Red Feather Lakes
 CO.....40°48N 105°35W **66 B5**
Randolph *ME*.....44°14N 69°46W **76 D3**
Red Head *FL*.....30°29N 85°51W **67 A3**
Randolph *MS*.....34°11N 89°10W **81 B4**
Red Hills *NY*.....41°55N 73°33W **89 D7**
Randolph *NY*.....42°10N 78°59W **89 C2**
Red Hook *NY*.....42°0N 73°53W **89 D7**
Randolph *NE*.....42°23N 97°22W **84 B8**
Red L. *AZ*.....35°40N 114°4W **62 B1**
Randolph *UT*.....41°40N 111°11W **100 B4**
Red L. *SD*.....43°44N 99°13W **91 G6**
Randolph *VT*.....43°55N 72°40W **86 C2**
Red Lake *MN*.....47°53N 95°1W **80 C3**
Randolph Air Force Base
 TX.....29°32N 98°16W **117 B4**
Red Lake County ☆
 MN.....47°50N 96°0W **80 C3**
Randolph Center *VT* 43°57N 72°36W **86 C2**
Red Lake Falls *MN* 47°53N 96°16W **80 C3**
Randolph County ☆
 AL.....33°20N 85°25W **60 C5**
Red Lake Indian Reservation
 MN.....48°30N 94°30W **80 B4**
Randolph County ☆
 AR.....36°20N 91°0W **63 B5**
Red Level *AL*.....31°24N 86°36W **60 E4**
Randolph County ☆
 GA.....31°45N 84°45W **68 E2**
Red Lion *PA*.....39°54N 76°36W **77 A4**
Randolph County ☆
 IL.....38°0N 89°50W **71 E4**
Red Lodge *MT*.....45°11N 109°15W **83 E8**
Randolph County ☆
 IN.....40°10N 85°0W **72 C6**
Red Mountain *CA*.. 35°37N 117°38W **65 H9**
Randolph County ☆
 MO.....39°25N 92°30W **82 B4**
Red Oak *GA*.....33°40N 84°30W **68 C2**
Randolph County ☆
 NC.....35°40N 79°50W **90 C6**
Red Oak *IA*.....41°1N 95°14W **73 D3**
Randolph County ☆
 WV.....38°40N 80°0W **102 C5**
Red Oak *NC*.....36°2N 77°54W **90 B8**
Random Lake *WI*.. 43°33N 87°58W **103 E6**
Red Oak *OK*.....34°57N 95°5W **93 D8**
Randville *MI*.....46°0N 88°3W **79 C2**
Red River *NM*.....36°42N 105°23W **88 A5**
Rangeley *ME*.....44°58N 70°39W **86 B4**
Red River ➤
 TX.....33°37N 95°3W **99 D12**
Rangeley L. *ME*.. 44°55N 70°43W **76 D3**
Red River Hot Springs
 ID.....45°47N 115°12W **70 D3**
Rangely *CO*.....40°5N 108°48W **66 B2**
Red River of the North ➤
 N. Amer......49°0N 97°15W **91 A8**
Ranger *GA*.....34°30N 84°43W **68 B2**
Red River Parish ☆
 LA.....32°1N 93°21W **75 B2**
Ranier *MN*.....48°36N 93°20W **80 B5**
Red River Valley *MN* 49°0N 97°0W **80 C2**
Rankin *IL*.....40°28N 87°54W **71 C6**
Red Rock *AZ*.....32°34N 111°19W **62 E4**
Rankin *TX*.....31°13N 101°56W **98 F6**
Red Rock *OK*.....36°28N 97°11W **93 B6**
Rankin County ☆ *MS* 32°15N 90°0W **81 D4**
Red Rock Canyon Nat.
 Conservation Area ○
 NV.....36°6N 115°28W **85 E5**
Ransom *IL*.....41°9N 88°39W **71 C5**
Red Rock Cr. ➤ *MT* 44°35N 111°50W **83 E7**
Ransom *KS*.....38°38N 99°56W **74 C4**
Red Rock Cr. ➤ *OK* 36°30N 96°59W **93 B7**
Ransom County ☆
 ND.....46°30N 97°40W **91 D7**
Red Rock Lakes Nat. Wildlife
 Refuge ○ *MT*.. 44°38N 111°45W **83 F6**
Ranson *WV*.....39°18N 77°52W **77 A3**
Rantoul *KS*.....38°33N 95°7W **74 C8**
Rantoul *IL*.....40°19N 88°9W **71 C5**
Rapelje *MT*.....45°59N 109°15W **83 D8**
Rapid ➤ *MN*.....48°42N 94°26W **80 B4**
Rapid City *SD*.....44°5N 103°14W **91 F2**
Rapid River *MI*.. 45°55N 86°58W **79 D4**
Rapides Parish ☆ *LA* 31°15N 92°30W **75 C3**
Rappahannock ➤
 VA.....37°34N 76°18W **77 C4**
Rappahannock County ☆
 VA.....38°40N 78°10W **102 C6**

Red Springs *NC* . . . . . 34°49N 79°11W **90 D6**
Red Springs *TX* . . . . . 33°37N 99°25W **99 D8**
Red Willow County ☆
    NE. . . . . . 40°15N 100°30W **84 D5**
Red Willow Cr. →
    NE. . . . . . 40°13N 100°29W **84 D5**
Red Wing *MN* . . . . . 44°34N 92°31W **80 F6**
Redbay *FL.* . . . . . 30°35N 85°57W **67 A3**
Redbird *WY* . 43°15N 104°17W **104 C8**
Reddell *LA* . . . . . 30°40N 92°25W **75 D3**
Reddick *FL* . . . . . 29°22N 82°12W **67 B6**
Redding *CA* . . . . . 41°6N 88°15W **71 B5**
Redding *CA* . . 40°35N 122°24W **64 C4**
Redding *CT* . . . . . 41°18N 73°23W **78 C1**
Redding *IA* . . . . . 40°46N 117°11W **73 E4**
Redding Ridge *CT* . 41°19N 73°21W **78 C1**
Redfield *AR* . . . . . 34°27N 92°11W **63 D3**
Redfield *IA* . . . . . 41°35N 94°12W **73 D4**
Redfield *KS.* . . . . 37°50N 94°53W **74 D9**
Redfield *SD.* . . . . 44°53N 98°31W **91 F7**
Redfort *IL* . . . . . 41°6N 88°15W **71 B5**
Rediq *SD* . . . . . 45°16N 103°33W **91 E2**
Redington Beach
    FL. . . . 27°48N 82°48W **119 C2**
Redington Shores
    FL. . . . 27°49N 82°49W **119 C2**
Redkey *IN.* . . . . 40°21N 85°9W **72 C5**
Redlands *CA* . . 34°4N 117°11W **65 J9**
Redman Point Bar
    TN. . . . 35°13N 90°55W **112 A1**
Redmesa *CO.* . . 37°6N 108°11W **66 E2**
Redmon *IL* . . . 39°39N 87°52W **71 D6**
Redmond *OR* . . 44°17N 121°11W **94 C4**
Redmond *UT.* . . 39°0N 111°52W **100 D4**
Redmond *WA* . . 47°40N 122°7W **118 B5**
Redondo Beach
    CA. . . . 33°50N 118°23W **111 D2**
Redoubt Volcano
    AK. . . . 60°29N 152°45W **61 F9**
Redrock *NM* . . 32°41N 108°44W **88 E2**
Redstone *CO.* . . 39°11N 107°14W **66 C3**
Redstone Arsenal
    AL. . . . 34°35N 86°41W **60 B4**
Redstone Cr. → *SD.* . . 44°4N 98°5W **91 F7**
Redwater → *MT.* . 48°3N 105°13W **83 B12**
Redwood *MS.* . . 32°29N 90°48W **81 D3**
Redwood *NY.* . . 44°34N 95°5W **80 F3**
Redwood City *CA* . 37°30N 122°15W **64 F4**
Redwood County ☆
    MN. . . . 44°20N 95°15W **80 F3**
Redwood Cr. → *CA* . 41°18N 124°5W **64 B2**
Redwood Falls *MN* . 44°32N 95°7W **80 F3**
Redwood Nat. Park △
    CA. . . . 41°40N 124°5W **64 B2**
Redwood Regional Park
    CA. . . . 37°48N 122°9W **118 B3**
Ree Heights *SD* . . 44°31N 99°12W **91 F6**
Reece *KS.* . . . 37°48N 96°27W **74 D7**
Reed *KY.* . . . 37°51N 87°21W **96 C5**
Reed *OK.* . . . 34°54N 99°42W **93 D4**
Reeder *ND* . . . 46°7N 102°57W **91 D3**
Reedley *CA* . . 36°36N 119°27W **65 G7**
Reeds *MO* . . . 37°7N 94°10W **82 C2**
Reeds Pk. *NM.* . . 33°9N 107°51W **88 D4**
Reeds Spring *MO.* . 36°45N 93°23W **82 E3**
Reedsburg *WI* . . 43°32N 90°0W **103 E3**
Reedsport *OR* . . 43°42N 124°6W **94 D1**
Reedsville *WV.* . . 39°31N 79°48W **102 B5**
Reedville *VA.* . . 37°51N 76°17W **77 C4**
Reedy *WV* . . . 38°54N 81°26W **102 C3**
Reedy Creek Park
    NC. . . . 35°16N 80°42W **107 A2**
Reelfoot L. *TN* . . 36°25N 89°22W **96 D3**
Reese *MI.* . . . 43°27N 83°42W **79 F8**
Reese → *NV.* . . 40°48N 117°4W **85 C6**
Reeves *LA* . . . 30°31N 93°3W **75 D2**
Reeves County ☆
    TX. . . . 31°13N 103°45W **98 F4**
Reeves Hill *MA* . 42°20N 71°20W **106 A1**
Reform *AL.* . . . 33°23N 88°1W **60 C2**
Refugio *TX* . . . 28°18N 97°17W **99 J10**
Refugio County ☆
    TX. . . . 28°14N 97°20W **99 J10**
Regan *ND* . . . 47°10N 100°32W **91 C5**
Regan *ND.* . . . 46°25N 102°33W **91 D3**
Regina *NM* . . . 36°11N 106°57W **88 A4**
Register *GA.* . . 32°22N 81°53W **68 D5**
Rego Park *NY.* . . 40°43N 73°51W **114 B3**
Rehoboth *MA.* . . 41°50N 71°15W **78 C3**
Rehoboth *NM.* . . 35°32N 108°39W **88 B2**
Rehoboth Beach *DE.* . 38°40N 75°6W **77 B5**
Rehoboth Beach *DE* . 38°43N 75°15W **77 B5**
Reidland *KY.* . . 37°1N 88°32W **96 C4**
Reidsville *GA.* . . 32°6N 82°7W **68 D4**
Reidsville *NC.* . . 36°21N 79°40W **90 B6**
Reinbeck *IA* . . . 42°19N 92°36W **73 C6**
Reisterstown *MD.* . . 39°28N 76°50W **77 A4**
Reliance *DE.* . . . 38°38N 75°43W **77 B5**
Reliance *SD.* . . . 43°53N 99°36W **91 G6**
Reliance *WY.* . . . 41°40N 109°12W **104 E3**
Rembrandt *IA.* . . . 42°50N 95°10W **73 C3**
Remer *MN* . . . 47°4N 93°55W **80 E5**
Remington *IN.* . . 40°46N 87°9W **72 C3**
Remington *VA.* . . 38°32N 77°49W **102 C7**
Remmel Mt. *WA.* . 48°54N 120°9W **101 B5**
Remsen *IA.* . . . 42°49N 95°58W **73 C3**
Remsen *NY* . . . 43°20N 75°11W **89 B5**
Rend Lake *IL.* . . 38°2N 88°58W **71 E5**
Renfroe *GA.* . . . 32°14N 84°43W **68 D2**
Renfrow *OK.* . . . 36°56N 97°39W **93 B6**
Renick *WV.* . . . 38°1N 80°22W **102 C4**
Reno *NV.* . . . . 39°31N 119°48W **85 C1**
Reno ✕ (RNO) *NV* . 39°30N 119°46W **85 C1**
Reno County ☆ *KS.* . . 38°0N 98°0W **74 C5**
Renovo *PA* . . . 41°20N 77°45W **95 C5**
Rensselaer *IN.* . . 40°57N 87°9W **72 C3**
Rensselaer *NY.* . . 42°38N 73°45W **89 C7**
Rensselaer County ☆
    NY. . . . 42°40N 73°30W **89 C7**
Rentiesville *OK* . . 35°35N 95°30W **93 C8**
Renton *WA* . . . 47°28N 122°12W **118 D4**
Rentz *GA.* . . . 32°25N 82°59W **68 D4**
Renville *MN.* . . . 44°48N 95°13W **80 F3**
Renville County ☆
    MN. . . . 44°45N 95°0W **80 F4**
Renville County ☆
    ND. . . . 48°37N 101°35W **91 B4**
Renwick *IA.* . . . 42°50N 93°59W **73 C5**
Repton *AL.* . . . 31°25N 87°14W **60 D4**
Republic *KS.* . . . 39°55N 97°49W **74 B6**
Republic *MI.* . . . 46°25N 87°59W **79 C3**
Republic *OH.* . . . 41°8N 83°1W **92 B3**
Republic *WA.* . . . 48°39N 118°44W **101 B7**
Republic County ☆
    KS. . . . 39°50N 97°40W **74 B6**
Republican → *KS.* . 39°4N 96°48W **74 B7**
Republican City *NE.* . 40°6N 99°13W **84 D6**
Reseda *CA.* . . . 34°12N 118°32W **111 A1**
Reserve *KS.* . . . 39°59N 95°34W **74 B8**
Reserve *LA.* . . . 30°3N 90°33W **75 D5**
Reserve *NM.* . . . 33°43N 108°45W **88 D2**
Reston *VA.* . . . 38°57N 77°20W **102 C7**
Retsil *WA.* . . . 47°32N 122°36W **118 C2**
Reva *SD.* . . . . 45°32N 103°5W **91 E2**
Revere *MA.* . . . 42°25N 71°0W **106 A3**
Revere *MO.* . . . 40°35N 91°41W **82 A5**
Revillo *SD.* . . . 45°1N 96°34W **91 E9**
Rewey *WI.* . . . 42°51N 90°24W **103 E3**
Rexburg *ID* . . . 43°49N 111°47W **70 F7**
Rexford *KS.* . . . 39°28N 100°45W **74 B3**

Rexford *MT.* . . . 48°53N 115°12W **83 B2**
Rexton *MI.* . . . 46°10N 85°14W **79 C6**
Reydon *OK.* . . . 35°39N 99°55W **93 C4**
Reyes Pk. *CA.* . . 38°0N 123°0W **64 D3**
Reyno *AR* . . . . 36°22N 90°45W **63 B5**
Reynolds *GA.* . . . 32°33N 84°6W **68 D2**
Reynolds *IL.* . . . 41°20N 90°40W **71 B3**
Reynolds *IN* . . . 40°45N 86°52W **72 C4**
Reynolds *ND.* . . . 47°40N 97°7W **91 C8**
Reynolds *NE.* . . . 40°6N 97°20W **84 D8**
Reynolds County ☆
    NY. . . . 40°35N 73°40W **114 C4**
Reynolds County *MO* . 37°20N 91°0W **82 D6**
Reynoldsville *OH.* . 39°57N 82°48W **92 D4**
Reynoldsville *PA.* . 41°6N 78°53W **95 C4**
Rhame *ND.* . . . 46°14N 103°39W **91 D2**
Rhea County ☆ *TN.* . 35°30N 85°0W **97 E8**
Rheem Valley *CA.* . 37°51N 122°7W **118 A4**
Rhine *GA* . . . . 31°59N 83°12W **68 E3**
Rhinebeck *NY.* . . 41°56N 73°55W **89 D7**
Rhinelander *WI.* . . 45°38N 89°25W **103 C4**
Rhode Island *RI.* . 41°30N 71°15W **78 C3**
Rhode Island □
    U.S.A. . . . 41°40N 71°30W **78 C3**
Rhode Island Sd. *RI.* . 41°20N 71°10W **78 C3**
Rhodes Pk. *ID.* . . 46°40N 114°47W **70 C4**
Rhodhiss *N.C.* . . 35°47N 81°26W **90 C4**
Rhododendron *OR.* . 45°20N 121°55W **94 B4**
Rhome *TX.* . . . 33°3N 97°28W **99 D10**
Rib Lake *WI* . . . 45°19N 90°12W **103 C3**
Ribera *NM.* . . . 35°23N 105°27W **88 B5**
Ricardo *TX.* . . . 27°25N 97°51W **98 K10**
Rice *CA* . . . . 34°5N 114°51W **65 J12**
Rice *MN.* . . . . 45°45N 94°13W **80 E4**
Rice *TX.* . . . . 32°14N 96°30W **99 E11**
Rice *WA.* . . . . 47°17N 78°18W **102 D6**
Rice County ☆ *KS.* . 38°25N 98°10W **74 C5**
Rice County ☆ *MN.* . 44°20N 93°15W **80 F5**
Rice Lake *WI* . . . 45°30N 91°44W **103 C2**
Ricebro *GA.* . . . 31°44N 81°26W **68 E5**
Riceville *IA.* . . . 43°22N 92°33W **73 B6**
Riceville *TN.* . . . 35°23N 84°42W **97 E8**
Rich *MS.* . . . . 34°7N 90°27W **81 B3**
Rich County ☆ *UT.* . 41°30N 111°10W **100 B4**
Rich Fountain *MO.* . 38°24N 91°53W **82 C5**
Rich Hill *MO.* . . 38°6N 94°22W **82 C2**
Rich Square *NC.* . . 36°16N 77°17W **90 B8**
Richard B. Russell L.
    GA. . . . 34°5N 82°38W **68 B4**
Richards *MO.* . . . 37°54N 94°33W **82 C2**
Richards *TX.* . . . 30°32N 95°51W **99 G12**
Richardson *TX.* . . 32°56N 96°43W **109 A5**
Richardson County ☆
    NE. . . . 40°15N 95°45W **84 D10**
Richardson Lakes
    ME. . . . 44°46N 70°58W **86 B4**
Richardton *ND.* . . 46°53N 102°19W **91 D3**
Richboro *PA* . . . 40°13N 75°1W **87 B1**
Richey *MT.* . . . 47°39N 105°4W **83 C11**
Richfield *ID.* . . . 43°3N 114°9W **70 F4**
Richfield *KS.* . . . 37°16N 101°47W **74 D2**
Richfield *MN.* . . . 44°53N 93°16W **113 B2**
Richfield *PA.* . . . 40°41N 77°7W **95 D5**
Richfield *UT.* . . . 38°46N 112°5W **100 E3**
Richfield Springs *NY* . 42°51N 74°59W **89 C6**
Richford *NY.* . . . 42°21N 76°11W **89 C5**
Richford *VT.* . . . 45°0N 72°40W **86 B2**
Richgrove *CA.* . . 35°48N 119°7W **65 H7**
Richland *GA.* . . . 32°5N 84°40W **68 D2**
Richland *MI.* . . . 42°22N 85°27W **79 G6**
Richland *MS.* . . . 32°14N 90°10W **81 D3**
Richland *MO.* . . . 37°51N 92°26W **82 D4**
Richland *OR.* . . . 44°46N 117°10W **94 C8**
Richland *TX.* . . . 31°57N 96°26W **99 F11**
Richland *WA.* . . . 46°17N 119°18W **101 D6**
Richland Center *WI* . 43°21N 90°23W **103 E3**
Richland Chambers Res.
    TX. . . . 32°0N 96°12W **99 F11**
Richland County ☆ *IL* . 38°45N 88°5W **71 E5**
Richland County ☆
    MT. . . . 47°48N 104°40W **83 C13**
Richland County ☆
    ND. . . . 46°15N 97°0W **91 D9**
Richland County ☆
    OH. . . . 40°45N 82°31W **92 C4**
Richland County ☆
    SC. . . . 34°10N 81°0W **90 D5**
Richland County ☆
    WI. . . . 43°20N 90°30W **103 E3**
Richland Cr. → *TN.* . 35°2N 86°50W **96 D6**
Richland Hills *TX.* . 32°48N 97°13W **109 B2**
Richland Parish ☆
    LA . . . . 32°25N 91°52W **75 B4**
Richland Springs *TX* . 31°16N 98°57W **99 F9**
Richlands *NC* . . . 34°54N 77°34W **90 D8**
Richlands *VA.* . . . 37°6N 81°48W **102 D3**
Richmond *CA.* . . . 37°46N 122°27W **118 A4**
Richmond *IL.* . . . 39°50N 84°53W **72 D6**
Richmond *KS.* . . . 38°24N 95°15W **74 C8**
Richmond *KY.* . . . 37°45N 84°18W **97 C8**
Richmond *ME.* . . . 44°5N 69°48W **76 D4**
Richmond *MO.* . . . 39°17N 93°58W **82 B3**
Richmond *TX.* . . . 29°35N 95°46W **99 H12**
Richmond *UT.* . . . 41°56N 111°48W **100 B4**
Richmond *VA.* . . . 37°33N 77°27W **102 D7**
Richmond ✕ (RIC)
    VA. . . . 37°30N 77°19W **102 D7**
Richmond County ☆
    GA. . . . 33°15N 82°5W **68 C4**
Richmond County ☆
    NC. . . . 35°0N 79°45W **90 D6**
Richmond County ☆
    NY. . . . 40°40N 74°15W **89 E6**
Richmond County ☆
    VA. . . . 37°58N 76°46W **102 D8**
Richmond Heights
    FL. . . . 25°38N 80°23W **67 F8**
Richmond Heights
    MO. . . . 38°38N 90°19W **117 B2**
Richmond Hill *GA.* . 31°56N 81°18W **68 E5**
Richmond Hill *NY.* . 40°41N 73°49W **114 B3**
Richmond Valley
    NY. . . . 40°31N 74°13W **114 C1**
Richmondville *NY.* . 42°38N 74°34W **89 C6**
Richton *MS.* . . . 31°16N 88°56W **81 E5**
Richville *MN.* . . . 46°31N 95°38W **80 D3**
Richville *NY.* . . . 44°25N 75°22W **89 A5**
Richwood *LA.* . . . 32°27N 92°5W **75 B3**
Richwood *OH.* . . . 40°26N 83°18W **92 C3**
Richwood *WV.* . . . 38°14N 80°32W **102 C4**
Richwoods *MO.* . . 38°10N 90°50W **82 C6**
Rickets Glen State Park
    PA. . . . 41°19N 76°16W **95 C6**
Rico *CO.* . . . . 37°41N 108°2W **66 E2**
Riddle *ID.* . . . . 42°11N 116°7W **70 G2**
Riddle *OR.* . . . . 42°57N 123°22W **94 D2**
Riderwood *MD.* . . 39°24N 76°38W **107 A2**
Ridge *MD.* . . . . 38°7N 76°24W **77 B4**
Ridge Farm *IL.* . . 39°54N 87°39W **71 D6**
Ridge Spring *SC.* . . 33°51N 81°40W **90 D5**
Ridgecrest *CA.* . . 35°38N 117°40W **65 H9**
Ridgefield *CT.* . . 41°17N 73°30W **78 C1**
Ridgefield *NJ.* . . . 40°49N 74°0W **114 B2**
Ridgefield *WA.* . . 45°49N 122°45W **101 E3**
Ridgefield Park *NJ.* . 40°52N 74°1W **114 A2**
Ridgeland *MS.* . . . 32°26N 90°8W **81 D3**

Ridgeland *SC* . . . 32°29N 80°59W **90 F5**
Ridgeland *WI* . . . 45°12N 91°54W **103 C2**
Ridgely *TN* . . . . 36°16N 89°29W **96 D3**
Ridgeville *IN* . . . 40°18N 85°2W **72 C5**
Ridgeville *SC.* . . . 33°6N 80°19W **90 E5**
Ridgeway *IA* . . . 43°18N 91°59W **73 B7**
Ridgeway *MO* . . . 40°23N 93°57W **82 A3**
Ridgeway *OH* . . . 40°31N 83°35W **92 C3**
Ridgeway *SC.* . . . 34°18N 80°58W **90 D5**
Ridgeway *VA.* . . . 36°35N 79°52W **102 E5**
Ridgeway *WI.* . . . 43°1N 90°1W **103 E3**
Ridgewood *NJ.* . . 40°59N 74°7W **87 B2**
Ridgwood *NJ.* . . . 40°42N 73°53W **114 B3**
Ridgway *CO.* . . . 38°9N 107°46W **66 D3**
Ridgway *IL.* . . . . 37°48N 88°16W **71 F5**
Ridgway *PA.* . . . 41°25N 78°44W **95 C4**
Rienzi *MS.* . . . . 34°46N 88°32W **81 B5**
Rieth *OR.* . . . . 45°40N 118°54W **94 B7**
Riffe, L. *WA.* . . . 46°32N 122°26W **101 D3**
Rifle *CO.* . . . . 39°32N 107°47W **66 C3**
Rifle → *MI.* . . . . 43°58N 83°49W **79 E8**
Rigby *ID* . . . . 43°40N 111°55W **70 F7**
Riggins *ID.* . . . . 45°25N 116°19W **70 D2**
Rikers I. *NY.* . . . 40°47N 73°53W **114 B3**
Riley *IN.* . . . . . 39°23N 87°18W **72 D3**
Riley *KS.* . . . . . 39°18N 96°50W **74 B7**
Riley *OR.* . . . . . 43°32N 119°28W **94 D6**
Riley County ☆ *KS.* . 39°20N 96°40W **74 B7**
Rileyville *VA.* . . . 38°46N 78°23W **77 B2**
Rilito *AZ.* . . . . 32°25N 111°9W **62 E4**
Rimersburg *PA.* . . 41°3N 79°30W **95 C3**
Rimrock *WA.* . . . 46°40N 121°7W **101 D4**
Rinard *IA.* . . . . 42°20N 94°29W **73 C4**
Rincon
    Puerto Rico . . 18°20N 67°15W **105 G15**
Rincon *GA.* . . . . 32°18N 81°14W **68 D5**
Rindge *NH.* . . . . 42°45N 72°1W **86 D2**
Rineyville *KY.* . . . 37°45N 85°58W **97 C7**
Ringgold *GA.* . . . 34°55N 85°7W **68 B1**
Ringgold *LA.* . . . 32°20N 93°17W **75 B2**
Ringgold *NE.* . . . 41°59N 100°46W **84 C4**
Ringgold County ☆
    IA. . . . 40°45N 94°15W **73 E4**
Ringling *MT* . . . 46°16N 110°49W **83 D7**
Ringling *OK.* . . . 34°11N 97°36W **93 D6**
Ringoes *NJ.* . . . . 40°26N 74°52W **87 B2**
Ringsted *IA.* . . . . 43°18N 94°31W **73 B4**
Ringwood *NJ.* . . . 41°7N 74°15W **87 A2**
Ringwood *OK.* . . . 36°23N 98°15W **93 B5**
Rio *IL.* . . . . . . 41°7N 90°24W **71 B3**
Rio *WI.* . . . . . 43°27N 89°14W **103 E4**
Rio Arriba County ☆
    NM. . . . 36°30N 106°45W **88 A4**
Rio Blanco *CO.* . . 39°44N 107°57W **66 C3**
Rio Blanco County ☆
    CO. . . . 40°0N 108°15W **66 C2**
Rio Communities
    NM. . . . 34°40N 106°43W **88 C4**
Rio Dell *CA* . . . . 40°30N 124°6W **64 C2**
Rio Grande
    N. Amer. . . . 25°58N 97°9W **98 M10**
Rio Grande *NJ* . . . 39°1N 74°53W **87 C2**
Rio Grande *OH* . . . 38°56N 82°21W **92 E4**
Rio Grande →
    Puerto Rico . . 18°23N 65°50W **105 G17**
Rio Grande City *TX.* . 26°23N 98°49W **98 L9**
Rio Grande County ☆
    CO. . . . 37°40N 106°20W **66 E4**
Rio Grande Nat. Forest
    CO. . . . 37°30N 106°30W **66 E4**
Rio Hondo *TX.* . . 26°14N 97°35W **98 L10**
Rio Rancho *NM.* . . 35°14N 106°41W **88 B4**
Rio Vista *CA.* . . . 38°10N 121°42W **64 E5**
Ripley *CA.* . . . . 33°32N 114°39W **65 K12**
Ripley *IL.* . . . . 40°1N 90°38W **71 C3**
Ripley *MS.* . . . . 34°44N 88°57W **81 B5**
Ripley *NY.* . . . . 42°16N 79°43W **95 C1**
Ripley *OH.* . . . . 38°45N 83°51W **92 E3**
Ripley *OK.* . . . . 36°1N 96°54W **93 B7**
Ripley *TN.* . . . . 35°45N 89°32W **96 D3**
Ripley *WV.* . . . . 38°49N 81°43W **102 C3**
Ripley County ☆ *IN.* . 39°5N 85°15W **72 D5**
Ripley County ☆ *MO* . 36°40N 90°50W **82 E6**
Ripogenus Dam *ME.* . 45°53N 69°11W **76 C4**
Ripon *CA.* . . . . 37°44N 121°7W **64 F4**
Ripon *WI.* . . . . 43°51N 88°50W **103 E5**
Rippey *IA.* . . . . 41°56N 94°12W **73 D4**
Rippon *WV.* . . . . 39°13N 77°54W **77 A3**
Ririe *ID.* . . . . . 43°38N 111°47W **70 F7**
Ririe Res. *ID.* . . . 43°30N 111°43W **70 F7**
Risco *MO.* . . . . 36°33N 89°49W **82 E7**
Rising City *NE* . . . 41°12N 97°18W **84 C8**
Rising Fawn *GA.* . . 34°46N 85°32W **68 B1**
Rising Star *TX.* . . 32°6N 98°58W **99 E9**
Rising Sun *IN.* . . 38°57N 84°51W **72 E6**
Rising Sun *MD.* . . 39°42N 76°4W **77 A4**
Rison *AR.* . . . . 33°58N 92°11W **63 E3**
Rita Blanca Cr. →
    TX. . . . 35°40N 102°29W **98 B5**
Rita Blanca Nat. Grassland
    TX. . . . 36°20N 102°30W **98 A5**
Ritchie *MD.* . . . . 38°52N 76°51W **119 B4**
Ritchie County ☆
    WV. . . . 39°13N 81°3W **102 B3**
Ritidian Pt. *Guam.* . 13°39N 144°51E **105 b**
Ritter, Mt. *CA.* . . 37°41N 119°12W **64 F7**
Rittman *OH.* . . . 40°58N 81°47W **92 C5**
Ritzville *WA.* . . . 47°8N 118°23W **101 C7**
Riva *MD* . . . . . 38°57N 76°35W **119 B4**
Rivanna → *VA.* . . 37°45N 78°10W **102 D6**
River Edge *NJ.* . . 40°56N 74°1W **114 A2**
River Falls *AL.* . . 31°22N 86°32W **60 E4**
River Falls *WI.* . . 44°52N 92°38W **103 D1**
River Forest *IL.* . . 41°53N 87°49W **108 B2**
River Grove *IL.* . . 41°55N 87°50W **108 B1**
River Hills *WI* . . . 43°9N 87°55W **112 B2**
River Ridge *LA.* . . 29°57N 90°12W **113 C1**
River Rouge *MI* . . 42°16N 83°8W **109 A1**
Riverbank *CA* . . . 37°44N 120°56W **64 F6**
Riverdale *CA.* . . . 36°26N 119°52W **65 G7**
Riverdale *GA.* . . . 33°34N 84°25W **68 C3**
Riverdale *MD.* . . . 38°57N 76°54W **119 B4**
Riverdale *ND.* . . . 47°30N 101°22W **91 C4**
Riverdale *NY.* . . . 40°59N 74°17W **114 A3**
Riverdale *NE* . . . 40°47N 99°10W **84 D6**
Riverhead *NY.* . . 40°55N 72°40W **78 D2**
Riverside *CA.* . . . 33°59N 117°22W **65 K9**
Riverside *IA.* . . . 41°29N 91°35W **73 D7**
Riverside *IL.* . . . 41°50N 87°49W **108 C1**
Riverside *NJ.* . . . 40°2N 74°58W **87 B2**
Riverside *NM.* . . . 32°50N 104°17W **88 E6**
Riverside *TX.* . . . 30°51N 95°24W **99 G12**
Riverside *WA.* . . . 48°30N 119°30W **101 B6**
Riverside *WY.* . . . 41°13N 106°47W **104 E6**
Riverside County ☆
    CA. . . . 33°45N 116°0W **65 K11**
Riverside Park *NY.* . 39°48N 86°11W **110 B1**
Riverside Res. *CO.* . 40°20N 104°15W **66 B6**
Riverton *IL.* . . . . 39°51N 89°33W **71 D4**
Riverton *IA.* . . . . 40°41N 95°34W **73 E3**
Riverton *NE.* . . . . 40°5N 98°46W **84 D7**
Riverton *UT.* . . . . 40°31N 111°59W **100 C7**
Riverton *WV.* . . . . 38°45N 79°26W **102 C5**
Riverton *WY* . . . . 43°2N 108°23W **104 D5**
Riverview *FL.* . . . 27°52N 82°20W **67 D6**

Riverview *MO.* . . . 38°44N 90°12W **117 A2**
Riverview *WY.* . . . 43°25N 104°12W **104 C8**
Riverview Park *PA.* . 40°28N 80°1W **116 B1**
Riveside *WV* . . . . 39°32N 80°7W **102 B4**
Riviera *CA.* . . . . 35°4N 114°35W **62 B1**
Riviera *TX.* . . . . 27°18N 97°49W **98 K10**
Riviera Beach *FL.* . 26°47N 80°3W **67 E8**
Riviera Beach *MD.* . 39°10N 76°31W **77 A4**
Rixeyville *VA.* . . . 38°35N 77°59W **102 C7**
Roach L. *NV.* . . . 35°41N 115°22W **85 G5**
Roachdale *IN.* . . . 39°51N 86°48W **72 D4**
Road Town
    Br. Virgin Is. . 18°27N 64°37W **105 G18**
Roan Cliffs *CO.* . . 39°20N 108°40W **66 C2**
Roan Cliffs *UT.* . . 39°20N 110°0W **100 D6**
Roan Cr. → *CO.* . . 39°26N 108°13W **66 C2**
Roan Mountain *TN.* . 36°12N 82°4W **97 D10**
Roan Plateau *CO.* . 39°22N 109°20W **100 D6**
Roan Plateau *UT.* . 39°11N 72°29W **86 C2**
Roane County ☆ *TN* . 35°52N 84°31W **97 E8**
Roane County ☆
    WV. . . . 38°48N 81°21W **102 C3**
Roanoke *AL.* . . . 33°9N 85°22W **60 C5**
Roanoke *IL.* . . . . 40°48N 89°12W **71 C4**
Roanoke *IN.* . . . . 40°58N 85°22W **72 C5**
Roanoke *TX.* . . . . 33°0N 97°10W **99 D10**
Roanoke *VA.* . . . . 37°16N 79°56W **102 D5**
Roanoke County ☆
    VA. . . . 37°16N 79°56W **102 D5**
Roanoke I. *NC* . . . 35°53N 75°39W **90 C10**
Roanoke Rapids *NC* . 36°28N 77°40W **90 B8**
Roanoke Rapids L.
    NC. . . . 36°29N 77°40W **90 B8**
Roaring Spring *PA.* . 40°20N 78°24W **95 D4**
Roaring Springs *TX* . 33°54N 100°52W **98 D7**
Robards *KY.* . . . 37°41N 87°33W **96 C5**
Robbins *IL.* . . . . 41°38N 87°42W **108 D2**
Robbins *NC.* . . . 35°26N 79°35W **90 C6**
Robbins *TN.* . . . 36°21N 84°35W **97 D8**
Robbinsdale *MN.* . . 45°1N 93°19W **113 A2**
Robbinsville *NC.* . . 35°19N 83°48W **90 C2**
Roboc L. *TN.* . . . 35°0N 90°7W **112 B1**
Robersonville *NC.* . 35°50N 77°15W **90 C8**
Robert E. Lee Park
    MD. . . . 39°23N 76°39W **107 A2**
Robert Lee *TX.* . . 31°54N 100°29W **98 F7**
Robert S. Kerr L. *OK* . 35°21N 94°47W **93 C9**
Roberta *GA.* . . . 32°43N 84°1W **68 D2**
Roberts *ID.* . . . . 43°43N 112°8W **70 F6**
Roberts *MT.* . . . . 45°22N 109°10W **83 E8**
Roberts, Mt. *AK.* . . 60°2N 166°16W **61 F6**
Roberts County ☆
    SD. . . . 35°55N 100°55W **98 B7**
Roberts County ☆
    TX. . . . 35°55N 100°55W **98 B7**
Robertson County ☆
    KY. . . . 38°30N 84°5W **97 B8**
Robertson County ☆
    TN. . . . 31°2N 86°29W **96 D6**
Robertson County ☆
    TX. . . . 31°2N 96°29W **99 F11**
Robertsdale *AL.* . . 30°33N 87°43W **60 F3**
Robertson *WY* . . . 41°11N 110°25W **104 E2**
Robertsville *NJ.* . . 40°21N 74°17W **87 B2**
Robeson County ☆
    NC. . . . 34°30N 79°10W **90 D6**
Robesonia *PA.* . . 40°21N 76°8W **95 D6**
Robins *IA.* . . . . 42°4N 91°40W **73 C7**
Robinson *IL.* . . . . 39°0N 87°44W **71 E6**
Robinson *ND.* . . . 47°9N 99°49W **91 C6**
Robinson *KS.* . . . 39°49N 95°25W **74 B8**
Robinson, L. *SC.* . . 34°30N 80°12W **90 D5**
Robinsonville *MS.* . 34°49N 90°19W **81 B3**
Robstown *TX.* . . . 27°47N 97°40W **99 K10**
Roby *MO.* . . . . 37°31N 92°8W **82 D4**
Roby *TX.* . . . . 32°45N 100°23W **98 E7**
Roca *NE.* . . . . 40°39N 96°40W **84 D9**
Rochdale *MA.* . . . 42°12N 71°54W **78 B3**
Rochelle *GA.* . . . 31°57N 83°27W **68 E3**
Rochelle *IL.* . . . . 41°56N 89°4W **71 B4**
Rochelle *TX.* . . . 31°14N 99°13W **98 F8**
Rochelle Park *NJ.* . 40°54N 74°4W **114 A2**
Rochester *IL.* . . . 39°45N 89°32W **71 D4**
Rochester *IN.* . . . 41°4N 86°13W **72 B4**
Rochester *KY.* . . . 37°13N 86°53W **96 C6**
Rochester *MA.* . . . 41°44N 70°49W **78 C4**
Rochester *MN.* . . . 44°1N 92°28W **80 F6**
Rochester *NH.* . . . 43°18N 70°59W **86 D4**
Rochester *NY.* . . . 43°10N 77°37W **89 B3**
Rochester *OH.* . . . 41°8N 82°18W **92 B4**
Rochester *PA.* . . . 40°42N 80°17W **95 C1**
Rochester *TX.* . . . 33°19N 99°51W **99 D8**
Rochester *VT.* . . . 43°51N 72°48W **86 C2**
Rochester Hills *MI.* . 42°41N 83°8W **109 A5**
Rochester Park *TX.* . 32°43N 96°44W **109 B5**
Rock *MI.* . . . . . 46°4N 87°10W **79 C4**
Rock *WV.* . . . . 41°29N 90°37W **102 E3**
Rock Cave *WV.* . . 38°50N 80°21W **102 C4**
Rock County ☆ *MN.* . 43°45N 96°15W **80 G2**
Rock County ☆ *NE.* . 42°30N 99°30W **84 B6**
Rock County ☆ *WI* . 42°43N 89°10W **103 F4**
Rock Cr. → *DC.* . . 38°54N 77°3W **119 B3**
Rock Cr. → *IL.* . . 41°42N 90°3W **71 B3**
Rock Cr. → *MT.* . . 46°43N 113°40W **83 D4**
Rock Cr. → *MT.* . . 48°27N 107°6W **83 B10**
Rock Cr. → *NV.* . . 40°39N 116°55W **85 B4**
Rock Cr. → *OR.* . . 44°34N 120°25W **94 B5**
Rock Cr. → *SD.* . . 43°44N 97°58W **91 G8**
Rock Cr. → *UT.* . . 40°17N 110°30W **100 C5**
Rock Creek *MN* . . 45°46N 92°58W **80 E6**
Rock Creek *WY.* . . 41°41N 106°12W **104 E6**
Rock Creek Butte
    OR. . . . 44°49N 118°7W **94 C7**
Rock Creek Park *DC* . 38°56N 77°2W **119 B3**
Rock Falls *IL.* . . . 41°47N 89°41W **71 B4**
Rock Falls *IA.* . . . 43°13N 93°5W **73 B5**
Rock Hall *MD.* . . . 39°8N 76°14W **77 A4**
Rock Hill *MO.* . . . 38°37N 90°23W **117 B1**
Rock Hill *SC.* . . . 34°56N 81°1W **90 D4**
Rock Is. *WI.* . . . 45°25N 86°49W **103 C7**
Rock Island *IL.* . . 41°30N 90°34W **71 B3**
Rock Island County ☆
    IL. . . . 41°25N 90°30W **71 B3**
Rock Island Dam
    WA. . . . 47°23N 120°4W **101 C5**
Rock L. *ND.* . . . . 48°50N 99°12W **91 B6**
Rock L. *WA.* . . . 47°11N 117°4W **101 C8**
Rock Point *AZ.* . . 36°43N 109°38W **62 A6**
Rock Port *MO.* . . 40°25N 95°31W **82 A1**
Rock Rapids *IA.* . . 43°26N 96°10W **73 B2**
Rock Spring *GA.* . . 34°50N 85°15W **68 B1**
Rock Springs *MT.* . 46°49N 106°6W **83 D10**
Rock Springs *WY* . . 41°35N 109°14W **104 E3**
Rock Valley *IA.* . . 43°12N 96°18W **73 B2**
Rockaway Beach
    OR. . . . 45°37N 123°57W **94 B2**
Rockaway Inlet *NY* . 40°34N 73°54W **114 C3**
Rockaway Pt. *NY.* . 40°33N 73°57W **114 C3**
Rockbridge County ☆
    VA. . . . 37°50N 79°20W **102 D5**
Rockcastle → *KY.* . 36°58N 84°21W **97 D8**

Rockcastle County ☆
    KY. . . . 37°20N 84°20W **97 C8**
Rockdale *TX.* . . . 30°39N 97°0W **99 G11**
Rockdale County ☆
    GA. . . . 33°40N 84°0W **68 C2**
Rockefeller Center
    NY. . . . 40°45N 73°58W **114 B3**
Rockefeller Park
    OH. . . . 41°31N 81°37W **107 A2**
Rockford *AL.* . . . 32°53N 86°13W **60 D4**
Rockford *IA.* . . . 42°16N 89°6W **71 A4**
Rockford *IL.* . . . 43°3N 92°57W **73 B6**
Rockford *MI.* . . . 43°7N 85°34W **79 F6**
Rockford *MN.* . . . 45°5N 93°44W **80 E5**
Rockford *OH.* . . . 40°41N 84°39W **92 C2**
Rockford *WA.* . . . 47°27N 117°8W **101 C8**
Rockham *SD.* . . . 44°55N 98°49W **91 F7**
Rockingham *NC.* . . 34°57N 79°46W **90 D6**
Rockingham *VT.* . . 43°11N 72°29W **86 C2**
Rockingham County ☆
    NC. . . . 36°20N 79°50W **90 B6**
Rockingham County ☆
    NH. . . . 43°0N 71°10W **86 D3**
Rockingham County ☆
    VA. . . . 38°27N 78°52W **102 C6**
Rocklake *ND* . . . 48°47N 99°15W **91 B6**
Rockland *ID.* . . . 42°34N 112°53W **70 G6**
Rockland *ME.* . . . 44°6N 69°7W **76 D4**
Rockland *MA.* . . . 42°8N 70°55W **78 B4**
Rockland *MI.* . . . 46°44N 89°11W **79 C2**
Rockland *WI.* . . . 43°54N 90°55W **103 E3**
Rockland County ☆
    NY. . . . 41°10N 74°5W **89 D6**
Rockledge *FL.* . . . 28°20N 80°43W **67 C8**
Rockledge *PA.* . . . 40°4N 75°5W **116 A2**
Rocklin *CA.* . . . . 38°48N 121°14W **64 E5**
Rockmart *GA.* . . . 34°0N 85°3W **68 B1**
Rockport *CA.* . . . 39°44N 123°49W **64 D3**
Rockport *IN.* . . . 37°53N 87°3W **72 F3**
Rockport *MA.* . . . 42°39N 70°37W **78 B4**
Rockport *TX.* . . . 28°2N 97°3W **99 J10**
Rockport *WA.* . . . 48°29N 121°36W **101 B4**
Rocksprings *TX.* . . 30°1N 100°13W **98 G7**
Rockton *IL.* . . . . 42°27N 89°4W **71 A4**
Rockville *CT.* . . . 41°52N 72°28W **78 C2**
Rockville *IN.* . . . 39°46N 87°14W **72 D3**
Rockville *MD.* . . . 39°5N 77°9W **77 A3**
Rockville *NE.* . . . 41°7N 98°50W **84 C7**
Rockville *UT.* . . . 37°10N 113°2W **100 F2**
Rockville Centre
    NY. . . . 40°39N 73°38W **114 C5**
Rockwall *TX.* . . . 32°56N 96°28W **99 E11**
Rockwall County ☆
    TX. . . . 32°56N 96°28W **99 E11**
Rockwell *IA* . . . 42°59N 93°11W **73 C5**
Rockwell *NC.* . . . 35°33N 80°25W **90 C5**
Rockwell City *IA* . 42°24N 94°38W **73 C4**
Rockwood *ME.* . . 45°41N 69°45W **76 C4**
Rockwood *PA.* . . 39°55N 79°9W **95 E3**
Rockwood *TN.* . . 35°52N 84°41W **97 E8**
Rockwood → *MN.* . 45°9N 93°33W **84 D9**
Rocky *OK.* . . . . 35°9N 99°3W **93 C4**
Rocky → *NC.* . . . 35°57N 79°33W **90 C6**
Rocky Boy *MT* . . 48°16N 109°47W **83 B8**
Rocky Boy's Indian Reservation
    MT. . . . 48°16N 109°30W **83 B8**
Rocky Comfort Cr. →
    GA. . . . 32°59N 82°25W **68 D4**
Rocky Ford *CO* . . 38°3N 103°43W **66 D7**
Rocky Ford *GA* . . 32°40N 81°50W **68 D5**
Rocky Fork L. *OH.* . 39°11N 83°26W **92 D3**
Rocky Hill *CT.* . . 41°40N 72°39W **78 C2**
Rocky Mount *NC.* . 35°57N 77°48W **90 C8**
Rocky Mount *VA.* . 37°0N 79°53W **102 D5**
Rocky Mountain Arsenal Nat.
    Wildlife Area △
    CO. . . . 39°50N 104°50W **109 A2**
Rocky Mountain Nat. Park △
    CO. . . . 40°25N 105°45W **66 B5**
Rocky Mts. *N. Amer.* . 49°0N 115°0W **58 G10**
Rocky Reach Dam
    WA. . . . 47°32N 120°18W **101 C5**
Rocky Ridge *MT.* . 47°48N 112°23W **83 C4**
Rocky Ridge *OH* . . 41°31N 83°27W **92 B3**
Rocky Ridge *UT.* . 39°56N 111°50W **100 D4**
Rocky Ripple *IN.* . 39°50N 86°10W **110 A2**
Rocky Run → *VA.* . 38°58N 77°14W **119 B2**
Rocky Top *OR.* . . 44°47N 122°17W **94 C3**
Rockyport *MO* . . 44°47N 122°14W **94 C3**
Rodeo *CA.* . . . 38°2N 122°16W **118 A4**
Rodeo *NM.* . . . 31°50N 109°2W **88 F1**
Rodeo Cove *CA.* . 37°49N 122°32W **118 B1**
Rodessa *LA.* . . . 32°58N 93°59W **75 B2**
Rodgers Forge *MD* . 39°22N 76°36W **107 A2**
Rodman *IA.* . . . 43°23N 92°43W **73 B4**
Rodney *IA.* . . . 42°12N 95°57W **73 C3**
Rodney *MS.* . . . 31°50N 91°1W **81 D2**
Roebling *NJ.* . . . 40°7N 74°47W **87 B2**
Roeland Park *KS.* . 39°2N 94°37W **116 D2**
Roff *OK.* . . . . 34°38N 96°50W **93 D7**
Roger Mills County ☆
    OK. . . . 35°45N 99°45W **93 C4**
Roger Williams Park Zoo
    RI. . . . 41°46N 71°24W **78 C3**
Rogers *AR.* . . . 36°20N 94°7W **63 B1**
Rogers *ND.* . . . 47°4N 98°12W **91 C7**
Rogers *NE.* . . . 41°28N 96°55W **84 C9**
Rogers *TX.* . . . 30°56N 97°14W **99 G10**
Rogers City *MI.* . . 45°25N 83°49W **79 D8**
Rogers County ☆ *OK* . 36°40N 81°33W **102 E3**
Rogers, Mt. *VA.* . . 36°40N 81°33W **102 E3**
Rogers Park *IL.* . . 42°0N 87°40W **108 A3**
Rogerson *ID.* . . . 42°13N 114°36W **70 G4**
Rogersville *AL.* . . 34°50N 87°18W **60 B3**
Rogersville *MO.* . . 37°7N 93°3W **82 D3**
Rogersville *TN.* . . 36°24N 83°1W **97 D9**
Roggen *CO.* . . . 40°10N 104°22W **66 B6**
Rogue → *OR.* . . . 42°26N 124°26W **94 E1**
Rogue River *OR.* . . 42°26N 123°10W **94 E2**
Rogue River Nat. Forest
    OR. . . . 42°54N 122°22W **94 E3**
Rohnerville *CA.* . . 40°34N 124°8W **64 C2**
Roland *IA.* . . . . 42°10N 93°30W **73 C5**
Roland *OK.* . . . . 35°25N 94°31W **93 C9**
Roland, L. *MD.* . . 39°22N 76°38W **107 A2**
Rolette *ND.* . . . 48°40N 99°51W **91 B6**
Rolette County ☆
    ND. . . . 48°45N 99°55W **91 B6**
Rolfe *IA.* . . . . 42°49N 94°32W **73 C4**
Roll *AZ.* . . . . 32°45N 113°59W **62 E2**
Rolla *KS.* . . . . 37°7N 101°38W **74 D2**
Rolla *MO.* . . . . 37°57N 91°46W **82 D5**
Rolla *ND.* . . . . 48°52N 99°37W **91 B6**
Rolling Fork *MS.* . . 32°55N 90°53W **81 D3**
Rolling Fork → *KY.* . 37°51N 85°50W **97 C7**
Rolling Hills Estates
    CA. . . . 33°47N 118°21W **111 D2**
Roma *TX.* . . . . 26°24N 99°1W **98 L8**
Roma-Los Saenz *TX.* . 26°24N 99°1W **98 L8**
Romano, C. *FL.* . . 25°51N 81°41W **67 F7**
Romano, C. *AK.* . . 61°49N 166°6W **61 F6**
Rome *GA.* . . . . 34°15N 85°10W **68 B1**
Rome *IL.* . . . . 40°53N 89°30W **71 C4**
Rome *NY.* . . . . 43°13N 75°27W **89 B5**
Rome City *IN.* . . 41°30N 85°22W **72 B5**
Romeo *CO* . . . 37°10N 105°59W **66 E5**
Romeo *MI.* . . . 42°49N 83°1W **79 G8**
Romeoville *IL.* . . 41°39N 88°5W **71 B5**
Romero *TX.* . . . 35°44N 102°56W **98 B5**
Romeroville *NM.* . 35°31N 105°15W **88 B5**

Romney *WV* . . . 39°21N 78°45W **77 A2**
Ronald Reagan National,
    Washington ✕ (DCA)
    VA. . . . 38°51N 77°2W **119 B3**
Ronan *MT.* . . . 47°32N 114°6W **83 C3**
Ronceverte *WV.* . . 37°45N 80°28W **102 D4**
Ronkonkoma *NY.* . . 40°48N 73°7W **87 B3**
Roodhouse *IL.* . . 39°29N 90°24W **71 D3**
Roof Butte *AZ.* . . 36°28N 109°5W **62 A6**
Rooks County ☆ *KS* . 39°22N 99°5W **74 B4**
Roopville *GA.* . . 33°27N 85°8W **68 C1**
Roosevelt *AZ.* . . 33°41N 111°9W **62 D4**
Roosevelt *MN.* . . 48°48N 95°6W **80 B3**
Roosevelt *OK.* . . 34°51N 99°1W **93 D5**
Roosevelt *UT.* . . 40°18N 109°59W **100 C6**
Roosevelt County ☆
    MT. . . . 48°20N 105°20W **83 B12**
Roosevelt County ☆
    NM. . . . 34°0N 103°30W **88 D7**
Roosevelt Nat. Forest
    CO. . . . 40°45N 105°40W **66 B5**
Roosevelt Park *PA.* . 39°54N 75°10W **116 B1**
Root → *MN.* . . . 43°46N 91°51W **80 G7**
Root River Parkway
    WI. . . . 42°55N 88°0W **112 C1**
Roper *NC.* . . . . 35°53N 76°37W **90 C9**
Roper, Mt. *NV.* . . 39°21N 119°55W **85 C1**
Ropesville *TX.* . . 33°26N 102°9W **98 D5**
Rosalia *WA.* . . . 47°14N 117°22W **101 C8**
Rosamond *CA.* . . 34°52N 118°10W **65 J8**
Rosamond L. *CA.* . 34°50N 118°4W **65 J8**
Rosburg *WA.* . . 46°20N 123°38W **101 D2**
Roscoe *IL.* . . . . 42°25N 89°1W **71 A4**
Roscoe *SD.* . . . 45°27N 99°20W **91 E6**
Roscoe *TX.* . . . 32°27N 100°32W **98 E7**
Roscommon *MI* . . 44°30N 84°35W **79 E7**
Roscommon County ☆
    MI. . . . 44°15N 84°40W **79 E7**
Rose, L. *FL.* . . . 28°32N 81°30W **115 A1**
Rose, Mt. *NV.* . . 39°21N 119°55W **85 C1**
Rose Bowl *CA.* . . 34°9N 118°10W **111 B4**
Rose City *MI.* . . 44°25N 84°7W **79 E7**
Rose Creek *MN.* . 43°36N 92°50W **80 G6**
Rose Hill *IL.* . . . 39°6N 88°9W **71 D5**
Rose Hill *IA* . . . 41°19N 92°33W **73 D6**
Rose Hill *KS.* . . 37°34N 97°7W **74 D6**
Rose Hill *NC.* . . 34°50N 78°2W **90 D7**
Rose Hill *VA.* . . 36°40N 83°22W **102 E1**
Rose Pk. *AZ.* . . . 33°25N 109°21W **62 D6**
Roseau *MN.* . . . 48°51N 95°46W **80 B3**
Roseau → *MN.* . . 49°0N 96°30W **80 B2**
Roseau County ☆
    MN. . . . 48°45N 95°50W **80 B3**
Roseboro *NC.* . . 34°58N 78°31W **90 D7**
Rosebud *MO.* . . 38°23N 91°24W **82 C5**
Rosebud *SD.* . . 43°14N 100°51W **91 G5**
Rosebud *TX.* . . 31°4N 96°59W **99 F11**
Rosebud County ☆
    MT. . . . 46°16N 106°29W **83 D11**
Rosebud Creek →
    MT. . . . 46°16N 106°29W **83 D11**
Rosebud Indian Reservation
    SD. . . . 43°10N 101°0W **91 G5**
Roseburg *OR* . . 43°13N 123°20W **94 D2**
Rosebush *MI.* . . 43°42N 84°46W **79 F7**
Rosedale *IN.* . . 39°38N 87°17W **72 D3**
Rosedale *MD.* . . 39°19N 76°30W **107 B2**
Rosedale *MS.* . . 33°51N 91°2W **81 C2**
Rosedale *NY.* . . 40°39N 73°44W **114 C4**
Rosedale *OK.* . . 34°55N 97°11W **93 D6**
Roseglen *ND.* . . 47°45N 101°50W **91 C4**
Roseland *IL.* . . . 41°42N 87°37W **108 D3**
Roseland *LA.* . . 30°46N 90°31W **75 D5**
Roseland *NJ.* . . 40°49N 74°17W **114 B1**
Roseland *NE.* . . 40°28N 98°34W **84 D7**
Roselle *IL.* . . . 41°39N 74°15W **108 B1**
Roselle *NJ.* . . . 40°39N 74°15W **114 D1**
Roselle Park *NJ* . 40°39N 74°15W **114 D1**
Rosemead *CA.* . . 34°4N 118°5W **111 B4**
Rosemont *IL.* . . 41°59N 87°53W **108 B1**
Rosemont *MD* . . 39°20N 77°3W **119 A1**
Rosemount *MN* . . 44°45N 93°8W **80 F5**
Rosenberg *TX.* . . 29°34N 95°49W **99 H12**
Rosenhayn *NJ.* . . 39°29N 75°8W **87 C1**
Rosepine *LA.* . . 30°55N 93°17W **75 D2**
Rosette *UT* . . . 41°49N 113°25W **100 B2**
Roseville *CA* . . . 38°45N 121°17W **64 E5**
Roseville *IL.* . . . 40°44N 90°40W **71 C3**
Roseville *MN* . . 45°0N 93°9W **113 A2**
Roseville *OH.* . . 39°49N 82°5W **92 D4**
Roseville *PA.* . . 41°52N 76°58W **95 C6**
Rosharon *TX.* . . 29°21N 95°28W **99 H12**
Rosholt *SD.* . . . 45°52N 96°44W **91 E9**
Rosholt *WI* . . . 44°38N 89°18W **103 D4**
Rosiclare *IL.* . . . 37°26N 88°21W **71 F5**
Rosie *AR* . . . . 35°32N 91°30W **63 C4**
Rosier *GA.* . . . 32°59N 82°18W **68 D4**
Roslindale *MA* . . 42°17N 71°7W **106 B3**
Roslyn *SD.* . . . 45°29N 97°30W **91 E8**
Roslyn *WA* . . . 47°13N 120°59W **101 C5**
Roslyn Estates *NY.* . 40°47N 73°39W **114 B5**
Roslyn Harbor *NY.* . 40°48N 73°39W **114 B5**
Rosman *NC.* . . . 35°9N 82°49W **90 C3**
Rosnan *NC* . . . 41°39N 102°33W **98 B3**
Ross *IA* . . . . . 41°46N 92°54W **116 C3**
Ross Barnett Res. *MS* . 32°24N 90°4W **81 D3**
Ross County ☆ *OH* . 39°20N 82°59W **92 D4**
Ross L. *WA.* . . . 48°44N 121°4W **101 B4**
Ross Lake Nat. Recr. Area →
    WA. . . . 48°43N 121°4W **101 B4**
Rossford *OH.* . . 41°36N 83°34W **92 C3**
Rossie *IA* . . . . 43°1N 95°11W **73 B3**
Rositer *PA.* . . . 40°52N 78°56W **95 D4**
Rosslyn *VA* . . . 38°53N 77°4W **119 B3**
Rosslyn Farms *PA* . 40°25N 80°5W **116 B1**
Rossmoor *CA.* . . 33°47N 118°5W **111 D4**
Rossmoor *NJ* . . 40°19N 74°28W **87 B2**
Rosston *AR.* . . . 33°36N 93°17W **63 E2**
Rosston *OK.* . . . 36°49N 99°56W **93 A4**
Rossville *GA.* . . 34°58N 85°17W **68 B1**
Rossville *IL.* . . . 40°23N 87°40W **71 C6**
Rossville *IN* . . . 40°25N 86°36W **72 C4**
Rossville *KY* . . . 40°33N 74°12W **114 D1**
Roswell *GA.* . . . 34°2N 84°22W **68 B2**
Roswell *NM* . . . 33°24N 104°32W **88 D6**
Rota N. Marianas . . 14°9N 145°12E **105 a**
Rotan *TX.* . . . . 32°51N 100°28W **98 E7**
Rothsay *MN* . . . 46°28N 96°17W **80 D2**
Rothschild *WI* . . 44°54N 89°37W **103 D4**
Rotonda *FL.* . . . 26°53N 82°17W **67 E6**
Rotterdam *NY* . . 42°48N 74°1W **89 C6**
Rough → *KY* . . . 37°32N 86°34W **96 C6**
Rough River L. *KY.* . 37°37N 86°30W **96 C6**
Roulette *PA.* . . . 41°46N 78°9W **95 C4**
Round Hill *VA.* . . 39°8N 77°46W **77 A3**
Round Mountain *NV* . 38°43N 117°4W **85 D3**
Round Mt. *TX.* . . 30°26N 98°21W **99 G9**
Round Oak *GA* . . 33°5N 83°37W **68 C3**
Round Rock *AZ* . . 36°31N 109°28W **62 A6**
Round Rock *TX.* . . 30°31N 97°41W **99 G10**
Round Top *TX.* . . 30°4N 96°42W **99 G11**
Round Top Regional Park
    CA. . . . 37°50N 122°11W **118 A3**

Round Valley Indian Reservation
CA ...... 39°50N 123°20W **64 D3**
Round Valley Res.
NJ ...... 40°37N 74°51W **87 B2**
Roundup MT ...... 46°27N 108°33W **83 D9**
Rouses Point NY ...... 44°59N 73°22W **86 B1**
Rouseville PA ...... 41°28N 79°42W **95 C3**
Routt County CO ...... 40°30N 107°00W **66 B4**
Routt Nat. Forest CO ...... 40°45N 107°00W **66 B4**
Rouzerville PA ...... 39°44N 77°32W **77 A3**
Rover TN ...... 35°40N 86°36W **96 E6**
Rowan IA ...... 42°45N 93°33W **73 C5**
Rowan County ☆ KY ...... 38°10N 83°25W **97 B9**
Rowan County ☆ NC ...... 35°40N 80°30W **90 C5**
Rowe NM ...... 35°30N 105°41W **88 B5**
Rowena TX ...... 31°39N 100°33W **99 F7**
Rowland NC ...... 34°32N 79°18W **90 D6**
Rowlesburg WV ...... 39°21N 79°40W **102 B5**
Rowley IA ...... 42°22N 91°51W **73 C7**
Rowley UT ...... 40°54N 112°24W **100 C3**
Roxana DE ...... 38°30N 75°10W **77 B7**
Roxboro NC ...... 36°24N 78°59W **90 B7**
Roxbury PA ...... 41°45N 73°11W **78 C1**
Roxbury KS ...... 38°33N 97°26W **74 C6**
Roxbury MA ...... 42°19N 71°5W **106 B3**
Roxbury NY ...... 40°33N 73°53W **114 C3**
Roxbury NY ...... 42°17N 74°34W **99 C6**
Roxbury VT ...... 44°8N 72°44W **86 B2**
Roxie MS ...... 31°30N 91°4W **81 E2**
Roxton TX ...... 33°33N 95°44W **99 D12**
Roy MT ...... 47°20N 108°58W **83 C9**
Roy NM ...... 35°57N 104°12W **88 B6**
Roy UT ...... 41°10N 112°2W **100 B3**
Roy WA ...... 47°0N 122°33W **101 D3**
Royal IA ...... 43°4N 95°17W **73 B3**
Royal Center IN ...... 40°52N 86°30W **72 C4**
Royal City WA ...... 46°54N 119°38W **101 D6**
Royal Oak MD ...... 38°44N 76°11W **77 B4**
Royal Oak MI ...... 42°30N 83°9W **79 G8**
Royal Palm Beach
FL ...... 26°42N 80°14W **67 E8**
Royale, Isle MI ...... 48°0N 88°54W **79 B3**
Royalston MA ...... 42°40N 72°12W **78 B2**
Royalton MN ...... 45°50N 94°18W **80 E4**
Royalty TX ...... 31°22N 102°52W **98 F5**
Royersford PA ...... 40°11N 75°33W **87 B1**
Royse City TX ...... 32°59N 96°20W **99 E11**
Royston GA ...... 34°17N 83°7W **68 B3**
Roza Canal WA ...... 46°35N 120°23W **101 D5**
Rozel KS ...... 38°12N 99°24W **74 C4**
Rozet WY ...... 44°17N 105°12W **104 B7**
Rubonia FL ...... 27°34N 82°33W **119 D3**
Ruby AK ...... 64°45N 155°30W **61 C9**
Ruby Beach = Jacksonville Beach
FL ...... 30°17N 81°24W **67 A7**
Ruby Dome NV ...... 40°37N 115°28W **85 B5**
Ruby L. NV ...... 40°10N 115°28W **85 B5**
Ruby Lake Nat. Wildlife Refuge ○
NV ...... 40°12N 115°28W **85 B5**
Ruby Mts. NV ...... 40°30N 115°20W **85 B5**
Ruby Valley NV ...... 40°30N 115°21W **85 B5**
Rudolph WI ...... 44°30N 89°48W **103 D4**
Rudy AR ...... 35°31N 94°16W **63 C1**
Rudyard MI ...... 46°14N 84°36W **79 C7**
Rudyard MT ...... 48°34N 110°33W **83 B7**
Ruffling Pt.
Br. Virgin Is. ...... 18°44N 64°27W **105 G18**
Rufus OR ...... 45°42N 120°44W **94 B5**
Rugby ND ...... 48°22N 100°0W **91 B6**
Rugby TN ...... 36°21N 90°0W **112 A2**
Ruidosa TX ...... 29°59N 104°41W **98 H3**
Ruidoso NM ...... 33°20N 105°41W **88 E5**
Ruidoso Downs NM 33°20N 105°32W **88 D5**
Rule TX ...... 33°11N 99°54W **99 D8**
Ruleville MS ...... 33°44N 90°33W **81 C3**
Rulo NE ...... 40°3N 95°26W **84 D10**
Rum → MN ...... 45°11N 93°23W **80 E5**
Rumbley MD ...... 38°6N 75°51W **77 B5**
Rumford ME ...... 44°33N 70°33W **86 B4**
Rumney NH ...... 43°47N 71°48W **86 C3**
Rump Mt. ME ...... 45°12N 71°4W **86 A3**
Rumson NJ ...... 40°23N 74°0W **87 B3**
Runge TX ...... 28°53N 97°43W **99 H10**
Runnells IA ...... 41°31N 93°21W **73 D5**
Runnels County ☆
TX ...... 31°51N 99°57W **99 F8**
Running Water →
TX ...... 34°0N 101°30W **98 C6**
Rupert ID ...... 42°37N 113°41W **70 G5**
Rupert VT ...... 43°16N 73°12W **86 C1**
Rupert WV ...... 37°58N 80°41W **102 D4**
Rural Retreat VA ...... 36°54N 81°17W **102 E3**
Rush KY ...... 38°20N 82°46W **97 B10**
Rush Center KS ...... 38°28N 99°19W **74 C4**
Rush City MN ...... 45°41N 92°58W **80 E6**
Rush County ☆ IN ...... 39°35N 85°30W **72 D5**
Rush County ☆ KS ...... 38°30N 99°15W **74 C4**
Rush Cr. → CO ...... 38°23N 102°33W **66 D8**
Rush Springs OK ...... 34°47N 97°58W **93 D6**
Rush Valley UT ...... 40°22N 112°27W **100 C3**
Rushford MN ...... 43°48N 91°46W **80 G7**
Rushmore, Mt. SD ...... 43°53N 103°28W **56 D3**
Rushville IL ...... 40°7N 90°34W **71 C3**
Rushville IN ...... 39°37N 85°27W **72 D5**
Rushville NE ...... 42°43N 102°28W **84 B3**
Rush TX ...... 31°48N 95°9W **99 F12**
Rusk TX ...... 31°48N 95°9W **99 F12**
Rusk County ☆ TX ...... 32°5N 94°40W **99 E12**
Rusk County ☆ WI ...... 45°25N 91°10W **103 C2**
Ruskin FL ...... 27°43N 82°26W **119 C4**
Ruskin NE ...... 40°9N 97°52W **84 D8**
Ruso ND ...... 47°50N 100°56W **91 C5**
Russell KS ...... 38°54N 98°52W **74 C5**
Russell IA ...... 40°59N 93°12W **73 E5**
Russell KY ...... 38°31N 82°42W **97 B10**
Russell MN ...... 44°19N 95°57W **80 F3**
Russell Cave Nat. Monument ○
AL ...... 34°59N 85°49W **60 B5**
Russell County ☆
AL ...... 32°18N 85°10W **60 D5**
Russell County ☆ KS ...... 39°0N 98°45W **74 C5**
Russell County ☆ VA ...... 37°0N 85°0W **97 C7**
Russell County ☆ VA ...... 37°0N 82°0W **102 E3**
Russell Cr. → KY ...... 37°14N 85°30W **97 C7**
Russell L. = Richard B. Russell L.
GA ...... 34°5N 82°38W **68 B4**
Russell Springs KS ...... 38°55N 101°11W **74 C2**
Russell Springs KY ...... 37°3N 85°5W **97 C7**
Russellville AL ...... 34°30N 87°44W **60 B3**
Russellville AR ...... 35°17N 93°8W **63 C2**
Russellville KY ...... 36°51N 86°53W **96 D6**
Russellville MO ...... 38°31N 92°26W **82 C4**
Russellville OH ...... 38°52N 83°47W **92 E3**
Russellville PA ...... 39°51N 75°57W **77 A5**
Russellville TN ...... 36°15N 83°12W **97 D9**
Russian → CA ...... 38°27N 123°8W **64 D3**
Russian Mission AK 61°47N 161°19W **61 F7**
Russiaville IN ...... 40°25N 86°16W **72 C4**
Rustburg VA ...... 37°17N 79°6W **102 D5**
Ruston LA ...... 32°32N 92°38W **75 B3**
Ruth MS ...... 31°23N 90°19W **81 E3**
Ruth NV ...... 39°17N 114°59W **85 C6**
Rutherford NJ ...... 40°49N 74°6W **114 B2**
Rutherford TN ...... 36°8N 88°59W **96 C3**
Rutherford County ☆
NC ...... 35°20N 81°50W **90 C4**
Rutherford County ☆
TN ...... 35°51N 86°24W **96 E6**
Rutherford Fork →
TN ...... 36°16N 89°11W **96 D3**
Rutherfordton NC ...... 35°22N 81°58W **90 C4**
Ruthsburg MD ...... 39°0N 75°58W **77 B5**

Ruthton MN ...... 44°11N 96°6W **80 F2**
Ruthven IA ...... 43°8N 94°54W **73 B4**
Rutland IL ...... 40°59N 89°3W **71 C4**
Rutland MA ...... 42°23N 71°57W **78 B3**
Rutland ND ...... 46°3N 97°30W **91 D8**
Rutland OH ...... 39°3N 82°8W **92 D4**
Rutland VT ...... 43°37N 72°58W **86 C2**
Rutland County ☆ VT 43°35N 73°0W **86 C1**
Rutledge GA ...... 33°38N 83°37W **68 C3**
Rutledge MN ...... 46°16N 92°52W **80 E6**
Rutledge TN ...... 36°17N 83°31W **97 D9**
Ruxton MD ...... 39°24N 76°38W **107 A2**
Ryan IA ...... 42°21N 91°29W **73 C7**
Ryan Park WY ...... 41°19N 106°31W **104 E6**
Ryde AR ...... 33°45N 91°59W **63 D4**
Ryderwood WA ...... 46°23N 123°3W **101 D2**
Rye AR ...... 33°45N 91°59W **63 D4**
Rye CO ...... 37°55N 104°56W **66 E6**
Rye NH ...... 43°2N 70°50W **86 C4**
Rye Beach NH ...... 42°59N 70°46W **86 C4**
Rye Patch Res. NV ...... 40°28N 118°19W **85 B2**
Ryegate MT ...... 46°18N 109°15W **83 D8**

S

Sabana Grande
Puerto Rico ...... 18°5N 66°58W **105 G16**
Sabaneta Pt.
N. Marianas ...... 15°17N 145°49E **105 c**
Sabetha KS ...... 39°54N 95°48W **74 B8**
Sabin MN ...... 46°47N 96°39W **80 D2**
Sabina OH ...... 39°29N 83°38W **92 D3**
Sabinal TX ...... 29°19N 99°28W **99 H8**
Sabine → LA ...... 29°59N 93°47W **75 E2**
Sabine County ☆
TX ...... 31°20N 93°51W **99 F14**
Sabine L. LA ...... 29°53N 93°51W **75 E2**
Sabine Nat. Forest
TX ...... 31°38N 94°0W **99 F14**
Sabine Nat. Wildlife Refuge ○
LA ...... 29°52N 93°30W **75 E2**
Sabine Parish ☆ LA ...... 31°38N 93°30W **75 C3**
Sabine Pass TX ...... 29°44N 93°54W **99 H14**
Sable, C. FL ...... 25°9N 81°8W **67 F7**
Sabula IA ...... 42°4N 90°10W **73 C8**
Sabula MO ...... 38°1N 93°43W **82 D6**
Sac → MO ...... 38°1N 93°43W **82 C3**
Sac and Fox Indian Reservation
U.S.A. ...... 39°59N 95°31W **74 B8**
Sac and Fox/Mesquakie Indian
Reservation IA ...... 41°59N 92°39W **73 D6**
Sac City IA ...... 42°25N 95°0W **73 C3**
Sacajawea, L. WA ...... 46°20N 118°45W **101 D7**
Sacajawea Peak OR ...... 45°15N 117°17W **94 D8**
Sacaton AZ ...... 33°5N 111°44W **62 D4**
Sackets Harbor NY ...... 43°57N 76°7W **89 B4**
Saco AL ...... 31°57N 85°49W **60 E5**
Saco ME ...... 43°30N 70°27W **86 D4**
Saco MT ...... 48°28N 107°21W **83 B10**
Saco → ME ...... 43°28N 70°22W **86 D4**
Sacramento CA ...... 38°35N 121°29W **64 E5**
Sacramento KY ...... 37°25N 87°16W **96 C5**
Sacramento NM ...... 32°48N 105°34W **88 E5**
Sacramento → CA ...... 38°3N 121°56W **64 E5**
Sacramento County ☆
CA ...... 38°20N 121°20W **64 E5**
Sacramento Int. ✈ (SMF)
CA ...... 38°42N 121°35W **64 E5**
Sacramento Mts.
NM ...... 32°30N 105°30W **88 E5**
Sacramento Valley
CA ...... 39°30N 122°0W **64 D5**
Sacramento Wash →
AZ ...... 34°43N 114°28W **62 C1**
Saddle Brook NJ ...... 40°53N 74°5W **114 A2**
Saddle Mt. OR ...... 45°58N 123°41W **94 B2**
Saddle Mt. WY ...... 44°43N 109°59W **104 B3**
Saddle Mts. WA ...... 46°55N 120°0W **101 D5**
Saddle Rock NY ...... 40°47N 73°44W **114 B4**
Sadieville KY ...... 38°23N 84°32W **97 B8**
Sadorus IL ...... 39°58N 88°21W **71 D5**
Saegertown PA ...... 41°43N 80°9W **95 C2**
Safety Harbor FL ...... 27°59N 82°41W **119 A2**
Safford AZ ...... 32°50N 109°43W **62 E6**
Sag Harbor NY ...... 41°0N 72°18W **78 D2**
Sagadahoc County ☆
ME ...... 44°0N 70°0W **86 C4**
Sagamore MA ...... 41°45N 70°33W **78 C4**
Sagamore Hill Nat. Historic Site ○
NY ...... 40°53N 73°30W **89 E7**
Sagamore Hills OH ...... 41°18N 81°34W **107 B2**
Saganashkee Slough
IL ...... 41°41N 87°53W **108 C1**
Sagavanirktok →
AK ...... 70°19N 147°53W **61 A11**
Sage WY ...... 41°49N 110°58W **104 E2**
Sage → MT ...... 47°16N 109°43W **83 C8**
Sagerton TX ...... 33°5N 99°58W **99 D8**
Sageville IA ...... 42°36N 90°43W **73 C8**
Saginaw MI ...... 43°26N 83°56W **79 F8**
Saginaw TX ...... 32°51N 97°21W **109 A1**
Saginaw → MI ...... 43°39N 83°51W **79 F8**
Saginaw B. MI ...... 43°50N 83°40W **79 F8**
Saginaw County ☆ MI 43°20N 84°0W **79 F7**
Sagola MI ...... 46°5N 88°5W **79 C4**
Saguache CO ...... 38°5N 106°8W **66 D4**
Saguache County ☆
CO ...... 38°10N 106°15W **66 D4**
Saguaro Nat. Park ○
AZ ...... 32°12N 110°38W **62 E5**
Sahuarita AZ ...... 31°57N 110°58W **62 F5**
Sailor Springs IL ...... 38°46N 88°29W **71 E5**
Sailor's Creek Battlefield Historic
State Park → VA ...... 37°17N 78°14W **102 D6**
St. Albans NY ...... 40°41N 73°45W **114 B4**
St. Albans VT ...... 44°49N 73°5W **86 B1**
St. Albans WV ...... 38°23N 81°50W **102 C3**
St. Andrew Sd. GA ...... 30°58N 81°25W **68 F5**
St. Andrews SC ...... 32°47N 80°0W **90 F5**
St. Andrews B. FL ...... 30°5N 85°32W **67 A3**
St. Anne IL ...... 41°1N 87°43W **71 B6**
St. Ansgar IA ...... 43°23N 92°55W **73 B6**
St. Anthony ID ...... 43°58N 111°41W **70 F7**
St. Anthony MN ...... 45°1N 93°13W **113 A2**
St. Augustine Beach
FL ...... 29°54N 81°19W **67 B7**
St. Augustine Shores
FL ...... 29°49N 81°19W **67 B7**
St. Benedict KS ...... 39°53N 96°6W **74 B7**
St. Bernard LA ...... 29°52N 89°51W **113 C3**
St. Bernard OH ...... 39°10N 84°29W **107 B2**
St. Bernard Parish ☆
LA ...... 29°55N 89°20W **75 E6**
St. Catherines I. GA ...... 31°40N 81°10W **68 E5**
St. Charles ID ...... 42°7N 111°23W **70 G7**
St. Charles IL ...... 41°54N 88°19W **71 B5**
St. Charles IA ...... 41°17N 93°49W **73 D5**
St. Charles KY ...... 37°11N 87°33W **96 C5**
St. Charles MI ...... 43°18N 84°9W **79 F7**
St. Charles MN ...... 43°58N 92°4W **80 G6**
St. Charles MO ...... 38°47N 90°29W **82 C6**
St. Charles SD ...... 43°5N 99°6W **91 G6**
St. Charles VA ...... 36°48N 83°4W **102 E1**

St. Charles County ☆
MO ...... 38°45N 90°40W **82 C6**
St. Charles Parish ☆
LA ...... 29°59N 90°25W **75 E5**
St. Clair GA ...... 33°9N 82°13W **68 C4**
St. Clair MI ...... 42°50N 82°30W **79 F9**
St. Clair MO ...... 44°5N 93°51W **80 F5**
St. Clair PA ...... 40°43N 76°12W **95 D6**
St. Clair → MI ...... 42°38N 82°31W **79 G9**
St. Clair, L. N. Amer. ...... 42°27N 82°39W **79 G9**
St. Clair County ☆
AL ...... 33°35N 86°17W **60 C4**
St. Clair County ☆ IL 38°30N 89°55W **71 E4**
St. Clair County ☆ MI 43°0N 82°45W **79 F9**
St. Clair County ☆
MO ...... 38°0N 93°45W **82 C3**
St. Clair Shores MI ...... 42°30N 82°53W **79 G9**
St. Clairsville OH ...... 40°5N 80°54W **92 C6**
St. Cloud FL ...... 28°15N 81°17W **67 C7**
St. Cloud MN ...... 45°34N 94°10W **80 E4**
St. Croix → WI ...... 44°45N 92°48W **103 D1**
St. Croix, L. WI ...... 44°55N 92°39W **103 D1**
St. Croix County ☆
WI ...... 45°0N 92°20W **103 C1**
St. Croix Falls WI ...... 45°24N 92°38W **103 C1**
St. Croix Flowage
WI ...... 46°15N 91°56W **103 B2**
St. Croix I.
Puerto Rico ...... 17°45N 64°45W **105 H18**
St. Croix Indian Reservation
N. Amer. ...... 45°30N 92°20W **103 C1**
St. Croix Island Int. Historic Site ○
N. Amer. ...... 45°8N 67°8W **76 C5**
St. Croix Nat. Scenic Riverway ○
WI ...... 46°6N 91°23W **103 B2**
St. David AZ ...... 31°54N 110°13W **62 F5**
St. David IL ...... 40°30N 90°3W **71 C3**
St. Donatus IA ...... 42°22N 90°33W **73 C8**
St. Edward NE ...... 41°34N 97°52W **84 C8**
St. Elias, Mt. AK ...... 60°18N 140°56W **61 F12**
St. Elias Mts.
N. Amer. ...... 60°33N 139°28W **61 F13**
St. Elizabeth MO ...... 38°15N 92°16W **82 C4**
St. Elmo IL ...... 39°2N 88°51W **71 D5**
St. Ferdinand = Florissant
MO ...... 38°47N 90°19W **117 A1**
St. Francis SD ...... 43°9N 100°54W **91 G5**
St. Francis KS ...... 39°47N 101°48W **74 B2**
St. Francis ME ...... 47°10N 68°54W **76 A5**
St. Francis MN ...... 45°23N 93°22W **80 E5**
St. Francis WI ...... 42°58N 87°53W **112 C2**
St. Francis → AR ...... 34°38N 90°36W **63 D5**
St. Francis County ☆
AR ...... 35°1N 90°47W **63 C5**
St. Francisville IL ...... 38°36N 87°39W **71 E6**
St. Francisville LA ...... 30°47N 91°23W **75 D4**
St. Francois County ☆
MO ...... 37°50N 90°30W **82 D6**
St. Francois Mts. MO 37°30N 90°35W **82 D6**
St. Froid, L. ME ...... 46°58N 68°37W **76 B5**
St. Gabriel LA ...... 30°16N 91°6W **75 D4**
St. Gaudens Nat. Historic Park ○
NH ...... 43°30N 72°22W **86 C2**
St. Genevieve County ☆
MO ...... 37°50N 90°0W **82 D6**
St. George GA ...... 30°31N 82°2W **68 F4**
St. George KS ...... 39°12N 96°25W **74 B7**
St. George SC ...... 33°11N 80°35W **90 E5**
St. George UT ...... 37°6N 113°35W **100 F2**
St. George, C. FL ...... 29°40N 85°5W **67 B3**
St. George, Pt. CA ...... 41°47N 124°15W **64 B2**
St. George I. AK ...... 56°35N 169°35W **61 H5**
St. George I. FL ...... 29°35N 84°55W **67 B4**
St. George Island MD 38°7N 76°29W **77 B4**
St. Helen MI ...... 44°22N 84°25W **79 E7**
St. Helena CA ...... 38°30N 122°28W **64 E4**
St. Helena MD ...... 42°49N 97°15W **84 B8**
St. Helena Parish ☆
LA ...... 30°50N 90°40W **75 D5**
St. Helena Sd. SC ...... 32°15N 80°20W **90 F5**
St. Helens OR ...... 45°52N 122°48W **94 B3**
St. Helens, Mt. WA 46°12N 122°12W **101 D3**
St. Henry OH ...... 40°25N 84°38W **92 C2**
St. Hilaire MN ...... 48°1N 96°14W **80 B2**
St. Ignace MI ...... 45°52N 84°44W **79 D7**
St. Ignatius MT ...... 47°19N 114°6W **83 C3**
St. James MI ...... 45°45N 85°31W **79 D6**
St. James MN ...... 43°59N 94°38W **80 G4**
St. James MO ...... 38°0N 91°37W **82 D5**
St. James NY ...... 40°53N 73°9W **78 D1**
St. James City FL ...... 26°29N 82°5W **67 E6**
St. James Parish ☆ LA 30°5N 90°50W **75 D5**
St. Jean AZ ...... 42°22N 83°0W **109 A3**
St. Jo TX ...... 33°42N 97°31W **99 D10**
St. Joe AR ...... 36°2N 92°48W **63 B3**
St. Joe → ID ...... 47°19N 116°21W **70 B2**
St. Joe → ID ...... 47°24N 116°45W **70 B2**
St. Joe Mt. ID ...... 47°25N 116°0W **70 B2**
St. Joe Nat. Forest ID 47°5N 115°30W **70 B3**
St. John KS ...... 38°0N 98°46W **74 C5**
St. John MO ...... 38°42N 90°20W **117 A1**
St. John ND ...... 48°57N 99°43W **91 B6**
St. John WA ...... 47°6N 117°35W **101 C8**
St. John → N. Amer. ...... 45°12N 66°5W **76 C7**
St. John I.
U.S. Virgin Is. ...... 18°20N 64°42W **105 G18**
St. John the Baptist Parish ☆
LA ...... 30°3N 90°33W **75 D5**
St. Johns AZ ...... 34°30N 109°22W **62 C6**
St. Johns MI ...... 43°0N 84°33W **79 F7**
St. Johns OR ...... 45°35N 122°45W **116 A1**
St. Johns → FL ...... 30°24N 81°24W **67 A7**
St. Johns County ☆
FL ...... 29°45N 81°25W **67 B7**
St. Johnsbury VT ...... 44°25N 72°1W **86 B2**
St. Joseph IL ...... 40°7N 88°2W **71 C5**
St. Joseph LA ...... 31°55N 91°14W **75 C4**
St. Joseph MI ...... 42°6N 86°29W **79 G5**
St. Joseph MN ...... 45°34N 94°19W **80 E4**
St. Joseph MO ...... 39°46N 94°50W **82 B2**
St. Joseph TN ...... 35°2N 87°30W **96 E5**
St. Joseph → IN ...... 41°5N 85°8W **72 B5**
St. Joseph → MI ...... 42°7N 86°29W **79 G5**
St. Joseph B. FL ...... 29°47N 85°21W **67 B3**
St. Joseph County ☆
IN ...... 41°35N 86°15W **72 B4**
St. Joseph Pen. FL ...... 29°51N 85°25W **67 B3**
St. Joseph Sound FL 28°5N 82°48W **119 A2**
St. Landry Parish ☆
LA ...... 30°40N 92°0W **75 D4**
St. Lawrence SD ...... 44°31N 98°56W **91 F7**
St. Lawrence County ☆
NY ...... 44°30N 75°0W **89 A6**
St. Leo MN ...... 44°43N 96°3W **80 F2**
St. Leonard MD ...... 38°29N 76°31W **77 B4**
St. Libory NE ...... 41°5N 98°21W **84 C7**
St. Louis MO ...... 38°37N 90°11W **117 B2**
St. Louis MI ...... 43°25N 84°36W **79 F7**
St. Louis OK ...... 35°5N 96°52W **93 D7**
St. Louis → MN ...... 46°44N 92°9W **80 D6**
St. Louis County ☆
MN ...... 47°40N 92°20W **80 C6**
St. Louis County ☆
MO ...... 38°36N 76°56W **82 C6**
St. Louis Lambert Int. ✈ (STL)
MO ...... 38°45N 90°22W **82 C6**
St. Louis Park MN ...... 45°56N 93°21W **113 B1**
St. Louisville OH ...... 40°10N 82°27W **92 C4**
St. Lucie FL ...... 27°29N 80°20W **67 D8**

St. Lucie Canal FL ...... 27°10N 80°18W **67 D8**
St. Lucie County ☆
FL ...... 27°25N 80°30W **67 D8**
St. Maries ID ...... 47°19N 116°35W **70 B2**
St. Maries → ID ...... 47°19N 116°35W **70 B2**
St. Marks FL ...... 30°9N 84°12W **67 A4**
St. Marks → FL ...... 30°8N 84°12W **67 A4**
St. Marks Nat. Wildlife Refuge ○
FL ...... 30°7N 84°17W **67 A4**
St. Martin L. ...... 45°36N 86°46W **79 D5**
St. Martin Parish ☆
LA ...... 30°7N 91°50W **75 D4**
St. Martinville LA ...... 30°7N 91°50W **75 D4**
St. Mary MO ...... 37°53N 89°57W **82 D7**
St. Mary L. MT ...... 48°39N 113°34W **83 B4**
St. Mary Parish ☆ LA 29°48N 91°30W **75 E4**
St. Mary's AK ...... 62°4N 163°10W **61 E7**
St. Marys GA ...... 30°44N 81°33W **68 F5**
St. Marys IA ...... 41°19N 93°44W **73 D5**
St. Marys KS ...... 39°12N 96°4W **74 B7**
St. Marys OH ...... 40°33N 84°24W **92 C2**
St. Marys PA ...... 41°26N 78°34W **95 C4**
St. Marys WV ...... 39°23N 81°12W **102 B3**
St. Marys → GA ...... 30°43N 81°27W **68 F5**
St. Marys → IN ...... 41°5N 85°8W **72 B5**
St. Marys → MN ...... 46°0N 83°55W **79 D8**
St. Mary's City MD ...... 38°11N 76°26W **77 B4**
St. Marys County ☆
MD ...... 38°15N 76°40W **77 B4**
St. Matthew I. AK ...... 60°24N 172°42W **61 F4**
St. Matthews KY ...... 38°15N 85°39W **97 B7**
St. Matthews SC ...... 33°40N 80°46W **90 E5**
St. Meinrad IN ...... 38°10N 86°49W **72 E4**
St. Michael AK ...... 63°29N 162°2W **61 E7**
St. Michael MN ...... 45°13N 93°40W **80 E5**
St. Michaels MD ...... 38°47N 76°14W **77 B4**
St. Nazianz WI ...... 44°0N 87°55W **103 E6**
St. Olaf IA ...... 43°10N 91°14W **104 C1**
St. Onge SD ...... 44°33N 103°43W **91 F2**
St. Paris OH ...... 40°8N 83°58W **92 C2**
St. Patrick Peak MT 46°59N 114°51W **83 D3**
St. Paul AK ...... 57°7N 170°17W **61 H5**
St. Paul KS ...... 37°31N 95°10W **74 D8**
St. Paul MN ...... 44°56N 93°5W **113 B3**
St. Paul NE ...... 41°13N 98°27W **84 C7**
St. Paul I. AK ...... 57°10N 170°15W **61 H5**
St. Pauls NC ...... 34°48N 78°58W **90 D7**
St. Pete Beach FL ...... 27°43N 82°44W **119 C2**
St. Peter IL ...... 38°52N 88°51W **71 E5**
St. Peter MN ...... 44°20N 93°57W **80 F5**
St. Peters MO ...... 38°48N 90°37W **82 C6**
St. Petersburg FL ...... 27°46N 82°41W **119 B2**
St. Petersburg-Clearwater Int. ✈
(PIE) FL ...... 27°54N 82°41W **119 B2**
St. Phillip TN ...... 46°50N 104°9W **83 D13**
St. Regis MT ...... 47°18N 115°6W **83 C2**
St. Regis Falls NY ...... 44°41N 74°33W **89 A6**
St. Regis Indian Reservation
N. Amer. ...... 44°59N 74°39W **89 A6**
St. Robert MO ...... 37°50N 92°11W **82 D4**
St. Simons I. GA ...... 31°12N 81°15W **68 E5**
St. Simons Island GA 31°9N 81°22W **68 E5**
St. Stephen SC ...... 33°24N 79°55W **90 E6**
St. Tammany Parish ☆
LA ...... 30°29N 90°2W **75 D5**
Ste. → Charlotte Amalie
U.S. Virgin Is. ...... 18°21N 64°56W **105 G18**
St. Thomas ND ...... 38°23N 92°13W **82 C4**
St. Thomas ND ...... 48°37N 97°27W **91 B8**
St. Thomas I.
U.S. Virgin Is. ...... 18°20N 64°55W **105 G18**
St. Vincent MN ...... 48°58N 97°14W **80 B1**
St. Vincent I. FL ...... 29°42N 85°3W **67 B3**
St. Vrain → CO ...... 40°11N 104°32W **66 B6**
St. Xavier University
IL ...... 41°42N 87°42W **108 C2**
Ste. Genevieve MO ...... 37°59N 90°2W **82 D6**
Ste. Marie L. ...... 38°56N 88°1W **71 E5**
Saipan N. Marianas ...... 15°12N 145°45E **105 c**
Saipan Channel
N. Marianas ...... 15°5N 145°41E **105 c**
Sakakawea, L. ND ...... 47°30N 101°25W **91 C4**
Saks AL ...... 33°42N 85°50W **60 C5**
Salado, Rio → NM ...... 34°16N 106°52W **88 C4**
Salamanca NY ...... 42°10N 78°43W **89 C2**
Salamonia IN ...... 40°23N 84°52W **72 C6**
Salamonie, L. IN ...... 40°46N 85°37W **72 C5**
Sale City GA ...... 31°16N 84°1W **68 E2**
Sale Creek TN ...... 35°23N 85°7W **97 E7**
Salem AL ...... 32°36N 85°14W **60 D5**
Salem AR ...... 36°22N 91°50W **63 B4**
Salem CT ...... 41°28N 72°16W **78 C2**
Salem FL ...... 29°53N 83°25W **67 B5**
Salem IL ...... 38°38N 88°57W **71 E5**
Salem IN ...... 38°36N 86°6W **72 E4**
Salem KY ...... 37°16N 88°15W **96 C4**
Salem MA ...... 42°31N 70°53W **78 B4**
Salem MO ...... 37°39N 91°32W **82 D5**
Salem NC ...... 35°42N 81°42W **90 C4**
Salem NJ ...... 39°34N 75°28W **87 C1**
Salem NM ...... 32°42N 107°13W **88 E3**
Salem NY ...... 43°10N 73°20W **86 C1**
Salem NE ...... 40°5N 95°43W **84 D10**
Salem VA ...... 36°47N 76°7W **115 B3**
Salem OH ...... 40°54N 80°52W **92 C6**
Salem OR ...... 44°56N 123°2W **94 C2**
Salem SD ...... 43°44N 97°23W **91 F8**
Salem UT ...... 40°3N 111°40W **100 C4**
Salem WV ...... 39°17N 80°34W **102 B4**
Salem County ☆ NJ ...... 39°40N 75°20W **87 C1**
Salem Plateau MO ...... 37°30N 91°30W **82 D5**
Salina AZ ...... 36°1N 109°52W **62 A6**
Salina KS ...... 38°50N 97°37W **74 C6**
Salina OK ...... 36°18N 95°9W **93 B8**
Salina UT ...... 38°58N 111°51W **100 D4**
Salinas Puerto Rico 17°59N 66°18W **105 H16**
Salinas CA ...... 36°40N 121°39W **64 G5**
Salinas → CA ...... 36°45N 121°48W **64 G5**
Salinas, Sierra de
CA ...... 36°20N 121°20W **65 G5**
Salinas Pk. NM ...... 33°18N 106°32W **88 D4**
Salinas Pueblo Missions Nat.
Monument ○ U.S.A. 34°6N 106°4W **88 C4**
Saline Valley CA ...... 36°15N 117°45W **65 G9**
Saline LA ...... 32°10N 92°59W **75 B3**
Saline MI ...... 42°10N 83°47W **79 G8**
Saline → AR ...... 33°10N 92°8W **63 E3**
Saline → AR ...... 33°44N 93°58W **63 D2**
Saline → IL ...... 37°35N 88°8W **71 F5**
Saline → KS ...... 38°52N 97°30W **74 C6**
Saline Bayou → LA 31°45N 92°58W **75 C3**
Saline County ☆ AR ...... 34°30N 92°40W **63 D3**
Saline County ☆ IL ...... 37°45N 88°40W **71 F5**
Saline County ☆ KS ...... 38°45N 97°40W **74 C6**
Saline County ☆ MO ...... 39°10N 93°10W **82 B3**
Saline County ☆ NE ...... 40°30N 97°10W **84 D8**
Saline L. LA ...... 31°50N 92°30W **75 C3**
Saline Valley CA ...... 36°50N 117°50W **65 G9**
Salineno TX ...... 26°31N 99°7W **98 L8**
Salineville OH ...... 40°37N 80°50W **92 C6**
Salisbury CT ...... 41°59N 73°25W **78 C1**

Salisbury MA ...... 42°51N 70°49W **78 B4**
Salisbury MD ...... 38°22N 75°36W **77 B5**
Salisbury MO ...... 39°25N 92°48W **82 B4**
Salisbury NC ...... 35°40N 80°29W **90 C5**
Salisbury PA ...... 39°45N 79°5W **77 A1**
Salisbury VT ...... 43°53N 73°6W **86 C1**
Salisbury Heights NH 43°24N 71°44W **86 C3**
Salish Mts. MT ...... 48°20N 115°0W **83 B3**
Salipa AL ...... 31°37N 88°1W **60 E2**
Salix IA ...... 42°19N 96°17W **73 C2**
Salkehatchie → SC ...... 32°37N 80°53W **90 F5**
Salkum WA ...... 46°32N 122°38W **101 D3**
Salladasburg PA ...... 41°17N 77°14W **95 C5**
Sallisaw OK ...... 35°28N 94°47W **93 C9**
Salmon ID ...... 45°11N 113°54W **70 D5**
Salmon → NH ...... 43°12N 70°50W **86 C4**
Salmon Falls Cr. →
ID ...... 42°43N 114°51W **70 G4**
Salmon Middle Fork →
ID ...... 45°18N 114°36W **70 D4**
Salmon Mt. NH ...... 45°14N 71°8W **86 A3**
Salmon, Mts. CA ...... 41°0N 123°30W **64 B3**
Salmon Nat. Forest
ID ...... 45°0N 114°30W **70 D4**
Salmon River Mts.
ID ...... 44°50N 115°30W **70 E3**
Salmon River Res.
NY ...... 43°32N 75°55W **89 B5**
Salmon South Fork →
ID ...... 45°23N 115°31W **70 D3**
Salome AZ ...... 33°47N 113°37W **62 D2**
Salt → AZ ...... 33°23N 112°19W **62 D3**
Salt → KY ...... 38°0N 85°57W **97 B7**
Salt → MO ...... 39°28N 91°4W **82 B5**
Salt → WY ...... 43°10N 111°4W **104 C1**
Salt Basin TX ...... 31°42N 105°2W **98 F2**
Salt Cr. → IL ...... 40°8N 89°56W **71 C4**
Salt Cr. → NM ...... 33°30N 104°35W **88 D6**
Salt Cr. → OH ...... 38°58N 83°1W **92 E3**
Salt Cr. → WY ...... 43°41N 106°20W **104 C6**
Salt Draw → TX ...... 31°19N 103°28W **98 F4**
Salt Flat TX ...... 31°45N 105°5W **98 F2**
Salt Fork → TX ...... 33°16N 100°0W **98 D7**
Salt Fork Arkansas →
OK ...... 36°36N 97°3W **93 B6**
Salt Fork L. OH ...... 40°3N 81°30W **92 C5**
Salt Fork Red → OK 34°27N 99°21W **93 D4**
Salt Fork State Park ○
OH ...... 40°7N 81°30W **92 C5**
Salt L. HI ...... 21°21N 157°55W **69 K14**
Salt L. NM ...... 32°18N 104°0W **88 E7**
Salt L. NM ...... 34°5N 103°4W **88 C7**
Salt Lake City UT ...... 40°45N 111°53W **117 B1**
Salt Lake City Int. ✈ (SLC)
UT ...... 40°47N 111°58W **117 B1**
Salt Lake County ☆
UT ...... 40°40N 112°0W **100 C3**
Salt Lick KY ...... 38°7N 83°37W **97 B9**
Salt Marsh L. UT ...... 39°29N 113°55W **100 D2**
Salt Plains Nat. Wildlife Refuge ○
OK ...... 36°44N 98°13W **93 B5**
Salt River Canyon
AZ ...... 33°50N 110°40W **62 D5**
Salt River Indian Reservation
AZ ...... 33°30N 111°50W **62 D4**
Salt Springs FL ...... 29°21N 81°44W **67 B7**
Saltillo MS ...... 34°23N 88°41W **81 B5**
Saltillo PA ...... 40°13N 78°1W **95 D4**
Saltillo TN ...... 35°23N 88°12W **96 E4**
Salton City CA ...... 33°18N 115°57W **65 K11**
Salton Sea CA ...... 33°15N 115°45W **65 K11**
Saltville VA ...... 36°53N 81°46W **102 E3**
Saluda NC ...... 34°0N 81°46W **90 D4**
Saluda SC ...... 34°1N 81°46W **90 D4**
Saluda VA ...... 37°36N 76°36W **102 D8**
Saluda → SC ...... 34°1N 81°4W **90 D4**
Saluda County ☆
SC ...... 34°0N 81°45W **90 D4**
Saluda AR ...... 35°44N 93°24W **63 C2**
Salvador, L. LA ...... 29°43N 90°15W **113 D1**
Salyersville KY ...... 37°45N 83°4W **97 C9**
Sam Houston Nat. Forest
TX ...... 30°32N 95°29W **99 G12**
Sam Rayburn Res. TX 31°4N 94°5W **99 F13**
Samaria ID ...... 42°7N 112°20W **70 G6**
Samburg TN ...... 36°23N 89°21W **96 C3**
Samish B. WA ...... 48°36N 122°31W **101 B3**
Sammamish, L. WA ...... 47°36N 122°5W **118 C5**
Samoset FL ...... 27°28N 82°33W **67 D6**
Sampson County ☆
NC ...... 35°0N 78°30W **90 C7**
Samson AL ...... 31°7N 86°3W **60 E4**
Samuel R. McKelvie Nat. Forest
NE ...... 42°40N 101°0W **84 B4**
San Acacia NM ...... 34°15N 106°54W **88 D4**
San Agustin, Plains of
NM ...... 33°45N 108°15W **88 D2**
San Andreas CA ...... 38°12N 120°41W **64 E6**
San Andres Mts. NM 33°0N 106°30W **88 E4**
San Andres Pk. NM 32°41N 106°32W **88 E4**
San Angelo TX ...... 31°28N 100°26W **98 F7**
San Anselmo CA ...... 37°59N 122°34W **64 F4**
San Antonio NM ...... 33°55N 106°52W **88 D4**
San Antonio TX ...... 29°25N 98°29W **117 C3**
San Antonio, L. CA ...... 35°48N 120°53W **65 H6**
San Antonio, B. TX ...... 28°20N 96°45W **99 J11**
San Antonio Int. ✈ (SAT)
TX ...... 29°32N 98°28W **117 B3**
San Antonio Missions Nat.
Historical Park ○
TX ...... 29°23N 98°29W **117 C3**
San Ardo CA ...... 36°1N 120°54W **65 G6**
San Augustine TX ...... 31°32N 94°7W **99 F13**
San Augustine County ☆
TX ...... 31°30N 94°8W **99 F13**
San Benito TX ...... 26°8N 97°38W **98 L10**
San Benito County ☆
CA ...... 36°30N 121°0W **65 G6**
San Bernardino Nat. Forest
CA ...... 34°10N 116°50W **65 J10**
San Bernard → TX ...... 28°52N 95°27W **99 J12**
San Bernard Nat. Wildlife
Refuge ○ TX ...... 28°51N 95°31W **99 J12**
San Bernardino CA ...... 34°7N 117°19W **65 J9**
San Bernardino County ☆
CA ...... 34°50N 116°0W **65 J11**
San Bernardino Mts.
CA ...... 34°10N 116°45W **65 J10**
San Blas, C. FL ...... 29°40N 85°21W **67 B3**
San Bruno CA ...... 37°38N 122°25W **64 F4**
San Bruno Mt. CA ...... 37°41N 122°26W **118 E2**
San Buenaventura = Ventura
CA ...... 34°17N 119°18W **65 J7**
San Carlos CA ...... 34°11N 110°27W **62 D5**
San Carlos AZ ...... 33°21N 110°27W **62 D5**
San Carlos Indian Reservation
AZ ...... 33°15N 110°30W **62 D6**
San Carlos L. AZ ...... 33°11N 110°32W **62 D5**
San Carlos Park FL ...... 26°28N 81°49W **67 E6**
San Clemente CA ...... 33°26N 117°37W **65 K9**
San Clemente I. CA ...... 32°54N 118°30W **65 L8**
San Clemente Island
San Cristobal NM ...... 36°36N 105°39W **88 A5**
San Cristobal Wash →
AZ ...... 32°45N 113°45W **62 E2**
San Diego CA ...... 32°42N 117°9W **117 B2**
San Diego TX ...... 27°46N 98°14W **99 K9**
San Diego Bay CA ...... 32°39N 117°8W **117 C2**

San Diego County ☆
CA ...... 33°0N 117°15W **65 K10**
San Diego Int. ✈ (SAN)
CA ...... 32°44N 117°11W **117 B2**
San Elizario TX ...... 31°35N 106°16W **98 F1**
San Felipe → CA ...... 33°10N 115°49W **65 K11**
San Felipe Indian Reservation
NM ...... 35°26N 106°31W **88 B4**
San Felipe Pueblo
NM ...... 35°26N 106°27W **88 B4**
San Fernando CA ...... 34°17N 118°26W **65 J8**
San Fernando Valley
CA ...... 34°10N 118°31W **111 A1**
San Fidel NM ...... 35°5N 107°36W **88 B3**
San Francisco CA ...... 37°46N 122°23W **64 F4**
San Francisco → AZ ...... 32°59N 109°22W **62 E6**
San Francisco B.
CA ...... 37°39N 122°14W **118 E3**
San Francisco County ☆
CA ...... 37°47N 122°25W **64 F4**
San Francisco Cr. →
TX ...... 29°53N 102°19W **98 H5**
San Francisco Int. ✈ (SFO)
CA ...... 37°37N 122°22W **64 F4**
San Francisco Mts.
AZ ...... 35°15N 111°45W **62 B4**
San Francisco Peaks
NM ...... 33°45N 108°58W **88 D2**
San Gabriel CA ...... 34°5N 118°5W **111 B4**
San Gabriel → CA ...... 33°58N 118°6W **111 C4**
San Gabriel → TX ...... 30°46N 97°1W **99 G10**
San Gabriel Mts.
CA ...... 34°17N 117°38W **111 A3**
San German
Puerto Rico ...... 18°4N 67°4W **105 G15**
San Gorgonio Mt.
CA ...... 34°6N 116°50W **65 J10**
San Ildefonso Indian Reservation
NM ...... 35°53N 106°8W **88 B4**
San Isabel Nat. Forest
CO ...... 38°0N 105°2W **66 D5**
San Isidro TX ...... 26°43N 98°27W **98 L8**
San Jacinto CA ...... 33°47N 116°57W **65 K10**
San Jacinto County ☆
TX ...... 30°36N 95°8W **99 G12**
San Jacinto Mts.
CA ...... 33°45N 116°40W **65 K10**
San Joaquin CA ...... 36°36N 120°11W **64 G6**
San Joaquin → CA ...... 38°4N 121°51W **64 E5**
San Joaquin County ☆
CA ...... 37°50N 121°15W **64 F5**
San Joaquin Valley
CA ...... 37°20N 121°0W **64 F6**
San Jon NM ...... 35°6N 103°20W **88 C7**
San Jose N. Marianas ...... 14°58N 145°37E **105 c**
San Jose CA ...... 37°20N 121°53W **64 F5**
San Jose IL ...... 40°18N 89°36W **71 C4**
San Jose NM ...... 35°26N 105°28W **88 C5**
San Jose → CA ...... 37°2N 121°17W **64 F5**
San Jose Int. ✈ (SJC)
CA ...... 37°22N 121°55W **64 F5**
San Juan
Puerto Rico ...... 18°28N 66°7W **105 G16**
San Juan → UT ...... 37°16N 110°26W **100 F5**
San Juan Basin NM 36°20N 108°10W **88 A2**
San Juan Bautista
CA ...... 36°51N 121°32W **64 G5**
San Juan Capistrano
CA ...... 33°30N 117°40W **65 K9**
San Juan County ☆
CO ...... 37°50N 107°40W **66 E3**
San Juan County ☆
NM ...... 36°30N 108°30W **88 A2**
San Juan County ☆
UT ...... 38°0N 109°30W **100 F6**
San Juan County ☆
WA ...... 48°32N 123°5W **101 B2**
San Juan Cr. → CA ...... 35°40N 120°22W **65 H6**
San Juan I. WA ...... 48°32N 123°5W **101 B2**
San Juan Indian Reservation
NM ...... 36°3N 106°4W **88 A4**
San Juan Island Nat. Historical
Park ○ WA ...... 48°35N 123°8W **101 B2**
San Juan Luis Munoz Marin Int. ✈
(SJU)
Puerto Rico ...... 18°26N 66°0W **105 G16**
San Juan Nat. Forest
CO ...... 37°30N 108°0W **66 E3**
San Juan Pueblo NM ...... 36°3N 106°4W **88 A4**
San Leandro CA ...... 37°42N 122°9W **118 D3**
San Leandro Bay
CA ...... 37°44N 122°13W **118 B3**
San Lorenzo CA ...... 37°40N 122°7W **118 B3**
San Lorenzo NM ...... 32°49N 107°55W **88 E3**
San Lucas CA ...... 36°8N 121°1W **65 G5**
San Luis AZ ...... 32°29N 114°47W **62 E1**
San Luis CO ...... 37°12N 105°25W **66 E5**
San Luis Obispo CA 35°17N 120°40W **65 H6**
San Luis Obispo County ☆
CA ...... 35°15N 120°30W **65 H6**
San Luis Peak CO ...... 37°59N 106°56W **66 E4**
San Luis Rey → CA ...... 33°12N 117°24W **65 K9**
San Luis Valley CO 37°45N 105°50W **66 E5**
San Manuel AZ ...... 32°36N 110°38W **62 E5**
San Marcos CA ...... 33°9N 117°10W **65 K9**
San Marcos TX ...... 29°53N 97°56W **99 H10**
San Marino CA ...... 34°7N 118°5W **111 B4**
San Martin CA ...... 37°5N 121°37W **64 F5**
San Martin, C. CA ...... 35°53N 121°28W **65 H5**
San Mateo CA ...... 37°34N 122°19W **64 F4**
San Mateo NM ...... 35°20N 107°39W **88 B3**
San Mateo County ☆
CA ...... 37°30N 122°25W **64 F4**
San Mateo Mts. NM 33°45N 107°25W **88 D3**
San Miguel CA ...... 35°45N 120°42W **65 H6**
San Miguel → AZ ...... 32°30N 111°0W **62 E4**
San Miguel → CO ...... 38°23N 108°48W **66 D2**
San Miguel County ☆
CO ...... 38°0N 108°30W **66 E2**
San Miguel County ☆
NM ...... 35°30N 105°0W **88 B6**
San Miguel I. CA ...... 34°2N 120°23W **65 J6**
San Nicolas Island
CA ...... 33°15N 119°30W **65 K7**
San Pablo CA ...... 37°58N 122°21W **118 A2**
San Pablo B. CA ...... 38°5N 122°20W **64 E4**
San Patricio NM ...... 33°25N 105°20W **88 D5**
San Patricio County ☆
TX ...... 28°2N 97°31W **99 J10**
San Pedro TX ...... 27°48N 97°41W **99 K10**
San Pedro → AZ ...... 32°59N 110°47W **62 E5**
San Pedro Bay CA ...... 33°44N 118°12W **111 D3**
San Pedro Channel
CA ...... 33°35N 118°25W **65 K8**
San Perlita TX ...... 26°30N 97°39W **98 L10**
San Pitch → UT ...... 39°5N 111°51W **100 D4**
San Rafael CA ...... 37°58N 122°32W **64 F4**
San Rafael NM ...... 35°7N 107°53W **88 B3**
San Rafael → UT ...... 38°47N 110°7W **100 D5**
San Rafael Desert
UT ...... 38°41N 110°26W **100 E5**
San Rafael Hills
CA ...... 34°11N 118°12W **111 A3**
San Rafael Mts. CA 34°40N 119°50W **65 J7**
San Rafael Swell
UT ...... 38°45N 110°45W **100 E5**

San Saba *TX* . . . . . . 31°12N 98°43W **99 F9**
San Saba → *TX* . . . . 31°15N 98°36W **99 F9**
San Saba County ☆
  TX . . . . . . 31°13N 98°40W **99 F9**
San Sebastián
  Puerto Rico . . . . 18°20N 66°59W **105 G16**
San Simeon *CA* . . 35°39N 121°11W **65 H5**
San Simon *AZ* . . . 32°16N 109°14W **62 E6**
San Simon → *AZ* . . 32°50N 109°39W **62 E6**
San Simon Wash →
  AZ . . . . . . 32°11N 112°25W **62 F3**
San Xavier Tohono O'odham
  Indian Reservation
  AZ . . . . . . 32°10N 111°0W **62 E4**
San Ygnacio *TX* . . 27°3N 99°26W **98 K8**
San Ysidro *CA* . . 32°33N 117°2W **117 C2**
San Ysidro *NM* . . 35°34N 106°46W **88 B4**
Sanak I. *AK* . . . . 54°25N 162°40W **61 J7**
Sanatoga *PA* . . . . 40°15N 75°36W **87 B1**
Sanborn *IA* . . . . 43°11N 95°39W **73 B3**
Sanborn *ND* . . . . 46°57N 98°14W **91 D7**
Sanborn County ☆ *SD*. 44°0N 98°0W **91 G7**
Sanbornville *NH* . . 43°33N 71°2W **86 C3**
Sand Arroyo Cr. →
  U.S.A. . . . . 37°22N 102°8W **94 D1**
Sand Cr. → *IN* . . . 39°3N 85°51W **72 D5**
Sand Cr. → *SD* . . . 45°7N 103°17W **91 E2**
Sand Cr. → *WY* . . 43°20N 105°2W **104 C7**
Sand Draw *WY* . . . 42°46N 108°11W **104 B4**
Sand Fork *WV* . . . 38°55N 80°45W **102 C4**
Sand Hill → *MN* . . 47°35N 96°50W **80 C2**
Sand Hills *NE* . . . 42°10N 101°30W **84 B4**
Sand Hills *CA* . . . 32°50N 115°0W **65 L11**
Sand I. *HI* . . . . . 21°19N 157°53W **69 K14**
Sand I. *OR* . . . . . 45°35N 122°33W **104 A1**
Sand I. *WI* . . . . . 46°59N 90°58W **103 B3**
Sand Key *FL* . . . . 27°54N 82°50W **119 B1**
Sand Key Park *FL* . 27°58N 82°50W **119 B1**
Sand Lake *MI* . . . 43°18N 85°31W **79 F6**
Sand Lake *NY* . . . 42°38N 73°32W **78 B1**
Sand Lake Nat. Wildlife Refuge △
  SD . . . . . . 45°48N 98°13W **91 E7**
Sand Point *AK* . . . 55°20N 160°30W **61 J7**
Sand Pt. *MI* . . . . 43°55N 83°24W **79 F8**
Sand Springs *OK* . . 36°9N 96°7W **93 B7**
Sand Tank Mts. *AZ* 32°45N 112°30W **62 E3**
Sandborn *IN* . . . . 38°54N 87°11W **72 E3**
Sanders *AZ* . . . . . 35°13N 109°20W **62 B6**
Sanders County ☆
  MT . . . . . . 47°40N 115°30W **83 C2**
Sanderson *FL* . . . 30°15N 82°16W **68 A5**
Sanderson *TX* . . . 30°9N 102°24W **98 G5**
Sandersville *GA* . . 32°59N 82°48W **68 D4**
Sandersville *MS* . . 31°47N 89°2W **81 E4**
Sandia *TX* . . . . . 28°1N 97°53W **99 J10**
Sandia Indian Reservation
  NM . . . . . . 35°15N 106°33W **88 B4**
Sandoval *IL* . . . . 38°37N 89°7W **71 E4**
Sandoval County ☆
  NM . . . . . . 35°45N 106°45W **88 B4**
Sandpoint *ID* . . . 48°17N 116°33W **70 A2**
Sands Point *NY* . . . 40°52N 73°41W **114 A4**
Sands Point Preserve
  NY . . . . . . 40°51N 73°43W **114 A4**
Sandston *VA* . . . . 37°31N 77°19W **102 D7**
Sandstone *MN* . . . 46°8N 92°52W **80 D6**
Sandtown *DE* . . . . 39°4N 75°44W **77 A5**
Sandusky *MI* . . . . 43°25N 82°50W **79 F9**
Sandusky *OH* . . . . 41°27N 83°0W **92 B3**
Sandusky B. *OH* . . . 41°27N 83°0W **92 B3**
Sandusky County ☆
  OH . . . . . . 41°21N 83°7W **92 B3**
Sandwich *IL* . . . . 41°39N 88°37W **71 B5**
Sandwich *MA* . . . . 41°46N 70°30W **78 C4**
Sandy *OR* . . . . . 45°24N 122°16W **94 B3**
Sandy *PA* . . . . . 41°6N 78°46W **95 C4**
Sandy *UT* . . . . . 40°32N 111°50W **117 C2**
Sandy Cr. → *WY* . . 41°51N 109°47W **104 E3**
Sandy Creek *MT* . . 44°41N 112°10W **83 F5**
Sandy Creek *NY* . . 43°39N 76°5W **89 B4**
Sandy Creek *PA* . . 40°28N 79°50W **116 B2**
Sandy Hook *KY* . . . 38°5N 83°8W **97 B9**
Sandy Hook *MS* . . . 31°2N 89°49W **81 E4**
Sandy Lake Indian Reservation
  MN . . . . . . 46°51N 93°19W **80 D5**
Sandy Pond *NY* . . . 42°26N 71°58W **98 C6**
Sandy Springs *GA* . 33°56N 84°23W **68 C2**
Sandy Valley *NV* . . 35°49N 115°38W **85 G5**
Sandyville *WV* . . . 38°54N 81°40W **102 C3**
Sanford *CO* . . . . 37°16N 105°54W **66 E5**
Sanford *FL* . . . . 28°48N 81°16W **67 C7**
Sanford *ME* . . . . 43°27N 70°47W **86 C4**
Sanford *NC* . . . . 35°29N 79°10W **90 B6**
Sanford *TX* . . . . 35°42N 101°32W **98 B6**
Sanford, Mt. *AK* . . 62°13N 144°8W **61 E11**
Sangamon → *IL* . . 40°1N 90°26W **71 C3**
Sangamon County ☆
  IL . . . . . . 39°45N 89°40W **71 D4**
Sangchris L. *IL* . . 39°39N 89°29W **71 D4**
Sanger *CA* . . . . . 36°42N 119°33W **65 G7**
Sanger *TX* . . . . . 33°22N 97°10W **99 D10**
Sangre de Cristo
  NM . . . . . . 36°40N 105°15W **88 A5**
Sangre de Cristo Mts.
  U.S.A. . . . . 37°30N 105°20W **66 E5**
Sanibel *FL* . . . . 26°27N 82°1W **67 E6**
Sanibel I. *FL* . . . 26°26N 82°6W **67 E6**
Sanilac County ☆ *MI* 43°25N 82°50W **79 F9**
Sanostee *NM* . . . 36°25N 108°52W **88 A2**
Sanpete County ☆
  UT . . . . . . 39°30N 111°40W **100 D4**
Sanpoil → *WA* . . . 47°57N 118°41W **101 C7**
Sans Bois Mts. *OK* . 35°1N 95°13W **93 C8**
Sansom Park *TX* . . 32°48N 97°24W **109 B1**
Sant Joseph County ☆
  MI . . . . . . 41°50N 85°30W **79 H6**
Santa *ID* . . . . . 47°9N 116°27W **70 B2**
Santa Ana *CA* . . . 33°46N 117°52W **65 K9**
Santa Ana Indian Reservation
  NM . . . . . . 35°26N 106°37W **88 B4**
Santa Ana John Wayne ✈ (SNA)
  CA . . . . . . 33°41N 117°52W **65 K9**
Santa Ana Mts. *CA* . 33°40N 117°30W **65 K9**
Santa Ana Pueblo
  NM . . . . . . 35°26N 106°37W **88 B4**
Santa Anna *TX* . . . 31°45N 99°20W **99 F8**
Santa Barbara *CA* . 34°25N 119°42W **65 J7**
Santa Barbara Channel
  CA . . . . . . 34°15N 120°0W **65 J7**
Santa Barbara County ☆
  CA . . . . . . 34°40N 120°0W **65 H5**
Santa Barbara I. *CA*. 33°29N 119°2W **65 K7**
Santa Catalina, Gulf of
  CA . . . . . . 33°10N 117°50W **65 K9**
Santa Catalina I. *CA* 33°23N 118°25W **65 K8**
Santa Catalina Mts.
  AZ . . . . . . 32°35N 110°50W **62 E5**
Santa Clara *CA* . . 37°21N 121°57W **118 B4**
Santa Clara *NM* . . 32°47N 108°9W **88 E2**
Santa Clara *UT* . . 37°8N 113°39W **100 F2**
Santa Clara → *CA* . 34°14N 119°16W **65 J7**
Santa Clara County ☆
  CA . . . . . . 37°15N 121°40W **64 F5**
Santa Clara Indian Reservation
  NM . . . . . . 35°59N 106°11W **88 B4**
Santa Clara Pueblo
  NM . . . . . . 35°58N 106°5W **88 B4**
Santa Clara Valley
  CA . . . . . . 36°50N 121°30W **64 G5**
Santa Clarita *CA* . 34°24N 118°33W **65 J8**

Santa Claus *IN* . . . 38°7N 86°55W **72 E4**
Santa Cruz *CA* . . 36°58N 122°1W **64 G4**
Santa Cruz County ☆
  AZ . . . . . . 31°30N 110°45W **62 F5**
Santa Cruz County ☆
  CA . . . . . . 37°0N 122°0W **64 G5**
Santa Cruz I. *CA* . 34°1N 119°43W **65 J7**
Santa Cruz Mts. *CA* . 37°15N 122°0W **64 F4**
Santa Cruz Wash →
  AZ . . . . . . 33°23N 112°12W **62 D3**
Santa Elena *TX* . . 26°46N 98°29W **98 L9**
Santa Fe *NM* . . . 35°41N 105°57W **88 B5**
Santa Fe Baldy *NM* . 35°50N 105°46W **88 B5**
Santa Fe County ☆
  NM . . . . . . 35°30N 106°0W **88 B4**
Santa Fe L. *FL* . . 29°45N 82°5W **67 B6**
Santa Fe Nat. Forest
  NM . . . . . . 36°3N 106°42W **88 A4**
Santa Fe Springs *CA* 33°56N 118°3W **111 C4**
Santa Isabel
  Puerto Rico . . 17°58N 66°24W **105 H16**
Santa Lucia Range
  CA . . . . . . 36°0N 121°20W **65 H5**
Santa Margarita L.
  CA . . . . . . 35°20N 120°30W **65 H6**
Santa Maria *AZ* . . 33°25N 112°12W **116 C1**
Santa Maria *CA* . . 34°57N 120°26W **65 J6**
Santa Maria → *AZ* . 34°19N 114°31W **62 C1**
Santa Monica *CA* . 34°1N 118°29W **111 B2**
Santa Monica B. *CA* 33°56N 118°28W **65 K8**
Santa Monica Mountains Nat. Recr.
  Area → *CA* . . 34°4N 118°44W **65 J8**
Santa Monica Mts.
  CA . . . . . . 34°6N 118°29W **111 B2**
Santa Monica Municipal ✈ (SMO)
  CA . . . . . . 34°0N 118°27W **111 B2**
Santa Paula *CA* . . 34°21N 119°4W **65 J7**
Santa Rita *AZ* . . 13°23N 144°40E **105 b**
Santa Rita *MT* . . . 48°42N 112°19W **83 B7**
Santa Rosa *AZ* . . 32°19N 112°22W **62 E3**
Santa Rosa *CA* . . 38°26N 122°43W **64 E4**
Santa Rosa *NM* . . 34°57N 104°41W **88 C6**
Santa Rosa *TX* . . 26°16N 97°50W **98 L10**
Santa Rosa, Mt.
  Guam . . . . . 13°32N 144°55E **105 b**
Santa Rosa and San Jacinto
  Mountains Nat. Monument →
  U.S.A. . . . . 33°28N 116°20W **65 J8**
Santa Rosa Beach *FL* 30°22N 86°14W **67 A2**
Santa Rosa County ☆
  FL . . . . . . 30°45N 87°0W **67 A2**
Santa Rosa I. *CA* . 33°58N 120°6W **65 K6**
Santa Rosa I. *FL* . 30°20N 86°50W **67 A2**
Santa Rosa Indian Reservation
  CA . . . . . . 33°34N 116°32W **65 K10**
Santa Rosa L. *NM* . 35°22N 104°41W **88 B6**
Santa Rosa Mts.
  CA . . . . . . 33°20N 116°15W **65 K10**
Santa Rosa Range
  NV . . . . . . 41°45N 117°40W **85 A3**
Santa Rosa Wash →
  AZ . . . . . . 33°0N 112°0W **62 E4**
Santa Teresa *NM* . 31°51N 106°38W **88 F4**
Santa Ynez *CA* . . 34°37N 120°5W **65 J6**
Santa Ynez → *CA* . 34°41N 120°36W **65 J6**
Santa Ynez Mts. *CA*. 34°30N 120°0W **65 J7**
Santa Ysabel Indian Reservation
  CA . . . . . . 33°10N 116°40W **65 K10**
Santaquin *UT* . . . 39°59N 111°47W **100 D4**
Santa's Village *NH*. 44°27N 71°32W **86 B3**
Sante Genevieve *MO*. 37°59N 90°3W **82 D6**
Santee *CA* . . . . . 32°50N 116°58W **117 A2**
Santee *NE* . . . . . 42°51N 97°50W **84 B8**
Santee *SC* . . . . . 33°29N 80°29W **90 D5**
Santee → *SC* . . . . 33°7N 79°17W **90 E6**
Santee Indian Reservation
  NE . . . . . . 42°50N 97°50W **84 B8**
Santee Lakes *CA* . 32°50N 117°0W **117 A2**
Santiago Mts. *TX* . 29°55N 103°22W **98 H4**
Santiago Peak *TX* . 29°55N 103°22W **98 H4**
Santiam Pass *OR* . 44°25N 121°55W **94 C4**
Santo Domingo Indian Reservation
  NM . . . . . . 35°30N 106°30W **88 B4**
Santo Domingo Pueblo
  NM . . . . . . 35°31N 106°22W **88 B4**
Sapello *NM* . . . . 35°46N 105°15W **88 B5**
Sapelo I. *GA* . . . 31°25N 81°12W **68 E5**
Sapelo Island *GA* . 31°23N 81°17W **68 E5**
Sapelo Sound *GA* . 31°30N 81°10W **68 E5**
Sappa → *NE* . . . 40°7N 99°39W **84 D6**
Sappho *WA* . . . . 48°4N 124°16W **101 B1**
Sapulpa *OK* . . . . 35°59N 96°5W **93 C7**
Sara, L. *IL* . . . . 39°8N 88°36W **71 D5**
Saragosa *TX* . . . 31°2N 103°39W **98 H4**
Sarah *MS* . . . . . 34°34N 90°13W **81 B3**
Saraland *AL* . . . . 30°50N 88°4W **67 A8**
Saranac *MI* . . . . 42°56N 85°13W **79 G6**
Saranac → *NY* . . 44°39N 73°45W **89 A7**
Saranac L. *NY* . . 44°20N 74°8W **89 B6**
Saranac Lake *NY* . 44°20N 74°10W **89 A6**
Saranac Lakes *NY* . 44°20N 74°28W **89 A6**
Sarasota *FL* . . . . 27°20N 82°32W **67 E6**
Sarasota County ☆
  FL . . . . . . 27°15N 82°20W **67 D6**
Saratoga *CA* . . . 37°16N 122°2W **64 F4**
Saratoga *IN* . . . . 40°14N 84°55W **72 C6**
Saratoga *TX* . . . 30°17N 94°31W **99 G13**
Saratoga *WY* . . . 41°27N 106°49W **104 E6**
Saratoga County ☆
  NY . . . . . . 43°10N 73°50W **89 B7**
Saratoga L. *NY* . . 43°1N 73°45W **89 B7**
Saratoga Nat. Historical Park →
  NY . . . . . . 43°0N 73°38W **89 C7**
Saratoga Springs *NY*. 43°5N 73°47W **89 C7**
Sarcobatus Flat *NV* 37°10N 116°58W **85 E4**
Sarcoxie *MO* . . . 37°3N 94°7W **82 D2**
Sardinia *OH* . . . 39°0N 83°49W **92 D3**
Sardis *AL* . . . . . 32°17N 86°59W **60 D4**
Sardis *GA* . . . . . 32°58N 81°46W **68 D4**
Sardis *MS* . . . . . 34°26N 89°55W **81 B4**
Sardis *TN* . . . . . 35°27N 88°18W **96 E4**
Sardis L. *MS* . . . 34°25N 89°48W **81 B4**
Sardis L. *OK* . . . 34°40N 95°25W **93 D8**
Sarepta *LA* . . . . 32°54N 93°27W **75 B2**
Sargeant *MS* . . . 34°7N 89°17W **81 B4**
Sargent *MN* . . . . 43°48N 92°48W **80 G6**
Sargent *NE* . . . . 41°39N 99°22W **84 B6**
Sargent County ☆ *ND* 46°3N 97°45W **91 D8**
Sargents *CO* . . . 38°25N 106°24W **66 D4**
Sarigan N. Marianas. 16°43N 145°47E **105 a**
Sarles *ND* . . . . . 48°58N 99°0W **91 B7**
Sarpy County ☆ *NE*. 41°10N 96°10W **84 C9**
Sartartia *MS* . . . 32°34N 90°49W **81 D3**
Sartell *MN* . . . . 45°37N 94°12W **80 E4**
Sasabe *AZ* . . . . . 31°29N 111°33W **62 F4**
Sasakwa *OK* . . . . 34°57N 96°31W **93 D7**
Sasamoro *TX* . . . 29°14N 98°17W **117 D4**
Sassafras *KY* . . . 37°22N 83°6W **97 C9**
Sassafras Mt. *SC* . 35°4N 82°47W **90 C3**
Satanta *KS* . . . . 37°26N 100°59W **74 D3**
Satellite Beach *FL* . 28°10N 80°36W **67 C8**
Satilla → *GA* . . . 30°59N 81°29W **68 F5**
Satolah *GA* . . . . 34°59N 83°11W **68 B3**
Satsuma *TX* . . . . 29°59N 88°4W **60 F2**
Satus Pass *WA* . . 45°59N 120°39W **101 E5**
Sauceda Mts. *AZ* . 32°35N 112°35W **62 E3**
Saucier *MS* . . . . 30°39N 89°8W **81 F4**
Saugatuck *MI* . . . 42°40N 86°12W **79 G5**
Saugatuck → *CT* . 41°7N 73°22W **78 C1**
Saugerties *NY* . . 42°5N 73°57W **89 C7**

Sauget *IL* . . . . . 38°35N 90°11W **117 B3**
Saugus *MA* . . . . 42°28N 71°0W **106 A3**
Saugus → *MA* . . 42°27N 70°58W **106 A3**
Sauk → *WA* . . . 48°29N 121°36W **101 B4**
Sauk Centre *MN* . . 45°44N 94°57W **80 E4**
Sauk City *WI* . . . 43°17N 89°43W **103 E4**
Sauk Rapids *MN* . . 45°35N 94°10W **80 E4**
Saukville *WI* . . . 43°23N 87°56W **103 E6**
Saulsbury *TN* . . . 35°3N 89°5W **96 E3**
Sault Ste. Marie *MI* . 46°30N 84°21W **79 C7**
Saunders County ☆
  NE . . . . . . 41°15N 96°40W **84 C9**
Saunemin *IL* . . . 40°54N 88°24W **71 C5**
Sauquoit *NY* . . . 43°0N 75°16W **89 C5**
Sausalito *CA* . . . 37°51N 122°29W **118 A2**
Savage *MD* . . . . 39°8N 76°50W **77 A4**
Savage *MS* . . . . 34°38N 90°13W **81 B3**
Savage *MT* . . . . 47°27N 104°21W **83 C13**
Savage River State Forest
  MD . . . . . . 39°41N 79°12W **77 A1**
Savanna *IL* . . . . 42°5N 90°8W **71 A3**
Savanna *OK* . . . 34°50N 95°51W **93 D8**
Savannah *GA* . . . 32°5N 81°6W **68 D5**
Savannah *MO* . . . 39°56N 94°50W **82 B2**
Savannah *OH* . . . 38°40N 85°43W **72 E5**
Savannah *TN* . . . 35°14N 88°15W **96 E4**
Savannah → *GA* . 32°2N 80°53W **90 F5**
Savannah Beach = Tybee Island
  GA . . . . . . 32°1N 80°51W **68 D6**
Savannah River Plant
  SC . . . . . . 33°15N 81°35W **90 E4**
Savanurg *KS* . . . 63°42N 170°29W **61 E5**
Savoy *IL* . . . . . 40°3N 88°15W **71 C5**
Savoy *TX* . . . . . 33°35N 96°22W **99 D12**
Sawkill Range *CO* . 39°0N 106°30W **66 D4**
Sawpit *CO* . . . . 37°56N 108°6W **66 E2**
Sawtooth City *ID* . 43°54N 114°50W **70 F4**
Sawtooth Mts. *MN* . 47°30N 91°0W **80 C8**
Sawtooth Nat. Forest
  UT . . . . . . 41°54N 113°29W **70 H5**
Sawtooth Nat. Recr. Area →
  ID . . . . . . 44°10N 114°50W **70 E4**
Sawtooth Range *ID* . 44°3N 114°58W **70 E4**
Sawtooth Wilderness
  ID . . . . . . 43°59N 115°4W **70 F3**
Sawyer *KS* . . . . 37°30N 98°41W **74 D5**
Sawyer *MI* . . . . 41°53N 86°35W **79 H5**
Sawyer *ND* . . . . 48°5N 101°3W **91 B4**
Sawyer *OK* . . . . 34°1N 95°23W **93 D8**
Sawyer County ☆ *WI* 45°50N 91°0W **103 C3**
Saxe *VA* . . . . . 36°56N 78°40W **102 E6**
Saxis *VA* . . . . . 37°55N 75°43W **77 C5**
Saxonburg *PA* . . . 40°45N 79°49W **95 D3**
Saxonville *MA* . . 42°19N 71°24W **106 B1**
Saxton *KY* . . . . 36°38N 84°7W **97 D8**
Saxton *PA* . . . . 40°13N 78°15W **95 D4**
Saybrook *IL* . . . . 40°26N 88°32W **71 C5**
Sayers *TX* . . . . 29°22N 98°17W **117 C4**
Saylorsburg *PA* . . 40°54N 75°19W **87 B1**
Sayre *AL* . . . . . 33°44N 86°58W **60 C3**
Sayre *OK* . . . . . 35°18N 99°38W **93 C4**
Sayre *PA* . . . . . 41°59N 76°32W **95 C6**
Sayreville *NJ* . . . 40°28N 74°22W **87 B2**
Sayville *NY* . . . . 40°44N 73°5W **87 B3**
Scaggsville *MD* . . 39°9N 76°54W **77 A4**
Scales Mound *IL* . 42°29N 90°15W **71 A3**
Scammon *KS* . . . 37°17N 94°49W **74 D9**
Scammon Bay *AK* . 61°51N 165°35W **61 F6**
Scandia *KS* . . . . 39°48N 97°47W **74 B6**
Scandinavia *WI* . . 44°27N 89°9W **103 D4**
Scanlon *MN* . . . . 46°42N 92°26W **80 D6**
Scappoose *OR* . . 45°45N 122°53W **94 B3**
Scarborough *ME* . . 43°35N 70°19W **76 E3**
Scarsdale *NY* . . . 29°50N 89°58W **113 C3**
Scarsdale *NY* . . . 40°59N 73°49W **87 B3**
Scarville *IA* . . . . 43°28N 93°40W **73 B6**
Scenic *SD* . . . . . 43°47N 102°33W **91 G3**
Scenic Woods *TX* . 29°51N 95°18W **110 A3**
Schaller *IA* . . . . 42°30N 95°18W **73 C4**
Schaumburg *IL* . . 42°2N 88°5W **71 A5**
Schell City *MO* . . 38°1N 94°7W **82 C2**
Schell Creek Ra. *NV* 39°25N 114°40W **85 C6**
Schellsburg *PA* . . 40°3N 78°39W **95 D4**
Schenectady *NY* . . 42°49N 73°57W **89 C7**
Schenectady County ☆
  NY . . . . . . 42°50N 74°0W **89 C7**
Schenley Park *PA* . 40°25N 79°56W **116 B2**
Schererville *IN* . . 41°29N 87°27W **72 B3**
Scherr *WV* . . . . 39°12N 79°10W **77 A1**
Schertz *TX* . . . . 29°33N 98°16W **117 B4**
Schiller Park *IL* . . 41°56N 87°52W **108 B1**
Schiller Woods *IL* . 41°57N 87°51W **108 B1**
Schlater *MS* . . . 33°39N 90°21W **81 C3**
Schleicher County ☆
  TX . . . . . . 30°52N 100°36W **98 G7**
Schleswig *IA* . . . 42°10N 95°26W **73 C3**
Schley County ☆ *GA* 32°15N 84°15W **68 D2**
Schoenchen *KS* . . 38°43N 99°20W **74 C4**
Schofield *WI* . . . 44°54N 89°37W **103 D4**
Schofield Barracks
  HI . . . . . . 21°29N 158°7W **69 K13**
Schoharie *NY* . . . 42°40N 74°19W **89 C6**
Schoharie County ☆
  NY . . . . . . 42°35N 74°30W **89 C6**
Schoharie Cr. → *NY* 42°57N 74°18W **89 C6**
Scholls *OR* . . . . 45°24N 122°56W **94 a**
Schoodic Res. *NY* . 42°23N 68°5W **76 D5**
Schoodic L. *ME* . . 45°13N 68°56W **76 C5**
Schoolcraft *MI* . . 42°7N 85°38W **79 G6**
Schoolcraft County ☆
  MI . . . . . . 46°10N 86°15W **79 C5**
Schriever *LA* . . . 29°45N 90°49W **75 E5**
Schroon → *NY* . . 43°47N 73°47W **89 B7**
Schroon Lake *NY* . 43°50N 73°46W **89 B7**
Schulenburg *TX* . . 29°41N 96°54W **99 H11**
Schurz *NV* . . . . 38°57N 118°49W **85 D3**
Schuyler *NE* . . . 41°27N 97°4W **84 C8**
Schuyler *VA* . . . 37°47N 78°42W **102 D6**
Schuyler County ☆
  IL . . . . . . 40°10N 90°40W **71 C3**
Schuyler County ☆
  MO . . . . . . 40°25N 92°30W **82 A4**
Schuyler County ☆
  NY . . . . . . 42°20N 76°50W **89 C4**
Schuylkill County ☆
  PA . . . . . . 40°35N 76°12W **95 E7**
Schuylkill Haven *PA* 40°37N 76°11W **95 D6**
Schwatka Mts. *AK* . 67°15N 156°30W **61 C7**
Schweitzer Mt. *ID* . 48°23N 116°37W **70 A2**
Science and Industry, Museum of
  IL . . . . . . 41°47N 87°34W **108 C3**
Science Hill *KY* . . 37°11N 84°38W **97 C8**
Scio *OH* . . . . . 40°24N 81°5W **92 C5**
Scio *OR* . . . . . 44°42N 122°51W **94 C3**
Scioto → *OH* . . . 38°44N 83°1W **92 E3**
Scioto County ☆ *OH* 38°50N 83°0W **107 A1**
Scipio *IN* . . . . . 39°3N 95°58W **93 C8**
Scipio *OK* . . . . 35°3N 95°58W **93 C8**
Scipio *UT* . . . . . 39°15N 112°6W **100 D3**
Scitrek Museum *GA* . 33°46N 84°22W **106 B2**
Scituate *MA* . . . 42°12N 70°44W **78 B4**
Scituate Res. *RI* . . 41°45N 71°33W **78 C3**
Scobey *MT* . . . . 48°47N 105°25W **83 B12**
Scofield *UT* . . . 39°44N 111°10W **100 D4**
Scofield Res. *UT* . 39°49N 111°8W **100 D4**
Scotch Plains *NJ* . 40°39N 74°24W **87 B2**
Scotchtown *NY* . . 41°29N 74°22W **87 A2**
Scotia *CA* . . . . . 40°29N 124°6W **64 C2**

Scotia *NY* . . . . 42°50N 73°58W **89 C7**
Scotia *NE* . . . . 41°28N 98°42W **84 C7**
Scotland *AR* . . . 35°32N 92°37W **63 C3**
Scotland *CT* . . . 41°42N 72°7W **78 C2**
Scotland *MD* . . . 38°5N 76°22W **77 B4**
Scotland *SD* . . . 43°9N 97°43W **91 H8**
Scotland County ☆
  MO . . . . . . 40°25N 92°10W **82 A4**
Scotland County ☆
  NC . . . . . . 34°50N 79°30W **90 D6**
Scotland Neck *NC* . 36°8N 77°25W **90 A8**
Scotlandville *LA* . 30°31N 91°11W **75 D4**
Scotrun *PA* . . . . 41°4N 75°19W **87 A1**
Scott *LA* . . . . . 34°42N 92°6W **63 D3**
Scott *MS* . . . . . 33°36N 91°5W **81 C2**
Scott, Mt. *OR* . . 45°27N 122°32W **94 a**
Scott, Mt. *OR* . . 42°55N 122°1W **94 E3**
Scott Air Force Base
  IL . . . . . . 38°34N 89°51W **71 E4**
Scott Bar Mts. *CA* . 41°50N 123°0W **64 B4**
Scott City *KS* . . 38°29N 100°54W **74 C3**
Scott City *MO* . . 37°13N 89°31W **82 D7**
Scott County ☆ *AR* . 34°54N 94°5W **63 D1**
Scott County ☆ *IL* . 39°40N 90°30W **71 D3**
Scott County ☆ *IN* . 38°40N 85°45W **72 E5**
Scott County ☆ *IA* . 41°35N 90°35W **73 D8**
Scott County ☆ *KS* . 38°30N 101°0W **74 C3**
Scott County ☆ *KY* . 38°15N 84°35W **97 B8**
Scott County ☆ *MN*. 44°40N 93°30W **80 F5**
Scott County ☆ *MS* . 32°22N 89°29W **81 D4**
Scott County ☆ *TN* . 36°25N 84°29W **97 D8**
Scott County ☆ *VA* . 36°55N 82°45W **97 D10**
Scott Mts. *CA* . . 41°15N 122°45W **64 B4**
Scott Peak *ID* . . 44°21N 112°49W **70 E6**
Scottdale *GA* . . . 33°47N 84°16W **106 B3**
Scottdale *PA* . . . 40°6N 79°35W **95 D3**
Scotts Bluff County ☆
  NE . . . . . . 41°50N 103°45W **84 C2**
Scotts Bluff Nat. Monument ☆
  NE . . . . . . 41°50N 103°40W **84 C2**
Scotts Hill *TN* . . 35°31N 88°15W **96 E4**
Scotts Valley *CA* . 37°3N 122°1W **64 F4**
Scottsbluff *NE* . . 41°52N 103°40W **84 C2**
Scottsboro *AL* . . 34°40N 86°2W **60 B4**
Scottsburg *IN* . . 38°41N 85°47W **72 E5**
Scottsburg *VA* . . 36°45N 78°48W **102 E6**
Scottsville *KY* . . 36°45N 86°11W **96 D6**
Scottsville *NY* . . 43°2N 77°47W **89 C4**
Scottsville *VA* . . 37°48N 78°30W **102 D6**
Scottville *MI* . . . 43°58N 86°17W **79 F5**
Scotty's Junction *NV* 37°17N 117°6W **85 E4**
Scranton *AR* . . . 35°19N 93°33W **63 C2**
Scranton *IA* . . . 42°1N 94°33W **73 C4**
Scranton *KS* . . . 38°48N 95°44W **74 C8**
Scranton *ND* . . . 46°9N 103°9W **91 D2**
Scranton *PA* . . . 41°25N 75°40W **87 A1**
Scranton *SC* . . . 33°55N 79°45W **90 E6**
Screven *GA* . . . 31°29N 82°1W **68 E4**
Screven County ☆
  GA . . . . . . 32°45N 81°40W **68 D5**
Scribner *NE* . . . 41°40N 96°40W **84 C9**
Scurry *TX* . . . . 32°44N 100°55W **98 E7**
Scurry County ☆
  TX . . . . . . 32°44N 100°55W **98 E7**
Sea Breeze *NJ* . . 39°18N 75°20W **87 C1**
Sea Bright *NJ* . . 40°22N 73°59W **87 B3**
Sea Cliff *NY* . . . 40°50N 73°38W **114 A5**
Sea Isle City *NJ* . 39°9N 74°42W **87 C2**
Sea World *CA* . . 32°46N 117°14W **65 L9**
Seaboard *NC* . . . 36°29N 77°26W **90 A8**
Seabrook *NH* . . . 42°53N 70°52W **86 C4**
Seabrook *TX* . . . 29°34N 95°2W **99 H12**
Seabrook Island *SC* 32°35N 80°10W **90 F5**
Seaford *DE* . . . 38°39N 75°37W **77 B5**
Seaford *MN* . . . 44°29N 95°20W **80 F3**
Seagate *NY* . . . 40°34N 74°0W **114 C2**
Seagraves *TX* . . 32°57N 102°34W **98 E5**
Seagrove *NC* . . . 35°33N 79°46W **90 B6**
Seal Beach Nat. Wildlife Refuge △
  CA . . . . . . 33°44N 118°4W **111 D4**
Seale *AL* . . . . . 32°18N 85°6W **60 D5**
Sealy *TX* . . . . . 29°47N 96°9W **99 H11**
Seaman *OH* . . . 38°57N 83°34W **92 E3**
Searchlight *NV* . . 35°28N 114°55W **85 G6**
Searcy *AR* . . . . 35°15N 91°44W **63 C4**
Searcy County ☆ *AR* 35°55N 92°48W **63 C3**
Searles L. *CA* . . 35°44N 117°21W **65 H9**
Searsboro *IA* . . . 41°35N 92°42W **73 D6**
Searsburg *VT* . . . 42°52N 72°58W **86 B2**
Searsmont *ME* . . 44°28N 68°56W **76 D5**
Seaside *CA* . . . 36°37N 121°50W **64 G5**
Seaside *OR* . . . 46°0N 123°56W **94 B2**
Seaside Heights *NJ*. 39°55N 74°4W **87 C2**
Seaside Park *NJ* . 39°55N 74°5W **87 C2**
Seat Pleasant *MD* . 38°53N 76°53W **119 B4**
SeaTac *WA* . . . 47°27N 122°19W **118 C4**
Seattle *WA* . . . 47°36N 122°20W **118 C3**
Seattle-Tacoma Int. ✈ (SEA)
  WA . . . . . . 47°27N 122°18W **118 D4**
Sebago L. *ME* . . 43°52N 70°34W **86 C4**
Sebastian *FL* . . . 27°49N 80°28W **67 D8**
Sebastian, C. *OR* . 42°20N 124°26W **94 E1**
Sebastian County ☆
  AR . . . . . . 35°10N 94°10W **63 C1**
Sebastopol *CA* . . 38°24N 122°49W **64 E4**
Sebastopol *MS* . . 32°34N 89°20W **81 D4**
Sebec L. *ME* . . . 45°18N 69°15W **76 C4**
Sebeka *MN* . . . 46°38N 95°5W **80 D3**
Sebewaing *MI* . . 43°44N 83°27W **79 F8**
Seboeis *ME* . . . 45°22N 68°43W **76 C5**
Seboeis → *ME* . . 45°56N 69°51W **76 C5**
Seboomook L. *ME* . 45°56N 69°51W **76 C4**
Sebree *KY* . . . . 37°36N 87°32W **96 C5**
Sebrell *VA* . . . . 36°47N 77°8W **102 E7**
Sebring *FL* . . . . 27°30N 81°27W **67 D7**
Secaucus *NJ* . . . 40°47N 74°3W **114 B2**
Second Connecticut L.
  NH . . . . . . 45°9N 71°10W **86 A3**
Second Mesa *AZ* . 35°48N 110°30W **62 B5**
Secretary *MD* . . . 38°37N 75°57W **77 B5**
Section *AL* . . . . 34°35N 85°59W **60 B5**
Security *CO* . . . 38°45N 104°45W **66 D6**
Sedalia *CO* . . . . 39°26N 104°58W **66 C6**
Sedalia *MO* . . . 38°42N 93°14W **82 C3**
Sedan *KS* . . . . 37°8N 96°11W **74 D7**
Sedan *MN* . . . . 45°34N 95°13W **80 E3**
Sedan *NM* . . . . 36°9N 103°8W **88 A7**
Sedgwick, Mt. *NM* . 35°11N 108°6W **88 B2**
Sedgwick *CO* . . . 40°56N 102°32W **66 B8**
Sedgwick *KS* . . . 37°55N 97°26W **74 D6**
Sedgwick County ☆
  CO . . . . . . 40°50N 102°15W **66 B8**
Sedgwick County ☆
  KS . . . . . . 37°30N 97°20W **74 D6**
Sedona *AZ* . . . . 34°52N 111°46W **62 C4**
Sedro-Woolley *WA*. 48°30N 122°14W **101 B3**
Seedskadee Nat. Wildlife Refuge △
  WY . . . . . . 41°49N 109°48W **104 E3**

Seekonk *MA* . . . 41°49N 71°20W **78 C3**
Seeley Lake *MT* . . 47°11N 113°29W **83 C4**
Seelyville *IN* . . . 39°30N 87°16W **72 D3**
Seguam *AK* . . . 52°19N 172°30W **61 K4**
Seguam Pass *AK* . 52°0N 172°30W **61 K4**
Seguin *TX* . . . . 29°34N 97°58W **99 H10**
Seibert *CO* . . . . 39°18N 102°53W **66 C8**
Seiling *OK* . . . . 36°9N 98°56W **93 B5**
Selah *WA* . . . . 46°39N 120°32W **101 D5**
Selawik *AK* . . . . 66°36N 160°0W **61 C7**
Selawik Nat. Wildlife Refuge △
  AK . . . . . . 66°35N 159°0W **61 C8**
Selby *SD* . . . . . 45°31N 100°2W **91 E5**
Selbyville *DE* . . 38°28N 75°14W **77 B5**
Selbyville *VA* . . 43°1N 73°1W **86 C1**
Selden *KS* . . . . 39°33N 100°34W **74 B3**
Selden *NY* . . . . 40°52N 73°2W **114 B5**
Seldovia *AK* . . . 59°26N 151°43W **61 G10**
Selfridge *ND* . . . 46°2N 100°56W **91 D5**
Seligman *AZ* . . . 35°20N 112°53W **62 B3**
Seligman *MO* . . . 36°31N 93°56W **82 E3**
Selinsgrove *PA* . . 40°48N 76°52W **95 D6**
Selkirk *MB* . . . . 50°10N 96°55W **82 B3**
Selkirk Mts. *ID* . . 48°30N 116°40W **70 A2**
Sellers *SC* . . . . 34°17N 79°28W **90 D6**
Sellersburg *IN* . . 38°24N 85°45W **72 E5**
Sells *AZ* . . . . . 31°55N 111°53W **62 F4**
Selma *CA* . . . . 36°34N 119°37W **65 G7**
Selma *AL* . . . . 32°25N 87°1W **60 D3**
Selma *AR* . . . . 33°42N 91°34W **63 E4**
Selma *IL* . . . . . 42°9N 89°44W **71 A4**
Selma *NC* . . . . 35°32N 78°17W **90 C7**
Selma *TX* . . . . 36°34N 119°37W **65 G7**
Selman *OK* . . . . 36°48N 99°30W **93 B4**
Selmer *TN* . . . . 35°10N 88°36W **96 E4**
Selway → *ID* . . . 46°9N 115°36W **70 C3**
Selway-Bitterroot Wilderness
  ID . . . . . . 46°1N 114°49W **70 C4**
Selz *ND* . . . . . 47°52N 99°54W **91 C6**
Semichi Is. *AK* . . 52°42N 174°0E **61 K1**
Seminary *MS* . . . 31°34N 89°30W **81 E4**
Seminoe Dam *WY* . 42°8N 106°54W **104 D6**
Seminoe Res. *WY* . 42°9N 106°55W **104 D6**
Seminole *FL* . . . 27°50N 82°47W **119 B2**
Seminole *OK* . . . 35°14N 96°41W **93 C7**
Seminole *TX* . . . 32°43N 102°39W **98 E5**
Seminole, L. *GA* . 30°43N 84°52W **68 F2**
Seminole County ☆
  FL . . . . . . 28°40N 81°15W **67 C7**
Seminole County ☆
  GA . . . . . . 31°0N 84°55W **68 F2**
Seminole County ☆
  OK . . . . . . 35°10N 96°40W **93 C7**
Seminole Draw →
  TX . . . . . . 32°27N 102°20W **98 E5**
Semisopochnoi I. *AK* 51°55N 179°36E **61 L2**
Semmes *AL* . . . 30°47N 88°16W **60 F2**
Senachwine L. *IL* . 41°10N 89°18W **71 B4**
Senath *MO* . . . . 36°8N 90°10W **82 E6**
Senatobia *MS* . . 34°37N 89°58W **81 B4**
Seneca *IL* . . . . 41°19N 88°37W **71 B5**
Seneca *KS* . . . . 39°50N 96°4W **74 B7**
Seneca *MO* . . . 36°51N 94°37W **82 E2**
Seneca *NE* . . . . 42°3N 100°50W **84 B5**
Seneca *OR* . . . 44°8N 118°58W **94 C6**
Seneca *SC* . . . . 34°41N 82°57W **90 D3**
Seneca *SD* . . . . 45°4N 99°31W **91 E6**
Seneca County ☆ *NY* 42°45N 76°45W **89 C4**
Seneca County ☆ *OH* 41°7N 83°11W **92 B3**
Seneca Falls *NY* . 42°55N 76°48W **89 C4**
Seneca L. *NY* . . 42°40N 76°54W **89 C4**
Seneca Rocks *WV* . 38°50N 79°23W **102 C5**
Senecaville L. *OH* . 39°55N 81°25W **92 D5**
Seney *MI* . . . . 46°21N 85°57W **79 C6**
Seney Nat. Wildlife Refuge △
  MI . . . . . . 46°16N 86°6W **79 C5**
Senoia *GA* . . . . 33°18N 84°33W **68 C2**
Sentinel *AZ* . . . 32°52N 113°13W **62 E2**
Sentinel *OK* . . . 35°9N 99°11W **93 C4**
Sentinel Butte *ND* . 46°56N 103°51W **91 D2**
Separ *NM* . . . . 32°12N 108°25W **88 E2**
Sepulga → *AL* . . 31°3N 87°5W **60 F3**
Sepulveda *CA* . . 34°13N 118°28W **111 A2**
Sepulveda Flood Control Basin
  CA . . . . . . 34°11N 118°28W **111 A2**
Sequatchie → *TN*. . 35°1N 85°23W **97 E7**
Sequatchie County ☆
  TN . . . . . . 35°26N 85°23W **97 E7**
Sequim *WA* . . . 48°5N 123°6W **101 B2**
Sequoia Nat. Forest
  CA . . . . . . 36°30N 118°20W **65 G8**
Sequoia Nat. Park △
  CA . . . . . . 36°30N 118°30W **65 G8**
Sequoyah County ☆
  OK . . . . . . 35°30N 94°45W **93 C9**
Sequoyah Nat. Wildlife Refuge △
  OK . . . . . . 35°37N 95°1W **93 C8**
Serafina *NM* . . . 35°24N 105°19W **88 B5**
Sergeant Bluff *IA* . 42°24N 96°22W **73 C2**
Serpent Mound *OH* . 39°1N 83°26W **92 D3**
Serramonte *CA* . . 37°39N 122°28W **118 C2**
Sesser *IL* . . . . . 38°5N 89°1W **71 E4**
Seth Ward *TX* . . 34°13N 101°42W **98 C6**
Seward County ☆
  KS . . . . . . 37°15N 100°45W **74 D3**
Seward County ☆
  NE . . . . . . 40°55N 97°6W **84 C8**
Seward Peninsula
  AK . . . . . . 65°30N 166°0W **61 D6**
Sewaren *NJ* . . . 40°33N 74°15W **114 C1**
Sewell *NJ* . . . . 39°43N 75°16W **87 C1**
Sewickley *PA* . . 40°32N 80°12W **116 A1**
Seward *AK* . . . . 60°7N 149°27W **61 F10**
Seward *IL* . . . . 42°14N 89°22W **71 A4**
Seward *NE* . . . . 40°55N 97°6W **84 C8**
Seward *PA* . . . . 40°25N 79°1W **95 D3**
Sewickley *PA* . . 41°24N 73°14W **114 a**
Seymour *CT* . . . 42°36N 72°45W **78 B2**
Seymour *IN* . . . 38°58N 85°53W **72 E5**
Seymour *IA* . . . 40°40N 93°9W **73 D5**
Seymour *MO* . . . 37°9N 92°46W **82 D4**
Seymour *TN* . . . 35°53N 83°43W **97 E9**
Seymour *TX* . . . 33°35N 99°16W **98 D8**
Seymour *WI* . . . 44°31N 88°20W **103 D5**
Seymour, L. *WA* . 30°16N 91°14W **75 D4**
Seymourville *LA* . 30°16N 91°14W **75 D4**

Shackelford County ☆
  TX . . . . . . 32°45N 99°18W **99 E8**
Shadehill Res. *SD* . 45°45N 102°12W **91 E3**
Shady Cove *OR* . . 42°37N 122°49W **94 E3**
Shady Dale *GA* . . 33°24N 83°36W **68 C3**
Shady Grove *FL* . 30°17N 83°38W **67 A5**
Shady Grove *KY* . 37°20N 87°53W **96 C5**
Shady Point *OK* . 35°5N 94°40W **93 C9**
Shady Side *MD* . . 38°50N 76°31W **77 B4**
Shady Spring *WV* . 37°42N 81°6W **102 D3**
Shadyside *OH* . . 39°58N 80°45W **92 D6**
Shafer, L. *IN* . . . 40°46N 86°46W **72 C4**
Shafter *AK* . . . 66°35N 159°10W **61 C8**
Shafter *CA* . . . 35°30N 119°16W **65 H7**
Shafter *TX* . . . 29°49N 104°18W **98 H3**
Shageluk *AK* . . . 62°41N 159°34W **61 E8**
Shaker Heights *OH* . 41°28N 81°32W **107 B1**
Shakopee *MN* . . 44°48N 93°32W **80 F5**
Shaktoolik *AK* . . 64°20N 161°9W **61 D7**
Shallotte *NC* . . . 33°58N 78°23W **90 E7**
Shallow Water *CA* . 38°23N 100°55W **74 C3**
Shallowater *TX* . 33°36N 102°0W **98 D5**
Shambaugh *IA* . . 40°42N 95°3W **73 E3**
Shamokin *PA* . . 40°47N 76°34W **95 D6**
Shamrock *OK* . . 35°56N 96°35W **93 C7**
Shamrock *TX* . . 35°13N 100°15W **98 B7**
Shandon *CA* . . . 35°39N 120°23W **65 H6**
Shaniko *OR* . . . 45°0N 120°45W **94 B5**
Shannon *GA* . . . 34°20N 85°4W **68 B1**
Shannon *IL* . . . 42°9N 89°44W **71 A4**
Shannon *MS* . . . 34°7N 88°43W **81 B5**
Shannon *NC* . . . 35°32N 78°17W **90 C7**
Shannon *TN* . . . 36°14N 88°50W **96 D4**
Shannon *TX* . . . 33°47N 72°22W **96 D4**
Shannon *WI* . . . 42°30N 88°44W **103 F5**
Shannon Hill *PA* . 39°54N 75°16W **116 B1**
Shannon County ☆
  MO . . . . . . 37°10N 91°20W **82 D5**
Shannon County ☆
  SD . . . . . . 43°15N 102°35W **91 G3**
Shannontown *SC* . 33°53N 80°21W **90 D5**
Shapleigh *ME* . . 43°32N 70°51W **86 C4**
Sharkey County ☆
  MS . . . . . . 32°55N 90°53W **81 D3**
Sharon *CT* . . . . 41°53N 73°29W **78 C1**
Sharon *KS* . . . . 37°15N 98°25W **74 D5**
Sharon *MA* . . . 42°7N 71°11W **78 B3**
Sharon *ND* . . . 47°36N 97°54W **91 C8**
Sharon *OK* . . . 36°17N 99°20W **93 B4**
Sharon *PA* . . . . 41°14N 80°31W **95 C2**
Sharon *TN* . . . 36°14N 88°50W **96 D4**
Sharon *VT* . . . . 43°47N 72°25W **86 C2**
Sharon *WI* . . . . 42°30N 88°44W **103 F5**
Sharon Springs *KS* . 38°54N 101°45W **74 C2**
Sharon Springs *NY* . 42°48N 74°37W **89 C6**
Sharonville *OH* . . 39°16N 84°25W **92 D2**
Sharp County ☆ *AR* 36°4N 91°37W **63 B4**
Sharpe, L. *SD* . . 44°1N 99°23W **91 F6**
Sharpes *FL* . . . 28°26N 80°46W **67 C8**
Sharps *VA* . . . . 37°49N 76°42W **77 C4**
Sharpsburg *IA* . . 40°48N 94°38W **73 E4**
Sharpsburg *KY* . . 38°12N 83°56W **97 B9**
Sharpsburg *MD* . . 39°28N 77°45W **77 A3**
Sharpsburg *NC* . . 35°53N 77°50W **90 B8**
Sharpsville *IN* . . 40°23N 86°5W **72 C4**
Sharpsville *PA* . . 41°15N 80°29W **95 C2**
Sharptown *MD* . . 38°35N 75°45W **77 B5**
Shasta *CA* . . . . 40°36N 122°29W **64 D4**
Shasta County ☆ *CA* 40°40N 122°0W **64 C5**
Shasta Dam *CA* . . 40°43N 122°25W **64 C4**
Shasta L. *CA* . . . 40°43N 122°25W **64 C4**
Shasta Lake *CA* . . 40°41N 122°22W **64 C4**
Shasta Nat. Forest
  CA . . . . . . 41°10N 122°20W **64 B4**
Shavano Park *TX* . 29°35N 98°33W **117 B2**
Shaver L. *CA* . . 37°9N 119°18W **65 F7**
Shaw *MS* . . . . 33°36N 90°47W **81 C3**
Shawangunk Mts. *NY* 41°35N 74°30W **89 D6**
Shawano *WI* . . . 44°47N 88°36W **103 D5**
Shawano County ☆
  WI . . . . . . 44°45N 88°40W **103 D5**
Shawnee *KS* . . . 39°1N 94°43W **74 B9**
Shawnee *OH* . . 39°36N 82°13W **92 D4**
Shawnee *OK* . . . 35°20N 96°55W **93 C7**
Shawnee *KS* . . . 39°0N 95°5W **74 B8**
Shawnee Nat. Forest
  IL . . . . . . 37°40N 88°20W **71 F5**
Shawnee State Forest
  OH . . . . . . 38°43N 83°13W **92 E3**
Shawneetown *IL* . 37°42N 88°8W **71 F5**
Shea Stadium *NY* . 40°45N 73°51W **114 B3**
Sheboygan *WI* . . 43°46N 87°45W **103 E6**
Sheboygan County ☆
  WI . . . . . . 43°45N 87°50W **103 E6**
Sheboygan Falls *WI* 43°44N 87°49W **103 E6**
Sheen, L. *FL* . . . 28°25N 81°31W **118 B5**
Sheenjek → *AK* . . 66°45N 144°33W **61 C11**
Sheep Hole Mts.
  CA . . . . . . 34°10N 115°40W **65 J11**
Sheep Mt. *CO* . . 39°55N 107°8W **66 C3**
Sheep Mt. *WY* . . 43°31N 110°28W **104 C2**
Sheep Range *NV* . 36°35N 115°15W **85 F5**
Sheep Springs *NM* . 36°9N 108°42W **88 A2**
Sheepshead Bay *NY* 40°35N 73°56W **114 C3**
Sheepshead Mts. *OR* 42°54N 118°9W **94 E7**
Sheffield *AL* . . . 34°46N 87°41W **60 B3**
Sheffield *IL* . . . 41°21N 89°44W **71 B4**
Sheffield *IA* . . . 42°54N 93°13W **73 C5**
Sheffield *MA* . . 42°6N 73°21W **78 B1**
Sheffield *PA* . . . 41°42N 79°3W **95 C3**
Sheffield *TX* . . . 30°41N 101°49W **98 G6**
Shelbiana *KY* . . 37°26N 82°30W **97 C10**
Shelbina *MO* . . 39°47N 92°2W **82 B4**
Shelburn *IN* . . . 39°11N 87°24W **72 D3**
Shelburne *VT* . . 44°23N 73°14W **86 B1**
Shelburne Falls *MA* . 42°36N 72°45W **78 B2**
Shelburne Museum
  VT . . . . . . 44°23N 73°14W **86 B1**
Shelby *IA* . . . . 41°31N 95°27W **73 D3**
Shelby *MI* . . . . 43°37N 86°22W **79 F5**
Shelby *MS* . . . . 33°57N 90°46W **81 C3**
Shelby *MT* . . . . 48°30N 111°51W **83 B6**
Shelby *NC* . . . . 35°17N 81°32W **90 C4**
Shelby *NE* . . . . 41°12N 97°26W **84 C8**
Shelby *OH* . . . . 40°53N 82°40W **92 C4**
Shelby County ☆ *AL* 33°15N 86°40W **60 C4**
Shelby County ☆ *IL* 39°30N 88°50W **71 D4**
Shelby County ☆ *IN* 39°30N 85°45W **72 D5**
Shelby County ☆ *IA* 41°40N 95°20W **73 D3**
Shelby County ☆ *KY* 38°10N 85°10W **97 B7**
Shelby County ☆ *MO* 39°50N 92°0W **82 B4**
Shelby County ☆ *OH* 40°17N 84°9W **92 C2**
Shelby County ☆
  TX . . . . . . 31°48N 94°11W **99 F13**
Shelbyville *IL* . . 39°24N 88°48W **71 D5**
Shelbyville *IN* . . 39°31N 85°47W **72 D5**
Shelbyville *KY* . . 38°13N 85°14W **97 B7**
Shelbyville *MO* . 39°48N 92°2W **82 B4**
Shelbyville *TN* . . 35°29N 86°28W **96 E6**
Shelbyville *TX* . . 31°46N 94°5W **99 F13**
Shelbyville, L. *IL* . 39°26N 88°46W **71 D5**
Sheldon *IA* . . . 43°11N 95°51W **73 B3**
Sheldon *IL* . . . 40°46N 87°34W **71 C6**
Sheldon *MO* . . . 37°39N 94°18W **82 D2**
Sheldon *ND* . . . 46°35N 97°30W **91 D8**
Sheldon *VT* . . . 44°54N 72°57W **86 A2**
Sheldon *WI* . . . 45°19N 90°58W **103 C3**
Sheldon Nat. Wildlife Refuge △
  NV . . . . . . 41°48N 119°12W **85 A1**

Sheldon Point *AK* . . . 62°32N 164°52W **61 E6**
Shelikof Strait *AK* . . . 57°30N 155°0W **61 H9**
Shell *WY* . . . 44°32N 107°47W **104 B5**
Shell Beach = Huntington Beach
 CA . . . . 33°40N 118°5W **65 K8**
Shell Lake *WI* . . . 45°45N 91°55W **103 C2**
Shell Rock *IA* . . . 42°43N 112°7W **73 C6**
Shell Rock → *IA* . . . 42°35N 92°25W **73 C6**
Shelley *ID* . . . 43°23N 112°7W **70 F6**
Shellman *GA* . . . 31°46N 84°37W **68 E2**
Shellman Bluff *GA* . . 31°35N 81°19W **68 E5**
Shellsburg *IA* . . . 42°6N 91°52W **73 C7**
Shelltown *MD* . . . 37°58N 75°40W **77 C5**
Shelly *MN* . . . 47°28N 96°49W **80 C2**
Shelter I. *NY* . . . 41°4N 72°20W **78 C7**
Shelton *CT* . . . 41°19N 73°5W **78 C1**
Shelton *NE* . . . 40°47N 98°44W **84 D7**
Shelton *WA* . . . 47°13N 123°6W **101 C2**
Shenandoah *IA* . . . 40°46N 95°22W **73 E3**
Shenandoah *PA* . . . 40°49N 76°12W **95 D6**
Shenandoah *VA* . . . 38°29N 78°37W **102 C6**
Shenandoah → *VA* . . 39°19N 77°44W **102 B7**
Shenandoah County ☆
 VA . . . . 38°53N 78°30W **102 C6**
Shenandoah Mts.
 VA . . . . 38°40N 79°15W **102 C5**
Shenandoah Nat. Park △
 VA . . . . 38°35N 78°22W **77 B2**
Shepherd *MI* . . . 43°32N 84°41W **79 F7**
Shepherd *MT* . . . 45°57N 108°21W **83 E9**
Shepherd *TX* . . . 30°31N 95°1W **99 G12**
Shepherdstown *WV* . . 39°26N 77°48W **77 A3**
Shepherdsville *KY* . . 37°59N 85°43W **97 C7**
Sheppard Air Force Base
 TX . . . . 33°57N 98°30W **99 D9**
Sherando *VA* . . . 37°59N 78°57W **102 D6**
Sherard *MS* . . . 34°13N 90°42W **81 B3**
Sherburn *MN* . . . 43°39N 94°43W **80 G4**
Sherburne *NY* . . . 42°41N 75°30W **89 C5**
Sherburne *VT* . . . 43°40N 72°49W **86 C2**
Sherburne County ☆
 MN . . . . 45°20N 93°45W **80 E5**
Sheridan *AR* . . . 34°19N 92°24W **63 D3**
Sheridan *CO* . . . 39°38N 105°1W **109 C1**
Sheridan *IL* . . . 41°32N 88°41W **71 B5**
Sheridan *IN* . . . 40°8N 86°13W **72 C4**
Sheridan *MI* . . . 43°13N 85°4W **79 F6**
Sheridan *MO* . . . 40°31N 94°37W **82 A2**
Sheridan *MT* . . . 45°27N 112°12W **83 E5**
Sheridan *OR* . . . 45°6N 123°24W **94 B2**
Sheridan *WY* . . . 44°48N 106°58W **104 B6**
Sheridan County ☆
 KS . . . . 39°20N 100°30W **74 B3**
Sheridan County ☆
 MT . . . . 48°48N 104°30W **83 B13**
Sheridan County ☆
 ND . . . . 47°45N 100°20W **91 C5**
Sheridan County ☆
 NE . . . . 42°30N 102°20W **84 B3**
Sheridan County ☆
 WY . . . . 44°50N 106°45W **104 B6**
Sheridan Lake *CO* . . 38°28N 102°18W **66 D8**
Sheridan Park *WI* . . 42°34N 87°49W **112 C2**
Sherman *CT* . . . 41°35N 73°30W **78 C1**
Sherman *IL* . . . 39°54N 89°36W **71 D4**
Sherman *MS* . . . 34°22N 88°50W **81 B5**
Sherman *NY* . . . 42°9N 79°35W **88 B2**
Sherman *TX* . . . 33°38N 96°36W **99 D11**
Sherman County ☆
 KS . . . . 39°20N 101°45W **74 B2**
Sherman County ☆
 NE . . . . 41°15N 99°0W **84 C7**
Sherman County ☆
 OR . . . . 45°30N 120°40W **94 B5**
Sherman County ☆
 TX . . . . 36°10N 101°58W **98 A6**
Sherman Oaks *CA* . . 34°8N 118°29W **111 B2**
Sherman Park *IL* . . 41°47N 87°39W **108 C2**
Sherman Pk. *ID* . . 42°38N 111°33W **70 G7**
Sherman Res. *NE* . . 41°18N 98°55W **84 C7**
Sherman Station *ME* . . 45°54N 68°26W **76 C5**
Sherrard *IL* . . . 41°19N 90°31W **71 B3**
Sherrelwood *CO* . . 39°50N 105°0W **109 A1**
Sherrill *AR* . . . 34°23N 91°57W **63 D4**
Sherwood *AR* . . . 34°48N 92°16W **63 D3**
Sherwood *MD* . . . 38°46N 76°19W **77 B4**
Sherwood *ND* . . . 48°57N 101°38W **91 B4**
Sherwood *OH* . . . 41°17N 84°33W **92 B2**
Sherwood *OR* . . . 45°21N 122°50W **94 B3**
Sherwood *TN* . . . 35°5N 85°56W **97 E7**
Sherwood, L. *FL* . . 28°33N 81°29W **115 A2**
Shetek, L. *MN* . . 44°7N 95°42W **80 F3**
Shetucket → *CT* . . 41°39N 72°6W **78 C2**
Shevlin *MN* . . . 47°32N 95°15W **80 C3**
Sheyenne *ND* . . . 47°50N 99°7W **91 C6**
Sheyenne → *ND* . . 47°2N 96°50W **91 C9**
Sheyenne L. *ND* . . 47°42N 100°12W **91 C5**
Sheyenne Nat. Grassland
 ND . . . . 46°25N 97°20W **91 D8**
Shiawassee → *MI* . . 43°23N 83°58W **79 F8**
Shiawassee County ☆
 MI . . . . 42°55N 84°10W **79 G7**
Shiawassee Nat. Wildlife Refuge
 MI . . . . 43°21N 84°1W **79 F7**
Shickley *NE* . . . 40°25N 97°43W **84 D8**
Shickshinny *PA* . . 41°9N 76°9W **95 C6**
Shidler *OK* . . . 36°47N 96°40W **93 B7**
Shidler Res. *OK* . . 36°56N 96°40W **93 B7**
Shields *KS* . . . 38°37N 100°27W **74 C3**
Shields *MI* . . . 43°23N 84°3W **79 F7**
Shillington *PA* . . 40°18N 75°58W **95 D7**
Shiloh *GA* . . . 32°49N 84°42W **68 D2**
Shiloh *NJ* . . . 39°28N 75°18W **87 C1**
Shiloh *OH* . . . 40°58N 82°36W **92 C4**
Shiloh Nat. Military Park △
 TN . . . . 35°8N 88°20W **96 E4**
Shin Pond *ME* . . 46°6N 68°33W **76 B4**
Shiner *TX* . . . 29°26N 97°10W **99 H10**
Shinglehouse *PA* . . 41°58N 78°12W **95 C4**
Shingler *GA* . . . 31°35N 83°47W **68 E3**
Shingleton *MI* . . 46°21N 86°28W **79 C5**
Shingletown *CA* . . 40°30N 121°53W **64 C5**
Shinnston *WV* . . 39°24N 80°18W **102 B4**
Shiocton *WI* . . . 44°27N 88°35W **103 D5**
Ship Bottom *NJ* . . 39°39N 74°11W **87 C2**
Ship I. *MS* . . . 30°13N 88°55W **81 F6**
Ship Rock *NM* . . 36°41N 108°50W **88 A2**
Shipman *IL* . . . 39°7N 90°3W **71 D3**
Shipman *VA* . . . 37°43N 78°51W **102 D6**
Shippensburg *PA* . . 40°3N 77°31W **95 D5**
Shippenville *PA* . . 41°15N 79°28W **95 C3**
Shiprock *NM* . . . 36°47N 108°41W **88 A2**
Shipshewana *IN* . . 41°41N 85°35W **72 B5**
Shirley *AR* . . . 35°39N 92°19W **63 C3**
Shirley *IN* . . . 39°53N 85°35W **72 D5**
Shirley *MA* . . . 42°33N 71°39W **78 B3**
Shirley Basin *WY* . . 42°20N 106°10W **104 D8**
Shirley City = Woodlawn
 MD . . . . 39°19N 76°43W **107 B1**
Shirley Mills *ME* . . 45°22N 69°37W **76 C4**
Shishaldin Volcano
 AK . . . . 54°45N 163°58W **61 J7**
Shishmaref *AK* . . 66°15N 166°4W **61 C6**
Shively *KY* . . . 38°12N 85°49W **97 B7**
Shivwits Plateau *AZ* . . 36°15N 113°30W **62 A2**
Shoal Cr. → *IL* . . 38°28N 89°35W **71 E4**
Shoal Cr. → *MO* . . 39°44N 93°32W **82 B3**
Shoal Cr. → *TN* . . 34°50N 87°33W **96 F5**
Shoals *IN* . . . 38°40N 86°47W **72 E4**
Shoalwater Indian Reservation
 WA . . . . 46°40N 75°58W **95 D7**
Shoals *PA* . . . 41°59N 75°58W **95 D7**
Shonto *AZ* . . . 36°36N 110°39W **62 A5**

Shopville *KY* . . . 37°9N 84°29W **97 C8**
Shoreacres *TX* . . 29°36N 95°1W **99 H12**
Shoreham *VT* . . . 43°54N 73°19W **86 C1**
Shoreline *WA* . . . 47°45N 122°18W **118 B3**
Shorewood *WI* . . 43°5N 87°53W **112 B2**
Short Gap *WV* . . 39°33N 78°49W **77 A2**
Shorter *AL* . . . 32°24N 85°57W **60 D5**
Shorterville *AL* . . 31°34N 85°6W **60 E5**
Shortsville *NY* . . 42°57N 77°14W **89 C3**
Shoshone *CA* . . . 35°58N 116°16W **65 H10**
Shoshone *ID* . . . 42°56N 114°25W **70 G4**
Shoshone → *WY* . . 44°52N 108°11W **104 B4**
Shoshone Basin *WY* . . 41°53N 108°5W **104 E4**
Shoshone County ☆
 ID . . . . 47°30N 116°0W **70 B3**
Shoshone Falls *ID* . . 42°36N 114°24W **70 G4**
Shoshone L. *WY* . . 44°22N 110°43W **104 B2**
Shoshone Mts. *NV* . . 39°20N 117°25W **85 C3**
Shoshone Nat. Forest
 WY . . . . 44°20N 109°45W **104 B3**
Shoshoni *WY* . . . 43°14N 108°7W **104 D5**
Shoup *ID* . . . 45°23N 114°17W **70 D7**
Shoveltown MO . . 38°48N 90°16W **117 A2**
Show Low *AZ* . . . 34°15N 110°2W **62 C5**
Showell *MD* . . . 38°24N 75°13W **77 B5**
Shreve *OH* . . . 40°41N 82°1W **92 C4**
Shreveport *LA* . . 32°31N 93°45W **75 B2**
Shrewsbury *MA* . . 42°18N 71°43W **78 B3**
Shrewsbury *PA* . . 39°46N 76°41W **77 A4**
Shubuta *MS* . . . 31°52N 88°42W **81 E5**
Shuksan, Mt. *WA* . . 48°50N 121°36W **101 B4**
Shullsburg *WI* . . 42°35N 90°13W **103 F3**
Shumagin Is. *AK* . . 55°7N 160°30W **61 J7**
Shungnak *AK* . . 66°52N 157°9W **61 C8**
Shuqualak *MS* . . 32°59N 88°34W **81 D5**
Shushan *NY* . . . 43°5N 73°21W **86 C1**
Shutesbury *MA* . . 42°32N 72°25W **78 B2**
Shuyak I. *AK* . . . 58°31N 152°30W **61 G9**
Siasconset *MA* . . 41°16N 69°58W **78 C5**
Sibley *IA* . . . 43°24N 95°45W **73 B3**
Sibley *LA* . . . 32°33N 93°18W **75 B2**
Sibley *MS* . . . 31°23N 91°24W **81 E2**
Sibley County ☆ *MN* . . 44°35N 94°15W **80 F4**
Sicily Island *LA* . . 31°51N 91°40W **75 C4**
Sidell *IL* . . . 39°55N 87°49W **71 D6**
Sidnaw *MI* . . . 46°30N 88°43W **79 C3**
Sidney *AR* . . . 36°0N 91°40W **63 B4**
Sidney *IA* . . . 40°45N 95°39W **73 E3**
Sidney *KS* . . . 37°11N 99°39W **74 D4**
Sidney *MT* . . . 47°43N 104°9W **83 C13**
Sidney *NY* . . . 42°19N 75°24W **89 C5**
Sidney *NE* . . . 41°8N 102°59W **84 C3**
Sidney *OH* . . . 40°17N 84°9W **92 C2**
Sidney Lanier, L. *GA* . . 34°25N 84°4W **68 B2**
Sidon *MS* . . . 33°25N 90°12W **81 C3**
Sierra Blanca *TX* . . 31°11N 105°22W **98 G2**
Sierra Blanca Peak
 NM . . . . 33°23N 105°49W **88 D5**
Sierra City *CA* . . 39°34N 120°38W **64 D6**
Sierra County ☆ *CA* . . 39°40N 121°30W **64 D5**
Sierra County ☆ *NM* . . 33°0N 107°0W **88 D3**
Sierra Madre *CA* . . 34°9N 118°3W **111 B4**
Sierra Madre Mts.
 CA . . . . 34°54N 119°51W **65 J7**
Sierra Nat. Forest
 CA . . . . 37°15N 119°10W **65 F7**
Sierra Nevada *CA* . . 39°0N 120°30W **64 D6**
Sierra Vista *AZ* . . 31°33N 110°18W **62 F5**
Sierraville *CA* . . 39°36N 120°22W **64 D6**
Siesta Key *FL* . . 27°16N 82°33W **67 D6**
Signal Hill *CA* . . 33°48N 118°10W **111 D3**
Signal Mountain *TN* . . 35°7N 85°21W **97 D7**
Signal Pk. *AZ* . . 33°20N 114°2W **62 D1**
Signal Pk. *UT* . . 37°19N 113°20W **100 F2**
Sigourney *IA* . . 41°20N 92°12W **73 D6**
Sigsbee *GA* . . 31°16N 83°52W **68 E3**
Sigurd *UT* . . . 38°50N 111°58W **100 E4**
Sikes *LA* . . . 32°5N 92°29W **75 B3**
Sikeston *MO* . . 36°53N 89°35W **82 G9**
Sil Nakya *AZ* . . 32°13N 111°49W **62 E4**
Silas *AL* . . . 31°46N 88°20W **60 D6**
Siler City *NC* . . 35°44N 79°28W **90 C6**
Siletz *OR* . . . 44°43N 123°55W **94 C2**
Siletz → *OR* . . . 44°54N 124°1W **94 C1**
Siletz Indian Reservation
 OR . . . . 44°47N 123°48W **94 C2**
Silo *OK* . . . 34°3N 96°29W **93 D7**
Siloam Springs *AR* . . 36°11N 94°32W **63 B2**
Silsbee *TX* . . . 30°21N 94°11W **99 G13**
Silsbee *TX* . . . 30°21N 94°11W **99 G13**
Silver *TX* . . . 32°4N 100°40W **98 E7**
Silver, L. *FL* . . 28°35N 81°23W **115 A2**
Silver Bay *MN* . . 47°18N 91°16W **80 C7**
Silver Bell *AZ* . . 32°23N 111°30W **62 E4**
Silver City *IA* . . 41°7N 95°39W **73 D3**
Silver City *MS* . . 33°6N 90°30W **81 C3**
Silver City *NM* . . 32°46N 108°17W **88 D2**
Silver Cliff *CO* . . 38°8N 105°27W **66 D5**
Silver Cr. → *AZ* . . 34°44N 110°2W **62 C5**
Silver Cr. → *OR* . . 43°16N 119°13W **94 D6**
Silver Creek *MS* . . 31°36N 89°59W **81 E4**
Silver Creek *NY* . . 42°33N 79°10W **89 C1**
Silver Creek *NE* . . 41°19N 97°40W **84 C8**
Silver Dollar City
 MO . . . . 36°40N 93°20W **82 E3**
Silver Fork *UT* . . 40°37N 111°36W **117 C4**
Silver Grove *OH* . . 39°2N 84°23W **107 B2**
Silver Hill *MA* . . 42°24N 71°18W **106 A2**
Silver Hill *MD* . . 38°49N 76°55W **119 C4**
Silver L. *NH* . . 43°52N 71°10W **86 C3**
Silver L. *OR* . . 43°12N 119°25W **94 D6**
Silver L. *WA* . . 46°17N 122°47W **101 D3**
Silver Lake *CA* . . 35°21N 116°7W **65 H10**
Silver Lake *KS* . . 39°6N 95°52W **74 B8**
Silver Lake *MN* . . 44°54N 94°12W **80 F4**
Silver Lake *OR* . . 43°8N 121°3W **94 D4**
Silver Lake Res. *CA* . . 34°5N 118°15W **111 B3**
Silver Peak *NV* . . 37°45N 117°38W **85 E3**
Silver Peak Ra.
 U.S.A. . . . . . . 37°45N 117°45W **85 E3**
Silver Run *MD* . . 39°42N 77°3W **77 A3**
Silver Spring *MD* . . 38°59N 77°2W **119 A3**
Silver Springs *FL* . . 29°13N 82°3W **67 B6**
Silver Springs *NV* . . 39°25N 119°14W **85 D1**
Silverdale *WA* . . 47°3N 96°54W **74 D7**
Silverthorne *CO* . . 39°38N 106°4W **66 C4**
Silverton *CO* . . 37°49N 107°40W **66 E3**
Silverton *NJ* . . 40°1N 74°8W **87 B2**
Silverton *OR* . . 45°1N 122°47W **94 C3**
Silverton *TX* . . 34°28N 101°19W **98 C6**
Silverton *WA* . . 48°5N 121°35W **101 B4**
Silverwood *ID* . . 43°34N 119°0W **94 D6**
Silvies → *OR* . . 43°34N 119°0W **94 D6**
Silvis *IL* . . . 41°30N 90°25W **71 B3**
Simi Valley *CA* . . 34°16N 118°47W **65 J8**
Simla *CO* . . . 39°9N 104°5W **66 C6**
Simmesport *LA* . . 30°59N 91°49W **75 D4**
Simmler *CA* . . 35°21N 119°59W **65 H7**
Simms *MT* . . . 47°30N 111°56W **83 C6**

Simnasho *OR* . . . 44°58N 121°21W **94 C4**
Simonton Lake *IN* . . 41°44N 85°59W **72 B5**
Simpson *KS* . . . 39°23N 97°56W **74 B6**
Simpson *LA* . . . 31°16N 93°1W **75 C2**
Simpson County ☆
 KY . . . . 36°45N 86°35W **96 D6**
Simpson County ☆
 MS . . . . 31°53N 89°58W **81 E4**
Simpson Park Mts.
 NV . . . . 39°50N 116°35W **85 C4**
Simpsonville *SC* . . 34°44N 82°15W **90 D3**
Sims *IL* . . . 38°22N 88°32W **71 E5**
Simsbury *CT* . . . 41°53N 72°48W **78 C2**
Sinai *SD* . . . 44°15N 97°3W **91 F8**
Sinclair *WY* . . . 41°47N 107°7W **104 E6**
Sinclair, L. *GA* . . 33°8N 83°12W **68 C3**
Sinclairville *NY* . . 42°16N 79°16W **89 C1**
Sing Sing = Ossining
 NY . . . . 41°10N 73°55W **87 A3**
Singac *NJ* . . . 40°53N 74°14W **114 A1**
Singer *LA* . . . 30°39N 93°25W **75 D2**
Sinking Spring *OH* . . 39°4N 83°23W **92 D3**
Sinnemahoning *PA* . . 41°19N 78°6W **95 C4**
Sinton *TX* . . . 28°2N 97°31W **99 J10**
Sioux Center *IA* . . 43°5N 96°11W **73 B2**
Sioux City *IA* . . 42°30N 96°24W **73 C2**
Sioux County ☆ *IA* . . 43°5N 96°10W **73 B2**
Sioux County ☆ *ND* . . 46°0N 101°0W **91 D5**
Sioux County ☆ *NE* . . 42°30N 103°45W **84 B2**
Sioux Falls *SD* . . 43°33N 96°44W **91 G9**
Sioux Rapids *IA* . . 42°53N 95°9W **73 C3**
Sipsey → *AL* . . . 33°0N 88°10W **60 C2**
Siren *WI* . . . 45°47N 92°24W **103 C1**
Sirmans *FL* . . . 30°21N 83°39W **67 A5**
Siskiyou County ☆
 CA . . . . 41°30N 122°40W **64 B4**
Siskiyou Mts. *U.S.A.* . . 42°0N 122°40W **64 B3**
Siskiyou Nat. Forest
 OR . . . . 42°20N 124°0W **94 E2**
Siskiyou Summit *OR* . . 42°3N 122°48W **94 E3**
Sisquoc → *CA* . . 34°54N 120°18W **65 J6**
Sisseton *SD* . . . 45°40N 97°3W **91 E8**
Sisseton Indian Reservation = Lake Traverse Indian Reservation
 ND . . . . 46°0N 97°10W **91 E8**
Sisson = Mount Shasta
 CA . . . .
Sissonville *WV* . . 38°32N 81°38W **102 C3**
Sister Bay *WI* . . 45°11N 87°7W **103 C6**
Sisters *OR* . . . 44°18N 121°33W **94 C4**
Sistersville *WV* . . 39°34N 80°59W **102 B4**
Sitka *AK* . . . 57°3N 135°20W **61 H14**
Sitka *KS* . . . 37°11N 99°39W **74 D4**
Sitka → *AK* . . . 57°10N 135°20W **61 H14**
Sitka Nat. Historical Park △
 U.S.A. . . . . . . 57°3N 135°19W **61 H14**
Sitkinak I. *AK* . . 56°33N 154°10W **61 H9**
Siufaalete Pt.
 Amer. Samoa . . 14°17S 169°29W **105 f**
Siuslaw → *OR* . . 44°1N 124°8W **94 C1**
Siuslaw Nat. Forest
 OR . . . . 44°15N 123°50W **94 C2**
Six Flags Great Adventure
 NJ . . . . 40°10N 74°27W **87 B2**
Six Gun City *NH* . . 44°25N 71°29W **86 B3**
Six Rivers Nat. Forest
 CA . . . . 41°0N 123°30W **64 C2**
Skagit → *WA* . . 48°23N 122°22W **101 B3**
Skagit B. *WA* . . 48°20N 122°34W **101 B3**
Skagit County ☆
 WA . . . . 48°30N 121°30W **101 B4**
Skagway *AK* . . . 59°28N 135°19W **61 G14**
Skagway-Hoonah-Angoon ☆
 AK . . . . 58°45N 136°15W **61 G13**
Skamania County ☆
 WA . . . . 46°0N 122°0W **101 D4**
Skaneateles *NY* . . 42°57N 76°26W **89 C4**
Skanee *MI* . . . 46°52N 88°13W **79 C3**
Skedee *OK* . . . 36°23N 96°42W **93 B7**
Skellytown *TX* . . 35°34N 101°11W **98 B6**
Skiatook *OK* . . 36°20N 96°0W **93 B7**
Skiatook L. *OK* . . 36°20N 96°10W **93 B7**
Skidmore *MO* . . 40°17N 95°5W **82 A1**
Skidmore *TX* . . 28°15N 97°41W **99 J10**
Skidway Lake *MI* . . 44°11N 84°2W **79 E7**
Skillet Fork → *IL* . . 38°5N 88°5W **71 E5**
Skokie *IL* . . . 42°3N 87°46W **108 A2**
Skokie *IL* . . . 42°3N 87°46W **108 A2**
Skokie Heritage Museum
 IL . . . . 42°0N 123°3W **64 C2**
Skowhegan *ME* . . 44°46N 69°43W **76 D4**
Skull Valley *AZ* . . 34°30N 112°41W **62 C3**
Skull Valley Indian Reservation
 UT . . . . 40°25N 112°45W **100 C3**
Skuna → *MS* . . 33°54N 89°41W **81 C4**
Skunk → *IA* . . 40°42N 91°7W **73 E7**
Sky Lake *FL* . . 28°27N 81°23W **115 B2**
Skykomish *WA* . . 47°42N 121°22W **101 C4**
Skykomish → *WA* . . 47°49N 121°23W **101 C3**
Skyland *AL* . . . 33°53N 84°19W **106 A3**
Skyline *AL* . . . 34°49N 86°7W **60 B4**
Skyway *WA* . . . 47°29N 122°15W **118 C4**
Slagle *LA* . . . 31°12N 93°9W **75 C2**
Slanesville *WV* . . 39°22N 78°31W **77 A2**
Slate Creek *ID* . . 45°38N 116°17W **70 D2**
Slate Spring *MS* . . 33°44N 89°22W **81 C4**
Slater *IA* . . . 41°53N 93°41W **73 D5**
Slater *MO* . . . 39°13N 93°4W **82 B3**
Slater *WY* . . . 42°49N 104°49W **104 E8**
Slatington *PA* . . 40°45N 75°37W **87 B1**
Slaton *TX* . . . 33°26N 101°39W **98 D6**
Slaughter *LA* . . 30°43N 91°9W **75 D4**
Slaughter Beach *DE* . . 38°52N 75°18W **77 B5**
Slaughters *KY* . . 37°29N 87°30W **96 C5**
Slaughterville *OK* . . 35°5N 97°20W **93 C6**
Slayton *MN* . . . 43°59N 95°45W **80 G3**
Sledge *MS* . . . 34°26N 90°13W **81 B3**
Sleeper *MO* . . . 37°36N 92°36W **82 D4**
Sleeping Bear Dunes Nat. Lakeshore
 MI . . . . 44°50N 86°5W **79 E5**
Sleeping Bear Pt. *MI* . . 44°55N 86°3W **79 E5**
Sleepy Eye *MN* . . 44°18N 94°43W **80 F4**
Sleetmute *AK* . . 61°42N 157°10W **61 F8**
Slemp *KY* . . . 37°5N 83°6W **97 C9**
Slick *OK* . . . 35°47N 96°16W **93 C7**
Slick Rock *CO* . . 38°3N 108°54W **66 D2**
Slide Mt. *NY* . . 42°0N 74°25W **89 D6**
Slidell *LA* . . . 30°17N 89°47W **75 D6**
Sligo *PA* . . . 41°6N 79°29W **95 C3**
Slim Buttes *SD* . . 45°20N 103°15W **91 E2**
Slippery Rock *PA* . . 41°4N 80°3W **95 C2**
Sloan *IA* . . . 42°14N 96°14W **73 C2**
Sloan *NV* . . . 35°57N 115°13W **85 G8**
Sloat *CA* . . . 39°52N 120°44W **64 D6**
Slocomb *AL* . . . 31°7N 85°36W **60 E5**
Slocum *RI* . . . 41°32N 71°31W **78 C3**
Slope County ☆ *ND* . . 46°20N 103°30W **91 D2**
Smackover *AR* . . 33°22N 92°44W **63 E3**
Small, C. *ME* . . 43°42N 69°51W **76 E4**
Smarr *GA* . . . 32°59N 83°53W **68 D3**
Smarts Mt. *NH* . . 43°48N 72°3W **86 C3**
Smethport *PA* . . 41°49N 78°27W **95 C4**
Smiley *TX* . . . 29°16N 97°38W **99 H10**
Smith *NV* . . . 38°47N 119°21W **85 D2**
Smith → *NC* . . 36°27N 79°43W **90 B6**
Smith B. *AK* . . 70°30N 154°20W **61 A9**
Smith Center *KS* . . 39°47N 98°47W **74 B5**
Smith County ☆ *KS* . . 39°47N 98°45W **74 B5**
Smith County ☆ *MS* . . 32°1N 89°23W **81 D4**
Smith County ☆ *TN* . . 36°5N 85°57W **97 D7**

Smith County ☆ *TX* . . 32°21N 95°18W **99 E12**
Smith Forest Preserve
 IL . . . . 41°59N 87°45W **108 B2**
Smith I. *MD* . . . 38°0N 76°0W **77 B4**
Smith I. *NC* . . . 33°53N 77°59W **90 E8**
Smith I. *VA* . . . 37°9N 75°53W **102 D9**
Smith Lake *OR* . . 45°36N 122°43W **116 A1**
Smith Mountain L.
 VA . . . . 37°2N 79°30W **102 D5**
Smith River *CA* . . 41°56N 124°9W **64 B1**
Smith River Nat. Recr. Area □
 CA . . . . 41°55N 123°50W **64 B2**
Smithburg *NJ* . . 40°13N 74°21W **87 B2**
Smithburg *WV* . . 39°17N 80°44W **102 B4**
Smithdale *MS* . . 31°20N 90°41W **81 E3**
Smithfield *NC* . . 35°31N 78°21W **90 C7**
Smithfield *RI* . . 41°55N 71°33W **78 C3**
Smithfield *UT* . . 41°50N 111°50W **100 B4**
Smithfield *VA* . . 36°59N 76°38W **102 E8**
Smithland *IA* . . 42°14N 95°56W **73 C3**
Smithland *KY* . . 37°9N 88°24W **96 C4**
Smiths *AL* . . . 32°32N 85°6W **60 D5**
Smiths Ferry *ID* . . 44°18N 116°5W **70 F2**
Smiths Grove *KY* . . 37°3N 86°12W **96 C6**
Smithsburg *MD* . . 39°39N 77°35W **77 A3**
Smithton *MO* . . 38°41N 93°5W **82 C3**
Smithton *PA* . . 40°9N 79°44W **95 D3**
Smithville *GA* . . 31°54N 84°15W **68 E2**
Smithville *MD* . . 38°46N 75°45W **77 B5**
Smithville *MS* . . 34°4N 88°23W **81 B5**
Smithville *OK* . . 34°28N 94°39W **93 D9**
Smithville *TN* . . 35°58N 85°49W **97 E7**
Smithville *TX* . . 30°1N 97°10W **99 G10**
Smithville *WV* . . 39°4N 81°6W **102 B3**
Smoaks *SC* . . . 33°5N 80°49W **90 E5**
Smoke Creek Desert
 NV . . . . 40°30N 119°40W **85 B1**
Smokey Point *WA* . . 48°9N 122°11W **101 B3**
Smoky Dome *ID* . . 43°30N 114°56W **70 F4**
Smoky Hill → *KS* . . 39°4N 96°48W **74 B7**
Smoky Hills *KS* . . 39°15N 99°30W **74 B4**
Smoky Mts. *ID* . . 43°40N 114°38W **70 F4**
Smolan *KS* . . . 38°44N 97°41W **74 C6**
Smoot *WY* . . . 42°37N 110°55W **104 D2**
Smugglers Notch Resort
 VT . . . . 44°33N 72°47W **86 B2**
Smyrna *DE* . . . 39°18N 75°36W **77 A5**
Smyrna *GA* . . . 33°53N 84°31W **68 C2**
Smyrna *TN* . . . 35°59N 86°31W **96 E6**
Smyrna Mills *ME* . . 46°8N 68°10W **76 B5**
Smyth County ☆
 VA . . . . 36°55N 81°25W **102 E3**
Snail Lake *MN* . . 45°4N 93°7W **113 A3**
Snake → *ID* . . 46°12N 119°2W **101 D6**
Snake → *MN* . . 48°26N 97°7W **80 B1**
Snake → *MN* . . 45°49N 92°46W **80 E6**
Snake Creek Canal
 FL . . . . 25°57N 80°19W **112 C2**
Snake Mts. *NV* . . 41°25N 115°0W **85 A6**
Snake Range *NV* . . 39°0N 114°20W **85 D6**
Snake River Birds of Prey Nat.
Conservation Area □
 ID . . . . 43°0N 116°19W **70 F2**
Snake River Plain *ID* . . 42°50N 114°0W **70 G4**
Snake Valley *UT* . . 39°30N 113°55W **100 D2**
Snakenden Branch →
 VA . . . . 38°55N 77°18W **119 B1**
Sneads Ferry *NC* . . 34°33N 77°24W **90 D8**
Sneedville *TN* . . 36°32N 83°13W **97 D9**
Snelling *CA* . . . 37°31N 120°26W **64 F4**
Snellville *GA* . . 33°51N 84°1W **68 C2**
Snohomish *WA* . . 47°55N 122°6W **101 C3**
Snohomish County ☆
 WA . . . . 48°0N 121°30W **101 B4**
Snoqualmie *WA* . . 47°31N 121°49W **101 C4**
Snoqualmie Pass
 WA . . . . 47°25N 121°25W **101 C4**
Snover *MI* . . . 43°28N 82°58W **79 F9**
Snow Hill *AL* . . 32°0N 87°0W **60 D4**
Snow Hill *MD* . . 38°11N 75°24W **77 B5**
Snow Hill *NC* . . 35°27N 77°40W **90 C8**
Snow L. *WY* . . 43°6N 109°46W **104 C4**
Snow Mt. *CA* . . 39°23N 122°45W **64 D4**
Snow Mt. *ME* . . 45°18N 70°48W **76 C3**
Snow Pk. *WA* . . 48°35N 118°29W **101 B7**
Snow Shoe *PA* . . 41°2N 77°57W **95 C5**
Snow Water L. *NV* . . 40°48N 114°59W **85 B6**
Snowball *AR* . . 35°55N 92°49W **63 C3**
Snowdon *AL* . . 32°15N 86°18W **60 D4**
Snowflake *AZ* . . 34°30N 110°5W **62 C5**
Snowmass *CO* . . 39°20N 106°59W **66 C4**
Snowmass Mt. *CO* . . 39°8N 107°5W **66 C3**
Snowshoe *WV* . . 38°24N 80°0W **102 C4**
Snowshoe Ski Resort
 WV . . . . 38°25N 80°0W **102 C4**
Snowville *UT* . . 41°58N 112°43W **100 B3**
Snowy Mt. *NY* . . 43°42N 74°23W **89 B6**
Snowyside Pk. *ID* . . 43°57N 114°58W **70 F4**
Snug Harbor *FL* . . 27°12N 82°13W **119 B3**
Snyder *NE* . . . 41°42N 96°48W **84 C9**
Snyder *OK* . . . 34°40N 98°57W **93 D5**
Snyder *TX* . . . 32°44N 100°55W **98 E7**
Snyder County ☆ *PA* . . 40°50N 77°0W **95 D5**
Soap Lake *WA* . . 47°23N 119°29W **101 C6**
Socastee *SC* . . 33°41N 78°59W **90 E7**
Social Circle *GA* . . 33°39N 83°43W **68 C3**
Society Hill *AL* . . 32°26N 85°27W **60 D5**
Society Hill *SC* . . 34°31N 79°51W **90 D6**
Socorro *TX* . . . 31°39N 106°18W **98 H1**
Socorro County ☆ *NM* . . 34°0N 107°0W **88 C4**
Socorro *NM* . . 34°4N 106°54W **88 C4**
Soda L. *CA* . . 35°10N 116°4W **65 H10**
Soda Springs *CA* . . 39°20N 120°23W **64 D6**
Soda Springs *ID* . . 42°39N 111°36W **70 G7**
Sodaville *OR* . . 44°29N 122°52W **94 C3**
Soddy-Daisy *TN* . . 35°17N 85°10W **97 D7**
Sodus *NY* . . . 43°14N 77°4W **89 B3**
Sodus Point *NY* . . 43°16N 76°59W **89 B3**
Sol Duc → *WA* . . 48°3N 124°1W **101 C1**
Solana Beach *CA* . . 32°58N 117°16W **65 L9**
Solano County ☆
 CA . . . . 38°21N 121°50W **64 E5**
Soldier *KS* . . . 39°35N 95°46W **73 D3**
Soldier *KS* . . . 39°32N 95°58W **74 B8**
Soldier Summit *UT* . . 39°56N 111°5W **100 D4**
Soldiers Grove *WI* . . 43°24N 90°47W **103 E3**
Soldotna *AK* . . 60°29N 151°3W **61 F10**
Soledad *CA* . . 36°26N 121°20W **64 G4**
Solen *ND* . . . 46°23N 100°48W **91 D5**
Solomon *AZ* . . 32°49N 109°38W **62 E6**
Solomon → *KS* . . 39°29N 98°26W **74 B6**
Solomon, N. Fork →
 KS . . . . 39°25N 99°12W **74 B4**
Solomon, S. Fork →
 KS . . . . 39°29N 98°26W **74 B6**
Solomons *MD* . . 38°19N 76°27W **77 B4**
Solon *ME* . . . 44°57N 69°52W **76 D4**
Solon *IA* . . . 41°48N 91°29W **73 D7**
Solon Springs *WI* . . 46°22N 91°49W **103 B2**
Solsberry *IN* . . 39°4N 86°59W **72 D4**
Solvang *CA* . . 34°36N 120°8W **65 J6**
Solvay *NY* . . . 43°3N 76°13W **89 B4**
Somers *IA* . . . 41°59N 72°27W **78 C2**
Somers *MT* . . 48°5N 114°13W **83 B3**
Somers Point *NJ* . . 39°20N 74°36W **87 C2**
Somerset *CO* . . 38°56N 107°28W **66 C3**
Somerset *KY* . . 37°5N 84°36W **97 C8**

Somerset *MA* . . . 41°47N 71°8W **78 C3**
Somerset *MI* . . . 38°57N 77°5W **118 B3**
Somerset *MI* . . . 42°3N 84°23W **79 G7**
Somerset *OH* . . . 39°48N 82°18W **92 D4**
Somerset *PA* . . . 40°1N 79°5W **95 D3**
Somerset *TX* . . . 29°14N 98°40W **99 H9**
Somerset County ☆
 ME . . . . 45°30N 70°0W **76 C4**
Somerset County ☆
 MD . . . . 38°10N 75°50W **77 B5**
Somerset County ☆
 NJ . . . . 40°35N 74°35W **87 B2**
Somerset County ☆ *PA* . . 40°0N 79°0W **95 E4**
Somerset Res. *VT* . . 43°0N 72°57W **86 C2**
Somersworth *NH* . . 43°16N 70°52W **86 C4**
Somerton *AZ* . . 32°36N 114°43W **62 E1**
Somervell County ☆
 TX . . . . 32°14N 97°45W **99 E10**
Somerville *AL* . . 34°22N 71°5W **106 A3**
Somerville *NJ* . . 40°35N 74°38W **87 B2**
Somerville *OH* . . 39°34N 84°38W **92 D2**
Somerville *TN* . . 35°15N 89°21W **96 E3**
Somerville *TX* . . 30°21N 96°32W **99 G11**
Somerville, L. *TX* . . 30°19N 96°31W **99 G11**
Somes Bar *CA* . . 41°23N 123°29W **64 B3**
Sondheimer *LA* . . 32°33N 91°11W **75 B4**
Sonny Bono Nat. Wildlife Refuge □ *CA* . . 33°15N 115°40W **65 K11**
Sonoma *CA* . . . 38°18N 122°28W **64 E4**
Sonoma, L. *CA* . . 38°43N 123°1W **64 E3**
Sonoma County ☆
 CA . . . . 38°30N 123°0W **64 E4**
Sonoma Peak *NV* . . 40°52N 117°36W **85 B3**
Sonora *CA* . . . 37°59N 120°23W **64 F6**
Sonora *KY* . . . 37°32N 85°54W **97 C7**
Sonora *TX* . . . 30°34N 100°39W **98 G7**
Sonoran Desert *AZ* . . 33°40N 113°30W **62 D2**
Sonoran Desert Nat. Monument □
 AZ . . . . 33°10N 112°45W **62 D3**
Sontag *MS* . . . 31°39N 90°12W **81 E3**
Sony Picture Studio
 CA . . . . 34°1N 118°4W **111 B2**
Sooner L. *OK* . . 36°28N 95°53W **93 B8**
Sopchoppy *FL* . . 30°4N 84°29W **67 A4**
Soper *OK* . . . 34°2N 95°42W **93 D8**
Soperton *GA* . . 32°23N 82°35W **68 D4**
Sophia *WV* . . . 37°42N 81°15W **102 D3**
Sorento *IL* . . . 39°1N 89°35W **71 D4**
Sorrento *LA* . . 30°11N 90°51W **75 D5**
Soso *MS* . . . 31°45N 89°17W **81 E4**
Souderton *PA* . . 40°19N 75°19W **87 B1**
Sougahatchee Cr. →
 AL . . . . 32°36N 85°54W **60 D5**
Souhegan → *NH* . . 42°51N 71°29W **86 D3**
Sound Beach *NY* . . 40°49N 73°53W **114 B3**
Soundview *NY* . . 40°49N 73°53W **114 B3**
Sour Lake *TX* . . 30°9N 94°25W **99 G13**
Souris → *N. Amer.* . . 48°55N 100°40W **91 B5**
Souris → *N. Amer.* . . 49°40N 99°34W **56 A4**
Souris → *N. Amer.* . . 49°0N 100°57W **91 B5**
South → *NC* . . 34°20N 78°33W **90 D7**
South Amboy *NJ* . . 40°29N 74°18W **87 B2**
South Anna → *VA* . . 37°48N 77°25W **102 D7**
South Ashburnham
 MA . . . . 42°37N 71°57W **78 B3**
South Baldy Pk. *NM* . . 34°0N 107°11W **88 C3**
South Baltimore
 MD . . . . 39°16N 76°36W **107 B2**
South Barre *MA* . . 42°23N 72°6W **78 B2**
South Bass I. *OH* . . 41°39N 82°49W **92 B4**
South Bay *FL* . . 26°40N 80°43W **67 E8**
South Beach *FL* . . 25°46N 80°7W **112 D3**
South Beach *NY* . . 40°34N 74°4W **114 C2**
South Beach *WA* . . 47°34N 122°30W **118 C3**
South Beloit *IL* . . 42°29N 89°2W **71 A4**
South Bend *IN* . . 41°41N 86°15W **72 B4**
South Bend *WA* . . 46°40N 123°48W **101 D2**
South Bend Park
 GA . . . . 33°42N 84°23W **106 B2**
South Berwick *ME* . . 43°14N 70°49W **86 C4**
South Bloomfield
 OH . . . . 39°43N 82°59W **92 D4**
South Boardman *MI* . . 44°38N 85°17W **79 E6**
South Boston *MA* . . 42°20N 71°2W **106 A4**
South Boston *VA* . . 36°42N 78°54W **102 E6**
South Branch Potomac →
 WV . . . . 39°32N 78°35W **102 B6**
South Branch Two →
 MN . . . . 48°46N 96°56W **80 B2**
South Burlington *VT* . . 44°28N 73°13W **86 B1**
South C. = Kalae *HI* . . 18°55N 155°41W **69 E6**
South Carolina □
 U.S.A. . . . . . . 34°0N 81°0W **90 D5**
South Carthage *TN* . . 36°15N 85°57W **97 D7**
South Carver *MA* . . 41°51N 70°54W **78 C4**
South Chaplin *CT* . . 41°46N 72°9W **78 C2**
South Charleston
 OH . . . . 39°50N 83°38W **92 D3**
South Charleston
 WV . . . . 38°22N 81°44W **102 C3**
South Charlestown
 NH . . . . 43°12N 72°26W **86 C2**
South China *ME* . . 44°24N 69°34W **76 D4**
South Cle Elum
 WA . . . . 47°11N 120°57W **101 C5**
South Coffeyville *OK* . . 36°59N 95°37W **93 B8**
South Colton *NY* . . 44°31N 74°53W **89 A6**
South Congaree *SC* . . 33°53N 81°9W **90 D4**
South Dakota □
 U.S.A. . . . . . . 44°15N 100°0W **91 F6**
South Dartmouth
 MA . . . . 41°31N 70°57W **78 C4**
South Dayton *NY* . . 42°21N 79°4W **89 C1**
South Daytona *FL* . . 29°10N 81°0W **67 B7**
South Decatur *GA* . . 33°44N 84°16W **106 B3**
South Deerfield *MA* . . 42°29N 72°37W **78 B2**
South Deering *IL* . . 41°42N 87°33W **108 C3**
South Easton *MA* . . 42°3N 71°5W **78 B3**
South Egremont *MA* . . 42°10N 73°25W **78 C1**
South El Monte *CA* . . 34°3N 118°2W **111 B4**
South English *IA* . . 41°27N 92°5W **73 D6**
South Fabius → *MO* . . 39°54N 91°30W **82 B5**
South Fallsburg *NY* . . 41°43N 74°38W **89 D6**
South Floral Park
 NY . . . . 40°43N 73°42W **114 B4**
South Fork *CO* . . 37°40N 106°37W **66 E4**
South Fork *PA* . . 40°22N 78°48W **95 D4**
South Fork American →
 CA . . . . 38°57N 120°59W **64 E6**
South Fork Edisto →
 SC . . . . 33°16N 80°54W **90 E5**
South Fork Forked Deer →
 TN . . . . 36°0N 89°26W **96 E3**
South Fork Grand →
 SD . . . . 45°43N 102°17W **91 E3**
South Fork Indian Reservation
 NV . . . . 40°45N 115°40W **85 B5**
South Fork John Day →
 OR . . . . 44°29N 119°31W **94 C6**
South Fork Kentucky →
 KY . . . . 37°34N 83°43W **97 C9**
South Fork Milk →
 MT . . . . 48°4N 106°19W **83 B11**
South Fork Moreau →
 SD . . . . 45°0N 102°50W **91 E3**
South Fork Obion →
 TN . . . . 36°12N 88°56W **96 D4**
South Fork Owyhee →
 ID . . . . 42°16N 116°53W **70 G2**
South Fork Powder →
 WY . . . . 43°40N 106°30W **104 C6**

South Fork Republican →
 NE . . . . 40°3N 101°31W **74 A2**
South Fork Sappa Cr. →
 KS . . . . 39°47N 100°35W **74 B3**
South Fork Selway →
 ID . . . . 46°10N 115°58W **70 C3**
South Fork Shenandoah →
 VA . . . . 38°57N 78°12W **102 C6**
South Fork Shoshone →
 WY . . . . 44°22N 109°14W **104 B3**
South Fork Solomon →
 KS . . . . 39°28N 98°26W **74 B5**
South Fork South Branch Potomac → *WV* . . 39°5N 78°59W **102 B6**
South Fork Spring →
 AR . . . . 36°19N 91°30W **63 B4**
South Fox I. *MI* . . 45°25N 85°51W **79 D6**
South Fulton *TN* . . 36°30N 88°52W **96 D4**
South Gate *CA* . . 33°56N 118°12W **111 C3**
South Gorin *MO* . . 40°22N 92°1W **82 A4**
South Grand → *MO* . . 38°17N 93°25W **82 C3**
South Greensburg
 PA . . . . 40°17N 79°33W **95 D3**
South Hadley *MA* . . 42°16N 72°35W **78 B2**
South Hadley Falls
 MA . . . . 42°14N 72°36W **78 B2**
South Hamilton *MA* . . 42°37N 70°53W **78 B4**
South Haven *KS* . . 37°3N 97°24W **74 D6**
South Haven *MI* . . 42°24N 86°16W **79 G5**
South Heart *ND* . . 46°52N 102°59W **91 D3**
South Hempsted *NY* . . 40°40N 73°36W **114 B5**
South Hero *VT* . . 44°39N 73°19W **86 B1**
South Hill *VA* . . 36°44N 78°8W **102 E6**
South Holston L. *TN* . . 36°31N 82°5W **97 D10**
South Hooksett *NH* . . 43°2N 71°26W **86 D3**
South Hutchinson *KS* . . 38°2N 97°56W **74 C6**
South I. *SC* . . . 33°10N 79°11W **90 E6**
South Jacksonville *IL* . . 39°42N 90°14W **71 D3**
South Jordan *UT* . . 40°33N 111°55W **117 C2**
South Lake Tahoe
 CA . . . . 38°57N 119°59W **64 E7**
South Lancaster *MA* . . 42°27N 71°41W **78 B3**
South Lawn *MD* . . 38°47N 77°0W **119 C3**
South Lebanon *OH* . . 39°22N 84°13W **92 D2**
South Lincoln *MA* . . 42°24N 71°19W **106 A2**
South Loup → *NE* . . 41°4N 98°39W **84 C7**
South Lyon *MI* . . 42°28N 83°39W **79 G8**
South Manitou I. *MI* . . 45°2N 86°8W **79 D5**
South Marsh I. *MD* . . 38°6N 76°2W **77 B4**
South Merrimack
 NH . . . . 42°49N 71°34W **86 D3**
South Miami *FL* . . 25°42N 80°17W **112 D1**
South Middleboro
 MA . . . . 41°45N 70°50W **78 C4**
South Milwaukee
 WI . . . . 42°55N 87°52W **103 F6**
South Mountain *AZ* . . 33°22N 112°4W **116 C2**
South Mountain *MD* . . 39°27N 77°40W **77 A3**
South Mountain *PA* . . 39°51N 77°29W **77 A3**
South Mountain *UT* . . 40°28N 112°2W **117 D1**
South Mountain Park
 AZ . . . . 33°20N 112°8W **116 C2**
South Mountain Reservation
 NJ . . . . 40°45N 74°17W **114 B1**
South Mountains
 AZ . . . . 33°19N 112°4W **116 C2**
South Mt. *ID* . . 42°44N 116°54W **70 G2**
South Newport *GA* . . 31°38N 81°24W **68 E5**
South Newtane *VT* . . 42°55N 72°48W **86 D2**
South Ogden *UT* . . 41°12N 111°58W **100 B4**
South Orange *NJ* . . 40°44N 74°15W **114 B1**
South Otselic *NY* . . 42°39N 75°47W **89 C5**
South Ozone Park
 NY . . . . 40°41N 73°49W **114 B4**
South Paris *ME* . . 44°14N 70°31W **76 D3**
South Park *PA* . . 40°18N 79°59W **116 C1**
South Pasadena *CA* . . 34°7N 118°8W **111 B4**
South Pasadena *FL* . . 27°45N 82°44W **119 C2**
South Pass *LA* . . 29°3N 89°12W **75 E6**
South Pass → *WY* . . 42°22N 108°55W **104 D4**
South Pass City
 WY . . . . 42°28N 108°48W **104 D4**
South Pekin *IL* . . 40°30N 89°39W **71 C4**
South Pittsburg *TN* . . 35°1N 85°42W **97 E7**
South Platte → *NE* . . 41°7N 100°42W **84 C5**
South Point *OH* . . 38°25N 82°35W **92 E4**
South Pomfret *VT* . . 43°40N 72°33W **86 C2**
South Ponte Vedra Beach
 FL . . . . 30°3N 81°20W **67 A7**
South Portland *ME* . . 43°38N 70°15W **76 E3**
South Range *MI* . . 47°4N 88°38W **79 B3**
South Res. *MA* . . 42°26N 71°6W **106 A4**
South River *NJ* . . 40°27N 74°23W **87 B2**
South Royalton *VT* . . 43°49N 72°32W **86 C2**
South St. Paul *MN* . . 44°53N 93°2W **113 B3**
South St. Paul Municipal ✈
 MN . . . . 44°51N 93°1W **113 B3**
South Salt Lake
 UT . . . . 40°43N 111°53W **117 B2**
South San Francisco
 CA . . . . 37°38N 122°26W **118 C2**
South San Gabriel →
 CA . . . . 34°3N 118°6W **111 B4**
South Sanford *ME* . . 43°25N 70°45W **86 C4**
South Seaville *NJ* . . 39°11N 74°46W **87 C2**
South Shore *KY* . . 38°43N 82°59W **97 B9**
South Shore *SD* . . 45°7N 96°56W **91 E9**
South Shore Park
 WI . . . . 42°57N 87°52W **112 C2**
South Sioux City *NE* . . 42°28N 96°24W **84 B9**
South Sister *OR* . . 44°4N 121°51W **94 C4**
South Skunk → *IA* . . 41°15N 92°3W **73 D6**
South Stoddard *NH* . . 43°4N 72°7W **86 C2**
South Strafford *VT* . . 43°49N 72°23W **86 C2**
South Sudbury *MA* . . 42°21N 71°26W **106 A1**
South Sulphur →
 TX . . . . 33°23N 95°18W **99 D12**
South Torrington
 WY . . . . 42°3N 104°11W **104 D8**
South Tucson *AZ* . . 32°12N 110°58W **62 E5**
South Umpqua →
 OR . . . . 43°16N 123°27W **94 D2**
South Valley *NM* . . 35°1N 106°41W **88 B4**
South Valley Stream
 NY . . . . 40°39N 73°43W **114 C4**
South Venice *FL* . . 27°3N 82°25W **67 D6**
South Wayne *WI* . . 42°34N 89°53W **103 F4**
South Weare *NH* . . 43°5N 71°45W **86 C3**
South Webster *OH* . . 38°49N 82°44W **92 E4**
South Wellfleet *MA* . . 41°55N 69°58W **78 C5**
South West City *MO* . . 36°31N 94°37W **82 E2**
South Whitley *IN* . . 41°5N 85°38W **72 B5**
South Williamson
 KY . . . . 37°40N 82°17W **97 C10**
South Williamsport
 PA . . . . 41°13N 77°0W **95 C6**
South Windsor *CT* . . 41°49N 72°37W **78 C2**
South Woodstock *VT* . . 43°35N 72°31W **86 C2**
South Yarmouth *MA* . . 41°40N 70°10W **78 C4**
South Zanesville *OH* . . 39°53N 82°0W **92 D4**
Southampton *MA* . . 42°14N 72°44W **78 B2**
Southampton *NY* . . 40°53N 72°23W **78 C7**
Southampton County ☆
 VA . . . . 36°43N 77°4W **102 E7**
Southard *OK* . . 36°4N 98°29W **93 B5**
Southaven *MS* . . 34°59N 90°9W **81 A3**
Southbridge *MA* . . 42°5N 72°2W **78 B2**
Southbury *CT* . . 41°29N 73°13W **78 C1**
Southeast C. *AK* . . 62°56N 169°39W **61 E5**
Southeast Fairbanks ☆
 AK . . . . 63°45N 143°15W **61 E12**

Southern California, University of
  CA.... 34°1N 118°17W 111 B3
Southern Pines NC... 35°11N 79°24W 90 C6
Southern Ute Indian Reservation
  CO.... 37°10N 107°30W 66 E3
Southfield MI.... 42°28N 83°15W 109 A2
Southington CT.... 41°36N 72°53W 78 C2
Southlake TX.... 32°56N 97°8W 109 A3
Southland TX.... 33°22N 101°33W 98 D6
Southold NY.... 41°4N 72°26W 78 C2
Southport NC.... 33°55N 78°1W 90 E7
Southport NY.... 42°3N 76°49W 89 C4
Southside AL.... 33°55N 86°1W 60 C4
Southside WV.... 38°43N 81°58W 102 C3
Southside Place TX 29°42N 95°26W 110 B2
Southton TX.... 29°17N 98°25W 117 D3
Southwest Florida Int. ✈ (RSW)
  FL... 26°32N 81°45W 67 E7
Southwest Harbor
  ME... 44°17N 68°20W 76 D5
Southwest Museum
  CA... 34°6N 118°13W 111 B3
Southwest Pass LA. 29°56N 89°17W 75 E6
Southwest Pt.
  U.S. Virgin Is.. 17°40N 64°55W 105 H18
Southwick MA... 42°3N 72°46W 78 B2
Southwood Acres CT 41°59N 72°33W 78 C2
Southworth WA... 47°30N 122°30W 118 C2
Spalding ID.... 46°27N 116°49W 70 C2
Spalding NE.... 41°42N 98°22W 84 C7
Spalding County ☆
  GA... 33°15N 84°15W 68 C2
Spanaway WA... 47°6N 122°26W 101 C3
Spangle WA.... 47°26N 117°23W 101 C8
Spanish Fork UT.. 40°7N 111°39W 100 C4
Spanish Fort AL.. 30°40N 87°53W 60 F3
Spanish Lake MO.. 38°47N 90°12W 117 A2
Spanish Lake County Park ○
  MO... 38°47N 90°12W 117 A2
Spanish Town
  Br. Virgin Is.. 17°43N 64°26W 105 H18
Sparkman AR... 33°55N 92°51W 63 E3
Sparks GA.... 31°11N 83°26W 68 E3
Sparks NE.... 42°56N 100°15W 84 B5
Sparks PA.... 39°32N 119°45W 85 C1
Sparks OK.... 35°37N 96°50W 93 C7
Sparland IL.... 41°2N 89°26W 71 B4
Sparlingville MI.. 42°58N 82°32W 79 G9
Sparr FL.... 29°20N 82°7W 67 B6
Sparrows Point
  U.S.A... 39°13N 76°28W 107 B3
Sparrows Pt. MD.. 39°12N 76°29W 107 B3
Sparta GA.... 33°17N 82°58W 68 C4
Sparta IL.... 38°8N 89°42W 71 E4
Sparta KY.... 38°41N 84°54W 97 B8
Sparta MI.... 43°10N 85°42W 79 F6
Sparta MO.... 37°0N 93°5W 82 D3
Sparta NC.... 36°30N 81°7W 90 B4
Sparta NJ.... 41°2N 74°38W 87 B5
Sparta TN.... 35°56N 85°28W 97 E7
Sparta VA.... 38°0N 77°14W 77 C3
Sparta WI.... 43°56N 90°49W 103 E3
Spartanburg County ☆
  SC... 34°50N 82°0W 90 D4
Spartanburg PA.. 41°49N 79°41W 95 C3
Spaulding OK... 35°1N 96°26W 93 C7
Spavinaw OK... 36°23N 95°3W 93 B8
Speaks TX.... 29°15N 96°42W 99 H11
Spearfish SD... 44°30N 103°52W 91 F2
Spearman TX... 36°12N 101°12W 98 A6
Spearsville LA... 32°56N 92°36W 75 B3
Spearville KS... 37°51N 99°45W 74 D4
Spectacle I. MA.. 42°19N 70°59W 106 A4
Speculator NY... 43°30N 74°22W 89 B6
Speed KS.... 39°41N 99°25W 74 B4
Speedway IN... 39°48N 86°16W 110 B1
Spencer ID.... 44°22N 112°11W 70 E6
Spencer IN.... 39°17N 86°46W 72 D4
Spencer IA.... 43°9N 95°9W 73 B3
Spencer MA.... 42°15N 71°59W 78 B3
Spencer NY.... 42°13N 76°30W 89 C4
Spencer NE.... 42°53N 98°42W 84 B7
Spencer OH.... 41°6N 82°8W 94 B4
Spencer SD.... 43°44N 97°36W 91 G8
Spencer TN.... 35°45N 85°28W 97 E7
Spencer WV.... 38°48N 81°21W 102 C3
Spencer WI.... 44°46N 90°18W 103 D3
Spencer County ☆ IN. 38°0N 87°0W 72 F3
Spencer County ☆ KY 38°0N 85°20W 97 B7
Spencertown NY.. 42°19N 73°33W 78 B1
Spencerville OH.. 40°43N 84°21W 92 C2
Spencerville OK.. 34°8N 95°21W 93 D8
Sperry OK.... 36°18N 95°59W 93 B8
Sperryville VA... 38°39N 78°14W 102 C6
Spiceland IN... 39°50N 85°26W 72 D5
Spicer MN.... 45°14N 94°56W 80 E4
Spickard MO... 40°14N 93°36W 82 A3
Spink SD.... 42°51N 96°45W 91 H9
Spink County ☆ SD. 45°0N 98°18W 91 F7
Spirit L. IA... 43°29N 95°6W 73 B3
Spirit Lake ID... 47°58N 116°52W 70 B2
Spirit Lake IA... 43°26N 95°6W 73 B3
Spirit Lake Indian Reservation
  ND... 47°58N 99°0W 91 C7
Spiritwood ND... 46°56N 98°30W 91 D7
Spiro OK.... 35°15N 94°37W 93 C9
Splendora TX... 30°14N 95°10W 99 G12
Spofford TX.... 29°10N 100°25W 98 H7
Spokane
  WA... 47°40N 117°24W 101 C8
Spokane ➙ WA.. 47°54N 118°20W 101 C7
Spokane County ☆
  WA... 47°35N 117°25W 101 C8
Spokane Indian Reservation
  WA... 47°57N 118°0W 101 C7
Spokane Int. ✈ (GEG)
  WA... 47°37N 117°32W 101 C8
Spooner WI.... 45°50N 91°53W 103 C2
Spoon ➙ IL.... 40°19N 90°4W 71 C3
Sportsman Acres OK 36°15N 95°16W 93 B8
Spot Pond MA... 42°26N 71°4W 106 A3
Spotswood NJ... 40°23N 74°23W 87 B2
Spotsylvania VA.. 38°12N 77°36W 102 C7
Spotsylvania County ☆
  VA... 38°12N 77°36W 102 C7
Spotted Horse WY 44°43N 105°50W 104 B7
Spotted Ra. NV.. 36°48N 115°48W 85 F5
Sprague NE.... 40°38N 96°45W 84 D9
Sprague WA.... 47°18N 117°59W 101 C8
Sprague ➙ OR... 42°34N 121°51W 94 E4
Sprague River OR 42°27N 121°30W 94 E4
Spray OR.... 44°50N 119°48W 94 C6
Spring TX.... 30°5N 95°25W 99 G12
Spring ➙ MO... 36°57N 94°45W 82 D2
Spring Butte WY. 40°11N 73°53W 87 B1
Spring City PA... 40°11N 75°33W 87 B1
Spring City TN... 35°42N 84°52W 97 E8
Spring City UT... 39°29N 111°30W 100 D4
Spring Cr. ➙ CA. 40°54N 84°45W 68 F2
Spring Cr. ➙ ND.. 47°15N 101°48W 91 C4
Spring Cr. ➙ NE.. 40°20N 101°6W 84 D4
Spring Cr. ➙ NV.. 39°55N 117°40W 85 C3
Spring Cr. ➙ SD.. 45°45N 100°18W 91 E5
Spring Cr. ➙ SD.. 43°52N 102°42W 91 G3
Spring Creek NV. 40°44N 115°31W 85 B5
Spring Glen UT... 39°40N 110°51W 100 D5
Spring Green WI.. 43°11N 90°4W 103 E3
Spring Grove MN. 43°34N 91°38W 80 G7
Spring Grove PA.. 39°52N 76°52W 77 A4
Spring Hill AL... 31°42N 85°58W 60 E5
Spring Hill AR... 33°35N 93°39W 63 E2

Spring Hill FL.... 28°27N 82°41W 67 C6
Spring Hill IA.... 41°25N 93°39W 73 D5
Spring Hill MN... 45°32N 94°50W 80 E4
Spring Hill TN... 35°45N 86°56W 96 E6
Spring Hills IN... 39°50N 86°11W 110 A1
Spring Lake MI... 43°5N 86°12W 79 F5
Spring Lake NC... 35°10N 78°58W 90 C7
Spring Lake NJ... 40°9N 74°2W 87 B2
Spring Mts. NV... 36°0N 115°45W 85 F5
Spring Pond MA.. 42°29N 70°56W 106 A4
Spring Valley CA. 32°44N 116°59W 117 B2
Spring Valley IL.. 41°20N 89°12W 71 B4
Spring Valley MN. 43°41N 92°23W 80 G6
Spring Valley NV. 40°58N 114°25W 85 C6
Spring Valley NV. 36°6N 115°14W 110 C1
Spring Valley NY. 41°7N 74°3W 87 A2
Spring Valley WV. 39°10N 114°25W 85 C6
Spring Valley WI. 44°51N 92°14W 103 D1
Springbrook IA... 42°10N 90°29W 73 C8
Springdale AR... 36°11N 94°8W 63 B1
Springdale OH... 39°17N 84°29W 92 D2
Springdale UT... 37°10N 113°0W 100 F3
Springdale WA... 48°4N 117°45W 101 B8
Springer NM.... 36°22N 104°36W 88 A6
Springer OK.... 34°19N 97°8W 93 D6
Springerton IL... 38°11N 88°21W 71 E5
Springerville AZ.. 34°8N 109°17W 62 C6
Springfield CO... 37°24N 102°37W 66 E8
Springfield FL... 30°10N 85°37W 67 A3
Springfield GA... 32°22N 81°18W 68 D5
Springfield ID... 43°5N 112°41W 70 F6
Springfield IL... 39°48N 89°39W 71 D4
Springfield KY... 37°41N 85°13W 97 C7
Springfield LA... 30°26N 90°33W 75 D5
Springfield ME... 45°24N 68°8W 76 C5
Springfield MA... 42°6N 72°35W 78 B2
Springfield MN... 44°14N 94°59W 80 F4
Springfield MO... 37°13N 93°17W 82 D3
Springfield NE... 41°5N 96°8W 84 C9
Springfield NJ... 40°43N 74°18W 114 B1
Springfield OH... 39°55N 83°49W 92 D3
Springfield OR... 44°3N 123°1W 94 C2
Springfield PA... 39°56N 75°19W 87 C1
Springfield SD... 42°49N 97°54W 91 H8
Springfield TN... 36°31N 86°53W 96 D6
Springfield VA... 38°46N 77°10W 102 C7
Springfield VT... 43°18N 72°29W 86 C2
Springfield WV... 39°27N 78°42W 77 A2
Springfield, L. IL.. 39°46N 89°36W 71 D4
Springhill LA.... 33°0N 93°28W 75 B2
Springlake TX... 34°14N 102°18W 98 C5
Springport MI... 42°22N 84°42W 79 G7
Springs NY.... 41°1N 72°10W 78 C2
Springtown TX... 32°58N 97°41W 99 E10
Springvale GA... 31°50N 84°53W 68 E2
Springvale ME... 43°28N 70°48W 86 C4
Springview NE... 42°50N 99°45W 84 B6
Springville AL... 33°46N 86°29W 60 C4
Springville IA... 42°3N 91°27W 73 C7
Springville NY... 42°31N 78°40W 89 C2
Springville UT... 40°10N 111°37W 100 C4
Sproul State Forest
  PA... 41°11N 77°49W 95 C5
Spruce Knob WV.. 38°42N 79°32W 102 C5
Spruce Knob-Seneca Rocks Nat.
  Recr. Area ○ WV 38°50N 79°30W 102 C5
Spruce Mts. AZ.. 34°28N 112°24W 62 C3
Spruce Pine NC... 35°55N 82°4W 90 C3
Spur TX.... 33°28N 100°52W 98 D7
Spurlockville WV. 38°8N 82°3W 102 C2
Squa Pan L. ME.. 46°31N 68°13W 76 B5
Squam L. NH.... 43°45N 71°32W 86 C3
Squantum MA.... 42°17N 71°0W 106 B3
Square Butte Cr. ➙
  ND... 46°55N 100°55W 91 D5
Square L. ME.... 47°3N 68°20W 76 A5
Squaw Lake MN.. 47°38N 94°8W 80 C4
Squaw Peak Recreation Area
  AZ... 33°34N 112°0W 116 B2
Squaw Valley CA. 36°44N 119°15W 65 G7
Squaxin Island Indian Reservation
  WA... 47°12N 122°55W 101 C3
Squibnocket Point
  MA... 41°18N 70°47W 78 C4
Squire WV.... 37°14N 81°37W 102 D3
Squires MO.... 36°51N 92°37W 82 E4
Stacy MN.... 45°24N 92°59W 80 E6
Stacyville IA.... 43°26N 92°47W 73 B6
Stafford CT.... 41°59N 72°17W 78 C2
Stafford KS.... 37°58N 98°36W 74 D5
Stafford TX.... 29°36N 95°33W 110 C1
Stafford VA.... 38°25N 77°25W 102 C7
Stafford County ☆
  VA... 38°25N 77°25W 102 C7
Stafford Springs CT 41°57N 72°18W 78 C2
Stambaugh MI... 46°5N 88°38W 79 C3
Stamford CT.... 41°3N 73°32W 78 C1
Stamford NY.... 42°25N 74°38W 89 C6
Stamford NE.... 40°8N 99°36W 84 D6
Stamford SD.... 43°53N 101°5W 91 G4
Stamford TX.... 32°57N 99°48W 98 E8
Stamford, L. TX.. 33°4N 99°34W 98 D8
Stamps AR.... 33°22N 93°30W 63 E2
Standardsville VA. 38°18N 78°26W 102 C6
Stanberry MO... 40°13N 94°35W 82 A2
Standing Rock AK. 35°48N 108°22W 88 B2
Standing Rock Indian Reservation
  SD... 45°45N 101°0W 91 E4
Standing Stone State Park ○
  TN... 36°28N 85°25W 97 D7
Standish MI.... 43°59N 83°57W 79 F8
Stanfield AZ.... 32°53N 111°58W 62 E4
Stanfield OR.... 45°47N 119°13W 94 B6
Stanford KY.... 37°32N 84°40W 97 C8
Stanford MT.... 47°9N 110°13W 83 C7
Stanhope IA.... 42°17N 93°48W 73 C5
Stanhope NJ.... 40°54N 74°42W 87 B5
Stanislaus ➙ CA. 37°40N 121°14W 64 F4
Stanislaus County ☆
  CA... 37°30N 121°0W 64 F6
Stanislaus Nat. Forest
  CA... 38°10N 120°0W 64 E6
Stanley ID.... 44°13N 114°56W 70 E3
Stanley KS.... 38°51N 94°40W 74 C9
Stanley KY.... 37°50N 87°5W 96 C4
Stanley LA.... 31°58N 93°54W 75 C2
Stanley NC.... 35°21N 81°6W 90 C5
Stanley NM.... 35°9N 105°59W 88 B5
Stanley VA.... 38°35N 78°30W 102 C6
Stanley WI.... 44°58N 90°56W 103 D3
Stanley County ☆ SD 44°30N 100°50W 91 F4
Stanleyville NC... 36°12N 80°17W 90 B5
Stannards NY.... 42°5N 77°55W 89 C3
Stanley's I. UT... 40°50N 112°49W 100 C4
Stanton B. McKinney Nat. Wildlife
  Refuge ○ CT... 41°12N 73°7W 78 C1
Stanton KY.... 37°51N 83°52W 97 C9
Stanton MI.... 43°18N 85°5W 79 F6
Stanton MO.... 38°17N 91°6W 82 C5
Stanton ND.... 47°19N 101°23W 91 C4
Stanton NE.... 41°57N 97°14W 84 C8
Stanton TN.... 35°28N 89°24W 96 E3
Stanton TX.... 32°8N 101°48W 98 E6

Stanton County ☆
  KS... 37°30N 101°45W 74 D2
Stanton County ☆
  NE... 41°50N 97°10W 84 C8
Stanwood WA... 48°15N 122°23W 101 B3
Staplehurst NE... 40°58N 97°10W 84 D8
Staples MN.... 46°21N 94°48W 80 D4
Stapleton AL.... 30°45N 87°48W 60 F3
Stapleton CO... 39°46N 104°52W 109 B2
Stapleton NY.... 40°36N 74°5W 114 C2
Stapleton NE.... 41°29N 100°31W 84 C5
Star NC.... 35°24N 79°47W 90 C6
Star City AR.... 33°56N 91°51W 63 E4
Star City IN.... 40°58N 86°33W 72 C4
Star Lake NY.... 44°10N 75°2W 89 A5
Star Prairie WI... 45°12N 92°32W 103 C1
Starbuck MN.... 45°37N 95°32W 80 E3
Starbuck WA.... 46°31N 118°7W 101 D7
Stark KS.... 37°42N 95°9W 74 D8
Stark County ☆ ND 46°55N 102°30W 91 D3
Stark County ☆ OH 40°48N 81°15W 94 B5
Starke FL.... 29°57N 82°7W 67 B6
Starke County ☆ IN 41°15N 86°40W 72 C3
Starks LA.... 30°19N 93°40W 75 D2
Starkville CO.... 37°8N 104°30W 66 E6
Starkville MS.... 33°28N 88°49W 81 C5
Starkweather ND.. 48°27N 98°53W 91 B7
Starr County ☆ TX. 26°30N 98°50W 98 L9
Starrs Mill GA.... 33°19N 84°31W 68 C2
Starrucca PA.... 41°54N 75°28W 95 C7
Starvation Res. UT 40°15N 110°30W 100 C5
State Center IA... 42°1N 93°10W 73 C5
State College PA.. 40°48N 77°52W 95 D5
State Line MS.... 31°26N 88°28W 81 E5
Staten Island NY. 40°35N 74°9W 114 C2
Staten Island Zoo NY 40°38N 74°6W 114 C2
Statenville GA... 30°42N 83°2W 68 F3
Statesboro GA... 32°27N 81°47W 68 D5
Statesville NC... 35°47N 80°53W 90 C5
Statham GA.... 33°58N 83°35W 68 C3
Statue of Liberty NJ. 40°41N 74°2W 114 B2
Staunton IL.... 39°1N 89°47W 71 D4
Staunton VA.... 38°9N 79°4W 102 C5
Stayton OR.... 44°48N 122°48W 94 C3
Staytonville DE... 38°50N 75°32W 77 B5
Stead NM.... 36°6N 103°12W 88 A7
Steamboat Rock IA 42°25N 93°4W 73 C5
Steamboat Springs
  CO... 40°29N 106°50W 66 B4
Stearns County ☆
  MN... 45°35N 94°30W 80 E4
Stebbins AK.... 63°31N 162°17W 61 E7
Stedman NC.... 35°0N 78°41W 90 D7
Steele AL.... 33°56N 86°12W 60 C4
Steele MO.... 36°5N 89°50W 82 F7
Steele ND.... 46°51N 99°55W 91 D6
Steele, Mt. WY... 41°50N 107°0W 104 E5
Steele City NE... 40°2N 97°2W 84 D8
Steele County ☆ MN 44°0N 93°10W 80 F5
Steele County ☆ ND 47°27N 97°50W 91 C8
Steeleville IL.... 38°0N 89°40W 71 E4
Steelville MO.... 37°58N 91°22W 82 D5
Steens Mt. OR... 42°35N 118°40W 94 E7
Steer, L. FL.... 28°31N 81°30W 115 A2
Stegman ➙ Artesia
  NM... 32°51N 104°24W 88 E6
Steilacoom WA... 48°19N 120°39W 101 B5
Steinauer NE.... 40°12N 96°14W 84 D9
Steinhatchee FL.. 29°40N 83°23W 67 B5
Stella MO.... 36°46N 94°12W 82 E2
Stella NE.... 40°14N 95°46W 84 D10
Stemmers ➙ MD. 39°19N 76°28W 107 A2
Stephen MN.... 48°27N 96°53W 80 B2
Stephens AR.... 33°25N 93°4W 63 E2
Stephens City VA. 39°5N 78°13W 77 A4
Stephens County ☆
  GA... 34°35N 83°15W 68 B3
Stephens County ☆
  OK... 34°30N 97°50W 93 D6
Stephens County ☆
  TX... 32°45N 98°54W 99 E9
Stephens Knob KY. 36°37N 84°20W 97 D8
Stephenson MI... 45°25N 87°36W 79 D4
Stephenson County ☆
  IL... 42°20N 89°40W 71 A4
Stephentown NY.. 42°33N 73°22W 78 B1
Stephenville TX.. 32°13N 98°12W 99 E9
Steps Pt.
  Amer. Samoa... 14°23S 170°45W 105 e
Steptoe WA.... 47°0N 117°21W 101 D8
Steptoe Valley NV. 39°50N 114°45W 85 C6
Sterling AK.... 60°32N 150°46W 61 F10
Sterling CO.... 40°37N 103°13W 66 B7
Sterling GA.... 31°16N 81°34W 68 E5
Sterling ID.... 43°2N 112°44W 70 F6
Sterling IL.... 41°48N 89°42W 71 B4
Sterling KS.... 38°13N 98°12W 74 C5
Sterling MI.... 44°2N 84°2W 79 F7
Sterling NE.... 40°28N 96°23W 84 D9
Sterling OK.... 34°45N 98°10W 93 D5
Sterling UT.... 39°12N 111°42W 100 D4
Sterling VA.... 39°1N 77°4W 77 A3
Sterling City TX.. 31°51N 101°0W 98 F7
Sterling County ☆ TX 32°0N 101°0W 98 F7
Sterling Heights MI 42°35N 83°2W 79 G8
Sterling Park CA.. 37°41N 122°27W 118 B2
Sterling Res. CO.. 40°47N 103°16W 66 B7
Sterlington LA... 32°42N 92°5W 75 B3
Stetsonville WI... 45°4N 90°19W 103 D3
Steubenville KY.. 36°53N 84°48W 97 D8
Steubenville OH.. 40°22N 80°37W 92 C6
Stevens County ☆
  KS... 37°15N 101°20W 74 D2
Stevens County ☆
  MN... 45°40N 96°0W 80 E2
Stevens County ☆
  WA... 48°30N 118°0W 101 B8
Stevens Point WI. 44°31N 89°34W 103 D4
Stevens Pottery GA 32°53N 83°17W 68 D3
Stevens Village AK. 66°1N 149°6W 61 C10
Stevenson AL.... 34°52N 85°50W 60 B5
Stevenson MD... 39°24N 76°42W 107 A1
Stevenson WA... 45°42N 121°53W 101 E4
Stevensville MD.. 38°59N 76°19W 77 B4
Stevensville MI... 42°1N 86°31W 79 G5
Stevensville MT.. 46°30N 114°5W 83 D3
Steward IL.... 41°51N 89°1W 71 B4
Stewardson IL... 39°16N 88°38W 71 D5
Stewart ➙ GA... 33°25N 83°52W 68 C3
Stewart MN.... 44°43N 94°29W 80 F4
Stewart MS.... 33°27N 89°26W 81 C4
Stewart B. McKinney Nat. Wildlife
  Refuge ○ CT... 41°12N 73°7W 78 C1
Stewart County ☆ GA 32°0N 84°45W 68 D2
Stewart County ☆
  TN... 36°20N 87°55W 96 D5
Stewart Manor NY. 40°43N 73°41W 114 B4
Stewarts Point CA. 38°39N 123°24W 64 E3
Stewartstown NH. 45°0N 71°31W 86 B3
Stewartstown PA.. 39°45N 76°36W 77 A4

Stewartsville MO. 39°45N 94°30W 82 B2
Stewartville MN.. 43°51N 92°29W 80 G6
Stibnite ID.... 44°54N 115°20W 70 E3
Stickney IL.... 41°49N 87°46W 108 C2
Stickney SD.... 43°35N 98°26W 91 G7
Stigler OK.... 35°15N 95°8W 93 C8
Stiles TX.... 31°25N 101°34W 98 F6
Stilesville IN... 39°38N 86°38W 72 D4
Still Pond MD... 39°20N 76°3W 77 A4
Stillmore GA.... 32°27N 82°13W 68 D4
Stillwater MN... 45°3N 92°49W 80 E6
Stillwater NV... 39°31N 118°33W 85 C2
Stillwater OK... 36°7N 97°4W 93 B6
Stillwater County ☆
  MT... 45°48N 109°15W 83 E8
Stillwater Range NV 39°50N 118°5W 85 C2
Stillwater Res. NY. 43°54N 75°3W 89 B5
Stilwell GA.... 32°23N 81°15W 68 D5
Stilwell KS.... 38°46N 94°39W 74 C9
Stilwell OK.... 35°49N 94°38W 93 C9
Stinnett TX.... 35°50N 101°27W 98 B6
Stinson Lake NH.. 43°51N 71°48W 86 C3
Stirling City CA.. 39°54N 121°32W 64 D5
Stirrat WV.... 37°44N 82°0W 102 D3
Stites ID.... 46°6N 115°59W 70 C3
Stock Island FL.. 24°32N 81°34W 67 G7
Stockbridge GA.. 33°33N 84°14W 68 C2
Stockbridge MA.. 42°17N 73°19W 78 B1
Stockbridge-Munsee Indian
  Reservation WI. 44°50N 88°50W 103 D5
Stockett MT.... 47°21N 111°10W 83 C6
Stockholm ME... 47°3N 68°8W 76 A5
Stockholm SD... 45°6N 96°48W 91 E9
Stockholm WI... 44°29N 92°16W 103 D1
Stockland IL.... 40°37N 87°36W 71 C6
Stockley DE.... 38°40N 75°20W 77 B5
Stockport IA.... 40°51N 91°50W 73 E7
Stockton CA.... 37°58N 121°17W 64 F4
Stockton IL.... 42°21N 90°1W 71 A3
Stockton KS.... 39°26N 99°16W 74 B4
Stockton MD.... 38°3N 75°25W 77 B5
Stockton MO.... 37°42N 93°48W 82 D3
Stockton UT.... 40°27N 112°22W 100 C3
Stockton, L. MO.. 37°42N 93°46W 82 D3
Stockton Plateau
  TX... 30°30N 102°30W 98 G5
Stockville NE.... 40°32N 100°23W 84 D5
Stoddard WI.... 43°40N 91°13W 103 E2
Stoddard County ☆
  MO... 36°50N 90°0W 82 E7
Stokes County ☆ NC 36°20N 80°10W 90 B5
Stone ID.... 42°1N 112°42W 70 G6
Stone Canyon Res.
  CA... 34°6N 118°27W 111 B2
Stone County ☆ AR. 35°52N 92°9W 63 C3
Stone County ☆ MS. 30°47N 89°8W 81 E4
Stone County ☆ MO. 36°45N 93°25W 82 E3
Stone Harbor NJ.. 39°3N 74°45W 87 C2
Stone Mountain Park ○
  GA... 33°48N 84°8W 68 C2
Stone Park IL.... 41°53N 87°52W 108 B1
Stoneboro PA.... 41°20N 80°7W 95 C2
Stoneham CO.... 40°36N 103°40W 66 B7
Stoneham MA.... 42°29N 71°5W 106 A3
Stoner CO.... 37°35N 108°19W 66 E2
Stones River Nat. Battlefield
  TN... 35°53N 86°26W 96 E6
Stoneville NC... 36°28N 79°54W 90 B6
Stoneville SD... 44°44N 102°39W 91 F3
Stonewall LA.... 32°17N 93°50W 75 B2
Stonewall MS.... 32°8N 88°47W 81 D5
Stonewall OK.... 34°39N 96°32W 93 D7
Stonewall County ☆
  TX... 33°8N 100°14W 98 D7
Stonewall Jackson L.
  WV... 38°58N 80°29W 102 B4
Stonewood WV... 39°15N 80°19W 102 B4
Stonington CO... 37°18N 102°11W 66 E8
Stonington ME... 44°9N 68°40W 76 D5
Stony Brook NY.. 40°56N 73°8W 89 E7
Stony Brook Res.
  MA... 42°15N 71°8W 106 B3
Stony Creek VA.. 36°57N 77°24W 90 B6
Stony Creek ➙ IL. 41°38N 87°41W 108 C2
Stony Point NC... 35°52N 81°3W 90 C4
Stony Point NY... 41°14N 73°59W 87 A3
Stony Pt. NY.... 43°50N 76°18W 89 B4
Stony Ridge OH.. 41°31N 83°30W 92 B3
Stony River AK... 61°47N 156°35W 61 F8
Stonyford CA.... 39°23N 122°33W 64 E4
Stoughton MA.... 42°7N 71°6W 106 B3
Stoughton WI.... 42°55N 89°13W 103 F4
Stout IA.... 42°32N 92°43W 73 C6
Stoutland MO... 37°49N 92°31W 82 D4
Stoutsville MO... 39°33N 91°51W 82 B5
Stoutsville OH... 39°36N 82°50W 92 D4
Stovall NC.... 36°27N 78°35W 90 B7
Stover MO.... 38°27N 92°59W 82 C4
Stow OH.... 41°10N 81°27W 92 B5
Stowe PA.... 40°15N 75°41W 87 B1
Stowe VT.... 44°28N 72°41W 86 B2
Stowell TX.... 29°47N 94°23W 99 H13
Stoystown PA... 40°6N 78°57W 95 D4
Strabane NH.... 43°19N 71°32W 86 C3
Strafford MO.... 37°16N 93°7W 82 D3
Strafford County ☆
  NH... 43°20N 71°0W 86 C3
Strandburg SD... 45°3N 96°46W 91 E9
Strandquist MN... 48°30N 96°27W 80 B2
Strang NE.... 40°25N 97°35W 84 D8
Strasburg CO.... 39°44N 104°0W 66 C6
Strasburg IL.... 39°22N 88°36W 71 D5
Strasburg ND.... 46°8N 100°10W 91 D5
Strasburg OH.... 40°36N 81°32W 92 C5
Strasburg PA.... 39°59N 76°11W 77 A4
Strasburg VA.... 38°59N 78°22W 102 C6
Stratford CA.... 36°11N 119°49W 65 G7
Stratford CT.... 41°12N 73°8W 78 C1
Stratford IA.... 42°16N 93°56W 73 C5
Stratford NH.... 44°42N 71°36W 86 B3
Stratford OK.... 34°48N 96°58W 93 D7
Stratford SD.... 45°19N 98°18W 91 E7
Stratford TX.... 36°20N 102°4W 98 A5

Stratford WI.... 44°48N 90°4W 103 D3
Stratham NH.... 43°3N 70°55W 86 C4
Strathcona MN... 48°33N 96°10W 80 B2
Strathmore CA... 36°9N 119°4W 65 G7
Strathmore CO... 39°19N 102°36W 66 C8
Stratton CO.... 39°18N 102°36W 66 C8
Stratton ME.... 45°8N 70°26W 76 C3
Stratton NE.... 40°9N 101°14W 84 D4
Straughn IN.... 39°48N 85°18W 72 D5
Strawberry AR... 35°58N 91°19W 63 C4
Strawberry CA... 38°48N 120°9W 64 E6
Strawberry ➙ AR. 35°53N 91°13W 63 C4
Strawberry Mt. OR 44°19N 118°43W 94 C7
Strawberry Point IA 42°41N 91°32W 73 C7
Strawberry Res. UT 40°8N 111°9W 100 C4
Strawn IL.... 40°39N 88°24W 71 C5
Strawn TX.... 32°33N 98°30W 99 E9
Strong AR.... 33°7N 92°21W 63 E3
Strong ME.... 44°49N 70°14W 76 C3
Strong ➙ MS... 31°51N 90°8W 81 E3
Strong City KS... 38°24N 96°32W 74 C8
Strong City OK... 35°40N 99°36W 93 C4
Stronghurst IL... 40°45N 90°55W 71 C3
Strongsville OH.. 41°19N 81°50W 92 B5
Stroud OK.... 35°45N 96°40W 93 C7
Stroudsburg PA.. 40°59N 75°12W 87 B1
Strum WI.... 44°33N 91°24W 103 D2
Struthers OH.... 41°4N 80°39W 92 B6
Stryker MT.... 48°41N 114°46W 83 B3
Stryker OH.... 41°30N 84°25W 92 B2
Stuart FL.... 27°12N 80°15W 67 D8
Stuart IA.... 41°30N 94°19W 73 D4
Stuart NE.... 42°36N 99°8W 84 B6
Stuart OK.... 34°54N 96°6W 93 D7
Stuart VA.... 36°38N 80°16W 90 B4
Stuart, Mt. WA... 47°29N 120°54W 101 C5
Stuarts Draft VA.. 38°2N 79°2W 102 C5
Studio City CA... 34°8N 118°24W 111 B2
Studley KS.... 39°21N 100°31W 74 B3
Study Butte TX... 29°19N 103°31W 98 H4
Stump L. ND.... 47°54N 98°24W 91 C7
Stumpy Lake VA.. 36°45N 76°8W 115 B3
Sturgeon MO.... 39°14N 92°17W 82 B4
Sturgeon ➙ MI... 45°24N 84°38W 79 D7
Sturgeon ➙ MI... 47°2N 88°30W 79 C3
Sturgeon B. MI... 45°45N 85°0W 79 D6
Sturgeon Bay WI.. 44°50N 87°23W 103 D6
Sturgeon Lake MN. 46°23N 92°49W 80 D6
Sturgeon Pt. MI.. 44°43N 83°16W 79 E8
Sturgis KY.... 37°33N 87°59W 96 C5
Sturgis MI.... 41°48N 85°25W 79 H6
Sturgis MS.... 33°21N 89°3W 81 C4
Sturgis SD.... 44°25N 103°31W 91 F2
Sturtevant WI... 42°42N 87°54W 103 F6
Stutsman County ☆ ND 47°0N 99°0W 91 C6
Stuttgart AR.... 34°30N 91°33W 63 D4
Styx ➙ AL.... 30°31N 87°27W 60 F3
Sublett Ra. ID.... 42°18N 112°55W 70 G6
Sublette IL.... 41°39N 89°14W 71 B4
Sublette KS.... 37°29N 100°51W 74 D3
Sublette County ☆
  WY... 43°0N 110°0W 104 D3
Sucarnoochee ➙ AL. 32°25N 88°22W 60 D2
Success AR.... 36°27N 90°43W 63 B5
Success, L. CA... 36°4N 118°55W 65 G8
Success, Mt. NH.. 44°27N 71°5W 86 B3
Sudan TX.... 34°4N 102°31W 98 C5
Sudbury MA.... 42°22N 71°24W 106 A1
Sudlersville MD.. 39°11N 75°52W 77 A5
Sue, L. FL.... 28°34N 81°21W 115 A2
Suffern NY.... 41°7N 74°9W 87 A2
Suffield CT.... 41°59N 72°39W 78 C2
Suffolk VA.... 36°44N 76°35W 102 E8
Suffolk County ☆ MA 42°21N 71°5W 78 B3
Suffolk County ☆ NY 40°50N 73°0W 89 E8
Sugar ➙ IL.... 42°26N 89°12W 71 A4
Sugar ➙ NH.... 43°24N 72°24W 86 C2
Sugar City CO... 38°14N 103°40W 66 D7
Sugar City ID.... 43°52N 111°45W 70 F7
Sugar Cr. ➙ IL.. 40°9N 89°38W 71 C4
Sugar Cr. ➙ IN.. 39°51N 87°21W 72 D3
Sugar Grove OH.. 39°38N 82°33W 92 D4
Sugar Grove PA.. 41°59N 79°20W 95 C3
Sugar Hill GA.... 34°6N 84°2W 68 B2
Sugar Land TX... 29°37N 95°38W 99 H12
Sugar Mountain NC 36°8N 81°52W 90 B4
Sugar Notch PA.. 41°11N 75°59W 95 C7
Sugarcreek PA... 41°25N 79°53W 95 C3
Sugarloaf Mt. ME. 45°2N 70°19W 76 C3
Sugartown LA.... 30°50N 93°1W 75 D2
Sugarville UT.... 39°28N 112°39W 100 D3
Suisun B. CA.... 38°5N 122°2W 64 E4
Suisun City CA... 38°15N 122°2W 64 E4
Suitland MD.... 38°50N 76°55W 119 B4
Sulligent AL.... 33°54N 88°8W 60 C2
Sullivan IL.... 39°36N 88°37W 71 D5
Sullivan IN.... 39°6N 87°24W 72 D3
Sullivan KY.... 37°30N 87°57W 96 C5
Sullivan MO.... 38°13N 91°10W 82 C5
Sullivan County ☆ IN 39°5N 87°25W 72 D3
Sullivan County ☆
  MO... 40°10N 93°5W 82 A3
Sullivan County ☆
  NH... 43°20N 72°15W 86 C2
Sullivan County ☆
  NY... 41°45N 74°45W 89 D6
Sullivan County ☆
  PA... 41°30N 76°35W 95 C6
Sullivan County ☆
  TN... 36°32N 82°19W 97 D10
Sully IA.... 41°34N 92°50W 73 D5
Sulphur LA.... 30°14N 93°23W 75 D2
Sulphur OK.... 34°31N 96°58W 93 D7
Sulphur ➙ U.S.A.. 33°7N 93°52W 63 E2
Sulphur Cr. ➙ SD. 44°45N 102°0W 91 F3
Sulphur Draw ➙
  TX... 33°12N 102°17W 98 D5
Sulphur Rock AR.. 35°45N 91°28W 63 C4
Sulphur Springs AR 36°29N 94°28W 63 B1
Sulphur Springs IN 40°0N 85°27W 72 C5
Sulphur Springs TX 33°8N 95°36W 99 D12
Sulphur Springs Draw ➙
  TX... 32°12N 101°36W 98 E6
Sulphur Springs Range
  NV... 40°15N 116°0W 85 B5
Sultan WA.... 47°52N 121°49W 101 C4
Sumas WA.... 48°59N 122°16W 101 B3
Sumatra FL.... 30°1N 84°59W 67 A4
Sumatra MT.... 46°37N 107°33W 83 D10
Summer I. MI.... 45°34N 86°39W 79 D5
Summer L. OR.... 42°50N 120°45W 94 E5
Summer Lake OR.. 42°58N 120°47W 94 E5
Summerdale AL... 30°29N 87°42W 60 F3
Summerfield FL... 29°0N 82°4W 67 C6

Summerfield NC.. 36°13N 79°54W 90 B6
Summerfield OH.. 39°48N 81°20W 92 D5
Summerfield TX.. 34°44N 102°31W 98 C5
Summerland Key FL 24°40N 81°27W 67 G7
Summers County ☆
  WV... 37°40N 80°54W 102 D4
Summersville MO. 37°11N 91°40W 82 D5
Summersville WV. 38°17N 80°51W 102 C4
Summerville L. WV 38°13N 80°53W 102 C4
Summerton SC... 33°36N 80°20W 90 D5
Summertown TN.. 35°26N 87°18W 96 E5
Summerville GA.. 34°29N 85°21W 68 B1
Summerville OR.. 45°29N 118°0W 94 B7
Summerville SC.. 33°1N 80°11W 90 E5
Summit AK.... 63°20N 149°7W 61 E10
Summit IL.... 41°47N 87°47W 108 C2
Summit MS.... 31°17N 90°28W 81 E3
Summit NJ.... 40°43N 74°22W 87 B2
Summit OK.... 35°40N 95°26W 93 C8
Summit OR.... 44°38N 123°35W 94 C2
Summit SD.... 45°18N 97°2W 91 E8
Summit UT.... 37°48N 112°56W 100 F3
Summit County ☆
  CO... 39°30N 106°0W 66 C4
Summit County ☆ OH 41°8N 81°20W 92 B5
Summit County ☆
  UT... 40°55N 111°0W 100 C4
Summit L. NV.... 41°31N 119°4W 85 A1
Summit Lake Indian Reservation
  NV... 41°33N 119°2W 85 A1
Summit Mt. NV... 39°23N 116°28W 85 C4
Summit Peak CO.. 37°21N 106°42W 66 E4
Summit Point UT.. 38°3N 109°7W 100 F6
Sumner IA.... 42°51N 92°6W 73 C6
Sumner IL.... 38°42N 87°53W 71 D6
Sumner MO.... 39°39N 93°15W 82 B3
Sumner NE.... 40°57N 99°31W 84 D6
Sumner L. NM... 34°40N 104°25W 88 C6
Sumner County ☆
  KS... 37°15N 97°20W 74 D6
Sumner County ☆
  TN... 36°24N 86°27W 96 D6
Sumpter OR.... 44°45N 118°12W 94 C7
Sumrall MS.... 31°25N 89°33W 81 E4
Sumter SC.... 33°55N 80°21W 90 E5
Sumter County ☆
  AL... 32°35N 88°11W 60 D2
Sumter County ☆ FL 28°45N 82°10W 67 C6
Sumter County ☆ GA 32°0N 84°10W 68 D2
Sumter County ☆ SC 33°50N 80°30W 90 D5
Sumter Nat. Forest SC 34°50N 83°0W 90 D2
Sun LA.... 30°39N 89°54W 75 D6
Sun ➙ MT.... 47°29N 111°19W 83 C6
Sun City AZ.... 33°35N 112°16W 116 A2
Sun City CA.... 33°42N 117°11W 65 K9
Sun City FL.... 27°43N 82°55W 119 C4
Sun City Center FL 27°43N 82°21W 67 D6
Sun City West AZ. 33°40N 112°20W 62 D3
Sun Lakes AZ.... 33°10N 111°52W 62 D4
Sun Prairie WI... 43°11N 89°13W 103 E4
Sun River MT.... 47°31N 111°43W 83 C6
Sun Valley CA... 34°13N 118°22W 111 A2
Sun Valley ID.... 43°42N 114°21W 70 F4
Sun Valley NV... 39°36N 119°46W 85 C1
Sunapee NH.... 43°23N 72°7W 86 C2
Sunapee L. NH... 43°23N 72°5W 86 C2
Sunbright TN.... 36°15N 84°40W 97 D8
Sunburg MN.... 45°21N 95°14W 80 E3
Sunburst MT.... 48°53N 111°55W 83 B6
Sunbury OH.... 40°15N 82°52W 92 C4
Sunbury PA.... 40°52N 76°48W 95 D6
Suncook NH.... 43°8N 71°27W 86 C3
Suncook ➙ NH... 43°12N 71°28W 86 C3
Sundance WY.... 44°24N 104°23W 104 B8
Sunderland MD... 38°40N 76°36W 77 B4
Sunfish Lake MN.. 44°52N 93°5W 113 B3
Sunfish Park MN.. 45°0N 92°56W 113 A4
Sunflower MS... 33°33N 90°32W 81 C3
Sunflower, Mt. KS. 39°6N 102°2W 74 B1
Sunflower County ☆
  MS... 33°44N 90°33W 81 C3
Sunland Park NM. 31°50N 106°40W 88 F4
Sunman IN.... 39°14N 85°6W 72 D5
Sunny Side TX... 29°39N 95°22W 110 B2
Sunnyside UT.... 39°34N 110°23W 100 D5
Sunnyside NV... 38°25N 115°1W 85 D5
Sunnyside WA... 46°20N 120°0W 101 D6
Sunnyslope AZ... 33°34N 112°4W 116 B2
Sunnyvale CA... 37°23N 122°2W 64 F4
Sunol CA.... 37°36N 121°52W 118 D5
Sunray OK.... 34°25N 97°58W 93 D6
Sunray TX.... 36°1N 101°49W 98 A6
Sunrise FL.... 26°8N 80°14W 112 B2
Sunrise Manor NV. 36°12N 115°4W 110 B2
Sunrise Mountain Natural Area
  NV... 36°12N 114°58W 110 B3
Sunrise Mt. NV... 36°13N 114°58W 110 B3
Sunset AR.... 35°13N 90°12W 63 C5
Sunset LA.... 30°24N 92°4W 75 D3
Sunset TX.... 33°27N 97°47W 99 D10
Sunset Beach CA.. 33°42N 118°4W 111 D4
Sunset Crater Volcano Nat.
  Monument ○ AZ. 35°20N 111°20W 62 B4
Sunset Park NV... 36°3N 115°9W 110 C2
Suntrana AK.... 63°52N 148°51W 61 E10
Supai AZ.... 36°15N 112°41W 62 A3
Superior AZ.... 33°18N 111°6W 62 D4
Superior IA.... 43°26N 94°57W 73 B4
Superior MT.... 47°12N 114°53W 83 C2
Superior NE.... 40°1N 98°4W 84 D7
Superior WI.... 46°44N 92°6W 103 B1
Superior WY.... 41°46N 108°58W 104 E4
Superior, L. N. Amer. 47°0N 87°0W 79 B4
Superior Nat. Forest
  MN... 47°50N 91°30W 80 C6
Suquamish WA... 47°43N 122°33W 118 B2
Sur, Pt. CA.... 36°18N 121°54W 64 G5
Surf City NC.... 34°26N 77°33W 90 D8
Surf City NJ.... 39°40N 74°10W 87 C2
Surfside Beach SC 33°37N 78°59W 90 E7
Surgoinsville TN.. 36°28N 82°51W 97 D10
Suring WI.... 44°59N 88°22W 103 D5
Surprise AZ.... 33°38N 112°19W 62 D3
Surprise ➙ NE... 41°6N 97°19W 84 C8
Surrency GA.... 31°44N 82°12W 68 E4
Surrey ND.... 48°14N 101°6W 91 B4
Surry ME.... 44°29N 68°29W 76 D5
Surry VA.... 37°8N 76°50W 102 D8
Surry County ☆ NC. 36°20N 80°45W 90 B5
Surry County ☆ VA. 37°8N 76°50W 102 D8
Susank KS.... 38°38N 98°46W 74 C5
Susanville CA.... 40°25N 120°39W 64 C5
Susquehanna PA.. 41°57N 75°36W 95 C7
Susquehanna ➙ PA 39°33N 76°5W 77 A4
Susquehanna County ☆
  PA... 41°55N 75°50W 95 B7
Susquehannock State Forest
  PA... 41°35N 77°47W 95 C5
Sussex NJ.... 41°13N 74°37W 87 A2
Sussex VA.... 36°55N 77°17W 102 E7
Sussex WI.... 43°8N 88°13W 103 E5
Sussex WY.... 43°42N 106°18W 104 C6
Sussex County ☆ DE 38°45N 75°20W 77 B5
Sussex County ☆ NJ. 41°15N 74°45W 87 A2

Sussex County ☆
  VA .... 36°55N 77°17W **102 E7**
Sutcliffe NV .... 39°57N 119°36W **85 C1**
Sutherland IA ...... 42°58N 95°29W **73 C3**
Sutherland NE ..... 41°10N 101°08W **84 C4**
Sutherland Res. NE .. 41°6N 101°10W **84 C4**
Sutherlin OR .... 43°23N 123°19W **94 D2**
Sutter CA .... 39°10N 121°45W **64 D5**
Sutter Buttes CA ... 39°12N 121°45W **64 D5**
Sutter County ☆ CA . 39°0N 121°45W **64 D5**
Sutter Creek CA .... 38°24N 120°48W **64 D5**
Suttle AL .... 32°32N 87°11W **60 D3**
Sutton MA .... 42°9N 71°46W **78 B3**
Sutton ND .... 47°24N 98°27W **91 C7**
Sutton VT .... 44°36N 97°52W **84 D8**
Sutton VT .... 44°39N 72°3W **86 B2**
Sutton WV .... 38°40N 80°43W **102 C4**
Sutton B. MI .... 44°59N 85°37W **79 E6**
Sutton County ☆
  TX .... 30°34N 100°39W **98 G7**
Sutton L. WV .... 38°40N 80°41W **102 C4**
Sutwik I. AK .... 56°34N 157°12W **61 H8**
Suwannee ← FL ..... 29°20N 83°9W **67 B5**
Suwannee → FL ..... 29°17N 83°10W **67 B5**
Suwannee County ☆
  FL .... 30°15N 83°0W **67 A4**
Suwannee Sd. FL ... 29°20N 83°15W **67 B5**
Swain AR .... 35°51N 93°20W **63 C2**
Swain County ☆ NC . 35°30N 83°30W **69 C2**
Swaledale IA .... 42°55N 93°20W **73 B4**
Swampscott MA ..... 42°28N 70°53W **106 A4**
Swan Cr. → MO .... 36°41N 93°6W **82 A5**
Swan L. MT .... 47°56N 113°51W **83 C4**
Swan Lake MT ...... 47°56N 113°51W **83 C4**
Swan R. MT .... 48°0N 113°45W **83 C4**
Swan River MN ..... 47°5N 93°12W **80 C5**
Swan Valley ID ..... 43°27N 111°21W **70 F8**
Swandale WV .... 38°30N 80°57W **102 C4**
Swannanoa NC ..... 35°36N 82°24W **90 C3**
Swanquarter NC .... 35°25N 76°20W **90 C9**
Swans I. ME .... 44°10N 68°26W **76 D5**
Swansboro NC ...... 34°39N 77°7W **90 D8**
Swansea SC .... 33°44N 81°9W **90 E4**
Swanson L. NE ..... 40°10N 101°4W **84 D4**
Swanton MD .... 39°27N 79°14W **77 A1**
Swanton VT .... 44°55N 73°8W **86 B1**
Swanville MN ...... 45°55N 94°38W **80 E4**
Swarthmore PA ..... 39°54N 75°21W **87 C1**
Swartswood NJ ..... 41°8N 74°50W **87 A2**
Swartz Creek MI .... 42°58N 83°50W **79 G8**
Swasey Peak UT .... 39°23N 113°19W **100 D2**
Swayzee IN .... 40°30N 85°49W **73 D8**
Swea City IA .... 43°23N 94°19W **73 B4**
Swedeborg MO ..... 37°55N 92°20W **82 D4**
Sweden ME .... 46°57N 68°8W **76 B5**
Swedesboro NJ ..... 39°45N 75°19W **87 C1**
Swedish Knoll UT ... 39°16N 111°26W **100 D4**
Sweeny TX .... 29°3N 95°42W **99 H12**
Sweet Air MD ...... 39°31N 76°32W **77 A4**
Sweet Briar Station
  VA .... 37°33N 79°4W **102 D5**
Sweet Grass MT .... 48°59N 111°58W **83 B6**
Sweet Grass County ☆
  MT .... 46°0N 110°0W **83 E8**
Sweet Home AR ..... 34°41N 92°15W **63 D3**
Sweet Home OR ..... 44°24N 122°44W **94 C3**
Sweet Springs MO .. 38°58N 93°25W **82 C3**
Sweet Springs WV .. 37°38N 80°14W **102 D4**
Sweet Water AL .... 32°6N 87°52W **60 D3**
Sweetwater TN ..... 35°36N 84°29W **97 E8**
Sweetwater TX ..... 32°28N 100°25W **98 E7**
Sweetwater → WY .. 42°31N 107°22W **104 D5**
Sweetwater County ☆
  WY .... 42°0N 109°0W **104 E4**
Sweetwater L. ND .. 48°13N 98°50W **91 C7**
Sweetwater Marsh Nat. Wildlife
  Refuge CA ... 32°41N 117°6W **117 C2**
Sweetwater Res. CA 32°41N 117°0W **117 B3**
Sweetwater Station
  WY .... 42°32N 108°11W **104 D4**
Swenson TX .... 33°13N 100°19W **98 D7**
Swift County ☆ MN .. 45°15N 95°45W **80 E3**
Swift Res. WA ...... 46°4N 122°3W **101 D3**
Swifton AR .... 35°49N 91°8W **63 C4**
Swinburne I. NY .... 40°33N 74°3W **114 C2**
Swink CO .... 38°1N 103°38W **66 D7**
Swink OK .... 34°1N 95°12W **93 D9**
Swinomish Indian Reservation
  WA .... 48°23N 122°32W **101 B4**
Swisher IA .... 41°50N 91°42W **73 D7**
Swisher County ☆
  TX .... 34°32N 101°46W **98 C6**
Swisshome OR ...... 44°4N 123°48W **94 C2**
Swissvale PA .... 40°25N 79°52W **116 B2**
Switzerland County ☆
  IN .... 38°50N 85°0W **72 E6**
Swords CO .... 33°33N 83°18W **68 C3**
Swoyerville PA ..... 41°18N 75°53W **95 C7**
Sycamore IL .... 41°59N 88°41W **71 B5**
Sycamore KS .... 37°20N 95°43W **74 D8**
Sycamore OH .... 40°57N 83°10W **92 C3**
Sycan Marsh OR .... 42°45N 121°5W **94 E4**
Sydney ND .... 46°44N 98°46W **91 D7**
Sykeston ND .... 47°28N 99°24W **91 C6**
Sykesville MD ...... 39°22N 76°58W **77 A4**
Sykesville PA .... 41°3N 78°50W **95 C4**
Sylacauga AL ...... 33°10N 86°15W **60 C4**
Sylva NC .... 35°23N 83°13W **90 C2**
Sylvan PA .... 39°45N 78°1W **77 A2**
Sylvan Grove KS ... 39°1N 98°24W **74 B5**
Sylvania GA .... 32°45N 81°38W **68 D5**
Sylvania OH .... 41°43N 83°42W **92 B3**
Sylvarena MS ...... 32°1N 89°23W **81 D4**
Sylvester GA ...... 31°32N 83°50W **68 E3**
Sylvester TX .... 32°43N 100°15W **98 E7**
Sylvia KS .... 37°57N 98°25W **74 D5**
Symerton IL .... 41°20N 88°3W **71 B5**
Symmes Cr. → OH .. 38°26N 82°27W **92 E4**
Symsonia KY .... 36°55N 88°31W **96 D4**
Syracuse IN .... 41°26N 85°45W **72 B5**
Syracuse KS .... 37°59N 101°45W **74 D2**
Syracuse MO .... 38°40N 92°53W **82 C4**
Syracuse NY .... 43°3N 76°9W **89 B4**
Syracuse NE .... 40°39N 96°11W **84 D9**
Syracuse ✈ (SYR) NY . 43°7N 76°6W **89 B4**
Syria VA .... 38°29N 78°20W **102 C6**

T

T.O. Fuller State Park
  TN .... 35°3N 90°7W **112 B1**
Tabernash CO ...... 39°57N 105°52W **66 C5**
Tabiona UT .... 40°17N 110°43W **100 C5**
Table Mt. AZ .... 32°49N 110°31W **112 E5**
Table Mt. NE ...... 45°55N 103°48W **91 E2**
Table Rock WY ..... 41°37N 108°22W **104 E4**
Table Rock L. MO .. 36°36N 93°19W **82 E3**
Table Top AZ ...... 32°45N 112°8W **112 E3**
Tabor IA .... 40°54N 95°40W **73 D2**
Tabor MN .... 48°5N 96°52W **80 B2**
Tabor SD .... 42°57N 97°40W **91 H8**
Tabor City NC ..... 34°10N 78°52W **90 D7**
Tacna AZ .... 32°42N 113°59W **62 E2**
Tacoma WA .... 47°14N 122°26W **101 C3**
Taconic Mt. U.S.A. . 42°40N 73°18W **78 B1**
Taconite Harbor MN 47°32N 90°55W **80 C8**
Taft CA .... 35°8N 119°29W **65 H7**
Taft FL .... 28°25N 81°21W **115 B2**
Taylor OK .... 35°46N 95°32W **93 C8**
Taft OK .... 35°1N 86°43W **96 E6**
Taft TX .... 27°59N 97°24W **99 K10**
Tafton PA .... 41°24N 75°11W **87 A1**
Tagpochau, Mt.
  N. Marianas .. 15°11N 145°44E **105 c**
Tahgong Pt.
  N. Marianas .. 15°6N 145°39E **105 c**
Tahlequah OK ...... 35°55N 94°58W **93 C9**
Tahoe, L. U.S.A. ... 39°6N 120°2W **64 D4**
Tahoe City CA ..... 39°10N 120°9W **64 D4**
Tahoe Nat. Forest
  CA .... 39°20N 120°30W **64 D4**
Taholah WA .... 47°21N 124°17W **101 C1**
Tahquamenon → MI . 46°34N 85°2W **79 C6**
Taibun NM .... 34°26N 104°1W **88 C6**
Taijque NM .... 34°45N 106°17W **88 C4**
Takoma Park MD ... 38°58N 77°0W **119 B3**
Takotna AK .... 62°59N 156°4W **61 E8**
Talaia AK .... 36°32N 95°42W **93 B8**
Talala OK .... 36°32N 95°42W **93 B8**
Talbot County ☆ GA . 32°45N 84°40W **68 D2**
Talbot County ☆ MD . 38°45N 76°0W **77 B4**
Talbotton GA .... 32°41N 84°32W **68 D2**
Talco TX .... 33°22N 95°6W **99 D12**
Talent OR .... 42°15N 122°47W **94 E3**
Taliaferro County ☆
  GA .... 33°35N 82°50W **68 C4**
Taliesin WI .... 43°8N 90°4W **103 E3**
Talihina OK .... 34°45N 95°3W **93 D8**
Talkeetna AK ...... 62°20N 150°6W **61 E10**
Talking Rock GA ... 34°31N 84°30W **68 B2**
Talladega AL ...... 33°26N 86°6W **60 C4**
Talladega County ☆
  AL .... 33°26N 86°6W **60 C4**
Talladega Cr. → AL . 33°18N 86°22W **60 C4**
Talladega Nat. Forest
  AL .... 32°55N 87°15W **60 D3**
Tallahala Cr. → MS . 31°12N 89°5W **81 E4**
Tallahassee FL ..... 30°27N 84°17W **67 A4**
Tallahatchie → MS .. 33°33N 90°10W **81 C3**
Tallahatchie County ☆
  MS .... 33°58N 90°22W **81 C3**
Tallapoosa GA ..... 33°45N 85°17W **68 C1**
Tallapoosa → AL ... 32°30N 86°16W **60 D4**
Tallapoosa County ☆
  AL .... 32°50N 85°46W **60 D5**
Tallassee AL .... 32°32N 85°54W **60 D5**
Talleyville DE ...... 39°48N 75°33W **77 A5**
Tallgrass Prairie Nat. Preserve
  KS .... 38°26N 96°34W **74 C7**
Tallmadge OH ...... 41°6N 81°27W **92 B5**
Tallula IL .... 39°56N 89°56W **71 D4**
Tallulah LA .... 32°25N 91°11W **75 B4**
Tallulah Falls GA .. 34°44N 83°24W **68 B3**
Talmage KS .... 39°2N 97°16W **74 B6**
Talmage NE .... 40°32N 96°1W **84 D9**
Talofofo Guam ..... 13°21N 144°45E **105 b**
Taloga OK .... 36°2N 98°58W **93 B5**
Talpa TX .... 31°47N 99°43W **99 F8**
Talquin, L. FL ..... 30°23N 84°39W **67 A4**
Tama IA .... 41°58N 92°35W **73 D6**
Tama County ☆ IA .. 42°5N 92°30W **73 C6**
Tamaha OK .... 35°20N 94°59W **93 C9**
Tamaqua PA .... 40°48N 75°58W **95 D7**
Tamarac Nat. Wildlife Refuge
  MN .... 47°2N 95°36W **80 C3**
Tamarack ID .... 44°57N 116°23W **70 E2**
Tamarack MN ...... 46°39N 93°8W **80 D5**
Tamaroa IL .... 38°8N 89°14W **71 E4**
Tamiami Canal FL .. 25°50N 81°0W **67 F8**
Tamms IL .... 37°14N 89°16W **71 F4**
Tamora NE .... 40°54N 97°14W **84 D8**
Tampa FL .... 27°56N 82°27W **119 B3**
Tampa KS .... 38°33N 97°9W **74 C6**
Tampa B. FL .... 27°50N 82°30W **119 C3**
Tampa Int. ✈ (TPA)
  FL .... 41°38N 89°47W **71 B4**
Tampico IL .... 41°38N 89°47W **71 B4**
Tamuning Guam .... 13°29N 144°47E **105 b**
Tamworth NH ...... 43°50N 71°18W **86 C3**
Tanacross AK ...... 63°23N 143°21W **61 E12**
Tanaga I. AK ...... 51°48N 177°53W **61 L1**
Tanaga Volcano AK . 51°53N 178°8W **61 L3**
Tanana AK .... 65°10N 152°4W **61 D9**
Tanana → AK ...... 65°10N 151°58W **61 D9**
Tanapag N. Marianas 15°14N 145°45E **105 c**
Taney County ☆ MO . 36°40N 93°0W **82 E3**
Taneytown MD ..... 39°40N 77°11W **77 A3**
Taneyville MO ..... 36°44N 93°2W **82 E3**
Tangelo Park FL ... 28°27N 81°26W **115 B2**
Tangent OR .... 44°33N 123°7W **94 C2**
Tangier AR .... 37°49N 75°59W **77 C5**
Tangier I. VA ...... 37°55N 75°59W **77 C5**
Tangier Sd. MD .... 38°0N 75°57W **77 B5**
Tangipahoa → LA .. 30°53N 90°31W **75 D5**
Tangipahoa → LA .. 30°30N 90°16W **75 D5**
Tangipahoa Parish ☆
  LA .... 30°30N 90°30W **75 D5**
Tankersley TX ..... 31°21N 100°39W **98 F7**
Tanner WV .... 38°59N 80°57W **102 C4**
Tanner Point VA ... 36°59N 76°19W **115 A2**
Tanners Lake MN .. 44°57N 92°58W **113 B4**
Taopi MN .... 43°34N 92°38W **80 G6**
Taos NM .... 36°24N 105°35W **88 A5**
Taos → NM .... 36°24N 105°35W **88 A5**
Taos County ☆ NM . 36°30N 105°40W **88 A5**
Taos Indian Reservation
  NM .... 36°35N 105°25W **88 A5**
Taos Pueblo NM ... 36°24N 105°33W **88 A5**
Tappahannock VA .. 37°56N 76°52W **77 C4**
Tappan L. OH ...... 40°21N 81°14W **92 C5**
Tappen ND .... 46°52N 99°38W **91 D6**
Taputapu, C.
  Amer. Samoa .. 14°20S 170°51W **105 e**
Tar → NC .... 35°33N 77°6W **90 C8**
Tarboro NC .... 35°1N 81°48W **68 C5**
Tarboro NC .... 35°54N 77°32W **90 C8**
Targhee Nat. Forest
  ID .... 44°30N 111°30W **70 E7**
Targhee Pass U.S.A. 44°40N 111°6W **70 E7**
Tarkio MO .... 40°27N 95°23W **82 A1**
Tarkio → MO ...... 40°14N 95°37W **82 A1**
Tarkio → MO ...... 40°27N 95°23W **82 A1**
Tarlton OH .... 39°33N 82°47W **92 D4**
Tarnov NE .... 41°37N 97°30W **84 C8**
Tarpon Springs FL . 28°9N 82°45W **67 C6**
Tarrant AL .... 33°34N 86°47W **60 C4**
Tarrant County ☆
  TX .... 32°44N 97°7W **99 E10**
Tarryall CO .... 39°7N 105°29W **66 C5**
Tarryall → CO ..... 39°15N 105°19W **66 C5**
Tarrytown NY ...... 41°4N 73°52W **87 A3**
Tarzan TX .... 32°18N 101°58W **98 E6**
Tarzana CA .... 34°10N 118°33W **111 A1**
Tate GA .... 34°25N 84°23W **68 B2**
Tate County ☆ MS .. 34°37N 89°58W **81 B4**
Tatitlek AK .... 60°52N 146°41W **61 F11**
Tatum NM .... 33°16N 103°19W **88 D7**
Tatum TX .... 32°19N 94°31W **99 E13**
Tatum Cr. → AR .... 30°43N 82°32W **68 F4**
Tatums OK .... 34°29N 97°28W **93 D6**
Ta'ū Amer. Samoa .. 14°15S 169°30W **105 f**
Taum Sauk Mt. MO . 37°34N 90°44W **82 E6**
Taunton MA .... 41°54N 71°6W **78 C3**
Taunton Lake NJ .. 39°51N 74°52W **87 C2**
Tavernier FL .... 25°1N 80°31W **67 F8**
Tawakoni, L. TX ... 32°49N 95°55W **99 E12**
Tawas City MI ..... 44°16N 83°31W **79 E8**
Taylor AR .... 33°6N 93°28W **63 E2**
Taylor MI .... 42°14N 83°16W **79 G8**
Taylor MS .... 34°18N 89°35W **81 B4**
Taylor ND .... 46°54N 102°26W **91 D3**
Taylor TX .... 30°34N 97°25W **99 G10**
Taylor WI .... 44°19N 91°7W **103 D2**
Taylor → CO .... 38°32N 106°55W **66 D4**
Taylor, Mt. NM .... 35°14N 107°37W **88 B3**
Taylor County ☆ FL . 30°0N 83°30W **67 A5**
Taylor County ☆ GA . 32°35N 84°15W **68 D2**
Taylor County ☆ IA . 40°45N 94°40W **73 E4**
Taylor County ☆ KY . 37°20N 85°20W **97 C7**
Taylor County ☆ TX . 32°21N 99°53W **99 E8**
Taylor County ☆ WV . 39°21N 80°2W **102 B4**
Taylor County ☆ WI 45°10N 90°30W **103 C3**
Taylor Mill KY .... 38°59N 84°29W **107 B1**
Taylor Park Res.
  CO .... 38°49N 106°36W **66 D4**
Taylor Ridge GA ... 34°35N 85°12W **68 B1**
Taylors SC .... 34°55N 82°18W **90 D3**
Taylors Bridge DE . 39°23N 75°36W **77 A5**
Taylors Island MD . 38°28N 76°18W **77 B4**
Taylorsville IN .... 39°18N 85°57W **72 D5**
Taylorsville KY .... 38°2N 85°21W **97 B7**
Taylorsville MD .... 39°27N 77°3W **77 A3**
Taylorsville MS .... 31°50N 89°26W **81 E4**
Taylorsville NC .... 35°55N 81°11W **90 C4**
Taylorsville UT .... 40°40N 111°56W **117 C2**
Taylorville IL ...... 39°33N 89°18W **71 D4**
Tazewell TN .... 36°27N 83°34W **97 D9**
Tazewell VA .... 37°7N 81°31W **102 D3**
Tazewell County ☆
  VA .... 37°7N 81°31W **102 D3**
Tazlina AK .... 62°4N 146°27W **61 E11**
Tchula AK .... 33°11N 90°13W **81 C3**
Tea SD .... 43°27N 96°50W **91 G9**
Teague TX .... 31°38N 96°17W **99 F11**
Teahwhit Head
  WA .... 47°52N 124°37W **101 C1**
Teaneck NJ .... 40°53N 74°1W **114 A2**
Teasdale UT .... 38°17N 111°29W **100 E4**
Tecolote Canyon Natural Park
  CA .... 32°46N 117°11W **117 A2**
Tecopa CA .... 35°51N 116°13W **65 H10**
Tecumseh MI ...... 42°0N 83°57W **79 G8**
Tecumseh NE ...... 40°22N 96°11W **84 D9**
Tecumseh OK ...... 35°15N 96°56W **93 C7**
Tecumseh, Mt. NH . 43°57N 71°34W **86 C3**
Ted Williams Tunnel
  MA .... 42°21N 71°1W **106 A3**
Tee Nos Pos AZ .... 36°55N 109°6W **62 A6**
Tehachapi CA ...... 35°8N 118°27W **65 J8**
Tehachapi Mts. CA . 35°0N 118°30W **65 J8**
Tehachapi Pass CA . 35°6N 118°18W **65 J8**
Tehama CA .... 40°2N 122°7W **64 C4**
Tehama County ☆
  CA .... 40°5N 122°15W **64 C4**
Tejon Pass CA ..... 34°49N 118°53W **65 J8**
Tekamah NE .... 41°47N 96°13W **84 C9**
Tekoa WA .... 47°14N 117°4W **101 C8**
Tekonsha MI .... 42°5N 84°59W **79 G7**
Telescope Pk. CA .. 36°10N 117°5W **65 G9**
Telfair County ☆ GA . 31°55N 83°0W **68 E4**
Telida AK .... 63°23N 153°16W **61 E9**
Tell City IN .... 37°57N 86°46W **72 E4**
Teller AK .... 65°16N 166°22W **61 D6**
Teller County ☆
  CO .... 38°50N 105°0W **66 D5**
Tellico L. TN ...... 35°21N 84°17W **97 E8**
Tellico Plains TN .. 35°22N 84°18W **97 E8**
Telluride CO .... 37°56N 107°49W **66 D3**
Telocaset OR ...... 45°5N 117°49W **94 C7**
Telogia FL .... 30°21N 84°49W **67 A4**
Temblor Range CA . 35°20N 119°50W **65 H7**
Temecula CA ...... 37°51N 122°14W **118 A3**
Tempe AZ .... 33°24N 111°54W **116 C3**
Temperance MI .... 41°47N 83°34W **79 H8**
Temperanceville VA 37°54N 75°33W **77 C5**
Tempiute NV ...... 37°39N 115°38W **85 E5**
Temple NH .... 42°50N 71°49W **86 D3**
Temple OK .... 34°16N 98°14W **93 D5**
Temple TX .... 31°6N 97°21W **99 F10**
Temple City CA .... 34°6N 118°3W **111 B4**
Temple Hill KY .... 36°58N 85°51W **97 D7**
Temple Hills MD ... 38°48N 76°56W **119 C4**
Temple Terrace FL . 28°2N 82°23W **67 C6**
Templeton CA ..... 35°33N 120°42W **65 H6**
Templeton MA ..... 42°33N 72°4W **78 B2**
Ten Sleep WY ..... 44°2N 107°27W **104 B5**
Ten Thousand Is. FL 25°55N 81°45W **67 F7**
Tenafly NJ .... 40°54N 73°58W **114 A3**
Tenaha TX .... 31°57N 94°15W **99 F13**
Tenakee Springs
  AK .... 57°47N 135°13W **61 H14**
Tendoy ID .... 44°57N 113°38W **70 E5**
Tenino WA .... 46°51N 122°51W **101 D3**
Tenkiller Ferry L. OK 35°35N 95°2W **93 C8**
Tennant CA .... 41°35N 95°26W **73 D3**
Tennessee → TN ... 34°4N 88°34W **96 C4**
Tennessee □ U.S.A. . 36°0N 86°30W **96 C4**
Tennessee Pass CO . 39°22N 106°19W **66 C4**
Tennessee Ridge TN 36°19N 87°47W **96 D5**
Tennessee-Tombigbee Waterway
  U.S.A. .... 32°50N 88°10W **81 D5**
Tennille GA .... 32°56N 82°48W **68 D4**
Tennyson IN .... 38°5N 87°7W **72 E3**
Tennyson WI ...... 42°41N 90°41W **103 F3**
Tensas → LA ...... 31°38N 91°49W **75 C4**
Tensas Parish ☆ LA . 32°0N 91°10W **75 B4**
Tensas River Nat. Wildlife
  Refuge → LA .. 32°10N 91°27W **75 B4**
Tensaw → AL ...... 30°41N 88°0W **60 F3**
Tensed ID .... 47°10N 116°55W **70 B2**
Tenstrike MN ...... 47°39N 94°41W **80 C4**
Terlingua TX ...... 29°19N 103°36W **98 H4**
Terlingua Cr. → TX . 29°10N 103°36W **98 H4**
Terlton OK .... 36°8N 96°29W **93 B7**
Terra Alta WV ..... 39°27N 79°33W **77 A1**
Terra Bella CA .... 35°58N 119°3W **65 H7**
Terra Ceia FL ..... 27°34N 82°34W **119 D3**
Terral OK .... 33°54N 97°57W **93 E6**
Terre Haute IN .... 39°28N 87°25W **72 D3**
Terrebonne OR .... 44°21N 121°11W **94 C4**
Terrebonne B. LA .. 29°5N 90°35W **75 E5**
Terrebonne Parish ☆
  LA .... 29°20N 91°0W **75 E4**
Terrell TX .... 32°44N 96°17W **99 E11**
Terrell County ☆ GA . 31°50N 84°25W **68 E2**
Terrell County ☆ TX . 30°0N 102°0W **98 G6**
Terrell Hills TX .... 29°28N 98°27W **117 B3**
Terreton ID .... 43°50N 112°26W **70 F6**
Terril IA .... 43°18N 94°58W **73 B4**
Terry MS .... 32°6N 90°18W **81 D3**
Terry MT .... 46°47N 105°19W **83 D12**
Terry County ☆ TX . 33°11N 102°18W **98 D5**
Terry Pk. SD ...... 44°19N 103°49W **91 E2**
Terrytown LA ...... 29°54N 90°1W **113 C2**
Terrytown NE ...... 41°51N 103°40W **84 C2**
Teshekpuk L. AK ... 70°35N 153°26W **61 A9**
Tesuque NM .... 35°46N 105°55W **88 B5**
Tesuque Indian Reservation
  NM .... 35°48N 105°58W **88 B5**
Teterboro ✈ (TEB)
  NJ .... 40°51N 74°3W **114 A2**
Tetlin AK .... 63°8N 142°31W **61 E12**
Tetlin Junction AK . 63°19N 142°36W **61 E12**
Tetlin Nat. Wildlife Refuge
  AK .... 62°40N 141°50W **61 E12**
Teton ID .... 43°53N 111°40W **70 F7**
Teton → MT .... 47°56N 110°31W **83 C7**
Teton County ☆ ID . 43°45N 111°5W **70 F7**
Teton County ☆ MT . 47°52N 112°20W **83 C5**
Teton County ☆
  WY .... 44°0N 110°30W **104 C2**
Teton Pass WY .... 43°30N 110°57W **104 C2**
Teton Range WY ... 43°45N 111°0W **104 C2**
Teton Village WY .. 43°35N 110°50W **104 C2**
Tetonia ID .... 43°49N 111°10W **70 F7**
Teutopolis IL ...... 39°8N 88°29W **71 D5**
Tewaukon L. ND ... 46°0N 97°22W **91 E8**
Tewksbury MA ..... 42°37N 71°14W **78 B3**
Texana, L. TX ...... 29°0N 96°35W **99 J11**
Texarkana AR ..... 33°26N 94°2W **63 E1**
Texarkana TX ..... 33°26N 94°3W **99 D13**
Texas □ U.S.A. .... 31°40N 98°30W **99 F9**
Texas City TX ..... 29°24N 94°54W **99 H13**
Texas County ☆ MO . 37°20N 91°50W **82 D5**
Texas County ☆ OK . 36°45N 101°30W **93 B2**
Texas Point Nat. Wildlife
  TX .... 29°42N 93°54W **99 H14**
Texhoma OK .... 36°30N 101°47W **93 B2**
Texico NM .... 34°24N 103°3W **88 C7**
Texline TX .... 36°23N 103°2W **98 A4**
Texola OK .... 35°12N 99°59W **93 C3**
Texoma, L. TX ..... 33°50N 96°34W **99 D11**
Texon TX .... 31°13N 101°42W **98 F6**
Thackerville OK ... 33°48N 97°9W **93 E6**
Thalia TX .... 33°59N 99°32W **99 D8**
Thalmann GA ...... 31°18N 81°41W **68 E5**
Thames → CT ...... 41°18N 72°5W **78 C2**
Thatcher AZ .... 32°51N 109°46W **62 E6**
Thatcher CO .... 37°33N 104°7W **66 E6**
Thawville IL .... 40°41N 88°7W **71 C5**
Thaxton MS .... 34°18N 89°11W **81 B4**
Thayer IL .... 39°32N 89°45W **71 D4**
Thayer KS .... 37°29N 95°28W **74 D8**
Thayer MO .... 36°31N 91°33W **82 E5**
Thayer NE .... 40°28N 97°30W **84 D8**
Thayer County ☆ NE 40°15N 97°40W **84 D8**
Thebes IL .... 37°13N 89°28W **71 F4**
Thedford NE .... 41°59N 100°35W **84 C5**
Theodore AL ...... 30°33N 88°10W **60 F2**
Theodore Roosevelt L.
  AZ .... 33°46N 111°0W **62 D4**
Theodore Roosevelt Nat. Park △
  ND .... 47°0N 103°25W **91 D2**
Theodore Wirth Regional Park
  MN .... 44°59N 93°19W **113 B2**
Theodosia MO ..... 36°35N 92°39W **82 E4**
Theresa NY .... 44°13N 75°48W **89 A5**
Theressa FL .... 29°50N 82°4W **67 B6**
Theriot LA .... 29°28N 90°45W **75 E5**
Therma = Eagle Nest
  NM .... 36°33N 105°16W **88 A5**
Thermal CA .... 33°39N 116°9W **65 K10**
Thermalito CA ..... 39°31N 121°36W **64 D4**
Thermopolis WY ... 43°39N 108°13W **104 C4**
Thibodaux LA ..... 29°48N 90°49W **75 E5**
Thief → MN .... 48°7N 96°10W **80 B2**
Thief L. MN .... 48°30N 95°58W **80 B3**
Thief River Falls MN 48°7N 96°10W **80 B2**
Thielsen, Mt. OR .. 43°9N 122°4W **94 E4**
Thirtymile Cr. →
  ND .... 46°22N 102°4W **91 D3**
Thistle UT .... 39°59N 111°30W **100 D4**
Thomas MD .... 38°36N 76°18W **77 B4**
Thomas OK .... 35°45N 98°45W **93 C5**
Thomas WV .... 39°9N 79°30W **77 A1**
Thomas A. Edison, L.
  CA .... 37°25N 119°0W **65 F7**
Thomas County ☆
  GA .... 30°50N 83°55W **68 F3**
Thomas County ☆
  KS .... 39°20N 101°0W **74 B2**
Thomas County ☆
  NE .... 41°50N 100°30W **84 C5**
Thomas Hill Res.
  MO .... 39°34N 92°39W **82 B4**
Thomasboro IL ..... 40°15N 88°11W **71 C5**
Thomaston AL ..... 32°16N 87°38W **60 D3**
Thomaston CT ..... 41°41N 73°4W **78 C1**
Thomaston GA ..... 32°53N 84°20W **68 D2**
Thomaston ME ..... 44°5N 69°11W **76 D4**
Thomaston NY ..... 40°47N 73°42W **114 B4**
Thomasville AL .... 31°55N 87°44W **60 D3**
Thomasville GA .... 30°50N 83°59W **68 F3**
Thomasville NC .... 35°53N 80°5W **90 C5**
Thompson IA ...... 43°22N 93°46W **73 B5**
Thompson ND ..... 47°47N 97°6W **91 C8**
Thompson → MO .. 39°46N 93°37W **82 B3**
Thompson, L. SD .. 44°17N 97°26W **91 F8**
Thompson Falls MT 47°36N 115°21W **83 C2**
Thompson L. MA .. 42°19N 70°59W **106 B4**
Thompson Pk. CA .. 41°0N 123°2W **64 B3**
Thompson Springs
  UT .... 38°58N 109°43W **100 D5**
Thompsons Cr. →
  MS .... 31°10N 88°55W **81 F5**
Thompsonville IL ... 37°55N 88°46W **71 F5**
Thompsonville MI .. 44°31N 85°56W **79 E6**
Thomson GA .... 33°28N 82°30W **68 C4**
Thomson IL .... 41°58N 90°6W **71 B3**
Thoreau NM .... 35°24N 108°13W **88 B2**
Thornburg IA ...... 41°27N 92°20W **73 D5**
Thornburg VA ..... 38°7N 77°31W **77 C3**
Thorndale TX ...... 30°37N 97°12W **99 G10**
Thornhurst PA ..... 41°11N 75°35W **87 A1**
Thornton CO ...... 39°52N 104°58W **109 A2**
Thornton ID .... 43°45N 111°51W **70 F7**
Thornton IA .... 42°57N 93°23W **73 C5**
Thornton MS ...... 33°5N 90°19W **81 C3**
Thornton TX ...... 31°25N 96°34W **99 F11**
Thornton WV ...... 40°8N 86°36W **72 C4**
Thornville OH ..... 39°54N 82°25W **92 D4**
Thorny Mt. MO .... 37°35N 91°1W **82 D5**
Thorp WA .... 47°4N 120°40W **101 C5**
Thorp WI .... 44°58N 90°48W **103 D3**
Thorsby AL .... 32°55N 86°43W **60 D4**
Thousand Hills State Park
  MO .... 40°11N 92°39W **82 A4**
Thousand Islands NY 44°20N 76°0W **89 A4**
Thousand Oaks CA . 34°10N 118°50W **65 J8**
Thousand Springs Cr. →
  U.S.A. .... 41°17N 113°51W **100 B2**
Thrall TX .... 30°35N 97°18W **99 G10**
Three Creek ID .... 42°4N 115°10W **70 G3**
Three Forks MT .... 45°54N 111°33W **83 E6**
Three Lakes WI .... 45°48N 89°10W **103 C4**
Three Oaks MI .... 41°48N 86°36W **79 H6**
Three Rivers CA ... 36°26N 118°54W **65 G8**
Three Rivers MI ... 41°57N 85°38W **79 H6**
Three Rivers NM ... 33°19N 106°5W **88 D4**
Throckmorton TX .. 33°11N 99°11W **99 D8**
Throckmorton County ☆
  TX .... 33°10N 99°0W **99 D8**
Throgs Neck NY ... 40°48N 73°49W **114 B4**
Thunder B. MI ..... 45°0N 83°20W **79 E8**
Thunder Basin Nat. Grassland
  WY .... 43°45N 105°5W **104 C7**
Thunder Butte SD .. 45°19N 101°53W **91 E4**
Thunder Hawk SD .. 45°56N 101°58W **91 E4**
Thunderbird, L. OK . 35°14N 97°18W **93 C6**
Thunderbird Park
  AZ .... 33°41N 112°11W **116 A1**
Thunderbolt GA ... 32°1N 81°4W **68 D5**
Thunderhead, L. MO 40°30N 93°1W **82 A3**
Thurman IA .... 40°49N 95°45W **73 E3**
Thurmont MD ..... 39°37N 77°25W **77 A3**
Thurston NE .... 42°11N 96°42W **84 B9**
Thurston OH ...... 39°50N 82°33W **92 D4**
Thurston County ☆
  NE .... 42°15N 96°40W **84 B9**
Thurston County ☆
  WA .... 46°58N 122°55W **101 D3**
Tibbie AL .... 31°22N 88°15W **60 E2**
Tiber Res. MT ..... 48°19N 111°6W **83 B6**
Tibet, L. FL .... 28°27N 81°31W **115 B1**
Tiburon CA .... 37°52N 122°27W **118 A2**
Ticaboo UT .... 37°40N 110°42W **100 F5**
Tice FL .... 26°40N 81°49W **67 E7**
Tichnor AR .... 34°0N 91°12W **63 D4**
Tickfaw → LA ..... 30°21N 90°28W **75 D5**
Ticonderoga NY ... 43°51N 73°26W **86 C1**
Tidewater OR ...... 44°25N 123°54W **94 C2**
Tidioute PA .... 41°41N 79°24W **95 B3**
Tidmore = Seminole
  OK .... 35°14N 96°41W **93 C7**
Tie Plant MS ...... 33°44N 89°47W **81 C4**
Tie Siding WY ..... 41°5N 105°30W **104 F7**
Tierra Amarilla NM 36°42N 106°33W **88 A4**
Tierra Blanca Cr. →
  TX .... 34°58N 101°55W **98 C6**
Tierra Verde FL ... 27°41N 82°43W **119 C2**
Tierrasanta CA .... 32°49N 117°6W **117 B2**
Tieton WA .... 46°42N 120°46W **101 D5**
Tiffany CO .... 37°2N 107°32W **66 E3**
Tiffany Mt. WA .... 48°40N 119°56W **101 B6**
Tiffin IA .... 41°42N 91°40W **73 D7**
Tiffin → OH .... 41°7N 83°11W **92 B3**
Tiffin OH .... 41°7N 83°11W **92 B3**
Tift County ☆ GA .. 31°30N 83°30W **68 E3**
Tifton GA .... 31°27N 83°31W **68 E3**
Tigalda I. AK ...... 54°6N 165°1W **61 J6**
Tiger WA .... 48°42N 117°24W **101 B8**
Tignall GA .... 33°52N 82°44W **68 C4**
Tijeras NM .... 35°5N 106°23W **88 B4**
Tijuana → CA ..... 32°33N 117°6W **117 C2**
Tikchik Lakes AK .. 60°0N 159°0W **61 G8**
Tilden IL .... 38°13N 89°41W **71 E4**
Tilden NE .... 42°3N 97°50W **84 B8**
Tilden TX .... 28°28N 98°33W **99 J9**
Tilghman MD ...... 38°43N 76°20W **77 B4**
Tiline KY .... 37°11N 88°15W **96 D4**
Tillamook → OR ... 45°27N 123°51W **94 B2**
Tillamook OR ...... 45°27N 123°51W **94 B2**
Tillamook B. OR ... 45°30N 123°55W **94 B2**
Tillamook County ☆
  OR .... 45°20N 123°45W **94 B2**
Tillamook Head OR . 45°57N 124°0W **94 B1**
Tillar AR .... 33°43N 91°27W **63 E4**
Tiller OR .... 42°56N 122°57W **94 E3**
Tillery, L. NC ...... 35°12N 80°4W **90 C5**
Tillman County ☆ OK 34°25N 99°0W **93 D4**
Tillmans Corner AL . 30°46N 88°6W **60 F2**
Tilton GA .... 34°40N 84°56W **68 B2**
Tilton IL .... 40°6N 87°39W **71 C6**
Tilton NH .... 43°27N 71°36W **86 C3**
Timbalier B. LA .... 29°5N 90°20W **75 E5**
Timbalier I. LA .... 29°9N 90°13W **75 E5**
Timber Lake SD ... 45°26N 101°5W **91 E4**
Timberville VA ..... 38°38N 78°46W **102 C6**
Timbo AR .... 35°52N 92°9W **63 C3**
Timken KS .... 38°29N 99°11W **74 C4**
Timken Wildlife Management Area
  LA .... 29°48N 90°12W **113 D1**
Timmonsville SC ... 34°8N 79°57W **90 D6**
Timms Hill WI ..... 45°27N 90°11W **103 C3**
Timnath CO .... 40°32N 104°59W **66 B6**
Timpas CO .... 37°49N 103°46W **66 E6**
Timpson TX .... 31°54N 94°24W **99 F13**
Tims Ford L. TN ... 35°15N 86°10W **96 E6**
Timucuan Ecological and Historical
  Preserve □ U.S.A. 30°27N 81°27W **67 A7**
Tin Mt. CA .... 36°50N 117°10W **65 G9**
Tina MO .... 39°32N 93°27W **82 B3**
Tina NM .... 40°10N 93°36W **82 A3**
Tinemaha Res. CA . 37°3N 118°13W **65 F8**
Tingley IA .... 40°51N 94°12W **73 E4**
Tingmerkpuk Mt.
  AK .... 68°34N 162°87W **61 A7**
Tinian N. Marianas . 15°0N 145°38E **105 c**
Tinian Channel
  N. Marianas .. 14°54N 145°36E **105 c**
Tinmouth VT ...... 43°25N 73°2W **86 D1**
Tinnie NM .... 33°22N 105°14W **88 D5**
Tinsley MS .... 32°44N 90°28W **81 D3**
Tinsman AR .... 33°38N 92°21W **63 E3**
Tintah MN .... 46°1N 96°19W **80 D2**
Tinton Falls NJ .... 40°18N 74°6W **87 B3**
Tioga LA .... 31°24N 92°30W **75 C4**
Tioga ND .... 48°24N 102°56W **91 B3**
Tioga PA .... 41°55N 77°8W **95 B5**
Tioga TX .... 33°28N 96°55W **99 D11**
Tioga County ☆ NY . 42°10N 76°10W **89 C4**
Tioga County ☆ PA . 41°50N 77°10W **95 C5**
Tioga Pass CA ..... 37°54N 119°15W **64 E5**
Tionesta CA .... 41°30N 79°28W **95 E3**
Tionesta PA .... 41°30N 79°28W **95 C3**
Tipler WI .... 45°58N 88°38W **103 C5**
Tipp City OH ...... 39°58N 84°11W **92 D2**
Tippah County ☆ MS 34°44N 88°55W **81 B5**
Tippecanoe → IN .. 40°30N 86°45W **72 C4**
Tippecanoe County ☆
  IN .... 40°25N 86°55W **72 C4**
Tipton CA .... 36°4N 119°19W **65 G7**
Tipton IN .... 40°17N 86°2W **72 C4**
Tipton IA .... 41°46N 91°8W **73 D7**
Tipton KS .... 39°21N 98°28W **74 B5**
Tipton MO .... 38°39N 92°47W **82 C4**
Tipton OK .... 34°30N 99°8W **93 D4**
Tipton County ☆ IN . 40°20N 86°5W **72 C4**
Tipton County ☆ TN . 35°29N 89°43W **96 E3**
Tipton Mt. AZ ..... 35°32N 114°12W **62 B1**
Tiptonville TN ..... 36°23N 89°29W **96 D3**
Tiqua Indian Reservation
  TX .... 31°41N 106°19W **98 F1**
Tishomingo MS .... 34°41N 88°13W **81 B5**
Tishomingo OK ... 34°14N 96°41W **93 D7**
Tishomingo County ☆
  MS .... 34°49N 88°12W **81 B5**
Tishomingo Nat. Wildlife Refuge
  OK .... 34°11N 96°39W **93 D7**
Titonka IA .... 43°14N 94°3W **73 B4**
Tittabawassee → MI 43°23N 83°59W **79 F8**
Titus County ☆ TX . 33°9N 94°58W **99 D13**
Titusville FL ...... 28°37N 80°49W **67 C8**
Titusville PA ...... 41°38N 79°41W **95 B3**
Tiverton RI .... 41°38N 71°12W **78 C3**
Tiverton Four Corners
  RI .... 41°34N 71°11W **78 C3**
Tivoli TX .... 28°28N 96°53W **99 J11**
Toana Range NV ... 40°50N 114°20W **85 B6**
Toano VA .... 37°22N 76°48W **102 D8**
Toast NC .... 36°30N 80°38W **90 B5**
Tobias NE .... 40°25N 97°20W **84 D8**
Tobin MT .... 40°23N 117°31W **85 B3**
Tobin Range NV ... 40°20N 117°30W **85 B3**
Tobyhanna PA ..... 41°11N 75°25W **87 A1**
Toccoa GA .... 34°35N 83°19W **68 B3**
Toccopola MS ..... 34°15N 89°14W **81 B4**
Toco Hills GA ..... 33°49N 84°20W **106 B2**
Todd County ☆ KY . 36°50N 87°10W **96 D6**
Todd County ☆ MN . 46°10N 94°50W **80 D4**
Todd County ☆ SD . 43°5N 101°0W **91 G4**
Toddville MD ...... 38°18N 76°4W **77 B4**
Todt Hill NY .... 40°36N 74°6W **114 C2**
Tofte MN .... 47°35N 90°50W **80 C8**
Togiak AK .... 59°4N 160°24W **61 G7**
Togiak Nat. Wildlife Refuge →
  AK .... 59°20N 160°5W **61 G7**
Togowotee Pass WY 43°45N 110°4W **104 C3**
Tohatchi NM ...... 35°52N 108°47W **88 B2**
Tohono O'odham Indian
  Reservation △ AZ 32°15N 112°0W **62 E4**
Tohopekaliga, East L.
  FL .... 28°18N 81°15W **67 C7**
Tohopekaliga, L. FL 28°12N 81°24W **67 C7**
Toiyabe Range NV . 39°30N 117°0W **85 C3**
Tok AK .... 63°20N 142°59W **61 E12**
Tokeland WA ...... 46°42N 123°59W **101 D2**
Toksook Bay AK ... 60°32N 165°6W **61 F6**
Tolageak AK .... 70°3N 162°27W **61 A7**
Tolar NM .... 34°27N 103°56W **88 C7**
Tolbert TX .... 34°13N 99°24W **99 C8**
Tolchester Beach
  MD .... 39°13N 76°14W **77 A4**
Toledo IA .... 39°16N 81°54W **71 D5**
Toledo IL .... 39°16N 88°15W **71 D5**
Toledo OH .... 41°39N 83°33W **92 B3**
Toledo WA .... 46°26N 122°51W **101 D3**
Toledo Bend Res.
  LA .... 31°11N 93°34W **75 C2**
Toledo Bend Res. Dam
  LA .... 31°12N 93°34W **75 C2**
Tolland CT .... 41°52N 72°22W **78 C2**
Tolland County ☆
  CT .... 41°45N 72°20W **78 C2**
Tollesboro KY ..... 38°34N 83°34W **97 B9**
Tolleson AZ .... 33°27N 112°15W **116 C1**
Tolley ND .... 48°44N 101°50W **91 B4**
Tolna ND .... 47°50N 98°5W **91 C7**
Tolono IL .... 39°59N 88°16W **71 D5**
Tolu KY .... 37°26N 88°15W **96 C4**
Tom NM .... 33°44N 94°35W **93 E9**
Tom Bass Regional Park
  TX .... 29°35N 95°22W **110 C2**
Tom Green County ☆
  TX .... 31°28N 100°26W **98 F7**
Tom Steed Res. OK . 34°46N 98°50W **93 D5**
Tomah WI .... 43°59N 90°30W **103 E3**
Tomahawk WI ..... 45°28N 89°44W **103 C4**
Tomahawk L. OR .. 45°36N 122°39W **116 A2**
Tomales Pt. CA .... 38°14N 122°59W **64 E4**
Tomball TX .... 30°6N 95°37W **99 G12**
Tombigbee → AL ... 31°8N 87°57W **60 D4**
Tombigbee Nat. Forest
  MS .... 33°15N 89°15W **81 C4**
Tombstone AZ ..... 31°43N 110°4W **62 F5**
Tome NM .... 34°44N 106°44W **88 C4**
Tomichi → CO ..... 38°31N 106°58W **66 D4**
Tompkins County ☆
  NY .... 42°30N 76°30W **89 C4**
Tompkinsville KY .. 36°42N 85°41W **97 D7**
Tompkinsville MD .. 38°18N 76°54W **77 B4**
Toms → NJ .... 39°57N 74°7W **87 C2**
Toms Brook VA .... 38°57N 78°26W **77 B2**
Toms River NJ .... 39°58N 74°12W **87 C2**
Tonalea AZ .... 36°19N 110°56W **62 A4**
Tonasket WA ...... 48°42N 119°26W **101 B6**
Tonawanda Indian Reservation
  NY .... 43°5N 78°32W **89 B2**
Tonganoxie KS .... 39°7N 95°5W **74 B8**
Tongass Nat. Forest
  AK .... 54°45N 133°0W **61 J14**
Tongue → MT ..... 46°25N 105°52W **83 D12**
Tongue → ND ..... 48°56N 97°18W **91 B8**
Tongue River Res.
  MT .... 45°8N 106°46W **83 E11**
Tonica IL .... 41°13N 89°4W **71 B4**
Tonkawa OK ...... 36°41N 97°18W **93 B6**
Tonopah AZ .... 33°30N 112°56W **62 D2**
Tonopah NV .... 38°4N 117°14W **85 D3**
Tonsina AK .... 61°39N 145°11W **61 F11**
Tontitown AR ..... 36°11N 94°14W **63 B1**
Tonto → AZ .... 33°45N 111°10W **62 D4**
Tonto Nat. Forest
  AZ .... 34°0N 111°20W **62 D4**
Tonto Nat. Monument △
  AZ .... 33°39N 111°7W **62 D4**
Tony WI .... 45°29N 91°0W **103 C3**
Tooele UT .... 40°32N 112°18W **100 C3**
Tooele County ☆
  UT .... 40°25N 113°0W **100 C3**
Toole County ☆ MT . 48°48N 111°50W **83 B6**
Toombs County ☆
  GA .... 32°10N 82°15W **68 D4**
Toomsboro GA .... 32°50N 83°5W **68 D3**
Toone TN .... 35°21N 88°57W **96 E4**
Topanga State Park
  CA .... 34°7N 118°31W **111 B1**
Topawa AZ .... 31°48N 111°51W **62 F4**
Topaz L. NV .... 38°41N 119°33W **85 D1**
Topeka IN .... 41°32N 85°32W **72 B5**
Topeka KS .... 39°3N 95°40W **74 B8**
Topock AZ .... 34°46N 114°29W **62 C1**
Toponas CO .... 40°6N 106°48W **66 B4**
Toppenish WA ..... 46°23N 120°19W **101 D5**
Topsfield ME ...... 45°25N 67°44W **76 C6**
Topsfield MA ...... 42°38N 70°57W **78 B4**
Topton PA .... 40°30N 75°41W **95 D7**
Toquerville UT .... 37°15N 113°17W **100 F2**
Toquima Range NV 38°55N 116°50W **85 D3**
Tornillo TX .... 31°26N 106°5W **98 F1**
Tornillo L. NM .... 31°48N 105°47W **88 E5**
Toro L. → NM ..... 36°42N 103°57W **88 A7**
Toro, L. → NM .... 36°42N 103°57W **88 A7**
Toronto IA .... 41°54N 90°52W **73 D8**
Toronto KS .... 37°48N 95°57W **74 D8**
Toronto OH .... 40°28N 80°36W **92 C6**
Toronto SD .... 44°34N 96°39W **91 F9**
Toronto Lake KS ... 37°46N 95°57W **74 D8**
Torrance CA .... 33°50N 118°19W **111 C3**
Torrance County ☆
  NM .... 34°40N 106°0W **88 C5**
Torreon NM .... 35°49N 107°13W **88 B3**
Torres Martinez Indian Reservation
  CA .... 33°29N 116°5W **65 K10**
Torrey UT .... 38°18N 111°25W **100 E4**
Torrington CT ..... 41°48N 73°7W **78 C1**
Torrington WY .... 42°4N 104°11W **104 D8**
Tortilla Flat AZ ... 33°31N 111°23W **62 D4**
Tortola
  Br. Virgin Is. .. 18°19N 64°45W **105 G18**
Toston MT .... 46°11N 111°26W **83 D6**
Totowa NJ .... 40°54N 74°12W **114 A1**
Touchet → WA .... 46°2N 118°40W **101 D7**
Toughy NE .... 41°8N 96°50W **84 C9**
Toulon IL .... 41°6N 89°52W **71 B4**
Tournament Players Club of
  Michigan MI ... 42°37N 83°18W **109 B1**
Toutle → WA ...... 46°19N 122°55W **101 D3**
Towanda IL .... 40°34N 88°54W **71 C5**
Towanda KS .... 37°48N 97°0W **74 D7**
Towanda PA .... 41°46N 76°27W **95 B6**
Towaoc CO .... 37°12N 108°44W **66 E2**
Tower City ND ..... 46°56N 97°40W **91 D8**
Tower City PA ..... 40°35N 76°33W **95 D6**
Tower Hill IL ...... 39°23N 88°58W **71 D5**
Tower Junction
  WY .... 44°55N 110°25W **104 B2**

Town Creek AL .... 34°41N 87°24W 60 B3
Towner CO ...... 38°28N 102°55W 66 D8
Towner ND ..... 48°21N 100°25W 91 B5
Towner County ☆
 ND ...... 48°45N 99°10W 91 B6
Townley NJ ..... 40°41N 74°14W 114 B2
Towns GA ...... 32°0N 82°45W 68 D4
Towns County ☆ GA 34°55N 83°45W 68 B3
Townsend DE..... 39°24N 75°41W 77 A5
Townsend GA..... 31°33N 81°31W 68 E5
Townsend MA..... 42°40N 71°42W 106 B1
Townsend MT..... 46°19N 111°31W 83 D6
Townshend VT ..... 43°3N 72°42W 86 C2
Townville PA ..... 41°41N 79°53W 95 C3
Towson MD...... 39°24N 76°36W 107 A2
Toxey AL....... 31°55N 88°19W 60 E2
Toyah TX ...... 31°19N 103°48W 98 F4
Toyah Cr. ☆ TX .. 31°18N 103°27W 98 F4
Toyah L. TX..... 31°15N 103°20W 98 F4
Toyahvale TX .... 30°57N 103°47W 98 G4
Tracy CA .... 37°44N 121°26W 64 F5
Tracy MN....... 44°14N 95°37W 80 F3
Tracy City TN .... 35°16N 85°44W 97 E7
Tracyton WA ..... 47°36N 122°39W 118 C2
Tradewater → KY.. 37°31N 88°3W 96 C4
Traer IA .... 42°12N 92°28W 73 C6
Trafalgar IN..... 39°25N 86°9W 72 D4
Trail MN....... 47°47N 95°42W 80 C3
Trail of Tears Nat. Historic Trail
 AR....... 35°45N 93°30W 63 C2
Traill County ☆ ND.. 47°30N 97°20W 91 C8
Trammel VA ..... 37°1N 82°18W 102 D2
Trammel Cr. → KY.. 36°53N 86°23W 96 C6
Tranquillity CA .... 36°39N 120°15W 65 G6
Trans-Alaska Pipeline
 AK...... 70°11N 148°27W 61 A10
Transylvania LA.... 32°31N 91°11W 75 B4
Transylvania County ☆
 NC....... 35°10N 82°50W 90 C3
Trappe MD ...... 38°40N 76°4W 77 B4
Trapper Pk. MT ... 45°54N 114°18W 83 E3
Trask Mt. OR .... 45°22N 123°27W 94 B2
Traskwood AR .... 34°27N 92°39W 63 D3
Travelers Rest SC... 34°58N 82°27W 90 D3
Traverse, L. U.S.A... 45°46N 96°38W 80 E2
Traverse City MI... 44°46N 85°38W 79 E6
Traverse County ☆
 MN....... 45°45N 96°25W 80 E2
Traverse Mountains
 UT....... 40°29N 111°49W 117 D3
Traverse Pt. MI.... 47°9N 88°14W 79 B3
Travis NY...... 40°35N 74°11W 114 C1
Travis, L. TX .... 30°24N 97°55W 99 G10
Travis County ☆
 TX....... 30°17N 97°45W 99 G10
Treasure County ☆
 MT....... 46°15N 107°20W 83 D10
Treasure I. CA .... 37°49N 122°22W 118 B2
Treasure I. TN.... 30°5N 90°6W 112 B1
Treasure Island FL.. 27°46N 82°46W 112 C2
Tree Tops Park FL.. 26°4N 80°16W 112 C2
Treece KS ...... 37°0N 94°51W 74 D9
Trego County ☆ KS.. 38°55N 99°50W 74 C4
Trementina NM ... 35°28N 104°32W 88 B6
Tremont IL ..... 40°28N 89°29W 71 C4
Tremont MS ..... 34°14N 88°16W 81 B5
Tremont NY..... 40°50N 73°52W 114 A3
Tremonton UT .... 41°43N 112°10W 86 C2
Trempeleau WI.... 44°0N 91°26W 103 D2
Trempealeau County ☆
 WI ...... 44°15N 91°20W 103 D2
Trenary MT ..... 46°12N 86°58W 79 C5
Trent SD ...... 43°54N 96°39W 91 G9
Trent → NC ..... 35°5N 77°2W 90 C8
Trenton FL ..... 29°37N 82°49W 67 B6
Trenton GA ..... 34°52N 85°31W 68 B1
Trenton IL...... 38°36N 89°41W 71 A4
Trenton KY ..... 36°43N 87°16W 96 D5
Trenton ME...... 44°27N 68°22W 76 D5
Trenton MI ..... 42°8N 83°11W 79 C8
Trenton MO ..... 40°5N 93°37W 82 A3
Trenton NC ..... 35°4N 77°21W 90 C8
Trenton ND ..... 48°4N 103°51W 91 B2
Trenton NJ ..... 40°14N 74°46W 87 B2
Trenton TN ..... 40°11N 101°1W 84 D4
Trenton OH ..... 39°29N 84°28W 92 C6
Trenton TN ..... 35°59N 88°56W 96 E4
Trenton UT ..... 41°55N 111°57W 100 B4
Trentwood WA .... 47°42N 117°13W 101 C8
Tres Piedras NM... 36°39N 105°58W 88 A5
Tres Pinos CA .... 36°48N 121°19W 64 G5
Treutlen County ☆
 GA ...... 32°25N 82°30W 68 D4
Trevorton PA ..... 40°47N 76°41W 95 D6
Trexlertown PA ... 40°33N 75°36W 87 B1
Treynor IA...... 41°14N 95°36W 73 D3
Tri-City OR ..... 42°59N 123°19W 94 E2
Triangle VA...... 38°33N 77°20W 77 B3
Tribbey OK ..... 35°7N 97°4W 93 C6
Tribly FL ...... 28°28N 82°12W 67 C6
Tribune KS ..... 38°28N 101°45W 74 C2
Trident MT ..... 45°57N 111°28W 83 E6
Trident Peak NV ... 41°54N 118°24W 85 B3
Trigg County ☆ KY.. 36°50N 87°55W 96 D5
Trigo Mountains AZ.. 33°15N 114°40W 62 D1
Trimble MO ..... 39°28N 94°34W 82 B2
Trimble MN ..... 36°12N 89°11W 96 D3
Trimble County KY.. 38°35N 85°20W 96 B7
Trimont MN ..... 43°46N 94°43W 80 G4
Trinchera CO .... 37°2N 104°3W 66 E6
Trinidad CA ..... 41°4N 124°9W 64 B2
Trinidad CO ..... 37°10N 104°31W 66 E6
Trinidad DC ..... 38°54N 76°59W 119 B4
Trinidad TX..... 32°9N 96°5W 99 E11
Trinidad Head CA .. 41°3N 124°9W 64 B2
Trinity NC ..... 35°54N 79°59W 90 C6
Trinity TX ..... 30°57N 95°22W 99 G12
Trinity → CA .... 41°11N 123°42W 64 B3
Trinity → TX .... 29°45N 94°43W 99 H13
Trinity Center CA .. 40°59N 122°41W 64 C4
Trinity County ☆ CA 40°40N 123°0W 64 C4
Trinity County ☆ TX. 31°4N 95°8W 99 F12
Trinity Dam CA ... 40°48N 122°46W 64 C4
Trinity Is. AK .... 56°33N 154°25W 61 H9
Trinity Mt. ID .... 43°36N 115°26W 70 F3
Trinity Mts. CA ... 40°50N 122°40W 64 C4
Trinity Nat. Forest
 CA ...... 40°40N 123°15W 64 C3
Trinity Range NV... 40°10N 118°40W 85 B2
Trinity River Greenbelt Park
 TX....... 32°45N 96°48W 109 B4
Trinway OH ..... 40°9N 82°1W 92 C4
Trion GA ...... 34°33N 85°19W 68 B1
Triplett MO ..... 39°30N 93°12W 82 B3
Tripoli IA...... 42°49N 92°16W 73 B6
Tripp SD ...... 43°13N 97°58W 91 G8
Tripp County ☆ SD.. 43°20N 100°0W 91 G6
Triumph LA ..... 29°20N 89°30W 75 E6
Trona CA ...... 35°46N 117°23W 65 H8
Tropic UT ..... 37°37N 112°5W 100 F3
Trotwood OH .... 39°48N 84°18W 92 D2
Troup TX....... 32°9N 95°7W 99 E12
Troup County ☆ GA. 33°0N 85°0W 68 C1
Trousdale KS .... 37°49N 99°5W 74 D4
Trousdale County ☆
 TN....... 36°23N 86°9W 96 D6
Trout Cr. → OR... 42°23N 118°33W 94 E7
Trout Cr. → OR.. 45°42N 120°30W 94 C5
Trout Creek MI ... 46°29N 89°1W 79 C2
Trout Creek MT ... 47°50N 115°36W 83 C2
Trout Creek UT ... 39°42N 113°50W 100 D2

Trout Creek Mts. OR 42°6N 118°18W 94 E7
Trout Lake MI .... 46°12N 85°1W 79 C6
Trout Lake WA .... 46°0N 121°32W 101 E4
Trout Pk. WY .... 44°36N 109°32W 104 B3
Troutdale OR .... 45°32N 122°23W 94 B3
Troutdale VA .... 36°42N 81°26W 102 E3
Troutman NC .... 35°42N 80°53W 90 C5
Troutmans NC .... 35°42N 80°53W 90 C5
Troutville VA .... 37°25N 79°53W 102 D5
Troy AL .... 31°48N 85°58W 60 D5
Troy ID .... 46°44N 116°46W 70 C2
Troy IN .... 37°59N 86°55W 72 F4
Troy KS .... 39°47N 95°5W 74 B8
Troy MI .... 42°37N 83°9W 79 G8
Troy MO .... 38°59N 90°59W 82 C6
Troy MT .... 48°28N 115°53W 83 B2
Troy NC .... 35°22N 79°53W 90 C6
Troy NH .... 42°49N 72°11W 86 D2
Troy NY .... 42°44N 73°41W 78 B1
Troy OH .... 40°2N 84°12W 92 C2
Troy OR .... 45°57N 117°27W 94 B8
Troy PA .... 41°47N 76°47W 95 C6
Troy SD .... 45°2N 96°52W 91 E9
Troy TN .... 36°20N 89°10W 96 D3
Troy TX .... 31°12N 97°18W 99 F10
Troy VT .... 44°59N 72°25W 86 B2
Troy Peak NV .... 38°19N 115°30W 85 D5
Truchas NM ..... 36°3N 105°49W 88 A5
Truchas Pk. NM ... 35°58N 105°39W 88 B5
Truckee CA ..... 39°20N 120°11W 64 D6
Truckee → NV ... 39°51N 119°24W 85 C1
Truesdale LA ... 32°44N 95°11W 73 C3
Truesdale IA .... 42°44N 95°1W 73 C3
Truesdale MO .... 38°51N 91°5W 82 C5
Trujillo NM ..... 35°32N 104°42W 88 B6
Trujillo Alto
 Puerto Rico ... 18°21N 66°1W 105 G16
Truman MN ..... 43°50N 94°26W 80 G4
Truman AR ..... 35°41N 90°31W 63 C5
Trumansburg NY... 42°33N 76°40W 89 C4
Trumbull CT .... 41°15N 73°12W 78 C1
Trumbull NE .... 40°41N 98°16W 84 D7
Trumbull, Mt. AZ.. 36°25N 113°19W 62 A2
Trumbull County ☆
 OH....... 41°14N 80°49W 92 B6
Truro MA ...... 42°0N 70°3W 78 C4
Truscott TX..... 33°45N 99°49W 99 D8
Trussville AL .... 33°37N 86°35W 60 C4
Truth or Consequences
 NM....... 33°8N 107°15W 88 D3
Truxton AZ ..... 35°29N 113°34W 62 B2
Tryon NE ...... 41°33N 100°57W 84 C4
Tryon OK ...... 35°52N 96°58W 93 C7
Tryon Creek State Park ☆
 OR....... 45°25N 122°40W 116 E3
Tsaile AZ ...... 36°17N 109°14W 62 A6
Tsala Apopka L. FL.. 28°53N 82°19W 67 C6
Tschida, L. ND ... 46°37N 101°55W 91 C4
Tualatin OR..... 45°23N 122°45W 116 F3
Tuba City AZ .... 36°8N 111°14W 62 A4
Tubac AZ ...... 31°37N 111°3W 62 F4
Tucannon → WA.. 46°33N 118°11W 101 D7
Tuckahoe NJ.... 39°17N 74°45W 87 C2
Tuckahoe → MD... 38°59N 75°56W 77 B5
Tuckaway Park NJ.. 35°6N 80°49W 107 B2
Tucker AR ...... 34°26N 91°57W 63 D4
Tucker GA ...... 33°51N 84°13W 68 C2
Tucker County ☆
 WV ...... 39°9N 79°30W 102 B5
Tuckerman AR ... 35°44N 91°12W 63 C4
Tuckernuck Island
 MA ...... 41°18N 70°15W 78 C4
Tuckerton NJ .... 39°36N 74°20W 87 C2
Tucson AZ ...... 32°13N 110°58W 62 E5
Tucson Int. ✈ (TUS)
 AZ....... 32°7N 110°56W 62 E5
Tucumcari NM ... 35°10N 103°44W 88 B7
Tucumcari Cr. →
 NM....... 35°20N 103°15W 88 B7
Tuftonboro NH.... 43°42N 71°13W 86 C3
Tufts University MA.. 42°24N 71°7W 106 A3
Tug Fork → WV.. 38°7N 82°36W 102 C2
Tugidak I. AK ... 56°30N 154°40W 61 H9
Tukwila WA .... 47°28N 122°15W 118 C3
Tula Amer. Samoa.. 14°15S 170°34W 105 e
Tula MS .... 34°14N 89°22W 81 B4
Tulalip Indian Reservation
 WA....... 48°4N 122°13W 101 B3
Tulare CA ...... 36°13N 119°21W 65 G7
Tulare SD ...... 44°44N 98°31W 91 F7
Tulare County ☆
 CA....... 36°10N 118°50W 65 G8
Tulare Lake Bed CA.. 36°0N 119°48W 65 H7
Tularosa NM .... 33°5N 106°1W 88 D4
Tularosa Valley NM. 32°45N 106°0W 88 E4
Tule → CA ..... 36°3N 119°50W 65 G7
Tule Cr. → TX ... 34°40N 101°14W 98 C6
Tule L. CA ..... 41°53N 121°30W 64 B5
Tule Lake Nat. Wildlife Refuge ◌
 CA....... 41°52N 121°30W 64 B5
Tule River Indian Reservation
 CA....... 36°0N 118°50W 65 H8
Tule Valley UT ... 39°25N 113°30W 100 D2
Tulelake CA ..... 41°57N 121°29W 98 C6
Tulia TX....... 34°32N 101°46W 98 C6
Tullahassee OK ... 35°50N 95°25W 93 C8
Tullahoma TN ... 35°22N 86°13W 96 E6
Tulloch Res. CA ... 37°53N 120°36W 64 F6
Tullos LA ...... 31°49N 92°19W 75 C3
Tully NY .... 42°48N 76°7W 89 C4
Tulsa OK ...... 36°10N 95°55W 93 B8
Tulsa County ☆ OK. 36°10N 95°50W 93 B8
Tulsa Int. ✈ (TUL)
 OK....... 36°12N 95°53W 93 B8
Tuluksak AK .... 61°6N 160°58W 61 F7
Tumacacori Nat. Historic Park ◌
 AZ....... 31°35N 111°6W 62 F4
Tumbledown Mt. ME 45°27N 70°28W 76 C3
Tumon B. Guam... 13°31N 144°48E 105 b
Tumwater WA .... 47°1N 122°54W 101 C3
Tunica LA ...... 30°56N 91°33W 75 D4
Tunica MS ...... 34°41N 90°23W 81 B3
Tunica County ☆ MS 34°41N 90°23W 81 B3
Tunica-Biloxi Indian Reservation
 LA....... 31°7N 92°23W 75 C3
Tunis MD ...... 38°49N 76°10W 77 B4
Tunkhannock PA .. 41°32N 75°57W 95 C7
Tunnel Hill IL.... 37°32N 88°50W 71 F5
Tunnelton WV.... 39°24N 79°45W 102 B5
Tuntutuliak AK... 60°22N 162°38W 61 F7
Tununak AK .... 60°37N 165°15W 61 F6
Tuolumne CA .... 37°58N 120°15W 64 F6
Tuolumne → CA... 37°36N 121°10W 64 F5
Tuolumne County ☆
 CA....... 38°0N 120°0W 64 E7
Tupelo MS ...... 34°16N 88°43W 81 B5
Tupelo OK ...... 34°36N 96°26W 93 D7
Tupelo Nat. Battlefield ◌
 MS....... 34°15N 88°14W 81 B5
Tupper L. NY .... 44°14N 74°28W 89 A6
Tupper Lake NY... 44°14N 74°28W 89 A6
Turbeville SC .... 33°54N 80°1W 90 D5
Turbeville VA .... 36°37N 79°2W 102 E5
Turin IA .... 42°1N 95°58W 73 C3
Turkey TX ...... 34°24N 100°54W 98 C7
Turkey → IA .... 42°43N 91°2W 73 C7
Turkey Cr. → OK.. 35°53N 97°56W 93 C6
Turkey Creek LA .. 30°53N 92°25W 75 D3
Turkey Creek Park
 FL....... 28°30N 81°28W 115 A2
Turkey Mt. LA ... 29°22N 100°12W 98 H7
Turkey Ridge SD .. 43°26N 97°10W 91 G8
Turlock CA ..... 37°30N 120°51W 64 F6

Turlock L. CA .... 37°37N 120°35W 64 F6
Turner MI...... 44°9N 83°47W 79 E8
Turner MT...... 48°51N 108°24W 83 B9
Turner OR...... 44°51N 122°57W 94 C3
Turner WA...... 46°25N 117°51W 101 D8
Turner County ☆ GA 31°45N 83°45W 68 E3
Turner County ☆ SD. 43°17N 97°5W 91 G8
Turner Field GA... 33°44N 84°23W 106 B2
Turners Falls MA.. 42°36N 72°33W 78 B2
Turnerville WY... 42°52N 110°54W 104 D2
Turon KS ...... 37°48N 98°26W 74 D5
Turpin OK ...... 36°52N 100°52W 93 B3
Turpin Hills OH ... 39°6N 84°22W 107 B2
Turrell AR ...... 35°23N 90°15W 63 C5
Turtle → ND .... 48°19N 97°8W 91 B8
Turtle → SD .... 44°55N 98°29W 91 F7
Turtle-Flambeau Flowage
 WI....... 46°4N 90°14W 103 B3
Turtle Lake MN ... 45°5N 93°7W 113 A3
Turtle Lake ND ... 47°31N 100°53W 91 C5
Turtle Lake WI ... 45°24N 92°8W 103 C1
Turtle Mountain Indian
 Reservation ND.. 48°58N 99°58W 91 B6
Turtle Mountains ND 48°58N 100°0W 91 B6
Turtle River → WI.. 47°35N 94°46W 80 C4
Tusayan AZ..... 35°58N 112°9W 62 B3
Tuscaloosa AL ... 33°12N 87°34W 60 C3
Tuscaloosa, L. AL.. 33°16N 87°30W 60 C3
Tuscaloosa County ☆
 AL....... 33°11N 87°27W 60 C3
Tuscarawas → OH.. 40°24N 81°25W 92 C5
Tuscarawas County ☆
 OH....... 40°22N 81°26W 92 C5
Tuscarora NV .... 41°19N 116°14W 85 A4
Tuscarora Indian Reservation
 NY....... 43°10N 78°55W 89 B2
Tuscarora Mt. PA.. 40°55N 77°55W 95 D5
Tuscarora Mts. NV.. 41°0N 116°20W 85 A4
Tuscola IL ...... 39°48N 88°17W 71 D5
Tuscola TX...... 32°12N 99°48W 99 E8
Tuscola County ☆ MI 43°25N 83°20W 79 F8
Tuscumbia AL ... 34°44N 87°42W 60 B3
Tuscumbia MO... 38°14N 92°28W 82 C4
Tuskahoma OK ... 34°37N 95°17W 93 D8
Tushka OK ..... 34°19N 96°10W 93 D7
Tuskegee AL .... 32°25N 85°42W 60 D5
Tuskegee Nat. Forest
 AL....... 32°29N 85°35W 60 D5
Tutuila Amer. Samoa 14°19S 170°50W 105 e
Tutwiler MS..... 34°1N 90°26W 81 B3
Tuweep AZ ..... 36°25N 113°4W 62 A2
Tuxedo Park NY... 41°12N 74°11W 87 A2
Tuzigoot Nat. Monument △
 AZ....... 34°46N 112°2W 62 C3
Twain Harte CA .. 38°2N 120°14W 64 E6
Twentynine Palms CA 34°8N 116°3W 65 J10
Twentynine Palms Indian
 Reservation CA.. 34°7N 116°3W 65 J10
Twiggs County ☆
 GA....... 32°40N 83°30W 68 D3
Twin Bridges MT.. 45°33N 112°20W 83 E5
Twin Brooks SD... 45°12N 96°47W 91 E9
Twin Buttes Res. TX 31°22N 100°32W 98 F7
Twin City GA .... 32°35N 82°10W 68 D4
Twin Falls ID .... 42°34N 114°28W 70 G4
Twin Falls County ☆
 ID....... 42°30N 114°45W 70 G4
Twin Hills AK .... 59°23N 159°58W 61 G8
Twin Lake MI .... 43°22N 86°10W 79 F5
Twin Lakes CO ... 39°5N 106°23W 66 C4
Twin Lakes GA ... 30°43N 83°13W 68 E3
Twin Lakes MN... 43°34N 93°51W 80 G5
Twin Lakes WI ... 42°31N 88°15W 103 E5
Twin Lakes NM... 35°43N 108°46W 88 B2
Twin Lakes PA ... 41°32N 75°34W 87 A2
Twin Mountain NH.. 44°16N 71°32W 86 B3
Twin Peaks MT ... 45°25N 114°29W 70 F4
Twin Peaks CA... 37°45N 122°26W 118 B2
Twin Peaks ID ... 40°35N 114°43W 117 C3
Twin Peaks Wilderness
 UT....... 40°35N 111°43W 117 C3
Twin Rivers NJ ... 40°15N 74°32W 87 B2
Twin Valley MN .. 47°16N 96°16W 80 C2
Twinsburg OH ... 41°19N 81°26W 92 B5
Twisp WA ...... 48°22N 120°7W 101 B5
Twitchell Res. CA.. 34°59N 120°19W 65 J6
Twitty TX ...... 35°19N 100°14W 98 B7
Two Butte Cr. → CO 38°2N 102°9W 66 E8
Two Buttes CO ... 37°34N 102°24W 66 E8
Two Buttes Res. CO 37°38N 102°32W 66 E8
Two Harbors MN.. 47°2N 91°40W 80 C7
Two Medicine →
 MT....... 48°29N 112°14W 83 B5
Two Rivers WI ... 44°9N 87°34W 103 D6
Two Rivers Nat. Wildlife Refuge ◌
 IL....... 38°57N 90°31W 71 E3
Two Taverns PA... 39°47N 77°11W 77 A3
Ty Ty GA ...... 31°28N 83°39W 68 E3
Tyaskin MD ..... 38°18N 75°52W 77 B5
Tybee Island GA .. 32°1N 80°51W 68 D6
Tye TX .... 32°27N 99°52W 99 E8
Tygart L. WV .... 39°19N 80°2W 102 B4
Tygart Valley → WV 39°28N 81°0W 102 B4
Tyger → SC .... 34°28N 81°26W 90 D4
Tygh Valley OR ... 45°15N 121°10W 94 B4
Tyler TX....... 32°21N 95°18W 99 E12
Tyler MN ...... 44°17N 96°8W 80 F2
Tyler County ☆ TX. 30°47N 94°23W 99 G13
Tyler County ☆ WV 39°30N 80°54W 102 B3
Tylertown MS .... 31°7N 90°9W 81 E3
Tymochtee → OH.. 40°57N 83°16W 92 C3
Tynan TX ...... 28°10N 97°48W 99 J10
Tyndall SD ..... 43°0N 97°50W 91 G8
Tyndall Air Force Base
 FL....... 30°3N 85°40W 67 A3
Tyngsborough MA.. 42°40N 71°25W 78 B3
Tyonek AK ..... 61°4N 151°8W 61 F10
Tyro KS .... 37°2N 95°49W 74 D8
Tyrone NM ..... 32°40N 108°22W 88 D2
Tyrone OK ..... 36°57N 101°4W 93 B2
Tyrone PA ...... 40°40N 78°14W 95 D5
Tyronza AR ..... 35°29N 90°22W 63 C5
Tyronza → AR ... 35°9N 90°22W 63 C5
Tyrrell County ☆ NC 35°50N 76°10W 90 C9
Tyson VT ...... 43°27N 72°44W 86 C2
Tysons Corner VA.. 38°55N 77°13W 119 B2

U

U.L. Bend Nat. Wildlife Refuge ◌
 MT....... 47°40N 107°57W 83 C10
U.S.A. = United States of
 America ■ N. Amer. 37°0N 96°0W 52 C7
U.S. Air Force Academy
 CO....... 38°59N 104°51W 66 D6
U.S. Cellular Field
 IL....... 41°50N 87°37W 108 C3
U.S.S. Arizona Memorial ◌
 HI....... 21°22N 157°57W 69 K14
Ucross WY...... 44°34N 106°32W 104 B6
Udall KS ...... 37°23N 97°7W 74 D6
Udell IA....... 40°47N 92°45W 73 E6
Uehling NE ..... 41°44N 96°30W 84 C9
Uhrichsville OH .. 40°24N 81°21W 92 C5
Uinta → UT .... 40°9N 109°51W 100 C6
Uinta Mts. UT ... 40°45N 110°30W 100 C5
Uinta County ☆
 UT....... 40°20N 109°30W 100 C6
Uintah UT ..... 41°9N 111°58W 100 C4
Uintah and Ouray Indian
 Reservation UT... 40°20N 109°30W 100 C6
Ukiah OR ...... 45°8N 118°56W 94 B7
Ulak I. AK ..... 51°22N 178°57W 61 L3
Ulen MN ...... 47°5N 96°16W 80 C2
Ullin IL .... 37°17N 89°11W 71 F4
Ulster County ☆ NY 41°50N 74°15W 89 D7
Ulupalakua Ranch
 HI....... 20°39N 156°24W 69 C5
Ulysses KS ..... 37°35N 101°22W 74 D2
Ulysses NE ..... 41°4N 97°12W 84 C8
Ulysses PA...... 41°54N 77°46W 95 C5
Ulysses S. Grant Nat. Historic
 Site △ MO .... 38°33N 90°28W 82 C6
Umatac Guam.... 13°18N 144°39E 105 b
Umatilla OR .... 45°55N 119°21W 94 B6
Umatilla FL..... 28°55N 81°40W 67 C6
Umatilla, L. WA .. 45°53N 119°40W 101 E6
Umatilla County ☆
 OR....... 45°41N 118°31W 94 B7
Umatilla Indian Reservation
 OR....... 45°38N 118°11W 94 B7
Umatilla Nat. Forest
 OR....... 45°38N 118°11W 94 B7
Umbagog L. NH... 44°46N 71°3W 86 B3
Umbarger TX .... 34°57N 102°7W 98 C5
Umiat AK ...... 69°22N 152°8W 61 B9
Umnak I. AK .... 53°15N 168°20W 61 K5
Umpire AR ..... 34°17N 94°3W 63 D1
Umpqua → OR... 43°22N 124°12W 94 D1
Umpqua Nat. Forest
 OR....... 43°10N 122°40W 94 D3
Unadilla GA ..... 32°16N 83°44W 68 D3
Unadilla NY..... 42°20N 75°19W 89 C5
Unadilla → NY... 42°41N 96°16W 84 D7
Unalakleet AK ... 63°52N 160°47W 61 E7
Unalaska AK .... 53°53N 166°32W 61 K6
Unalaska I. AK ... 53°35N 166°50W 61 K6
Uncompahgre → CO 38°45N 108°6W 66 D2
Uncompahgre Nat. Forest
 CO....... 38°30N 108°30W 66 D2
Uncompahgre Peak
 CO....... 38°4N 107°28W 66 D3
Uncompahgre Plateau
 CO....... 38°20N 108°15W 66 D2
Underground Atlanta
 GA....... 33°45N 84°24W 106 B2
Underhill VT .... 44°33N 72°56W 86 B2
Underwood IL .... 38°32N 81°20W 115 A3
Underwood IA ... 41°23N 95°41W 73 D3
Underwood ND ... 47°27N 101°9W 91 C4
Unga I. AK ..... 55°15N 160°40W 61 J7
Unicoi TN ...... 36°12N 82°21W 97 C10
Unicoi County ☆ TN 36°9N 82°25W 97 C10
Unimak I. AK ... 54°45N 164°0W 61 J7
Unimak Pass AK.. 54°15N 164°30W 61 J6
Union AL....... 32°59N 87°54W 60 D3
Union IL .... 42°15N 93°4W 73 C5
Union ME ...... 44°13N 69°17W 76 D4
Union MS ...... 32°34N 89°7W 81 D4
Union MO ...... 38°27N 91°0W 82 C5
Union NJ ...... 40°42N 74°15W 114 B1
Union NE ...... 40°49N 95°55W 84 D10
Union OR ...... 45°13N 117°52W 94 B8
Union SC ...... 34°43N 81°37W 90 D4
Union WV ...... 37°36N 80°33W 102 D4
Union → IN .... 41°10N 84°55W 72 B6
Union County ☆ FL. 37°40N 87°55W 96 C5
Union County ☆ GA. 34°54N 84°0W 68 B3
Union County ☆ IL. 37°30N 89°15W 71 F4
Union County ☆ IN. 39°35N 84°55W 72 D6
Union County ☆ KY 37°40N 87°55W 96 C5
Union County ☆ MS. 34°29N 89°0W 81 B4
Union County ☆ NC. 35°0N 80°40W 90 D5
Union County ☆ NJ. 40°40N 74°20W 87 B2
Union County ☆
 NM....... 36°30N 103°30W 88 A7
Union County ☆ OH. 40°20N 83°22W 92 C3
Union County ☆ PA. 41°0N 77°0W 95 D6
Union County ☆ SC. 34°40N 81°35W 90 D4
Union County ☆ SD. 42°55N 96°45W 91 H9
Union County ☆ TN 36°15N 83°48W 97 C9
Union Creek OR .. 42°52N 122°27W 94 E3
Union Dale PA ... 41°43N 75°30W 95 C7
Union Flat Cr. →
 U.S.A. ..... 46°49N 118°0W 101 D8
Union Gap WA ... 46°33N 120°28W 101 D5
Union Grove WI .. 42°41N 88°3W 103 E5
Union Hills AZ ... 33°43N 112°3W 116 A2
Union L. NJ ..... 39°22N 75°3W 87 C1
Union Parish ☆ LA. 32°47N 92°24W 75 B3
Union Point GA... 33°37N 83°4W 68 C3
Union Port NY ... 40°48N 73°51W 114 B3
Union Slough Nat. Wildlife
 Refuge → IA ... 43°17N 94°7W 73 B4
Union Springs AL.. 32°9N 85°43W 60 D5
Union Springs NY.. 42°51N 76°42W 89 C4
Union Star MO ... 39°59N 94°36W 82 B2
Union Valley Res.
 TX....... 32°52N 120°26W 64 E6
Uniondale IN .... 40°50N 85°15W 72 C5
Uniondale AL .... 32°27N 87°31W 60 D3
Uniontown KS ... 37°51N 94°59W 74 D9
Uniontown KY ... 37°51N 87°56W 96 C5
Uniontown PA ... 39°54N 79°44W 95 E3
Uniontown WA ... 46°32N 117°5W 101 D8
Unionville CT.... 41°45N 72°53W 78 C2
Unionville MI .... 43°39N 83°28W 79 F8
Unionville MN ... 40°49N 92°42W 73 E6
Unionville MI .... 43°39N 83°28W 79 F8
Unionville MO ... 40°29N 93°1W 82 A3
Unionville NY ... 41°18N 74°34W 87 A2
Unionville PA ... 39°54N 79°44W 95 B2
Unionville VA ... 38°16N 77°50W 77 A3
Uniopolis OH .... 40°36N 84°5W 92 C2
United Center IL .. 41°53N 87°41W 108 C2

United States of America ■
 N. Amer. .... 37°0N 96°0W 52 C7
Unity ME ...... 44°37N 69°20W 76 D4
Unity MD ...... 39°13N 77°5W 77 A3
Unity OR ...... 44°26N 118°12W 94 C7
Unity WI ...... 44°51N 90°19W 103 D3
Universal City TX.. 29°32N 98°17W 117 B4
Universal Studios
 CA....... 34°9N 118°21W 111 B2
University City CA 32°51N 117°12W 117 A1
University City MO 38°39N 90°18W 117 A2
University Gardens
 NY....... 40°46N 73°43W 114 B4
University Park IL.. 41°25N 87°44W 71 B6
University Park MD 38°58N 76°56W 119 B4
University Park NM 32°17N 106°45W 88 E4
University Park TX 32°51N 96°48W 109 A5
University Place
 WA....... 47°14N 122°33W 101 C3
Upatoi Cr. → GA.. 32°22N 84°58W 68 D2
Upham ND ..... 48°35N 100°44W 91 B5
Upland CA ..... 34°6N 117°39W 65 J9
Upland IN ..... 40°28N 85°30W 72 C5
Upland NE ..... 40°18N 98°54W 84 D7
Upolu Pt. HI .... 20°16N 155°52W 69 C6
Upper Alkali L. CA 41°47N 120°8W 64 B6
Upper Arlington OH 40°0N 83°4W 92 C3
Upper B. NY .... 40°40N 74°3W 114 C2
Upper Crossroads
 MD....... 39°33N 76°29W 77 A4
Upper Darby PA .. 39°55N 75°16W 116 B1
Upper Delaware Scenic & Recr.
 River → NY ... 41°40N 75°3W 89 D5
Upper Iowa → IA.. 43°29N 91°14W 73 B7
Upper Klamath L.
 OR....... 42°25N 121°55W 94 E4
Upper Lake CA ... 39°10N 122°54W 64 D4
Upper Marlboro MD 38°49N 76°45W 77 B4
Upper Mississippi River Nat.
 Wildlife & Fish Refuge →
 IA....... 42°57N 91°9W 73 C7
Upper Missouri Breaks Nat.
 Monument → MT 47°50N 109°55W 83 C8
Upper New York B. = Upper B.
 NY....... 40°40N 74°3W 114 C2
Upper Ouachita Nat. Wildlife
 Refuge → LA ... 32°57N 92°8W 75 B3
Upper Peoria L. IL.. 40°55N 89°27W 71 C4
Upper Red L. MN.. 48°8N 94°45W 80 B4
Upper St. Clair PA.. 40°20N 80°5W 116 C1
Upper San Leandro Res.
 CA....... 37°45N 122°5W 118 B3
Upper Sandusky OH 40°50N 83°17W 92 C3
Upper Sioux Indian Reservation
 MN....... 44°46N 95°31W 80 F3
Upper Souris Nat. Wildlife
 Refuge → ND ... 48°35N 101°38W 91 B4
Upper Tract WV... 38°47N 79°17W 102 C5
Upperville VA .... 39°0N 77°53W 77 B3
Upshur County ☆
 TX....... 32°45N 94°57W 99 E13
Upshur County ☆ WV 39°0N 80°8W 102 C4
Upson AL ...... 32°24N 94°9W 99 D3
Upson County ☆ GA 32°50N 84°20W 68 D2
Upton KY ...... 37°28N 85°54W 97 C7
Upton MA ...... 42°11N 71°36W 78 C3
Upton ME ...... 44°42N 71°1W 76 D2
Upton WY ...... 44°6N 104°38W 104 B8
Upton County ☆ TX 31°15N 102°0W 98 F6
Urania LA ...... 31°52N 92°18W 75 C3
Uravan CO ..... 38°22N 108°44W 66 D2
Urbana IL ...... 40°7N 88°12W 71 C5
Urbana IA ...... 42°13N 91°52W 73 C7
Urbana MO ..... 37°51N 93°10W 82 D3
Urbana OH ..... 40°7N 83°45W 92 C3
Urbandale IA .... 41°38N 93°43W 73 D5
Urbank MN ..... 46°8N 95°31W 80 D3
Uriah AL ...... 31°18N 87°30W 60 E3
Urich MO ...... 38°28N 94°2W 82 C2
Uroyan, Montanas de
 Puerto Rico ... 18°12N 67°0W 105 G16
Ursa IL .... 40°4N 91°22W 71 C2
Ursina PA ...... 39°49N 79°17W 102 C5
Ursine NV ...... 37°59N 114°13W 85 E6
Usher FL ...... 29°24N 82°49W 67 B6
Usk WA ...... 48°19N 117°17W 101 B8
Utah □ U.S.A. ... 39°20N 111°30W 100 D4
Utah L. UT ..... 40°12N 111°48W 100 C4
Utah Test Range North
 UT....... 41°7N 113°11W 100 B2
Utah Test Range South
 UT....... 40°30N 113°50W 100 C2
Ute Creek → NM.. 35°21N 103°50W 88 B7
Ute L. NM...... 35°21N 103°22W 88 B7
Ute Mountain Indian Reservation
 CO....... 37°11N 108°41W 66 E2
Ute Park NM .... 36°34N 105°9W 88 A5
Utica IN ...... 38°30N 100°10W 74 C3
Utica KS ...... 32°7N 90°37W 81 D3
Utica NY ...... 43°6N 75°14W 89 B5
Utica NE ...... 40°54N 97°21W 84 D8
Utica OH ...... 40°14N 82°27W 92 C4
Utica SD ...... 42°59N 97°30W 91 H8
Utleyville CO .... 37°11N 103°4W 66 E7
Utopia TX ...... 29°37N 99°32W 99 H8
Utuado
 Puerto Rico ... 18°16N 66°42W 105 G16
Uvada UT ...... 37°43N 114°3W 100 F1
Uvalde TX...... 29°13N 99°47W 99 H8
Uvalde County ☆ TX 29°30N 99°43W 99 H8
Uvas, Sierra de las
 NM....... 32°29N 107°12W 88 E3
Uwharrie → NC... 35°23N 80°3W 90 C5
Uwharrie Nat. Forest
 NC....... 35°20N 80°0W 90 C6
Uxbridge MA .... 42°5N 71°38W 78 B3
Uyak AK ...... 57°38N 154°0W 61 H9

V

Vacaville CA .... 38°21N 121°59W 64 E5
Vacherie LA ..... 30°0N 90°48W 75 E5
Vader WA ...... 46°24N 122°58W 101 D3
Vadnais, L. MN... 45°3N 93°5W 113 A3
Vadnais Heights MN 45°3N 93°4W 113 A3
Vado NM ...... 32°7N 106°40W 88 E4
Vaiden MS ..... 33°20N 89°45W 81 C4
Vail AZ .... 32°3N 110°43W 62 E5
Vail CO .... 39°40N 106°20W 66 C4
Vail IA .... 42°4N 95°12W 73 C3
Valatie NY...... 42°25N 73°41W 89 C7
Valatie NY...... 44°4N 73°53W 103 D6
Valdez AK ...... 61°7N 146°16W 61 F11
Valdosta GA .... 30°50N 83°17W 68 F3
Valdese NC ..... 35°44N 81°34W 90 C4
Vale OR .... 43°59N 117°15W 94 D8
Vale SD .... 44°37N 103°24W 91 E3
Valencia NM .... 34°48N 106°43W 88 C4
Valencia County ☆
 NM....... 34°45N 107°0W 88 C4
Valentine AZ .... 35°23N 113°40W 62 B2

Valentine NE .... 42°52N 100°33W 84 B5
Valentine TX .... 30°35N 104°30W 98 G3
Valentine Nat. Wildlife Refuge ◌
 NE....... 42°36N 100°36W 84 B5
Valentine Falls KS. 39°21N 95°28W 74 B8
Valentines VA .... 36°35N 77°50W 102 E7
Valeria IA ...... 41°44N 93°20W 73 D5
Valier IL ...... 38°1N 89°3W 71 E4
Valier MT ...... 48°18N 112°16W 83 B5
Vallecito CA .... 37°23N 107°35W 66 E3
Vallecito Res. CO.. 37°23N 107°34W 66 E3
Vallejo CA ..... 38°7N 122°14W 64 E4
Valles Mines MO.. 38°2N 90°30W 82 C6
Valley AL ...... 32°49N 85°11W 60 D5
Valley NE ...... 41°19N 96°21W 84 C9
Valley WA ...... 48°11N 117°44W 101 B8
Valley Center KS.. 37°50N 97°22W 74 D6
Valley Center CA.. 33°13N 117°2W 65 K9
Valley City ND ... 46°55N 98°0W 91 D8
Valley Falls ☆ AR.. 34°45N 115°30W 76 D3
Valley County ☆
 ID....... 48°45N 106°30W 83 B11
Valley County ☆ NE 41°30N 99°0W 84 C7
Valley Falls KS ... 39°21N 95°28W 74 B8
Valley Falls OR .. 42°54N 73°34W 94 E5
Valley Falls RI ... 41°54N 71°24W 78 C2
Valley Forge Nat. Historical Park ◌
 PA....... 40°6N 75°27W 95 D7
Valley Grove WV.. 40°6N 80°34W 102 A4
Valley Head AL... 34°34N 85°37W 60 B5
Valley Head WV.. 38°33N 80°2W 102 C4
Valley Junction = West Des Moines
 IA....... 41°35N 93°43W 73 D5
Valley Lee MD ... 38°12N 76°31W 77 B4
Valley Mills TX ... 31°40N 97°28W 99 F10
Valley of Fire State Park ◌
 NV....... 36°26N 114°29W 85 F6
Valley Park MS ... 32°38N 90°52W 81 D3
Valley Park MO .. 38°33N 90°29W 82 C6
Valley Springs CA.. 38°12N 120°50W 64 E6
Valley Station KY.. 38°6N 85°52W 97 B7
Valley Stream NY.. 40°39N 73°42W 114 C4
Valley Stream State Park ◌
 NY....... 40°40N 73°41W 114 B4
Valley View OH .. 41°23N 81°36W 107 B2
Valley View PA ... 40°39N 76°33W 95 D6
Valley View TX ... 33°29N 97°10W 99 D10
Valliant OK ..... 34°0N 95°6W 93 E8
Valmeyer IL ..... 38°18N 90°19W 71 E3
Valmy NV ...... 35°49N 114°55W 85 B3
Valmy WV ..... 40°48N 117°8W 85 B3
Valparaiso FL .... 30°29N 86°30W 67 A2
Valparaiso IN .... 41°28N 87°4W 72 B3
Valparaiso NE ... 41°5N 96°50W 84 C9
Van TX .... 32°31N 95°38W 99 E12
Van Alstyne TX... 33°25N 96°35W 99 D11
Van Buren = Kettering
 OH....... 39°41N 84°10W 92 D2
Van Buren AR ... 35°26N 94°21W 63 C1
Van Buren IN ... 40°37N 85°30W 72 C5
Van Buren ME ... 47°10N 67°58W 76 A6
Van Buren MO ... 37°0N 91°1W 82 E5
Van Buren OH ... 41°8N 83°39W 92 B3
Van Buren County ☆
 AR....... 35°36N 92°28W 63 C3
Van Buren County ☆
 IA....... 40°45N 91°55W 73 E7
Van Buren County ☆
 MI....... 42°15N 86°0W 79 G6
Van Buren County ☆
 TN....... 35°45N 85°28W 97 E7
Van Horn TX .... 31°3N 104°50W 98 F3
Van Horne IA ... 42°1N 92°6W 73 C6
Van Meter IA ... 41°32N 93°57W 73 D5
Van Nuys CA ... 34°11N 118°26W 111 A2
Van Nuys ✈ (VNY)
 CA....... 34°12N 118°29W 111 A2
Van Tassell WY .. 42°40N 104°5W 104 D8
Van Vleet MS ... 33°59N 88°54W 81 C5
Van Wert IA .... 40°52N 93°48W 73 E5
Van Wert OH ... 40°52N 84°35W 92 C2
Van Wert County ☆
 OH....... 40°52N 84°35W 92 C2
Van Zandt County ☆
 TX....... 32°33N 95°52W 99 E12
Vance County ☆ NC 36°15N 78°20W 90 B7
Vanceboro ME ... 45°34N 67°26W 76 C6
Vanceboro NC ... 35°19N 77°9W 90 C8
Vanceburg KY ... 38°36N 83°19W 97 B9
Vancleave MS ... 30°32N 88°42W 81 F5
Vancleve KY .... 37°38N 83°25W 97 C9
Vancorum CO ... 38°22N 108°36W 66 D2
Vancourt TX .... 31°21N 100°11W 98 F7
Vancouver WA .. 45°38N 122°40W 101 E3
Vancouver, Mt. AK 60°20N 139°41W 61 F13
Vandalia IL ..... 38°58N 89°6W 71 E4
Vandalia MO.... 39°19N 91°29W 82 B5
Vandalia OH .... 39°54N 84°12W 92 D2
Vandemere NC .. 35°11N 76°41W 90 C9
Vandenberg Air Force Base
 CA....... 34°47N 120°32W 65 J6
Vandenberg Village
 CA....... 34°43N 120°28W 65 J6
Vander NC ..... 35°2N 78°48W 90 C7
Vanderbilt MI ... 45°9N 84°40W 79 D7
Vanderburgh County ☆
 IN....... 38°0N 87°35W 72 F3
Vandercook Lake MI 42°12N 84°23W 79 G7
Vandergrift PA ... 40°36N 79°34W 95 D3
Vanderpool TX... 29°45N 99°33W 99 H8
Vanduser MO ... 36°59N 89°42W 82 E7
Vanndale AR .... 35°13N 90°30W 63 C5
Vanoss OK ..... 34°46N 96°52W 93 D7
Vardaman MS ... 33°53N 89°11W 81 C4
Varina IA ...... 42°40N 94°54W 73 C4
Varna IL .... 41°2N 89°14W 71 B4
Varnado LA ..... 30°54N 89°50W 75 D6
Varnville SC .... 32°51N 81°5W 90 E4
Vashon WA ..... 47°27N 122°28W 118 C3
Vashon Heights
 WA....... 47°30N 122°27W 118 C3
Vashon Island WA 47°25N 122°28W 118 D3
Vass NC .... 35°15N 79°17W 90 C6
Vassar KS ...... 38°42N 95°37W 74 C8
Vassar MI ...... 43°22N 83°35W 79 F8
Vatia Amer. Samoa.. 14°15S 170°40W 105 e
Vaughan MS .... 32°48N 90°3W 81 D3
Vaughn MT ..... 47°33N 111°33W 83 C5
Vaughn WA ..... 34°36N 105°13W 88 C5
Vaughnsville OH.. 40°53N 84°2W 92 C2
Veblen SD ..... 45°52N 97°17W 91 E8
Veedersburg IN .. 40°7N 87°16W 72 C3
Vega TX....... 35°15N 102°26W 98 B5
Vega Alta
 Puerto Rico ... 18°25N 66°20W 105 G16
Vega Baja
 Puerto Rico ... 18°27N 66°23W 105 G16
Vegas Verde = North Las Vegas
 NV....... 36°11N 115°7W 110 B1
Veguita NM ..... 34°31N 106°46W 88 C4
Velma OK ...... 34°28N 97°40W 93 D6
Velva ND ...... 48°4N 100°56W 91 B5
Venango County ☆
 PA....... 41°20N 79°50W 95 C3
Venedocia OH ... 40°47N 84°28W 92 C2
Veneta OR ..... 44°3N 123°21W 94 C2
Venetian Islands FL 25°47N 80°9W 112 D3
Venetie AK ..... 67°1N 146°25W 61 C11
Venice CA ...... 33°59N 118°27W 111 C2
Venice FL ...... 27°6N 82°27W 67 D6
Venice IL ...... 38°40N 90°10W 117 B3
Venice LA ...... 29°17N 89°22W 75 E6
Venice NE ...... 41°16N 96°7W 84 C9
Ventnor City NJ... 39°20N 74°29W 87 C2

Venton MD ...... 38°12N 75°18W **77 B5**
Ventucopa CA ..... 34°50N 119°29W **65 J7**
Ventura CA ..... 34°17N 119°18W **65 J7**
Ventura County ☆
  CA ..... 34°30N 119°0W **65 J7**
Venus FL ..... 27°4N 81°22W **67 D7**
Vera OK ..... 36°27N 95°53W **93 B8**
Verda LA ..... 31°42N 92°46W **75 C3**
Verdel NE ..... 42°49N 98°12W **84 B7**
Verden OK ..... 35°5N 98°5W **93 C5**
Verdi NV ..... 39°31N 119°59W **85 C1**
Verdigre NE ..... 42°36N 98°2W **84 B7**
Verdigris → OK ..... 35°48N 95°19W **93 D8**
Verdon NE ..... 40°9N 95°43W **84 D10**
Verdugo Mts. CA ..... 34°10N 118°16W **111 B3**
Vergas MN ..... 46°40N 95°48W **80 D3**
Vergennes VT ..... 44°10N 73°15W **86 B1**
Vermejo → NM ..... 36°35N 104°30W **88 A6**
Vermilion IL ..... 39°35N 87°35W **71 D6**
Vermilion OH ..... 41°25N 82°22W **92 B4**
Vermilion → IL ..... 41°19N 89°44W **71 B4**
Vermilion B. LA ..... 29°42N 92°0W **75 E4**
Vermilion Cliffs
  UT ..... 37°10N 112°30W **100 F3**
Vermilion Cliffs Nat. Monument
  AZ ..... 36°54N 112°5W **62 A3**
Vermilion County ☆
  IL ..... 40°10N 87°45W **71 C6**
Vermilion Is. MN ..... 47°53N 92°26W **80 C6**
Vermilion Parish ☆
  LA ..... 29°55N 92°15W **75 E3**
Vermilion Ra. MN ..... 47°50N 92°0W **80 C7**
Vermillion SD ..... 42°47N 96°56W **91 H9**
Vermillion → SD ..... 42°44N 96°53W **91 H9**
Vermillion Bluffs
  CO ..... 40°50N 108°20W **66 B2**
Vermillion County ☆
  IN ..... 39°50N 87°30W **72 E3**
Vermont □ U.S.A. ..... 44°0N 73°0W **86 B2**
Verna FL ..... 27°23N 82°16W **67 D6**
Verndale MN ..... 46°24N 95°1W **80 D3**
Vernal UT ..... 40°27N 109°32W **100 C6**
Vernon AL ..... 33°45N 88°7W **60 C2**
Vernon CA ..... 34°0N 118°13W **111 B3**
Vernon CT ..... 41°50N 72°28W **78 C2**
Vernon FL ..... 30°37N 85°43W **67 A3**
Vernon IL ..... 38°48N 89°5W **71 E4**
Vernon IN ..... 39°1N 85°36W **72 E5**
Vernon NJ ..... 41°12N 74°29W **87 A2**
Vernon TX ..... 34°9N 99°17W **99 C8**
Vernon UT ..... 40°6N 112°26W **100 C3**
Vernon Center MN ..... 43°58N 94°10W **80 G4**
Vernon County ☆
  MO ..... 37°50N 94°20W **82 D2**
Vernon County ☆
  WI ..... 43°30N 90°50W **103 E3**
Vernon L. LA ..... 31°11N 93°22W **75 C2**
Vernon Parish ☆ LA ..... 31°9N 93°16W **75 C2**
Vernonia OR ..... 45°52N 123°11W **94 B2**
Vernor MI ..... 42°19N 83°7W **79 G9**
Vero Beach FL ..... 27°38N 80°24W **67 D8**
Verona MS ..... 34°12N 88°43W **81 B5**
Verona ND ..... 46°22N 98°4W **91 D7**
Verona NJ ..... 40°49N 74°14W **114 B1**
Verona PA ..... 40°30N 79°50W **116 A2**
Verona WI ..... 42°59N 89°32W **103 F4**
Verrazano Narrows Bridge
  NY ..... 40°36N 74°2W **114 C2**
Verret L. LA ..... 29°53N 91°10W **75 E4**
Versailles CT ..... 41°36N 72°2W **78 C2**
Versailles IL ..... 39°53N 90°39W **71 D3**
Versailles IN ..... 39°4N 85°15W **72 E5**
Versailles KY ..... 38°3N 84°44W **97 B8**
Versailles MO ..... 38°26N 92°51W **82 C4**
Versailles OH ..... 40°13N 84°29W **92 C2**
Vesper KS ..... 39°2N 98°17W **74 B5**
Vesper WI ..... 44°29N 89°58W **103 D4**
Vesta CA ..... 33°58N 82°56W **68 C4**
Vesta NE ..... 40°20N 96°20W **84 D9**
Vestavia Hills AL ..... 33°27N 86°47W **60 C4**
Vesuvius VA ..... 43°13N 101°23W **91 G4**
Veterans Memorial County Park
  MO ..... 38°48N 90°15W **117 A2**
Vevay IN ..... 38°45N 85°4W **72 E5**
Vian OK ..... 35°30N 94°58W **93 C9**
Viborg SD ..... 43°10N 97°5W **91 G8**
Viburnum MO ..... 37°43N 91°8W **82 D5**
Vicco KY ..... 37°13N 83°4W **97 C9**
Vicente, Pt. CA ..... 33°44N 118°24W **111 D2**
Vici OK ..... 36°9N 99°18W **93 B4**
Vick AR ..... 33°20N 92°6W **63 E3**
Vicksburg MS ..... 32°21N 90°51W **81 D3**
Vicksburg MI ..... 42°7N 85°32W **79 G6**
Vicksburg Nat. Military Park
  MS ..... 32°21N 90°51W **81 D3**
Victor CO ..... 38°43N 105°9W **66 D5**
Victor ID ..... 43°36N 111°7W **70 F7**
Victor IA ..... 41°44N 92°18W **73 D6**
Victor MT ..... 46°25N 114°9W **83 D3**
Victor NY ..... 42°59N 77°25W **89 C6**
Victoria KS ..... 38°52N 99°9W **74 C4**
Victoria TX ..... 28°48N 97°0W **99 H11**
Victoria VA ..... 36°59N 78°8W **102 E6**
Victoria County ☆
  TX ..... 28°45N 96°55W **99 J11**
Victorville CA ..... 34°32N 117°18W **65 J9**
Vidal CA ..... 34°7N 114°31W **65 J12**
Vidal Junction CA ..... 34°11N 114°34W **65 J12**
Vidalia GA ..... 32°13N 82°25W **68 D4**
Vidalia LA ..... 31°34N 91°26W **75 C4**
Vidauri TX ..... 28°26N 97°8W **99 J10**
Vidette GA ..... 32°52N 82°15W **68 C4**
Vidor TX ..... 30°7N 94°1W **99 G13**
Vieja, Sierra TX ..... 30°35N 104°40W **98 G3**
Vienna GA ..... 32°6N 83°47W **68 D3**
Vienna IL ..... 37°25N 88°54W **71 F5**
Vienna MD ..... 38°29N 75°50W **77 B5**
Vienna MO ..... 38°11N 91°57W **82 C5**
Vienna SD ..... 44°42N 97°30W **91 F8**
Vienna VA ..... 38°54N 77°16W **119 B2**
Vienna WV ..... 39°20N 81°33W **102 B3**
Vieques Puerto Rico 18°8N 65°25W **105 G17**
Vietnam Veterans Memorial
  DC ..... 38°53N 77°2W **119 B3**
Vietnam War Museum
  IL ..... 41°58N 87°39W **108 B3**
Vieux Desert, L. MI ..... 46°8N 89°7W **79 C2**
View Park CA ..... 34°0N 118°20W **111 B3**
Vigo County ☆ IN ..... 39°25N 87°25W **72 D3**
Vigo Park TX ..... 34°39N 101°30W **98 C6**
Viking MN ..... 48°13N 96°24W **80 B2**
Vilas CO ..... 37°22N 102°27W **66 E8**
Vilas SD ..... 44°1N 97°36W **91 F8**
Vilas County ☆ WI ..... 46°0N 89°30W **103 B4**
Villa Grove CO ..... 38°15N 105°59W **66 D5**
Villa Grove IL ..... 39°52N 88°10W **71 D5**
Villa Hills KY ..... 39°3N 84°35W **107 B1**
Villa Rica GA ..... 33°44N 84°55W **68 C2**
Village, The OK ..... 35°35N 97°33W **93 C6**
Village of Superior
  WI ..... 46°40N 92°6W **103 B1**
Villalba Puerto Rico 18°8N 66°30W **105 G16**
Villanueva NM ..... 35°16N 105°22W **88 B5**
Villard MN ..... 45°43N 95°16W **80 E3**
Villas NJ ..... 39°2N 74°56W **87 D2**
Villegreen CO ..... 37°18N 103°31W **66 E7**

Villisca IA ..... 40°56N 94°59W **73 E4**
Vilonia AR ..... 35°5N 92°13W **63 C3**
Vina AL ..... 34°23N 88°4W **60 B2**
Vinalhaven ME ..... 44°3N 68°50W **76 D5**
Vinalhaven I. ME ..... 44°5N 68°51W **76 D5**
Vincennes IN ..... 38°41N 87°32W **72 E3**
Vincent AL ..... 33°23N 86°25W **60 C4**
Vincent IA ..... 42°36N 94°1W **73 C4**
Vincentown NJ ..... 39°56N 74°45W **87 C2**
Vine Grove KY ..... 37°49N 85°59W **97 C7**
Vineland FL ..... 28°23N 81°30W **115 B1**
Vineland NJ ..... 39°29N 75°2W **87 C1**
Vineyard Haven MA 41°27N 70°36W **78 C4**
Vineyard Sd. MA ..... 41°25N 70°45W **78 C4**
Vinings GA ..... 33°53N 84°29W **106 A2**
Vinita OK ..... 36°39N 95°9W **93 B8**
Vinita Park MO ..... 38°41N 90°20W **117 B1**
Vinson OK ..... 34°54N 99°52W **93 D4**
Vinton IA ..... 42°10N 92°1W **73 C6**
Vinton LA ..... 30°11N 93°35W **75 D2**
Vinton OH ..... 38°59N 82°21W **92 E4**
Vinton VA ..... 37°17N 79°54W **102 D5**
Vinton County ☆
  OH ..... 39°15N 82°29W **92 D4**
Viola AR ..... 36°24N 91°59W **63 B4**
Viola DE ..... 39°5N 75°34W **77 A5**
Viola IL ..... 41°12N 90°35W **71 B3**
Viola KS ..... 37°29N 97°39W **74 D6**
Viola TN ..... 35°32N 85°52W **97 E7**
Viola WI ..... 43°31N 90°40W **103 E3**
Violet LA ..... 29°53N 89°53W **113 C3**
Virden IL ..... 39°30N 89°46W **71 D4**
Virden NM ..... 32°41N 109°0W **88 D1**
Virgil KS ..... 37°59N 96°1W **74 D7**
Virgil SD ..... 44°17N 98°26W **91 F7**
Virgilina VA ..... 36°33N 78°47W **102 E6**
Virgin UT ..... 37°12N 113°11W **100 F2**
Virgin → NV ..... 36°28N 114°21W **85 F6**
Virgin Gorda
  Br. Virgin Is. .. 18°30N 64°26W **105 G18**
  W. Indies ..... 18°30N 64°30W **105 G18**
Virgin Is. (British) ☒
  W. Indies ..... 18°30N 64°30W **105 G18**
Virgin Is. (U.S.) ☒
  W. Indies ..... 18°20N 65°0W **105 G18**
Virgin Islands Nat. Park △
  U.S. Virgin Is. 18°21N 64°43W **105 G18**
Virginia AZ ..... 36°45N 113°45W **62 A2**
Virginia ID ..... 42°30N 112°10W **70 G6**
Virginia IL ..... 39°57N 90°13W **71 D3**
Virginia MN ..... 47°31N 92°32W **80 C6**
Virginia □ U.S.A. .... 37°30N 78°45W **102 D6**
Virginia, L. FL ..... 28°53N 81°20W **115 A2**
Virginia Beach VA ... 36°44N 76°0W **102 E8**
Virginia City MT ..... 45°18N 111°56W **83 E6**
Virginia City NV ..... 39°19N 119°39W **85 C1**
Virginia Gardens
  FL ..... 25°48N 80°18W **112 B1**
Virginia Key FL ..... 25°44N 80°8W **112 D3**
Virginia Mts. NV ..... 39°58N 119°55W **85 B1**
Viroqua WI ..... 43°34N 90°53W **103 E3**
Visalia CA ..... 36°20N 119°18W **65 G7**
Visitacion Valley
  CA ..... 37°42N 122°23W **118 B2**
Vista CA ..... 33°12N 117°14W **65 K9**
Vista MO ..... 37°58N 93°40W **82 D3**
Vista Grove GA ..... 33°51N 84°16W **106 A3**
Vivian LA ..... 32°53N 93°59W **75 B2**
Vivian SD ..... 43°56N 100°18W **91 G5**
Volborg MT ..... 45°51N 105°41W **83 E12**
Volcano CA ..... 38°27N 120°38W **64 E4**
Volcano HI ..... 19°26N 155°14W **69 D6**
Volga IA ..... 42°48N 91°33W **73 C7**
Volga SD ..... 44°19N 96°56W **91 F9**
Volin SD ..... 42°58N 97°11W **91 H8**
Voluntown CT ..... 41°34N 71°52W **78 C3**
Volusia County ☆ FL 29°0N 81°15W **67 B7**
Von Ormy TX ..... 29°17N 98°38W **117 D2**
Vona CO ..... 39°18N 102°45W **66 C8**
Vonore TN ..... 35°36N 84°14W **97 D8**
Voorheesville NY ..... 42°39N 73°56W **89 C7**
Voyageurs Nat. Park △
  MN ..... 48°32N 93°0W **80 B6**
Vulcan MI ..... 45°47N 87°53W **79 D4**
Vulture Mts. AZ ..... 33°45N 112°50W **62 D3**
Vya NV ..... 41°35N 119°52W **85 A1**

W

W. Kerr Scott Res.
  NC ..... 36°10N 81°20W **90 B4**
Wabash IN ..... 40°48N 85°49W **72 C5**
Wabash → IN ..... 37°48N 88°2W **72 F2**
Wabash County ☆ IL 38°30N 87°50W **71 E6**
Wabash County ☆ IN 40°50N 85°50W **72 C5**
Wabasha MN ..... 44°23N 92°2W **80 F6**
Wabasha County ☆
  MN ..... 44°15N 92°15W **80 F6**
Wabasso FL ..... 27°45N 80°26W **67 D8**
Wabasso MN ..... 44°24N 95°15W **80 F3**
Wabaunsee KS ..... 39°9N 96°21W **74 B7**
Wabaunsee County ☆
  KS ..... 39°0N 96°15W **74 B7**
Wabeno WI ..... 45°26N 88°39W **103 C5**
Wabuska NV ..... 39°9N 119°11W **85 C1**
Waccamaw, L. NC ..... 34°18N 78°31W **90 D7**
Waccasassa B. FL ..... 29°10N 82°50W **67 B6**
Wachapreague VA .. 37°36N 75°42W **102 D9**
Wachuset Res. MA .. 42°24N 71°41W **78 B3**
Wacissa FL ..... 30°21N 83°59W **67 A5**
Waco NE ..... 40°54N 97°28W **84 D8**
Waco TX ..... 31°33N 97°9W **99 F10**
Waco L. TX ..... 31°35N 97°12W **99 F10**
Waconda Lake KS .. 39°26N 98°19W **74 B5**
Waconia MN ..... 44°51N 93°47W **80 F5**
Waddington NY ..... 44°52N 75°12W **89 A7**
Wade Hampton ☆
  AK ..... 62°15N 163°0W **61 E7**
Wadena MN ..... 46°26N 95°8W **80 D3**
Wadena County ☆
  MN ..... 46°26N 95°0W **80 D3**
Wadesboro NC ..... 34°58N 80°5W **90 D4**
Wading River NJ ..... 39°38N 74°31W **87 C2**
Wadley AL ..... 33°7N 85°34W **60 C5**
Wadley GA ..... 32°52N 82°24W **68 D4**
Wadsworth NV ..... 39°38N 119°17W **85 C1**
Wadsworth OH ..... 41°2N 81°44W **92 C5**
Wadsworth TX ..... 28°50N 95°56W **99 J12**
Wadsworth Atheneum
  CT ..... 41°46N 72°41W **78 C2**
Waelder TX ..... 29°42N 97°18W **99 H10**
Wagener SC ..... 33°39N 81°22W **90 D4**
Waggaman LA ..... 29°55N 90°12W **113 C1**
Wagner SD ..... 43°5N 98°18W **91 G7**
Wagon Mound NM .. 36°1N 104°42W **88 A6**
Wagon Wheel Gap
  CO ..... 37°46N 106°49W **66 E4**
Wagoner OK ..... 35°58N 95°22W **93 C8**
Wagoner County ☆
  OK ..... 36°0N 95°30W **93 B8**
Wagontire OR ..... 43°15N 119°53W **94 D6**
Wagontire Mt. OR .. 43°21N 119°52W **94 D6**
Wah Wah Mts. UT .. 38°25N 113°40W **100 E2**
Wahiawā HI ..... 21°30N 158°2W **69 K13**
Wahiawā District □
  HI ..... 21°30N 157°58W **69 J14**
Wahiawā Res. HI ... 21°30N 158°3W **69 K13**
Wahkiakum County ☆
  WA ..... 46°10N 123°30W **101 D2**
Wahkon MN ..... 46°7N 93°31W **80 D5**

Wahoo NE ..... 41°13N 96°37W **84 C9**
Wahpeton ND ..... 46°16N 96°36W **91 D9**
Wai'ale'ale HI ..... 22°4N 159°30W **69 A2**
Waialua HI ..... 21°41N 158°8W **69 J13**
Waialua B. HI ..... 21°34N 158°8W **69 J13**
Waialua B. HI ..... 21°35N 158°5W **69 J13**
Waialua District □
  HI ..... 21°35N 158°5W **69 J13**
Wai'anae HI ..... 21°27N 158°11W **69 K13**
Wai'anae Coast HI 21°26N 158°11W **69 K13**
Wai'anae District □
  HI ..... 21°28N 158°10W **69 K13**
Wai'anae Range
  HI ..... 21°30N 158°10W **69 K13**
Waiehu HI ..... 20°56N 156°30W **69 C5**
Waihee-Waiehu HI 20°56N 156°31W **69 C5**
Waikīkī HI ..... 21°17N 157°50W **69 K14**
Waikoloa Village
  HI ..... 19°55N 155°49W **69 D6**
Wailea-Makena HI. 20°40N 156°27W **69 C5**
Wailua HI ..... 22°3N 159°20W **69 A2**
Wailua HI ..... 20°51N 156°8W **69 C5**
Wailuku HI ..... 20°53N 156°30W **69 C5**
Wailuku → HI ..... 21°24N 157°57W **69 K14**
Waimānalo HI ..... 21°21N 157°43W **69 K14**
Waimānalo B. HI ... 21°21N 157°43W **69 K14**
Waimea HI ..... 21°57N 159°40W **69 B2**
Waimea HI ..... 21°39N 158°3W **69 J13**
Waimea B. HI ..... 21°40N 158°5W **69 J13**
Waimea Canyon HI 22°0N 159°39W **69 A2**
Wainwright AK ..... 70°38N 160°2W **61 A7**
Waipahu HI ..... 21°23N 158°1W **69 K13**
Waipi'o HI ..... 21°25N 158°0W **69 K13**
Waipi'o Acres HI ... 21°28N 158°1W **69 K13**
Waipi'o Peninsula
  HI ..... 21°21N 157°42W **69 K14**
Waita Res. HI ..... 21°55N 159°28W **69 B2**
Waite ME ..... 45°20N 67°42W **76 C6**
Waite Park MN ..... 45°33N 94°14W **80 E4**
Waiteville WV ..... 37°28N 80°25W **102 D4**
Waits → VT ..... 44°2N 72°9W **86 C2**
Waitsburg WA ..... 46°16N 118°9W **101 D7**
Waitsfield VT ..... 44°12N 72°50W **86 C2**
Waka TX ..... 36°17N 101°3W **98 A6**
Wakarusa IN ..... 41°32N 86°1W **72 B4**
Wake County ☆ NC .. 35°40N 78°45W **90 C7**
Wake Forest NC ..... 35°59N 78°30W **90 C7**
Wake I. Pac. Oc. ..... 19°18N 166°36E **105 C5**
Wakeeney KS ..... 39°1N 99°53W **74 B4**
Wakefield KS ..... 39°13N 97°1W **74 B6**
Wakefield MA ..... 42°30N 71°5W **106 A3**
Wakefield MI ..... 46°29N 89°56W **79 C2**
Wakefield NE ..... 42°16N 96°52W **84 B9**
Wakefield NH ..... 43°35N 71°4W **86 C3**
Wakefield RI ..... 41°26N 71°30W **78 D3**
Wakefield VA ..... 36°58N 76°59W **102 E8**
Wakita OK ..... 36°53N 97°55W **93 B6**
Wakpala SD ..... 45°40N 100°32W **91 E5**
Wakulla FL ..... 30°14N 84°14W **67 A4**
Wakulla Beach FL .. 30°6N 84°16W **67 A4**
Wakulla County ☆
  FL ..... 30°15N 84°20W **67 A4**
Walcott IA ..... 41°35N 90°47W **73 D8**
Walcott ND ..... 46°33N 96°56W **91 D9**
Walcott, L. ID ..... 42°40N 113°20W **70 G5**
Walden CO ..... 40°44N 106°17W **66 B4**
Walden NY ..... 41°34N 74°11W **89 D6**
Walden TN ..... 35°10N 85°14W **97 E7**
Walden Res. CO ..... 40°43N 106°17W **66 B4**
Walden Ridge TN .. 35°30N 85°15W **97 E7**
Waldo AR ..... 33°21N 93°18W **63 E2**
Waldo FL ..... 29°48N 82°10W **67 B6**
Waldo ME ..... 44°31N 69°5W **76 D4**
Waldo OH ..... 40°28N 83°5W **92 C3**
Waldo County ☆ ME 44°25N 69°0W **76 D4**
Waldo L. OR ..... 43°44N 122°2W **94 D3**
Waldoboro ME ..... 44°6N 69°23W **76 D4**
Waldorf MN ..... 43°56N 93°42W **80 G5**
Waldorf MD ..... 38°38N 76°55W **77 B4**
Waldport OR ..... 44°26N 124°4W **94 C1**
Waldron AR ..... 34°54N 94°5W **63 D1**
Waldron IN ..... 39°27N 85°40W **72 D5**
Waldron MI ..... 41°44N 84°25W **79 H7**
Wales AK ..... 65°37N 168°5W **61 D5**
Wales MA ..... 42°4N 72°13W **78 B2**
Wales ND ..... 48°54N 98°36W **91 B7**
Wales UT ..... 39°29N 111°38W **100 D4**
Walford IA ..... 41°53N 91°50W **73 D7**
Walhalla ND ..... 48°55N 97°55W **91 B8**
Walhalla SC ..... 34°46N 83°4W **90 C2**
Walk, L. TX ..... 29°31N 100°59W **98 H7**
Walker IA ..... 42°17N 91°47W **73 C7**
Walker LA ..... 30°29N 90°51W **75 D5**
Walker MI ..... 42°58N 85°46W **79 G6**
Walker MN ..... 47°6N 94°35W **80 C4**
Walker MO ..... 37°54N 94°14W **82 D2**
Walker SD ..... 45°35N 101°5W **91 E4**
Walker → NV ..... 38°54N 118°45W **85 D2**
Walker County ☆ AL 33°50N 87°17W **60 C3**
Walker County ☆
  GA ..... 34°45N 85°15W **68 B1**
Walker County ☆
  TX ..... 30°43N 95°33W **99 G12**
Walker L. NV ..... 38°42N 118°43W **85 D2**
Walker River Indian Reservation
  NV ..... 43°21N 70°28W **76 E3**
Walkers Pt. ME ..... 43°21N 70°28W **76 E3**
Walkersville MD ..... 39°29N 77°21W **77 A3**
Walkerton IN ..... 41°28N 86°29W **72 B4**
Walkertown NC ..... 36°10N 80°10W **90 B5**
Walkerville MI ..... 43°43N 86°8W **79 F5**
Wall SD ..... 43°59N 102°14W **91 G3**
Wall TX ..... 31°22N 100°18W **98 F7**
Wall Lake IA ..... 42°16N 95°5W **73 C3**
Walla Walla WA .... 46°4N 118°20W **101 D7**
Walla Walla → WA .. 46°3N 118°55W **101 D7**
Walla Walla County ☆
  WA ..... 46°18N 118°37W **101 D7**
Wallace ID ..... 47°28N 115°56W **70 B3**
Wallace NC ..... 34°44N 77°59W **90 D8**
Wallace NE ..... 40°50N 101°10W **84 D4**
Wallace SD ..... 45°5N 97°29W **91 E8**
Wallace County ☆
  KS ..... 38°50N 101°45W **74 C2**
Walland TN ..... 35°44N 83°49W **97 E9**
Wallaston, L.
  PA ..... 41°25N 75°15W **87 A1**
Waller TX ..... 30°4N 95°56W **99 G12**
Waller County ☆ TX 30°0N 96°0W **99 G12**
Wallingford IA ..... 43°19N 94°48W **73 B4**
Wallingford CT ..... 41°27N 72°50W **78 C2**
Wallington NJ ..... 40°51N 74°6W **114 A2**
Wallis TX ..... 29°38N 96°4W **99 H11**
Wallisville L. TX ..... 29°57N 94°44W **99 H13**
Wallkill NY ..... 41°37N 74°11W **89 D6**
Wallkill → NY ..... 41°35N 74°3W **89 D6**
Walloon L. MI ..... 45°17N 85°0W **79 D7**
Wallops I. VA ..... 37°50N 75°30W **102 D9**
Wallowa OR ..... 45°34N 117°32W **94 B8**
Wallowa County ☆
  OR ..... 45°20N 117°30W **94 B8**
Wallowa Mts. OR .. 45°20N 117°30W **94 B8**

Wallowa-Whitman Nat. Forest
  OR ..... 45°15N 117°20W **94 B8**
Walls MS ..... 34°58N 90°9W **81 B3**
Wallsburg UT ..... 40°23N 111°25W **100 C4**
Wallula WA ..... 46°5N 118°54W **101 D7**
Wallula, L. WA ..... 46°5N 118°59W **101 D7**
Walnut CA ..... 34°2N 117°51W **111 B4**
Walnut IA ..... 41°29N 95°13W **73 D3**
Walnut IL ..... 41°33N 89°36W **71 B4**
Walnut KS ..... 37°36N 95°5W **63 B8**
Walnut MS ..... 34°57N 88°54W **81 B5**
Walnut → KS ..... 37°3N 97°0W **74 D6**
Walnut Canyon Nat. Monument
  AZ ..... 35°15N 111°20W **62 B4**
Walnut Cove NC ..... 36°18N 80°9W **90 B5**
Walnut Cr. → KS .... 38°21N 98°41W **74 C5**
Walnut Cr. → OH ... 39°41N 82°59W **92 D4**
Walnut Creek CA ... 37°54N 122°4W **64 F4**
Walnut Creek NC ... 35°18N 77°52W **90 C8**
Walnut Grove AL ... 34°4N 86°18W **60 B4**
Walnut Grove MS .. 32°36N 89°28W **81 D4**
Walnut Grove MO .. 37°25N 93°33W **82 D3**
Walnut Hill FL ..... 30°54N 87°26W **67 A1**
Walnut Park CA ..... 33°58N 118°13W **111 C3**
Walnut Ridge AR ... 36°4N 90°57W **63 B5**
Walnut Springs TX. 32°3N 97°45W **99 F10**
Walpole MA ..... 42°9N 71°15W **78 B3**
Walpole NH ..... 43°5N 72°26W **86 C2**
Walsenburg CO ..... 37°38N 104°47W **66 E6**
Walsh CO ..... 37°23N 102°17W **66 E8**
Walsh County ☆ ND 48°24N 97°45W **91 B8**
Walt Disney World
  FL ..... 28°22N 81°33W **115 B1**
Walter Chandler Park
  TN ..... 35°1N 90°3W **112 B1**
Walter D. Stone Memorial Zoo
  MA ..... 42°28N 71°6W **106 A3**
Walter F. George Res.
  U.S.A. ..... 31°38N 85°4W **60 E5**
Walterboro SC ..... 32°55N 80°40W **90 F5**
Walters OK ..... 34°22N 98°19W **93 D5**
Walterville OR ..... 44°4N 122°48W **94 C3**
Walthall MS ..... 33°37N 89°17W **81 C4**
Walthall County ☆ MS 31°7N 90°9W **81 E3**
Waltham ME ..... 44°43N 68°20W **76 D5**
Waltham MA ..... 42°23N 71°14W **106 A2**
Walthill NE ..... 42°9N 96°30W **84 B9**
Waltman WY ..... 43°4N 107°12W **104 C5**
Walton IN ..... 40°40N 86°15W **72 C4**
Walton KS ..... 38°7N 97°15W **74 C6**
Walton KY ..... 38°52N 84°37W **97 B8**
Walton → NV ..... 38°54N 118°45W **85 D2**
Walton County ☆ FL 30°30N 86°10W **67 A2**
Walton County ☆
  GA ..... 33°45N 83°45W **68 C3**
Waltonville IL ..... 38°13N 89°2W **71 E4**
Walworth County ☆
  SD ..... 45°30N 100°0W **91 E6**
Walworth County ☆
  WI ..... 42°40N 88°30W **103 F5**
Wamac IL ..... 38°31N 89°9W **71 E4**
Wamego KS ..... 39°12N 96°18W **74 B7**
Wampsville NY ..... 43°4N 75°42W **89 B5**
Wampum PA ..... 40°54N 80°21W **95 D2**
Wamsutter WY ..... 41°40N 107°58W **104 D4**
Wanamingo MN ..... 44°18N 92°47W **80 F6**
Wanapum Dam
  WA ..... 46°52N 119°58W **101 D6**
Wanaque NJ ..... 41°2N 74°18W **87 A2**
Wanaque Res. NJ ... 41°2N 74°18W **87 A2**
Wanatah IN ..... 41°26N 86°54W **72 B4**
Wanblee SD ..... 43°34N 101°40W **91 G4**
Wanchese NC ..... 35°51N 75°38W **90 C10**
Wanda MN ..... 44°19N 95°13W **80 F3**
Wanette OK ..... 34°58N 97°2W **93 D6**
Wango MD ..... 38°20N 75°25W **77 B5**
Wann OK ..... 36°55N 95°48W **93 B8**
Wapack Nat. Wildlife Refuge
  NH ..... 42°53N 71°52W **86 D3**
Wapakoneta OH ..... 40°34N 84°12W **92 C2**
Wapanucka OK ..... 34°22N 96°26W **93 D7**
Wapato WA ..... 46°27N 120°25W **101 D5**
Wapella IL ..... 40°11N 91°11W **73 D7**
Wapello County ☆ IA 41°11N 92°24W **73 D6**
Wapinitia Pass OR .. 45°14N 121°42W **94 B4**
Wapiti WY ..... 44°28N 109°26W **104 B3**
Wappapello L. MO .. 36°56N 90°17W **82 E6**
Wappingers Falls NY 41°36N 73°55W **89 D7**
Waspinicon → IA ... 41°44N 90°19W **73 D8**
War WV ..... 37°18N 81°41W **102 D3**
War in the Pacific Nat. Hist. Park △
  Guam ..... 13°24N 144°39E **105 b**
Ward AR ..... 35°2N 91°57W **63 C4**
Ward SD ..... 44°9N 96°28W **91 F9**
Ward County ☆ ND .. 48°5N 101°30W **91 B4**
Ward County ☆ TX .. 31°32N 103°8W **98 F4**
Wardell MO ..... 36°21N 89°49W **82 E7**
Warden WA ..... 46°58N 119°2W **101 D6**
Wardensville WV ... 39°5N 78°36W **77 A2**
Wardsville MO ..... 38°29N 92°11W **82 C4**
Ware MA ..... 42°16N 72°14W **78 B2**
Ware → MA ..... 42°11N 72°22W **78 B2**
Ware County ☆ GA .. 31°10N 82°20W **68 E4**
Ware Shoals SC ..... 34°24N 82°15W **90 D3**
Wareham MA ..... 41°46N 70°43W **78 C4**
Warehouse Point CT 41°56N 72°37W **78 C2**
Waresboro GA ..... 31°15N 82°29W **68 E4**
Warfield KY ..... 37°51N 82°25W **97 C10**
Warm Lake ID ..... 44°39N 115°40W **70 E3**
Warm Springs GA .. 32°53N 84°41W **68 C2**
Warm Springs NV .. 38°10N 116°20W **85 D4**
Warm Springs NV .. 38°12N 116°29W **85 D4**
Warm Springs OR .. 44°51N 121°17W **94 C4**
Warm Springs → OR 44°51N 121°4W **94 C4**
Warm Springs Indian Reservation
  OR ..... 45°0N 121°25W **94 C4**
Warm Springs Res.
  OR ..... 43°35N 118°13W **94 D7**
Warminster PA ..... 40°12N 75°6W **95 D7**
Warner NH ..... 43°17N 71°49W **86 C3**
Warner SD ..... 45°19N 98°30W **91 E7**
Warner → NH ..... 43°15N 71°50W **86 C3**
Warner Brothers Studios
  CA ..... 34°9N 118°20W **111 B2**
Warner Mts. CA ..... 41°40N 120°15W **64 B6**
Warner Robins GA. 32°37N 83°36W **68 D3**
Warner Springs
  CA ..... 33°17N 116°38W **65 K10**
Warner Valley OR .. 42°28N 119°50W **94 E6**
Warr Acres OK ..... 35°31N 97°37W **93 C6**
Warren AR ..... 33°37N 92°4W **63 E3**
Warren CT ..... 41°44N 73°21W **78 C1**
Warren ID ..... 45°16N 115°41W **70 D3**
Warren IL ..... 42°29N 90°0W **71 A4**
Warren IN ..... 40°41N 85°26W **72 C5**
Warren MA ..... 42°28N 83°1W **109 A2**
Warren MN ..... 48°12N 96°46W **80 B2**
Warren NH ..... 43°56N 71°54W **86 C3**
Warren OH ..... 41°14N 80°49W **92 B6**
Warren PA ..... 41°51N 79°9W **95 B3**
Warren RI ..... 41°44N 71°17W **78 C3**
Warren TX ..... 30°37N 94°24W **99 G13**
Warren VT ..... 44°7N 72°50W **86 B2**
Warren Air Force Base
  WY ..... 41°10N 104°54W **104 E8**
Warren County ☆
  GA ..... 33°20N 82°40W **68 C4**
Warren County ☆ IN 40°20N 87°20W **72 C3**
Warren County ☆ IA 41°20N 93°33W **73 D5**
Warren County ☆ KY 37°0N 86°25W **96 C6**
Warren County ☆
  MS ..... 32°21N 90°53W **81 D3**

Warren County ☆
  MO ..... 38°45N 91°10W **82 C5**
Warren County ☆ NC 36°15N 78°0W **90 B7**
Warren County ☆ NJ 40°50N 75°0W **87 B2**
Warren County ☆
  NY ..... 43°35N 73°45W **89 B7**
Warren County ☆
  OH ..... 39°26N 84°13W **92 D2**
Warren County ☆
  PA ..... 41°50N 79°15W **95 C3**
Warren County ☆
  TN ..... 35°41N 85°46W **97 E7**
Warren County ☆
  VA ..... 38°55N 78°12W **102 C6**
Warren Grove NJ ... 39°44N 74°22W **87 C2**
Warren Park IN ..... 39°46N 86°5W **116 B2**
Warren Pks. WY .... 44°29N 104°28W **104 B8**
Warrens WI ..... 44°8N 90°30W **103 D3**
Warrensburg IL ..... 39°56N 89°4W **71 D4**
Warrensburg MO ... 38°46N 93°44W **82 C3**
Warrensburg NY ... 43°29N 73°46W **89 B7**
Warrenton GA ..... 33°24N 82°40W **68 C4**
Warrenton MO ..... 38°49N 91°9W **82 C5**
Warrenton NC ..... 36°24N 78°9W **90 B7**
Warrenton OR ..... 46°10N 123°56W **94 A2**
Warrenton VA ..... 38°43N 77°48W **77 B3**
Warrenville SC ..... 33°33N 81°48W **90 E4**
Warrick County ☆ IN 38°5N 87°15W **72 E3**
Warrington FL ..... 30°23N 87°17W **67 A1**
Warrior AL ..... 33°49N 86°49W **60 C4**
Warroad MN ..... 48°54N 95°19W **80 B3**
Warsaw IL ..... 40°22N 91°26W **71 C2**
Warsaw IN ..... 41°14N 85°51W **72 B5**
Warsaw KY ..... 38°47N 84°54W **97 B8**
Warsaw MO ..... 38°15N 93°23W **82 C3**
Warsaw NC ..... 35°0N 78°5W **90 D7**
Warsaw NY ..... 42°45N 78°8W **89 C2**
Warthen GA ..... 33°6N 82°48W **68 C4**
Wartrace TN ..... 35°32N 86°20W **96 E6**
Warwick GA ..... 31°50N 83°57W **68 E3**
Warwick ND ..... 47°51N 98°43W **91 C7**
Warwick NY ..... 41°16N 74°22W **87 A2**
Warwick OK ..... 35°41N 97°0W **93 C7**
Warwick RI ..... 41°42N 71°28W **78 C3**
Wasatch-Cache Nat. Forest
  UT ..... 41°14N 111°25W **117 B3**
Wasatch County ☆
  UT ..... 40°20N 111°15W **100 C4**
Wasatch Plateau
  UT ..... 39°20N 111°30W **100 D4**
Wasatch Ra. UT .... 40°0N 111°30W **117 B2**
Wasco CA ..... 35°36N 119°20W **65 H7**
Wasco OR ..... 45°36N 120°42W **94 B4**
Wasco County ☆
  OR ..... 45°15N 121°15W **94 B4**
Waseca MN ..... 44°5N 93°30W **80 F5**
Waseca County ☆
  MN ..... 44°5N 93°30W **80 F5**
Washakie County ☆
  WY ..... 44°0N 107°40W **104 C5**
Washburn IL ..... 40°55N 89°17W **71 C4**
Washburn ME ..... 46°47N 68°9W **76 B5**
Washburn ND ..... 47°17N 101°2W **91 C4**
Washburn TX ..... 35°11N 101°34W **98 B6**
Washburn WI ..... 46°40N 90°54W **103 B3**
Washburn, Mt. WY 44°48N 110°26W **104 B2**
Washington AR ..... 33°47N 93°41W **63 E2**
Washington CT ..... 41°39N 73°19W **78 C1**
Washington DC ..... 38°53N 77°2W **119 B3**
Washington GA ..... 33°44N 82°44W **68 C4**
Washington IL ..... 40°42N 89°24W **71 C4**
Washington IN ..... 38°40N 87°10W **72 E3**
Washington IA ..... 41°18N 91°42W **73 D7**
Washington KS ..... 39°49N 97°3W **74 B6**
Washington KY ..... 38°37N 83°49W **97 B9**
Washington LA ..... 30°37N 92°4W **75 D3**
Washington ME ..... 44°17N 69°22W **76 D4**
Washington MO ..... 38°33N 91°1W **82 C5**
Washington NC ..... 35°33N 77°3W **90 C8**
Washington NJ ..... 40°46N 74°59W **87 B2**
Washington PA ..... 40°10N 80°15W **95 D2**
Washington UT ..... 37°8N 113°31W **100 F2**
Washington VA ..... 38°43N 78°10W **77 B2**
Washington □
  U.S.A. ..... 47°30N 120°30W **101 C5**
Washington, Lake
  WA ..... 47°37N 122°15W **118 B4**
Washington, Mt. NH 44°16N 71°18W **86 B3**
Washington County ☆
  AL ..... 31°22N 88°15W **60 E2**
Washington County ☆
  AR ..... 36°4N 94°10W **63 B1**
Washington County ☆
  CO ..... 40°0N 103°10W **66 C7**
Washington County ☆
  GA ..... 33°0N 82°50W **68 C4**
Washington County ☆
  ID ..... 44°30N 116°50W **70 E2**
Washington County ☆
  IL ..... 38°20N 89°25W **71 E4**
Washington County ☆
  IN ..... 38°35N 86°5W **72 E4**
Washington County ☆
  IA ..... 41°20N 91°40W **73 D7**
Washington County ☆
  KS ..... 39°45N 97°0W **74 B6**
Washington County ☆
  KY ..... 37°45N 85°10W **97 C7**
Washington County ☆
  ME ..... 45°0N 67°40W **76 C6**
Washington County ☆
  MD ..... 39°40N 78°0W **77 A3**
Washington County ☆
  MN ..... 45°10N 92°55W **80 E6**
Washington County ☆
  MS ..... 33°16N 90°53W **81 C3**
Washington County ☆
  MO ..... 38°0N 90°50W **82 D5**
Washington County ☆
  NC ..... 35°50N 76°30W **90 C9**
Washington County ☆
  NE ..... 41°24N 96°13W **84 C9**
Washington County ☆
  NY ..... 43°15N 73°25W **89 B7**
Washington County ☆
  OH ..... 39°27N 81°27W **92 D5**
Washington County ☆
  OK ..... 36°40N 95°55W **93 B8**
Washington County ☆
  OR ..... 45°30N 123°0W **94 B2**
Washington County ☆
  PA ..... 40°8N 80°8W **95 D2**
Washington County ☆
  RI ..... 41°30N 71°40W **78 C3**
Washington County ☆
  TN ..... 36°18N 82°29W **97 D10**
Washington County ☆
  TX ..... 30°10N 96°24W **99 G11**
Washington County ☆
  UT ..... 37°20N 113°30W **100 F2**
Washington County ☆
  VA ..... 36°55N 82°0W **102 E2**

Washington County ☆
  VT ..... 44°15N 72°40W **86 B2**
Washington County ☆
  WI ..... 43°20N 88°15W **103 E5**
Washington Court House
  OH ..... 39°32N 83°26W **92 D3**
Washington Dulles Int. ✈ (IAD)
  VA ..... 38°57N 77°27W **102 C7**
Washington Grove
  MD ..... 39°8N 77°11W **77 A3**
Washington Heights
  NY ..... 40°51N 73°56W **114 A3**
Washington I. WI ... 45°23N 86°54W **103 C7**
Washington Island
  LA ..... 30°15N 90°9W **75 D5**
Washington Park
  OR ..... 45°30N 122°42W **116 A1**
Washington Park WI 43°4N 87°58W **112 B2**
Washington Ronald Reagan
  National ✈ (DCA)
  VA ..... 38°51N 77°2W **119 B3**
Washington Terrace
  UT ..... 41°11N 111°59W **100 B4**
Washingtonville NY 41°26N 74°10W **87 A2**
Washita → OK ..... 34°8N 96°36W **93 D7**
Washita Battlefield Nat. Historic
  Site → TX ..... 35°7N 99°42W **93 C4**
Washita County ☆
  OK ..... 35°15N 99°0W **93 C5**
Washoe City NV ..... 39°19N 119°49W **85 C1**
Washoe County ☆
  NV ..... 40°16N 119°40W **85 B1**
Washoe L. NV ..... 39°16N 119°48W **85 C1**
Washougal WA ..... 45°35N 122°21W **101 E3**
Washta IA ..... 42°35N 95°43W **73 C3**
Washtenaw County ☆
  MI ..... 42°15N 83°50W **79 G8**
Washtucna WA ..... 46°45N 118°19W **101 D7**
Wasilla AK ..... 61°35N 149°26W **61 F10**
Waskom TX ..... 32°29N 94°4W **99 E13**
Wassaw I. GA ..... 31°53N 80°58W **68 E6**
Wassaw Sd. GA ..... 31°55N 80°55W **68 E6**
Wassuk Range NV .. 38°40N 118°50W **85 D2**
Wasta SD ..... 44°4N 102°27W **91 F3**
Watauga TN ..... 36°22N 82°18W **97 D10**
Watauga TX ..... 32°51N 97°15W **99 E10**
Watauga County ☆
  NC ..... 36°15N 81°45W **90 B4**
Watauga L. TN ..... 36°19N 82°7W **97 D10**
Water Valley KY .... 36°34N 88°49W **96 D4**
Water Valley MS ... 34°10N 89°38W **81 B4**
Waterboro ME ..... 43°32N 70°43W **86 C4**
Waterbury CT ..... 41°33N 73°3W **78 C1**
Waterbury VT ..... 44°20N 72°46W **86 B2**
Waterbury Center
  VT ..... 44°22N 72°43W **86 B2**
Wateree Res. VT .... 44°23N 72°46W **86 B2**
Wateree → SC ..... 33°45N 80°37W **90 D5**
Wateree, L. SC ..... 34°26N 80°54W **90 D5**
Waterflow NM ..... 36°45N 108°27W **88 A2**
Waterford CA ..... 37°38N 120°46W **64 F6**
Waterford CT ..... 41°20N 72°9W **78 D2**
Waterford MI ..... 42°45N 83°23W **79 G8**
Waterford MS ..... 34°39N 89°29W **81 B4**
Waterford NY ..... 42°48N 73°41W **78 B1**
Waterford PA ..... 41°57N 79°59W **95 C3**
Waterford WI ..... 42°46N 88°13W **103 F5**
Watergap KY ..... 37°38N 82°45W **97 C10**
Waterloo AL ..... 34°55N 88°4W **60 B2**
Waterloo AR ..... 33°3N 93°15W **63 E2**
Waterloo IL ..... 38°20N 90°9W **71 E3**
Waterloo IN ..... 41°26N 85°1W **72 B5**
Waterloo IA ..... 42°30N 92°21W **73 C6**
Waterloo KY ..... 38°37N 83°43W **97 B9**
Waterloo MT ..... 45°43N 112°12W **83 E5**
Waterloo NY ..... 42°54N 76°52W **89 C4**
Waterloo OR ..... 44°30N 122°49W **94 C3**
Waterman IL ..... 41°46N 88°47W **71 B5**
Waterproof LA ..... 31°48N 91°23W **75 C4**
Waters MI ..... 44°54N 84°42W **79 E7**
Watersmeet MI ..... 46°16N 89°11W **79 C2**
Watertown CT ..... 41°36N 73°7W **78 C1**
Watertown FL ..... 30°11N 82°36W **67 A6**
Watertown MA ..... 42°22N 71°10W **106 A2**
Watertown NY ..... 43°59N 75°55W **89 B5**
Watertown SD ..... 44°54N 97°7W **91 E8**
Watertown TN ..... 36°6N 86°8W **96 D6**
Watertown WI ..... 43°12N 88°43W **103 E5**
Waterville KS ..... 39°42N 96°45W **74 B7**
Waterville ME ..... 44°33N 69°38W **76 D4**
Waterville MN ..... 44°13N 93°34W **80 F5**
Waterville NY ..... 42°56N 75°23W **89 C5**
Waterville OH ..... 41°30N 83°43W **92 B3**
Waterville VT ..... 44°42N 72°47W **86 B2**
Waterville WA ..... 47°39N 120°4W **101 C5**
Waterville Valley NH 43°57N 71°30W **86 C3**
Watford City ND .... 47°48N 103°17W **91 C2**
Watkins MN ..... 45°19N 94°25W **80 E4**
Watkins Glen NY ... 42°23N 76°52W **89 C4**
Watkinsville GA ..... 33°52N 83°25W **68 C3**
Watonga OK ..... 35°51N 98°25W **93 C5**
Watonwan County ☆
  MN ..... 44°0N 94°40W **80 F4**
Watova OK ..... 36°37N 95°37W **93 B8**
Watrous NM ..... 35°48N 104°59W **88 B6**
Watseka IL ..... 40°47N 87°44W **71 C6**
Watson LA ..... 30°34N 91°15W **63 D3**
Watson MN ..... 45°0N 95°48W **80 E3**
Watson MO ..... 40°29N 95°37W **82 A1**
Watsontown PA ..... 41°5N 76°52W **95 C6**
Watsonville CA ..... 36°55N 121°45W **64 G3**
Watts Bar L. TN .... 35°37N 84°47W **97 E8**
Wattsburg PA ..... 42°0N 79°49W **95 B3**
Wattuppa Pond MA. 41°42N 71°6W **78 C2**
Waubay SD ..... 45°20N 97°18W **91 E8**
Waubay L. SD ..... 45°23N 97°24W **91 E8**
Waubun MN ..... 47°11N 95°57W **80 C3**
Wauchula FL ..... 27°33N 81°49W **67 D7**
Waucoma IA ..... 43°2N 92°1W **73 B6**
Waugoshance Pt. MI 45°46N 85°1W **79 D6**
Wauka L. KS ..... 38°45N 95°15W **74 C8**
Waukee IA ..... 41°37N 93°53W **73 D5**
Waukeenah FL ..... 30°25N 83°57W **67 A5**
Waukegan IL ..... 42°22N 87°50W **71 A6**
Waukesha WI ..... 43°1N 88°14W **103 F5**
Waukesha County ☆
  WI ..... 43°0N 88°15W **103 F5**
Waukomis OK ..... 36°17N 97°54W **93 B6**
Waukon IA ..... 43°16N 91°29W **73 B7**
Waupaca WI ..... 44°21N 89°5W **103 D4**
Waupaca County ☆
  WI ..... 44°25N 89°0W **103 D4**
Waupun WI ..... 43°38N 88°44W **103 E5**
Waurika L. OK ..... 34°10N 98°3W **93 D6**
Wausa NE ..... 42°30N 97°32W **84 B8**
Wausau FL ..... 30°38N 85°35W **67 A3**
Wausau WI ..... 44°58N 89°38W **103 D4**
Wausaukee WI ..... 45°23N 87°57W **103 C6**

Wauseon OH........ 41°33N 84°8W 92 B2
Waushara County ☆
WI............ 44°10N 89°15W 103 D4
Wautoma WI........ 44°4N 89°18W 103 D4
Wauwatosa WI .... 43°2N 88°0W 112 B1
Wauzeka WI .... 43°5N 90°53W 103 E3
Waveland IN .... 39°53N 87°3W 72 D3
Waveland MS .... 30°17N 89°23W 81 F4
Waverley MA ..... 42°23N 71°10W 106 A2
Waverley Hall GA .. 32°41N 84°44W 68 D2
Waverly AL........ 32°44N 85°35W 60 D5
Waverly FL .... 27°59N 81°37W 67 D7
Waverly GA .... 31°6N 81°43W 68 E5
Waverly IL .... 39°36N 89°57W 71 D4
Waverly IA .... 42°44N 92°29W 73 C6
Waverly KS......... 38°23N 95°36W 74 C8
Waverly KY......... 37°43N 87°48W 96 C5
Waverly MO .... 39°13N 93°31W 82 B3
Waverly NY.......... 42°1N 76°32W 89 C4
Waverly NE......... 40°55N 96°32W 84 D9
Waverly TN......... 36°5N 87°48W 96 D5
Waverly VA.......... 37°2N 77°6W 77 C3
Waverly WA ...... 47°21N 117°14W 101 C8
Wawasee, L. IN...... 41°24N 85°42W 72 B5
Wawona CA ...... 37°32N 119°39W 64 F7
Waxahachie TX .... 32°24N 96°51W 99 E11
Waxhaw NC .... 34°56N 80°45W 90 D5
Wayan ID .... 42°58N 111°23W 70 G7
Waycross GA .... 31°13N 82°21W 68 E4
Wayland IA .... 41°8N 91°40W 73 D7
Wayland KY .... 37°27N 82°48W 97 C10
Wayland MA....... 42°21N 71°20W 106 A1
Wayland MI........ 42°40N 85°39W 79 G6
Wayland NY .... 42°34N 77°35W 89 C3
Wayne KS .... 39°43N 97°33W 74 B6
Wayne NJ .... 40°55N 74°16W 114 A1
Wayne NE.......... 42°14N 97°1W 84 B8
Wayne OH......... 41°18N 83°29W 92 B3
Wayne OK.......... 34°55N 97°19W 93 D6
Wayne WV.......... 38°13N 82°27W 102 C2
Wayne County ☆ GA 31°30N 82°0W 68 E5
Wayne County ☆ IL 38°25N 88°25W 71 E5
Wayne County ☆ IN . 39°50N 85°0W 72 D6
Wayne County ☆ IA 40°45N 93°20W 73 E5
Wayne County ☆ KY 36°45N 84°50W 97 D8
Wayne County ☆ MI 42°15N 83°15W 79 G8
Wayne County ☆ MS 31°40N 88°39W 81 E5
Wayne County ☆ MO 37°5N 90°30W 82 D6
Wayne County ☆ NC. 35°20N 78°0W 90 C7
Wayne County ☆ NY. 43°10N 77°0W 89 B4
Wayne County ☆ NE. 42°15N 97°5W 84 B8
Wayne County ☆ OH 40°48N 81°56W 92 C5
Wayne County ☆ PA 41°35N 75°15W 95 C7
Wayne County ☆ TN 35°10N 87°44W 96 E5
Wayne County ☆
UT.......... 38°15N 111°0W 100 E5
Wayne County ☆
WV .... 38°13N 82°27W 102 C2
Wayne County, Detroit ✈ (DTW)
MI.......... 42°13N 83°21W 79 G8
Wayne Nat. Forest
OH .... 39°33N 81°4W 92 D5
Waynesboro GA...... 33°6N 82°1W 68 C4
Waynesboro MS..... 31°40N 88°39W 81 E5
Waynesboro PA .... 39°45N 77°35W 77 A3
Waynesboro TN ..... 35°19N 87°46W 96 E5
Waynesboro VA .... 38°4N 78°53W 102 C6
Waynesburg PA ..... 39°54N 80°11W 95 E2
Waynesville IL ...... 40°15N 89°8W 71 C4
Waynesville MO .... 37°50N 92°12W 82 D4
Waynesville NC ..... 35°28N 82°58W 90 C3
Waynesville OH ..... 39°32N 84°5W 92 D2
Waynetown IN .... 40°5N 87°4W 72 C3
Waynoka OK .... 36°35N 98°53W 93 B5
Wayside GA .... 33°4N 83°37W 68 C3
Wayside MS......... 33°16N 91°2W 81 C2
Wayzata MN ...... 44°58N 93°30W 113 B1
Weakley County ☆
TN............. 36°14N 88°50W 96 D4
Weare NH .... 43°6N 71°44W 86 C3
Weatherby MO ...... 39°55N 94°14W 82 B2
Weatherford OK.... 35°32N 98°43W 93 C5
Weatherford TX... 32°46N 97°48W 99 E10
Weatherly PA ...... 40°57N 75°50W 87 B1
Weaubleau MO...... 37°54N 93°32W 82 D3
Weaverville CA.... 40°44N 122°56W 64 C4
Weaverville NC..... 35°42N 82°34W 90 C3
Webb IA .... 42°57N 95°1W 73 C3
Webb MS .... 33°57N 90°21W 81 C3
Webb City MO ...... 37°9N 94°28W 82 D2
Webb City OK ...... 36°48N 96°42W 93 B7
Webb County ☆ TX. 27°30N 99°10W 99 K8
Webber KS .... 39°56N 98°2W 74 B5
Webbers Falls OK .... 35°31N 95°8W 93 C8
Webbville KY ...... 38°11N 82°52W 97 B10
Weber ➜ U.S.A. .. 41°13N 112°8W 100 B3
Weber County ☆
UT........ 41°20N 111°40W 100 B4
Webster FL .... 28°37N 82°3W 67 C6
Webster IA .... 41°26N 92°10W 73 D6
Webster MA .... 42°3N 71°53W 78 B3
Webster ND .... 48°17N 98°53W 91 B7
Webster NY......... 43°13N 77°26W 89 B3
Webster SD .... 45°20N 97°31W 91 E8
Webster WI .... 45°53N 92°22W 103 C1
Webster City IA ..... 42°28N 93°49W 73 C5
Webster County ☆
GA .... 32°0N 84°35W 68 E2
Webster County ☆
IA .... 42°25N 94°10W 73 C4
Webster County ☆
KY............ 37°30N 87°40W 96 C5
Webster County ☆
MS .... 33°37N 89°17W 81 C4
Webster County ☆
MO .... 37°15N 92°50W 82 D4
Webster County ☆
NE............. 40°15N 98°30W 84 D7
Webster County ☆
WV .... 38°29N 80°25W 102 C4
Webster Groves
MO .... 38°35N 90°21W 117 B1
Webster Parish ☆ LA 32°40N 93°20W 75 B2
Webster Res. ID ..... 42°46N 111°11W 70 G7
Webster Res. KS .... 39°25N 99°26W 74 B4
Webster Springs WV 38°29N 80°25W 102 C4
Websters Mill PA .... 39°52N 78°2W 77 A2
Weddington NC ...... 35°1N 80°46W 90 C5
Wedowee AL .... 33°19N 85°29W 60 C5
Weed CA .... 41°25N 122°23W 64 B4
Weed NM .... 32°48N 105°31W 88 E5
Weed Heights NV.. 38°59N 119°13W 85 D1
Weedon Island Preserve
FL............ 27°50N 82°36W 119 B3
Weedsport NY .... 43°3N 76°34W 89 B4
Weedville PA .... 41°17N 78°30W 95 C4
Weehawken NJ ..... 40°45N 74°2W 114 B2
Weekapaug RI ...... 41°20N 71°45W 78 C3
Weekstown NJ ..... 39°37N 74°37W 87 C2
Weeping Water NE .. 40°52N 96°8W 84 D9
Weigelstown PA.... 39°59N 76°49W 95 E6
Weimar CA .... 39°2N 120°59W 64 D6
Weimar TX .... 29°42N 96°47W 99 H11
Weinberg-King State Park ⌂
IL .... 40°14N 90°54W 71 C3
Weiner AR.......... 35°37N 90°54W 63 C5
Weippe ID .... 46°23N 115°56W 70 C3
Weir KS .... 37°19N 94°46W 74 D9
Weir KY .... 37°7N 87°13W 96 C5
Weir MS .... 33°16N 89°18W 81 C4
Weir, L. FL .... 29°0N 81°57W 67 B7
Weirsdale FL........ 28°59N 81°55W 67 C7
Weirton WV .... 40°24N 80°35W 102 A4
Weiser ID .... 44°15N 116°58W 70 E2
Weiser ➜ ID........ 44°14N 116°58W 70 E2
Weiss L. AL......... 34°8N 85°48W 60 B5
Weissert NE .... 41°28N 99°27W 84 C6
Welby CO .... 39°50N 104°57W 109 A2
Welch OK .... 36°52N 95°6W 93 B8
Welch TX......... 32°56N 102°8W 98 E5
Welch WV .... 37°26N 81°35W 102 D3
Welcome MD .... 38°28N 77°8W 77 B3
Welcome MN .... 43°40N 94°37W 80 G4
Welcome NC......... 35°55N 80°15W 90 C5
Weld ME .... 44°42N 70°25W 76 D3
Weld County ☆ CO 40°45N 104°15W 66 B6
Welda KS.......... 38°10N 95°18W 74 C8
Weldon IL .... 40°7N 88°45W 71 C5
Weldon IA......... 40°54N 93°44W 73 E5
Weldon NC......... 36°25N 77°36W 90 B8
Weldon ➜ MO....... 40°6N 93°39W 82 A3
Weldon Spring MO . 38°43N 90°41W 82 C6
Weleetka OK .... 35°20N 96°8W 93 C7
Wellborn TX ...... 30°32N 96°18W 99 G11
Wellersburg PA .... 39°44N 78°51W 77 A2
Wellesley MA ..... 42°17N 71°17W 106 B2
Wellesley Falls MA 42°18N 71°18W 106 B2
Wellesley Hills MA 42°18N 71°16W 106 B2
Wellfleet MA .... 41°56N 70°2W 78 C4
Wellfleet NE ...... 40°45N 100°44W 84 D5
Wellford VA .... 37°53N 76°46W 77 C4
Wellington CO ..... 40°42N 105°0W 66 B5
Wellington IL ...... 40°32N 87°41W 71 C6
Wellington KS...... 37°16N 97°24W 74 D6
Wellington ME ...... 45°2N 69°36W 76 C4
Wellington MA..... 42°24N 71°5W 106 A3
Wellington MO...... 39°8N 93°59W 82 B3
Wellington NV ..... 38°45N 119°23W 85 D1
Wellington OH ...... 41°10N 82°13W 92 B4
Wellington TX ..... 34°51N 100°13W 98 C7
Wellington UT ... 39°32N 110°44W 100 D5
Wellman IA .... 41°28N 91°50W 73 D7
Wellman TX .... 33°3N 102°26W 98 D5
Wellpinit WA ..... 47°53N 117°59W 101 C8
Wells KS .... 39°5N 97°33W 74 B6
Wells ME........... 43°20N 70°35W 86 C4
Wells MN.......... 43°45N 93°44W 80 G5
Wells NY .... 43°24N 74°17W 89 B6
Wells NV .... 41°7N 114°58W 85 A6
Wells TX .... 31°29N 94°56W 99 F13
Wells VT .... 43°25N 73°10W 86 C1
Wells ➜ VT .... 44°10N 72°3W 86 B2
Wells County ☆ IN.. 40°45N 85°15W 72 C5
Wells County ☆ ND. 47°35N 99°45W 91 C6
Wells Dam WA.... 47°57N 119°52W 101 C6
Wellsboro PA ...... 41°45N 77°18W 95 C5
Wellsburg IA .... 42°26N 92°56W 73 C6
Wellsburg NY .... 42°1N 76°44W 89 C4
Wellsburg WV...... 40°16N 80°37W 102 A4
Wellsford KS........ 37°37N 99°2W 74 D4
Wellston = Warner Robins
GA .... 32°37N 83°36W 68 D3
Wellston MO....... 38°40N 90°17W 117 B2
Wellston OH........ 39°7N 82°32W 92 D4
Wellston OK........ 35°42N 97°4W 93 C6
Wellsville KS....... 38°43N 95°5W 74 C8
Wellsville MO ...... 39°4N 91°34W 82 B5
Wellsville NY ...... 42°7N 77°57W 89 C3
Wellsville OH ...... 40°36N 80°39W 92 C6
Wellsville PA ...... 40°3N 76°56W 95 D6
Wellsville UT..... 41°38N 111°56W 100 B4
Wellton AZ .... 32°40N 114°8W 62 E1
Welsh LA.......... 30°14N 92°49W 75 D3
Welton IA .... 41°55N 90°36W 73 D8
Wenatchee WA.... 47°25N 120°19W 101 C5
Wenatchee ➜ WA 47°27N 120°19W 101 C5
Wenatchee Mts.
WA .... 47°15N 120°30W 101 C5
Wenatchee Nat. Forest
WA .... 47°55N 120°55W 101 C5
Wendell ID ...... 42°47N 114°42W 70 G4
Wendell MN .... 46°2N 96°6W 80 D2
Wendell NH .... 43°22N 72°9W 86 C2
Wenden AZ........ 33°49N 113°33W 62 D2
Wendover UT...... 40°44N 114°2W 100 C1
Wenona IL .... 41°3N 89°3W 71 B4
Wenona MD .... 38°8N 75°57W 77 B5
Wentworth MO...... 36°59N 94°4W 82 E2
Wentworth NC ..... 36°24N 79°46W 90 B6
Wentworth NH ...... 43°52N 71°55W 86 C3
Wentworth SD ...... 43°59N 96°57W 91 G9
Wentworth, L. NH .... 43°35N 71°9W 86 C3
Wentzville MO ...... 38°49N 90°51W 82 C6
Weott CA .... 40°20N 123°55W 64 C3
Werley WI .... 43°1N 90°46W 103 E3
Weskan KS ...... 38°52N 101°57W 74 C2
Weslaco TX .... 26°10N 97°58W 98 L10
Wesley GA .... 32°29N 82°20W 68 D4
Wesley IA .... 43°5N 93°59W 73 B5
Wesley ME .... 44°57N 67°40W 76 D6
Wesleyville PA .... 42°9N 80°1W 95 B3
Wessington SD ..... 44°27N 98°42W 91 F7
Wessington Springs SD 44°5N 98°34W 91 F7
Wesson AR .... 33°7N 92°46W 63 E3
Wesson MS .... 31°42N 90°24W 81 E3
West MS........... 33°12N 89°47W 81 C4
West TX.......... 31°48N 97°6W 99 F10
West ➜ VT .... 42°52N 72°33W 86 D2
West Alexandria OH 39°45N 84°32W 92 D2
West Allis WI .... 43°1N 88°0W 112 B1
West Arlington VT.... 43°8N 73°12W 86 C1
West Arm Grand Traverse B.
MI............ 44°50N 85°40W 79 E6
West B. FL .... 30°10N 85°45W 67 A3
West B. LA .... 29°3N 89°22W 75 E6
West B. TX .... 29°14N 95°0W 99 H13
West Babylon NY.... 40°42N 73°21W 87 B3
West Baton Rouge Parish ☆
LA .... 30°27N 91°12W 75 D4
West Bedford MA .. 42°28N 71°18W 106 A2
West Bend IA .... 42°57N 94°27W 73 C4
West Bend WI....... 43°25N 88°11W 103 E5
West Blocton AL ...... 33°7N 87°7W 60 C3
West Bountiful UT 40°53N 111°54W 117 A2
West Boylston MA.. 42°22N 71°47W 78 B3
West Branch IA .... 41°40N 91°20W 73 D7
West Branch MI ..... 44°17N 84°14W 79 E7
West Branch Susquehanna ➜
PA.......... 40°53N 76°48W 95 D6
West Bridgewater MA. 42°1N 71°0W 78 B4
West Brookfield MA . 42°14N 72°9W 78 B2
West Burke VT..... 44°39N 71°59W 86 B3
West Burlington IA .. 40°49N 91°9W 73 E7
West Caldwell NJ.. 40°50N 74°18W 114 A1
West Campton NH... 43°40N 71°41W 86 C3
West Canaan NH ..... 43°40N 72°2W 86 C2
West Cape May NJ.. 38°56N 74°56W 87 D2
West Carroll Parish ☆
LA .... 32°48N 91°27W 75 B4
West Carthage NY.. 43°59N 75°37W 89 B5
West Chazy NY..... 44°49N 73°28W 86 B1
West Chester IA ..... 41°20N 91°49W 73 D7
West Chester PA .... 39°58N 75°36W 87 C1
West Columbia SC... 33°59N 81°4W 90 E4
West Columbia TX.. 29°9N 95°39W 99 H12
West Concord MA . 42°27N 71°24W 106 A1
West Concord MN ... 44°9N 92°54W 80 F6
West Cote Blanche B.
LA .... 29°45N 91°55W 75 E4
West Covina CA ..... 34°4N 117°54W 65 J9
West Creek NJ ...... 39°38N 74°18W 87 C2
West Cummington
MA .... 42°29N 72°57W 78 B2
West Delta Park
OR .... 45°35N 122°42W 116 A1
West Des Moines IA 41°35N 93°43W 73 D5
West Dover VT..... 42°56N 72°51W 86 D2
West Dummerston
VT............ 42°55N 72°38W 86 D2
West Elk Mts. CO.. 38°35N 107°15W 66 D3
West Elkton OH.... 39°35N 84°33W 92 D2
West Fairlee VT .... 43°54N 72°16W 86 C2
West Fargo ND ..... 46°52N 96°54W 91 D9
West Feliciana Parish ☆
LA .... 30°50N 91°23W 75 D4
West Fork ➜ WV... 39°28N 80°9W 102 B4
West Fork Amite ➜
U.S.A........... 31°0N 90°50W 81 E3
West Fork Poplar ➜
MT .... 48°31N 105°22W 83 B12
West Fork Trinity ➜
TX............ 32°48N 96°54W 99 E11
West Forks ME..... 45°20N 69°58W 76 C4
West Frankfort IL .. 37°54N 88°55W 71 F5
West Glacier MT ... 48°30N 113°59W 83 B4
West Grand L. ME.. 45°14N 67°51W 76 C6
West Green GA ..... 31°37N 82°44W 68 E4
West Grove PA...... 39°49N 75°49W 95 E7
West Hamlin WV .. 38°17N 82°12W 102 C2
West Hartford CT... 41°45N 72°44W 78 C2
West Haven CT ..... 41°17N 72°57W 78 C2
West Hebron NY .... 43°14N 73°23W 86 C1
West Helena AR..... 34°33N 90°38W 63 D5
West Hempstead
NY............ 40°42N 73°39W 114 B5
West Hollywood CA 34°5N 118°21W 111 B2
West Homestead
PA........... 40°23N 79°54W 116 B2
West Jefferson NC.. 36°24N 81°30W 90 B4
West Jordan UT .. 40°36N 111°56W 117 C1
West Kingston RI... 41°29N 71°34W 78 C3
West Lafayette IN .. 40°27N 86°55W 72 C4
West Lebanon IN ... 40°16N 87°23W 72 C3
West Liberty IA ..... 41°34N 91°16W 73 D7
West Liberty KY.... 37°55N 83°16W 97 C9
West Liberty OH ... 40°15N 83°45W 92 C3
West Liberty WV .. 40°10N 80°36W 102 A4
West Line MO ...... 38°38N 94°35W 82 C2
West Linn OR.... 45°21N 122°36W 116 B2
West Los Angeles, University of
CA .... 34°7N 118°23W 111 C2
West Louisville KY . 37°42N 87°17W 96 C5
West Lynn MA .... 42°27N 70°58W 106 A4
West Mansfield OH . 40°24N 83°33W 92 C3
West Mayfield PA .. 40°47N 80°20W 95 D2
West Medford MA .. 42°25N 71°7W 106 A3
West Memphis AR .. 35°8N 90°11W 112 B1
West Miami FL .... 25°45N 80°17W 112 D1
West Mifflin PA .... 40°21N 79°52W 116 B2
West Milan NH....... 44°37N 71°18W 86 B3
West Milford NJ ...... 41°8N 74°22W 87 A2
West Milford WV .. 39°12N 80°24W 102 B4
West Millgrove OH .. 41°15N 83°30W 92 B3
West Milton OH..... 39°58N 84°20W 92 D2
West Milwaukee WI. 43°0N 87°58W 112 B2
West Mineral KS ... 37°17N 94°55W 74 D9
West Monroe LA .... 32°31N 92°9W 75 B3
West Mts. ID ...... 44°28N 116°14W 70 E2
West New York NJ. 40°46N 74°1W 114 B2
West Newbury MA.. 42°48N 71°0W 78 B4
West Newfield ME.. 43°39N 70°55W 86 C4
West Nishnabotna ➜
IA .... 40°39N 95°38W 73 E3
West Nueces ➜ TX. 29°16N 99°56W 99 H8
West Odessa TX.... 31°50N 102°30W 98 F5
West of Twin Peaks
CA .... 37°43N 122°27W 118 B2
West Okoboji L. IA .. 43°23N 95°9W 73 B3
West Orange NJ .... 40°47N 74°14W 114 B1
West Orange TX.... 30°5N 93°46W 99 G14
West Ossipee NH.... 43°48N 71°12W 86 C3
West Palm Beach FL. 26°43N 80°3W 67 E8
West Palm Beach Canal
FL............ 26°40N 80°15W 67 E8
West Palm Beach Int. ✈ (PBI)
FL............ 26°41N 80°6W 67 E8
West Park PA .... 40°28N 80°4W 116 B1
West Paterson NJ.. 40°53N 74°11W 114 A1
West Pawlet VT .... 43°21N 73°15W 86 C1
West Pensacola FL.. 30°25N 87°16W 67 A1
West Plains MO .... 36°44N 91°51W 82 E5
West Plymouth NH . 43°45N 71°45W 86 C3
West Point CA ..... 38°24N 120°32W 64 E6
West Point GA ...... 32°53N 85°11W 68 D1
West Point IL ...... 40°15N 91°11W 71 C2
West Point IA ...... 40°43N 91°27W 73 E7
West Point KY ..... 37°59N 85°57W 97 C7
West Point MS ...... 33°36N 88°39W 81 C5
West Point NY ...... 41°24N 73°58W 89 D7
West Point NE ...... 41°51N 96°43W 84 C9
West Point VA ...... 37°32N 76°48W 102 D8
West Point L. GA.... 33°8N 85°0W 68 C1
West Point Military Academy
NY........... 41°23N 73°57W 89 D7
West Portland OR 45°27N 122°43W 116 B1
West Richland WA 46°18N 119°20W 101 D6
West Rindge NH .... 42°47N 72°3W 86 D2
West River MD..... 38°52N 76°31W 77 B4
West Roxbury MA.. 42°16N 71°9W 106 B3
West Rutland VT .... 43°36N 73°3W 86 C1
West Sacramento
CA .... 38°35N 121°32W 64 E5
West St. Paul MN... 44°54N 93°5W 113 B3
West Salem IL....... 38°31N 88°1W 71 E5
West Salem OH ..... 40°58N 82°7W 92 C4
West Salem WI ..... 43°54N 91°5W 103 E2
West Seneca NY .... 42°51N 78°48W 89 C2
West Siloam Springs
OK .... 36°12N 94°39W 93 B9
West Slope OR .... 45°29N 122°45W 116 B1
West Springfield MA . 42°6N 72°38W 78 B2
West Springfield VA 38°47N 77°13W 119 C2
West Stewartstown
NH .... 44°59N 71°32W 86 B3
West Tavaputs Plateau
UT............ 39°50N 110°20W 100 D5
West Terre Haute IN 39°28N 87°27W 72 D3
West Thompson Res.
CT............ 41°57N 71°54W 78 C3
West Thorton NH.... 43°55N 71°42W 86 C3
West Thumb WY . 44°25N 110°34W 104 B2
West Tisbury MA .... 41°23N 70°41W 78 C4
West Topsham VT ..... 44°7N 72°19W 86 B2
West Town IL....... 41°53N 87°42W 108 B2
West Union IA ..... 42°57N 91°49W 73 C7
West Union MN ..... 45°48N 95°5W 80 E3
West Union OH ..... 38°48N 83°33W 92 E3
West Union WV .... 39°18N 80°47W 102 B4
West Unity OH...... 41°35N 84°26W 92 B2
West University Place
TX............. 29°43N 95°26W 110 B2
West Valley City
UT........... 40°42N 111°58W 117 B1
West View PA....... 40°31N 80°2W 116 A1
West Virginia ☐
U.S.A.......... 38°45N 80°30W 102 C4
West Warwick RI .... 41°43N 71°32W 78 C3
West Wendover NV. 40°44N 114°4W 85 B6
West Winfield NY ... 42°53N 75°12W 89 C5
West Yarmouth MA. 41°39N 70°15W 78 C4
West Yellowstone
MT .... 44°40N 111°6W 83 F6
West York PA ...... 39°57N 76°46W 95 E6
Westbay FL......... 30°18N 85°52W 67 A3
Westboro MO ...... 40°32N 95°19W 82 A1
Westborough MA .. 42°16N 71°37W 78 B3
Westbrook CT....... 41°17N 72°27W 78 C2
Westbrook ME ...... 43°41N 70°22W 76 E3
Westbrook MN ..... 44°3N 95°26W 80 F3
Westbrook TX ...... 32°21N 101°1W 98 E6
Westby MT .... 48°52N 104°3W 83 B13
Westby WI.......... 43°39N 90°51W 103 E3
Westchester CA .. 33°57N 118°23W 111 C2
Westchester IL .... 41°51N 87°53W 108 B1
Westchester NY ... 40°51N 73°51W 114 A3
Westchester County ☆
NY............ 41°40N 73°45W 89 D7
Westcliffe CO ...... 38°9N 105°28W 66 D5
Westend CA ...... 35°42N 117°24W 65 H9
Westerly RI .... 41°22N 71°50W 78 C3
Western NE........ 40°24N 97°12W 84 D8
Western Addition
CA .... 37°47N 122°25W 118 B2
Western Grove AR... 36°6N 92°57W 63 B3
Westernport MD .... 39°29N 79°3W 77 A1
Westerville NE ..... 41°24N 99°23W 84 C6
Westerville OH...... 40°8N 82°56W 92 C4
Westfall OR....... 43°59N 117°48W 94 D8
Westfield IL .... 39°27N 88°0W 71 D5
Westfield IN .... 40°2N 86°8W 72 C4
Westfield IA .... 42°45N 96°36W 73 C2
Westfield ME ...... 46°34N 67°55W 76 B6
Westfield MA .... 42°7N 72°45W 78 B2
Westfield NJ .... 40°39N 74°21W 87 B2
Westfield NY .... 42°20N 79°35W 89 C1
Westfield PA .... 41°55N 77°32W 95 C5
Westfield WI....... 43°53N 89°30W 103 E4
Westfield ➜ MA ..... 42°5N 72°35W 78 B2
Westfir OR .... 43°46N 122°31W 94 D3
Westford MA ...... 42°35N 71°26W 78 B3
Westgate IA.......... 42°46N 92°0W 73 C6
Westgate MD ...... 38°57N 77°6W 119 B3
Westhoff TX ...... 29°12N 97°28W 99 H10
Westhope ND .... 48°55N 101°1W 91 B4
Westlake CA ..... 37°42N 122°29W 118 B2
Westlake LA .... 30°15N 93°59W 75 D2
Westland MI .... 42°15N 83°20W 79 G8
Westminster CA ... 33°45N 118°0W 111 D4
Westminster CO .... 39°50N 105°2W 109 A1
Westminster MA.... 42°33N 71°55W 78 B3
Westminster MD ... 39°34N 76°59W 77 A4
Westminster SC ..... 34°40N 83°6W 90 D2
Westminster VT ..... 43°5N 72°28W 86 C2
Westmont NJ........ 39°54N 75°2W 116 B2
Westmont PA ...... 40°19N 78°58W 95 D4
Westmore VT .... 44°50N 72°3W 86 B2
Westmoreland KS... 39°24N 96°25W 74 B7
Westmoreland NH .. 42°57N 72°25W 86 D2
Westmoreland TN ... 36°34N 86°15W 96 D6
Westmoreland VA .... 38°4N 76°34W 77 B4
Westmoreland County ☆
PA............ 40°20N 79°25W 95 D3
Westmoreland County ☆
VA .... 38°6N 76°50W 102 C8
Westmorland CA .. 33°2N 115°37W 65 K11
Weston CO .... 37°8N 104°48W 66 E6
Weston MA ..... 42°22N 71°16W 106 A2
Weston MO .... 39°25N 94°54W 82 B2
Weston NE .... 41°12N 96°45W 84 C9
Weston OR ..... 45°49N 118°26W 94 B7
Weston VT......... 43°18N 72°38W 86 C2
Weston WV........ 39°2N 80°28W 102 B4
Weston WY...... 44°38N 105°20W 104 B7
Weston County ☆
WY .... 43°55N 104°35W 104 C8
Weston Res. MA.... 42°20N 71°11W 106 A2
Westover MD ...... 38°7N 75°42W 77 B5
Westover PA .... 40°45N 78°40W 95 D4
Westover WV ...... 39°38N 79°58W 102 B5
Westover Air Reserve Base
MA .... 42°13N 72°29W 78 B2
Westphalia MI....... 42°56N 84°48W 79 G7
Westphalia MO...... 38°26N 92°0W 82 C4
Westpoint TN .... 35°8N 87°32W 96 E5
Westport CA ..... 39°38N 123°47W 64 D3
Westport CT .... 41°9N 73°22W 78 C1
Westport IN........ 39°11N 85°34W 72 D5
Westport KY ...... 38°29N 85°28W 97 B7
Westport MN ...... 45°43N 95°10W 80 E3
Westport NH........ 42°49N 72°20W 86 D2
Westport NY .... 44°11N 73°26W 86 B1
Westport OK........ 36°8N 96°20W 93 B7
Westport OR ..... 46°8N 123°23W 94 A2
Westport WA .... 46°53N 124°6W 101 D1
Westview MD ..... 39°17N 76°44W 107 B1
Westville FL........ 30°46N 85°51W 67 A3
Westville IL.......... 40°2N 87°38W 71 C6
Westville IN........ 41°32N 86°54W 72 B4
Westville NJ .... 39°52N 75°7W 116 B2
Westville OK....... 35°58N 94°40W 93 C9
Westville SC .... 34°27N 80°36W 90 D5
Westwego LA .... 29°54N 90°8W 113 C2
Westwood CA ..... 40°18N 121°0W 64 C6
Westwood KY...... 38°30N 82°50W 97 B10
Westwood KS ...... 39°2N 94°37W 75 C2
Westwood MA ..... 42°13N 71°14W 78 B3
Westwood MD .... 38°40N 76°45W 77 B4
Westwood NJ ...... 40°58N 74°2W 87 B2
Westwood Lakes FL 25°44N 80°23W 67 F8
Westwood Village
CA .... 34°3N 118°26W 111 B2
Westwood Village
TX......... 29°24N 98°37W 117 C2
Wet Mts. CO..... 38°0N 105°10W 66 E5
Wethersfield CT .... 41°42N 72°40W 78 C2
Wetmore CO....... 38°14N 105°5W 66 D5
Wetmore KS........ 39°38N 95°49W 74 B8
Wetumka OK .... 35°14N 96°15W 93 C7
Wetumpka AL ...... 32°32N 86°13W 60 D4
Wetzel County ☆
WV .... 39°34N 80°41W 102 B4
Wevok AK......... 68°53N 166°13W 61 B6
Wewahitchka FL .... 30°7N 85°12W 67 A3
Wewoka OK .... 35°9N 96°30W 93 C7
Wexford County ☆
MI........... 44°20N 85°40W 79 E6
Weyauwega WI..... 44°19N 88°56W 103 D5
Weyerhaeuser WI .. 45°26N 91°25W 103 C2
Weymouth MA ...... 42°13N 70°58W 78 B4
Whalan MN......... 43°44N 91°55W 80 G7
Whaleysville MD ... 38°24N 75°18W 77 B5
Wharncliffe WV .... 37°33N 81°58W 102 D3
Wharton NJ .... 40°54N 74°35W 87 B2
Wharton OH .... 40°52N 83°28W 92 C3
Wharton TX .... 29°19N 96°6W 99 H11
Wharton County ☆
TX........... 29°12N 96°16W 99 H11
Wharton State Forest
NJ............ 39°45N 74°40W 87 C2
What Cheer IA ...... 41°24N 92°21W 73 D6
Whatcom = Bellingham
WA .... 48°46N 122°29W 101 B3
Whatcom, L. WA . 48°44N 122°20W 101 B3
Whatcom County ☆
WA .... 48°56N 122°0W 101 B4
Whately MA .... 42°26N 72°38W 78 B2
Whatley AL......... 31°39N 87°42W 60 E3
Wheat Ridge CO .. 39°45N 105°4W 109 B1
Wheatcroft KY ...... 37°30N 87°52W 96 C5
Wheatland CA ..... 39°1N 121°25W 64 D5
Wheatland IN .... 38°40N 87°19W 72 E3
Wheatland IA .... 41°50N 90°51W 73 D8
Wheatland MO..... 37°57N 93°24W 82 D3
Wheatland WY ... 42°3N 104°58W 104 D8
Wheatland County ☆
MT .... 46°30N 109°50W 83 D8
Wheatland Res. No.2
WY .... 41°50N 105°38W 104 E7
Wheatley AR........ 34°55N 91°7W 63 D4
Wheaton IL.......... 41°52N 88°6W 71 B5
Wheaton KS .... 39°30N 96°19W 74 B7
Wheaton MD .... 39°3N 77°3W 77 A3
Wheaton MN....... 45°48N 96°30W 80 E2
Wheaton MO .... 36°46N 94°3W 82 E2
Wheeler IL .... 39°3N 88°19W 71 D5
Wheeler KS........ 39°46N 101°43W 74 B2
Wheeler MS........ 34°35N 88°37W 81 B5
Wheeler OR ...... 45°41N 123°53W 94 B2
Wheeler TX........ 35°27N 100°16W 98 B7
Wheeler WI......... 45°3N 91°55W 103 C2
Wheeler County ☆
GA .... 32°5N 82°45W 68 D4
Wheeler County ☆
NE............. 41°50N 98°30W 84 C7
Wheeler County ☆
OR .... 44°45N 120°0W 94 C6
Wheeler County ☆
TX........... 35°30N 100°15W 98 B7
Wheeler L. AL ...... 34°48N 87°23W 60 B3
Wheeler Pk. CA ..... 40°26N 120°41W 64 C6
Wheeler Pk. NM... 36°34N 105°25W 88 A5
Wheeler Pk. NV .... 38°57N 114°15W 85 D6
Wheeler Ridge CA .. 35°0N 118°57W 65 H8
Wheelersburg OH .. 38°44N 82°51W 92 E4
Wheeling IL .... 42°8N 87°55W 71 A6
Wheeling WV ...... 40°4N 80°43W 102 A4
Wheelock ND ..... 48°18N 103°15W 91 B2
Wheelwright KY.. 37°20N 82°43W 97 C10
Whelen Springs AR .. 33°50N 93°7W 63 E2
Whidbey I. WA .. 48°12N 122°17W 101 B3
Whigham GA ...... 30°53N 84°19W 68 F2
Whiskey Pk. WY.. 42°18N 107°35W 104 D5
Whiskeytown-Shasta-Trinity Nat.
Recr. Area ⌂ CA 40°45N 122°15W 64 C4
Whispering Pines NC 35°17N 79°26W 90 C6
Whitaker PA .... 40°23N 79°53W 116 B2
Whitakers NC ...... 36°6N 77°43W 90 B8
White GA .... 34°17N 84°45W 68 B2
White SD .... 44°26N 96°39W 91 F9
White ➜ AZ .... 33°44N 110°13W 62 D5
White ➜ AR .... 33°57N 91°5W 63 E4
White ➜ IN .... 38°25N 87°45W 72 E3
White ➜ NV .... 37°19N 115°8W 85 E5
White ➜ OR ...... 45°14N 121°4W 94 B4
White ➜ SD .... 43°42N 99°27W 91 G6
White ➜ TX .... 33°14N 100°56W 98 D7
White ➜ UT ...... 40°4N 109°41W 100 C6
White ➜ VT .... 43°37N 72°20W 86 C2
White ➜ WA ..... 47°50N 120°48W 101 C5
White ➜ WA ..... 47°12N 122°15W 101 C3
White Bear L. MN . 45°4N 92°58W 113 A4
White Bear Lake MN. 45°4N 93°0W 113 A3
White Bird ID .... 45°46N 116°18W 70 D2
White Bluff TN....... 36°6N 87°13W 96 D5
White Butte ND .... 46°23N 103°18W 91 D2
White Butte SD.... 45°56N 102°22W 91 E3
White Canyon UT 37°49N 110°26W 100 F5
White Castle LA ..... 30°10N 91°9W 75 D4
White Center WA. 47°31N 122°21W 118 C3
White City FL...... 29°53N 85°13W 67 B3
White City FL...... 27°22N 80°20W 67 D8
White City KS ...... 38°48N 96°44W 74 C7
White City OR ... 42°26N 122°51W 94 E3
White Cloud KS ..... 39°59N 95°18W 74 B8
White Cloud MI ..... 43°33N 85°46W 79 F6
White County ☆ AR 35°15N 91°44W 63 C4
White County ☆ GA 34°40N 83°45W 68 B3
White County ☆ IL .. 38°5N 88°10W 71 E5
White County ☆ IN . 40°45N 86°50W 72 C4
White County ☆ TN. 35°56N 85°28W 97 E7
White Deer TX..... 35°26N 101°10W 98 B6
White Earth ND .... 48°23N 102°46W 91 B3
White Earth ➜ ND. 48°9N 102°42W 91 B3
White Earth Indian Reservation
MN .... 47°20N 95°45W 80 C3
White Hall AL .... 32°20N 86°43W 60 D4
White Hall AR ...... 34°16N 92°5W 63 D3
White Hall IL .... 39°26N 90°24W 71 D3
White Haven PA ..... 41°4N 75°47W 87 A1
White Horse NJ .... 40°11N 74°42W 87 B2
White House TN..... 36°28N 86°39W 96 D6
White I. CA .... 33°45N 118°9W 111 D4
White L. LA .... 29°44N 92°30W 75 E3
White Lake NC...... 34°39N 78°30W 90 D7
White Lake SD...... 43°44N 98°43W 91 G7
White Lake WI ..... 45°10N 88°46W 103 C5
White Lakes NM .. 35°12N 105°47W 88 B5
White Mountain
AK .... 64°41N 163°24W 61 D7
White Mountain Nat. Forest
NH .... 44°35N 71°23W 86 B3
White Mountain Peak
CA .... 37°38N 118°15W 65 F8
White Mountains Nat. Recr.
Area ⌂ AK ... 65°30N 147°40W 61 D11
White Mts. AK ..... 65°30N 146°30W 61 D11
White Mts. AZ ..... 34°0N 109°40W 62 D6
White Mts. CA .... 37°30N 118°15W 65 F8
White Mts. NH ...... 44°15N 71°15W 86 B3
White Oak GA .... 31°2N 81°43W 68 E5
White Oak OH ...... 39°12N 84°35W 107 A1
White Oak TX .... 32°32N 94°52W 99 E13
White Oak Cr. ➜
TX........... 33°14N 94°42W 99 D13
White Oak Lake AR . 33°42N 93°5W 63 E2
White Owl SD...... 44°36N 102°26W 91 F3
White Pass WA .... 46°38N 121°24W 101 D4
White Pigeon MI .... 41°48N 85°39W 79 H6
White Pine MI....... 46°45N 89°35W 79 C2
White Pine MT ..... 47°45N 115°29W 83 C2
White Pine TN ...... 36°7N 83°17W 97 D9
White Pine County ☆
NV............ 39°30N 115°0W 85 C6
White Pine Range
NV......... 39°10N 115°20W 85 C5
White Plains GA ..... 33°28N 83°1W 68 C3
White Plains MD ... 38°36N 76°55W 77 B4
White Plains NY ..... 41°2N 73°46W 87 A3
White River SD .... 43°34N 100°45W 91 G5
White River Junction
VT............ 43°39N 72°19W 86 C2
White River Nat. Forest
CO .... 39°20N 106°45W 66 C4
White River Nat. Wildlife
Refuge ⌂ AR ..... 34°18N 91°5W 63 D4
White River Res. TX 33°27N 101°5W 98 D6
White River Valley
NV............ 38°6N 114°58W 85 D6
White Rock KY ..... 36°40N 83°27W 97 D9
White Rock NM ... 35°50N 106°12W 88 B4
White Rock Cr. ➜
KS .... 39°55N 97°50W 74 B6
White Rock Lake
TX.......... 32°48N 96°43W 109 A5
White Rocks Nat. Recr. Area ⌂
VT........... 43°22N 72°55W 86 C2
White Salmon WA 45°44N 121°29W 101 E4
White Sands NM... 32°23N 106°29W 88 E4
White Sands Missile Range
NM .... 33°0N 106°25W 88 E4
White Sands Nat. Monument ⌂
NM .... 32°46N 106°20W 88 D4
White Shield ND .. 47°40N 101°51W 91 C4
White Signal NM .. 32°33N 108°22W 88 E2
White Springs FL... 30°20N 82°45W 67 A6
White Stone VA .... 37°39N 76°23W 102 D8
White Sulphur Springs
MT .... 46°33N 110°54W 83 D7
White Sulphur Springs
WV .... 37°48N 80°18W 102 D4
White Swan WA .. 46°23N 120°44W 101 D5
White Woman Cr. ➜
U.S.A.......... 38°26N 100°54W 74 C3
Whiteburg MD ...... 38°12N 75°32W 77 B5
Whiteclay NE ...... 42°57N 102°33W 84 B3
Whiteface TX ...... 33°36N 102°37W 98 D5
Whiteface ➜ MN.... 46°58N 92°48W 80 D6
Whiteface Mt. NY.... 44°22N 73°54W 89 A7
Whiteface Res. MN . 47°17N 92°11W 80 C6
Whitefield ME ...... 44°10N 69°38W 76 D4
Whitefield NH...... 44°23N 71°37W 86 B3
Whitefish MT ..... 48°25N 114°20W 83 B3
Whitefish ➜ MI.... 45°55N 86°57W 79 D5
Whitefish B. MI .... 46°40N 84°55W 79 C7
Whitefish B. WI .... 43°7N 87°53W 112 B2
Whitefish Bay WI .. 43°6N 87°54W 112 B2
Whitefish Point MI.. 46°45N 84°59W 79 C7
Whitefish Pt. MI .... 46°46N 84°57W 79 C7
Whiteford MD ..... 39°42N 76°21W 77 A4
Whitehall AR .... 35°29N 90°44W 63 C5
Whitehall MI .... 43°24N 86°21W 79 F5
Whitehall MT ..... 45°52N 112°6W 83 E5
Whitehall NY .... 43°33N 73°24W 86 C1
Whitehall PA...... 40°21N 79°59W 116 B2
Whitehall PA........ 40°38N 75°30W 87 B1
Whitehall WI....... 44°22N 91°19W 103 D2
Whitehorse SD .... 45°16N 100°53W 91 E5
Whitehouse OH ...... 41°31N 83°48W 92 B3
Whiteland IN........ 39°33N 86°5W 72 D4
Whitelaw WI....... 44°9N 87°49W 103 D6
Whiteleysburg DE .. 38°57N 75°45W 77 B5
Whiteriver AZ...... 33°50N 109°58W 62 D6
Whiterocks UT.... 40°28N 109°56W 100 C6
Whites City NM ... 32°11N 104°22W 88 E6
Whitesboro NY...... 43°7N 75°18W 89 B5
Whitesboro OK...... 34°41N 94°53W 93 D9
Whitesboro TX..... 33°39N 96°54W 99 D11
Whitesburg KY...... 37°7N 82°49W 97 C10
Whiteside County ☆
IL .... 41°45N 89°55W 71 B4
Whitestone NY .... 40°47N 73°49W 114 B4
Whitestown IN ...... 40°0N 86°21W 72 D4
Whitesville KY ..... 37°41N 86°52W 96 C6
Whitesville WV..... 37°59N 81°32W 102 D3
Whitetail MT...... 48°54N 105°10W 83 B12
Whiteville NC ...... 34°20N 78°42W 90 D7
Whiteville TN ...... 35°20N 89°9W 96 E3
Whitewater KS ...... 37°58N 97°9W 74 D6
Whitewater MO .... 37°14N 89°48W 82 D7
Whitewater MT ... 48°46N 107°38W 83 B10
Whitewater WI ..... 42°50N 88°44W 103 F5
Whitewater B. FL.... 25°15N 81°0W 67 F8
Whitewater Baldy
NM .... 33°20N 108°39W 88 D2
Whitewood SD ..... 44°28N 103°39W 91 F2
Whitewright TX ... 33°31N 96°24W 99 D11
Whitfield County ☆
GA .... 34°50N 84°55W 68 B2
Whiting IN......... 41°41N 87°30W 72 B3
Whiting IA.......... 42°8N 96°9W 73 C2
Whiting KS .... 39°35N 95°37W 74 B8
Whiting ME........ 44°48N 67°11W 76 D6
Whiting NJ........ 39°57N 74°23W 87 C2
Whiting VT .... 43°50N 73°12W 86 C1
Whiting WI .... 44°30N 89°34W 103 D4
Whitinsville MA ..... 42°7N 71°40W 78 B3
Whitlash MT ...... 48°55N 111°15W 83 B6
Whitley City KY ... 36°44N 84°28W 97 D8
Whitley County ☆ IN 41°10N 85°30W 72 B5
Whitley County ☆
KY............ 36°45N 84°10W 97 D8
Whitman MA .... 42°5N 70°56W 78 B4
Whitman NE ...... 42°3N 101°31W 84 B4
Whitman Air Force Base
MO .... 38°44N 93°31W 82 C3
Whitman County ☆
WA .... 47°0N 117°30W 101 D8
Whitman Mission Nat. Historic
Site ⌂ WA...... 46°2N 118°28W 101 D7
Whitmire SC .... 34°30N 81°37W 90 D4
Whitmore Lake MI . 42°20N 83°45W 79 G8
Whitmore Village HI 21°31N 158°1W 69 J13
Whitney NE........ 42°47N 103°15W 84 B2
Whitney NV......... 36°4N 115°5W 110 C2
Whitney TX........ 31°57N 97°19W 99 F10
Whitney, L. TX..... 31°52N 97°22W 99 F10
Whitney, Mt. CA.. 36°35N 118°18W 65 G8
Whitney Point NY . 42°20N 75°58W 89 C5
Whitsett TX........ 28°38N 98°16W 99 J9
Whittemore IA ...... 43°4N 94°26W 73 B4
Whittemore MI..... 44°14N 83°48W 79 E8
Whittier AK .... 60°47N 148°41W 61 F10
Whittier CA .... 33°58N 118°2W 111 C4
Whittier Narrows Flood Control
Basin CA .... 34°1N 118°4W 111 B4
Whittlesey, Mt. WI. 46°18N 90°37W 103 B3
Whitwell TN .... 35°12N 85°31W 97 E7
Wibaux MT ...... 46°59N 104°11W 83 D13
Wibaux County ☆
MT .... 46°50N 104°20W 83 D13
Wichita KS......... 37°42N 97°20W 74 D6
Wichita ➜ TX .... 34°4N 98°10W 99 C9
Wichita County ☆
KS............. 38°30N 101°20W 74 C2
Wichita County ☆
TX............ 33°57N 98°40W 99 D9
Wichita Falls TX.... 33°54N 98°30W 99 D9
Wichita Mountains Nat. Wildlife
Refuge ⌂ OK ..... 34°46N 98°42W 93 D5
Wichita Mts. OK.... 34°50N 98°45W 93 D5
Wick WV .... 39°25N 80°58W 102 B4
Wickenburg AZ .... 33°58N 112°44W 62 D3
Wickes AR .... 34°18N 94°20W 63 D1
Wickiup Res. OR .. 43°41N 121°41W 94 D4
Wickliffe KY .... 36°58N 89°5W 96 D3
Wickliffe OH........ 41°36N 81°28W 92 B5
Wicomico ➜ MD.... 38°13N 75°55W 77 B5
Wicomico Church
VA .... 37°49N 76°23W 77 C4
Wicomico County ☆
MD .... 38°25N 75°45W 77 B5
Wiggins CO .... 40°14N 104°4W 66 B6
Wiggins MS .... 30°51N 89°8W 81 F4
Wiggins MS .... 32°42N 89°38W 81 D4
Wilbarger County ☆
TX............. 34°9N 99°17W 99 C8
Wilber NE .... 40°29N 96°58W 84 D9
Wilbraham MA ...... 42°7N 72°26W 78 B2
Wilbur OR .... 43°19N 123°21W 94 D2
Wilbur WA ...... 47°46N 118°42W 101 C7
Wilburton OK ...... 34°55N 95°19W 93 D8
Wilcox NE .... 40°22N 99°10W 84 D6
Wilcox PA .... 41°35N 78°41W 95 C4
Wilcox County ☆ AL 31°59N 87°17W 60 E3
Wilcox County ☆ GA 32°0N 83°25W 68 D3
Wild Animal Park
CA .... 33°6N 116°59W 65 K10
Wild Horse CO...... 38°50N 103°0W 66 D8
Wild Horse Hill NE 41°55N 101°56W 84 C4
Wild Horse Res. NV 41°41N 115°51W 85 A5
Wild Rice ➜ MN.... 47°20N 96°50W 80 C2
Wild Rice ➜ ND ... 46°45N 96°47W 91 D9
Wild Rose WI ...... 44°11N 89°15W 103 D4
Wildcat Cr. ➜ IN.... 40°28N 86°52W 72 C4
Wilder ID........ 43°41N 116°55W 70 F2
Wilder KY .... 39°3N 84°29W 107 B2
Wilder MN......... 43°50N 95°12W 80 G3
Wilder VT .... 43°40N 72°15W 86 C2
Wildersville TN...... 35°47N 88°22W 96 E4
Wilderville OR .... 42°23N 123°28W 94 E2
Wildhorse Cr. ➜ OK 34°32N 97°10W 93 D6
Wildorado TX...... 35°13N 102°12W 98 B5
Wildrose ND ...... 48°38N 103°11W 91 B2
Wildwood FL ...... 28°52N 82°2W 67 C6
Wildwood NJ....... 38°59N 74°50W 87 D2
Wildwood Crest NJ . 38°58N 74°50W 87 D2
Wiley CO.......... 38°10N 102°40W 66 D8
Wiley City WA .... 46°33N 120°41W 101 D5
Wilkes-Barre PA ... 41°15N 75°53W 95 C7
Wilkes County ☆ GA 33°50N 82°45W 68 C4
Wilkes County ☆ NC 36°10N 81°10W 90 B4
Wilkesboro NC....... 36°9N 81°10W 90 B4
Wilkesboro Res. = W. Kerr Scott
Res. NC .... 36°10N 81°20W 90 B4

Wilkin County ☆ MN .... 46°20N 96°25W 80 D2
Wilkinsburg PA .. 40°26N 79°52W 116 B2
Wilkinson County ☆ GA .... 32°45N 83°10W 68 D3
Wilkinson County ☆ MS .... 31°6N 91°18W 81 E2
Will County ☆ IL . 41°25N 88°0W 71 B6
Will Rogers, Oklahoma City ✕ (OKC) OK ... 35°24N 97°36W 93 C6
Will Rogers State Historical Park ⌂ CA .... 34°2N 118°30W 111 B1
Willacoochee GA . 31°20N 83°3W 68 E3
Willacy County ☆ TX .... 26°29N 97°47W 98 L10
Willamette → OR . 45°39N 122°46W 94 B3
Willamette Heights OR .... 45°32N 122°42W 116 A1
Willamette Nat. Forest OR .... 44°20N 122°10W 94 C3
Willapa B. WA ... 46°40N 124°0W 101 D1
Willard CO .... 40°33N 103°39W 66 B7
Willard MO .... 37°18N 93°26W 82 D3
Willard NM .... 34°36N 106°2W 88 C4
Willard OH .... 41°3N 82°44W 92 B4
Willard UT .... 41°25N 112°2W 100 B3
Willards MD ... 38°24N 75°21W 77 B5
Willcox AZ .... 32°15N 109°50W 62 E6
Willcox Playa AZ . 32°8N 109°51W 62 E6
Willernie MN ... 45°3N 92°57W 113 A4
Willey IA ..... 41°59N 94°49W 73 D4
William B. Bankhead Nat. Forest AL .... 34°10N 87°15W 60 B3
William 'Bill' Dannelly Res. AL .... 32°6N 87°24W 60 D3
William P. Hobby, Houston ✕ (HOU) TX ... 29°38N 95°16W 110 C3
Williams AZ ... 35°15N 112°11W 62 B3
Williams CA ... 39°9N 122°9W 64 D4
Williams MN ... 48°45N 94°54W 80 A4
Williams → VT .. 43°12N 72°27W 86 C2
Williams County ☆ ND .... 48°20N 103°30W 91 B4
Williams County ☆ OH .... 41°35N 84°37W 92 B2
Williams Creek IN . 39°53N 86°9W 110 A2
Williams Fork → CO .... 40°28N 107°40W 66 B3
Williams Fork Res. CO .... 40°0N 106°8W 66 C4
Williamsbridge NY 40°52N 73°51W 114 A3
Williamsburg FL . 28°24N 81°26W 115 D3
Williamsburg IA . 41°40N 92°1W 73 D6
Williamsburg KS . 38°29N 95°28W 74 C8
Williamsburg KY . 36°44N 84°10W 97 D8
Williamsburg MA . 42°23N 72°44W 78 B2
Williamsburg MD . 38°40N 75°50W 77 B5
Williamsburg OH . 39°3N 84°4W 92 D2
Williamsburg PA . 40°28N 78°12W 95 D4
Williamsburg VA . 37°16N 76°43W 102 D8
Williamsburg County ☆ SC .... 33°40N 90°6W 90 E6
Williamsfield IL . 40°55N 90°1W 71 C3
Williamson GA .. 33°11N 84°22W 68 C2
Williamson IA .. 41°5N 93°15W 73 D5
Williamson NY .. 43°14N 77°11W 89 B3
Williamson WV .. 37°41N 82°17W 102 D2
Williamson → WI . 42°28N 121°57W 94 E4
Williamson County ☆ IL .... 37°40N 88°55W 71 F5
Williamson County ☆ TN .... 35°55N 86°52W 96 E6
Williamson County ☆ TX .... 30°38N 97°41W 99 G10
Williamsport IN . 40°17N 87°17W 72 C3
Williamsport MD . 39°37N 77°50W 77 A3
Williamsport OH . 39°35N 83°7W 92 D3
Williamsport PA . 41°15N 77°1W 95 C5
Williamston MI .. 42°41N 84°17W 79 G7
Williamston NC .. 35°51N 77°4W 90 C8
Williamston SC .. 34°37N 82°29W 90 D3
Williamstown KY . 38°38N 84°34W 97 B8
Williamstown MA . 42°43N 73°12W 78 B1
Williamstown NJ . 39°40N 74°59W 87 C2
Williamstown NY . 43°26N 75°53W 89 B5
Williamstown WV . 39°24N 81°27W 102 B3
Williamsville IL . 39°57N 89°33W 71 D4
Williamsville MO . 36°58N 90°33W 82 E6
Williford AR ... 36°15N 91°21W 63 B4
Willimantic CT .. 41°43N 72°13W 78 C2
Willimantic → CT . 41°43N 72°12W 78 C2
Willingboro NJ .. 40°3N 74°54W 87 B2
Willis KS ..... 39°43N 95°31W 74 B8
Willis TX ..... 30°25N 95°29W 99 G12
Willis, L. FL ... 28°23N 81°28W 115 B2
Williston FL ... 29°23N 82°27W 67 B3
Williston MD ... 38°48N 75°52W 77 B5
Williston ND ... 48°9N 103°37W 91 B2
Williston SC ... 33°24N 81°25W 90 E4
Williston TN ... 35°9N 89°22W 96 E3
Williston VT ... 44°25N 73°10W 86 B2
Williston Park NY 40°45N 73°38W 114 B5
Willisville IL .. 37°59N 89°35W 71 F4
Willits CA ..... 39°25N 123°21W 64 D3
Willmar MN .... 45°7N 95°3W 80 E3
Willmore Park MN. 38°34N 90°17W 117 B2
Willoughby OH .. 41°39N 81°24W 92 B5
Willoughby, L. VT . 44°45N 72°34W 86 B2
Willoughby Bay VA 36°57N 76°17W 115 A2
Willoughby Spit VA 36°58N 76°16W 115 A2
Willow AK ..... 61°45N 150°3W 61 F10
Willow AR ..... 34°8N 92°45W 63 D3
Willow OK ..... 35°3N 99°31W 93 C4
Willow City ND .. 48°36N 100°18W 91 B5
Willow Cr. → OR . 45°48N 120°1W 94 B5
Willow Cr. → UT . 40°2N 109°45W 100 C6
Willow Creek → .. 40°56N 123°38W 64 D3
Willow Creek Res. NV .... 41°14N 116°32W 85 A4
Willow Grove OH . 39°38N 79°39W 77 A5
Willow Grove PA . 40°9N 75°7W 87 B1
Willow L. WY ... 43°0N 109°52W 104 C3
Willow Lake SD . 44°38N 97°18W 91 F8
Willow Ranch CA . 41°54N 120°21W 64 B6
Willow Res. WI .. 45°43N 89°51W 103 C4
Willow River MN . 46°19N 92°51W 80 D6
Willow Springs IL. 41°44N 87°51W 108 C1
Willow Springs MO 37°0N 91°58W 82 E5
Willowbrook CA .. 33°55N 118°15W 111 C3
Willowbrook KS . 38°8N 97°57W 74 C6
Willowbrook NY . 40°36N 74°8W 114 C2
Willowdale OR .. 44°48N 120°24W 94 C5
Willowick OH ... 41°38N 81°28W 92 B5
Willows CA .... 39°31N 122°12W 64 D4
Wills Cr. → OH .. 40°9N 81°54W 92 C5
Wills Point TX .. 32°43N 96°1W 99 E11
Willsboro NY ... 44°21N 73°24W 86 B2
Willshire OH ... 40°45N 84°48W 92 C2
Wilma FL ..... 30°9N 84°58W 67 A4
Wilmar AR ..... 33°38N 91°56W 63 E4
Wilmer AL ..... 30°49N 88°20W 60 E2
Wilmer TX ..... 32°35N 96°41W 109 C5
Wilmette IL .... 42°4N 87°42W 108 A4
Wilmington DE .. 39°45N 75°33W 77 A5
Wilmington IL .. 41°18N 88°9W 71 B5
Wilmington MA .. 42°33N 71°10W 78 B3
Wilmington NC .. 34°14N 77°55W 90 D8
Wilmington OH .. 39°27N 83°50W 92 D3
Wilmington VT .. 42°52N 72°52W 86 D2

Wilmot MN ..... 43°46N 95°50W 80 G3
Wilmore KS ..... 37°20N 99°13W 74 D4
Wilmore KY .... 37°52N 84°40W 97 C8
Wilmot AR ..... 33°4N 91°34W 63 E4
Wilmot KS ..... 37°10N 96°53W 74 D7
Wilmot SD ..... 45°25N 96°52W 91 E9
Wilsall MT ..... 45°59N 110°38W 83 E7
Wilsey KS ..... 38°38N 96°41W 74 C7
Wilson AR ..... 35°34N 90°3W 63 C5
Wilson KS ..... 38°50N 98°29W 74 C5
Wilson LA ..... 30°55N 91°7W 75 D4
Wilson NC ..... 35°44N 77°55W 90 C8
Wilson NY ..... 43°19N 78°50W 89 B2
Wilson OK ..... 34°10N 97°26W 93 D6
Wilson TX ..... 33°19N 101°44W 98 D6
Wilson → OR ... 45°29N 123°53W 94 B2
Wilson, Mt. CO . 37°50N 107°59W 66 E3
Wilson County ☆ NC. 35°45N 78°0W 90 C7
Wilson County ☆ TN 36°12N 86°18W 96 D6
Wilson County ☆ TX. 29°8N 98°10W 99 H9
Wilson Creek Ra. NV .... 38°12N 114°18W 85 D6
Wilson L. AL ... 34°48N 87°38W 60 B3
Wilson Lake KS . 38°58N 98°30W 74 C5
Wilsons Creek Nat. Battlefield ⌂ MO .... 37°6N 93°25W 82 D3
Wilsons Mills ME. 44°57N 71°2W 86 B3
Wilsonville AL .. 33°14N 86°29W 60 C4
Wilsonville NE .. 40°7N 100°7W 84 D5
Wilsonville OR .. 45°18N 122°46W 94 B3
Wilton AR ..... 33°45N 94°9W 63 E1
Wilton CT ..... 41°12N 73°26W 78 C1
Wilton IA ..... 41°35N 91°1W 73 D7
Wilton ME ..... 44°36N 70°14W 76 D3
Wilton MN ..... 47°30N 95°0W 80 C3
Wilton ND ..... 47°10N 100°47W 91 C5
Wilton NH ..... 42°51N 71°44W 86 D3
Wilton WI ..... 43°49N 90°32W 103 E3
Wilton Manors FL. 26°9N 80°8W 112 B3
Wimbledon ND .. 47°10N 98°28W 91 C7
Winamac IN .... 41°3N 86°36W 72 B4
Winchendon MA . 42°41N 72°3W 78 B2
Winchester AR .. 33°47N 91°29W 63 E4
Winchester ID .. 46°14N 116°38W 70 C2
Winchester IL .. 39°38N 90°27W 71 D3
Winchester IN .. 40°10N 84°59W 72 C6
Winchester KY .. 37°59N 84°11W 97 C8
Winchester MA .. 42°26N 71°8W 106 A3
Winchester NH .. 42°46N 72°23W 86 D2
Winchester NV .. 36°7N 115°7W 110 C2
Winchester OH .. 38°56N 83°39W 92 E3
Winchester TN .. 35°11N 86°7W 96 E6
Winchester VA .. 39°11N 78°10W 77 A2
Winchester WY .. 43°51N 108°10W 104 C4
Winchester Bay OR 43°41N 124°10W 94 C1
Wind → WY ... 43°12N 108°12W 104 C4
Wind Cave Nat. Park △ SD .... 43°32N 103°17W 91 G2
Wind Mt. NM ... 32°2N 105°31W 88 E5
Wind Point WI .. 42°47N 87°46W 103 F6
Wind River Indian Reservation WY .... 43°20N 109°30W 104 C4
Wind River Pk. WY 42°42N 109°7W 104 D3
Wind River Range WY .... 43°0N 109°30W 104 D3
Windber PA .... 40°14N 78°50W 95 D4
Windcrest TX ... 29°31N 98°19W 117 B3
Winder GA ..... 34°0N 83°45W 68 B3
Windermere FL .. 28°29N 81°32W 115 B1
Windfall IN .... 40°22N 85°57W 72 C5
Windham CT .... 41°42N 72°9W 78 C2
Windham County ☆ CT .... 41°45N 72°0W 78 C2
Windham County ☆ VT .... 43°0N 72°45W 86 D2
Windiga MI .... 45°55N 89°9W 79 B2
Winding Stair Mountain Nat. Recr. Area △ OK .. 34°44N 94°43W 93 D9
Windom KS ..... 38°23N 97°55W 74 C6
Windom MN ..... 43°52N 95°7W 80 G3
Window Rock AZ . 35°41N 109°3W 62 B6
Windsor CA .... 38°33N 122°49W 64 E4
Windsor CO .... 40°29N 104°54W 66 B6
Windsor CT .... 41°50N 72°39W 78 C2
Windsor IL ..... 39°26N 88°36W 71 D5
Windsor MO .... 38°32N 93°31W 82 C3
Windsor NC .... 36°0N 76°57W 90 C8
Windsor VA .... 36°49N 76°45W 102 E8
Windsor VT .... 43°29N 72°24W 86 C2
Windsor County ☆ VT .... 43°39N 72°40W 86 C2
Windsor Forest GA 31°59N 81°5W 68 E5
Windsor Hills CA . 33°59N 118°22W 111 C2
Windsor Locks CT. 41°56N 72°38W 78 C2
Windsor Park NC. 35°13N 80°45W 107 A2
Windthorst TX .. 33°34N 98°26W 99 D9
Windy Pk. WA .. 48°56N 119°58W 101 B6
Winema Nat. Forest OR .... 43°10N 121°50W 94 D4
Winfield AL .... 33°56N 87°49W 60 C3
Winfield IA .... 41°7N 91°26W 73 D7
Winfield KS .... 37°15N 96°59W 74 D7
Winfield MD .... 39°26N 77°4W 77 A3
Winfield MO .... 39°0N 90°44W 82 C6
Winfield NJ .... 40°38N 74°17W 114 C1
Winfield TN .... 36°33N 84°27W 97 D8
Winfield WV .... 38°32N 81°54W 102 C3
Winfred SD .... 44°0N 97°19W 91 G8
Wingate IN .... 40°10N 87°4W 72 C3
Wingate NC .... 34°59N 80°26W 90 D5
Wingdale NY .... 41°39N 73°34W 78 C1
Winger MN .... 47°32N 95°59W 80 C3
Wingo KY ..... 36°39N 88°44W 96 D4
Winifred MT .... 47°34N 109°23W 83 C7
Winigan MO .... 40°3N 92°54W 82 A4
Wink TX ...... 31°45N 103°9W 98 F4
Winkelman AZ .. 32°59N 110°46W 62 E5
Winkler County ☆ TX .... 31°52N 103°6W 98 F4
Winlock WA .... 46°30N 122°56W 101 D3
Winn Parish ☆ LA. 31°56N 92°38W 75 C3
Winnebago IL ... 42°16N 89°15W 71 A4
Winnebago MN .. 43°46N 94°10W 80 G4
Winnebago NE .. 42°14N 96°28W 84 C9
Winnebago, L. WI. 44°0N 88°26W 103 E5
Winnebago County ☆ IL .... 42°20N 89°10W 71 A4
Winnebago County ☆ IA .... 43°20N 93°40W 73 B5
Winnebago County ☆ WI .... 44°0N 88°45W 103 D5
Winnebago Indian Reservation NE .... 42°14N 96°40W 84 B9
Winneconne WI .. 44°7N 88°43W 103 D5
Winnemucca NV . 40°58N 117°44W 85 B3
Winnemucca L. NV. 40°7N 119°21W 85 B1
Winner SD ..... 43°22N 99°52W 91 G6
Winneshiek County ☆ IA .... 43°15N 91°50W 73 B7
Winnetka IL .... 42°7N 87°58W 108 A4
Winnett MT .... 47°0N 108°21W 83 D9
Winnfield LA ... 31°56N 92°38W 75 C3
Winnibigoshish, L. MN .... 47°27N 94°13W 80 C4
Winnipesaukee NH 43°38N 71°21W 86 C3
Winnipesaukee, L. NH .... 43°38N 71°21W 86 C3
Winnsquam L. NH. 43°32N 71°31W 86 C3

Winnsboro LA ... 32°10N 91°43W 75 B4
Winnsboro SC ... 34°23N 81°5W 90 D4
Winnsboro TX ... 32°58N 95°17W 99 E12
Winona KS ..... 39°4N 101°15W 74 B2
Winona MN ..... 44°3N 91°39W 80 F7
Winona MS ..... 33°29N 89°44W 81 C4
Winona MO ..... 37°1N 91°20W 82 D5
Winona WA ..... 46°57N 117°48W 101 D8
Winona County ☆ MN .... 44°0N 91°50W 80 G7
Winona Lake IN . 41°14N 85°49W 72 B5
Winooski VT .... 44°29N 73°11W 86 B1
Winooski → VT .. 44°29N 73°17W 86 B1
Winside NE .... 42°10N 97°10W 84 B8
Winslow = Bainbridge Island WA .... 47°38N 122°32W 118 C2
Winslow AZ .... 35°2N 110°42W 62 B5
Winslow AR .... 35°48N 94°8W 63 C1
Winslow IN .... 38°23N 87°13W 72 E2
Winslow ME .... 44°33N 69°37W 76 D4
Winslow NJ .... 39°37N 74°52W 87 C2
Winsted CT .... 41°55N 73°4W 78 C1
Winsted MN .... 44°58N 94°3W 80 F4
Winston NM .... 33°20N 107°39W 88 D3
Winston OR .... 43°7N 123°25W 94 D2
Winston County ☆ AL 34°9N 87°24W 60 B3
Winston County ☆ MS 33°7N 89°3W 81 C4
Winston-Salem NC. 36°6N 80°15W 90 B5
Winter WI ..... 45°49N 91°1W 103 C2
Winter Garden FL. 28°34N 81°35W 67 C7
Winter Harbor ME. 44°24N 68°5W 76 D5
Winter Haven FL. 28°1N 81°44W 67 C7
Winter Park CO . 39°53N 105°46W 66 C5
Winter Park FL . 28°36N 81°20W 67 C7
Winterhaven CA . 32°44N 114°38W 65 L12
Winters CA .... 38°32N 121°58W 64 E5
Winters TX .... 31°58N 99°58W 99 F8
Winterset IA ... 41°20N 94°1W 73 D4
Wintersville OH . 40°23N 80°42W 92 C6
Winterville GA .. 33°58N 83°17W 68 B3
Winterville NC .. 35°32N 77°24W 90 C8
Winthrop AR .... 33°50N 94°21W 63 E1
Winthrop IA .... 42°28N 91°44W 73 C7
Winthrop ME .... 44°18N 69°58W 76 D4
Winthrop MA .... 42°22N 70°58W 106 A4
Winthrop MN .... 44°32N 94°22W 80 F4
Winthrop WA .... 48°28N 120°10W 101 B5
Winthrop Harbor IL 42°29N 87°50W 71 A6
Winton CA ..... 37°23N 120°37W 64 F6
Winton MN ..... 47°56N 91°48W 80 C7
Winton NC ..... 36°24N 76°56W 90 B9
Wiota IA ..... 41°24N 94°54W 73 D4
Wirt County ☆ WV. 39°4N 81°24W 102 B3
Wiscasset ME ... 44°0N 69°40W 76 E4
Wisconsin □ U.S.A. 44°45N 89°30W 103 D4
Wisconsin → WI . 43°0N 91°15W 103 E2
Wisconsin, L. WI . 43°25N 89°44W 103 E4
Wisconsin Dells WI 43°38N 89°46W 103 E4
Wisconsin Rapids WI .... 44°23N 89°49W 103 D4
Wise VA ..... 36°59N 82°35W 102 E2
Wise County ☆ TX. 33°14N 97°35W 99 D10
Wise County ☆ VA. 37°0N 82°45W 102 E2
Wise River MT .. 45°48N 112°57W 83 E5
Wishek ND .... 46°16N 99°33W 91 D6
Wishon Res. CA . 36°30N 119°5W 65 G8
Wishram WA .... 45°40N 120°58W 101 E5
Wisner LA ..... 31°59N 91°39W 75 C4
Wisner NE ..... 41°59N 96°55W 84 C9
Wissota L. WI .. 44°56N 91°20W 103 D2
Witch Lake MI .. 46°1N 88°1W 79 C3
Withee WI ..... 44°57N 90°36W 103 D3
Witherbee NY ... 44°5N 73°32W 86 B1
Withlacoochee → FL. 29°0N 82°45W 67 C6
Withlacoochee → FL .... 30°24N 83°0W 67 A5
Withrow Nature Preserve OH .... 39°3N 84°23W 107 B2
Witt IL ..... 39°15N 89°21W 71 D4
Witten SD ..... 43°26N 100°5W 91 G5
Wittenberg WI .. 44°49N 89°10W 103 D4
Wittman AZ .... 38°48N 76°18W 77 B4
Wittmann AZ ... 33°47N 112°32W 62 D3
Wixom MI ..... 42°32N 83°32W 79 G8
Wixom L. MI ... 43°50N 84°20W 79 F7
Woburn MA .... 42°29N 71°9W 106 A3
Wolbach NE .... 41°24N 98°24W 84 C7
Wolcott CO .... 39°42N 106°40W 66 C4
Wolcott CT .... 41°36N 72°59W 78 C2
Wolcott IN .... 40°46N 87°3W 72 C3
Wolcott NY .... 43°13N 76°49W 89 B4
Wolcottville IN . 41°32N 85°22W 72 B5
Wold Cr. → SD . 44°42N 98°40W 91 F7
Wolf NE ..... 30°22N 89°18W 81 F4
Wolf → TN .... 35°10N 89°54W 96 E3
Wolf → WI .... 44°8N 88°41W 103 D5
Wolf Cr. → OK .. 36°34N 99°34W 93 B4
Wolf Creek OR .. 42°42N 123°24W 94 E2
Wolf Creek Pass CO 37°29N 106°48W 66 E4
Wolf Lake IL ... 43°15N 86°7W 79 F5
Wolf Lake MI ... 43°15N 86°7W 79 F5
Wolf Mts. MT ... 45°12N 107°8W 83 E10
Wolf Point MT .. 48°5N 105°39W 83 B12
Wolf Trap Farm Park VA .... 38°56N 77°17W 119 B2
Wolfdale PA .... 40°12N 80°17W 95 D2
Wolfe City TX .. 33°22N 96°4W 99 D11
Wolfeboro NH ... 43°35N 71°13W 86 C3
Wolford ND .... 48°30N 99°42W 91 B6
Wolfsville MD .. 39°37N 77°35W 77 A3
Wollaston MA ... 42°15N 71°2W 106 B3
Wolsey SD ..... 44°21N 98°28W 91 F7
Wolverine MI ... 45°17N 84°36W 79 D7
Wolverine Peak WY .... 42°59N 109°22W 104 D3
Wolverton MN ... 46°34N 96°44W 80 D2
Wonalancet NH .. 43°54N 71°21W 86 C3
Wood SD ..... 43°30N 100°29W 91 G5
Wood → NE .... 41°22N 98°55W 84 C7
Wood County ☆ OH. 41°23N 83°39W 92 B3
Wood County ☆ TX. 32°48N 95°25W 99 E12
Wood County ☆ WV .... 39°14N 81°34W 102 B3
Wood Dale IL ... 41°58N 87°59W 108 B2
Wood Lake MN .. 44°39N 95°32W 80 F3
Wood Ridge NJ .. 40°50N 74°4W 114 A2
Wood River IL .. 38°52N 90°5W 71 D3
Wood River NE .. 40°49N 98°36W 84 C7
Woodall Mt. MS . 34°47N 88°15W 81 B5
Woodbine GA ... 30°58N 81°44W 68 E5
Woodbine IA ... 41°44N 95°43W 73 D2
Woodbine KS ... 38°48N 96°57W 74 C7
Woodbine KY ... 36°54N 84°5W 97 D8
Woodbine MD ... 39°22N 77°4W 77 A3
Woodbine NJ ... 39°14N 74°49W 87 C2
Woodbourne NY . 41°46N 74°36W 89 D6
Woodbridge CT .. 41°21N 73°12W 78 C1
Woodbridge NJ .. 40°33N 74°17W 114 C1
Woodbridge VA .. 38°40N 77°15W 77 B3
Woodburn IA ... 41°1N 93°36W 73 D5

Woodburn IA ... 41°1N 93°36W 73 D5
Woodburn KY ... 36°50N 86°32W 96 D6
Woodburn OR ... 45°9N 122°51W 94 B3
Woodbury CT ... 41°33N 73°13W 78 C1
Woodbury GA ... 32°59N 84°35W 68 D2
Woodbury KY ... 37°11N 86°38W 96 C6
Woodbury NJ ... 39°50N 75°9W 87 C2
Woodbury TN ... 35°50N 86°4W 96 E6
Woodbury County ☆ IA .... 42°25N 96°0W 73 C2
Woodfin NC .... 35°38N 82°36W 90 C3
Woodfords CA ... 38°47N 119°50W 64 E7
Woodford County ☆ IL .... 40°43N 89°13W 71 C4
Woodford County ☆ KY .... 38°2N 84°45W 97 B8
Woodhaven NY ... 40°41N 73°51W 114 B3
Woodhaven MI ... 42°8N 83°14W 79 H8
Woodlake CA ... 36°25N 119°6W 65 G7
Woodland CA ... 38°41N 121°46W 64 E5
Woodland IL ... 40°43N 87°44W 71 C6
Woodland ME ... 45°9N 67°25W 76 C6
Woodland MS ... 33°47N 89°3W 81 C4
Woodland TX ... 33°6N 95°50W 99 D12
Woodland WA ... 45°54N 122°45W 101 E3
Woodland Beach DE 39°20N 75°28W 77 A5
Woodland Park CO 38°57N 105°12W 66 D5
Woodlands, The TX. 30°9N 95°29W 99 G12
Woodlawn KY ... 36°35N 84°28W 107 B2
Woodlawn MD ... 39°19N 76°43W 115 A3
Woodlynne NJ ... 39°54N 75°5W 116 B2
Woodman WI ... 43°7N 90°48W 103 E3
Woodmont MD ... 39°20N 77°14W 119 A6
Woodmoor MD ... 39°20N 76°44W 107 B5
Woodrow NY .... 40°32N 74°11W 114 C1
Woodruff SC ... 34°44N 82°2W 90 D3
Woodruff UT ... 41°31N 111°10W 100 B4
Woodruff WI ... 45°54N 89°42W 103 C4
Woodruff County ☆ AR .... 35°9N 91°21W 63 C4
Woodruff Narrows Res. WY .... 41°31N 111°1W 104 E1
Woods, L. of the MN. 49°0N 95°0W 80 A4
Woods County ☆ OK 36°45N 98°50W 93 B5
Woods Cross UT . 40°52N 111°53W 117 A2
Woods Hole MA . 41°31N 70°40W 78 C4
Woods Landing WY. 41°7N 106°1W 104 E6
Woods Res. TN .. 35°18N 86°5W 97 E7
Woodsboro MD .. 39°32N 77°19W 77 A3
Woodsboro TX .. 28°14N 97°20W 99 J10
Woodsfield OH .. 39°46N 81°7W 92 D5
Woodside NY ... 40°44N 73°54W 114 B3
Woodson AR .... 34°32N 92°13W 63 D3
Woodson TX .... 33°1N 99°3W 99 D8
Woodson County ☆ KS .... 37°50N 95°45W 74 D8
Woodson Terrace MO .... 38°43N 90°21W 117 A2
Woodstock AK .. 67°25N 150°6W 61 C10
Woodstock CT .. 41°56N 72°5W 78 C2
Woodstock GA .. 34°6N 84°31W 68 B2
Woodstock IL .. 42°19N 88°27W 71 A5
Woodstock NH .. 43°57N 71°42W 86 C3
Woodstock NY .. 42°2N 74°7W 89 C6
Woodstock VT .. 43°37N 72°31W 86 C2
Woodstock VA .. 38°53N 78°30W 77 B2
Woodston KS ... 39°27N 99°6W 74 B4
Woodsville NH .. 44°9N 72°2W 86 B2
Woodville AL ... 34°38N 86°17W 60 B4
Woodville FL ... 30°19N 84°15W 67 A4
Woodville GA ... 33°40N 83°7W 68 C3
Woodville MS ... 31°6N 91°18W 81 E2
Woodville OK ... 33°59N 96°38W 93 D7
Woodville TX ... 30°47N 94°25W 99 G13
Woodward IA ... 41°51N 93°55W 73 D5
Woodward OK ... 36°26N 99°24W 93 B4
Woodward County ☆ OK .... 36°25N 99°15W 93 B4
Woodworth LA .. 31°9N 92°30W 75 C3
Woodworth ND .. 47°9N 99°18W 91 C6
Woody Creek CO. 39°17N 106°54W 66 C4
Woolen's Garden IN 39°55N 86°6W 110 A2
Woolridge MO .. 38°55N 92°32W 82 C4
Woolstock IA ... 42°34N 93°51W 73 C5
Woolwine VA ... 36°47N 80°17W 102 E4
Woonsocket RI .. 42°0N 71°31W 78 B4
Woonsocket SD . 44°3N 98°17W 91 F7
Wooster AR .... 35°12N 92°27W 63 C3
Wooster OH .... 40°48N 81°56W 92 C5
Wooton KY .... 37°12N 83°18W 97 D9
Worcester MA .. 42°16N 71°48W 78 B3
Worcester NY .. 42°36N 74°45W 89 C6
Worcester VT .. 44°20N 72°34W 86 B2
Worcester County ☆ MA .... 42°25N 72°0W 78 B2
Worcester County ☆ MD .... 38°15N 75°20W 77 B5
Worcester Mts. VT. 44°27N 72°39W 86 B2
Worden IL ..... 38°56N 89°50W 71 E4
Worden MT .... 45°58N 108°10W 83 E9
Worland WY ... 44°1N 107°57W 104 B5
World Trade Center, site of former NY .... 40°42N 74°0W 114 B3
World's End MA . 42°16N 70°52W 106 B4
Worley ID ..... 47°24N 116°55W 70 B2
Woronoco MA ... 42°10N 72°52W 78 B2
Worth IL ..... 41°41N 87°47W 108 C3
Worth MO ..... 40°24N 94°27W 82 A2
Worth County ☆ GA. 31°33N 83°51W 68 E3
Worth County ☆ IA. 43°20N 93°15W 73 B5
Worth County ☆ MO 40°30N 94°25W 82 A2
Wortham TX .... 31°47N 96°28W 99 F11
Worthing SD ... 43°20N 96°46W 91 G9
Worthington IN . 39°7N 86°59W 72 D4
Worthington MN . 43°37N 95°36W 80 G3
Worthington OH . 40°5N 83°1W 92 C3
Worthington WV . 39°27N 80°18W 102 B4
Wounded Knee SD 43°8N 102°22W 91 G3
Wrangell AK .... 56°28N 132°23W 61 H14
Wrangell Mts. AK. 61°30N 142°0W 61 F12
Wrangell-Petersburg AK .... 56°30N 133°0W 61 H14
Wrangell-St. Elias Nat. Park and Preserve △ AK. 61°0N 142°0W 61 F12
Wray CO ..... 40°5N 102°13W 66 B8
Wren AL ..... 34°28N 87°18W 60 B3
Wren OH ..... 40°48N 84°47W 92 C2
Wrens GA ..... 33°12N 82°24W 68 C4
Wren's Nest GA . 33°44N 84°25W 106 B2
Wrenshall MN .. 46°37N 92°23W 80 D6
Wright FL ..... 30°27N 86°38W 67 A2
Wright KS ..... 37°47N 99°54W 74 D4
Wright WY .... 43°45N 105°28W 104 C7
Wright Brothers Nat. Memorial = NC .... 36°1N 75°40W 90 B10
Wright City MO . 38°50N 91°1W 82 C5
Wright City OK . 34°5N 95°0W 93 D9

Wright County ☆ MN 45°10N 94°0W 80 E3
Wright County ☆ MO .... 37°15N 92°30W 82 D4
Wright Patman L. TX .... 33°19N 94°10W 99 D13
Wrightson, Mt. AZ. 31°42N 110°51W 62 F5
Wrightstown WI . 44°20N 88°10W 103 D5
Wrightsville AR . 34°36N 92°13W 63 D3
Wrightsville GA . 32°44N 82°43W 68 D4
Wrightsville Beach NC .... 34°12N 77°48W 90 D8
Wrightwood CA . 34°22N 117°38W 65 J8
Wrigley TN .... 35°54N 87°21W 96 E5
Wrigley Field IL . 41°56N 87°39W 108 B3
Wupatki Nat. Monument = AZ .... 35°35N 111°22W 62 B4
Wyaconda MO .. 40°24N 91°55W 82 A5
Wyalusing PA ... 41°40N 76°16W 95 C6
Wyandot County ☆ OH .... 40°50N 83°17W 92 C3
Wyandotte MI ... 42°12N 83°9W 79 G8
Wyandotte OK .. 36°48N 94°44W 93 B9
Wyandotte County ☆ KS .... 39°10N 94°45W 74 B9
Wyarno WY .... 44°49N 106°46W 104 B6
Wyatt LA ..... 32°9N 92°42W 75 B3
Wyatt MO ..... 36°55N 89°13W 82 E7
Wyeville WI .... 44°0N 90°28W 103 D3
Wykoff MN ..... 43°42N 92°16W 80 G6
Wylie TX ..... 33°1N 96°33W 99 D11
Wylie, L. SC ... 35°1N 81°1W 90 C4
Wylliesburg VA . 36°51N 78°35W 102 E6
Wymore NE .... 40°7N 96°40W 84 D9
Wyncote PA .... 40°5N 75°8W 116 A2
Wyndmere ND .. 46°16N 97°8W 91 D8
Wynne AR ..... 35°14N 90°47W 63 C5
Wynnedale IN .. 39°49N 86°11W 110 A2
Wynnewood OK . 34°39N 97°10W 93 D6
Wynnewood PA . 40°0N 75°16W 116 B1
Wynona OK .... 36°33N 96°20W 93 B7
Wynot NE ..... 42°45N 97°10W 84 B8
Wyocena WI .... 43°30N 89°17W 103 E4
Wyoconda → MO. 40°2N 91°34W 82 A5
Wyodak WY .... 44°17N 105°22W 104 B7
Wyoming DE ... 39°7N 75°34W 77 A5
Wyoming IL .... 41°4N 89°47W 71 C4
Wyoming MI ... 42°54N 85°42W 79 G6
Wyoming MN ... 45°21N 92°59W 80 E5
Wyoming □ U.S.A. 43°0N 107°30W 104 C5
Wyoming County ☆ NY .... 42°40N 78°15W 89 C2
Wyoming County ☆ PA .... 41°30N 76°5W 95 C6
Wyoming County ☆ WV .... 37°35N 81°32W 102 D3
Wyoming Pk. WY. 42°36N 110°37W 104 D2
Wyoming Range WY .... 42°55N 110°52W 104 D2
Wyomissing PA . 40°20N 75°59W 95 D7
Wythe County ☆ VA. 37°0N 81°5W 102 E3
Wytheville VA ... 36°57N 81°5W 102 E3

X

X.L. Ranch Indian Reservation CA .... 41°34N 120°26W 64 B6
Xenia IL ..... 38°38N 88°38W 71 E5
Xenia OH ..... 39°41N 83°56W 92 D3

Y

Yaak MT ..... 48°50N 115°43W 83 B2
Yabucoa Puerto Rico .. 18°3N 65°53W 105 G17
Yachats OR .... 44°19N 124°6W 94 C1
Yacolt WA ..... 45°51N 122°24W 101 E3
Yadkin → NC ... 35°23N 80°4W 90 C5
Yadkin County ☆ NC 36°10N 80°40W 90 B5
Yadkinville NC .. 36°8N 80°39W 90 B5
Yah-Tah-Hey NM. 35°38N 108°47W 88 B2
Yakama Indian Reservation WA .... 46°10N 120°30W 101 D5
Yakima WA .... 46°36N 120°31W 101 D5
Yakima → WA .. 46°15N 119°14W 101 D6
Yakima County ☆ WA .... 46°30N 120°30W 101 D5
Yakima Training Center WA .... 46°38N 120°25W 101 D5
Yakutat AK .... 59°33N 139°44W 61 G13
Yakutat B. AK .. 59°45N 140°45W 61 G12
Yale IA ..... 41°47N 94°21W 73 D4
Yale IL ..... 39°7N 88°2W 71 D5
Yale MI ..... 43°8N 82°48W 79 F9
Yale OK ..... 36°7N 96°42W 93 B7
Yale SD ..... 44°26N 97°59W 91 F8
Yale VA ..... 36°51N 77°17W 102 E7
Yale, L. FL ... 28°47N 81°47W 115 A1
Yalobusha → MS. 33°33N 90°10W 81 C3
Yalobusha County ☆ MS .... 33°59N 89°41W 81 C4
Yamhill County ☆ OR .... 45°15N 123°10W 94 B2
Yampa CO ..... 40°9N 106°55W 66 B4
Yampa → CO ... 40°32N 108°59W 66 B3
Yamsay Mt. OR . 42°56N 121°22W 94 E4
Yancey County ☆ NC .... 35°50N 82°20W 90 C3
Yanceyville NC . 36°24N 79°20W 90 B6
Yankee Stadium NY 40°49N 73°55W 114 B3
Yankton SD .... 42°53N 97°23W 91 H8
Yankton County ☆ SD .... 43°0N 97°30W 91 G8
Yankton Indian Reservation SD .... 43°5N 98°20W 91 G7
Yanush OK ..... 34°43N 95°19W 93 D8
Yaquina B. OR . 44°37N 124°0W 94 C1
Yaquina Head OR. 44°41N 124°5W 94 C1
Yarbo AL ..... 31°32N 88°17W 60 E2
Yardville NJ ... 40°11N 74°40W 87 B2
Yarmouth ME ... 43°48N 70°11W 76 E3
Yarnell AZ .... 34°13N 112°45W 62 C3
Yarrow Point WA. 47°38N 122°12W 118 C4
Yates City KS .. 37°53N 95°44W 74 D8
Yates City IL .. 40°47N 90°1W 71 C3
Yatesboro PA ... 40°46N 79°19W 95 D3
Yatesville L. KY. 38°8N 82°41W 97 B10
Yauco Puerto Rico. 18°2N 66°51W 105 G16
Yavapai County ☆ AZ .... 34°30N 112°30W 62 C3
Yazoo → MS ... 32°22N 90°54W 81 D3
Yazoo City MS .. 32°51N 90°25W 81 D3
Yazoo County ☆ MS 32°50N 90°25W 81 D3
Yeadon PA .... 39°56N 75°16W 116 B1
Yeager OK ..... 35°10N 96°22W 93 C7
Yeehaw Junction FL 27°42N 80°54W 67 D8
Yell County ☆ AR. 35°0N 93°24W 63 C2
Yellow → FL ... 30°30N 87°0W 67 A2
Yellow → IN ... 41°16N 86°37W 72 B4
Yellow → WI ... 44°13N 91°6W 103 D2
Yellow Jacket CO. 37°32N 108°43W 66 E2
Yellow Medicine County ☆ MN .... 44°44N 95°45W 80 F3
Yellow Pine ID . 44°58N 115°30W 70 E3
Yellow Spring WV. 39°11N 78°31W 77 A2

Yellow Springs OH. 39°48N 83°53W 92 D3
Yellowstone → MT .... 47°59N 103°59W 83 C14
Yellowstone County ☆ MT .... 46°0N 108°0W 83 D10
Yellowstone L. WY 44°27N 110°22W 104 B2
Yellowstone Nat. Park △ WY .... 44°40N 110°30W 104 B2
Yellville AR .... 36°14N 92°41W 63 B3
Yelm WA ..... 46°57N 122°36W 101 D3
Yemassee SC ... 32°41N 80°51W 90 F5
Yeoman IN ..... 40°40N 86°44W 72 C4
Yerington NV ... 38°59N 119°10W 65 E9
Yermo CA ..... 34°54N 116°50W 65 J10
Yeso NM ..... 34°26N 104°37W 88 C5
Yetter IA ..... 42°19N 94°51W 73 C4
Yigo Guam .... 13°32N 144°53E 105 b
Yoakum TX .... 29°17N 97°9W 99 H10
Yoakum County ☆ TX .... 33°11N 102°50W 98 D5
Yockanookany → MS .... 32°40N 89°41W 81 D4
Yocona → MS ... 34°11N 90°10W 81 B3
Yoder WY ..... 41°55N 104°18W 104 E8
Yolo County ☆ CA. 38°45N 121°50W 64 E5
Yona Guam .... 13°25N 144°46E 105 b
Yoncalla OR ... 43°36N 123°17W 94 D2
Yonkers NY .... 40°56N 73°52W 114 A3
York AL ..... 32°29N 88°18W 60 D2
York ND ..... 48°19N 99°34W 91 B6
York NE ..... 40°52N 97°36W 84 D8
York PA ..... 39°58N 76°44W 95 E6
York SC ..... 35°0N 81°12W 90 C4
York → VA .... 37°15N 76°23W 102 D8
York County ☆ ME. 43°25N 70°50W 76 E3
York County ☆ NE. 40°45N 97°30W 84 D8
York County ☆ PA. 39°55N 76°45W 95 E6
York County ☆ SC. 34°55N 81°10W 90 C4
York County ☆ VA. 37°14N 76°30W 102 D8
York Springs PA. 40°0N 77°7W 95 D5
York Village ME . 43°9N 70°39W 76 E3
Yorktown AR ... 34°1N 91°49W 63 D4
Yorktown IN ... 40°10N 85°30W 72 C5
Yorktown TX ... 28°59N 97°30W 99 J10
Yorktown VA ... 37°14N 76°30W 102 D8
Yorktown Heights NY .... 41°16N 73°47W 87 A3
Yorkville GA ... 33°55N 84°58W 68 C2
Yorkville IL .... 41°38N 88°27W 71 B5
Yosemite KY ... 37°20N 84°49W 97 C8
Yosemite Nat. Park △ CA .... 37°45N 119°40W 64 F7
Yosemite Village CA .... 37°45N 119°35W 64 F7
Yost UT ..... 41°58N 113°33W 100 B2
Youghiogheny → PA .... 40°22N 79°52W 95 D3
Youghiogheny River Lake MD .... 39°48N 79°22W 95 D3
Young County ☆ TX. 33°12N 98°44W 99 D9
Young Harris GA . 34°56N 83°51W 68 A3
Youngs, Lake WA. 47°25N 122°6W 118 C5
Youngstown FL . 30°22N 85°26W 67 A3
Youngstown NY . 43°15N 79°3W 89 B1
Youngstown OH . 41°6N 80°39W 92 B6
Youngsville LA .. 30°6N 92°0W 75 D3
Youngsville NC . 36°1N 78°29W 90 B7
Youngsville NM . 36°11N 106°34W 88 A4
Youngsville PA . 41°51N 79°19W 95 B3
Youngtown AZ .. 33°35N 112°18W 116 B1
Youngwood PA .. 40°14N 79°34W 95 D3
Yountville CA ... 38°24N 122°22W 64 E4
Ypsilanti MI ... 42°14N 83°37W 79 G8
Ypsilanti ND ... 46°47N 98°34W 91 D7
Yreka CA ..... 41°44N 122°38W 64 B4
Yuba → CA .... 39°8N 121°36W 64 D5
Yuba City CA ... 39°8N 121°37W 64 D5
Yuba County ☆ CA. 39°15N 121°25W 64 D5
Yucca AZ ..... 34°52N 114°9W 62 C1
Yucca House Nat. Monument = CO .... 37°16N 108°38W 66 E2
Yucca L. NV ... 36°57N 116°2W 85 F4
Yucca Valley CA . 34°8N 116°27W 65 J10
Yukon OK ..... 35°31N 97°45W 93 C6
Yukon → AK ... 62°32N 163°54W 61 E7
Yukon-Charley Rivers Nat. Preserve △ AK. 65°15N 144°0W 61 D12
Yukon Delta Nat. Wildlife Refuge △ AK.. 61°0N 163°0W 61 F7
Yukon Flats AK . 66°40N 145°45W 61 C11
Yukon Harbor WA 47°31N 122°32W 118 C2
Yukon-Koyukuk ☆ AK .... 65°42N 152°43W 61 D9
Yulee FL ..... 30°38N 81°36W 67 A7
Yuma AZ ..... 32°43N 114°37W 62 E1
Yuma CO ..... 40°8N 102°43W 66 B8
Yuma County ☆ AZ. 33°0N 114°0W 62 E2
Yuma County ☆ CO 40°0N 102°30W 66 C8
Yuma Desert AZ. 32°25N 114°40W 62 E1
Yunaska I. AK .. 52°38N 170°40W 61 K5
Yutan NE ..... 41°15N 96°24W 84 C9

Z

Zacata VA ..... 38°7N 76°47W 77 B4
Zachary LA .... 30°39N 91°9W 75 D4
Zahl ND ..... 48°34N 103°42W 91 B2
Zaleski OH .... 39°17N 82°24W 92 D4
Zalma MO ..... 37°9N 90°5W 82 D6
Zamperini Field ✕ CA .... 33°48N 118°20W 111 D2
Zanesville OH .. 39°56N 82°1W 92 C4
Zap ND ..... 47°17N 101°55W 91 C4
Zapata TX ..... 26°55N 99°16W 98 L8
Zapata County ☆ TX. 27°0N 99°16W 98 K8
Zavala County ☆ TX .... 28°50N 99°45W 99 J8
Zavalla TX .... 31°10N 94°26W 99 F13
Zearing IA .... 42°10N 93°18W 73 C5
Zebulon GA .... 33°6N 84°21W 68 C2
Zebulon NC .... 35°49N 78°19W 90 C7
Zeeland MI .... 42°49N 86°1W 79 G5
Zeeland ND .... 45°58N 99°50W 91 E6
Zeigler IL ..... 37°54N 89°3W 71 F4
Zelienople PA .. 40°48N 80°8W 95 D2
Zell SD ..... 44°54N 98°44W 91 F7
Zenda KS ..... 37°27N 98°17W 74 D5
Zephyr Cove NV. 39°0N 119°57W 85 C1
Zephyr Field LA . 30°1N 90°9W 113 C1
Zephyrhills FL .. 28°14N 82°11W 67 C7
Zia Indian Reservation NM .... 35°30N 106°50W 88 B4
Ziebach County ☆ SD .... 45°0N 101°50W 91 E4
Zillah WA ..... 46°24N 120°16W 101 D5
Zimmerman MN . 45°37N 93°34W 80 E5
Zion IL ..... 42°27N 87°50W 71 A6
Zion Nat. Park △ UT .... 37°15N 113°5W 100 F2
Zion Res. AZ ... 34°37N 109°29W 62 C6
Zirkel, Mt. CO .. 40°49N 106°43W 66 B4
Zolfo Springs FL. 27°30N 81°48W 67 D7
Zumbro Falls MN. 44°17N 92°25W 80 F6
Zumbrota MN ... 44°17N 92°40W 80 F6
Zuni → AZ .... 34°39N 109°4W 62 C6
Zuni Indian Reservation NM .... 35°10N 108°50W 88 B2
Zuni Mts. NM .. 35°10N 108°10W 88 B2
Zuni Pueblo NM. 35°4N 108°51W 88 B2
Zurich KS ..... 39°14N 99°26W 74 B4
Zwingle IA .... 42°18N 90°41W 73 C8
Zwolle LA ..... 31°38N 93°39W 75 C2